monitoring the future

questionnaire responses from the nation's high school seniors

1984

Jerald G. Bachman, Lloyd D. Johnston, and
Patrick M. O'Malley

Survey Research Center • Institute for Social Research
The University of Michigan
Ann Arbor, Michigan

ISR Code Number 4675
ISSN 0190-9185
ISBN 0-87944-306-5
Library of Congress Catalog Card Number 79-640937

Published in 1985 by:
Institute for Social Research,
The University of Michigan, Ann Arbor, Michigan

6 5 4 3 2 1

Printed in the United States of America

Table of Contents

Preface   vii
  Purposes of this Series of Publications   vii
  A Guide for the Reader   viii
  Availability of Archived Data   ix
  Other Publications from the Study   ix
  Acknowledgements   x

Introduction   1
  The Need for Social Indicators   2
  Research Design and Procedures   2
    Reasons for Focusing on High School Seniors   2
    Sampling Procedures   3
    School Recruiting Procedures   4
    Advance Contact with Teachers and Students   4
    Questionnaire Administrations   4
    Procedures for Protecting Confidentiality   5
  Content Areas and Questionnaire Design   5
  Representativeness and Validity   5
    School Participation   5
    Student Participation   7
    Validity of Self-Report Data   7
    Accuracy of the Sample   7
    Consistency and the Measurements of Trends   8
  Caveats to Users of the Data   8
    Estimation of Sampling Errors   8
    Subgroup Definitions   8
    Missing Data Notes   8
    Characterizing Heroin Users   8
    Interpreting Racial Differences   9

Descriptive Results   13
  Introduction to the Table Format and Conventions   13
  Questionnaire Form 1-5   16
    Section C (all Forms): Demographic Variables, Family Background, etc. 16
    Section B (all Forms): Drug Use   25
  Questionnaire Form 1   33
    Section A   33
    Section B (Detailed Drug Use)   40
    Section D   82

Questionnaire Form 2   89
    Section A   89
    Section D   104
    Section E   111
Questionnaire Form 3   119
    Section A   119
    Section D   133
    Section E   136
Questionnaire Form 4   146
    Section A   146
    Section D   160
    Section E   166
Questionnaire Form 5   174
    Section A   174
    Section D   188
    Section E   194

Cross-Time Index of Questionnaire Items   205
    Introduction to the Indexing Conventions   205
    Question Index   211

Appendices

    Appendix A: Sampling Error Estimates and Tables   247
    Appendix B: Procedures Used to Derive Design Effects
        and Sampling Errors   257
    Appendix C: Questionnaire Covers, Instructions, and
        Sample Page   271

References   275

Tables

    Table 1: Sample Sizes and Student Response Rates   4
    Table 2: Measurement Content Areas   6
    Table 3: Subject Area Key   208
    Table A-1: Confidence Intervals (95%) Level) Around Percentage Values   251
    Table A-2: Confidence Intervals for Differences Between Two Percentages
        (95% Confidence Level)   253
    Table B-1: Sample Sizes (Unweighted and Weighted) in Subgroups by Year   265
    Table B-2: Sample Sizes (Unweighted and Weighted) in Subgroups by Year
        for Questions on a Single Form   266
    Table B-3: Guidelines for Computing Design Effects (DEFFs) for
        Percentages and Means Derived from Monitoring the Future Samples   268

Figures

    Figure 1: Guide to Table Format   15
    Figure 2: Guide to Cross-Time Index   207
    Figure B-1: Design Effects for Single Percentages   261
    Figure B-2: Design Effects for Differences Between Percentages   263

Preface

This volume is the latest in a series which presents descriptive statistical results from a national survey of young people entitled Monitoring the Future: A continuing Study of the Lifestyles and Values of Youth. Each year the study surveys a large sample of high school seniors, located in approximately 125 schools nationwide, and drawn to be representative of all seniors in the coterminous United States.

The first four volumes in this series, dealing with the high school classes of 1975, 1976, 1977, and 1978 were published simultaneously early in 1980. Additional volumes appear on an annual basis. The most important contribution of this series is likely to be the opportunity it provides for the exploration of trends, a process that obviously involves the use of several different volumes. With that in mind, we have kept the format highly consistent from one volume to another, and we have developed an index (described below) which should facilitate the process of matching data across years. It should be noted that the volume presenting 1975 data is different from the others in several respects.*

Although we designed the volumes to fit together as a series, we also saw distinct advantages in having each volume able to stand alone — to be usable without reference to any of the others. For that reason, the introductory material on research design and questionnaire content, the instructions for accessing the data tables, and the appendices on sampling errors are all included in each volume. Thus, the small price we pay for making each volume self-contained is that much of the text portion is repeated each year.

Purposes of this Series of Publications

Monitoring the Future, which is conducted by the University of Michigan's Institute for Social Research and receives its core funding from the National Institute on Drug Abuse, is an unusually comprehensive research project in several respects: surveys are conducted annually on an ongoing basis; the samples are large and nationally representative; and the subject matter is very broad, encompassing some 1,300 variables per year. Many people — scholars, policy makers, educators, and so on — will have an interest in the results.

The principal investigators are already writing for a number of these audiences and will continue to do so. Because of the limitations in our own time, interests, and expertise, however, there is an enormous amount of valuable information which may never be utilized if the initiative to digest and disseminate all of it must come from us alone. Further, since the project is in part a social indicator series, its value rests to a considerable degree on *timely* dissemination of the results. For these reasons, we wish to share the study's results with others in a number of fields on a rapid and regular basis. We have chosen to provide two major and complementary vehicles for doing this: (a) these annual reference volumes of descriptive results, and (b) machine-readable data archives for direct analysis by others.

We believe that many potential users who would not mount the effort required to conduct computer analyses of archived data will be able to get most of

---

*The 1975 volume does not include comparison data for black and white subgroups, nor does it include data for the subgroups who did and did not plan to complete four years of college. Also, somewhat fewer questionnaire items appear than in the other volumes. These restrictions are the result primarily of missing data problems that occurred only in the 1975 survey. In most respects, however, those seeking to compare different classes of high school seniors will find the 1975 data useful.

what they want from these volumes of descriptive results. The user of any one of these volumes can estimate – usually with considerable accuracy – a wide variety of characteristics of the high school class described in that volume. To take just one example, the user of the 1984 volume can ascertain that 40.0 percent of seniors in the high school class of 1984 reported using marijuana at least once during the preceding year. Further, by utilizing two or more of these volumes the reader can describe recent trends in any such characteristic. To continue with the same example, the volume describing the high school class of 1975 also indicates that 40.0 percent of these seniors reported marijuana use during the preceding year; and when that is combined with the data from the intervening years the reader is able to discern a steady increase between 1975 and 1979 (50.8 percent of that class reported having used marijuana at least once in the preceding year), and a subsequent steady decrease back down to the 1975 level. The figures for the years 1975 to 1984 are:

1975: 40.0	1980: 48.8
1976: 44.5	1981: 46.1
1977: 47.6	1982: 44.3
1978: 50.2	1983: 42.3
1979: 50.8	1984: 40.0

A similar examination of trends can be carried out for over 1,300 different variables dealing with a wide variety of subject areas (listed in Table 2 of the Introduction). A simple indexing system (described below) has been developed which makes it quite straightforward for the reader wishing to do trend analyses to locate the results for a given question for any year of the study. The index in the present volume lists the location of all items included in the surveys from 1976 onward, as well as most items included in 1975.

Analyses such as those illustrated above need not be limited to the total sample. The data provided in these volumes also permit examination of a variety of subgroups (e.g., males, females, those from different regions, those with different levels of drug use experience).

We recognize that providing ready access to essentially undigested data carries certain risks, particularly the risk of mistaken interpretations based on inadequate controls, lack of awareness of sample limitations, etc. More than offsetting the risks, in our view, are the advantages of prompt and widespread dissemination of these nationally representative survey indicator data. Although we are unable to eliminate the risks, we hope to reduce them by providing the reader with an extensive list of caveats presented at the end of the Introduction section. We ask all who use the data to read these caveats carefully and take them seriously.

A Guide for the Reader

This volume is divided into three main parts: (1) the introductory section, (2) the section giving the descriptive results from the current year's survey, and (3) the cross-time item reference index.

Introductory Section. The introduction contains a description of the study — its purposes, major content areas, design, field procedures, response rates, and methods of publication and data dissemination. Since most of this material remains unchanged from year to year, anyone having read another of the volumes may wish to skim this section. We do, however, suggest reviewing the caveats, located at the end of the introductory section, which deal with interpreting and extrapolating from these data.

Descriptive Results Section. In this section all questions contained in this year's survey are presented along with percentagized frequency distributions of answers for the entire sample and for selected subgroups. The questions in this section are organized according to the number of the questionnaire form in which they were contained (forms one through five) and according to the order in which the questions occurred. There is one important exception, however. A major segment of questions common to all five forms of the questionnaire (dealing with drug use, background characteristics, and some other subjects) is presented only once, at the beginning of the Descriptive Results section, using the data from respondents on all five forms.

The first portion of the descriptive results section contains detailed definitions of all subgroups for whom data are presented. It also describes the statistical conventions used in generating the tables.

Cross-Time Index of Questionnaire Items. Beginning with the 1982 volume, this index is ordered by subject area. (It was ordered by item reference number prior to 1982.) The index is intended to serve two purposes.

First, it should be useful in locating items dealing with a subject area of interest. The subject area key at the beginning of the cross-time item index shows the alphabetical code assigned to various subject areas (e.g., "politics" or "work and leisure"). Having selected a subject area of interest, one can then go to that section of the index to locate all questions in any of the surveys which deal with that subject. (The procedure is slightly different in volumes prior to 1982, as described in those volumes.) To locate the results for any given question in this volume, simply look in column two of the item index for its page location.

The cross-time index can also be used to determine in which other years an item was used and where to locate it. If, in reviewing the Descriptive Results section, one locates an interesting item and would like to know in which of the other annual surveys of seniors it has appeared, it may be found in the cross-time index by the unique "item reference number" within the relevant subject area. The index will indicate all years in which that same item appeared and show the questionnaire form, section, and item number for each year. This information thus can be used to decide which other volumes in this series might be of relevance; and the same item may be readily located by its reference number in the index of any other volume prior to the 1982 volume, and by its subject area and reference number in any volume from 1982 on.

Sampling Appendices. Appendix A is provided for those wishing to determine the confidence limits around a percentage estimate, or to test the statistical significance of an observed difference between two groups, or to test the significance of a change from one year to another. It gives the necessary procedures and tables for such tests and provides the appropriate factors by which to correct for the fact that the study makes use of a multi-stage probability sample clustered in a limited number of schools (usually about 125). Appendix B provides further detail on sample design effects and the procedures which were used to derive the sampling error estimates.

Availability of Archived Data

As was mentioned earlier, this series of volumes is complemented by an archiving of the raw data set for direct analysis by others not associated with the project. The present volumes should be a considerable help to those wishing to access the archived data since they provide a verbatim statement of items and answer categories, and also because they include basic univariate and bivariate frequency distributions for all items, as well as the missing data rates. The cross-time index of items contained in each of these volumes also provides an efficient way to identify the relevant variables in various content areas, as well as to determine when they were measured and their questionnaire locations. In fact, we hope that the availability of this series will not only facilitate the use of the archived data but actually stimulate interest in their use.

The individual level data which are summarized in this and previous volumes are available from:

The Interuniversity Consortium for Political and Social Research (ICPSR)
Institute for Social Research
P.O. Box 1248
Ann Arbor, Michigan 48106

The ICPSR archive makes individual-level data available to interested investigators for analysis. A few variables have been modified or deleted to ensure that the answers of an individual respondent cannot be located through pattern recognition (i.e., using various descriptor variables in combination to make a unique identification). The changed or deleted variables include month of birth, race, and the sampling weight, which adjusts for selection probability.

Other Publications from the Study

A number of different forms of publications based on Monitoring the Future data have been developed or are being planned. One series of reports, dealing with trends in drug use and drug-related attitudes and beliefs, is being published by the National Institute on Drug Abuse. The first report in that series, *Drug Use Among American High School Students 1975-1977* (Johnston, Bachman, and O'Malley), was published in late 1977. Subsequent reports have been issued annually.

An Occasional Paper series has been launched by the project. It includes papers on design and methodological issues as well as special substantive analyses and early, and sometimes more detailed, drafts of articles planned for journal publication. The first occasional paper, "The Monitoring the Future Project Design and Procedures" (Bachman and Johnston, 1978), provides a detailed description of the study and its underlying rationale.

The present series of reference volumes is being published by the Institute for Social Research. A new volume will be added to this series each year.

To request particular papers, reprints, or periodic notification of publications available from the study, write to Monitoring the Future, Room 2030, Institute for Social Research, The University of Michigan, Box 1248, Ann Arbor, Michigan 48106.

*Single copies of these reports may be ordered without cost from the National Clearinghouse for Drug Abuse Information, National Institute on Drug Abuse, 5600 Fishers Lane, Rockville, Maryland 20857. See References for a complete list of reports.

Acknowledgements

A great many people have contributed to the launching and development of this research effort. We are indebted to a number of officials of the National Institute on Drug Abuse and the Special Action Office for Drug Abuse Prevention for their encouragement and advice at the outset — in particular, Richard Bucher, Robert DuPont, William Pollin, and Louise Richards.

Our colleagues at the Institute for Social Research and elsewhere who shared their insights, and often their most cherished instrumentation, are too numerous to mention; but their contributions are greatly appreciated. To the former director of the Survey Research Center's Sampling Section, Irene Hess, and to her colleagues we owe a particular debt for the creativity of the sampling design for the study. The contributions of the SRC Field Section also have been very valuable.

Major contributions to the production of this particular volume were made by staff members Jerome Hiniker, Dawn Bare, and Ginger Maggio. We would also like to thank the staff of the Publishing Division of the Institute for Social Reserch for their work in arranging publication.

The present and former members of the project staff (listed below) have, of course, contributed greatly to the building of this large and complex research series.

Finally, we would like to acknowledge the tens of thousands of high school seniors, their teachers, and their principals, whose cooperation and generous contributions of time make the Monitoring the Future project possible.

JERALD G. BACHMAN
LLOYD D. JOHNSTON
PATRICK M. O'MALLEY

Present and Former Members of the Project Staff

Donna Ando	Michael Fisher	John Miller
Margaret Bailey	Henry Freeman	Marion Morse
Dawn Bare	Walter Gruhn	Jim Neveaux
Ellen Berger	Lana Harrison	Dorothy Paulette
Mary Lou Bewley	James Hersey	Susan Pauls
Katherine Blatt	A. Regula Herzog	Sharon Pietila
Mary Lea Bonucchi	Jerome Hiniker	Joseph Pleck
Katheryn Boris	Pamela Kittel	Deborah Poinier
Marcy Breslow	Mark Krell	Judith Redmond
Susan Burek	Zenon Kuzmyn	Barbara Renaud
Mary Danneffel-Mashruwala	Carol Larsen	Don Rubinstein
Mary Lou Davis	Sally Lawson	Maria Sanchez
Mary Dempsy	Ludmilla Litus	Tina Smith
William Diedrich	A. Kathryn Loker	Ann Taylor
Robert Doljanac	Regina Lumbard	Richard Taylor
Karen Donahue	Mary Lutz	Lynda Tolen
Leslie Eveland	Ginger Maggio	Sandra Wronski
Halford Fairchild	Oksana Malanchuk	Thelma Wurzelbacher
Maureen Ferrell	Wayne McCulloch	Daniel Zahs
Marjorie Fisher	Joan McGraw	

Introduction

The Monitoring the Future project is designed to explore changes in many important values, behaviors, and lifestyle orientations of contemporary American youth. Two general types of tasks may be distinguished. The first is to provide a systematic and accurate *description* of the youth population of interest in a given year, and to quantify the direction and rate of the changes taking place among them over time. The second task, more analytic than descriptive, involves the *explanation* of the relationships and trends observed to exist.

The task of description may be subdivided into three parts: (1) the description of static conditions (which may be accomplished through a single cross-sectional study); (2) the description of cross-cohort or, in longer time-spans, generational changes (usually accomplished using repeated cross sections of the same age groups); and (3) the description of changes with aging (usually accomplished by means of longitudinal studies). The Monitoring the Future project has the capacity to provide each of these three types of description, since it incorporates all three types of research design into a single study. (This complex design, in which multiple cohorts are followed longitudinally, has been referred to as a cohort-sequential design.)

The content of this volume exemplifies the first of these types of description in that it contains cross-sectional data on a single high school class. When the data in this volume are used in combination with data from other such volumes in the series, the nature, direction, and rates of change from one cohort of seniors to another also may be described — the type of reporting which is often labeled as the social indicator approach. The third class of description — dealing with the maturational changes which occur during the years after high school — will not be dealt with in this series of volumes but will be reported in other publications from the study.*

The accurate characterization of American young people and the description of important changes occurring among them is but one class of objectives for the study. The second class of objectives involves the development of a greater understanding of what causes these young people to be as they are, and why the changes being documented are occurring. Explanation will be sought through both the analysis of change at the aggregate level and at the individual level. The results of these explorations will be disseminated via the various publications discussed in the Preface.

The merging of the social indicator approach and the analysis of relationships (particularly longitudinal relations) into a single cohort-sequential design is, in our view, synergistic: the effectiveness of the two approaches combined is greater than if the two were undertaken separately. Because the present series of volumes deals with senior year data only, our remarks here focus primarily on the project's social indicator contributions — the accurate description of high

---

* Panels of students from each graduating class are being randomly selected and followed longitudinally for up to ten years. Thus it soon will be possible to characterize the changes which seem to take place consistently with aging during the early adult years. Not only will longitudinal development in the years after high school be studied, but once enough of these longitudinal panels have accumulated, it will also be possible to characterize cross-sectionally most American young people aged 18 to 28, (at least the major segment of the population who completed high school — roughly 80-85 percent), and to describe the changing characteristics of that age group each year.

school seniors and the documentation of trends over time. It is worth noting, however, that even the limited amount of bivariate data included in the present volumes will suggest promising directions for relational analyses, many of which can be carried out using the archived data tapes from the project.

The Need for Social Indicators

The fundamental argument for developing social indicators is that there are considerable scientific and practical benefits derived from having accurate information about current social realities and the way those realities have been changing. For the scientific community such indicators provide a rich set of information against which existing theory may be tested and from which new theory may be suggested. For the community at large, social indicators permit the "reality testing" of common perceptions and beliefs about the nation and its people. Past experience has demonstrated that widely held conceptions, which themselves may serve to create or exacerbate problems, can be most inaccurate. One example is the exaggerated popular conception of the size and nature of the "gap" between generations (see Adelson, 1970, 1979); another is the mistaken assumption that most young people condone the use of a variety of illegal drugs (Johnston, 1973; Johnston, Bachman, and O'Malley, 1977; 1979 a, b; 1981).

While deflating exaggerated perceptions, a continual monitoring of indicators on youth also can reveal the beginning of new problems and thus give rise to corrective efforts at a relatively early stage. For instance, most would view with concern the emergence of new types of drug use. Monitoring the Future has already documented and reported a sharp increase in regular marijuana use among high school seniors, and as a result more attention has been paid to the issue by policy makers, the media, and the general public. The discovery of such trends may trigger more intense efforts to discover the causes, consequences, and (when appropriate) preventatives of such behaviors.

Although social indicators seldom translate directly into specific policy decisions, the availability of descriptive information can substantially enhance the decision-making capabilities of policy makers. These data provide considerable insight into the size and nature of problems, the rate of change occurring nationally and in subgroups, and in some instances information about related factors and even the likely impacts of major social interventions (such as changed drug laws, or new incentives for recruitment into the military, to name but two). They also provide the possibility of feedback on the consequences of some social interventions as well as major historical events.

The particular topics included in our monitoring system are summarized later in this introduction and, of course, they are presented fully in the complete set of data tables. For present purposes, it is enough to indicate that the range of topics is very broad. This breadth is partly due to the wide interests of the principal investigators; but it also reflects our conviction that the concurrent examination of trends in a variety of areas is not only much more cost efficient but also more scientifically productive.

Research Design and Procedures*

The basic research design involves annual data collections from high school seniors during the spring of each year, beginning with the class of 1975. Each data collection takes place in approximately 125 public and private high schools selected to provide an accurate cross section of high school seniors throughout the coterminous United States. The design also provides for the longitudinal study of a subsample from each class of participating seniors; but since the focus of this series of volumes is exclusively on the data collected annually from seniors, the follow-up procedures will not be discussed here.

Reasons for Focusing on High School Seniors. There are several reasons for choosing the senior year of high school as an optimal point for monitoring the behaviors and attitudes of youth. One is that the completion of high school represents the end of an important developmental stage in this society, since it demarcates both the end of universal public education and, for many, the end of living in the parental home. Therefore, it is a logical point at which to take stock of the accumulated influences of these two environments on American youth.

Further, the completion of high school represents the jumping off point from which young people diverge into widely differing social environments, including college, business firms, military service, and homemaking. But these environmental transitions are not the only important changes which coincide with the end of high school. Most young men and women now reach the formal age of adulthood shortly before or after graduation; more significantly, they begin to assume adult roles, including financial self-support, marriage, and parenthood.

Finally, there are some important practical advantages to building a system of data collections around samples of high school seniors. The last year of high school constitutes the final point at which a reasonably good national sample of an age-specific cohort can be drawn and studied economically. The need for systematically repeated, large-scale samples from which to make reliable estimates of change requires

---

*A more extensive description of the research design and procedures may be found in Bachman and Johnston (1978).

that considerable stress be laid on efficiency and feasibility; the present design meets those requirements.

One limitation in the design is that it does not include in the target population those young men and women who drop out of high school before graduation (or before the last few months of the senior year, to be more precise). This excludes a relatively small proportion of each age cohort — between 15 and 20 percent (Dearman and Plisko, 1982) — though not an unimportant segment, since we know that certain behaviors such as illicit drug use (Johnston, 1973) and delinquency (Bachman, O'Malley, and Johnston, 1978) tend to be higher than average in this group. However, the addition of a representative sample of dropouts would increase the cost of the present research enormously, because of their dispersion and generally higher level of resistance to being located and interviewed.

For the purposes of estimating characteristics of the entire age group, the omission of high school dropouts does introduce certain biases; however, their small proportion sets outer limits on the bias (Johnston, O'Malley, and Bachman, 1985, Appendix). For the purposes of estimating *changes* from one cohort of high school seniors to another, the omission of dropouts represents a problem only if different cohorts have considerably different proportions who drop out. We have no reason to expect dramatic changes in those rates for the foreseeable future, and recently published government statistics indicate a great deal of stability in dropout rates since 1970 (Dearman and Plisko, 1982, p. 4).

Some may use our high school data to draw conclusions about changes for the entire age group. While we do not encourage such extrapolation, we suspect that the conclusions reached often would be valid, since over 80 percent of the age group is in the surveyed segment of the population *and* we expect that change among those not in school are very likely to parallel the changes among those who are. Nevertheless, for purposes of characterizing the entire age group we would urge the user to check the results emanating from the present monitoring system against those emerging from other data collection systems using different methods, such as household interviews. (It is encouraging to note that when we have compared drug use data for this age group from the present study with those from interview studies, the findings have shown a high degree of similarity.)

Sampling Procedures. The procedure for securing a nationwide sample of high school seniors is a multistage one. Stage 1 is the selection of particular geographic areas, Stage 2 is the selection of one or more high schools in each area, and Stage 3 is the selection of seniors within each high school.

Stage 1: Geographic Areas. The geographic areas used in this study are the primary sampling units

(PSUs) developed by the Sampling Section of the Survey Research Center for use in the Center's nationwide interview studies. These consist of 74 primary areas throughout the coterminous United States — including the 12 largest metropolitan areas, which contain about 30 percent of the nation's population. Of the 62 other primary areas, 10 are in the Northeast, 18 in the North Central area, 24 in the South, and 10 in the West. Because these same PSUs are used for personal interview studies by the Survey Research Center (SRC), local field representatives can be assigned to administer the data collections in practically all schools.

Stage 2: Schools. In the major metropolitan areas more than one high school is often included in the sampling design; in most other sampling areas a single high school is sampled. In all cases, the selections of high schools are made such that the probability of drawing a school is proportionate to the size of its senior class. The larger the senior class (according to recent records), the higher the selection probability assigned to the high school. When a sampled school is unwilling to participate, a replacement school as similar to it as possible is selected from the same geographic area.

Stage 3: Students. Within each selected school, up to about 400 seniors may be included in the data collection. In schools with fewer than 400 seniors, the usual procedure is to include all of them in the data collection. In larger schools, a subset of seniors is selected either by randomly sampling classrooms or by some other random method that is convenient for the school and judged to be unbiased. Sample weights are assigned to each respondent so as to take account of variations in the sizes of samples from one school to another, as well as the (smaller) variations in selection probabilities occurring at the earlier stages of sampling.

The three-stage sampling procedure described above yielded the number of participating schools and students indicated in Table 1.

One other important feature of the base-year sampling procedure should be noted here. All schools (except for half of the initial 1975 sample) are asked to participate in two data collections, thereby permitting replacement of half of the total sample of schools each year. One motivation for requesting that schools participate for two years is administrative efficiency; it is a costly and time-consuming procedure to secure the cooperation of schools, and a two-year period of participation cuts down that effort substantially. Another important advantage is that whenever an appreciable shift in scores from one graduating class to the next is observed, it is possible to check whether the shift might be attributable to some differences in the newly sampled schools. This is done simply by repeating the analysis using only the 60 or so schools which participated both years. Thus far, the half-sample approach

Table 1

Sample Sizes and Student Response Rates

	1975	1976	1977	1978	1979	1980	1981	1982	1983	1984
Number of Public Schools	111	108	108	111	111	107	109	116	112	117
Number of Private Schools	14	15	16	20	20	20	19	21	22	17
Total Number of Schools	125	123	124	131	131	127	128	137	134	134
Total Number of Students*	15791	16678	18436	18924	16662	16524	18267	18348	16947	16499
Student Response Rate**	78%	77%	79%	83%	82%	82%	81%	83%	84%	83%

* Sample weights are assigned to each respondent to correct for unequal probabilities of selection which arise in the multi-stage sampling procedure.

** The student response rate is derived by dividing the attained sample by the target sample (both based on weighted numbers of cases). The target sample is based upon listings provided by schools. Since such listings may fail to take account of recent student attrition, the actual response rate may be slightly underestimated.

has worked quite well; and examination of drug prevalance data from the "matched half-samples" showed that the half samples of repeat schools yielded drug prevalence trends which were virtually identical to trends based on all schools.

School Recruiting Procedures. Early during the fall semester an initial contact is made with each sampled school. First a letter is sent to the principal describing the study and requesting permission to survey seniors. The letter is followed by a telephone call from a project staff member, who attempts to deal with any questions or problems and (when necessary) makes arrangements to contact and seek permission from other school district officials. Basically the same procedures are followed for schools asked to participate for the second year.

Once the school's agreement to participate is obtained, arrangements are made by phone for administering the questionnaires. A specific date for the survey is mutually agreed upon and a local SRC representative is assigned to carry out the administration.

Advance Contact with Teachers and Students. The local SRC representative is instructed to visit the school two weeks ahead of the actual date of administration. This visit serves as an occasion to meet the teachers whose classes will be affected and to provide them with a brochure describing the study, a brief set of guidelines about the questionnaire administration, and a supply of flyers to be distributed to the students a week to 10 days in advance of the questionnaire administration. The guidelines to the teachers include

a suggested announcement to students at the time the flyers are distributed.

From the students' standpoint, the first information about the study usually consists of the teacher's announcement and the short descriptive flyer. In announcing the study, the teachers are asked to stress that the questionnaires used in the survey are not tests, and that there are no right or wrong answers. The flyer tells students that they will be invited to participate in the study, points out that their participation is strictly voluntary, and stresses confidentiality (including a reference to the fact that the Monitoring the Future project has a special government grant of confidentiality which allows their answers to be protected). The flyer also serves as an informative document which the students can show to their parents.

Questionnaire Administrations. The questionnaire administration in each school is carried out by the local SRC representatives and their assistants, following standardized procedures detailed in a project instruction manual. The questionnaires are administered in classrooms during normal class periods whenever possible, although circumstances in some schools require the use of larger group administrations. Teachers are not asked to do anything more than introduce the SRC staff members and (in most cases) remain in the classroom to help guarantee an orderly atmosphere for the survey. Teachers are urged to avoid walking around the room, so that students may feel free to write their answers without fear of being observed.

The actual process of completing the questionnaires is quite straightforward. Respondents are given sharpened pencils and asked to use them because the questionnaires are designed for automatic scanning. Most respondents can finish within a 45-minute class period; for those who cannot, an effort is made to provide a few minutes of additional time.

Procedures for Protecting Confidentiality. In any study that relies on voluntary reporting of drug use or other illegal acts, it is essential to develop procedures which guarantee the confidentiality of such reports. It is also desirable that these procedures be described adequately to respondents so that they are comfortable about providing honest answers.

We noted that the first information given to students about the survey consists of a descriptive flyer stressing confidentiality and voluntary participation. This theme is repeated at the start of the questionnaire administration. Each participating student is instructed to read the message on the cover of the questionnaire, which stresses the importance and value of the study, notes that answers will be kept strictly confidential, states that the study is completely voluntary, and tells the student "If there is any question you or your parents would find objectionable for any reason, just leave it blank." The instructions then point out that in a few months a summary of nationwide results will be mailed to all participants and also that a follow-up questionnaire will be sent to some students after a year. The cover message explains that these are the reasons for asking that name and address be written on a special form which will be removed from the questionnaire and handed in separately. The message also points out that the two different code numbers (one on the questionnaire and one on the tear-out form) cannot be matched except by a special computer tape at The University of Michigan. (The content of the inside and outside of the standard questionnaire cover, including the tear-out form, may be found in Appendix C.)

Content Areas and Questionnaire Design

Drug use and related attitudes are the topics which receive the most extensive coverage in the Monitoring the Future project; but the questionnaires also deal with a wide range of other subject areas, including attitudes about government, social institutions, race relations, changing roles for women, educational aspirations, occupational aims, and marital and family plans, as well as a variety of background and demographic factors.* (Table 2 provides an outline of the 20 general subject areas into which all items are categorized in the Question Index toward the end of this volume.) Given this breadth of content, the study is not presented to respondents as a "drug use study," nor do they tend to view it as such.

Because many questions are needed to cover all of these topic areas, much of the questionnaire content is divided into five different questionnaire forms which are distributed to participants in an ordered sequence that produces five virtually identical subsamples. About one-third of each questionnaire form consists of key or "core" variables which are common to all forms. All demographic variables and some measures of drug use are included in this "core" set of measures. This use of the full sample for drug and demographic measures provides a more accurate estimation on these dimensions and also makes it possible to link them statistically to all of the other measures which are included in a single form only.**

Representativeness and Validity

The samples for this study are intended to be representative of high school seniors throughout the 48 coterminous states. We have already discussed the fact that this definition of the sample excludes one important portion of the age cohort: those who have dropped out of high school before nearing the end of the senior year. But given the aim of representing high school seniors, it will now be useful to consider the extent to which the obtained samples of schools and students are likely to be representative of all seniors and the degree to which the data obtained are likely to be valid.

We can distinguish at least four ways in which survey data of this sort might fall short of being fully accurate. First, some sampled schools refuse to participate, which could introduce some bias. Second, the failure to obtain questionnaire data from 100 percent of the students sampled in participating schools would also introduce bias. Third, the answers provided by participating students are open to both conscious and unconscious distortions which could reduce validity. Finally, limitations in sample size and/or design could place limits on the accuracy of estimates. Each of these issues is treated extensively elsewhere (Johnston, Bachman, and O'Malley, 1979a, especially Appendices A and B), so in this section we will present only the highlights of each of those discussions.

School Participation. As noted in the description of the sampling design, schools are invited to participate

---

*An example of analyses relating background, demographic, and lifestyle factors to drug use is Bachman, Johnston, and O'Malley (1981); a much broader array of other subject areas included in the study is treated by Bachman and Johnston (1979).

**These core variables are the first ones on which data are presented in the Descriptive Results Section.

Table 2

Measurement Content Areas

A. Drugs. Drug use and related attitudes and beliefs, drug availability and exposure, surrounding conditions and social meanings of drug use. Views of significant others regarding drugs.

B. Education. Educational lifestyle, values, experiences, and environments.

C. Work and Leisure. Vocational values, meaning of work and leisure, work and leisure activities, preferences regarding occupational characteristics and type of work setting.

D. Sex Roles and Family. Values, attitudes, and expectations about marriage, family structure, sex roles, and sex discrimination.

E. Population Concerns. Values and attitudes about overpopulation and birth control.

F. Conservation, Materialism, Equity, etc. Values, attitudes, and expectations related to conservation, pollution, materialism, equity, and the sharing of resources. Preferences regarding type of dwelling and urbanicity.

G. Religion. Religious affiliation, practices, and views.

H. Politics. Political affiliation, activities, and views.

I. Social Change. Values, attitudes, and expectations about social change.

J. Social Problems. Concern with various social problems facing the nation and the world.

K. Major Social Institutions. Confidence in and commitment to various major social institutions (business, unions, branches of government, press, organized religion, military, etc.).

L. Military. Views about the armed services and the use of military force. Personal plans for military service.

M. Interpersonal Relationships. Qualitative and quantitative characteristics of cross-age and peer relationships. Interpersonal conflict.

N. Race Relations. Attitudes toward and experiences with other racial groups.

O. Concern for Others. Concern for others; voluntary and charitable activities.

P. Happiness. Happiness and life satisfaction, overall and in specific life domains.

Q. Other Personality Variables. Attitudes about self (including self-esteem), locus of control, loneliness, risk-taking, trust in others, importance placed on various life goals, counter-culture orientation, hostility.

R. Background. Demographic and family background characteristics, living arrangements.

S. Deviant Behavior and Victimization. Delinquent behaviors, driving violations and accidents (including those under the influence of drugs), victimization experiences.

T. Health Habits and Symptoms. Health habits, somatic symptoms, medical experiences.

in the study for a two-year period. With very few exceptions, each school which has participated for one data collection has agreed to participate for a second. Thus far, from 66 percent to 80 percent of the schools initially invited to participate have agreed to do so each year; for each school refusal, a similar school (in terms of size, geographic area, urbanicity, etc.) was recruited as a replacement. The selection of replacement schools almost entirely removes problems of bias in region, urbanicity, and the like that might result from certain schools refusing to participate. Other potential biases are more subtle, however. For example, if it turned out that most schools with "drug problems" refused to participate, that could seriously bias the drug estimates derived from the sample. And if any other single factor were dominant in most refusals, that also might suggest a source of serious bias. In fact, however, the reasons for schools' refusals to participate are varied and largely a function of happenstance events of the particular year. Thus, we feel fairly confident that school refusals have not seriously biased the surveys.

Student Participation. Completed questionnaires are obtained from three-fourths to four-fifths of all students sampled. The single most important reason that students are missed is that they are absent from class at the time of data collection, and in most cases it is not workable to schedule a special follow-up data collection for them. Students with fairly high rates of absenteeism also report above-average rates of drug use; therefore, there is some degree of bias introduced by missing the absentees. That bias could be largely corrected through the use of special weighting; however, this course was not chosen because the bias in estimates (for drug use, where the potential effect was hypothesized to be largest) was determined to be quite small and because the necessary weighting procedures would have introduced undesirable complications (see Johnston et al., 1977).

In addition to absenteeism, student nonparticipation occurs because of schedule conflicts with school trips and other activities which tend to be more frequent than usual during the final months of the senior year. Of course, some students refuse to complete or turn in a questionnaire. However, the SRC representatives in the field estimate this proportion to be only about one percent.

Validity of Self-Report Data. Survey measures of delinquency and of drug use depend upon respondents reporting what are, in many cases, illegal acts. Thus, a critical question is whether such self-reports are likely to be valid. Like most studies dealing with

these areas, we have no direct, objective validation of the present measures; however, the considerable amount of inferential evidence which exists strongly suggests that the self-report questions produce largely valid data. A number of factors have given us reasonable confidence about the validity of the responses to what are presumably among the most sensitive questions in the study: a low nonresponse on the drug questions; a large proportion admitting to some illicit drug use; the consistency of findings across several years of the present study; strong evidence of construct validity (based on relationships observed between variables); a close match between our data and the findings from other studies using other methods; and the findings from several methodological studies which have used objective validation methods.*

As for others of the measures, a few have a long and venerable history — as scholars of the relevant literatures will recognize — though some of these measures have been modified to fit the present questionnaire format. Many (probably most) questions, however, have been developed specifically for this project through a careful process of question writing, pilot testing, pretesting, and question revision or elimination. Some already have been included in other publications from the study, but many have not; therefore, there currently exists little *empirical* evidence of their validity and reliability. On the other hand, the fact that virtually all results presented in this volume are based on individual items, rather than indexes or abstract concepts, should make it easy for the reader to judge the degree to which each item has "face validity" and also the degree to which there is some evidence of construct validity in the bivariate results.

Accuracy of the Sample. A sample survey never can provide the same level of accuracy as would be obtained if the entire target population were to participate in the survey — in the case of the present study, about three million seniors per year. But perfect accuracy of this sort would be extremely expensive and certainly not worthwhile considering the fact that a high level of accuracy can be provided by a carefully designed probability sample. The accuracy of the sample in this study is affected both by the size of the student sample and by the number of schools in which they are clustered. Appendix B presents a discussion of the ways in which this clustering and other aspects of the sampling design are taken into account in computing the precision or accuracy of the samples. For the purposes of this introduction, it is sufficient to note that virtually all estimates based on the total sample have confidence intervals of ±1.5 percentage points or smaller — sometimes considerably smaller.

---

* A more detailed discussion of the evidence for validity of the measures of illicit drug use may be found in Johnston et al. (1977; 1979a), Appendix A. An analysis of inconsistencies in students' reports of monthly versus yearly drug use is provided by Bachman and O'Malley (1981).

This means that, had we been able to invite all schools and all seniors in the 48 coterminous states to participate, the results from such a massive survey would be within an estimated 1.5 percentage points of our present sample findings at least 95 times out of 100. We consider this to be a quite high level of accuracy, and one that permits the detection of fairly small trends from one year to the next.

Consistency and the Measurement of Trends. One other point is worth noting in a discussion of the validity of our findings. The Monitoring the Future project is, by intention, a study designed to be sensitive to changes from one time to another. Accordingly, the measures and procedures have been standardized and applied consistently across each data collection. To the extent that any biases remain because of limits in school and/or student participation, and to the extent that there are distortions (lack of validity) in the responses of some students, it seems very likely that such problems will exist in much the same way from one year to the next. In other words, biases in the survey estimates should tend to be consistent from one year to another, which means that the measurement of *trends* should be affected very little by any such biases.

Caveats to Users of the Data

In attempting to understand and interpret the statistical results contained in this volume, the reader should keep in mind the several considerations discussed below.

Estimation of Sampling Errors. Appendix A provides figures which allow the reader to determine the 95 percent confidence interval around any observed percentage for both the total sample and the several subgroups for which statistics are given. Appendix A also provides tables and guidelines for testing the statistical significance of observed differences between subgroups (e.g., males vs. females) and the significance of year-to-year changes for the entire sample and for the various subgroups on any given variable. Estimates based on subgroups containing relatively few cases (e.g., those who have used heroin) will have substantially larger margins of error than those subgroups with large numbers of cases.

Subgroup Definitions. At the beginning of the Descriptive Results section there is a careful definition of each of the subgroups analyzed in this series of volumes. It is important for the reader to read these definitions so as not to be misled by the necessarily abbreviated descriptions given in the column headings of the data tables. For example, the column labeled "4-year college plans" includes data only for seniors who

expect to be graduated from a four-year college, which is only a subset of all who expect to receive some college training. To take another example, several column headings in the lifetime illicit drug use index use the term "pills"; however, these categories contain people who indicate that they used any of a number of drugs — including some which usually are not taken in pill form (e.g., cocaine and narcotics other than heroin).

Missing Data Notes. Each column of percentages for a given variable adds to 100 percent (with slight variations due to rounding), whether based on the entire sample or any one of the subgroups being described. Missing data were not included in computing these percentages, so it is up to the reader to determine whether an exceptional level of missing data exists on any given question. This can be done by comparing the weighted number of cases on which those percentages were based (given in italics under each percentage distribution) with the total number of weighted cases who took the questionnaire (given at the top of the same column). As would be expected, the missing data rate tends to rise modestly toward the end of each questionnaire. Occasionally there is an exceptional level of nonresponse for some other reason, the most common being that the respondent has been branched around a question or set of questions which are inappropriate for him or her. In this case the percentages are based only on those for whom the question was appropriate *and* who answered. A footnote has been entered to help call attention to the fact that completing a particular question is contingent upon the answer on a prior question. Most such cases are contained in Form 1 of the questionnaire, which has several sets of detailed questions about drug use which are answered only by those respondents who have used a particular class of drug during the past year.

Characterizing Heroin Users. Because this project places a special emphasis on the study of drug use, one set of columns distinguishes respondents according to the extent to which they have been involved with illicit drugs. The five drug use categories are based on an index of seriousness of involvement. The index has Guttman-like properties — that is, anyone classified at a given level is also very likely to have exhibited any drug-using behaviors which are associated with the lower levels in the index.

The most extreme category in the index is defined in terms of the respondent's ever having used heroin during his or her lifetime. However, any interpretations made about heroin users from these data must be tempered with extreme caution, not only because the small number of cases makes estimation in a given year relatively unreliable, but also because heroin users are probably the most selectively represented of all of the subgroups presented here. Heroin users — especially continuing users — are among those most likely to drop out of high school (Johnston, 1973). Therefore, we feel that heroin users are particularly underrepresented in a sample of high school seniors. Furthermore, most of those included in the study report only very occasional heroin use. Frequent users — addicts, if you will — are not well represented in these data.

Given these problems with the representation of heroin users, the readers may wonder why it was decided to present them as a separate category of drug users. There are two reasons for doing so. First, because even occasional heroin use represents such an extreme point on the continuum of drug involvement, it seems preferable that the heroin users not be mixed in with the next highest category of use (the "more pills" category). It remains quite possible, of course, for anyone to *combine* any two or more categories in the drug use continuum (by computing means of percentages weighted by the number of cases in each category); therefore, those wishing to incorporate heroin users with the next category can do so whenever they wish. The second reason for keeping them separate is that we suspect the data based on high school seniors provide some indication of the characteristics which might be found among heavier heroin users who dropped out of school. Some variables in the study are strongly correlated with the drug use continuum, and the present heroin user category provides both an end point for that continuum and an indication of the direction (further out on the continuum) in which heavier heroin users are likely to lie.

In sum, the reporting of separate percentages for heroin users among high school seniors permits greater clarity in analyzing other levels of drug use and provides data which may be suggestive about the larger population of young heroin users. But the particular data are clearly limited and should be interpreted with these cautions in mind.

Interpreting Racial Differences. Data are given for the two largest racial/ethnic subgroups in the population — those who identify themselves as white or Caucasian and those who identify themselves as black or Afro-American. Data are not given for the other ethnic categories (American Indians, Asian Americans, Mexican Americans, Puerto Ricans, or other Latin Americans) since each of these groups comprises less than three percent of the sample in any given year, which means that their small Ns (in combination with their clustered groupings in a limited number of schools) would yield estimates which would be too unreliable. In fact, even blacks — who constitute approximately 12 percent of each year's sample — are represented by only 350 to 425 respondents per year on any single questionnaire form. Further, because our sample is a stratified clustered sam-

ple, it yields less accuracy than would be yielded by a pure random sample of equal size (see Appendix B for details). Therefore, because of the limited number of cases, the margin of sampling error around any statistic describing blacks is larger than for most other subgroups described in this volume.

There exists, however, a quick way to determine the replicability of any finding involving racial comparisons. Since most questions are repeated from year to year, one can readily establish the degree to which a finding is replicated by looking at the results for the same question in prior or subsequent years. Given the relatively small Ns for blacks, the reader is urged to seek such replication before putting much faith in the reliability of any particular racial comparison.

There are factors in addition to unreliability, however, which could be misleading in the interpretation of racial differences. Given the social importance which has been placed on various racial differences reported in the social science literature, we would like to caution the reader to consider the various factors which could account for differences. These factors fall into three categories: differential representation in the sample, differential response tendencies, and the confounding of race with a number of other background and demographic characteristics.

Differential Representation. Census data characterizing American young people in the approximate age range of those in our sample show that somewhat lower proportions of blacks than whites remain in school through the end of twelfth grade (Dearman and Plisko, 1982, p. 23). Therefore, a slightly different segment of the black population than of the white population resides in our target population of high school seniors. Further, our samples appear to underrepresent slightly those black males who, according to census figures, *are* in high school at the twelfth grade level. Identified black males comprise about 6 percent of our sample, whereas census data suggest that they should comprise around 7 percent (U.S. Bureau of the Census, 1978). Therefore, it appears that we are losing more black males from our target population than white males or females of either race. This may be due to generally poorer attendance rates on the part of some black males and/or an unwillingness on the part of some to participate in data collections of this sort.

In sum, a smaller segment of the black population than of the white population of high school age is represented by the data contained here. Insofar as any characteristic is associated with being a school dropout or absentee, it is likely to be somewhat disproportionately underrepresented among blacks in our sample.

Differential Response Tendencies. In examining our full range of variables, we have noted certain racial differences in response tendencies. First, the tendency to state agreement in response to agree-disagree questions is generally somewhat greater among blacks than among whites. For example, blacks tend to agree more with the positively worded items in our index of self-esteem, but they also tend to agree more with the negatively worded items. As it happens, that particular index has an equal number of positively and negatively worded items, so that any overall "agreement bias" should be self-cancelling when the index score is computed. Since all data in this volume are based on single items, however, group differences in agreement bias are likely to affect results on questions employing the agree-disagree format. Fortunately, most of our questions are not of that type.

We have also observed a somewhat greater than average tendency for black respondents to select extreme answer categories on attitudinal scales. For example, even if the same proportion of blacks as whites felt positively (or negatively) about some subject, fewer of the whites are likely to say they feel *very* positively (or *very* negatively). We do not have any ready explanations for these differences in response styles, but what seems important for our present purposes is that, in the process of interpreting racial differences, the reader should be aware that differences in responses to particular questions may be related to these more general tendencies.

A somewhat separate issue in response tendency is a respondent's willingness to answer particular questions. The missing data rate, which can be determined by dividing the number responding to a question by the number taking the questionnaire (given at the top of each page), may reflect willingness to answer particular questions. If a particular question or set of questions has a missing data rate higher than is true for the prior or subsequent questions, then presumably more respondents than usual were unwilling (or perhaps unable) to answer it. We have observed such an exaggerated missing data rate for black males on the set of questions dealing with the respondent's own use of illicit drugs. Clearly a respondent's willingness to be candid on such questions depends on his or her trust of the research process and of the researchers themselves. We interpret the exaggerated missing data rates for black males in these sections as possibly reflecting, at least in part, less trust. The reader is advised to check for exceptional levels of missing data when making comparisons on any variable in which candor is likely to be reduced by lower system trust. One bit of additional evidence related to trust in the research process is that higher proportions of blacks than whites indicated that if they had used marijuana or heroin they would not have been willing to report it in the survey.

Covariance with Other Factors. Some characteristics such as race are highly confounded (correlated) with other variables — variables which may in fact explain some observed racial differences. Put another way, at the aggregate level we might observe a consid-

erable racial difference on some characteristic, but once we control for some background characteristics such as socio-economic level or region of the country — that is, once we compare the black respondents with whites who come from similar backgrounds — there may be no racial difference at all.

Race happens to be correlated with important background and demographic variables much more than some of the other variables dealt with here (like the respondent's sex). When we compare males and females in this sample we know that observed differences between them are not likely to be explained by differences in their family background (such as the socioeconomic level of their families, the region of the country, or the size of the cities in which they grew up) because males and females on the average come from extremely similar backgrounds. A perusal of Section C of Questionnaire Forms 1 through 5, however, will illustrate that on the average the black subgroup in this sample is quite different from the white subgroup in a number of such respects. A higher proportion of blacks live in the South and a higher proportion grew up in families with the father and/or mother absent, and more had mothers who worked while they were growing up. A substantially higher proportion of blacks are Baptists, and blacks tend to attribute more importance to religion in their lives than do whites. Fewer are enrolled in a college-preparatory curriculum (though a higher proportion say they plan to attend some type of college). A slightly higher proportion of black respondents are married and have children, and on the average they are slightly older than the white sample. As was mentioned earlier, black males are more underrepresented in our sample than black females, with the result that each year roughly 58 percent of our black sample is female versus roughly 51 percent of the white sample.

We note these differences in demographic, background, and ascriptive characteristics because, in any attempt to understand *why* a racial difference exists, one would want to be able to examine the role of these covarying characteristics. It is not possible, given the amount of data contained in this volume, to "factor out" the contribution of most of these covarying characteristics when interpreting racial differences. Therefore, while the data here may provide a relatively accurate *description* of racial differences (keeping in mind our earlier cautions about representativeness and response style), they do not by themselves yield a great deal by way of explanation.

However, since the full data sets now reside in an archive, described in the Preface, it is possible for the reader to conduct a more in depth exploration of observed differences—or nondifferences, for that matter. We particularly encourage readers interested in racial comparisons to make further explorations in the data in order to determine the possible role of the other variables discussed here.

Users of the data are also encouraged to contact the principal investigators for information on the most recent analyses of racial differences, some of which are already underway.

Given the long list of caveats about interpreting racial differences, one might ask why we chose to publish the statistics for racial subgroups at all. After considerable deliberation among ourselves as well as with colleagues more knowledgeable in the field of race relations, we concluded that the expected benefits of making these data available (along with this cautionary discussion) outweigh the potential costs of having them misused. Unfortunately, because blacks constitute a relatively small proportion of the American population, they constitute too small a number in most surveys to be characterized separately. Because the sample sizes in the present survey are large in comparison to most, we have at least sufficient numbers of cases to consider publishing data on blacks separately. Further, given the iterative nature of the series, we are also able to provide checks for replication of findings on different samples each year. While there may be some risk that findings will be taken out of context or used carelessly in ways that might tend to increase racial misunderstandings, there is substantially greater risk that valuable information concerning the races (and relative to their well-being) will be lost if it were not included here.

A note on the questions about amphetamine use. Prior to the 1982 survey, we discovered that some respondents' answers to questions on amphetamine use erroneously included use of over-the-counter stay-awake and diet pills, as well as some "look-alike" pills. In the 1982 survey, we introduced some new questions on the use of amphetamines in order to make more clear to the respondents that "look-alike" pills and over-the-counter products should be excluded. We also kept the old version of the questions in two questionnaire forms in the 1982 and 1983 surveys so that it would be possible to "splice" the trend lines resulting from the old and new questions.

As a result of these changes, the reader who uses these volumes to examine trends in amphetamine use must be careful not to make inappropriate comparisons. The response distributions shown in the combined Forms 1 to 5 section (pages 28–29) from 1975 to 1981 contain the responses for Forms 1 through 5. In 1982 and 1983, that section contains two sets of responses. The first set is for Forms 1, 2, and 4 (with Form 1 double-weighted); these provide what we believe to be the best estimates of current amphetamine use and of trends from 1982 on. The second set of responses are based on Forms 3 and 5, the old versions of the questions; thus, these questions provide the best comparisons for looking at trends over time from 1975 to 1983 (although there is reason to be cautious about these trends because of the erroneous inclusion of non-amphetamines, as described above). Beginning with 1984, all forms use the new versions of the questions.

---

* An exended analysis and discussion of black-white differences in response styles may be found in Bachman and O'Malley (1984).

Descriptive Results

Introduction to the Table Format and Conventions

Univariate and selected bivariate percentage distributions are given in this section for all questions asked of this year's senior class. The definitions of column headings and the source of the standard contents for each table are given below under the numbers indicated in Figure 1.

Definitions of Column Headings

(1) **Questionnaire Form.** The form from which all data on the page were derived is given here. When the designation "Forms 1-5" is used, it indicates that responses from students completing all five questionnaires have been combined; accordingly, the numbers of respondents in each column are five times as large for questions contained in a single form only.

(2) **Total Sample.** Univariate percentage distributions based on the total sample of respondents are given in this column.

(3) **Sex.** Percentage distributions are given separately for males (M) and females (F). Respondents with missing data on the question asking the respondent's sex (Question C03) are omitted from both groupings.

(4) **Race.** Percentage distributions are given separately for those describing themselves as "White or Caucasian" (W) and "Black or Afro-American" (B) in answer to Question C04. Comparable columns for the other racial or ethnic groups (Mexican Americans, Asian Americans, American Indians, etc.) are not shown because of the low number of cases in each group. *Note:* See the caveats regarding the interpretation of racial differences in the introduction section of this volume.

(5) **Region.** Percentage distributions are given separately for respondents living in each of four mutually exclusive regions of the country. The regional classifications are based on Census categories and are defined as follows:

Northeast (NE): Census classifications of New England and Middle Atlantic states; includes Maine, New Hampshire, Vermont, Massachusetts, Rhode Island, Connecticut, New York, New Jersey, and Pennsylvania.

North Central (NC): Census classifications of East North Central and West North Central states; includes Ohio, Indiana, Illinois, Michigan, Wisconsin, Minnesota, Iowa, Missouri, North Dakota, South Dakota, Nebraska, and Kansas.

South (S): Census classifications of South Atlantic, East South Central, and West South Central states; includes Delaware, Maryland, District of Columbia, Virginia, West Virginia, North Carolina, South Carolina, Georgia, Florida, Kentucky, Tennessee, Alabama, Mississippi, Arkansas, Louisiana, Oklahoma, and Texas.

West (W): Census classifications of Mountain and Pacific states; includes Montana, Idaho, Wyoming, Colorado, New Mexico, Arizona, Utah, Nevada, Washington, Oregon, and California.

(6) **Four-Year College Plans.** Percentage distributions are given separately for (1) respondents who indicate that they "definitely will" or "probably will" graduate from a four-year college program and (2) those who say that they "definitely won't" or "probably won't" graduate from a four-year college program, based on responses to Question C21d. Respondents not answering question C21d are omitted from both columns. (A number of those who do not expect to complete a four-year college program *do* expect to get some post-secondary education, as may be seen in

the tables for questions C21a and c.)

(7) **Illicit Drug Use: Lifetime.** Percentage distributions are given separately for five mutually exclusive subgroups differentiated by their degree of involvement with illicit drugs. Eligibility for each category is defined below.

None. This column contains data from those respondents who indicated that they had not used marijuana at any time and did not report use of any of the following illicit drugs in their lifetime: LSD, other psychedelics, cocaine, amphetamines, tranquilizers, methaqualone, barbiturates, heroin, or other narcotics.*

Marijuana Only. This column contains data from other respondents who indicated that they had used marijuana (or hashish) but had never used any of the other illicit drugs just listed.

Few Pills. This column contains data from those respondents who indicated having used one or more of the above listed drugs (other than marijuana) but who had not used any one class of them on three or more occasions *and* who had not used heroin at all.

More Pills. This column contains data from respondents who had used any of the above listed drugs (other than marijuana) on three or more occasions but who had never used heroin.

Any Heroin. This column contains data from those respondents who indicated having used heroin on one or more occasions in their lifetime.

(8) **N(Weighted Number of Cases).** This row contains the number of students who turned in questionnaires in each of the categories indicated by the column headings. The number of cases is stated in terms of the weighted number of respondents rather than the actual number, since all percentages in the tables have been calculated using weighted cases. The actual number of respondents generally is about 15 percent higher than the weighted number for data collected in 1975, 1976, and 1977. (A comparison of weighted and unweighted numbers is provided in Tables B-1 and B-2 in Appendix B.) For data collected in 1978 or later, the actual number of respondents is roughly equal to the weighted number. Weighting is used to improve the accuracy of estimates by correcting for unequal probabilities of selection which arise in the multi-stage sampling procedures.

(9) **Percentage of Weighted Total.** This row indicates the percentage of the total number of respondents who fall into the category indicated by each column heading. Unlike all other percentages on the page, which can be summed vertically, these percentages sum horizontally. To the extent that the subcate-

gories in a column (e.g., Males and Females) fail to sum to 100 percent, cases have been eliminated because of missing data on the variable in question (e.g., Sex), or, in the case of Race, because several subcategories have been omitted intentionally.

Table Contents

(10) **Questions and Answers.** Each question along with its accompanying answer alternatives is presented verbatim. The alphanumeric prefix to the question indicates the section of the questionnaire in which it is located and its sequence within that section. So, for example, a prefix of B12c indicates that the item was question 12c in the B Section of the questionnaire.

(11) **Item Reference Number.** This is a unique identification number permanently assigned to each question. Any question may be located in the Question Index of the 1975–1981 volumes by using this number, and in the Question Index of all subsequent volumes by using this number in conjunction with the subject area code.

(12) **Subject Area Code.** Every question has been classified into one or more subject areas; the alphanumeric code indicates the subject area (or areas) applicable to the question shown. The complete listing of subject areas is presented in Table 3 (at the beginning of the Question Index near the end of this volume). Starting with the 1982 volume, the Question Index is ordered first by subject area, and then (within areas) by item reference number.

(13) **Percentage Distribution.** Each column of numbers beside a question gives the percentage of each group (defined by the column heading) who chose each answer alternative, rounded to the nearest tenth of a percent. These figures add vertically to 100 percent (with some rounding error). Nonrespondents to the question are excluded from the percentage calculations.

(14) **Number of Weighted Cases Answering (N).** The number of students in the relevant group (defined by the column heading) who answered the question is given just below the percentage distribution. The number of nonrespondents may be determined by subtracting this weighted number answering from the weighted number taking the questionnaire, shown at the top of the same column. Nonresponse may be due to the subject not answering the question, even though it pertains to him or her, or to the subject skipping inappropriate questions as instructed on a prior item.

---

*Inhalants (including the amyl and butyl nitrites) are not included in this list of illicit drugs because the relevant questions are not contained in all questionnaire forms nor in all years of the study. Similarly, the use of PCP is counted only if it was reported under "other psychedelics" use, because specific questions about PCP are not included in all forms or years. This results in a few apparent inconsistencies in the tables relating the drug use index to specific questions about these drugs.

Figure 1
Guide to Table Format

QUESTIONNAIRE FORM 1-5 1982	TOTAL	SEX		RACE		REGION				4YR COLLEGE PLANS		ILLICIT DRUG USE: LIFETIME				
		M	F	White	Black	NE	NC	S	W	Yes	No	None	Mari-juana Only	Few Pills	More Pills	Any Her-oin
N (Weighted No. of Cases):	18348	8828	8788	13887	2080	4741	5383	5551	2672	9360	7507	6328	4040	2439	4839	210
% of Weighted Total:	100.0	48.1	47.9	75.7	11.3	25.8	29.3	30.3	14.6	51.0	40.9	34.5	22.0	13.3	26.4	1.1

These next questions ask for some background information about yourself.

C01: In what year were you born?

	TOTAL	M	F	White	Black	NE	NC	S	W	Yes	No	None	Mari. Only	Few Pills	More Pills	Any Heroin
1. Before '62	.3	.3	.3	.1	.6	.2	.3	.4	.2	.2	.4	.4	.1	.3	.2	1.1
2. 1962	2.0	2.6	1.4	1.3	3.9	1.5	2.0	2.7	1.5	1.0	2.9	2.0	1.9	2.2	1.4	5.3
3. 1963	23.3	26.6	19.6	21.8	26.1	15.2	27.2	25.6	24.4	19.4	27.1	23.4	23.9	23.4	22.0	25.4
4. 1964	72.8	69.3	76.6	75.6	66.3	80.5	69.5	69.9	72.2	77.3	68.6	72.2	72.2	72.7	75.2	67.9
5. 1965	1.6	1.1	2.1	1.2	3.0	2.5	1.0	1.4	1.6	2.1	1.0	1.8	1.9	1.3	1.2	.2
6. 1966	-	*	*	*	*	*	*	*	-	*	*	.1	-	-	-	-
7. 1967	-	-	-	-	-	-	*	*	-	-	-	*	-	-	-	-
8. After 1967	*	*	*	*	*	-	*	*	-	*	*	*	*	*	*	-
Item 10 Subject R01 N	17899	8816	8787	13882	2079	4572	5306	5428	2593	9324	7466	6259	3986	2408	4718	207

C02: In what month were you born?

	TOTAL	M	F	White	Black	NE	NC	S	W	Yes	No	None	Mari. Only	Few Pills	More Pills	Any Heroin
01. January	8.0	8.0	8.3	7.7	10.0	8.4	8.0	8.4	6.9	8.2	7.9	8.2	7.3	9.1	7.5	11.6
02. February	7.3	7.3	7.5	7.2	7.8	7.4	7.2	7.8	6.6	7.4	7.4	7.4	7.6	7.1	7.2	7.0
03. March	7.8	8.2	7.5	7.8	7.7	8.4	7.6	7.0	8.8	8.0	7.6	7.2	8.3	7.2	8.7	4.3
04. April	7.7	7.7	7.7	7.8	7.3	8.1	7.5	7.4	8.1	7.8	7.7	7.5	7.8	7.7	7.6	12.1
05. May	8.2	8.2	8.1	8.4	7.2	8.6	8.5	7.4	8.9	8.4	8.0	8.3	8.2	7.8	8.6	8.4
06. June	8.2	8.7	7.9	8.6	7.4	7.3	8.9	8.2	8.5	7.9	8.8	7.8	8.0	8.1	9.0	6.1
07. July	9.0	9.1	8.9	9.1	9.2	8.6	9.2	8.9	9.3	9.1	8.8	8.9	9.1	9.2	8.7	13.4
08. August	9.1	9.5	8.6	9.1	9.1	9.3	8.9	9.4	8.9	8.9	9.5	9.7	9.4	8.9	8.5	8.4
09. September	9.2	8.7	9.8	9.2	10.0	9.3	9.2	9.5	8.3	8.9	9.5	9.5	8.4	9.8	9.4	4.9
10. October	8.9	8.6	9.0	8.9	8.0	8.6	8.8	9.6	8.5	9.0	8.8	9.2	9.0	9.0	8.5	7.4
11. November	8.1	8.0	7.9	8.2	7.3	7.8	8.0	8.4	8.2	8.0	8.4	8.0	8.2	8.4	8.2	5.4
12. December	8.3	8.0	8.7	8.0	8.8	8.1	8.3	8.0	9.0	8.6	7.8	8.4	8.5	7.8	8.1	11.0
Item 20 Subject R01 N	17871	8802	8779	13863	2079	4566	5294	5420	2591	9312	7455	6253	3986	2398	4706	207

C03: What is your sex?

	TOTAL	M	F	White	Black	NE	NC	S	W	Yes	No	None	Mari. Only	Few Pills	More Pills	Any Heroin
1. Male	50.1	100.0	-	50.9	43.2	49.8	50.6	50.0	49.9	50.0	48.7	47.8	55.3	48.7	48.7	62.6
2. Female	49.9	-	100.0	49.1	56.8	50.2	49.4	50.0	50.1	50.0	51.3	52.2	44.7	51.3	51.3	37.4
Item 30 Subject R01 N	17616	8828	8788	13676	2047	4511	5214	5339	2552	9216	7324	6177	3913	2370	4650	202

C04: How do you describe yourself?

	TOTAL	M	F	White	Black	NE	NC	S	W	Yes	No	None	Mari. Only	Few Pills	More Pills	Any Heroin
1. American Indian	1.4	1.5	1.2	-	-	.8	1.2	1.6	2.4	.6	2.2	.8	1.5	1.4	1.7	3.2
2. Black or Afro-American	11.7	10.1	13.3	-	100.0	10.2	5.1	21.9	6.3	11.3	10.5	13.7	16.1	11.4	4.3	13.1
3. Mexican American or Chicano	2.2	2.3	2.1	-	-	.2	1.0	.9	10.9	1.7	2.4	2.2	2.1	2.4	1.9	2.5
4. Puerto Rican or other Latin American	1.9	1.8	2.0	-	-	4.1	.5	1.4	1.6	2.1	1.3	2.2	2.0	1.3	1.6	1.5
5. Oriental or Asian American	1.8	1.9	1.7	-	-	2.4	1.3	.3	5.1	3.0	.4	3.4	1.0	.8	.8	1.6
6. White or Caucasian	78.1	79.4	76.9	100.0	-	78.9	87.7	72.4	69.3	78.7	80.0	74.7	74.3	79.8	87.3	68.5
7. Other	2.9	3.1	2.7	-	-	3.4	3.3	1.5	4.4	2.6	3.1	3.0	3.0	2.9	2.4	9.6
Item 40 Subject R01 N	17775	8763	8729	13887	2080	4534	5272	5406	2562	9286	7412	6215	3961	2392	4688	203

C05: Where did you grow up mostly?

	TOTAL	M	F	White	Black	NE	NC	S	W	Yes	No	None	Mari. Only	Few Pills	More Pills	Any Heroin
1. On a farm	7.9	8.3	7.4	8.9	4.0	2.7	9.7	11.7	5.2	5.3	11.3	10.1	6.7	7.2	6.1	4.1
2. In the country, not on a farm		15.4	13.7	14.8	17.0	12.3	13.1	19.5	11.5	11.1	19.2	16.0	14.2	14.6	12.8	14.0
3. In a small ci...					20.8	34.5	31.4	26.4	24.4	29.0	31.0	30.3	28.4	29.4	30.2	30.1

QUESTIONNAIRE FORM 1-5 1984	TOTAL	SEX		RACE		REGION				4YR COLLEGE PLANS		ILLICIT DRUG USE: LIFETIME				
		M	F	White	Black	NE	NC	S	W	Yes	No	None	Mari-juana Only	Few Pills	More Pills	Any Her-oin
N (Weighted No. of Cases):	16499	7800	8029	12337	2244	3387	4612	5568	2932	9103	6124	6199	3529	2196	3936	207
% of Weighted Total:	100.0	47.3	48.7	74.8	13.6	20.5	28.0	33.7	17.8	55.2	37.1	37.6	21.4	13.3	23.9	1.3

These next questions ask for some background information about yourself.

C01: In what year were you born?

1. Before '64	0.4	0.4	0.3	0.1	1.0	0.3	0.2	0.5	0.3	0.2	0.5	0.3	0.3	0.4	0.3	1.9
2. 1964	2.2	2.8	1.5	1.5	4.1	1.9	1.8	2.8	1.8	1.3	3.2	2.3	2.2	1.8	1.7	3.1
3. 1965	22.6	26.1	18.9	22.1	22.8	17.1	27.1	23.1	20.8	18.9	27.4	22.1	22.7	21.9	23.0	28.5
4. 1966	73.1	69.4	77.1	75.0	68.8	77.5	69.9	72.0	75.3	77.3	68.0	73.4	73.1	74.6	73.2	64.9
5. 1967	1.7	1.3	2.1	1.2	3.2	3.0	0.9	1.4	1.8	2.2	0.9	1.8	1.7	1.2	1.7	1.2
6. 1968	*	*	0.1	*	0.1	0.1	*	*	*	0.1	*	0.1	*	0.1	-	0.5
7. 1969	*	*	*	*	0.1	*	*	0.1	-	*	-	0.1	-	-	*	-
8. After 1969	*	*	*	-	0.1	*	*	*	*	*	*	-	-	0.1	*	-
Item 10 Subject R01 N	16127	7788	8028	12323	2242	3264	4559	5420	2884	9062	6088	6145	3484	2169	3831	203

C02: In what month were you born?

01. January	8.0	8.1	7.9	7.8	9.0	7.2	8.2	8.3	7.9	7.7	8.3	8.3	7.6	7.0	8.4	7.8
02. February	7.3	7.5	7.2	7.2	7.7	7.1	7.5	7.2	7.4	7.4	7.2	7.4	7.0	7.6	7.2	4.2
03. March	8.6	8.1	9.1	8.6	9.0	8.9	8.1	8.7	8.6	8.8	8.3	8.5	8.5	8.5	8.6	9.9
04. April	8.2	7.8	8.5	8.3	7.2	7.7	8.7	7.8	8.4	8.4	7.8	8.4	8.1	7.6	8.3	9.6
05. May	7.8	7.9	7.8	7.9	7.0	8.4	7.5	7.4	8.5	7.7	7.8	8.0	7.8	7.7	7.8	7.1
06. June	8.3	8.4	8.5	8.6	7.7	8.4	8.8	7.4	9.1	8.5	8.0	8.2	7.8	8.8	8.2	14.7
07. July	9.3	9.8	8.5	9.3	8.6	9.2	9.5	9.0	9.4	9.0	9.6	8.9	10.2	8.0	9.5	10.2
08. August	9.0	8.9	8.9	9.0	9.7	9.1	8.5	9.5	8.8	8.5	9.9	9.2	8.6	8.9	9.3	4.6
09. September	9.1	9.9	8.8	9.2	9.0	9.5	9.3	8.9	9.0	9.4	8.8	9.0	9.5	10.6	8.2	10.6
10. October	8.1	7.4	8.5	7.9	8.4	7.8	7.8	8.8	7.5	8.1	7.9	7.9	8.3	8.7	7.8	7.7
11. November	8.3	8.4	8.1	8.2	8.3	8.6	8.3	8.3	8.2	8.5	8.2	8.2	8.7	8.1	8.6	6.1
12. December	8.0	8.0	8.3	8.0	8.4	8.2	7.8	8.6	7.2	8.0	8.2	8.0	7.9	8.2	8.0	7.4
Item 20 Subject R01 N	16105	7778	8027	12311	2241	3262	4551	5413	2880	9054	6078	6137	3480	2167	3825	204

C03: What is your sex?

1. Male	49.3	100.0	-	49.9	43.2	50.0	49.3	46.8	53.0	48.1	49.4	46.6	54.2	47.1	48.9	60.5
2. Female	50.7	-	100.0	50.1	56.8	50.0	50.7	53.2	47.0	51.9	50.6	53.4	45.8	52.9	51.1	39.5
Item 30 Subject R01 N	15830	7800	8030	12131	2182	3216	4474	5316	2824	8941	5938	6048	3406	2135	3756	197

C04: How do you describe yourself?

1. American Indian	1.5	1.5	1.6	-	-	0.8	1.7	1.7	1.6	0.7	2.6	1.0	1.6	1.3	2.1	6.0
2. Black or Afro-American	14.0	12.2	15.6	-	100.0	11.5	7.6	24.3	7.7	14.2	12.3	16.1	20.7	12.1	4.3	9.9
3. Mexican American or Chicano	2.1	2.1	2.0	-	-	0.2	1.2	1.6	6.8	1.7	2.5	1.9	2.1	2.7	1.9	6.5
4. Puerto Rican or other Latin American	1.3	1.4	1.2	-	-	3.1	0.4	1.2	0.6	1.2	1.2	1.4	1.1	1.6	1.0	1.9
5. Oriental or Asian American	1.6	2.0	1.3	-	-	1.1	0.9	0.9	4.6	2.4	0.5	2.3	1.3	1.0	1.1	1.3
6. White or Caucasian	77.0	78.2	76.2	100.0	-	79.7	86.3	68.8	74.8	77.8	78.0	74.9	71.3	79.0	87.1	65.0
7. Other	2.4	2.7	2.2	-	-	3.5	2.0	1.4	3.9	2.0	2.9	2.5	1.8	2.4	2.5	9.4
Item 40 Subject R01 N	16014	7741	7972	12337	2244	3238	4540	5376	2860	9010	6053	6106	3461	2146	3810	202

C05: Where did you grow up mostly?

1. On a farm	7.5	8.5	6.5	8.6	3.1	2.2	12.4	8.3	4.4	5.2	11.2	9.7	5.6	5.4	6.7	13.0
2. In the country, not on a farm	13.0	14.4	11.4	13.7	10.9	12.1	14.5	15.1	7.5	9.5	18.0	13.7	12.3	12.7	12.4	12.9
3. In a small city or town (under 50,000 people)	32.5	32.4	32.9	34.6	23.1	38.5	34.4	27.4	32.1	31.5	34.4	32.4	31.7	33.4	33.5	28.9
4. In a medium-sized city (50,000 - 100,000)	16.3	15.2	17.2	15.7	18.8	14.8	13.6	16.8	21.4	17.8	14.0	15.0	17.3	17.2	17.2	13.5
5. In a suburb of a medium-sized city	8.0	7.2	8.8	8.3	6.3	10.9	6.0	8.5	7.1	8.8	6.6	6.6	8.7	8.6	9.3	9.8
6. In a large city (100,000 - 500,000)	8.2	7.9	8.6	5.9	17.6	6.9	5.1	9.7	11.8	9.0	6.7	8.0	9.3	7.8	7.3	8.8
7. In a suburb of a large city	6.3	5.8	6.8	6.7	4.7	6.9	6.8	5.9	5.5	7.9	4.0	6.1	6.6	6.9	6.3	3.3
8. In a very large city (over 500,000)	4.4	4.4	4.3	2.6	12.1	3.2	3.9	4.4	6.5	5.3	2.9	4.7	4.7	4.2	3.6	3.3
9. In a suburb of a very large city	3.8	4.2	3.4	3.9	3.4	4.3	3.3	4.0	3.7	5.0	2.2	3.7	3.9	3.8	3.6	6.5
Item 50 Subject R03 N	14941	7239	7371	11472	2066	3043	4302	4952	2643	8432	5651	5694	3263	2010	3527	175

C06: What is your present marital status?

1. Married	2.2	1.9	2.3	1.8	2.8	1.8	2.0	2.6	1.9	1.5	2.9	2.5	1.9	1.8	1.9	4.2
2. Engaged	6.2	3.5	8.8	6.1	5.3	5.8	6.2	7.1	5.0	3.2	10.7	4.4	5.7	6.4	8.9	12.0
3. Separated/divorced	0.7	0.8	0.6	0.4	2.0	0.6	0.5	0.7	1.0	0.5	0.9	0.6	0.7	0.7	0.5	4.1
4. Single	90.9	93.8	88.3	91.7	90.0	91.8	91.3	89.5	92.0	94.8	85.6	92.4	91.6	91.0	88.7	79.7
Item 60 Subject D01,R01 N	16096	7742	7998	12286	2226	3261	4555	5405	2875	9068	6083	6118	3482	2163	3839	201

*=less than .05 per cent.

QUESTIONNAIRE FORM 1-5 1984	TOTAL	SEX		RACE		REGION				4YR COLLEGE PLANS		ILLICIT DRUG USE: LIFETIME				
		M	F	White	Black	NE	NC	S	W	Yes	No	None	Mari-juana Only	Few Pills	More Pills	Any Her-oin
N (Weighted No. of Cases):	16499	7800	8029	12337	2244	3387	4612	5568	2932	9103	6124	6199	3529	2196	3936	207
% of Weighted Total:	100.0	47.3	48.7	74.8	13.6	20.5	28.0	33.7	17.8	55.2	37.1	37.6	21.4	13.3	23.9	1.3

C07: How many brothers and sisters do you have? (Include step brothers and sisters and half-brothers and sisters.)

C07A: Older brothers and sisters

0. None	26.1	26.4	26.0	27.3	21.2	25.2	24.4	26.9	28.1	29.7	21.8	29.5	24.1	27.1	22.3	24.7
1. One	26.3	26.9	25.8	27.6	21.3	25.4	26.3	26.5	27.1	26.7	25.9	25.8	27.0	25.7	26.8	19.9
2. Two	17.6	17.1	18.0	17.8	15.8	19.4	17.8	17.0	16.4	16.6	18.9	15.9	18.3	18.9	19.4	13.8
3. Three	11.5	11.7	11.2	11.5	11.7	12.2	12.3	10.8	10.6	10.6	12.6	10.6	11.8	11.1	12.6	13.7
4. Four	6.9	6.8	7.0	6.6	8.1	6.3	7.3	7.1	6.4	6.3	7.4	7.1	6.1	6.3	7.4	8.4
5. Five	4.2	4.4	4.2	3.6	7.2	4.3	4.5	4.3	3.5	4.1	4.2	4.5	4.5	3.4	3.9	5.7
6. Six or more	7.4	6.8	7.9	5.6	14.7	7.1	7.3	7.4	7.9	6.0	9.2	6.6	8.1	7.4	7.5	13.8
Item 75 Subject R02 N	15043	7222	7491	11448	2102	3069	4299	5016	2660	8446	5736	5723	3269	2027	3568	194

C07B: Younger brothers and sisters

0. None	29.3	29.6	29.1	30.7	24.9	31.5	28.8	28.8	28.5	29.6	29.3	27.1	30.0	29.6	32.0	32.5
1. One	34.8	35.6	34.0	36.0	30.5	35.3	33.8	35.6	34.4	36.3	32.5	35.5	34.1	35.1	34.7	32.1
2. Two	19.6	19.2	20.1	19.4	19.5	19.0	20.3	19.0	20.1	19.2	20.3	20.1	19.8	20.0	18.3	14.8
3. Three	8.9	8.3	9.4	8.2	11.5	8.2	9.4	9.2	8.1	8.4	9.4	9.3	9.2	8.8	8.0	8.6
4. Four	3.8	3.6	4.0	3.2	5.9	3.2	4.2	3.6	4.4	3.4	4.1	4.3	3.2	3.3	3.9	2.9
5. Five	1.7	1.8	1.6	1.3	3.2	1.3	1.8	1.7	2.0	1.3	2.2	1.7	1.9	1.9	1.5	1.4
6. Six or more	1.9	1.9	1.8	1.3	4.6	1.5	1.7	2.0	2.4	1.6	2.2	1.9	1.8	1.4	1.7	7.7
Item 76 Subject R02 N	14561	6999	7259	11110	1998	2922	4146	4884	2609	8307	5478	5595	3141	1973	3413	184

C07C: Which of the following people live in the same household with you? (Mark ALL that apply.)

A. I live alone	0.7	0.8	0.5	0.5	1.0	0.7	0.5	0.7	1.2	0.5	1.0	0.6	0.7	0.6	0.9	2.6
B. Father (or male guardian)	76.7	77.6	76.4	82.0	50.9	77.0	82.0	73.5	74.1	79.1	74.3	80.5	74.1	74.6	75.8	65.0
C. Mother (or female guardian)	90.8	89.8	92.1	92.4	86.7	92.2	92.5	89.4	89.1	93.0	88.3	92.6	90.7	90.8	89.2	78.6
D. Brother(s) and/or sister(s)	73.2	72.7	74.1	73.9	68.8	77.3	73.9	71.3	71.1	75.0	71.6	76.2	73.3	71.6	69.9	66.6
E. Grandparent(s)	5.0	4.9	5.1	4.1	9.0	6.2	3.4	6.5	3.2	4.9	5.1	5.0	4.9	5.6	4.7	6.7
F. My husband/wife	0.9	0.6	1.2	0.7	1.3	0.6	0.8	1.4	0.6	0.3	1.7	0.9	0.8	0.7	1.0	3.3
G. My children	1.2	0.3	2.1	0.7	4.0	1.0	1.2	1.7	0.5	0.6	2.0	1.0	1.4	1.1	1.1	3.8
H. Other relative(s)	4.5	4.1	4.8	3.2	10.0	5.4	3.2	5.1	4.2	4.2	4.7	4.2	4.7	4.4	4.9	4.8
I. Non-relative(s)	2.8	2.4	3.1	2.7	2.2	3.3	2.1	2.1	4.5	2.6	3.1	1.9	2.4	2.8	4.1	9.7
Item 80-160 Subject R03 N	16042	7691	7995	12253	2213	3241	4544	5386	2871	9058	6068	6112	3464	2159	3821	200

The next three questions ask about your parents. If you were raised mostly by foster parents, step-parents, or others, answer for them. For example, if you have both a step-father and a natural father, answer for the one that was most important in raising you.

C08: What is the highest level of schooling your father completed?

1. Completed grade school or less	5.5	5.0	6.0	4.2	8.6	4.3	5.9	6.7	4.2	3.7	8.1	6.2	5.1	5.1	4.9	8.9
2. Some high school	14.5	13.9	14.7	13.5	17.3	14.8	15.6	15.6	10.1	9.2	22.0	13.0	14.1	15.4	16.2	17.6
3. Completed high school	31.0	31.3	30.5	31.4	32.8	33.2	37.4	27.7	24.5	26.1	38.0	30.7	30.3	30.0	32.6	27.9
4. Some college	14.7	15.5	14.2	15.6	12.0	12.5	13.9	14.6	18.7	17.5	10.7	15.2	14.2	15.0	14.3	15.9
5. Completed college	17.4	17.7	17.0	19.2	10.4	18.1	14.5	17.3	21.1	22.7	9.8	17.3	18.2	17.3	17.4	13.7
6. Graduate or professional school after college	11.4	11.8	11.2	12.7	4.9	12.2	8.3	11.2	16.1	16.9	3.7	11.6	11.6	12.2	10.8	10.8
7. Don't know, or does not apply	5.5	4.7	6.2	3.5	14.0	4.9	4.4	6.9	5.2	3.8	7.7	5.9	6.6	5.0	3.8	5.3
Item 310 Subject R02 N	15996	7683	7953	12242	2186	3224	4543	5364	2865	9045	6069	6082	3460	2157	3815	200

C09: What is the highest level of schooling your mother completed?

1. Completed grade school or less	3.1	2.3	3.7	2.1	3.7	3.2	2.9	3.3	2.9	2.1	4.3	3.3	2.6	3.5	2.6	5.7
2. Some high school	13.4	12.1	14.6	11.6	19.9	11.1	13.1	17.4	9.2	9.0	19.9	12.8	13.7	13.6	13.8	12.0
3. Completed high school	40.7	41.9	39.7	42.9	35.6	45.5	47.5	36.7	31.8	35.1	48.8	39.6	40.0	39.5	43.9	39.1
4. Some college	17.1	17.0	17.2	17.6	16.1	13.4	15.1	17.2	24.0	21.2	11.3	16.8	17.4	18.1	16.8	18.8
5. Completed college	15.5	16.6	14.4	16.6	11.4	15.4	13.4	14.6	20.4	20.5	8.2	16.8	15.6	15.6	13.8	9.9
6. Graduate or professional school after college	7.3	7.2	7.5	7.2	8.0	8.5	5.6	7.2	8.9	10.2	3.2	7.2	7.6	7.4	7.0	9.1
7. Don't know, or does not apply	3.0	3.0	2.9	2.1	5.2	2.9	2.4	3.6	2.8	2.0	4.2	3.4	3.1	2.4	2.1	5.3
Item 320 Subject R02 N	16013	7685	7968	12248	2194	3228	4542	5376	2868	9057	6080	6091	3464	2159	3818	200

QUESTIONNAIRE FORM 1-5 1984	TOTAL	SEX		RACE		REGION				4YR COLLEGE PLANS		ILLICIT DRUG USE: LIFETIME				
		M	F	White	Black	NE	NC	S	W	Yes	No	None	Marijuana Only	Few Pills	More Pills	Any Heroin
N (Weighted No. of Cases):	16499	7800	8029	12337	2244	3387	4612	5568	2932	9103	6124	6199	3529	2196	3936	207
% of Weighted Total:	100.0	47.3	48.7	74.8	13.6	20.5	28.0	33.7	17.8	55.2	37.1	37.6	21.4	13.3	23.9	1.3
C10: Did your mother have a paid job (half-time or more) during the time you were growing up?																
1. No	26.8	26.6	27.0	29.1	11.3	27.6	29.2	24.4	26.7	27.4	26.6	30.4	25.0	25.1	24.4	26.5
2. Yes, some of the time when I was growing up	29.5	30.4	28.7	31.7	20.2	31.5	32.2	26.5	28.8	28.9	30.0	29.1	28.9	29.6	30.8	31.7
3. Yes, most of the time	18.0	18.9	17.1	17.4	20.5	18.2	17.5	18.0	18.4	17.4	18.9	16.2	18.5	19.7	19.3	16.9
4. Yes, all or nearly all of the time	25.6	24.2	27.2	21.8	47.9	22.7	21.1	31.0	26.1	26.2	24.6	24.3	27.6	25.7	25.5	25.0
Item 330 Subject R02 N	15983	7674	7951	12227	2186	3218	4531	5367	2867	9062	6075	6079	3467	2155	3812	198
C11: How would you describe your political preference?																
1. Strongly Republican	8.9	11.8	6.1	10.2	2.9	7.5	7.5	10.7	9.1	10.1	7.0	9.7	8.3	8.3	8.1	11.4
2. Mildly Republican	14.9	15.9	13.9	17.4	4.0	12.4	15.0	15.1	17.1	17.5	11.4	16.1	13.8	14.9	14.3	10.1
3. Mildly Democrat	14.3	14.0	14.8	13.7	18.5	13.3	14.3	14.6	14.9	15.2	13.0	14.1	15.6	15.1	13.6	8.8
4. Strongly Democrat	11.3	10.2	12.2	7.2	34.7	9.2	9.2	15.0	10.0	11.6	10.5	11.0	13.6	10.9	9.5	10.3
5. American Independent Party	1.3	1.3	1.2	1.2	1.2	2.6	0.9	1.0	0.9	1.1	1.5	0.8	1.1	1.2	1.8	5.1
6. No preference, independent	21.6	23.4	19.8	23.5	12.0	24.4	25.3	17.9	19.6	20.9	22.8	21.5	19.2	21.8	24.2	21.4
7. Other	1.3	1.8	0.8	1.1	1.3	1.4	1.3	1.0	1.9	1.1	1.6	1.1	1.0	0.8	1.9	8.4
8. Don't know, haven't decided	26.5	21.5	31.2	25.8	25.5	29.2	26.5	24.8	26.5	22.6	32.3	25.6	27.3	27.0	26.5	24.5
Item 340 Subject H01 N	15933	7641	7936	12192	2183	3200	4519	5359	2855	9054	6054	6072	3449	2144	3792	197
C12: How would you describe your political beliefs?																
1. Very conservative	3.4	4.3	2.4	2.9	5.0	2.8	2.2	4.8	3.5	3.3	3.3	4.0	3.1	3.1	2.6	8.1
2. Conservative	13.3	16.1	10.8	13.9	11.6	11.7	12.7	14.5	13.7	14.7	11.1	15.7	12.5	12.2	11.1	7.7
3. Moderate	31.7	31.8	31.7	33.1	28.3	29.8	32.5	33.0	30.3	34.2	28.4	32.9	32.9	31.2	29.8	24.7
4. Liberal	14.6	13.6	15.8	14.0	17.4	14.2	13.4	13.9	18.5	17.0	11.3	11.7	15.8	18.2	16.7	10.4
5. Very liberal	3.1	3.5	2.7	2.9	4.2	3.4	2.7	2.7	4.1	3.6	2.2	2.6	2.5	2.9	4.2	3.3
6. Radical	2.9	4.3	1.3	2.8	2.4	3.5	2.8	2.3	3.1	2.6	3.1	1.7	2.3	2.3	5.1	9.7
8. None of the above, or don't know	31.0	26.3	35.4	30.4	31.2	34.7	33.6	28.8	26.6	24.6	40.5	31.4	30.9	30.1	30.5	36.1
Item 350 Subject H01 N	15897	7625	7917	12159	2179	3199	4513	5340	2846	9044	6055	6051	3448	2140	3783	197
C13: The next three questions are about religion.																
C13A: What is your religious preference?																
01. Baptist	22.6	21.4	23.7	17.3	58.3	10.0	14.8	42.5	11.8	20.2	25.7	24.0	24.4	22.0	18.3	21.4
02. Churches of Christ	5.6	6.1	5.1	5.2	7.2	5.3	5.3	5.1	7.6	4.8	6.8	4.9	5.7	5.9	6.4	4.1
03. Disciples of Christ	0.4	0.3	0.4	0.4	0.2	0.2	0.5	0.3	0.3	0.4	0.3	0.4	0.3	0.2	0.4	-
04. Episcopal	1.8	1.6	2.0	2.1	0.9	2.4	0.8	2.1	2.3	2.3	1.1	1.4	1.9	1.8	2.5	2.0
05. Lutheran	5.8	5.6	6.0	7.2	0.5	3.0	13.0	2.1	4.4	5.6	6.3	5.4	5.7	6.9	6.0	4.8
06. Methodist	8.5	8.0	9.1	9.0	9.5	7.3	9.6	10.9	3.7	8.9	8.2	9.6	8.4	8.3	7.0	5.9
07. Presbyterian	4.0	4.1	3.9	4.7	1.3	4.4	3.5	4.4	3.6	4.7	3.2	4.7	3.4	4.3	3.2	3.5
08. United Church of Christ	0.8	0.8	0.7	0.9	0.7	0.9	1.4	0.5	0.2	0.9	0.8	0.7	0.8	0.8	0.8	1.4
09. Other Protestant	4.1	4.0	4.1	4.6	1.4	5.9	4.8	2.2	4.4	3.9	4.2	4.8	3.0	3.7	4.0	5.3
10. Unitarian	0.1	0.1	0.2	0.2	*	0.2	0.1	0.1	0.1	0.1	0.1	0.1	*	0.3	0.2	-
11. Roman Catholic	27.6	26.9	28.5	29.9	4.9	44.2	29.7	16.4	26.7	30.1	24.0	25.9	29.0	29.0	29.4	22.5
12. Eastern Orthodox	0.3	0.3	0.4	0.4	-	0.8	0.3	0.2	0.1	0.4	0.2	0.4	0.2	0.2	0.4	1.0
13. Jewish	0.9	0.9	0.9	1.1	*	1.8	0.3	0.5	1.5	1.4	0.2	0.5	1.3	0.9	1.2	0.3
16. Latter Day Saints	1.5	1.4	1.6	1.8	0.1	0.1	0.3	0.6	6.7	1.7	1.2	2.2	0.8	1.0	1.1	2.7
14. Other religion	5.7	5.2	6.0	4.6	8.2	4.4	6.2	5.2	7.0	4.9	6.9	6.9	4.4	5.4	4.8	8.7
15. None	10.3	13.2	7.4	10.7	6.9	9.1	9.3	6.9	19.5	9.8	10.8	8.0	10.6	9.3	14.2	16.4
Item 360 Subject G N	15821	7578	7892	12114	2174	3170	4495	5342	2813	9001	6023	6047	3414	2118	3769	198
C13B: How often do you attend religious services?																
1. Never	10.2	12.2	8.3	10.9	5.9	12.0	9.1	7.1	16.0	8.3	12.9	7.8	9.9	8.6	14.9	19.3
2. Rarely	35.8	38.2	33.1	35.6	33.5	39.5	33.7	32.7	40.8	31.8	41.1	26.5	39.6	39.6	45.0	37.4
3. Once or twice a month	16.2	15.8	16.8	15.4	22.7	14.8	16.1	19.2	12.6	17.3	14.4	15.2	17.0	18.3	16.1	15.8
4. About once a week or more	37.7	33.8	41.8	38.1	38.0	33.7	41.1	41.0	30.6	42.5	31.5	50.5	33.5	33.6	24.1	27.4
Item 370 Subject G N	15978	7658	7963	12227	2190	3220	4536	5371	2851	9075	6098	6087	3456	2145	3809	199

*=less than .05 per cent.

QUESTIONNAIRE FORM 1-5 1984	TOTAL	SEX		RACE		REGION				4YR COLLEGE PLANS		ILLICIT DRUG USE: LIFETIME				
		M	F	White	Black	NE	NC	S	W	Yes	No	None	Mari- juana Only	Few Pills	More Pills	Any Her- oin
N (Weighted No. of Cases):	16499	7800	8029	12337	2244	3387	4612	5568	2932	9103	6124	6199	3529	2196	3936	207
% of Weighted Total:	100.0	47.3	48.7	74.8	13.6	20.5	28.0	33.7	17.8	55.2	37.1	37.6	21.4	13.3	23.9	1.3
C13C: How important is religion in your life?																
1. Not important	11.0	14.1	7.9	12.3	3.8	14.0	9.6	6.4	18.4	10.6	11.4	8.3	10.9	9.6	16.0	18.1
2. A little important	26.7	29.8	23.8	28.8	16.8	32.3	27.8	21.9	27.5	24.0	31.1	19.9	28.4	30.1	34.1	33.2
3. Pretty important	32.6	31.0	34.2	32.8	32.5	31.6	35.0	33.6	28.3	33.0	31.6	32.0	34.2	34.3	31.7	21.8
4. Very important	29.7	25.1	34.1	26.1	46.9	22.0	27.6	38.2	25.9	32.3	25.8	39.8	26.4	26.0	18.2	27.0
Item 380 Subject G N	15970	7646	7967	12213	2194	3222	4523	5372	2853	9077	6090	6094	3444	2145	3806	199
C14: When are you most likely to graduate from high school?																
1. By this June	98.2	97.6	98.8	98.7	96.8	98.6	98.3	97.9	98.1	99.0	97.3	98.9	98.2	98.5	97.2	94.7
2. July to January	1.5	2.0	1.0	1.2	3.0	0.9	1.4	1.8	1.7	0.8	2.3	0.9	1.5	1.3	2.6	1.3
3. After next January	-	-	-	-	-	-	-	-	-	-	-	-	-	-	-	-
6. Don't expect to graduate	0.3	0.3	0.2	0.2	0.2	0.5	0.3	0.2	0.2	0.2	0.4	0.2	0.3	0.1	0.3	4.0
Item 390 Subject B01 N	15931	7627	7935	12194	2168	3208	4523	5358	2842	9086	6113	6081	3442	2131	3790	198
C15: Which of the following best describes your present high school program?																
1. Academic or college prep	48.5	46.7	50.9	50.7	43.1	54.3	43.7	48.8	48.8	70.3	17.7	56.7	48.1	47.2	38.7	29.8
2. General	30.1	29.2	30.5	29.3	32.9	23.6	30.6	31.0	34.7	21.1	42.7	24.1	31.5	32.5	36.5	36.4
3. Vocational, technical, or commercial	14.4	17.0	11.6	14.3	14.1	17.8	17.2	12.7	9.3	5.3	27.3	12.1	13.5	13.5	18.7	20.6
4. Other, or don't know	7.1	7.0	7.0	5.8	9.8	4.2	8.5	7.5	7.2	3.3	12.3	7.2	6.9	6.8	6.1	13.3
Item 400 Subject B01 N	15823	7578	7880	12122	2146	3186	4501	5325	2812	9058	6073	6053	3411	2111	3768	195
C16: Compared with others your age throughout the country, how do you rate yourself on school ability?																
1. Far below average	0.6	0.8	0.3	0.5	1.1	0.8	0.6	0.6	0.3	0.3	1.0	0.5	0.5	0.3	0.7	4.1
2. Below average	1.8	2.2	1.3	1.7	1.8	1.8	2.2	1.7	1.4	0.8	3.1	1.5	1.5	1.6	2.5	2.8
3. Slightly below average	5.2	5.9	4.5	4.9	5.9	4.8	6.4	4.9	4.5	3.0	8.6	3.9	5.4	5.1	6.9	8.8
4. Average	36.9	35.3	38.0	34.0	48.1	38.2	36.4	39.0	32.4	26.7	51.5	32.3	38.6	41.0	39.7	41.2
5. Slightly above average	24.0	23.1	25.0	24.8	21.9	24.4	23.6	23.8	24.4	25.8	21.5	23.0	24.8	24.1	25.1	17.6
6. Above average	25.7	25.7	26.1	27.9	18.0	24.1	26.1	24.7	28.9	35.0	12.6	31.1	24.1	23.0	21.2	20.7
7. Far above average	5.7	7.0	4.7	6.2	3.3	5.9	4.7	5.2	8.2	8.5	1.7	7.7	5.1	4.8	4.0	4.7
Item 410 Subject B01 N	15601	7481	7764	11977	2099	3141	4444	5226	2791	8980	5985	5990	3370	2079	3701	190
C17: How intelligent do you think you are compared with others your age?																
1. Far below average	0.4	0.6	0.3	0.3	0.9	0.4	0.5	0.6	0.1	0.2	0.8	0.4	0.5	0.1	0.3	2.1
2. Below average	1.3	1.4	1.2	1.2	1.1	1.4	1.8	0.9	1.0	0.5	2.2	1.1	1.2	1.2	1.5	3.2
3. Slightly below average	4.1	3.9	4.1	3.9	3.3	3.8	4.7	3.9	3.5	2.0	7.0	3.3	4.1	4.4	4.7	4.7
4. Average	35.2	32.0	38.0	34.0	39.4	34.4	36.5	37.8	29.3	24.8	50.5	31.7	36.2	39.4	37.3	41.2
5. Slightly above average	24.1	22.9	25.2	24.4	23.8	25.3	23.3	23.7	24.6	26.0	21.4	23.5	24.1	24.2	25.2	20.0
6. Above average	27.8	30.2	25.9	29.3	23.1	27.8	27.8	25.8	31.7	36.8	14.9	31.6	27.7	24.6	24.6	19.4
7. Far above average	7.1	9.0	5.4	6.9	8.4	6.9	5.4	7.3	9.7	9.7	3.2	8.3	6.2	6.4	6.3	9.3
Item 420 Subject B01 N	15612	7461	7798	11977	2105	3137	4451	5234	2791	9002	5996	5985	3369	2091	3709	186
C18: During the LAST FOUR WEEKS, how many whole days of school have you missed . . .																
C18A: Because of illness																
1. None	57.4	64.1	51.0	57.9	57.9	51.5	59.3	60.0	56.2	60.5	53.8	64.7	57.4	54.3	48.3	45.1
2. 1 day	17.8	15.9	19.6	18.3	14.5	19.2	17.7	17.4	17.2	17.8	17.8	16.2	17.7	19.7	19.4	16.5
3. 2 days	10.6	8.8	12.5	10.5	10.7	12.8	10.1	9.7	11.0	9.8	11.8	8.8	11.0	10.9	13.3	14.3
4. 3 days	6.0	4.9	7.1	5.8	6.9	7.1	5.6	5.4	6.6	5.2	7.0	4.6	6.0	6.2	8.5	2.9
5. 4-5 days	5.1	4.1	6.1	4.8	6.0	5.9	4.6	4.5	6.1	4.3	6.1	3.5	5.3	4.9	7.0	10.0
6. 6-10 days	1.9	1.5	2.5	1.8	2.2	2.2	1.8	1.9	1.8	1.6	2.3	1.5	1.7	2.8	2.1	5.8
7. 11 or more	1.1	0.9	1.2	0.8	1.7	1.3	0.9	1.0	1.1	0.8	1.3	0.7	0.9	1.3	1.4	5.4
Item 430 Subject B06 N	15411	7360	7703	11825	2073	3067	4406	5181	2758	8889	5943	5918	3312	2071	3660	186

QUESTIONNAIRE FORM 1-5 1984	TOTAL	SEX		RACE		REGION				4YR COLLEGE PLANS		ILLICIT DRUG USE: LIFETIME				
		M	F	White	Black	NE	NC	S	W	Yes	No	None	Mari- juana Only	Few Pills	More Pills	Any Her- oin
N (Weighted No. of Cases):	16499	7800	8029	12337	2244	3387	4612	5568	2932	9103	6124	6199	3529	2196	3936	207
% of Weighted Total:	100.0	47.3	48.7	74.8	13.6	20.5	28.0	33.7	17.8	55.2	37.1	37.6	21.4	13.3	23.9	1.3

C18B: Because you skipped or "cut"

1. None	73.6	72.2	75.0	73.1	78.8	71.5	77.5	76.5	64.3	76.9	69.1	86.3	74.4	69.1	56.6	43.8
2. 1 day	12.0	12.4	11.6	12.5	10.1	11.7	11.0	12.2	13.5	11.6	12.8	7.6	12.6	15.1	16.9	10.8
3. 2 days	6.0	6.1	5.7	6.0	5.2	6.8	5.1	5.1	8.0	5.0	7.2	3.0	5.9	7.2	9.6	13.4
4. 3 days	3.5	3.7	3.2	3.5	2.9	3.8	2.9	2.7	5.4	2.8	4.4	1.5	3.3	3.8	6.4	5.1
5. 4-5 days	2.9	3.0	2.7	3.0	1.8	3.4	2.0	2.4	4.7	2.4	3.4	1.1	2.3	3.0	5.8	10.0
6. 6-10 days	1.2	1.4	1.0	1.2	0.6	1.7	0.8	0.6	2.2	0.8	1.7	0.3	0.8	1.2	2.6	6.9
7. 11 or more	0.9	1.1	0.7	0.8	0.7	1.1	0.7	0.6	1.8	0.5	1.4	0.1	0.6	0.8	2.0	10.0
Item 440 Subject B06 N	14988	7179	7482	11553	1992	2989	4311	4999	2689	8664	5803	5734	3229	2022	3580	178

C18C: For other reasons

1. None	58.0	60.6	55.5	57.8	59.3	54.4	60.4	59.3	55.7	57.4	59.3	61.5	57.1	56.5	54.8	46.1
2. 1 day	20.1	18.7	21.6	21.0	17.1	20.4	20.1	20.1	19.9	21.1	18.7	20.1	20.4	21.2	19.5	21.3
3. 2 days	10.4	9.7	11.1	10.5	10.4	11.6	9.3	10.3	11.0	10.4	10.3	9.1	11.1	10.6	11.7	11.5
4. 3 days	5.5	5.2	5.7	5.1	7.1	5.7	4.8	5.6	6.4	5.4	5.6	4.8	5.4	5.1	6.8	6.2
5. 4-5 days	3.7	3.6	3.8	3.6	3.5	5.2	3.2	2.9	4.4	3.7	3.7	3.0	4.0	4.8	3.8	6.9
6. 6-10 days	1.5	1.4	1.6	1.5	1.6	1.9	1.3	1.2	2.0	1.5	1.6	1.1	1.3	1.2	2.3	4.4
7. 11 or more	0.7	0.7	0.7	0.6	1.0	0.8	0.8	0.6	0.7	0.6	0.9	0.3	0.7	0.5	1.2	3.6
Item 450 Subject B06 N	15161	7241	7581	11662	2028	3027	4360	5068	2705	8791	5833	5841	3278	2034	3576	183

C19: During the last four weeks, how often have you gone to school, but skipped a class when you weren't supposed to?

1. Not at all	68.0	65.1	70.8	68.5	69.6	64.0	73.2	76.1	48.7	68.4	67.9	80.5	66.2	61.8	54.2	45.8
2. 1 or 2 times	19.5	20.9	18.1	19.3	19.1	21.1	17.8	15.6	27.8	19.3	19.4	13.5	20.8	25.4	24.3	21.9
3. 3-5 times	7.5	8.3	6.9	7.5	6.9	8.5	6.1	4.8	13.9	7.5	7.5	3.7	8.3	7.8	12.5	15.4
4. 6-10 times	2.9	3.3	2.6	2.9	1.8	3.4	1.6	1.9	6.3	3.0	2.8	1.2	2.8	3.1	5.6	7.8
5. 11-20 times	1.1	1.3	0.9	1.0	1.0	1.4	0.6	0.6	2.3	1.0	1.2	0.3	1.0	1.1	2.1	5.0
6. More than 20 times	1.0	1.2	0.8	0.8	1.5	1.5	0.7	0.9	1.1	0.8	1.2	0.8	0.9	0.9	1.2	4.2
Item 460 Subject B06 N	15787	7547	7879	12113	2137	3167	4491	5308	2821	9075	6115	6052	3403	2111	3749	194

C20: Which of the following best describes your average grade so far in high school?

9. A (93-100)	9.0	7.1	10.8	10.1	4.2	8.5	7.9	9.9	9.4	13.1	3.1	13.7	7.1	6.8	4.7	5.5
8. A- (90-92)	9.6	7.5	11.8	10.8	4.5	9.9	9.1	9.0	11.4	12.9	5.2	12.5	8.4	8.4	7.4	5.7
7. B+ (87-89)	16.5	14.2	19.1	17.5	12.2	16.3	16.2	16.3	17.5	19.2	12.5	18.8	16.3	16.6	13.5	12.9
6. B (83-86)	20.0	19.3	20.8	20.2	19.4	21.7	18.6	19.3	21.7	21.1	18.7	20.8	18.9	20.3	19.8	18.7
5. B- (80-82)	15.2	16.9	13.6	14.8	18.6	16.5	14.8	15.4	14.1	14.4	16.6	12.7	16.6	15.3	18.1	17.2
4. C+ (77-79)	14.3	16.3	12.1	12.3	22.9	13.3	14.3	15.5	12.8	10.8	18.9	10.9	16.3	15.7	15.9	19.0
3. C (73-76)	10.0	11.7	8.0	9.4	11.4	8.6	11.9	9.6	8.9	6.3	15.0	7.1	10.4	11.4	13.0	10.7
2. C- (70-72)	4.2	5.3	2.9	3.8	5.4	4.0	5.5	3.7	3.1	1.9	7.3	2.8	4.7	4.0	5.8	4.2
1. D (69 or below)	1.3	1.6	0.8	1.2	1.4	1.0	1.6	1.2	1.0	0.4	2.6	0.7	1.2	1.3	1.9	6.3
Item 470 Subject B01 N	15723	7508	7852	12066	2127	3153	4481	5288	2801	9059	6079	6034	3386	2103	3725	194

C21: How likely is it that you will do each of the following things after high school?

C21A: Attend a technical or vocational school

1. Definitely won't	45.4	40.2	50.9	46.8	42.0	57.3	42.0	45.3	37.9	59.8	25.7	49.6	46.2	44.5	39.5	35.3
2. Probably won't	27.4	29.6	25.4	27.9	24.8	21.3	27.9	27.7	32.8	27.5	27.6	27.7	25.9	27.6	28.7	24.1
3. Probably will	18.0	20.6	15.0	16.4	22.3	14.0	18.1	18.9	20.5	8.8	30.3	14.6	18.1	18.8	21.6	27.7
4. Definitely will	9.2	9.6	8.8	8.9	10.8	7.3	12.1	8.1	8.8	3.8	16.4	8.0	9.8	9.1	10.2	13.0
Item 480 Subject B09,C03 N	15059	7141	7571	11589	2007	3004	4331	5046	2678	8775	6091	5823	3232	1994	3564	185

C21B: Serve in the armed forces

1. Definitely won't	60.2	43.1	76.8	62.5	49.8	62.5	61.5	56.7	62.0	63.6	56.0	61.7	57.9	60.2	60.6	51.0
2. Probably won't	23.9	32.3	15.8	24.8	18.2	23.6	23.7	24.0	24.3	24.4	23.2	24.2	22.8	25.2	23.7	24.8
3. Probably will	9.2	13.2	5.3	7.0	18.9	8.7	8.1	11.2	7.9	7.0	12.3	7.7	11.7	8.6	9.1	14.3
4. Definitely will	6.8	11.4	2.1	5.7	13.1	5.2	6.8	8.1	5.8	5.0	8.6	6.4	7.6	6.0	6.5	10.0
Item 490 Subject B09,L01 N	14572	6907	7343	11333	1887	2893	4206	4875	2598	8605	5817	5648	3133	1941	3448	164

QUESTIONNAIRE FORM 1-5 1984	TOTAL	SEX		RACE		REGION				4YR COLLEGE PLANS		ILLICIT DRUG USE: LIFETIME				
		M	F	White	Black	NE	NC	S	W	Yes	No	None	Marijuana Only	Few Pills	More Pills	Any Heroin
N (Weighted No. of Cases):	16499	7800	8029	12337	2244	3387	4612	5568	2932	9103	6124	6199	3529	2196	3936	207
% of Weighted Total:	100.0	47.3	48.7	74.8	13.6	20.5	28.0	33.7	17.8	55.2	37.1	37.6	21.4	13.3	23.9	1.3

C21C: Graduate from a two-year college program

	TOTAL	M	F	White	Black	NE	NC	S	W	Yes	No	None	Mari. Only	Few Pills	More Pills	Any Her-oin
1. Definitely won't	38.2	38.2	38.2	39.4	33.8	47.2	38.4	38.2	27.7	43.3	31.8	41.4	38.2	33.4	35.6	38.0
2. Probably won't	27.8	30.2	25.5	29.0	24.2	22.5	31.3	28.6	26.4	27.8	28.5	28.8	26.7	29.1	27.2	23.8
3. Probably will	21.5	20.6	22.3	19.3	29.5	17.2	19.9	22.2	27.7	17.0	27.3	18.5	22.6	23.7	23.8	26.8
4. Definitely will	12.5	10.9	14.1	12.3	12.6	13.1	10.4	11.0	18.2	11.9	12.4	11.3	12.6	13.8	13.4	11.4
Item 500 Subject B09 N	14980	7095	7540	11529	1994	2977	4331	5011	2662	8695	6086	5779	3215	1992	3553	181

C21D: Graduate from college (four-year program)

	TOTAL	M	F	White	Black	NE	NC	S	W	Yes	No	None	Mari. Only	Few Pills	More Pills	Any Her-oin
1. Definitely won't	22.7	22.8	22.4	23.1	18.3	25.7	26.8	21.1	16.1	-	56.6	17.8	21.6	23.5	30.4	36.8
2. Probably won't	17.5	17.8	16.9	17.2	18.5	13.0	19.4	18.3	17.9	-	43.4	15.4	17.8	17.2	20.7	15.2
3. Probably will	21.1	22.4	19.8	20.5	23.4	19.1	19.7	20.9	26.1	35.3	-	20.9	21.6	23.9	19.2	22.5
4. Definitely will	38.7	37.0	40.9	39.2	39.8	42.2	34.2	39.8	39.9	64.7	-	45.8	39.0	35.3	29.7	25.5
Item 510 Subject B09 N	15228	7235	7644	11729	2030	3036	4378	5102	2712	9104	6124	5887	3295	2029	3575	182

C21E: Attend graduate or professional school after college

	TOTAL	M	F	White	Black	NE	NC	S	W	Yes	No	None	Mari. Only	Few Pills	More Pills	Any Her-oin
1. Definitely won't	31.2	31.6	30.6	31.6	26.6	32.8	35.3	30.3	24.4	10.8	60.7	25.8	31.0	31.5	38.7	43.2
2. Probably won't	32.4	33.2	31.5	33.4	30.9	28.5	34.2	32.6	33.7	34.0	30.7	32.1	34.2	34.0	30.9	26.8
3. Probably will	25.4	24.4	26.6	25.4	25.9	27.1	21.7	25.3	29.9	39.0	5.9	28.7	25.0	24.7	21.7	16.2
4. Definitely will	11.0	10.8	11.3	9.6	16.7	11.6	8.8	11.9	12.1	16.2	2.7	13.4	9.7	9.8	8.7	13.8
Item 520 Subject B09 N	14953	7084	7530	11511	1981	2965	4308	5006	2675	8744	6083	5791	3204	1993	3529	181

C22: Suppose you could do just what you'd like and nothing stood in your way. How many of the following things would you WANT to do? (Mark ALL that apply)

	TOTAL	M	F	White	Black	NE	NC	S	W	Yes	No	None	Mari. Only	Few Pills	More Pills	Any Her-oin
A. Attend a technical or vocational school	25.4	29.0	21.6	24.7	26.2	20.6	29.5	24.0	26.7	11.7	45.8	21.6	26.1	25.8	30.2	32.6
B. Serve in the armed forces	16.0	22.2	9.8	13.9	26.4	14.0	15.3	19.8	12.4	13.6	19.6	14.7	18.6	14.7	16.1	22.0
C. Graduate from a two-year college program	24.8	20.7	28.7	24.3	25.4	21.3	24.6	23.3	31.7	17.3	35.8	22.1	24.8	29.6	26.9	22.2
D. Graduate from college (four year program)	63.2	62.5	64.6	63.8	64.2	62.3	59.5	63.7	69.0	90.2	24.8	68.7	63.9	63.7	54.8	49.5
E. Attend graduate or professional school after college	40.9	39.0	43.1	41.0	41.8	41.6	38.0	41.1	44.6	56.9	17.4	44.9	39.6	42.0	36.4	27.8
F. None of the above	8.0	8.2	7.7	8.4	4.8	10.1	8.2	7.7	6.1	2.5	16.4	7.0	7.8	6.2	10.4	15.0
Item 530-580 Subject B09,C03 N	15500	7385	7753	11909	2088	3085	4431	5208	2775	9027	6025	5980	3342	2076	3655	184

C23: On the average over the school year, how many hours per week do you work in a paid or unpaid job?

	TOTAL	M	F	White	Black	NE	NC	S	W	Yes	No	None	Mari. Only	Few Pills	More Pills	Any Her-oin
1. None	25.1	22.9	27.0	20.8	45.8	21.7	24.8	28.6	22.7	25.5	24.1	28.7	25.1	23.0	19.9	22.3
2. 5 or less hours	10.2	10.5	9.9	10.5	9.5	8.3	12.2	9.5	10.4	11.5	8.4	11.6	10.0	11.0	7.8	6.2
3. 6 to 10 hours	9.9	10.0	9.8	10.3	8.2	9.9	11.0	8.2	11.4	10.8	8.6	10.9	10.1	10.1	8.2	8.7
4. 11 to 15 hours	10.4	10.0	10.9	11.6	4.9	12.1	10.6	8.6	11.4	11.6	8.9	10.5	11.2	10.2	9.7	9.1
5. 16 to 20 hours	15.3	14.5	16.4	16.4	10.5	18.4	15.0	13.9	15.1	16.0	14.4	13.7	16.4	16.2	16.9	12.9
6. 21 to 25 hours	11.4	11.5	11.2	12.5	6.9	12.3	10.8	11.1	11.6	10.6	12.3	9.6	10.5	13.4	13.9	11.0
7. 26 to 30 hours	8.2	8.7	7.8	8.5	6.5	8.2	6.8	9.2	8.8	7.1	9.9	6.9	8.1	7.7	10.9	10.5
8. More than 30 hours	9.5	11.9	7.2	9.5	7.8	9.1	8.7	10.8	8.6	6.8	13.4	8.0	8.6	8.3	12.8	19.4
Item 590 Subject C01 N	15511	7388	7764	11931	2076	3077	4441	5209	2783	9019	6043	5979	3341	2077	3661	185

C24: During an average week, how much money do you get from . . .

C24A: A job or other work

	TOTAL	M	F	White	Black	NE	NC	S	W	Yes	No	None	Mari. Only	Few Pills	More Pills	Any Her-oin
1. None	28.7	26.6	30.8	25.4	46.1	23.3	31.2	31.2	26.2	30.0	27.1	33.5	28.3	26.8	22.7	22.0
2. $1-5	3.5	3.2	3.9	3.8	1.8	2.8	5.1	2.7	3.5	3.6	3.5	4.1	3.2	3.6	3.0	2.8
3. $6-10	4.4	4.0	4.6	4.5	3.7	3.8	5.0	3.9	4.8	4.2	4.6	4.6	4.4	4.7	3.6	6.4
4. $11-20	5.4	5.4	5.4	5.7	4.1	4.7	6.9	4.3	5.9	5.8	4.9	6.0	5.0	4.7	5.0	4.7
5. $21-35	8.7	8.3	9.1	9.5	5.9	10.3	10.0	7.0	8.0	9.6	7.4	8.6	9.2	9.0	7.8	12.8
6. $36-50	11.3	11.1	11.6	12.2	7.0	14.6	11.2	9.4	11.2	12.5	9.6	10.3	11.9	12.6	12.3	5.4
7. $51-75	15.8	15.3	16.4	16.9	10.9	18.6	14.1	15.3	16.2	15.8	15.5	14.6	15.9	16.7	17.7	12.1
8. $76-125	16.0	17.6	14.5	16.3	13.5	16.1	12.5	18.1	17.6	13.5	19.5	13.4	15.9	16.4	20.1	17.4
9. $126+	6.2	8.5	3.9	5.8	7.0	5.7	3.9	8.2	6.6	5.0	7.7	5.0	6.2	5.5	7.7	16.5
Item 600 Subject C02 N	14865	7110	7423	11531	1915	2967	4268	4966	2665	8662	5819	5758	3183	1984	3517	176

QUESTIONNAIRE FORM 1-5 1984	TOTAL	SEX		RACE		REGION				4YR COLLEGE PLANS		ILLICIT DRUG USE: LIFETIME				
		M	F	White	Black	NE	NC	S	W	Yes	No	None	Marijuana Only	Few Pills	More Pills	Any Heroin
N (Weighted No. of Cases):	16499	7800	8029	12337	2244	3387	4612	5568	2932	9103	6124	6199	3529	2196	3936	207
% of Weighted Total:	100.0	47.3	48.7	74.8	13.6	20.5	28.0	33.7	17.8	55.2	37.1	37.6	21.4	13.3	23.9	1.3
C24B: Other sources (allowances, etc.)																
1. None	33.8	32.8	34.8	35.9	21.6	38.8	34.8	30.1	33.5	31.5	37.5	34.8	34.5	31.4	32.9	31.6
2. $1-5	17.2	16.1	18.2	18.0	13.3	16.2	20.2	14.8	17.6	17.8	16.1	19.7	16.8	15.5	14.8	8.8
3. $6-10	19.5	18.9	20.1	20.1	17.6	19.8	20.1	18.7	19.5	20.6	17.7	19.1	18.6	21.8	20.0	13.1
4. $11-20	14.9	15.9	14.1	13.7	21.5	14.0	13.2	17.1	14.8	15.7	13.9	13.9	16.4	15.5	14.7	19.2
5. $21-35	7.0	7.7	6.3	6.2	12.1	4.7	6.0	9.1	7.3	7.3	6.6	6.4	6.9	7.5	8.1	5.6
6. $36-50	3.2	3.6	2.8	2.5	5.9	2.4	2.3	4.5	2.9	3.1	3.2	2.6	2.7	3.8	4.0	7.5
7. $51-75	1.6	1.8	1.4	1.3	2.7	1.6	1.2	2.1	1.3	1.5	1.8	1.2	1.7	1.7	2.0	4.0
8. $76-125	1.2	1.3	1.1	1.0	2.4	1.1	1.0	1.4	1.3	1.1	1.5	0.9	0.9	1.5	1.6	2.5
9. $126+	1.6	1.9	1.3	1.3	2.9	1.4	1.1	2.2	1.8	1.4	1.8	1.4	1.5	1.4	2.0	7.8
Item 610 Subject C02 N	14613	6938	7346	11296	1937	2852	4234	4902	2625	8592	5649	5653	3172	1951	3433	174
C25: During a typical week, on how many evenings do you go out for fun and recreation?																
1. Less than one	8.7	7.2	10.1	7.6	12.0	7.5	8.8	8.9	9.4	8.1	9.5	12.8	6.7	6.1	5.1	9.3
2. One	14.3	12.6	15.9	13.4	17.6	12.1	14.0	15.3	15.4	14.5	14.1	19.4	13.1	12.1	9.0	4.9
3. Two	29.9	28.9	31.0	30.3	28.6	28.1	30.7	29.3	31.9	32.3	26.3	32.2	31.9	30.6	24.4	22.2
4. Three	25.9	27.1	24.9	26.7	23.8	25.6	24.8	26.4	27.3	27.0	24.4	21.6	28.5	29.6	28.7	25.1
5. Four or five	14.7	16.2	13.2	15.9	10.1	17.2	15.3	14.0	12.1	13.5	16.3	10.5	13.6	15.9	21.7	19.5
6. Six or seven	6.5	8.1	4.8	6.0	7.9	9.5	6.5	6.1	3.8	4.6	9.4	3.5	6.2	5.7	11.2	19.0
Item 620 Subject C07,M01 N	15496	7379	7758	11931	2065	3074	4438	5214	2769	9017	6029	5983	3332	2068	3660	187
C26: On the average, how often do you go out with a date (or your spouse, if you are married)?																
1. Never	13.7	13.8	13.3	11.9	19.9	14.0	14.0	12.0	15.8	12.9	15.1	20.2	10.9	9.2	7.7	13.9
2. Once a month or less	18.6	19.6	17.5	19.0	17.3	16.9	20.0	18.3	19.1	20.7	15.7	22.0	17.5	17.6	15.5	8.5
3. 2 or 3 times a month	18.7	21.5	16.3	18.6	21.4	17.1	18.8	19.1	19.8	20.3	16.4	18.3	21.0	18.6	18.1	11.4
4. Once a week	16.1	16.6	15.8	16.1	17.4	15.1	15.4	16.7	17.2	16.4	15.4	14.3	18.1	18.5	15.8	18.7
5. 2 or 3 times a week	21.9	20.0	23.9	22.9	16.6	21.9	21.7	23.0	20.2	21.2	22.9	18.8	21.2	24.0	26.3	27.5
6. Over 3 times a week	10.9	8.5	13.2	11.5	7.4	15.0	10.1	10.8	7.9	8.4	14.6	6.4	11.2	12.0	16.6	20.1
Item 630 Subject C07,M01 N	15339	7295	7690	11837	2017	3033	4414	5137	2755	8890	5977	5900	3302	2058	3633	185
C27: During an average week, how much do you usually drive a car, truck, or motorcycle?																
1. Not at all	14.9	9.9	19.5	10.3	35.8	24.0	10.8	13.6	14.0	13.2	17.1	16.4	14.9	13.4	13.0	18.7
2. 1 to 10 miles	12.7	9.6	15.6	11.1	19.8	12.4	13.9	11.0	12.3	12.4	13.1	15.0	11.9	9.8	4.8
3. 11 to 50 miles	30.6	27.3	34.0	31.7	26.7	29.8	33.9	28.2	30.7	33.0	27.4	32.4	31.4	32.2	26.7	24.1
4. 51 to 100 miles	21.1	25.4	17.2	23.4	10.2	16.8	22.7	21.5	22.5	21.8	20.1	19.1	20.8	22.0	24.8	14.0
5. 100 to 200 miles	13.5	17.7	9.5	15.5	4.2	10.1	12.1	16.6	14.0	13.5	13.5	11.9	13.7	13.3	15.7	22.2
6. More than 200 miles	7.1	10.2	4.1	7.9	3.3	5.1	6.6	9.1	6.5	6.1	8.7	5.2	7.3	6.8	10.0	16.2
Item 640 Subject F07 N	15458	7359	7744	11904	2051	3054	4446	5185	2774	8974	6006	5962	3322	2079	3647	187
C28: Within the LAST 12 MONTHS, how many times, if any, have you received a ticket (OR been stopped and warned) for moving violations such as speeding, running a stop light, or improper passing?																
0. None–GO TO Q.C30	73.5	63.5	83.1	70.7	89.2	81.1	72.1	72.7	68.9	73.5	73.2	80.9	72.2	70.7	64.7	59.3
1. Once	16.7	21.2	12.4	18.3	7.9	11.7	17.6	17.3	19.5	17.3	16.0	13.2	17.6	19.3	20.3	15.3
2. Twice	6.0	8.8	3.2	6.7	2.0	4.6	6.3	6.0	6.9	5.9	6.2	3.9	6.2	6.2	8.7	7.7
3. Three times	2.0	3.2	0.8	2.3	0.6	1.3	2.0	2.3	2.2	1.9	2.2	1.0	2.3	2.3	3.0	6.2
4. Four or more times	1.9	3.2	0.5	2.0	0.4	1.3	2.0	1.7	2.5	1.4	2.5	0.9	1.7	1.5	3.3	11.4
Item 650 Subject S02 N	15136	7207	7593	11728	1950	2987	4360	5053	2736	8840	5838	5868	3257	2040	3560	180
C29: How many of these tickets or warnings occurred after you were . . .																
C29A: Drinking alcoholic beverages?																
0. None	83.1	80.7	87.9	82.6	92.5	82.6	78.8	84.9	86.6	85.6	79.3	92.5	85.4	81.5	74.7	58.9
1. One	12.7	14.5	9.3	13.2	5.6	12.1	16.0	11.9	9.8	11.0	15.2	6.2	11.0	15.6	18.7	15.2
2. Two	2.7	3.0	2.1	2.7	1.0	2.7	4.1	1.6	2.5	2.3	3.4	1.0	2.3	2.1	4.1	12.7
3. Three	0.8	1.0	0.3	0.9	-	1.3	0.6	1.0	0.6	0.6	1.2	0.1	0.7	0.6	1.6	3.0
4. Four or more	0.7	0.8	0.5	0.6	0.9	1.2	0.5	0.7	0.5	0.5	1.0	0.1	0.6	0.2	0.9	10.1
Item 660 Subject A07a,S02 N★	3997	2612	1288	3425	216	564	1208	1372	853	2342	1549	1120	909	597	1244	73

★=excludes respondents for whom question was inappropriate.

QUESTIONNAIRE FORM 1-5 1984	TOTAL	SEX		RACE		REGION				4YR COLLEGE PLANS		ILLICIT DRUG USE: LIFETIME				
		M	F	White	Black	NE	NC	S	W	Yes	No	None	Mari- juana Only	Few Pills	More Pills	Any Her- oin
N (Weighted No. of Cases):	16499	7800	8029	12337	2244	3387	4612	5568	2932	9103	6124	6199	3529	2196	3936	207
% of Weighted Total:	100.0	47.3	48.7	74.8	13.6	20.5	28.0	33.7	17.8	55.2	37.1	37.6	21.4	13.3	23.9	1.3
C29B: Smoking marijuana or hashish?																
0. None	94.6	93.8	96.4	94.5	96.7	90.5	94.6	95.8	95.5	96.2	92.4	100.0	98.8	96.8	87.6	56.1
1. One	3.9	4.4	2.7	4.1	2.1	5.1	4.2	3.2	3.6	2.8	5.5	-	0.7	2.8	9.1	25.4
2. Two	0.9	1.1	0.5	0.9	-	2.7	0.5	0.7	0.5	0.7	1.1	-	-	0.3	2.0	11.3
3. Three	0.2	0.3	0.1	0.2	0.5	0.6	0.2	0.2	0.1	0.2	0.3	-	0.2	-	0.6	-
4. Four or more	0.4	0.4	0.4	0.3	0.7	1.0	0.5	0.2	0.3	0.2	0.8	-	0.3	-	0.7	7.2
Item 670 Subject A07a,S02 N★	3914	2552	1273	3363	207	557	1172	1346	839	2302	1509	1108	887	581	1216	73
C29C: Using other illegal drugs?																
0. None	98.0	97.9	98.5	98.2	99.0	95.7	98.0	98.9	98.2	98.7	97.1	100.0	99.5	99.8	95.6	75.2
1. One	1.3	1.4	1.0	1.2	0.3	2.4	1.6	0.5	1.4	0.8	2.2	-	0.2	0.2	3.3	11.4
2. Two	0.3	0.3	0.1	0.3	-	0.8	0.2	0.2	0.2	0.2	0.3	-	-	-	0.7	3.4
3. Three	0.1	0.2	*	0.1	0.2	0.3	-	0.2	0.1	0.1	0.1	-	-	-	0.3	2.1
4. Four or more	0.3	0.2	0.4	0.2	0.5	0.8	0.3	0.2	0.1	0.2	0.3	-	0.3	-	0.2	7.9
Item 680 Subject A07a,S02 N★	3897	2538	1271	3349	206	551	1169	1338	840	2297	1499	1107	885	580	1204	72
C30: We are interested in any accidents which occurred while you were driving a car, truck, or motorcycle. ("Accidents" means a collision involving property damage or personal injury– not bumps or scratches in parking lots.) During the LAST 12 MONTHS, how many ac- cidents have you had while you were driving (whether or not you were responsible)?																
0. None–GO TO Q.C32	77.3	72.2	81.9	74.9	89.3	77.9	77.8	76.4	77.5	76.6	78.1	83.3	77.8	74.3	69.2	65.2
1. One	17.6	20.9	14.6	19.5	8.5	16.7	17.0	18.6	17.6	18.2	16.9	14.0	17.4	20.2	22.2	18.9
2. Two	3.9	5.1	2.7	4.3	1.7	4.1	3.7	3.9	3.9	4.0	3.7	2.1	3.6	4.4	6.3	8.6
3. Three	0.9	1.3	0.5	1.0	0.2	1.1	1.1	0.8	0.8	0.8	1.0	0.5	0.8	0.8	1.7	3.7
4. Four or more	0.3	0.5	0.2	0.4	0.2	0.2	0.4	0.3	0.3	0.3	0.3	0.1	0.3	0.3	0.6	3.6
Item 690 Subject S02 N	14985	7138	7518	11626	1926	2932	4327	5013	2713	8763	5767	5827	3241	2006	3518	177
C31: How many of these accidents occurred after you were . . .																
C31A: Drinking alcoholic beverages?																
0. None	87.8	86.0	90.8	87.3	95.9	87.2	84.4	89.8	89.9	89.2	85.5	96.4	90.0	89.0	79.4	64.6
1. One	10.4	11.7	8.2	11.0	3.1	9.6	14.0	8.7	8.9	9.5	11.9	3.6	8.6	9.5	17.8	15.7
2. Two	1.2	1.6	0.6	1.2	-	2.2	1.0	0.9	1.1	0.7	2.1	*	0.9	1.4	2.1	8.3
3. Three	0.2	0.3	0.1	0.2	0.5	0.2	0.2	0.3	-	0.1	0.3	-	-	-	0.4	1.6
4. Four or more	0.4	0.4	0.3	0.3	0.5	0.8	0.4	0.2	0.1	0.5	0.2	-	0.5	-	0.3	9.8
Item 700 Subject A07a,S02 N★	3396	1985	1351	2910	206	649	960	1183	604	2041	1263	983	716	515	1079	63
C31B: Smoking marijuana or hashish?																
0. None	96.0	94.9	97.7	96.1	97.9	94.4	95.2	97.3	96.2	97.1	94.1	100.0	98.8	98.2	90.6	71.9
1. One	3.2	4.1	1.6	3.2	1.0	3.7	3.9	2.2	3.3	2.4	4.4	-	0.9	1.5	7.6	18.1
2. Two	0.6	0.7	0.4	0.5	-	1.2	0.4	0.5	0.3	0.2	1.1	-	-	0.3	1.4	4.3
3. Three	0.1	0.1	*	*	0.5	-	0.2	-	0.1	*	0.1	-	-	-	0.2	-
4. Four or more	0.2	0.2	0.3	0.2	0.5	0.7	0.3	-	0.1	0.2	0.2	-	0.3	-	0.2	5.7
Item 710 Subject A07a,S02 N★	3327	1933	1337	2856	203	636	935	1167	589	2006	1235	968	704	506	1048	61
C31C: Using other illegal drugs?																
0. None	98.5	98.2	98.8	98.5	98.6	97.5	97.9	99.1	99.2	99.1	97.4	100.0	100.0	99.6	97.5	76.6
1. One	1.0	1.4	0.6	1.2	0.3	1.7	1.4	0.6	0.5	0.5	2.0	-	-	0.1	1.8	15.8
2. Two	0.1	0.1	*	*	-	0.1	0.1	*	-	-	0.1	-	-	-	0.1	0.7
3. Three	0.2	0.1	0.3	0.2	0.5	-	0.4	0.1	0.3	0.2	0.3	-	-	0.3	0.4	-
4. Four or more	0.2	0.2	0.3	0.1	0.5	0.7	0.3	0.1	-	0.2	0.2	-	-	-	0.1	6.8
Item 720 Subject A07a,S02 N★	3318	1919	1341	2848	204	629	939	1162	589	2004	1230	968	706	506	1037	60

*=less than .05 per cent.   ★=excludes respondents for whom question was inappropriate.

QUESTIONNAIRE FORM 1-5 1984	TOTAL	SEX		RACE		REGION				4YR COLLEGE PLANS		ILLICIT DRUG USE: LIFETIME				
		M	F	White	Black	NE	NC	S	W	Yes	No	None	Mari-juana Only	Few Pills	More Pills	Any Heroin
N (Weighted No. of Cases): % of Weighted Total:	16499 100.0	7800 47.3	8029 48.7	12337 74.8	2244 13.6	3387 20.5	4612 28.0	5568 33.7	2932 17.8	9103 55.2	6124 37.1	6199 37.6	3529 21.4	2196 13.3	3936 23.9	207 1.3
C32: If you have not entered military service, and do not expect to enter, GO TO PART D.																
What is, or will be, your branch of service?																
1. Army	25.1	25.2	24.0	24.0	29.5	18.3	26.9	27.9	21.8	23.0	27.2	25.9	24.9	26.8	22.9	14.3
2. Navy	17.2	19.0	12.4	19.8	10.2	21.0	17.7	14.5	19.3	17.2	17.1	17.0	14.2	15.8	21.6	15.1
3. Marine Corps	12.0	14.5	4.5	12.4	9.4	13.5	13.2	10.5	12.1	9.7	13.7	11.3	10.8	14.2	12.7	12.4
4. Air Force	30.5	26.8	41.7	28.9	35.7	28.3	27.9	32.0	33.5	36.2	25.8	29.6	34.9	31.2	27.5	37.4
5. Coast Guard	2.2	2.5	1.5	2.6	1.0	5.6	1.3	1.3	2.7	2.1	2.5	2.3	2.4	1.9	2.4	2.2
6. Uncertain	13.0	12.0	15.9	12.4	14.2	13.3	13.0	13.8	10.6	11.8	13.7	13.9	12.8	10.1	12.9	18.7
Item 730 Subject L01 N★	2677	1923	660	1719	624	453	728	1083	413	1215	1323	917	632	339	666	48
C33: Do you expect to be an officer?																
1. No	15.1	15.2	13.5	14.8	13.6	14.1	20.2	12.1	15.5	9.4	19.6	14.6	12.9	13.6	17.2	14.4
2. Uncertain	43.5	42.7	45.5	44.2	42.9	43.9	48.0	41.6	40.2	31.8	54.8	38.3	45.2	49.3	47.7	33.2
3. Yes	41.4	42.1	41.0	40.9	43.5	42.0	31.8	46.4	44.2	58.7	25.6	47.1	42.0	37.1	35.0	52.4
Item 740 Subject L01 N★	2693	1935	659	1735	627	454	724	1101	414	1224	1332	921	638	336	671	51
C34: Do you expect to have a career in the Armed Forces?																
1. No	24.3	25.1	23.0	25.5	20.7	29.0	25.9	21.4	23.8	26.3	21.4	23.8	24.3	19.8	26.9	21.1
2. Uncertain	48.7	49.2	47.2	52.5	41.1	50.1	52.2	44.6	52.2	49.1	50.5	45.5	48.8	59.0	49.3	41.4
3. Yes	27.0	25.7	29.8	22.0	38.2	20.8	21.9	34.0	24.0	24.6	28.2	30.6	26.8	21.2	23.9	37.5
Item 750 Subject L01 N★	2666	1921	647	1722	614	451	714	1087	413	1212	1320	907	634	331	666	53

★=excludes respondents for whom question was inappropriate.

QUESTIONNAIRE FORM 1-5 1984	TOTAL	SEX M	F	RACE White	Black	REGION NE	NC	S	W	4YR COLLEGE PLANS Yes	No	ILLICIT DRUG USE: LIFETIME None	Marijuana Only	Few Pills	More Pills	Any Heroin
N (Weighted No. of Cases):	16499	7800	8029	12337	2244	3387	4612	5568	2932	9103	6124	6199	3529	2196	3936	207
% of Weighted Total:	100.0	47.3	48.7	74.8	13.6	20.5	28.0	33.7	17.8	55.2	37.1	37.6	21.4	13.3	23.9	1.3

The following questions are about CIGARETTE SMOKING.

B01: Have you ever smoked cigarettes?

1. Never	30.3	32.9	28.5	28.7	40.2	28.1	27.4	31.8	34.7	35.3	23.5	56.1	15.9	18.6	10.3	13.0
2. Once or twice	30.7	32.8	28.7	29.6	36.8	28.0	30.8	31.2	32.9	32.6	28.8	29.9	41.5	34.9	20.8	15.8
3. Occasionally but not regularly	17.0	15.1	18.8	17.9	13.0	15.9	17.9	17.1	16.8	17.2	16.9	8.6	22.5	22.6	22.0	16.7
4. Regularly in the past	6.9	6.4	7.3	7.5	3.4	8.4	7.3	6.0	6.1	5.7	8.2	2.6	7.1	8.1	12.2	19.3
5. Regularly now	15.1	12.7	16.7	16.4	6.6	19.5	16.7	13.9	9.5	9.2	22.5	2.8	13.0	15.9	34.7	35.2
Item 760 Subject A01a N	16132	7654	7925	12187	2165	3292	4528	5432	2880	8986	6003	6087	3482	2180	3890	197

B02: How frequently have you smoked cigarettes during the past 30 days?

1. Not at all - incl. (1) in B01	70.7	74.1	68.1	69.0	82.4	66.5	68.6	71.4	77.1	77.3	62.1	90.6	70.2	66.2	43.8	44.1
2. Less than one cigarette per day	10.6	9.9	11.4	10.9	8.6	9.9	11.0	10.9	10.4	10.8	10.7	5.3	13.2	13.7	14.6	11.9
3. One to five cigarettes per day	6.4	5.0	7.6	6.5	5.3	6.2	7.4	6.4	5.0	5.4	7.6	2.0	7.2	8.5	11.1	11.4
4. About one-half pack per day	5.7	4.5	6.7	6.1	2.9	7.9	5.9	5.2	3.9	3.4	8.5	1.2	5.1	7.0	12.4	10.4
5. About one pack per day	5.1	5.1	4.8	5.8	0.4	7.4	5.5	4.6	2.9	2.3	8.6	0.6	3.6	3.5	14.0	14.1
6. About one and one-half packs per day	1.2	1.1	1.2	1.3	0.2	1.8	1.1	1.2	0.5	0.6	2.0	0.1	0.7	0.9	3.3	4.8
7. Two packs or more per day	0.3	0.4	0.2	0.3	0.2	0.3	0.4	0.3	0.1	0.2	0.5	0.1	0.1	0.2	0.7	3.3
Item 780 Subject A01c N	16110	7637	7916	12165	2167	3286	4524	5419	2881	8978	5985	6083	3468	2175	3890	197

B03: Next we want to ask you about drinking alcoholic beverages, including beer, wine, and liquor.

Have you ever had any beer, wine, or liquor to drink?

1. No	7.2	7.0	7.5	5.5	14.9	4.8	5.8	8.7	9.3	7.6	6.3	16.5	1.2	1.9	0.8	2.5
2. Yes	92.8	93.0	92.5	94.5	85.1	95.2	94.2	91.3	90.7	92.4	93.7	83.5	98.8	98.1	99.2	97.5
Item 790 Subject A01a N	12588	5998	6210	9658	1602	2579	3542	4223	2243	7117	4741	4821	2644	1751	3073	157

B04: On how many occasions have you had alcoholic beverages to drink . . .

B04A: . . . in your lifetime?

1. 0 occasions - incl. (1) in B03	7.4	7.1	7.8	5.6	15.7	4.5	6.0	9.4	9.3	7.7	6.7	16.8	1.3	1.7	1.0	3.2
2. 1-2	7.1	5.6	8.5	5.2	17.8	4.9	6.4	9.4	6.3	7.4	6.6	13.8	4.6	3.8	0.8	2.5
3. 3-5	8.1	6.5	9.6	6.8	14.5	6.6	7.5	9.4	8.4	8.4	7.7	14.0	7.0	6.2	1.2	1.2
4. 6-9	8.4	6.8	9.9	7.8	11.7	7.2	8.8	9.0	7.8	8.9	7.8	12.7	8.4	6.9	2.6	2.6
5. 10-19	12.5	11.0	14.0	12.6	13.2	11.2	12.9	12.5	13.2	13.3	11.6	14.9	13.7	14.5	7.0	3.5
6. 20-39	14.0	12.7	15.6	14.9	10.7	15.1	14.9	12.0	15.2	14.8	13.5	10.9	19.4	17.7	12.6	6.6
7. 40 or more	42.5	50.3	34.5	47.1	16.4	50.4	43.5	38.4	39.8	39.5	46.0	16.8	45.5	49.3	75.0	80.5
Item 810 Subject A01a N	15599	7411	7670	11942	1977	3201	4418	5186	2794	8784	5739	5959	3348	2097	3805	193

B04B: . . . during the last 12 months?

1. 0 occasions - incl. (1) in B03	14.0	12.8	15.3	10.9	29.9	8.7	12.5	17.6	15.8	14.5	13.2	28.4	6.6	6.4	2.5	4.6
2. 1-2	14.1	11.2	17.0	12.0	25.7	12.3	13.6	15.8	13.9	14.2	14.0	22.6	13.0	11.3	3.8	7.0
3. 3-5	12.4	10.3	14.3	11.9	14.6	11.8	12.2	12.7	12.8	13.3	11.1	15.7	13.4	12.9	6.6	5.6
4. 6-9	11.3	10.7	12.1	11.6	9.8	12.2	11.2	10.9	11.1	11.2	11.9	11.4	13.9	12.4	8.6	4.0
5. 10-19	16.5	16.2	16.8	18.0	9.9	17.8	17.6	14.3	17.4	17.1	15.8	11.1	20.3	22.4	18.6	15.4
6. 20-39	13.2	13.7	12.6	14.9	5.1	15.4	14.0	11.4	12.7	13.2	13.3	5.8	14.8	17.5	21.0	15.6
7. 40 or more	18.5	25.1	11.8	20.7	4.9	21.8	18.9	17.2	16.3	16.5	20.6	5.0	18.0	17.2	38.9	47.8
Item 820 Subject A01b N	15529	7380	7630	11914	1947	3187	4389	5159	2794	8741	5718	5890	3351	2094	3803	190

B04C: . . . during the last 30 days?

1. 0 occasions - incl. (1) in B03	32.8	28.6	37.2	27.9	57.9	26.4	29.4	37.9	36.4	34.3	31.0	55.2	26.4	22.1	10.6	13.9
2. 1-2	22.7	20.2	25.3	23.0	22.0	23.0	23.3	21.7	23.3	23.7	21.6	24.0	25.7	26.9	16.5	12.0
3. 3-5	18.5	19.3	17.8	20.6	10.1	19.3	20.0	16.5	18.6	19.3	17.5	12.4	22.2	22.9	22.5	12.0
4. 6-9	12.4	14.5	10.2	13.7	4.8	14.8	13.3	10.5	11.4	12.0	13.0	5.5	13.7	15.3	20.3	13.4
5. 10-19	8.8	10.8	6.8	9.9	3.2	9.9	9.7	8.1	7.5	7.2	10.8	2.0	8.3	8.5	19.1	25.5
6. 20-39	2.8	3.6	2.0	3.0	1.3	3.4	2.7	3.2	1.8	2.3	3.4	0.5	2.3	3.0	6.5	10.8
7. 40 or more	2.0	3.0	0.7	1.9	0.7	3.1	1.6	2.1	1.0	1.3	2.6	0.4	1.5	1.4	4.5	12.3
Item 830 Subject A01c N	15570	7414	7636	11962	1940	3197	4406	5168	2799	8759	5744	5902	3358	2104	3816	192

QUESTIONNAIRE FORM 1-5 1984	TOTAL	SEX		RACE		REGION				4YR COLLEGE PLANS		ILLICIT DRUG USE: LIFETIME				
		M	F	White	Black	NE	NC	S	W	Yes	No	None	Marijuana Only	Few Pills	More Pills	Any Heroin
N (Weighted No. of Cases):	16499	7800	8029	12337	2244	3387	4612	5568	2932	9103	6124	6199	3529	2196	3936	207
% of Weighted Total:	100.0	47.3	48.7	74.8	13.6	20.5	28.0	33.7	17.8	55.2	37.1	37.6	21.4	13.3	23.9	1.3

B05: On the occasions that you drink alcoholic beverages, how often do you drink enough to feel pretty high?

	TOTAL	M	F	White	Black	NE	NC	S	W	Yes	No	None	Marijuana Only	Few Pills	More Pills	Any Heroin
1. On none of the occasions	24.1	20.1	28.2	20.4	44.8	21.4	22.1	28.2	22.7	27.2	19.7	48.7	15.7	15.6	4.8	8.3
2. On few of the occasions	32.1	29.4	34.8	31.8	33.3	31.2	31.4	33.5	31.4	31.3	33.6	30.5	39.0	36.0	26.2	17.9
3. On about half of the occasions	17.1	18.0	16.1	18.6	9.3	18.2	18.6	14.9	17.3	16.8	17.5	9.8	18.7	19.4	24.1	16.3
4. On most of the occasions	17.8	20.6	14.9	19.5	7.0	19.9	18.3	15.1	19.5	17.0	18.3	7.9	17.7	20.3	28.8	27.1
5. On nearly all of the occasions	9.1	12.0	5.9	9.6	5.6	9.4	9.6	8.3	9.2	7.6	10.9	3.1	8.8	8.7	16.1	30.3
Item 840 Subject A01e N★	11862	5672	5811	9237	1415	2508	3379	3904	2071	6653	4539	4061	2662	1752	3098	165

B06: Think back over the LAST TWO WEEKS. How many times have you had five or more drinks in a row? (A "drink" is a glass of wine, a bottle of beer, a shot glass of liquor, or a mixed drink.)

	TOTAL	M	F	White	Black	NE	NC	S	W	Yes	No	None	Marijuana Only	Few Pills	More Pills	Any Heroin
1. None - incl. (1) in B03	61.3	52.5	70.4	57.1	85.2	57.1	55.7	66.5	65.5	65.4	56.5	83.3	58.3	54.3	34.9	28.4
2. Once	12.8	13.7	12.1	14.4	5.9	12.6	15.1	11.0	12.6	12.8	12.7	7.8	15.9	16.7	16.2	6.5
3. Twice	10.1	12.3	7.8	11.2	4.0	10.7	11.3	8.8	9.5	9.0	11.3	4.6	11.7	12.7	15.6	12.3
4. Three to five times	10.8	14.2	7.3	12.1	3.3	12.5	12.7	9.3	8.5	9.2	12.6	3.4	10.5	11.9	21.5	21.8
5. Six to nine times	3.0	4.4	1.5	3.2	0.8	4.0	3.3	2.5	2.6	2.4	3.9	0.4	2.3	2.7	7.1	16.7
6. Ten or more times	2.0	2.9	0.9	2.0	0.8	3.1	1.9	2.0	1.3	1.2	3.0	0.4	1.3	1.6	4.7	14.4
Item 850 Subject A01d N	15448	7295	7647	11869	1940	3179	4380	5111	2778	8736	5661	5894	3337	2076	3758	189

The next major section of this questionnaire deals with various other drugs. There is a lot of talk these days about this subject, but very little accurate information. Therefore, we still have a lot to learn about the actual experiences and attitudes of people your age.

We hope that you can answer all questions; but if you find one which you feel you cannot answer honestly, we would prefer that you leave it blank.

Remember that your answers will be kept strictly confidential: they are never connected with your name or your class.

B07: On how many occasions (if any) have you used marijuana (grass, pot) or hashish (hash, hash oil) . . .

B07A: . . . in your lifetime?

	TOTAL	M	F	White	Black	NE	NC	S	W	Yes	No	None	Marijuana Only	Few Pills	More Pills	Any Heroin
1. 0 occasions	45.1	42.1	48.7	44.3	49.9	36.0	47.7	50.9	40.2	50.3	39.3	100.0	-	27.4	9.6	5.4
2. 1-2	12.3	12.1	12.5	12.0	14.3	10.9	13.0	12.5	12.4	11.9	13.2	-	39.4	15.0	6.2	5.0
3. 3-5	7.6	7.3	7.8	7.6	8.0	7.7	8.1	6.9	7.8	7.5	7.6	-	19.3	11.9	6.8	4.6
4. 6-9	5.4	5.3	5.4	5.6	4.5	6.5	5.2	4.7	5.5	5.7	5.0	-	10.9	10.2	6.3	5.0
5. 10-19	7.3	7.4	7.3	7.4	6.2	8.4	7.0	6.2	8.7	6.8	7.9	-	13.1	12.2	11.3	6.2
6. 20-39	5.7	5.6	5.8	5.9	5.3	7.4	5.1	4.6	6.9	5.1	6.4	-	8.0	8.8	10.5	12.9
7. 40 or more	16.7	20.2	12.5	17.1	11.8	23.2	13.8	14.2	18.5	12.6	20.7	-	9.3	14.5	49.2	61.0
Item 860 Subject A01a N	15905	7560	7826	12091	2102	3240	4491	5329	2845	8912	5910	6199	3505	2147	3834	199

B07B: . . . during the last 12 months?

	TOTAL	M	F	White	Black	NE	NC	S	W	Yes	No	None	Marijuana Only	Few Pills	More Pills	Any Heroin
1. 0 occasions	60.0	56.8	64.0	59.0	65.8	50.4	63.6	64.4	56.8	64.1	55.8	100.0	41.0	47.5	21.3	19.0
2. 1-2	11.2	11.2	11.1	11.4	10.3	11.8	11.6	10.3	11.4	11.5	10.7	-	26.1	17.8	12.1	10.0
3. 3-5	6.8	6.8	6.7	6.9	6.5	7.7	6.1	6.4	7.6	6.7	6.9	-	13.7	11.0	9.4	5.3
4. 6-9	4.6	4.3	4.9	4.8	3.9	6.0	3.9	3.9	5.6	4.1	5.1	-	6.7	6.8	9.0	7.4
5. 10-19	5.4	5.8	5.0	5.7	4.8	7.3	4.5	4.8	6.0	5.0	6.2	-	6.7	7.2	11.9	10.3
6. 20-39	3.7	3.8	3.6	3.7	4.4	5.0	2.9	3.3	4.4	3.1	4.4	-	3.0	4.6	9.5	14.3
7. 40 or more	8.3	11.4	4.7	8.5	4.3	11.7	7.3	6.9	8.3	5.5	10.7	-	2.9	5.1	26.8	33.7
Item 870 Subject A01b N	15818	7518	7797	12055	2082	3215	4469	5306	2829	8871	5888	6199	3459	2134	3806	198

★=excludes respondents for whom question was inappropriate.

QUESTIONNAIRE FORM 1-5 1984	TOTAL	SEX		RACE		REGION				4YR COLLEGE PLANS		ILLICIT DRUG USE: LIFETIME				
		M	F	White	Black	NE	NC	S	W	Yes	No	None	Mari- juana Only	Few Pills	More Pills	Any Her- oin
N (Weighted No. of Cases):	16499	7800	8029	12337	2244	3387	4612	5568	2932	9103	6124	6199	3529	2196	3936	207
% of Weighted Total:	100.0	47.3	48.7	74.8	13.6	20.5	28.0	33.7	17.8	55.2	37.1	37.6	21.4	13.3	23.9	1.3
B07C: ... during the last 30 days?																
1. 0 occasions	74.8	71.8	78.9	74.7	77.2	66.7	77.9	77.6	74.1	79.1	70.8	100.0	71.1	70.6	42.0	32.2
2. 1-2	9.5	9.7	9.1	9.7	9.2	11.1	8.6	8.8	10.5	9.4	9.4	-	18.1	13.8	14.6	13.6
3. 3-5	4.4	4.5	4.3	4.5	4.4	6.2	3.7	3.9	4.7	3.8	5.2	-	5.2	6.3	9.7	7.7
4. 6-9	2.8	2.9	2.6	2.7	2.8	4.4	2.3	2.5	2.2	2.2	3.5	-	2.5	3.7	6.8	7.1
5. 10-19	3.5	4.1	2.7	3.5	3.3	4.2	3.3	3.1	3.7	2.7	4.3	-	1.6	3.2	10.5	10.9
6. 20-39	2.5	3.2	1.6	2.6	1.5	3.9	2.0	2.1	2.2	1.5	3.3	-	0.7	1.6	8.0	11.2
7. 40 or more	2.5	3.8	1.0	2.4	1.6	3.6	2.4	2.0	2.5	1.4	3.6	-	0.8	0.9	8.2	17.4
Item 880 Subject A01c N	15810	7517	7791	12051	2075	3219	4467	5296	2828	8871	5884	6199	3457	2129	3804	197
B08: On how many occasions (if any) have you used LSD ("acid") ...																
B08A: ... in your lifetime?																
1. 0 occasions	92.0	90.4	94.1	91.2	98.9	89.1	92.0	94.0	91.3	94.4	89.8	100.0	100.0	95.1	72.9	33.1
2. 1-2	3.8	4.3	3.1	4.2	0.8	4.6	3.5	2.9	4.7	3.0	4.4	-	-	4.9	11.8	19.1
3. 3-5	1.9	2.2	1.4	2.0	0.2	2.6	1.9	1.3	2.0	1.1	2.6	-	-	-	7.0	13.5
4. 6-9	0.9	1.1	0.6	1.0	-	1.5	0.8	0.6	0.8	0.5	1.3	-	-	-	3.3	8.8
5. 10-19	0.7	1.0	0.5	0.8	0.1	0.9	0.9	0.6	0.4	0.5	1.0	-	-	-	2.6	7.9
6. 20-39	0.4	0.5	0.2	0.4	*	0.6	0.3	0.3	0.4	0.3	0.4	-	-	-	1.4	5.8
7. 40 or more	0.4	0.5	0.1	0.4	0.1	0.6	0.5	0.2	0.3	0.2	0.5	-	-	-	1.1	11.7
Item 890 Subject A01a N	16096	7653	7929	12195	2174	3269	4542	5413	2872	8994	6028	6167	3509	2174	3884	200
B08B: ... during the last 12 months?																
1. 0 occasions	95.3	94.2	96.9	94.9	99.5	93.0	95.6	96.5	95.5	96.9	93.9	100.0	100.0	98.6	83.6	58.6
2. 1-2	3.0	3.5	2.3	3.3	0.3	4.3	2.7	2.3	3.1	2.0	4.0	-	-	1.4	10.6	18.2
3. 3-5	0.8	1.1	0.5	1.0	0.1	1.3	0.8	0.6	0.8	0.6	1.1	-	-	-	3.2	6.7
4. 6-9	0.4	0.5	0.2	0.4	-	0.7	0.3	0.3	0.5	0.3	0.5	-	-	-	1.5	3.3
5. 10-19	0.3	0.5	0.1	0.3	0.1	0.5	0.4	0.2	0.1	0.2	0.4	-	-	-	0.8	7.5
6. 20-39	0.1	0.1	*	0.1	-	0.1	0.1	0.1	*	0.1	0.1	-	-	-	0.2	3.4
7. 40 or more	0.1	0.1	-	0.1	-	0.1	0.1	*	*	*	0.1	-	-	-	0.2	2.3
Item 900 Subject A01b N	16076	7646	7925	12179	2177	3263	4534	5408	2871	8993	6024	6168	3510	2172	3863	200
B08C: ... during the last 30 days?																
1. 0 occasions	98.5	97.8	99.3	98.4	99.8	97.4	98.6	98.7	99.1	99.0	98.0	100.0	100.0	99.4	95.2	76.9
2. 1-2	1.1	1.5	0.7	1.3	0.1	1.8	1.0	1.0	0.8	0.7	1.5	-	-	0.6	3.9	10.0
3. 3-5	0.2	0.3	-	0.2	-	0.4	0.2	0.2	*	0.1	0.3	-	-	-	0.6	4.4
4. 6-9	0.1	0.2	*	0.1	0.1	0.1	0.2	0.1	*	0.1	0.1	-	-	-	0.1	6.8
5. 10-19	*	*	*	*	-	0.1	-	-	*	*	*	-	-	-	*	0.9
6. 20-39	*	*	-	-	-	0.1	-	-	-	*	*	-	-	-	*	0.5
7. 40 or more	*	0.1	-	*	-	0.1	*	*	*	-	0.1	-	-	-	0.1	0.5
Item 910 Subject A01c N	16074	7646	7924	12181	2176	3264	4533	5408	2869	8994	6023	6168	3509	2172	3863	201
B09: On how many occasions (if any) have you used psychedelics other than LSD (like mesca- line, peyote, psilocybin, PCP) ...																
B09A: ... in your lifetime?																
1. 0 occasions	93.4	92.3	94.9	92.8	98.9	87.1	94.5	96.5	92.9	94.9	92.1	100.0	100.0	95.8	77.8	44.5
2. 1-2	2.9	3.2	2.5	3.2	0.7	4.9	2.6	1.8	3.3	2.4	3.5	-	-	4.2	8.9	16.4
3. 3-5	1.2	1.3	1.0	1.3	0.1	2.4	0.8	0.6	1.6	1.0	1.2	-	-	-	4.5	8.2
4. 6-9	0.8	1.0	0.6	0.8	0.2	1.9	0.5	0.2	0.9	0.7	0.8	-	-	-	2.9	5.5
5. 10-19	0.7	0.9	0.5	0.8	0.2	1.5	0.5	0.3	0.8	0.5	0.9	-	-	-	2.7	5.6
6. 20-39	0.5	0.7	0.2	0.5	-	1.1	0.4	0.3	0.3	0.2	0.7	-	-	-	1.6	7.5
7. 40 or more	0.5	0.7	0.3	0.5	-	1.3	0.5	0.3	0.3	0.3	0.8	-	-	-	1.6	12.2
Item 920 Subject A01a N	16054	7637	7911	12176	2160	3261	4523	5396	2874	8982	6016	6159	3498	2166	3871	200
B09B: ... during the last 12 months?																
1. 0 occasions	96.2	95.2	97.3	95.7	99.3	91.6	97.1	98.5	95.5	97.0	95.5	100.0	100.0	98.6	86.6	64.7
2. 1-2	2.1	2.4	1.7	2.4	0.4	4.2	1.5	0.8	2.9	1.8	2.3	-	-	1.4	7.2	12.0
3. 3-5	0.7	0.9	0.5	0.8	0.1	1.6	0.5	0.2	1.0	0.6	0.7	-	-	-	2.6	6.0
4. 6-9	0.5	0.7	0.3	0.5	0.1	1.3	0.5	0.2	0.3	0.3	0.7	-	-	-	1.7	9.2
5. 10-19	0.3	0.4	0.2	0.3	0.1	0.7	0.3	0.1	0.2	0.2	0.4	-	-	-	1.1	2.8
6. 20-39	0.1	0.2	0.1	0.1	-	0.3	0.1	0.1	0.1	0.1	0.1	-	-	-	0.4	3.7
7. 40 or more	0.1	0.2	*	0.1	-	0.3	*	0.1	*	*	0.2	-	-	-	0.3	1.6
Item 930 Subject A01b N	16036	7630	7907	12165	2162	3255	4516	5390	2874	8978	6009	6159	3499	2166	3853	198

*=less than .05 per cent.

QUESTIONNAIRE FORM 1-5 1984	TOTAL	SEX		RACE		REGION				4YR COLLEGE PLANS		ILLICIT DRUG USE: LIFETIME				
		M	F	White	Black	NE	NC	S	W	Yes	No	None	Mari- juana Only	Few Pills	More Pills	Any Her- oin
N (Weighted No. of Cases):	16499	7800	8029	12337	2244	3387	4612	5568	2932	9103	6124	6199	3529	2196	3936	207
% of Weighted Total:	100.0	47.3	48.7	74.8	13.6	20.5	28.0	33.7	17.8	55.2	37.1	37.6	21.4	13.3	23.9	1.3
B09C: . . . during the last 30 days?																
1. 0 occasions	98.4	97.9	99.1	98.4	99.6	96.3	98.6	99.3	98.9	98.8	98.1	100.0	100.0	99.7	94.7	79.9
2. 1-2	1.1	1.4	0.6	1.1	0.3	2.4	1.0	0.4	1.0	0.8	1.2	-	-	0.3	3.8	10.6
3. 3-5	0.3	0.3	0.2	0.3	0.1	0.8	0.1	0.1	0.1	0.2	0.3	-	-	-	0.9	3.7
4. 6-9	0.1	0.2	*	0.1	0.1	0.3	0.2	0.1	-	0.1	0.2	-	-	-	0.3	4.7
5. 10-19	*	0.1	*	0.1	-	0.1	*	*	0.1	*	0.1	-	-	-	0.2	0.6
6. 20-39	*	*	*	*	-	*	-	*	-	*	*	-	-	-	*	-
7. 40 or more	*	0.1	-	*	-	0.1	*	*	-	-	0.1	-	-	-	0.1	0.5
Item 940 Subject A01c N	16032	7626	7907	12163	2162	3253	4516	5390	2873	8980	6005	6159	3499	2167	3852	197
B10: On how many occasions (if any) have you use cocaine (sometimes called "coke") . . .																
B10A: . . . in your lifetime?																
1. 0 occasions	83.9	81.3	87.2	83.5	90.3	75.2	90.6	88.5	74.7	86.7	81.4	100.0	100.0	76.9	50.4	17.6
2. 1-2	6.8	7.7	5.8	6.7	6.4	8.4	5.4	5.6	9.7	6.0	7.8	-	-	23.1	14.4	20.1
3. 3-5	2.9	3.5	2.2	3.1	1.4	4.4	1.6	1.9	5.0	2.4	3.3	-	-	-	11.5	9.0
4. 6-9	1.6	1.9	1.3	1.8	0.4	2.6	0.7	1.3	2.9	1.3	2.2	-	-	-	6.4	9.0
5. 10-19	1.8	2.0	1.4	2.0	0.7	3.3	0.7	1.1	3.1	1.5	2.0	-	-	-	6.9	11.3
6. 20-39	1.1	1.3	0.9	1.1	0.4	2.2	0.4	0.5	2.3	0.9	1.2	-	-	-	4.3	7.9
7. 40 or more	1.8	2.3	1.2	1.8	0.4	4.0	0.6	1.1	2.3	1.3	2.1	-	-	-	6.1	25.0
Item 950 Subject A01a N	16027	7642	7921	12194	2157	3250	4533	5375	2869	8994	6012	6157	3485	2168	3857	195
B10B: . . . during the last 12 months?																
1. 0 occasions	88.4	86.2	90.9	87.7	95.2	80.5	94.2	92.3	80.7	90.3	86.8	100.0	100.0	89.0	60.9	36.1
2. 1-2	5.2	6.1	4.2	5.5	3.1	7.0	3.4	3.8	8.6	4.7	5.7	-	-	11.0	14.7	16.6
3. 3-5	2.3	2.6	1.9	2.5	0.6	4.0	1.2	1.4	3.7	1.9	2.7	-	-	-	9.0	10.8
4. 6-9	1.5	1.8	1.0	1.6	0.5	2.4	0.4	1.0	2.9	1.3	1.6	-	-	-	5.7	8.6
5. 10-19	1.2	1.3	1.0	1.3	0.2	2.7	0.3	0.7	1.7	0.9	1.4	-	-	-	4.5	8.9
6. 20-39	0.9	1.1	0.6	0.9	0.2	1.9	0.3	0.3	1.6	0.7	0.9	-	-	-	3.1	10.8
7. 40 or more	0.6	0.8	0.4	0.6	0.2	1.4	0.2	0.4	0.9	0.4	0.8	-	-	-	2.2	8.2
Item 960 Subject A01b N	15993	7623	7915	12175	2152	3237	4527	5362	2867	8975	6009	6158	3487	2155	3838	190
B10C: . . . during the last 30 days?																
1. 0 occasions	94.2	93.0	95.6	94.0	97.6	89.0	97.7	96.0	91.0	95.4	93.1	100.0	100.0	97.1	79.4	57.4
2. 1-2	3.2	3.8	2.6	3.4	1.5	5.5	1.4	2.3	5.2	2.7	3.7	-	-	2.9	11.1	15.0
3. 3-5	1.2	1.4	0.9	1.3	0.3	2.4	0.3	0.9	1.8	0.9	1.4	-	-	-	4.7	6.4
4. 6-9	0.7	0.9	0.5	0.7	0.3	1.4	0.3	0.3	1.3	0.5	0.9	-	-	-	2.5	9.2
5. 10-19	0.5	0.6	0.3	0.5	0.1	1.1	0.3	0.3	0.4	0.4	0.5	-	-	-	1.5	7.6
6. 20-39	0.1	0.1	0.1	0.1	0.1	0.2	0.1	0.1	0.1	0.1	0.1	-	-	-	0.3	2.6
7. 40 or more	0.2	0.2	0.1	0.1	0.1	0.3	0.1	0.1	0.2	0.1	0.3	-	-	-	0.6	1.6
Item 970 Subject A01c N	15991	7622	7914	12173	2150	3237	4526	5365	2863	8977	6005	6158	3486	2155	3837	192
B11: Amphetamines can be prescribed by doctors to help people lose weight or to give people more energy. They are sometimes called uppers, ups, speed, bennies, dexies, pep pills, and diet pills. Drugstores are not supposed to sell them without a prescription from a doctor. Amphetamines do NOT include any non-prescription drugs, such as over-the-counter diet pills (like Dexatrim) or stay-awake pills (like No-Doz), or any mail-order drugs. On how many occasions (if any) have you taken amphetamines on your own–that is, without a doctor telling you to take them...																
B11A: . . . in your lifetime?																
1. 0 occasions	72.1	74.0	70.7	68.6	91.5	70.2	69.3	75.6	72.1	77.3	65.5	100.0	100.0	47.2	17.7	26.3
2. 1-2	8.9	8.2	9.6	9.6	4.8	8.8	9.3	8.2	9.5	8.4	9.3	-	-	52.8	6.8	8.7
3. 3-5	4.6	4.4	4.8	5.3	1.4	4.7	4.9	4.1	5.1	4.1	5.4	-	-	-	19.0	4.1
4. 6-9	3.1	2.9	3.3	3.5	0.9	3.7	3.1	2.8	3.1	2.7	3.8	-	-	-	12.5	7.9
5. 10-19	3.6	3.3	3.8	4.2	0.6	3.9	4.1	2.8	3.7	2.7	4.7	-	-	-	14.4	8.9
6. 20-39	2.7	2.2	3.1	3.2	0.5	3.4	3.2	2.2	2.3	1.9	3.9	-	-	-	10.9	8.5
7. 40 or more	5.0	5.0	4.7	5.7	0.3	5.3	6.1	4.2	4.2	3.1	7.4	-	-	-	18.7	35.7
Item 980 Subject A01a N	16028	7641	7924	12198	2166	3263	4532	5359	2875	8994	6003	6143	3471	2160	3867	197

*=less than .05 per cent.

DESCRIPTIVE RESULTS: 1984

29

QUESTIONNAIRE FORM 1-5 1984	TOTAL	SEX		RACE		REGION				4YR COLLEGE PLANS		ILLICIT DRUG USE: LIFETIME				
		M	F	White	Black	NE	NC	S	W	Yes	No	None	Mari- juana Only	Few Pills	More Pills	Any Her- oin
N (Weighted No. of Cases):	16499	7800	8029	12337	2244	3387	4612	5568	2932	9103	6124	6199	3529	2196	3936	207
% of Weighted Total:	100.0	47.3	48.7	74.8	13.6	20.5	28.0	33.7	17.8	55.2	37.1	37.6	21.4	13.3	23.9	1.3
B11B: . . . during the last 12 months?																
1. 0 occasions	82.3	83.2	81.8	79.8	95.8	81.0	79.7	84.9	83.1	85.8	77.8	100.0	100.0	83.0	38.8	41.6
2. 1-2	6.6	6.3	6.9	7.5	2.3	6.8	7.4	5.6	7.2	6.0	7.5	-	-	17.0	17.8	8.2
3. 3-5	3.3	3.1	3.4	3.7	0.9	3.6	3.2	3.0	3.5	2.7	4.2	-	-	-	13.2	7.4
4. 6-9	2.5	2.6	2.4	2.9	0.5	3.0	2.7	2.0	2.4	2.1	3.0	-	-	-	9.5	16.0
5. 10-19	2.3	2.1	2.2	2.6	0.3	2.5	3.1	1.8	1.5	1.5	3.1	-	-	-	9.1	6.9
6. 20-39	1.5	1.3	1.6	1.7	0.1	1.8	1.4	1.4	1.2	0.9	2.1	-	-	-	5.6	9.4
7. 40 or more	1.6	1.5	1.6	1.8	0.1	1.3	2.5	1.3	1.1	1.0	2.4	-	-	-	6.1	10.5
Item 990 Subject A01b N	15984	7624	7903	12165	2167	3251	4521	5346	2866	8980	5984	6144	3472	2139	3841	197
B11C: . . . during the last 30 days?																
1. 0 occasions	91.7	92.2	91.4	90.7	98.1	91.5	89.9	92.8	92.6	93.8	89.0	100.0	100.0	96.3	69.8	54.3
2. 1-2	3.7	3.6	3.8	4.2	1.1	3.9	4.2	3.3	3.4	3.0	4.6	-	-	3.7	12.5	17.0
3. 3-5	1.8	1.7	1.8	2.0	0.4	1.6	2.3	1.4	1.8	1.2	2.5	-	-	-	6.8	9.7
4. 6-9	1.1	0.9	1.1	1.2	0.1	1.2	1.2	0.9	0.9	0.7	1.4	-	-	-	4.1	6.0
5. 10-19	1.1	1.0	1.2	1.2	0.2	1.1	1.5	1.0	0.8	0.8	1.5	-	-	-	4.2	8.0
6. 20-39	0.4	0.4	0.5	0.5	*	0.3	0.8	0.3	0.3	0.2	0.8	-	-	-	1.7	2.7
7. 40 or more	0.2	0.2	0.2	0.2	-	0.3	0.1	0.3	0.2	0.1	0.3	-	-	-	0.8	2.3
Item 1000 Subject A01c N	15982	7620	7903	12163	2165	3250	4521	5348	2863	8981	5981	6145	3471	2141	3837	197
B12: On how many occasions (if any) have you used quaaludes (quads, soapers, methaqualone) on your own–that is, without a doctor telling you to take them . . .																
B12A: . . . in your lifetime?																
1. 0 occasions	91.7	90.9	93.0	90.7	98.8	90.4	92.4	91.1	93.4	93.9	89.5	100.0	100.0	93.6	72.3	39.1
2. 1-2	4.3	4.6	3.8	4.8	0.6	5.0	3.6	4.5	4.1	3.6	5.0	-	-	6.4	13.4	15.7
3. 3-5	1.4	1.4	1.3	1.6	0.1	1.7	1.4	1.5	1.0	1.1	1.8	-	-	-	5.4	8.1
4. 6-9	1.0	1.0	0.8	1.1	0.2	1.0	1.0	1.1	0.5	0.4	1.5	-	-	-	3.5	8.8
5. 10-19	0.7	0.9	0.5	0.8	0.1	0.8	0.6	0.8	0.6	0.5	1.0	-	-	-	2.6	7.0
6. 20-39	0.5	0.6	0.4	0.5	0.1	0.6	0.6	0.5	0.3	0.3	0.7	-	-	-	1.7	9.7
7. 40 or more	0.4	0.6	0.2	0.4	0.1	0.4	0.4	0.6	0.1	0.2	0.6	-	-	-	1.1	11.6
Item 1010 Subject A01a N	16053	7669	7936	12218	2174	3257	4544	5379	2874	9002	6031	6148	3481	2170	3858	202
B12B: . . . during the last 12 months?																
1. 0 occasions	96.2	95.3	97.3	95.8	99.4	95.6	96.2	95.7	97.9	97.6	94.7	100.0	100.0	98.8	87.0	59.1
2. 1-2	2.2	2.6	1.6	2.4	0.4	2.5	2.2	2.2	1.5	1.6	2.9	-	-	1.2	7.5	17.1
3. 3-5	0.8	1.0	0.5	0.9	-	1.1	0.6	1.0	0.3	0.4	1.2	-	-	-	2.8	8.3
4. 6-9	0.3	0.4	0.2	0.3	*	0.4	0.3	0.4	0.2	0.1	0.5	-	-	-	1.2	3.8
5. 10-19	0.3	0.4	0.2	0.3	0.1	0.2	0.4	0.3	0.1	0.2	0.3	-	-	-	0.8	7.0
6. 20-39	0.1	0.1	0.1	0.2	-	0.2	0.2	0.1	*	*	0.2	-	-	-	0.5	1.5
7. 40 or more	0.1	0.1	*	0.1	-	0.1	0.1	0.2	-	0.1	0.2	-	-	-	0.3	3.2
Item 1020 Subject A01b N	16040	7661	7936	12203	2178	3252	4540	5378	2870	8998	6031	6148	3482	2168	3843	202
B12C: . . . during the last 30 days?																
1. 0 occasions	98.9	98.6	99.3	98.9	99.6	99.0	98.7	98.6	99.6	99.3	98.4	100.0	100.0	99.7	96.4	81.3
2. 1-2	0.7	0.8	0.4	0.7	0.2	0.7	0.8	0.7	0.2	0.4	0.9	-	-	0.3	2.2	7.4
3. 3-5	0.2	0.3	0.2	0.2	0.1	0.2	0.3	0.3	*	0.2	0.3	-	-	-	0.7	4.4
4. 6-9	0.1	0.2	0.1	0.1	-	0.1	0.1	0.2	*	*	0.2	-	-	-	0.3	3.1
5. 10-19	0.1	0.1	*	0.1	0.1	0.1	0.1	0.1	0.1	0.1	0.2	-	-	-	0.3	1.7
6. 20-39	*	*	-	*	-	-	-	*	-	*	*	-	-	-	-	0.6
7. 40 or more	*	*	-	*	-	-	-	0.1	-	*	*	-	-	-	*	1.4
Item 1030 Subject A01c N	16038	7659	7935	12202	2177	3253	4539	5376	2869	8999	6028	6148	3481	2169	3840	204
B13: Barbiturates are sometimes prescribed by doctors to help people relax or get to sleep. They are sometimes called downs, downers, goofballs, yellows, reds, blues, rainbows. On how many occasions (if any) have you taken barbiturates on your own–that is, without a doctor telling you to take them...																

*=less than .05 per cent.

QUESTIONNAIRE FORM 1-5 1984	TOTAL	SEX		RACE		REGION				4YR COLLEGE PLANS		ILLICIT DRUG USE: LIFETIME				
		M	F	White	Black	NE	NC	S	W	Yes	No	None	Marijuana Only	Few Pills	More Pills	Any Heroin
N (Weighted No. of Cases):	16499	7800	8029	12337	2244	3387	4612	5568	2932	9103	6124	6199	3529	2196	3936	207
% of Weighted Total:	100.0	47.3	48.7	74.8	13.6	20.5	28.0	33.7	17.8	55.2	37.1	37.6	21.4	13.3	23.9	1.3

B13A: . . . in your lifetime?

1. 0 occasions	90.1	89.4	91.1	89.2	96.6	88.8	90.4	90.0	91.1	92.4	87.5	100.0	100.0	89.2	68.2	31.8
2. 1-2	4.5	4.6	4.3	4.8	1.9	4.6	4.4	4.4	4.6	3.8	5.3	-	-	10.8	11.9	12.2
3. 3-5	1.9	1.9	1.8	2.0	0.8	2.2	1.7	2.0	1.5	1.5	2.4	-	-	-	7.2	9.5
4. 6-9	1.3	1.6	1.0	1.5	0.3	1.4	1.3	1.3	1.4	1.0	1.6	-	-	-	4.9	13.8
5. 10-19	1.0	1.0	0.9	1.1	0.2	1.4	1.0	0.9	0.6	0.6	1.4	-	-	-	3.6	9.4
6. 20-39	0.6	0.7	0.5	0.7	0.1	0.8	0.5	0.5	0.7	0.4	0.8	-	-	-	2.1	6.1
7. 40 or more	0.7	0.9	0.4	0.8	0.1	0.8	0.7	0.9	0.2	0.4	1.0	-	-	-	2.1	17.2
Item 1040 Subject A01a N	15984	7635	7909	12182	2155	3251	4526	5348	2859	8974	6009	6131	3468	2164	3827	201

B13B: . . . during the last 12 months?

1. 0 occasions	95.1	94.5	96.0	94.7	98.3	94.9	95.1	94.8	95.8	96.3	93.8	100.0	100.0	96.7	83.7	53.3
2. 1-2	2.5	2.7	2.2	2.7	1.1	2.1	2.6	2.6	2.7	1.9	3.3	-	-	3.3	8.0	13.7
3. 3-5	1.1	1.3	0.9	1.2	0.4	1.4	1.0	1.2	0.8	0.9	1.4	-	-	-	4.0	13.2
4. 6-9	0.6	0.7	0.4	0.7	0.1	1.0	0.5	0.7	0.3	0.4	0.6	-	-	-	2.2	7.0
5. 10-19	0.4	0.4	0.3	0.4	-	0.3	0.4	0.3	0.4	0.2	0.5	-	-	-	1.3	4.2
6. 20-39	0.2	0.2	0.1	0.2	*	0.2	0.2	0.2	0.1	0.1	0.3	-	-	-	0.6	1.8
7. 40 or more	0.2	0.2	0.1	0.1	0.1	0.1	0.2	0.2	*	0.1	0.2	-	-	-	0.3	6.7
Item 1050 Subject A01b N	15969	7629	7901	12166	2155	3246	4526	5340	2856	8968	6003	6131	3469	2160	3813	200

B13C: . . . during the last 30 days?

1. 0 occasions	98.3	98.1	98.7	98.2	99.3	98.3	98.1	98.1	98.8	98.7	98.0	100.0	100.0	99.5	94.6	72.9
2. 1-2	1.1	1.2	0.9	1.2	0.5	1.1	1.2	1.2	0.8	0.9	1.2	-	-	0.5	3.6	14.5
3. 3-5	0.2	0.3	0.2	0.3	0.1	0.2	0.2	0.3	0.2	0.1	0.3	-	-	-	0.8	3.7
4. 6-9	0.2	0.2	0.2	0.2	-	0.2	0.2	0.2	0.1	0.1	0.2	-	-	-	0.6	3.7
5. 10-19	0.1	0.2	*	0.1	0.1	0.1	0.2	0.1	0.1	0.1	0.2	-	-	-	0.4	3.3
6. 20-39	*	*	*	*	-	-	*	0.1	-	*	*	-	-	-	0.1	1.3
7. 40 or more	*	-	*	*	-	-	-	*	*	*	-	-	-	-	*	0.7
Item 1060 Subject A01c N	15962	7623	7901	12164	2155	3246	4526	5337	2854	8967	6000	6131	3468	2160	3811	199

B14: Tranquilizers are sometimes prescribed by doctors to calm people down, quiet their nerves, or relax their muscles. Librium, Valium, and Miltown are all tranquilizers. On how many occasions (if any) have you taken tranquilizers on your own–that is, without a doctor telling you to take them...

B14A: . . . in your lifetime?

1. 0 occasions	87.6	88.1	87.5	86.5	95.3	86.3	88.9	86.9	88.6	89.4	85.3	100.0	100.0	78.0	63.9	36.6
2. 1-2	6.3	5.4	7.2	6.8	3.4	6.8	5.6	6.7	6.4	5.7	7.2	-	-	22.0	13.4	13.7
3. 3-5	2.4	2.4	2.3	2.7	0.6	2.2	2.1	2.6	2.6	2.2	2.6	-	-	-	9.4	12.3
4. 6-9	1.3	1.4	1.2	1.5	0.3	1.6	1.2	1.4	1.0	1.0	1.7	-	-	-	5.2	6.6
5. 10-19	1.0	1.1	0.9	1.2	0.1	1.1	1.0	1.1	0.7	0.8	1.3	-	-	-	3.8	8.0
6. 20-39	0.6	0.7	0.5	0.6	0.2	0.8	0.5	0.6	0.4	0.4	0.8	-	-	-	1.9	10.2
7. 40 or more	0.7	0.9	0.5	0.8	0.1	1.1	0.8	0.7	0.3	0.5	1.0	-	-	-	2.4	12.6
Item 1070 Subject A01a N	15989	7645	7927	12191	2172	3243	4524	5358	2864	8999	6018	6142	3471	2161	3825	193

B14B: . . . during the last 12 months?

1. 0 occasions	93.9	93.7	94.2	93.1	98.3	93.2	94.4	93.1	95.1	94.8	92.6	100.0	100.0	93.3	80.2	56.3
2. 1-2	3.5	3.3	3.7	4.0	1.2	3.7	3.0	4.1	3.1	3.2	4.0	-	-	6.7	10.3	13.6
3. 3-5	1.1	1.2	1.0	1.3	0.2	1.3	1.0	1.3	1.0	0.9	1.4	-	-	-	4.4	7.6
4. 6-9	0.7	0.8	0.4	0.8	0.1	0.8	0.5	0.8	0.4	0.5	0.8	-	-	-	2.3	8.0
5. 10-19	0.4	0.5	0.3	0.4	0.1	0.4	0.5	0.4	0.2	0.3	0.6	-	-	-	1.4	6.9
6. 20-39	0.3	0.4	0.2	0.3	*	0.4	0.4	0.3	0.2	0.2	0.5	-	-	-	1.0	5.6
7. 40 or more	0.1	0.1	0.1	0.1	0.1	0.2	0.1	0.1	*	0.1	0.1	-	-	-	0.4	1.9
Item 1080 Subject A01b N	15961	7630	7916	12162	2170	3240	4519	5345	2858	8981	6009	6144	3472	2146	3807	193

B14C: . . . during the last 30 days?

1. 0 occasions	97.9	97.7	98.3	97.8	99.3	97.7	97.8	97.8	98.7	98.5	97.2	100.0	100.0	98.8	93.4	74.5
2. 1-2	1.3	1.3	1.2	1.4	0.5	1.5	1.1	1.5	0.8	0.9	1.8	-	-	1.2	4.0	13.0
3. 3-5	0.4	0.6	0.2	0.5	0.1	0.5	0.5	0.3	0.3	0.3	0.5	-	-	-	1.5	4.0
4. 6-9	0.2	0.3	0.1	0.2	0.1	*	0.4	0.2	0.1	0.2	0.3	-	-	-	0.7	4.1
5. 10-19	0.1	0.1	*	0.1	0.1	0.1	*	0.2	*	0.1	0.2	-	-	-	0.3	3.1
6. 20-39	*	-	0.1	*	-	*	0.1	-	*	*	*	-	-	-	0.1	0.7
7. 40 or more	*	*	-	*	-	0.1	-	*	-	*	*	-	-	-	0.1	0.5
Item 1090 Subject A01c N	15956	7626	7914	12160	2170	3238	4519	5343	2857	8982	6007	6142	3471	2147	3805	193

*=less than .05 per cent.

QUESTIONNAIRE FORM 1-5 1984	TOTAL	SEX		RACE		REGION				4YR COLLEGE PLANS		ILLICIT DRUG USE: LIFETIME				
		M	F	White	Black	NE	NC	S	W	Yes	No	None	Mari-juana Only	Few Pills	More Pills	Any Her-oin
N (Weighted No. of Cases):	16499	7800	8029	12337	2244	3387	4612	5568	2932	9103	6124	6199	3529	2196	3936	207
% of Weighted Total:	100.0	47.3	48.7	74.8	13.6	20.5	28.0	33.7	17.8	55.2	37.1	37.6	21.4	13.3	23.9	1.3

B15: On how many occasions (if any) have you used heroin (smack, horse, skag) . . .

B15A: . . . in your lifetime?

	TOTAL	M	F	White	Black	NE	NC	S	W	Yes	No	None	Mari-juana Only	Few Pills	More Pills	Any Her-oin
1. 0 occasions	98.7	98.5	99.0	98.9	99.2	98.4	98.7	98.9	98.9	99.0	98.5	100.0	100.0	100.0	100.0	-
2. 1-2	0.8	0.8	0.7	0.7	0.5	0.9	0.7	0.6	0.9	0.6	0.9	-	-	-	-	60.2
3. 3-5	0.1	0.2	0.1	0.1	0.1	0.2	0.2	0.1	0.2	0.1	0.2	-	-	-	-	11.7
4. 6-9	0.1	0.2	*	0.1	*	0.1	0.1	0.1	*	*	0.2	-	-	-	-	8.8
5. 10-19	0.1	0.1	*	0.1	0.1	0.1	0.1	0.1	-	*	0.1	-	-	-	-	5.1
6. 20-39	0.1	0.1	0.1	0.1	-	*	0.1	0.1	*	0.1	0.1	-	-	-	-	5.7
7. 40 or more	0.1	0.2	*	0.1	0.1	0.3	*	0.1	*	0.1	0.1	-	-	-	-	8.5
Item 1100 Subject A01a N	15964	7642	7926	12187	2165	3237	4512	5350	2864	8991	6014	6136	3460	2157	3821	200

B15B: . . . during the last 12 months?

	TOTAL	M	F	White	Black	NE	NC	S	W	Yes	No	None	Mari-juana Only	Few Pills	More Pills	Any Her-oin
1. 0 occasions	99.5	99.3	99.7	99.6	99.6	99.4	99.4	99.5	99.6	99.6	99.4	100.0	100.0	100.0	100.0	58.1
2. 1-2	0.2	0.3	0.2	0.2	0.2	0.2	0.3	0.2	0.3	0.2	0.3	-	-	-	-	19.4
3. 3-5	0.1	0.1	*	0.1	0.1	0.1	0.1	0.1	*	0.1	0.1	-	-	-	-	5.6
4. 6-9	0.1	0.2	*	0.1	0.1	0.1	0.1	0.1	*	*	0.1	-	-	-	-	7.7
5. 10-19	*	0.1	*	*	0.1	0.1	*	0.1	-	*	*	-	-	-	-	3.6
6. 20-39	*	0.1	*	*	-	*	*	*	*	*	*	-	-	-	-	2.7
7. 40 or more	*	*	*	*	-	0.1	*	*	*	*	*	-	-	-	-	2.9
Item 1110 Subject A01b N	15970	7647	7927	12188	2167	3241	4513	5352	2864	8992	6016	6136	3461	2158	3822	202

B15C: . . . during the last 30 days?

	TOTAL	M	F	White	Black	NE	NC	S	W	Yes	No	None	Mari-juana Only	Few Pills	More Pills	Any Her-oin
1. 0 occasions	99.7	99.5	99.9	99.8	99.8	99.5	99.7	99.7	99.9	99.7	99.7	100.0	100.0	100.0	100.0	73.9
2. 1-2	0.2	0.2	0.1	0.1	0.2	0.2	0.2	0.2	0.1	0.1	0.2	-	-	-	-	12.3
3. 3-5	0.1	0.2	*	0.1	*	0.1	0.1	0.1	*	0.1	0.1	-	-	-	-	8.5
4. 6-9	*	*	-	*	-	*	-	-	-	*	*	-	-	-	-	1.2
5. 10-19	*	*	*	*	-	*	-	-	-	*	*	-	-	-	-	0.5
6. 20-39	*	*	*	*	-	0.1	*	*	-	*	*	-	-	-	-	2.1
7. 40 or more	*	*	-	*	-	*	-	*	-	*	*	-	-	-	-	1.5
Item 1120 Subject A01c N	15968	7646	7927	12189	2167	3240	4514	5350	2865	8994	6016	6136	3460	2159	3822	201

B16: There are a number of narcotics other than heroin, such as methadone, opium, morphine, codeine, demerol, paregoric, talwin, and laudanum. These are sometimes prescribed by doctors. On how many occasions (if any) have you taken narcotics other than heroin on your own–that is, without a doctor telling you to take them...

B16A: . . . in your lifetime?

	TOTAL	M	F	White	Black	NE	NC	S	W	Yes	No	None	Mari-juana Only	Few Pills	More Pills	Any Her-oin
1. 0 occasions	90.3	89.1	91.6	89.1	96.9	87.7	91.1	92.0	89.0	91.8	88.5	100.0	100.0	88.3	70.0	24.9
2. 1-2	4.5	4.9	4.2	5.2	1.6	5.9	4.3	3.6	5.1	4.1	5.1	-	-	11.7	11.4	18.3
3. 3-5	1.9	2.0	1.8	2.2	0.4	2.6	1.6	1.6	2.2	1.7	2.3	-	-	-	7.4	13.0
4. 6-9	1.2	1.5	0.9	1.4	0.4	1.4	1.1	1.1	1.3	1.1	1.3	-	-	-	4.6	6.7
5. 10-19	0.9	1.2	0.6	1.0	0.2	1.0	0.8	0.6	1.4	0.6	1.2	-	-	-	2.8	15.8
6. 20-39	0.5	0.6	0.4	0.5	0.1	0.7	0.6	0.3	0.4	0.3	0.8	-	-	-	1.6	9.4
7. 40 or more	0.7	0.9	0.4	0.6	0.5	0.6	0.6	0.7	0.7	0.5	0.8	-	-	-	2.1	12.0
Item 1130 Subject A01a N	15898	7640	7910	12180	2161	3220	4515	5319	2845	8963	5993	6111	3453	2159	3785	198

B16B: . . . during the last 12 months?

	TOTAL	M	F	White	Black	NE	NC	S	W	Yes	No	None	Mari-juana Only	Few Pills	More Pills	Any Her-oin
1. 0 occasions	94.8	93.8	95.8	94.2	98.4	93.3	95.2	95.5	94.7	95.7	93.9	100.0	100.0	96.2	83.1	47.8
2. 1-2	2.6	3.0	2.3	3.0	0.7	3.6	2.2	2.4	2.8	2.3	3.1	-	-	3.8	8.1	16.2
3. 3-5	1.0	1.2	0.9	1.1	0.2	1.3	1.1	0.9	1.0	0.9	1.2	-	-	-	3.9	9.4
4. 6-9	0.8	1.1	0.5	0.9	0.2	1.1	0.8	0.6	0.8	0.5	1.0	-	-	-	2.6	12.6
5. 10-19	0.4	0.5	0.3	0.4	0.1	0.5	0.4	0.3	0.4	0.3	0.5	-	-	-	1.3	6.3
6. 20-39	0.2	0.3	0.2	0.2	0.1	0.2	0.2	0.2	0.2	0.2	0.2	-	-	-	0.6	5.4
7. 40 or more	0.1	0.2	0.1	0.1	0.2	0.1	0.1	0.1	0.2	0.1	0.2	-	-	-	0.4	2.4
Item 1140 Subject A01b N	15880	7628	7907	12160	2163	3214	4513	5310	2842	8955	5982	6112	3454	2153	3772	196

*=less than .05 per cent.

QUESTIONNAIRE FORM 1-5 1984	TOTAL	SEX		RACE		REGION				4YR COLLEGE PLANS		ILLICIT DRUG USE: LIFETIME				
		M	F	White	Black	NE	NC	S	W	Yes	No	None	Mari- juana Only	Few Pills	More Pills	Any Her- oin
N (Weighted No. of Cases):	16499	7800	8029	12337	2244	3387	4612	5568	2932	9103	6124	6199	3529	2196	3936	207
% of Weighted Total:	100.0	47.3	48.7	74.8	13.6	20.5	28.0	33.7	17.8	55.2	37.1	37.6	21.4	13.3	23.9	1.3
B16C: . . . during the last 30 days?																
1. 0 occasions	98.2	97.8	98.6	98.0	99.2	98.0	98.2	98.3	98.2	98.6	97.8	100.0	100.0	99.5	94.2	70.4
2. 1-2	1.0	1.1	0.9	1.1	0.3	1.2	0.9	1.0	1.0	0.8	1.2	-	-	0.5	3.4	10.6
3. 3-5	0.5	0.6	0.3	0.5	0.2	0.3	0.6	0.4	0.4	0.3	0.7	-	-	-	1.4	9.9
4. 6-9	0.2	0.3	0.1	0.2	0.1	0.3	0.2	0.1	0.2	0.2	0.2	-	-	-	0.6	4.4
5. 10-19	0.1	0.1	*	0.1	0.2	0.1	*	0.1	0.1	0.1	0.1	-	-	-	0.2	3.6
6. 20-39	*	*	*	*	-	*	-	*	*	*	*	-	-	-	0.1	0.2
7. 40 or more	*	0.1	*	*	0.1	-	*	0.1	0.1	*	0.1	-	-	-	0.1	0.9
Item 1150 Subject A01c　　N	15875	7623	7907	12158	2163	3211	4513	5310	2841	8952	5981	6112	3453	2154	3768	196
B17: On how many occasions (if any) have you sniffed glue, or breathed the contents of aerosol spray cans, or inhaled any other gases or sprays in order to get high . . .																
B17A: . . . in your lifetime?																
1. 0 occasions	85.6	82.2	89.1	84.4	93.2	83.7	85.8	87.1	84.6	87.6	83.2	96.1	89.0	81.8	70.0	48.4
2. 1-2	9.0	10.6	7.5	9.7	4.8	9.5	8.4	8.2	10.7	7.8	10.5	3.0	8.5	13.3	16.1	15.8
3. 3-5	2.3	3.0	1.6	2.6	1.4	3.1	2.3	2.0	2.1	2.3	2.4	0.5	1.5	2.8	5.6	8.2
4. 6-9	1.2	1.6	0.7	1.3	0.1	1.5	1.3	1.1	0.8	0.9	1.7	0.1	0.6	1.2	3.0	7.8
5. 10-19	0.8	1.2	0.4	1.0	0.2	1.0	1.0	0.6	0.7	0.6	1.1	0.1	0.2	0.4	2.7	4.4
6. 20-39	0.5	0.6	0.3	0.6	0.1	0.8	0.6	0.4	0.2	0.5	0.4	*	0.1	0.4	1.4	4.3
7. 40 or more	0.6	0.8	0.3	0.5	0.3	0.4	0.5	0.5	0.9	0.4	0.8	0.2	0.1	0.2	1.3	11.0
Item 1160 Subject A01a　　N	12835	6188	6369	9858	1723	2617	3621	4306	2290	7259	4908	4920	2699	1804	3103	168
B17B: . . . during the last 12 months?																
1. 0 occasions	94.9	93.5	96.2	94.4	97.6	93.9	95.0	95.4	94.7	95.3	94.2	98.8	97.1	94.0	88.2	71.6
2. 1-2	3.1	3.8	2.4	3.4	1.7	3.8	2.8	2.9	3.1	2.7	3.6	0.8	2.1	4.3	6.6	8.6
3. 3-5	1.0	1.3	0.7	1.1	0.4	1.2	1.1	0.8	0.9	1.0	1.1	0.2	0.4	1.0	2.4	9.3
4. 6-9	0.5	0.6	0.4	0.6	-	0.7	0.6	0.4	0.4	0.4	0.6	-	0.1	0.6	1.5	3.0
5. 10-19	0.2	0.3	0.2	0.2	0.3	0.2	0.3	0.2	0.3	0.2	0.3	*	0.1	0.1	0.7	2.7
6. 20-39	0.2	0.2	0.1	0.2	-	0.1	0.2	0.1	0.2	0.2	0.1	0.1	0.1	*	0.3	1.3
7. 40 or more	0.2	0.2	*	0.1	0.1	0.1	0.1	0.1	0.3	0.2	0.1	0.1	0.1	*	0.3	3.4
Item 1170 Subject A01b　　N	12813	6174	6365	9842	1723	2609	3618	4302	2284	7248	4902	4917	2694	1800	3096	164
B17C: . . . during the last 30 days?																
1. 0 occasions	98.1	97.5	98.8	98.0	98.8	97.9	98.1	98.3	98.2	98.3	97.9	99.5	99.2	98.0	95.8	85.2
2. 1-2	1.3	1.8	0.8	1.4	0.9	1.8	1.3	1.2	1.0	1.3	1.4	0.3	0.7	1.4	3.0	7.6
3. 3-5	0.3	0.3	0.3	0.3	0.2	0.2	0.3	0.3	0.3	0.2	0.4	*	0.1	0.4	0.6	2.3
4. 6-9	0.1	0.2	*	0.1	0.1	0.1	0.1	0.1	0.1	*	0.1	-	-	0.2	0.2	1.6
5. 10-19	0.1	0.2	0.1	0.1	-	-	0.2	0.1	0.2	0.1	0.1	0.1	*	-	0.2	2.4
6. 20-39	0.1	0.1	*	*	0.1	*	*	*	0.1	0.1	*	0.1	*	-	0.1	0.3
7. 40 or more	*	0.1	-	*	-	0.1	0.1	-	0.1	*	0.1	*	-	*	0.1	0.6
Item 1180 Subject A01c　　N	12810	6172	6365	9839	1723	2608	3616	4301	2284	7249	4898	4917	2693	1800	3094	166

*=less than .05 per cent.

QUESTIONNAIRE FORM 1 1984	TOTAL	SEX		RACE		REGION				4YR COLLEGE PLANS		ILLICIT DRUG USE: LIFETIME				
		M	F	White	Black	NE	NC	S	W	Yes	No	None	Marijuana Only	Few Pills	More Pills	Any Heroin
N (Weighted No. of Cases):	3311	1534	1616	2414	478	670	941	1113	587	1772	1137	1223	794	381	765	32
% of Weighted Total:	100.0	46.3	48.8	72.9	14.4	20.2	28.4	33.6	17.7	53.5	34.3	36.9	24.0	11.5	23.1	1.0
A001: Taking all things together, how would you say things are these days–would you say you're very happy, pretty happy, or not too happy these days?																
3. Very happy	18.1	17.5	19.2	20.3	10.7	16.5	16.3	19.9	19.6	20.7	14.4	19.7	18.0	17.3	15.6	11.5
2. Pretty happy	70.0	71.7	68.7	70.5	70.4	71.8	72.2	66.8	70.4	68.9	73.0	69.0	70.5	70.4	71.3	74.4
1. Not too happy	11.9	10.8	12.2	9.2	18.8	11.8	11.4	13.3	10.0	10.4	12.6	11.4	11.4	12.3	13.1	14.1
Item 1190 Subject P01,Q01 N	3294	1526	1611	2406	474	668	940	1106	580	1767	1132	1218	789	381	762	32
A002: How much do you agree or disagree with each of the following statements?																
A002A: The nation needs much more long-range planning and coordination to be prepared for the future																
1. Disagree	2.5	3.2	1.8	1.9	4.1	2.5	1.9	3.2	2.2	2.2	2.3	2.6	1.9	3.2	1.9	4.7
2. Mostly disagree	4.3	3.9	4.4	4.5	2.9	5.0	4.7	3.8	3.9	3.8	4.4	3.6	5.3	4.2	4.2	3.0
3. Neither	11.3	11.1	11.2	12.0	8.5	12.2	12.1	9.0	13.3	10.7	11.8	10.2	11.8	12.5	11.9	25.7
4. Mostly agree	42.3	41.7	43.3	45.2	30.0	37.8	46.9	41.0	42.2	43.1	42.2	43.1	39.6	46.9	43.6	26.6
5. Agree	39.6	40.2	39.3	36.4	54.5	42.5	34.4	43.0	38.4	40.3	39.3	40.4	41.5	33.3	38.4	40.0
Item 1200 Subject I01 N	3260	1513	1599	2396	461	661	935	1089	575	1756	1126	1210	782	377	752	32
A002B: I enjoy the fast pace and changes of today's world																
1. Disagree	12.4	12.4	12.1	9.9	21.0	10.9	11.6	15.7	9.2	8.7	16.7	13.1	12.4	11.4	10.6	16.7
2. Mostly disagree	16.8	15.7	17.7	17.2	12.5	15.5	18.7	15.6	17.2	14.9	19.7	17.5	18.3	16.1	15.3	5.7
3. Neither	17.9	18.8	16.9	18.9	13.1	19.0	18.9	14.6	21.1	18.4	18.5	19.7	18.5	18.3	15.1	12.5
4. Mostly agree	33.7	32.4	35.4	35.5	29.9	35.5	33.8	32.3	34.2	37.9	28.8	31.7	32.4	34.2	37.2	44.1
5. Agree	19.3	20.7	17.9	18.5	23.5	19.0	17.0	21.8	18.3	20.1	16.4	18.0	18.4	20.0	21.9	21.1
Item 1210 Subject I03,Q02 N	3270	1515	1602	2397	464	661	937	1095	576	1753	1129	1211	784	378	755	32
A002C: Things change too quickly in today's world																
1. Disagree	14.3	15.2	13.3	14.0	17.0	15.7	11.3	17.2	11.9	15.7	12.1	13.2	13.4	15.1	16.5	25.2
2. Mostly disagree	22.2	23.9	21.4	24.9	15.4	21.6	23.9	20.2	24.1	26.9	16.5	20.4	23.5	24.7	23.7	20.4
3. Neither	18.9	19.4	18.4	20.7	12.1	19.8	19.5	16.1	22.3	20.2	16.7	18.6	17.9	20.2	19.8	14.2
4. Mostly agree	21.6	20.2	22.7	21.5	21.7	20.1	23.4	21.0	21.5	19.6	25.4	23.0	23.2	19.9	19.2	13.8
5. Agree	23.0	21.2	24.2	18.9	33.8	22.8	21.8	25.6	20.2	17.5	29.3	24.8	22.0	20.1	20.8	26.3
Item 1220 Subject I03,Q02 N	3265	1514	1601	2395	464	661	935	1096	573	1752	1131	1207	787	377	755	32
A002D: I think the times ahead for me will be tougher and less fun than things are now																
1. Disagree	18.7	17.8	19.5	19.9	15.6	18.6	18.1	18.0	21.0	20.4	16.8	17.7	21.9	16.9	17.3	22.0
2. Mostly disagree	19.3	18.8	20.1	21.9	11.0	15.2	19.8	18.7	24.7	22.5	15.1	20.2	17.0	20.7	20.0	24.4
3. Neither	11.8	12.8	11.5	13.0	6.9	12.0	11.7	11.2	13.0	13.0	11.0	12.8	12.1	10.2	11.7	13.8
4. Mostly agree	23.4	22.8	23.2	22.6	24.2	26.8	24.9	21.6	20.2	21.5	25.9	22.3	23.3	26.2	23.9	15.5
5. Agree	26.8	27.7	25.8	22.6	42.3	27.5	25.5	30.4	21.1	22.8	31.2	27.0	25.7	26.0	27.0	24.4
Item 1230 Subject I01,J N	3275	1518	1607	2402	466	664	938	1098	575	1761	1129	1213	787	376	759	31
A003: Of all the time you spend with other people, about how much is spent with people over 30?																
1. Very little	20.5	21.8	18.6	16.8	34.7	20.0	19.9	23.8	15.9	19.2	20.9	18.8	21.7	18.6	22.0	25.5
2. Some	41.0	44.0	38.2	43.3	32.1	46.1	39.1	37.1	45.8	43.8	38.3	39.4	43.3	41.8	42.5	40.3
3. About half	30.9	27.3	35.2	32.5	25.3	27.7	32.1	31.3	32.0	30.4	32.4	33.0	28.8	34.9	28.6	21.4
4. Most	5.8	5.7	6.0	6.1	5.1	5.3	6.4	6.3	4.6	5.5	6.3	7.0	5.3	3.9	5.7	1.9
5. Nearly all	1.7	1.2	2.0	1.3	2.8	1.0	2.5	1.5	1.6	1.2	2.1	1.8	0.8	0.8	1.2	10.9
Item 1240 Subject M02 N	3303	1532	1616	2412	478	667	941	1111	584	1771	1135	1223	793	381	762	32

QUESTIONNAIRE FORM 1 1984	TOTAL	SEX		RACE		REGION				4YR COLLEGE PLANS		ILLICIT DRUG USE: LIFETIME				
		M	F	White	Black	NE	NC	S	W	Yes	No	None	Mari-juana Only	Few Pills	More Pills	Any Her-oin
N (Weighted No. of Cases):	3311	1534	1616	2414	478	670	941	1113	587	1772	1137	1223	794	381	765	32
% of Weighted Total:	100.0	46.3	48.8	72.9	14.4	20.2	28.4	33.6	17.7	53.5	34.3	36.9	24.0	11.5	23.1	1.0

A004: Would you like to spend more time, or less time, with people over 30 if you could?

	TOTAL	M	F	White	Black	NE	NC	S	W	Yes	No	None	Mari-juana Only	Few Pills	More Pills	Any Her-oin
1. Much less time	3.2	3.6	2.5	2.8	4.6	2.8	4.3	2.8	2.5	2.6	3.6	2.6	3.0	2.1	4.9	3.2
2. Somewhat less time	6.8	6.7	6.3	6.6	6.9	6.7	7.1	6.8	6.6	5.5	7.7	4.4	8.2	7.6	7.9	3.7
3. About the same as now	69.2	69.7	69.3	71.6	61.3	71.8	70.3	67.3	68.3	70.2	69.2	70.9	69.7	69.4	68.0	63.1
4. Somewhat more time	17.7	17.5	18.4	17.2	19.9	16.4	16.4	18.8	19.0	18.5	16.9	18.8	16.7	17.4	17.2	23.0
5. Much more time	3.1	2.5	3.5	1.8	7.3	2.2	1.9	4.3	3.6	3.3	2.6	3.4	2.3	3.6	2.1	7.0
Item 1250 Subject M02 N	3294	1525	1613	2402	478	667	938	1111	577	1766	1136	1220	793	379	759	32

A005: Would you like to spend more time, or less time, working with or helping younger children?

	TOTAL	M	F	White	Black	NE	NC	S	W	Yes	No	None	Mari-juana Only	Few Pills	More Pills	Any Her-oin
1. Much less time	6.0	9.1	2.7	6.3	3.5	6.1	6.4	5.5	6.0	4.8	7.1	4.8	6.3	4.3	8.0	15.7
2. Somewhat less time	7.2	9.5	4.4	7.6	3.1	8.0	7.5	6.9	6.4	6.3	8.2	5.8	7.1	7.8	8.7	12.8
3. About the same as now	33.2	42.1	25.0	35.4	26.2	34.4	32.4	31.8	35.5	32.0	34.1	32.3	33.5	37.9	33.5	30.0
4. Somewhat more time	34.7	29.9	39.9	35.3	34.6	34.9	37.0	33.1	33.9	38.7	31.4	35.9	34.3	33.0	34.3	26.0
5. Much more time	18.9	9.3	28.1	15.4	32.6	16.5	16.7	22.7	18.2	18.3	19.2	21.3	18.8	17.0	15.4	15.5
Item 1260 Subject M02 N	3297	1527	1614	2406	478	666	936	1111	584	1769	1131	1217	793	381	762	32

A006: The next questions ask how satisfied or dissatisfied you are with several aspects of your life. For each question, mark the circle that shows best how you feel. If you are neutral about something, or are just as satisfied as you are dissatisfied, mark the middle answer.

How satisfied are you with...

A006A: Your job? (If you have no job, leave blank)

	TOTAL	M	F	White	Black	NE	NC	S	W	Yes	No	None	Mari-juana Only	Few Pills	More Pills	Any Her-oin
7. Completely satisfied	21.1	22.6	20.1	20.8	27.5	21.3	18.2	24.7	19.0	19.2	24.1	20.0	25.2	20.6	17.5	20.8
6.	18.8	18.3	19.6	20.8	8.4	16.2	19.1	19.7	20.0	20.1	16.8	20.8	17.5	19.7	18.0	14.3
5.	13.7	14.5	13.1	15.7	4.4	12.2	16.7	10.6	16.6	16.1	11.9	14.9	14.9	13.4	12.3	10.9
4. Neutral	27.8	25.7	29.4	24.8	43.9	31.5	24.0	29.6	25.9	24.6	30.0	25.9	26.3	25.2	32.8	26.0
3.	6.9	6.6	7.2	7.2	2.0	6.0	8.0	6.3	7.4	8.0	5.9	8.2	6.0	6.7	6.9	4.1
2.	4.4	4.8	3.9	4.7	2.5	5.3	6.1	2.5	4.5	5.8	3.2	4.0	4.2	7.3	4.3	3.2
1. Completely dissatisfied	7.2	7.5	6.7	6.0	11.3	7.5	7.9	6.6	6.6	6.2	8.0	6.2	5.8	7.2	8.3	20.7
Item 1270 Subject C01,P02 N	2001	975	923	1556	205	436	546	646	373	1070	685	695	477	243	497	25

A006B: The neighborhood where you live?

	TOTAL	M	F	White	Black	NE	NC	S	W	Yes	No	None	Mari-juana Only	Few Pills	More Pills	Any Her-oin
7. Completely satisfied	33.1	33.2	33.5	33.3	32.8	28.6	36.2	33.9	32.0	32.6	35.9	34.9	34.9	26.7	31.3	19.1
6.	18.7	20.8	17.0	21.4	8.5	16.6	20.9	16.7	21.6	20.8	16.9	20.2	18.0	21.5	16.9	12.5
5.	10.1	12.2	8.2	10.9	6.0	10.9	8.4	10.0	12.2	11.3	8.3	10.5	9.7	11.7	9.8	8.5
4. Neutral	23.6	20.2	26.4	20.5	36.6	26.8	21.2	24.9	21.4	21.8	24.3	20.5	24.3	26.2	25.0	42.3
3.	4.2	4.4	4.2	4.8	3.3	3.9	4.4	4.5	3.7	5.0	3.4	4.5	4.2	3.8	4.4	5.1
2.	3.8	3.7	3.8	3.9	2.2	6.0	2.8	3.5	3.7	3.7	3.8	3.6	2.8	4.2	5.6	5.7
1. Completely dissatisfied	6.3	5.4	6.8	5.1	10.5	7.3	6.0	6.4	5.3	4.8	7.4	5.9	6.0	5.8	7.0	6.9
Item 1280 Subject P02 N	3297	1527	1615	2411	476	666	939	1110	582	1769	1132	1219	790	381	763	32

A006C: Your personal safety in your neighborhood, on your job, and in your school–safety from being attacked and injured in some way?

	TOTAL	M	F	White	Black	NE	NC	S	W	Yes	No	None	Mari-juana Only	Few Pills	More Pills	Any Her-oin
7. Completely satisfied	41.9	47.4	37.5	43.6	36.4	38.8	46.0	40.9	40.6	42.8	40.3	41.2	43.4	42.0	41.9	36.8
6.	21.2	22.4	19.9	24.0	9.3	20.2	19.6	21.1	25.2	24.5	17.0	22.4	21.5	16.2	22.2	18.2
5.	7.9	6.5	9.3	8.0	8.2	8.4	8.3	6.2	10.3	8.5	7.7	8.5	6.9	9.7	7.6	13.1
4. Neutral	18.7	15.3	21.5	15.8	29.2	21.4	18.2	20.3	13.6	15.3	23.9	17.3	18.7	20.9	18.4	24.5
3.	3.8	2.9	4.6	3.9	2.9	2.7	3.7	4.2	4.5	4.0	3.1	4.5	2.3	4.4	4.4	-
2.	2.3	1.8	2.8	1.9	4.4	2.5	1.6	2.7	2.4	1.8	3.1	2.6	2.3	2.2	1.9	-
1. Completely dissatisfied	4.2	3.6	4.5	2.8	9.7	6.0	2.7	4.7	3.5	3.1	5.0	3.6	4.8	4.5	3.6	7.4
Item 1290 Subject P02 N	3297	1529	1613	2410	475	666	940	1108	583	1768	1134	1219	793	380	761	32

QUESTIONNAIRE FORM 1 1984	TOTAL	SEX		RACE		REGION				4YR COLLEGE PLANS		ILLICIT DRUG USE: LIFETIME				
		M	F	White	Black	NE	NC	S	W	Yes	No	None	Marijuana Only	Few Pills	More Pills	Any Heroin
N (Weighted No. of Cases):	3311	1534	1616	2414	478	670	941	1113	587	1772	1137	1223	794	381	765	32
% of Weighted Total:	100.0	46.3	48.8	72.9	14.4	20.2	28.4	33.6	17.7	53.5	34.3	36.9	24.0	11.5	23.1	1.0

A006D: The safety of things you own from being stolen or destroyed in your neighborhood, on your job, and in your school?

	TOTAL	M	F	White	Black	NE	NC	S	W	Yes	No	None	Marijuana Only	Few Pills	More Pills	Any Heroin
7. Completely satisfied	23.1	22.7	23.8	23.0	23.8	22.0	21.2	25.9	22.3	23.2	22.6	22.6	23.4	20.8	23.6	27.9
6.	18.6	20.4	17.4	21.7	8.3	16.7	20.5	15.8	22.7	21.3	15.9	19.7	17.8	17.5	19.2	4.2
5.	13.0	15.2	11.2	14.3	6.6	13.3	15.4	9.9	14.7	13.0	12.6	13.3	13.7	12.3	12.5	15.4
4. Neutral	21.4	19.3	22.8	19.1	30.1	21.6	21.0	23.4	17.9	18.0	25.8	22.2	21.1	22.1	19.4	21.9
3.	9.2	9.4	8.9	9.6	8.3	10.4	9.8	8.3	8.9	10.8	7.7	9.1	8.2	12.7	9.6	6.9
2.	5.0	4.6	5.3	5.3	3.8	4.8	3.8	5.0	6.8	5.8	4.0	4.7	4.5	5.3	5.5	11.3
1. Completely dissatisfied	9.7	8.3	10.7	7.1	19.1	11.2	8.2	11.7	6.8	8.0	11.5	8.3	11.3	9.3	10.1	12.3
Item 1300 Subject P02 N	3289	1525	1611	2406	470	665	940	1101	583	1768	1128	1216	790	381	758	32

A006E: Your educational experiences?

	TOTAL	M	F	White	Black	NE	NC	S	W	Yes	No	None	Marijuana Only	Few Pills	More Pills	Any Heroin
7. Completely satisfied	21.6	19.0	24.3	18.8	34.7	21.1	18.8	26.4	17.7	21.5	21.2	25.8	23.6	15.4	14.3	16.6
6.	25.2	26.8	24.7	28.1	15.4	21.1	28.5	23.0	28.6	30.1	19.4	29.3	23.1	27.3	22.1	18.3
5.	15.2	17.4	13.3	17.3	7.4	15.3	16.8	12.8	16.9	16.2	14.8	13.5	16.5	19.5	14.7	19.9
4. Neutral	24.2	23.7	23.8	21.9	30.0	27.5	22.5	25.0	21.5	19.8	29.5	21.1	24.3	22.1	28.4	31.5
3.	5.1	5.2	4.7	5.2	3.7	5.8	5.2	4.0	6.4	5.4	4.3	4.4	4.2	5.7	7.3	1.8
2.	3.7	3.4	4.2	4.1	2.3	3.7	3.7	3.5	4.0	3.9	3.9	3.0	3.0	5.6	5.0	-
1. Completely dissatisfied	5.1	4.5	5.0	4.6	6.4	5.4	4.6	5.3	4.8	3.1	6.9	2.9	5.2	4.4	8.3	12.0
Item 1310 Subject B01,P02 N	3280	1517	1608	2397	473	662	933	1104	581	1762	1128	1211	788	380	760	32

A006F: Your friends and other people you spend time with?

	TOTAL	M	F	White	Black	NE	NC	S	W	Yes	No	None	Marijuana Only	Few Pills	More Pills	Any Heroin
7. Completely satisfied	47.1	44.3	50.1	46.9	50.3	45.8	48.3	49.7	41.9	44.2	50.8	47.7	50.3	42.1	45.7	49.2
6.	25.8	28.8	23.4	29.1	11.8	26.1	25.0	22.6	32.8	28.6	23.2	25.7	26.1	27.8	26.2	31.5
5.	9.0	9.5	8.3	9.4	6.3	9.5	10.1	7.9	8.6	11.1	6.7	8.7	8.7	10.8	9.0	5.0
4. Neutral	12.0	11.4	11.7	8.6	23.9	12.6	10.2	13.6	11.1	10.0	13.5	12.5	10.2	12.4	10.8	8.0
3.	2.9	2.7	3.3	3.1	2.2	2.9	3.2	2.4	3.4	3.2	2.4	2.4	1.9	4.0	4.4	6.3
2.	1.3	1.0	1.5	1.3	1.6	1.3	1.8	1.1	0.9	1.6	1.0	1.1	1.2	1.7	1.4	-
1. Completely dissatisfied	1.9	2.3	1.6	1.6	4.0	1.9	1.4	2.8	1.3	1.4	2.6	1.9	1.6	1.1	2.6	-
Item 1320 Subject M04,P02 N	3294	1527	1613	2408	472	666	937	1107	584	1768	1131	1220	791	381	759	32

A006G: The way you get along with your parents?

	TOTAL	M	F	White	Black	NE	NC	S	W	Yes	No	None	Marijuana Only	Few Pills	More Pills	Any Heroin
7. Completely satisfied	34.2	33.9	34.9	31.7	45.4	35.1	32.0	37.9	29.6	32.4	36.1	37.4	36.8	29.4	28.4	30.1
6.	21.1	22.7	19.7	23.6	11.8	18.6	24.6	18.5	23.5	23.0	19.0	23.3	18.7	23.7	21.0	6.1
5.	11.4	14.2	9.4	12.9	5.7	11.2	12.1	10.4	12.7	13.4	9.5	11.6	11.5	12.3	11.3	14.5
4. Neutral	18.0	17.0	18.2	16.2	24.0	18.9	15.2	19.9	18.2	16.2	19.8	15.6	17.6	17.1	20.8	32.9
3.	5.5	5.1	5.7	6.0	4.3	5.7	4.9	5.1	7.0	6.1	5.4	4.9	5.1	7.9	5.4	5.9
2.	4.7	3.8	5.7	5.2	3.3	4.7	5.9	3.2	5.5	5.0	4.4	3.7	5.2	4.5	5.9	-
1. Completely dissatisfied	5.0	3.2	6.5	4.4	5.5	5.9	5.3	5.0	3.4	3.9	5.9	3.6	5.0	5.1	7.2	10.5
Item 1330 Subject M03,P02 N	3286	1521	1612	2402	471	664	939	1101	582	1767	1126	1218	789	381	758	32

A006H: Yourself?

	TOTAL	M	F	White	Black	NE	NC	S	W	Yes	No	None	Marijuana Only	Few Pills	More Pills	Any Heroin
7. Completely satisfied	31.2	35.6	26.9	26.5	52.7	33.9	26.0	36.8	25.8	27.4	34.9	30.0	35.7	30.2	27.0	17.9
6.	26.7	27.4	26.6	29.6	17.5	25.9	29.0	22.8	31.0	31.3	21.5	27.6	26.1	29.7	26.7	20.4
5.	12.9	13.1	13.2	15.3	3.9	10.9	15.6	11.2	14.2	14.3	11.5	14.3	11.1	11.3	13.6	11.3
4. Neutral	20.7	16.8	23.4	19.8	19.5	20.1	20.6	21.0	21.0	18.3	23.7	19.9	19.6	19.1	23.8	40.7
3.	3.9	3.8	4.1	4.6	1.5	4.5	3.9	3.7	3.8	4.5	3.6	4.0	4.2	5.0	3.1	3.2
2.	2.0	1.7	2.4	2.2	1.3	2.1	1.8	2.2	1.6	2.4	1.9	1.9	1.8	2.4	2.3	2.6
1. Completely dissatisfied	2.6	1.5	3.4	2.0	3.7	2.6	3.1	2.3	2.6	1.9	2.9	2.4	1.4	2.4	3.5	4.0
Item 1340 Subject P01,Q01 N	3267	1516	1602	2391	469	655	938	1097	577	1755	1122	1212	783	375	754	32

A006I: Your standard of living–the things you have like housing, car, furniture, recreation, and the like?

	TOTAL	M	F	White	Black	NE	NC	S	W	Yes	No	None	Marijuana Only	Few Pills	More Pills	Any Heroin
7. Completely satisfied	33.9	33.4	34.3	33.3	37.4	33.1	30.4	37.0	34.3	34.6	31.9	36.7	33.7	28.3	30.4	35.8
6.	25.7	28.2	23.6	29.1	14.6	27.0	28.4	22.1	26.9	28.1	23.5	25.8	27.3	24.0	25.8	26.3
5.	11.6	12.6	10.7	12.6	5.8	11.9	13.0	10.2	11.9	12.5	11.0	11.0	10.5	17.0	11.9	8.9
4. Neutral	16.6	14.4	18.6	14.1	26.2	16.4	16.2	18.3	14.1	13.8	20.4	15.6	16.3	17.6	17.8	12.7
3.	5.3	5.3	5.6	5.6	4.7	3.4	5.6	5.4	6.8	5.5	5.6	5.2	5.1	7.0	5.3	3.2
2.	2.6	2.3	2.9	2.4	3.5	3.3	2.4	2.6	2.3	2.6	2.3	3.1	2.3	1.6	3.2	1.9
1. Completely dissatisfied	4.2	3.9	4.2	2.9	7.7	4.9	4.0	4.3	3.7	3.0	5.4	2.7	4.9	4.5	5.6	11.2
Item 1350 Subject F01,P02 N	3291	1524	1614	2404	475	666	939	1105	581	1768	1132	1219	792	380	760	32

	TOTAL	SEX		RACE		REGION				4YR COLLEGE PLANS		ILLICIT DRUG USE: LIFETIME				
QUESTIONNAIRE FORM 1 1984		M	F	White	Black	NE	NC	S	W	Yes	No	None	Mari- juana Only	Few Pills	More Pills	Any Her- oin
N (Weighted No. of Cases):	3311	1534	1616	2414	478	670	941	1113	587	1772	1137	1223	794	381	765	32
% of Weighted Total:	100.0	46.3	48.8	72.9	14.4	20.2	28.4	33.6	17.7	53.5	34.3	36.9	24.0	11.5	23.1	1.0
A006J: The amount of time you have for doing things you want to do?																
7. Completely satisfied	16.4	16.6	15.9	15.3	18.5	17.4	15.6	17.9	13.6	14.5	17.7	14.4	18.3	16.5	16.6	26.5
6.	16.2	17.9	14.5	17.7	10.4	17.6	17.1	13.5	18.1	17.7	14.4	17.7	14.1	19.6	15.5	13.3
5.	15.3	17.5	13.6	16.8	9.2	12.9	17.8	12.4	19.5	17.5	13.2	16.3	16.0	17.2	13.0	-
4. Neutral	19.6	19.1	20.0	17.1	30.1	20.9	18.1	21.0	17.9	18.3	21.2	20.7	20.3	21.1	15.7	20.4
3.	11.9	11.9	12.0	14.3	4.7	10.6	13.0	11.5	12.3	12.9	10.4	12.5	10.2	8.5	15.4	3.2
2.	8.7	8.0	9.4	8.8	7.8	9.4	7.5	8.4	10.4	8.7	9.8	8.6	8.1	8.2	10.5	3.9
1. Completely dissatisfied	11.9	8.9	14.4	10.0	19.3	11.1	10.9	15.2	8.2	10.5	13.2	9.8	12.9	8.9	13.3	32.6
Item 1360 Subject P02 N	3293	1525	1613	2404	475	665	938	1108	582	1767	1131	1218	792	381	760	32
A006K: The way you spend your leisure time— recreation, relaxation, and so on?																
7. Completely satisfied	30.1	31.1	29.0	28.7	36.7	28.0	31.0	32.8	25.8	28.3	31.4	29.5	30.4	26.9	31.2	38.4
6.	21.1	21.9	21.3	24.3	10.4	21.2	21.3	19.1	24.5	23.3	19.3	20.9	23.0	22.4	21.0	8.3
5.	14.3	16.6	12.5	15.7	9.1	14.9	17.3	11.6	14.0	16.1	12.6	15.9	12.3	16.8	13.0	13.5
4. Neutral	18.2	15.9	19.6	15.9	24.5	20.6	15.7	19.6	16.8	16.6	20.1	17.5	19.3	18.9	16.4	18.0
3.	7.5	7.3	7.5	7.8	4.5	5.4	7.9	6.7	10.5	7.9	6.7	7.5	7.2	5.9	8.9	10.7
2.	3.7	3.5	3.9	4.1	2.9	4.3	3.2	3.7	3.6	3.3	4.3	3.8	2.5	4.3	4.2	1.9
1. Completely dissatisfied	5.2	3.7	6.3	3.5	11.9	5.5	3.6	6.5	4.9	4.6	5.7	4.8	5.4	4.9	5.3	9.3
Item 1370 Subject C08,P02 N	3290	1526	1610	2403	475	662	940	1107	581	1766	1131	1218	793	381	758	30
A006L: Your life as a whole these days?																
7. Completely satisfied	19.8	20.5	19.5	19.2	25.9	18.9	17.5	23.5	17.4	18.7	21.7	20.7	22.3	15.9	17.4	15.8
6.	26.9	29.0	25.5	30.1	14.0	26.6	29.9	23.2	29.8	30.5	22.8	28.8	26.0	31.4	24.2	24.1
5.	17.0	19.0	15.5	19.0	10.6	17.6	18.4	13.9	19.8	18.8	15.4	15.8	16.2	16.9	20.3	20.9
4. Neutral	23.7	21.2	25.0	20.2	36.8	23.4	21.4	27.4	20.5	20.7	26.4	23.8	23.9	19.8	24.4	25.0
3.	6.3	5.6	6.9	6.2	3.9	6.0	6.8	5.5	7.4	6.3	6.1	5.9	5.7	8.7	6.6	4.1
2.	2.5	2.2	3.0	2.5	2.0	2.3	2.2	3.0	2.3	2.4	2.9	1.7	2.3	4.0	3.0	2.7
1. Completely dissatisfied	3.8	2.6	4.6	2.9	6.9	5.2	3.9	3.6	2.8	2.7	4.7	3.2	3.6	3.3	4.1	7.3
Item 1380 Subject P01 N	3282	1522	1608	2401	473	660	938	1102	582	1763	1129	1217	791	379	757	30
A006M: The way our national government is operating?																
7. Completely satisfied	3.6	4.6	2.8	3.4	4.5	2.5	2.8	5.1	3.1	3.6	3.1	4.5	2.7	1.8	3.3	4.1
6.	6.1	8.9	3.7	7.1	2.1	4.6	5.4	6.8	7.5	7.0	4.2	6.3	5.8	8.4	5.1	-
5.	13.2	14.5	12.2	15.1	4.9	11.6	13.0	13.6	14.4	16.4	9.1	16.5	12.2	10.8	10.9	13.0
4. Neutral	40.2	35.6	44.7	40.0	40.0	41.5	38.8	40.0	41.4	39.7	42.1	38.2	43.3	37.0	43.1	49.3
3.	12.1	12.9	11.3	13.4	8.4	12.5	14.7	10.2	11.3	13.2	11.7	10.8	11.5	15.6	12.8	13.7
2.	8.4	8.6	8.4	8.4	8.7	9.7	8.5	6.7	9.8	8.3	8.9	8.3	7.5	10.9	8.0	1.8
1. Completely dissatisfied	16.4	15.0	17.0	12.6	31.4	17.5	16.7	17.6	12.4	11.7	20.9	15.5	16.9	15.5	16.8	18.1
Item 1390 Subject H02,K02 N	3287	1523	1610	2402	473	665	940	1103	579	1768	1128	1216	793	380	757	32
A006N: The amount of fun you are having?																
7. Completely satisfied	24.7	25.0	24.6	23.6	29.4	24.7	24.7	27.3	19.5	22.3	27.0	22.4	28.1	22.4	24.8	34.9
6.	24.9	26.3	23.8	27.9	12.7	23.5	27.9	21.5	27.9	27.9	21.5	26.5	24.0	27.3	24.1	9.8
5.	17.0	17.5	15.9	18.6	10.3	17.4	17.0	14.1	21.9	18.4	15.3	17.6	15.0	19.6	17.4	14.5
4. Neutral	19.7	18.9	20.6	17.1	33.0	18.3	17.1	23.5	18.6	17.7	22.8	20.0	20.2	15.7	19.5	21.2
3.	5.8	5.8	6.0	6.1	4.1	5.8	6.7	5.6	4.6	6.6	4.7	6.4	5.1	5.9	5.3	9.7
2.	3.1	3.2	3.2	3.5	1.7	3.8	2.1	3.0	4.2	2.9	3.8	2.6	2.9	3.6	4.1	3.6
1. Completely dissatisfied	4.9	3.3	5.8	3.3	8.8	6.5	4.6	4.9	3.3	4.1	5.0	4.4	4.7	5.5	4.8	6.2
Item 1400 Subject P02,Q01 N	3296	1525	1616	2406	477	667	940	1106	583	1769	1133	1218	793	381	762	32
A007: How important is each of the following to you in your life?																
A007A: Being successful in my line of work																
1. Not important	1.2	1.2	0.9	0.9	1.0	0.8	0.9	1.8	1.0	0.9	1.4	0.8	1.2	1.1	1.1	2.7
2. Somewhat important	8.5	8.5	7.2	8.5	6.3	10.6	7.6	7.4	9.4	6.5	11.1	7.3	9.3	7.5	8.5	6.6
3. Quite important	31.7	31.4	32.5	34.8	19.0	31.2	35.8	28.9	30.9	29.7	34.9	33.6	29.0	30.5	33.6	33.4
4. Extremely important	58.6	58.8	59.3	55.9	73.6	57.3	55.6	61.8	58.8	62.9	52.5	58.2	60.5	60.9	56.9	57.3
Item 1410 Subject C06,Q07 N	3274	1518	1600	2396	468	664	936	1097	577	1755	1123	1213	784	378	756	32

QUESTIONNAIRE FORM 1 1984	TOTAL	SEX		RACE		REGION				4YR COLLEGE PLANS		ILLICIT DRUG USE: LIFETIME				
		M	F	White	Black	NE	NC	S	W	Yes	No	None	Mari-juana Only	Few Pills	More Pills	Any Her-oin
N (Weighted No. of Cases):	3311	1534	1616	2414	478	670	941	1113	587	1772	1137	1223	794	381	765	32
% of Weighted Total:	100.0	46.3	48.8	72.9	14.4	20.2	28.4	33.6	17.7	53.5	34.3	36.9	24.0	11.5	23.1	1.0
A007B: Having a good marriage and family life																
1. Not important	4.7	6.2	2.7	4.0	5.6	4.5	4.0	4.1	6.9	4.1	4.6	4.4	3.2	5.6	5.5	11.6
2. Somewhat important	7.7	9.4	5.5	8.2	5.3	9.3	8.4	6.2	7.4	6.3	9.4	6.4	8.2	6.4	10.0	11.5
3. Quite important	14.8	17.0	12.7	14.1	17.8	15.0	16.4	13.9	13.8	15.2	14.8	13.9	14.9	14.9	15.4	12.4
4. Extremely important	72.8	67.4	79.1	73.7	71.3	71.2	71.2	75.8	72.0	74.5	71.1	75.2	73.7	73.0	69.1	64.5
Item 1420 Subject D03,Q07 N	3273	1512	1604	2391	469	666	936	1094	577	1754	1127	1211	783	378	759	30
A007C: Having lots of money																
1. Not important	5.6	5.1	5.9	5.8	3.6	4.4	4.7	7.1	5.5	5.3	6.3	6.7	5.3	3.7	4.2	9.4
2. Somewhat important	34.1	29.7	38.7	37.0	24.9	29.9	39.1	32.1	34.6	35.3	35.4	39.8	33.6	32.3	27.9	26.8
3. Quite important	35.8	36.4	36.0	36.4	34.6	36.5	36.2	34.3	37.3	36.8	34.9	34.6	36.2	40.5	36.8	20.7
4. Extremely important	24.5	28.8	19.3	20.7	37.0	29.3	20.0	26.6	22.6	22.6	23.3	18.9	24.9	23.5	31.1	43.1
Item 1430 Subject F01,Q07 N	3276	1515	1605	2396	469	664	934	1101	577	1756	1127	1212	785	380	758	32
A007D: Having plenty of time for recreation and hobbies																
1. Not important	3.0	1.9	3.5	1.8	7.1	3.6	2.6	2.6	3.7	2.3	3.4	2.9	3.4	3.6	1.7	-
2. Somewhat important	31.4	25.8	36.9	30.4	39.2	25.6	35.1	35.2	24.9	28.3	37.1	35.4	31.3	26.5	27.2	32.0
3. Quite important	40.4	41.0	40.5	41.4	35.0	40.4	40.5	38.5	43.8	43.3	36.9	40.2	42.2	42.6	39.5	27.2
4. Extremely important	25.2	31.2	19.2	26.3	18.7	30.5	21.8	23.6	27.6	26.1	22.5	21.4	23.1	27.3	31.7	40.8
Item 1440 Subject C08,Q07 N	3287	1521	1610	2400	473	666	937	1104	580	1763	1129	1219	788	381	758	32
A007E: Having strong friendships																
1. Not important	1.2	1.0	1.1	0.6	3.3	1.1	0.7	1.5	1.5	1.2	1.0	1.2	1.0	1.6	0.6	-
2. Somewhat important	8.0	7.6	8.5	6.4	18.0	6.4	8.2	9.8	6.4	6.5	10.9	8.1	8.6	6.5	6.5	1.8
3. Quite important	28.9	30.4	26.9	26.8	37.3	25.5	31.7	29.7	26.6	26.1	32.5	29.2	28.5	28.0	28.1	37.4
4. Extremely important	61.9	61.0	63.6	66.2	41.4	67.1	59.4	59.0	65.4	66.1	55.6	61.4	61.9	64.0	64.9	60.8
Item 1450 Subject M04,Q07 N	3280	1515	1609	2396	471	662	938	1102	578	1755	1130	1215	787	381	756	31
A007F: Being able to find steady work																
1. Not important	0.8	1.1	0.5	0.6	0.7	0.4	0.3	1.2	1.3	0.9	0.6	0.9	0.8	0.4	0.3	3.3
2. Somewhat important	3.8	3.6	4.0	4.1	3.4	4.3	2.9	4.8	2.9	4.2	3.5	3.6	3.8	4.1	3.9	2.6
3. Quite important	23.4	21.9	24.9	25.8	14.1	23.4	27.4	19.5	24.3	23.2	24.8	25.5	21.8	22.6	22.4	36.3
4. Extremely important	72.0	73.4	70.7	69.6	81.8	71.9	69.4	74.5	71.5	71.8	71.1	70.1	73.6	72.9	73.3	57.9
Item 1460 Subject C04,Q07 N	3285	1521	1608	2400	474	666	938	1102	579	1760	1130	1217	788	381	759	32
A007G: Making a contribution to society																
1. Not important	8.0	8.1	7.2	7.5	6.7	8.5	8.1	6.4	10.5	5.7	11.1	6.5	6.6	7.8	10.6	21.3
2. Somewhat important	40.7	39.1	42.2	41.8	40.1	42.1	46.2	37.9	35.4	36.0	47.7	40.2	40.7	35.6	45.2	38.2
3. Quite important	36.3	37.5	35.8	36.0	39.3	36.4	32.4	37.7	39.9	38.5	33.5	36.7	38.6	41.0	31.2	26.6
4. Extremely important	15.0	15.3	14.8	14.7	13.8	13.0	13.3	18.0	14.2	19.8	7.8	16.6	14.2	15.5	13.0	13.9
Item 1470 Subject O01,Q07 N	3274	1515	1603	2395	467	663	936	1098	578	1752	1128	1213	782	379	758	32
A007H: Being a leader in my community																
1. Not important	36.1	32.1	38.9	35.8	36.5	39.6	37.5	31.1	39.5	26.7	49.1	34.5	33.5	31.7	43.8	38.9
2. Somewhat important	39.3	40.0	39.8	40.8	35.1	39.3	40.6	40.2	35.6	42.9	35.7	40.9	41.5	39.5	35.6	36.1
3. Quite important	17.0	18.2	15.6	16.7	19.5	15.1	15.1	19.2	18.1	21.2	10.5	16.7	18.6	19.5	13.9	15.0
4. Extremely important	7.6	9.7	5.7	6.7	8.9	5.9	6.9	9.6	6.8	9.3	4.7	7.9	6.4	9.3	6.7	10.0
Item 1480 Subject M05,Q07 N	3279	1519	1605	2397	471	661	938	1103	576	1755	1130	1218	784	378	757	32
A007I: Being able to give my children better opportunities than I've had																
1. Not important	2.5	2.7	2.1	2.7	1.0	1.2	3.5	1.6	4.1	2.7	1.9	2.0	1.7	2.7	4.0	-
2. Somewhat important	10.6	10.8	10.0	11.9	4.9	11.9	12.4	7.6	12.0	11.1	9.9	12.9	8.8	10.7	8.7	11.8
3. Quite important	30.3	31.6	29.7	34.8	16.7	32.5	34.8	24.4	31.7	31.0	31.5	29.3	32.6	29.6	31.3	37.7
4. Extremely important	56.6	54.9	58.1	50.7	77.4	54.4	49.3	66.4	52.2	55.1	56.7	55.8	56.9	56.9	56.0	50.6
Item 1490 Subject Q07 N	3255	1510	1589	2378	466	661	932	1094	569	1744	1119	1207	781	375	748	32

QUESTIONNAIRE FORM 1 1984	TOTAL	SEX		RACE		REGION				4YR COLLEGE PLANS		ILLICIT DRUG USE: LIFETIME				
		M	F	White	Black	NE	NC	S	W	Yes	No	None	Mari-juana Only	Few Pills	More Pills	Any Her-oin
N (Weighted No. of Cases):	3311	1534	1616	2414	478	670	941	1113	587	1772	1137	1223	794	381	765	32
% of Weighted Total:	100.0	46.3	48.8	72.9	14.4	20.2	28.4	33.6	17.7	53.5	34.3	36.9	24.0	11.5	23.1	1.0
A007J: Living close to parents and relatives																
1. Not important	24.9	25.3	23.8	25.1	26.1	21.7	26.0	25.3	26.3	25.4	23.8	20.3	25.9	26.7	30.1	24.2
2. Somewhat important	42.2	43.8	41.0	42.6	43.9	43.6	42.9	40.4	42.6	42.1	42.8	42.2	44.3	40.8	42.1	38.6
3. Quite important	22.4	21.6	23.5	23.0	17.6	22.7	21.8	23.4	21.2	22.7	22.3	25.3	21.5	23.2	18.8	18.9
4. Extremely important	10.5	9.3	11.7	9.3	12.4	11.9	9.3	10.9	9.8	9.8	11.1	12.2	8.3	9.3	9.0	18.4
Item 1500 Subject M03,Q07 N	3281	1518	1609	2396	474	664	936	1102	578	1761	1127	1218	784	380	758	32
A007K: Getting away from this area of the country																
1. Not important	51.4	52.6	51.0	53.7	44.3	45.7	49.2	54.3	56.1	52.9	52.1	57.7	49.8	49.1	46.4	51.2
2. Somewhat important	23.3	22.9	23.2	22.7	24.9	24.7	23.0	23.5	21.8	22.8	22.2	21.3	24.3	27.0	23.4	18.4
3. Quite important	13.1	12.2	14.0	12.2	15.9	16.2	14.0	11.3	11.3	13.2	12.7	11.9	14.3	10.3	13.5	15.4
4. Extremely important	12.2	12.3	11.9	11.4	14.8	13.3	13.8	10.9	10.8	11.1	13.0	9.1	11.5	13.6	16.7	15.0
Item 1510 Subject Q07 N	3282	1521	1606	2399	473	666	937	1103	576	1760	1130	1217	786	381	757	32
A007L: Working to correct social and economic inequalities																
1. Not important	23.2	25.5	20.5	25.5	14.6	24.4	25.8	19.8	24.1	21.1	26.6	20.6	23.6	22.6	27.7	11.0
2. Somewhat important	46.4	45.8	48.0	49.4	38.5	47.0	48.3	46.2	43.2	46.5	48.3	46.3	47.1	44.2	46.9	55.9
3. Quite important	21.8	20.5	22.7	18.8	31.8	20.1	19.8	24.2	22.1	22.8	18.5	23.8	21.4	23.5	17.3	30.4
4. Extremely important	8.6	8.2	8.8	6.4	15.0	8.5	6.1	9.8	10.6	9.6	6.6	9.3	7.9	9.8	8.0	2.7
Item 1520 Subject N02,O01,Q07 N	3261	1508	1599	2381	469	661	932	1097	571	1746	1123	1206	779	378	758	32
A007M: Discovering new ways to experience things																
1. Not important	9.3	10.2	8.3	10.0	7.7	7.7	11.9	10.1	5.7	8.4	11.9	10.6	9.7	7.0	8.1	10.2
2. Somewhat important	36.4	36.4	36.6	38.1	32.6	35.4	40.7	33.8	35.6	35.3	40.5	39.6	35.9	38.5	32.3	35.6
3. Quite important	36.8	36.1	38.0	35.9	38.9	39.8	32.9	37.6	38.2	37.5	33.4	35.5	37.1	35.4	38.5	32.9
4. Extremely important	17.4	17.3	17.2	16.0	20.8	17.1	14.5	18.5	20.4	18.8	14.2	14.4	17.3	19.1	21.1	21.4
Item 1530 Subject Q07 N	3278	1517	1606	2394	472	663	935	1102	579	1758	1127	1215	784	380	759	32
A007N: Finding purpose and meaning in my life																
1. Not important	2.7	4.1	1.1	2.8	1.1	3.7	2.2	2.1	3.6	2.3	3.1	2.6	2.4	3.1	2.4	11.7
2. Somewhat important	11.0	14.0	7.8	12.6	6.6	12.1	12.7	8.6	11.7	10.5	12.5	12.3	10.4	12.3	9.0	16.1
3. Quite important	29.0	33.8	24.6	31.2	20.9	30.5	32.4	25.5	28.7	26.3	34.0	27.7	30.9	24.5	32.2	17.9
4. Extremely important	57.3	48.1	66.5	53.4	71.4	53.8	52.7	63.9	55.9	60.9	50.4	57.4	56.3	60.1	56.4	54.4
Item 1540 Subject Q07 N	3279	1517	1608	2394	474	665	936	1102	576	1758	1131	1217	785	378	758	32
A008: Generally speaking, would you say that most people can be trusted or that you can't be too careful in dealing with people?																
3. Most people can be trusted	27.5	29.8	25.7	31.5	12.4	24.3	32.9	24.1	29.0	31.3	23.6	30.5	27.9	25.4	22.9	22.5
2. Don't know, undecided	25.9	26.9	24.9	27.0	18.1	27.6	26.9	23.1	27.7	25.1	27.6	27.0	23.2	30.0	25.1	37.3
1. Can't be too careful	46.6	43.2	49.4	41.5	69.5	48.1	40.2	52.9	43.3	43.6	48.8	42.6	48.9	44.6	51.9	40.2
Item 1550 Subject Q05 N	3223	1485	1591	2365	464	653	923	1079	568	1745	1105	1198	772	373	749	29
A009: Would you say that most of the time people try to be helpful or that they are mostly just looking out for themselves?																
3. Try to be helpful	34.0	29.4	38.3	35.3	27.8	34.1	37.4	31.4	33.2	35.6	33.6	37.1	34.6	31.3	29.5	29.3
2. Don't know, undecided	31.1	34.3	28.5	32.4	24.8	33.2	31.1	28.8	32.8	30.8	31.1	27.6	31.3	37.2	33.7	37.5
1. Just looking out for themselves	35.0	36.3	33.3	32.4	47.4	32.7	31.5	39.8	34.0	33.6	35.3	35.3	34.1	31.5	36.8	33.2
Item 1560 Subject Q05 N	3274	1518	1605	2393	474	663	939	1099	574	1756	1130	1220	784	379	755	30
A010: Do you think most people would try to take advantage of you if they got a chance or would they try to be fair?																
3. Would try to be fair	26.3	24.5	27.8	29.0	11.8	26.1	30.0	22.4	27.9	29.0	23.2	29.5	25.4	28.6	21.5	26.0
2. Don't know, undecided	32.8	33.4	32.4	36.0	20.3	32.1	34.8	29.8	36.4	31.7	34.6	32.3	34.1	30.6	35.0	26.8
1. Would try to take advantage of you	40.9	42.1	39.8	35.0	67.9	41.8	35.3	47.8	35.8	39.2	42.2	38.2	40.5	40.7	43.5	47.2
Item 1570 Subject Q05 N	3278	1520	1606	2395	474	665	938	1101	574	1758	1131	1220	784	380	758	30

QUESTIONNAIRE FORM 1 1984	TOTAL	SEX		RACE		REGION				4YR COLLEGE PLANS		ILLICIT DRUG USE: LIFETIME				
		M	F	White	Black	NE	NC	S	W	Yes	No	None	Marijuana Only	Few Pills	More Pills	Any Heroin
N (Weighted No. of Cases):	3311	1534	1616	2414	478	670	941	1113	587	1772	1137	1223	794	381	765	32
% of Weighted Total:	100.0	46.3	48.8	72.9	14.4	20.2	28.4	33.6	17.7	53.5	34.3	36.9	24.0	11.5	23.1	1.0

A011: These next questions ask your opinions about a number of different topics. How much do you agree or disagree with each statement below?

A011A: I feel that you can't be a good citizen unless you always obey the law

	TOTAL	M	F	White	Black	NE	NC	S	W	Yes	No	None	Mari- juana Only	Few Pills	More Pills	Any Her- oin
1. Disagree	17.1	20.0	13.8	15.7	21.2	20.7	14.8	16.9	17.1	17.5	15.9	13.3	16.6	20.7	20.9	35.1
2. Mostly disagree	18.4	18.1	18.6	19.8	13.2	20.6	21.8	14.5	18.0	19.3	17.3	14.6	18.8	22.9	23.4	7.1
3. Neither	19.5	19.8	19.6	20.3	15.6	21.4	20.4	16.3	22.0	18.5	21.6	18.8	20.8	19.2	19.7	26.1
4. Mostly agree	33.1	30.9	35.4	34.4	27.9	29.6	33.3	35.2	32.6	34.3	32.4	38.0	33.6	27.6	27.9	29.4
5. Agree	11.9	11.2	12.6	9.7	22.1	7.7	9.7	17.2	10.3	10.4	12.9	15.4	10.2	9.6	8.1	2.3
Item 1580 Subject H03 N	3277	1520	1607	2399	471	663	939	1099	577	1760	1128	1221	782	381	757	32

A011B: I feel a good citizen should go along with whatever the government does even if he disagrees with it

	TOTAL	M	F	White	Black	NE	NC	S	W	Yes	No	None	Mari- juana Only	Few Pills	More Pills	Any Her- oin
1. Disagree	39.6	37.5	41.7	37.9	47.9	44.5	37.4	39.9	37.1	40.9	37.3	35.0	40.2	39.0	47.0	40.0
2. Mostly disagree	25.3	24.0	26.5	26.8	17.6	26.2	27.5	21.3	28.3	25.0	26.5	26.1	26.7	25.8	22.9	28.7
3. Neither	17.2	18.4	16.4	18.6	13.6	14.4	20.1	16.4	17.4	15.8	19.4	18.3	15.8	18.0	17.0	19.4
4. Mostly agree	12.5	13.8	11.2	12.7	11.0	12.0	11.0	13.9	12.7	13.2	11.1	15.0	10.2	13.3	9.5	4.9
5. Agree	5.4	6.3	4.2	4.1	9.9	2.9	4.0	8.6	4.4	5.0	5.8	5.4	7.2	3.9	3.6	7.0
Item 1590 Subject H03 N	3279	1517	1610	2396	474	664	938	1102	575	1759	1130	1219	785	379	758	32

A011C: I feel a good citizen tries to change the government policies he disagrees with

	TOTAL	M	F	White	Black	NE	NC	S	W	Yes	No	None	Mari- juana Only	Few Pills	More Pills	Any Her- oin
1. Disagree	7.6	6.3	8.3	5.8	13.6	6.2	5.5	9.9	8.2	6.7	8.1	7.1	7.4	7.2	7.9	2.5
2. Mostly disagree	9.9	9.3	10.5	9.8	9.4	10.2	10.4	9.5	9.3	9.2	11.1	9.2	10.4	11.8	10.1	-
3. Neither	25.8	23.2	28.0	26.4	25.1	26.4	29.7	23.0	24.0	22.9	30.2	24.2	25.9	28.3	26.7	32.5
4. Mostly agree	30.8	31.3	30.3	33.1	23.9	32.2	32.0	29.6	29.5	32.0	29.4	31.6	30.2	31.5	30.6	29.9
5. Agree	25.9	29.8	22.9	24.9	28.0	25.0	22.4	28.0	28.9	29.2	21.2	27.9	26.2	21.3	24.7	35.1
Item 1600 Subject H03 N	3259	1512	1600	2390	471	659	932	1094	575	1751	1125	1217	778	376	753	30

A011D: The way people vote has a major impact on how things are run in this country

	TOTAL	M	F	White	Black	NE	NC	S	W	Yes	No	None	Mari- juana Only	Few Pills	More Pills	Any Her- oin
1. Disagree	6.0	7.2	4.8	6.0	4.3	6.3	5.0	6.7	5.8	5.7	5.9	5.5	5.1	8.1	6.4	8.6
2. Mostly disagree	9.1	9.2	8.3	9.4	6.9	9.1	8.8	7.9	11.8	9.6	8.5	8.0	9.3	9.1	11.0	3.6
3. Neither	13.3	13.5	13.2	13.9	7.9	15.5	15.6	10.0	13.5	13.0	14.0	13.0	15.1	10.0	12.8	20.1
4. Mostly agree	33.2	32.2	34.6	34.5	29.7	32.8	38.1	30.4	31.1	34.2	33.0	34.1	32.9	31.2	34.3	32.2
5. Agree	38.4	37.8	39.1	36.3	51.2	36.4	32.5	44.9	37.8	37.6	38.6	39.2	37.6	41.5	35.5	35.6
Item 1610 Subject H05,I02 N	3270	1518	1604	2394	472	659	935	1098	577	1756	1128	1215	783	381	755	32

A011E: People who get together in citizen action groups to influence government policies can have a real effect

	TOTAL	M	F	White	Black	NE	NC	S	W	Yes	No	None	Mari- juana Only	Few Pills	More Pills	Any Her- oin
1. Disagree	3.5	4.2	2.5	3.2	3.2	4.2	2.7	4.1	2.7	2.9	3.6	3.1	3.7	4.4	3.7	6.5
2. Mostly disagree	8.7	9.2	8.2	8.8	7.5	8.5	9.0	8.1	9.7	8.1	9.4	6.9	11.5	10.4	8.3	6.3
3. Neither	27.6	27.9	27.1	29.7	18.5	29.0	31.6	24.6	25.5	26.3	30.9	24.8	28.3	28.5	31.3	20.5
4. Mostly agree	37.4	36.9	38.2	38.0	33.7	37.2	39.1	34.9	39.7	40.1	34.7	39.5	35.0	38.7	36.5	33.4
5. Agree	22.8	21.8	24.0	20.3	37.2	21.2	17.6	28.4	22.4	22.6	21.4	25.7	21.6	18.0	20.2	33.2
Item 1620 Subject H03,I02 N	3263	1513	1603	2389	472	659	932	1095	577	1755	1126	1214	782	381	751	32

A011F: Despite its many faults, our system of doing things is still the best in the world

	TOTAL	M	F	White	Black	NE	NC	S	W	Yes	No	None	Mari- juana Only	Few Pills	More Pills	Any Her- oin
1. Disagree	5.8	5.3	6.2	4.3	10.6	6.8	6.0	6.2	3.5	5.0	6.7	4.6	6.2	4.6	6.5	7.9
2. Mostly disagree	6.3	4.9	7.1	5.6	7.1	6.9	6.8	5.6	6.2	4.7	7.9	5.3	5.9	5.7	7.7	5.7
3. Neither	20.2	17.2	22.2	19.8	19.5	21.3	22.6	17.5	20.3	18.4	23.2	20.1	21.5	21.3	18.7	28.8
4. Mostly agree	31.3	30.2	32.9	32.7	27.1	34.6	33.8	26.8	32.2	31.7	32.0	31.5	30.7	35.3	31.6	24.1
5. Agree	36.4	42.4	31.5	37.6	35.7	30.4	30.7	44.0	37.9	40.2	30.2	38.4	35.7	33.2	35.5	33.4
Item 1630 Subject H04 N	3250	1506	1596	2376	470	655	927	1093	575	1746	1123	1206	777	381	752	32

QUESTIONNAIRE FORM 1 1984	TOTAL	SEX		RACE		REGION				4YR COLLEGE PLANS		ILLICIT DRUG USE: LIFETIME				
		M	F	White	Black	NE	NC	S	W	Yes	No	None	Mari- juana Only	Few Pills	More Pills	Any Her- oin
N (Weighted No. of Cases):	3311	1534	1616	2414	478	670	941	1113	587	1772	1137	1223	794	381	765	32
% of Weighted Total:	100.0	46.3	48.8	72.9	14.4	20.2	28.4	33.6	17.7	53.5	34.3	36.9	24.0	11.5	23.1	1.0

A011G: America needs growth to survive, and that is going to require some increase in pollution

	TOTAL	M	F	White	Black	NE	NC	S	W	Yes	No	None	Mari-juana Only	Few Pills	More Pills	Any Heroin
1. Disagree	37.1	37.8	37.2	37.2	37.7	38.3	36.5	36.9	37.0	38.8	35.4	37.5	35.8	39.5	38.3	26.5
2. Mostly disagree	21.9	20.9	23.2	23.8	17.6	23.7	21.6	21.3	21.5	25.4	17.6	22.4	22.8	21.7	22.0	14.8
3. Neither	22.1	20.8	23.1	22.5	19.2	21.7	23.1	20.9	22.8	20.2	24.9	21.2	22.2	21.5	23.4	26.4
4. Mostly agree	12.3	14.1	10.3	11.8	12.9	10.7	13.7	12.1	12.4	10.1	15.3	12.9	12.2	11.6	11.1	20.5
5. Agree	6.6	6.4	6.2	4.6	12.5	5.6	5.1	8.7	6.3	5.5	6.8	6.1	6.9	5.7	5.2	11.9
Item 1640 Subject F04 N	3259	1509	1603	2387	470	659	936	1089	575	1755	1125	1210	783	380	752	32

A011H: If we just leave things to God, they will turn out for the best

	TOTAL	M	F	White	Black	NE	NC	S	W	Yes	No	None	Mari-juana Only	Few Pills	More Pills	Any Heroin
1. Disagree	19.2	22.4	16.0	21.1	7.5	26.9	15.0	12.0	30.5	23.0	13.6	16.3	17.9	24.2	23.2	31.5
2. Mostly disagree	13.6	15.3	12.1	15.4	4.9	15.2	16.4	9.7	14.6	13.9	13.9	12.0	15.3	14.5	15.1	10.9
3. Neither	24.8	23.4	25.7	26.7	14.0	25.5	28.5	20.6	25.8	23.7	26.6	24.7	24.5	21.4	27.8	19.9
4. Mostly agree	18.1	18.9	18.1	17.5	26.2	14.3	19.1	22.0	13.7	18.9	17.7	19.8	17.6	20.2	14.0	9.2
5. Agree	24.3	20.1	28.1	19.2	47.5	18.0	20.9	35.7	15.4	20.5	28.2	27.2	24.8	19.7	19.9	28.5
Item 1650 Subject I02 N	3237	1498	1591	2372	466	656	925	1084	572	1740	1117	1198	778	376	749	32

A011I: Going to school has been an enjoyable experience for me

	TOTAL	M	F	White	Black	NE	NC	S	W	Yes	No	None	Mari-juana Only	Few Pills	More Pills	Any Heroin
1. Disagree	6.4	7.7	4.9	6.2	4.5	10.4	6.3	5.1	4.7	4.3	8.8	4.5	4.9	7.8	10.2	12.2
2. Mostly disagree	7.0	5.9	7.9	7.2	5.7	7.7	7.6	6.8	5.8	5.9	8.6	5.7	5.8	8.9	9.5	8.0
3. Neither	15.8	17.5	13.0	16.5	10.3	18.5	15.1	12.5	19.8	13.8	17.7	14.0	14.9	15.6	19.3	6.3
4. Mostly agree	39.8	41.7	39.6	41.6	37.8	40.0	41.3	38.1	40.1	43.1	36.7	41.6	40.5	35.1	38.4	50.6
5. Agree	31.0	27.2	34.6	28.5	41.7	23.3	29.7	37.4	29.6	32.9	28.3	34.2	33.9	32.6	22.6	22.9
Item 1660 Subject B01 N	3263	1512	1603	2385	472	660	931	1095	577	1754	1123	1217	779	379	753	32

A011J: Doing well in school is important for getting a good job

	TOTAL	M	F	White	Black	NE	NC	S	W	Yes	No	None	Mari-juana Only	Few Pills	More Pills	Any Heroin
1. Disagree	2.4	3.4	1.4	2.4	1.2	3.0	2.1	1.6	4.1	1.9	2.9	1.3	1.9	1.8	5.0	8.6
2. Mostly disagree	2.6	3.5	1.4	2.7	1.4	3.8	2.2	1.5	3.8	1.7	3.2	1.3	2.8	3.6	3.8	7.8
3. Neither	7.2	8.3	5.5	7.5	3.2	8.6	7.7	6.0	7.1	5.7	9.1	5.2	6.9	10.1	4.6	
4. Mostly agree	29.5	32.1	27.0	30.4	26.0	29.9	31.0	26.7	32.0	28.2	31.7	28.5	30.6	29.3	31.1	17.4
5. Agree	58.3	52.7	64.7	57.1	68.2	54.8	57.0	64.2	53.0	62.5	53.1	63.7	57.8	56.4	50.0	61.6
Item 1670 Subject B01 N	3274	1516	1607	2394	472	663	935	1100	577	1755	1131	1217	783	381	756	32

The following questions are about CIGARETTE SMOKING.

B001: Have you ever smoked cigarettes?

	TOTAL	M	F	White	Black	NE	NC	S	W	Yes	No	None	Mari-juana Only	Few Pills	More Pills	Any Heroin
1. Never–GO TO Q.B006	31.1	34.3	29.5	30.4	40.2	26.2	31.0	33.1	33.0	36.1	26.5	58.5	15.4	18.3	10.6	11.8
2. Once or twice	30.2	31.6	29.1	28.6	37.1	29.2	29.1	29.9	33.6	32.3	28.8	28.5	42.1	34.2	19.2	18.7
3. Occasionally but not regularly	16.7	14.7	18.2	17.1	13.3	16.9	16.6	17.4	15.3	17.1	15.0	7.6	22.4	20.8	22.2	16.9
4. Regularly in the past	6.6	6.6	6.7	7.6	2.7	7.0	6.7	5.3	8.5	5.7	8.1	2.7	7.1	8.2	11.3	14.1
5. Regularly now	15.4	12.8	16.5	16.2	6.7	20.7	16.7	14.2	9.7	8.9	21.5	2.7	12.9	18.4	36.8	38.5
Item 760 Subject A01a N	3245	1505	1595	2384	463	655	927	1085	577	1747	1118	1202	776	381	756	28

B002: When did you first smoke cigarettes on a daily basis?

	TOTAL	M	F	White	Black	NE	NC	S	W	Yes	No	None	Mari-juana Only	Few Pills	More Pills	Any Heroin
0. Never smoked daily	53.2	57.7	51.6	53.7	58.2	47.5	53.2	53.2	60.1	64.3	44.7	72.6	59.8	54.2	33.5	23.7
1. Grade 6 or earlier	6.2	7.2	4.9	6.3	5.1	7.8	7.7	5.5	3.0	4.4	7.1	4.5	5.9	5.4	7.9	16.2
2. Grade 7 or 8	12.1	9.8	12.8	11.7	11.0	16.1	12.2	10.5	10.1	7.3	16.0	7.0	9.2	9.6	19.1	21.1
3. Grade 9 (Freshman)	9.5	8.1	10.4	9.5	8.3	11.9	6.5	11.1	8.5	7.4	11.3	5.6	8.2	7.9	13.9	26.3
4. Grade 10 (Sophomore)	8.9	8.0	9.9	9.7	4.9	7.8	10.7	8.6	8.0	7.0	11.9	4.0	8.1	12.4	12.5	5.0
5. Grade 11 (Junior)	6.4	5.6	6.7	5.7	8.8	5.9	6.3	6.4	7.2	5.5	5.9	3.6	5.9	6.9	8.5	2.9
6. Grade 12 (Senior)	3.6	3.6	3.7	3.5	3.7	2.9	3.3	4.7	3.2	4.1	3.0	2.8	2.9	3.5	4.5	4.9
Item 1680 Subject A01g N★	2228	980	1124	1650	276	481	642	723	383	1110	818	498	654	307	674	25

★=excludes respondents for whom question was inappropriate.

QUESTIONNAIRE FORM 1 1984	TOTAL	SEX		RACE		REGION				4YR COLLEGE PLANS		ILLICIT DRUG USE: LIFETIME				
		M	F	White	Black	NE	NC	S	W	Yes	No	None	Mari-juana Only	Few Pills	More Pills	Any Her-oin
N (Weighted No. of Cases):	3311	1534	1616	2414	478	670	941	1113	587	1772	1137	1223	794	381	765	32
% of Weighted Total:	100.0	46.3	48.8	72.9	14.4	20.2	28.4	33.6	17.7	53.5	34.3	36.9	24.0	11.5	23.1	1.0

B003: How frequently have you smoked cigarettes during the past 30 days?

	TOTAL	M	F	White	Black	NE	NC	S	W	Yes	No	None	Mari-juana Only	Few Pills	More Pills	Any Her-oin
1. Not at all	59.9	62.7	58.7	58.4	72.4	56.1	57.9	59.0	69.6	67.4	54.5	80.8	67.3	58.2	39.0	42.9
2. Less than one cigarette per day	13.3	12.3	14.5	13.8	13.1	11.5	13.4	14.9	12.4	15.2	11.4	10.1	13.0	14.1	14.6	2.9
3. One to five cigarettes per day	8.9	8.5	9.1	9.2	7.2	8.7	10.8	8.6	6.2	7.3	10.3	4.9	8.9	9.7	11.7	15.9
4. About one-half pack per day	8.4	7.1	9.3	8.6	5.0	10.0	8.0	9.1	5.8	6.1	9.8	2.4	5.3	9.9	14.7	18.7
5. About one pack per day	7.3	7.1	6.6	7.7	1.8	10.2	7.7	6.1	5.3	3.3	10.1	1.2	3.8	6.2	15.8	10.6
6. About one and one-half packs per day	1.9	1.6	1.5	2.0	0.2	3.1	1.8	1.8	0.6	0.6	3.0	0.3	1.2	1.7	3.6	9.0
7. Two packs or more per day	0.4	0.6	0.3	0.3	0.3	0.4	0.4	0.6	*	0.2	0.9	0.3	0.4	0.1	0.6	-
Item 780 Subject A01c N★	2233	985	1125	1655	276	482	642	722	387	1114	819	498	654	311	677	25

B004: Have you ever tried to stop smoking and found that you could not?

	TOTAL	M	F	White	Black	NE	NC	S	W	Yes	No	None	Mari-juana Only	Few Pills	More Pills	Any Her-oin
1. Yes	17.0	14.1	18.4	16.4	15.6	21.0	17.5	17.1	10.8	11.2	22.1	7.7	11.9	16.4	26.2	45.0
2. No	83.0	85.9	81.6	83.6	84.4	79.0	82.5	82.9	89.2	88.8	77.9	92.3	88.1	83.6	73.8	55.0
Item 1690 Subject A01i N★	2119	938	1065	1586	253	458	609	684	367	1050	786	460	615	294	661	25

B005: Do you want to stop smoking now?

	TOTAL	M	F	White	Black	NE	NC	S	W	Yes	No	None	Mari-juana Only	Few Pills	More Pills	Any Her-oin
1. Yes	15.9	14.0	16.6	15.3	17.2	18.1	16.4	17.2	10.0	10.4	20.3	7.5	13.5	17.6	23.0	20.3
2. No	16.8	16.7	16.0	17.7	6.2	20.1	17.1	16.4	12.6	12.4	20.5	6.8	12.8	15.5	28.1	36.4
8. Don't smoke now	67.3	69.3	67.4	67.0	76.6	61.8	66.5	66.4	77.4	77.2	59.3	85.7	73.7	66.9	48.9	43.3
Item 1700 Subject A01i N★	2190	966	1103	1629	265	473	632	707	378	1086	809	484	636	305	673	25

B006: Do you think you will be smoking cigarettes five years from now?

	TOTAL	M	F	White	Black	NE	NC	S	W	Yes	No	None	Mari-juana Only	Few Pills	More Pills	Any Her-oin
1. I definitely will	1.1	1.2	0.7	0.8	0.8	1.2	1.1	0.9	1.2	0.9	1.0	0.4	0.9	0.8	2.2	3.2
2. I probably will	12.4	11.1	13.0	13.0	5.8	15.4	14.4	12.0	6.8	7.9	18.0	4.2	12.0	15.9	24.2	26.1
3. I probably will not	25.4	22.3	27.3	24.9	25.2	26.0	24.8	25.8	24.6	22.2	27.6	17.2	27.2	30.8	32.4	39.2
4. I definitely will not	61.1	65.4	59.0	61.3	68.2	57.4	59.6	61.3	67.4	69.0	53.4	78.3	60.0	52.5	41.3	31.5
Item 1710 Subject A04a N	3257	1510	1599	2385	468	656	926	1097	578	1756	1120	1208	784	379	753	32

The different questionnaire forms used in this study tend to emphasize somewhat different topics. The next major section in this form deals with alcohol and various other drugs. There is a lot of talk these days about these subjects, but very little accurate information. Therefore, we still have a lot to learn about the actual experiences and attitudes of people your age.

We hope that you can answer all questions; but if you find one which you feel you cannot answer honestly, we would prefer that you leave it blank.

Remember that your answers will be strictly confidential. We never connect them with your name or your class.

The next questions are about ALCOHOLIC BEVERAGES, including beer, wine, and liquor.

B007: On how many occasions (if any) have you had alcohol to drink . . .

B007A: . . . in your lifetime?

	TOTAL	M	F	White	Black	NE	NC	S	W	Yes	No	None	Mari-juana Only	Few Pills	More Pills	Any Her-oin
1. 0 occasions	7.8	7.2	8.5	6.0	16.4	3.2	6.5	11.2	8.9	7.5	8.3	17.5	1.7	0.8	1.5	7.3
2. 1-2	9.0	7.4	11.0	6.5	20.6	5.6	8.7	12.0	7.7	8.6	10.1	17.3	5.3	3.4	2.1	3.1
3. 3-5	8.2	6.4	10.2	7.1	15.2	5.7	7.3	10.0	9.3	9.1	8.1	14.9	7.2	2.8	1.2	-
4. 6-9	8.3	6.4	10.3	7.7	11.0	6.8	9.2	8.2	8.8	9.1	7.5	11.7	8.5	7.1	2.8	6.2
5. 10-19	13.7	11.4	16.2	14.0	13.5	13.3	15.4	11.1	16.2	14.2	13.6	15.2	15.8	19.5	7.1	-
6. 20-39	14.2	13.1	15.2	15.5	9.5	15.5	14.0	13.0	15.1	14.8	14.4	9.9	21.3	16.1	13.3	11.6
7. 40 or more	38.9	48.1	28.6	43.1	13.8	50.1	39.0	34.5	34.1	36.7	37.9	13.5	40.2	50.3	72.0	71.9
Item 810 Subject A01a N	3128	1457	1537	2322	434	632	898	1041	557	1706	1066	1181	743	363	738	30

*=less than .05 per cent.   ★=excludes respondents for whom question was inappropriate.

QUESTIONNAIRE FORM 1 1984	TOTAL	SEX		RACE		REGION				4YR COLLEGE PLANS		ILLICIT DRUG USE: LIFETIME				
		M	F	White	Black	NE	NC	S	W	Yes	No	None	Mari-juana Only	Few Pills	More Pills	Any Her-oin
N (Weighted No. of Cases):	3311	1534	1616	2414	478	670	941	1113	587	1772	1137	1223	794	381	765	32
% of Weighted Total:	100.0	46.3	48.8	72.9	14.4	20.2	28.4	33.6	17.7	53.5	34.3	36.9	24.0	11.5	23.1	1.0

B007B: . . . during the last 12 months?

1. 0 occasions	17.1	15.0	19.7	13.7	35.4	9.2	16.1	22.8	17.3	17.6	18.0	34.2	8.9	5.7	4.1	10.8
2. 1-2	14.1	11.9	16.7	12.4	24.0	12.0	11.9	16.2	16.0	13.2	16.3	21.2	14.8	8.9	4.3	3.5
3. 3-5	12.4	9.4	15.5	12.3	11.3	13.0	12.7	11.0	13.8	13.9	11.1	14.8	12.8	13.5	8.5	2.9
4. 6-9	12.2	11.1	13.1	12.8	9.6	13.8	12.8	10.5	12.3	12.3	11.9	12.6	14.4	14.2	8.5	11.5
5. 10-19	15.6	16.0	15.1	17.2	9.2	16.9	17.8	13.3	15.2	15.9	14.9	9.8	19.6	21.3	18.3	19.0
6. 20-39	12.5	14.4	10.2	13.4	7.1	14.3	14.1	11.1	10.5	12.9	11.8	3.9	14.9	19.4	20.4	14.6
7. 40 or more	16.1	22.2	9.7	18.1	3.4	20.9	14.6	15.1	14.9	14.3	15.9	3.6	14.6	17.0	35.8	37.6
Item 820 Subject A01b N	3124	1453	1535	2326	426	635	893	1034	562	1696	1067	1164	746	367	741	29

B007C: . . . during the last 30 days?

1. 0 occasions	36.5	32.4	41.8	31.7	60.4	27.2	32.3	44.0	40.1	37.6	38.3	60.5	29.9	23.7	12.5	12.3
2. 1-2	21.3	17.6	25.0	22.3	17.8	23.3	21.3	18.3	24.5	23.0	18.6	21.6	23.1	25.2	17.5	21.7
3. 3-5	17.4	19.4	15.8	19.8	9.5	17.9	22.1	13.9	15.9	17.5	17.5	10.4	23.5	18.1	22.5	18.6
4. 6-9	12.4	14.7	9.8	13.5	7.1	16.7	12.2	11.5	9.6	12.2	12.7	5.6	13.7	15.4	20.3	18.0
5. 10-19	7.8	9.9	5.1	8.4	3.1	9.2	7.6	7.7	6.9	6.1	8.4	0.9	5.9	11.6	18.2	9.3
6. 20-39	2.8	3.7	1.8	2.9	1.3	3.3	2.5	3.1	2.0	2.5	2.3	0.7	2.6	4.1	5.5	5.9
7. 40 or more	1.7	2.3	0.7	1.4	0.7	2.4	1.9	1.5	0.9	1.0	2.3	0.4	1.3	1.9	3.4	14.2
Item 830 Subject A01c N	3138	1467	1534	2340	428	633	904	1043	558	1699	1079	1166	752	372	743	30

IF YOU HAVE NOT HAD ANY BEER, WINE, OR LIQUOR IN THE LAST TWELVE MONTHS, GO TO Q.B017.

B008: When you used alcohol during the last year, how often did you use it in each of the following situations?

B008A: When you were alone

1. Not at all	69.8	61.8	79.5	71.3	66.9	69.1	69.3	69.0	73.0	73.6	67.1	82.3	70.3	66.7	58.4	56.1
2. A few of the times	23.1	28.2	16.7	22.0	25.7	23.8	23.1	23.6	21.3	21.1	22.6	14.4	23.6	26.2	30.8	24.3
3. Some of the times	5.6	8.0	2.9	5.3	5.3	5.2	6.4	6.1	4.1	3.8	8.4	1.9	4.8	7.1	8.9	15.9
4. Most of the times	1.0	1.3	0.7	0.9	1.2	1.0	1.1	0.8	1.1	1.0	1.3	0.7	1.1	-	1.3	-
5. Every time	0.5	0.7	0.2	0.5	0.9	0.9	0.1	0.5	0.5	0.5	0.6	0.6	0.2	-	0.7	3.7
Item 1720 Subject A05a N★	2619	1248	1243	2031	272	579	770	804	466	1403	891	778	691	346	718	27

B008B: With just 1 or 2 other people

1. Not at all	13.2	10.0	17.1	12.6	15.4	13.1	13.0	10.9	17.9	16.2	10.7	26.5	9.4	10.6	4.7	5.0
2. A few of the times	31.2	28.0	35.5	30.5	41.6	33.8	31.5	31.1	28.0	32.1	30.9	34.4	34.0	31.5	24.9	20.2
3. Some of the times	24.3	27.4	20.2	25.8	14.3	25.2	26.9	21.7	23.5	23.6	24.0	14.0	25.8	25.5	33.8	22.7
4. Most of the times	24.5	28.6	19.9	25.3	16.9	22.8	23.7	28.1	21.7	22.1	26.2	16.7	22.5	26.7	32.4	41.3
5. Every time	6.7	6.1	7.3	5.8	11.7	5.0	5.0	8.2	8.8	5.9	8.2	8.3	8.3	5.8	4.1	10.9
Item 1730 Subject A05b N★	2611	1240	1245	2026	270	575	770	801	466	1402	888	772	690	345	718	26

B008C: At a party

1. Not at all	12.9	10.0	15.9	11.8	21.6	9.8	12.5	15.4	12.9	12.7	13.9	24.5	9.5	10.5	4.7	9.0
2. A few of the times	18.3	16.6	20.8	16.9	28.8	16.3	15.4	20.1	22.8	18.8	18.6	23.4	20.5	14.1	13.0	9.0
3. Some of the times	16.6	17.4	15.5	16.7	16.6	14.7	18.8	17.0	14.9	17.1	15.7	16.4	18.7	17.6	14.2	19.2
4. Most of the times	30.6	31.9	29.6	33.4	17.5	35.7	30.0	27.0	31.8	33.3	26.5	22.5	31.6	37.1	36.1	25.9
5. Every time	21.5	24.1	18.1	21.2	15.5	23.6	23.3	20.6	17.6	18.0	25.4	13.2	19.6	20.8	32.0	36.9
Item 1740 Subject A05c N★	2603	1234	1242	2014	273	578	767	799	460	1398	882	769	690	339	716	27

B008D: When your date or spouse was present

1. Not at all	34.3	36.9	32.7	31.6	56.1	30.7	34.5	34.2	38.5	38.3	29.6	54.5	31.4	31.5	17.7	9.6
2. A few of the times	25.1	25.4	24.9	25.8	21.9	25.9	24.8	24.8	25.4	25.1	25.7	20.2	29.2	27.8	25.0	22.2
3. Some of the times	17.8	20.3	15.2	18.8	7.2	19.0	17.3	18.1	16.7	16.9	18.7	11.5	20.3	17.3	22.5	18.8
4. Most of the times	15.7	13.0	17.7	16.8	10.9	16.5	16.1	15.6	13.9	14.1	16.8	8.4	12.6	16.4	25.6	23.0
5. Every time	7.1	4.4	9.5	7.0	4.0	7.8	7.3	7.4	5.5	5.6	9.2	5.4	6.5	6.9	9.1	26.4
Item 1750 Subject A05b N★	2602	1232	1242	2019	270	573	765	800	463	1392	889	765	688	344	719	27

★=excludes respondents for whom question was inappropriate.

QUESTIONNAIRE FORM 1 1984	TOTAL	SEX		RACE		REGION				4YR COLLEGE PLANS		ILLICIT DRUG USE: LIFETIME				
		M	F	White	Black	NE	NC	S	W	Yes	No	None	Mari- juana Only	Few Pills	More Pills	Any Her- oin
N (Weighted No. of Cases):	3311	1534	1616	2414	478	670	941	1113	587	1772	1137	1223	794	381	765	32
% of Weighted Total:	100.0	46.3	48.8	72.9	14.4	20.2	28.4	33.6	17.7	53.5	34.3	36.9	24.0	11.5	23.1	1.0
B008E: When people over age 30 were present																
1. Not at all	29.6	27.3	32.1	27.6	47.1	23.2	31.9	32.7	28.5	29.3	33.0	35.3	34.0	24.7	22.3	3.7
2. A few of the times	39.5	40.7	38.4	41.0	31.5	40.8	38.8	39.0	39.9	41.3	36.0	34.7	42.0	40.4	42.5	37.6
3. Some of the times	17.2	19.4	14.8	17.6	11.3	19.6	16.4	15.9	17.9	15.0	18.1	11.9	14.2	22.8	22.3	35.0
4. Most of the times	8.8	8.8	8.7	9.3	5.6	11.5	7.6	8.2	8.7	8.8	8.9	9.3	7.7	8.6	9.1	11.4
5. Every time	4.9	3.8	5.9	4.5	4.5	4.9	5.4	4.2	5.0	5.6	3.9	8.8	2.1	3.5	3.7	12.2
Item 1760 Subject A05b N★	2611	1240	1246	2027	270	578	768	801	464	1401	888	771	688	346	718	27
B008F: During the daytime (before 4:00 p.m.)																
1. Not at all	59.1	50.0	70.5	57.5	78.8	55.2	61.0	60.0	59.3	63.7	56.6	76.0	61.9	54.3	42.5	24.0
2. A few of the times	28.8	33.7	22.8	30.8	14.6	30.5	29.0	27.2	29.3	26.2	29.9	18.1	28.5	32.2	38.6	38.7
3. Some of the times	9.8	13.4	5.7	9.7	4.6	11.6	8.3	10.1	9.5	8.5	10.8	4.4	8.3	13.0	14.6	23.6
4. Most of the times	1.5	2.0	0.6	1.3	1.0	2.0	0.9	2.0	1.3	1.2	1.5	1.1	1.2	0.5	2.8	5.4
5. Every time	0.8	0.9	0.4	0.6	1.0	0.7	0.8	0.8	0.6	0.4	1.2	0.4	0.2	-	1.5	8.3
Item 1770 Subject A05c N★	2610	1240	1242	2029	267	579	766	799	466	1401	887	770	688	346	719	27
B008G: At your home (or apartment or dorm)																
1. Not at all	36.6	32.5	42.1	36.5	42.0	32.1	38.0	37.6	37.9	39.1	35.8	49.2	37.6	30.5	24.8	25.2
2. A few of the times	34.4	35.9	32.1	34.4	34.8	33.5	34.0	35.6	34.4	33.3	34.1	27.1	37.4	36.0	39.6	19.3
3. Some of the times	16.2	19.2	12.7	16.7	6.9	19.6	15.0	15.4	15.0	15.0	17.0	10.7	14.6	21.2	20.5	32.0
4. Most of the times	8.7	8.8	8.4	8.3	11.2	10.3	8.6	7.8	8.4	8.5	8.6	6.8	8.2	8.3	11.1	19.8
5. Every time	4.2	3.6	4.7	4.1	5.1	4.6	4.4	3.6	4.3	4.2	4.5	6.2	2.1	4.0	3.9	3.7
Item 1780 Subject A05c N★	2607	1240	1240	2025	269	576	766	798	466	1402	887	773	688	346	714	27
B008H: At school																
1. Not at all	85.6	81.3	91.1	86.5	85.9	85.4	86.0	86.5	83.4	87.0	85.9	94.2	86.6	85.4	76.1	68.6
2. A few of the times	10.7	13.2	7.0	10.1	9.9	10.7	10.7	9.7	12.5	9.5	10.4	4.7	9.4	12.0	17.6	13.0
3. Some of the times	2.6	3.7	1.4	2.3	3.6	3.1	2.1	2.2	3.3	2.4	2.4	0.5	2.6	2.1	4.8	9.3
4. Most of the times	0.7	1.1	0.3	0.7	0.5	0.4	0.8	0.9	0.6	0.9	0.4	-	1.4	-	1.0	5.4
5. Every time	0.5	0.7	0.2	0.4	-	0.4	0.5	0.7	0.2	0.2	0.9	0.5	0.1	0.6	0.5	3.7
Item 1790 Subject A05c N★	2616	1244	1244	2031	270	579	769	802	466	1404	890	773	691	346	718	27
B008I: In a car																
1. Not at all	35.7	30.4	42.3	33.9	51.1	40.2	31.4	31.5	44.1	38.9	33.5	54.1	32.1	31.8	21.5	15.5
2. A few of the times	27.0	25.8	27.4	27.4	24.5	27.0	26.5	27.6	26.4	26.9	26.7	27.1	29.1	27.3	24.1	34.8
3. Some of the times	20.1	22.4	17.6	21.4	10.3	19.5	22.0	20.3	17.3	20.0	20.3	8.3	20.5	23.9	31.3	16.2
4. Most of the times	14.3	18.0	10.5	14.5	13.2	11.1	16.7	16.9	10.1	12.0	16.0	8.1	14.5	15.7	20.2	19.8
5. Every time	3.0	3.4	2.3	2.8	0.9	2.2	3.3	3.7	2.1	2.3	3.6	2.4	3.8	1.3	2.8	13.7
Item 1810 Subject A05c N★	2615	1242	1246	2032	269	577	770	802	466	1403	890	773	690	346	719	27
B009: What have been the most important reasons for your drinking alcoholic beverages? (Mark all that apply.)																
A. To experiment–to see what it's like	41.8	40.7	43.8	39.5	58.6	35.4	40.8	45.4	45.6	44.1	41.1	50.1	45.4	40.1	31.6	17.1
B. To relax or relieve tension	39.8	41.0	37.7	41.3	25.2	40.1	40.5	40.6	36.7	37.8	41.4	28.2	38.0	41.5	52.1	55.5
C. To feel good or get high	49.1	52.5	44.2	50.7	33.6	53.0	48.1	44.9	53.3	47.6	47.5	24.1	51.2	53.4	70.8	64.3
D. To seek deeper insights and understanding	3.9	5.3	2.3	3.8	3.6	4.8	3.5	4.1	3.2	3.4	3.9	2.3	3.3	4.1	5.5	15.9
E. To have a good time with my friends	74.0	78.6	69.2	76.5	55.3	75.3	75.2	70.8	76.0	73.6	74.3	61.7	78.5	78.0	80.9	79.1
F. To fit in with a group I like	10.5	12.3	9.0	11.2	5.9	7.6	14.0	10.3	8.9	10.7	10.6	10.2	11.0	10.3	10.4	11.8
G. To get away from my problems or troubles	22.1	19.5	23.7	22.6	15.8	19.0	26.0	22.4	18.9	20.1	25.2	12.8	22.0	26.2	29.2	33.2
H. Because of boredom, nothing else to do	22.1	24.3	19.6	21.8	21.6	20.8	20.7	23.2	24.2	22.4	20.5	13.2	21.5	29.0	29.0	44.4
I. Because of anger or frustration	19.5	18.7	19.9	19.8	12.3	17.5	20.5	20.9	17.9	17.2	21.1	11.1	16.8	26.3	26.9	30.4
J. To get through the day	1.7	1.9	1.2	1.3	0.9	1.4	1.6	1.7	2.4	1.3	1.5	0.4	1.3	3.2	2.4	10.4
K. To increase the effects of some other drug(s)	5.2	6.2	3.3	4.6	4.3	5.1	5.1	4.8	6.1	4.1	4.7	-	0.7	5.3	14.0	21.7
L. To decrease (offset) the effects of some other drug(s)	0.8	0.9	0.6	0.7	1.0	0.6	0.4	1.3	0.7	0.6	0.9	-	0.4	-	2.1	8.9
M. To get to sleep	6.5	7.0	5.4	5.3	11.5	6.4	5.8	6.8	7.5	5.7	6.5	3.1	6.7	7.3	9.3	10.1
N. Because it tastes good	48.0	47.7	48.1	50.0	31.1	49.9	48.5	46.8	46.7	49.2	46.0	40.3	47.8	49.8	56.5	45.2
O. Because I am "hooked"–I feel I have to drink	1.3	1.6	0.7	1.0	0.6	0.3	1.5	1.6	1.6	0.9	1.3	0.3	1.4	0.9	2.0	8.9
Item 1820-1960 Subject A06a N★	2574	1226	1222	1995	271	569	764	791	450	1380	876	742	686	342	718	26

★=excludes respondents for whom question was inappropriate.

QUESTIONNAIRE FORM 1 1984	TOTAL	SEX		RACE		REGION				4YR COLLEGE PLANS		ILLICIT DRUG USE: LIFETIME				
		M	F	White	Black	NE	NC	S	W	Yes	No	None	Mari-juana Only	Few Pills	More Pills	Any Her-oin
N (Weighted No. of Cases):	3311	1534	1616	2414	478	670	941	1113	587	1772	1137	1223	794	381	765	32
% of Weighted Total:	100.0	46.3	48.8	72.9	14.4	20.2	28.4	33.6	17.7	53.5	34.3	36.9	24.0	11.5	23.1	1.0

B010: When you drink alcoholic beverages, how high do you usually get?

	TOTAL	M	F	White	Black	NE	NC	S	W	Yes	No	None	Mari-juana Only	Few Pills	More Pills	Any Heroin
1. Not at all high	19.0	15.2	23.7	17.1	35.7	16.1	19.2	20.3	20.2	22.3	16.7	40.7	13.1	13.1	5.1	5.4
2. A little high	34.0	30.8	37.7	34.0	34.2	31.9	32.7	37.2	33.0	34.4	34.4	37.2	39.6	32.5	24.9	33.3
3. Moderately high	39.2	44.4	33.4	41.3	26.8	44.3	39.5	35.6	38.5	37.8	39.2	19.3	41.0	47.1	55.6	45.1
4. Very high	7.8	9.5	5.2	7.5	3.4	7.7	8.5	6.9	8.3	5.5	9.6	2.8	6.2	7.3	14.3	16.1
Item 1970 Subject A01e **N★**	2601	1232	1240	2015	273	578	763	800	460	1394	888	766	692	344	715	26

B011: When you drink alcoholic beverages, how long do you usually stay high?

	TOTAL	M	F	White	Black	NE	NC	S	W	Yes	No	None	Mari-juana Only	Few Pills	More Pills	Any Heroin
1. Usually don't get high	20.3	16.5	24.8	18.0	37.1	16.2	20.3	22.3	22.1	23.2	18.3	42.9	14.1	14.9	5.5	10.4
2. One to two hours	42.2	40.3	44.9	43.3	41.2	41.4	39.7	47.4	38.5	43.0	42.2	39.5	50.8	45.9	34.9	39.1
3. Three to six hours	33.1	38.7	26.3	34.3	20.0	37.7	33.5	27.1	36.9	30.6	33.4	15.9	32.2	35.3	51.4	39.9
4. Seven to 24 hours	4.0	4.1	3.9	4.1	1.7	4.6	6.0	2.9	2.1	2.9	5.9	1.3	2.8	3.7	7.9	4.9
5. More than 24 hours	0.3	0.5	0.1	0.2	-	-	0.5	0.3	0.4	0.3	0.2	0.4	0.1	0.2	0.3	5.7
Item 1980 Subject A01f **N★**	2588	1226	1234	2008	270	569	761	795	464	1389	881	756	689	344	715	26

The following questions ask about how much you have to drink on the occasions when you drink alcoholic beverages. For these questions, a "drink" means any of the following: A 12-ounce can (or bottle) of beer, a 4-ounce glass of wine, a mixed drink or shot glass of liquor.

B012: Think back over the LAST TWO WEEKS. How many times have you had five or more drinks in a row?

	TOTAL	M	F	White	Black	NE	NC	S	W	Yes	No	None	Mari-juana Only	Few Pills	More Pills	Any Heroin
1. None	58.4	47.3	71.1	55.4	83.2	55.6	51.7	63.0	64.9	63.4	55.5	79.8	57.7	57.7	37.0	37.5
2. Once	13.5	15.0	12.3	15.3	7.2	12.5	17.8	10.6	12.7	14.0	12.5	9.9	15.1	11.4	17.6	-
3. Twice	11.2	14.5	7.4	11.8	3.7	11.8	12.7	11.0	8.4	9.7	11.7	5.9	12.3	12.7	14.5	16.7
4. 3 to 5 times	12.1	16.2	7.4	13.3	4.3	13.7	12.9	11.2	10.4	9.3	15.0	3.9	10.7	14.2	21.9	16.2
5. 6 to 9 times	3.0	4.9	1.1	3.1	0.9	3.2	3.9	2.4	2.6	2.7	3.0	0.1	3.1	2.8	5.4	17.0
6. 10 or more times	1.8	2.1	0.8	1.2	0.8	3.2	1.1	1.7	1.1	0.8	2.3	0.4	1.2	1.3	3.6	12.6
Item 850 Subject A01d **N★**	2585	1222	1236	2007	271	569	761	795	460	1392	877	763	683	344	711	26

B013: During the last two weeks, how many times have you had 3 or 4 drinks in a row (but no more than that)?

	TOTAL	M	F	White	Black	NE	NC	S	W	Yes	No	None	Mari-juana Only	Few Pills	More Pills	Any Heroin
1. None	57.8	51.6	65.9	55.3	81.6	53.5	55.9	60.4	62.0	61.2	57.6	79.6	58.2	52.1	37.2	37.4
2. Once	18.1	18.1	17.9	19.4	10.6	21.1	17.9	16.6	17.0	18.7	16.4	10.8	18.8	22.9	23.6	14.2
3. Twice	11.7	13.6	9.3	12.4	3.4	11.7	12.3	12.0	10.1	10.5	12.1	6.1	12.0	11.8	17.4	12.6
4. 3 to 5 times	9.4	12.3	5.7	10.1	3.5	10.9	10.7	7.7	8.1	7.8	9.8	3.2	8.6	9.2	16.0	28.1
5. 6 to 9 times	1.9	3.1	0.7	2.0	0.4	1.7	2.1	1.8	2.1	1.3	2.2	0.3	1.6	2.5	3.6	2.9
6. 10 or more times	1.1	1.4	0.6	0.8	0.4	1.2	1.1	1.5	0.6	0.5	1.8	-	0.9	1.5	2.3	4.7
Item 1990 Subject A01d **N★**	2592	1228	1240	2015	271	571	766	795	461	1398	879	769	687	346	706	26

B014: During the last two weeks, how many times have you had two drinks in a row (but no more than that)?

	TOTAL	M	F	White	Black	NE	NC	S	W	Yes	No	None	Mari-juana Only	Few Pills	More Pills	Any Heroin
1. None	57.9	54.1	62.9	57.7	66.2	52.5	57.6	60.9	59.9	60.0	58.9	76.5	55.6	52.6	42.9	53.8
2. Once	20.8	21.9	19.7	21.2	19.9	24.9	19.0	19.8	20.5	20.9	19.5	13.5	22.1	25.3	25.2	34.2
3. Twice	10.6	11.5	9.6	10.5	8.3	10.4	12.0	9.4	10.8	10.3	9.7	5.6	11.9	10.7	14.7	4.5
4. 3 to 5 times	7.3	8.6	5.6	7.5	4.4	9.7	8.0	5.5	6.7	6.2	8.2	3.5	7.8	6.5	11.5	4.4
5. 6 to 9 times	1.8	2.4	1.3	2.1	0.4	1.3	1.6	2.8	1.2	1.6	1.8	0.9	1.3	2.9	3.0	-
6. 10 to 19 times	1.3	1.4	0.8	1.0	0.7	1.0	1.7	1.4	0.9	1.0	1.5	0.1	1.2	1.9	2.4	3.1
7. 20 or more times	0.1	0.2	0.1	0.1	0.2	0.2	0.1	0.1	-	-	0.3	-	0.1	-	0.3	-
Item 2000 Subject A01d **N★**	2541	1199	1216	1975	264	554	754	784	450	1379	849	760	673	331	697	25

★=excludes respondents for whom question was inappropriate.

QUESTIONNAIRE FORM 1 1984	TOTAL	SEX		RACE		REGION				4YR COLLEGE PLANS		ILLICIT DRUG USE: LIFETIME				
		M	F	White	Black	NE	NC	S	W	Yes	No	None	Mari- juana Only	Few Pills	More Pills	Any Her- oin
N (Weighted No. of Cases):	3311	1534	1616	2414	478	670	941	1113	587	1772	1137	1223	794	381	765	32
% of Weighted Total:	100.0	46.3	48.8	72.9	14.4	20.2	28.4	33.6	17.7	53.5	34.3	36.9	24.0	11.5	23.1	1.0
B015: During the last two weeks, how many times have you had just one drink?																
1. None	57.0	57.2	57.4	56.9	58.8	57.0	56.2	56.9	58.3	58.1	57.4	65.2	54.8	55.6	52.1	66.9
2. Once	24.9	22.7	26.8	25.8	21.0	25.5	25.4	24.9	23.5	23.7	24.5	23.8	25.4	22.8	25.7	23.3
3. Twice	8.8	9.4	8.4	8.5	10.8	9.0	9.4	8.2	8.3	9.3	8.3	7.1	11.1	6.1	9.9	2.1
4. 3 to 5 times	5.9	6.3	5.3	5.6	7.6	6.9	5.2	5.5	6.4	6.4	5.9	3.0	6.5	9.6	6.1	7.8
5. 6 to 9 times	2.2	2.9	1.6	2.4	0.8	1.4	2.3	3.0	1.9	1.8	2.4	0.6	1.6	4.1	3.8	-
6. 10 to 19 times	0.9	1.1	0.4	0.7	0.8	0.2	1.0	1.2	1.4	0.6	1.2	0.3	0.5	1.4	1.9	-
7. 20 or more times	0.3	0.3	0.2	0.2	0.2	-	0.6	0.2	0.2	0.2	0.4	-	0.2	0.5	0.5	-
Item 2010 Subject A01d N★	2485	1182	1181	1948	254	544	733	767	441	1356	828	736	652	333	685	25
B016: Have you ever tried to stop using alcoholic beverages and found that you couldn't stop?																
1. Yes	4.0	4.5	3.3	3.7	4.5	4.6	5.4	3.5	2.0	2.9	5.2	3.2	3.5	5.7	4.1	6.6
2. No	96.0	95.5	96.7	96.3	95.5	95.4	94.6	96.5	98.0	97.1	94.8	96.8	96.5	94.3	95.9	93.4
Item 2020 Subject A01i N★	2575	1225	1222	2003	266	569	756	789	460	1380	878	754	685	345	713	27
B017: Do you think you will be drinking alcoholic beverages five years from now?																
1. I definitely will	16.0	19.6	12.6	18.4	3.4	22.9	17.5	11.6	14.1	16.9	14.4	7.9	16.1	23.1	26.1	25.1
2. I probably will	53.0	52.5	53.2	56.7	37.9	58.3	55.9	47.3	52.8	53.1	52.1	45.2	57.0	59.5	59.1	57.6
3. I probably will not	15.7	13.8	17.6	12.8	27.9	10.9	13.0	19.6	18.0	15.7	16.3	21.5	15.3	9.2	8.9	13.5
4. I definitely will not	15.4	14.1	16.7	12.1	30.8	7.9	13.6	21.5	15.1	14.3	17.1	25.4	11.6	8.2	5.9	3.8
Item 2030 Subject A04a N	3254	1514	1595	2390	466	655	929	1095	576	1757	1115	1206	786	380	756	32

The next questions are about MARIJUANA and HASHISH.

Marijuana is sometimes called: grass, pot, dope.

Hashish is sometimes called: hash, hash oil.

B018: On how many occasions (if any) have you used hashish . . .

B018A: . . . in your lifetime?

	TOTAL	M	F	White	Black	NE	NC	S	W	Yes	No	None	Mari- juana Only	Few Pills	More Pills	Any Her- oin
1. 0 occasions	74.7	70.4	81.0	73.2	88.0	66.0	76.5	80.0	71.6	79.9	72.8	100.0	76.8	65.8	37.2	24.5
2. 1-2	10.9	11.7	10.2	11.8	6.1	9.9	12.2	8.9	13.8	9.3	12.8	-	15.6	22.1	18.0	25.5
3. 3-5	4.8	5.9	3.2	5.4	2.1	7.6	3.2	3.7	6.3	4.7	4.3	-	4.4	6.3	12.2	8.8
4. 6-9	2.6	2.9	2.2	2.8	1.0	4.0	1.3	3.1	1.9	1.9	2.9	-	0.7	3.8	7.9	9.0
5. 10-19	2.9	3.8	1.5	3.2	0.8	4.7	2.8	1.5	3.5	2.1	2.4	-	0.9	0.9	10.7	3.7
6. 20-39	1.3	1.6	0.8	1.3	0.5	2.7	0.9	0.9	1.2	0.7	1.2	-	0.5	0.5	4.2	13.1
7. 40 or more	2.8	3.8	1.1	2.3	1.5	5.1	3.0	1.9	1.7	1.4	3.6	-	1.1	0.7	9.8	15.4
Item 2040 Subject A01a N	3224	1503	1581	2381	456	652	921	1077	574	1744	1108	1223	790	378	752	31

B018B: . . . during the last 12 months?

	TOTAL	M	F	White	Black	NE	NC	S	W	Yes	No	None	Mari- juana Only	Few Pills	More Pills	Any Her- oin
1. 0 occasions	87.7	85.0	92.2	87.7	93.8	82.4	88.3	90.3	87.8	90.9	87.9	100.0	90.5	87.8	65.5	57.4
2. 1-2	6.4	7.3	4.7	6.7	2.9	6.7	6.5	5.3	8.0	5.2	6.5	-	6.6	10.1	14.2	17.3
3. 3-5	2.4	3.5	1.0	2.5	1.0	4.0	1.7	2.2	2.3	2.1	1.6	-	0.9	1.0	8.8	7.4
4. 6-9	1.2	1.7	0.6	1.2	0.9	2.8	1.1	0.7	0.5	0.5	1.5	-	0.9	0.8	3.5	6.9
5. 10-19	1.0	1.2	0.6	1.0	0.5	1.6	1.1	0.8	0.9	0.7	0.9	-	0.2	-	3.9	7.4
6. 20-39	0.5	0.4	0.6	0.5	0.3	1.1	0.4	0.4	0.1	0.4	0.5	-	0.2	0.2	1.6	3.6
7. 40 or more	0.7	0.8	0.3	0.4	0.6	1.5	0.8	0.4	0.4	0.2	1.0	-	0.6	-	2.5	-
Item 2050 Subject A01b N	3216	1497	1582	2377	455	650	917	1078	572	1738	1106	1223	789	377	747	29

B018C: . . . during the last 30 days?

	TOTAL	M	F	White	Black	NE	NC	S	W	Yes	No	None	Mari- juana Only	Few Pills	More Pills	Any Her- oin
1. 0 occasions	96.0	95.1	97.9	96.5	96.7	93.5	95.3	97.0	98.1	97.6	95.6	100.0	97.0	96.6	89.0	77.3
2. 1-2	2.2	2.8	1.3	2.0	2.1	3.8	2.7	1.4	1.4	1.7	2.3	-	1.9	3.0	5.3	14.3
3. 3-5	0.6	0.6	0.3	0.6	0.2	0.5	0.7	0.8	0.1	0.3	0.7	-	0.3	0.4	1.6	8.4
4. 6-9	0.3	0.5	0.1	0.4	-	0.8	0.4	0.2	-	0.1	0.3	-	-	-	1.5	-
5. 10-19	0.3	0.3	0.2	0.2	0.4	0.7	0.2	0.3	0.2	0.2	0.2	-	0.1	-	1.1	-
6. 20-39	0.1	0.1	0.1	0.1	-	-	0.2	0.1	-	0.1	0.1	-	0.1	-	0.3	-
7. 40 or more	0.4	0.6	0.1	0.2	0.6	0.8	0.6	0.2	0.2	0.1	0.8	-	0.6	-	1.2	-
Item 2060 Subject A01c N	3211	1494	1579	2375	452	651	916	1074	571	1736	1103	1223	787	376	747	29

★=excludes respondents for whom question was inappropriate.

QUESTIONNAIRE FORM 1 1984	TOTAL	SEX		RACE		REGION				4YR COLLEGE PLANS		ILLICIT DRUG USE: LIFETIME				
		M	F	White	Black	NE	NC	S	W	Yes	No	None	Mari-juana Only	Few Pills	More Pills	Any Her-oin
N (Weighted No. of Cases):	3311	1534	1616	2414	478	670	941	1113	587	1772	1137	1223	794	381	765	32
% of Weighted Total:	100.0	46.3	48.8	72.9	14.4	20.2	28.4	33.6	17.7	53.5	34.3	36.9	24.0	11.5	23.1	1.0

B019: On how many occasions (if any) have you used marijuana . . .

B019A: . . . in your lifetime?

1. 0 occasions	44.0	41.4	48.1	44.2	48.1	32.8	49.3	48.4	40.0	49.9	40.7	100.0	1.5	21.5	10.8	17.3
2. 1-2	12.1	11.5	12.9	11.5	16.1	14.1	11.6	12.1	10.6	11.7	13.3	-	36.4	14.4	4.7	7.1
3. 3-5	7.7	6.8	8.4	7.7	8.6	7.0	8.3	7.8	7.1	8.0	7.7	-	20.0	9.4	6.3	7.6
4. 6-9	5.5	5.7	5.3	5.5	4.2	6.7	4.7	4.9	6.2	5.2	5.7	-	11.3	10.3	6.1	-
5. 10-19	6.5	7.1	5.8	6.4	4.9	5.8	5.9	5.5	9.9	6.7	6.1	-	12.6	12.2	7.9	6.4
6. 20-39	6.3	5.9	6.7	6.7	5.0	8.4	5.0	5.8	7.2	5.6	6.6	-	7.9	9.7	13.0	9.0
7. 40 or more	18.0	21.6	12.7	18.0	13.2	25.1	15.3	15.4	19.0	12.9	20.0	-	10.3	22.5	51.3	52.6
Item 2070 Subject A01a N	3186	1490	1559	2359	441	648	908	1058	572	1726	1095	1223	791	378	749	29

B019B: . . . during the last 12 months?

1. 0 occasions	60.0	57.2	64.9	60.1	64.8	51.8	64.9	62.9	56.1	64.0	60.2	100.0	41.8	43.4	23.8	34.5
2. 1-2	11.5	11.4	11.5	11.5	12.7	12.9	10.8	10.3	13.2	12.1	10.3	-	26.5	16.8	11.6	12.3
3. 3-5	6.4	6.3	6.4	6.3	6.3	6.5	5.1	7.3	6.9	6.5	6.4	-	13.4	10.9	7.6	6.9
4. 6-9	4.3	3.8	4.6	4.4	2.6	5.9	2.7	3.8	5.9	3.8	3.8	-	5.8	7.8	7.9	5.2
5. 10-19	5.3	5.9	4.7	6.0	3.3	6.4	5.5	4.0	6.1	5.4	5.3	-	6.4	6.7	12.1	3.5
6. 20-39	3.9	3.9	3.8	3.4	5.9	5.0	2.7	4.6	3.1	3.0	4.8	-	2.9	6.7	8.8	16.2
7. 40 or more	8.7	11.6	4.0	8.3	4.3	11.6	8.2	7.2	8.7	5.2	9.2	-	3.2	7.7	28.1	21.4
Item 2080 Subject A01b N	3172	1484	1552	2354	440	644	904	1053	571	1721	1088	1223	783	375	744	29

B019C: . . . during the last 30 days?

1. 0 occasions	74.2	71.6	79.3	75.0	76.1	67.2	76.5	76.8	73.9	78.8	73.5	100.0	71.0	65.2	42.0	41.8
2. 1-2	10.1	9.6	10.2	10.3	9.4	11.2	9.2	9.3	11.5	10.1	8.9	-	18.8	14.2	15.2	18.0
3. 3-5	3.7	4.2	3.2	3.7	3.8	5.6	3.0	2.7	4.5	3.5	4.0	-	4.2	6.2	7.8	1.9
4. 6-9	3.1	3.4	2.5	2.7	3.9	4.7	2.6	3.0	1.9	2.0	4.2	-	2.5	6.1	6.9	6.8
5. 10-19	3.6	3.9	3.1	3.5	4.0	3.9	2.9	4.0	3.7	2.9	3.4	-	1.9	3.7	10.7	14.7
6. 20-39	2.4	3.0	1.1	2.4	0.5	3.2	2.4	1.9	2.4	1.0	3.0	-	1.0	2.8	7.1	8.3
7. 40 or more	2.9	4.3	0.7	2.4	2.3	4.2	3.4	2.2	2.1	1.7	2.9	-	0.6	1.8	10.3	8.6
Item 2090 Subject A01c N	3167	1482	1548	2351	437	645	903	1050	570	1720	1085	1223	777	375	744	31

IF YOU HAVE NOT USED MARIJUANA OR HASHISH IN THE LAST TWELVE MONTHS, GO TO Q.B028.

B020: When you used marijuana or hashish during the last year, how often did you use it in each of the following situations?

B020A: When you were alone

1. Not at all	65.8	59.5	75.3	68.4	61.7	66.3	65.5	66.1	65.0	72.9	61.9	-	83.6	69.3	51.3	55.3
2. A few of the times	19.8	22.4	17.1	19.5	22.8	19.0	18.6	20.0	22.0	17.0	23.1	-	10.8	22.1	26.2	13.4
3. Some of the times	11.1	14.4	5.6	9.6	10.3	12.1	12.3	9.7	10.4	7.7	11.4	-	3.8	6.9	17.8	22.2
4. Most of the times	2.2	2.2	1.7	1.8	3.6	1.3	2.7	3.1	1.5	1.9	2.3	-	1.3	1.2	3.3	4.1
5. Every time	1.1	1.5	0.3	0.7	1.6	1.3	0.9	1.0	1.1	0.5	1.3	-	0.5	0.5	1.3	4.9
Item 2100 Subject A05a N★	1267	626	547	932	157	311	321	383	252	614	429	-	454	212	564	21

B020B: With just 1 or 2 other people

1. Not at all	7.0	8.2	6.3	7.2	7.4	5.1	7.4	5.9	10.5	8.3	6.3	-	10.1	6.1	4.8	6.3
2. A few of the times	31.2	28.0	36.1	30.2	40.1	33.8	31.6	30.3	28.7	34.1	29.1	-	41.9	35.5	21.3	30.8
3. Some of the times	17.1	18.8	13.8	17.6	13.5	18.2	14.2	19.4	15.9	15.0	17.0	-	9.5	23.9	20.0	26.4
4. Most of the times	33.3	34.7	31.3	34.6	26.8	31.9	37.8	32.0	31.3	30.5	36.0	-	22.8	24.5	45.6	20.8
5. Every time	11.4	10.3	12.5	10.4	12.2	11.0	9.0	12.4	13.6	12.2	11.6	-	15.7	10.0	8.3	15.7
Item 2110 Subject A05b N★	1271	627	550	936	157	312	321	387	252	617	432	-	457	214	563	21

B020C: At a party

1. Not at all	25.3	21.3	32.1	23.5	37.6	22.9	22.4	29.5	25.7	29.4	25.3	-	38.3	28.5	14.1	15.6
2. A few of the times	23.8	26.1	23.1	25.6	20.2	21.2	28.5	19.7	27.5	27.2	22.2	-	28.7	28.2	18.7	15.4
3. Some of the times	17.4	17.9	15.4	17.7	14.5	20.5	15.9	17.0	16.2	17.1	15.9	-	14.8	13.2	21.2	22.7
4. Most of the times	18.4	19.0	17.3	19.8	12.1	19.2	19.8	17.6	17.0	15.0	19.7	-	9.0	19.4	25.6	22.7
5. Every time	15.0	15.7	12.0	13.3	15.6	16.1	13.5	16.2	13.5	11.3	16.9	-	9.3	10.7	20.4	23.6
Item 2120 Subject A05c N★	1268	626	546	934	155	311	320	384	253	616	429	-	455	214	561	21

★=excludes respondents for whom question was inappropriate.

QUESTIONNAIRE FORM 1 1984	TOTAL	SEX		RACE		REGION				4YR COLLEGE PLANS		ILLICIT DRUG USE: LIFETIME				
		M	F	White	Black	NE	NC	S	W	Yes	No	None	Mari- juana Only	Few Pills	More Pills	Any Her- oin
N (Weighted No. of Cases):	3311	1534	1616	2414	478	670	941	1113	587	1772	1137	1223	794	381	765	32
% of Weighted Total:	100.0	46.3	48.8	72.9	14.4	20.2	28.4	33.6	17.7	53.5	34.3	36.9	24.0	11.5	23.1	1.0
B020D: When your date or spouse was present																
1. Not at all	49.0	57.3	43.0	49.6	58.3	46.2	46.1	50.5	54.1	57.7	42.2	-	65.8	56.0	33.4	39.2
2. A few of the times	22.0	19.1	24.6	22.9	16.3	20.0	26.3	21.4	19.9	19.9	23.8	-	16.7	20.2	27.4	8.9
3. Some of the times	13.9	15.5	10.9	13.6	9.6	16.0	13.6	12.8	13.3	10.9	16.7	-	8.3	13.3	18.1	27.4
4. Most of the times	9.0	5.4	12.2	8.1	9.4	9.5	8.2	9.2	9.3	7.2	9.3	-	3.9	8.6	13.4	10.2
5. Every time	6.0	2.7	9.4	5.7	6.3	8.3	5.9	6.1	3.3	4.4	8.1	-	5.3	1.8	7.7	14.3
Item 2130 Subject A05b N★	1270	625	550	933	156	313	320	385	251	615	432	-	456	215	562	21
B020E: When people over age 30 were present																
1. Not at all	66.7	61.6	76.1	68.1	68.4	67.0	71.8	64.5	63.2	74.1	64.2	-	81.5	67.1	55.8	40.9
2. A few of the times	21.2	25.8	13.6	20.0	22.8	20.3	18.3	21.6	25.2	17.5	21.7	-	12.7	24.8	26.3	27.0
3. Some of the times	8.3	8.6	7.1	8.5	4.8	7.8	7.9	8.9	8.5	6.2	9.2	-	3.2	5.0	13.5	15.4
4. Most of the times	2.2	2.6	1.7	2.3	2.7	2.4	0.9	3.5	1.8	0.9	3.0	-	1.6	2.1	2.5	6.6
5. Every time	1.6	1.4	1.5	1.1	1.4	2.5	1.0	1.6	1.3	1.3	2.0	-	1.0	1.0	1.8	10.1
Item 2140 Subject A05b N★	1264	624	547	930	156	310	320	382	253	611	431	-	455	212	560	21
B020F: During the daytime (before 4:00 p.m.)																
1. Not at all	40.2	36.4	47.4	39.6	52.4	34.9	42.5	43.2	39.5	46.1	37.7	-	59.1	42.3	24.4	29.9
2. A few of the times	25.6	26.0	25.0	26.7	20.6	24.8	26.4	22.4	30.6	26.5	25.3	-	25.0	31.4	24.8	12.5
3. Some of the times	19.8	24.0	14.4	20.9	14.2	23.8	18.0	19.1	18.4	16.4	20.7	-	9.2	21.5	28.3	18.5
4. Most of the times	10.5	9.5	10.3	9.7	9.1	11.2	10.9	11.5	7.7	8.6	11.6	-	4.3	3.6	17.3	29.3
5. Every time	3.7	4.2	2.8	3.1	3.7	5.3	2.2	3.8	3.7	2.4	4.7	-	2.4	1.1	5.4	9.8
Item 2150 Subject A05c N★	1269	626	548	932	157	312	321	383	253	615	431	-	456	215	561	21
B020G: At your home (or apartment or dorm)																
1. Not at all	52.3	50.3	57.7	53.6	55.6	50.9	55.9	52.9	48.7	57.7	49.1	-	71.0	54.1	37.0	26.8
2. A few of the times	22.6	23.1	21.5	21.5	25.5	21.8	18.2	23.8	27.3	21.6	25.4	-	19.1	28.2	23.9	14.7
3. Some of the times	14.0	15.5	10.1	14.3	9.6	15.2	15.9	12.8	12.1	10.5	14.3	-	6.7	9.5	21.5	19.6
4. Most of the times	6.9	7.0	6.5	6.7	5.6	7.4	6.7	5.7	8.6	6.8	5.7	-	1.3	4.9	11.9	20.4
5. Every time	4.1	4.0	4.2	3.9	3.8	4.8	3.2	4.9	3.3	3.5	5.5	-	1.9	3.2	5.6	18.6
Item 2160 Subject A05c N★	1271	626	550	934	157	312	320	386	253	616	432	-	457	214	563	21
B020H: At school																
1. Not at all	66.6	61.7	74.3	68.5	64.6	60.8	63.4	73.6	67.5	73.8	62.1	-	82.6	71.5	52.7	55.7
2. A few of the times	16.3	18.6	14.1	16.9	13.3	20.3	18.8	11.9	15.1	15.0	18.9	-	9.2	16.4	22.0	23.2
3. Some of the times	9.9	12.2	6.0	8.9	11.8	11.3	10.6	8.1	9.9	6.3	11.0	-	4.3	8.0	14.8	7.8
4. Most of the times	5.3	5.7	4.5	4.5	8.9	5.2	5.9	4.6	5.8	3.7	5.9	-	2.6	2.7	8.6	8.4
5. Every time	1.8	1.8	1.1	1.1	1.4	2.4	1.4	1.8	1.8	1.2	2.0	-	1.3	1.3	2.0	4.9
Item 2170 Subject A05c N★	1272	628	549	935	157	313	321	385	253	617	432	-	456	216	563	21
B020I: In a car																
1. Not at all	23.0	21.4	26.6	24.9	17.3	23.5	20.8	19.5	30.7	30.2	17.1	-	33.4	24.0	15.1	11.3
2. A few of the times	25.5	23.8	29.1	24.8	32.2	19.7	29.4	25.1	28.2	26.7	27.2	-	29.4	31.4	19.9	26.9
3. Some of the times	23.1	25.8	18.8	23.4	20.4	24.5	21.9	22.7	23.4	21.3	23.7	-	18.5	25.8	26.4	8.8
4. Most of the times	21.9	21.9	20.0	22.0	18.1	24.6	23.2	24.6	12.5	17.2	24.6	-	13.8	14.3	30.5	46.1
5. Every time	6.5	7.0	5.4	5.0	12.0	7.7	4.7	8.1	5.1	4.6	7.3	-	5.0	4.6	8.1	7.0
Item 2190 Subject A05c N★	1270	625	550	934	157	312	321	384	253	617	431	-	456	214	563	21
B021: How many of the times when you used marijuana or hashish during the last year did you use it along with alcohol–that is, so that their effects overlapped?																
1. Not at all	30.3	26.2	35.6	26.9	49.1	29.5	23.6	33.9	34.5	32.7	30.7	-	45.9	33.3	17.4	18.7
2. A few of the times	32.2	32.7	32.3	33.0	30.7	29.8	33.7	28.6	38.6	35.4	29.3	-	35.3	39.4	26.9	31.9
3. Some of the times	18.0	18.8	16.6	19.0	9.2	20.0	21.2	14.9	16.6	14.8	19.1	-	8.3	14.2	27.3	21.3
4. Most of the times	13.0	15.2	10.4	14.6	5.8	13.3	14.7	14.6	8.0	12.1	13.6	-	5.7	8.6	20.4	10.3
5. Every time	6.5	7.0	5.1	6.6	5.2	7.5	6.8	8.1	2.4	5.0	7.3	-	4.9	4.5	8.0	17.8
Item 2200 Subject A01h N★	1243	615	538	924	147	302	315	376	250	608	419	-	444	212	554	19

★=excludes respondents for whom question was inappropriate.

QUESTIONNAIRE FORM 1 1984	TOTAL	SEX		RACE		REGION				4YR COLLEGE PLANS		ILLICIT DRUG USE: LIFETIME				
		M	F	White	Black	NE	NC	S	W	Yes	No	None	Marijuana Only	Few Pills	More Pills	Any Heroin
N (Weighted No. of Cases):	3311	1534	1616	2414	478	670	941	1113	587	1772	1137	1223	794	381	765	32
% of Weighted Total:	100.0	46.3	48.8	72.9	14.4	20.2	28.4	33.6	17.7	53.5	34.3	36.9	24.0	11.5	23.1	1.0

B022: What have been the most important reasons for your using marijuana or hashish? (Mark all that apply.)

	TOTAL	M	F	White	Black	NE	NC	S	W	Yes	No	None	Mari-juana Only	Few Pills	More Pills	Any Heroin
A. To experiment–to see what it's like	60.2	60.9	61.6	60.3	61.1	56.1	63.8	60.3	60.8	67.5	56.6	-	75.1	62.0	49.2	27.8
B. To relax or relieve tension	40.9	42.4	37.7	41.3	31.3	43.8	37.6	40.6	41.9	35.8	44.4	-	24.7	38.6	54.8	49.8
C. To feel good or get high	74.6	79.0	69.5	75.9	65.7	78.9	72.8	71.2	76.7	72.7	75.2	-	60.4	78.0	85.0	78.7
D. To seek deeper insights and understanding	11.4	13.9	7.9	10.8	13.2	15.6	8.8	11.3	9.7	9.8	12.4	-	4.2	16.7	14.7	20.4
E. To have a good time with my friends	64.9	69.4	59.8	66.2	54.1	66.0	64.1	61.1	70.4	62.5	68.0	-	54.8	69.9	71.6	64.0
F. To fit in with a group I like	12.4	14.3	9.8	12.1	11.2	9.0	16.0	12.5	11.8	12.0	12.9	-	14.1	13.1	10.6	13.3
G. To get away from my problems or troubles	22.3	20.9	23.3	21.0	25.0	21.0	22.0	25.2	19.9	15.8	29.0	-	15.4	26.0	26.1	28.7
H. Because of boredom, nothing else to do	25.6	28.5	21.6	24.6	25.6	25.8	22.6	25.2	29.7	25.0	24.9	-	15.7	32.7	31.3	31.2
I. Because of anger or frustration	16.0	15.0	16.3	14.4	17.4	16.4	13.8	19.1	13.4	11.2	21.3	-	9.6	18.5	20.1	25.3
J. To get through the day	8.9	8.6	7.2	7.6	3.9	10.0	7.4	9.2	9.1	5.5	10.1	-	2.3	6.6	14.2	28.5
K. To increase the effects of some other drug(s)	11.2	13.8	7.5	11.9	6.7	11.6	12.3	9.4	12.1	10.2	9.6	-	2.1	8.0	19.3	28.4
L. To decrease (offset) the effects of some other drug(s)	1.8	1.8	1.5	1.8	1.0	2.0	1.3	2.0	2.0	1.5	1.7	-	0.5	0.6	3.1	9.2
M. Because I am "hooked"–I have to have it	3.0	3.5	1.7	2.3	3.2	4.4	1.4	3.3	2.6	1.2	3.8	-	0.1	0.9	5.3	11.8
Item 2210-2330 Subject A06a N★	*1264*	*622*	*548*	*930*	*158*	*310*	*316*	*386*	*253*	*614*	*430*	*-*	*455*	*213*	*558*	*21*

B023: When you use marijuana or hashish how high do you usually get?

	TOTAL	M	F	White	Black	NE	NC	S	W	Yes	No	None	Mari-juana Only	Few Pills	More Pills	Any Heroin
1. Not at all high	6.8	6.4	7.7	6.3	9.1	6.0	6.2	7.9	6.5	8.4	6.4	-	12.8	2.3	3.6	-
2. A little high	29.0	26.7	33.1	27.2	39.0	23.7	34.9	26.3	31.9	34.3	24.6	-	41.3	36.4	16.5	16.6
3. Moderately high	36.9	36.6	35.3	37.7	29.1	43.6	33.6	33.9	37.5	34.2	38.1	-	31.2	32.8	43.3	42.7
4. Very high	27.4	30.4	23.9	28.8	22.8	26.6	25.3	31.8	24.1	23.0	31.0	-	14.7	28.4	36.7	40.8
Item 2340 Subject A01e N★	*1264*	*622*	*549*	*929*	*158*	*309*	*320*	*385*	*250*	*612*	*433*	*-*	*456*	*210*	*559*	*21*

B024: When you use marijuana or hashish, how long do you usually stay high?

	TOTAL	M	F	White	Black	NE	NC	S	W	Yes	No	None	Mari-juana Only	Few Pills	More Pills	Any Heroin
1. Usually don't get high	9.6	9.3	10.8	9.1	10.8	8.4	7.8	11.0	11.0	12.0	8.0	-	17.8	6.7	4.3	-
2. One to two hours	51.7	50.6	52.1	52.4	42.2	54.7	53.7	45.3	55.0	53.0	47.7	-	53.0	55.6	48.9	57.2
3. Three to six hours	33.1	34.9	31.1	33.7	38.8	31.3	32.9	37.4	29.1	30.5	37.2	-	26.1	30.9	39.8	31.7
4. Seven to 24 hours	5.0	4.6	5.5	4.4	6.9	4.7	5.2	5.2	4.9	4.3	5.9	-	2.6	6.4	6.3	11.2
5. More than 24 hours	0.7	0.6	0.4	0.4	1.3	1.0	0.3	1.1	-	0.2	1.2	-	0.5	0.4	0.7	-
Item 2350 Subject A01f N★	*1268*	*626*	*549*	*932*	*159*	*311*	*319*	*386*	*251*	*614*	*433*	*-*	*454*	*214*	*559*	*21*

B025: During the LAST MONTH, about how many marijuana cigarettes (joints, reefers), or the equivalent, did you smoke a day, on the average? (If you shared them with other people, count only the amount YOU smoked.)

	TOTAL	M	F	White	Black	NE	NC	S	W	Yes	No	None	Mari-juana Only	Few Pills	More Pills	Any Heroin
1. None	42.6	39.6	49.5	45.2	37.6	38.1	41.9	42.2	49.8	50.8	39.2	-	58.8	48.8	29.4	13.6
2. Less than 1 a day	33.9	35.9	32.8	35.7	31.5	35.2	33.6	32.5	34.8	35.6	31.9	-	30.2	33.1	37.7	32.3
3. 1 a day	8.5	9.8	6.6	8.0	9.6	8.5	9.4	8.7	6.7	6.7	10.2	-	5.4	4.4	11.5	22.1
4. 2 - 3 a day	9.4	8.8	7.5	6.8	12.4	11.9	8.7	10.1	6.0	4.4	11.0	-	3.9	9.8	12.8	19.9
5. 4 - 6 a day	2.8	3.0	1.8	2.4	2.4	2.6	3.2	3.7	1.1	1.0	3.9	-	1.2	2.0	4.1	2.8
6. 7 - 10 a day	1.5	1.7	0.5	0.4	5.1	1.4	0.9	2.2	1.5	1.1	1.4	-	-	1.6	2.4	-
7. 11 or more a day	1.4	1.2	1.2	1.5	1.4	2.4	2.4	0.6	-	0.3	2.3	-	0.6	0.3	2.1	9.3
Item 2360 Subject A01d N★	*1186*	*594*	*505*	*874*	*149*	*289*	*304*	*362*	*231*	*576*	*403*	*-*	*413*	*199*	*535*	*20*

B026: Do you know how much marijuana you have used (in ounces) during the LAST MONTH?

	TOTAL	M	F	White	Black	NE	NC	S	W	Yes	No	None	Mari-juana Only	Few Pills	More Pills	Any Heroin
8. Don't know	22.9	18.4	26.6	21.5	28.8	22.4	24.1	25.0	18.5	20.9	23.7	-	22.2	18.9	24.8	18.4
1. None	37.9	35.4	44.2	39.6	38.6	35.3	37.9	38.2	40.6	43.8	36.5	-	54.0	42.8	25.2	13.6
2. Less than 1/2 ounce	18.6	21.8	15.6	18.0	18.6	20.2	14.3	15.7	26.9	21.0	16.8	-	17.7	21.0	18.3	12.6
3. About 1/2 ounce	6.1	7.5	4.5	6.8	4.5	4.7	6.9	5.6	7.4	5.6	6.2	-	2.3	4.8	9.2	13.6
4. About 1 ounce	6.9	8.7	3.7	7.3	4.2	6.1	9.7	7.6	3.3	4.1	7.5	-	1.7	5.7	11.2	15.3
5. About 2 ounces	4.4	4.5	3.4	4.3	1.5	5.9	5.0	4.4	1.7	3.0	4.2	-	1.1	4.1	6.5	21.5
6. 3 to 5 ounces	1.8	1.7	1.2	1.3	1.3	4.4	0.6	1.9	-	0.6	2.6	-	0.7	1.4	2.7	-
7. 6 or more ounces	1.4	2.0	0.8	1.2	2.6	1.0	1.5	1.4	1.7	1.0	2.5	-	0.3	1.4	2.2	5.1
Item 2370 Subject A01d N★	*1190*	*597*	*506*	*879*	*149*	*292*	*304*	*362*	*231*	*579*	*404*	*-*	*414*	*199*	*539*	*20*

★=excludes respondents for whom question was inappropriate.

QUESTIONNAIRE FORM 1 1984	TOTAL	SEX M	F	RACE White	Black	REGION NE	NC	S	W	4YR COLLEGE PLANS Yes	No	ILLICIT DRUG USE: LIFETIME None	Mari- juana Only	Few Pills	More Pills	Any Her- oin
N (Weighted No. of Cases):	3311	1534	1616	2414	478	670	941	1113	587	1772	1137	1223	794	381	765	32
% of Weighted Total:	100.0	46.3	48.8	72.9	14.4	20.2	28.4	33.6	17.7	53.5	34.3	36.9	24.0	11.5	23.1	1.0

B027: Have you ever tried to stop using marijuana or hashish and found that you couldn't stop?

	TOTAL	M	F	White	Black	NE	NC	S	W	Yes	No	None	Mari- juana Only	Few Pills	More Pills	Any Her- oin
1. Yes	6.2	6.4	5.5	4.3	13.9	6.2	3.8	7.8	7.0	4.6	7.3	-	5.7	5.5	5.9	16.7
2. No	93.8	93.6	94.5	95.7	86.1	93.8	96.2	92.2	93.0	95.4	92.7	-	94.3	94.5	94.1	83.3
Item 2380 Subject A01i N★	1266	624	550	932	157	307	319	388	253	614	433	-	451	214	561	21

B028: Thinking back over your whole life, has there ever been a period when you used marijuana or hashish on a daily, or almost daily, basis for at least a month?

1. No–GO TO QUESTION B032.	83.8	82.9	87.2	83.9	89.6	76.2	87.2	86.1	82.4	89.3	81.2	100.0	92.7	81.0	53.1	32.8
2. Yes	16.2	17.1	12.8	16.1	10.4	23.8	12.8	13.9	17.6	10.7	18.8	-	7.3	19.0	46.9	67.2
Item 21180 Subject A01a N	3136	1474	1528	2319	442	627	904	1044	561	1700	1082	1149	770	368	746	28

B029: How old were you when you first smoked marijuana or hashish that frequently?

1. Grade 6 or earlier	10.0	10.7	7.3	9.2	8.8	11.9	11.4	9.7	5.7	9.0	8.6	-	5.6	6.8	11.6	14.0
2. Grade 7 or 8	27.7	32.1	23.4	28.9	23.2	32.6	26.6	22.7	30.0	29.8	26.5	-	19.7	33.0	28.7	41.3
3. Grade 9(Freshman)	23.3	22.0	26.6	24.5	22.8	24.5	20.5	20.1	30.7	21.8	22.5	-	23.0	18.9	23.8	34.9
4. Grade 10(Sophomore)	19.8	19.0	21.0	19.7	21.7	15.3	20.2	23.8	19.3	22.9	19.6	-	17.5	31.7	18.8	5.2
5. Grade 11(Junior)	13.1	10.3	15.9	12.3	17.2	9.2	15.3	16.8	10.0	12.6	15.7	-	22.9	7.5	12.4	4.7
6. Grade 12(Senior)	6.1	6.0	5.9	5.5	6.2	6.5	6.1	6.8	4.3	3.8	7.2	-	11.4	2.1	4.7	-
Item 21190 Subject A01g N★	633	306	254	433	83	179	136	206	113	225	252	-	107	82	392	20

B030: How recently did you use marijuana or hashish on a daily, or almost daily, basis for at least a month?

1. During the past month	25.3	28.8	18.1	22.9	28.3	23.2	28.5	29.5	17.3	21.5	27.0	-	19.0	21.9	26.1	22.5
2. 2 months ago	6.9	7.9	4.3	6.4	7.8	6.4	8.9	7.6	4.1	6.0	6.1	-	13.0	5.7	6.0	5.2
3. 3 to 9 months ago	12.3	10.8	14.6	13.5	13.6	11.7	7.6	13.0	17.6	10.0	15.4	-	14.7	9.1	11.8	19.2
4. About 1 year ago	18.4	17.8	18.0	16.9	16.1	18.1	16.0	19.6	19.5	17.1	17.5	-	11.0	17.3	21.1	5.5
5. About 2 years ago	16.9	17.2	20.6	20.6	9.2	16.7	18.1	14.4	20.1	21.4	16.4	-	16.0	17.9	18.0	18.1
6. 3 or more years ago	20.2	17.4	24.4	19.8	25.0	23.8	20.9	16.0	21.3	24.1	17.6	-	26.3	28.2	16.9	29.6
Item 21200 Subject A01a N★	587	285	233	409	71	166	129	184	108	203	238	-	88	80	374	20

B031: Over your whole lifetime, during how many months have you used marijuana or hashish on a daily or near-daily basis?

1. Less than 3 months	39.0	38.7	43.0	39.7	46.7	36.3	30.9	48.7	35.3	42.0	43.5	-	67.2	55.7	28.8	15.4
2. 3 to 9 months	16.1	13.8	19.1	16.6	12.5	17.8	16.7	12.8	18.4	21.5	11.6	-	10.7	8.7	19.2	23.2
3. About 1 year	12.8	12.0	13.6	12.9	13.0	10.6	17.3	13.5	9.8	14.0	11.9	-	10.5	13.3	13.9	11.8
4. About 1 and 1/2 years	6.4	6.2	6.1	6.7	4.7	7.7	7.0	5.6	5.1	4.4	7.6	-	-	1.7	9.1	-
5. About 2 years	9.1	11.6	6.9	10.3	5.7	10.3	6.4	7.2	13.6	7.9	10.3	-	3.1	7.9	10.9	10.5
6. About 3 to 5 years	12.2	11.9	9.3	10.0	13.3	12.9	11.4	9.1	17.2	8.9	10.2	-	7.1	12.8	13.2	27.7
7. 6 to 9 years	3.7	4.8	1.8	3.3	2.4	4.3	8.7	2.1	-	1.4	3.7	-	1.4	-	4.3	9.1
8. 10 or more years	0.7	1.1	0.2	0.5	1.8	-	1.5	0.9	0.6	-	1.3	-	-	-	0.6	2.2
Item 21210 Subject A01a N★	571	276	229	400	71	163	119	182	107	202	234	-	81	78	366	20

B032: Do you think you will be using marijuana or hashish five years from now?

1. I definitely will	2.6	2.7	2.3	2.6	2.3	3.5	2.3	2.6	2.3	2.2	2.7	0.4	0.8	1.3	8.2	17.9
2. I probably will	12.7	13.1	10.4	11.6	9.5	17.6	10.9	11.3	12.8	10.1	12.3	0.2	11.5	17.7	31.3	28.1
3. I probably will not	22.1	23.5	20.6	21.7	24.5	24.4	19.8	21.3	25.0	21.5	22.5	7.5	34.7	33.5	27.0	20.9
4. I definitely will not	62.6	60.7	66.7	64.1	63.8	54.5	67.1	64.8	59.9	66.3	62.5	91.8	53.0	47.5	33.6	33.1
Item 2390 Subject A04a N	3202	1490	1582	2357	467	633	919	1077	573	1737	1105	1200	773	371	745	29

The next questions are about LSD, the psychedelic drug which is sometimes called "acid".

B033: On how many occasions (if any) have you taken LSD . . .

★=excludes respondents for whom question was inappropriate.

QUESTIONNAIRE FORM 1 1984	TOTAL	SEX		RACE		REGION				4YR COLLEGE PLANS		ILLICIT DRUG USE: LIFETIME				
		M	F	White	Black	NE	NC	S	W	Yes	No	None	Mari-juana Only	Few Pills	More Pills	Any Her-oin
N (Weighted No. of Cases):	3311	1534	1616	2414	478	670	941	1113	587	1772	1137	1223	794	381	765	32
% of Weighted Total:	100.0	46.3	48.8	72.9	14.4	20.2	28.4	33.6	17.7	53.5	34.3	36.9	24.0	11.5	23.1	1.0

B033A: . . . in your lifetime?

	TOTAL	M	F	White	Black	NE	NC	S	W	Yes	No	None	Mari-juana Only	Few Pills	More Pills	Any Heroin
1. 0 occasions	91.6	90.6	94.0	91.3	98.1	88.4	92.4	93.6	90.0	94.8	91.6	100.0	100.0	91.7	70.4	44.6
2. 1-2	3.9	4.1	3.4	4.2	1.5	5.3	2.9	3.5	4.8	2.9	3.7	-	-	8.3	12.0	11.0
3. 3-5	2.1	2.6	1.2	2.3	-	3.3	1.9	1.3	2.4	1.3	2.2	-	-	-	8.0	20.3
4. 6-9	0.7	0.8	0.5	0.8	-	0.9	1.1	0.4	0.6	0.1	1.0	-	-	-	3.1	3.4
5. 10-19	0.7	0.9	0.4	0.7	-	0.7	1.0	0.4	0.7	0.6	0.6	-	-	-	2.7	4.4
6. 20-39	0.5	0.4	0.2	0.4	0.1	0.8	0.4	0.5	0.4	0.1	0.3	-	-	-	2.0	2.8
7. 40 or more	0.6	0.7	0.3	0.4	0.3	0.6	0.4	0.4	1.1	0.2	0.7	-	-	-	1.8	13.5
Item 890 Subject A01a N	3169	1479	1562	2357	445	627	918	1053	572	1719	1105	1200	780	367	743	30

B033B: . . . during the last 12 months?

	TOTAL	M	F	White	Black	NE	NC	S	W	Yes	No	None	Mari-juana Only	Few Pills	More Pills	Any Heroin
1. 0 occasions	94.8	93.6	97.2	94.6	99.6	92.0	94.9	96.5	94.6	97.0	94.4	100.0	100.0	97.5	80.3	68.8
2. 1-2	3.3	4.2	2.0	3.8	0.2	5.2	2.8	2.6	3.4	2.1	3.8	-	-	2.5	12.4	14.4
3. 3-5	0.9	1.0	0.4	0.8	-	1.2	1.2	0.3	1.0	0.4	1.0	-	-	-	3.6	1.4
4. 6-9	0.5	0.5	0.3	0.5	-	0.8	0.5	0.1	0.9	0.4	0.3	-	-	-	2.0	2.5
5. 10-19	0.3	0.4	-	0.2	0.1	0.4	0.3	0.3	0.2	-	0.2	-	-	-	1.2	2.8
6. 20-39	0.1	0.1	0.1	0.1	-	-	0.1	0.3	-	0.1	-	-	-	-	0.4	4.9
7. 40 or more	0.1	0.2	-	0.1	-	0.4	0.1	-	-	-	0.2	-	-	-	0.2	5.2
Item 900 Subject A01b N	3163	1477	1559	2353	445	625	915	1051	572	1719	1103	1201	780	366	736	30

B033C: . . . during the last 30 days?

	TOTAL	M	F	White	Black	NE	NC	S	W	Yes	No	None	Mari-juana Only	Few Pills	More Pills	Any Heroin
1. 0 occasions	98.2	97.8	99.1	98.2	99.6	96.9	97.9	98.5	99.3	99.2	97.9	100.0	100.0	98.3	93.8	79.8
2. 1-2	1.4	1.6	0.9	1.6	0.2	2.4	1.8	0.9	0.6	0.7	1.5	-	-	1.7	4.8	9.2
3. 3-5	0.2	0.2	-	0.1	-	0.4	0.1	0.3	-	-	0.3	-	-	-	0.8	2.8
4. 6-9	0.1	0.2	-	*	0.1	-	0.1	0.3	0.1	0.1	0.1	-	-	-	0.4	4.9
5. 10-19	-	-	-	-	-	-	-	-	-	-	-	-	-	-	-	-
6. 20-39	-	-	-	-	-	-	-	-	-	-	-	-	-	-	-	-
7. 40 or more	0.1	0.1	-	0.1	-	0.3	0.1	-	-	-	0.2	-	-	-	0.2	3.4
Item 910 Subject A01c N	3164	1478	1559	2355	445	625	915	1053	571	1719	1104	1201	780	366	737	30

IF YOU HAVE NOT TAKEN LSD IN THE LAST TWELVE MONTHS, GO TO Q.B041.

B034: When you used LSD during the last year, how often did you use it in each of the following situations?

B034A: When you were alone

	TOTAL	M	F	White	Black	NE	NC	S	W	Yes	No	None	Mari-juana Only	Few Pills	More Pills	Any Heroin
1. Not at all	83.8	85.7	86.2	84.6	76.6	83.2	78.1	90.4	84.7	89.7	83.0	-	-	90.9	84.9	54.2
2. A few of the times	11.3	7.4	11.4	11.1	-	12.9	15.1	5.8	10.1	7.5	8.0	-	-	9.1	11.2	19.5
3. Some of the times	2.9	4.5	-	1.7	23.4	2.0	4.1	3.8	1.7	2.8	3.5	-	-	-	2.3	15.6
4. Most of the times	-	-	-	-	-	-	-	-	-	-	-	-	-	-	-	-
5. Every time	2.0	2.4	2.4	2.6	-	2.0	2.7	-	3.4	-	5.5	-	-	-	1.6	10.8
Item 2400 Subject A05a N★	167	92	47	126	2	51	44	39	33	53	60	-	-	9	144	9

B034B: With just 1 or 2 other people

	TOTAL	M	F	White	Black	NE	NC	S	W	Yes	No	None	Mari-juana Only	Few Pills	More Pills	Any Heroin
1. Not at all	21.3	25.1	17.5	22.1	76.6	28.9	15.7	29.1	8.4	18.5	23.7	-	-	11.6	19.2	29.6
2. A few of the times	33.0	31.2	29.0	29.9	-	25.7	39.1	37.9	29.9	29.2	31.9	-	-	44.1	34.1	18.4
3. Some of the times	11.3	11.7	7.0	12.6	23.4	6.9	17.4	8.2	12.7	5.1	16.3	-	-	-	12.1	13.5
4. Most of the times	15.3	13.4	17.6	14.1	-	14.5	17.4	11.3	18.2	17.9	11.6	-	-	7.9	15.7	21.5
5. Every time	19.2	18.7	28.9	21.3	-	24.1	10.4	13.5	30.9	29.3	16.5	-	-	36.5	18.8	16.9
Item 2410 Subject A05b N★	171	97	47	131	2	52	48	38	33	53	64	-	-	9	149	9

B034C: At a party

	TOTAL	M	F	White	Black	NE	NC	S	W	Yes	No	None	Mari-juana Only	Few Pills	More Pills	Any Heroin
1. Not at all	38.5	34.6	42.8	36.9	76.6	37.9	33.9	29.1	56.8	44.7	38.6	-	-	92.9	35.5	13.8
2. A few of the times	22.5	21.5	26.0	23.2	-	27.0	21.5	20.2	19.8	25.3	15.9	-	-	7.1	25.4	-
3. Some of the times	17.2	19.9	11.1	17.6	-	15.0	21.4	22.7	8.4	10.7	19.6	-	-	-	17.9	27.8
4. Most of the times	5.4	6.1	5.4	6.0	23.4	7.4	5.9	1.4	6.3	2.2	7.6	-	-	-	5.5	10.5
5. Every time	16.3	17.9	14.6	16.4	-	12.7	17.4	26.5	8.7	17.1	18.3	-	-	-	15.6	47.9
Item 2420 Subject A05c N★	170	96	46	130	2	51	48	38	33	53	63	-	-	8	149	9

*=less than .05 per cent.   ★=excludes respondents for whom question was inappropriate.

QUESTIONNAIRE FORM 1 1984	TOTAL	SEX		RACE		REGION				4YR COLLEGE PLANS		ILLICIT DRUG USE: LIFETIME				
		M	F	White	Black	NE	NC	S	W	Yes	No	None	Marijuana Only	Few Pills	More Pills	Any Heroin
N (Weighted No. of Cases):	3311	1534	1616	2414	478	670	941	1113	587	1772	1137	1223	794	381	765	32
% of Weighted Total:	100.0	46.3	48.8	72.9	14.4	20.2	28.4	33.6	17.7	53.5	34.3	36.9	24.0	11.5	23.1	1.0

B034D: When your date or spouse was present

1. Not at all	67.3	74.0	58.0	69.6	76.6	62.3	79.3	67.5	56.7	64.3	70.9	-	-	72.5	67.3	48.9
2. A few of the times	12.3	12.3	9.6	9.7	-	12.7	9.8	11.1	16.6	12.3	9.3	-	-	7.1	13.7	-
3. Some of the times	6.2	5.0	3.5	4.2	23.4	7.7	2.3	10.7	4.1	2.8	7.1	-	-	11.1	4.8	26.1
4. Most of the times	3.5	1.7	5.3	3.6	-	6.7	2.7	3.0	-	2.3	3.4	-	-	-	4.0	-
5. Every time	10.9	7.0	23.6	12.9	-	10.6	5.9	7.7	22.5	18.2	9.3	-	-	9.3	10.3	25.0
Item 2430 Subject A05b N★	167	93	47	128	2	51	48	37	31	53	62	-	-	8	145	9

B034E: When people over age 30 were present

1. Not at all	71.8	70.2	78.3	72.4	100.0	64.9	71.7	69.6	84.7	80.6	69.8	-	-	81.8	73.2	29.1
2. A few of the times	14.8	17.5	10.7	13.4	-	19.4	15.1	14.9	7.3	12.0	13.2	-	-	18.2	13.6	36.9
3. Some of the times	6.5	6.6	2.8	7.1	-	9.3	5.0	9.0	1.7	1.4	10.4	-	-	-	6.2	19.7
4. Most of the times	4.0	4.2	4.3	4.7	-	4.8	5.8	-	4.6	2.3	4.8	-	-	-	4.0	8.1
5. Every time	2.9	1.4	3.8	2.4	-	1.5	2.3	6.4	1.8	3.7	1.8	-	-	-	2.9	6.2
Item 2440 Subject A05b N★	169	95	46	129	2	50	48	38	33	53	63	-	-	8	147	9

B034F: During the daytime (before 4:00 p.m.)

1. Not at all	56.6	54.3	59.1	58.4	76.6	54.4	54.3	69.3	49.0	57.7	58.1	-	-	100.0	54.4	37.2
2. A few of the times	21.5	24.5	14.3	19.3	-	23.8	21.4	10.3	31.0	26.6	16.1	-	-	-	23.4	19.7
3. Some of the times	12.5	12.3	15.1	13.3	23.4	11.9	8.9	17.4	13.0	10.1	12.0	-	-	-	12.6	26.1
4. Most of the times	5.1	4.8	5.2	4.7	-	7.1	8.0	3.0	-	2.3	8.5	-	-	-	5.8	-
5. Every time	4.3	4.1	6.4	4.3	-	2.9	7.4	-	7.0	3.4	5.3	-	-	-	3.9	16.9
Item 2450 Subject A05c N★	167	95	46	129	2	50	48	37	33	53	63	-	-	8	146	9

B034G: At your home (or apartment or dorm)

1. Not at all	58.0	61.9	52.0	58.5	76.6	54.7	54.7	61.0	64.9	66.4	66.7	-	-	72.5	58.2	29.1
2. A few of the times	21.6	17.6	26.1	20.7	-	34.2	17.4	21.8	7.2	13.8	17.5	-	-	18.2	21.5	33.7
3. Some of the times	11.8	14.6	3.2	10.7	23.4	5.2	20.7	14.0	6.7	4.8	8.6	-	-	-	12.1	20.2
4. Most of the times	3.6	1.6	9.6	4.6	-	0.8	1.1	-	15.8	9.6	-	-	-	-	4.1	-
5. Every time	5.0	4.3	9.1	5.6	-	5.0	6.1	3.2	5.3	5.5	7.3	-	-	9.3	4.1	16.9
Item 2460 Subject A05c N★	169	96	47	131	2	52	48	37	32	53	63	-	-	8	148	9

B034H: At school

1. Not at all	76.1	71.5	81.4	76.8	71.1	69.5	67.1	89.6	83.9	81.6	75.7	-	-	88.9	76.0	57.0
2. A few of the times	15.2	17.2	13.4	15.5	-	20.6	22.2	3.2	10.0	12.9	12.8	-	-	-	16.3	16.7
3. Some of the times	5.5	6.3	5.3	4.0	21.7	6.1	6.1	4.0	5.5	5.1	6.1	-	-	11.1	4.7	15.6
4. Most of the times	1.9	3.4	-	2.5	-	1.7	2.3	3.2	-	-	2.8	-	-	-	2.2	-
5. Every time	1.4	1.7	-	1.2	7.2	2.0	2.3	-	0.6	0.4	2.5	-	-	-	0.9	10.8
Item 2470 Subject A05c N★	169	95	47	130	3	51	48	37	33	53	64	-	-	8	148	9

B034I: In a car

1. Not at all	51.1	51.8	58.2	51.5	71.1	57.1	41.8	48.4	58.5	57.0	54.3	-	-	76.5	48.7	48.0
2. A few of the times	23.6	23.6	16.5	22.8	28.9	20.2	34.0	17.5	20.6	21.1	17.3	-	-	17.0	25.3	10.8
3. Some of the times	7.2	7.0	-	5.6	-	11.5	4.7	10.8	-	2.1	8.0	-	-	-	8.2	-
4. Most of the times	9.8	9.0	12.6	10.7	-	4.3	11.7	16.9	6.9	11.0	11.1	-	-	-	9.2	30.5
5. Every time	8.4	8.7	12.6	9.4	-	6.9	7.8	6.4	13.9	8.8	9.3	-	-	6.5	8.6	10.8
Item 2490 Subject A05c N★	167	95	46	129	3	50	48	38	32	53	64	-	-	8	146	9

B035: How many of the times when you used LSD during the last year did you use it along with each of the following drugs–that is, so that their effects overlapped?

B035A: With alcohol

1. Not at all	28.7	26.9	40.3	31.3	71.1	32.1	18.8	31.4	34.9	37.1	28.8	-	-	49.6	25.5	30.9
2. A few of the times	26.1	29.9	23.3	26.8	7.2	20.3	39.6	20.2	22.2	27.6	27.7	-	-	25.0	27.6	15.3
3. Some of the times	9.5	10.3	1.1	8.1	21.7	12.5	8.6	2.6	14.0	5.0	6.8	-	-	-	10.2	10.5
4. Most of the times	10.5	6.9	14.4	9.1	-	7.8	16.8	6.1	10.7	8.4	9.2	-	-	9.0	11.6	-
5. Every time	25.1	26.0	21.0	24.7	-	27.2	16.1	39.7	18.3	21.7	27.5	-	-	16.4	25.1	43.4
Item 2500 Subject A01h N★	169	96	46	130	3	51	48	38	32	52	64	-	-	8	148	9

★=excludes respondents for whom question was inappropriate.

QUESTIONNAIRE FORM 1 1984	TOTAL	SEX		RACE		REGION				4YR COLLEGE PLANS		ILLICIT DRUG USE: LIFETIME				
		M	F	White	Black	NE	NC	S	W	Yes	No	None	Marijuana Only	Few Pills	More Pills	Any Heroin
N (Weighted No. of Cases):	3311	1534	1616	2414	478	670	941	1113	587	1772	1137	1223	794	381	765	32
% of Weighted Total:	100.0	46.3	48.8	72.9	14.4	20.2	28.4	33.6	17.7	53.5	34.3	36.9	24.0	11.5	23.1	1.0
B035B: With marijuana																
1. Not at all	28.6	20.6	48.9	28.9	76.6	31.0	18.0	34.7	33.4	39.2	27.7	-	-	74.0	23.6	42.1
2. A few of the times	13.3	15.4	12.3	15.0	-	15.3	15.4	12.2	8.6	12.2	20.9	-	-	8.3	14.5	4.6
3. Some of the times	17.9	22.8	6.2	18.4	23.4	13.9	27.0	8.5	21.5	14.6	12.8	-	-	-	19.0	21.5
4. Most of the times	10.0	11.1	7.1	7.3	-	2.5	17.5	10.8	9.5	8.3	11.3	-	-	-	10.8	9.0
5. Every time	30.2	30.1	25.4	30.4	-	37.2	22.2	33.8	26.9	25.7	27.3	-	-	17.7	32.1	22.9
Item 2510 Subject A01h N★	169	95	46	129	2	50	48	38	32	53	61	-	-	7	148	9
B036: What have been the most important reasons for your taking LSD? (Mark all that apply.)																
A. To experiment–to see what it's like	80.1	81.5	83.0	80.7	100.0	80.6	81.9	76.8	80.4	83.8	86.4	-	-	90.4	80.0	74.0
B. To relax or relieve tension	12.3	10.3	10.8	11.1	-	13.1	10.8	23.0	1.7	15.6	8.8	-	-	11.8	10.6	39.9
C. To feel good or get high	72.0	74.7	66.5	67.7	100.0	80.5	72.6	66.2	63.8	71.9	65.3	-	-	46.4	72.5	83.0
D. To seek deeper insights and understanding	26.7	29.8	21.8	23.1	-	23.9	23.8	33.9	27.7	26.7	22.1	-	-	17.5	26.3	41.2
E. To have a good time with my friends	55.2	58.8	48.1	52.5	-	51.1	63.3	48.0	57.9	65.4	45.4	-	-	42.7	54.8	70.8
F. To fit in with a group I like	5.7	4.9	4.9	4.1	-	4.1	-	11.4	10.3	9.2	3.3	-	-	11.8	4.8	15.6
G. To get away from my problems or troubles	12.7	13.4	13.0	11.5	-	13.4	8.1	22.0	8.1	14.6	10.3	-	-	-	12.3	29.1
H. Because of boredom, nothing else to do	19.8	28.2	4.8	18.4	-	10.2	34.6	19.2	14.5	23.6	18.0	-	-	-	19.6	38.5
I. Because of anger or frustration	7.4	9.1	6.1	7.2	-	9.9	2.5	15.4	1.7	7.0	7.3	-	-	21.7	4.9	35.3
J. To get through the day	5.3	4.6	-	2.1	-	2.0	2.7	18.6	-	2.8	3.7	-	-	9.6	3.8	26.4
K. To increase the effects of some other drug(s)	13.1	12.5	8.3	10.4	-	16.8	7.9	15.4	12.0	13.6	8.2	-	-	-	12.3	35.3
L. To decrease (offset) the effects of some other drug(s)	3.2	4.7	-	2.2	-	1.7	-	8.0	4.7	2.8	2.5	-	-	-	2.5	15.6
M. Because I am "hooked"–I have to have it	4.4	4.7	-	2.2	-	3.7	2.8	11.5	-	2.8	4.7	-	-	11.8	2.6	26.4
Item 2520-2640 Subject A06a N★	164	92	47	129	1	51	46	35	32	52	60	-	-	7	148	9
B037: When you take LSD how high do you usually get?																
1. Not at all high	2.5	3.0	-	0.8	76.6	2.0	-	8.8	-	1.4	3.4	-	-	-	1.6	-
2. A little high	5.6	5.8	8.2	6.0	-	10.4	3.4	1.5	6.0	5.5	10.2	-	-	33.3	4.6	-
3. Moderately high	24.8	22.2	25.8	25.1	23.4	30.1	29.6	8.2	28.5	15.9	29.6	-	-	29.4	24.3	34.1
4. Very high	67.1	69.0	65.9	68.2	-	57.5	67.0	81.6	65.5	77.2	56.8	-	-	37.2	69.6	65.9
Item 2650 Subject A01e N★	168	96	46	129	2	50	48	37	32	53	63	-	-	8	148	9
B038: When you take LSD how long do you usually stay high?																
1. Usually don't get high	3.2	4.2	-	0.8	76.6	2.0	2.3	8.8	-	1.4	5.1	-	-	-	2.4	-
2. One to two hours	2.5	-	7.4	2.2	-	7.4	-	1.5	-	-	5.4	-	-	36.8	1.0	-
3. Three to six hours	29.4	28.9	23.7	31.3	23.4	28.2	31.3	22.7	36.0	22.2	28.6	-	-	23.8	29.3	39.9
4. Seven to 24 hours	60.9	65.8	62.4	62.6	-	60.7	61.6	57.5	64.0	75.4	57.4	-	-	32.5	63.2	60.1
5. More than 24 hours	4.0	1.1	6.5	3.2	-	1.7	4.8	9.6	-	1.0	3.5	-	-	7.0	4.2	-
Item 2660 Subject A01f N★	168	96	46	129	2	50	48	37	32	53	63	-	-	8	148	9
B039: Have you ever had a "bad trip" on LSD?																
1. No	66.2	69.9	57.8	65.0	76.6	60.1	67.7	66.7	73.2	70.7	59.5	-	-	66.3	67.3	37.2
2. Yes, once	25.1	20.8	32.0	26.0	23.4	30.8	22.9	23.1	21.5	22.0	29.0	-	-	24.7	25.4	29.1
3. Yes, more than once	8.7	9.3	10.2	8.9	-	9.1	9.5	10.2	5.2	7.2	11.5	-	-	9.0	7.3	33.7
Item 2670 Subject A01k N★	171	97	47	131	2	52	48	38	32	53	63	-	-	8	149	9
B040: Have you ever tried to stop using LSD and found that you couldn't stop?																
1. Yes	3.2	1.6	3.4	2.4	-	3.7	2.9	2.7	3.5	-	3.4	-	-	27.2	1.2	15.3
2. No	96.8	98.4	96.6	97.6	100.0	96.3	97.1	97.3	96.5	100.0	96.6	-	-	72.8	98.8	84.7
Item 2680 Subject A01i N★	167	95	46	130	2	51	48	37	32	53	63	-	-	8	148	9

★=excludes respondents for whom question was inappropriate.

QUESTIONNAIRE FORM 1 1984	TOTAL	SEX		RACE		REGION				4YR COLLEGE PLANS		ILLICIT DRUG USE: LIFETIME				
		M	F	White	Black	NE	NC	S	W	Yes	No	None	Mari-juana Only	Few Pills	More Pills	Any Her-oin
N (Weighted No. of Cases):	3311	1534	1616	2414	478	670	941	1113	587	1772	1137	1223	794	381	765	32
% of Weighted Total:	100.0	46.3	48.8	72.9	14.4	20.2	28.4	33.6	17.7	53.5	34.3	36.9	24.0	11.5	23.1	1.0

B041: Do you think you will be using LSD five years from now?

1. I definitely will	0.9	0.7	0.9	0.9	0.8	1.5	0.8	0.8	0.6	0.7	1.2	0.4	0.9	0.8	1.7	3.6
2. I probably will	1.1	1.3	0.7	1.1	0.1	2.2	0.8	0.9	1.0	0.6	1.3	-	0.2	0.8	3.9	7.3
3. I probably will not	7.8	8.2	6.1	8.1	3.7	10.4	7.4	6.3	8.4	6.2	7.5	2.2	4.3	8.7	20.0	31.1
4. I definitely will not	90.2	89.7	92.2	90.0	95.4	85.9	91.0	92.1	90.0	92.4	89.9	97.4	94.7	89.7	74.4	58.0
Item 2690 Subject A04a N	3132	1462	1551	2319	450	614	905	1053	560	1709	1087	1189	764	355	713	28

The next questions are about PSYCHEDELICS OTHER THAN LSD.

This group would include the following drugs: Mescaline, Peyote, Psilocybin, PCP.

B042: On how many occasions (if any) have you taken psychedelics other than LSD . . .

B042A: . . . in your lifetime?

1. 0 occasions	92.6	92.0	94.0	92.4	98.1	85.2	93.7	96.6	91.9	94.9	92.3	100.0	100.0	93.9	74.1	38.2
2. 1-2	2.7	2.8	2.4	2.8	1.0	4.9	2.3	1.5	3.2	2.4	2.8	-	-	6.1	8.3	9.3
3. 3-5	1.4	1.5	1.2	1.6	0.2	3.0	1.4	0.3	1.6	0.9	0.9	-	-	-	5.7	7.4
4. 6-9	1.0	1.2	0.8	1.1	0.2	2.2	0.6	0.2	1.5	0.7	0.9	-	-	-	3.8	8.9
5. 10-19	1.1	1.5	0.5	1.0	0.4	2.2	0.9	0.7	1.0	0.7	1.5	-	-	-	4.1	16.3
6. 20-39	0.5	0.4	0.4	0.5	-	0.9	0.4	0.2	0.7	0.1	0.8	-	-	-	1.8	7.2
7. 40 or more	0.6	0.6	0.7	0.7	-	1.6	0.6	0.4	0.1	0.3	0.9	-	-	-	2.2	12.7
Item 920 Subject A01a N	3130	1463	1547	2337	434	620	902	1038	571	1708	1093	1192	770	361	729	32

B042B: . . . during the last 12 months?

1. 0 occasions	95.2	94.5	96.2	94.9	98.5	89.8	95.7	98.3	94.4	96.9	94.4	100.0	100.0	97.4	82.3	57.6
2. 1-2	2.6	2.9	2.3	2.9	1.1	5.6	2.2	0.8	3.3	1.8	2.9	-	-	2.6	9.0	22.1
3. 3-5	0.8	1.0	0.4	0.8	-	0.9	0.7	0.1	1.9	0.6	0.7	-	-	-	3.3	-
4. 6-9	0.7	0.9	0.5	0.6	0.3	1.7	0.6	0.5	0.2	0.5	0.7	-	-	-	2.6	8.4
5. 10-19	0.5	0.5	0.3	0.4	0.2	1.3	0.5	0.2	0.2	0.1	0.8	-	-	-	2.0	4.6
6. 20-39	0.2	0.2	0.2	0.2	-	0.5	0.1	0.1	-	0.1	0.2	-	-	-	0.6	4.2
7. 40 or more	0.1	0.1	-	0.1	-	0.2	0.1	-	-	-	0.2	-	-	-	0.2	3.2
Item 930 Subject A01b N	3126	1461	1545	2336	434	619	899	1038	571	1706	1091	1192	770	361	725	32

B042C: . . . during the last 30 days?

1. 0 occasions	97.9	97.3	98.7	98.0	99.1	95.3	97.9	98.9	98.7	98.8	97.4	100.0	100.0	99.2	92.1	79.6
2. 1-2	1.4	1.7	0.9	1.3	0.6	3.0	1.4	0.5	1.3	0.8	1.5	-	-	0.8	5.6	3.6
3. 3-5	0.5	0.5	0.3	0.4	0.3	1.2	0.3	0.4	-	0.4	0.5	-	-	-	1.6	8.4
4. 6-9	0.2	0.2	0.1	0.2	-	0.3	0.3	0.1	-	-	0.4	-	-	-	0.4	8.3
5. 10-19	0.1	0.1	-	0.1	-	0.1	-	0.1	-	-	0.2	-	-	-	0.2	-
6. 20-39	-	-	-	-	-	-	-	-	-	-	-	-	-	-	-	-
7. 40 or more	*	0.1	-	*	-	-	0.1	-	-	-	0.1	-	-	-	0.2	-
Item 940 Subject A01c N	3127	1462	1545	2336	434	618	899	1038	572	1707	1091	1192	770	360	726	32

IF YOU HAVE NOT TAKEN ANY PSYCHE-DELICS OTHER THAN LSD IN THE LAST TWELVE MONTHS, GO TO Q.B046.

B043: When you take psychedelics other than LSD how high do you usually get?

1. Not at all high	4.9	5.1	5.6	4.4	25.6	3.2	2.7	18.8	2.0	2.7	8.0	-	-	8.5	2.8	13.6
2. A little high	10.8	8.8	12.7	10.4	11.1	10.5	11.2	5.1	14.6	14.1	10.6	-	-	13.9	11.3	4.4
3. Moderately high	38.0	36.9	36.7	39.4	28.4	43.9	33.8	46.0	25.4	33.3	34.9	-	-	29.8	39.0	38.2
4. Very high	46.3	49.2	45.0	45.8	34.8	42.3	52.3	30.1	58.0	49.9	46.5	-	-	47.7	46.9	43.8
Item 2700 Subject A01e N★	153	79	61	118	9	65	40	20	29	54	60	-	-	10	129	13

*=less than .05 per cent.   ★=excludes respondents for whom question was inappropriate.

QUESTIONNAIRE FORM 1 1984	TOTAL	SEX		RACE		REGION				4YR COLLEGE PLANS		ILLICIT DRUG USE: LIFETIME				
		M	F	White	Black	NE	NC	S	W	Yes	No	None	Mari- juana Only	Few Pills	More Pills	Any Her- oin
N (Weighted No. of Cases):	3311	1534	1616	2414	478	670	941	1113	587	1772	1137	1223	794	381	765	32
% of Weighted Total:	100.0	46.3	48.8	72.9	14.4	20.2	28.4	33.6	17.7	53.5	34.3	36.9	24.0	11.5	23.1	1.0
B044: When you take psychedelics other than LSD how long do you usually stay high?																
1. Usually don't get high	4.0	3.4	5.6	3.4	23.5	3.2	-	17.7	2.0	4.2	4.4	-	-	8.5	2.0	13.6
2. One to two hours	8.9	7.2	9.9	7.9	11.5	6.4	9.8	12.1	10.9	7.3	8.9	-	-	13.9	9.0	4.4
3. Three to six hours	48.7	55.5	40.5	53.3	23.6	56.7	40.5	38.2	48.7	46.8	52.6	-	-	43.3	51.2	31.4
4. Seven to 24 hours	36.0	30.4	42.1	32.0	41.5	31.8	45.9	25.9	38.3	38.1	32.1	-	-	26.8	35.7	47.4
5. More than 24 hours	2.5	3.5	1.9	3.3	-	1.8	3.8	5.9	-	3.6	1.9	-	-	7.5	2.1	3.2
Item 2710 Subject A01f N★	153	79	61	118	9	65	40	19	29	55	59	-	-	10	129	13
B045: What psychedelics other than LSD have you taken during the last year? (Mark all that apply.)																
A. Mescaline	61.0	57.9	60.9	60.7	50.7	85.2	63.3	23.5	28.9	54.7	58.1	-	-	49.7	62.1	57.7
B. Peyote	12.2	18.2	4.8	11.4	-	10.2	5.5	14.2	24.4	20.0	6.9	-	-	-	10.7	34.9
C. Psilocybin	15.1	19.9	9.1	13.8	-	11.1	-	7.9	49.8	21.5	10.6	-	-	6.7	15.0	21.8
D. PCP	25.3	33.8	16.2	25.8	7.9	21.8	27.2	45.4	17.0	14.3	30.1	-	-	5.0	25.3	57.7
E. Concentrated THC	17.7	23.1	9.4	16.5	7.9	13.6	21.9	17.1	21.4	18.9	12.3	-	-	6.1	15.4	47.8
F. Other	30.2	21.2	35.5	26.4	16.2	22.7	31.5	37.4	39.9	24.2	25.1	-	-	24.2	26.8	67.0
G. Don't know the names of some I have used	18.9	18.3	21.4	17.8	41.0	18.9	14.3	33.3	15.9	21.3	19.3	-	-	30.6	15.6	42.9
Item 2720-2780 Subject A01l N★	153	78	62	119	7	64	41	19	29	53	57	-	-	9	130	13

The next questions are about some non-prescription drugs.

B046: Some types of diet pills (also called appetite suppressants) can be sold legally without a doctor's prescription by drugstores, through the mail, etc. These "over-the-counter" drugs include Dexatrim, Dietac, Prolamine, and others.

On how many occasions (if any) have you taken such non-prescription diet pills ...

B046A: ... in your lifetime?	TOTAL	M	F	White	Black	NE	NC	S	W	Yes	No	None	Mari- juana Only	Few Pills	More Pills	Any Her- oin
1. 0 occasions	70.3	85.2	56.9	67.6	86.6	69.5	65.7	71.9	75.7	72.1	68.7	86.1	76.9	64.2	41.8	46.1
2. 1-2	10.7	6.1	14.7	10.9	7.6	11.8	12.7	9.2	8.8	9.9	12.2	7.2	11.4	19.5	11.5	14.5
3. 3-5	4.1	1.8	6.3	4.6	0.6	5.0	3.9	4.4	3.0	4.0	4.3	2.1	3.2	4.9	8.0	8.9
4. 6-9	3.1	1.9	4.3	3.5	0.7	2.0	3.5	3.5	2.8	2.7	3.0	1.1	2.2	3.1	7.1	6.6
5. 10-19	3.7	1.7	5.7	4.2	2.4	3.6	4.1	4.0	2.6	3.7	3.6	1.3	2.9	3.5	8.0	4.7
6. 20-39	2.7	1.1	4.1	3.1	0.8	2.9	3.6	1.8	2.8	2.7	2.7	0.8	1.6	3.2	7.0	-
7. 40 or more	5.4	2.2	8.0	6.0	1.4	5.2	6.5	5.2	4.2	5.0	5.5	1.4	1.8	1.6	16.5	19.1
Item 21220 Subject A01a N	3196	1491	1584	2373	449	640	924	1055	576	1732	1112	1203	774	368	750	31
B046B: ... during the last 12 months?																
1. 0 occasions	81.2	90.8	72.5	79.0	91.9	81.6	79.8	80.4	84.3	81.3	81.8	92.7	85.6	81.0	58.2	71.5
2. 1-2	7.0	3.9	10.0	7.6	4.0	6.8	6.8	7.5	6.6	7.0	7.3	3.4	7.2	9.5	11.9	4.9
3. 3-5	2.3	1.0	3.7	2.7	0.6	2.3	2.1	2.6	2.0	2.2	2.5	0.8	2.7	2.3	4.2	7.8
4. 6-9	2.4	1.5	3.3	2.6	1.4	1.6	3.0	3.1	1.5	2.2	2.5	0.8	1.2	1.8	6.8	2.0
5. 10-19	2.9	1.4	4.0	3.3	0.4	4.4	2.7	2.6	2.5	3.3	1.4	1.1	1.6	3.8	7.4	1.5
6. 20-39	2.0	0.9	3.2	2.4	1.0	1.6	2.1	2.0	2.4	2.1	2.2	0.4	1.3	1.4	5.3	6.9
7. 40 or more	2.1	0.6	3.3	2.4	0.7	1.7	3.5	1.7	0.8	1.9	2.2	0.9	0.5	0.3	6.2	5.5
Item 21230 Subject A01b N	3184	1487	1578	2366	450	637	921	1050	576	1728	1107	1201	773	366	744	30
B046C: ... during the last 30 days?																
1. 0 occasions	90.1	95.2	85.8	89.2	95.8	89.5	88.8	90.2	92.7	90.6	90.1	96.5	94.4	92.5	74.4	76.4
2. 1-2	4.1	2.6	5.5	4.4	1.9	4.5	4.5	4.1	3.2	3.5	4.9	1.8	2.8	4.2	9.4	7.2
3. 3-5	1.7	0.8	2.4	1.9	0.8	1.4	1.6	1.8	1.7	1.8	1.6	0.3	0.9	1.0	4.9	6.9
4. 6-9	1.5	0.8	2.0	1.6	0.2	1.7	1.8	1.3	1.0	1.7	0.6	0.2	0.8	1.4	3.9	6.7
5. 10-19	1.5	0.3	2.3	1.7	0.6	2.1	1.5	1.5	1.1	1.3	1.7	0.9	0.7	0.7	4.0	-
6. 20-39	0.9	0.2	1.6	1.1	0.4	0.7	1.5	0.6	0.4	0.8	1.0	0.3	0.4	0.2	2.6	-
7. 40 or more	0.2	0.1	0.3	0.2	0.3	-	0.2	0.5	*	0.3	0.1	-	-	-	0.8	2.8
Item 21240 Subject A01c N	3186	1488	1578	2368	449	637	922	1051	576	1730	1108	1201	774	366	745	30

*=less than .05 per cent.   ★=excludes respondents for whom question was inappropriate.

QUESTIONNAIRE FORM 1 1984	TOTAL	SEX		RACE		REGION				4YR COLLEGE PLANS		ILLICIT DRUG USE: LIFETIME				
		M	F	White	Black	NE	NC	S	W	Yes	No	None	Mari-juana Only	Few Pills	More Pills	Any Her-oin
N (Weighted No. of Cases):	3311	1534	1616	2414	478	670	941	1113	587	1772	1137	1223	794	381	765	32
% of Weighted Total:	100.0	46.3	48.8	72.9	14.4	20.2	28.4	33.6	17.7	53.5	34.3	36.9	24.0	11.5	23.1	1.0

B047: Some stay-awake pills can be sold legally without a doctor's prescription by drugstores, through the mail, etc. These non-prescription or "over-the-counter" drugs include No-Doz, Vivarin, Wake, Caffedrine, and others.

On how many occasions (if any) have you taken such non-prescription stay-awake pills...

B047A: . . . in your lifetime?

	TOTAL	M	F	White	Black	NE	NC	S	W	Yes	No	None	Mari-juana Only	Few Pills	More Pills	Any Heroin
1. 0 occasions	77.3	76.8	78.3	73.7	95.2	80.9	74.1	79.4	74.5	77.3	79.5	90.3	82.8	71.0	55.0	38.9
2. 1-2	10.3	10.2	10.3	11.8	3.3	6.9	12.5	9.9	11.0	11.2	8.4	6.2	11.2	15.4	12.9	12.2
3. 3-5	3.7	4.7	2.9	4.5	0.5	3.4	3.2	3.5	5.1	4.3	2.9	2.0	2.2	4.2	8.0	1.9
4. 6-9	2.6	2.5	2.4	2.8	0.4	2.9	2.1	2.2	3.6	1.9	2.9	1.0	1.2	3.5	5.5	16.3
5. 10-19	2.4	2.1	2.8	3.0	0.2	2.3	3.2	2.1	1.9	2.6	1.8	0.2	1.4	2.8	6.5	15.7
6. 20-39	1.6	1.5	1.7	2.0	0.4	1.9	1.8	1.2	1.8	1.6	1.7	0.2	0.7	1.2	5.0	2.7
7. 40 or more	2.1	2.2	1.7	2.1	-	1.6	3.0	1.6	2.1	1.1	2.9	*	0.5	1.8	7.1	12.4
Item 21250 Subject A01a N	3198	1490	1587	2376	449	640	925	1062	571	1736	1112	1207	776	367	745	32

B047B: . . . during the last 12 months?

	TOTAL	M	F	White	Black	NE	NC	S	W	Yes	No	None	Mari-juana Only	Few Pills	More Pills	Any Heroin
1. 0 occasions	86.1	84.6	87.5	84.0	96.7	88.1	83.7	88.0	84.0	86.0	87.5	94.4	89.7	83.2	70.5	65.9
2. 1-2	6.6	7.3	6.0	7.7	1.6	4.1	7.8	5.6	9.1	7.2	5.3	3.9	6.1	8.8	10.3	2.8
3. 3-5	2.2	2.2	2.4	2.6	1.0	2.6	2.0	1.9	2.9	2.2	2.2	0.8	1.8	3.3	4.6	3.8
4. 6-9	1.9	2.2	1.5	2.2	0.4	2.8	1.8	1.6	1.8	1.5	2.0	0.5	0.8	0.9	5.2	18.6
5. 10-19	1.7	2.0	1.4	1.9	0.2	1.0	2.5	2.0	0.5	1.7	1.4	0.2	1.1	1.4	4.9	2.5
6. 20-39	1.0	0.9	1.0	1.2	0.2	1.3	1.1	0.6	1.4	1.0	1.0	0.1	0.2	2.2	2.9	1.4
7. 40 or more	0.5	0.8	0.3	0.4	-	0.2	1.0	0.4	0.3	0.4	0.6	-	0.3	-	1.7	4.9
Item 21260 Subject A01b N	3185	1484	1584	2367	452	637	919	1058	571	1731	1111	1206	776	365	737	30

B047C: . . . during the last 30 days?

	TOTAL	M	F	White	Black	NE	NC	S	W	Yes	No	None	Mari-juana Only	Few Pills	More Pills	Any Heroin
1. 0 occasions	94.2	93.8	94.5	93.1	99.3	95.7	91.6	95.2	94.7	94.6	94.1	98.8	95.8	93.1	85.7	78.7
2. 1-2	3.2	3.3	3.2	3.9	0.6	1.9	4.2	2.8	3.8	3.2	3.0	1.1	2.8	5.8	5.8	4.8
3. 3-5	1.1	1.1	1.0	1.3	0.1	1.0	1.2	0.9	1.1	0.7	1.3	*	0.6	1.1	2.9	10.3
4. 6-9	0.7	0.9	0.5	0.9	-	0.6	1.4	0.5	0.1	0.7	0.8	-	0.5	-	2.6	-
5. 10-19	0.5	0.4	0.4	0.5	-	0.4	0.8	0.5	0.2	0.5	0.5	*	-	0.1	1.7	6.3
6. 20-39	0.2	0.2	0.2	0.2	-	0.3	0.3	*	0.1	0.1	0.1	-	-	-	0.7	-
7. 40 or more	0.2	0.3	0.1	0.1	-	0.1	0.5	0.1	-	0.2	0.3	-	0.3	-	0.5	-
Item 21270 Subject A01c N	3183	1482	1584	2367	451	639	918	1057	570	1731	1108	1203	775	366	737	30

B048: In addition to non-prescription diet and stay-awake pills, there are other stimulants and pep pills which can be sold legally in most states without a prescription–usually by mail. These are sometimes called "fake pep pills," "imitation speed," or "look-alikes," because they look like prescription amphetamines and sometimes have similar names.

Other than diet pills and stay-awake pills you have already told us about, on how many occasions (if any) have you taken other non-prescription stimulants or pep pills ...

B048A: . . . in your lifetime?

	TOTAL	M	F	White	Black	NE	NC	S	W	Yes	No	None	Mari-juana Only	Few Pills	More Pills	Any Heroin
1. 0 occasions	84.7	85.9	84.8	83.3	94.0	83.0	83.8	85.6	86.3	89.6	81.1	99.3	94.6	80.0	53.9	47.4
2. 1-2	5.1	4.7	5.3	5.3	3.5	4.9	5.1	5.1	5.3	3.4	6.3	0.5	3.7	13.3	9.9	14.2
3. 3-5	2.5	2.2	2.7	2.9	0.6	2.4	2.4	2.3	3.0	2.1	2.3	0.1	0.5	2.7	8.1	13.3
4. 6-9	2.1	2.3	1.9	2.3	0.9	2.5	1.3	2.7	1.8	1.8	2.2	0.1	0.9	1.5	7.0	1.8
5. 10-19	1.4	0.9	1.9	1.6	0.7	1.9	1.5	1.3	1.2	0.8	2.1	-	0.1	0.8	5.7	2.6
6. 20-39	1.5	1.1	1.7	1.8	0.1	2.8	1.8	1.0	0.7	1.1	2.4	-	0.3	0.5	5.7	7.1
7. 40 or more	2.6	2.9	1.8	2.8	0.2	2.5	4.0	2.0	1.7	1.2	3.5	0.1	0.1	1.2	9.6	13.7
Item 21280 Subject A01a N	3185	1474	1590	2368	449	635	915	1063	572	1734	1105	1206	772	366	739	32

*=less than .05 per cent.

QUESTIONNAIRE FORM 1 1984	TOTAL	SEX		RACE		REGION				4YR COLLEGE PLANS		ILLICIT DRUG USE: LIFETIME				
		M	F	White	Black	NE	NC	S	W	Yes	No	None	Mari-juana Only	Few Pills	More Pills	Any Her-oin
N (Weighted No. of Cases):	3311	1534	1616	2414	478	670	941	1113	587	1772	1137	1223	794	381	765	32
% of Weighted Total:	100.0	46.3	48.8	72.9	14.4	20.2	28.4	33.6	17.7	53.5	34.3	36.9	24.0	11.5	23.1	1.0

B048B: ... during the last 12 months?

	TOTAL	M	F	White	Black	NE	NC	S	W	Yes	No	None	Mari-juana Only	Few Pills	More Pills	Any Heroin
1. 0 occasions	90.3	90.3	91.5	89.5	97.0	89.3	89.1	91.0	92.4	93.0	88.8	99.5	97.0	90.9	68.7	70.8
2. 1-2	3.7	3.7	3.3	3.9	1.9	4.0	3.8	3.1	4.2	2.8	4.0	0.4	2.1	6.8	8.9	10.6
3. 3-5	1.7	2.0	1.4	1.9	0.2	1.2	1.8	2.2	1.4	1.5	1.7	-	0.3	0.4	6.9	4.1
4. 6-9	1.4	1.3	1.3	1.6	0.3	1.9	1.1	1.3	1.3	0.8	2.1	0.1	0.5	0.4	5.0	-
5. 10-19	1.3	1.0	1.1	1.2	0.6	2.2	1.3	1.1	0.5	0.9	1.3	-	0.1	0.5	4.4	11.8
6. 20-39	1.0	0.8	0.9	1.1	-	1.5	1.3	0.7	0.3	0.7	1.1	-	0.1	1.0	3.5	-
7. 40 or more	0.6	0.9	0.4	0.8	-	-	1.5	0.6	-	0.3	0.9	-	-	-	2.6	2.7
Item 21290 Subject A01b N	3182	1472	1589	2367	449	637	914	1059	572	1734	1106	1208	771	365	735	32

B048C: ... during the last 30 days?

	TOTAL	M	F	White	Black	NE	NC	S	W	Yes	No	None	Mari-juana Only	Few Pills	More Pills	Any Heroin
1. 0 occasions	95.6	95.5	96.2	94.9	99.5	95.1	93.9	96.2	97.5	96.9	94.8	99.8	98.9	98.1	84.2	86.2
2. 1-2	1.6	2.0	1.1	1.9	0.5	2.2	1.5	1.3	1.7	1.3	1.7	0.2	0.8	1.3	5.2	3.2
3. 3-5	1.2	0.9	1.3	1.5	-	1.1	1.3	1.4	0.7	0.6	1.8	-	0.3	0.3	4.2	3.3
4. 6-9	0.6	0.4	0.6	0.6	-	1.0	0.9	0.4	-	0.4	0.6	-	-	0.2	2.3	4.7
5. 10-19	0.6	0.7	0.5	0.7	-	0.5	1.4	0.3	-	0.6	0.6	-	-	0.2	2.6	-
6. 20-39	0.2	0.2	0.2	0.2	-	-	0.5	0.1	-	*	0.2	-	-	-	0.8	-
7. 40 or more	0.2	0.3	0.1	0.2	-	-	0.4	0.2	-	0.1	0.2	-	-	-	0.7	2.7
Item 21300 Subject A01c N	3182	1473	1588	2366	450	636	912	1061	572	1734	1105	1207	772	365	735	32

The next questions are about AMPHETA-MINES, which doctors can prescribe to help people lose weight or to give people more energy. Drugstores are not supposed to sell them without a prescription from a doctor.

Amphetamines are sometimes called: uppers, ups, speed, bennies, dexies, pep pills, diet pills. They include the following drugs: Benzedrine, Dexedrine, Methedrine, Ritalin, Preludin, Dexamyl, Methamphetamine.

IN YOUR ANSWERS ABOUT AMPHETA-MINES, DO NOT INCLUDE ANY NON-PRESCRIPTION OR OVER-THE-COUNTER DRUGS.

B049: Have you ever taken amphetamines because a doctor told you to use them?

	TOTAL	M	F	White	Black	NE	NC	S	W	Yes	No	None	Mari-juana Only	Few Pills	More Pills	Any Heroin
1. No	92.9	92.7	93.8	92.9	96.2	93.2	92.5	92.3	94.2	93.2	93.7	96.8	95.1	90.0	87.0	65.5
2. Yes, but I had already tried them on my own	2.5	2.4	1.7	2.1	0.5	3.4	2.0	2.7	2.0	1.6	1.9	-	0.2	2.5	8.0	25.4
3. Yes, and it was the first time I took any	4.6	4.9	4.5	5.0	3.3	3.3	5.5	5.0	3.8	5.2	4.4	3.2	4.7	7.5	5.0	9.1
Item 2790 Subject A01j N	3181	1478	1583	2369	444	636	923	1050	571	1726	1116	1198	771	364	747	30

B050: On how many occasions (if any) have you taken amphetamines on your own–that is, without a doctor telling you to take them ...

B050A: ... in your lifetime?

	TOTAL	M	F	White	Black	NE	NC	S	W	Yes	No	None	Mari-juana Only	Few Pills	More Pills	Any Heroin
1. 0 occasions	76.4	79.1	75.2	73.8	94.3	72.9	74.8	79.3	77.3	81.2	73.5	100.0	100.0	56.5	23.6	25.6
2. 1-2	6.5	6.4	6.5	6.8	2.6	8.1	6.7	5.1	7.0	5.7	6.7	-	-	43.5	6.0	12.5
3. 3-5	3.6	2.8	4.4	4.2	0.4	4.0	3.2	4.0	3.2	3.0	4.6	-	-	-	15.1	5.9
4. 6-9	2.9	2.4	3.3	3.2	1.0	3.5	2.5	3.0	2.8	2.7	2.9	-	-	-	12.1	9.7
5. 10-19	3.6	3.3	3.8	4.0	1.3	3.4	4.4	3.3	3.3	2.7	4.4	-	-	-	15.1	8.5
6. 20-39	2.6	2.0	2.6	2.9	0.4	3.4	3.2	1.7	2.3	2.0	2.8	-	-	-	10.6	9.9
7. 40 or more	4.4	4.1	4.3	5.1	0.1	4.6	5.2	3.7	4.1	2.9	5.1	-	-	-	17.5	27.8
Item 980 Subject A01a N	3167	1471	1580	2360	443	635	915	1040	577	1729	1102	1200	772	361	742	32

B050B: ... during the last 12 months?

	TOTAL	M	F	White	Black	NE	NC	S	W	Yes	No	None	Mari-juana Only	Few Pills	More Pills	Any Heroin
1. 0 occasions	85.9	86.5	86.5	84.3	97.3	83.1	84.1	88.3	87.6	88.4	85.6	100.0	100.0	88.1	47.3	54.1
2. 1-2	4.8	4.3	4.8	5.3	0.8	7.1	5.0	2.7	5.5	3.8	5.4	-	-	11.9	14.3	8.8
3. 3-5	2.7	2.9	2.2	2.9	0.6	2.5	2.8	2.9	2.2	2.3	2.8	-	-	-	11.0	7.8
4. 6-9	2.4	2.9	2.0	2.6	0.8	2.3	2.6	2.5	2.2	2.4	2.0	-	-	-	9.8	15.7
5. 10-19	1.8	1.3	1.6	1.9	0.4	2.2	2.5	1.5	0.8	1.2	1.8	-	-	-	7.3	9.1
6. 20-39	1.4	1.1	1.7	1.7	-	2.6	0.9	1.3	1.2	1.1	1.2	-	-	-	5.9	1.8
7. 40 or more	1.1	1.0	1.2	1.3	0.1	0.3	2.2	0.8	0.5	0.9	1.3	-	-	-	4.5	2.7
Item 990 Subject A01b N	3157	1465	1577	2352	443	635	911	1036	576	1726	1097	1201	772	355	737	32

*=less than .05 per cent.

QUESTIONNAIRE FORM 1 1984	TOTAL	SEX		RACE		REGION				4YR COLLEGE PLANS		ILLICIT DRUG USE: LIFETIME				
		M	F	White	Black	NE	NC	S	W	Yes	No	None	Mari- juana Only	Few Pills	More Pills	Any Her- oin
N (Weighted No. of Cases):	3311	1534	1616	2414	478	670	941	1113	587	1772	1137	1223	794	381	765	32
% of Weighted Total:	100.0	46.3	48.8	72.9	14.4	20.2	28.4	33.6	17.7	53.5	34.3	36.9	24.0	11.5	23.1	1.0
B050C: . . . during the last 30 days?																
1. 0 occasions	93.0	93.6	92.8	92.1	98.6	91.8	91.5	93.8	95.3	94.6	92.6	100.0	100.0	96.0	73.4	66.5
2. 1-2	3.0	3.2	3.0	3.3	0.8	3.9	3.0	2.9	2.5	2.5	3.5	-	-	4.0	10.1	23.3
3. 3-5	1.4	1.0	1.5	1.5	0.3	1.5	1.7	1.2	1.1	0.9	1.3	-	-	-	5.8	3.7
4. 6-9	0.9	1.0	0.8	1.1	-	1.0	1.4	0.8	0.4	0.6	0.9	-	-	-	3.8	3.8
5. 10-19	1.0	0.9	1.0	1.2	0.3	1.6	1.2	0.7	0.5	0.9	0.9	-	-	-	4.3	-
6. 20-39	0.5	0.2	0.8	0.7	-	0.2	1.0	0.4	0.2	0.4	0.7	-	-	-	2.1	2.7
7. 40 or more	0.1	0.1	0.1	0.1	-	-	0.2	0.2	-	0.2	0.1	-	-	-	0.5	-
Item 1000 Subject A01c　　N	3159	1467	1578	2355	443	635	912	1037	576	1728	1097	1202	772	355	738	32

IF YOU HAVE NOT TAKEN AMPHETAMINES IN THE LAST TWELVE MONTHS, GO TO Q.B059.

THE FOLLOWING QUESTIONS REFER ONLY TO TAKING AMPHETAMINES WITHOUT A DOCTOR'S ORDERS. IF YOU HAVE NOT DONE THIS IN THE LAST TWELVE MONTHS, GO TO Q.B059

B051: When you used amphetamines during the last year, how often did you use them in each of the following situations?

	TOTAL	M	F	White	Black	NE	NC	S	W	Yes	No	None	Mari- juana Only	Few Pills	More Pills	Any Her- oin
B051A: When you were alone																
1. Not at all	45.6	49.4	43.6	44.5	32.2	44.0	46.9	39.3	56.3	49.7	43.2	-	-	80.1	41.9	36.2
2. A few of the times	25.0	25.4	23.0	25.3	37.0	28.0	21.8	26.3	24.7	22.3	29.1	-	-	10.6	27.2	8.9
3. Some of the times	11.0	11.3	9.7	10.7	3.5	7.1	14.2	12.7	7.3	8.8	9.3	-	-	3.9	11.7	16.1
4. Most of the times	9.8	7.4	11.8	9.9	14.6	12.5	10.1	10.3	4.2	8.0	11.7	-	-	3.2	9.9	27.8
5. Every time	8.6	6.5	11.8	9.7	12.7	8.4	7.0	11.3	7.5	11.1	6.6	-	-	2.3	9.3	11.1
Item 2800 Subject A05a　N★	434	190	207	351	16	102	138	123	70	191	155	-	-	36	375	14
B051B: With just 1 or 2 other people																
1. Not at all	24.9	22.5	26.6	23.9	55.4	22.6	27.5	26.9	19.7	29.2	20.7	-	-	29.7	23.4	22.3
2. A few of the times	33.1	38.4	29.8	32.7	17.8	31.3	30.9	32.9	40.4	32.1	34.2	-	-	49.0	31.9	31.0
3. Some of the times	22.8	23.4	20.2	23.0	3.5	22.9	25.5	21.5	19.9	20.7	19.4	-	-	5.9	24.6	31.6
4. Most of the times	11.7	8.9	14.4	12.1	23.3	14.6	10.0	13.9	6.9	10.3	17.4	-	-	-	13.2	8.0
5. Every time	7.5	6.8	9.1	8.4	-	8.6	6.0	4.8	13.2	7.6	8.4	-	-	15.3	6.9	7.0
Item 2810 Subject A05b　N★	432	190	205	349	16	101	138	122	71	191	154	-	-	37	373	14
B051C: At a party																
1. Not at all	45.8	41.3	50.5	44.2	62.5	47.6	45.8	45.4	44.3	48.3	47.8	-	-	71.4	43.1	31.9
2. A few of the times	17.0	19.3	15.8	18.0	7.9	15.9	20.1	14.0	17.5	14.2	19.3	-	-	19.4	16.9	11.8
3. Some of the times	17.5	17.3	16.9	18.7	12.4	18.7	15.5	17.2	20.3	16.3	17.6	-	-	7.5	18.9	16.3
4. Most of the times	12.3	13.4	10.8	12.5	4.7	12.8	10.8	14.8	10.5	13.3	9.9	-	-	-	13.9	9.1
5. Every time	7.3	8.6	6.0	6.5	12.5	5.1	7.8	8.5	7.4	7.9	5.5	-	-	1.7	7.2	31.0
Item 2820 Subject A05c　N★	427	186	205	345	16	98	136	123	70	191	150	-	-	36	370	13
B051D: When your date or spouse was present																
1. Not at all	61.9	62.6	62.6	61.8	82.9	63.9	53.2	69.7	62.5	68.2	58.6	-	-	92.5	58.3	57.5
2. A few of the times	16.7	14.5	16.5	17.0	2.7	15.9	21.6	12.2	16.1	11.9	19.2	-	-	3.9	18.3	16.9
3. Some of the times	14.1	17.3	12.0	14.0	9.7	12.1	16.9	13.2	12.8	14.2	11.7	-	-	-	15.8	13.2
4. Most of the times	4.9	4.2	5.1	5.0	4.7	4.2	5.0	4.5	6.1	4.8	6.4	-	-	1.7	5.4	-
5. Every time	2.4	1.5	3.8	2.2	-	3.8	3.2	0.3	2.6	0.9	4.1	-	-	2.0	2.1	12.3
Item 2830 Subject A05b　N★	431	188	206	348	16	101	138	123	69	191	152	-	-	36	373	14
B051E: When people over age 30 were present																
1. Not at all	67.7	64.6	74.1	69.3	80.8	71.4	60.0	68.4	76.7	75.3	68.7	-	-	100.0	65.0	48.5
2. A few of the times	14.7	16.9	12.4	14.5	7.9	18.7	17.6	12.2	7.6	9.0	17.6	-	-	-	16.1	14.1
3. Some of the times	11.0	13.1	7.7	10.5	6.2	3.9	15.9	12.6	8.4	9.0	8.3	-	-	-	11.9	19.2
4. Most of the times	5.5	4.9	4.4	5.1	5.1	3.9	4.5	6.8	7.3	5.9	3.9	-	-	-	5.9	11.1
5. Every time	1.1	0.5	1.3	0.7	-	2.1	2.0	-	-	0.8	1.4	-	-	-	1.0	7.0
Item 2840 Subject A05b　N★	433	190	206	350	16	101	138	123	70	191	154	-	-	36	374	14

★=excludes respondents for whom question was inappropriate.

QUESTIONNAIRE FORM 1 1984	TOTAL	SEX		RACE		REGION				4YR COLLEGE PLANS		ILLICIT DRUG USE: LIFETIME				
		M	F	White	Black	NE	NC	S	W	Yes	No	None	Mari-juana Only	Few Pills	More Pills	Any Her-oin
N (Weighted No. of Cases):	3311	1534	1616	2414	478	670	941	1113	587	1772	1137	1223	794	381	765	32
% of Weighted Total:	100.0	46.3	48.8	72.9	14.4	20.2	28.4	33.6	17.7	53.5	34.3	36.9	24.0	11.5	23.1	1.0

B051F: During the daytime (before 4:00 p.m.)

	TOTAL	M	F	White	Black	NE	NC	S	W	Yes	No	None	Mari-juana Only	Few Pills	More Pills	Any Her-oin
1. Not at all	23.0	25.7	20.7	20.3	53.2	19.9	18.7	31.8	20.7	24.3	21.5	-	-	39.7	19.9	19.7
2. A few of the times	23.2	25.5	21.6	22.5	20.2	25.4	22.7	14.3	36.3	23.5	26.7	-	-	43.3	22.0	13.8
3. Some of the times	18.9	21.2	15.3	18.9	14.4	18.7	16.7	22.0	18.4	18.6	14.6	-	-	9.3	20.5	13.9
4. Most of the times	22.5	19.7	24.6	24.8	-	21.9	29.2	17.9	18.0	21.5	26.3	-	-	5.8	23.9	40.9
5. Every time	12.4	7.8	17.9	13.5	12.1	14.0	12.8	14.1	6.6	12.2	10.9	-	-	1.9	13.8	11.7
Item 2850 Subject A05c N★	433	189	208	350	16	102	139	122	70	192	154	-	-	38	375	14

B051G: At your home (or apartment or dorm)

	TOTAL	M	F	White	Black	NE	NC	S	W	Yes	No	None	Mari-juana Only	Few Pills	More Pills	Any Her-oin
1. Not at all	39.8	44.3	37.9	39.1	39.6	45.7	36.0	35.0	46.9	40.8	42.9	-	-	69.5	36.1	35.5
2. A few of the times	23.0	23.0	22.3	23.5	18.8	24.4	23.3	21.1	23.5	21.5	24.8	-	-	27.7	22.8	17.6
3. Some of the times	18.0	19.8	14.4	17.9	12.4	18.0	19.9	18.7	13.0	18.9	12.5	-	-	-	20.3	14.2
4. Most of the times	12.5	11.5	13.9	13.2	17.1	8.5	13.9	13.8	13.0	13.8	12.3	-	-	2.8	13.0	32.6
5. Every time	6.8	1.4	11.5	6.3	12.1	3.4	6.9	11.5	3.6	5.0	7.5	-	-	-	7.9	-
Item 2860 Subject A05c N★	434	189	208	351	16	102	139	123	70	192	154	-	-	38	376	13

B051H: At school

	TOTAL	M	F	White	Black	NE	NC	S	W	Yes	No	None	Mari-juana Only	Few Pills	More Pills	Any Her-oin
1. Not at all	32.1	31.1	34.0	29.6	63.8	27.6	27.6	41.5	31.2	32.3	34.0	-	-	69.3	27.2	27.8
2. A few of the times	25.1	26.2	25.5	26.8	16.6	19.3	22.1	26.1	24.2	27.3	24.2	-	-	20.2	26.3	19.5
3. Some of the times	18.0	22.2	12.0	18.4	12.4	22.7	18.1	12.7	20.0	18.1	14.7	-	-	5.9	19.6	17.3
4. Most of the times	18.1	15.4	19.7	19.0	7.2	22.6	23.0	15.7	5.8	14.9	21.0	-	-	2.8	19.6	27.5
5. Every time	6.7	5.1	8.8	6.1	-	7.8	9.2	3.9	5.3	7.3	6.1	-	-	1.9	7.3	7.9
Item 2880 Subject A05c N★	434	189	208	351	16	102	139	123	70	192	154	-	-	38	376	13

B051I: In a car

	TOTAL	M	F	White	Black	NE	NC	S	W	Yes	No	None	Mari-juana Only	Few Pills	More Pills	Any Her-oin
1. Not at all	50.3	47.9	55.3	49.5	75.7	58.4	47.4	49.7	45.8	53.1	50.0	-	-	70.0	47.5	49.7
2. A few of the times	21.0	16.4	23.4	21.4	10.7	18.5	20.0	22.0	24.7	16.2	26.2	-	-	15.8	22.1	14.8
3. Some of the times	18.2	24.4	12.4	19.7	10.9	15.2	20.0	18.5	18.6	17.8	15.1	-	-	6.0	19.7	20.2
4. Most of the times	7.0	7.3	5.7	6.5	2.7	7.5	5.6	6.9	9.2	8.8	5.4	-	-	5.2	7.4	4.4
5. Every time	3.5	4.1	3.2	2.9	-	0.4	7.0	2.9	1.8	4.1	3.3	-	-	3.0	3.3	11.0
Item 2890 Subject A05c N★	432	189	207	349	16	100	139	123	70	191	153	-	-	36	375	13

B052: How many of the times when you used amphetamines during the last year did you use them along with each of the following drugs– that is, so that their effects overlapped?

B052A: With alcohol

	TOTAL	M	F	White	Black	NE	NC	S	W	Yes	No	None	Mari-juana Only	Few Pills	More Pills	Any Her-oin
1. Not at all	42.3	41.6	45.0	40.9	67.3	46.1	36.1	46.5	41.8	46.0	43.5	-	-	62.1	40.5	18.0
2. A few of the times	21.3	19.9	20.8	23.5	-	23.6	19.3	18.5	26.6	16.8	25.1	-	-	25.2	20.9	26.9
3. Some of the times	16.9	14.2	19.3	17.2	9.4	13.8	21.9	11.3	21.2	18.7	11.7	-	-	3.4	18.5	17.3
4. Most of the times	13.3	17.4	10.1	13.6	6.7	7.1	17.8	16.1	8.7	11.4	15.6	-	-	5.8	14.2	13.5
5. Every time	6.2	6.9	4.8	4.9	16.6	9.4	5.0	7.5	1.8	7.1	4.1	-	-	3.5	5.8	24.3
Item 2900 Subject A01h N★	432	189	208	352	15	102	139	119	71	192	156	-	-	38	374	14

B052B: With marijuana

	TOTAL	M	F	White	Black	NE	NC	S	W	Yes	No	None	Mari-juana Only	Few Pills	More Pills	Any Her-oin
1. Not at all	51.8	45.0	61.1	51.0	62.6	52.8	49.5	53.0	53.1	59.2	52.1	-	-	76.2	49.7	30.5
2. A few of the times	17.1	18.1	14.6	17.7	7.9	18.5	13.5	19.4	18.4	14.2	20.0	-	-	16.5	17.4	9.4
3. Some of the times	14.3	14.2	13.7	14.9	3.5	12.6	16.3	13.3	14.7	12.0	11.6	-	-	5.8	15.6	10.8
4. Most of the times	12.1	15.9	8.0	12.7	7.2	10.0	15.3	10.8	11.3	9.0	14.4	-	-	1.6	12.6	34.5
5. Every time	4.6	6.8	2.7	3.8	18.7	6.1	5.4	3.5	2.6	5.5	1.9	-	-	-	4.7	14.7
Item 2910 Subject A01h N★	431	190	206	350	16	101	139	121	70	192	153	-	-	38	373	14

B052C: With LSD

	TOTAL	M	F	White	Black	NE	NC	S	W	Yes	No	None	Mari-juana Only	Few Pills	More Pills	Any Her-oin
1. Not at all	94.4	91.8	98.3	94.9	96.2	95.3	93.1	95.6	93.8	94.2	97.2	-	-	100.0	94.9	66.9
2. A few of the times	2.4	2.4	1.0	2.2	-	2.6	2.6	2.0	2.4	1.8	2.2	-	-	-	2.4	' 8.9
3. Some of the times	1.9	3.6	-	1.3	3.8	-	1.8	2.4	3.9	2.9	-	-	-	-	1.8	10.2
4. Most of the times	0.3	-	0.6	0.4	-	-	0.9	-	-	-	-	-	-	-	0.4	-
5. Every time	1.0	2.2	-	1.2	-	2.1	1.5	-	-	1.1	0.7	-	-	-	0.6	14.1
Item 2920 Subject A01h N★	424	187	202	346	15	99	137	118	71	192	150	-	-	37	367	14

★=excludes respondents for whom question was inappropriate.

QUESTIONNAIRE FORM 1 1984	TOTAL	SEX		RACE		REGION				4YR COLLEGE PLANS		ILLICIT DRUG USE: LIFETIME				
		M	F	White	Black	NE	NC	S	W	Yes	No	None	Mari-juana Only	Few Pills	More Pills	Any Her-oin
N (Weighted No. of Cases):	3311	1534	1616	2414	478	670	941	1113	587	1772	1137	1223	794	381	765	32
% of Weighted Total:	100.0	46.3	48.8	72.9	14.4	20.2	28.4	33.6	17.7	53.5	34.3	36.9	24.0	11.5	23.1	1.0
B052D: With psychedelics other than LSD																
1. Not at all	94.8	93.0	97.3	95.5	90.5	89.5	95.5	97.5	96.1	95.3	97.0	-	-	100.0	95.3	67.2
2. A few of the times	2.1	1.8	1.6	2.0	-	5.3	1.5	1.2	-	1.8	1.0	-	-	-	2.4	-
3. Some of the times	1.4	2.1	0.6	1.3	4.1	1.2	2.9	-	0.8	1.1	0.8	-	-	-	1.3	8.5
4. Most of the times	1.3	2.0	0.4	0.6	5.5	1.9	-	1.3	3.1	1.9	0.5	-	-	-	1.1	10.2
5. Every time	0.5	1.1	-	0.6	-	2.1	-	-	-	-	0.7	-	-	-	-	14.1
Item 2930 Subject A01h N★	422	185	204	345	14	99	137	115	71	192	150	-	-	37	365	14
B053: What have been the most important reasons for your taking amphetamines without a doctor's orders? (Mark all that apply.)																
A. To experiment–to see what it's like	48.4	54.8	44.1	48.9	28.6	50.6	43.1	48.5	55.6	51.6	50.8	-	-	65.0	46.6	55.6
B. To relax or relieve tension	15.6	13.2	17.5	13.7	28.4	16.0	15.9	19.2	8.1	12.4	20.3	-	-	17.9	14.6	35.7
C. To feel good or get high	45.2	49.0	40.8	45.7	44.2	41.4	40.2	50.0	52.1	39.5	53.6	-	-	37.0	46.0	49.8
D. To seek deeper insights and understanding	3.2	5.4	0.4	2.9	-	5.3	1.7	4.5	1.4	2.8	3.2	-	-	-	2.8	23.1
E. To have a good time with my friends	29.6	32.2	27.0	30.6	28.8	32.6	22.9	33.3	32.1	28.1	29.4	-	-	21.9	30.2	36.8
F. To fit in with a group I like	3.9	5.4	2.9	4.1	-	3.3	4.9	5.0	1.1	3.6	6.0	-	-	6.8	3.0	20.8
G. To get away from my problems or troubles	11.5	5.8	17.0	11.3	4.1	10.9	13.5	11.8	7.6	7.9	17.3	-	-	16.7	10.4	24.3
H. Because of boredom, nothing else to do	19.0	22.6	14.8	17.7	44.4	19.3	19.6	17.7	19.3	18.2	21.1	-	-	24.3	18.0	31.1
I. Because of anger or frustration	9.0	7.3	10.7	8.4	4.1	8.9	12.5	8.3	3.2	6.1	13.1	-	-	20.1	7.5	17.2
J. To get through the day	31.6	31.1	32.1	32.9	16.6	30.3	32.6	27.7	38.0	29.6	34.2	-	-	13.0	32.6	49.2
K. To increase the effects of some other drug(s)	11.3	13.4	8.3	10.6	17.2	8.2	11.2	10.1	18.0	12.2	7.3	-	-	11.9	10.2	38.3
L. To decrease (offset) the effects of some other drug(s)	5.0	8.8	1.1	4.6	-	4.9	3.3	4.8	8.6	3.8	7.0	-	-	-	4.2	38.8
M. To stay awake	61.6	63.4	59.2	63.7	31.6	62.5	68.0	52.4	63.0	63.2	59.5	-	-	37.9	63.5	69.9
N. To get more energy	69.4	74.7	66.2	70.8	40.6	62.0	76.9	65.8	71.4	70.0	72.7	-	-	59.6	70.4	68.1
O. To help me lose weight	41.0	18.7	62.0	44.6	14.3	40.7	39.8	46.4	34.6	42.8	41.6	-	-	12.4	43.4	57.3
P. Because I am "hooked"–I feel I have to have them	2.4	1.7	3.1	2.0	4.1	1.7	2.1	3.4	2.4	2.3	2.7	-	-	-	2.1	17.2
Item 2940-3090 Subject A06a N★	423	183	208	350	14	100	136	117	70	190	152	-	-	38	369	14
B054: When you take amphetamines, how high do you usually get?																
1. Not at all high	9.3	9.0	9.1	8.1	28.1	8.3	7.4	14.5	6.1	12.1	5.9	-	-	23.3	7.3	4.1
2. A little high	34.8	39.7	31.6	35.0	23.2	41.8	34.0	30.4	33.9	35.7	38.7	-	-	44.8	35.0	16.9
3. Moderately high	29.5	30.8	28.7	30.8	19.0	25.1	29.8	30.5	33.4	28.8	30.2	-	-	8.6	31.8	36.2
4. Very high	3.5	4.2	2.4	2.8	-	4.1	0.8	4.3	6.6	4.2	1.6	-	-	3.1	3.1	17.2
5. I don't take them to get high	22.8	16.4	28.1	23.3	29.7	20.7	28.1	20.4	20.0	19.2	23.6	-	-	20.2	23.0	25.6
Item 3100 Subject A01e N★	418	185	199	342	15	99	134	115	70	185	151	-	-	37	361	14
B055: When you take amphetamines how long do you usually stay high?																
1. Usually don't get high	25.3	17.9	31.3	23.4	50.1	24.2	24.3	29.9	21.0	26.4	21.3	-	-	30.6	24.8	4.2
2. One to two hours	27.0	31.3	26.3	29.2	-	31.2	20.5	27.9	32.6	32.0	29.8	-	-	36.4	26.7	17.5
3. Three to six hours	35.7	40.7	29.2	36.0	43.3	30.8	44.5	32.9	29.7	28.8	38.7	-	-	27.7	36.1	55.3
4. Seven to 24 hours	11.9	10.1	12.9	11.2	6.6	13.1	10.7	9.3	16.6	12.5	10.3	-	-	5.4	12.2	23.0
5. More than 24 hours	0.2	-	0.3	0.2	-	0.7	-	-	-	0.4	-	-	-	-	0.2	-
Item 3110 Subject A01f N★	424	184	206	349	13	100	139	116	69	188	153	-	-	37	370	13
B056: What amphetamines have you taken during the last year without a doctor's orders? (Mark all that apply.)																
A. Benzedrine	12.5	14.9	7.8	11.0	9.2	18.6	10.9	11.9	8.2	9.5	11.7	-	-	4.2	12.2	43.4
B. Dexedrine	12.4	11.6	12.2	11.3	3.1	12.8	15.2	10.0	10.0	10.8	12.1	-	-	7.0	11.6	45.7
C. Methedrine	22.2	19.8	22.5	22.0	4.3	26.1	20.6	20.0	23.6	19.3	27.0	-	-	30.9	20.5	46.5
D. Ritalin	2.5	3.1	1.3	2.4	-	4.3	0.4	1.8	5.5	2.3	1.1	-	-	-	2.5	10.0
E. Preludin	4.1	4.5	3.0	4.2	-	4.8	3.2	4.7	4.0	3.6	3.5	-	-	-	4.4	7.0
F. Dexamyl	6.6	4.9	5.8	5.4	-	8.4	6.3	5.1	6.8	4.7	6.6	-	-	4.0	5.9	29.7
G. Methamphetamine	15.5	12.2	16.3	14.2	8.7	21.0	11.8	11.9	21.2	11.1	16.2	-	-	9.5	15.4	35.5
H. Other	32.1	31.4	31.5	30.0	71.2	27.2	31.3	37.1	32.4	25.3	35.8	-	-	16.5	32.7	49.7
I. Don't know the names of some amphetamines I have used	60.8	62.0	60.5	63.2	12.9	65.9	55.7	56.7	70.3	66.4	56.4	-	-	53.9	61.9	55.1
Item 3120-3200 Subject A01I N★	416	183	202	343	14	98	135	114	69	187	148	-	-	36	364	14

★=excludes respondents for whom question was inappropriate.

QUESTIONNAIRE FORM 1 1984	TOTAL	SEX		RACE		REGION				4YR COLLEGE PLANS		ILLICIT DRUG USE: LIFETIME				
		M	F	White	Black	NE	NC	S	W	Yes	No	None	Marijuana Only	Few Pills	More Pills	Any Heroin
N (Weighted No. of Cases):	3311	1534	1616	2414	478	670	941	1113	587	1772	1137	1223	794	381	765	32
% of Weighted Total:	100.0	46.3	48.8	72.9	14.4	20.2	28.4	33.6	17.7	53.5	34.3	36.9	24.0	11.5	23.1	1.0
B057: What methods have you used for taking amphetamines? (Mark all that apply.)																
A. By mouth	98.2	96.6	99.3	97.8	100.0	97.0	97.8	100.0	97.6	97.1	98.5	-	-	100.0	97.9	100.0
B. Injection	1.1	1.9	0.6	0.8	4.1	0.8	0.4	2.4	0.8	0.8	1.0	-	-	-	0.3	24.4
C. Other	14.7	20.5	8.1	15.3	-	18.5	14.9	7.6	20.7	13.5	14.1	-	-	1.1	16.1	14.2
Item 3210-3230 Subject A05d N★	426	186	206	350	14	101	139	116	70	190	153	-	-	37	373	14
B058: Have you ever tried to stop using amphetamines and found that you couldn't stop?																
1. Yes	6.4	5.5	7.6	6.9	-	5.6	7.5	6.7	4.7	6.6	7.6	-	-	7.0	5.8	20.2
2. No	93.6	94.5	92.4	93.1	100.0	94.4	92.5	93.3	95.3	93.4	92.4	-	-	93.0	94.2	79.8
Item 3240 Subject A01i N★	425	185	207	350	15	101	137	117	70	190	153	-	-	37	372	14
B059: Do you think you will be using amphetamines without a doctor's orders five years from now?																
1. I definitely will	0.8	0.4	1.1	0.7	0.8	0.6	0.7	1.2	0.5	0.7	0.7	0.2	0.5	0.5	1.8	8.8
2. I probably will	5.5	4.3	6.2	5.9	1.9	6.6	5.3	5.5	4.6	4.3	5.8	0.5	0.4	5.1	19.2	12.7
3. I probably will not	21.7	21.6	21.0	23.1	14.1	25.1	22.2	18.4	23.2	20.2	23.0	12.0	16.4	29.9	39.4	36.0
4. I definitely will not	72.0	73.6	71.7	70.3	83.3	67.6	71.8	74.9	71.8	74.7	70.5	87.3	82.7	64.5	39.5	42.5
Item 3250 Subject A04a N	3193	1488	1595	2374	459	629	925	1065	574	1743	1112	1202	776	367	738	28

The next questions are about QUAALUDES (Methaqualone), which are sometimes prescribed by doctors. Drugstores are not supposed to sell them without a prescription.

Quaaludes are sometimes called: soapers, quads.

B060: On how many occasions (if any) have you taken quaaludes on your own–that is, without a doctor telling you to take them . . .

B060A: . . . in your lifetime?

	TOTAL	M	F	White	Black	NE	NC	S	W	Yes	No	None	Marijuana Only	Few Pills	More Pills	Any Heroin
1. 0 occasions	91.7	91.6	92.6	90.8	98.8	90.0	93.8	90.7	92.2	93.9	90.5	100.0	100.0	93.9	69.6	49.9
2. 1-2	4.3	4.3	4.1	4.9	0.4	5.0	2.3	4.9	5.4	4.0	4.4	-	-	6.1	14.9	13.8
3. 3-5	1.4	1.6	1.0	1.5	0.3	1.7	1.3	1.4	1.0	0.9	1.7	-	-	-	5.7	5.4
4. 6-9	1.1	0.9	1.1	1.2	0.3	1.2	0.8	1.7	0.4	0.4	1.5	-	-	-	4.4	9.4
5. 10-19	0.7	0.7	0.7	0.9	-	0.7	0.9	0.3	0.9	0.5	0.9	-	-	-	2.5	9.4
6. 20-39	0.5	0.5	0.3	0.3	0.2	1.0	0.4	0.5	0.1	0.1	0.6	-	-	-	2.2	-
7. 40 or more	0.3	0.4	0.2	0.3	-	0.2	0.4	0.5	-	0.1	0.4	-	-	-	0.8	12.0
Item 1010 Subject A01a N	3145	1475	1564	2353	442	622	913	1040	569	1724	1098	1198	770	361	730	32

B060B: . . . during the last 12 months?

	TOTAL	M	F	White	Black	NE	NC	S	W	Yes	No	None	Marijuana Only	Few Pills	More Pills	Any Heroin
1. 0 occasions	96.5	96.0	97.6	96.3	99.3	95.8	96.9	95.5	98.6	97.8	95.9	100.0	100.0	98.9	86.5	76.7
2. 1-2	2.0	2.3	1.5	2.2	0.7	2.5	1.8	2.6	0.6	1.6	2.2	-	-	1.1	7.8	7.9
3. 3-5	0.8	0.8	0.5	0.9	-	1.1	0.4	1.2	0.5	0.5	0.9	-	-	-	3.4	3.6
4. 6-9	0.4	0.4	0.2	0.3	-	0.5	0.7	0.1	0.2	-	0.7	-	-	-	1.4	5.7
5. 10-19	0.1	0.1	*	0.1	-	0.1	-	0.1	-	*	0.1	-	-	-	0.2	1.4
6. 20-39	0.1	0.1	0.1	0.1	-	-	0.2	0.1	-	-	0.1	-	-	-	0.5	-
7. 40 or more	0.1	0.2	-	0.1	-	-	-	0.3	-	0.1	0.1	-	-	-	0.2	4.7
Item 1020 Subject A01b N	3141	1471	1564	2350	442	621	911	1040	568	1723	1098	1198	770	361	726	32

B060C: . . . during the last 30 days?

	TOTAL	M	F	White	Black	NE	NC	S	W	Yes	No	None	Marijuana Only	Few Pills	More Pills	Any Heroin
1. 0 occasions	98.9	98.4	99.4	98.9	100.0	99.1	98.4	98.7	99.8	99.5	98.4	100.0	100.0	99.9	95.8	86.5
2. 1-2	0.7	0.8	0.4	0.6	-	0.8	1.1	0.6	0.2	0.4	0.7	-	-	0.1	2.7	4.2
3. 3-5	0.3	0.5	0.2	0.3	-	0.2	0.5	0.3	-	-	0.8	-	-	-	1.1	4.6
4. 6-9	0.1	0.1	*	0.1	-	-	0.1	0.1	-	-	-	-	-	-	0.3	-
5. 10-19	*	0.1	-	0.1	-	-	-	0.1	-	-	0.1	-	-	-	0.2	-
6. 20-39	-	-	-	-	-	-	-	-	-	-	-	-	-	-	-	-
7. 40 or more	*	0.1	-	-	-	-	-	0.1	-	0.1	-	-	-	-	-	4.7
Item 1030 Subject A01c N	3140	1470	1564	2348	442	622	911	1039	568	1723	1097	1198	770	362	725	32

*=less than .05 per cent.   ★=excludes respondents for whom question was inappropriate.

QUESTIONNAIRE FORM 1 1984	TOTAL	SEX		RACE		REGION				4YR COLLEGE PLANS		ILLICIT DRUG USE: LIFETIME				
		M	F	White	Black	NE	NC	S	W	Yes	No	None	Marijuana Only	Few Pills	More Pills	Any Heroin
N (Weighted No. of Cases):	3311	1534	1616	2414	478	670	941	1113	587	1772	1137	1223	794	381	765	32
% of Weighted Total:	100.0	46.3	48.8	72.9	14.4	20.2	28.4	33.6	17.7	53.5	34.3	36.9	24.0	11.5	23.1	1.0

IF YOU HAVE NOT TAKEN QUAALUDES IN THE LAST TWELVE MONTHS, GO TO Q.B063.

THE FOLLOWING QUESTIONS REFER ONLY TO TAKING QUAALUDES WITHOUT A DOCTOR'S ORDERS. IF YOU HAVE NOT DONE THIS IN THE LAST TWELVE MONTHS, GO TO Q.B063.

B061: When you take quaaludes how high do you usually get?

	TOTAL	M	F	White	Black	NE	NC	S	W	Yes	No	None	Mar. Only	Few Pills	More Pills	Any Heroin
1. Not at all high	5.1	9.6	-	3.5	30.7	8.0	3.9	2.6	13.8	5.6	3.6	-	-	-	5.7	-
2. A little high	21.1	23.7	24.6	23.0	44.6	19.4	26.2	23.1	-	24.7	25.5	-	-	35.9	21.1	13.8
3. Moderately high	40.3	30.2	54.3	43.2	-	46.6	31.5	36.2	69.9	33.0	45.8	-	-	64.1	38.3	54.5
4. Very high	30.0	36.4	15.2	27.7	24.8	22.8	33.6	34.6	16.2	36.7	20.0	-	-	-	31.0	31.6
5. I don't take them to get high	3.5	-	5.9	2.6	-	3.2	4.8	3.6	-	-	5.2	-	-	-	3.9	-
Item 3260 Subject A01e N★	109	58	38	86	3	27	26	47	8	39	43	-	-	4	97	7

B062: When you take quaaludes how long do you usually stay high?

	TOTAL	M	F	White	Black	NE	NC	S	W	Yes	No	None	Mar. Only	Few Pills	More Pills	Any Heroin
1. Usually don't get high	6.1	8.6	4.5	4.8	30.7	8.0	6.0	5.0	6.8	5.6	6.2	-	-	-	6.8	-
2. One to two hours	20.6	19.3	26.9	21.0	44.6	14.2	10.9	32.1	7.1	18.1	26.5	-	-	71.2	18.5	21.9
3. Three to six hours	56.2	54.6	57.6	61.2	24.8	58.6	54.9	53.8	65.4	60.4	53.6	-	-	28.8	58.3	42.4
4. Seven to 24 hours	16.6	17.6	10.9	12.9	-	17.1	28.2	9.0	20.7	15.9	13.7	-	-	-	15.7	35.7
5. More than 24 hours	0.5	-	-	-	-	2.1	-	-	-	-	-	-	-	-	0.6	-
Item 3270 Subject A01f N★	108	58	37	85	3	27	26	46	8	39	42	-	-	4	97	7

B063: The next questions are about BARBITURATES, which doctors sometimes prescribe to help people relax or get to sleep. Drugstores are not supposed to sell them without a prescription.

Barbiturates are sometimes called: downs, downers, goofballs, yellows, reds, blues, rainbows.

They include the following drugs: Phenobarbital, Seconal, Tuinal, Nembutal, Luminal, Desbutal, Amytal.

Have you ever taken barbiturates because a doctor told you to use them?

	TOTAL	M	F	White	Black	NE	NC	S	W	Yes	No	None	Mar. Only	Few Pills	More Pills	Any Heroin
1. No	92.7	93.0	93.0	92.1	95.7	92.4	93.1	92.1	93.7	92.5	93.3	96.5	95.7	89.3	85.6	74.4
2. Yes, but I had already tried them on my own.	1.7	2.0	1.2	1.8	0.6	2.3	1.2	1.5	1.9	1.2	1.6	-	-	1.1	5.5	23.8
3. Yes, and it was the first time I took any	5.6	5.1	5.8	6.1	3.7	5.3	5.7	6.3	4.3	6.3	5.1	3.5	4.3	9.6	8.9	1.9
Item 3280 Subject A01j N	3094	1436	1555	2323	429	614	899	1027	554	1698	1084	1176	748	355	724	32

B064: On how many occasions (if any) have you taken barbiturates on your own–that is, without a doctor telling you to take them . . .

B064A: . . . in your lifetime?

	TOTAL	M	F	White	Black	NE	NC	S	W	Yes	No	None	Mar. Only	Few Pills	More Pills	Any Heroin
1. 0 occasions	91.2	91.5	91.6	90.2	97.8	89.6	91.6	92.4	90.2	93.4	91.3	100.0	100.0	91.8	68.0	47.8
2. 1-2	3.7	3.5	3.9	4.2	1.1	4.4	3.8	2.5	5.1	3.0	3.9	-	-	8.2	11.8	8.3
3. 3-5	1.3	1.3	1.4	1.6	0.2	1.8	0.9	1.5	1.1	1.2	1.2	-	-	-	5.6	6.2
4. 6-9	1.5	1.5	1.3	1.7	0.3	1.1	1.4	1.8	1.5	0.9	1.5	-	-	-	5.6	19.2
5. 10-19	1.3	1.2	1.0	1.3	0.4	2.0	1.2	1.1	0.8	1.0	1.1	-	-	-	5.2	6.3
6. 20-39	0.6	0.7	0.4	0.7	0.2	0.4	0.5	0.4	1.2	0.1	0.8	-	-	-	2.3	3.3
7. 40 or more	0.4	0.3	0.4	0.3	-	0.7	0.5	0.3	0.2	0.4	0.2	-	-	-	1.4	8.9
Item 1040 Subject A01a N	3086	1441	1544	2319	428	614	899	1016	558	1701	1075	1181	758	357	708	30

★=excludes respondents for whom question was inappropriate.

QUESTIONNAIRE FORM 1 1984	TOTAL	SEX		RACE		REGION				4YR COLLEGE PLANS		ILLICIT DRUG USE: LIFETIME				
		M	F	White	Black	NE	NC	S	W	Yes	No	None	Mari-juana Only	Few Pills	More Pills	Any Her-oin
N (Weighted No. of Cases):	3311	1534	1616	2414	478	670	941	1113	587	1772	1137	1223	794	381	765	32
% of Weighted Total:	100.0	46.3	48.8	72.9	14.4	20.2	28.4	33.6	17.7	53.5	34.3	36.9	24.0	11.5	23.1	1.0

B064B: . . . during the last 12 months?

1. 0 occasions	95.9	95.8	96.8	95.6	98.9	95.2	95.7	96.3	96.3	97.0	96.8	100.0	100.0	98.2	84.4	68.1
2. 1-2	1.9	2.1	1.5	2.1	0.4	1.6	2.2	1.3	2.5	1.5	1.7	-	-	1.8	7.0	6.5
3. 3-5	1.1	1.0	1.0	1.1	0.5	1.6	1.2	1.1	0.4	0.8	1.0	-	-	-	4.7	3.5
4. 6-9	0.7	0.8	0.5	0.8	0.3	1.1	0.3	1.1	0.4	0.4	0.4	-	-	-	2.5	17.0
5. 10-19	0.3	0.2	0.2	0.3	-	0.5	0.4	-	0.3	0.3	0.1	-	-	-	1.1	-
6. 20-39	*	-	-	-	-	-	0.1	-	-	-	-	-	-	-	0.1	-
7. 40 or more	0.1	0.1	0.1	0.1	-	-	0.1	0.1	-	0.1	-	-	-	-	0.2	5.0
Item 1050 Subject A01b N	3080	1438	1541	2313	428	612	898	1015	556	1699	1073	1181	758	356	704	29

B064C: . . . during the last 30 days?

1. 0 occasions	98.4	98.2	98.9	98.2	99.7	98.3	97.7	98.9	98.8	98.9	98.5	100.0	100.0	99.8	94.1	75.5
2. 1-2	1.3	1.4	0.9	1.5	-	1.4	2.2	0.4	1.1	1.0	1.0	-	-	0.2	4.9	11.0
3. 3-5	0.2	0.2	0.2	0.2	0.3	0.2	-	0.4	0.1	0.1	0.3	-	-	-	0.7	3.5
4. 6-9	0.1	0.2	*	0.1	-	0.2	-	0.2	-	-	0.2	-	-	-	0.2	5.0
5. 10-19	-	-	-	-	-	-	-	-	-	-	-	-	-	-	-	-
6. 20-39	0.1	0.1	-	-	-	-	0.1	0.1	-	0.1	-	-	-	-	0.1	5.0
7. 40 or more	-	-	-	-	-	-	-	-	-	-	-	-	-	-	-	-
Item 1060 Subject A01c N	3079	1437	1541	2311	428	612	898	1014	555	1697	1073	1181	758	356	703	29

IF YOU HAVE NOT TAKEN BARBITURATES IN THE LAST TWELVE MONTHS, GO TO Q.B072.

THE FOLLOWING QUESTIONS REFER ONLY TO TAKING BARBITURATES WITHOUT A DOCTOR'S ORDERS. IF YOU HAVE NOT DONE THIS IN THE LAST TWELVE MONTHS, GO TO Q.B072

B065: When you used barbiturates during the last year, how often did you use them in each of the following situations?

B065A: When you were alone

1. Not at all	41.3	43.8	43.8	41.2	48.9	52.0	38.8	34.2	41.7	45.7	41.2	-	-	77.7	38.2	41.1
2. A few of the times	27.5	27.0	27.2	27.7	27.7	23.1	22.7	28.7	42.8	27.8	25.7	-	-	-	30.0	19.7
3. Some of the times	10.9	8.7	10.8	7.7	23.4	14.9	6.2	17.1	3.2	11.6	13.1	-	-	-	10.1	28.3
4. Most of the times	6.1	6.9	4.4	6.2	-	3.7	3.0	10.6	8.2	3.2	7.4	-	-	-	7.0	-
5. Every time	14.2	13.4	13.8	17.2	-	6.2	29.3	9.4	4.0	11.7	12.6	-	-	22.3	14.7	10.9
Item 3290 Subject A05a N★	121	59	48	100	5	30	39	33	18	49	35	-	-	3	105	9

B065B: With just 1 or 2 other people

1. Not at all	29.0	34.6	22.3	30.3	42.7	25.4	45.2	20.9	16.4	32.2	23.4	-	-	-	28.1	19.1
2. A few of the times	33.5	35.1	35.5	36.5	11.4	33.6	26.6	26.9	58.9	35.6	36.5	-	-	25.8	35.9	22.0
3. Some of the times	18.0	11.7	17.9	16.8	-	21.3	11.4	25.8	12.1	11.4	22.3	-	-	-	19.4	13.7
4. Most of the times	11.8	9.1	18.7	9.2	45.9	12.4	7.8	17.9	8.4	16.2	6.3	-	-	-	10.5	34.2
5. Every time	7.7	9.5	5.5	7.2	-	7.3	9.0	8.5	4.3	4.6	11.5	-	-	74.2	6.1	10.9
Item 3300 Subject A05b N★	121	60	47	99	6	31	38	33	19	49	35	-	-	2	106	9

B065C: At a party

1. Not at all	45.4	51.2	40.6	45.7	72.3	34.6	56.9	43.1	44.5	48.8	41.2	-	-	100.0	45.8	12.4
2. A few of the times	21.2	20.5	25.7	23.5	-	25.3	16.6	14.5	35.1	25.5	21.2	-	-	-	23.1	11.2
3. Some of the times	12.7	4.2	21.1	11.3	27.7	22.4	3.4	17.9	6.0	9.6	13.6	-	-	-	12.7	19.1
4. Most of the times	13.7	11.7	12.6	13.7	-	10.9	12.8	16.8	14.4	6.7	19.1	-	-	-	13.8	19.7
5. Every time	7.0	12.4	-	5.9	-	6.7	10.3	7.7	-	9.4	4.9	-	-	-	4.7	37.6
Item 3310 Subject A05c N★	120	58	47	98	5	30	37	33	19	48	35	-	-	2	105	9

B065D: When your date or spouse was present

1. Not at all	65.4	72.1	55.9	67.4	48.9	73.2	74.9	47.9	65.6	69.0	67.2	-	-	100.0	67.8	20.0
2. A few of the times	15.2	11.8	23.8	14.3	51.1	7.1	7.8	29.8	17.0	14.7	18.6	-	-	-	14.8	28.3
3. Some of the times	6.2	4.3	6.7	5.9	-	9.7	5.4	3.9	6.0	2.4	6.5	-	-	-	6.0	10.9
4. Most of the times	6.7	5.4	5.1	4.6	-	4.1	5.3	14.5	-	6.6	3.1	-	-	-	5.7	21.8
5. Every time	6.4	6.4	8.4	7.9	-	5.9	6.6	3.9	11.5	7.3	4.6	-	-	-	5.6	19.1
Item 3320 Subject A05b N★	120	58	47	98	5	30	37	33	19	48	35	-	-	2	105	9

*=less than .05 per cent. ★=excludes respondents for whom question was inappropriate.

QUESTIONNAIRE FORM 1 1984	TOTAL	SEX		RACE		REGION				4YR COLLEGE PLANS		ILLICIT DRUG USE: LIFETIME				
		M	F	White	Black	NE	NC	S	W	Yes	No	None	Marijuana Only	Few Pills	More Pills	Any Heroin
N (Weighted No. of Cases):	3311	1534	1616	2414	478	670	941	1113	587	1772	1137	1223	794	381	765	32
% of Weighted Total:	100.0	46.3	48.8	72.9	14.4	20.2	28.4	33.6	17.7	53.5	34.3	36.9	24.0	11.5	23.1	1.0
B065E: When people over age 30 were present																
1. Not at all	77.6	79.3	74.9	77.0	100.0	67.2	86.6	75.2	80.6	79.4	77.4	-	-	66.9	82.2	23.3
2. A few of the times	8.2	8.2	9.1	8.2	-	10.2	6.7	9.5	5.7	5.7	9.3	-	-	-	6.6	30.9
3. Some of the times	5.3	5.5	6.7	5.0	-	5.9	3.5	4.6	9.3	5.5	3.8	-	-	-	3.7	26.7
4. Most of the times	4.7	1.9	5.0	4.7	-	9.3	1.5	6.9	-	5.6	3.1	-	-	-	4.7	8.2
5. Every time	4.1	5.0	4.2	5.1	-	7.4	1.6	3.8	4.4	3.8	6.4	-	-	33.1	2.9	10.9
Item 3330 Subject A05b N★	118	57	47	96	5	30	37	32	18	48	35	-	-	2	103	9
B065F: During the daytime (before 4:00 p.m.)																
1. Not at all	44.9	44.5	46.7	44.6	72.3	28.0	47.7	61.9	37.7	43.7	51.9	-	-	66.9	45.2	20.6
2. A few of the times	21.6	20.4	26.8	24.5	-	27.6	13.0	15.9	38.1	29.7	15.8	-	-	-	22.1	26.7
3. Some of the times	16.5	17.9	12.8	15.4	27.7	24.7	16.1	7.0	20.0	6.5	21.2	-	-	-	16.4	26.0
4. Most of the times	7.9	3.6	7.4	5.4	-	10.0	10.3	8.1	-	5.2	8.2	-	-	-	7.6	15.8
5. Every time	9.1	13.6	6.4	10.1	-	9.6	12.9	7.2	4.3	14.9	2.9	-	-	33.1	8.6	10.9
Item 3340 Subject A05c N★	118	57	47	97	5	30	37	32	19	48	35	-	-	2	104	9
B065G: At your home (or apartment or dorm)																
1. Not at all	35.5	42.1	35.7	37.4	64.0	45.9	29.6	33.6	33.9	36.9	49.6	-	-	-	37.4	12.0
2. A few of the times	23.1	24.2	23.3	23.1	12.6	23.6	16.4	17.8	44.8	25.7	20.0	-	-	13.9	23.0	36.0
3. Some of the times	13.9	7.0	15.8	11.5	-	13.8	11.6	14.6	17.1	10.3	9.5	-	-	-	13.8	26.4
4. Most of the times	9.5	10.9	6.9	8.5	23.4	6.5	7.6	19.7	-	11.0	12.7	-	-	-	9.8	13.7
5. Every time	18.0	15.8	18.2	19.5	-	10.3	34.7	14.4	4.3	16.0	8.3	-	-	86.1	16.0	12.0
Item 3350 Subject A05c N★	120	57	50	99	5	30	37	34	19	47	34	-	-	5	104	9
B065H: At school																
1. Not at all	63.5	59.2	70.6	65.2	76.6	54.7	59.6	70.0	73.6	61.6	61.1	-	-	100.0	65.7	19.1
2. A few of the times	13.9	13.5	13.8	14.8	-	18.4	12.2	9.7	17.5	13.7	15.2	-	-	-	13.4	26.7
3. Some of the times	12.1	15.4	5.1	11.7	-	16.8	16.8	6.1	6.0	10.6	12.9	-	-	-	12.4	15.1
4. Most of the times	7.7	6.1	10.5	6.0	23.4	6.7	5.2	14.2	3.0	12.1	7.9	-	-	-	6.3	28.3
5. Every time	2.8	5.7	-	2.4	-	3.4	6.2	-	-	2.1	2.9	-	-	-	2.2	10.9
Item 3360 Subject A05c N★	120	58	47	98	5	30	37	33	19	48	35	-	-	2	105	9
B065I: In a car																
1. Not at all	64.2	61.3	72.1	64.4	100.0	53.5	61.3	68.4	79.5	71.6	57.9	-	-	100.0	65.4	31.5
2. A few of the times	12.2	10.2	14.1	12.9	-	20.4	11.9	7.1	8.6	9.2	19.3	-	-	-	12.8	11.2
3. Some of the times	14.6	12.8	12.5	13.7	-	18.5	17.1	11.4	9.1	8.5	15.1	-	-	-	14.4	24.6
4. Most of the times	4.8	8.0	-	3.8	-	4.2	-	11.9	2.9	4.6	3.1	-	-	-	3.6	21.8
5. Every time	4.2	7.6	1.3	5.2	-	3.4	9.8	1.3	-	6.1	4.6	-	-	-	3.8	10.9
Item 3380 Subject A05c N★	120	58	47	98	5	30	37	33	19	48	35	-	-	2	105	9
B066: How many of the times when you used barbiturates during the last year did you use them along with each of the following drugs–that is, so that their effects overlapped?																
B066A: With alcohol																
1. Not at all	38.0	38.4	45.7	39.4	72.7	24.3	34.0	43.5	58.5	48.2	45.6	-	-	100.0	37.9	11.2
2. A few of the times	25.8	26.5	22.7	27.4	-	41.3	16.6	21.0	27.4	27.9	17.2	-	-	-	27.2	21.8
3. Some of the times	15.0	3.6	25.1	14.2	-	16.8	16.0	14.3	11.2	4.7	15.9	-	-	-	15.0	21.9
4. Most of the times	12.9	18.8	2.5	11.1	27.3	11.8	20.3	11.4	2.9	5.6	16.7	-	-	-	13.0	18.4
5. Every time	8.2	12.7	4.1	8.0	-	5.7	13.1	9.8	-	13.6	4.6	-	-	-	6.9	26.7
Item 3390 Subject A01h N★	119	58	47	98	4	30	37	33	19	47	35	-	-	2	105	9
B066B: With marijuana																
1. Not at all	42.2	48.4	32.9	42.0	40.5	48.3	40.6	31.5	54.0	51.0	30.5	-	-	100.0	41.4	24.0
2. A few of the times	24.8	20.9	34.1	24.7	32.3	20.9	14.1	31.7	39.2	29.2	27.8	-	-	-	26.1	22.0
3. Some of the times	9.7	4.8	15.5	10.1	-	8.8	11.2	12.2	3.8	2.0	13.5	-	-	-	9.5	15.5
4. Most of the times	14.3	15.0	9.3	13.4	27.3	16.3	13.9	19.4	2.9	6.6	21.8	-	-	-	13.7	27.5
5. Every time	9.0	10.9	8.2	9.8	-	5.7	20.3	5.3	-	11.2	6.4	-	-	-	9.2	10.9
Item 3400 Subject A01h N★	117	58	45	96	4	30	35	33	19	47	35	-	-	2	103	9

★=excludes respondents for whom question was inappropriate.

QUESTIONNAIRE FORM 1 1984	TOTAL	SEX		RACE		REGION				4YR COLLEGE PLANS		ILLICIT DRUG USE: LIFETIME				
		M	F	White	Black	NE	NC	S	W	Yes	No	None	Marijuana Only	Few Pills	More Pills	Any Heroin
N (Weighted No. of Cases):	3311	1534	1616	2414	478	670	941	1113	587	1772	1137	1223	794	381	765	32
% of Weighted Total:	100.0	46.3	48.8	72.9	14.4	20.2	28.4	33.6	17.7	53.5	34.3	36.9	24.0	11.5	23.1	1.0
B066C: With LSD																
1. Not at all	89.9	83.8	99.0	91.3	100.0	87.0	89.0	87.8	100.0	92.7	85.2	-	-	100.0	93.3	48.7
2. A few of the times	3.7	6.6	1.0	4.4	-	-	11.0	1.3	-	4.1	5.7	-	-	-	3.7	4.7
3. Some of the times	2.7	2.1	-	1.2	-	6.2	-	3.7	-	-	3.6	-	-	-	3.0	-
4. Most of the times	2.9	5.8	-	1.9	-	3.4	-	7.2	-	3.2	2.5	-	-	-	-	35.8
5. Every time	0.9	1.8	-	1.1	-	3.4	-	-	-	-	3.0	-	-	-	-	10.9
Item 3410 Subject A01h N★	117	58	45	96	4	30	35	32	19	47	34			2	103	9
B066D: With psychedelics other than LSD																
1. Not at all	90.2	87.1	95.5	91.6	100.0	84.5	90.8	89.1	100.0	92.7	88.6	-	-	100.0	93.1	53.3
2. A few of the times	4.9	4.8	4.5	5.0	-	5.4	9.2	2.6	-	4.1	4.8	-	-	-	4.7	9.1
3. Some of the times	4.0	6.4	-	2.3	-	6.7	-	8.3	-	3.2	3.6	-	-	-	2.2	26.7
4. Most of the times	-	-	-	-	-	-	-	-	-	-	-	-	-	-	-	-
5. Every time	0.9	1.8	-	1.1	-	3.4	-	-	-	-	3.0	-	-	-	-	10.9
Item 3420 Subject A01h N★	117	58	45	96	4	30	35	32	19	47	34			2	103	9
B066E: With amphetamines																
1. Not at all	84.9	81.9	91.4	85.6	100.0	87.0	88.8	81.3	79.8	81.3	84.9	-	-	100.0	87.6	48.4
2. A few of the times	6.5	6.4	6.2	6.7	-	3.4	7.5	7.2	8.6	8.7	5.9	-	-	-	5.9	15.8
3. Some of the times	2.5	1.5	-	2.0	-	2.9	-	6.5	-	-	6.0	-	-	-	2.0	9.1
4. Most of the times	4.1	6.3	2.4	3.3	-	3.4	-	4.9	11.6	10.0	-	-	-	-	3.2	15.8
5. Every time	2.0	4.0	-	2.4	-	3.4	3.7	-	-	-	3.2	-	-	-	1.3	10.9
Item 3430 Subject A01h N★	114	58	43	96	3	30	35	30	19	47	32			2	100	9
B066F: With quaaludes																
1. Not at all	83.1	77.7	90.9	84.3	100.0	86.2	78.6	77.3	97.1	88.0	76.5	-	-	100.0	84.6	59.6
2. A few of the times	8.6	11.2	3.4	8.3	-	10.3	10.2	10.4	-	8.8	10.3	-	-	-	8.5	13.7
3. Some of the times	5.7	6.8	5.7	6.3	-	-	9.9	7.7	2.9	-	10.2	-	-	-	6.4	-
4. Most of the times	-	-	-	-	-	-	-	-	-	-	-	-	-	-	-	-
5. Every time	2.6	4.3	-	1.1	-	3.5	1.4	4.6	-	3.2	3.0	-	-	-	0.5	26.7
Item 3440 Subject A01h N★	116	58	45	96	4	29	36	32	19	47	34			2	102	9
B067: What are the most important reasons for your taking barbiturates without a doctor's orders? (Mark all that apply.)																
A. To experiment–to see what it's like	48.1	54.9	42.0	48.3	36.7	43.7	39.2	53.4	63.2	67.7	30.6	-	-	22.2	47.8	65.0
B. To relax or relieve tension	59.0	58.6	63.9	57.1	80.2	61.3	46.2	60.0	78.9	59.1	66.4	-	-	55.6	57.6	76.8
C. To feel good or get high	50.0	54.6	41.5	47.4	80.2	62.9	42.3	52.0	41.8	46.3	50.7	-	-	-	48.9	88.4
D. To seek deeper insights and understanding	9.6	13.3	5.7	7.6	-	16.4	6.9	10.3	2.9	9.6	5.6	-	-	-	7.6	38.0
E. To have a good time with my friends	31.8	39.6	22.4	31.6	-	53.5	27.9	22.0	23.2	41.6	19.2	-	-	-	29.9	70.2
F. To fit in with a group I like	7.2	9.9	6.1	7.1	-	3.0	3.3	12.9	11.6	9.9	11.4	-	-	-	5.9	26.5
G. To get away from my problems or troubles	18.8	14.1	24.5	18.0	-	6.2	17.6	28.4	23.8	9.4	27.0	-	-	46.0	16.6	31.4
H. Because of boredom, nothing else to do	19.4	18.5	20.7	16.1	80.2	22.7	3.8	41.6	6.1	18.2	21.2	-	-	30.5	17.2	39.7
I. Because of anger or frustration	19.8	24.0	16.6	18.6	-	19.3	16.9	24.8	17.0	18.5	20.7	-	-	-	19.1	38.0
J. To get through the day	10.8	10.6	11.9	10.4	-	10.6	11.1	11.7	9.1	10.4	15.6	-	-	15.5	7.9	43.0
K. To increase the effects of some other drug(s)	13.9	20.3	4.6	11.2	36.7	13.0	15.9	13.8	11.6	11.1	22.0	-	-	-	10.4	63.2
L. To decrease (offset) the effects of some other drug(s)	10.9	14.5	2.2	7.9	-	15.8	-	13.5	20.1	14.3	5.6	-	-	-	8.0	49.9
M. To get to sleep	49.1	43.6	56.4	50.1	19.8	33.7	55.8	45.9	65.6	44.2	60.5	-	-	82.1	47.6	49.9
N. To relieve physical pain	36.4	40.0	37.3	38.5	36.7	37.1	27.5	36.9	52.0	46.5	41.8	-	-	22.2	34.3	68.1
O. Because I am "hooked"–I have to have them	2.8	5.9	-	1.9	-	3.5	-	7.0	-	3.1	5.6	-	-	-	-	38.0
Item 3450-3580 Subject A06a N★	118	57	48	99	3	29	37	33	19	48	33			5	105	9
B068: When you take barbiturates how high do you usually get?																
1. Not at all high	11.8	13.3	13.3	10.9	40.5	2.9	17.2	11.3	16.5	10.7	19.4	-	-	31.8	11.0	-
2. A little high	25.6	25.7	29.2	26.0	59.5	36.4	24.9	19.6	20.8	25.9	34.1	-	-	-	26.9	30.1
3. Moderately high	33.8	39.5	26.7	37.4	-	31.0	35.1	36.2	31.2	35.2	33.2	-	-	-	37.1	20.3
4. Very high	7.9	9.5	6.0	6.5	-	10.3	-	10.6	14.4	3.1	5.4	-	-	-	4.8	49.6
5. I don't take them to get high	20.9	12.0	24.8	19.3	-	19.3	22.8	22.2	17.0	25.2	7.9	-	-	68.2	20.2	-
Item 3590 Subject A01e N★	117	57	47	97	4	30	35	34	18	48	35			5	102	9

★=excludes respondents for whom question was inappropriate.

QUESTIONNAIRE FORM 1 1984	TOTAL	SEX		RACE		REGION				4YR COLLEGE PLANS		ILLICIT DRUG USE: LIFETIME				
		M	F	White	Black	NE	NC	S	W	Yes	No	None	Marijuana Only	Few Pills	More Pills	Any Heroin
N (Weighted No. of Cases):	3311	1534	1616	2414	478	670	941	1113	587	1772	1137	1223	794	381	765	32
% of Weighted Total:	100.0	46.3	48.8	72.9	14.4	20.2	28.4	33.6	17.7	53.5	34.3	36.9	24.0	11.5	23.1	1.0

B069: When you take barbiturates how long do you usually stay high?

	TOTAL	M	F	White	Black	NE	NC	S	W	Yes	No	None	Marijuana Only	Few Pills	More Pills	Any Heroin
1. Usually don't get high	25.8	23.4	27.1	26.4	19.8	13.4	39.2	24.3	19.8	28.6	18.1	-	-	77.8	25.7	-
2. One to two hours	28.0	27.2	25.9	26.8	43.5	33.2	26.5	24.1	30.8	26.4	32.1	-	-	22.2	29.3	16.8
3. Three to six hours	38.2	38.3	42.5	40.2	36.7	42.6	34.4	44.2	29.2	41.9	38.5	-	-	-	38.5	54.8
4. Seven to 24 hours	7.9	11.2	4.5	6.5	-	10.8	-	7.5	20.2	3.1	11.3	-	-	-	6.5	28.4
5. More than 24 hours	-	-	-	-	-	-	-	-	-	-	-	-	-	-	-	-
Item 3600 Subject A01f N★	116	56	47	97	3	27	37	33	19	47	32	-	-	5	103	9

B070: What barbiturates have you taken during the last year without a doctor's orders? (Mark all that apply.)

	TOTAL	M	F	White	Black	NE	NC	S	W	Yes	No	None	Marijuana Only	Few Pills	More Pills	Any Heroin
A. Phenobarbital	23.3	26.7	15.5	21.5	5.7	30.9	20.9	13.5	32.3	21.3	28.0	-	-	25.7	21.7	43.0
B. Seconal	20.6	24.4	15.1	17.5	-	23.7	24.7	24.2	3.1	7.4	37.0	-	-	-	18.8	52.9
C. Tuinal	10.2	11.3	9.8	11.4	-	6.9	16.0	12.4	-	4.2	25.3	-	-	-	9.0	29.6
D. Nembutal	6.5	6.3	2.3	2.5	18.7	14.7	-	12.1	-	3.2	7.8	-	-	20.0	2.8	48.6
E. Luminal	10.9	9.2	10.3	8.9	-	13.3	6.0	14.6	11.6	8.0	14.7	-	-	-	7.5	58.5
F. Desbutal	6.8	7.7	3.9	6.4	-	10.3	6.0	9.4	-	-	16.9	-	-	-	5.3	29.6
G. Amytal	6.7	6.4	0.9	4.2	-	14.7	3.3	8.1	-	-	8.9	-	-	-	5.1	29.6
H. Adrenocal	4.5	6.3	3.5	3.8	-	6.9	-	11.3	-	3.2	8.4	-	-	-	0.9	52.9
I. Other	28.5	26.0	32.6	30.1	34.6	24.4	19.5	43.3	29.5	35.8	27.8	-	-	31.9	27.5	39.0
J. Don't know the names of some that I have used	60.1	61.3	63.3	63.8	41.0	59.7	55.4	60.4	69.2	67.9	55.7	-	-	22.3	59.3	85.0
Item 3610-3700 Subject A01l N★	110	53	46	92	3	26	37	28	19	46	32	-	-	3	99	8

B071: Have you ever tried to stop using barbiturates and found that you couldn't stop?

	TOTAL	M	F	White	Black	NE	NC	S	W	Yes	No	None	Marijuana Only	Few Pills	More Pills	Any Heroin
1. Yes	4.3	6.6	2.8	2.3	32.3	3.6	-	12.3	-	3.1	10.6	-	-	-	2.5	28.4
2. No	95.7	93.4	97.2	97.7	67.7	96.4	100.0	87.7	100.0	96.9	89.4	-	-	100.0	97.5	71.6
Item 3710 Subject A01i N★	118	56	49	97	4	28	37	33	20	48	34	-	-	5	103	9

B072: Do you think you will be using barbiturates without a doctor's prescription five years from now?

	TOTAL	M	F	White	Black	NE	NC	S	W	Yes	No	None	Marijuana Only	Few Pills	More Pills	Any Heroin
1. I definitely will	0.7	0.4	0.9	0.6	0.4	0.7	0.4	1.1	0.5	0.7	0.5	0.3	0.6	1.4	1.0	8.8
2. I probably will	1.7	1.4	1.7	1.9	0.5	2.3	1.7	1.5	1.2	0.7	2.3	0.1	0.3	2.0	5.8	1.5
3. I probably will not	16.8	18.5	14.7	18.0	9.6	20.8	16.1	15.1	16.9	15.6	17.6	8.1	11.3	18.8	36.1	41.3
4. I definitely will not	80.8	79.7	82.7	79.5	89.5	76.2	81.8	82.3	81.5	83.0	79.6	91.6	87.9	77.9	57.1	48.3
Item 3720 Subject A04a N	3158	1477	1586	2357	457	621	911	1057	569	1738	1103	1199	772	359	719	28

The next questions are about TRANQUILIZERS, which doctors sometimes prescribe to calm people down, quiet their nerves, or relax their muscles.

They include the following drugs: Librium, Valium, Miltown, Equanil, Meprobamate, Serax, Atarax, Tranxene, Vistaril.

B073: Have you ever taken tranquilizers because a doctor told you to use them?

	TOTAL	M	F	White	Black	NE	NC	S	W	Yes	No	None	Marijuana Only	Few Pills	More Pills	Any Heroin
1. No	89.4	89.2	89.8	88.3	96.3	91.2	88.9	88.8	89.5	89.1	90.4	94.5	94.3	80.8	80.8	66.1
2. Yes, but I had already tried them on my own.	1.6	1.6	1.3	1.5	0.4	2.2	1.3	1.7	1.1	1.3	1.3	-	-	1.0	5.3	21.9
3. Yes, and it was the first time I took any	9.0	9.2	9.0	10.2	3.3	6.6	9.8	9.4	9.4	9.6	8.3	5.5	5.7	18.2	14.0	12.0
Item 3730 Subject A01j N	3130	1463	1579	2354	446	613	913	1038	566	1732	1096	1198	761	356	718	31

B074: On how many occasions (if any) have you taken tranquilizers on your own–that is, without a doctor telling you to take them . . .

★=excludes respondents for whom question was inappropriate.

QUESTIONNAIRE FORM 1 1984	TOTAL	SEX		RACE		REGION				4YR COLLEGE PLANS		ILLICIT DRUG USE: LIFETIME				
		M	F	White	Black	NE	NC	S	W	Yes	No	None	Mari-juana Only	Few Pills	More Pills	Any Her-oin
N (Weighted No. of Cases):	3311	1534	1616	2414	478	670	941	1113	587	1772	1137	1223	794	381	765	32
% of Weighted Total:	100.0	46.3	48.8	72.9	14.4	20.2	28.4	33.6	17.7	53.5	34.3	36.9	24.0	11.5	23.1	1.0

B074A: . . . in your lifetime?

	TOTAL	M	F	White	Black	NE	NC	S	W	Yes	No	None	Mari-juana Only	Few Pills	More Pills	Any Her-oin
1. 0 occasions	89.3	91.1	88.3	88.2	97.3	86.5	91.2	89.1	90.0	90.5	89.3	100.0	100.0	74.7	67.8	53.6
2. 1-2	5.6	4.2	6.9	6.4	1.2	7.7	4.4	5.2	6.3	4.9	6.1	-	-	25.3	11.5	13.4
3. 3-5	1.9	1.6	2.0	2.2	0.6	1.9	1.4	2.2	1.8	2.1	1.3	-	-	-	8.0	4.4
4. 6-9	1.4	1.6	0.9	1.5	-	1.8	1.7	0.9	1.0	0.9	1.3	-	-	-	5.7	5.8
5. 10-19	0.8	0.5	1.0	0.9	0.3	0.8	0.6	1.3	0.2	0.8	0.6	-	-	-	3.3	7.0
6. 20-39	0.5	0.3	0.6	0.5	0.4	0.4	0.6	0.5	0.4	0.3	0.8	-	-	-	2.1	3.8
7. 40 or more	0.5	0.7	0.3	0.4	0.1	0.9	0.1	0.7	0.2	0.4	0.5	-	-	-	1.6	12.2
Item 1070 Subject A01a N	3103	1454	1562	2334	441	610	901	1027	565	1726	1084	1196	761	356	703	31

B074B: . . . during the last 12 months?

	TOTAL	M	F	White	Black	NE	NC	S	W	Yes	No	None	Mari-juana Only	Few Pills	More Pills	Any Her-oin
1. 0 occasions	95.6	96.0	95.6	95.0	99.2	94.4	96.2	95.0	97.1	95.9	95.8	100.0	100.0	93.1	85.1	75.3
2. 1-2	2.4	2.0	2.7	2.7	0.4	3.2	1.5	2.8	2.2	2.1	2.6	-	-	6.9	7.0	6.3
3. 3-5	0.8	0.9	0.8	1.1	-	1.1	0.9	0.9	0.4	0.8	0.7	-	-	-	3.4	6.0
4. 6-9	0.7	0.6	0.5	0.8	-	0.5	1.1	0.6	0.3	0.6	0.7	-	-	-	3.0	-
5. 10-19	0.2	*	0.4	0.2	0.3	0.5	0.1	0.3	-	0.3	0.2	-	-	-	0.6	7.5
6. 20-39	0.2	0.3	0.1	0.1	-	0.3	0.2	0.3	-	0.2	0.1	-	-	-	0.6	5.0
7. 40 or more	*	0.1	-	*	0.1	0.1	-	0.1	-	*	-	-	-	-	0.2	-
Item 1080 Subject A01b N	3094	1448	1558	2326	440	607	898	1026	563	1721	1081	1196	761	350	701	30

B074C: . . . during the last 30 days?

	TOTAL	M	F	White	Black	NE	NC	S	W	Yes	No	None	Mari-juana Only	Few Pills	More Pills	Any Her-oin
1. 0 occasions	98.4	98.3	98.7	98.2	99.6	97.6	98.1	98.3	99.8	98.4	98.6	100.0	100.0	99.0	94.2	78.1
2. 1-2	1.0	1.1	0.8	1.3	-	1.6	1.0	1.1	0.2	0.8	1.2	-	-	1.0	3.6	9.4
3. 3-5	0.4	0.5	0.4	0.5	-	0.7	0.8	0.1	-	0.5	0.2	-	-	-	1.8	-
4. 6-9	0.2	0.1	0.1	0.1	0.4	0.1	0.1	0.3	*	0.2	-	-	-	-	0.3	7.5
5. 10-19	*	0.1	-	-	-	-	-	0.1	-	0.1	-	-	-	-	-	5.0
6. 20-39	-	-	-	-	-	-	-	-	-	-	-	-	-	-	-	-
7. 40 or more	-	-	-	-	-	-	-	-	-	-	-	-	-	-	-	-
Item 1090 Subject A01c N	3093	1448	1558	2326	440	607	898	1025	563	1721	1081	1196	761	350	699	30

IF YOU HAVE NOT TAKEN TRANQUILIZERS IN THE LAST TWELVE MONTHS, GO TO Q.B082.

THE FOLLOWING QUESTIONS REFER ONLY TO TAKING TRANQUILIZERS WITHOUT A DOCTOR'S ORDERS. IF YOU HAVE NOT DONE THIS IN THE LAST TWELVE MONTHS, GO TO Q.B082.

B075: When you used tranquilizers during the last year, how often did you use them in each of the following situations?

B075A: When you were alone

	TOTAL	M	F	White	Black	NE	NC	S	W	Yes	No	None	Mari-juana Only	Few Pills	More Pills	Any Her-oin
1. Not at all	45.5	39.1	52.5	47.3	56.5	56.6	30.2	49.5	42.8	42.4	44.7	-	-	62.3	43.6	35.8
2. A few of the times	24.9	25.5	20.9	24.1	43.5	23.3	32.8	20.0	27.2	23.2	30.3	-	-	3.3	28.2	15.8
3. Some of the times	7.8	14.6	2.0	5.6	-	5.4	7.1	9.6	9.1	8.9	7.7	-	-	-	8.6	20.1
4. Most of the times	8.3	4.3	11.7	8.1	-	5.3	5.9	11.7	8.5	5.6	7.8	-	-	-	9.6	14.5
5. Every time	13.4	16.4	12.9	14.8	-	9.3	24.0	9.2	12.4	19.9	9.4	-	-	34.3	10.0	13.8
Item 3740 Subject A05a N★	119	51	59	100	4	30	31	46	13	60	43	-	-	17	92	7

B075B: With just 1 or 2 other people

	TOTAL	M	F	White	Black	NE	NC	S	W	Yes	No	None	Mari-juana Only	Few Pills	More Pills	Any Her-oin
1. Not at all	35.1	28.5	46.5	34.5	53.7	34.9	27.4	40.1	36.8	47.2	26.7	-	-	64.7	31.4	21.9
2. A few of the times	23.2	29.5	16.5	24.3	11.1	24.0	36.8	15.3	16.0	16.3	28.0	-	-	22.0	23.9	28.4
3. Some of the times	13.3	5.1	15.0	14.1	-	9.6	12.8	16.0	13.2	4.8	26.1	-	-	-	17.0	-
4. Most of the times	14.7	20.9	9.4	11.2	35.1	18.9	10.8	16.2	9.7	13.5	13.1	-	-	-	13.5	35.9
5. Every time	13.7	16.0	12.6	15.8	-	12.7	12.2	12.4	24.4	18.3	6.1	-	-	13.3	14.3	13.8
Item 3750 Subject A05b N★	116	50	57	96	4	29	31	44	13	58	41	-	-	15	91	7

*=less than .05 per cent.   ★=excludes respondents for whom question was inappropriate.

QUESTIONNAIRE FORM 1 1984	TOTAL	SEX		RACE		REGION				4YR COLLEGE PLANS		ILLICIT DRUG USE: LIFETIME				
		M	F	White	Black	NE	NC	S	W	Yes	No	None	Mari-juana Only	Few Pills	More Pills	Any Her-oin
N (Weighted No. of Cases):	3311	1534	1616	2414	478	670	941	1113	587	1772	1137	1223	794	381	765	32
% of Weighted Total:	100.0	46.3	48.8	72.9	14.4	20.2	28.4	33.6	17.7	53.5	34.3	36.9	24.0	11.5	23.1	1.0
B075C: At a party																
1. Not at all	71.1	65.6	76.1	72.6	88.3	58.1	71.5	79.1	74.2	74.5	64.2	-	-	91.7	72.8	27.3
2. A few of the times	11.5	13.2	10.5	12.1	-	15.9	2.3	11.9	21.4	11.0	15.0	-	-	-	13.5	14.5
3. Some of the times	2.9	3.4	2.9	3.5	-	6.0	2.3	2.0	-	-	3.8	-	-	-	1.7	24.2
4. Most of the times	8.1	9.1	6.5	6.4	11.7	9.1	15.1	3.6	4.4	6.6	12.1	-	-	-	7.9	-
5. Every time	6.4	8.7	4.0	5.4	-	10.9	8.8	3.5	-	8.0	5.0	-	-	8.3	4.1	33.9
Item 3760　Subject A05c	*N★*	*115*	*51*	*55*	*95*	*4*	*30*	*30*	*43*	*13*	*58*	*41*	*-*	*-*	*15*	*90*	*7*
B075D: When your date or spouse was present																
1. Not at all	76.6	75.9	80.1	78.2	88.9	73.0	83.5	76.1	70.2	83.2	82.4	-	-	95.1	75.6	41.9
2. A few of the times	11.9	14.3	11.7	12.3	11.1	8.1	10.1	10.5	29.8	10.8	6.1	-	-	-	14.2	13.8
3. Some of the times	4.3	4.4	1.5	1.7	-	6.7	2.3	5.4	-	3.9	2.1	-	-	-	3.9	20.1
4. Most of the times	2.0	1.1	-	1.7	-	-	4.1	2.6	-	-	2.7	-	-	-	2.6	-
5. Every time	5.1	4.3	6.7	6.2	-	12.2	-	5.4	-	2.1	6.7	-	-	4.9	3.7	24.2
Item 3770　Subject A05b	*N★*	*114*	*50*	*56*	*94*	*4*	*29*	*30*	*43*	*13*	*57*	*41*	*-*	*-*	*15*	*89*	*7*
B075E: When people over age 30 were present																
1. Not at all	69.6	74.2	69.4	70.1	74.8	70.6	70.8	65.4	78.4	76.7	61.6	-	-	73.2	70.2	41.9
2. A few of the times	8.4	6.3	10.4	9.4	-	12.8	9.4	4.6	8.9	6.2	9.2	-	-	3.8	9.0	13.8
3. Some of the times	7.0	8.5	2.6	5.6	-	4.3	5.1	10.8	4.3	3.6	11.4	-	-	-	7.3	20.1
4. Most of the times	5.6	2.9	5.5	4.6	-	2.7	6.4	6.2	8.4	1.9	7.6	-	-	7.3	5.2	10.4
5. Every time	9.4	8.1	12.1	10.3	25.2	9.5	8.2	13.0	-	11.6	10.2	-	-	15.8	8.3	13.8
Item 3780　Subject A05b	*N★*	*113*	*50*	*55*	*94*	*4*	*28*	*30*	*43*	*13*	*56*	*41*	*-*	*-*	*15*	*88*	*7*
B075F: During the daytime (before 4:00 p.m.)																
1. Not at all	50.0	42.5	54.3	46.9	95.1	49.0	51.4	47.5	57.4	53.3	49.7	-	-	77.6	45.4	26.2
2. A few of the times	19.1	20.6	20.9	20.6	4.9	21.1	14.9	21.3	18.0	10.3	31.9	-	-	17.8	19.6	25.3
3. Some of the times	9.9	16.0	6.0	10.8	-	12.2	15.9	3.0	12.7	12.2	8.0	-	-	-	12.7	-
4. Most of the times	11.1	7.4	10.7	9.8	-	11.7	4.0	17.8	4.6	7.9	8.0	-	-	-	12.7	20.1
5. Every time	9.9	13.5	8.2	12.0	-	6.0	13.8	10.4	7.3	16.3	2.5	-	-	4.6	9.7	28.4
Item 3790　Subject A05c	*N★*	*115*	*50*	*56*	*96*	*4*	*29*	*31*	*43*	*13*	*58*	*41*	*-*	*-*	*15*	*90*	*7*
B075G: At your home (or apartment or dorm)																
1. Not at all	32.6	41.9	24.6	32.3	28.5	30.5	46.1	21.3	42.2	29.8	39.2	-	-	36.0	32.2	-
2. A few of the times	19.5	16.8	22.6	20.9	4.9	16.0	13.7	26.0	19.4	16.3	16.6	-	-	7.3	21.9	25.3
3. Some of the times	7.8	8.9	4.0	6.7	-	8.8	6.2	10.7	-	7.0	9.1	-	-	-	8.5	20.1
4. Most of the times	12.8	8.6	17.4	11.1	41.3	21.8	7.5	10.2	13.5	12.1	9.9	-	-	11.0	12.5	26.2
5. Every time	27.3	23.8	31.4	29.1	25.2	22.8	26.5	31.7	24.9	34.7	25.2	-	-	45.7	24.9	28.4
Item 3800　Subject A05c	*N★*	*116*	*51*	*56*	*97*	*4*	*30*	*31*	*43*	*13*	*58*	*42*	*-*	*-*	*16*	*90*	*7*
B075H: At school																
1. Not at all	74.3	73.6	74.4	75.2	69.8	74.1	76.5	73.2	73.4	78.6	74.4	-	-	94.9	74.3	21.9
2. A few of the times	12.4	13.5	11.0	13.6	-	14.4	13.0	9.9	14.7	6.3	18.9	-	-	5.1	13.9	13.8
3. Some of the times	2.3	3.8	1.3	2.8	-	2.5	6.3	-	-	3.4	1.7	-	-	-	2.9	-
4. Most of the times	7.0	4.6	8.9	4.0	30.2	5.5	2.3	13.4	-	8.1	1.1	-	-	-	6.0	35.9
5. Every time	4.0	4.4	4.3	4.4	-	3.5	2.0	3.4	11.9	3.6	3.9	-	-	-	2.8	28.4
Item 3810　Subject A05c	*N★*	*115*	*50*	*56*	*95*	*4*	*29*	*31*	*43*	*13*	*57*	*41*	*-*	*-*	*15*	*90*	*7*
B075I: In a car																
1. Not at all	80.7	75.5	86.4	80.8	88.9	73.2	85.6	80.4	86.5	78.9	83.2	-	-	100.0	78.0	66.1
2. A few of the times	6.8	6.0	8.6	8.2	-	11.0	-	6.9	13.5	7.9	8.1	-	-	-	8.7	-
3. Some of the times	2.7	3.8	-	2.0	-	4.2	6.3	-	-	3.4	-	-	-	-	3.5	-
4. Most of the times	4.5	4.6	3.1	3.0	-	3.0	-	10.1	-	4.9	3.8	-	-	-	4.1	20.1
5. Every time	5.3	10.0	1.8	5.9	11.1	8.6	8.1	2.6	-	5.0	5.0	-	-	-	5.6	13.8
Item 3830　Subject A05c	*N★*	*115*	*50*	*56*	*95*	*4*	*29*	*31*	*43*	*13*	*57*	*41*	*-*	*-*	*15*	*90*	*7*
B076: How many of the times when you used tranquilizers during the last year did you use them along with each of the following drugs– that is, so that their effects overlapped?																

★=excludes respondents for whom question was inappropriate.

QUESTIONNAIRE FORM 1 1984	TOTAL	SEX		RACE		REGION				4YR COLLEGE PLANS		ILLICIT DRUG USE: LIFETIME				
		M	F	White	Black	NE	NC	S	W	Yes	No	None	Marijuana Only	Few Pills	More Pills	Any Heroin
N (Weighted No. of Cases):	3311	1534	1616	2414	478	670	941	1113	587	1772	1137	1223	794	381	765	32
% of Weighted Total:	100.0	46.3	48.8	72.9	14.4	20.2	28.4	33.6	17.7	53.5	34.3	36.9	24.0	11.5	23.1	1.0

B076A: With alcohol

	TOTAL	M	F	White	Black	NE	NC	S	W	Yes	No	None	Mar. Only	Few Pills	More Pills	Any Heroin
1. Not at all	59.0	50.6	64.5	60.1	53.7	55.8	51.9	67.2	55.2	63.6	53.0	-	-	82.0	58.6	26.0
2. A few of the times	15.1	18.7	14.2	17.2	-	16.2	15.5	8.2	34.4	13.2	18.5	-	-	10.1	16.6	13.8
3. Some of the times	10.7	9.4	12.3	8.1	30.2	10.4	14.0	10.5	4.3	4.4	16.5	-	-	-	9.2	26.2
4. Most of the times	4.4	6.1	0.3	4.4	4.9	2.4	4.7	5.2	6.1	3.2	5.7	-	-	-	5.7	-
5. Every time	10.9	15.2	8.7	10.2	11.1	15.3	13.9	8.9	-	15.7	6.3	-	-	7.9	9.9	33.9
Item 3840 Subject A01h N★	115	51	56	95	4	30	30	43	13	57	42	-	-	15	89	7

B076B: With marijuana

	TOTAL	M	F	White	Black	NE	NC	S	W	Yes	No	None	Mar. Only	Few Pills	More Pills	Any Heroin
1. Not at all	62.2	62.9	68.1	61.6	58.7	53.6	63.2	63.2	77.0	66.8	64.1	-	-	89.9	57.8	42.0
2. A few of the times	19.2	15.2	21.3	21.9	-	27.5	12.6	17.0	23.0	16.1	25.7	-	-	10.1	20.7	28.4
3. Some of the times	5.0	5.3	3.5	4.8	-	6.3	6.0	5.0	-	2.3	-	-	-	-	6.5	-
4. Most of the times	5.5	3.4	5.1	4.7	30.2	2.7	4.6	9.9	-	5.3	6.3	-	-	-	5.8	15.8
5. Every time	8.0	13.3	2.0	6.9	11.1	9.9	13.6	5.0	-	9.5	3.9	-	-	-	9.2	13.8
Item 3850 Subject A01h N★	117	52	56	97	4	31	31	43	13	58	42	-	-	15	91	7

B076C: With LSD

	TOTAL	M	F	White	Black	NE	NC	S	W	Yes	No	None	Mar. Only	Few Pills	More Pills	Any Heroin
1. Not at all	95.5	91.1	98.7	96.1	100.0	93.9	93.6	96.5	100.0	94.1	95.8	-	-	95.3	97.8	66.1
2. A few of the times	1.7	3.9	-	2.0	-	-	6.4	-	-	3.4	-	-	-	-	2.2	-
3. Some of the times	0.6	-	1.3	0.8	-	2.5	-	-	-	-	1.8	-	-	4.7	-	-
4. Most of the times	1.3	3.0	-	-	-	-	-	3.5	-	2.6	-	-	-	-	-	20.1
5. Every time	0.9	2.1	-	1.1	-	3.6	-	-	-	-	2.5	-	-	-	-	13.8
Item 3860 Subject A01h N★	114	50	56	94	4	29	30	43	13	57	41	-	-	15	88	7

B076D: With psychedelics other than LSD

	TOTAL	M	F	White	Black	NE	NC	S	W	Yes	No	None	Mar. Only	Few Pills	More Pills	Any Heroin
1. Not at all	97.8	95.0	100.0	98.9	100.0	96.4	100.0	96.5	100.0	97.4	97.5	-	-	100.0	100.0	66.1
2. A few of the times	-	-	-	-	-	-	-	-	-	-	-	-	-	-	-	-
3. Some of the times	-	-	-	-	-	-	-	-	-	-	-	-	-	-	-	-
4. Most of the times	1.3	3.0	-	-	-	-	-	3.5	-	2.6	-	-	-	-	-	20.1
5. Every time	0.9	2.1	-	1.1	-	3.6	-	-	-	-	2.5	-	-	-	-	13.8
Item 3870 Subject A01h N★	114	50	56	94	4	29	30	43	13	57	41	-	-	15	88	7

B076E: With amphetamines

	TOTAL	M	F	White	Black	NE	NC	S	W	Yes	No	None	Mar. Only	Few Pills	More Pills	Any Heroin
1. Not at all	91.9	83.1	98.5	91.8	100.0	93.5	91.3	94.0	82.9	86.9	95.8	-	-	100.0	92.3	66.1
2. A few of the times	4.2	9.7	-	5.1	-	-	8.7	-	17.1	7.2	1.7	-	-	-	5.5	-
3. Some of the times	2.3	5.2	-	1.2	-	-	-	6.0	-	4.5	-	-	-	-	1.3	20.1
4. Most of the times	-	-	-	-	-	-	-	-	-	-	-	-	-	-	-	-
5. Every time	1.6	2.1	1.5	2.0	-	6.5	-	-	-	1.5	2.5	-	-	-	0.9	13.8
Item 3880 Subject A01h N★	114	50	56	94	4	29	30	43	13	57	41	-	-	15	88	7

B076F: With quaaludes

	TOTAL	M	F	White	Black	NE	NC	S	W	Yes	No	None	Mar. Only	Few Pills	More Pills	Any Heroin
1. Not at all	94.0	87.5	98.7	94.3	100.0	93.9	91.4	94.0	100.0	92.1	94.3	-	-	100.0	95.0	66.1
2. A few of the times	2.3	3.9	1.3	2.8	-	2.5	6.5	-	-	3.4	1.8	-	-	-	3.0	-
3. Some of the times	1.5	3.5	-	1.8	-	-	2.1	2.6	-	1.9	1.5	-	-	-	2.0	-
4. Most of the times	-	-	-	-	-	-	-	-	-	-	-	-	-	-	-	-
5. Every time	2.2	5.1	-	1.1	-	3.6	-	3.5	-	2.6	2.5	-	-	-	-	33.9
Item 3890 Subject A01h N★	113	49	56	94	4	29	29	43	13	57	41	-	-	15	87	7

B076G: With barbiturates

	TOTAL	M	F	White	Black	NE	NC	S	W	Yes	No	None	Mar. Only	Few Pills	More Pills	Any Heroin
1. Not at all	91.9	86.7	96.4	92.5	100.0	92.9	91.1	92.0	91.1	90.1	95.4	-	-	100.0	93.5	52.3
2. A few of the times	3.6	6.0	2.0	4.3	-	3.6	6.5	-	8.9	5.4	-	-	-	-	3.5	13.8
3. Some of the times	3.6	5.3	1.5	2.1	-	-	2.4	8.0	-	4.5	2.1	-	-	-	3.0	20.1
4. Most of the times	-	-	-	-	-	-	-	-	-	-	-	-	-	-	-	-
5. Every time	0.9	2.1	-	1.1	-	3.6	-	-	-	-	2.5	-	-	-	-	13.8
Item 3900 Subject A01h N★	113	49	56	94	4	29	29	43	13	57	41	-	-	15	87	7

★=excludes respondents for whom question was inappropriate.

QUESTIONNAIRE FORM 1 1984	TOTAL	SEX		RACE		REGION				4YR COLLEGE PLANS		ILLICIT DRUG USE: LIFETIME				
		M	F	White	Black	NE	NC	S	W	Yes	No	None	Marijuana Only	Few Pills	More Pills	Any Heroin
N (Weighted No. of Cases):	3311	1534	1616	2414	478	670	941	1113	587	1772	1137	1223	794	381	765	32
% of Weighted Total:	100.0	46.3	48.8	72.9	14.4	20.2	28.4	33.6	17.7	53.5	34.3	36.9	24.0	11.5	23.1	1.0

B077: What have been the most important reasons for taking tranquilizers without a doctor's orders? (Mark all that apply.)

	TOTAL	M	F	White	Black	NE	NC	S	W	Yes	No	None	Marijuana Only	Few Pills	More Pills	Any Heroin
A. To experiment–to see what it's like	41.8	52.2	34.7	43.2	64.7	52.4	41.2	34.7	41.7	40.5	40.5	-	-	31.7	43.2	60.1
B. To relax or relieve tension	64.9	60.9	66.2	63.6	93.1	60.3	56.5	72.1	73.5	77.1	53.7	-	-	62.1	67.1	64.2
C. To feel good or get high	33.4	39.8	26.4	31.3	64.7	46.2	29.4	29.8	23.6	32.2	34.7	-	-	15.1	34.1	74.0
D. To seek deeper insights and understanding	4.9	8.8	2.2	3.9	-	6.2	-	9.0	-	5.0	6.7	-	-	5.4	2.6	33.9
E. To have a good time with my friends	17.3	17.6	16.4	13.8	64.7	13.5	17.5	20.7	14.3	16.5	18.1	-	-	9.7	15.6	60.1
F. To fit in with a group I like	5.3	8.3	3.4	4.3	-	5.7	-	9.0	4.8	5.0	7.8	-	-	-	4.0	33.9
G. To get away from my problems or troubles	16.7	12.7	18.2	17.2	-	14.8	12.7	21.4	15.0	17.3	20.6	-	-	-	18.6	34.6
H. Because of boredom, nothing else to do	15.1	22.0	9.0	13.4	42.2	12.3	23.4	14.0	4.8	14.2	18.9	-	-	-	15.4	49.7
I. Because of anger or frustration	18.3	19.4	18.9	16.8	-	14.3	15.9	21.2	24.3	17.4	24.9	-	-	4.5	17.5	33.9
J. To get through the day	14.8	19.4	13.1	14.8	-	20.2	14.0	14.4	4.8	17.3	14.9	-	-	4.3	14.3	48.4
K. To increase the effects of some other drug(s)	7.2	14.2	2.0	5.4	57.8	4.7	10.1	8.8	-	11.1	4.2	-	-	-	5.2	49.7
L. To decrease (offset) the effects of some other drug(s)	5.8	11.4	1.8	5.4	-	6.6	-	6.1	17.8	7.9	5.0	-	-	-	4.7	33.9
M. To get to sleep	46.3	49.5	43.9	46.8	-	46.7	42.8	44.8	59.5	47.2	49.9	-	-	49.4	46.9	45.4
N. To relieve physical pain	37.3	41.1	33.0	37.9	42.2	34.4	37.8	42.4	26.0	32.1	45.9	-	-	41.8	35.5	61.2
O. Because I am "hooked"–I have to have them	2.1	4.9	-	1.0	-	3.3	-	3.5	-	2.5	2.5	-	-	-	-	33.9
Item 3910-4040　Subject A06a　N★	117	51	57	98	3	31	31	43	12	60	41	-	-	16	91	7

B078: When you take tranquilizers how high do you usually get?

	TOTAL	M	F	White	Black	NE	NC	S	W	Yes	No	None	Marijuana Only	Few Pills	More Pills	Any Heroin
1. Not at all high	16.7	13.7	21.5	17.8	53.7	16.0	8.6	22.3	17.8	14.4	21.6	-	-	35.1	14.1	-
2. A little high	29.9	27.2	32.9	31.2	4.9	15.3	27.6	31.6	65.1	24.3	31.9	-	-	9.7	37.3	-
3. Moderately high	21.4	28.7	15.0	22.5	30.2	38.2	21.3	12.1	12.5	18.9	20.2	-	-	7.5	22.0	53.9
4. Very high	7.7	10.3	2.7	4.1	11.1	10.7	11.3	5.4	-	6.5	10.0	-	-	-	5.9	20.1
5. I don't take them to get high	24.3	20.1	27.8	24.4	-	19.9	31.2	28.5	4.6	35.9	16.3	-	-	47.7	20.8	26.0
Item 4050　Subject A01e　N★	115	52	56	96	4	31	29	43	13	59	42	-	-	16	88	7

B079: When you take tranquilizers how long do you usually stay high?

	TOTAL	M	F	White	Black	NE	NC	S	W	Yes	No	None	Marijuana Only	Few Pills	More Pills	Any Heroin
1. Usually don't get high	36.9	30.6	43.9	38.1	35.3	30.5	38.2	42.4	30.8	41.4	34.9	-	-	62.4	36.4	-
2. One to two hours	25.7	23.4	25.4	24.5	6.9	17.3	24.7	27.0	43.3	24.7	18.9	-	-	16.7	30.1	-
3. Three to six hours	27.8	30.2	25.7	29.1	57.8	42.3	25.5	21.2	21.7	24.1	36.9	-	-	13.3	25.4	66.1
4. Seven to 24 hours	9.5	15.9	5.0	8.3	-	9.9	11.6	9.4	4.3	9.9	9.3	-	-	7.7	8.1	33.9
5. More than 24 hours	-	-	-	-	-	-	-	-	-	-	-	-	-	-	-	-
Item 4060　Subject A01f　N★	114	51	56	96	3	29	31	41	13	58	41	-	-	16	89	7

B080: What tranquilizers have you taken during the last year without a doctor's orders? (Mark all that apply.)

	TOTAL	M	F	White	Black	NE	NC	S	W	Yes	No	None	Marijuana Only	Few Pills	More Pills	Any Heroin
A. Librium	12.9	17.4	9.5	13.1	-	12.9	11.1	11.6	21.7	11.7	15.5	-	-	-	12.6	47.7
B. Valium	79.3	78.1	81.0	80.4	64.7	97.0	59.1	80.2	82.9	74.2	83.0	-	-	62.9	82.4	100.0
C. Miltown	1.9	4.3	-	2.2	-	3.5	-	2.7	-	1.9	2.6	-	-	-	1.2	13.8
D. Equanil	3.9	9.0	-	3.1	-	3.5	6.4	3.6	-	5.9	2.6	-	-	-	2.2	33.9
E. Meprobamate	3.2	6.3	1.0	2.3	-	3.5	-	3.6	8.9	3.5	4.0	-	-	-	1.3	33.9
F. Serax	4.9	11.3	-	5.8	-	3.5	11.5	2.7	-	5.2	6.4	-	-	-	5.2	13.8
G. Atarax	3.1	5.1	1.8	1.1	-	3.5	-	6.1	-	4.4	2.6	-	-	6.7	-	33.9
H. Tranxene	5.7	6.6	5.6	6.8	-	3.5	-	13.1	-	6.0	4.7	-	-	6.8	4.9	13.8
I. Vistaril	5.1	6.3	4.6	3.5	35.3	6.3	2.0	7.9	-	4.0	8.7	-	-	-	3.7	33.9
J. Don't know the names of some tranquilizers I have used	38.7	43.9	31.0	36.8	-	25.5	60.7	30.5	44.2	36.4	42.2	-	-	37.0	36.0	55.8
Item 4070-4160　Subject A01l　N★	113	49	57	95	3	29	30	41	13	58	40	-	-	16	88	7

B081: Have you ever tried to stop using tranquilizers and found that you couldn't stop?

	TOTAL	M	F	White	Black	NE	NC	S	W	Yes	No	None	Marijuana Only	Few Pills	More Pills	Any Heroin
1. Yes	4.0	9.1	-	3.1	-	8.7	6.4	-	-	6.3	2.4	-	-	-	4.0	13.8
2. No	96.0	90.9	100.0	96.9	100.0	91.3	93.6	100.0	100.0	93.7	97.6	-	-	100.0	96.0	86.2
Item 4170　Subject A01i　N★	113	50	56	94	4	30	30	41	12	56	42	-	-	14	89	7

★=excludes respondents for whom question was inappropriate.

QUESTIONNAIRE FORM 1 1984	TOTAL	SEX		RACE		REGION				4YR COLLEGE PLANS		ILLICIT DRUG USE: LIFETIME				
		M	F	White	Black	NE	NC	S	W	Yes	No	None	Mari- juana Only	Few Pills	More Pills	Any Her- oin
N (Weighted No. of Cases):	3311	1534	1616	2414	478	670	941	1113	587	1772	1137	1223	794	381	765	32
% of Weighted Total:	100.0	46.3	48.8	72.9	14.4	20.2	28.4	33.6	17.7	53.5	34.3	36.9	24.0	11.5	23.1	1.0
B082: Do you think you will be using tranquilizers without a doctor's orders five years from now?																
1. I definitely will	0.4	0.3	0.5	0.3	0.6	0.2	0.1	0.9	0.3	0.5	0.2	0.1	0.6	-	0.7	9.1
2. I probably will	2.5	2.0	2.9	2.6	1.5	2.9	1.7	3.0	2.4	1.9	3.1	0.6	0.6	2.1	7.5	19.6
3. I probably will not	23.5	23.1	23.3	24.8	13.8	27.1	24.8	21.4	21.3	23.4	23.4	14.5	19.9	31.3	39.4	30.7
4. I definitely will not	73.6	74.6	73.3	72.4	84.1	69.8	73.4	74.6	76.0	74.2	73.3	84.8	78.9	66.6	52.4	40.5
Item 4180　Subject A04a　N	3120	1465	1576	2340	451	610	903	1041	566	1728	1100	1195	767	354	699	27

The next questions are about COCAINE, which is sometimes called "coke".

B083: On how many occasions (if any) have you taken cocaine . . .

B083A: . . . in your lifetime?

	TOTAL	M	F	White	Black	NE	NC	S	W	Yes	No	None	Mari- juana Only	Few Pills	More Pills	Any Her- oin
1. 0 occasions	83.5	80.2	87.9	83.2	91.5	75.9	90.4	87.7	73.2	86.8	82.6	100.0	100.0	68.8	47.5	23.5
2. 1-2	7.1	8.4	5.5	6.8	5.1	8.7	4.8	5.9	11.1	6.1	7.9	-	-	31.2	14.0	23.1
3. 3-5	2.7	3.7	1.7	3.0	1.0	3.9	1.8	1.9	4.4	2.0	2.3	-	-	-	11.5	6.4
4. 6-9	1.8	2.3	1.1	1.9	0.2	2.5	1.1	1.4	2.9	1.3	2.3	-	-	-	7.5	2.8
5. 10-19	1.8	2.3	1.2	1.9	1.4	3.4	0.8	1.3	2.6	1.2	2.2	-	-	-	7.2	13.6
6. 20-39	1.3	1.2	1.1	1.2	0.4	2.8	0.7	0.4	2.5	0.9	1.2	-	-	-	5.5	5.0
7. 40 or more	1.8	2.0	1.4	1.9	0.5	2.9	0.5	1.4	3.4	1.6	1.5	-	-	-	6.7	25.8
Item 950　Subject A01a　N	3134	1478	1570	2363	439	618	910	1034	571	1731	1101	1197	763	362	728	29

B083B: . . . during the last 12 months?

	TOTAL	M	F	White	Black	NE	NC	S	W	Yes	No	None	Mari- juana Only	Few Pills	More Pills	Any Her- oin
1. 0 occasions	88.0	85.7	91.2	87.7	93.9	79.8	93.5	91.7	81.6	90.5	87.5	100.0	100.0	83.9	58.5	44.0
2. 1-2	5.4	6.2	4.4	5.4	3.8	8.7	3.6	3.8	7.4	4.5	5.8	-	-	16.1	14.5	17.5
3. 3-5	2.3	3.3	1.3	2.5	0.7	3.8	1.4	1.7	3.3	1.5	2.6	-	-	-	9.9	3.7
4. 6-9	1.4	2.1	0.7	1.5	0.9	1.9	0.8	1.2	2.4	1.3	1.2	-	-	-	6.2	-
5. 10-19	1.2	1.0	1.1	1.3	0.3	3.0	0.1	0.7	2.1	0.9	1.5	-	-	-	4.6	19.7
6. 20-39	1.1	1.1	1.0	1.1	0.3	2.2	0.4	0.4	2.5	1.1	0.8	-	-	-	4.6	8.0
7. 40 or more	0.5	0.6	0.2	0.5	0.1	0.6	0.3	0.5	0.6	0.3	0.5	-	-	-	1.8	7.0
Item 960　Subject A01b　N	3126	1474	1569	2359	438	617	909	1028	572	1726	1102	1197	763	359	724	28

B083C: . . . during the last 30 days?

	TOTAL	M	F	White	Black	NE	NC	S	W	Yes	No	None	Mari- juana Only	Few Pills	More Pills	Any Her- oin
1. 0 occasions	93.9	92.8	95.7	94.0	96.7	88.8	97.4	95.8	90.3	95.3	93.8	100.0	100.0	94.7	77.8	55.9
2. 1-2	3.1	4.1	2.0	2.9	1.9	5.7	1.3	2.1	5.1	2.5	3.3	-	-	5.3	10.5	11.5
3. 3-5	1.7	1.7	1.3	1.8	0.8	3.1	0.5	1.1	2.9	1.2	1.6	-	-	-	6.8	9.8
4. 6-9	0.8	0.7	0.7	0.8	0.3	1.3	0.4	0.4	1.6	0.6	0.7	-	-	-	3.2	8.2
5. 10-19	0.3	0.4	0.2	0.3	0.2	1.0	0.2	0.2	0.1	0.4	0.3	-	-	-	1.0	11.7
6. 20-39	0.1	0.1	*	0.1	0.1	0.2	0.1	0.1	-	*	0.1	-	-	-	0.2	3.0
7. 40 or more	0.1	0.2	-	0.1	-	-	0.2	0.2	-	-	0.3	-	-	-	0.5	-
Item 970　Subject A01c　N	3125	1473	1569	2358	438	617	908	1028	572	1727	1100	1197	763	359	724	28

IF YOU HAVE NOT TAKEN COCAINE IN THE LAST TWELVE MONTHS, GO TO Q.B091.

B084: When you used cocaine during the last year, how often did you use it in each of the following situations?

B084A: When you were alone

	TOTAL	M	F	White	Black	NE	NC	S	W	Yes	No	None	Mari- juana Only	Few Pills	More Pills	Any Her- oin
1. Not at all	78.6	75.8	85.0	81.9	66.0	76.2	72.7	82.4	81.5	79.1	78.4	-	-	91.5	77.8	48.3
2. A few of the times	13.2	12.7	12.5	10.8	14.5	19.8	8.6	9.8	10.7	11.4	14.7	-	-	7.2	13.1	36.1
3. Some of the times	5.7	9.0	1.7	5.1	19.5	3.0	12.9	3.5	6.7	7.3	3.5	-	-	1.3	6.4	6.9
4. Most of the times	0.9	0.6	-	0.9	-	1.0	1.2	1.4	-	-	1.8	-	-	-	1.1	-
5. Every time	1.7	1.9	0.8	1.3	-	-	4.6	2.9	1.1	2.2	1.6	-	-	-	1.6	8.7
Item 4190　Subject A05a　N★	364	203	134	279	27	122	56	85	101	156	135	-	-	53	291	17

*=less than .05 per cent.　★=excludes respondents for whom question was inappropriate.

QUESTIONNAIRE FORM 1 1984	TOTAL	SEX		RACE		REGION				4YR COLLEGE PLANS		ILLICIT DRUG USE: LIFETIME				
		M	F	White	Black	NE	NC	S	W	Yes	No	None	Mari-juana Only	Few Pills	More Pills	Any Her-oin
N (Weighted No. of Cases):	3311	1534	1616	2414	478	670	941	1113	587	1772	1137	1223	794	381	765	32
% of Weighted Total:	100.0	46.3	48.8	72.9	14.4	20.2	28.4	33.6	17.7	53.5	34.3	36.9	24.0	11.5	23.1	1.0
B084B: With just 1 or 2 other people																
1. Not at all	8.3	7.2	10.6	7.8	8.3	7.3	8.7	9.6	8.1	9.7	8.3	-	-	11.0	7.2	4.8
2. A few of the times	32.4	30.8	32.5	31.6	38.6	32.8	15.6	39.9	34.7	31.6	31.8	-	-	52.9	28.5	39.1
3. Some of the times	12.0	11.4	11.7	11.5	20.5	14.8	16.0	7.1	10.6	8.8	14.1	-	-	3.9	13.9	7.2
4. Most of the times	26.4	28.4	25.0	27.3	16.0	26.6	30.4	20.7	29.0	24.0	28.6	-	-	3.0	30.3	38.8
5. Every time	20.9	22.2	20.1	21.8	16.6	18.4	29.2	22.7	17.6	25.9	17.2	-	-	29.2	20.1	10.1
Item 4200 Subject A05b N★	367	206	133	282	27	120	57	88	102	158	134	-	-	54	294	16
B084C: At a party																
1. Not at all	36.1	36.6	36.4	33.6	61.0	37.9	45.6	37.5	27.5	33.7	40.9	-	-	77.3	28.0	30.7
2. A few of the times	20.3	20.1	22.6	21.6	5.7	22.2	15.6	11.0	28.8	24.4	16.5	-	-	6.7	22.9	24.0
3. Some of the times	12.6	16.1	7.2	12.7	11.2	15.6	6.7	10.6	14.0	10.1	12.9	-	-	1.8	15.0	9.5
4. Most of the times	18.0	16.7	20.3	19.4	19.8	12.1	24.1	22.6	17.8	16.7	18.7	-	-	3.2	21.1	16.3
5. Every time	12.9	10.6	13.6	12.7	2.2	12.2	8.0	18.3	11.9	15.1	11.0	-	-	11.0	13.0	19.5
Item 4210 Subject A05c N★	363	202	133	277	28	122	55	87	100	156	134	-	-	55	289	16
B084D: When your date or spouse was present																
1. Not at all	60.2	73.2	43.1	59.3	65.5	58.3	71.0	70.4	48.1	56.6	65.5	-	-	85.9	56.5	31.9
2. A few of the times	12.7	12.0	12.2	11.3	10.0	14.2	9.3	7.4	17.4	11.4	12.1	-	-	3.5	14.3	19.1
3. Some of the times	8.5	6.0	11.6	8.3	15.5	7.0	4.2	4.1	16.5	7.9	7.8	-	-	1.9	9.4	17.7
4. Most of the times	9.2	7.0	12.1	10.7	2.8	8.5	6.1	10.0	10.8	13.3	6.7	-	-	1.3	10.5	12.8
5. Every time	9.4	1.7	20.9	10.5	6.3	12.0	9.3	8.1	7.2	10.8	7.9	-	-	7.4	9.3	18.5
Item 4220 Subject A05b N★	361	200	134	275	28	121	55	85	100	156	133	-	-	55	288	16
B084E: When people over age 30 were present																
1. Not at all	67.9	63.7	75.4	67.9	75.8	62.8	67.3	70.2	72.4	72.2	67.7	-	-	96.0	64.2	32.9
2. A few of the times	12.2	12.9	11.1	13.3	6.4	14.7	10.0	9.2	12.9	12.7	9.4	-	-	1.4	13.9	20.2
3. Some of the times	10.0	10.1	9.0	9.7	10.6	14.5	8.5	9.1	6.3	5.7	11.6	-	-	-	11.1	26.3
4. Most of the times	6.5	10.6	1.0	6.1	4.6	3.1	11.0	10.2	4.6	5.7	8.4	-	-	-	7.3	14.1
5. Every time	3.4	2.7	3.5	3.0	2.6	4.8	3.3	1.3	3.7	3.7	2.8	-	-	2.6	3.5	6.5
Item 4230 Subject A05b N★	365	204	134	280	28	120	57	87	101	158	134	-	-	55	291	16
B084F: During the daytime (before 4:00 p.m.)																
1. Not at all	59.3	56.3	64.9	57.0	84.8	57.8	62.2	63.8	55.6	56.5	66.4	-	-	90.7	54.1	40.2
2. A few of the times	20.6	20.9	18.2	20.1	13.1	26.6	9.8	18.1	21.9	22.8	16.3	-	-	-	23.9	34.9
3. Some of the times	11.5	12.7	11.1	13.5	2.1	7.8	20.2	10.0	12.4	10.3	9.9	-	-	-	14.4	-
4. Most of the times	5.0	6.4	2.6	5.4	-	5.3	1.1	5.9	6.0	5.5	4.8	-	-	3.0	4.7	18.3
5. Every time	3.6	3.8	3.2	4.1	-	2.6	6.7	2.2	4.1	4.9	2.6	-	-	6.3	2.9	6.7
Item 4240 Subject A05c N★	364	204	133	280	27	119	57	87	101	157	134	-	-	54	291	16
B084G: At your home (or apartment or dorm)																
1. Not at all	55.4	56.1	59.8	58.6	56.1	51.7	62.4	55.8	55.6	56.9	60.9	-	-	73.9	54.0	10.1
2. A few of the times	18.4	16.7	16.4	16.9	9.7	20.8	10.7	19.4	18.9	13.1	21.4	-	-	11.7	17.9	52.4
3. Some of the times	12.4	15.4	7.9	13.5	12.3	11.1	11.4	10.3	16.5	13.9	6.8	-	-	3.1	14.8	3.5
4. Most of the times	8.1	7.0	10.1	6.4	15.6	9.3	9.1	10.1	4.3	10.7	4.1	-	-	1.1	8.5	25.1
5. Every time	5.7	4.9	5.9	4.7	6.3	7.1	6.5	4.4	4.7	5.3	6.8	-	-	10.2	4.7	9.0
Item 4250 Subject A05c N★	367	206	134	282	28	121	57	87	102	159	134	-	-	55	293	16
B084H: At school																
1. Not at all	80.5	79.8	83.8	81.1	81.5	82.3	81.3	80.9	77.8	75.9	86.8	-	-	96.0	79.3	46.4
2. A few of the times	9.8	10.5	9.3	9.6	8.6	11.2	3.0	9.2	12.5	14.3	5.8	-	-	-	10.6	31.7
3. Some of the times	5.4	5.3	5.1	6.2	5.7	5.2	9.6	3.4	5.1	6.0	3.6	-	-	-	6.5	5.3
4. Most of the times	2.8	3.3	0.9	1.9	4.2	1.4	2.7	5.1	2.5	2.5	3.0	-	-	-	2.6	16.6
5. Every time	1.5	1.1	0.9	1.2	-	-	3.4	1.5	2.1	1.4	0.9	-	-	4.0	1.1	-
Item 4260 Subject A05c N★	365	204	134	280	28	120	56	87	102	157	134	-	-	55	291	16

★=excludes respondents for whom question was inappropriate.

QUESTIONNAIRE FORM 1 1984	TOTAL	SEX		RACE		REGION				4YR COLLEGE PLANS		ILLICIT DRUG USE: LIFETIME				
		M	F	White	Black	NE	NC	S	W	Yes	No	None	Mari-juana Only	Few Pills	More Pills	Any Her-oin
N (Weighted No. of Cases):	3311	1534	1616	2414	478	670	941	1113	587	1772	1137	1223	794	381	765	32
% of Weighted Total:	100.0	46.3	48.8	72.9	14.4	20.2	28.4	33.6	17.7	53.5	34.3	36.9	24.0	11.5	23.1	1.0

B084I: In a car

1. Not at all	51.5	50.9	54.2	49.8	77.1	46.4	52.4	58.6	51.0	59.9	47.3	-	-	88.8	45.0	40.9
2. A few of the times	21.9	23.3	19.1	21.5	10.4	27.8	16.3	17.3	21.8	17.9	21.9	-	-	9.9	24.1	19.2
3. Some of the times	16.2	15.4	18.0	18.5	2.6	13.5	20.7	13.3	19.6	13.4	21.1	-	-	-	20.4	-
4. Most of the times	6.3	5.5	5.9	5.5	8.4	8.3	2.0	7.2	5.6	5.4	5.2	-	-	-	6.3	28.9
5. Every time	4.0	4.8	2.9	4.7	1.5	4.0	8.6	3.6	2.0	3.4	4.4	-	-	1.3	4.2	11.0
Item 4280 Subject A05c N★	369	205	136	281	29	123	56	88	102	158	135	-	-	55	293	17

B085: How many of the times when you used cocaine during the last year did you use it along with each of the following drugs–that is, so that their effects overlapped?

B085A: With alcohol

1. Not at all	34.9	32.9	38.0	32.2	55.4	31.4	37.0	36.3	36.8	34.2	34.5	-	-	59.5	30.2	32.9
2. A few of the times	24.9	22.5	28.8	26.7	23.1	32.4	22.5	20.8	20.9	26.0	26.2	-	-	28.6	24.9	14.7
3. Some of the times	10.4	10.7	8.1	10.4	6.0	13.7	3.3	12.2	8.9	9.8	10.7	-	-	-	11.8	19.7
4. Most of the times	16.3	17.7	17.1	17.1	10.9	8.5	24.6	12.6	24.0	15.8	15.3	-	-	1.1	19.6	10.5
5. Every time	13.4	16.3	8.0	13.5	4.6	14.0	12.4	18.1	9.4	14.2	13.3	-	-	10.8	13.5	22.2
Item 4290 Subject A01h N★	362	204	132	280	26	118	57	86	101	158	131	-	-	54	291	16

B085B: With marijuana

1. Not at all	39.6	39.0	43.4	39.2	42.8	41.2	32.1	31.9	48.1	44.2	37.3	-	-	60.9	34.9	46.8
2. A few of the times	22.9	21.2	24.6	24.1	10.3	27.2	12.6	25.0	21.6	19.6	24.3	-	-	29.5	22.3	11.3
3. Some of the times	12.8	13.1	11.2	14.0	7.9	10.6	6.6	17.2	15.0	15.2	9.8	-	-	-	15.6	7.0
4. Most of the times	12.2	15.0	8.4	11.1	23.8	9.0	30.8	11.7	6.5	8.9	16.2	-	-	3.2	13.2	28.1
5. Every time	12.5	11.7	12.4	11.6	15.2	12.0	17.9	14.2	8.8	12.2	12.4	-	-	6.4	14.0	6.8
Item 4300 Subject A01h N★	359	202	132	277	27	119	54	84	101	159	132	-	-	55	288	15

B085C: With LSD

1. Not at all	95.2	92.9	98.1	94.9	98.0	98.2	91.8	92.4	95.7	96.6	93.6	-	-	100.0	95.0	80.8
2. A few of the times	2.6	3.5	1.9	3.4	-	0.5	3.8	4.3	3.1	2.4	3.3	-	-	-	3.3	-
3. Some of the times	0.8	1.4	-	0.8	2.0	1.4	1.1	-	0.6	-	1.3	-	-	-	0.4	9.9
4. Most of the times	1.2	2.2	-	0.9	-	-	2.0	3.3	0.6	0.9	1.8	-	-	-	1.0	9.3
5. Every time	0.2	-	-	-	-	-	1.3	-	-	-	-	-	-	-	0.3	-
Item 4310 Subject A01h N★	349	194	132	269	28	116	55	81	97	157	127	-	-	52	279	16

B085D: With psychedelics other than LSD

1. Not at all	96.3	95.0	98.1	96.9	97.2	96.0	91.7	97.1	98.5	98.0	94.8	-	-	98.9	96.8	79.5
2. A few of the times	1.2	1.6	0.8	1.0	-	1.8	1.1	-	1.5	0.6	1.2	-	-	-	1.5	-
3. Some of the times	0.8	1.0	0.6	1.0	-	1.5	-	1.1	-	-	1.4	-	-	-	0.3	11.2
4. Most of the times	1.4	2.1	0.6	1.0	2.8	0.7	4.8	1.8	-	0.9	2.6	-	-	-	1.2	9.3
5. Every time	0.4	0.3	-	0.2	-	-	2.4	-	-	0.4	-	-	-	1.1	0.2	-
Item 4320 Subject A01h N★	353	197	132	273	27	116	55	82	100	156	132	-	-	54	282	16

B085E: With amphetamines

1. Not at all	93.9	96.5	90.3	94.3	95.1	96.8	88.1	95.6	92.3	91.8	95.7	-	-	100.0	92.9	90.7
2. A few of the times	3.3	1.6	5.6	3.1	2.1	1.7	-	3.3	7.1	5.6	1.4	-	-	-	3.6	9.3
3. Some of the times	1.3	1.0	2.0	1.2	-	0.9	5.5	-	0.6	1.7	0.5	-	-	-	1.6	-
4. Most of the times	1.3	0.9	2.1	1.4	2.8	0.7	5.1	1.1	-	0.9	2.4	-	-	-	1.6	-
5. Every time	0.2	-	-	-	-	-	1.3	-	-	-	-	-	-	-	0.2	-
Item 4330 Subject A01h N★	352	196	132	272	27	115	55	82	100	157	130	-	-	54	281	16

B085F: With quaaludes

1. Not at all	96.7	96.2	97.5	96.8	100.0	99.1	94.7	91.3	99.4	98.8	94.9	-	-	97.5	97.1	88.0
2. A few of the times	1.6	1.1	2.5	1.8	-	-	1.1	5.2	0.6	0.3	2.1	-	-	2.5	1.3	2.7
3. Some of the times	0.7	1.2	-	0.9	-	0.9	-	1.6	-	-	1.8	-	-	-	0.8	-
4. Most of the times	0.4	0.8	-	0.6	-	-	2.8	-	-	-	1.2	-	-	-	0.5	-
5. Every time	0.6	0.8	-	-	-	-	1.3	1.8	-	0.9	-	-	-	-	0.2	9.3
Item 4340 Subject A01h N★	351	196	132	272	27	116	54	82	100	157	130	-	-	54	281	16

★=excludes respondents for whom question was inappropriate.

QUESTIONNAIRE FORM 1 1984	TOTAL	SEX		RACE		REGION				4YR COLLEGE PLANS		ILLICIT DRUG USE: LIFETIME				
		M	F	White	Black	NE	NC	S	W	Yes	No	None	Mari- juana Only	Few Pills	More Pills	Any Her- oin
N (Weighted No. of Cases):	3311	1534	1616	2414	478	670	941	1113	587	1772	1137	1223	794	381	765	32
% of Weighted Total:	100.0	46.3	48.8	72.9	14.4	20.2	28.4	33.6	17.7	53.5	34.3	36.9	24.0	11.5	23.1	1.0

B085G: With barbiturates

	TOTAL	M	F	White	Black	NE	NC	S	W	Yes	No	None	Mari- juana Only	Few Pills	More Pills	Any Her- oin
1. Not at all	98.2	97.8	100.0	98.7	100.0	98.9	94.5	98.2	99.4	99.1	97.7	-	-	100.0	98.3	90.7
2. A few of the times	0.9	1.0	-	0.5	-	1.1	-	1.8	0.6	0.9	0.9	-	-	-	0.6	9.3
3. Some of the times	0.4	0.6	-	0.5	-	-	2.3	-	-	-	0.5	-	-	-	0.4	-
4. Most of the times	0.3	0.6	-	0.4	-	-	2.0	-	-	-	0.8	-	-	-	0.4	-
5. Every time	0.2	-	-	-	-	-	1.3	-	-	-	-	-	-	-	0.2	-
Item 4350 Subject A01h N★	352	196	132	272	27	115	55	82	100	157	130	-	-	54	281	16

B085H: With tranquilizers

	TOTAL	M	F	White	Black	NE	NC	S	W	Yes	No	None	Mari- juana Only	Few Pills	More Pills	Any Her- oin
1. Not at all	98.9	98.7	99.4	99.7	98.4	99.6	98.7	97.2	99.4	98.8	99.3	-	-	100.0	99.1	90.7
2. A few of the times	0.8	1.0	0.6	0.3	-	-	-	2.8	0.6	0.9	0.7	-	-	-	0.5	9.3
3. Some of the times	-	-	-	-	-	-	-	-	-	-	-	-	-	-	-	-
4. Most of the times	-	-	-	-	-	-	-	-	-	-	-	-	-	-	-	-
5. Every time	0.3	0.2	-	-	1.6	0.4	1.3	-	-	0.3	-	-	-	-	0.4	-
Item 4360 Subject A01h N★	350	195	132	271	27	115	54	82	100	157	129	-	-	54	280	16

B086: What have been the most important reasons for your taking cocaine? (Mark all that apply.)

	TOTAL	M	F	White	Black	NE	NC	S	W	Yes	No	None	Mari- juana Only	Few Pills	More Pills	Any Her- oin
A. To experiment–to see what it's like	76.6	76.4	77.5	77.7	80.8	70.5	79.1	84.8	75.8	79.4	73.0	-	-	96.9	73.3	64.8
B. To relax or relieve tension	19.7	20.5	18.3	18.6	27.7	24.7	20.1	22.1	11.3	13.0	25.5	-	-	7.1	20.3	53.5
C. To feel good or get high	67.3	69.7	62.6	69.9	41.2	71.0	66.1	59.7	69.8	64.5	68.8	-	-	25.7	74.9	76.2
D. To seek deeper insights and understanding	6.9	7.0	6.0	6.5	-	10.9	4.8	4.3	5.1	4.9	6.8	-	-	1.4	6.7	29.2
E. To have a good time with my friends	49.5	49.5	51.8	52.3	31.4	48.1	44.6	44.1	58.4	53.5	48.0	-	-	16.6	54.1	83.3
F. To fit in with a group I like	6.4	5.4	8.6	4.7	-	4.4	2.5	8.0	9.4	5.5	8.0	-	-	5.0	5.4	30.0
G. To get away from my problems or troubles	10.2	9.8	10.1	9.9	8.2	13.8	7.8	10.0	7.1	6.1	14.2	-	-	6.1	10.4	20.0
H. Because of boredom, nothing else to do	9.7	11.2	5.4	8.8	8.6	8.2	7.2	13.9	9.1	7.5	10.5	-	-	4.3	10.0	23.2
I. Because of anger or frustration	6.8	6.9	5.8	5.6	11.5	9.7	-	11.0	2.9	2.8	10.3	-	-	-	6.8	29.2
J. To get through the day	7.7	9.3	4.8	7.8	6.9	12.0	5.1	9.1	2.7	7.4	9.6	-	-	-	7.8	34.2
K. To increase the effects of some other drug(s)	11.4	13.2	9.4	10.1	14.5	7.0	16.0	14.5	11.8	12.2	10.1	-	-	2.8	11.5	39.2
L. To decrease (offset) the effects of some other drug(s)	3.9	4.8	2.8	3.7	-	3.6	-	4.3	5.9	4.3	4.4	-	-	1.3	3.4	22.6
M. To stay awake	21.7	16.8	26.1	22.0	9.4	22.6	18.2	19.6	24.2	20.1	23.3	-	-	3.9	24.5	35.2
N. To get more energy	33.5	29.4	38.9	34.7	16.2	31.9	31.6	28.2	40.8	35.0	36.6	-	-	4.2	38.9	38.9
O. Because I am "hooked"–I have to have it	2.5	3.8	-	2.1	-	2.1	2.7	5.8	-	0.9	4.8	-	-	-	1.7	24.9
Item 4370-4510 Subject A06a N★	356	201	131	277	26	121	49	86	100	157	128	-	-	56	284	16

B087: When you take cocaine how high do you usually get?

	TOTAL	M	F	White	Black	NE	NC	S	W	Yes	No	None	Mari- juana Only	Few Pills	More Pills	Any Her- oin
1. Not at all high	6.0	6.7	6.2	5.8	9.2	3.7	6.2	7.4	7.5	8.5	4.3	-	-	20.3	3.2	-
2. A little high	23.5	25.2	21.2	23.6	17.8	24.8	20.6	22.2	24.5	21.1	22.5	-	-	41.8	20.9	7.7
3. Moderately high	39.3	38.1	38.8	40.4	25.1	44.5	37.1	40.2	33.1	38.8	35.0	-	-	23.3	43.1	30.3
4. Very high	28.4	28.8	29.0	28.6	35.2	23.0	32.5	28.7	32.7	28.1	34.6	-	-	8.5	31.2	49.0
5. I don't take it to get high	2.8	1.3	4.8	1.6	12.7	3.9	3.6	1.5	2.2	3.5	3.5	-	-	6.1	1.6	12.9
Item 4520 Subject A01e N★	362	205	132	278	27	121	53	89	99	157	132	-	-	56	288	17

B088: When you take cocaine how long do you usually stay high?

	TOTAL	M	F	White	Black	NE	NC	S	W	Yes	No	None	Mari- juana Only	Few Pills	More Pills	Any Her- oin
1. Usually don't get high	9.7	10.8	9.4	9.4	9.8	8.0	5.3	11.3	12.3	12.1	9.3	-	-	27.6	5.6	12.9
2. One to two hours	43.7	47.6	40.7	45.3	33.7	46.8	51.0	43.2	37.2	46.7	40.0	-	-	46.4	45.0	15.5
3. Three to six hours	33.6	31.4	35.5	34.0	42.4	28.9	35.1	31.6	40.4	30.6	36.5	-	-	20.0	36.1	39.7
4. Seven to 24 hours	11.8	9.5	13.8	10.4	14.1	14.7	6.3	12.8	10.1	10.6	12.5	-	-	5.9	11.8	31.9
5. More than 24 hours	1.1	0.7	0.7	0.9	-	1.7	2.3	1.1	-	-	1.6	-	-	-	1.4	-
Item 4530 Subject A01f N★	360	204	133	280	27	120	47	90	103	159	132	-	-	57	285	17

B089: Have you ever tried to stop using cocaine and found that you couldn't stop?

	TOTAL	M	F	White	Black	NE	NC	S	W	Yes	No	None	Mari- juana Only	Few Pills	More Pills	Any Her- oin
1. Yes	4.5	4.7	3.6	3.7	4.8	3.6	-	11.2	1.8	3.8	5.7	-	-	0.3	4.1	25.6
2. No	95.5	95.3	96.4	96.3	95.2	96.4	100.0	88.8	98.2	96.2	94.3	-	-	99.7	95.9	74.4
Item 4540 Subject A01i N★	362	206	132	281	28	120	49	90	103	160	131	-	-	56	288	17

★=excludes respondents for whom question was inappropriate.

QUESTIONNAIRE FORM 1 1984	TOTAL	SEX		RACE		REGION				4YR COLLEGE PLANS		ILLICIT DRUG USE: LIFETIME				
		M	F	White	Black	NE	NC	S	W	Yes	No	None	Marijuana Only	Few Pills	More Pills	Any Heroin
N (Weighted No. of Cases):	3311	1534	1616	2414	478	670	941	1113	587	1772	1137	1223	794	381	765	32
% of Weighted Total:	100.0	46.3	48.8	72.9	14.4	20.2	28.4	33.6	17.7	53.5	34.3	36.9	24.0	11.5	23.1	1.0

B090: What methods have you used for taking cocaine? (Mark all that apply.)

	TOTAL	M	F	White	Black	NE	NC	S	W	Yes	No	None	Marijuana Only	Few Pills	More Pills	Any Heroin
A. Sniffing or "snorting"	96.5	97.1	96.0	98.4	85.2	96.2	100.0	94.2	97.3	97.3	96.1	-	-	87.4	98.9	87.1
B. Smoking	30.2	29.2	31.3	27.0	34.8	30.7	30.8	21.7	36.9	23.4	33.3	-	-	16.7	31.7	50.3
C. Injection	4.0	4.7	2.1	3.8	-	4.1	3.5	8.6	-	1.2	5.6	-	-	1.7	2.3	39.4
D. By mouth	45.1	43.3	47.8	45.7	39.7	51.6	39.2	41.0	43.9	44.4	47.0	-	-	24.4	47.7	70.7
E. Other	4.8	5.5	4.5	5.1	-	7.4	3.3	2.3	4.5	4.2	6.0	-	-	-	5.2	13.8
Item 4550-4590 Subject A05d N★	362	207	133	283	27	121	49	90	103	160	132	-	-	57	288	17

B091: Do you think you will be using cocaine five years from now?

	TOTAL	M	F	White	Black	NE	NC	S	W	Yes	No	None	Marijuana Only	Few Pills	More Pills	Any Heroin
1. I definitely will	1.3	1.2	1.1	1.0	0.9	3.3	0.6	0.8	1.2	0.9	1.3	0.3	0.6	0.8	3.7	10.0
2. I probably will	6.5	7.0	5.6	6.8	2.9	10.2	3.5	4.6	10.6	5.5	6.3	0.4	1.8	5.7	21.6	26.1
3. I probably will not	14.0	16.0	11.8	15.0	8.2	19.6	11.6	11.7	16.3	13.1	14.3	4.0	12.9	19.0	30.2	24.4
4. I definitely will not	78.2	75.7	81.5	77.1	88.0	66.9	84.3	82.9	72.0	80.5	78.1	95.4	84.7	74.5	44.4	39.6
Item 4600 Subject A04a N	3132	1475	1583	2349	457	612	904	1047	569	1731	1104	1189	768	353	714	30

The next questions are about HEROIN, which is sometimes called smack, horse, skag.

B092: On how many occasions (if any) have you taken heroin . . .

B092A: . . . in your lifetime?

	TOTAL	M	F	White	Black	NE	NC	S	W	Yes	No	None	Marijuana Only	Few Pills	More Pills	Any Heroin
1. 0 occasions	99.0	99.3	98.7	99.1	99.5	98.6	99.7	98.9	98.3	99.2	99.2	100.0	100.0	100.0	100.0	-
2. 1-2	0.6	0.2	0.9	0.5	0.5	0.5	0.3	0.7	1.4	0.6	0.4	-	-	-	-	62.3
3. 3-5	0.1	-	0.1	0.1	-	-	-	0.1	0.2	0.1	-	-	-	-	-	6.1
4. 6-9	0.1	0.1	0.1	*	-	0.2	-	0.1	-	-	0.2	-	-	-	-	6.3
5. 10-19	0.1	0.1	*	0.1	-	0.3	-	*	-	-	0.1	-	-	-	-	7.3
6. 20-39	0.1	0.1	0.1	0.1	-	0.1	-	0.1	-	-	0.1	-	-	-	-	6.5
7. 40 or more	0.1	0.2	*	0.1	-	0.3	-	0.1	0.1	0.1	-	-	-	-	-	11.6
Item 1100 Subject A01a N	3083	1451	1563	2333	438	604	892	1024	563	1718	1084	1195	755	353	699	32

B092B: . . . during the last 12 months?

	TOTAL	M	F	White	Black	NE	NC	S	W	Yes	No	None	Marijuana Only	Few Pills	More Pills	Any Heroin
1. 0 occasions	99.5	99.5	99.6	99.7	99.5	99.2	100.0	99.4	99.5	99.6	99.8	100.0	100.0	100.0	100.0	53.9
2. 1-2	0.2	0.1	0.3	0.1	0.5	0.1	-	0.3	0.4	0.3	-	-	-	-	-	20.6
3. 3-5	-	-	-	-	-	-	-	-	-	-	-	-	-	-	-	-
4. 6-9	0.1	0.1	*	0.1	-	0.2	-	0.1	-	-	0.1	-	-	-	-	7.6
5. 10-19	0.1	0.1	*	0.1	-	0.5	-	-	-	-	0.1	-	-	-	-	9.3
6. 20-39	0.1	0.1	*	*	-	0.1	-	0.1	-	0.1	-	-	-	-	-	6.7
7. 40 or more	*	*	-	*	-	-	-	-	0.1	*	-	-	-	-	-	2.0
Item 1110 Subject A01b N	3082	1451	1563	2333	438	605	892	1023	563	1718	1084	1195	755	354	699	30

B092C: . . . during the last 30 days?

	TOTAL	M	F	White	Black	NE	NC	S	W	Yes	No	None	Marijuana Only	Few Pills	More Pills	Any Heroin
1. 0 occasions	99.7	99.6	99.7	99.8	100.0	99.3	100.0	99.7	99.6	99.8	99.8	100.0	100.0	100.0	100.0	69.1
2. 1-2	0.1	0.1	0.2	0.1	-	0.3	-	*	0.4	0.1	-	-	-	-	-	13.9
3. 3-5	0.1	0.2	*	0.1	-	0.3	-	0.2	-	0.1	0.1	-	-	-	-	13.6
4. 6-9	-	-	-	-	-	-	-	-	-	-	-	-	-	-	-	-
5. 10-19	*	0.1	-	*	-	0.2	-	-	-	-	0.1	-	-	-	-	3.4
6. 20-39	-	-	-	-	-	-	-	-	-	-	-	-	-	-	-	-
7. 40 or more	-	-	-	-	-	-	-	-	-	-	-	-	-	-	-	-
Item 1120 Subject A01c N	3083	1452	1563	2333	438	605	892	1023	563	1718	1084	1195	755	355	699	30

The next questions are about NARCOTICS OTHER THAN HEROIN, which are sometimes prescribed by doctors. Drugstores are not supposed to sell them without a prescription. These include:

Methadone, Codeine, Talwin, Morphine, Opium, Demerol, Laudanum, Paregoric.

*=less than .05 per cent.   ★=excludes respondents for whom question was inappropriate.

QUESTIONNAIRE FORM 1 1984	TOTAL	SEX		RACE		REGION				4YR COLLEGE PLANS		ILLICIT DRUG USE: LIFETIME				
		M	F	White	Black	NE	NC	S	W	Yes	No	None	Marijuana Only	Few Pills	More Pills	Any Heroin
N (Weighted No. of Cases):	3311	1534	1616	2414	478	670	941	1113	587	1772	1137	1223	794	381	765	32
% of Weighted Total:	100.0	46.3	48.8	72.9	14.4	20.2	28.4	33.6	17.7	53.5	34.3	36.9	24.0	11.5	23.1	1.0

B093: Have you ever taken any narcotics other than heroin because a doctor told you to use them?

	TOTAL	M	F	White	Black	NE	NC	S	W	Yes	No	None	Marijuana Only	Few Pills	More Pills	Any Heroin
1. No	81.4	82.3	80.3	77.9	95.9	81.2	80.6	83.7	78.9	79.5	83.6	87.7	86.2	74.5	69.7	60.8
2. Yes, but I had already tried them on my own.	2.3	3.4	1.4	2.4	1.1	2.4	2.1	2.3	2.7	1.9	2.5	-	0.2	0.7	8.2	29.5
3. Yes, and it was the first time I took any	16.3	14.3	18.4	19.7	3.1	16.4	17.3	14.1	18.5	18.6	14.0	12.3	13.6	24.8	22.2	9.7
Item 5020 Subject A01j N	3034	1428	1542	2306	428	589	892	1004	549	1699	1073	1166	744	350	690	29

B094: On how many occasions (if any) have you taken narcotics other than heroin on your own–that is, without a doctor telling you to take them . . .

B094A: . . . in your lifetime?

	TOTAL	M	F	White	Black	NE	NC	S	W	Yes	No	None	Marijuana Only	Few Pills	More Pills	Any Heroin
1. 0 occasions	90.8	89.4	92.3	89.4	97.8	88.5	91.8	93.3	87.2	90.9	92.0	100.0	100.0	84.9	69.8	38.8
2. 1-2	4.0	4.7	3.2	4.6	1.1	5.6	3.4	2.8	5.4	4.0	3.6	-	-	15.1	9.0	24.0
3. 3-5	2.2	2.1	2.3	2.6	-	2.5	1.3	2.1	3.7	2.4	2.0	-	-	-	9.4	8.7
4. 6-9	1.1	1.6	0.7	1.2	0.8	1.8	1.0	1.1	0.4	1.0	0.9	-	-	-	4.6	3.8
5. 10-19	0.9	1.2	0.5	1.0	-	0.7	0.9	0.3	2.0	1.0	0.5	-	-	-	3.3	12.0
6. 20-39	0.5	0.4	0.6	0.6	-	0.7	0.8	0.2	0.2	0.3	0.6	-	-	-	1.9	6.5
7. 40 or more	0.5	0.7	0.4	0.6	0.3	0.1	0.7	0.3	1.1	0.4	0.4	-	-	-	2.1	6.2
Item 1130 Subject A01a N	3063	1453	1543	2323	435	601	895	1013	554	1708	1079	1183	751	357	691	31

B094B: . . . during the last 12 months?

	TOTAL	M	F	White	Black	NE	NC	S	W	Yes	No	None	Marijuana Only	Few Pills	More Pills	Any Heroin
1. 0 occasions	95.5	94.4	96.7	94.8	99.2	93.4	95.3	97.0	95.3	95.7	96.2	100.0	100.0	94.5	84.0	72.9
2. 1-2	2.4	3.1	1.7	2.7	0.2	3.7	2.0	1.6	3.3	2.4	2.1	-	-	5.5	7.6	8.0
3. 3-5	0.9	1.1	0.6	1.1	-	1.6	0.9	0.7	0.4	0.8	0.9	-	-	-	3.9	-
4. 6-9	0.5	0.9	0.2	0.6	0.3	0.7	0.8	0.3	0.4	0.5	0.3	-	-	-	2.3	3.8
5. 10-19	0.3	0.3	0.4	0.4	-	0.5	0.6	*	0.2	0.2	0.4	-	-	-	1.0	10.5
6. 20-39	0.3	0.2	0.4	0.3	0.3	0.1	0.3	0.3	0.3	0.3	0.1	-	-	-	1.2	-
7. 40 or more	*	0.1	-	-	-	-	-	0.1	-	0.1	-	-	-	-	-	4.8
Item 1140 Subject A01b N	3060	1452	1541	2320	435	601	893	1012	554	1706	1078	1183	751	356	688	31

B094C: . . . during the last 30 days?

	TOTAL	M	F	White	Black	NE	NC	S	W	Yes	No	None	Marijuana Only	Few Pills	More Pills	Any Heroin
1. 0 occasions	98.5	98.3	98.7	98.3	99.4	99.0	97.8	98.8	98.4	98.8	98.5	100.0	100.0	99.7	94.3	80.9
2. 1-2	0.8	0.9	0.7	1.0	-	0.4	1.0	0.7	1.3	0.7	0.8	-	-	0.3	3.5	-
3. 3-5	0.4	0.5	0.3	0.4	0.3	0.1	0.8	0.3	0.1	0.2	0.5	-	-	-	1.3	7.7
4. 6-9	0.1	0.1	0.1	0.1	-	0.2	0.2	-	0.1	0.1	-	-	-	-	0.3	3.3
5. 10-19	0.2	0.2	0.1	0.1	0.3	0.3	0.2	0.2	-	0.1	0.2	-	-	-	0.4	8.1
6. 20-39	*	-	*	*	-	-	-	0.1	-	*	-	-	-	-	0.1	-
7. 40 or more	-	-	-	-	-	-	-	-	-	-	-	-	-	-	-	-
Item 1150 Subject A01c N	3058	1450	1541	2318	435	599	893	1012	554	1704	1078	1183	751	356	686	31

IF YOU HAVE NOT TAKEN NARCOTICS OTHER THAN HEROIN IN THE LAST TWELVE MONTHS, GO TO Q.B103.

THE FOLLOWING QUESTIONS REFER ONLY TO TAKING NARCOTICS OTHER THAN HEROIN WITHOUT A DOCTOR'S ORDERS. IF YOU HAVE NOT DONE THIS IN THE LAST TWELVE MONTHS, GO TO Q.B103.

B095: When you used narcotics other than heroin during the last year, how often did you use them in each of the following situations?

B095A: When you were alone

	TOTAL	M	F	White	Black	NE	NC	S	W	Yes	No	None	Marijuana Only	Few Pills	More Pills	Any Heroin
1. Not at all	46.2	48.1	41.3	48.8	24.3	55.1	53.5	20.0	52.9	40.1	54.4	-	-	75.6	41.9	39.7
2. A few of the times	29.4	29.3	32.6	32.1	31.6	27.7	27.1	37.1	26.6	29.2	30.1	-	-	20.8	32.9	5.6
3. Some of the times	9.6	7.9	13.1	9.2	44.1	5.6	10.3	15.4	7.2	13.6	2.6	-	-	-	9.0	35.7
4. Most of the times	7.8	9.3	6.2	5.1	-	7.4	1.3	12.4	13.2	7.3	7.4	-	-	-	8.1	19.0
5. Every time	7.0	5.4	6.8	4.8	-	4.2	7.8	15.1	-	9.8	5.6	-	-	3.6	8.1	-
Item 5030 Subject A05a N★	123	72	46	106	5	33	37	28	24	65	40	-	-	14	100	8

*=less than .05 per cent.   ★=excludes respondents for whom question was inappropriate.

QUESTIONNAIRE FORM 1 1984	TOTAL	SEX		RACE		REGION				4YR COLLEGE PLANS		ILLICIT DRUG USE: LIFETIME				
		M	F	White	Black	NE	NC	S	W	Yes	No	None	Marijuana Only	Few Pills	More Pills	Any Heroin
N (Weighted No. of Cases):	3311	1534	1616	2414	478	670	941	1113	587	1772	1137	1223	794	381	765	32
% of Weighted Total:	100.0	46.3	48.8	72.9	14.4	20.2	28.4	33.6	17.7	53.5	34.3	36.9	24.0	11.5	23.1	1.0

B095B: With just 1 or 2 other people

1. Not at all	26.8	22.7	32.6	26.6	24.3	20.8	24.1	44.5	19.2	29.6	16.2	-	-	43.9	23.3	30.5
2. A few of the times	33.2	32.6	32.9	34.3	-	35.7	31.1	21.3	46.4	29.6	40.1	-	-	38.3	35.4	-
3. Some of the times	16.0	13.3	22.0	17.2	31.6	16.0	18.1	11.3	18.4	19.3	9.1	-	-	-	18.2	18.7
4. Most of the times	15.6	23.1	5.0	14.7	44.1	15.1	19.6	16.7	8.8	12.3	25.9	-	-	-	16.5	34.0
5. Every time	8.5	8.3	7.4	7.2	-	12.5	7.1	6.2	7.3	9.2	8.6	-	-	17.8	6.6	16.8
Item 5040 Subject A05b N★	123	73	45	107	5	34	37	27	24	65	40	-	-	14	101	8

B095C: At a party

1. Not at all	56.4	53.0	61.8	54.1	50.1	46.0	59.2	72.4	48.5	67.2	41.0	-	-	77.3	55.1	31.8
2. A few of the times	17.0	17.9	12.9	18.6	-	28.3	8.0	7.6	25.7	12.8	25.4	-	-	6.6	19.4	5.6
3. Some of the times	9.2	12.9	4.4	10.7	-	13.7	8.8	4.1	9.5	4.6	17.3	-	-	-	10.3	13.1
4. Most of the times	10.1	8.2	14.1	10.3	31.6	6.9	19.2	5.8	4.9	9.7	13.2	-	-	-	11.5	9.8
5. Every time	7.3	8.1	6.7	6.3	18.3	5.1	4.8	10.1	11.4	5.8	3.0	-	-	16.1	3.7	39.7
Item 5050 Subject A05c N★	122	72	45	105	5	33	37	27	24	64	40	-	-	13	100	8

B095D: When your date or spouse was present

1. Not at all	80.0	80.3	77.6	81.6	74.2	77.6	77.5	84.6	82.4	85.0	80.9	-	-	86.9	81.8	43.1
2. A few of the times	9.1	6.8	13.4	8.3	25.8	10.3	10.8	4.3	9.9	5.7	7.8	-	-	6.5	9.0	15.0
3. Some of the times	4.7	6.4	2.5	4.0	-	5.6	1.4	5.5	7.7	5.4	4.2	-	-	6.5	2.3	32.1
4. Most of the times	4.0	4.8	3.3	4.7	-	2.1	7.0	5.6	-	2.8	4.0	-	-	-	4.9	-
5. Every time	2.2	1.7	3.2	1.4	-	4.3	3.2	-	-	1.1	3.2	-	-	-	1.9	9.8
Item 5060 Subject A05b N★	120	70	45	104	5	33	37	27	22	64	38	-	-	13	98	8

B095E: When people over age 30 were present

1. Not at all	56.6	66.5	36.4	57.3	24.3	55.7	58.6	58.4	52.7	53.9	63.5	-	-	77.1	53.5	43.0
2. A few of the times	21.4	17.6	29.6	23.2	25.8	23.4	15.4	24.2	24.5	22.2	20.6	-	-	16.7	22.2	28.2
3. Some of the times	7.5	7.2	8.6	4.9	31.6	10.1	5.2	1.4	14.4	8.3	4.9	-	-	6.3	8.5	-
4. Most of the times	8.3	3.7	16.4	8.8	18.3	4.7	18.1	6.7	-	6.9	5.9	-	-	-	9.5	9.8
5. Every time	6.3	5.0	9.0	5.9	-	6.1	2.7	9.3	8.4	8.9	5.1	-	-	-	6.3	19.0
Item 5070 Subject A05b N★	125	75	46	108	5	34	37	29	25	65	41	-	-	14	101	8

B095F: During the daytime (before 4:00 p.m.)

1. Not at all	44.3	46.1	39.3	43.4	42.7	55.2	24.8	42.1	61.9	40.8	47.5	-	-	85.3	37.6	34.4
2. A few of the times	22.6	21.4	26.8	24.3	31.6	21.2	34.6	18.5	11.1	27.0	17.0	-	-	8.4	25.6	17.8
3. Some of the times	22.5	21.8	22.5	22.6	25.8	14.8	21.1	34.2	21.5	24.8	17.6	-	-	6.3	25.2	26.0
4. Most of the times	7.5	7.9	7.7	7.4	-	3.7	16.3	5.1	2.2	6.1	10.6	-	-	-	7.8	21.9
5. Every time	3.0	2.8	3.6	2.4	-	5.2	3.2	-	3.3	1.3	7.3	-	-	-	3.7	-
Item 5080 Subject A05c N★	124	74	46	107	5	33	37	29	25	65	40	-	-	14	101	7

B095G: At your home (or apartment or dorm)

1. Not at all	39.0	45.2	28.4	39.4	24.3	55.8	30.1	28.3	42.6	37.5	45.1	-	-	47.7	36.2	34.4
2. A few of the times	20.8	27.6	11.8	23.6	-	25.7	19.0	19.1	19.0	24.3	12.1	-	-	29.4	21.3	6.4
3. Some of the times	10.9	10.4	12.9	10.6	49.9	4.9	16.3	6.7	15.4	6.8	17.4	-	-	-	12.1	20.1
4. Most of the times	12.9	8.3	18.4	10.1	25.8	2.6	9.9	29.4	12.2	15.2	9.9	-	-	6.5	12.4	39.1
5. Every time	16.4	8.6	28.5	16.3	-	11.0	24.7	16.4	10.7	16.2	15.5	-	-	16.4	18.0	-
Item 5090 Subject A05c N★	123	73	45	105	5	32	37	28	25	64	40	-	-	13	100	7

B095H: At school

1. Not at all	64.9	59.6	70.2	65.2	42.7	67.8	58.1	63.7	72.7	65.9	63.1	-	-	93.5	60.0	66.0
2. A few of the times	18.7	19.4	19.3	21.7	-	23.4	19.2	16.1	14.3	19.3	17.1	-	-	6.5	22.3	-
3. Some of the times	10.8	15.2	4.8	10.5	25.8	8.8	14.3	9.7	9.8	10.0	11.4	-	-	-	12.3	15.0
4. Most of the times	3.0	2.6	4.0	0.8	31.6	-	5.1	6.6	-	3.0	3.5	-	-	-	2.3	19.0
5. Every time	2.5	3.1	1.8	1.8	-	-	3.2	3.9	3.3	1.7	5.0	-	-	-	3.1	-
Item 5100 Subject A05c N★	124	74	46	107	5	34	37	28	25	64	41	-	-	13	100	8

★=excludes respondents for whom question was inappropriate.

QUESTIONNAIRE FORM 1 1984	TOTAL	SEX		RACE		REGION				4YR COLLEGE PLANS		ILLICIT DRUG USE: LIFETIME				
		M	F	White	Black	NE	NC	S	W	Yes	No	None	Mari- juana Only	Few Pills	More Pills	Any Her- oin
N (Weighted No. of Cases):	3311	1534	1616	2414	478	670	941	1113	587	1772	1137	1223	794	381	765	32
% of Weighted Total:	100.0	46.3	48.8	72.9	14.4	20.2	28.4	33.6	17.7	53.5	34.3	36.9	24.0	11.5	23.1	1.0
B095I: In a car																
1. Not at all	72.5	65.7	84.2	71.9	100.0	70.5	73.0	77.3	69.1	73.8	73.4	-	-	94.5	69.0	69.4
2. A few of the times	19.5	21.7	14.6	20.2	-	27.3	23.0	5.3	19.9	19.4	15.8	-	-	-	23.4	8.7
3. Some of the times	2.6	4.4	-	3.1	-	-	-	9.4	2.4	2.4	1.5	-	-	-	3.2	-
4. Most of the times	4.3	7.2	-	3.6	-	-	4.0	8.0	6.2	3.5	7.6	-	-	-	3.8	21.9
5. Every time	1.1	1.0	1.3	1.2	-	2.2	-	-	2.4	0.9	1.8	-	-	5.5	0.6	-
Item 5120 Subject A05c N★	123	73	46	106	5	33	37	28	25	64	40	-	-	13	100	7
B096: How many of the times when you used narcotics other than heroin during the last year did you use them along with each of the following drugs–that is, so that their effects over- lapped?																
B096A: With alcohol																
1. Not at all	54.1	48.9	60.8	55.9	24.3	57.1	52.8	65.9	39.6	54.6	56.0	-	-	75.1	52.2	16.8
2. A few of the times	17.1	18.3	17.5	18.2	-	4.8	20.8	16.6	27.0	20.9	13.1	-	-	3.5	20.6	5.6
3. Some of the times	10.7	12.8	8.6	10.7	44.1	11.9	11.2	12.4	6.4	8.2	6.5	-	-	-	11.6	24.8
4. Most of the times	11.6	11.8	8.1	8.7	31.6	9.7	12.6	-	24.7	6.2	21.8	-	-	21.4	10.7	7.6
5. Every time	6.6	8.2	5.1	6.5	-	16.4	2.6	5.1	2.2	10.1	2.6	-	-	-	4.9	45.2
Item 5130 Subject A01h N★	128	76	46	109	5	33	40	29	27	64	40	-	-	16	102	8
B096B: With marijuana																
1. Not at all	54.7	50.0	62.6	53.1	55.9	55.8	42.1	71.3	54.4	67.1	38.0	-	-	90.4	49.8	38.7
2. A few of the times	15.6	14.2	15.3	16.0	-	24.9	7.6	13.1	18.3	10.0	21.7	-	-	4.2	18.2	6.1
3. Some of the times	7.2	9.6	3.8	8.3	-	4.5	10.8	-	13.6	5.2	4.6	-	-	-	8.9	-
4. Most of the times	13.1	17.9	6.2	14.1	25.8	5.1	28.4	7.1	6.3	6.6	25.9	-	-	-	13.2	41.0
5. Every time	9.4	8.3	12.1	8.5	18.3	9.6	11.1	8.5	7.3	11.0	9.8	-	-	5.5	9.8	14.2
Item 5140 Subject A01h N★	127	78	45	110	5	35	40	28	24	65	41	-	-	13	104	7
B096C: With LSD																
1. Not at all	96.8	95.8	98.2	97.8	100.0	97.6	95.7	94.7	100.0	97.7	95.9	-	-	100.0	98.4	66.8
2. A few of the times	1.9	2.1	1.8	2.2	-	2.4	4.3	-	-	-	4.1	-	-	-	1.6	11.3
3. Some of the times	-	-	-	-	-	-	-	-	-	-	-	-	-	-	-	-
4. Most of the times	1.2	2.1	-	-	-	-	-	5.3	-	2.3	-	-	-	-	-	21.9
5. Every time	-	-	-	-	-	-	-	-	-	-	-	-	-	-	-	-
Item 5150 Subject A01h N★	119	71	44	104	3	31	35	28	25	63	37	-	-	14	96	7
B096D: With psychedelics other than LSD																
1. Not at all	96.7	94.4	100.0	97.6	100.0	96.9	95.8	94.4	100.0	97.7	93.5	-	-	100.0	98.4	67.9
2. A few of the times	1.2	2.1	-	-	-	-	-	5.6	-	2.3	-	-	-	-	-	19.0
3. Some of the times	-	-	-	-	-	-	-	-	-	-	-	-	-	-	-	-
4. Most of the times	1.3	2.1	-	1.5	-	-	4.2	-	-	-	3.9	-	-	-	1.6	-
5. Every time	0.8	1.4	-	1.0	-	3.1	-	-	-	-	2.6	-	-	-	-	13.1
Item 5160 Subject A01h N★	120	72	44	104	4	33	36	27	25	64	39	-	-	13	97	8
B096E: With amphetamines																
1. Not at all	92.7	94.2	89.4	92.9	100.0	97.3	85.8	92.0	97.6	87.6	97.7	-	-	100.0	92.5	78.1
2. A few of the times	4.8	3.7	7.0	5.6	-	2.7	9.9	2.7	2.4	7.7	2.3	-	-	-	5.9	-
3. Some of the times	0.4	-	1.1	0.5	-	-	1.3	-	-	0.8	-	-	-	-	0.5	-
4. Most of the times	1.2	2.0	-	-	-	-	-	5.2	-	2.3	-	-	-	-	-	21.9
5. Every time	0.9	-	2.5	1.1	-	-	3.0	-	-	1.7	-	-	-	-	1.1	-
Item 5170 Subject A01h N★	121	72	44	104	5	32	36	28	25	64	38	-	-	13	98	7
B096F: With quaaludes																
1. Not at all	92.2	88.4	98.0	92.4	100.0	94.0	87.7	89.0	100.0	96.5	87.1	-	-	100.0	92.8	67.9
2. A few of the times	2.6	3.1	2.0	3.0	-	3.0	1.6	5.7	-	1.2	6.4	-	-	-	3.2	-
3. Some of the times	2.0	3.2	-	2.3	-	-	6.6	-	-	-	-	-	-	-	2.5	-
4. Most of the times	1.2	2.0	-	1.4	-	-	4.1	-	-	-	3.9	-	-	-	1.5	-
5. Every time	2.0	3.3	-	0.9	-	3.0	-	5.2	-	2.3	2.6	-	-	-	-	32.1
Item 5180 Subject A01h N★	124	77	43	108	3	34	37	28	25	64	39	-	-	13	101	8

★=excludes respondents for whom question was inappropriate.

QUESTIONNAIRE FORM 1 1984	TOTAL	SEX		RACE		REGION				4YR COLLEGE PLANS		ILLICIT DRUG USE: LIFETIME				
		M	F	White	Black	NE	NC	S	W	Yes	No	None	Marijuana Only	Few Pills	More Pills	Any Heroin
N (Weighted No. of Cases):	3311	1534	1616	2414	478	670	941	1113	587	1772	1137	1223	794	381	765	32
% of Weighted Total:	100.0	46.3	48.8	72.9	14.4	20.2	28.4	33.6	17.7	53.5	34.3	36.9	24.0	11.5	23.1	1.0
B096G: With barbiturates																
1. Not at all	95.3	93.4	98.1	95.9	100.0	96.9	93.6	91.5	100.0	97.7	95.2	-	-	100.0	96.7	67.9
2. A few of the times	0.7	-	1.9	0.8	-	-	-	3.1	-	-	2.2	-	-	-	0.8	-
3. Some of the times	2.0	3.3	-	2.3	-	-	6.4	-	-	-	-	-	-	-	2.5	-
4. Most of the times	1.2	2.0	-	-	-	-	-	5.4	-	2.3	-	-	-	-	-	19.0
5. Every time	0.8	1.4	-	1.0	-	3.1	-	-	-	-	2.6	-	-	-	-	13.1
Item 5190 Subject A01h N★	124	75	44	107	5	33	39	27	25	64	39	-	-	13	100	8
B096H: With tranquilizers																
1. Not at all	97.1	97.9	95.7	98.1	100.0	100.0	100.0	87.6	100.0	95.9	97.7	-	-	100.0	98.0	78.1
2. A few of the times	2.9	2.1	4.3	1.9	-	-	-	12.4	-	4.1	2.3	-	-	-	2.0	21.9
3. Some of the times	-	-	-	-	-	-	-	-	-	-	-	-	-	-	-	-
4. Most of the times	-	-	-	-	-	-	-	-	-	-	-	-	-	-	-	-
5. Every time	-	-	-	-	-	-	-	-	-	-	-	-	-	-	-	-
Item 5200 Subject A01h N★	119	70	44	102	5	32	35	27	24	63	38	-	-	13	96	7
B096I: With cocaine																
1. Not at all	87.0	86.6	90.7	88.8	81.7	94.0	86.9	86.1	79.3	91.4	86.1	-	-	85.3	88.3	67.9
2. A few of the times	7.6	5.8	6.9	5.6	-	3.0	1.6	11.0	18.5	6.9	7.6	-	-	14.7	5.9	19.0
3. Some of the times	3.0	4.3	1.1	2.7	18.3	-	7.6	2.9	-	0.8	-	-	-	-	3.7	-
4. Most of the times	1.7	2.0	1.3	1.9	-	-	3.9	-	2.2	0.9	3.8	-	-	-	2.1	-
5. Every time	0.8	1.3	-	0.9	-	3.0	-	-	-	-	2.5	-	-	-	-	13.1
Item 5210 Subject A01h N★	128	77	44	108	5	34	39	28	27	64	40	-	-	15	102	8
B096J: With heroin																
1. Not at all	97.9	96.6	100.0	99.0	100.0	96.9	100.0	94.6	100.0	97.7	97.4	-	-	100.0	100.0	67.9
2. A few of the times	-	-	-	-	-	-	-	-	-	-	-	-	-	-	-	-
3. Some of the times	-	-	-	-	-	-	-	-	-	-	-	-	-	-	-	-
4. Most of the times	1.2	2.0	-	-	-	-	-	5.4	-	2.3	-	-	-	-	-	19.0
5. Every time	0.8	1.4	-	1.0	-	3.1	-	-	-	-	2.6	-	-	-	-	13.1
Item 5220 Subject A01h N★	121	72	44	104	5	33	36	27	25	64	39	-	-	13	98	8
B097: What have been the most important reasons for your using narcotics other than heroin without a doctor's orders? (Mark all that apply.)																
A. To experiment–to see what it's like	50.4	58.9	34.8	51.1	58.3	60.6	48.4	37.5	52.9	48.9	49.4	-	-	67.1	46.0	79.3
B. To relax or relieve tension	44.6	37.5	55.1	40.5	75.8	32.4	42.4	45.8	65.0	54.2	42.8	-	-	21.7	46.9	52.7
C. To feel good or get high	48.1	58.7	31.3	48.7	75.8	51.7	46.4	40.2	54.5	38.1	63.1	-	-	36.0	46.7	86.8
D. To seek deeper insights and understanding	2.9	4.8	-	1.9	-	3.0	-	5.7	4.2	4.0	2.6	-	-	-	1.0	32.1
E. To have a good time with my friends	23.9	30.0	16.4	24.0	34.1	36.5	16.0	22.5	20.1	26.5	19.1	-	-	15.2	21.5	70.0
F. To fit in with a group I like	1.8	2.0	1.5	0.6	-	2.0	-	5.7	-	3.5	-	-	-	-	0.7	19.0
G. To get away from my problems or troubles	13.6	10.5	20.1	12.8	41.7	13.0	14.9	18.5	6.8	15.7	16.2	-	-	17.4	11.3	37.7
H. Because of boredom, nothing else to do	8.5	14.2	-	8.3	-	9.3	6.7	5.7	13.3	8.5	10.4	-	-	-	7.8	32.1
I. Because of anger or frustration	9.8	6.9	15.5	8.4	41.7	5.1	8.1	19.0	9.1	12.7	10.1	-	-	17.4	7.1	32.1
J. To get through the day	8.7	6.9	12.7	7.3	41.7	8.5	8.1	5.7	13.5	9.3	12.2	-	-	-	7.5	39.7
K. To increase the effects of some other drug(s)	9.9	14.3	3.7	8.8	34.1	7.6	11.7	16.3	3.2	12.1	8.0	-	-	-	8.3	47.1
L. To decrease (offset) the effects of some other drug(s)	2.7	4.5	-	1.7	-	3.0	-	5.7	3.2	2.4	4.4	-	-	-	0.7	32.1
M. To get to sleep	23.2	14.7	37.2	23.2	-	20.7	11.5	38.6	29.3	19.0	27.7	-	-	13.4	23.8	32.1
N. As a substitute for heroin	3.7	5.6	1.0	2.8	-	3.0	4.0	7.4	-	2.4	6.4	-	-	-	1.5	37.7
O. To relieve physical pain	47.8	43.9	53.5	47.1	34.1	41.2	42.6	57.7	55.3	51.1	42.0	-	-	24.5	49.5	64.5
P. To control coughing	16.1	12.4	23.9	15.0	-	14.3	21.2	20.9	5.1	16.1	18.5	-	-	4.6	15.8	39.7
Q. Because I am "hooked"–I have to have it	-	-	-	-	-	-	-	-	-	-	-	-	-	-	-	-
Item 5230-5370 Subject A06a N★	121	72	44	106	3	34	38	26	23	61	40	-	-	13	101	8

★=excludes respondents for whom question was inappropriate.

QUESTIONNAIRE FORM 1 1984	TOTAL	SEX		RACE		REGION				4YR COLLEGE PLANS		ILLICIT DRUG USE: LIFETIME				
		M	F	White	Black	NE	NC	S	W	Yes	No	None	Mari-juana Only	Few Pills	More Pills	Any Her-oin
N (Weighted No. of Cases):	3311	1534	1616	2414	478	670	941	1113	587	1772	1137	1223	794	381	765	32
% of Weighted Total:	100.0	46.3	48.8	72.9	14.4	20.2	28.4	33.6	17.7	53.5	34.3	36.9	24.0	11.5	23.1	1.0

B098: When you take narcotics other than heroin how high do you usually get?

1. Not at all high	7.5	7.5	8.2	6.9	24.3	7.5	8.4	9.9	3.2	11.7	4.5	-	-	12.0	5.8	-
2. A little high	29.4	24.7	35.8	30.2	25.8	28.1	24.4	32.8	35.8	23.8	33.0	-	-	6.5	34.0	15.0
3. Moderately high	28.1	34.0	21.0	29.6	49.9	38.2	29.0	22.0	18.8	26.5	26.6	-	-	18.9	28.5	45.3
4. Very high	12.5	16.9	6.3	11.5	-	10.6	18.3	8.5	9.7	10.6	20.6	-	-	-	12.8	32.1
5. I don't take them to get high	22.5	16.9	28.7	21.8	-	15.5	19.9	26.7	32.5	27.4	15.3	-	-	62.6	18.9	7.6
Item 5380 Subject A01e N★	125	76	45	108	5	35	40	26	24	64	40	-	-	13	102	8

B099: When you take narcotics other than heroin how long do you usually stay high?

1. Usually don't get high	23.2	19.7	27.8	21.2	24.3	23.2	22.7	29.2	17.1	29.1	16.9	-	-	51.1	19.9	7.6
2. One to two hours	29.3	30.4	23.9	31.8	-	29.3	28.5	23.9	36.6	25.3	29.7	-	-	30.1	30.5	16.8
3. Three to six hours	38.1	39.3	40.2	39.7	25.8	41.7	35.9	33.9	41.5	39.2	39.6	-	-	9.6	41.4	51.0
4. Seven to 24 hours	8.8	10.7	6.6	6.6	49.9	3.7	12.9	13.0	4.8	5.3	13.8	-	-	9.3	7.6	24.6
5. More than 24 hours	0.6	-	1.5	0.6	-	2.0	-	-	-	1.1	-	-	-	-	0.7	-
Item 5390 Subject A01f N★	121	72	45	105	5	33	37	27	24	63	40	-	-	13	99	8

B100: What narcotics other than heroin have you taken during the last year without a doctor's orders? (Mark all that apply.)

A. Methadone	12.9	12.9	14.2	13.3	-	14.2	14.4	9.9	12.2	14.0	12.5	-	-	-	10.5	62.6
B. Opium	39.9	46.6	28.7	38.2	65.9	42.7	45.0	30.9	38.5	33.2	53.1	-	-	21.2	40.6	60.6
C. Morphine	20.0	16.3	28.0	18.8	41.7	26.9	20.1	11.6	19.5	24.5	18.9	-	-	7.4	18.7	55.1
D. Codeine	85.2	85.8	89.8	85.5	58.3	75.6	82.8	87.6	100.0	85.4	84.9	-	-	80.7	85.6	86.9
E. Demerol	19.5	18.2	21.4	17.0	58.3	23.0	8.9	27.5	22.2	22.6	12.3	-	-	8.5	19.1	41.3
F. Paregoric	3.1	5.2	-	2.1	-	3.2	-	10.0	-	4.3	2.7	-	-	-	1.1	32.1
G. Talwin	7.4	8.7	6.1	4.4	75.8	6.4	10.9	10.2	-	4.4	11.5	-	-	-	4.0	60.2
H. Laudanum	3.5	5.8	-	2.5	-	3.2	4.3	5.7	-	2.4	6.7	-	-	-	1.6	32.1
I. Other	10.2	11.0	10.0	11.7	-	9.5	6.9	12.3	13.9	9.5	14.6	-	-	-	11.2	13.1
J. Don't know the names of some I have used	14.7	10.5	18.3	14.7	-	28.2	6.7	9.0	14.5	15.0	13.2	-	-	-	14.3	42.0
Item 5400-5490 Subject A01l N★	116	69	42	101	3	32	36	26	22	60	38	-	-	12	96	8

B101: Have you ever tried to stop using narcotics other than heroin and found that you couldn't stop?

1. Yes	3.1	3.5	2.8	2.2	-	3.1	3.5	5.5	-	2.3	5.8	-	-	-	1.3	32.1
2. No	96.9	96.5	97.2	97.8	100.0	96.9	96.5	94.5	100.0	97.7	94.2	-	-	100.0	98.7	67.9
Item 5500 Subject A01i N★	122	72	46	105	5	33	37	27	25	64	40	-	-	13	99	8

B102: What methods have you used for taking any of these narcotics other than heroin? (Mark all that apply.)

A. Sniffing or "snorting"	17.6	19.1	16.8	14.5	100.0	27.8	15.6	15.1	8.3	12.8	15.8	-	-	9.7	14.1	75.6
B. Smoking	31.6	38.2	19.2	31.2	24.2	32.5	41.9	21.8	23.6	26.0	40.4	-	-	19.7	31.8	47.5
C. Injection	7.1	8.2	5.9	5.4	41.7	13.8	5.2	7.4	-	2.3	12.9	-	-	-	3.9	60.6
D. By mouth	84.0	83.4	87.7	83.1	58.3	66.9	85.4	90.1	100.0	85.6	78.0	-	-	80.3	84.6	81.3
E. Other	6.8	9.8	2.5	7.7	-	8.4	13.9	-	-	6.1	5.2	-	-	6.9	6.3	13.1
Item 5510-5550 Subject A05d N★	123	74	44	108	3	35	39	26	23	63	39	-	-	13	103	8

B103: Do you think you will be using any narcotics other than heroin without a doctor's orders five years from now?

1. I definitely will	0.7	0.4	0.8	0.4	0.7	0.6	0.5	1.0	0.4	0.5	0.7	0.4	0.6	0.5	1.0	9.2
2. I probably will	1.3	1.7	1.0	1.0	1.0	1.1	1.0	1.6	0.9	1.1	1.4	*	0.3	-	5.3	4.3
3. I probably will not	15.6	16.3	14.4	16.8	9.9	19.7	12.5	15.1	17.1	14.4	16.1	6.0	11.1	20.3	34.5	39.0
4. I definitely will not	82.5	81.6	83.8	81.3	89.1	78.1	86.1	82.3	81.7	84.1	81.8	93.6	88.0	79.2	59.2	47.5
Item 5560 Subject A04a N	3140	1492	1591	2369	459	609	914	1049	568	1748	1109	1200	773	355	706	27

B104: When (if ever) did you FIRST do each of the following things? Don't count anything you took because a doctor told you to.

*=less than .05 per cent.   ★=excludes respondents for whom question was inappropriate.

QUESTIONNAIRE FORM 1 1984	TOTAL	SEX		RACE		REGION				4YR COLLEGE PLANS		ILLICIT DRUG USE: LIFETIME				
		M	F	White	Black	NE	NC	S	W	Yes	No	None	Mari-juana Only	Few Pills	More Pills	Any Her-oin
N (Weighted No. of Cases):	3311	1534	1616	2414	478	670	941	1113	587	1772	1137	1223	794	381	765	32
% of Weighted Total:	100.0	46.3	48.8	72.9	14.4	20.2	28.4	33.6	17.7	53.5	34.3	36.9	24.0	11.5	23.1	1.0

B104A: Smoke cigarettes on a daily basis

8. Never	64.3	67.8	61.1	63.1	74.2	59.3	62.8	66.0	68.7	72.0	55.7	86.9	62.7	54.9	34.3	31.3
1. Grade 6 or below	6.1	6.8	5.2	6.2	4.3	7.8	7.1	4.9	4.9	4.6	7.4	3.1	6.2	7.5	9.6	13.1
2. Grade 7 or 8	9.2	8.7	9.8	9.7	5.7	12.1	9.6	7.3	8.9	6.8	12.1	3.3	8.4	13.2	16.7	25.1
3. Grade 9 (Freshman)	7.0	5.1	8.8	7.2	5.4	9.0	5.2	7.7	6.7	5.6	8.4	2.4	7.5	4.9	15.2	23.9
4. Grade 10 (Sophomore)	6.9	6.1	7.7	7.4	4.4	6.1	8.1	7.3	5.3	5.1	9.5	2.0	7.8	9.5	13.4	-
5. Grade 11 (Junior)	3.9	3.3	4.4	3.7	4.3	3.9	4.2	3.8	3.5	3.5	4.0	1.4	4.4	5.6	6.7	2.5
6. Grade 12 (Senior)	2.6	2.3	3.0	2.8	1.8	1.8	3.0	3.1	2.1	2.4	2.9	0.8	2.9	4.5	4.1	4.2
Item 5570 Subject A01g N	2982	1419	1517	2290	416	578	870	984	550	1677	1041	1146	718	336	685	29

B104B: Try an alcoholic beverage–more than just a few sips

8. Never	7.6	6.8	8.3	5.9	15.2	2.8	6.5	10.4	9.0	7.6	8.3	18.2	1.4	0.4	1.1	7.7
1. Grade 6 or below	11.0	15.3	7.2	11.1	10.1	12.7	11.1	9.3	12.3	9.9	11.8	6.0	11.0	10.4	18.2	27.9
2. Grade 7 or 8	21.7	23.3	20.0	23.2	13.5	29.2	20.0	18.8	21.8	21.7	20.2	11.8	22.0	30.2	32.5	29.8
3. Grade 9 (Freshman)	23.4	23.2	23.9	25.4	13.5	26.2	24.5	21.6	22.0	23.5	24.0	15.9	29.0	30.4	26.3	20.1
4. Grade 10 (Sophomore)	17.5	16.2	18.6	18.0	18.6	17.0	17.2	18.6	16.4	18.3	17.4	19.6	18.4	15.2	14.9	11.1
5. Grade 11 (Junior)	12.7	10.5	14.8	11.6	16.0	7.9	15.3	13.8	11.4	12.8	12.1	17.9	13.9	9.1	5.1	-
6. Grade 12 (Senior)	6.1	4.7	7.2	4.7	13.0	4.2	5.4	7.4	7.0	6.2	6.2	10.7	4.2	4.3	1.9	3.3
Item 5580 Subject A01g N	2879	1370	1460	2234	384	562	848	945	524	1606	1019	1020	734	338	693	28

B104C: Try marijuana or hashish

8. Never	45.7	42.5	48.9	45.0	50.1	34.2	50.4	50.9	41.1	50.7	42.0	100.0	0.2	24.1	10.8	17.3
1. Grade 6 or below	4.3	5.5	2.9	4.5	2.7	6.1	4.0	3.3	4.8	3.3	5.4	-	4.8	4.2	10.9	17.3
2. Grade 7 or 8	14.8	18.5	11.4	15.3	12.7	19.4	11.1	12.3	20.2	13.6	15.1	-	19.6	26.4	29.4	36.4
3. Grade 9 (Freshman)	12.7	12.2	13.5	13.6	8.7	16.6	12.8	11.1	11.3	10.5	14.4	-	21.9	16.8	22.7	17.1
4. Grade 10 (Sophomore)	10.8	10.3	11.2	10.9	10.1	13.7	9.8	10.7	9.9	9.8	12.2	-	22.1	17.0	15.1	5.8
5. Grade 11 (Junior)	7.1	7.0	6.8	6.6	8.9	5.3	7.0	7.1	8.9	7.5	6.2	-	18.5	7.2	7.6	-
6. Grade 12 (Senior)	4.5	4.0	5.2	4.1	6.7	4.7	4.9	4.6	3.7	4.6	4.7	-	12.9	4.2	3.5	6.1
Item 5590 Subject A01g N	2970	1410	1514	2282	415	570	876	978	548	1680	1035	1163	696	324	696	29

B104D: Try LSD

8. Never	93.1	91.5	94.7	92.0	99.3	91.3	93.7	95.5	90.1	95.0	92.8	100.0	100.0	94.7	74.6	43.1
1. Grade 6 or below	0.1	-	0.1	0.1	-	-	0.1	0.1	-	-	0.1	-	-	-	0.3	-
2. Grade 7 or 8	0.6	0.8	0.5	0.7	0.1	0.5	0.7	0.5	1.0	0.5	0.8	-	-	0.4	1.8	21.5
3. Grade 9 (Freshman)	1.7	1.9	1.6	2.0	0.2	2.6	1.2	1.3	2.5	1.1	1.5	-	-	1.1	6.2	20.6
4. Grade 10 (Sophomore)	1.7	2.3	1.1	2.0	0.3	1.7	2.0	1.1	2.5	1.3	1.7	-	-	0.7	7.1	6.0
5. Grade 11 (Junior)	1.9	2.5	1.4	2.3	-	2.8	1.7	1.0	2.8	1.7	2.1	-	-	1.2	7.6	3.8
6. Grade 12 (Senior)	0.8	1.0	0.6	0.9	-	1.1	0.5	0.6	1.2	0.6	0.9	-	-	1.8	2.4	4.9
Item 5600 Subject A01g N	3034	1437	1549	2309	433	586	894	994	559	1706	1069	1170	743	341	686	27

B104E: Try any psychedelic other than LSD

8. Never	94.8	93.8	95.6	94.0	99.2	90.7	95.4	98.1	92.2	96.0	94.7	100.0	100.0	98.2	78.9	39.6
1. Grade 6 or below	*	0.1	-	*	-	0.2	-	-	-	-	0.1	-	-	-	-	4.6
2. Grade 7 or 8	0.7	0.6	0.7	0.8	0.1	1.3	0.4	0.5	0.7	0.3	0.8	-	-	0.4	2.1	20.9
3. Grade 9 (Freshman)	0.8	0.9	0.8	1.0	0.2	2.0	0.4	0.6	0.8	0.7	1.0	-	-	0.2	3.2	17.4
4. Grade 10 (Sophomore)	2.2	2.7	1.7	2.5	0.2	3.7	1.9	0.4	4.2	1.8	1.8	-	-	-	9.7	10.2
5. Grade 11 (Junior)	1.1	1.2	0.9	1.2	0.3	1.5	1.4	0.3	1.4	0.7	1.3	-	-	0.4	4.5	4.6
6. Grade 12 (Senior)	0.4	0.6	0.3	0.5	-	0.6	0.6	*	0.8	0.4	0.3	-	-	0.8	1.5	2.7
Item 5610 Subject A01g N	3003	1420	1535	2278	440	575	877	994	556	1697	1047	1175	749	340	647	22

B104F: Try amphetamines

8. Never	81.1	83.1	79.2	77.9	96.1	78.7	79.1	84.0	82.0	84.9	77.2	100.0	100.0	70.2	26.8	19.1
1. Grade 6 or below	0.4	0.5	0.4	0.3	-	0.4	0.8	0.2	0.5	0.2	0.7	-	-	-	1.7	10.4
2. Grade 7 or 8	2.2	2.5	1.9	2.7	0.7	2.6	1.9	2.2	2.2	1.7	2.5	-	-	2.1	8.5	20.5
3. Grade 9 (Freshman)	6.0	5.2	6.6	7.0	1.3	9.3	5.3	4.9	5.4	4.0	8.4	-	-	4.5	25.2	29.3
4. Grade 10 (Sophomore)	5.3	3.4	7.2	6.4	0.5	5.0	6.5	4.2	5.5	4.7	5.6	-	-	6.1	22.2	6.2
5. Grade 11 (Junior)	3.3	3.5	2.9	3.6	1.3	2.4	4.3	3.1	3.0	2.8	3.8	-	-	8.4	11.0	14.5
6. Grade 12 (Senior)	1.7	1.8	1.8	2.1	0.1	1.8	2.1	1.6	1.4	1.7	1.8	-	-	8.6	4.4	-
Item 5620 Subject A01g N	2880	1369	1467	2180	433	563	842	946	529	1634	1008	1164	746	276	599	26

*=less than .05 per cent.

QUESTIONNAIRE FORM 1 1984	TOTAL	SEX		RACE		REGION				4YR COLLEGE PLANS		ILLICIT DRUG USE: LIFETIME				
		M	F	White	Black	NE	NC	S	W	Yes	No	None	Mari-juana Only	Few Pills	More Pills	Any Her-oin
N (Weighted No. of Cases):	3311	1534	1616	2414	478	670	941	1113	587	1772	1137	1223	794	381	765	32
% of Weighted Total:	100.0	46.3	48.8	72.9	14.4	20.2	28.4	33.6	17.7	53.5	34.3	36.9	24.0	11.5	23.1	1.0

B104G: Try quaaludes

8. Never	92.8	92.4	93.2	91.5	99.1	92.4	94.4	91.2	93.7	94.4	91.8	100.0	100.0	94.7	72.6	50.1
1. Grade 6 or below	0.2	0.2	0.2	0.1	0.3	0.2	-	0.5	-	0.1	0.3	-	-	-	0.5	10.3
2. Grade 7 or 8	0.8	0.9	0.8	0.9	-	0.4	0.4	0.9	1.8	0.8	0.8	-	-	0.9	2.6	11.7
3. Grade 9 (Freshman)	2.4	2.8	2.0	3.1	-	3.2	1.8	2.6	1.9	1.7	2.4	-	-	0.6	9.2	21.4
4. Grade 10 (Sophomore)	2.0	1.8	2.3	2.3	0.2	1.6	2.0	2.5	1.6	1.4	2.6	-	-	1.7	8.0	4.2
5. Grade 11 (Junior)	1.4	1.6	1.1	1.7	-	2.0	1.1	1.6	0.7	1.2	1.7	-	-	1.9	5.1	2.2
6. Grade 12 (Senior)	0.4	0.4	0.5	0.4	0.5	0.2	0.3	0.7	0.3	0.4	0.4	-	-	0.2	1.9	-
Item 5630 Subject A01g N	3046	1441	1556	2313	440	586	895	1009	556	1710	1069	1174	750	347	678	26

B104H: Try barbiturates

8. Never	93.7	93.7	93.9	92.6	98.7	93.3	93.6	94.7	92.8	95.2	93.5	100.0	100.0	96.7	74.4	45.2
1. Grade 6 or below	0.1	0.2	0.1	0.2	-	0.2	-	0.3	-	0.1	0.1	-	-	0.4	0.4	-
2. Grade 7 or 8	0.9	1.0	0.8	1.1	-	0.3	0.6	0.9	1.9	0.7	1.2	-	-	-	3.7	14.7
3. Grade 9 (Freshman)	2.2	1.9	2.2	2.5	0.2	3.2	1.8	1.7	2.4	1.5	2.2	-	-	0.9	8.7	22.8
4. Grade 10 (Sophomore)	1.8	1.8	2.0	2.1	0.7	1.5	2.9	1.2	1.7	1.5	1.8	-	-	1.0	7.7	13.7
5. Grade 11 (Junior)	0.9	1.2	0.7	1.1	-	1.5	0.7	0.9	0.7	0.8	1.0	-	-	0.3	4.0	3.7
6. Grade 12 (Senior)	0.3	0.3	0.4	0.4	0.5	-	0.4	0.3	0.6	0.2	0.2	-	-	0.6	1.3	-
Item 5640 Subject A01g N	2968	1410	1511	2242	436	574	871	975	548	1677	1041	1172	750	330	619	28

B104I: Try tranquilizers

8. Never	92.4	93.9	91.0	91.2	98.4	90.0	92.7	92.3	94.6	93.6	91.6	100.0	100.0	82.7	75.5	52.2
1. Grade 6 or below	0.2	0.3	0.1	0.2	-	0.2	0.2	0.1	0.3	0.1	0.2	-	-	0.5	0.5	-
2. Grade 7 or 8	0.9	0.8	0.9	1.1	-	1.0	0.9	0.8	0.7	0.6	0.8	-	-	1.6	2.4	21.4
3. Grade 9 (Freshman)	1.9	1.8	2.1	2.3	0.4	3.5	1.3	1.7	1.7	1.6	1.8	-	-	3.3	6.8	16.7
4. Grade 10 (Sophomore)	1.6	1.1	2.2	1.8	0.8	1.9	1.5	1.8	1.2	1.2	2.3	-	-	4.1	5.1	9.7
5. Grade 11 (Junior)	2.0	1.5	2.4	2.5	0.3	2.5	2.2	2.3	0.9	2.1	2.1	-	-	3.2	7.7	-
6. Grade 12 (Senior)	0.9	0.5	1.3	0.9	-	1.0	1.1	1.0	0.6	0.8	1.3	-	-	4.6	1.9	-
Item 5650 Subject A01g N	2948	1390	1512	2230	437	574	873	972	530	1647	1049	1169	749	309	624	27

B104J: Try cocaine

8. Never	84.6	80.7	88.4	83.7	91.9	77.1	91.4	89.0	73.9	87.3	83.2	100.0	100.0	72.1	49.6	23.4
1. Grade 6 or below	0.1	0.1	0.1	0.1	-	0.2	0.2	*	-	0.1	0.2	-	-	0.1	0.4	-
2. Grade 7 or 8	0.6	0.8	0.5	0.8	-	0.4	0.2	0.6	1.6	0.4	0.9	-	-	0.2	2.2	12.5
3. Grade 9 (Freshman)	2.3	3.1	1.6	2.4	0.9	2.9	0.8	1.7	4.9	1.9	2.2	-	-	2.1	7.7	30.2
4. Grade 10 (Sophomore)	3.3	3.7	3.1	3.4	1.6	5.0	2.5	1.9	5.4	2.4	4.4	-	-	2.6	12.5	20.6
5. Grade 11 (Junior)	4.8	5.7	3.8	5.0	2.7	7.5	2.8	3.0	8.0	4.2	5.0	-	-	10.1	15.6	6.9
6. Grade 12 (Senior)	4.2	6.0	2.5	4.6	3.0	6.8	2.1	3.6	6.1	3.9	4.1	-	-	12.8	12.1	6.4
Item 5660 Subject A01g N	3059	1448	1562	2325	440	592	896	1010	561	1711	1081	1174	746	343	696	29

B104K: Try heroin

8. Never	99.3	99.5	99.1	99.3	99.8	98.8	99.9	99.2	98.8	99.4	99.5	100.0	100.0	100.0	100.0	-
1. Grade 6 or below	*	-	*	*	-	-	-	-	0.1	*	-	-	-	-	-	2.7
2. Grade 7 or 8	0.1	-	0.2	0.1	-	0.2	-	0.1	0.1	0.1	0.1	-	-	-	-	14.6
3. Grade 9 (Freshman)	0.3	0.2	0.4	0.3	0.2	0.3	-	0.3	0.6	0.2	0.2	-	-	-	-	37.1
4. Grade 10 (Sophomore)	0.1	0.1	0.1	0.1	-	0.1	-	0.2	-	0.1	0.1	-	-	-	-	12.4
5. Grade 11 (Junior)	0.2	0.2	0.1	0.2	-	0.6	-	0.1	-	0.1	0.1	-	-	-	-	21.0
6. Grade 12 (Senior)	0.1	-	0.1	*	-	-	0.1	-	0.3	0.1	-	-	-	-	-	12.2
Item 5670 Subject A01g N	3063	1453	1562	2330	442	592	898	1011	562	1715	1084	1172	750	350	698	22

B104L: Try any narcotic other than heroin

8. Never	93.4	91.8	95.0	92.1	98.9	91.1	94.4	95.0	91.3	93.7	93.8	100.0	100.0	92.9	75.2	38.0
1. Grade 6 or below	0.1	0.1	*	0.1	-	-	0.2	0.1	-	*	0.2	-	-	0.2	0.3	-
2. Grade 7 or 8	0.7	1.0	0.5	0.9	-	0.1	0.3	0.7	1.9	1.0	0.4	-	-	0.2	2.7	10.9
3. Grade 9 (Freshman)	1.5	2.0	1.0	1.7	-	2.6	0.7	1.2	2.1	1.3	1.4	-	-	-	5.9	25.4
4. Grade 10 (Sophomore)	1.7	1.6	1.8	2.0	1.1	1.6	1.7	1.6	1.8	1.7	1.5	-	-	1.9	6.4	12.9
5. Grade 11 (Junior)	1.6	2.0	1.2	2.0	-	2.4	2.0	0.6	2.2	1.6	1.6	-	-	1.9	6.6	4.3
6. Grade 12 (Senior)	1.0	1.5	0.5	1.2	-	2.1	0.8	0.7	0.7	0.8	1.0	-	-	2.9	2.9	8.6
Item 5680 Subject A01g N	2953	1405	1501	2233	436	569	864	987	532	1655	1050	1165	745	315	635	24

The next questions are about your experiences in school.

*=less than .05 per cent.

QUESTIONNAIRE FORM 1 1984	TOTAL	SEX		RACE		REGION				4YR COLLEGE PLANS		ILLICIT DRUG USE: LIFETIME				
		M	F	White	Black	NE	NC	S	W	Yes	No	None	Marijuana Only	Few Pills	More Pills	Any Heroin
N (Weighted No. of Cases):	3311	1534	1616	2414	478	670	941	1113	587	1772	1137	1223	794	381	765	32
% of Weighted Total:	100.0	46.3	48.8	72.9	14.4	20.2	28.4	33.6	17.7	53.5	34.3	36.9	24.0	11.5	23.1	1.0

D001: Some people like school very much. Others don't. How do you feel about going to school?

	TOTAL	M	F	White	Black	NE	NC	S	W	Yes	No	None	Mari-juana Only	Few Pills	More Pills	Any Heroin
5. I like school very much	14.7	13.3	15.9	12.6	22.2	12.6	13.4	16.2	16.1	17.7	10.4	17.8	16.0	12.5	7.5	26.1
4. I like school quite a lot	31.3	30.3	32.7	32.2	28.6	26.0	32.2	32.8	32.9	36.4	23.7	37.8	28.7	33.9	22.7	13.0
3. I like school some	39.6	42.9	36.6	40.4	40.0	42.0	40.9	39.2	35.6	35.9	45.3	34.4	43.1	38.5	45.0	35.4
2. I don't like school very much	10.4	9.5	10.7	10.8	5.9	13.7	9.1	9.2	10.8	7.5	14.3	8.1	8.5	10.6	17.2	11.6
1. I don't like school at all	4.1	4.0	4.1	3.9	3.3	5.8	4.4	2.6	4.6	2.4	6.4	1.9	3.8	4.5	7.7	13.9
Item 7630 Subject B01,Q08 N	2957	1382	1524	2245	429	570	869	984	534	1737	1091	1164	720	333	632	24

D002: How often do you feel that the school work you are assigned is meaningful and important?

	TOTAL	M	F	White	Black	NE	NC	S	W	Yes	No	None	Mari-juana Only	Few Pills	More Pills	Any Heroin
5. Almost always	13.5	11.0	15.7	10.4	28.0	9.6	10.5	19.1	12.1	15.5	9.8	17.1	11.4	13.2	7.8	13.4
4. Often	29.2	29.6	28.9	29.6	27.4	27.1	31.1	27.2	31.9	31.3	26.5	32.7	31.2	27.6	22.9	40.5
3. Sometimes	39.8	39.2	40.6	41.5	33.7	42.4	41.9	36.9	38.9	39.2	41.2	38.8	39.8	42.7	40.6	22.2
2. Seldom	15.3	17.7	12.6	16.1	8.8	17.8	14.6	14.1	15.7	12.6	18.6	10.3	15.3	15.7	24.0	15.5
1. Never	2.3	2.6	2.1	2.4	2.0	3.1	1.9	2.7	1.5	1.4	3.9	1.2	2.3	0.8	4.8	8.4
Item 5700 Subject B01 N	2945	1374	1520	2238	426	566	867	979	533	1736	1081	1164	717	330	629	23

D003: How interesting are most of your courses to you?

	TOTAL	M	F	White	Black	NE	NC	S	W	Yes	No	None	Mari-juana Only	Few Pills	More Pills	Any Heroin
5. Very exciting and stimulating	4.4	4.5	4.3	3.2	8.3	3.4	3.3	5.9	4.6	5.0	3.6	5.5	4.2	5.6	1.7	16.7
4. Quite interesting	31.3	28.2	34.5	29.7	39.1	23.2	34.4	31.6	34.2	34.6	26.6	37.5	31.7	28.3	20.4	15.4
3. Fairly interesting	45.4	46.5	44.7	46.9	38.2	48.8	44.7	44.6	44.7	44.4	47.5	44.7	44.3	48.8	47.5	43.0
2. Slightly dull	14.5	16.1	12.8	16.1	9.7	18.2	12.4	14.8	13.7	13.2	16.1	9.6	15.4	14.7	22.5	19.3
1. Very dull	4.3	4.7	3.7	4.2	4.7	6.3	5.2	3.2	2.8	2.9	6.3	2.8	4.4	2.6	8.0	5.6
Item 5710 Subject B01 N	2935	1371	1515	2231	424	562	867	973	533	1730	1079	1158	717	328	627	22

D004: How important do you think the things you are learning in school are going to be for your later life?

	TOTAL	M	F	White	Black	NE	NC	S	W	Yes	No	None	Mari-juana Only	Few Pills	More Pills	Any Heroin
5. Very important	22.4	20.9	23.7	18.8	39.3	14.8	22.4	28.2	19.7	24.0	19.0	25.5	22.6	20.2	16.7	16.6
4. Quite important	30.2	30.7	29.7	30.9	28.3	26.0	32.1	31.2	31.6	31.6	28.5	34.0	28.9	29.3	24.8	42.7
3. Fairly important	30.2	30.6	29.5	31.5	22.2	34.9	30.4	25.5	33.5	29.4	31.7	28.0	31.3	30.9	33.4	13.3
2. Slightly important	14.8	15.2	14.2	16.5	7.5	19.8	13.7	12.8	14.7	13.3	16.9	10.7	15.5	17.7	20.4	15.7
1. Not at all important	2.5	2.5	2.4	2.3	2.7	4.4	1.4	2.3	2.6	1.6	3.9	1.8	1.7	2.0	4.6	11.7
Item 5720 Subject B01 N	2932	1370	1513	2229	424	563	866	972	532	1728	1078	1157	716	329	623	23

D005: How much competition for grades is there among students at your school?

	TOTAL	M	F	White	Black	NE	NC	S	W	Yes	No	None	Mari-juana Only	Few Pills	More Pills	Any Heroin
1. None	5.9	6.5	5.2	5.7	5.8	7.5	4.9	5.9	5.8	3.6	9.1	4.7	6.2	2.9	9.1	24.0
2. A little	19.3	20.2	18.9	20.5	14.6	19.3	20.3	18.8	18.7	16.4	23.3	17.9	18.6	18.3	23.8	21.1
3. Some	33.4	35.2	31.3	34.1	29.2	31.9	34.5	31.0	37.7	31.5	37.6	30.8	36.3	35.9	32.8	34.4
4. Quite a bit	29.6	28.3	31.0	29.0	32.9	29.8	27.8	31.7	28.5	33.4	23.7	32.4	28.7	32.4	25.0	8.1
5. A great deal	11.7	9.8	13.6	10.7	17.6	11.5	12.5	12.5	9.4	15.1	6.2	14.2	10.2	10.6	9.2	12.4
Item 5730 Subject B04 N	2920	1365	1506	2221	423	558	865	968	529	1726	1071	1155	713	327	622	22

D006: How do you think most of the students in your classes would feel if you cheated on a test?

	TOTAL	M	F	White	Black	NE	NC	S	W	Yes	No	None	Mari-juana Only	Few Pills	More Pills	Any Heroin
1. They would like it very much	2.5	4.1	1.0	1.9	4.1	3.4	1.6	2.9	2.0	2.3	2.6	1.6	3.1	2.6	2.5	20.6
2. They would like it	2.2	2.6	1.6	1.8	3.9	2.4	1.0	2.8	2.8	2.0	2.4	1.7	1.8	2.0	3.1	-
3. They would not care	77.8	78.2	77.3	79.0	75.7	79.9	77.5	79.0	74.1	76.7	79.9	74.0	78.2	80.7	84.0	52.8
4. They would dislike it	13.9	12.1	15.6	14.1	11.6	11.0	15.8	12.2	16.7	15.4	11.5	17.9	13.4	11.6	8.5	16.6
5. They would dislike it very much	3.7	3.0	4.4	3.1	4.7	3.3	4.1	3.1	4.5	3.7	3.7	4.8	3.5	3.1	2.0	10.0
Item 5740 Subject B04 N	2919	1367	1501	2220	420	555	864	968	532	1722	1069	1155	710	328	621	22

QUESTIONNAIRE FORM 1 1984	TOTAL	SEX		RACE		REGION				4YR COLLEGE PLANS		ILLICIT DRUG USE: LIFETIME				
		M	F	White	Black	NE	NC	S	W	Yes	No	None	Marijuana Only	Few Pills	More Pills	Any Heroin
N (Weighted No. of Cases):	3311	1534	1616	2414	478	670	941	1113	587	1772	1137	1223	794	381	765	32
% of Weighted Total:	100.0	46.3	48.8	72.9	14.4	20.2	28.4	33.6	17.7	53.5	34.3	36.9	24.0	11.5	23.1	1.0

D007: How do you think most of the students in your classes would feel if you intentionally did things to make your teachers angry?

1. They would like it very much	4.2	6.0	2.4	3.7	6.0	6.3	4.5	3.7	2.2	3.2	5.7	3.2	4.6	3.4	5.4	17.7
2. They would like it	11.5	15.0	8.2	11.3	12.7	15.2	9.1	12.4	9.6	10.6	11.9	10.3	12.8	11.6	12.5	-
3. They would not care	43.1	42.9	42.9	42.5	46.0	45.0	46.9	44.1	32.9	39.8	49.1	40.1	43.4	43.4	48.5	39.6
4. They would dislike it	33.6	30.9	36.5	35.3	26.6	28.0	31.7	33.0	43.6	38.5	26.5	37.5	32.6	35.4	27.1	28.0
5. They would dislike it very much	7.7	5.2	10.0	7.1	8.8	5.4	7.7	6.8	11.6	8.0	6.9	8.9	6.6	6.2	6.5	14.7
Item 5750 Subject B04 N	2907	1361	1495	2210	419	553	863	962	529	1718	1061	1152	709	327	614	22

D008: How often do you find that your friends encourage you to do things which your teachers wouldn't like?

1. Never	37.6	24.9	49.8	33.9	53.9	37.7	30.7	38.7	46.9	39.2	35.3	39.7	40.9	32.2	32.1	50.5
2. Seldom	33.7	34.6	32.2	36.2	22.5	30.0	36.4	34.1	32.5	35.1	30.9	35.0	32.7	34.5	34.5	14.8
3. Sometimes	20.0	27.6	13.3	20.9	17.5	22.4	22.4	19.5	14.6	18.9	22.5	18.8	19.1	23.5	20.9	2.3
4. Often	7.1	10.8	3.7	7.7	3.8	8.1	8.2	6.4	5.6	5.8	9.3	5.3	5.8	8.9	10.7	24.6
5. Almost always	1.5	2.1	0.9	1.3	2.4	1.7	2.3	1.3	0.4	1.0	2.0	1.2	1.5	0.9	1.8	7.8
Item 5760 Subject B04 N	2910	1359	1501	2214	418	553	860	968	529	1719	1065	1155	708	326	616	22

D009: Have you ever been in a work-study program–that is, a program where you work on a job as part of your schooling?

1. No, not ever	77.9	79.2	77.1	79.6	72.2	84.3	79.7	73.3	76.6	83.5	69.0	80.5	79.4	76.6	73.8	87.1
2. Yes, for a half year or less	8.1	7.4	8.4	7.2	11.7	5.4	8.0	7.7	11.8	6.5	10.6	8.0	6.2	8.6	9.0	2.7
3. Yes, for about a year	9.6	8.0	11.1	9.2	9.8	6.6	8.5	12.3	9.4	6.9	13.4	7.6	9.4	10.8	12.3	10.2
4. Yes, for about two years	2.7	3.6	2.0	2.6	3.5	1.4	2.1	4.7	1.5	1.8	4.4	2.3	2.8	3.7	2.7	-
5. Yes, for more than two years	1.7	1.9	1.4	1.4	2.9	2.2	1.7	2.0	0.7	1.2	2.6	1.6	2.1	0.2	2.2	-
Item 5770 Subject B02,C01 N	2894	1351	1493	2201	418	548	850	967	529	1716	1056	1146	705	324	615	22

D010: How many times this school year have you seen a counselor individually?

1. No times	16.5	15.0	17.9	17.4	13.0	15.1	16.2	19.9	12.3	12.9	22.6	16.9	15.5	13.5	18.1	23.1
2. 1 time	14.1	15.0	13.4	14.6	13.9	14.0	14.7	15.4	11.0	13.1	16.3	14.9	13.6	12.7	14.8	4.1
3. 2 times	19.6	20.1	19.3	20.5	16.5	21.3	20.4	19.1	17.5	18.0	21.4	19.2	22.3	17.2	17.7	18.8
4. 3 or 4 times	27.1	26.9	27.6	27.1	26.5	26.3	28.7	25.6	28.2	28.7	24.3	26.4	26.4	31.5	27.1	12.5
5. 5 - 7 times	12.1	12.2	11.9	10.9	16.5	11.1	11.5	10.8	16.4	14.7	8.1	12.2	11.5	14.3	12.6	14.7
6. 8 - 10 times	4.7	4.7	4.6	4.5	5.3	5.8	3.7	4.1	6.3	5.3	4.0	4.7	4.1	4.7	5.5	9.5
7. 11 or more times	5.8	6.2	5.4	5.0	8.2	6.3	4.7	5.1	8.3	7.3	3.2	5.7	6.6	6.2	4.2	17.3
Item 5780 Subject B05 N	2887	1346	1490	2201	414	546	855	961	525	1708	1055	1144	701	320	615	23

D011: How many times this school year have you seen a counselor as a part of a group of other students?

1. No times	54.5	52.7	56.0	55.7	50.1	58.6	53.6	51.5	57.1	52.0	59.1	54.4	54.6	54.7	54.8	44.7
2. 1 time	14.9	14.8	14.9	15.2	15.5	12.6	15.7	15.2	15.3	15.0	15.0	14.4	15.6	17.2	14.1	14.9
3. 2 times	12.9	14.4	11.8	13.2	10.2	12.7	13.7	14.1	9.5	13.4	11.1	13.2	11.3	10.1	15.2	11.3
4. 3 or 4 times	11.2	11.0	11.1	10.4	13.1	7.9	10.9	13.4	10.9	12.3	9.1	11.4	10.9	11.2	11.0	13.7
5. 5 - 7 times	3.4	3.4	3.5	3.0	5.2	4.0	3.3	3.4	3.0	3.6	3.2	3.1	3.9	5.0	2.9	5.3
6. 8 - 10 times	1.3	1.3	1.4	0.9	3.6	1.8	1.4	0.9	1.4	1.7	0.9	1.3	1.9	0.4	0.7	10.0
7. 11 or more times	1.8	2.3	1.4	1.6	2.3	2.5	1.2	1.5	2.7	2.0	1.6	2.2	1.9	1.5	1.2	-
Item 5790 Subject B05 N	2874	1338	1487	2191	413	537	855	958	524	1705	1048	1144	700	318	610	22

D012: Would you have preferred to see a counselor more or less often than you have during the past year?

5. Much more often	8.7	8.0	8.9	6.8	14.5	8.0	9.1	8.9	8.3	8.2	8.8	7.0	9.7	8.2	10.0	6.7
4. A little more often	23.5	23.4	23.8	22.7	28.7	20.8	22.2	25.9	24.2	24.9	21.8	25.1	19.4	26.0	23.8	11.8
3. About as often	51.7	52.4	51.2	55.2	40.9	53.3	52.8	50.1	51.0	55.7	45.4	54.1	54.7	50.8	47.0	34.9
2. A little less often	6.1	5.6	6.5	5.9	6.1	7.0	5.9	4.9	7.7	4.4	8.9	6.2	5.2	6.7	6.3	4.6
1. Much less often	10.0	10.6	9.6	9.4	9.7	10.9	10.0	10.2	8.9	6.8	15.1	7.7	10.9	8.3	12.9	42.0
Item 5800 Subject B05 N	2837	1326	1462	2167	407	530	845	944	518	1685	1033	1131	690	313	606	22

QUESTIONNAIRE FORM 1 1984	TOTAL	SEX		RACE		REGION				4YR COLLEGE PLANS		ILLICIT DRUG USE: LIFETIME				
		M	F	White	Black	NE	NC	S	W	Yes	No	None	Mari-juana Only	Few Pills	More Pills	Any Her-oin
N (Weighted No. of Cases):	3311	1534	1616	2414	478	670	941	1113	587	1772	1137	1223	794	381	765	32
% of Weighted Total:	100.0	46.3	48.8	72.9	14.4	20.2	28.4	33.6	17.7	53.5	34.3	36.9	24.0	11.5	23.1	1.0
D013: How helpful have your sessions with a counselor been to you?																
5.　Extremely helpful	11.9	11.0	12.5	8.8	26.0	9.1	9.6	14.6	13.5	12.3	11.1	12.6	13.6	11.0	7.8	9.2
4.　Quite helpful	23.3	22.8	23.6	22.2	27.1	23.3	22.8	23.1	24.4	25.3	20.1	25.8	21.5	25.2	20.3	24.6
3.　Somewhat helpful	22.8	23.7	22.0	23.2	19.8	20.7	23.9	21.6	25.1	24.1	20.0	24.6	22.7	21.0	21.3	6.0
2.　A little helpful	19.3	20.0	19.1	21.0	12.9	21.9	20.3	16.7	19.8	19.1	20.3	15.4	22.3	20.5	22.6	27.3
1.　Not at all helpful	11.9	13.3	10.4	12.8	7.9	14.4	11.8	12.0	9.2	10.3	14.4	10.2	10.5	13.1	15.9	24.2
8.　Did not see a counselor this year	10.9	9.2	12.5	12.1	6.4	10.6	11.6	12.0	8.0	8.9	14.2	11.5	9.5	9.2	12.2	8.6
Item 5810　Subject B05　　N	2902	1347	1499	2213	413	537	866	968	530	1697	1038	1150	703	322	620	23
D014: Would you have preferred more or less of each of the following types of counseling in the last year?																
D014A: Choosing what courses to take																
5.　Much more	18.7	17.9	19.3	15.2	34.7	18.2	18.0	22.0	14.4	17.4	20.3	16.7	18.8	17.8	21.0	27.8
4.　A little more	24.2	24.6	24.1	25.6	18.3	22.6	24.7	23.0	27.4	25.4	22.8	22.8	23.8	26.9	26.4	25.1
3.　About right	47.8	47.8	47.8	50.6	38.3	49.4	47.8	45.4	50.6	50.3	44.6	51.9	49.9	46.9	40.2	22.4
2.　A little less	3.7	4.1	3.4	3.3	3.7	4.5	3.4	3.7	3.3	3.4	4.3	3.6	2.9	4.5	4.4	-
1.　Much less	5.6	5.6	5.4	5.3	5.1	5.5	6.1	6.0	4.3	3.6	8.0	4.9	4.6	3.9	7.9	24.6
Item 5811　Subject B05　　N	2852	1327	1470	2174	410	516	856	957	523	1680	1014	1135	690	316	607	24
D014B: Discussing problems with course work																
5.　Much more	12.8	12.6	12.7	9.2	29.8	13.8	11.3	14.7	10.8	12.2	13.7	11.4	12.6	12.6	15.2	15.7
4.　A little more	24.0	23.6	24.5	23.8	26.6	23.8	22.7	25.0	24.2	23.9	23.8	24.4	21.8	19.9	26.5	24.8
3.　About right	50.6	50.7	51.0	54.8	33.0	50.3	52.4	46.8	54.9	54.5	45.2	53.5	52.6	55.0	42.3	34.0
2.　A little less	4.8	6.2	3.4	4.7	4.3	5.8	4.2	5.6	3.5	3.8	6.7	4.1	5.6	5.2	5.2	6.4
1.　Much less	7.8	7.0	8.4	7.5	6.3	6.4	9.3	7.9	6.7	5.7	10.6	6.5	7.5	7.3	10.7	19.0
Item 5812　Subject B05　　N	2823	1315	1455	2153	408	513	849	947	514	1658	1012	1120	686	311	603	23
D014C: Discussing any trouble you've gotten into																
5.　Much more	7.7	8.2	7.0	5.0	18.1	6.2	5.3	10.9	7.3	6.0	10.0	6.2	7.7	8.7	9.0	10.1
4.　A little more	11.7	13.9	9.8	11.0	12.5	11.9	11.5	11.0	13.2	10.9	12.8	9.6	11.7	12.3	14.0	14.5
3.　About right	58.1	56.7	59.8	62.9	41.5	59.8	59.3	54.5	61.0	64.6	48.9	63.7	59.1	58.6	49.6	37.5
2.　A little less	5.4	6.2	4.4	5.4	5.1	5.4	5.9	5.0	5.4	4.5	6.8	4.6	5.7	4.9	6.8	6.4
1.　Much less	17.0	15.0	19.0	15.7	22.9	16.7	18.0	18.6	13.0	14.0	21.4	15.9	15.8	15.5	20.6	31.4
Item 5813　Subject B05　　N	2752	1281	1417	2103	395	497	839	915	502	1610	995	1086	667	311	591	23
D014D: Discussing military plans																
5.　Much more	5.3	7.3	3.6	3.6	14.9	4.8	2.9	8.6	3.9	3.9	7.2	4.8	6.6	5.8	4.4	-
4.　A little more	7.3	10.0	4.7	6.8	8.4	5.4	6.3	9.6	6.7	6.7	8.2	7.3	7.3	6.2	8.0	5.4
3.　About right	43.8	43.5	44.2	47.4	28.1	46.5	44.8	39.8	46.8	49.3	35.0	47.9	43.5	42.6	38.0	37.7
2.　A little less	6.3	6.9	5.4	6.2	6.3	6.1	5.6	6.7	6.7	5.7	7.6	5.8	6.8	9.6	5.2	-
1.　Much less	37.3	32.2	42.1	36.0	42.1	37.3	40.4	35.3	35.9	34.4	42.0	34.2	35.8	35.8	44.4	56.9
Item 5814　Subject B05　　N	2706	1273	1381	2066	389	482	820	912	492	1580	981	1071	648	304	584	23
D014E: Discussing education or training plans																
5.　Much more	22.9	19.5	25.5	19.8	37.6	19.1	20.6	26.6	23.9	25.5	19.0	22.4	23.4	24.1	22.6	23.8
4.　A little more	31.1	32.8	30.2	31.9	28.8	28.2	32.7	30.4	32.8	34.3	27.2	33.7	29.2	35.0	27.3	23.5
3.　About right	35.5	36.2	34.9	38.4	24.1	40.0	37.5	32.0	34.3	33.7	38.0	35.8	37.0	32.7	36.5	20.1
2.　A little less	3.3	4.2	2.5	3.1	3.5	4.8	2.3	3.6	3.1	2.5	4.8	2.6	2.6	3.7	5.1	5.3
1.　Much less	7.0	7.3	6.8	6.7	6.0	7.9	6.9	7.4	5.9	4.0	11.0	5.6	7.9	4.5	8.4	27.3
Item 5815　Subject B05　　N	2805	1305	1447	2145	402	505	848	939	513	1652	1001	1112	680	310	601	23
D014F: Discussing career plans or job choice																
5.　Much more	27.6	24.1	30.1	23.6	44.5	25.1	25.6	30.8	27.2	29.6	25.0	27.6	25.4	26.1	28.7	24.8
4.　A little more	32.0	31.7	32.9	33.4	27.5	30.7	35.8	30.1	30.8	34.9	28.3	34.1	32.8	34.7	28.1	29.9
3.　About right	32.1	34.9	29.6	35.2	19.7	35.5	31.2	30.1	33.9	30.7	33.8	31.1	34.1	30.8	33.3	12.1
2.　A little less	2.5	3.0	2.0	2.5	2.5	2.6	2.4	2.5	2.5	1.6	3.7	1.8	2.6	3.7	2.3	8.2
1.　Much less	5.9	6.4	5.4	5.4	5.8	6.1	5.1	6.5	5.7	3.2	9.2	5.4	5.1	4.7	7.7	24.9
Item 5816　Subject B05　　N	2811	1307	1454	2147	404	509	842	947	513	1654	1004	1113	682	310	605	22

QUESTIONNAIRE FORM 1 1984	TOTAL	SEX		RACE		REGION				4YR COLLEGE PLANS		ILLICIT DRUG USE: LIFETIME				
		M	F	White	Black	NE	NC	S	W	Yes	No	None	Mari-juana Only	Few Pills	More Pills	Any Her-oin
N (Weighted No. of Cases):	3311	1534	1616	2414	478	670	941	1113	587	1772	1137	1223	794	381	765	32
% of Weighted Total:	100.0	46.3	48.8	72.9	14.4	20.2	28.4	33.6	17.7	53.5	34.3	36.9	24.0	11.5	23.1	1.0
D014G: Discussing personal problems																
5. Much more	8.7	7.5	9.6	6.7	15.4	9.1	7.9	9.7	7.8	7.4	10.4	7.8	6.3	11.7	10.5	1.2
4. A little more	10.4	9.8	11.0	10.6	9.5	8.1	12.5	9.1	12.0	10.2	11.5	9.7	10.1	9.2	12.9	7.9
3. About right	51.5	53.5	49.9	55.5	36.7	54.2	51.9	47.8	54.7	56.3	44.1	55.5	54.7	51.5	42.8	46.6
2. A little less	6.5	7.4	5.8	6.5	7.6	5.8	6.4	7.3	6.0	6.5	6.2	6.3	6.5	6.7	7.2	-
1. Much less	22.9	21.8	23.7	20.7	30.8	22.7	21.3	26.2	19.4	19.6	27.9	20.6	22.4	21.0	26.6	44.3
Item 5817 Subject B05 N	2739	1275	1411	2094	392	498	827	917	497	1607	984	1078	665	308	590	23

These last questions concern your health.

D015: During the LAST 30 DAYS, on how many days (if any) did you have the following problems or symptoms?

	TOTAL	M	F	White	Black	NE	NC	S	W	Yes	No	None	Mari-juana Only	Few Pills	More Pills	Any Her-oin
D015A: Headache																
1. None	18.9	29.4	8.8	16.5	29.9	16.6	16.2	21.3	21.2	17.6	19.4	21.3	20.7	15.9	14.0	8.4
2. One day	18.9	22.4	15.8	17.4	25.5	20.2	15.2	20.7	20.6	18.4	20.2	20.0	21.0	18.8	14.8	3.2
3. Two days	21.9	21.8	22.3	21.9	20.3	25.4	21.9	20.2	21.5	22.9	20.8	20.7	22.6	22.9	21.6	39.2
4. 3 to 5 days	22.9	17.6	28.1	25.0	15.1	21.5	25.5	21.4	22.9	23.1	23.0	21.7	22.1	24.6	26.2	23.8
5. 6 to 9 days	9.6	5.9	13.2	10.8	5.7	9.7	11.6	8.4	8.5	10.2	9.1	8.8	8.2	11.1	12.8	10.5
6. 10 to 19 days	5.1	1.9	7.8	5.9	1.4	3.9	6.3	5.2	4.1	5.6	4.0	5.5	2.7	4.8	6.7	8.8
7. 20+ days	2.6	1.0	4.1	2.5	2.2	2.7	3.3	2.7	1.3	2.2	3.5	1.9	2.8	1.9	4.0	6.1
Item 21310 Subject T N	2865	1336	1473	2194	407	523	864	956	522	1676	1026	1134	699	316	613	24
D015B: Sore throat or hoarse voice																
1. None	38.7	44.8	33.0	35.5	53.4	34.1	36.0	44.1	37.8	36.6	41.1	42.9	41.2	30.4	32.9	28.9
2. One day	15.9	17.4	14.6	16.8	12.2	18.7	16.5	15.0	13.6	15.3	16.3	15.6	15.4	18.1	15.5	10.4
3. Two days	16.5	17.4	15.8	17.2	13.2	16.1	17.0	15.9	17.1	18.0	15.3	15.5	17.6	17.1	18.0	15.6
4. 3 to 5 days	17.7	13.7	21.2	18.6	14.5	18.2	19.2	14.6	20.4	17.9	17.7	16.6	16.8	21.2	18.3	23.0
5. 6 to 9 days	7.2	3.6	10.6	7.9	5.0	7.3	7.3	7.5	6.5	8.4	5.5	6.6	5.6	10.2	8.6	8.1
6. 10 to 19 days	2.9	2.3	3.4	3.0	0.7	4.2	2.8	1.9	3.5	2.9	2.9	2.2	2.9	2.3	4.8	3.8
7. 20+ days	1.1	0.7	1.3	0.9	1.1	1.3	1.1	1.1	1.2	0.9	1.2	0.7	0.5	0.8	2.0	10.1
Item 21320 Subject T N	2865	1334	1476	2191	410	525	864	954	522	1674	1026	1134	698	317	613	25
D015C: Trouble with sinus congestion, runny nose, or sneezing																
1. None	27.2	30.2	24.5	23.9	42.3	31.5	21.5	31.6	24.3	25.1	30.4	29.0	30.3	22.7	22.5	17.2
2. One day	11.3	12.1	10.6	11.3	11.1	11.4	10.0	11.8	12.5	11.5	10.9	12.0	10.2	11.6	10.5	9.4
3. Two days	13.5	14.6	12.4	14.3	8.9	12.2	17.4	11.4	11.9	13.8	13.4	12.5	16.3	12.7	13.5	10.6
4. 3 to 5 days	20.2	18.7	21.6	20.9	18.5	20.1	20.7	21.7	17.0	20.2	19.9	22.1	19.0	17.8	18.3	28.8
5. 6 to 9 days	14.5	12.1	16.5	15.1	11.9	12.3	18.2	12.1	14.7	15.0	13.8	13.6	13.3	18.0	16.0	16.7
6. 10 to 19 days	7.2	5.7	8.6	7.8	3.8	8.2	4.8	6.5	11.7	8.3	5.8	5.7	5.9	9.8	10.9	4.8
7. 20+ days	6.1	6.5	5.7	6.7	3.5	4.2	7.5	4.9	7.9	6.2	5.9	5.1	5.0	7.3	8.4	12.4
Item 21330 Subject T N	2861	1334	1472	2189	409	524	863	953	522	1675	1023	1135	696	315	614	24
D015D: Coughing spells																
1. None	56.6	60.7	53.1	55.3	61.1	56.2	55.8	58.0	55.6	57.7	55.0	61.2	60.1	51.4	47.6	41.9
2. One day	12.8	14.4	11.4	13.8	10.2	12.8	13.6	12.2	12.5	12.1	13.8	11.5	12.1	14.8	14.6	17.1
3. Two days	10.4	8.1	12.3	10.4	9.8	9.9	10.5	9.8	11.9	10.6	9.4	9.9	10.7	9.5	11.3	21.4
4. 3 to 5 days	10.6	9.6	11.6	11.0	9.7	11.3	10.7	10.6	9.9	10.8	11.2	10.2	8.9	13.7	11.5	4.6
5. 6 to 9 days	5.7	4.2	6.9	5.8	5.8	5.3	6.1	5.6	5.4	5.4	5.8	4.6	4.5	5.4	9.2	2.5
6. 10 to 19 days	2.7	1.8	3.6	2.5	2.2	3.5	2.4	2.4	2.7	2.4	3.3	2.1	2.9	3.1	3.3	6.4
7. 20+ days	1.3	1.3	1.3	1.1	1.2	1.1	0.9	1.4	2.0	1.0	1.4	0.6	0.9	2.1	2.4	6.1
Item 21340 Subject T N	2855	1330	1470	2186	410	520	860	952	523	1673	1020	1133	693	314	613	24
D015E: Chest colds																
1. None	73.5	76.2	71.3	73.7	75.3	70.1	72.4	75.0	76.2	73.7	74.2	76.9	75.3	66.2	70.4	58.9
2. One day	7.7	8.9	6.7	8.0	5.5	8.6	8.6	6.8	7.0	7.3	7.6	5.6	9.0	12.8	7.5	15.0
3. Two days	6.9	6.6	6.8	6.7	6.3	8.1	6.9	6.9	5.4	6.8	6.1	6.6	5.3	8.1	7.4	9.9
4. 3 to 5 days	7.1	4.5	9.6	7.2	7.2	9.0	6.7	6.7	6.5	7.3	7.3	7.0	6.6	7.4	7.7	10.1
5. 6 to 9 days	2.9	2.2	3.6	3.0	3.2	3.4	3.2	2.6	2.5	3.2	2.7	2.1	2.9	2.8	4.7	-
6. 10 to 19 days	1.4	1.0	1.7	1.3	1.8	0.7	1.8	1.7	1.1	1.2	1.8	1.5	0.9	1.9	1.7	-
7. 20+ days	0.5	0.5	0.4	0.2	0.7	-	0.4	0.4	1.3	0.5	0.2	0.3	0.1	0.7	0.7	6.1
Item 21350 Subject T N	2831	1316	1460	2169	404	519	850	943	519	1664	1011	1126	690	311	605	24

QUESTIONNAIRE FORM 1 1984	TOTAL	SEX		RACE		REGION				4YR COLLEGE PLANS		ILLICIT DRUG USE: LIFETIME				
		M	F	White	Black	NE	NC	S	W	Yes	No	None	Mari- juana Only	Few Pills	More Pills	Any Her- oin
N (Weighted No. of Cases):	3311	1534	1616	2414	478	670	941	1113	587	1772	1137	1223	794	381	765	32
% of Weighted Total:	100.0	46.3	48.8	72.9	14.4	20.2	28.4	33.6	17.7	53.5	34.3	36.9	24.0	11.5	23.1	1.0

D015F: Coughing up phlegm or blood

1. None	83.5	83.5	83.6	82.4	89.5	84.3	80.3	85.3	84.5	82.8	84.9	87.4	85.5	77.7	76.9	75.7
2. One day	3.9	4.9	2.9	4.2	2.4	3.5	5.3	3.2	3.3	3.6	3.5	2.7	3.3	6.7	5.2	-
3. Two days	3.2	2.8	3.6	3.3	2.1	4.4	2.9	3.2	2.9	3.4	3.2	3.0	3.0	3.4	4.0	5.1
4. 3 to 5 days	4.7	4.8	4.7	5.2	2.8	4.0	5.2	5.0	3.9	5.5	3.8	3.8	4.3	4.6	6.9	6.7
5. 6 to 9 days	1.8	2.2	1.4	2.2	0.6	1.8	2.2	1.1	2.5	2.0	1.3	1.0	1.7	2.2	3.4	-
6. 10 to 19 days	1.6	0.6	2.6	1.7	1.0	1.1	2.5	0.9	2.3	1.5	2.1	1.3	1.3	2.7	2.1	6.4
7. 20+ days	1.2	1.3	1.0	1.0	1.6	1.0	1.7	1.3	0.5	1.2	1.3	0.8	0.8	2.6	1.5	6.1
Item 21360 Subject T N	2841	1324	1462	2175	404	523	856	946	515	1666	1016	1131	694	310	603	24

D015G: Shortness of breath when you were not exercising

1. None	85.3	88.9	82.0	85.4	85.1	84.0	85.0	85.0	87.5	86.5	83.7	88.7	86.9	83.2	79.1	60.5
2. One day	4.3	3.4	5.1	4.5	3.8	4.2	4.3	4.5	4.3	3.7	4.9	4.0	3.5	3.6	6.0	6.0
3. Two days	3.7	2.9	4.6	3.7	4.2	5.0	2.9	3.6	4.0	3.7	3.9	2.7	3.4	4.5	5.0	9.7
4. 3 to 5 days	3.4	2.5	4.3	3.4	3.5	2.9	4.0	4.1	1.8	3.4	3.6	2.9	3.2	4.8	4.1	8.4
5. 6 to 9 days	1.4	1.0	1.9	1.4	1.2	1.4	2.0	1.1	1.2	1.1	1.7	1.0	1.0	2.2	2.3	5.1
6. 10 to 19 days	0.8	0.4	1.1	0.7	1.2	0.8	0.7	0.9	0.9	0.7	0.8	0.3	1.0	0.9	1.5	-
7. 20+ days	1.0	0.9	0.9	0.8	1.0	1.7	1.1	0.9	0.4	0.7	1.5	0.4	1.0	0.8	2.0	10.4
Item 21370 Subject T N	2849	1327	1467	2179	407	523	857	948	521	1673	1019	1133	693	313	608	24

D015H: Wheezing or gasping

1. None	89.9	91.6	88.4	90.1	89.0	86.7	90.8	90.6	90.6	90.0	90.2	92.9	91.3	88.8	84.9	65.4
2. One day	2.9	2.8	3.0	2.8	2.8	4.6	1.7	2.8	3.2	2.9	2.7	1.9	2.1	3.6	4.7	2.5
3. Two days	2.2	1.7	2.8	2.2	3.0	2.4	1.8	2.5	2.4	2.7	1.4	1.3	2.1	3.3	3.2	14.8
4. 3 to 5 days	2.4	2.0	2.8	2.5	2.9	3.0	3.4	1.7	1.5	2.3	2.6	2.3	2.4	0.5	3.0	6.9
5. 6 to 9 days	1.0	0.8	1.2	0.8	1.4	1.2	1.3	0.9	0.3	0.8	1.2	0.4	1.2	1.8	1.2	-
6. 10 to 19 days	0.9	0.4	1.1	1.0	0.3	1.0	0.3	1.0	1.3	1.0	0.7	0.7	0.9	0.6	1.4	-
7. 20+ days	0.7	0.8	0.6	0.6	0.7	1.2	0.8	0.5	0.7	0.4	1.2	0.3	0.1	1.4	1.6	10.4
Item 21380 Subject T N	2844	1323	1466	2176	406	521	855	948	520	1669	1019	1133	694	310	607	24

D015I: Trouble remembering new things

1. None	72.0	73.6	71.1	72.3	73.8	73.7	70.1	73.6	70.6	73.8	70.2	77.7	75.9	67.5	61.4	51.5
2. One day	9.3	9.7	9.2	9.1	9.6	8.2	10.1	8.3	10.8	8.7	9.7	8.4	9.4	11.2	9.6	13.7
3. Two days	6.3	6.3	6.3	6.4	5.8	5.8	6.2	6.4	7.1	6.0	6.3	5.0	5.1	9.5	8.0	9.1
4. 3 to 5 days	5.5	4.7	6.0	5.7	3.9	6.0	5.6	5.7	4.2	5.4	6.0	4.8	4.0	5.2	8.8	6.0
5. 6 to 9 days	3.0	3.0	3.1	3.2	2.1	2.4	3.8	1.8	4.6	3.1	3.0	2.2	3.2	3.3	4.6	-
6. 10 to 19 days	1.9	1.5	2.0	1.9	1.4	1.7	2.4	1.7	1.4	1.8	2.0	1.0	1.0	1.7	4.2	9.3
7. 20+ days	2.0	1.4	2.3	1.5	3.4	2.2	1.7	2.4	1.3	1.4	2.8	1.1	1.4	1.5	3.5	10.4
Item 21390 Subject T N	2847	1326	1466	2178	408	521	858	948	520	1668	1020	1130	691	315	608	24

D015J: Difficulty thinking or concentrating

1. None	53.5	61.3	46.6	52.3	65.0	54.9	50.9	57.4	48.9	51.4	56.8	56.1	57.9	50.9	45.4	38.8
2. One day	13.5	12.5	14.6	13.2	11.3	10.6	14.2	13.7	15.1	13.5	13.4	13.0	13.1	13.6	14.6	10.5
3. Two days	12.1	10.3	13.8	13.1	7.5	12.4	13.3	10.4	12.8	13.3	9.9	13.2	10.5	12.1	12.7	9.9
4. 3 to 5 days	10.9	8.5	12.7	11.8	7.4	12.0	11.2	9.4	11.8	12.1	9.0	10.0	11.4	12.4	11.3	13.7
5. 6 to 9 days	4.8	3.6	5.9	4.3	5.0	4.6	5.1	4.1	6.1	5.1	4.6	3.9	3.2	6.5	7.4	5.9
6. 10 to 19 days	3.1	2.3	4.0	3.4	1.7	2.2	3.5	3.3	3.2	2.9	3.3	1.9	2.6	3.0	5.6	4.1
7. 20+ days	2.1	1.5	2.4	1.8	2.0	3.3	1.8	1.8	2.1	1.7	3.0	2.0	1.3	1.5	3.0	17.1
Item 21400 Subject T N	2844	1323	1468	2179	409	520	860	948	517	1667	1019	1131	692	314	608	21

D015K: Trouble learning new things

1. None	71.0	73.5	68.9	71.5	72.9	69.4	65.8	76.0	72.2	70.9	71.4	72.1	74.8	71.3	66.5	68.2
2. One day	11.0	10.1	11.9	10.4	11.2	9.1	12.4	10.9	10.8	10.3	11.5	10.4	11.5	9.8	11.8	12.1
3. Two days	7.5	7.3	7.7	7.8	6.4	10.4	8.2	5.5	7.0	7.8	6.9	8.2	5.6	6.8	8.1	8.5
4. 3 to 5 days	5.7	4.9	6.2	5.8	4.3	5.2	8.2	3.5	6.0	6.6	4.6	5.5	3.8	7.3	7.1	2.5
5. 6 to 9 days	2.2	2.4	2.2	2.2	2.1	2.6	1.9	2.2	2.4	2.5	1.8	1.8	2.6	2.2	2.7	4.2
6. 10 to 19 days	1.2	1.0	1.4	1.2	1.5	1.3	1.6	1.4	0.3	1.1	1.3	1.2	0.6	1.8	1.5	-
7. 20+ days	1.3	0.8	1.6	1.1	1.5	2.0	1.8	0.5	1.3	0.7	2.5	0.9	1.1	0.9	2.2	4.4
Item 21410 Subject T N	2837	1320	1463	2171	403	521	859	940	516	1664	1014	1127	694	313	601	24

QUESTIONNAIRE FORM 1 1984	TOTAL	SEX		RACE		REGION				4YR COLLEGE PLANS		ILLICIT DRUG USE: LIFETIME				
		M	F	White	Black	NE	NC	S	W	Yes	No	None	Mari- juana Only	Few Pills	More Pills	Any Her- oin
N (Weighted No. of Cases):	3311	1534	1616	2414	478	670	941	1113	587	1772	1137	1223	794	381	765	32
% of Weighted Total:	100.0	46.3	48.8	72.9	14.4	20.2	28.4	33.6	17.7	53.5	34.3	36.9	24.0	11.5	23.1	1.0
D015L: Trouble sleeping																
1. None	41.9	47.6	36.4	39.4	56.2	41.7	36.7	48.0	39.7	40.6	43.7	45.4	45.5	39.2	34.4	19.2
2. One day	13.9	14.8	13.1	13.5	14.2	14.6	11.2	14.5	16.3	14.2	13.0	13.0	14.1	16.3	13.0	-
3. Two days	16.3	15.5	17.3	16.7	13.8	15.4	18.3	15.4	15.6	17.3	15.5	17.0	17.1	12.3	16.2	27.8
4. 3 to 5 days	14.9	11.8	17.5	16.7	7.2	14.2	17.8	10.9	16.8	14.7	15.3	12.9	14.2	14.5	19.1	27.1
5. 6 to 9 days	6.3	5.2	7.4	6.9	4.3	6.1	7.2	5.6	5.9	6.8	5.5	6.9	4.9	7.7	6.0	7.8
6. 10 to 19 days	3.7	2.9	4.5	4.2	0.6	3.8	5.2	2.2	3.8	3.7	3.7	2.3	2.7	5.4	6.4	8.0
7. 20+ days	3.1	2.2	3.8	2.6	3.7	4.3	2.7	3.4	1.9	2.7	3.4	2.5	1.5	4.5	4.9	10.1
Item 21420 Subject T N	2842	1322	1465	2175	406	522	858	945	516	1667	1014	1127	692	314	606	25
D015M: Trouble getting started in the morning																
1. None	32.4	38.3	26.7	29.4	45.6	31.6	27.8	36.9	32.3	30.0	35.7	36.9	32.8	26.7	25.2	19.0
2. One day	10.1	10.7	9.9	9.6	11.1	7.8	10.5	10.4	11.2	9.7	10.7	10.0	12.7	7.8	8.1	17.7
3. Two days	12.1	10.6	13.4	12.5	10.6	11.5	13.5	11.1	12.4	12.2	12.1	13.4	12.1	12.5	11.0	5.8
4. 3 to 5 days	14.0	12.5	15.6	14.9	10.8	14.5	14.8	13.0	14.2	15.0	13.0	14.0	13.4	14.7	14.1	12.7
5. 6 to 9 days	9.7	9.3	10.2	10.7	6.1	10.3	10.3	8.4	10.4	11.1	7.6	9.0	10.2	9.9	9.9	9.2
6. 10 to 19 days	7.6	5.8	9.1	8.2	4.0	8.1	7.7	7.4	7.4	8.3	6.4	5.7	5.6	13.5	11.2	8.1
7. 20+ days	14.1	12.8	15.2	14.6	11.7	16.2	15.5	12.7	12.1	13.7	14.4	11.0	13.3	15.0	20.4	27.5
Item 21430 Subject T N	2845	1324	1466	2177	408	520	858	950	518	1668	1018	1134	692	313	604	24
D015N: Stayed home most or all of a day because you were not feeling well																
1. None	58.8	67.9	50.9	57.8	64.9	56.2	58.0	63.3	54.7	58.6	59.5	65.9	60.1	51.6	48.8	28.7
2. One day	18.7	15.4	21.4	19.2	15.3	18.8	17.3	17.9	22.2	19.6	17.0	16.2	20.2	20.6	20.1	28.9
3. Two days	11.1	8.8	13.1	11.8	8.1	13.9	12.1	8.3	11.7	11.1	11.2	9.6	9.5	12.4	14.6	18.0
4. 3 to 5 days	7.5	5.2	9.8	8.0	5.5	7.0	8.6	6.9	7.5	7.3	7.9	5.9	7.9	9.7	9.7	4.8
5. 6 to 9 days	2.2	1.7	2.6	1.9	3.8	2.0	2.5	2.4	1.8	1.9	2.7	1.4	1.6	3.7	3.7	-
6. 10 to 19 days	1.0	0.3	1.6	1.0	0.8	1.2	1.0	0.8	1.2	0.9	0.9	0.8	0.4	1.1	2.0	4.2
7. 20+ days	0.6	0.6	0.7	0.3	1.5	1.0	0.5	0.5	0.8	0.5	0.8	0.2	0.4	0.9	1.2	15.3
Item 21440 Subject T N	2848	1324	1470	2180	407	521	859	948	521	1671	1018	1134	693	312	607	24
D016: In the LAST 12 MONTHS, how many times (if any) have you seen a doctor or other professional for each of the following?																
D016A: For a routine physical check-up																
1. None	47.2	48.4	46.5	49.6	30.9	39.7	51.7	47.1	47.5	44.5	52.2	49.9	47.4	40.3	46.3	45.9
2. Once	38.3	38.1	38.0	38.5	41.1	40.6	34.4	37.9	42.9	40.6	34.1	38.6	40.4	38.0	35.4	32.2
3. Twice	11.1	11.2	11.1	9.2	21.4	15.9	10.0	11.8	6.9	11.6	10.6	9.2	8.1	17.4	14.4	10.5
4. 3 to 5 times	2.3	1.7	2.7	2.0	3.4	1.8	2.9	2.0	2.4	2.4	1.7	1.8	2.8	2.2	2.3	11.4
5. 6 to 9 times	0.5	0.2	0.9	0.3	2.1	0.7	0.3	0.8	0.3	0.5	0.6	0.3	0.6	1.3	0.7	-
6. 10+ times	0.6	0.4	0.7	0.5	1.1	1.3	0.7	0.4	-	0.3	0.8	0.2	0.6	0.8	1.0	-
Item 21450 Subject T N	2847	1322	1470	2174	409	516	862	952	516	1663	1022	1131	692	313	606	25
D016B: For an injury suffered in a fight, assault, or auto accident																
1. None	91.7	89.0	94.2	92.0	91.6	91.8	93.1	90.5	91.4	92.7	90.4	95.7	92.2	88.1	86.1	84.5
2. Once	4.7	5.7	3.6	4.6	4.5	4.9	3.6	5.5	4.7	4.2	5.2	2.9	5.0	5.7	6.9	9.3
3. Twice	2.0	2.9	1.3	2.0	1.8	1.9	1.8	2.0	2.6	1.6	2.5	1.0	1.6	1.8	4.2	-
4. 3 to 5 times	1.0	1.6	0.5	0.8	1.4	1.2	0.8	1.1	1.2	0.9	1.3	0.2	0.7	3.5	1.6	-
5. 6 to 9 times	0.1	0.3	-	0.2	-	-	0.3	0.2	-	0.1	0.1	-	0.2	0.4	0.2	-
6. 10+ times	0.4	0.5	0.4	0.4	0.6	0.3	0.5	0.6	0.1	0.5	0.4	0.2	0.2	0.5	1.0	6.1
Item 21460 Subject T N	2833	1317	1462	2167	405	516	859	943	514	1658	1019	1124	692	313	602	24
D016C: For any other accidental injury																
1. None	79.9	73.4	86.0	78.7	85.7	76.6	78.3	83.4	79.5	79.2	81.3	82.3	81.0	74.9	76.3	77.8
2. Once	10.9	15.0	7.1	11.4	8.6	11.7	12.3	8.7	11.8	11.2	10.1	10.4	10.1	12.7	12.6	7.8
3. Twice	5.1	6.4	3.8	5.2	3.8	6.4	5.0	4.9	4.4	5.5	4.3	4.5	5.3	5.6	5.4	1.1
4. 3 to 5 times	2.3	2.9	1.8	2.7	0.9	3.3	2.0	2.0	2.5	2.6	2.1	1.7	2.1	3.5	3.1	7.2
5. 6 to 9 times	0.6	0.6	0.6	0.6	0.5	0.7	1.0	0.3	0.4	0.4	0.9	0.2	0.9	0.5	1.0	-
6. 10+ times	1.2	1.6	0.6	1.3	0.5	1.2	1.5	0.7	1.5	1.1	1.3	0.8	0.6	2.8	1.6	6.1
Item 21470 Subject T N	2822	1311	1459	2160	403	511	854	939	518	1653	1016	1126	685	313	597	24

QUESTIONNAIRE FORM 1 1984	TOTAL	SEX		RACE		REGION				4YR COLLEGE PLANS		ILLICIT DRUG USE: LIFETIME				
		M	F	White	Black	NE	NC	S	W	Yes	No	None	Marijuana Only	Few Pills	More Pills	Any Heroin
N (Weighted No. of Cases):	3311	1534	1616	2414	478	670	941	1113	587	1772	1137	1223	794	381	765	32
% of Weighted Total:	100.0	46.3	48.8	72.9	14.4	20.2	28.4	33.6	17.7	53.5	34.3	36.9	24.0	11.5	23.1	1.0
D016D: For some physical illness or symptom																
1. None	59.8	67.1	53.0	58.5	65.6	61.6	57.8	60.8	59.4	56.9	63.8	63.6	63.7	49.6	53.7	46.3
2. Once	18.6	17.5	19.7	19.1	17.1	17.0	19.8	18.6	18.4	20.1	15.9	20.0	15.7	22.0	17.5	16.7
3. Twice	11.2	8.3	14.0	11.3	9.8	11.1	10.5	11.3	12.4	12.3	10.2	8.3	13.3	11.9	14.2	10.3
4. 3 to 5 times	7.3	4.9	9.4	7.8	6.2	7.7	7.7	7.4	6.4	7.8	6.9	5.5	6.0	11.1	10.1	9.7
5. 6 to 9 times	1.7	1.4	1.9	1.8	0.6	1.7	1.7	1.3	2.3	1.4	1.8	1.2	0.5	3.4	3.0	4.2
6. 10+ times	1.4	0.7	2.0	1.5	0.7	1.0	2.5	0.8	1.2	1.4	1.4	1.4	0.9	1.9	1.4	12.8
Item 21480 Subject T N	2821	1303	1464	2161	399	510	858	937	515	1652	1010	1120	688	311	601	24
D016E: For some emotional or psychological problem or symptom																
1. None	95.1	95.5	94.7	95.4	94.6	95.8	95.3	94.3	95.4	95.3	95.3	96.7	96.1	93.5	92.2	80.2
2. Once	2.3	2.4	2.2	2.0	3.8	1.5	2.5	2.6	2.4	2.2	2.0	1.9	2.5	3.9	2.2	4.2
3. Twice	0.6	0.7	0.6	0.6	0.6	0.7	0.7	0.7	0.4	0.6	0.6	0.4	0.8	1.3	0.2	-
4. 3 to 5 times	0.8	0.7	0.8	0.8	0.3	0.8	0.6	1.1	0.7	0.7	0.8	0.8	0.3	0.2	1.7	-
5. 6 to 9 times	0.3	0.1	0.6	0.3	0.4	0.5	0.4	-	0.6	0.3	0.5	0.1	0.1	0.2	1.0	5.2
6. 10+ times	0.8	0.6	1.1	1.0	0.3	0.7	0.6	1.3	0.6	0.9	0.9	0.1	0.2	0.9	2.8	10.4
Item 21490 Subject T N	2825	1309	1462	2162	401	509	859	941	516	1652	1016	1122	689	311	602	24
D017: In the LAST 12 MONTHS, how many times (if any) have you spent one or more nights in the hospital . . .																
D017A: Because of an injury																
1. None	95.1	92.9	97.1	95.2	94.7	93.8	95.5	94.4	96.8	95.6	94.6	95.8	94.7	95.7	94.1	86.8
2. Once	2.8	4.1	1.5	2.8	2.9	3.4	2.4	3.0	2.3	2.8	2.4	2.3	2.9	2.5	3.9	-
3. Twice	0.9	1.4	0.5	1.0	1.0	1.2	1.0	0.9	0.6	0.7	1.1	0.7	1.6	-	0.5	7.2
4. 3 to 5 times	0.6	1.0	0.3	0.6	0.6	1.2	0.6	0.6	0.1	0.5	0.9	0.8	0.6	-	0.8	-
5. 6 to 9 times	0.2	-	0.3	0.1	0.4	-	0.2	0.2	0.2	0.1	0.3	-	0.1	0.5	0.4	-
6. 10+ times	0.4	0.7	0.2	0.4	0.5	0.4	0.3	0.9	-	0.3	0.7	0.3	-	1.3	0.3	6.0
Item 21500 Subject T N	2816	1312	1454	2157	403	514	853	938	512	1650	1015	1119	687	308	601	25
D017B: Because of some physical illness																
1. None	93.8	94.8	92.8	94.4	92.5	93.0	93.3	92.6	97.7	94.9	92.0	94.9	93.9	93.0	92.6	84.7
2. Once	3.5	2.9	4.0	3.3	3.3	4.2	3.9	4.1	1.1	3.0	4.2	3.4	3.3	4.2	4.0	-
3. Twice	0.9	0.8	1.1	0.8	1.3	0.8	0.9	1.1	0.8	0.8	1.2	0.5	1.3	1.0	0.7	9.1
4. 3 to 5 times	0.8	0.5	1.1	0.7	1.5	0.8	0.7	1.3	0.1	0.8	1.0	0.7	0.9	0.4	1.0	-
5. 6 to 9 times	0.4	0.3	0.5	0.3	0.6	0.6	0.4	0.3	0.3	0.1	1.0	0.3	0.1	0.5	1.0	-
6. 10+ times	0.5	0.6	0.5	0.5	0.8	0.6	0.7	0.6	-	0.5	0.6	0.2	0.6	0.9	0.8	6.1
Item 21510 Subject T N	2815	1311	1454	2159	402	516	852	937	510	1647	1017	1118	687	310	599	24
D018: Overall, relative to other people your age, do you think your physical health over the past year has been . . .																
1. Much poorer than average	2.3	1.9	2.6	2.0	4.2	2.9	2.0	2.3	2.1	1.6	3.2	2.2	1.4	4.1	2.7	-
2. Somewhat poorer than average	8.9	6.0	11.5	9.3	8.6	9.3	9.6	8.4	8.3	8.6	9.3	7.4	7.2	14.3	10.8	4.8
3. About average	36.0	28.0	42.8	36.3	32.3	38.1	34.7	37.2	33.8	31.9	41.4	33.3	34.1	34.5	44.6	42.8
4. Somewhat better than average	29.4	33.7	25.5	29.2	30.2	28.6	31.1	27.8	30.4	31.2	27.6	29.9	33.7	25.8	25.3	24.4
5. Much better than average	23.4	30.3	17.5	23.2	24.7	21.2	22.7	24.2	25.4	26.7	18.4	27.2	23.6	21.2	16.5	28.1
Item 21520 Subject T N	2821	1306	1464	2162	402	514	853	936	518	1661	1009	1127	685	311	597	25

QUESTIONNAIRE FORM 2 1984		TOTAL	SEX		RACE		REGION				4YR COLLEGE PLANS		ILLICIT DRUG USE: LIFETIME				
			M	F	White	Black	NE	NC	S	W	Yes	No	None	Mari-juana Only	Few Pills	More Pills	Any Her-oin
N (Weighted No. of Cases):		3322	1624	1580	2491	453	681	929	1119	593	1855	1265	1285	662	479	773	51
% of Weighted Total:		100.0	48.9	47.5	75.0	13.6	20.1	28.0	33.7	17.9	55.8	38.1	38.7	19.9	14.4	23.3	1.5
A01: Taking all things together, how would you say things are these days–would you say you're very happy, pretty happy, or not too happy these days?																	
3. Very happy		17.9	16.8	19.1	19.4	13.3	18.4	14.2	18.7	21.4	21.2	13.1	20.0	18.0	16.4	15.8	14.3
2. Pretty happy		71.4	71.9	71.1	71.1	71.6	70.1	73.4	71.8	68.7	70.0	74.3	70.8	72.0	72.1	71.3	66.6
1. Not too happy		10.7	11.3	9.8	9.5	15.2	11.5	12.3	9.4	9.9	8.8	12.7	9.2	10.0	11.5	12.9	19.1
Item 1190 Subject P01,Q01	N	3227	1571	1551	2422	449	663	892	1095	577	1819	1219	1254	652	471	744	49
A02: The next questions ask about the kinds of things you might do. How often do you do each of the following?																	
A02A: Watch TV																	
5. Almost everyday		72.6	75.8	69.2	71.3	79.3	66.9	75.3	77.7	65.3	70.4	76.0	73.1	75.9	71.3	70.0	63.5
4. At least once a week		22.6	19.7	25.9	23.4	17.9	27.2	20.9	19.3	26.4	24.5	20.5	22.9	19.8	24.3	23.5	29.0
3. Once or twice a month		3.5	3.4	3.6	4.0	1.9	4.6	2.9	1.7	6.8	4.1	2.5	2.7	3.2	3.8	5.0	2.2
2. A few times a year		0.7	0.6	0.8	0.8	0.5	0.6	0.7	0.6	0.8	0.8	0.4	0.7	1.0	0.3	0.6	2.7
1. Never		0.6	0.5	0.5	0.5	0.5	0.7	0.2	0.7	0.7	0.2	0.6	0.5	0.1	0.3	0.9	2.6
Item 5820 Subject C07	N	3307	1616	1574	2485	446	680	926	1111	590	1850	1257	1284	658	475	770	50
A02B: Go to movies																	
5. Almost everyday		0.4	0.7	0.2	0.4	0.6	0.3	0.5	0.3	0.7	0.4	0.3	0.1	0.2	0.9	0.5	4.6
4. At least once a week		12.2	13.2	11.1	12.1	9.7	12.4	11.3	11.6	14.4	12.1	12.6	12.0	13.2	11.1	11.2	12.7
3. Once or twice a month		54.8	53.1	57.3	58.0	43.3	54.9	54.9	53.6	57.1	56.6	53.4	52.1	58.1	57.3	56.7	44.6
2. A few times a year		30.9	31.0	30.1	28.4	42.3	30.7	32.0	32.1	26.8	29.6	31.5	33.3	28.0	29.5	30.1	33.7
1. Never		1.7	2.0	1.3	1.1	4.1	1.8	1.2	2.4	1.1	1.3	2.1	2.5	0.5	1.1	1.5	4.4
Item 5830 Subject C07	N	3298	1609	1572	2481	445	675	926	1109	588	1845	1255	1280	656	472	770	50
A02C: Go to rock concerts																	
5. Almost everyday		0.2	0.3	-	0.2	-	0.7	0.1	0.1	-	0.2	0.1	-	-	0.1	0.6	-
4. At least once a week		0.2	0.4	0.1	0.2	0.2	0.1	-	0.4	0.2	*	0.4	0.1	0.2	0.4	0.4	-
3. Once or twice a month		5.0	6.5	3.2	5.4	1.2	5.7	3.3	4.4	8.0	3.9	6.4	2.3	2.8	4.5	10.5	17.8
2. A few times a year		50.0	50.8	49.7	54.5	37.2	50.7	51.5	49.6	47.8	54.2	44.5	37.7	57.4	49.8	64.8	53.1
1. Never		44.6	42.0	47.1	39.7	61.5	42.8	45.2	45.5	44.0	41.7	48.7	60.0	39.6	45.3	23.7	29.1
Item 5845 Subject C07	N	3310	1620	1576	2489	445	680	927	1112	590	1850	1262	1279	661	478	773	51
A02D: Ride around in a car (or motorcycle) just for fun																	
5. Almost everyday		34.0	39.7	27.2	34.0	30.1	34.9	34.3	37.9	25.4	27.1	43.0	24.1	35.2	35.4	46.1	64.2
4. At least once a week		34.2	33.8	34.8	34.4	36.7	32.8	34.6	35.5	32.9	34.2	34.8	31.9	35.6	42.1	33.4	18.7
3. Once or twice a month		14.6	12.7	17.2	15.3	13.7	13.5	15.2	12.6	18.6	17.4	11.0	18.2	14.8	9.5	11.4	17.1
2. A few times a year		10.4	9.0	11.9	10.4	10.3	10.7	11.2	8.2	12.9	13.0	6.7	15.2	8.6	8.8	5.5	-
1. Never		6.8	4.9	8.9	5.8	9.3	8.1	4.7	5.8	10.2	8.2	4.4	10.6	5.7	4.2	3.5	-
Item 5850 Subject C07	N	3305	1615	1573	2481	450	677	927	1110	591	1849	1259	1279	659	476	772	50
A02E: Participate in community affairs or volunteer work																	
5. Almost everyday		2.6	3.1	2.0	2.3	4.1	3.0	2.1	2.7	2.9	2.7	2.5	2.5	2.3	4.3	1.7	-
4. At least once a week		7.4	6.5	8.3	6.5	10.1	7.7	7.7	7.8	6.0	8.8	5.3	10.0	7.3	6.7	3.4	10.7
3. Once or twice a month		14.1	13.2	15.4	14.8	12.5	12.5	16.5	13.9	12.5	16.2	12.0	17.2	11.9	15.3	10.4	10.5
2. A few times a year		44.9	40.1	49.8	46.1	43.0	42.6	42.5	46.4	48.6	48.9	40.0	44.9	48.8	41.5	45.8	28.2
1. Never		31.0	37.2	24.4	30.3	30.3	34.2	31.2	29.2	30.1	23.3	40.2	25.4	29.8	32.1	38.7	50.6
Item 5860 Subject C07,O02	N	3302	1613	1572	2481	450	677	924	1110	591	1841	1264	1274	659	477	772	50
A02F: Play a musical instrument or sing																	
5. Almost everyday		30.0	24.0	36.7	29.8	32.0	28.2	32.6	27.5	32.4	34.9	24.5	33.7	28.1	27.5	27.7	41.7
4. At least once a week		9.3	8.1	10.8	8.7	13.8	8.7	10.1	9.7	8.0	9.8	8.6	10.6	7.5	10.4	7.6	10.7
3. Once or twice a month		5.1	4.8	5.1	4.7	6.4	3.8	5.7	5.8	4.2	6.1	3.3	6.4	3.8	5.5	3.5	7.8
2. A few times a year		11.8	12.1	11.5	11.4	13.3	7.9	11.1	13.1	15.1	13.1	10.2	11.9	10.1	12.3	12.9	10.6
1. Never		43.8	51.0	36.0	45.4	34.5	51.5	40.4	43.9	40.3	36.2	53.5	37.3	50.6	44.4	48.3	29.2
Item 5870 Subject C07	N	3299	1613	1569	2478	446	676	921	1109	592	1843	1259	1271	656	477	774	51

*=less than .05 per cent.

QUESTIONNAIRE FORM 2 1984	TOTAL	SEX		RACE		REGION				4YR COLLEGE PLANS		ILLICIT DRUG USE: LIFETIME				
		M	F	White	Black	NE	NC	S	W	Yes	No	None	Mari-juana Only	Few Pills	More Pills	Any Her-oin
N (Weighted No. of Cases):	3322	1624	1580	2491	453	681	929	1119	593	1855	1265	1285	662	479	773	51
% of Weighted Total:	100.0	48.9	47.5	75.0	13.6	20.1	28.0	33.7	17.9	55.8	38.1	38.7	19.9	14.4	23.3	1.5

A02G: Do creative writing

5. Almost everyday	5.8	6.0	5.8	5.0	8.3	3.7	6.6	4.2	10.1	7.7	3.4	5.9	6.4	5.6	5.5	5.8
4. At least once a week	12.2	11.4	13.0	11.5	16.8	11.5	7.5	15.2	15.0	15.4	7.9	13.1	10.7	12.0	12.2	11.5
3. Once or twice a month	19.1	16.2	22.4	19.5	19.2	19.7	18.1	18.4	21.0	23.7	12.6	21.6	16.2	17.2	19.0	23.3
2. A few times a year	27.5	25.4	29.8	27.2	29.1	28.0	27.2	27.7	27.2	30.0	24.7	27.9	28.0	28.1	26.8	13.8
1. Never	35.3	41.0	29.0	36.8	26.5	37.1	40.6	34.5	26.7	23.2	51.3	31.5	38.6	37.0	36.5	45.5
Item 5880 Subject C07 N	3290	1614	1562	2472	445	677	918	1104	591	1842	1252	1271	654	478	768	51

A02H: Actively participate in sports, athletics or exercising

5. Almost everyday	44.0	54.3	33.2	44.2	42.9	47.4	44.9	38.3	49.7	51.0	33.6	44.5	46.1	41.9	43.1	36.8
4. At least once a week	24.5	19.9	29.6	24.8	22.8	25.6	22.8	25.7	23.4	24.1	26.1	22.8	25.4	28.4	24.6	19.0
3. Once or twice a month	12.6	9.1	16.2	13.0	11.7	9.4	13.8	14.5	10.9	11.7	13.7	13.0	12.0	12.0	12.6	19.1
2. A few times a year	11.4	10.0	12.7	10.4	15.1	9.9	11.0	13.3	10.2	8.8	14.9	12.3	9.9	9.6	11.5	17.0
1. Never	7.5	6.7	8.3	7.7	7.4	7.8	7.6	8.2	5.8	4.4	11.8	7.4	6.7	8.0	8.2	8.1
Item 5890 Subject C07 N	3305	1619	1570	2485	448	680	927	1108	591	1849	1261	1277	658	478	772	51

A02I: Do art or craft work

5. Almost everyday	12.1	14.1	9.8	11.2	12.0	10.9	14.6	10.9	11.8	10.5	14.5	10.6	10.5	11.8	16.3	11.2
4. At least once a week	10.4	10.4	9.9	10.1	8.9	10.4	9.8	8.5	14.7	10.5	9.4	9.4	10.5	8.8	11.1	18.9
3. Once or twice a month	16.3	14.6	18.2	18.0	13.2	15.7	15.9	16.2	18.0	16.9	16.0	17.1	16.9	14.2	16.7	14.0
2. A few times a year	30.9	28.7	33.7	31.9	27.5	29.8	30.7	30.8	32.7	34.5	25.5	33.6	31.0	32.5	26.6	18.1
1. Never	30.3	32.2	28.3	28.9	38.4	33.1	29.0	33.5	22.8	27.6	34.6	29.2	31.2	32.7	29.3	37.9
Item 5900 Subject C07 N	3293	1617	1558	2472	447	679	921	1104	588	1842	1255	1271	660	475	767	50

A02J: Work around the house, yard, garden, car, etc.

5. Almost everyday	41.2	35.1	47.2	38.7	54.4	36.5	46.7	42.0	36.4	38.1	46.4	41.9	40.0	45.5	37.7	49.7
4. At least once a week	37.3	40.1	34.6	39.0	29.2	36.9	33.6	36.6	44.7	39.3	34.3	35.7	40.0	35.3	40.2	22.4
3. Once or twice a month	14.9	18.1	11.8	15.6	9.8	17.8	13.3	14.1	15.6	16.5	12.5	15.8	14.9	13.5	14.0	17.8
2. A few times a year	5.1	5.0	5.2	5.1	5.2	7.0	5.0	5.4	2.3	5.0	4.7	5.2	4.1	4.3	5.9	8.7
1. Never	1.6	1.7	1.3	1.5	1.4	1.8	1.4	1.9	1.0	1.1	2.1	1.5	1.0	1.3	2.2	1.4
Item 5910 Subject C07 N	3308	1618	1576	2486	448	678	926	1112	592	1851	1261	1281	659	478	770	50

A02K: Get together with friends, informally

5. Almost everyday	47.5	51.3	42.9	48.9	44.4	52.0	46.9	44.9	48.1	47.7	46.5	38.1	53.0	50.1	56.6	62.0
4. At least once a week	39.4	38.0	41.3	39.7	36.3	35.9	40.2	40.9	39.6	41.2	37.9	43.5	37.5	39.2	35.8	31.0
3. Once or twice a month	9.3	7.3	11.8	8.7	12.4	8.6	9.5	9.8	9.1	8.5	10.7	13.2	7.2	8.1	5.9	2.0
2. A few times a year	2.9	2.5	3.4	2.3	5.2	3.0	2.8	3.4	2.0	2.1	3.9	3.9	2.2	2.4	1.0	3.5
1. Never	0.8	0.8	0.7	0.4	1.6	0.5	0.6	0.9	1.2	0.5	1.1	1.3	0.1	0.2	0.6	1.4
Item 5920 Subject C07,M04 N	3300	1614	1572	2483	445	676	923	1111	589	1844	1259	1276	654	477	773	51

A02L: Go shopping or window-shopping

5. Almost everyday	3.3	1.6	5.1	2.4	7.8	3.2	3.4	3.7	2.8	3.0	3.9	3.4	3.7	4.0	2.8	2.1
4. At least once a week	37.8	25.4	50.6	37.4	40.4	42.7	36.6	38.7	32.5	38.3	37.6	36.5	39.1	41.1	38.5	24.0
3. Once or twice a month	43.5	47.0	40.0	44.2	42.0	38.9	44.8	43.5	46.9	46.2	40.4	44.8	43.5	41.2	41.8	53.7
2. A few times a year	11.1	18.2	3.8	11.7	7.1	11.1	10.5	9.6	14.8	11.2	10.4	12.0	10.8	8.4	11.5	7.2
1. Never	4.2	7.8	0.5	4.3	2.7	4.1	4.7	4.5	3.1	1.4	7.7	3.5	2.8	5.2	5.4	13.1
Item 5930 Subject C07,F01 N	3304	1615	1572	2481	448	677	924	1113	589	1850	1256	1277	658	477	771	51

A02M: Spend at least an hour of leisure time alone

5. Almost everyday	43.5	42.1	45.3	42.2	49.9	44.9	42.1	45.1	40.9	45.5	40.9	41.6	45.9	42.0	45.5	46.9
4. At least once a week	35.8	35.7	36.1	37.0	33.7	37.7	35.2	33.3	39.0	37.1	34.3	37.8	33.6	34.5	35.9	27.7
3. Once or twice a month	11.5	11.8	11.5	12.3	7.3	9.8	14.6	9.1	13.2	11.1	12.2	10.7	12.6	11.3	11.8	10.1
2. A few times a year	4.9	5.7	3.7	5.0	4.0	3.2	5.6	6.1	3.4	3.4	6.3	4.8	5.0	6.5	3.4	9.0
1. Never	4.4	4.7	3.4	3.6	5.1	4.3	2.5	6.4	3.5	2.8	6.4	5.2	2.9	5.6	3.5	6.3
Item 5940 Subject C07 N	3307	1617	1573	2484	449	679	925	1112	591	1851	1259	1277	659	477	774	51

QUESTIONNAIRE FORM 2 1984	TOTAL	SEX		RACE		REGION				4YR COLLEGE PLANS		ILLICIT DRUG USE: LIFETIME				
		M	F	White	Black	NE	NC	S	W	Yes	No	None	Mari-juana Only	Few Pills	More Pills	Any Her-oin
N (Weighted No. of Cases):	3322	1624	1580	2491	453	681	929	1119	593	1855	1265	1285	662	479	773	51
% of Weighted Total:	100.0	48.9	47.5	75.0	13.6	20.1	28.0	33.7	17.9	55.8	38.1	38.7	19.9	14.4	23.3	1.5
A02N: Read books, magazines, or newspapers																
5. Almost everyday	52.8	52.2	53.9	53.4	54.6	57.0	54.2	48.5	53.8	59.3	44.1	55.4	52.0	50.9	52.3	40.9
4. At least once a week	29.5	29.2	29.7	29.2	28.5	28.3	28.3	30.9	29.8	27.9	31.4	27.1	30.6	33.1	30.6	27.5
3. Once or twice a month	11.5	11.0	11.8	11.2	12.2	9.1	10.7	13.3	12.0	9.8	14.2	11.7	12.0	9.2	10.7	12.2
2. A few times a year	4.6	5.3	3.6	4.3	3.4	4.6	5.1	4.9	3.1	2.3	7.2	4.1	5.0	5.4	3.9	14.0
1. Never	1.7	2.3	1.0	1.8	1.4	0.9	1.8	2.4	1.2	0.7	3.1	1.7	0.5	1.4	2.6	5.4
Item 5950 Subject C07 N	*3304*	*1616*	*1572*	*2482*	*448*	*677*	*927*	*1110*	*590*	*1847*	*1260*	*1280*	*659*	*477*	*770*	*50*
A02O: Go to taverns, bars or nightclubs																
5. Almost everyday	2.1	3.5	0.6	2.2	1.3	2.8	2.6	1.9	1.0	0.9	3.5	0.9	1.7	2.4	3.6	14.3
4. At least once a week	13.6	15.0	11.8	13.7	13.1	14.8	15.6	14.2	7.9	12.7	15.0	6.4	14.3	15.9	23.0	23.3
3. Once or twice a month	18.3	18.9	17.5	19.4	13.0	19.2	16.6	21.0	14.7	18.5	17.9	11.4	20.2	20.6	26.6	26.5
2. A few times a year	21.0	21.7	20.7	21.8	18.6	24.4	20.7	20.4	18.8	21.3	20.9	19.0	21.1	25.0	21.2	22.5
1. Never	45.0	41.0	49.4	43.0	54.0	38.9	44.4	42.5	57.7	46.6	42.8	62.5	42.7	36.1	25.6	13.5
Item 5960 Subject C07 N	*3308*	*1621*	*1571*	*2484*	*449*	*677*	*928*	*1112*	*591*	*1849*	*1261*	*1278*	*660*	*478*	*774*	*51*
A02P: Go to parties or other social affairs																
5. Almost everyday	3.1	4.7	1.3	3.1	2.2	4.9	3.3	2.4	2.2	2.0	4.5	0.9	1.5	4.3	6.2	19.3
4. At least once a week	34.5	37.0	31.5	35.5	32.3	36.6	36.1	32.0	34.1	34.7	34.4	20.5	40.6	39.2	49.1	44.7
3. Once or twice a month	36.6	33.5	40.2	37.1	35.8	36.2	34.5	36.5	40.3	39.4	32.8	39.1	38.4	36.5	32.8	19.5
2. A few times a year	21.1	19.7	22.7	20.0	23.3	18.7	21.1	23.7	19.1	21.2	21.1	31.4	16.3	16.9	10.4	15.2
1. Never	4.7	5.1	4.3	4.3	6.4	3.6	5.0	5.4	4.2	2.7	7.2	8.0	3.2	3.1	1.5	1.4
Item 5970 Subject C07 N	*3316*	*1621*	*1577*	*2490*	*450*	*680*	*928*	*1114*	*593*	*1854*	*1263*	*1282*	*661*	*478*	*774*	*51*
A03: How much do you agree or disagree with each of the following statements?																
A03A: In the United States, we put too much emphasis on making profits and not enough on human well-being																
1. Disagree	5.4	7.8	2.8	5.3	5.9	6.6	5.2	5.3	4.8	5.6	5.0	5.2	4.8	6.5	5.4	7.7
2. Mostly disagree	11.6	14.4	8.8	12.3	8.4	10.1	11.9	12.2	11.6	13.4	9.8	12.4	11.7	9.3	12.1	7.8
3. Neither	17.7	20.4	15.4	18.9	10.3	16.8	18.6	16.9	19.0	17.7	17.9	16.0	16.8	21.2	18.9	27.2
4. Mostly agree	42.7	35.9	50.3	44.4	35.4	43.2	43.3	41.1	44.2	43.5	41.6	44.8	42.0	43.3	39.8	39.2
5. Agree	22.6	21.5	22.7	19.0	40.0	23.3	21.1	24.5	20.5	19.7	25.7	21.5	24.7	19.7	23.8	18.0
Item 5990 Subject F03,O03 N	*3285*	*1605*	*1563*	*2467*	*448*	*676*	*919*	*1102*	*588*	*1841*	*1251*	*1271*	*652*	*476*	*768*	*51*
A03B: People are too much concerned with material things these days																
1. Disagree	3.5	4.2	2.5	3.3	5.0	3.8	2.1	4.7	3.1	2.9	4.2	2.8	3.6	4.1	4.0	6.0
2. Mostly disagree	7.4	9.7	5.2	8.4	4.8	7.2	8.1	7.4	6.7	8.1	6.3	6.9	7.3	8.6	7.3	16.8
3. Neither	11.3	13.5	8.8	11.9	6.4	9.8	14.8	8.7	12.5	10.1	12.9	9.8	12.0	9.2	13.6	21.2
4. Mostly agree	37.9	38.0	38.7	40.3	29.7	35.8	39.4	36.5	40.4	40.1	36.0	38.0	39.7	39.5	35.9	30.6
5. Agree	39.9	34.5	44.7	36.2	54.1	43.4	35.6	42.8	37.3	38.8	40.6	42.4	37.5	38.7	39.3	25.3
Item 6000 Subject F02 N	*3300*	*1608*	*1575*	*2477*	*450*	*677*	*923*	*1108*	*591*	*1848*	*1259*	*1277*	*655*	*479*	*769*	*51*
A03C: Since it helps the economy to grow, people should be encouraged to buy more																
1. Disagree	18.3	15.9	20.2	15.7	26.6	21.3	16.0	18.3	18.5	14.3	23.2	16.6	19.2	17.7	19.0	25.0
2. Mostly disagree	21.9	18.0	26.0	22.5	20.0	19.4	20.4	23.8	23.4	22.6	20.9	22.1	19.0	24.2	23.4	10.1
3. Neither	29.9	28.9	31.7	32.0	22.4	31.1	30.1	29.4	29.2	33.7	24.6	30.1	29.8	28.7	31.6	28.5
4. Mostly agree	20.8	24.2	17.1	21.5	18.5	18.4	25.6	18.0	21.2	21.1	21.1	22.6	20.1	18.1	19.3	35.1
5. Agree	9.1	13.0	4.9	8.3	12.5	9.8	7.9	10.5	7.6	8.3	10.2	8.5	11.9	11.2	6.7	1.3
Item 6010 Subject F02 N	*3291*	*1608*	*1569*	*2473*	*446*	*675*	*922*	*1104*	*590*	*1842*	*1257*	*1274*	*655*	*475*	*770*	*51*

QUESTIONNAIRE FORM 2 1984	TOTAL	SEX		RACE		REGION				4YR COLLEGE PLANS		ILLICIT DRUG USE: LIFETIME				
		M	F	White	Black	NE	NC	S	W	Yes	No	None	Mari-juana Only	Few Pills	More Pills	Any Her-oin
N (Weighted No. of Cases):	3322	1624	1580	2491	453	681	929	1119	593	1855	1265	1285	662	479	773	51
% of Weighted Total:	100.0	48.9	47.5	75.0	13.6	20.1	28.0	33.7	17.9	55.8	38.1	38.7	19.9	14.4	23.3	1.5

A03D: There is nothing wrong with advertising that gets people to buy things they don't really need

1. Disagree	32.9	31.2	34.4	32.7	35.4	33.0	29.4	36.3	31.8	33.4	32.0	35.1	32.2	28.4	32.8	37.6
2. Mostly disagree	24.2	23.8	25.2	26.3	13.2	24.3	26.6	22.1	24.3	26.5	20.8	25.7	23.2	24.9	22.6	19.6
3. Neither	15.6	15.6	15.6	16.7	14.3	14.3	18.0	14.3	15.6	14.9	17.4	13.6	14.9	17.2	18.6	12.9
4. Mostly agree	14.0	14.0	14.2	13.6	16.4	13.9	14.5	12.7	15.9	14.0	14.1	14.2	14.8	13.4	13.1	19.2
5. Agree	13.3	15.4	10.6	10.7	20.8	14.5	11.5	14.5	12.4	11.1	15.7	11.4	14.9	16.1	12.9	10.6
Item 6020 Subject F02 N	3297	1610	1572	2478	448	677	922	1107	592	1847	1257	1275	656	477	771	51

A03E: There will probably be more shortages in the future, so Americans will have to learn how to be happy with fewer "things"

1. Disagree	8.7	10.7	6.4	8.2	10.4	9.8	7.2	9.8	7.5	8.6	8.4	8.6	8.5	9.4	7.6	13.0
2. Mostly disagree	11.9	12.2	11.6	12.6	8.5	9.6	10.8	12.5	14.8	13.2	10.2	11.8	10.6	13.6	12.1	14.0
3. Neither	15.9	15.4	16.4	17.1	11.7	17.9	16.3	13.4	17.5	17.7	14.0	15.6	16.6	14.9	15.7	24.3
4. Mostly agree	29.6	28.0	31.6	30.4	26.0	29.1	32.3	28.7	27.7	30.5	28.2	30.8	29.7	28.0	30.1	16.3
5. Agree	34.0	33.7	34.0	31.7	43.3	33.5	33.3	35.7	32.5	30.0	39.2	33.2	34.7	34.1	34.5	32.4
Item 6030 Subject F02 N	3302	1609	1576	2479	451	677	921	1111	593	1851	1258	1275	658	478	771	51

A04: Below are several ways that people have used to protest about serious social issues. How much do you approve or disapprove of these actions?

A04A: Signing petitions

4. Strongly approve	22.5	22.9	22.2	22.9	21.2	24.6	20.5	21.2	25.9	27.3	16.2	23.2	22.4	22.7	22.5	20.5
3. Approve	46.5	48.2	45.3	49.6	36.2	45.2	49.5	44.2	47.8	48.5	45.3	45.2	47.7	47.3	47.5	39.9
2. Disapprove	3.0	3.7	2.0	2.6	4.4	3.0	3.3	2.9	2.8	2.4	3.5	3.0	2.9	2.0	3.7	1.0
1. Strongly disapprove	0.9	0.9	0.8	0.9	1.3	1.1	0.5	1.4	0.6	0.5	1.2	0.9	0.9	0.5	0.9	4.6
8. Don't know, or it depends	27.0	24.2	29.7	23.9	36.9	26.2	26.3	30.4	22.8	21.3	33.7	27.7	26.2	27.4	25.4	34.0
Item 6040 Subject I02 N	3294	1610	1570	2475	447	675	922	1106	591	1847	1258	1280	653	475	768	51

A04B: Boycotting certain products or stores

4. Strongly approve	13.4	15.1	11.7	13.2	14.3	17.6	10.9	10.3	18.4	16.6	8.6	14.7	13.2	11.0	13.3	4.4
3. Approve	32.8	35.5	29.1	33.5	30.7	36.8	30.2	32.8	32.2	36.2	27.8	30.6	34.7	34.5	33.1	34.3
2. Disapprove	15.3	15.6	14.8	15.8	13.1	12.7	17.7	15.6	14.1	14.7	16.3	16.0	14.3	13.5	16.1	18.9
1. Strongly disapprove	4.0	4.3	3.7	3.5	5.0	3.4	4.6	4.5	2.8	2.7	6.1	4.5	4.3	2.7	3.5	8.3
8. Don't know, or it depends	34.5	29.4	40.7	34.0	36.9	29.6	36.6	36.8	32.6	29.7	41.2	34.2	33.5	38.2	34.0	34.1
Item 6050 Subject I02 N	3283	1610	1560	2467	446	672	921	1101	588	1844	1252	1274	653	474	766	50

A04C: Lawful demonstrations

4. Strongly approve	16.6	18.7	14.7	16.5	17.2	18.9	13.9	16.0	19.5	19.1	13.0	16.4	14.9	17.7	18.0	16.6
3. Approve	45.5	46.7	44.6	47.7	38.9	45.0	48.1	42.0	48.8	49.8	40.2	44.8	47.0	43.4	47.4	40.7
2. Disapprove	9.6	9.9	8.9	9.4	8.4	9.4	9.0	11.5	7.2	7.4	12.6	10.7	8.9	8.4	8.7	10.5
1. Strongly disapprove	4.3	5.1	3.7	4.2	4.5	3.6	5.2	4.7	3.2	3.2	6.3	4.5	4.0	4.3	4.3	7.6
8. Don't know, or it depends	23.9	19.6	28.1	22.1	31.0	23.1	23.8	25.7	21.3	20.6	28.0	23.7	25.2	26.2	21.6	24.5
Item 6060 Subject I02 N	3278	1605	1563	2467	445	673	919	1101	584	1840	1252	1267	651	474	769	51

A04D: Occupying buildings or factories

4. Strongly approve	5.2	5.8	4.2	4.3	9.3	6.2	3.8	6.0	4.7	4.8	5.7	4.6	6.4	5.7	4.2	5.7
3. Approve	21.9	20.9	22.8	21.0	24.7	21.1	22.4	23.6	19.1	17.7	27.1	19.3	22.4	20.9	26.0	21.3
2. Disapprove	25.1	27.3	23.1	27.1	18.4	24.1	26.4	23.8	26.8	27.7	22.3	28.1	23.8	22.0	23.8	17.9
1. Strongly disapprove	10.2	12.4	7.8	10.9	6.3	9.2	9.1	10.3	12.7	11.5	8.2	10.7	9.9	9.8	10.5	8.8
8. Don't know, or it depends	37.6	33.6	42.0	36.7	41.2	39.3	38.4	36.4	36.6	38.3	36.7	37.4	37.5	41.6	35.5	46.4
Item 6070 Subject I02 N	3265	1602	1552	2458	442	668	918	1095	585	1835	1249	1271	651	466	761	50

A04E: Wildcat strikes

4. Strongly approve	3.1	4.3	1.8	2.7	2.7	3.8	2.7	2.9	3.6	2.1	4.5	2.5	2.5	2.5	3.8	15.3
3. Approve	10.2	13.9	6.3	10.2	8.7	11.9	11.4	8.5	9.9	9.9	10.8	8.0	7.7	11.9	14.3	19.2
2. Disapprove	28.2	28.9	28.0	28.6	27.2	28.6	27.0	30.0	26.6	30.2	25.8	30.2	29.8	25.1	26.8	16.0
1. Strongly disapprove	16.8	17.2	15.8	17.1	17.4	15.8	17.6	17.6	15.1	16.3	17.0	18.3	14.8	20.2	13.9	14.8
8. Don't know, or it depends	41.6	35.7	48.2	41.4	44.1	39.9	41.4	41.1	44.9	41.5	41.8	41.0	45.2	40.4	41.2	34.8
Item 6080 Subject I02 N	3243	1600	1534	2441	439	657	913	1092	581	1818	1243	1255	647	464	761	51

QUESTIONNAIRE FORM 2 1984	TOTAL	SEX		RACE		REGION				4YR COLLEGE PLANS		ILLICIT DRUG USE: LIFETIME				
		M	F	White	Black	NE	NC	S	W	Yes	No	None	Mari-juana Only	Few Pills	More Pills	Any Her-oin
N (Weighted No. of Cases):	3322	1624	1580	2491	453	681	929	1119	593	1855	1265	1285	662	479	773	51
% of Weighted Total:	100.0	48.9	47.5	75.0	13.6	20.1	28.0	33.7	17.9	55.8	38.1	38.7	19.9	14.4	23.3	1.5
A04F: Blocking traffic																
4. Strongly approve	2.2	2.2	1.7	1.9	2.7	2.7	1.2	2.4	2.4	1.4	2.9	1.7	2.6	1.5	2.3	5.1
3. Approve	4.0	5.3	2.6	3.2	4.7	5.8	3.0	2.9	5.2	3.5	4.3	3.1	5.1	1.9	5.4	9.5
2. Disapprove	38.3	36.5	40.9	39.1	37.1	39.0	41.0	38.8	32.5	39.1	38.0	39.9	37.7	36.1	39.0	27.2
1. Strongly disapprove	42.6	43.5	41.6	43.9	39.2	39.2	41.0	44.4	45.5	43.9	40.7	43.9	42.6	45.3	39.6	30.4
8. Don't know, or it depends	13.0	12.5	13.2	11.9	16.2	13.3	13.8	11.4	14.3	12.1	14.2	11.5	12.1	15.2	13.7	27.9
Item 6090 Subject I02 N	3288	1611	1564	2473	443	672	923	1101	592	1841	1256	1277	654	473	767	51
A04G: Damaging things																
4. Strongly approve	2.4	2.8	2.1	1.9	3.3	2.9	1.6	3.0	2.2	1.3	3.9	2.1	2.7	2.4	2.0	8.2
3. Approve	2.0	2.8	0.9	1.6	2.2	2.5	1.8	1.8	2.2	1.2	2.7	0.9	2.2	2.2	2.6	13.9
2. Disapprove	21.0	23.6	17.7	19.8	23.2	20.7	19.3	23.4	19.3	18.3	24.7	21.5	18.0	20.5	23.7	10.7
1. Strongly disapprove	67.8	63.1	73.7	70.8	61.4	65.8	71.5	64.9	69.4	73.4	60.7	70.3	70.2	67.1	63.9	43.1
8. Don't know, or it depends	6.9	7.8	5.6	5.9	9.8	8.1	5.8	6.9	6.9	5.7	8.1	5.2	6.9	7.9	7.8	24.1
Item 6100 Subject I02 N	3295	1613	1569	2478	447	676	924	1105	590	1850	1255	1279	656	473	770	51
A04H: Personal violence																
4. Strongly approve	3.0	3.9	2.0	2.3	4.4	3.1	2.0	3.7	2.9	1.6	4.4	2.9	2.9	3.1	2.2	9.5
3. Approve	3.4	5.2	1.0	2.9	2.9	3.4	3.3	3.0	4.1	1.8	4.8	2.0	2.8	3.4	5.1	16.5
2. Disapprove	18.6	20.4	16.2	16.9	25.3	19.8	18.3	18.5	17.9	15.6	22.5	17.4	18.0	18.9	20.8	15.8
1. Strongly disapprove	66.3	59.6	74.5	70.0	57.8	62.5	68.5	66.3	67.0	74.3	56.9	70.9	67.9	63.3	62.3	30.3
8. Don't know, or it depends	8.8	10.9	6.3	8.0	9.5	11.1	7.8	8.5	8.1	6.6	11.4	6.8	8.4	11.3	9.6	27.9
Item 6110 Subject I02 N	3301	1614	1574	2481	449	677	926	1107	592	1850	1260	1281	656	477	769	51
A05: Do you think that you would prefer having a mate for most of your life, or would you prefer not having a mate?																
5. Definitely prefer to have a mate	58.8	54.1	64.2	61.2	51.6	55.8	58.3	60.3	60.4	59.8	58.5	59.4	61.4	60.6	56.5	54.5
4. Probably prefer to have a mate	26.6	29.9	23.4	25.8	28.8	30.3	26.0	24.6	27.2	27.4	25.6	27.4	25.3	26.7	27.2	11.4
3. Not sure	10.8	12.1	9.2	9.8	15.3	9.9	11.9	11.7	8.5	9.3	12.2	9.8	10.5	9.6	11.8	20.1
2. Probably prefer not to have a mate	2.7	2.7	2.5	2.5	2.9	3.0	3.1	1.9	3.4	2.7	2.6	2.1	2.1	2.4	4.1	7.7
1. Definitely prefer not to have a mate	1.0	1.2	0.7	0.8	1.4	1.1	0.7	1.4	0.6	0.8	1.1	1.3	0.7	0.6	0.4	6.3
Item 6120 Subject D01 N	3300	1613	1571	2480	447	677	923	1113	588	1846	1256	1279	657	476	769	51
A06: Which do you think you are most likely to choose in the long run?																
3. Getting married	76.1	71.7	82.1	78.6	64.8	73.8	74.3	76.7	80.3	79.5	73.1	77.6	79.9	78.0	72.5	58.6
2. I have no idea	17.3	21.6	11.9	15.6	24.5	19.9	18.3	15.8	15.5	14.7	19.7	16.9	15.2	15.6	19.0	18.6
1. Not getting married	5.7	6.2	4.6	4.8	9.8	5.8	6.6	5.9	3.9	5.4	5.7	4.9	4.2	5.8	6.8	19.8
8. Am already married	0.9	0.4	1.4	1.0	0.9	0.5	0.8	1.6	0.3	0.3	1.6	0.6	0.7	0.6	1.7	3.1
Item 6130 Subject D01 N	3249	1585	1552	2451	439	668	911	1091	578	1822	1237	1259	646	469	760	49
A07: If you did get married (or are married) . . .																
A07A: How likely do you think it is that you would stay married to the same person for life?																
5. Very likely	61.1	55.1	67.6	62.3	55.4	60.1	60.0	61.5	63.3	63.1	59.2	67.8	62.6	57.1	52.7	42.6
4. Fairly likely	23.4	27.6	19.3	24.4	19.7	22.5	26.8	22.0	21.4	23.9	23.1	19.9	23.0	27.6	27.9	23.4
3. Uncertain	13.0	13.9	11.4	11.1	22.4	15.3	10.5	13.8	12.8	10.9	14.5	10.9	13.4	12.7	15.1	13.6
2. Fairly unlikely	1.6	2.0	1.3	1.5	1.6	1.4	2.1	1.4	1.6	1.4	2.0	0.9	0.5	1.6	3.0	13.1
1. Very unlikely	0.9	1.4	0.4	0.7	0.9	0.6	0.6	1.4	0.9	0.7	1.2	0.5	0.5	1.0	1.3	7.3
Item 6140 Subject D01 N	3171	1548	1518	2376	428	633	894	1080	563	1768	1214	1219	641	460	732	50
A07B: How likely is it that you would want to have children?																
5. Very likely	62.4	60.9	64.3	63.4	59.8	65.6	58.5	63.4	63.1	66.0	57.7	63.8	63.9	61.2	60.6	45.6
4. Fairly likely	18.7	20.7	16.6	19.0	17.9	16.8	22.1	16.1	20.5	18.5	19.2	17.6	19.7	19.4	19.4	14.0
3. Uncertain	11.1	11.8	10.2	10.5	11.2	11.6	11.6	11.7	8.4	9.2	13.1	11.4	8.8	12.1	11.5	18.0
2. Fairly unlikely	2.8	2.2	3.2	3.0	2.5	1.7	2.6	3.2	3.4	2.9	2.6	2.8	2.3	2.1	3.6	5.6
1. Very unlikely	3.5	3.7	3.3	3.1	4.2	3.6	3.3	3.7	3.5	3.0	4.5	3.1	2.5	4.5	3.8	15.4
8. Already have child(ren)	1.5	0.7	2.3	1.0	4.5	0.7	1.9	1.8	1.1	0.4	3.0	1.2	2.9	0.6	1.1	1.4
Item 6150 Subject D02 N	3192	1554	1530	2393	434	641	895	1089	567	1780	1223	1234	641	462	738	49

QUESTIONNAIRE FORM 2 1984	TOTAL	SEX		RACE		REGION				4YR COLLEGE PLANS		ILLICIT DRUG USE: LIFETIME				
		M	F	White	Black	NE	NC	S	W	Yes	No	None	Mari- juana Only	Few Pills	More Pills	Any Her- oin
N (Weighted No. of Cases):	3322	1624	1580	2491	453	681	929	1119	593	1855	1265	1285	662	479	773	51
% of Weighted Total:	100.0	48.9	47.5	75.0	13.6	20.1	28.0	33.7	17.9	55.8	38.1	38.7	19.9	14.4	23.3	1.5

The questions in the next column ask you to imagine different kinds of married life that you might have. We want you to think about different ways you might share responsibilities for working, taking care of the home, and taking care of children. Please indicate how acceptable for you each of the different arrangements would be.

A08: Imagine you are married and have no children–how would you feel about each of the following working arrangements?

A08A: Husband works full-time, wife doesn't work

	TOTAL	M	F	White	Black	NE	NC	S	W	Yes	No	None	Mari-juana Only	Few Pills	More Pills	Any Heroin
1. Not at all acceptable	25.4	13.6	37.8	22.6	40.6	30.5	21.6	26.2	24.1	28.1	22.1	24.1	27.6	27.6	25.8	11.7
2. Somewhat acceptable	32.7	30.1	35.5	32.7	32.5	32.1	32.7	32.6	33.7	31.4	34.4	33.4	32.6	26.8	35.0	33.2
3. Acceptable	33.9	45.0	22.0	36.6	19.9	31.0	38.3	32.7	32.7	33.1	34.7	33.8	32.5	38.2	32.2	38.7
4. Desirable	7.9	11.2	4.7	8.1	7.1	6.5	7.4	8.5	9.4	7.4	8.8	8.8	7.3	7.4	7.0	16.4
Item 6160　Subject C05,D04　N	*3286*	*1609*	*1565*	*2478*	*442*	*674*	*919*	*1109*	*584*	*1842*	*1253*	*1273*	*655*	*474*	*768*	*51*

A08B: Husband works full-time, wife works about half-time

	TOTAL	M	F	White	Black	NE	NC	S	W	Yes	No	None	Mari-juana Only	Few Pills	More Pills	Any Heroin
1. Not at all acceptable	4.4	3.3	5.0	3.2	9.3	5.1	2.7	5.5	4.0	3.7	4.8	4.5	5.1	3.4	3.4	13.0
2. Somewhat acceptable	22.3	18.5	26.4	20.5	28.3	24.8	20.0	22.9	21.6	23.4	21.1	23.7	23.5	21.0	19.2	21.8
3. Acceptable	58.5	62.5	54.5	60.2	52.4	55.3	63.2	58.2	55.3	57.8	59.3	58.3	58.7	59.4	58.2	52.0
4. Desirable	14.9	15.7	14.1	16.0	9.9	14.7	14.1	13.4	19.1	15.2	14.8	13.5	12.7	16.3	19.3	13.2
Item 6170　Subject C05,D04　N	*3285*	*1606*	*1567*	*2477*	*443*	*675*	*918*	*1109*	*584*	*1841*	*1253*	*1271*	*654*	*475*	*768*	*51*

A08C: Both work full-time

	TOTAL	M	F	White	Black	NE	NC	S	W	Yes	No	None	Mari-juana Only	Few Pills	More Pills	Any Heroin
1. Not at all acceptable	13.3	18.2	8.0	12.0	13.5	12.6	11.4	15.2	13.5	10.6	16.7	12.3	13.4	13.9	13.2	19.5
2. Somewhat acceptable	18.0	20.2	15.9	17.8	17.6	16.3	18.1	18.5	18.5	17.3	18.6	18.8	17.3	19.7	16.3	13.9
3. Acceptable	46.8	43.3	49.8	48.1	43.7	47.3	48.9	45.3	45.5	47.5	46.2	47.1	47.1	45.1	46.8	45.8
4. Desirable	22.0	18.3	26.3	22.2	25.1	23.8	21.6	20.9	22.5	24.6	18.5	21.8	22.2	21.3	23.7	20.9
Item 6180　Subject C05,D04　N	*3264*	*1595*	*1556*	*2459*	*436*	*670*	*909*	*1102*	*582*	*1824*	*1245*	*1257*	*649*	*473*	*767*	*51*

A08D: Both work about half-time

	TOTAL	M	F	White	Black	NE	NC	S	W	Yes	No	None	Mari-juana Only	Few Pills	More Pills	Any Heroin
1. Not at all acceptable	42.1	43.5	41.0	39.5	55.3	42.0	37.8	49.3	35.6	38.9	46.8	42.0	42.4	40.5	42.1	37.9
2. Somewhat acceptable	28.7	28.5	28.8	30.5	22.6	26.9	32.4	25.5	30.7	30.1	27.3	28.5	28.7	29.4	29.0	29.4
3. Acceptable	21.5	20.3	22.9	22.3	15.6	24.2	22.6	18.0	23.1	22.8	19.5	21.7	21.3	22.4	20.6	26.4
4. Desirable	7.7	7.6	7.3	7.7	6.5	6.9	7.2	7.2	10.5	8.2	6.4	7.7	7.5	7.7	8.3	6.3
Item 6190　Subject C05,D04　N	*3261*	*1596*	*1554*	*2459*	*437*	*667*	*917*	*1095*	*582*	*1831*	*1240*	*1264*	*649*	*470*	*761*	*51*

A08E: Husband works about half-time, wife works full-time

	TOTAL	M	F	White	Black	NE	NC	S	W	Yes	No	None	Mari-juana Only	Few Pills	More Pills	Any Heroin
1. Not at all acceptable	51.4	56.6	45.7	49.4	57.7	50.0	46.5	57.7	49.0	47.0	56.9	49.8	53.7	52.9	51.0	49.4
2. Somewhat acceptable	27.1	22.4	32.4	28.7	20.9	26.5	29.4	24.5	29.0	30.1	23.9	29.2	26.2	25.6	26.7	16.0
3. Acceptable	17.9	16.4	19.7	18.9	15.6	19.6	21.0	13.9	18.5	19.9	14.9	17.7	16.2	19.0	19.1	19.1
4. Desirable	3.6	4.6	2.3	3.0	5.8	3.9	3.1	3.9	3.5	3.0	4.3	3.3	4.0	2.5	3.1	15.6
Item 6200　Subject C05,D04　N	*3271*	*1597*	*1564*	*2467*	*440*	*672*	*912*	*1104*	*583*	*1833*	*1248*	*1268*	*650*	*474*	*764*	*51*

A08F: Husband doesn't work, wife works full-time

	TOTAL	M	F	White	Black	NE	NC	S	W	Yes	No	None	Mari-juana Only	Few Pills	More Pills	Any Heroin
1. Not at all acceptable	77.2	77.1	77.6	75.7	84.0	73.6	72.7	83.6	76.2	76.1	79.0	76.0	78.7	80.1	76.9	62.1
2. Somewhat acceptable	12.8	10.9	15.1	14.4	7.5	14.4	15.4	9.2	13.7	14.8	10.6	14.3	12.3	10.7	13.3	7.8
3. Acceptable	7.0	7.7	6.1	7.6	3.9	8.7	8.9	4.3	7.0	7.4	6.2	6.7	5.5	7.9	7.6	15.1
4. Desirable	3.0	4.3	1.3	2.3	4.6	3.3	2.9	2.9	3.0	1.8	4.1	3.0	3.6	1.2	2.2	14.9
Item 6210　Subject C05,D04　N	*3272*	*1599*	*1561*	*2468*	*440*	*668*	*916*	*1106*	*582*	*1836*	*1246*	*1270*	*651*	*472*	*764*	*51*

A09: Imagine you are married and have one or more pre-school children. How would you feel about each of the following working arrangements?

QUESTIONNAIRE FORM 2 1984	TOTAL	SEX		RACE		REGION				4YR COLLEGE PLANS		ILLICIT DRUG USE: LIFETIME				
		M	F	White	Black	NE	NC	S	W	Yes	No	None	Marijuana Only	Few Pills	More Pills	Any Heroin
N (Weighted No. of Cases):	3322	1624	1580	2491	453	681	929	1119	593	1855	1265	1285	662	479	773	51
% of Weighted Total:	100.0	48.9	47.5	75.0	13.6	20.1	28.0	33.7	17.9	55.8	38.1	38.7	19.9	14.4	23.3	1.5

A09A: Husband works full-time, wife doesn't work

1. Not at all acceptable	9.0	5.5	12.1	6.7	20.9	9.6	6.3	10.6	9.4	8.6	8.9	9.6	8.9	9.4	7.8	9.9
2. Somewhat acceptable	18.4	14.5	22.3	15.6	29.1	19.1	14.9	20.5	19.1	19.0	17.5	15.9	21.4	17.7	20.6	14.7
3. Acceptable	39.6	41.1	38.8	40.5	34.7	39.3	43.2	37.5	38.4	36.9	42.7	38.6	38.6	41.1	40.5	42.0
4. Desirable	33.0	38.9	26.8	37.2	15.2	32.0	35.5	31.4	33.2	35.5	30.8	35.9	31.1	31.9	31.0	33.5
Item 6220 Subject C05,D04 N	3285	1608	1566	2478	443	673	919	1109	584	1842	1251	1275	655	474	766	51

A09B: Husband works full-time, wife works about half-time

1. Not at all acceptable	8.9	11.7	5.5	8.6	7.2	12.5	8.2	8.7	6.1	7.3	11.3	8.6	9.1	10.1	7.5	13.9
2. Somewhat acceptable	25.3	28.7	22.0	25.1	24.3	27.2	25.4	24.9	23.4	25.1	25.9	27.8	25.4	22.2	22.6	40.5
3. Acceptable	52.8	48.8	57.1	53.2	53.9	48.7	54.3	53.3	54.4	53.9	50.7	50.1	52.4	57.7	55.1	38.1
4. Desirable	13.0	10.9	15.3	13.1	14.6	11.6	12.1	13.0	16.0	13.6	12.2	13.5	13.1	10.0	14.7	7.4
Item 6230 Subject C05,D04 N	3288	1607	1569	2479	445	672	921	1111	584	1842	1253	1273	657	475	768	51

A09C: Both work full-time

1. Not at all acceptable	58.4	62.3	54.5	61.8	38.8	64.8	59.8	53.2	58.5	58.8	58.4	60.3	55.8	60.5	58.1	41.4
2. Somewhat acceptable	20.9	17.7	24.4	21.6	20.1	17.7	21.5	21.3	22.6	22.4	19.3	20.2	21.7	21.7	21.5	19.9
3. Acceptable	14.9	13.9	15.5	12.6	25.7	12.7	12.5	18.0	15.3	13.9	15.7	13.3	15.4	12.6	16.7	26.1
4. Desirable	5.9	6.1	5.6	4.0	15.5	4.9	6.1	7.5	3.5	4.9	6.5	6.2	7.1	5.2	3.7	12.6
Item 6240 Subject C05,D04 N	3278	1604	1563	2476	439	669	916	1107	586	1840	1248	1270	654	474	767	51

A09D: Both work about half-time

1. Not at all acceptable	41.7	44.6	38.3	39.5	49.7	39.6	38.7	48.6	35.5	37.6	46.7	41.2	40.7	42.3	42.0	33.7
2. Somewhat acceptable	33.0	31.8	34.7	34.3	27.4	34.5	33.0	30.9	35.4	35.0	31.0	34.6	33.5	30.4	32.6	32.2
3. Acceptable	19.2	17.5	20.9	20.3	16.6	20.0	21.9	15.6	20.8	20.2	17.6	18.1	19.5	20.9	19.6	24.1
4. Desirable	6.2	6.1	6.1	6.0	6.3	5.9	6.4	4.9	8.4	7.1	4.7	6.2	6.2	6.4	5.7	9.9
Item 6250 Subject C05,D04 N	3259	1592	1555	2464	432	667	912	1101	579	1827	1244	1264	649	472	761	51

A09E: Husband works about half-time, wife works full-time

1. Not at all acceptable	58.8	60.7	56.7	58.9	56.8	58.5	55.4	63.4	55.6	55.0	64.3	57.8	59.2	60.3	59.5	48.9
2. Somewhat acceptable	24.3	22.6	26.4	24.3	26.7	23.3	25.6	22.6	26.3	27.2	20.6	26.6	24.6	22.2	22.2	29.0
3. Acceptable	14.1	13.6	14.5	14.5	11.7	14.9	16.2	10.9	15.8	15.3	12.1	12.7	12.8	14.9	16.3	15.0
4. Desirable	2.9	3.0	2.4	2.2	4.8	3.3	2.8	3.0	2.3	2.5	3.0	2.9	3.3	2.6	2.0	7.0
Item 6260 Subject C05,D04 N	3279	1606	1563	2477	439	671	917	1107	584	1840	1250	1270	655	472	767	51

A09F: Husband doesn't work, wife works full-time

1. Not at all acceptable	70.9	71.3	70.5	69.4	78.6	67.6	66.8	78.4	66.6	67.0	76.8	69.3	73.0	73.0	71.6	52.1
2. Somewhat acceptable	14.6	13.0	16.7	15.7	9.9	15.7	16.0	11.3	17.6	17.4	10.6	15.7	13.1	12.8	14.9	19.9
3. Acceptable	10.4	10.9	10.1	11.2	7.0	11.6	13.0	7.2	11.0	11.7	8.7	10.5	9.4	11.7	9.9	14.9
4. Desirable	4.1	4.9	2.8	3.7	4.5	5.1	4.3	3.1	4.8	3.9	3.9	4.5	4.4	2.4	3.6	13.1
Item 6270 Subject C05,D04 N	3275	1602	1562	2474	439	669	918	1108	580	1839	1247	1269	655	472	767	50

A10: Imagine you are married and have one or more pre-school children. Imagine also that the husband is working full-time and the wife does not have a job outside the home. How would you feel about each of these arrangements for the day-to-day care of the child(ren)?

A10A: Wife does all child care

1. Not at all acceptable	32.7	26.0	39.8	32.8	33.0	35.6	33.0	31.4	31.2	36.1	28.8	31.9	33.3	33.5	34.2	27.0
2. Somewhat acceptable	29.1	29.4	28.2	29.5	27.0	26.2	30.4	29.2	30.3	28.0	31.1	30.5	29.8	28.0	27.7	23.3
3. Acceptable	28.3	30.8	26.2	27.9	31.6	27.7	27.6	29.4	28.0	26.4	29.7	27.5	27.2	27.0	29.0	36.2
4. Desirable	9.9	13.8	5.8	9.8	8.4	10.5	9.0	10.1	10.5	9.5	10.4	10.1	9.7	11.4	9.1	13.6
Item 6280 Subject D04 N	3278	1602	1566	2472	442	673	917	1107	580	1842	1248	1272	653	473	767	51

QUESTIONNAIRE FORM 2 1984	TOTAL	SEX		RACE		REGION				4YR COLLEGE PLANS		ILLICIT DRUG USE: LIFETIME				
		M	F	White	Black	NE	NC	S	W	Yes	No	None	Mari-juana Only	Few Pills	More Pills	Any Her-oin
N (Weighted No. of Cases):	3322	1624	1580	2491	453	681	929	1119	593	1855	1265	1285	662	479	773	51
% of Weighted Total:	100.0	48.9	47.5	75.0	13.6	20.1	28.0	33.7	17.9	55.8	38.1	38.7	19.9	14.4	23.3	1.5

A10B: Wife does most of it

1. Not at all acceptable	9.3	9.1	9.1	7.6	11.8	9.8	8.4	9.0	10.4	9.1	9.1	9.4	9.4	11.2	7.7	10.7
2. Somewhat acceptable	31.4	29.4	33.4	30.2	38.1	30.4	33.4	32.3	27.6	29.8	34.0	29.1	33.2	31.4	32.4	38.8
3. Acceptable	45.1	45.9	44.3	46.5	39.5	45.5	45.9	44.4	44.6	44.8	45.6	46.0	44.3	45.0	46.1	29.7
4. Desirable	14.3	15.6	13.3	15.8	10.6	14.3	12.2	14.3	17.4	16.3	11.3	15.5	13.1	12.4	13.7	20.8
Item 6290 Subject D04 N	3280	1604	1566	2473	443	672	919	1107	582	1841	1249	1274	653	473	766	51

A10C: Both do it equally

1. Not at all acceptable	4.7	5.5	3.6	3.7	5.9	4.4	3.1	6.2	4.5	4.2	5.0	4.1	4.4	6.0	4.5	10.7
2. Somewhat acceptable	16.7	18.9	14.3	16.1	18.9	14.5	16.3	18.7	15.8	15.5	17.4	16.8	13.8	19.0	17.6	11.1
3. Acceptable	41.4	43.4	38.9	40.7	46.2	44.2	40.9	41.7	38.3	40.1	43.7	41.7	42.2	38.6	39.7	58.2
4. Desirable	37.3	32.2	43.2	39.5	28.9	36.9	39.7	33.4	41.4	40.3	33.9	37.4	39.6	36.4	38.2	20.0
Item 6300 Subject D04 N	3277	1599	1568	2467	444	669	918	1106	584	1840	1247	1273	655	472	763	51

A10D: Husband does most of it

1. Not at all acceptable	46.3	44.2	48.0	44.3	49.9	44.2	41.7	51.6	46.1	46.4	46.0	46.1	44.9	50.4	45.9	38.6
2. Somewhat acceptable	40.5	42.6	39.3	42.7	38.6	40.6	44.0	37.0	41.5	42.0	39.4	40.2	42.5	36.8	41.3	46.7
3. Acceptable	10.7	11.0	10.3	11.2	7.3	11.7	12.0	8.8	11.4	10.3	11.1	11.5	10.3	9.7	11.0	5.9
4. Desirable	2.4	2.3	2.4	1.7	4.2	3.5	2.3	2.6	1.0	1.4	3.6	2.2	2.4	3.1	1.8	8.8
Item 6310 Subject D04 N	3266	1595	1561	2465	440	669	914	1103	580	1834	1245	1268	651	472	763	50

A10E: Husband does all of it

1. Not at all acceptable	85.7	84.6	87.5	86.8	84.0	84.0	84.3	87.5	86.3	88.3	83.2	86.6	85.2	85.6	86.0	72.5
2. Somewhat acceptable	8.4	9.2	7.5	8.3	8.6	9.5	9.0	7.0	8.9	7.4	9.6	7.5	10.2	8.0	8.2	11.9
3. Acceptable	3.4	3.8	3.0	3.3	3.2	3.3	3.8	3.3	3.3	3.1	3.5	3.3	3.0	3.0	4.3	-
4. Desirable	2.5	2.4	2.1	1.6	4.2	3.3	2.9	2.1	1.5	1.3	3.7	2.7	1.6	3.5	1.5	15.6
Item 6320 Subject D04 N	3273	1600	1562	2469	441	671	916	1105	580	1837	1248	1272	652	472	763	51

The next section of this questionnaire is about government and public affairs.

A11: Some people think about what's going on in government very often, and others are not that interested. How much of an interest do you take in government and current events?

1. No interest at all	4.9	5.0	4.4	4.9	5.0	6.1	5.2	4.1	4.7	2.6	8.0	4.0	4.0	5.4	5.7	26.2
2. Very little interest	17.9	13.5	22.3	17.9	14.6	19.6	19.2	16.8	16.1	13.6	24.2	15.7	21.5	16.0	19.5	16.1
3. Some interest	47.1	43.6	51.7	46.9	49.9	48.1	48.2	45.4	47.6	46.1	48.6	46.6	45.8	50.8	47.5	43.2
4. A lot of interest	21.8	26.1	17.0	22.0	22.9	18.9	20.9	24.1	21.9	27.0	14.8	24.7	20.9	19.7	20.2	9.4
5. A very great interest	8.3	11.8	4.5	8.3	7.6	7.3	6.5	9.6	9.7	10.6	4.5	9.0	7.8	8.1	7.2	5.1
Item 6330 Subject H01,Q08 N	3295	1612	1570	2477	446	674	921	1111	589	1846	1252	1278	657	476	765	51

A12: Do you think some of the people running the government are crooked or dishonest?

1. Most of them are crooked or dishonest	10.0	10.6	8.8	9.0	14.7	12.5	9.2	11.2	6.2	7.3	13.1	9.6	10.7	8.4	10.3	16.8
2. Quite a few are	30.0	30.5	30.0	29.6	32.5	31.1	27.7	33.3	26.1	30.4	29.4	29.1	27.4	32.2	31.7	35.3
3. Some are	53.5	52.1	55.5	55.5	45.5	51.6	57.7	49.1	57.4	56.3	50.8	54.7	55.9	51.8	52.3	44.4
4. Hardly any are	5.8	6.7	4.8	5.7	5.8	4.5	4.8	5.6	9.4	5.6	6.0	6.1	5.2	6.9	5.3	3.6
5. None at all are crooked or dishonest	0.6	0.2	0.9	0.3	1.5	0.3	0.5	0.8	1.0	0.4	0.7	0.5	0.9	0.6	0.4	-
Item 6340 Subject H04,K01 N	3286	1612	1563	2474	442	673	919	1108	586	1843	1247	1274	657	476	763	51

A13: Do you think the government wastes much of the money we pay in taxes?

1. Nearly all tax money is wasted	6.9	7.3	6.1	6.5	8.2	7.5	6.7	7.1	6.3	4.9	9.8	5.5	7.2	7.4	8.2	11.1
2. A lot of tax money is wasted	45.5	48.6	43.1	46.6	42.5	50.2	47.5	42.3	42.8	46.1	44.4	46.6	43.5	46.7	44.4	58.7
3. Some tax money is wasted	38.0	34.1	41.7	38.9	34.9	35.5	37.5	39.3	38.9	39.5	36.4	37.6	41.1	35.6	38.8	20.9
4. A little tax money wasted	8.7	9.0	8.2	7.6	12.6	5.5	7.9	10.4	10.3	8.5	8.6	8.8	7.4	9.9	8.3	7.4
5. No tax money is wasted	1.0	1.1	0.9	0.5	1.8	1.4	0.4	0.9	1.6	1.1	0.8	1.5	0.9	0.4	0.3	2.0
Item 6350 Subject H04,K01 N	3282	1609	1561	2469	443	672	920	1104	586	1842	1246	1272	656	475	762	51

QUESTIONNAIRE FORM 2 1984	TOTAL	SEX		RACE		REGION				4YR COLLEGE PLANS		ILLICIT DRUG USE: LIFETIME				
		M	F	White	Black	NE	NC	S	W	Yes	No	None	Marijuana Only	Few Pills	More Pills	Any Heroin
N (Weighted No. of Cases):	3322	1624	1580	2491	453	681	929	1119	593	1855	1265	1285	662	479	773	51
% of Weighted Total:	100.0	48.9	47.5	75.0	13.6	20.1	28.0	33.7	17.9	55.8	38.1	38.7	19.9	14.4	23.3	1.5

A14: How much of the time do you think you can trust the government in Washington to do what is right?

	TOTAL	M	F	White	Black	NE	NC	S	W	Yes	No	None	Marijuana Only	Few Pills	More Pills	Any Heroin
1. Almost always	8.7	9.5	7.7	9.3	5.0	8.6	6.6	9.5	10.7	9.7	6.9	9.2	7.8	10.7	8.0	2.6
2. Often	38.8	41.5	36.6	42.0	23.8	35.0	39.0	38.1	44.4	45.1	-30.7	40.3	38.1	35.6	40.7	23.8
3. Sometimes	39.8	36.7	43.1	38.1	48.6	43.5	42.5	38.5	34.0	36.2	45.3	39.5	41.7	40.2	38.4	45.2
4. Seldom	10.7	10.0	11.2	9.1	20.1	10.7	9.8	12.5	9.0	7.8	14.8	8.8	11.1	12.5	10.8	22.2
5. Never	1.9	2.3	1.3	1.4	2.6	2.3	2.1	1.5	1.9	1.3	2.2	2.2	1.4	0.9	2.1	6.3
Item 6360 Subject H04,K01 N	3285	1610	1563	2471	444	673	916	1109	587	1841	1248	1274	654	476	764	51

A15: Do you feel that the people running the government are smart people who usually know what they are doing?

	TOTAL	M	F	White	Black	NE	NC	S	W	Yes	No	None	Marijuana Only	Few Pills	More Pills	Any Heroin
1. They almost always know what they are doing	13.7	15.3	11.8	13.0	14.8	12.0	12.0	15.0	16.0	15.0	11.4	14.0	12.9	16.2	12.5	10.2
2. They usually know what they are doing	52.2	52.3	52.6	55.2	38.3	49.9	55.8	49.2	55.0	55.8	47.0	53.9	51.2	50.1	53.6	36.7
3. They sometimes know what they are doing	27.6	25.2	30.2	26.2	36.7	30.0	25.5	30.2	23.3	24.7	32.7	26.3	30.5	27.1	27.1	34.3
4. They seldom know what they are doing	5.5	5.8	5.0	4.8	8.8	6.8	5.8	5.0	4.4	3.9	7.7	5.0	4.9	5.7	5.9	8.5
5. They never know what they are doing	1.0	1.4	0.4	0.8	1.4	1.4	0.9	0.6	1.3	0.6	1.2	0.9	0.6	0.9	0.9	10.4
Item 6370 Subject H04,K01 N	3282	1611	1559	2471	441	674	915	1107	586	1840	1246	1271	654	476	764	51

A16: Would you say the government is pretty much run for a few big interests looking out for themselves, or is it run for the benefit of all the people?

	TOTAL	M	F	White	Black	NE	NC	S	W	Yes	No	None	Marijuana Only	Few Pills	More Pills	Any Heroin
1. Nearly always run for a few big interests	7.0	8.4	5.6	5.9	10.3	8.8	7.2	6.7	5.5	5.8	8.5	6.2	6.8	7.7	7.3	9.1
2. Usually run for a few big interests	20.5	20.8	20.0	20.5	22.1	21.3	20.4	19.9	20.7	18.8	22.4	18.2	20.5	20.8	23.4	30.3
3. Run some for the big interests, some for the people	48.4	46.1	51.2	48.5	49.6	49.7	47.3	49.3	47.1	49.5	47.1	48.5	50.5	49.7	46.9	38.3
4. Usually run for the benefit of all the people	19.7	20.2	19.1	20.6	14.9	16.4	21.2	19.3	21.8	21.3	18.1	21.9	18.5	17.4	18.5	18.4
5. Nearly always run for the benefit of all the people	4.4	4.5	4.1	4.4	3.1	3.8	3.9	4.8	4.9	4.6	3.9	5.2	3.7	4.4	3.9	3.9
Item 6380 Subject H04,K01 N	3272	1608	1554	2467	440	670	912	1106	584	1835	1243	1267	654	472	764	51

A17: Have you ever done, or do you plan to do, the following things?

A17A: Vote in a public election

	TOTAL	M	F	White	Black	NE	NC	S	W	Yes	No	None	Marijuana Only	Few Pills	More Pills	Any Heroin
1. I probably won't do this	3.8	4.2	3.5	3.2	5.0	3.9	3.4	3.8	4.2	1.9	6.4	3.5	2.3	3.4	4.6	15.9
2. Don't know	8.4	7.4	9.2	6.3	10.3	7.6	9.4	7.5	9.3	4.7	12.4	7.6	7.5	8.4	9.2	18.1
3. I probably will do this	82.2	81.4	83.3	85.7	75.0	81.8	80.6	83.5	82.7	87.5	76.0	83.7	83.0	82.0	81.3	62.2
4. I have already done this	5.6	7.0	4.0	4.8	9.7	6.7	6.6	5.2	3.8	5.9	5.2	5.2	7.2	6.2	4.8	3.8
Item 6390 Subject H05,I02 N	3287	1607	1569	2475	447	672	919	1111	585	1840	1253	1274	656	476	764	51

A17B: Write to public officials

	TOTAL	M	F	White	Black	NE	NC	S	W	Yes	No	None	Marijuana Only	Few Pills	More Pills	Any Heroin
1. I probably won't do this	24.0	22.7	24.9	22.9	25.7	23.6	26.4	23.7	21.0	15.2	35.8	22.9	23.0	24.2	25.7	32.4
2. Don't know	45.9	45.4	47.1	46.4	45.4	42.4	46.9	47.2	46.1	46.4	45.6	46.5	45.8	45.8	44.9	41.7
3. I probably will do this	19.9	20.9	18.4	19.9	20.3	20.1	17.4	21.4	20.7	25.3	12.2	19.9	20.2	21.0	19.5	14.3
4. I have already done this	10.2	10.9	9.6	10.9	8.6	13.8	9.2	7.7	12.3	13.0	6.4	10.7	10.9	9.0	9.9	11.6
Item 6400 Subject H05,I02 N	3284	1608	1567	2476	444	672	918	1109	586	1840	1254	1273	655	475	765	51

A17C: Give money to a political candidate or cause

	TOTAL	M	F	White	Black	NE	NC	S	W	Yes	No	None	Marijuana Only	Few Pills	More Pills	Any Heroin
1. I probably won't do this	37.6	40.2	34.7	36.6	40.4	38.5	39.1	35.1	39.2	31.1	46.4	33.6	38.1	38.2	41.6	62.9
2. Don't know	40.2	38.8	42.2	41.0	36.4	42.1	39.1	40.7	38.8	42.0	38.0	45.1	37.2	37.5	38.2	18.6
3. I probably will do this	19.1	18.0	20.3	19.2	20.7	16.2	19.3	20.5	19.3	23.6	13.2	18.8	20.0	21.2	17.5	18.5
4. I have already done this	3.1	3.0	2.9	3.2	2.5	3.2	2.5	3.6	2.8	3.4	2.4	2.5	4.8	3.1	2.7	-
Item 6410 Subject H05,I02 N	3277	1606	1564	2474	440	670	916	1107	585	1836	1253	1272	652	474	764	51

QUESTIONNAIRE FORM 2 1984	TOTAL	SEX		RACE		REGION				4YR COLLEGE PLANS		ILLICIT DRUG USE: LIFETIME				
		M	F	White	Black	NE	NC	S	W	Yes	No	None	Marijuana Only	Few Pills	More Pills	Any Heroin
N (Weighted No. of Cases):	3322	1624	1580	2491	453	681	929	1119	593	1855	1265	1285	662	479	773	51
% of Weighted Total:	100.0	48.9	47.5	75.0	13.6	20.1	28.0	33.7	17.9	55.8	38.1	38.7	19.9	14.4	23.3	1.5
A17D: Work in a political campaign																
1. I probably won't do this	49.4	50.3	48.1	49.8	45.6	50.3	51.9	45.5	51.5	40.9	61.1	47.5	50.1	47.1	53.1	60.1
2. Don't know	35.5	35.2	36.3	35.2	37.2	35.9	33.5	37.7	34.1	39.5	30.0	37.5	34.3	36.6	33.2	27.1
3. I probably will do this	9.3	8.1	10.3	8.6	14.2	8.5	6.6	11.7	9.8	12.1	5.2	9.4	10.3	8.9	8.1	8.1
4. I have already done this	5.8	6.3	5.4	6.4	3.0	5.2	8.0	5.1	4.6	7.6	3.6	5.6	5.2	7.5	5.6	4.7
Item 6420 Subject H05,I02 N	3272	1602	1563	2470	440	669	916	1102	585	1839	1247	1269	654	474	761	51
A17E: Participate in a lawful demonstration																
1. I probably won't do this	37.7	34.2	40.8	38.3	38.4	35.6	37.6	40.3	35.2	32.1	46.0	40.0	35.9	36.2	36.8	32.6
2. Don't know	44.9	47.1	43.3	44.7	42.9	42.8	45.3	46.5	43.7	47.4	40.7	45.1	46.4	46.8	41.9	42.2
3. I probably will do this	14.7	15.5	13.8	14.4	16.4	18.4	15.3	11.4	16.0	17.3	11.5	13.1	15.1	14.3	17.6	15.8
4. I have already done this	2.7	3.1	2.1	2.7	2.3	3.2	1.9	1.9	5.1	3.2	1.8	1.8	2.6	2.7	3.7	9.4
Item 6430 Subject H05,I02 N	3276	1604	1565	2470	443	671	914	1108	583	1837	1251	1273	651	473	764	51
A17F: Boycott certain products or stores																
1. I probably won't do this	40.5	36.3	44.9	41.1	37.0	35.7	41.4	44.5	37.0	36.8	46.7	40.3	39.7	41.8	41.0	41.2
2. Don't know	42.9	46.0	39.9	43.6	40.8	43.5	43.8	43.1	40.7	42.7	41.8	41.9	43.2	45.3	43.5	35.5
3. I probably will do this	12.5	13.2	11.7	10.9	20.0	16.6	10.9	10.0	14.7	15.3	8.8	13.9	12.6	10.3	11.0	17.0
4. I have already done this	4.1	4.5	3.5	4.5	2.2	4.2	3.9	2.3	7.7	5.2	2.7	3.9	4.5	2.6	4.6	6.3
Item 6440 Subject H05,I02 N	3280	1608	1565	2474	443	672	916	1107	584	1841	1250	1273	652	474	765	51
A18: How much do you agree or disagree with each of the following statements?																
A18A: The U.S. should begin a gradual program of disarming whether other countries do or not																
1. Disagree	40.1	50.5	29.4	41.4	34.2	39.0	34.4	48.3	35.1	42.3	37.6	40.8	35.9	40.9	41.4	54.5
2. Mostly disagree	17.7	17.2	18.3	18.6	14.4	20.1	20.3	15.6	15.1	18.7	17.1	17.9	19.9	16.9	16.2	15.8
3. Neither	19.5	14.1	25.1	18.4	23.3	16.5	23.0	17.1	21.8	17.1	23.1	18.6	19.5	21.6	20.0	14.6
4. Mostly agree	14.3	10.5	18.4	13.8	18.3	14.8	15.7	11.5	16.8	13.5	14.1	13.7	16.2	12.1	15.2	12.7
5. Agree	8.4	7.7	8.9	7.9	9.8	9.7	6.6	7.5	11.3	8.5	8.2	9.0	8.6	8.5	7.2	2.3
Item 6450 Subject H02,L03 N	3260	1604	1550	2458	440	671	915	1095	580	1835	1238	1267	648	471	761	50
A18B: There may be times when the U.S. should go to war to protect the rights of other countries																
1. Disagree	22.2	19.3	24.9	20.8	28.0	23.8	21.3	21.4	23.2	20.4	25.1	19.7	22.7	21.8	26.2	21.8
2. Mostly disagree	22.4	21.0	24.2	23.6	18.6	24.8	23.0	20.5	22.3	22.2	23.0	20.2	23.8	23.9	24.5	14.7
3. Neither	19.0	18.5	19.7	19.3	17.5	20.5	23.4	16.9	14.5	17.8	20.5	19.0	18.3	21.4	17.5	34.5
4. Mostly agree	23.0	24.1	22.0	23.8	20.5	19.0	22.5	24.7	25.0	26.5	17.7	25.6	23.2	21.0	20.4	17.2
5. Agree	13.4	17.2	9.2	12.5	15.5	11.9	9.8	16.5	15.0	13.0	13.8	15.6	12.0	11.9	11.4	11.7
Item 5690 Subject H02,L03 N	3275	1609	1560	2468	442	671	917	1102	584	1841	1245	1273	650	475	764	51
A18C: The U.S. should be willing to go to war to protect its own economic interests																
1. Disagree	9.5	7.9	10.9	8.0	14.3	11.4	9.3	7.7	10.9	8.5	11.0	9.4	10.7	9.7	8.5	3.1
2. Mostly disagree	13.6	12.7	14.5	14.0	10.2	15.0	14.3	10.5	16.5	14.3	12.6	13.3	14.0	12.8	13.8	19.8
3. Neither	20.4	19.4	21.7	21.4	13.2	20.9	22.1	17.9	21.6	20.8	19.8	20.5	20.5	22.5	18.4	24.1
4. Mostly agree	31.5	30.8	32.0	32.9	27.7	32.9	33.8	31.4	26.4	32.0	30.0	33.0	30.2	29.1	32.9	19.3
5. Agree	25.1	29.1	20.9	23.6	34.6	19.8	20.5	32.5	24.5	24.4	26.6	23.8	24.6	25.9	26.4	33.7
Item 6460 Subject H02,L03 N	3268	1606	1556	2466	439	667	918	1099	585	1836	1243	1271	648	473	764	50
A18D: The only good reason for the U.S. to go to war is to defend against an attack on our own country																
1. Disagree	8.3	9.0	7.4	7.8	8.1	7.5	8.3	8.4	8.8	8.5	8.0	10.3	5.6	6.5	7.9	8.1
2. Mostly disagree	11.4	13.6	9.4	12.0	9.2	11.3	11.7	11.0	11.7	13.0	9.3	13.0	10.1	12.0	9.8	6.9
3. Neither	8.8	8.0	9.8	9.0	6.9	8.2	9.7	8.9	7.8	8.7	9.2	9.1	7.1	9.2	8.3	18.6
4. Mostly agree	30.8	29.6	32.3	32.4	28.0	30.5	31.9	31.1	29.2	32.5	28.4	30.4	35.2	27.1	31.7	19.2
5. Agree	40.7	39.8	41.1	38.8	47.8	42.5	38.5	40.6	42.5	37.4	45.1	37.2	42.0	45.2	42.3	47.3
Item 6470 Subject H02,L03 N	3271	1607	1557	2465	442	669	915	1102	586	1840	1241	1270	650	474	764	51

QUESTIONNAIRE FORM 2 1984	TOTAL	SEX		RACE		REGION				4YR COLLEGE PLANS		ILLICIT DRUG USE: LIFETIME				
		M	F	White	Black	NE	NC	S	W	Yes	No	None	Mari-juana Only	Few Pills	More Pills	Any Her-oin
N (Weighted No. of Cases):	3322	1624	1580	2491	453	681	929	1119	593	1855	1265	1285	662	479	773	51
% of Weighted Total:	100.0	48.9	47.5	75.0	13.6	20.1	28.0	33.7	17.9	55.8	38.1	38.7	19.9	14.4	23.3	1.5

A18E: The U.S. does not need to have greater military power than the Soviet Union

1. Disagree	34.2	36.5	31.4	32.4	42.2	32.8	27.4	45.1	25.7	31.8	37.2	33.9	32.5	34.3	34.5	41.9
2. Mostly disagree	24.1	23.1	25.3	24.4	22.4	21.6	26.4	23.2	25.1	24.7	23.1	24.2	22.5	26.6	23.8	22.6
3. Neither	16.4	14.6	17.9	16.9	15.5	16.5	18.2	14.2	17.7	16.5	16.0	17.2	15.7	16.5	15.5	14.1
4. Mostly agree	13.3	12.7	14.2	13.9	9.3	15.0	15.3	9.4	15.6	13.1	14.0	13.2	16.4	11.0	13.3	8.7
5. Agree	12.0	13.0	11.1	12.3	10.6	14.1	12.8	8.1	16.0	13.8	9.7	11.5	13.0	11.5	12.9	12.7
Item 6480 Subject H02,L03 N	3263	1601	1557	2464	437	666	914	1098	584	1838	1241	1267	649	474	760	51

A18F: The U.S. ought to have much more military power than any other nation in the world

1. Disagree	17.0	16.2	18.1	17.2	14.5	22.1	18.1	10.8	21.3	18.8	14.4	17.1	18.8	15.5	17.3	15.8
2. Mostly disagree	19.4	19.4	19.5	21.1	11.8	20.4	21.5	16.8	19.5	21.1	17.5	22.0	22.1	14.7	17.2	6.2
3. Neither	25.0	22.4	27.4	25.2	23.6	22.7	26.6	24.2	26.7	23.9	26.3	25.6	22.2	28.3	24.3	25.5
4. Mostly agree	18.5	19.5	17.8	18.4	22.5	16.9	19.2	19.8	16.9	18.3	18.7	17.2	18.9	20.4	18.6	20.9
5. Agree	20.1	22.5	17.3	18.1	27.7	18.0	14.6	28.4	15.5	17.9	23.1	18.1	18.0	21.1	22.6	31.6
Item 6490 Subject H02,L03 N	3267	1604	1556	2467	439	669	913	1101	584	1838	1243	1272	649	472	763	48

A18G: Our present foreign policy is based on our own narrow economic and power interests

1. Disagree	5.8	7.0	4.4	5.5	5.0	7.9	5.1	5.4	5.3	6.1	5.5	5.7	5.2	4.6	7.0	5.8
2. Mostly disagree	12.2	12.8	11.4	13.0	8.7	12.0	12.9	12.5	10.6	13.2	10.8	13.4	11.1	10.4	12.2	10.6
3. Neither	44.0	39.0	49.8	45.9	37.9	42.0	48.3	41.9	43.8	41.6	47.8	41.9	45.6	48.8	42.8	46.6
4. Mostly agree	26.4	27.8	25.1	25.7	31.1	24.6	25.5	27.3	27.9	27.8	24.1	27.1	27.4	24.9	27.0	9.5
5. Agree	11.6	13.4	9.3	9.8	17.3	13.5	8.2	12.9	12.5	11.3	11.7	12.0	10.6	11.3	11.0	27.4
Item 6500 Subject H02,L03 N	3210	1589	1519	2421	434	655	902	1077	576	1809	1220	1242	636	469	754	50

A18H: Servicemen should obey orders without question

1. Disagree	13.1	12.2	13.8	10.4	23.2	16.3	11.6	11.6	14.5	13.4	12.3	13.4	13.6	12.4	11.5	18.5
2. Mostly disagree	18.8	15.3	22.7	18.9	18.5	20.5	18.4	18.8	17.3	21.5	15.0	19.5	18.1	17.7	19.7	11.9
3. Neither	21.2	20.0	22.7	22.4	15.7	20.2	23.9	19.8	20.8	20.8	21.2	21.9	21.3	22.0	20.1	15.2
4. Mostly agree	29.6	31.7	27.3	31.8	22.3	25.5	30.9	30.0	31.6	29.6	30.7	28.4	29.0	31.0	32.5	23.3
5. Agree	17.4	20.9	13.6	16.4	20.3	17.5	15.3	19.8	15.8	14.7	20.9	16.8	18.0	17.0	16.3	31.1
Item 6510 Subject L03 N	3254	1600	1548	2453	439	664	911	1097	582	1827	1242	1264	646	471	760	51

A19: This section deals with activities which may be against the rules or against the law. We hope you will answer all of these questions. However, if you find a question which you cannot answer honestly, we would prefer that you leave it blank. Remember, your answers will never be connected with your name. During the LAST 12 MONTHS, how often have you...

A19A: Argued or had a fight with either of your parents

1. Not at all	12.5	14.9	9.7	7.4	33.2	9.8	10.0	16.7	11.5	11.3	13.4	17.0	12.8	9.7	5.7	13.8
2. Once	9.9	11.1	8.5	9.4	11.9	8.7	10.1	10.8	9.4	9.7	10.0	11.9	9.3	9.2	7.6	8.8
3. Twice	11.6	12.6	10.6	11.6	10.1	9.9	10.5	11.6	15.2	11.4	12.5	12.3	10.2	13.7	10.6	8.6
4. 3 or 4 times	24.3	23.4	25.7	25.5	22.7	27.0	23.4	23.5	24.3	25.8	22.6	24.5	26.8	25.0	22.9	11.9
5. 5 or more times	41.7	38.1	45.5	46.2	22.1	44.6	46.0	37.4	39.6	41.8	41.4	34.3	40.9	42.4	53.3	57.0
Item 6520 Subject M03,S01 N	3278	1604	1568	2466	448	668	916	1105	589	1845	1244	1278	657	474	767	51

A19B: Hit an instructor or supervisor

1. Not at all	96.6	94.7	98.8	96.7	98.1	96.0	96.6	96.4	97.6	97.9	95.2	97.5	97.6	97.8	95.2	78.2
2. Once	2.4	3.5	1.1	2.3	1.4	1.9	2.6	2.6	2.0	1.5	3.4	1.9	1.5	2.2	3.2	7.4
3. Twice	0.5	0.8	0.1	0.4	0.3	0.9	0.3	0.5	0.1	0.2	0.7	0.3	0.8	-	0.5	2.0
4. 3 or 4 times	0.2	0.5	*	0.3	-	0.5	0.2	0.1	0.2	0.2	0.3	0.1	0.1	-	0.2	8.6
5. 5 or more times	0.3	0.6	-	0.3	0.2	0.6	0.4	0.3	-	0.2	0.3	0.1	-	-	0.9	3.9
Item 6530 Subject M02,S01 N	3287	1610	1572	2477	446	670	922	1106	590	1849	1253	1282	658	477	768	51

*=less than .05 per cent.

QUESTIONNAIRE FORM 2 1984	TOTAL	SEX		RACE		REGION				4YR COLLEGE PLANS		ILLICIT DRUG USE: LIFETIME				
		M	F	White	Black	NE	NC	S	W	Yes	No	None	Mari- juana Only	Few Pills	More Pills	Any Her- oin
N (Weighted No. of Cases):	3322	1624	1580	2491	453	681	929	1119	593	1855	1265	1285	662	479	773	51
% of Weighted Total:	100.0	48.9	47.5	75.0	13.6	20.1	28.0	33.7	17.9	55.8	38.1	38.7	19.9	14.4	23.3	1.5
A19C: Gotten into a serious fight in school or at work																
1. Not at all	82.6	78.3	88.0	82.4	87.4	76.9	82.3	85.5	84.3	86.8	76.8	88.8	84.7	81.4	73.8	50.7
2. Once	10.1	11.9	8.1	10.5	7.8	13.3	10.8	8.9	7.7	8.4	12.5	7.4	9.1	12.1	14.0	14.8
3. Twice	3.5	4.4	2.3	3.6	2.8	4.8	2.6	2.6	5.1	2.6	4.7	1.7	3.2	3.9	6.6	4.3
4. 3 or 4 times	2.4	3.2	1.2	2.3	1.1	2.4	2.7	2.2	2.2	1.4	3.9	1.6	2.3	1.9	3.1	11.5
5. 5 or more times	1.4	2.1	0.3	1.2	0.8	2.5	1.5	0.8	0.8	0.8	2.1	0.5	0.7	0.8	2.5	18.8
Item 6540　Subject B07,C01,S01　N	3286	1609	1571	2475	446	670	921	1105	590	1850	1252	1280	657	477	769	51
A19D: Taken part in a fight where a group of your friends were against another group																
1. Not at all	82.1	76.5	88.7	83.1	81.9	78.1	81.2	82.7	86.6	84.6	78.8	88.2	83.3	80.9	74.3	43.7
2. Once	10.1	12.7	7.0	9.8	9.8	10.9	10.9	10.0	8.2	8.8	11.6	7.2	9.9	11.6	14.5	10.6
3. Twice	4.0	4.6	3.0	3.4	4.9	5.2	4.0	4.2	2.3	3.6	4.4	2.7	2.8	3.7	5.8	18.4
4. 3 or 4 times	2.4	3.6	1.0	2.4	2.2	3.5	2.4	1.9	1.9	1.8	3.3	1.3	2.5	3.2	3.2	7.2
5. 5 or more times	1.4	2.5	0.3	1.3	1.2	2.3	1.4	1.2	1.0	1.1	1.9	0.5	1.5	0.5	2.3	20.0
Item 6550　Subject S01　N	3285	1608	1572	2473	447	668	922	1106	590	1850	1249	1280	659	476	768	51
A19E: Hurt someone badly enough to need bandages or a doctor																
1. Not at all	89.4	82.9	96.7	90.0	91.2	85.9	90.1	90.6	89.8	91.7	87.0	94.7	91.3	90.5	81.4	50.1
2. Once	6.3	9.8	2.3	6.0	6.0	7.6	5.6	6.0	6.5	5.5	6.7	3.4	5.3	5.6	11.3	19.6
3. Twice	2.2	3.4	0.8	2.3	0.8	3.6	1.6	1.6	2.5	1.6	2.7	0.9	1.8	1.6	4.6	6.5
4. 3 or 4 times	1.1	2.0	0.1	0.8	1.1	1.1	1.3	1.1	0.7	0.6	1.8	0.7	0.8	1.8	1.1	6.9
5. 5 or more times	1.1	1.9	0.1	0.9	0.9	1.9	1.5	0.7	0.5	0.6	1.7	0.3	0.8	0.5	1.6	16.9
Item 6560　Subject S01　N	3286	1607	1572	2475	446	668	922	1106	590	1847	1253	1279	659	477	767	51
A19F: Used a knife or gun or some other thing (like a club) to get something from a person																
1. Not at all	96.8	95.2	98.7	97.3	96.1	95.4	97.6	96.3	98.0	97.9	96.0	98.2	98.4	97.2	95.6	65.5
2. Once	1.7	2.4	0.7	1.2	3.0	1.7	1.0	2.4	1.2	1.3	1.6	1.3	0.5	2.0	1.6	14.6
3. Twice	0.5	0.6	0.4	0.5	0.5	0.9	0.2	0.5	0.4	0.3	0.8	0.2	0.2	0.5	1.1	2.5
4. 3 or 4 times	0.5	0.8	0.2	0.4	0.4	0.7	0.4	0.6	0.1	0.2	0.9	0.1	0.6	0.3	0.6	4.0
5. 5 or more times	0.6	1.0	-	0.6	-	1.3	0.7	0.2	0.2	0.3	0.8	0.1	0.3	-	1.0	13.4
Item 6570　Subject S01　N	3287	1610	1572	2475	447	670	921	1107	590	1850	1252	1280	659	477	769	51
A19G: Taken something not belonging to you worth under $50																
1. Not at all	69.7	62.0	78.4	67.9	80.8	63.5	68.5	75.5	67.8	70.8	68.3	82.1	69.9	63.5	55.0	29.3
2. Once	13.3	15.6	10.2	13.5	9.5	13.6	13.6	12.3	14.1	12.1	14.8	8.9	14.6	17.0	16.9	21.4
3. Twice	7.2	9.1	5.2	8.2	3.5	7.6	7.8	6.0	7.9	7.2	6.9	4.5	5.8	9.0	11.3	8.9
4. 3 or 4 times	5.1	6.7	3.6	5.6	2.7	8.3	5.5	2.9	5.2	5.4	4.6	2.0	4.6	6.1	9.1	22.9
5. 5 or more times	4.8	6.6	2.7	4.8	3.4	7.0	4.7	3.3	5.0	4.5	5.3	2.5	5.1	4.4	7.7	17.5
Item 6580　Subject S01　N	3270	1600	1565	2463	445	666	913	1102	589	1841	1243	1275	654	474	764	51
A19H: Taken something not belonging to you worth over $50																
1. Not at all	93.3	89.2	97.9	93.3	95.2	90.6	93.6	94.7	93.2	95.0	91.8	97.9	95.1	93.0	87.3	47.5
2. Once	4.0	6.4	1.3	3.9	3.5	5.3	3.7	2.9	4.8	3.1	4.6	1.0	3.7	5.0	7.2	22.4
3. Twice	0.9	1.4	0.2	0.9	0.3	1.6	0.8	0.4	1.3	0.6	1.1	0.3	0.2	0.7	2.2	7.9
4. 3 or 4 times	0.9	1.3	0.5	0.9	0.5	0.5	0.9	1.2	0.6	0.7	1.1	0.4	0.8	0.5	1.6	6.8
5. 5 or more times	1.0	1.6	0.2	0.9	0.5	2.0	1.0	0.8	0.2	0.5	1.5	0.4	0.2	0.7	1.7	15.5
Item 6590　Subject S01　N	3270	1595	1572	2469	440	666	915	1103	586	1840	1245	1273	651	475	767	51
A19I: Taken something from a store without paying for it																
1. Not at all	73.2	69.3	78.6	74.2	74.3	67.5	73.9	77.8	70.3	76.5	69.5	85.7	74.1	66.7	58.4	45.5
2. Once	12.4	12.8	11.3	11.3	14.4	13.3	11.8	10.9	15.0	10.8	13.9	8.4	13.1	13.7	17.0	15.4
3. Twice	5.0	5.8	4.0	5.1	3.7	5.7	5.3	3.6	6.0	4.3	5.6	2.7	4.8	7.3	7.2	6.0
4. 3 or 4 times	5.0	5.9	3.8	4.8	5.0	7.7	4.2	4.1	4.8	4.4	6.0	1.8	4.3	7.4	9.1	12.3
5. 5 or more times	4.4	6.3	2.4	4.6	2.6	5.8	4.8	3.6	4.0	4.0	5.0	1.5	3.8	4.9	8.3	20.9
Item 6600　Subject S01　N	3279	1601	1571	2470	445	666	917	1104	591	1844	1247	1279	656	475	766	51

QUESTIONNAIRE FORM 2 1984	TOTAL	SEX		RACE		REGION				4YR COLLEGE PLANS		ILLICIT DRUG USE: LIFETIME				
		M	F	White	Black	NE	NC	S	W	Yes	No	None	Mari-juana Only	Few Pills	More Pills	Any Her-oin
N (Weighted No. of Cases):	3322	1624	1580	2491	453	681	929	1119	593	1855	1265	1285	662	479	773	51
% of Weighted Total:	100.0	48.9	47.5	75.0	13.6	20.1	28.0	33.7	17.9	55.8	38.1	38.7	19.9	14.4	23.3	1.5

A19J: Taken a car that didn't belong to someone in your family without permission of the owner

	TOTAL	M	F	White	Black	NE	NC	S	W	Yes	No	None	Mari-juana Only	Few Pills	More Pills	Any Her-oin
1. Not at all	94.2	92.4	96.3	94.5	95.8	93.5	94.1	95.4	92.8	95.3	92.9	96.7	93.9	94.6	91.4	71.6
2. Once	3.5	4.0	2.9	3.4	2.5	2.9	4.2	2.7	4.6	3.1	4.0	2.0	2.8	4.2	5.5	15.5
3. Twice	1.3	2.0	0.5	1.4	0.3	2.5	0.7	1.1	1.3	0.8	1.9	0.8	2.2	0.7	1.4	5.9
4. 3 or 4 times	0.5	0.8	0.1	0.3	0.9	-	0.6	0.3	1.0	0.4	0.5	0.2	0.6	0.4	0.6	5.1
5. 5 or more times	0.5	0.9	0.1	0.4	0.5	1.2	0.4	0.4	0.2	0.4	0.8	0.3	0.5	0.1	1.1	2.0
Item 6610 Subject S01 N	3286	1608	1573	2475	447	670	919	1107	590	1849	1251	1282	659	475	766	51

A19K: Taken part of a car without permission of the owner

	TOTAL	M	F	White	Black	NE	NC	S	W	Yes	No	None	Mari-juana Only	Few Pills	More Pills	Any Her-oin
1. Not at all	93.6	89.4	98.3	93.2	96.0	91.7	93.3	95.1	93.3	95.8	91.1	97.3	94.5	93.3	87.8	77.2
2. Once	3.7	6.2	1.1	4.1	2.3	3.6	3.9	3.1	4.5	2.4	5.4	1.6	3.6	4.1	6.7	6.6
3. Twice	1.1	1.7	0.2	1.0	0.6	1.4	1.2	0.8	0.9	0.6	1.3	0.3	0.9	1.5	2.0	3.6
4. 3 or 4 times	0.8	1.3	0.2	0.9	0.3	1.8	0.7	0.4	0.6	0.7	0.8	0.3	0.6	1.1	1.4	5.3
5. 5 or more times	0.9	1.4	0.2	0.8	0.8	1.5	1.0	0.6	0.6	0.5	1.4	0.5	0.4	-	2.1	7.3
Item 6620 Subject S01 N	3281	1606	1568	2473	445	666	918	1106	590	1845	1251	1279	658	476	766	51

A19L: Gone into some house or building when you weren't supposed to be there

	TOTAL	M	F	White	Black	NE	NC	S	W	Yes	No	None	Mari-juana Only	Few Pills	More Pills	Any Her-oin
1. Not at all	74.8	68.5	81.7	73.8	81.1	71.3	75.9	76.1	74.4	76.5	72.5	84.0	77.2	71.2	62.0	39.8
2. Once	12.3	13.6	10.7	12.6	9.5	12.0	12.2	12.5	12.5	10.4	15.3	8.8	9.8	14.9	17.4	38.4
3. Twice	6.1	8.5	3.6	6.3	5.0	7.1	5.1	5.8	7.0	6.1	5.9	4.5	5.9	6.2	8.3	6.0
4. 3 or 4 times	3.9	5.4	2.5	4.5	1.5	5.8	4.8	2.9	2.5	4.0	3.6	1.6	4.1	4.4	7.0	9.9
5. 5 or more times	2.9	4.0	1.5	2.8	2.9	3.7	2.1	2.7	3.6	3.1	2.7	1.1	3.0	3.2	5.3	5.8
Item 6630 Subject S01 N	3282	1604	1572	2473	447	667	919	1106	590	1845	1251	1279	656	475	769	51

A19M: Set fire to someone's property on purpose

	TOTAL	M	F	White	Black	NE	NC	S	W	Yes	No	None	Mari-juana Only	Few Pills	More Pills	Any Her-oin
1. Not at all	98.1	96.7	99.8	98.4	97.8	97.1	97.7	98.5	99.3	98.7	97.9	99.1	98.5	99.4	96.3	83.4
2. Once	1.1	1.8	0.1	0.8	1.6	1.5	1.3	1.0	0.4	0.6	1.6	0.7	0.6	0.2	2.1	10.9
3. Twice	0.4	0.7	-	0.4	0.3	0.5	0.6	0.2	0.1	0.4	0.1	0.1	0.2	-	0.8	4.2
4. 3 or 4 times	0.1	0.2	-	*	-	-	0.1	0.1	0.3	*	0.1	0.1	0.2	0.2	-	1.4
5. 5 or more times	0.4	0.5	*	0.3	0.2	1.0	0.3	0.2	-	0.3	0.2	*	0.6	0.2	0.8	-
Item 6640 Subject S01 N	3289	1610	1572	2478	447	670	920	1107	591	1849	1253	1282	659	476	769	50

A19N: Damaged school property on purpose

	TOTAL	M	F	White	Black	NE	NC	S	W	Yes	No	None	Mari-juana Only	Few Pills	More Pills	Any Her-oin
1. Not at all	85.9	79.9	92.4	85.4	89.2	84.1	83.3	89.4	85.7	86.9	84.8	93.2	86.6	83.5	76.9	55.7
2. Once	7.3	9.8	4.6	7.1	7.3	7.3	9.2	5.1	8.5	7.4	6.8	4.2	7.6	9.8	10.4	15.2
3. Twice	3.1	4.3	1.8	3.4	2.1	3.6	2.9	2.4	4.0	2.9	3.4	1.2	3.2	3.7	5.5	5.8
4. 3 or 4 times	1.8	2.7	0.8	2.1	0.3	2.2	2.7	1.5	0.7	1.5	2.2	0.4	1.7	2.2	3.8	5.7
5. 5 or more times	1.9	3.2	0.4	1.9	1.1	2.8	2.0	1.6	1.2	1.3	2.7	1.1	0.8	0.8	3.5	17.6
Item 6650 Subject B07,S01 N	3277	1607	1566	2468	445	666	920	1100	591	1845	1246	1277	657	474	766	51

A19O: Damaged property at work on purpose

	TOTAL	M	F	White	Black	NE	NC	S	W	Yes	No	None	Mari-juana Only	Few Pills	More Pills	Any Her-oin
1. Not at all	95.0	91.4	99.0	94.9	97.5	93.3	95.7	94.8	96.4	96.3	93.3	97.9	95.3	93.5	92.2	74.0
2. Once	2.4	3.8	0.7	2.4	1.6	3.3	2.2	2.0	2.3	1.7	3.0	0.7	2.6	3.7	3.9	7.4
3. Twice	1.2	2.3	0.2	1.2	0.7	1.2	0.9	1.8	0.8	1.1	1.5	0.6	0.6	2.0	2.2	4.9
4. 3 or 4 times	0.7	1.1	*	0.8	-	0.8	1.0	0.5	0.3	0.4	1.1	0.4	1.2	0.5	0.7	1.4
5. 5 or more times	0.7	1.4	-	0.7	0.2	1.4	0.3	0.9	0.3	0.5	1.1	0.4	0.2	0.3	1.0	12.3
Item 6660 Subject C01,S01 N	3281	1606	1568	2470	446	670	917	1105	588	1845	1250	1279	658	474	766	51

A19P: Gotten into trouble with police because of something you did

	TOTAL	M	F	White	Black	NE	NC	S	W	Yes	No	None	Mari-juana Only	Few Pills	More Pills	Any Her-oin
1. Not at all	79.5	72.1	87.2	77.7	89.3	81.0	73.6	84.2	78.0	81.6	76.5	89.4	81.6	77.4	65.1	40.9
2. Once	13.2	15.8	10.7	14.5	7.6	12.0	16.4	10.1	15.7	12.8	14.0	8.3	13.0	14.8	20.6	10.8
3. Twice	4.0	6.4	1.6	4.2	1.5	3.7	5.9	3.0	3.3	3.2	5.2	1.2	3.1	4.9	7.9	20.7
4. 3 or 4 times	2.2	3.8	0.4	2.5	0.7	1.9	2.6	1.7	2.6	1.7	2.7	0.8	1.5	2.5	4.3	10.9
5. 5 or more times	1.1	2.0	0.2	1.1	0.8	1.4	1.6	1.0	0.4	0.7	1.7	0.3	0.7	0.4	2.1	16.6
Item 6670 Subject S01 N	3287	1609	1572	2476	446	667	921	1107	591	1849	1253	1282	658	477	768	51

*=less than .05 per cent.

QUESTIONNAIRE FORM 2 1984	TOTAL	SEX		RACE		REGION				4YR COLLEGE PLANS		ILLICIT DRUG USE: LIFETIME				
		M	F	White	Black	NE	NC	S	W	Yes	No	None	Mari-juana Only	Few Pills	More Pills	Any Her-oin
N (Weighted No. of Cases):	3322	1624	1580	2491	453	681	929	1119	593	1855	1265	1285	662	479	773	51
% of Weighted Total:	100.0	48.9	47.5	75.0	13.6	20.1	28.0	33.7	17.9	55.8	38.1	38.7	19.9	14.4	23.3	1.5

A20: The next questions are about some things which may have happened TO YOU. During the LAST 12 MONTHS, how often...

A20A: Has something of yours (worth under $50) been stolen?

1. Not at all	56.0	51.7	61.0	57.6	47.5	56.2	58.9	58.0	47.4	54.6	58.5	61.3	54.8	56.1	48.9	45.3
2. Once	25.8	25.9	25.2	24.8	30.6	24.4	25.5	26.6	26.3	25.9	25.6	23.8	26.4	26.7	27.7	26.6
3. Twice	10.9	12.5	9.3	10.5	13.1	11.4	9.7	8.8	16.1	12.1	8.9	8.8	12.4	9.2	13.7	24.2
4. 3 or 4 times	5.4	7.1	3.5	5.2	7.0	5.7	4.0	5.6	6.9	5.7	4.8	4.7	4.8	5.2	6.9	3.9
5. 5 or more times	2.0	2.8	1.0	1.8	1.9	2.2	1.9	1.1	3.3	1.7	2.1	1.4	1.5	2.8	2.8	-
Item 6680 Subject S03　　N	3260	1594	1562	2453	444	662	911	1096	591	1831	1247	1268	655	474	765	50

A20B: Has something of yours (worth over $50) been stolen?

1. Not at all	83.6	79.5	88.5	86.2	75.6	83.5	86.3	83.9	79.1	83.3	84.9	86.8	83.2	84.5	80.2	67.1
2. Once	12.0	14.6	9.2	10.3	18.2	12.3	10.4	11.6	15.1	12.3	11.4	11.1	11.7	12.2	12.4	25.2
3. Twice	2.8	3.8	1.5	2.0	5.1	1.8	1.9	3.2	4.3	3.0	2.2	1.3	3.8	2.3	4.4	2.2
4. 3 or 4 times	1.2	1.6	0.7	1.1	1.0	2.0	0.8	1.0	1.0	1.2	1.0	0.7	1.0	1.0	1.9	5.5
5. 5 or more times	0.4	0.5	0.1	0.3	-	0.4	0.5	0.2	0.5	0.2	0.4	0.1	0.3	-	1.3	-
Item 6690 Subject S03　　N	3273	1600	1568	2465	444	665	916	1101	591	1840	1251	1277	657	476	766	50

A20C: Has someone deliberately damaged your property (your car, clothing, etc.)?

1. Not at all	69.1	62.1	76.4	69.6	69.7	70.0	69.1	71.1	64.5	70.2	67.7	76.5	68.1	65.1	61.0	51.1
2. Once	18.7	22.0	15.0	18.7	18.3	18.1	19.2	17.5	21.0	17.6	19.9	14.3	19.0	20.4	24.6	27.1
3. Twice	6.8	8.7	5.2	6.8	6.7	6.5	6.8	6.6	7.7	7.4	6.2	5.3	6.9	7.2	8.4	15.0
4. 3 or 4 times	3.6	4.9	2.4	3.5	3.4	4.0	3.0	3.3	4.6	3.5	3.9	2.5	3.4	6.6	3.8	4.8
5. 5 or more times	1.7	2.3	1.0	1.4	1.8	1.4	1.9	1.6	2.1	1.3	2.2	1.4	2.6	0.7	2.1	2.0
Item 6700 Subject S03　　N	3271	1598	1571	2460	448	667	917	1098	590	1840	1249	1275	657	477	766	50

A20D: Has someone injured you with a weapon (like a knife, gun, or club)?

1. Not at all	94.8	92.4	97.7	95.6	94.3	94.6	94.3	95.2	95.0	96.2	93.4	96.1	96.3	96.7	91.2	80.0
2. Once	3.7	5.3	1.9	3.3	4.2	3.3	4.0	3.8	3.8	2.9	4.7	3.0	2.3	3.1	6.1	12.6
3. Twice	1.0	1.5	0.2	0.6	1.3	1.2	1.2	0.6	0.9	0.7	1.0	0.8	0.6	0.1	1.6	6.0
4. 3 or 4 times	0.3	0.4	0.2	0.3	0.2	0.5	0.4	0.1	0.1	0.1	0.4	0.1	0.4	-	0.5	1.4
5. 5 or more times	0.3	0.4	-	0.2	-	0.5	0.2	0.2	0.1	0.1	0.4	0.1	0.3	-	0.7	-
Item 6710 Subject S03　　N	3274	1599	1570	2465	446	666	916	1101	591	1843	1250	1278	657	476	767	49

A20E: Has someone threatened you with a weapon, but not actually injured you?

1. Not at all	83.4	77.2	90.7	84.8	77.9	82.7	83.5	83.7	83.4	86.0	80.8	89.0	82.9	81.7	78.1	46.0
2. Once	10.3	13.9	6.2	9.5	14.7	10.7	10.1	10.6	9.8	8.4	12.2	6.7	12.5	10.8	12.7	27.4
3. Twice	3.2	4.8	1.5	3.2	4.2	3.4	3.0	2.7	4.4	3.1	3.4	2.3	2.1	4.3	4.7	8.7
4. 3 or 4 times	1.7	2.3	0.9	1.5	1.8	1.6	1.9	1.7	1.5	1.6	1.7	1.6	1.4	1.7	1.9	7.6
5. 5 or more times	1.4	1.7	0.6	1.0	1.5	1.6	1.5	1.4	0.8	0.8	1.9	0.4	1.1	1.5	2.7	10.3
Item 6720 Subject S03　　N	3270	1597	1570	2464	446	666	916	1099	590	1841	1248	1277	658	473	766	50

A20F: Has someone injured you on purpose without using a weapon?

1. Not at all	83.4	81.8	85.7	83.4	86.0	83.0	82.3	86.5	80.1	85.0	81.3	90.0	85.0	81.7	74.1	63.2
2. Once	9.6	9.9	9.0	9.7	9.5	9.1	9.5	8.4	12.6	8.6	10.5	5.7	9.9	10.2	15.0	12.6
3. Twice	3.4	4.0	2.8	3.4	2.5	3.6	3.5	2.6	4.5	3.3	3.9	2.2	3.1	2.8	5.2	10.7
4. 3 or 4 times	2.2	2.5	1.6	2.3	0.6	2.0	3.0	1.6	2.0	1.7	3.1	1.5	0.6	4.3	3.1	6.8
5. 5 or more times	1.4	1.7	1.0	1.2	1.5	2.3	1.7	1.0	0.8	1.5	1.3	0.6	1.4	1.1	2.7	6.7
Item 6730 Subject S03　　N	3270	1597	1570	2463	446	665	916	1099	590	1838	1250	1275	658	475	766	50

QUESTIONNAIRE FORM 2 1984	TOTAL	SEX		RACE		REGION				4YR COLLEGE PLANS		ILLICIT DRUG USE: LIFETIME				
		M	F	White	Black	NE	NC	S	W	Yes	No	None	Mari- juana Only	Few Pills	More Pills	Any Her- oin
N (Weighted No. of Cases):	3322	1624	1580	2491	453	681	929	1119	593	1855	1265	1285	662	479	773	51
% of Weighted Total:	100.0	48.9	47.5	75.0	13.6	20.1	28.0	33.7	17.9	55.8	38.1	38.7	19.9	14.4	23.3	1.5

A20G: Has an unarmed person threatened you with injury, but not actually injured you?

1. Not at all	72.4	65.4	80.0	72.4	74.1	70.7	70.9	74.4	73.1	73.3	71.1	79.2	72.5	69.1	64.9	51.5
2. Once	13.3	14.6	11.7	13.3	13.5	13.5	11.6	14.4	13.8	12.9	14.0	11.4	14.8	14.5	14.9	2.1
3. Twice	5.3	6.9	3.7	5.1	6.2	6.2	5.8	4.8	4.4	6.0	4.1	3.7	4.9	6.4	6.0	26.1
4. 3 or 4 times	4.5	6.1	2.8	4.7	3.1	5.0	5.4	3.6	4.4	3.9	5.5	2.9	4.5	5.6	6.3	8.0
5. 5 or more times	4.4	6.9	1.8	4.4	3.0	4.6	6.2	2.9	4.3	3.9	5.3	2.7	3.3	4.5	7.9	12.3
Item 6740 Subject S03 N	3275	1600	1570	2466	446	668	915	1101	591	1842	1250	1277	658	476	766	50

A21: The following questions concern ciga- rettes, alcohol, and a number of other drugs. How difficult do you think it would be for you to get each of the following types of drugs, if you wanted some?

A21A: Marijuana (pot, grass)

1. Probably impossible	6.9	5.2	8.5	4.6	13.7	4.3	6.0	9.7	6.0	5.0	9.5	14.2	1.6	4.1	0.7	3.5
2. Very difficult	3.0	2.6	3.2	2.3	3.4	1.0	3.3	3.7	3.5	2.9	2.9	4.8	2.3	2.5	1.0	1.4
3. Fairly difficult	5.5	5.4	5.8	5.4	4.1	4.1	6.4	6.0	4.6	5.6	5.7	8.2	4.9	4.8	2.2	2.0
4. Fairly easy	28.2	26.8	30.1	29.4	25.4	27.1	27.0	29.9	27.9	29.7	26.1	34.5	28.2	25.9	21.0	10.0
5. Very easy	56.5	60.0	52.4	58.4	53.1	63.5	57.3	50.7	58.0	56.8	55.8	38.3	63.0	62.7	75.2	83.1
Item 6750 Subject A03a N	3269	1604	1562	2464	446	665	918	1097	589	1836	1246	1272	659	477	768	50

A21B: LSD

1. Probably impossible	23.3	20.0	26.6	17.7	44.2	18.6	21.6	28.0	22.7	19.4	28.8	28.3	27.9	22.3	13.0	3.1
2. Very difficult	19.0	19.0	19.0	20.2	15.5	18.1	19.7	19.3	18.5	19.1	19.1	18.7	21.8	20.0	17.2	8.3
3. Fairly difficult	27.0	28.9	25.6	29.4	19.4	30.4	28.1	25.2	25.1	30.3	22.7	27.2	26.8	28.5	27.1	25.8
4. Fairly easy	22.6	22.4	23.1	24.7	15.0	23.0	22.2	20.4	27.2	24.6	20.3	20.1	18.3	22.0	31.0	21.7
5. Very easy	7.9	9.7	5.8	8.0	5.9	9.9	8.4	7.2	6.4	6.6	9.4	5.7	5.3	7.2	11.7	41.1
Item 6760 Subject A03a N	3223	1585	1535	2431	437	652	904	1084	582	1807	1235	1247	649	471	765	50

A21C: Some other psychedelic (mescaline, peyote, psilocybin, PCP, etc.)

1. Probably impossible	27.0	23.2	30.4	21.9	47.6	20.0	25.2	32.2	27.7	23.0	32.2	31.4	33.4	27.1	14.6	11.7
2. Very difficult	22.2	22.7	22.2	23.5	18.3	17.8	24.4	23.8	20.7	23.9	19.7	22.3	22.3	23.9	22.2	6.0
3. Fairly difficult	24.2	25.2	23.2	26.1	15.4	23.2	25.4	23.7	24.2	26.3	21.8	24.0	23.1	23.2	26.8	17.9
4. Fairly easy	18.7	19.0	18.6	20.6	12.5	24.0	18.4	14.3	21.7	19.7	17.7	16.5	16.8	18.9	24.0	23.5
5. Very easy	7.9	9.9	5.5	7.9	6.0	15.0	6.6	5.9	5.7	7.1	8.6	5.9	4.4	6.8	12.3	40.9
Item 6770 Subject A03a N	3209	1580	1527	2421	434	647	900	1081	580	1796	1235	1238	647	471	761	50

A21D: Amphetamines (uppers, pep pills, ben- nies, speed)

1. Probably impossible	12.4	9.9	14.4	7.2	33.4	9.3	10.4	16.2	11.9	10.2	14.9	19.6	13.6	8.2	1.5	5.8
2. Very difficult	7.1	7.8	6.4	6.2	10.1	5.9	6.8	8.1	6.9	7.9	5.5	9.8	7.9	6.9	1.7	1.1
3. Fairly difficult	12.4	14.6	10.3	12.0	15.0	11.6	10.4	13.7	14.0	13.6	10.9	14.1	14.0	15.1	7.5	-
4. Fairly easy	34.7	35.4	34.7	38.1	22.4	38.3	35.3	29.9	38.6	37.5	31.9	34.1	38.3	35.3	34.2	16.1
5. Very easy	33.5	32.3	34.3	36.5	19.2	34.8	37.2	32.2	28.7	30.8	36.8	22.4	26.2	34.5	55.1	77.0
Item 6780 Subject A03a N	3234	1587	1545	2442	438	658	905	1090	581	1809	1245	1254	654	472	764	49

A21E: Barbiturates (downers, goofballs, reds, yellows, etc.)

1. Probably impossible	16.0	13.3	18.1	10.3	37.5	12.1	14.8	20.1	14.5	12.9	20.0	21.3	19.9	12.5	5.8	10.2
2. Very difficult	12.3	13.8	11.1	12.1	13.6	9.8	13.5	12.9	12.2	13.2	10.5	13.4	14.0	15.9	7.1	2.5
3. Fairly difficult	19.8	20.6	19.2	20.6	15.2	21.5	20.7	16.9	21.8	20.8	18.4	18.1	20.3	21.1	22.0	13.9
4. Fairly easy	30.7	31.4	30.7	34.1	19.5	35.5	29.5	27.9	32.3	32.8	29.2	30.7	30.3	28.2	33.6	22.1
5. Very easy	21.3	20.9	20.9	22.8	14.2	21.1	21.5	22.2	19.3	20.3	21.9	16.6	15.5	22.4	31.5	51.2
Item 6790 Subject A03a N	3216	1579	1534	2427	435	653	900	1087	576	1799	1239	1243	650	472	760	49

A21F: Tranquilizers

1. Probably impossible	15.8	13.9	17.3	9.9	37.3	12.4	15.1	19.5	13.9	11.8	21.0	19.8	19.7	14.4	7.2	3.1
2. Very difficult	10.3	11.4	9.1	10.0	12.2	8.5	10.7	9.8	12.5	10.0	10.6	9.0	9.9	14.4	10.1	1.1
3. Fairly difficult	19.4	20.8	18.0	20.5	16.6	22.7	19.7	17.8	18.0	19.7	18.7	17.2	19.3	18.8	22.6	29.3
4. Fairly easy	28.7	27.7	29.7	31.4	17.8	31.6	29.0	27.1	28.0	30.6	27.2	30.1	30.4	25.2	29.0	12.4
5. Very easy	25.8	26.3	25.9	28.3	16.1	24.8	25.4	25.8	27.6	27.9	22.5	23.9	20.8	27.1	31.1	54.2
Item 6800 Subject A03a N	3218	1584	1532	2431	434	653	905	1083	577	1800	1237	1246	648	468	765	50

QUESTIONNAIRE FORM 2 1984	TOTAL	SEX		RACE		REGION				4YR COLLEGE PLANS		ILLICIT DRUG USE: LIFETIME				
		M	F	White	Black	NE	NC	S	W	Yes	No	None	Marijuana Only	Few Pills	More Pills	Any Heroin
N (Weighted No. of Cases):	3322	1624	1580	2491	453	681	929	1119	593	1855	1265	1285	662	479	773	51
% of Weighted Total:	100.0	48.9	47.5	75.0	13.6	20.1	28.0	33.7	17.9	55.8	38.1	38.7	19.9	14.4	23.3	1.5

A21G: Cocaine

	TOTAL	M	F	White	Black	NE	NC	S	W	Yes	No	None	Mar.	Few	More	Her.
1. Probably impossible	20.4	18.5	22.1	16.7	34.3	11.6	25.7	24.6	14.2	16.9	24.8	27.6	24.1	16.3	8.2	6.1
2. Very difficult	15.3	14.8	15.7	16.2	10.6	8.8	20.4	16.3	12.7	16.6	13.6	18.5	16.3	16.9	9.0	1.1
3. Fairly difficult	19.4	20.9	18.1	21.1	13.7	18.5	19.8	20.7	17.3	21.0	18.0	21.8	18.8	18.1	17.5	18.1
4. Fairly easy	25.4	25.1	26.0	27.1	18.9	30.9	22.7	22.4	28.9	27.4	23.1	20.4	24.1	28.8	33.0	21.9
5. Very easy	19.6	20.7	18.1	18.8	22.5	30.2	11.5	16.0	27.0	18.1	20.5	11.8	16.7	19.9	32.3	52.8
Item 6810 Subject A03a N	3222	1585	1535	2432	438	659	901	1082	581	1805	1237	1244	653	471	762	50

A21H: Heroin (smack, horse)

	TOTAL	M	F	White	Black	NE	NC	S	W	Yes	No	None	Mar.	Few	More	Her.
1. Probably impossible	32.8	31.2	34.0	28.6	47.4	24.5	36.9	35.4	30.8	28.4	38.3	33.8	37.8	33.8	27.5	9.3
2. Very difficult	24.2	24.9	24.0	26.4	16.0	24.0	23.3	24.3	25.8	26.4	21.8	23.5	21.3	26.0	28.0	7.3
3. Fairly difficult	23.1	24.2	22.1	25.6	14.3	27.0	21.1	21.9	23.8	24.7	21.6	21.3	24.0	21.7	26.3	15.8
4. Fairly easy	13.6	13.3	14.1	14.2	10.4	15.2	13.6	11.9	14.9	14.9	11.7	15.1	11.9	12.3	12.1	39.0
5. Very easy	6.3	6.5	5.8	5.2	11.8	9.3	5.1	6.5	4.6	5.6	6.6	6.3	4.9	6.2	6.1	28.7
Item 6820 Subject A03a N	3200	1578	1520	2420	431	648	900	1077	574	1787	1234	1232	649	468	760	49

A21I: Some other narcotic (methadone, opium, codeine, paregoric, etc.)

	TOTAL	M	F	White	Black	NE	NC	S	W	Yes	No	None	Mar.	Few	More	Her.
1. Probably impossible	26.3	24.0	28.3	20.8	46.8	19.6	27.9	30.9	22.8	23.2	30.2	31.1	33.5	24.8	13.9	9.6
2. Very difficult	19.1	19.5	19.0	19.9	18.6	18.5	19.9	20.0	16.8	20.4	17.4	20.1	19.0	21.9	16.5	10.8
3. Fairly difficult	22.5	22.5	22.8	24.9	11.6	26.5	23.2	20.3	20.9	24.2	20.1	21.6	23.8	20.8	25.1	13.3
4. Fairly easy	20.2	21.1	19.2	22.0	14.2	21.1	18.2	18.3	25.5	21.4	19.1	18.2	16.8	19.0	27.5	15.3
5. Very easy	12.0	13.0	10.6	12.3	8.7	14.3	10.7	10.5	14.0	10.8	13.2	9.0	6.9	13.5	17.0	51.0
Item 6830 Subject A03a N	3201	1579	1520	2419	431	651	897	1076	577	1790	1233	1231	648	470	761	50

This section asks for your views and feelings about a number of different things.

D01: How satisfied are you with your life as a whole these days?

	TOTAL	M	F	White	Black	NE	NC	S	W	Yes	No	None	Mar.	Few	More	Her.
1. Completely dissatisfied	2.4	2.8	2.1	2.2	2.7	2.6	1.8	2.9	2.2	2.0	2.8	2.7	2.0	2.1	2.1	5.8
2. Quite dissatisfied	8.6	7.9	9.5	8.9	9.2	9.5	10.3	7.0	8.0	9.6	7.2	9.0	8.5	9.3	7.7	3.1
3. Somewhat dissatisfied	11.5	11.2	11.2	10.9	16.0	11.5	11.3	11.5	11.8	11.0	11.8	10.4	12.2	10.7	13.4	7.8
4. Neither, or mixed feelings	13.2	12.6	14.2	12.4	14.4	13.1	13.6	13.3	12.3	11.3	16.3	11.7	12.9	13.0	15.8	11.9
5. Somewhat satisfied	24.4	26.0	22.9	24.5	20.3	26.7	26.6	21.8	23.3	23.8	25.4	23.7	23.8	23.4	26.0	39.0
6. Quite satisfied	33.5	32.3	34.4	35.6	26.9	30.9	31.2	35.5	36.1	36.2	29.9	36.4	33.6	35.1	28.7	23.7
7. Completely satisfied	6.5	7.1	5.8	5.6	10.4	5.7	5.1	8.1	6.4	6.1	6.6	6.2	7.1	6.4	6.3	8.7
Item 6840 Subject P01,Q01 N	3119	1517	1527	2387	423	615	894	1045	565	1821	1216	1236	624	449	716	48

D02: These next questions ask you to guess how well you might do in several different situations. How good do you think you would be...

D02A: As a husband or wife?

	TOTAL	M	F	White	Black	NE	NC	S	W	Yes	No	None	Mar.	Few	More	Her.
1. Poor	0.7	1.1	0.2	0.4	1.1	1.0	0.8	0.6	0.1	0.5	0.9	0.7	0.6	0.4	0.7	2.2
2. Not so good	1.8	2.0	1.5	1.8	1.6	1.5	2.1	2.3	1.0	1.7	2.1	1.5	1.5	2.5	1.7	4.7
3. Fairly good	9.3	11.5	7.3	9.6	8.7	8.5	10.5	8.8	9.4	7.9	11.2	8.8	9.2	10.1	10.6	2.7
4. Good	35.0	36.2	33.6	36.1	28.3	32.4	36.9	35.5	34.0	35.1	35.2	35.6	32.6	35.4	35.2	41.8
5. Very good	49.5	44.9	54.2	48.7	56.1	54.1	45.3	48.9	52.1	51.3	46.6	49.8	52.8	46.9	47.9	43.4
8. Don't know	3.7	4.2	3.2	3.4	4.2	2.5	4.4	4.0	3.3	3.4	4.1	3.5	3.3	4.7	3.9	5.2
Item 6850 Subject D01,Q01 N	3114	1515	1524	2383	421	611	892	1042	568	1823	1209	1238	621	449	714	47

D02B: As a parent?

	TOTAL	M	F	White	Black	NE	NC	S	W	Yes	No	None	Mar.	Few	More	Her.
1. Poor	1.3	1.3	1.3	1.2	1.3	1.6	1.4	1.4	1.0	1.1	1.8	1.1	0.8	1.8	1.8	3.2
2. Not so good	3.2	3.5	2.7	3.4	2.2	1.5	4.9	2.9	2.8	2.9	3.7	2.8	2.9	4.0	3.7	2.2
3. Fairly good	10.1	11.4	9.0	10.6	7.5	7.3	9.2	12.6	9.5	9.1	11.5	8.5	9.9	11.7	11.6	10.5
4. Good	32.4	35.4	29.4	33.7	26.2	36.1	33.4	29.4	32.3	32.9	31.2	34.1	31.5	31.3	31.7	27.2
5. Very good	48.3	43.0	53.8	46.5	58.4	51.2	45.8	47.8	50.2	49.9	46.1	48.4	50.8	47.1	46.4	47.0
8. Don't know	4.7	5.5	3.9	4.7	4.5	2.3	5.3	5.9	4.2	4.0	5.8	5.1	4.1	4.1	4.9	9.9
Item 6860 Subject D02,Q01 N	3100	1510	1517	2375	415	606	891	1037	567	1818	1204	1235	617	448	708	47

QUESTIONNAIRE FORM 2 1984	TOTAL	SEX		RACE		REGION				4YR COLLEGE PLANS		ILLICIT DRUG USE: LIFETIME				
		M	F	White	Black	NE	NC	S	W	Yes	No	None	Marijuana Only	Few Pills	More Pills	Any Heroin
N (Weighted No. of Cases):	3322	1624	1580	2491	453	681	929	1119	593	1855	1265	1285	662	479	773	51
% of Weighted Total:	100.0	48.9	47.5	75.0	13.6	20.1	28.0	33.7	17.9	55.8	38.1	38.7	19.9	14.4	23.3	1.5

D02C: As a worker on a job?

1. Poor	0.1	0.2	-	0.1	0.3	0.1	-	0.4	*	0.1	0.3	0.1	0.2	0.2	0.2	-
2. Not so good	0.3	0.3	0.4	0.3	0.7	0.1	0.4	0.5	0.2	0.4	0.3	-	0.6	0.6	0.4	-
3. Fairly good	4.4	4.4	4.4	4.4	3.7	5.3	4.1	4.6	3.4	3.2	5.8	3.7	3.2	4.4	6.4	5.7
4. Good	30.0	29.8	30.4	31.6	20.7	27.0	34.2	30.7	25.5	28.3	32.6	32.3	26.2	29.8	29.8	26.1
5. Very good	64.0	64.1	63.7	62.8	73.4	66.4	59.5	63.3	69.5	66.7	60.1	62.2	69.4	63.9	62.3	66.9
8. Don't know	1.1	1.1	1.1	0.8	1.2	1.1	1.8	0.5	1.3	1.2	0.9	1.7	0.4	1.1	0.9	1.3
Item 6870 Subject C03,Q01 N	3095	1506	1515	2370	415	609	891	1032	564	1814	1201	1232	617	446	708	45

D03: Some people think a lot about the social problems of the nation and the world, and about how they might be solved. Others spend little time thinking about these issues. How much do you think about such things?

1. Never	5.5	6.3	4.4	5.1	5.1	6.8	4.6	6.1	4.3	2.6	9.3	5.3	3.7	5.2	6.7	11.5
2. Seldom	22.4	22.2	22.7	23.0	21.8	22.3	23.3	22.5	20.9	20.1	26.7	19.1	23.5	23.4	26.0	38.9
3. Sometimes	49.2	47.4	51.2	50.3	45.3	47.0	52.9	47.6	49.1	50.0	48.1	51.6	51.0	47.4	46.5	30.5
4. Quite often	18.1	18.6	17.5	17.1	21.9	19.6	15.3	18.5	20.0	21.1	13.3	19.2	17.6	18.2	16.9	11.1
5. A great deal	4.8	5.4	4.1	4.4	5.9	4.2	3.9	5.3	5.8	6.1	2.6	4.8	4.2	5.8	4.0	7.9
Item 6880 Subject J,Q08 N	3091	1502	1514	2366	419	605	886	1035	565	1811	1201	1233	614	443	709	47

D04: Now we'd like you to make some ratings of how honest and moral the people are who run the following organizations. To what extent are there problems of dishonesty and immorality in the leadership of...

D04A: Large corporations?

1. Not at all	3.5	4.3	2.7	2.7	5.2	2.9	3.9	3.4	3.9	2.6	5.2	3.9	3.1	2.8	2.7	9.0
2. Slight	17.1	18.1	15.8	17.1	15.8	17.8	17.9	16.0	17.1	17.3	16.8	18.2	14.6	17.7	16.6	25.2
3. Moderate	37.2	39.7	34.8	39.0	31.5	33.1	39.2	38.5	35.7	38.5	35.4	35.9	39.5	40.2	37.6	11.0
4. Considerable	20.6	20.3	21.1	21.6	18.8	25.2	19.3	19.2	20.1	22.3	17.8	21.0	18.8	17.3	23.0	21.2
5. Great	4.9	4.2	5.6	4.3	6.6	5.4	3.8	5.3	5.3	5.4	4.2	5.3	4.1	4.0	5.5	7.2
8. No opinion	16.7	13.3	20.0	15.3	22.0	15.7	15.8	17.5	17.9	13.9	20.7	15.7	19.9	18.0	14.7	26.6
Item 6890 Subject K01 N	3001	1464	1465	2306	393	585	871	995	549	1762	1154	1206	592	433	686	45

D04B: Major labor unions?

1. Not at all	4.4	5.7	3.2	4.2	4.7	3.8	4.6	5.2	3.3	2.5	7.6	5.2	3.4	4.5	3.8	3.5
2. Slight	17.6	19.1	16.3	17.8	18.1	17.1	18.3	16.5	19.3	17.9	17.5	16.4	15.4	19.9	19.7	19.2
3. Moderate	32.3	32.9	32.0	34.3	23.5	33.8	34.4	31.6	28.7	33.5	30.1	31.2	36.7	31.0	32.6	21.4
4. Considerable	19.6	20.9	18.3	19.8	19.2	21.3	18.0	19.5	20.6	21.1	17.6	20.9	18.8	16.5	19.7	26.0
5. Great	6.1	7.2	4.8	6.0	5.3	6.0	6.3	5.0	7.9	6.2	5.9	6.5	4.2	6.1	6.9	4.2
8. No opinion	19.9	14.3	25.5	18.0	29.2	18.0	18.3	22.3	20.2	18.8	21.2	19.8	21.7	21.9	17.2	25.7
Item 6900 Subject K01 N	2995	1465	1458	2304	389	579	872	997	549	1758	1153	1206	585	434	685	45

D04C: The nation's colleges and universities?

1. Not at all	7.0	7.8	6.1	6.9	4.9	5.8	6.5	7.8	7.6	6.3	7.7	7.2	7.5	5.4	6.6	10.6
2. Slight	30.2	32.2	28.4	33.1	20.5	30.3	32.9	27.6	30.3	34.6	24.6	30.2	29.2	33.4	29.9	21.3
3. Moderate	23.1	23.4	22.6	22.8	24.5	26.0	22.5	21.0	25.1	23.8	21.9	23.6	25.0	18.8	22.5	23.0
4. Considerable	17.0	15.3	18.7	16.6	18.1	17.6	17.3	18.0	14.4	15.3	19.4	16.7	16.3	16.1	20.1	10.0
5. Great	7.7	7.9	7.3	6.7	12.0	5.8	6.6	9.6	7.8	8.0	6.9	7.8	6.4	10.3	6.5	10.6
8. No opinion	15.0	13.3	16.9	14.0	20.1	14.5	14.3	16.1	14.9	12.0	19.4	14.5	15.7	16.1	14.4	24.5
Item 6910 Subject B10,K01 N	2975	1457	1447	2295	382	576	867	988	544	1751	1142	1197	583	428	682	45

D04D: The nation's public schools?

1. Not at all	7.7	8.9	6.6	7.7	5.5	6.4	9.2	7.4	7.1	6.8	9.1	7.4	9.5	6.6	6.7	10.7
2. Slight	28.7	28.7	28.4	30.1	22.4	28.1	29.8	27.0	30.6	31.4	24.6	29.2	26.1	28.0	29.8	34.7
3. Moderate	26.6	27.4	25.8	26.9	26.6	30.7	25.8	26.2	24.1	26.2	27.4	26.8	27.8	26.5	26.7	11.4
4. Considerable	18.5	16.9	20.3	18.5	18.3	16.6	20.3	18.4	18.0	18.8	18.3	18.6	19.1	15.4	20.7	8.3
5. Great	7.7	7.9	7.3	6.3	13.7	6.9	5.3	10.1	7.9	7.8	7.4	7.6	6.4	10.6	6.0	16.3
8. No opinion	10.8	10.3	11.6	10.5	13.4	11.2	9.5	10.9	12.2	8.9	13.2	10.3	11.1	12.8	10.1	18.5
Item 6920 Subject B10,K01 N	2957	1451	1437	2283	381	568	867	986	537	1744	1132	1191	577	429	676	43

*=less than .05 per cent.

QUESTIONNAIRE FORM 2 1984	TOTAL	SEX		RACE		REGION				4YR COLLEGE PLANS		ILLICIT DRUG USE: LIFETIME				
		M	F	White	Black	NE	NC	S	W	Yes	No	None	Marijuana Only	Few Pills	More Pills	Any Heroin
N (Weighted No. of Cases):	3322	1624	1580	2491	453	681	929	1119	593	1855	1265	1285	662	479	773	51
% of Weighted Total:	100.0	48.9	47.5	75.0	13.6	20.1	28.0	33.7	17.9	55.8	38.1	38.7	19.9	14.4	23.3	1.5

D04E: Churches and religious organizations?

	TOTAL	M	F	White	Black	NE	NC	S	W	Yes	No	None	Mari-juana Only	Few Pills	More Pills	Any Heroin
1. Not at all	15.9	17.1	14.7	16.8	8.6	15.9	18.1	13.1	17.7	15.0	16.8	15.7	18.1	13.3	15.2	21.3
2. Slight	28.0	29.0	27.0	30.5	19.7	29.8	27.5	26.9	28.7	31.1	23.7	29.4	25.5	25.6	29.8	27.1
3. Moderate	15.6	14.8	16.4	15.0	18.0	16.3	14.5	14.9	18.1	17.1	13.5	15.9	15.9	16.5	14.6	2.3
4. Considerable	14.1	14.2	14.0	13.6	17.1	13.0	13.2	15.7	13.7	13.8	14.7	14.0	13.2	15.4	14.8	13.0
5. Great	14.1	13.5	14.7	12.5	20.4	10.8	14.9	17.3	10.5	13.3	15.3	13.8	13.8	16.3	13.1	24.4
8. No opinion	12.3	11.5	13.1	11.6	16.3	14.3	11.8	12.0	11.3	9.8	16.0	11.2	13.5	12.9	12.5	12.0
Item 6930 Subject G,K01 N	2981	1459	1451	2296	386	574	870	992	544	1755	1144	1202	580	432	681	45

D04F: The national news media (TV, magazines, news services)?

	TOTAL	M	F	White	Black	NE	NC	S	W	Yes	No	None	Mari-juana Only	Few Pills	More Pills	Any Heroin
1. Not at all	4.4	4.6	4.0	4.1	3.4	5.1	3.5	5.2	3.7	3.3	6.3	3.9	3.6	4.4	5.5	7.2
2. Slight	20.5	21.3	19.7	21.6	15.6	19.6	20.2	21.8	19.4	20.6	20.4	21.5	20.7	18.2	19.9	21.7
3. Moderate	29.9	30.5	30.2	30.6	27.6	32.7	30.8	27.4	30.3	32.3	26.8	30.7	31.6	27.5	29.8	17.8
4. Considerable	22.0	21.1	22.7	22.3	21.3	21.2	21.8	21.6	23.9	23.2	20.1	22.9	20.2	21.4	22.9	11.7
5. Great	12.7	12.7	12.3	11.8	16.8	10.7	14.0	13.1	12.0	11.8	13.9	11.9	10.9	16.3	11.9	30.9
8. No opinion	10.5	9.9	11.1	9.6	15.4	10.7	9.8	10.9	10.7	8.9	12.5	9.1	12.9	12.2	10.0	10.7
Item 6940 Subject K01 N	2972	1454	1449	2289	384	575	865	991	542	1755	1135	1201	582	424	680	44

D04G: The Presidency and the administration?

	TOTAL	M	F	White	Black	NE	NC	S	W	Yes	No	None	Mari-juana Only	Few Pills	More Pills	Any Heroin
1. Not at all	5.8	7.3	4.3	5.3	5.5	5.8	5.8	5.9	5.6	4.6	7.6	5.7	5.0	5.9	5.5	15.8
2. Slight	23.7	27.2	20.2	24.4	19.9	24.4	22.6	23.8	24.6	25.5	20.8	23.2	20.1	28.9	25.1	16.5
3. Moderate	30.6	29.7	31.1	31.7	26.2	28.5	32.7	29.8	30.8	32.8	27.9	33.3	32.6	23.7	28.7	21.1
4. Considerable	19.3	17.0	21.3	20.1	19.1	20.9	19.7	18.8	17.6	20.1	18.1	19.0	19.5	19.3	20.2	16.1
5. Great	7.9	8.3	7.8	7.1	11.4	9.5	7.3	8.0	7.3	6.8	9.7	7.4	8.1	7.7	8.6	14.1
8. No opinion	12.7	10.4	15.2	11.5	17.9	10.8	11.9	13.7	14.2	10.2	16.0	11.4	14.7	14.5	12.0	16.3
Item 6950 Subject H04,K01 N	2965	1447	1447	2281	385	573	866	987	539	1750	1132	1193	581	427	679	44

D04H: Congress–that is, the U.S. Senate and House of Representatives?

	TOTAL	M	F	White	Black	NE	NC	S	W	Yes	No	None	Mari-juana Only	Few Pills	More Pills	Any Heroin
1. Not at all	5.1	5.9	4.2	4.4	4.8	5.3	5.4	4.8	4.8	3.4	7.8	4.5	4.1	5.2	5.3	13.0
2. Slight	21.4	24.1	18.5	21.9	18.3	21.2	20.7	21.1	23.0	22.2	19.8	19.9	21.8	23.9	22.6	17.3
3. Moderate	31.9	31.1	32.5	33.2	28.5	29.0	34.0	31.2	32.8	34.9	27.4	34.3	33.9	26.7	30.5	11.9
4. Considerable	19.1	19.3	19.1	19.2	18.7	22.8	18.5	19.8	14.7	20.4	17.5	19.3	17.5	18.6	20.2	28.6
5. Great	7.7	7.8	7.3	7.5	8.5	7.7	7.1	7.5	9.0	6.9	8.7	7.9	5.8	8.1	8.4	10.0
8. No opinion	14.9	11.8	18.4	13.8	21.2	14.1	14.2	15.5	15.8	12.2	18.9	14.0	16.8	17.5	12.9	19.3
Item 6960 Subject H04,K01 N	2962	1449	1443	2281	382	573	861	990	539	1750	1130	1193	578	427	679	44

D04I: The U.S. Supreme Court?

	TOTAL	M	F	White	Black	NE	NC	S	W	Yes	No	None	Mari-juana Only	Few Pills	More Pills	Any Heroin
1. Not at all	13.1	15.6	10.2	13.6	7.4	12.0	14.8	11.2	14.8	13.6	12.4	13.4	11.3	12.6	13.0	19.1
2. Slight	26.7	29.3	24.0	28.4	20.6	29.5	26.8	24.0	28.7	28.8	23.8	27.1	23.1	28.1	29.1	31.5
3. Moderate	20.6	18.7	22.4	21.2	19.2	20.5	19.2	23.3	18.0	20.4	21.1	20.8	20.6	18.1	22.8	8.5
4. Considerable	14.1	13.5	14.8	13.7	16.4	16.1	14.5	13.1	13.4	14.0	14.2	14.0	15.9	13.2	13.0	13.5
5. Great	8.6	9.2	8.1	7.4	12.6	6.5	8.7	10.0	8.1	8.5	8.5	8.4	10.7	8.4	7.1	14.0
8. No opinion	16.9	13.7	20.5	15.7	23.9	15.3	16.0	18.4	17.1	14.7	20.1	16.2	18.4	19.5	15.0	13.5
Item 6970 Subject H04,K01 N	2948	1440	1437	2265	384	568	858	987	535	1741	1127	1193	576	427	668	44

D04J: All the courts and the justice system in general?

	TOTAL	M	F	White	Black	NE	NC	S	W	Yes	No	None	Mari-juana Only	Few Pills	More Pills	Any Heroin
1. Not at all	6.5	7.4	5.7	6.4	5.4	6.4	7.9	5.7	6.0	5.2	8.4	6.6	4.5	7.6	5.9	18.2
2. Slight	26.5	27.9	24.8	27.4	19.9	26.2	26.2	25.0	30.2	28.6	24.1	26.7	24.6	26.1	29.0	22.8
3. Moderate	28.1	28.8	27.6	29.9	22.2	31.0	28.6	27.1	25.9	29.9	25.5	29.0	28.8	25.7	28.6	17.7
4. Considerable	17.0	16.2	17.4	16.4	20.6	16.1	17.7	16.8	17.2	16.7	17.1	17.6	17.8	15.8	16.1	9.4
5. Great	6.3	6.4	6.2	5.7	8.6	6.6	6.0	6.7	5.6	6.2	6.3	6.2	6.7	6.0	5.3	17.8
8. No opinion	15.6	13.3	18.3	14.1	23.2	13.7	13.5	18.8	15.2	13.4	18.7	14.0	17.5	18.9	15.0	14.1
Item 6980 Subject H04,K01 N	2955	1442	1442	2274	382	571	863	984	537	1745	1129	1195	575	424	676	44

QUESTIONNAIRE FORM 2 1984	TOTAL	SEX		RACE		REGION				4YR COLLEGE PLANS		ILLICIT DRUG USE: LIFETIME				
		M	F	White	Black	NE	NC	S	W	Yes	No	None	Marijuana Only	Few Pills	More Pills	Any Heroin
N (Weighted No. of Cases):	3322	1624	1580	2491	453	681	929	1119	593	1855	1265	1285	662	479	773	51
% of Weighted Total:	100.0	48.9	47.5	75.0	13.6	20.1	28.0	33.7	17.9	55.8	38.1	38.7	19.9	14.4	23.3	1.5
D04K: The police and other law enforcement agencies?																
1. Not at all	5.2	6.2	4.0	4.5	5.5	4.9	5.3	6.0	3.8	3.3	7.9	4.9	3.6	5.4	5.2	16.7
2. Slight	22.7	23.0	22.4	23.4	18.8	21.3	23.5	22.3	24.0	23.5	22.0	22.0	25.1	22.1	22.5	23.2
3. Moderate	32.4	32.0	32.7	34.1	27.8	30.8	34.9	31.1	32.2	36.4	26.3	35.4	31.0	31.9	30.0	13.3
4. Considerable	20.2	20.3	20.7	20.5	18.5	24.1	18.7	19.7	19.3	20.7	19.4	20.5	20.4	18.9	21.1	11.0
5. Great	9.1	9.7	8.2	8.2	13.9	10.2	8.7	9.1	8.7	7.6	11.6	7.3	8.9	8.6	12.2	22.7
8. No opinion	10.4	8.9	12.0	9.3	15.6	8.8	8.9	11.8	12.0	8.5	12.7	10.0	10.9	13.1	9.0	13.1
Item 6990 Subject K01 N	2960	1446	1444	2278	384	572	860	988	541	1746	1133	1196	576	425	677	44
D04L: The U.S. military?																
1. Not at all	7.5	7.4	7.5	7.2	6.2	7.6	6.6	8.1	7.5	6.3	9.4	7.6	6.1	7.6	7.4	10.1
2. Slight	24.4	24.9	23.7	26.4	15.6	24.4	23.3	24.6	25.8	26.1	22.3	24.5	22.9	24.9	26.2	19.2
3. Moderate	25.3	26.8	24.0	26.2	23.2	28.4	25.9	22.0	27.3	28.0	21.0	26.4	26.1	23.7	24.8	14.5
4. Considerable	16.2	17.4	15.0	16.1	15.5	14.1	19.1	15.8	14.7	16.1	16.2	16.3	13.8	16.1	17.9	17.5
5. Great	8.4	9.4	7.1	6.8	15.3	7.4	6.5	10.8	7.9	7.3	10.1	7.8	9.9	7.6	7.8	16.1
8. No opinion	18.2	14.1	22.6	17.3	24.2	18.2	18.6	18.7	16.8	16.1	21.0	17.5	21.2	20.1	15.9	22.6
Item 7000 Subject K01,L04 N	2955	1443	1442	2275	383	567	856	991	542	1739	1134	1193	577	424	677	44
D05: How much do you agree or disagree with each of the following statements?																
D05A: There is too much competition in this society																
1. Disagree	9.7	12.2	7.1	9.5	10.1	8.9	8.1	11.2	10.3	10.9	8.0	10.3	10.1	8.9	8.2	10.9
2. Mostly disagree	14.0	17.5	10.8	16.0	7.7	13.5	13.2	15.1	13.5	16.1	10.9	14.2	13.7	12.8	15.0	10.6
3. Neither	23.9	27.3	20.5	24.4	21.6	21.8	27.2	23.0	22.5	23.4	24.9	24.9	22.3	25.9	22.3	22.6
4. Mostly agree	33.6	28.8	38.5	33.7	34.2	34.6	36.2	31.3	32.6	33.8	33.8	33.2	32.7	35.6	33.5	45.2
5. Agree	18.9	14.3	23.1	16.4	26.4	21.2	15.3	19.4	21.2	15.8	22.3	17.5	21.2	16.8	21.0	10.6
Item 7010 Subject Q08 N	2999	1455	1473	2311	389	580	878	996	545	1761	1153	1211	585	432	683	45
D05B: Too many young people are sloppy about their grooming and clothing, and just don't care how they look																
1. Disagree	16.1	17.7	14.2	15.5	16.8	14.7	16.9	16.8	15.1	15.4	17.2	13.6	20.0	15.4	17.2	22.3
2. Mostly disagree	29.7	29.3	30.2	31.6	23.7	32.6	30.2	26.0	32.3	33.0	25.0	30.3	28.9	29.7	29.3	25.8
3. Neither	20.9	22.9	19.2	21.5	17.1	19.6	22.2	20.9	20.5	20.8	21.2	22.7	19.6	19.5	20.4	19.1
4. Mostly agree	21.5	19.0	23.8	21.5	20.4	22.6	20.5	22.0	21.1	20.9	22.1	21.8	20.2	21.0	22.8	13.9
5. Agree	11.7	11.0	12.6	9.9	22.0	10.5	10.2	14.2	11.1	9.8	14.5	11.6	11.4	14.4	10.3	18.9
Item 7020 Subject Q08 N	2998	1453	1474	2309	388	579	879	995	546	1757	1155	1212	584	433	683	44
D05C: There is too much hard rock music on the radio these days																
1. Disagree	40.4	43.0	37.3	44.5	24.1	39.4	42.9	39.7	38.4	37.5	45.2	28.9	42.1	42.3	57.8	56.5
2. Mostly disagree	22.0	19.6	24.8	23.0	19.3	21.4	24.3	21.0	20.9	24.4	18.9	23.5	24.3	22.6	17.6	10.9
3. Neither	17.7	17.7	17.7	15.8	23.6	18.5	16.4	18.2	18.1	18.1	17.1	21.1	17.9	15.6	13.4	11.3
4. Mostly agree	10.0	9.4	10.5	9.4	11.3	10.3	9.4	9.8	10.9	10.7	8.9	13.7	8.2	9.2	5.6	3.0
5. Agree	9.9	10.3	9.6	7.2	21.8	10.4	7.0	11.2	11.7	9.3	9.9	12.9	7.6	10.3	5.6	18.3
Item 7030 Subject Q08 N	2994	1450	1471	2305	386	577	877	994	546	1758	1151	1209	585	433	679	45
D05D: People should do their own thing, even if other people think it's strange																
1. Disagree	3.6	4.3	2.8	3.3	4.9	4.0	3.0	4.4	2.7	2.7	5.1	4.9	2.4	1.5	3.2	5.2
2. Mostly disagree	6.1	7.0	5.3	5.8	5.1	4.7	6.0	6.8	6.8	6.3	5.9	6.5	5.9	5.0	5.8	6.7
3. Neither	12.1	13.2	10.7	11.9	10.8	10.5	13.3	11.7	12.4	11.8	12.7	13.1	11.2	14.5	9.4	10.9
4. Mostly agree	34.9	34.2	36.2	37.2	28.5	32.2	37.5	34.1	35.2	36.7	31.9	36.5	33.6	36.2	33.7	19.3
5. Agree	43.3	41.3	45.0	41.9	50.7	48.4	40.3	43.0	43.0	42.6	44.4	39.0	46.8	42.9	47.9	57.9
Item 7040 Subject Q08 N	2985	1445	1469	2299	386	575	876	991	543	1753	1149	1206	579	433	679	45

QUESTIONNAIRE FORM 2 1984	TOTAL	SEX		RACE		REGION				4YR COLLEGE PLANS		ILLICIT DRUG USE: LIFETIME				
		M	F	White	Black	NE	NC	S	W	Yes	No	None	Marijuana Only	Few Pills	More Pills	Any Heroin
N (Weighted No. of Cases):	3322	1624	1580	2491	453	681	929	1119	593	1855	1265	1285	662	479	773	51
% of Weighted Total:	100.0	48.9	47.5	75.0	13.6	20.1	28.0	33.7	17.9	55.8	38.1	38.7	19.9	14.4	23.3	1.5

D05E: I get a real kick out of doing things that are a little dangerous

1. Disagree	24.0	15.4	32.6	20.9	41.8	24.3	21.2	28.7	19.8	23.5	24.2	32.8	21.8	18.9	14.4	12.0
2. Mostly disagree	17.9	15.9	20.2	19.1	16.3	14.3	18.6	19.8	17.1	19.4	15.8	19.5	18.7	17.2	14.7	10.7
3. Neither	26.8	29.2	24.7	27.7	21.9	25.8	28.5	26.9	25.0	26.5	27.6	25.4	30.6	27.8	27.3	7.5
4. Mostly agree	19.8	23.9	15.8	21.0	10.3	22.2	20.7	14.8	25.2	20.6	18.8	15.4	19.4	22.9	26.6	12.6
5. Agree	11.4	15.6	6.7	11.3	9.6	13.4	10.9	9.8	12.9	10.0	13.6	6.9	9.5	13.2	16.9	57.2
Item 7050 Subject Q04 N	2995	1452	1472	2306	388	576	879	994	546	1757	1153	1209	583	434	680	45

D05F: I like to test myself every now and then by doing something a little risky

1. Disagree	20.7	13.9	27.2	18.3	31.9	20.7	17.1	25.8	17.2	21.2	19.3	27.0	18.8	18.0	13.5	4.0
2. Mostly disagree	16.4	14.7	18.4	17.1	15.5	13.5	19.0	15.9	16.1	17.2	15.0	20.4	17.5	12.8	11.3	5.5
3. Neither	22.4	22.0	22.7	23.4	15.6	18.9	23.0	22.9	23.9	22.1	23.1	21.8	24.2	23.3	21.2	16.2
4. Mostly agree	26.7	31.0	22.7	28.1	19.6	30.6	28.2	22.3	28.2	26.9	26.6	21.1	25.9	30.6	35.4	19.0
5. Agree	13.9	18.4	8.9	13.1	17.4	16.3	12.7	13.1	14.6	12.5	15.9	9.6	13.5	15.3	18.5	55.3
Item 7060 Subject Q04 N	2955	1433	1453	2278	380	568	862	982	543	1746	1126	1200	576	424	668	45

D05G: I take a positive attitude toward myself

1. Disagree	3.0	2.6	3.1	3.0	2.4	3.6	3.9	2.7	1.5	2.0	4.5	2.7	2.9	4.3	2.8	5.0
2. Mostly disagree	6.7	5.0	8.6	7.2	4.1	8.1	7.2	6.1	5.8	5.7	8.1	5.8	6.7	5.8	8.5	10.5
3. Neither	11.5	9.9	12.7	12.0	5.2	12.7	13.1	9.4	11.4	10.3	13.4	10.1	10.2	11.1	14.8	20.8
4. Mostly agree	43.2	42.2	44.7	45.4	31.0	40.3	45.8	42.8	42.6	43.7	42.7	45.4	41.1	45.4	41.7	20.3
5. Agree	35.6	40.3	30.8	32.4	57.3	35.3	30.0	39.1	38.8	38.3	31.4	36.1	39.1	33.4	32.2	43.5
Item 12550 Subject Q01 N	2960	1433	1457	2285	379	567	868	986	539	1745	1132	1195	580	428	671	45

D05H: I feel I am a person of worth, on an equal plane with others

1. Disagree	1.8	1.6	1.7	1.6	1.6	2.1	2.1	1.6	1.3	1.2	2.4	1.8	1.1	3.0	1.4	2.9
2. Mostly disagree	3.7	3.0	4.5	4.1	2.0	4.7	4.9	2.5	3.1	3.1	4.8	3.1	5.3	2.2	3.9	8.0
3. Neither	10.9	10.2	11.6	10.8	6.4	11.4	11.7	10.4	9.7	9.4	13.2	9.1	9.8	11.1	14.6	16.4
4. Mostly agree	35.7	34.5	36.9	38.7	20.9	32.4	39.3	34.7	35.0	33.8	38.9	35.8	32.2	38.5	36.9	31.5
5. Agree	47.9	50.6	45.3	44.8	69.1	49.4	42.0	50.7	50.9	52.4	40.7	50.2	51.6	45.1	43.2	41.1
Item 12570 Subject Q01 N	2953	1425	1460	2277	382	568	865	982	537	1743	1130	1192	580	428	667	45

D05I: I am able to do things as well as most other people

1. Disagree	0.8	0.9	0.7	0.7	0.5	1.1	0.6	0.9	0.7	0.5	1.1	0.8	0.9	0.6	0.6	6.6
2. Mostly disagree	3.0	2.8	3.0	3.1	1.4	3.5	3.8	2.3	2.4	2.3	3.9	2.2	2.1	3.5	4.2	6.6
3. Neither	6.2	6.3	6.0	6.3	5.7	7.1	7.2	6.1	4.0	5.2	8.0	5.7	5.3	6.2	7.3	8.6
4. Mostly agree	41.3	37.6	44.5	44.3	26.1	36.8	47.8	40.0	37.9	38.2	46.1	41.4	41.1	39.3	43.1	33.6
5. Agree	48.7	52.3	45.8	45.7	66.4	51.6	40.6	50.6	55.1	53.8	40.8	49.9	50.5	50.4	44.8	44.6
Item 12580 Subject Q01 N	2950	1427	1458	2276	380	567	860	982	541	1744	1124	1196	578	427	663	45

D05J: On the whole, I'm satisfied with myself

1. Disagree	2.8	2.6	2.6	2.7	2.7	2.9	3.4	2.5	2.1	1.9	3.9	2.3	2.6	3.7	2.6	6.5
2. Mostly disagree	5.5	4.4	6.8	5.6	5.1	6.3	6.0	5.9	3.3	5.1	6.2	4.5	4.7	5.6	7.8	10.4
3. Neither	9.7	9.4	9.8	10.1	6.9	10.0	10.4	8.3	10.6	9.3	10.4	8.3	10.1	7.8	12.5	10.7
4. Mostly agree	39.4	36.7	42.2	41.0	32.5	38.0	41.0	40.4	36.7	38.9	40.3	40.8	36.4	42.8	38.8	25.7
5. Agree	42.6	47.0	38.5	40.7	52.9	42.8	39.2	42.9	47.4	44.8	39.3	44.1	46.2	40.1	38.2	46.6
Item 12620 Subject P01,Q01 N	2954	1427	1457	2279	380	566	865	982	541	1745	1127	1196	578	428	666	45

D05K: I feel I do not have much to be proud of

1. Disagree	43.7	42.1	44.9	42.4	54.0	45.0	37.5	46.6	47.1	46.7	38.8	47.9	44.3	42.4	37.5	31.8
2. Mostly disagree	30.3	32.5	28.7	32.5	20.3	31.5	33.2	28.0	28.5	30.0	31.4	28.0	29.9	32.4	34.7	21.2
3. Neither	11.7	10.6	12.7	11.8	7.0	10.9	12.7	10.4	13.0	10.8	13.1	10.6	11.4	10.5	14.0	12.9
4. Mostly agree	8.2	8.3	8.1	7.9	7.6	9.1	9.4	7.8	6.0	7.0	9.8	7.4	9.4	8.0	7.5	20.4
5. Agree	6.1	6.5	5.6	5.4	11.0	3.5	7.2	7.1	5.4	5.4	7.0	6.1	5.0	6.7	6.2	13.8
Item 12660 Subject Q01 N	2940	1423	1451	2271	376	566	861	974	539	1739	1120	1193	576	425	661	45

QUESTIONNAIRE FORM 2 1984	TOTAL	SEX		RACE		REGION				4YR COLLEGE PLANS		ILLICIT DRUG USE: LIFETIME				
		M	F	White	Black	NE	NC	S	W	Yes	No	None	Mari- juana Only	Few Pills	More Pills	Any Her- oin
N (Weighted No. of Cases):	3322	1624	1580	2491	453	681	929	1119	593	1855	1265	1285	662	479	773	51
% of Weighted Total:	100.0	48.9	47.5	75.0	13.6	20.1	28.0	33.7	17.9	55.8	38.1	38.7	19.9	14.4	23.3	1.5

D05L: Sometimes I think that I am no good at all

1. Disagree	37.8	41.8	34.0	35.6	50.4	39.0	33.9	38.9	40.8	40.1	33.9	39.5	41.9	35.6	32.6	31.4
2. Mostly disagree	22.1	23.5	21.1	23.4	16.3	22.5	21.0	21.6	24.6	22.9	21.8	21.8	20.9	23.7	23.3	18.2
3. Neither	17.5	16.8	18.3	18.4	11.1	17.1	21.4	15.6	15.2	16.0	19.6	16.9	16.8	18.6	19.1	17.0
4. Mostly agree	14.2	10.3	18.2	15.0	10.6	13.2	15.3	14.6	12.9	13.6	15.3	14.4	13.5	13.0	15.4	14.5
5. Agree	8.3	7.6	8.5	7.6	11.7	8.2	8.3	9.3	6.6	7.3	9.5	7.5	6.9	9.1	9.7	18.9
Item 12680 Subject Q01 N	2937	1421	1447	2270	372	563	862	973	539	1732	1125	1189	572	426	666	45

D05M: I feel that I can't do anything right

1. Disagree	47.5	50.1	45.3	46.5	57.2	51.0	42.0	48.2	51.5	50.7	42.4	48.0	50.5	46.6	45.2	42.1
2. Mostly disagree	25.4	24.8	26.3	27.2	16.7	23.9	27.8	24.5	25.0	25.8	25.6	26.8	23.9	28.9	23.8	10.3
3. Neither	14.9	13.8	15.4	14.8	10.4	14.9	15.9	13.7	15.2	13.3	17.1	13.1	15.0	14.9	17.6	24.4
4. Mostly agree	8.3	7.8	9.0	8.5	6.1	6.2	10.2	9.0	6.4	6.7	10.5	7.9	6.9	7.5	8.9	15.7
5. Agree	3.9	3.6	4.0	3.0	9.6	4.0	4.0	4.7	1.9	3.5	4.4	4.2	3.7	2.1	4.5	7.5
Item 12720 Subject Q01 N	2930	1417	1446	2266	373	559	859	976	536	1730	1122	1183	575	426	666	42

D05N: I feel that my life is not very useful

1. Disagree	59.4	61.1	57.9	58.5	66.7	60.4	53.8	59.8	66.6	62.5	54.2	62.5	60.0	60.7	52.9	50.0
2. Mostly disagree	20.4	20.8	20.2	21.7	14.9	19.4	23.5	19.4	18.5	20.3	21.3	19.3	20.2	19.0	25.2	9.6
3. Neither	11.0	10.1	11.6	11.2	7.3	9.8	13.2	11.5	7.7	9.1	14.1	10.0	11.0	10.0	12.8	13.2
4. Mostly agree	5.9	4.9	6.9	5.9	5.1	6.4	6.2	5.6	5.5	4.7	7.7	4.7	6.3	8.3	5.5	14.8
5. Agree	3.3	3.1	3.3	2.7	6.1	4.0	3.5	3.7	1.8	3.3	2.7	3.5	2.5	2.1	3.6	12.4
Item 12750 Subject Q01 N	2932	1418	1447	2266	373	558	860	975	539	1731	1121	1183	575	427	665	44

D06: How many of your friends would you estimate . . .

D06A: Smoke cigarettes?

1. None	14.0	13.7	14.5	11.9	22.9	10.6	11.4	12.9	23.8	15.9	10.9	21.7	12.5	11.6	4.3	1.3
2. A few	38.0	39.2	37.0	37.1	40.2	34.6	39.8	36.8	40.9	42.0	32.8	44.8	38.3	38.9	25.5	27.5
3. Some	28.8	30.7	27.0	30.6	24.2	27.5	29.2	31.9	24.1	28.6	28.4	25.2	31.7	31.6	31.8	24.7
4. Most	17.6	15.2	19.6	19.0	10.4	25.1	18.5	16.3	10.6	12.2	25.8	7.6	15.3	16.0	36.2	42.0
5. All	1.6	1.1	1.9	1.4	2.2	2.1	1.2	2.1	0.6	1.2	2.1	0.6	2.2	1.8	2.2	4.5
Item 7070 Subject A02a N	2945	1428	1449	2275	375	566	861	976	542	1734	1127	1190	579	428	666	45

D06B: Smoke marijuana (pot, grass) or hashish?

1. None	22.3	19.9	25.0	21.6	18.1	15.9	24.3	22.5	25.3	23.1	21.4	39.9	11.7	16.8	5.4	1.3
2. A few	34.3	33.7	34.4	35.6	33.4	33.3	34.1	36.1	32.5	38.2	28.3	39.3	42.2	34.9	20.3	7.7
3. Some	25.1	27.0	23.7	25.1	24.8	27.2	25.0	25.1	23.2	23.1	28.1	16.2	31.5	27.7	33.8	18.2
4. Most	15.7	16.8	14.2	15.6	18.7	20.2	15.3	13.0	16.6	13.9	18.4	4.0	13.0	18.0	35.2	47.2
5. All	2.6	2.6	2.6	2.1	4.9	3.4	1.4	3.5	2.4	1.8	3.9	0.6	1.5	2.6	5.4	25.6
Item 7080 Subject A02a N	2950	1427	1453	2277	375	565	862	979	544	1733	1134	1190	577	429	669	45

D06C: Take LSD?

1. None	76.1	75.0	78.1	74.8	84.8	73.7	75.4	77.2	77.7	79.1	71.4	85.2	83.3	78.3	56.0	28.9
2. A few	16.9	17.4	16.0	18.0	11.5	17.7	17.4	15.9	17.1	15.8	18.5	11.8	14.3	18.1	28.1	11.8
3. Some	5.0	5.7	4.1	5.2	2.7	6.6	4.8	4.5	4.5	3.9	6.7	2.3	2.2	2.4	10.6	42.0
4. Most	1.5	1.2	1.4	1.5	0.6	1.5	1.9	1.6	0.4	0.7	2.6	0.4	0.1	0.7	4.8	5.9
5. All	0.5	0.8	0.3	0.4	0.3	0.5	0.6	0.7	0.3	0.4	0.8	0.4	-	0.4	0.6	11.4
Item 7090 Subject A02a N	2934	1420	1444	2270	372	563	856	977	538	1723	1128	1177	577	427	669	45

D06D: Take other psychedelics (mescaline, peyote, PCP, etc.)?

1. None	78.7	77.3	80.8	78.0	85.4	71.7	77.6	81.5	82.7	81.5	74.6	86.9	86.5	78.7	61.6	29.0
2. A few	15.2	15.8	14.3	15.9	10.7	18.0	15.8	14.1	13.4	14.2	16.6	10.3	12.0	17.1	24.9	16.2
3. Some	4.3	5.3	3.1	4.3	3.6	6.8	4.6	3.3	3.1	3.0	6.2	2.2	1.4	3.6	8.7	35.8
4. Most	1.3	0.8	1.5	1.4	-	2.7	1.7	0.5	0.5	1.0	1.7	0.3	0.1	0.2	4.1	7.8
5. All	0.6	0.8	0.4	0.4	0.3	0.8	0.4	0.7	0.3	0.3	1.0	0.4	-	0.4	0.7	11.3
Item 7100 Subject A02a N	2929	1417	1443	2264	372	561	857	972	539	1728	1119	1177	574	424	670	45

QUESTIONNAIRE FORM 2 1984	TOTAL	SEX		RACE		REGION				4YR COLLEGE PLANS		ILLICIT DRUG USE: LIFETIME				
		M	F	White	Black	NE	NC	S	W	Yes	No	None	Mari-juana Only	Few Pills	More Pills	Any Her-oin
N (Weighted No. of Cases):	3322	1624	1580	2491	453	681	929	1119	593	1855	1265	1285	662	479	773	51
% of Weighted Total:	100.0	48.9	47.5	75.0	13.6	20.1	28.0	33.7	17.9	55.8	38.1	38.7	19.9	14.4	23.3	1.5
D06E: Take amphetamines (uppers, pep pills, bennies, speed)?																
1. None	54.9	54.5	55.4	51.3	74.2	53.7	48.8	58.5	59.2	58.8	48.7	72.7	62.0	51.1	21.3	15.7
2. A few	29.6	29.9	29.2	32.1	18.5	30.0	32.9	27.6	27.5	29.6	29.4	22.5	31.4	37.0	37.6	11.5
3. Some	11.0	11.1	11.0	11.8	5.5	12.2	12.0	9.8	10.1	8.7	14.7	3.7	5.3	10.2	27.9	38.1
4. Most	3.8	3.7	3.8	4.2	1.3	3.3	5.9	2.9	2.9	2.4	6.1	0.7	1.3	1.3	11.9	22.6
5. All	0.7	0.8	0.6	0.6	0.5	0.8	0.4	1.2	0.3	0.6	1.0	0.4	-	0.3	1.3	12.0
Item 7110 Subject A02a N	2925	1414	1444	2263	371	560	854	973	538	1726	1116	1178	575	423	664	45
D06F: Take quaaludes (quads, methaqualone)?																
1. None	73.9	71.4	76.8	72.2	84.2	72.3	75.5	70.5	78.9	76.7	69.7	83.8	79.6	76.0	53.7	24.3
2. A few	18.5	20.3	16.7	19.8	11.5	19.3	17.0	20.9	15.8	17.4	19.7	12.9	18.5	18.8	28.0	24.0
3. Some	5.9	6.3	5.3	6.4	2.8	6.4	6.2	6.0	4.8	4.6	8.2	2.7	1.9	4.2	14.3	31.6
4. Most	1.2	1.3	0.9	1.3	1.2	1.4	1.1	1.8	0.2	1.0	1.5	0.2	-	0.7	3.4	11.2
5. All	0.5	0.7	0.2	0.4	0.3	0.7	0.2	0.9	0.3	0.3	0.8	0.4	-	0.3	0.6	9.0
Item 7120 Subject A02a N	2926	1418	1439	2263	371	559	858	971	538	1724	1119	1174	573	425	670	45
D06G: Take barbiturates (downers, goofballs, reds, yellows, etc.)?																
1. None	73.4	71.5	76.1	72.2	81.9	73.2	72.4	72.6	76.5	76.3	68.9	82.1	80.2	74.7	54.5	23.0
2. A few	19.4	21.0	17.7	20.4	13.0	19.6	19.8	19.5	18.6	18.4	20.9	14.7	17.5	20.4	29.1	20.1
3. Some	5.5	5.4	5.1	5.8	3.5	5.3	6.0	6.0	3.9	4.1	7.8	2.5	2.0	4.5	12.1	32.5
4. Most	1.2	1.4	0.9	1.2	1.3	1.4	1.6	0.9	0.7	0.9	1.7	0.2	0.2	-	3.9	12.9
5. All	0.5	0.7	0.3	0.4	0.3	0.5	0.2	0.9	0.3	0.4	0.7	0.4	-	0.4	0.4	11.5
Item 7130 Subject A02a N	2932	1418	1444	2267	372	562	858	973	538	1725	1123	1179	575	424	670	44
D06H: Take tranquilizers?																
1. None	73.4	72.9	74.3	72.1	81.5	73.1	74.3	71.2	76.1	75.7	70.1	80.0	80.1	74.8	58.6	23.7
2. A few	20.6	20.1	20.7	21.8	14.0	22.0	19.5	21.4	19.3	19.8	21.2	16.8	18.2	21.7	28.9	24.3
3. Some	4.6	5.2	3.9	4.7	3.2	3.9	4.2	5.8	3.9	3.3	6.7	2.7	1.8	3.2	9.5	26.8
4. Most	1.0	1.2	0.7	1.0	0.9	0.6	1.5	1.0	0.4	0.8	1.3	0.1	-	-	2.6	16.3
5. All	0.5	0.6	0.4	0.4	0.3	0.4	0.4	0.6	0.3	0.3	0.7	0.4	-	0.4	0.3	9.0
Item 7140 Subject A02a N	2921	1412	1440	2264	369	559	858	968	536	1720	1119	1174	574	424	665	45
D06I: Take cocaine?																
1. None	61.1	59.6	62.5	61.0	63.2	48.5	71.9	63.8	51.8	62.7	59.0	79.0	66.0	55.7	31.7	13.1
2. A few	24.4	24.2	24.7	23.9	27.0	27.6	20.4	25.3	25.5	24.5	23.9	17.0	27.5	29.5	32.4	16.3
3. Some	9.5	10.5	8.3	9.7	7.7	15.0	5.6	7.8	12.8	8.7	10.3	2.8	6.1	12.6	20.3	34.6
4. Most	3.9	4.1	3.7	4.2	1.4	7.0	1.6	1.9	8.0	3.0	5.3	0.9	0.3	1.7	12.9	16.4
5. All	1.2	1.7	0.8	1.2	0.7	1.9	0.4	1.2	1.9	1.1	1.5	0.4	0.2	0.6	2.8	19.6
Item 7150 Subject A02a N	2926	1414	1442	2265	370	561	857	972	537	1723	1121	1179	574	424	667	44
D06J: Take heroin (smack, horse)?																
1. None	87.0	86.4	88.1	87.3	87.1	85.1	88.1	86.0	89.2	88.4	85.1	88.9	90.1	89.1	83.4	43.9
2. A few	9.9	10.3	9.2	10.1	8.9	12.3	8.6	10.2	9.0	9.3	10.6	8.5	8.7	9.4	12.2	23.8
3. Some	2.2	2.3	1.9	1.9	3.2	1.9	2.3	2.8	1.2	1.7	2.9	1.7	1.2	1.1	3.0	25.4
4. Most	0.4	0.4	0.5	0.4	0.5	0.6	0.5	0.4	0.1	0.3	0.7	0.4	-	-	0.9	2.3
5. All	0.4	0.6	0.3	0.3	0.3	0.2	0.4	0.5	0.5	0.3	0.7	0.5	-	0.4	0.5	4.6
Item 7160 Subject A02a N	2913	1409	1435	2252	371	554	857	967	535	1717	1114	1173	572	422	664	44
D06K: Take other narcotics (methadone, opium, codeine, paregoric, etc.)?																
1. None	78.6	77.3	80.7	77.6	86.8	75.9	81.5	78.8	76.3	80.7	75.3	86.9	86.5	81.2	59.5	24.9
2. A few	15.6	16.1	14.9	17.0	9.5	18.4	13.0	14.8	18.5	15.2	16.3	10.5	11.4	15.7	28.3	23.2
3. Some	4.1	4.8	3.0	4.1	3.1	3.5	4.0	4.7	4.0	3.0	5.8	2.0	1.5	2.2	8.9	34.1
4. Most	1.0	1.1	0.9	0.9	0.2	1.9	1.0	0.8	0.7	0.5	1.9	0.2	0.4	0.5	2.6	8.6
5. All	0.6	0.6	0.5	0.5	0.3	0.4	0.4	0.9	0.5	0.5	0.7	0.5	0.2	0.4	0.7	9.1
Item 7170 Subject A02a N	2920	1415	1436	2258	370	557	856	969	538	1722	1115	1170	575	423	669	44

QUESTIONNAIRE FORM 2 1984	TOTAL	SEX		RACE		REGION				4YR COLLEGE PLANS		ILLICIT DRUG USE: LIFETIME				
		M	F	White	Black	NE	NC	S	W	Yes	No	None	Mari-juana Only	Few Pills	More Pills	Any Her-oin
N (Weighted No. of Cases):	3322	1624	1580	2491	453	681	929	1119	593	1855	1265	1285	662	479	773	51
% of Weighted Total:	100.0	48.9	47.5	75.0	13.6	20.1	28.0	33.7	17.9	55.8	38.1	38.7	19.9	14.4	23.3	1.5
D06L: Use inhalants (sniffing glue, aerosols, laughing gas, etc.)?																
1. None	80.7	78.7	83.4	80.1	86.3	79.4	80.9	80.6	81.8	83.1	76.7	85.4	84.3	78.6	73.7	45.7
2. A few	14.7	15.7	12.9	15.5	9.3	16.4	15.0	14.1	13.3	13.1	17.2	11.6	12.9	18.0	19.4	12.1
3. Some	3.5	4.2	2.7	3.3	3.4	3.2	3.2	3.7	3.9	2.9	4.4	2.5	1.9	2.9	5.1	27.9
4. Most	0.7	0.9	0.5	0.8	0.6	1.0	0.6	0.8	0.5	0.5	1.1	0.2	0.8	0.1	1.4	9.6
5. All	0.4	0.4	0.5	0.3	0.3	-	0.3	0.8	0.5	0.4	0.5	0.4	0.2	0.3	0.5	4.6
Item 7180 Subject A02a N	2915	1411	1435	2256	369	559	850	968	538	1720	1112	1170	572	421	670	45
D06M: Drink alcoholic beverages (liquor, beer, wine)?																
1. None	5.4	5.4	5.5	2.7	17.3	4.0	4.6	5.5	8.2	5.5	5.2	9.4	4.0	2.2	1.1	2.5
2. A few	11.3	9.1	13.3	9.1	20.8	10.3	9.4	12.2	14.0	11.5	10.8	18.9	10.2	6.6	2.2	2.8
3. Some	16.6	15.9	17.3	15.8	20.5	13.1	15.7	19.3	16.6	17.0	15.6	21.3	16.4	16.8	9.0	8.2
4. Most	41.8	45.1	39.0	45.0	29.9	39.6	44.1	43.4	37.7	43.6	39.8	39.7	45.1	45.3	41.7	37.6
5. All	24.8	24.5	24.9	27.3	11.6	33.1	26.2	19.6	23.5	22.4	28.6	10.7	24.4	29.0	46.0	48.9
Item 7190 Subject A02a N	2935	1420	1446	2267	372	562	858	975	540	1730	1124	1184	573	424	669	45
D06N: Get drunk at least once a week?																
1. None	18.5	15.5	21.3	14.9	36.1	18.0	16.7	17.2	24.0	19.8	16.6	29.3	15.3	13.7	5.5	3.8
2. A few	25.2	23.4	27.0	24.9	24.2	25.2	23.6	26.4	25.4	26.1	23.4	31.9	26.6	24.1	14.6	9.9
3. Some	26.7	28.5	25.0	28.5	20.5	25.5	27.7	26.8	26.2	27.0	26.5	22.0	31.8	27.6	30.4	19.0
4. Most	22.0	24.6	19.6	23.7	15.2	23.1	23.9	22.8	16.7	21.2	23.5	14.6	21.0	24.9	33.1	36.5
5. All	7.6	8.0	7.2	7.9	4.0	8.2	8.1	6.8	7.8	5.9	10.0	2.1	5.2	9.7	16.4	30.8
Item 7200 Subject A02a N	2942	1424	1449	2274	371	564	862	977	540	1730	1130	1187	576	425	670	45
Lately there has been increased attention paid to two types of drugs: PCP and amyl or butyl nitrite.																
E01: How many of your friends would you estimate . . .																
E01A: Take PCP (angel dust, crystal, peace pill, killer weed, supergrass, crystal cyclone)?																
1. None	85.8	85.2	86.9	86.0	87.8	85.9	86.3	84.9	86.7	87.8	82.9	91.0	90.7	88.1	75.8	30.6
2. A few	10.3	10.2	10.0	11.0	6.0	10.3	10.8	10.8	8.7	9.3	11.6	7.2	7.2	9.4	17.9	23.1
3. Some	2.8	3.1	2.5	2.1	5.0	2.4	2.0	3.6	3.0	2.1	3.8	1.2	1.8	2.1	5.0	26.0
4. Most	0.7	1.0	0.4	0.6	0.3	1.0	0.7	0.3	1.2	0.3	1.3	0.3	0.1	-	1.0	17.4
5. All	0.4	0.6	0.2	0.2	0.8	0.5	0.3	0.5	0.3	0.4	0.3	0.4	0.2	0.4	0.3	2.9
Item 7201 Subject A02a N	2909	1407	1432	2253	362	556	863	956	534	1712	1111	1170	569	424	662	44
E01B: Take amyl or butyl nitrites (poppers, snappers, Locker Room, Vaporole, Rush, Kick, Bullet)?																
1. None	85.0	83.6	86.8	84.6	90.2	86.4	84.2	84.7	85.3	87.3	81.8	92.0	91.6	81.7	72.9	38.5
2. A few	10.9	11.3	10.3	11.6	5.8	9.9	11.8	10.4	11.6	9.4	13.0	6.5	6.9	15.8	17.8	25.3
3. Some	2.9	3.9	1.8	2.7	2.7	2.9	2.5	3.4	2.7	2.4	3.7	1.0	1.1	1.5	6.9	27.8
4. Most	0.8	0.7	0.8	0.8	1.0	0.3	1.3	1.0	0.2	0.6	1.2	0.3	0.2	0.6	1.9	5.5
5. All	0.4	0.5	0.1	0.3	0.4	0.5	0.3	0.5	0.1	0.4	0.3	0.2	0.2	0.4	0.6	2.9
Item 7202 Subject A02a N	2894	1401	1423	2247	358	549	860	955	530	1707	1104	1167	565	420	659	44
E02: On how many occasions (if any) have you used PCP (angel dust, crystal, peace pill, killer weed, supergrass, crystal cyclone)?																
E02A: . . . in your lifetime?																
1. 0 occasions	95.0	93.2	96.9	95.0	96.8	94.0	95.6	95.6	94.2	96.3	93.4	99.7	98.6	96.4	86.6	30.4
2. 1-2	2.9	4.0	1.9	3.1	2.1	3.6	2.5	2.9	3.0	2.6	3.3	*	1.1	3.0	8.1	31.7
3. 3-5	0.5	0.7	0.3	0.4	0.2	1.0	0.4	0.2	1.0	0.1	1.0	0.1	-	0.5	1.7	1.7
4. 6-9	0.5	0.7	0.4	0.5	0.2	0.4	0.7	0.2	0.9	0.3	0.9	-	-	-	1.2	17.9
5. 10-19	0.3	0.4	0.2	0.3	-	0.4	0.1	0.4	-	0.2	0.4	-	0.1	-	0.9	-
6. 20-39	0.1	0.3	-	0.2	-	-	0.3	0.1	0.2	-	0.4	-	-	-	0.7	-
7. 40 or more	0.6	0.8	0.3	0.5	0.7	0.6	0.4	0.6	0.7	0.5	0.6	0.1	0.2	0.1	0.9	18.3
Item 1181 Subject A01a N	2896	1402	1426	2251	358	552	863	951	530	1706	1105	1176	569	419	656	40

*=less than .05 per cent.

QUESTIONNAIRE FORM 2 1984	TOTAL	SEX		RACE		REGION				4YR COLLEGE PLANS		ILLICIT DRUG USE: LIFETIME				
		M	F	White	Black	NE	NC	S	W	Yes	No	None	Mari-juana Only	Few Pills	More Pills	Any Her-oin
N (Weighted No. of Cases):	3322	1624	1580	2491	453	681	929	1119	593	1855	1265	1285	662	479	773	51
% of Weighted Total:	100.0	48.9	47.5	75.0	13.6	20.1	28.0	33.7	17.9	55.8	38.1	38.7	19.9	14.4	23.3	1.5

E02B: . . . during the last 12 months?

1. 0 occasions	97.7	96.9	98.7	97.8	98.2	97.7	98.1	97.7	97.1	98.1	97.3	99.8	99.4	98.9	93.8	64.5
2. 1-2	1.2	1.5	0.9	1.1	0.6	1.3	0.9	1.2	1.8	1.2	1.2	*	0.2	1.0	3.5	14.7
3. 3-5	0.2	0.3	0.1	0.2	-	0.3	0.1	0.4	-	0.1	0.4	-	-	-	0.5	6.5
4. 6-9	0.3	0.5	*	0.3	0.4	0.3	0.3	0.2	0.3	0.2	0.3	-	0.1	-	0.8	3.4
5. 10-19	0.2	0.3	0.1	0.2	-	0.2	0.3	0.1	-	0.1	0.2	-	-	-	0.3	5.9
6. 20-39	0.1	0.2	0.1	0.1	0.7	0.1	-	0.3	0.2	0.2	0.1	-	0.2	-	0.2	5.0
7. 40 or more	0.3	0.3	0.1	0.3	-	0.2	0.3	0.2	0.6	0.2	0.4	0.1	-	0.1	0.9	-
Item 1182 Subject A01b N	2898	1403	1427	2253	358	553	863	951	530	1707	1105	1176	569	420	658	39

E02C: . . . during the last 30 days?

1. 0 occasions	99.0	98.5	99.5	99.0	99.0	99.2	99.3	98.7	98.6	99.0	98.9	99.9	99.7	99.9	97.7	76.1
2. 1-2	0.4	0.5	0.2	0.4	-	0.5	0.1	0.5	0.4	0.4	0.4	-	-	-	0.9	9.7
3. 3-5	0.3	0.4	0.1	0.3	0.3	0.2	0.3	0.4	-	0.3	0.2	-	0.3	-	0.3	9.3
4. 6-9	0.2	0.4	-	0.2	0.6	-	-	0.2	0.8	0.1	0.3	-	-	-	0.6	3.9
5. 10-19	*	0.1	-	0.1	-	0.1	-	-	0.1	*	*	-	-	-	0.1	1.1
6. 20-39	-	-	-	-	-	-	-	-	-	-	-	-	-	-	-	-
7. 40 or more	0.1	0.1	0.1	0.2	-	-	0.3	0.2	-	0.1	0.2	0.1	-	0.1	0.3	-
Item 1183 Subject A01c N	2897	1403	1427	2253	358	552	863	951	530	1706	1106	1177	569	420	656	39

E03: On how many occasions (if any) have you used amyl or butyl nitrites (poppers, snappers, Locker Room, Vaporole, Rush, Kick, Bullet)?

E03A: . . . in your lifetime?

1. 0 occasions	91.9	89.8	94.6	90.8	98.1	91.7	91.2	93.6	90.2	93.0	90.5	99.7	97.9	92.0	76.4	36.4
2. 1-2	4.8	5.6	3.8	5.5	1.5	4.5	4.4	4.3	6.7	4.5	5.0	0.2	1.7	6.4	13.6	27.3
3. 3-5	1.3	1.6	0.8	1.3	0.2	1.0	1.6	0.9	1.7	1.2	1.4	-	0.3	1.2	3.6	12.1
4. 6-9	0.6	0.9	0.3	0.7	-	0.7	0.8	0.4	0.4	0.4	0.8	-	-	0.3	2.1	4.4
5. 10-19	0.5	0.6	0.4	0.6	-	1.0	0.4	0.3	0.2	0.3	0.8	-	0.1	0.2	1.8	1.9
6. 20-39	0.3	0.5	0.1	0.4	-	0.2	0.5	0.2	0.2	0.1	0.6	-	-	-	0.9	3.0
7. 40 or more	0.7	1.1	0.1	0.8	0.2	0.8	1.0	0.4	0.4	0.6	0.8	0.1	-	-	1.6	15.1
Item 1184 Subject A01a N	2891	1402	1420	2245	359	551	861	949	530	1704	1103	1172	567	420	653	41

E03B: . . . during the last 12 months?

1. 0 occasions	96.0	94.6	97.5	95.3	99.8	95.9	94.2	97.0	97.2	96.6	95.1	99.9	99.1	95.5	89.2	62.0
2. 1-2	2.2	2.6	1.8	2.6	-	1.8	3.0	2.0	1.8	2.2	2.1	-	0.9	3.3	5.8	13.9
3. 3-5	0.8	1.3	0.3	1.0	-	0.8	1.4	0.6	0.3	0.6	1.2	-	-	1.0	2.6	6.2
4. 6-9	0.3	0.4	0.1	0.3	-	1.1	0.1	0.1	-	0.2	0.5	-	-	0.2	0.2	13.2
5. 10-19	0.4	0.6	0.2	0.5	-	0.3	0.8	0.2	0.3	0.3	0.6	-	-	-	1.4	2.9
6. 20-39	0.1	0.2	-	0.1	-	-	0.3	-	-	-	0.2	-	-	-	0.3	-
7. 40 or more	0.2	0.3	0.1	0.2	0.2	0.1	0.2	0.3	0.3	0.2	0.2	0.1	-	-	0.4	1.7
Item 1185 Subject A01b N	2895	1404	1424	2243	360	551	863	950	531	1706	1106	1174	567	420	654	42

E03C: . . . during the last 30 days?

1. 0 occasions	98.6	97.9	99.5	98.4	99.8	99.3	97.4	99.0	98.9	98.8	98.2	99.9	99.8	98.8	96.7	81.3
2. 1-2	0.8	1.0	0.4	0.8	-	0.3	1.3	0.6	0.7	0.6	1.1	-	0.2	0.6	2.0	11.2
3. 3-5	0.3	0.6	*	0.4	-	0.2	0.7	0.2	0.2	0.4	0.3	-	-	0.6	0.5	7.5
4. 6-9	0.1	0.2	-	0.1	-	-	0.1	0.1	-	0.1	0.1	-	-	-	0.3	-
5. 10-19	0.1	0.1	0.1	0.1	0.2	-	0.2	-	0.1	*	0.2	-	-	-	0.4	-
6. 20-39	-	-	-	-	-	-	-	-	-	-	-	-	-	-	-	-
7. 40 or more	0.1	0.2	-	0.1	-	0.1	0.2	0.1	-	0.1	0.2	0.1	-	-	0.1	-
Item 1186 Subject A01c N	2892	1401	1423	2245	360	549	863	950	530	1704	1105	1174	567	420	653	41

E04: When (if ever) did you FIRST do each of the following things?

E04A: Try PCP

8. Never	96.2	95.0	97.4	95.9	98.1	94.7	96.4	97.0	96.2	97.2	94.8	99.8	99.8	98.4	89.3	31.8
1. Grade 6 or below	0.4	0.5	0.1	0.2	0.9	0.5	0.3	0.4	0.3	0.2	0.5	0.1	-	-	0.5	9.1
2. Grade 7 or 8	0.4	0.6	0.2	0.4	0.1	0.5	0.4	0.2	0.5	0.4	0.2	-	-	0.5	0.5	14.2
3. Grade 9 (Freshman)	1.0	1.7	0.4	1.1	0.2	1.1	1.1	0.8	1.1	0.7	1.5	-	0.2	0.2	2.9	20.8
4. Grade 10 (Sophomore)	0.9	1.0	0.8	1.0	0.5	1.2	0.9	0.5	1.2	0.5	1.5	0.1	-	0.3	3.0	11.7
5. Grade 11 (Junior)	0.8	0.9	0.7	0.9	0.3	1.2	0.6	0.8	0.6	0.5	1.2	-	-	0.5	2.6	9.1
6. Grade 12 (Senior)	0.4	0.4	0.3	0.4	-	0.9	0.3	0.3	0.2	0.4	0.3	0.1	-	0.2	1.2	3.4
Item 5686 Subject A01g N	2828	1355	1407	2204	349	539	847	925	516	1679	1071	1167	557	402	626	39

*=less than .05 per cent.

QUESTIONNAIRE FORM 2 1984	TOTAL	SEX		RACE		REGION				4YR COLLEGE PLANS		ILLICIT DRUG USE: LIFETIME				
		M	F	White	Black	NE	NC	S	W	Yes	No	None	Mari-juana Only	Few Pills	More Pills	Any Her-oin
N (Weighted No. of Cases):	3322	1624	1580	2491	453	681	929	1119	593	1855	1265	1285	662	479	773	51
% of Weighted Total:	100.0	48.9	47.5	75.0	13.6	20.1	28.0	33.7	17.9	55.8	38.1	38.7	19.9	14.4	23.3	1.5
E04B: Try amyl or butyl nitrites																
8. Never	93.8	91.7	95.9	92.6	99.0	93.5	93.4	94.7	92.9	94.3	93.0	99.8	98.4	94.9	80.8	40.2
1. Grade 6 or below	0.5	0.7	0.2	0.6	0.2	1.3	0.4	0.1	0.5	0.2	0.8	-	-	-	1.6	5.3
2. Grade 7 or 8	1.2	1.7	0.7	1.5	0.3	1.3	1.8	0.5	1.5	1.3	1.1	0.1	0.7	1.3	3.1	17.0
3. Grade 9 (Freshman)	1.3	1.5	1.0	1.4	0.2	1.4	1.2	1.5	1.0	0.7	2.2	0.1	0.1	0.5	3.7	21.9
4. Grade 10 (Sophomore)	1.3	1.9	0.7	1.5	-	1.2	0.9	0.8	2.7	1.3	1.2	-	0.4	-	5.1	4.0
5. Grade 11 (Junior)	1.0	1.3	0.7	1.3	0.3	1.1	0.3	1.4	1.5	1.2	0.8	-	0.2	2.1	2.7	6.7
6. Grade 12 (Senior)	1.0	1.2	0.8	1.1	-	0.3	2.0	1.0	-	1.0	1.0	0.1	0.2	1.3	3.0	4.9
Item 5687 Subject A01g N	2800	1350	1390	2181	347	531	835	921	513	1666	1059	1162	560	398	605	37
E05: What is your best guess about whether your parents think you drink alcoholic beverages (beer, wine, liquor)?																
1. They feel sure I don't drink	26.8	23.9	29.8	23.0	42.2	22.7	24.6	29.5	29.8	29.3	23.2	46.4	14.8	19.4	8.4	18.0
2. They think I probably don't drink	13.0	11.7	14.2	12.5	16.9	12.5	12.7	14.6	11.3	13.8	11.6	13.9	13.8	13.3	9.8	16.4
3. I don't know, or they differ in whether they think I do	9.5	10.2	9.0	9.4	9.6	8.8	8.9	9.5	11.3	9.6	9.4	9.3	10.8	8.9	9.5	4.3
4. They think I probably drink	16.7	17.9	15.4	17.8	13.1	20.3	15.2	17.7	13.5	16.1	18.0	11.9	21.5	17.8	19.7	17.4
5. They feel sure (or know) that I drink	33.9	36.3	31.6	37.3	18.2	35.7	38.6	28.6	34.0	31.3	37.9	18.5	39.1	40.6	52.6	43.9
Item 7510 Subject A09a N	2875	1388	1418	2229	357	544	856	950	525	1693	1097	1162	564	410	656	45
E06: What's your best guess about whether your parents think you smoke marijuana?																
1. They feel sure I don't	71.3	67.8	75.1	71.9	67.2	66.6	73.9	74.4	66.5	73.1	68.6	93.3	67.9	68.2	40.1	32.7
2. They think I probably don't	11.6	12.9	10.1	11.5	12.6	12.6	10.3	11.8	12.1	12.0	11.1	3.8	14.9	15.1	19.9	18.2
3. I don't know, or they differ in whether they think I do	6.1	6.7	5.6	5.6	7.5	8.6	5.1	4.8	7.5	5.9	6.6	1.5	8.1	7.1	11.8	4.5
4. They think I probably do	5.2	6.2	3.9	5.2	6.7	5.6	6.1	5.0	3.6	4.1	6.4	0.4	6.0	5.5	11.8	17.8
5. They feel sure (or know) that I do	5.8	6.4	5.3	5.8	6.0	6.7	4.6	3.9	10.2	4.9	7.3	1.1	3.1	4.2	16.4	26.8
Item 7520 Subject A09a N	2851	1373	1409	2205	359	538	846	942	525	1686	1083	1156	558	407	650	44
E07: Within the past three months, how often have you . . .																
E07A: Had arguments or quarrels with your parents or other older relatives?																
1. Not at all	18.9	23.5	14.0	14.8	38.2	15.0	17.7	21.7	19.8	18.0	20.2	21.7	19.6	14.9	15.1	15.9
2. Once or twice	45.6	46.9	44.6	46.5	43.6	47.1	44.4	45.1	47.2	45.4	45.8	47.5	47.4	49.4	39.5	28.6
3. Every month	14.9	13.1	16.6	16.3	7.7	14.6	17.4	12.9	14.6	15.1	14.7	13.8	15.3	15.2	16.8	13.9
4. Every week	14.4	12.3	16.5	15.7	6.5	16.5	13.6	15.1	12.2	15.5	12.7	12.5	12.2	15.1	18.9	25.0
5. Almost daily	6.3	4.1	8.3	6.6	4.0	6.9	7.0	5.3	6.2	6.0	6.6	4.4	5.4	5.4	9.8	16.5
Item 19530 Subject M03,Q09 N	2873	1384	1420	2232	355	543	855	946	529	1696	1096	1163	560	410	655	45
E07B: Had arguments or quarrels with people in positions of authority?																
1. Not at all	55.3	48.3	62.8	53.3	66.1	51.5	52.4	61.4	53.1	54.8	56.6	62.7	57.4	54.1	42.6	27.0
2. Once or twice	34.9	38.9	30.7	36.0	29.8	36.3	37.4	30.5	37.2	35.1	34.5	30.7	34.9	36.8	42.3	26.7
3. Every month	5.6	7.5	3.7	6.4	2.1	7.7	5.4	4.3	6.0	6.2	4.7	4.4	5.4	6.1	6.9	17.0
4. Every week	3.1	4.2	1.9	3.3	1.6	3.1	3.4	2.8	3.0	3.4	2.4	1.6	1.5	2.1	6.2	22.4
5. Almost daily	1.1	1.1	0.9	1.0	0.6	1.3	1.4	1.0	0.7	0.6	1.8	0.6	0.7	0.9	2.0	6.9
Item 19540 Subject Q09 N	2859	1379	1412	2222	351	539	850	944	527	1687	1091	1163	554	406	653	45
E07C: Been mad enough to feel like smashing something, but I didn't?																
1. Not at all	26.1	24.0	28.1	24.6	32.0	21.6	24.2	29.1	28.5	25.8	26.8	30.4	29.7	23.0	17.9	16.8
2. Once or twice	43.5	42.5	44.9	43.6	44.4	42.1	46.0	42.5	42.8	45.3	40.7	46.2	43.9	45.5	38.1	30.8
3. Every month	14.6	16.7	12.5	15.9	9.3	18.2	15.0	11.9	14.9	14.5	15.0	11.9	13.3	13.9	21.2	14.3
4. Every week	11.8	13.1	10.7	12.4	9.9	14.5	10.3	12.2	10.9	11.7	12.2	8.4	9.4	13.3	18.0	25.8
5. Almost daily	4.0	3.7	3.8	3.6	4.5	3.6	4.4	4.3	3.0	2.8	5.3	3.1	3.8	4.4	4.9	12.4
Item 19550 Subject Q09 N	2862	1375	1418	2222	355	539	853	946	524	1690	1091	1164	557	407	650	45

	TOTAL	SEX		RACE		REGION				4YR COLLEGE PLANS		ILLICIT DRUG USE: LIFETIME				
QUESTIONNAIRE FORM 2 **1984**		M	F	White	Black	NE	NC	S	W	Yes	No	None	Mari-juana Only	Few Pills	More Pills	Any Her-oin
N (Weighted No. of Cases):	3322	1624	1580	2491	453	681	929	1119	593	1855	1265	1285	662	479	773	51
% of Weighted Total:	100.0	48.9	47.5	75.0	13.6	20.1	28.0	33.7	17.9	55.8	38.1	38.7	19.9	14.4	23.3	1.5
E07D: Been mad enough so you actually did smash something?																
1. Not at all	72.5	64.3	81.5	71.9	78.7	69.5	72.4	74.9	71.7	76.3	67.4	81.4	75.7	69.7	58.0	42.1
2. Once or twice	20.5	26.4	14.1	21.0	15.4	21.5	20.3	18.9	22.4	17.6	25.0	14.2	18.4	23.0	31.8	17.2
3. Every month	4.4	5.9	2.6	4.6	3.1	5.5	4.9	3.5	4.2	4.0	4.7	2.6	4.1	5.4	6.5	16.6
4. Every week	1.5	1.9	1.2	1.5	2.4	2.5	0.8	2.3	0.5	1.4	1.4	1.3	1.2	0.5	2.4	10.5
5. Almost daily	1.0	1.5	0.5	1.0	0.4	1.0	1.6	0.5	1.2	0.7	1.5	0.5	0.5	1.4	1.3	13.7
Item 19560 Subject Q09 N	2853	1376	1409	2218	352	535	851	944	523	1687	1086	1161	553	405	651	45
E07E: Felt like getting into a fist fight with some-one, but didn't?																
1. Not at all	46.7	36.4	57.3	46.7	46.1	43.1	46.5	50.3	44.4	48.9	43.0	57.2	45.6	44.2	32.3	22.2
2. Once or twice	37.1	43.5	30.7	37.0	39.6	37.0	35.6	36.1	41.6	36.0	39.3	32.8	40.4	38.3	41.0	41.6
3. Every month	8.6	11.6	5.6	9.0	5.3	11.0	9.8	6.5	7.7	8.2	9.3	5.2	9.0	8.2	14.2	10.8
4. Every week	4.9	5.3	4.1	5.1	3.5	6.4	5.1	4.3	4.2	4.7	5.2	3.0	3.3	5.5	8.5	19.1
5. Almost daily	2.7	3.2	2.1	2.2	5.5	2.5	3.1	2.8	2.1	2.2	3.2	1.8	1.7	3.7	4.0	6.4
Item 19570 Subject Q09 N	2861	1376	1417	2223	354	539	850	945	527	1689	1092	1163	557	406	654	43
E07F: Actually got into a fight and hit some-body?																
1. Not at all	85.4	81.3	90.1	86.7	81.8	82.1	86.3	85.2	87.8	88.4	81.0	91.7	87.1	82.2	77.4	45.2
2. Once or twice	11.4	14.0	8.3	10.7	14.4	14.4	10.1	11.9	9.4	9.6	14.1	6.8	9.9	15.0	17.5	28.6
3. Every month	1.9	3.3	0.7	1.6	1.4	1.9	2.6	1.6	1.7	1.2	3.3	0.8	2.3	1.8	2.5	18.3
4. Every week	0.6	0.6	0.4	0.5	1.1	1.1	0.4	0.7	0.3	0.5	0.5	0.2	0.3	-	1.6	6.2
5. Almost daily	0.6	0.7	0.4	0.4	1.2	0.5	0.6	0.7	0.8	0.3	1.1	0.4	0.4	0.9	0.9	1.7
Item 19580 Subject Q09 N	2856	1376	1412	2219	352	539	849	943	526	1688	1087	1159	556	406	653	43

The next questions are about military service.

	TOTAL	M	F	White	Black	NE	NC	S	W	Yes	No	None	Mari-juana Only	Few Pills	More Pills	Any Her-oin
E08: Do you favor or oppose a military draft at the present time?																
1. Strongly oppose	22.4	27.2	18.0	21.9	23.5	26.1	22.0	19.6	24.6	21.5	23.6	18.1	27.4	23.1	24.5	36.2
2. Mostly oppose	19.6	19.9	19.4	21.2	15.3	20.0	21.2	17.7	20.1	20.0	19.0	21.0	18.2	17.2	20.4	12.1
3. No opinion, or mixed	38.8	29.8	47.5	37.1	45.7	35.9	40.6	41.3	34.4	37.8	40.8	40.1	37.2	39.3	38.4	38.0
4. Mostly favor	12.7	13.9	11.6	13.2	9.9	11.6	11.4	12.6	16.0	14.3	10.3	13.9	10.8	15.7	10.4	8.2
5. Strongly favor	6.4	9.3	3.6	6.5	5.7	6.4	4.7	8.8	4.9	6.4	6.4	7.0	6.4	4.7	6.3	5.5
Item 21060 Subject L02 N	2835	1373	1393	2202	351	537	836	943	518	1677	1079	1152	553	403	644	43
E09: Do you think any military draft in the U.S. should include women as well as men?																
1. No	27.9	17.6	38.5	26.7	36.9	27.6	26.1	30.7	26.1	27.5	27.7	30.0	28.0	28.6	25.0	16.0
2. Uncertain	33.4	27.4	39.3	33.3	29.9	30.8	33.7	34.3	34.1	32.4	35.3	33.2	31.0	33.7	36.2	31.5
3. Yes	38.7	55.1	22.3	39.9	33.2	41.6	40.3	35.1	39.8	40.1	36.9	36.9	41.0	37.8	38.8	52.5
Item 21070 Subject L02 N	2833	1369	1395	2201	351	535	836	944	518	1678	1075	1154	553	401	644	43

One idea for getting more high school grad-uates to serve in the military is to offer them a paid college education after three years of service in the armed forces. During the three years of military duty their pay would be fairly low, but afterward the government would pay their tuition plus $300 a month living expenses for up to four academic years.

	TOTAL	M	F	White	Black	NE	NC	S	W	Yes	No	None	Mari-juana Only	Few Pills	More Pills	Any Her-oin
E10: Do you think it would be a good idea for the U.S. to have such a program of paid college in return for military service?																
1. Definitely not	2.0	2.3	1.6	1.6	2.9	2.1	1.0	2.4	2.5	1.5	2.6	2.3	1.0	2.0	1.7	8.0
2. Probably not	3.2	3.8	2.7	3.2	2.6	2.5	3.2	3.4	3.5	3.3	3.2	3.7	1.3	2.3	4.1	8.5
3. No opinion or uncertain	17.8	16.4	19.4	17.1	19.0	16.9	18.2	19.1	15.9	12.9	25.6	18.5	18.3	19.1	15.5	13.9
4. Yes, probably	31.8	29.1	34.4	33.6	26.1	27.8	35.3	31.0	31.8	33.0	30.2	32.4	28.5	34.4	33.6	14.3
5. Yes, definitely	45.2	48.4	41.9	44.6	49.4	50.7	42.4	44.1	46.3	49.3	38.4	43.1	50.9	42.2	45.1	55.2
Item 21080 Subject L02 N	2806	1360	1379	2176	350	525	830	938	512	1665	1065	1147	547	396	636	43

QUESTIONNAIRE FORM 2 1984	TOTAL	SEX		RACE		REGION				4YR COLLEGE PLANS		ILLICIT DRUG USE: LIFETIME				
		M	F	White	Black	NE	NC	S	W	Yes	No	None	Mari-juana Only	Few Pills	More Pills	Any Her-oin
N (Weighted No. of Cases):	3322	1624	1580	2491	453	681	929	1119	593	1855	1265	1285	662	479	773	51
% of Weighted Total:	100.0	48.9	47.5	75.0	13.6	20.1	28.0	33.7	17.9	55.8	38.1	38.7	19.9	14.4	23.3	1.5
E11: If paid college in return for military service were available NOW, how likely is it that you would sign up for such a plan?																
1. Definitely would not	32.2	26.4	38.2	34.2	24.2	34.1	31.3	30.9	34.3	30.9	33.5	34.2	29.8	26.3	34.9	25.4
2. Probably would not	38.5	39.9	37.6	40.5	29.8	38.4	41.4	37.0	36.3	41.3	34.5	40.2	37.0	41.6	34.4	42.3
3. Probably would	22.7	24.4	20.4	19.9	34.3	20.0	22.0	24.6	23.1	21.1	25.3	20.1	24.7	24.7	24.4	21.1
4. Definitely would	6.6	9.3	3.7	5.4	11.6	7.5	5.3	7.5	6.3	6.7	6.6	5.5	8.5	7.3	6.4	11.2
Item 21090 Subject L02 N	2793	1352	1375	2166	350	523	830	934	506	1661	1056	1143	543	395	633	43
E12: Some people like school very much. Others don't. How do you feel about going to school?																
5. I like school very much	14.0	13.7	14.4	12.0	21.3	11.8	12.5	15.3	16.1	16.9	9.7	18.8	12.2	11.2	8.8	12.8
4. I like school quite a lot	29.5	29.2	30.1	30.8	26.5	25.1	31.6	29.0	31.7	34.2	22.5	34.1	30.3	30.1	21.8	21.0
3. I like school some	40.6	41.1	39.9	39.6	41.8	43.5	40.9	41.4	35.5	37.8	44.5	37.1	44.8	42.4	40.8	42.6
2. I don't like school very much	11.0	10.9	11.0	12.3	7.0	12.6	11.2	9.3	12.3	8.2	15.8	7.2	9.6	10.4	19.4	13.8
1. I don't like school at all	4.9	5.2	4.6	5.2	3.4	7.1	3.7	4.9	4.4	2.9	7.5	2.7	3.1	5.9	9.2	9.8
Item 7630 Subject B01,Q08 N	2875	1388	1419	2230	359	541	844	958	531	1700	1083	1169	558	397	665	44
E13: About how many hours do you spend in an average week on all your homework including both in school and out of school?																
1. 0 hours	6.9	9.5	4.4	7.2	5.1	10.6	6.5	6.4	4.8	3.2	12.5	4.4	7.7	5.4	9.6	21.7
2. 1-4 hours	43.0	45.6	39.6	43.3	43.2	45.5	38.6	44.4	44.8	36.7	52.1	39.3	41.5	47.4	47.4	46.3
3. 5-9 hours	23.7	21.5	25.9	23.9	22.3	20.8	24.1	23.5	26.3	26.3	20.2	22.6	23.7	25.6	24.8	22.4
4. 10-14 hours	12.4	11.7	13.4	12.1	12.6	11.0	13.1	12.7	12.2	16.2	6.8	15.0	12.8	10.9	9.5	2.6
5. 15-19 hours	6.2	5.6	7.0	6.3	7.5	4.9	9.1	5.1	4.9	7.9	3.6	8.4	5.3	5.7	3.8	3.0
6. 20-24 hours	3.6	3.4	3.9	3.1	4.6	4.1	3.8	3.1	3.7	4.3	2.6	5.1	3.4	2.8	1.8	1.0
7. 25 or more hours	4.2	2.6	5.7	4.0	4.7	3.1	4.8	4.9	3.2	5.3	2.2	5.1	5.6	2.0	3.0	2.9
Item 7640 Subject B01 N	2862	1380	1414	2219	358	540	840	953	529	1694	1075	1168	557	389	661	44
E14: In general, how much say or influence do you feel each of the following has on HOW YOUR SCHOOL IS RUN?																
E14A: The principal																
1. Little or no influence	12.2	14.2	10.1	10.8	16.8	11.5	12.9	12.1	11.7	9.6	15.9	10.3	11.4	12.3	14.0	32.8
2. Some influence	13.5	13.9	13.1	12.9	14.4	13.8	14.1	12.9	13.5	10.8	18.1	12.3	13.2	15.0	14.7	8.0
3. Moderate influence	13.9	15.9	11.9	14.7	10.2	11.4	18.0	12.2	12.6	12.9	15.1	14.1	13.4	13.1	13.8	29.5
4. Considerable influence	24.5	24.7	24.9	27.0	15.4	27.9	26.7	20.1	25.6	27.3	20.5	26.4	23.1	22.0	24.5	13.2
5. A great deal of influence	35.9	31.3	39.9	34.6	43.3	35.4	28.3	42.6	36.6	39.4	30.5	36.9	38.9	37.5	33.0	16.4
Item 7650 Subject B10 N	2827	1359	1402	2200	351	530	839	938	520	1677	1066	1157	546	385	655	44
E14B: The teachers																
1. Little or no influence	8.7	10.4	7.2	8.4	11.3	9.6	9.3	8.9	6.5	7.1	11.0	6.6	8.2	9.9	10.1	33.0
2. Some influence	20.9	21.3	20.5	20.7	20.8	20.2	22.5	21.8	17.6	18.2	25.2	21.2	17.9	21.8	22.3	16.3
3. Moderate influence	30.8	32.9	29.4	31.6	27.9	33.0	29.5	31.2	30.2	31.8	29.6	31.7	30.1	26.3	32.6	32.5
4. Considerable influence	29.9	25.5	33.5	30.7	28.0	28.5	28.9	28.5	35.2	32.8	25.2	30.8	34.1	32.5	25.2	15.3
5. A great deal of influence	9.7	9.9	9.4	8.6	11.9	8.7	9.7	9.6	10.6	10.0	9.0	9.8	9.7	9.5	9.8	2.9
Item 7660 Subject B10 N	2821	1356	1398	2200	345	528	837	934	521	1674	1062	1153	541	385	657	44
E14C: The students																
1. Little or no influence	30.8	32.8	29.3	32.0	28.5	34.2	33.3	30.7	23.5	29.8	32.2	29.0	28.8	30.9	35.1	26.8
2. Some influence	26.9	26.6	27.2	26.8	30.1	25.8	25.6	28.4	27.7	27.9	26.0	29.5	27.9	27.2	22.4	23.3
3. Moderate influence	19.5	18.4	20.3	19.9	16.6	18.6	17.7	18.8	24.6	20.4	18.2	20.5	19.9	16.6	20.6	15.4
4. Considerable influence	13.3	13.1	13.8	13.3	12.0	14.0	12.3	12.1	16.3	13.4	12.5	12.7	13.4	16.8	11.8	13.1
5. A great deal of influence	9.4	9.1	9.5	8.0	12.8	7.3	11.1	10.0	7.9	8.5	11.1	8.4	10.9	8.5	10.1	21.4
Item 7670 Subject B10 N	2813	1356	1392	2196	343	525	836	935	517	1671	1059	1153	537	384	655	44

QUESTIONNAIRE FORM 2 1984	TOTAL	SEX		RACE		REGION				4YR COLLEGE PLANS		ILLICIT DRUG USE: LIFETIME				
		M	F	White	Black	NE	NC	S	W	Yes	No	None	Mari- juana Only	Few Pills	More Pills	Any Her- oin
N (Weighted No. of Cases):	3322	1624	1580	2491	453	681	929	1119	593	1855	1265	1285	662	479	773	51
% of Weighted Total:	100.0	48.9	47.5	75.0	13.6	20.1	28.0	33.7	17.9	55.8	38.1	38.7	19.9	14.4	23.3	1.5
E14D: Parents of students																
1. Little or no influence	21.8	23.4	20.8	22.2	20.5	26.2	22.4	20.6	18.6	19.8	25.2	20.3	19.5	19.2	26.5	34.0
2. Some influence	30.9	30.5	30.6	32.4	24.6	31.9	30.6	32.3	27.5	31.2	30.5	31.8	32.7	27.3	29.8	24.3
3. Moderate influence	22.6	22.2	23.4	22.8	21.4	21.7	21.3	22.1	26.3	24.0	19.7	22.3	22.6	25.4	22.5	17.1
4. Considerable influence	14.1	14.7	13.5	14.2	13.8	14.3	14.4	13.0	15.5	15.3	12.4	14.6	13.4	16.3	13.1	11.7
5. A great deal of influence	10.6	9.2	11.7	8.4	19.7	5.9	11.2	11.9	12.2	9.6	12.2	11.0	11.8	11.7	8.1	12.9
Item 7680 Subject B10 N	2815	1354	1394	2199	343	526	836	933	519	1671	1060	1153	540	384	654	44
E15: Have you had any drug education courses or lectures in school?																
1. No–GO TO Q.E19	27.3	29.6	25.1	26.0	30.1	19.3	32.1	31.0	21.4	23.8	32.8	28.7	28.5	25.4	23.7	39.2
2. No, and I wish I had– GO TO Q.E19	3.4	2.8	4.1	3.4	2.4	2.9	3.4	4.1	2.9	3.7	3.2	3.8	2.7	3.2	3.9	1.3
3. Yes	69.2	67.6	70.8	70.6	67.4	77.8	64.5	64.9	75.8	72.5	64.0	67.5	68.8	71.4	72.4	59.5
Item 7690 Subject A10a N	2688	1287	1343	2121	317	510	796	885	497	1633	975	1100	517	375	622	41
E16: Would you say that the information about drugs that you received in school classes or programs has . . .																
1. Made you less interested in trying drugs	54.1	47.8	59.7	51.9	66.5	51.7	52.3	62.2	47.0	53.0	57.3	67.1	59.4	51.6	30.4	36.4
2. Not changed your interest in trying drugs	43.3	48.6	38.7	45.8	29.7	45.2	45.7	35.2	50.3	45.2	38.9	31.9	38.4	45.4	65.1	47.8
3. Made you more interested in trying drugs	2.5	3.6	1.6	2.3	3.8	3.1	2.0	2.5	2.7	1.8	3.8	1.0	2.2	2.9	4.6	15.8
Item 7840 Subject A10a N★	1865	873	949	1495	217	397	514	572	382	1176	637	740	358	268	454	24
E17: How many of the following drug education experiences have you had in high school? (Mark all that apply.)																
A. A special course about drugs	23.7	26.7	20.6	23.8	21.7	24.9	22.0	22.6	26.3	25.9	19.9	23.8	25.3	20.4	24.0	26.0
B. Films, lectures, or discussions in one of my regular courses	78.0	76.8	79.4	78.9	72.8	76.2	76.9	76.3	83.9	79.3	75.9	80.1	79.5	73.9	77.4	63.3
C. Films or lectures, outside of my regular courses	26.8	28.1	25.5	27.3	24.4	24.5	23.9	30.9	26.9	28.7	23.1	25.2	26.8	27.4	28.5	47.7
D. Special discussions ("rap" groups) about drugs	21.3	21.1	21.3	21.4	17.7	22.6	20.5	21.7	20.3	21.3	21.1	16.6	20.9	26.1	25.9	34.8
Item 7850-7880 Subject A10a N★	1841	859	938	1475	217	390	511	567	373	1160	632	732	359	268	440	23
E18: Overall, how valuable were the experiences to you?																
1. Little or no value	17.8	21.1	14.8	18.6	11.2	22.8	17.9	14.7	17.1	18.6	16.6	19.2	13.8	14.7	20.4	36.2
2. Some value	43.5	45.0	42.1	45.5	34.4	42.3	44.4	40.1	48.7	44.1	42.5	38.2	47.2	42.9	50.1	35.4
3. Considerable value	23.3	20.3	26.0	23.3	25.0	20.6	25.5	25.1	20.1	23.2	23.0	22.8	21.1	28.7	22.8	25.6
4. Great value	15.4	13.6	17.1	12.7	29.5	14.2	12.1	20.1	14.1	14.1	17.9	19.7	17.8	13.7	6.7	2.8
Item 7890 Subject A10a N★	1857	869	945	1488	219	395	514	571	376	1173	637	738	360	267	448	24
E19: During the LAST TWO WEEKS, how many times (if any) have you driven a car, truck, or motorcycle after . . .																
E19A: Drinking alcohol?																
1. None	68.8	60.8	76.8	65.1	87.3	74.7	64.0	67.0	73.6	70.1	66.8	83.6	69.2	60.1	49.2	32.5
2. Once	15.0	18.9	11.0	17.1	5.0	11.9	15.4	17.1	13.7	15.3	14.4	9.6	16.4	18.2	21.4	24.7
3. Twice	8.3	10.1	6.6	9.2	4.1	7.0	10.9	8.0	6.0	7.2	10.0	4.5	7.5	14.0	12.7	7.5
4. 3-5 times	5.4	7.1	3.6	6.3	1.1	3.9	7.0	5.3	4.3	5.1	6.0	1.6	4.2	6.3	10.9	24.8
5. 6-9 times	1.6	1.7	1.6	1.7	1.2	2.4	1.9	1.2	1.1	1.6	1.7	0.3	0.9	0.7	4.5	8.9
6. 10 or more	0.9	1.4	0.5	0.7	1.2	-	0.8	1.4	1.3	0.7	1.2	0.3	1.7	0.8	1.3	1.6
Item 1811 Subject A07a N	2810	1341	1400	2185	349	527	832	937	514	1669	1057	1154	546	384	642	44

★=excludes respondents for whom question was inappropriate.

QUESTIONNAIRE FORM 2 1984	TOTAL	SEX		RACE		REGION				4YR COLLEGE PLANS		ILLICIT DRUG USE: LIFETIME				
		M	F	White	Black	NE	NC	S	W	Yes	No	None	Mari-juana Only	Few Pills	More Pills	Any Her-oin
N (Weighted No. of Cases):	3322	1624	1580	2491	453	681	929	1119	593	1855	1265	1285	662	479	773	51
% of Weighted Total:	100.0	48.9	47.5	75.0	13.6	20.1	28.0	33.7	17.9	55.8	38.1	38.7	19.9	14.4	23.3	1.5
E19B: Having 5 or more drinks in a row?																
1. None	81.7	74.8	88.7	79.1	95.7	86.1	75.4	83.0	84.9	83.5	78.4	92.5	84.9	76.1	65.4	49.3
2. Once	9.0	11.7	6.3	10.5	2.3	7.3	11.4	8.9	7.2	8.4	10.1	4.5	8.7	10.2	16.0	18.6
3. Twice	4.2	6.0	2.6	4.7	0.9	2.6	6.1	3.6	3.8	3.3	5.6	2.2	2.4	8.4	6.9	-
4. 3-5 times	3.4	5.2	1.4	3.8	0.7	2.6	4.8	2.8	2.8	3.4	3.3	0.3	2.7	4.8	8.0	13.4
5. 6-9 times	1.0	1.2	0.8	1.1	-	0.8	1.1	1.0	1.1	1.0	1.1	0.1	1.0	0.3	2.5	5.8
6. 10 or more	0.7	1.1	0.2	0.7	0.5	0.7	1.0	0.7	0.3	0.3	1.4	0.3	0.3	0.1	1.1	12.9
Item 1812 Subject A07a N	2771	1323	1383	2164	343	521	824	921	504	1657	1037	1139	541	375	634	44
E20: During the LAST TWO WEEKS, how many times (if any) have you been a passenger in a car . . .																
E20A: When the driver had been drinking?																
1. None	55.8	56.5	55.9	53.7	66.4	57.1	50.8	57.3	59.6	59.0	50.8	72.4	54.9	46.1	34.0	39.4
2. Once	20.1	19.5	20.6	21.2	15.7	19.8	21.7	19.5	19.0	20.3	19.7	16.9	23.3	26.7	20.2	11.7
3. Twice	11.6	10.9	11.9	12.1	9.0	11.1	13.0	11.6	9.7	10.9	12.4	5.8	9.9	15.3	20.5	3.9
4. 3-5 times	8.2	8.8	7.5	8.8	5.2	6.5	10.5	7.4	7.5	6.7	10.6	3.3	7.1	8.6	17.1	16.5
5. 6-9 times	2.2	2.3	2.1	2.2	1.0	2.5	2.5	2.1	1.9	1.8	3.0	0.8	2.7	2.1	3.7	15.2
6. 10 or more	2.1	2.0	2.0	2.0	2.7	3.1	1.5	2.1	2.3	1.3	3.4	0.7	2.2	1.2	4.4	13.2
Item 1815 Subject A07a N	2809	1347	1395	2186	350	529	831	934	515	1673	1053	1148	547	385	645	44
E20B: When you think the driver had 5 or more drinks?																
1. None	74.6	72.5	77.4	72.3	86.0	76.8	68.7	76.8	78.2	77.6	69.5	87.4	76.4	68.1	55.6	53.6
2. Once	11.4	11.7	11.0	12.3	7.6	10.1	12.6	11.7	10.3	10.6	13.0	7.9	11.7	18.1	14.8	1.0
3. Twice	7.2	7.8	6.3	8.0	3.2	7.4	9.6	6.3	4.7	6.6	8.2	2.9	6.2	7.6	15.0	11.2
4. 3-5 times	4.9	6.4	3.4	5.4	2.1	3.5	7.2	3.4	5.3	3.9	6.5	1.0	4.2	5.1	10.8	20.0
5. 6-9 times	0.8	0.7	0.9	0.8	-	0.7	1.0	0.8	0.5	0.8	0.7	0.2	0.8	0.8	1.4	5.7
6. 10 or more	1.1	1.0	1.0	1.2	1.1	1.5	0.9	1.1	1.1	0.6	2.0	0.6	0.6	0.2	2.4	8.6
Item 1816 Subject A07a N	2777	1335	1376	2169	341	524	823	928	502	1656	1044	1142	540	378	633	44
E21: How often do you . . .																
E21A: Eat breakfast?																
1. Never	10.8	8.9	12.8	10.4	9.4	10.8	12.6	11.6	6.8	9.1	13.2	6.8	12.3	9.7	16.9	18.7
2. Seldom	27.5	23.3	32.0	27.1	29.7	28.0	28.9	26.2	27.2	24.9	31.5	24.7	27.1	28.3	33.6	22.0
3. Sometimes	15.8	13.8	17.3	15.0	20.5	16.8	12.1	17.9	17.2	16.0	15.4	15.0	17.4	14.9	16.4	8.7
4. Most days	9.4	9.5	9.3	9.0	11.2	10.4	7.0	11.3	8.9	9.9	9.0	9.7	9.3	10.1	8.1	16.0
5. Nearly every day	10.1	10.5	9.5	10.6	10.2	8.8	10.7	8.6	12.8	10.9	9.0	11.2	9.5	9.9	7.9	12.8
6. Every day	26.4	34.0	19.1	27.9	18.9	25.3	28.8	24.4	27.2	29.2	21.8	32.6	24.4	27.2	17.1	21.8
Item 20740 Subject T N	2823	1352	1402	2194	351	530	835	939	519	1678	1058	1157	546	385	651	44
E21B: Eat at least some green vegetables?																
1. Never	3.8	4.5	2.9	3.1	4.1	3.1	3.2	4.9	3.3	2.1	6.1	2.7	2.9	4.5	4.8	13.6
2. Seldom	11.7	11.8	11.9	10.6	16.1	11.4	13.3	11.4	10.0	8.5	16.9	8.7	14.9	11.1	13.6	18.5
3. Sometimes	20.3	18.4	22.3	19.4	23.0	18.3	19.7	22.7	19.0	19.0	23.0	18.5	18.7	23.8	22.4	23.3
4. Most days	21.9	21.5	22.1	22.3	21.5	24.3	21.9	20.4	22.2	21.7	22.1	20.2	22.5	23.6	24.9	11.6
5. Nearly every day	20.7	19.2	22.0	21.1	22.1	18.0	20.1	21.0	23.8	23.1	16.9	24.6	18.7	18.8	17.4	11.0
6. Every day	21.7	24.6	18.9	23.4	13.2	25.0	21.9	19.6	21.7	25.6	15.0	25.3	22.4	18.2	16.8	21.9
Item 20750 Subject T N	2811	1348	1396	2190	347	529	832	933	518	1675	1053	1149	545	382	652	43
E21C: Eat at least some fruit?																
1. Never	1.5	2.1	0.7	1.6	0.8	1.9	1.4	1.8	0.7	0.7	2.6	0.7	1.1	1.1	2.8	6.3
2. Seldom	10.2	10.0	10.3	9.4	14.1	9.5	12.0	10.2	8.1	6.7	15.9	8.1	11.3	11.1	11.6	12.9
3. Sometimes	25.4	23.3	27.4	25.3	26.9	27.0	22.3	28.8	22.5	22.3	30.4	23.4	23.9	29.6	28.9	12.8
4. Most days	23.6	22.3	25.0	23.1	25.2	22.9	21.6	25.6	23.9	25.3	21.3	23.3	23.9	25.8	23.4	14.6
5. Nearly every day	20.0	20.2	19.8	20.6	20.7	18.0	21.9	18.0	22.7	22.7	16.2	21.3	20.9	15.8	19.4	25.6
6. Every day	19.2	22.1	16.7	20.0	12.5	20.6	20.7	15.6	22.1	22.3	13.6	23.2	18.9	16.7	13.8	27.9
Item 20760 Subject T N	2812	1348	1396	2187	349	530	833	932	518	1675	1055	1154	545	382	648	44

QUESTIONNAIRE FORM 2 1984	TOTAL	SEX		RACE		REGION				4YR COLLEGE PLANS		ILLICIT DRUG USE: LIFETIME				
		M	F	White	Black	NE	NC	S	W	Yes	No	None	Mari-juana Only	Few Pills	More Pills	Any Her-oin
N (Weighted No. of Cases):	3322	1624	1580	2491	453	681	929	1119	593	1855	1265	1285	662	479	773	51
% of Weighted Total:	100.0	48.9	47.5	75.0	13.6	20.1	28.0	33.7	17.9	55.8	38.1	38.7	19.9	14.4	23.3	1.5
E21D: Exercise vigorously (jogging, swimming, calisthenics, or any other active sports)?																
1. Never	4.0	3.2	4.4	3.5	5.1	4.7	4.1	3.9	3.4	2.0	6.5	3.2	5.0	2.9	4.5	8.7
2. Seldom	16.6	13.6	19.9	15.4	23.9	15.3	15.7	20.2	12.8	13.6	22.0	16.1	14.9	18.8	17.4	17.6
3. Sometimes	25.6	20.1	31.1	26.5	23.0	24.2	26.1	26.0	25.8	25.7	25.5	25.5	25.0	25.5	26.8	20.2
4. Most days	16.3	16.6	16.1	16.9	12.6	17.7	15.8	14.8	18.5	15.8	17.3	14.5	17.9	18.8	17.0	7.8
5. Nearly every day	16.3	18.7	13.9	16.5	13.4	16.5	17.3	15.3	16.6	18.0	13.7	16.2	16.6	17.1	15.7	26.4
6. Every day	21.1	27.8	14.6	21.2	21.9	21.5	21.1	19.9	22.9	24.9	14.9	24.6	20.6	16.9	18.6	19.2
Item 20770 Subject T　　N	2809	1347	1394	2186	348	528	834	932	516	1673	1053	1152	542	381	650	44
E21E: Get at least seven hours of sleep?																
1. Never	1.7	1.9	1.3	1.6	1.4	2.6	0.9	1.8	1.7	1.2	2.2	1.0	1.5	1.5	3.0	1.0
2. Seldom	11.4	10.3	12.6	10.7	13.7	10.5	13.1	11.3	10.0	9.7	14.1	10.1	9.4	12.5	12.8	29.2
3. Sometimes	18.7	16.5	21.2	17.6	24.9	18.7	17.3	19.7	19.1	19.3	17.7	16.9	19.2	19.2	21.6	16.9
4. Most days	23.9	23.8	24.0	25.6	14.6	25.9	25.0	22.8	22.1	23.5	24.7	22.4	23.8	23.3	27.3	19.5
5. Nearly every day	23.0	23.3	22.4	23.3	21.0	20.6	23.6	22.7	24.8	25.7	19.0	24.8	27.4	20.6	17.5	20.6
6. Every day	21.4	24.1	18.6	21.1	24.3	21.8	20.1	21.7	22.3	20.5	22.3	24.7	18.6	22.9	17.9	12.7
Item 20780 Subject T　　N	2807	1344	1396	2182	349	527	834	931	515	1672	1051	1152	543	380	648	44
E21F: Get less sleep than you think you should?																
1. Never	8.8	9.5	8.2	7.8	13.5	8.5	7.7	10.2	8.6	7.4	11.0	10.0	9.8	6.3	6.9	8.8
2. Seldom	19.7	19.9	19.3	18.6	24.3	17.4	19.6	20.4	20.9	19.3	20.2	20.1	21.1	21.8	16.6	9.8
3. Sometimes	31.7	30.9	32.6	33.4	24.8	31.1	35.1	29.8	30.2	32.6	30.8	32.5	32.6	29.2	31.2	25.5
4. Most days	16.6	17.1	16.3	16.7	15.1	17.7	16.1	16.6	16.2	16.1	16.9	17.1	12.9	16.7	19.1	8.5
5. Nearly every day	12.7	11.5	13.8	13.2	11.5	14.4	12.8	11.1	13.8	13.9	10.8	10.8	14.2	14.1	13.8	27.6
6. Every day	10.5	11.1	9.9	10.4	10.8	10.8	8.8	12.0	10.4	10.8	10.2	9.4	9.4	11.8	12.4	19.9
Item 20790 Subject T　　N	2809	1346	1394	2184	349	527	833	933	515	1672	1052	1153	543	381	648	44

QUESTIONNAIRE FORM 3 1984	TOTAL	SEX		RACE		REGION				4YR COLLEGE PLANS		ILLICIT DRUG USE: LIFETIME				
		M	F	White	Black	NE	NC	S	W	Yes	No	None	Mari- juana Only	Few Pills	More Pills	Any Her- oin
N (Weighted No. of Cases):	3287	1532	1632	2482	442	675	914	1116	582	1823	1254	1211	735	430	791	41
% of Weighted Total:	100.0	46.6	49.6	75.5	13.4	20.5	27.8	33.9	17.7	55.5	38.1	36.8	22.4	13.1	24.1	1.3
A01: Taking all things together, how would you say things are these days-would you say you're very happy, pretty happy, or not too happy these days?																
3. Very happy	17.5	15.7	19.0	19.0	11.2	16.5	14.2	19.6	20.0	19.4	15.0	21.4	15.5	15.7	14.9	23.4
2. Pretty happy	70.7	72.4	70.0	71.4	72.1	71.0	74.5	68.6	68.3	70.7	71.8	68.7	73.5	71.6	71.8	50.9
1. Not too happy	11.8	11.9	11.0	9.6	16.7	12.5	11.3	11.8	11.7	9.9	13.2	9.9	11.0	12.7	13.2	25.7
Item 1190 Subject P01,Q01 N	3274	1523	1629	2475	439	666	914	1114	580	1819	1250	1207	734	429	788	41
A02: Some people think a lot about the so- cial problems of the nation and the world, and about how they might be solved. Others spend little time thinking about these issues. How much do you think about such things?																
1. Never	1.9	2.8	1.0	1.6	2.4	2.9	1.1	1.8	2.6	1.7	2.1	1.5	1.6	2.1	2.6	4.5
2. Seldom	14.9	14.0	15.9	15.8	12.0	20.6	15.6	11.7	13.4	13.8	16.8	14.4	15.6	13.2	15.7	14.0
3. Sometimes	53.1	51.6	54.9	53.4	49.8	49.1	55.4	53.7	52.9	50.9	56.9	51.3	54.3	59.4	51.7	43.3
4. Quite often	25.2	25.8	24.4	25.0	27.7	23.3	24.8	27.2	24.2	28.6	20.2	27.5	24.4	23.1	24.2	28.6
5. A great deal	4.8	5.9	3.7	4.3	8.1	4.0	3.2	5.6	6.9	5.0	4.0	5.2	4.0	2.1	5.8	9.7
Item 6880 Subject J,Q08 N	3276	1525	1629	2475	441	667	914	1113	581	1821	1249	1208	733	429	789	41
A03: The next questions ask your opinions about a number of different topics. How much do you agree or disagree with each statement below?																
A03A: Men and women should be paid the same money if they do the same work																
1. Disagree	1.9	3.0	0.6	1.5	2.0	2.9	1.8	1.5	1.4	0.8	2.8	1.7	1.8	1.0	2.0	2.5
2. Mostly disagree	1.8	3.1	0.5	1.6	1.0	2.5	1.2	1.4	2.4	1.8	1.6	1.8	1.2	2.4	1.9	-
3. Neither	1.5	2.7	0.3	1.2	1.7	1.3	1.1	1.6	2.5	1.3	1.2	1.6	0.5	1.0	2.0	10.6
4. Mostly agree	16.6	23.9	9.7	17.8	14.1	14.6	19.1	16.4	15.1	15.0	19.8	15.5	20.3	11.6	17.4	18.3
5. Agree	78.3	67.3	89.0	77.9	81.2	78.7	76.7	79.1	78.6	81.1	74.6	79.3	76.2	84.0	76.8	68.6
Item 7930 Subject D06 N	3280	1527	1632	2480	441	672	912	1114	582	1823	1250	1210	735	430	788	41
A03B: Women should be considered as seri- ously as men for jobs as executives or politi- cians																
1. Disagree	3.9	6.4	1.3	3.1	5.6	3.1	3.0	5.5	3.0	2.9	4.4	3.6	4.3	2.2	4.1	-
2. Mostly disagree	4.1	7.4	1.0	4.2	3.0	3.6	3.3	5.1	4.0	3.9	4.2	3.8	3.1	5.3	4.4	7.0
3. Neither	5.4	9.5	1.7	5.0	4.7	6.1	5.7	5.0	4.7	4.8	5.9	4.8	3.1	6.5	7.0	15.0
4. Mostly agree	25.5	32.9	18.3	26.5	21.6	21.3	29.7	25.9	23.0	24.0	28.0	24.0	29.0	26.8	23.5	29.3
5. Agree	61.2	43.7	77.8	61.2	65.1	66.0	58.2	58.5	65.3	64.5	57.4	63.8	60.6	59.2	61.1	48.7
Item 7940 Subject D06,H02 N	3278	1528	1629	2477	440	670	914	1113	581	1820	1251	1208	734	428	791	41
A03C: A woman should have exactly the same job opportunities as a man																
1. Disagree	7.4	12.2	2.4	6.7	8.4	6.5	6.1	8.2	8.9	5.8	8.5	6.8	7.5	5.7	8.2	9.6
2. Mostly disagree	6.5	11.3	2.2	6.9	4.3	4.9	7.1	6.4	7.4	6.6	6.4	6.5	6.8	6.2	6.0	13.8
3. Neither	5.0	6.8	3.3	5.4	2.8	5.0	6.4	4.6	3.5	3.8	6.4	4.1	6.2	4.0	5.7	7.3
4. Mostly agree	28.9	28.7	29.0	30.1	25.3	27.2	33.3	28.0	25.6	27.8	30.6	28.9	28.5	32.3	27.8	17.2
5. Agree	52.3	41.0	63.2	50.9	59.2	56.5	47.1	52.8	54.6	56.1	48.1	53.7	51.0	51.8	52.3	52.1
Item 7950 Subject D06 N	3259	1514	1624	2463	438	668	907	1104	579	1810	1243	1196	728	430	788	41
A03D: A woman should have exactly the same educational opportunities as a man																
1. Disagree	1.0	1.4	0.5	0.7	1.3	0.8	0.7	1.0	1.9	0.6	1.4	1.2	0.9	0.3	1.1	-
2. Mostly disagree	0.9	1.7	0.3	0.8	1.3	0.7	1.1	1.1	0.7	0.5	1.6	0.9	1.0	-	1.0	10.2
3. Neither	1.3	2.2	0.4	1.1	0.2	1.3	1.8	1.0	1.6	0.8	1.6	1.4	0.7	0.5	2.0	3.0
4. Mostly agree	9.0	11.2	6.6	8.1	12.5	8.9	9.7	10.0	6.1	5.9	12.7	8.6	9.6	6.8	9.1	14.6
5. Agree	87.7	83.4	92.1	89.2	84.7	88.4	86.8	87.0	89.8	92.2	82.7	87.9	87.8	92.4	86.9	72.1
Item 7960 Subject D06 N	3261	1519	1621	2462	438	670	907	1107	577	1812	1247	1201	733	428	782	41

QUESTIONNAIRE FORM 3 1984	TOTAL	SEX		RACE		REGION				4YR COLLEGE PLANS		ILLICIT DRUG USE: LIFETIME				
		M	F	White	Black	NE	NC	S	W	Yes	No	None	Mari-juana Only	Few Pills	More Pills	Any Her-oin
N (Weighted No. of Cases):	3287	1532	1632	2482	442	675	914	1116	582	1823	1254	1211	735	430	791	41
% of Weighted Total:	100.0	46.6	49.6	75.5	13.4	20.5	27.8	33.9	17.7	55.5	38.1	36.8	22.4	13.1	24.1	1.3
A03E: It is usually better for everyone involved if the man is the achiever outside the home and the woman takes care of the home and family																
1. Disagree	25.4	13.7	36.3	24.7	30.3	31.7	21.8	24.9	24.7	27.7	22.7	24.3	28.3	25.2	24.8	18.9
2. Mostly disagree	18.0	14.8	21.2	19.3	13.6	16.2	20.3	17.0	18.2	18.7	17.0	17.3	14.6	23.1	19.7	16.9
3. Neither	16.4	19.4	13.7	18.0	10.0	14.8	19.1	14.1	18.6	17.2	14.7	14.0	18.0	17.7	17.8	17.1
4. Mostly agree	23.1	26.2	20.4	22.4	25.1	20.4	23.2	24.0	24.6	22.4	24.7	27.3	20.9	20.8	20.3	20.6
5. Agree	17.1	26.0	8.3	15.6	21.1	17.0	15.6	20.0	13.8	14.0	20.8	17.1	18.1	13.3	17.4	26.5
Item 7970 Subject D05 N	3281	1531	1630	2480	441	671	914	1114	581	1822	1252	1210	735	429	790	41
A03F: A preschool child is likely to suffer if the mother works																
1. Disagree	17.0	12.3	20.9	13.7	31.2	17.5	14.1	17.8	19.3	16.0	17.8	15.8	19.1	14.6	17.6	10.9
2. Mostly disagree	18.1	11.7	24.6	18.4	19.7	17.5	18.2	18.4	18.3	19.2	17.2	17.0	18.3	20.6	18.9	23.8
3. Neither	14.1	13.9	14.4	15.2	10.2	13.7	16.3	12.4	14.3	16.2	11.1	15.1	11.0	16.3	13.4	13.9
4. Mostly agree	25.9	27.7	24.7	27.4	19.6	27.7	24.9	25.6	25.8	26.8	25.5	25.4	26.7	26.5	26.5	16.1
5. Agree	24.9	34.5	15.5	25.3	19.3	23.6	26.4	25.8	22.3	21.8	28.3	26.7	24.8	22.0	23.6	35.3
Item 7980 Subject D05 N	3258	1516	1623	2464	438	665	908	1105	580	1811	1246	1204	726	428	785	41
A03G: A working mother can establish just as warm and secure a relationship with her children as a mother who does not work																
1. Disagree	13.7	19.8	7.6	13.7	10.4	11.0	13.2	15.1	14.9	12.1	14.9	15.3	13.0	10.3	13.1	14.9
2. Mostly disagree	15.4	20.3	11.0	16.7	8.0	14.1	18.1	13.6	16.0	16.0	15.1	13.5	16.7	14.6	17.1	18.2
3. Neither	8.5	10.9	6.3	9.5	4.5	7.9	10.2	7.2	9.3	9.3	7.1	8.1	8.9	9.7	8.6	7.7
4. Mostly agree	29.3	26.8	31.8	30.6	22.4	28.3	31.3	29.3	27.2	30.2	28.5	30.8	27.9	31.9	27.9	25.8
5. Agree	33.1	22.2	43.2	29.5	54.7	38.7	27.2	34.9	32.7	32.4	34.4	32.3	33.5	33.6	33.3	33.4
Item 7990 Subject D05 N	3280	1529	1630	2479	441	672	913	1114	582	1823	1253	1209	735	430	789	41
A04: The next questions are about pollution and the environment. How much do you agree or disagree with each statement below?																
A04A: Pollution of most types has increased in the U.S. in the last ten years																
1. Disagree	3.0	4.6	1.4	2.7	3.8	2.7	4.2	2.3	2.5	2.6	3.4	2.4	3.1	3.2	3.6	2.4
2. Mostly disagree	6.6	8.7	4.4	6.7	6.3	6.0	8.5	6.0	5.8	6.6	6.3	5.5	7.7	6.4	6.6	8.3
3. Neither	8.3	8.5	7.9	8.9	4.1	6.5	11.0	7.2	8.4	8.7	7.8	7.6	9.5	8.1	8.9	6.6
4. Mostly agree	30.0	26.2	33.9	31.1	27.0	29.1	32.6	29.2	28.6	31.6	27.5	31.0	28.4	31.3	29.0	32.6
5. Agree	52.1	51.9	52.4	50.6	58.8	55.7	43.8	55.3	54.6	50.5	54.9	53.4	51.2	51.1	51.9	50.1
Item 8000 Subject F04 N	3265	1522	1623	2469	441	664	913	1111	578	1813	1247	1200	734	429	787	41
A04B: Government should take steps to deal with our environmental problems, even if it means that most of us pay higher prices or taxes																
1. Disagree	8.1	9.9	6.4	6.8	13.0	8.3	6.6	9.2	8.3	6.5	9.7	7.3	10.1	5.6	8.8	9.4
2. Mostly disagree	10.7	11.2	9.7	9.4	15.0	11.6	9.8	11.0	10.2	9.3	12.3	9.9	11.7	8.7	11.5	6.3
3. Neither	16.9	14.7	19.5	17.5	14.3	12.3	20.7	16.6	16.7	15.5	18.5	15.9	14.5	17.5	21.1	16.2
4. Mostly agree	38.7	34.8	42.9	40.9	31.1	38.8	38.7	38.1	40.0	41.7	36.4	39.8	38.4	43.6	35.3	41.6
5. Agree	25.6	29.5	21.5	25.4	26.7	28.9	24.2	25.1	24.8	27.0	23.1	27.1	25.3	24.6	23.4	26.5
Item 8010 Subject F04,H02 N	3274	1527	1626	2477	440	669	913	1112	580	1818	1250	1209	733	429	787	41
A04C: I would prefer to pay more money for things that will last a long time, rather than have them cost less and break sooner																
1. Disagree	1.4	1.9	0.7	1.0	2.1	1.5	0.4	1.4	2.6	0.9	1.7	1.2	1.5	0.8	1.3	5.5
2. Mostly disagree	1.2	1.5	0.8	1.1	1.3	0.6	2.2	0.6	1.2	0.7	1.7	1.4	0.6	0.4	1.3	11.7
3. Neither	3.4	3.5	3.4	3.6	2.7	3.6	4.3	2.8	3.2	3.3	3.6	3.1	3.3	2.4	4.4	1.4
4. Mostly agree	20.7	20.5	20.6	21.4	17.8	21.1	22.2	19.5	20.5	19.3	22.1	18.4	20.5	25.2	21.8	29.6
5. Agree	73.3	72.6	74.5	72.9	76.1	73.2	70.8	75.7	72.6	75.7	71.1	75.9	74.1	71.2	71.3	51.9
Item 8020 Subject F01 N	3271	1525	1627	2474	439	669	911	1110	580	1819	1246	1207	732	430	786	41

QUESTIONNAIRE FORM 3 1984	TOTAL	SEX		RACE		REGION				4YR COLLEGE PLANS		ILLICIT DRUG USE: LIFETIME				
		M	F	White	Black	NE	NC	S	W	Yes	No	None	Mari- juana Only	Few Pills	More Pills	Any Her- oin
N (Weighted No. of Cases):	3287	1532	1632	2482	442	675	914	1116	582	1823	1254	1211	735	430	791	41
% of Weighted Total:	100.0	46.6	49.6	75.5	13.4	20.5	27.8	33.9	17.7	55.5	38.1	36.8	22.4	13.1	24.1	1.3
A04D: I would probably be willing to use a bi- cycle or mass transit (if available) rather than a car to get to work																
1. Disagree	30.9	33.6	27.7	27.8	44.3	33.5	25.4	35.6	27.3	26.1	36.6	28.3	31.2	27.2	36.0	28.0
2. Mostly disagree	20.7	20.2	21.7	21.0	20.4	20.6	21.9	19.2	21.8	20.7	21.2	20.8	18.4	23.9	21.4	16.0
3. Neither	12.2	12.8	11.9	13.5	7.1	11.2	14.4	11.3	11.6	12.5	11.7	12.5	11.4	13.4	11.4	9.0
4. Mostly agree	20.4	18.6	21.9	21.2	15.1	19.1	20.7	20.3	21.4	22.8	17.2	21.4	22.0	20.8	18.0	21.1
5. Agree	15.8	14.8	16.7	16.5	13.0	15.6	17.5	13.5	17.8	17.8	13.1	17.1	17.0	14.6	13.2	25.8
Item 8030 Subject F07 N	3275	1524	1631	2476	441	670	913	1112	580	1819	1251	1206	734	430	789	41
A04E: I would be willing to eat less meat and more grains and vegetables, if it would help provide food for starving people																
1. Disagree	10.5	17.5	4.0	10.6	11.0	11.4	10.6	9.9	10.2	8.1	13.0	8.9	9.9	7.1	13.9	28.1
2. Mostly disagree	10.2	14.4	6.2	10.4	8.3	8.5	12.6	8.6	11.2	10.0	10.2	9.8	11.2	9.9	10.0	6.8
3. Neither	13.4	16.7	10.3	14.6	8.5	13.8	13.6	12.1	15.2	13.3	13.9	13.8	12.3	15.7	13.2	2.7
4. Mostly agree	30.1	28.1	32.4	30.8	28.1	30.3	31.9	30.5	25.9	31.3	28.8	29.7	29.0	37.0	28.5	30.9
5. Agree	35.9	23.3	47.2	33.6	44.1	35.9	31.2	38.9	37.4	37.3	34.0	37.8	37.6	30.4	34.5	31.6
Item 8040 Subject F03,O03 N	3265	1521	1626	2469	438	666	910	1109	580	1813	1249	1203	732	427	787	41
A05: In the following list you will find some statements about leisure time and work. Please show whether you agree or disagree with each statement.																
A05A: I like the kind of work you can forget about after the work day is over																
1. Disagree	11.8	13.3	10.4	9.8	22.1	12.6	9.7	13.2	11.5	12.9	10.2	13.2	11.5	9.1	11.4	9.1
2. Mostly disagree	14.1	12.7	15.5	14.5	13.9	12.6	16.1	11.9	16.8	16.4	11.1	16.5	13.6	13.8	12.0	11.2
3. Neither	12.9	12.6	13.7	13.3	10.4	14.6	12.4	11.7	14.7	15.0	10.2	14.9	10.6	14.1	11.7	14.6
4. Mostly agree	25.3	23.9	26.9	26.8	20.9	25.3	25.2	25.2	25.7	26.3	23.9	23.2	26.0	23.8	28.5	30.9
5. Agree	35.8	37.6	33.5	35.6	32.8	34.9	36.4	38.2	31.3	29.4	44.6	32.2	38.4	39.3	36.4	34.3
Item 8050 Subject C04 N	3273	1525	1629	2476	441	670	913	1111	578	1820	1251	1208	734	428	789	41
A05B: To me, work is nothing more than mak- ing a living																
1. Disagree	38.9	33.3	43.9	39.7	37.4	36.9	34.8	39.9	45.7	43.9	32.1	44.2	36.8	32.4	37.4	34.3
2. Mostly disagree	28.8	29.6	28.9	31.2	19.6	28.9	33.2	25.4	28.3	30.5	26.3	26.7	25.1	37.1	31.7	30.0
3. Neither	8.7	8.8	8.4	9.4	5.6	10.6	9.9	7.4	7.1	8.4	8.8	9.2	9.4	6.8	8.0	8.1
4. Mostly agree	12.5	15.1	9.9	11.6	15.9	12.4	12.5	13.5	10.9	10.5	15.9	10.9	16.9	12.7	10.4	16.6
5. Agree	11.1	13.1	8.9	8.3	21.4	11.2	9.7	13.8	7.9	6.7	16.9	9.0	11.7	11.0	12.5	11.1
Item 8060 Subject C06 N	3276	1527	1631	2478	441	670	914	1112	581	1822	1252	1208	735	430	789	41
A05C: I expect my work to be a very central part of my life																
1. Disagree	4.4	4.9	4.0	4.4	3.8	3.6	4.5	5.2	3.7	3.2	5.4	4.6	3.3	2.8	6.1	4.9
2. Mostly disagree	8.4	7.6	9.3	9.4	3.8	10.0	8.2	7.9	7.9	8.7	8.1	8.4	8.1	10.6	8.1	5.3
3. Neither	12.0	12.9	11.3	12.9	6.3	13.4	13.2	9.4	13.7	11.8	12.6	12.0	12.4	12.8	11.7	13.7
4. Mostly agree	38.8	37.3	40.7	41.5	28.4	36.9	42.0	36.5	40.5	39.8	38.7	36.9	37.5	46.3	39.3	33.8
5. Agree	36.2	37.2	34.8	31.8	57.8	36.0	32.1	40.9	34.1	36.5	35.2	38.1	38.7	27.5	34.8	42.3
Item 8070 Subject C06 N	3263	1522	1622	2470	441	665	911	1107	580	1812	1249	1202	733	428	788	41
A05D: I want to do my best in my job, even if this sometimes means working overtime																
1. Disagree	1.5	2.0	1.1	1.4	1.3	1.5	1.6	1.7	1.3	1.2	1.9	1.4	1.2	0.7	2.4	2.5
2. Mostly disagree	2.3	3.0	1.8	2.3	2.7	2.0	2.8	1.9	2.9	2.1	2.5	1.9	2.5	2.9	2.3	4.5
3. Neither	4.2	4.6	3.7	4.6	2.2	5.2	5.2	3.1	3.5	4.1	4.0	2.8	4.3	5.1	5.0	7.6
4. Mostly agree	31.3	30.7	32.6	32.8	24.6	33.1	33.0	28.1	32.7	31.3	32.1	30.8	31.4	31.7	32.8	19.1
5. Agree	60.7	59.7	60.8	58.9	69.2	58.2	57.5	65.2	59.6	61.3	59.5	63.0	60.5	59.6	57.5	66.4
Item 8080 Subject C06 N	3277	1528	1631	2479	440	670	914	1112	581	1821	1252	1208	735	430	790	41

QUESTIONNAIRE FORM 3 1984	TOTAL	SEX		RACE		REGION				4YR COLLEGE PLANS		ILLICIT DRUG USE: LIFETIME				
		M	F	White	Black	NE	NC	S	W	Yes	No	None	Mari- juana Only	Few Pills	More Pills	Any Her- oin
N (Weighted No. of Cases):	3287	1532	1632	2482	442	675	914	1116	582	1823	1254	1211	735	430	791	41
% of Weighted Total:	100.0	46.6	49.6	75.5	13.4	20.5	27.8	33.9	17.7	55.5	38.1	36.8	22.4	13.1	24.1	1.3
A05E: I would like to stay in the same job for most of my adult life																
1. Disagree	14.7	12.5	16.2	13.1	20.2	15.9	13.9	14.6	14.9	13.2	16.8	12.7	15.4	14.5	17.1	18.8
2. Mostly disagree	13.0	11.6	14.2	12.9	13.8	12.3	13.0	13.3	13.0	12.6	13.4	11.5	11.6	15.3	14.7	22.3
3. Neither	15.3	15.3	15.5	16.1	10.8	15.2	14.6	13.4	20.0	16.8	13.1	15.8	15.4	12.5	17.0	6.2
4. Mostly agree	27.4	26.5	28.7	28.5	25.4	26.2	30.6	25.7	27.0	28.9	26.3	27.9	28.1	29.5	25.0	20.3
5. Agree	29.6	34.0	25.4	29.4	29.8	30.4	27.8	32.9	25.1	28.5	30.5	32.1	29.5	28.2	26.1	32.4
Item 8090 Subject C03 N	3269	1526	1625	2475	438	667	912	1109	580	1821	1245	1205	734	429	787	40
A06: If you were to get enough money to live as comfortably as you'd like for the rest of your life, would you want to work?																
1. I would want to work	76.5	74.0	78.9	75.9	79.2	74.3	78.5	75.6	77.2	78.2	74.9	79.9	78.4	77.8	68.7	76.1
2. I would not want to work	23.5	26.0	21.1	24.1	20.8	25.7	21.5	24.4	22.8	21.8	25.1	20.1	21.6	22.2	31.3	23.9
Item 8100 Subject C06 N	3212	1490	1611	2443	430	650	896	1091	574	1790	1225	1193	719	423	770	39

The next questions are about living or work- ing with people of different races. Please rate each of the statements below using the follow- ing terms:

Not at all acceptable: I'd avoid this if I possibly could.

Somewhat acceptable: I could live with this, but not be happy about it.

Acceptable: This would be O.K., or I'd be neu- tral about this.

Desirable: I'd really like this.

A07: How would you feel about . . .

A07A: Having close personal friends of another race?

	TOTAL	M	F	White	Black	NE	NC	S	W	Yes	No	None	Mari- juana Only	Few Pills	More Pills	Any Her- oin
1. Not at all acceptable	2.1	3.3	0.8	2.3	0.1	2.4	1.5	2.8	1.6	1.0	3.2	1.4	1.9	0.6	3.4	12.5
2. Somewhat acceptable	5.5	6.6	4.4	6.0	3.9	6.2	5.0	7.0	2.8	3.7	8.0	4.8	6.3	6.0	5.6	2.8
3. Acceptable	56.9	58.9	55.3	60.4	47.3	59.0	63.7	54.4	48.4	55.4	60.1	54.9	56.4	60.1	59.2	62.8
4. Desirable	35.5	31.3	39.4	31.2	48.7	32.4	29.7	35.9	47.2	39.9	28.7	38.9	35.5	33.3	31.7	21.9
Item 8110 Subject N01 N	3261	1519	1625	2468	438	664	914	1104	580	1811	1250	1204	728	429	786	41
A07B: Having a job with a supervisor of a dif- ferent race?																
1. Not at all acceptable	2.5	3.5	1.4	2.5	1.2	2.2	2.5	3.2	1.6	1.8	3.1	1.7	3.2	1.1	3.5	8.5
2. Somewhat acceptable	9.0	11.0	7.1	9.7	6.0	8.8	7.6	12.0	5.5	7.3	10.9	7.7	7.4	10.2	11.2	17.5
3. Acceptable	69.8	69.8	69.4	71.2	67.0	71.3	76.7	66.1	64.2	70.5	69.5	70.0	70.4	69.6	69.7	67.5
4. Desirable	18.7	15.7	22.1	16.6	25.9	17.6	13.2	18.7	28.8	20.4	16.5	20.7	19.0	19.1	15.6	6.5
Item 8120 Subject C05,N01 N	3260	1518	1625	2468	438	663	914	1104	580	1811	1249	1203	728	429	787	41
A07C: Having a family of a different race (but same level of education and income) move next door to you?																
1. Not at all acceptable	5.3	7.0	3.4	5.6	2.7	5.5	6.0	6.0	2.8	3.4	7.2	4.0	4.9	5.5	6.2	24.4
2. Somewhat acceptable	11.4	14.1	9.1	12.2	7.7	9.5	13.2	13.8	6.2	8.6	15.2	9.6	10.7	10.8	14.7	17.9
3. Acceptable	57.2	58.9	55.9	59.7	52.7	60.8	58.0	56.9	52.3	59.0	55.7	58.3	55.6	58.0	57.6	45.0
4. Desirable	26.0	20.0	31.6	22.4	37.0	24.1	22.8	23.2	38.8	29.0	21.9	28.1	28.8	25.6	21.5	12.6
Item 8130 Subject N01 N	3260	1517	1625	2468	436	664	913	1103	581	1810	1249	1204	727	428	787	41
A07D: Having your (future) children's friends be all of your race?																
1. Not at all acceptable	17.9	15.8	19.7	15.8	26.0	17.6	14.1	19.1	21.8	20.5	13.9	19.4	17.6	16.4	16.6	17.5
2. Somewhat acceptable	21.0	20.4	21.6	21.5	20.3	18.8	23.6	19.1	23.1	22.4	18.8	21.1	19.7	19.7	22.3	22.8
3. Acceptable	42.3	43.1	41.8	42.8	39.4	48.2	43.1	39.2	40.1	41.5	43.9	42.0	44.7	44.3	41.0	25.1
4. Desirable	18.8	20.7	16.9	19.9	14.4	15.4	19.1	22.6	15.0	15.6	23.5	17.5	17.9	19.6	20.2	34.6
Item 8140 Subject N01 N	3229	1501	1612	2448	430	658	908	1093	570	1799	1236	1188	724	428	779	40

QUESTIONNAIRE FORM 3 1984	TOTAL	SEX		RACE		REGION				4YR COLLEGE PLANS		ILLICIT DRUG USE: LIFETIME				
		M	F	White	Black	NE	NC	S	W	Yes	No	None	Mari- juana Only	Few Pills	More Pills	Any Her- oin
N (Weighted No. of Cases):	3287	1532	1632	2482	442	675	914	1116	582	1823	1254	1211	735	430	791	41
% of Weighted Total:	100.0	46.6	49.6	75.5	13.4	20.5	27.8	33.9	17.7	55.5	38.1	36.8	22.4	13.1	24.1	1.3
A07E: Having some of your (future) children's friends be of other races?																
1. Not at all acceptable	3.4	4.5	2.1	3.4	2.3	4.5	3.3	3.0	2.9	2.0	4.9	2.3	3.3	4.1	3.5	7.6
2. Somewhat acceptable	8.6	10.9	6.5	9.1	4.9	6.5	9.2	11.2	5.1	6.3	11.9	8.0	7.3	9.1	9.8	19.5
3. Acceptable	52.0	54.1	49.9	54.3	45.1	54.6	55.4	50.5	46.5	49.8	54.6	49.7	51.7	52.6	55.8	46.8
4. Desirable	36.0	30.5	41.6	33.1	47.7	34.4	32.1	35.2	45.5	41.9	28.6	40.0	37.7	34.2	31.0	26.2
Item 8150 Subject N01 N	3243	1511	1617	2454	435	658	911	1097	577	1803	1242	1201	724	427	779	41
A08: How would you feel about having a job where . . .																
A08A: . . . all the employees are of your race?																
1. Not at all acceptable	6.9	5.2	8.3	3.8	20.6	7.4	4.0	8.1	8.6	7.3	5.4	6.7	7.5	6.7	5.8	4.4
2. Somewhat acceptable	16.0	16.0	15.6	13.5	26.7	14.2	14.3	16.9	19.1	16.7	14.5	16.7	15.5	13.1	15.1	38.9
3. Acceptable	53.9	52.2	55.6	56.5	44.2	58.3	54.1	50.1	55.5	57.0	50.7	55.8	54.9	54.0	52.4	37.0
4. Desirable	23.3	26.5	20.6	26.2	8.5	20.1	27.7	24.9	16.8	19.0	29.4	20.8	22.1	26.2	26.7	19.7
Item 8160 Subject C05,N01 N	3256	1519	1620	2466	435	665	912	1102	577	1809	1247	1203	724	428	788	41
A08B: . . . some employees are of a different race?																
1. Not at all acceptable	1.0	1.5	0.3	0.9	0.6	0.9	1.2	0.8	1.1	0.6	1.4	0.6	1.0	0.9	1.0	6.3
2. Somewhat acceptable	4.8	6.0	3.5	4.8	5.3	4.4	5.8	5.5	2.1	3.1	6.5	4.2	5.1	4.1	5.4	6.3
3. Acceptable	66.2	68.9	63.7	69.6	54.8	69.3	69.3	64.1	61.9	64.5	69.0	63.3	66.5	66.5	70.9	65.7
4. Desirable	28.0	23.6	32.5	24.7	39.3	25.4	23.7	29.7	34.8	31.8	23.1	31.8	27.4	28.4	22.6	21.6
Item 8170 Subject C05,N01 N	3251	1515	1620	2461	438	661	911	1101	578	1807	1245	1199	725	427	787	41
A08C: . . . most employees are of a different race?																
1. Not at all acceptable	10.4	11.9	9.2	11.8	5.4	10.6	8.7	14.0	6.1	9.6	11.5	9.3	8.5	10.8	13.4	15.0
2. Somewhat acceptable	32.5	33.2	32.7	36.8	19.3	31.2	38.8	32.1	24.9	32.1	34.2	30.3	31.8	37.6	34.6	29.4
3. Acceptable	47.1	46.4	46.9	45.6	54.8	50.0	45.4	43.6	53.1	49.6	43.4	49.3	48.8	40.5	46.3	42.4
4. Desirable	10.0	8.5	11.2	5.8	20.5	8.2	7.2	10.3	15.9	8.7	10.9	11.1	10.9	11.1	5.8	13.2
Item 8180 Subject C05,N01 N	3249	1517	1617	2461	435	661	910	1101	578	1808	1243	1201	724	426	785	41
A09: How would you feel about living in an area where . . .																
A09A: . . . all the neighbors are of your race?																
1. Not at all acceptable	4.4	4.1	4.6	2.3	11.4	4.4	2.4	4.1	8.0	4.9	2.9	4.4	4.7	3.8	4.0	4.4
2. Somewhat acceptable	10.0	10.1	9.4	7.8	18.7	9.6	8.9	10.1	12.3	10.0	9.2	11.0	9.9	9.3	8.5	9.9
3. Acceptable	52.7	52.0	53.5	53.1	54.0	60.0	51.7	46.2	58.4	56.5	48.3	53.1	53.2	50.4	53.6	56.6
4. Desirable	32.9	33.7	32.4	36.7	15.9	26.0	37.0	39.6	21.3	28.6	39.6	31.6	32.2	36.6	33.9	29.1
Item 8190 Subject N01 N	3251	1516	1620	2467	434	663	911	1102	574	1807	1246	1203	724	427	787	40
A09B: . . . some of the neighbors are of other races?																
1. Not at all acceptable	1.7	2.0	1.3	1.7	1.0	1.8	1.5	2.3	0.8	1.4	2.2	1.3	2.2	1.1	1.8	1.7
2. Somewhat acceptable	7.6	9.8	5.5	7.9	6.0	7.2	7.7	9.8	3.6	5.6	9.4	6.6	7.1	8.5	8.2	16.2
3. Acceptable	67.9	68.9	66.5	70.8	59.0	69.9	69.7	66.6	65.0	68.6	67.8	66.8	66.1	67.7	71.8	68.2
4. Desirable	22.9	19.3	26.6	19.6	34.0	21.1	21.1	21.3	30.6	24.4	20.6	25.3	24.6	22.6	18.2	13.9
Item 8200 Subject N01 N	3252	1516	1621	2462	437	661	909	1101	580	1810	1246	1201	726	427	787	40
A09C: . . . most of the neighbors are of other races?																
1. Not at all acceptable	18.7	20.3	17.3	21.1	8.5	19.5	17.3	24.5	9.2	17.5	20.3	17.0	16.4	18.4	23.4	28.6
2. Somewhat acceptable	36.5	38.2	35.3	40.9	27.0	34.4	42.5	34.9	32.7	36.2	38.4	34.1	38.3	40.1	37.5	29.8
3. Acceptable	37.6	35.2	39.5	33.8	51.1	39.7	34.8	34.3	45.8	39.1	34.8	40.7	38.0	32.4	35.4	29.3
4. Desirable	7.1	6.3	7.9	4.1	13.4	6.5	5.4	6.2	12.4	7.1	6.5	8.2	7.3	9.1	3.7	12.3
Item 8210 Subject N01 N	3248	1515	1618	2461	434	661	908	1101	578	1807	1242	1202	724	427	785	40
A10: How would you feel about having your (future) children go to schools where . . .																

QUESTIONNAIRE FORM 3 1984	TOTAL	SEX		RACE		REGION				4YR COLLEGE PLANS		ILLICIT DRUG USE: LIFETIME				
		M	F	White	Black	NE	NC	S	W	Yes	No	None	Marijuana Only	Few Pills	More Pills	Any Heroin
N (Weighted No. of Cases):	3287	1532	1632	2482	442	675	914	1116	582	1823	1254	1211	735	430	791	41
% of Weighted Total:	100.0	46.6	49.6	75.5	13.4	20.5	27.8	33.9	17.7	55.5	38.1	36.8	22.4	13.1	24.1	1.3
A10A: . . . all the children are of your race?																
1. Not at all acceptable	9.3	7.6	10.7	6.0	23.8	9.1	4.5	11.9	12.0	10.7	6.2	10.3	9.4	9.1	6.9	6.8
2. Somewhat acceptable	13.0	12.8	12.6	10.2	23.2	11.5	10.1	12.9	19.2	14.9	9.6	13.6	12.5	10.2	13.0	13.7
3. Acceptable	47.9	48.0	48.1	49.7	42.0	54.7	49.2	42.4	48.3	49.2	46.6	48.6	48.5	48.5	47.4	48.7
4. Desirable	29.9	31.6	28.6	34.0	10.9	24.7	36.2	32.8	20.4	25.2	37.6	27.5	29.6	32.2	32.7	30.7
Item 8220 Subject B03,N01 N	3247	1515	1618	2463	431	663	909	1098	578	1807	1243	1201	721	429	785	41
A10B: . . . some of the children are of other races?																
1. Not at all acceptable	1.0	1.3	0.5	0.9	0.8	1.4	0.7	1.0	1.1	0.7	1.2	1.2	1.0	0.2	0.9	-
2. Somewhat acceptable	5.7	7.7	3.7	6.0	5.0	6.4	6.6	6.6	1.6	3.9	7.7	5.7	5.5	4.1	6.4	9.1
3. Acceptable	64.0	67.0	61.0	66.0	56.3	65.9	66.6	62.1	61.1	61.8	67.2	60.7	65.0	63.4	68.7	69.5
4. Desirable	29.3	24.0	34.8	27.1	37.9	26.3	26.1	30.2	36.1	33.6	24.0	32.5	28.5	32.2	24.0	21.4
Item 8230 Subject B03,N01 N	3248	1515	1617	2460	435	662	906	1101	579	1807	1242	1201	722	427	785	41
A10C: . . . most of the children are of other races?																
1. Not at all acceptable	22.1	24.4	20.3	25.5	8.8	23.3	22.1	26.6	12.2	21.3	23.7	19.7	20.1	23.1	27.6	22.7
2. Somewhat acceptable	35.2	35.3	35.3	39.1	25.2	35.8	40.5	33.1	30.2	34.3	37.5	34.7	35.5	39.0	34.8	25.0
3. Acceptable	35.5	33.5	37.1	31.8	48.6	34.0	33.4	32.8	45.8	37.8	32.1	37.3	37.7	29.8	32.9	46.1
4. Desirable	7.1	6.8	7.4	3.6	17.3	6.9	3.9	7.5	11.7	6.7	6.8	8.4	6.7	8.1	4.7	6.2
Item 8240 Subject B03,N01 N	3244	1513	1616	2460	431	662	907	1097	578	1807	1241	1199	722	427	786	41
A11: What race are your close friends?																
1. All my race	31.5	29.9	33.8	35.7	20.7	30.3	47.7	26.2	17.5	31.3	32.6	32.0	32.2	32.6	29.9	27.6
2. Almost all my race	30.7	30.2	31.3	33.5	24.3	34.8	28.5	31.4	27.9	29.4	32.4	28.6	31.6	33.0	32.6	32.6
3. Mostly my race	20.8	22.4	18.7	21.0	20.9	18.6	15.9	23.0	26.6	22.6	17.9	19.7	19.0	20.4	23.9	15.5
4. About half my race	10.8	11.1	10.2	7.7	21.2	8.1	5.3	13.7	17.0	9.8	11.8	12.0	11.4	8.6	8.7	19.1
5. Mostly other race(s)	3.8	3.9	3.5	1.5	6.6	5.4	1.5	2.7	7.7	4.0	3.3	4.7	3.3	2.9	3.2	2.9
6. Almost all other race(s)	2.5	2.4	2.6	0.7	6.3	2.8	1.2	3.0	3.4	2.8	1.9	3.0	2.7	2.5	1.7	2.4
Item 8250 Subject N03 N	3239	1508	1616	2451	436	665	903	1098	573	1799	1239	1197	720	426	782	41
A12: What race are the people in your neighborhood?																
1. All my race	47.8	46.9	48.6	53.6	33.7	45.8	65.4	46.3	25.1	45.3	52.1	47.5	48.6	48.9	47.2	39.4
2. Almost all my race	26.0	26.9	25.8	28.7	19.7	26.5	21.5	25.7	33.0	27.3	24.0	26.3	25.5	25.1	26.8	32.3
3. Mostly my race	11.8	12.3	11.2	11.2	15.1	12.4	6.9	13.1	16.5	12.3	11.4	9.7	12.2	12.4	14.6	11.8
4. About half my race	6.4	5.1	7.1	3.8	15.6	6.3	3.1	7.7	9.2	5.9	6.5	5.8	7.0	4.6	7.4	3.3
5. Mostly other race(s)	4.9	5.1	4.7	2.1	8.5	5.7	1.3	4.3	10.8	5.5	3.9	7.1	4.4	5.1	1.8	4.5
6. Almost all other race(s)	3.1	3.6	2.6	0.6	7.4	3.3	1.8	2.9	5.5	3.7	2.0	3.8	2.4	3.9	2.1	8.7
Item 8260 Subject N03 N	3240	1508	1616	2452	436	663	907	1097	574	1802	1239	1199	719	426	783	41
A13: What race were the students in the elementary school where you spent the most time?																
1. All my race	33.1	31.4	35.0	37.5	18.6	34.2	53.5	22.5	20.0	31.5	36.6	33.6	31.7	36.1	33.3	23.0
2. Almost all my race	28.7	30.6	27.2	32.7	18.1	31.5	27.8	25.8	32.6	30.2	26.4	26.9	26.9	30.1	32.9	17.6
3. Mostly my race	14.0	14.3	13.9	15.4	11.0	13.4	8.4	17.2	17.3	14.7	13.3	13.2	15.5	14.1	14.5	16.4
4. About half my race	14.4	13.5	15.0	10.6	29.5	11.1	5.8	23.8	14.0	13.1	15.9	14.9	15.2	12.7	12.4	27.5
5. Mostly other race(s)	5.9	6.2	5.3	2.4	14.5	5.9	2.4	6.7	9.8	5.9	5.1	6.8	6.3	4.5	4.4	10.5
6. Almost all other race(s)	3.8	4.1	3.7	1.3	8.2	3.9	2.1	3.9	6.3	4.5	2.6	4.6	4.3	2.6	2.4	4.9
Item 8270 Subject B03,N03 N	3236	1509	1612	2450	435	663	906	1095	572	1798	1238	1198	718	426	780	41
A14: What race are the students in your present school (if you are in school)?																
1. All my race	12.2	13.5	11.6	14.3	3.2	8.6	29.4	4.4	4.2	10.7	14.5	12.7	10.8	9.1	14.3	17.5
2. Almost all my race	30.0	30.6	29.8	34.9	19.1	36.2	39.2	21.9	23.5	32.3	28.0	28.9	31.5	35.1	27.6	35.2
3. Mostly my race	23.5	24.2	23.2	26.7	14.4	28.2	17.5	22.9	28.6	24.9	21.2	22.1	21.0	25.8	28.5	17.2
4. About half my race	22.5	20.5	23.7	19.4	35.1	15.1	9.5	37.0	24.1	19.7	26.6	23.0	24.4	20.8	20.8	20.4
5. Mostly other race(s)	7.1	6.6	7.1	3.2	15.9	6.6	2.8	8.4	11.8	7.5	6.0	8.1	7.8	5.6	4.6	9.6
6. Almost all other race(s)	4.7	4.6	4.6	1.5	12.3	5.2	1.7	5.4	7.7	4.9	3.8	5.1	4.4	3.7	4.2	-
Item 8280 Subject B03,N03 N	3238	1507	1615	2452	435	663	906	1095	574	1801	1238	1198	719	426	782	41

QUESTIONNAIRE FORM 3 1984	TOTAL	SEX		RACE		REGION				4YR COLLEGE PLANS		ILLICIT DRUG USE: LIFETIME				
		M	F	White	Black	NE	NC	S	W	Yes	No	None	Mari- juana Only	Few Pills	More Pills	Any Her- oin
N (Weighted No. of Cases):	3287	1532	1632	2482	442	675	914	1116	582	1823	1254	1211	735	430	791	41
% of Weighted Total:	100.0	46.6	49.6	75.5	13.4	20.5	27.8	33.9	17.7	55.5	38.1	36.8	22.4	13.1	24.1	1.3
A15: What race are the people that you work with on your job (if you have a job)?																
1. All my race	41.8	41.7	42.1	49.8	10.0	43.2	58.3	32.0	31.9	40.6	44.5	43.2	41.7	40.4	42.3	42.2
2. Almost all my race	21.4	20.4	22.8	24.2	10.2	22.9	21.0	20.7	21.3	20.9	22.4	19.8	18.3	25.9	24.3	17.0
3. Mostly my race	14.9	15.1	14.9	16.0	9.7	13.1	10.4	18.1	18.1	16.3	14.0	13.3	15.2	14.5	16.9	23.8
4. About half my race	11.1	11.6	9.8	6.9	30.1	9.0	4.5	17.4	12.4	11.3	9.5	11.1	13.3	9.3	9.1	8.8
5. Mostly other race(s)	6.7	7.5	5.9	2.1	27.4	8.0	3.5	7.6	8.6	6.8	6.3	8.2	6.6	5.8	4.9	3.9
6. Almost all other race(s)	4.2	3.8	4.5	1.0	12.6	3.8	2.4	4.1	7.8	4.1	3.4	4.3	4.8	4.2	2.5	4.3
Item 8290 Subject N03 N	2658	1286	1278	2052	314	568	745	878	467	1485	1011	939	596	353	669	41
A16: How often do you do things (like having a conversation, eating together, playing sports) with people of other races?																
1. Not at all	10.6	9.4	11.8	11.7	5.8	9.9	19.1	7.2	4.4	8.7	14.1	9.2	12.4	8.7	11.8	13.8
2. A little	28.6	28.3	29.1	31.8	20.8	29.6	37.1	26.1	19.0	25.7	32.0	29.9	27.6	25.6	29.9	20.8
3. Some	37.7	37.8	37.7	38.2	38.1	38.3	30.9	41.2	41.3	39.4	35.7	35.9	37.1	46.2	36.4	35.1
4. A lot	23.1	24.5	21.4	18.3	35.4	22.2	12.9	25.6	35.3	26.2	18.2	25.0	22.9	19.4	21.9	30.3
Item 8300 Subject N03 N	3241	1510	1618	2453	437	662	907	1098	574	1802	1241	1201	721	425	783	41
A17: Generally, how do you feel about the experiences you have had with people of other races?																
5. Very good	27.8	24.0	31.4	25.8	32.4	26.1	27.5	24.6	36.6	30.3	24.7	32.9	25.1	26.2	24.2	23.6
4. Mostly good	40.6	40.6	40.5	40.6	43.3	42.5	42.0	38.1	41.1	42.9	37.1	40.4	43.2	43.8	37.2	36.6
3. Mixed	28.9	31.5	26.4	30.3	24.2	28.2	28.0	33.9	21.3	25.1	34.0	24.7	28.7	27.8	34.9	34.8
2. Mostly bad	1.9	2.8	1.2	2.5	-	2.2	2.0	2.4	0.6	1.2	3.0	1.7	2.1	1.8	2.3	1.7
1. Very bad	0.8	1.1	0.4	0.8	0.1	1.0	0.5	1.0	0.4	0.4	1.2	0.3	1.0	0.3	1.4	3.3
Item 8310 Subject N03 N	3236	1509	1614	2447	438	661	905	1096	575	1800	1237	1198	719	426	783	41
A18: The next questions are about some of your own plans. Are you married or engaged?																
1. Married–SKIP TO Q.A20	0.6	0.4	0.8	0.5	0.3	0.3	0.6	0.5	1.1	0.2	1.2	0.6	0.7	0.6	0.5	3.6
2. Engaged	7.7	4.8	10.4	7.4	7.6	7.1	6.8	9.7	6.2	3.9	13.4	4.7	7.7	8.7	10.8	20.7
3. Neither	91.7	94.8	88.8	92.1	92.2	92.5	92.6	89.8	92.7	95.9	85.5	94.7	91.6	90.7	88.8	75.7
Item 8320 Subject D01,R01 N	3052	1400	1550	2356	376	623	862	1013	554	1736	1141	1132	685	404	733	39
A19: If it were just up to you, what would be the ideal time for you to get married?																
1. Within the next year or so	7.0	4.0	9.8	7.0	6.3	5.1	7.1	8.6	5.8	2.8	13.3	5.2	6.3	7.2	8.6	17.2
2. Two or three years from now	17.7	12.3	22.9	18.7	12.7	13.6	19.7	20.6	13.9	10.3	29.4	17.7	14.4	20.6	19.3	9.9
3. Four or five years from now	34.3	33.9	34.6	36.8	24.2	30.6	40.7	31.5	33.4	36.9	30.7	37.0	35.5	34.8	30.2	30.5
4. Over five years from now	36.2	44.3	29.1	34.2	44.8	46.3	29.3	33.0	41.6	45.5	22.0	35.7	38.3	36.0	36.4	33.0
5. I don't want to marry	4.8	5.5	3.7	3.4	11.9	4.3	3.2	6.3	5.2	4.5	4.6	4.4	5.6	1.3	5.5	9.4
Item 8330 Subject D01 N ★	3098	1436	1559	2387	393	633	877	1035	552	1760	1157	1139	685	417	756	38
A20: Have you thought at all about whether you'd like to have children or how many you'd like to have?																
3. I've thought about it a lot	40.6	27.4	53.1	39.8	46.3	38.1	39.8	43.1	40.2	38.5	44.4	39.9	39.5	42.0	41.4	42.1
2. I've thought about it a little	49.4	57.5	42.2	50.7	43.6	50.0	51.0	46.7	50.9	51.5	45.8	50.1	49.2	51.2	48.8	35.9
1. I haven't thought about it at all	10.0	15.2	4.7	9.6	10.1	11.9	9.2	10.2	8.9	9.9	9.8	10.0	11.3	6.8	9.9	22.0
Item 8340 Subject D02 N	3169	1480	1575	2407	417	642	895	1068	564	1763	1215	1165	705	422	767	41
A21: All things considered, if you could have exactly the number of children you want, what number would you choose to have?																
1. None	4.0	4.0	4.1	3.8	4.9	5.1	2.9	4.5	3.3	3.6	4.1	3.1	4.9	2.4	5.0	4.8
2. One	6.6	5.1	7.6	5.8	10.8	3.1	5.6	9.2	7.4	6.5	6.4	5.1	6.0	7.2	9.1	8.8
3. Two	47.2	47.9	46.4	46.9	51.0	40.8	45.6	51.5	49.1	44.3	51.6	44.1	53.2	51.4	43.4	58.9
4. Three	20.3	21.4	19.7	21.5	14.4	24.4	22.1	17.2	18.5	21.4	19.1	21.0	18.4	21.9	20.9	7.0
5. Four	10.4	8.6	12.1	11.1	8.4	11.1	12.9	8.8	9.0	11.1	9.6	11.6	10.4	7.9	10.6	5.2
6. Five	2.1	2.0	2.1	2.1	1.0	2.2	2.6	1.3	2.6	2.4	1.6	2.8	1.5	1.8	1.4	-
7. Six or more	2.5	2.3	2.7	2.4	3.0	3.9	2.3	1.7	3.0	3.1	1.8	2.8	1.4	2.3	2.5	15.4
8. Don't know	6.9	8.8	5.2	6.4	6.5	9.5	6.0	5.9	7.1	7.6	5.8	9.5	4.3	5.3	6.7	-
Item 8350 Subject D02 N	3229	1502	1615	2447	434	658	908	1088	576	1798	1236	1196	723	424	775	41

★=excludes respondents for whom question was inappropriate.

QUESTIONNAIRE FORM 3 1984	TOTAL	SEX		RACE		REGION				4YR COLLEGE PLANS		ILLICIT DRUG USE: LIFETIME				
		M	F	White	Black	NE	NC	S	W	Yes	No	None	Mari- juana Only	Few Pills	More Pills	Any Her- oin
N (Weighted No. of Cases):	3287	1532	1632	2482	442	675	914	1116	582	1823	1254	1211	735	430	791	41
% of Weighted Total:	100.0	46.6	49.6	75.5	13.4	20.5	27.8	33.9	17.7	55.5	38.1	36.8	22.4	13.1	24.1	1.3

A22: If the "population explosion" were NOT a problem, would you choose to have a larger number of children?

4. Yes, I'm sure I would want more	5.9	5.5	6.4	6.0	4.1	6.7	6.8	5.1	4.9	5.3	6.6	6.3	4.0	4.7	7.2	10.7
3. I probably would want more	10.8	10.0	11.3	10.5	9.4	12.2	11.3	9.6	10.5	10.9	10.7	11.7	8.1	12.4	10.2	9.9
2. I probably would not want more	35.8	38.2	34.1	37.6	30.9	31.8	42.0	33.5	34.9	35.2	38.1	34.7	40.6	37.1	34.6	23.3
1. I'm sure I would not want more	31.0	27.4	33.9	30.2	37.5	27.1	25.7	36.5	33.7	32.8	28.4	27.6	33.5	29.6	34.3	37.2
8. Don't know, no idea	16.5	18.9	14.4	15.8	18.1	22.2	14.1	15.4	16.0	15.8	16.2	19.7	13.8	16.2	13.7	18.9
Item 8360 Subject D02,E01 N	3246	1514	1620	2460	437	664	910	1095	577	1807	1242	1199	725	427	786	41

A23: If it were just up to you, how soon after getting married would you want to have your first child?

1. I don't want to have children (or get married)	4.1	4.0	4.2	3.7	5.4	4.8	2.9	4.5	4.2	3.7	4.0	3.5	4.8	2.6	5.0	-
2. I wouldn't wait at all	5.1	7.9	2.5	4.9	6.7	5.3	5.2	5.0	4.7	5.4	4.6	5.0	4.7	5.1	5.2	8.2
3. I would wait one year	29.5	34.8	24.5	28.8	32.7	29.3	31.6	25.7	33.5	26.7	33.3	29.2	31.0	31.2	27.6	28.8
4. I would wait two years	29.8	25.5	34.2	31.1	25.2	29.8	31.9	29.1	27.7	31.3	28.7	31.6	28.3	28.1	30.2	21.7
5. I would wait three years	13.6	9.7	17.0	14.1	10.5	12.2	14.0	15.2	11.5	14.0	13.4	14.1	13.5	14.4	12.5	18.6
6. I would wait four or five years	7.0	4.8	8.9	7.8	3.7	5.8	4.9	9.6	6.7	7.9	5.5	6.3	7.5	8.2	7.3	2.2
7. I would wait more than five years	2.5	2.2	2.8	1.9	5.0	1.3	2.0	3.6	2.6	2.4	2.5	2.2	2.4	2.4	2.8	8.1
8. Don't know, or already have a child	8.5	11.0	5.9	7.7	10.9	11.4	7.5	7.3	9.0	8.6	7.9	8.0	7.8	8.1	9.3	12.3
Item 8370 Subject D02 N	3220	1497	1612	2441	432	654	905	1085	576	1792	1234	1195	718	427	771	41

A24: Now we'd like you to make some ratings of how good or bad a job you feel each of the following organizations is doing for the country as a whole. For each one, mark the circle that best describes how you feel.

How good or bad a job is being done for the country as a whole by...

A24A: Large corporations?

1. Very poor	2.1	2.9	1.2	1.9	2.2	3.2	2.1	1.8	1.7	2.0	1.9	1.7	2.2	0.9	3.1	12.2
2. Poor	6.0	7.7	4.2	5.8	6.0	8.0	5.3	5.8	5.1	6.9	4.6	5.9	5.5	6.0	6.3	3.8
3. Fair	30.7	33.7	27.8	30.9	31.4	29.0	32.7	29.3	32.3	29.2	33.1	30.0	31.5	33.2	31.0	18.1
4. Good	36.6	35.3	38.5	38.9	29.5	34.2	36.2	37.2	38.7	39.2	34.5	36.7	36.3	38.9	35.7	45.4
5. Very good	8.8	10.0	7.4	8.3	10.0	8.5	7.8	10.4	7.9	8.8	8.2	8.7	9.5	6.9	8.6	10.1
8. No opinion	15.7	10.4	20.9	14.2	20.9	17.0	15.9	15.6	14.3	13.9	17.7	17.0	15.1	14.2	15.2	10.5
Item 8380 Subject K02 N	3234	1513	1610	2454	435	655	907	1097	576	1798	1245	1196	724	425	779	41

A24B: Major labor unions?

1. Very poor	4.8	7.0	2.8	5.8	1.4	2.1	5.9	5.9	4.0	5.8	3.6	6.4	3.4	3.0	4.3	7.6
2. Poor	13.7	17.6	9.8	15.1	7.0	10.5	15.9	14.0	13.1	14.8	11.6	15.1	10.4	12.1	15.4	17.6
3. Fair	32.4	31.7	33.0	32.0	32.9	32.4	31.5	31.3	35.6	32.1	32.8	31.1	37.1	35.4	29.5	18.0
4. Good	25.2	24.7	25.9	25.0	27.1	29.3	24.9	23.3	24.6	25.6	25.3	25.2	24.4	24.3	25.5	27.6
5. Very good	6.4	7.4	5.2	5.4	8.9	8.2	4.9	6.3	7.1	5.9	6.8	4.7	6.1	7.8	7.8	19.2
8. No opinion	17.6	11.6	23.4	16.7	22.7	17.6	17.0	19.2	15.6	15.8	19.9	17.5	18.6	17.4	17.5	10.0
Item 8390 Subject K02 N	3235	1514	1612	2456	433	656	908	1094	577	1801	1244	1197	721	426	783	41

A24C: The nation's colleges and universities?

1. Very poor	0.7	1.3	0.1	0.6	1.1	0.9	0.8	0.7	0.3	0.5	1.0	0.5	0.6	0.5	0.9	3.6
2. Poor	2.0	2.6	1.3	1.9	2.1	2.5	2.3	1.7	1.5	1.2	2.8	2.0	1.8	1.6	2.1	5.0
3. Fair	13.9	14.5	12.9	12.9	16.8	13.2	13.9	15.2	12.1	11.3	17.1	13.9	13.9	13.7	13.9	13.4
4. Good	43.5	42.7	44.6	44.6	41.2	42.5	46.6	42.5	41.6	44.5	42.9	44.1	46.6	44.1	41.3	13.0
5. Very good	35.6	34.8	36.5	36.4	32.0	35.4	32.4	35.5	41.2	39.8	29.9	35.6	33.4	36.0	36.5	53.1
8. No opinion	4.3	4.2	4.6	3.6	6.8	5.6	4.0	4.4	3.3	2.6	6.3	3.9	3.6	4.1	5.3	12.0
Item 8400 Subject B10,K02 N	3239	1512	1617	2459	435	656	910	1095	578	1806	1244	1197	725	428	782	40

QUESTIONNAIRE FORM 3 1984	TOTAL	SEX		RACE		REGION				4YR COLLEGE PLANS		ILLICIT DRUG USE: LIFETIME				
		M	F	White	Black	NE	NC	S	W	Yes	No	None	Mari-juana Only	Few Pills	More Pills	Any Her-oin
N (Weighted No. of Cases):	3287	1532	1632	2482	442	675	914	1116	582	1823	1254	1211	735	430	791	41
% of Weighted Total:	100.0	46.6	49.6	75.5	13.4	20.5	27.8	33.9	17.7	55.5	38.1	36.8	22.4	13.1	24.1	1.3

A24D: The nation's public schools?

1. Very poor	5.1	5.3	5.0	5.3	5.3	6.3	4.0	5.7	4.6	5.2	5.1	5.8	4.4	3.5	5.6	9.6
2. Poor	13.5	13.8	13.3	14.5	9.3	14.4	13.0	12.1	16.1	15.1	11.6	13.1	13.5	11.1	14.8	29.4
3. Fair	34.4	33.9	35.2	35.5	29.7	32.7	36.5	32.2	37.5	35.8	32.1	32.9	38.0	36.0	34.0	20.3
4. Good	32.8	34.0	31.4	32.7	33.0	33.8	33.5	32.9	30.5	32.6	33.8	34.4	32.1	34.7	30.5	28.6
5. Very good	11.0	9.6	12.2	9.8	16.5	8.9	10.3	13.9	9.2	9.2	13.4	11.0	9.1	11.9	11.7	12.1
8. No opinion	3.1	3.4	2.8	2.1	6.3	4.0	2.7	3.3	2.2	2.1	4.0	2.8	2.9	2.8	3.4	-
Item 8410 Subject B10,K02 N	3234	1512	1612	2456	431	658	908	1091	577	1801	1241	1192	724	427	783	41

A24E: Churches and religious organizations?

1. Very poor	2.1	2.9	1.3	2.1	1.4	2.7	1.2	1.9	3.3	2.1	2.2	1.9	1.1	1.9	3.4	4.6
2. Poor	5.6	7.0	4.3	5.8	3.4	7.4	5.3	4.6	6.1	6.0	4.8	5.8	4.8	4.8	6.4	9.2
3. Fair	24.2	24.1	24.5	25.4	19.7	28.6	23.1	21.1	26.7	24.3	24.3	22.4	24.5	26.7	25.5	25.9
4. Good	35.0	33.2	37.2	36.1	31.3	36.8	38.3	32.7	32.3	36.5	33.5	35.8	38.1	36.0	31.6	21.0
5. Very good	21.3	20.1	22.1	18.8	33.4	12.8	20.3	28.9	18.0	20.9	21.7	24.5	20.4	18.8	17.2	27.8
8. No opinion	11.8	12.6	10.7	11.7	10.9	11.6	11.8	10.9	13.7	10.2	13.5	9.7	11.1	11.8	15.8	11.5
Item 8420 Subject G,K02 N	3243	1516	1615	2461	433	658	910	1097	578	1805	1247	1200	726	427	781	41

A24F: The national news media (TV, magazines, news services)?

1. Very poor	4.2	5.0	3.5	4.8	1.8	4.4	4.3	4.5	3.1	5.2	3.0	4.9	3.2	3.7	3.5	11.9
2. Poor	7.4	8.1	7.0	8.1	5.7	7.0	8.8	7.4	5.8	8.5	5.8	8.5	8.2	5.3	6.5	5.3
3. Fair	27.0	26.2	27.8	27.8	24.9	27.2	27.0	26.4	27.6	26.9	27.6	27.8	26.6	24.9	28.5	22.0
4. Good	35.9	35.4	36.7	36.9	30.2	36.8	35.9	33.9	38.8	35.5	36.7	35.8	36.2	36.5	35.2	37.7
5. Very good	20.7	21.1	19.6	18.3	29.8	20.3	18.7	22.8	20.0	20.7	20.4	18.6	21.4	24.5	20.7	18.4
8. No opinion	4.9	4.2	5.4	4.0	7.6	4.2	5.3	4.9	4.7	3.3	6.6	4.4	4.4	5.1	5.7	4.8
Item 8430 Subject K02 N	3244	1515	1618	2463	433	659	910	1098	577	1806	1247	1199	725	428	784	41

A24G: The President and his administration?

1. Very poor	7.8	7.4	7.6	5.9	17.0	9.8	7.5	6.7	7.9	7.2	8.0	6.1	10.2	5.3	8.9	9.6
2. Poor	10.6	10.1	10.8	8.2	21.7	11.7	12.2	9.4	9.0	9.1	12.6	8.8	12.8	8.5	11.7	20.0
3. Fair	28.3	27.1	30.2	27.5	31.1	29.4	32.0	25.3	26.9	26.5	31.2	27.6	29.3	30.4	28.4	12.5
4. Good	30.6	31.5	29.7	34.9	10.2	28.1	30.0	31.6	32.3	34.3	25.9	32.7	27.8	32.3	29.1	28.8
5. Very good	13.3	17.0	9.9	15.9	3.4	10.7	10.6	17.3	12.7	15.4	11.1	15.8	10.0	15.0	12.1	15.4
8. No opinion	9.5	7.0	11.9	7.6	16.6	10.3	7.7	9.6	11.2	7.5	11.2	9.0	10.0	8.6	9.7	13.7
Item 8440 Subject H04,K02 N	3238	1514	1614	2456	436	656	910	1095	578	1808	1240	1198	725	427	782	40

A24H: Congress–that is, the U.S. Senate and House of Representatives?

1. Very poor	4.4	6.4	2.5	4.4	4.6	5.4	4.6	3.9	3.9	3.8	5.0	3.6	5.1	2.3	5.9	13.2
2. Poor	9.9	11.2	8.3	9.5	11.9	8.6	11.3	10.1	8.7	10.1	9.9	10.0	10.4	8.3	9.0	17.2
3. Fair	37.3	37.2	37.7	36.6	39.5	37.6	36.6	37.6	37.5	36.8	38.8	38.1	36.6	35.4	38.6	29.3
4. Good	28.3	28.8	27.9	31.2	16.3	25.5	28.3	29.3	29.4	31.8	23.8	28.2	28.3	34.7	25.3	30.4
5. Very good	3.3	4.0	2.7	3.2	4.0	3.3	3.5	3.6	2.9	3.4	3.1	3.8	2.1	3.7	3.6	3.2
8. No opinion	16.7	12.3	20.9	15.2	23.8	19.6	15.7	15.5	17.6	14.1	19.4	16.3	17.5	15.6	17.7	6.6
Item 8450 Subject H04,K02 N	3239	1516	1612	2457	434	655	908	1098	578	1803	1245	1197	724	428	782	41

A24I: The U.S. Supreme Court?

1. Very poor	2.9	4.0	1.8	3.0	2.0	4.5	2.9	2.5	2.2	2.2	4.0	2.5	3.0	2.4	3.8	5.7
2. Poor	5.9	6.0	5.5	6.2	4.5	7.8	5.5	5.3	5.4	6.0	5.9	5.8	6.7	4.9	5.9	6.1
3. Fair	28.6	27.9	29.7	27.4	34.3	28.0	29.4	29.3	26.6	25.9	32.9	27.6	27.2	25.9	32.3	37.5
4. Good	34.3	35.3	33.3	36.7	24.6	34.1	32.4	35.2	35.6	38.9	28.2	36.9	32.9	38.5	30.4	24.3
5. Very good	8.8	10.9	6.7	8.5	10.9	5.9	9.3	9.7	9.4	9.6	7.3	9.1	8.9	8.1	7.4	13.2
8. No opinion	19.6	15.9	23.0	18.3	23.7	19.7	20.6	18.1	20.7	17.5	21.7	18.0	21.4	20.2	20.3	13.2
Item 8460 Subject H04,K02 N	3233	1514	1610	2455	433	656	909	1092	576	1804	1241	1196	723	428	780	41

A24J: All the courts and the justice system in general?

1. Very poor	5.7	7.4	4.0	5.8	4.7	8.6	5.1	4.7	5.1	5.5	6.2	5.7	5.2	4.1	6.8	18.3
2. Poor	15.0	15.9	14.2	15.8	11.5	17.8	14.4	14.1	14.4	15.7	13.8	14.0	15.8	17.5	14.7	16.2
3. Fair	37.3	36.3	38.5	37.1	40.1	32.0	39.4	40.8	33.6	37.6	37.5	36.3	35.3	38.2	23.2
4. Good	24.9	25.8	24.2	25.8	20.5	25.0	24.8	21.8	31.0	26.0	23.2	25.3	25.8	25.2	23.5	23.2
5. Very good	3.8	3.6	4.0	3.2	5.9	3.6	2.8	4.8	4.0	3.8	4.0	4.0	4.0	3.3	3.1	11.7
8. No opinion	13.2	10.9	15.0	12.2	17.4	13.0	13.5	13.9	12.0	11.4	15.3	12.4	12.8	14.6	13.7	13.9
Item 8470 Subject H04,K02 N	3232	1511	1613	2456	433	656	905	1095	576	1803	1240	1197	720	427	781	41

QUESTIONNAIRE FORM 3 1984	TOTAL	SEX		RACE		REGION				4YR COLLEGE PLANS		ILLICIT DRUG USE: LIFETIME				
		M	F	White	Black	NE	NC	S	W	Yes	No	None	Marijuana Only	Few Pills	More Pills	Any Heroin
N (Weighted No. of Cases):	3287	1532	1632	2482	442	675	914	1116	582	1823	1254	1211	735	430	791	41
% of Weighted Total:	100.0	46.6	49.6	75.5	13.4	20.5	27.8	33.9	17.7	55.5	38.1	36.8	22.4	13.1	24.1	1.3

A24K: The police and other law enforcement agencies?

	TOTAL	M	F	White	Black	NE	NC	S	W	Yes	No	None	Mar.	Few	More	Any
1. Very poor	5.9	7.7	4.1	5.4	7.9	8.6	4.6	5.3	6.2	5.3	6.6	4.0	6.4	5.2	8.7	11.2
2. Poor	13.5	12.6	14.0	13.5	14.4	13.1	12.8	15.4	11.4	12.8	14.3	12.4	14.6	11.1	15.4	16.3
3. Fair	39.0	37.3	41.3	39.8	38.9	40.7	41.2	37.1	37.2	39.5	38.7	42.1	37.8	41.4	35.8	15.4
4. Good	29.5	30.7	28.5	30.9	23.5	27.2	30.4	28.6	32.7	32.6	25.5	29.5	30.2	31.0	28.2	33.5
5. Very good	7.4	7.6	7.1	6.7	8.2	4.8	6.7	8.9	8.4	6.3	9.0	7.8	6.8	7.3	6.4	18.6
8. No opinion	4.7	4.1	5.1	3.7	7.0	5.6	4.4	4.7	4.1	3.5	5.8	4.1	4.3	4.1	5.5	5.0
Item 8480　Subject K02　　　N	3245	1517	1619	2463	436	657	912	1099	578	1805	1248	1200	726	428	785	40

A24L: The U.S. military?

	TOTAL	M	F	White	Black	NE	NC	S	W	Yes	No	None	Mar.	Few	More	Any
1. Very poor	2.4	2.9	1.8	2.5	1.1	3.4	2.0	1.4	3.7	2.3	2.2	1.8	2.6	1.4	3.6	4.6
2. Poor	3.2	3.9	2.7	3.3	2.8	4.4	3.3	2.4	3.2	4.2	1.9	3.5	1.9	3.8	3.6	5.5
3. Fair	22.2	23.1	21.5	21.9	23.9	22.1	25.4	18.5	24.3	22.5	21.9	24.2	22.1	18.1	21.5	23.0
4. Good	36.2	35.6	37.3	38.4	27.7	34.8	36.5	36.8	36.1	38.3	33.8	35.4	37.0	40.9	34.8	28.3
5. Very good	24.8	27.5	21.8	23.5	33.6	22.6	21.8	30.5	21.1	23.2	27.2	24.6	25.0	23.8	25.3	29.7
8. No opinion	11.2	7.0	15.0	10.3	10.9	12.6	10.9	10.3	11.6	9.5	12.9	10.6	11.3	12.0	11.1	8.9
Item 8490　Subject K02,L04　N	3238	1516	1612	2457	436	657	908	1096	578	1804	1244	1197	723	428	782	41

A25: All things considered, do you think the armed services presently have too much or too little influence on the way this country is run?

	TOTAL	M	F	White	Black	NE	NC	S	W	Yes	No	None	Mar.	Few	More	Any
1. Far too little	3.6	4.9	2.2	3.2	4.8	4.8	2.7	4.2	2.2	3.0	4.4	3.4	3.9	2.8	3.6	5.4
2. Too little	15.8	15.7	15.7	15.9	16.5	15.7	14.7	19.3	11.3	15.7	15.7	14.3	17.3	12.2	18.8	19.1
3. About right	62.3	61.5	63.6	63.3	57.6	59.2	63.4	64.1	60.8	62.2	63.3	62.8	59.3	69.1	61.2	54.5
4. Too much	14.7	13.6	15.7	14.4	15.9	16.1	15.8	10.3	19.6	15.8	13.1	16.2	15.8	13.2	12.3	12.6
5. Far too much	3.6	4.3	2.8	3.2	5.2	4.2	3.5	2.1	6.1	3.3	3.4	3.3	3.7	2.8	4.0	8.5
Item 8500　Subject K03,L04　N	3208	1503	1595	2430	433	650	900	1085	574	1790	1229	1190	722	422	765	40

A26: Do you think the U.S. spends too much or too little on the armed services?

	TOTAL	M	F	White	Black	NE	NC	S	W	Yes	No	None	Mar.	Few	More	Any
1. Far too little	4.9	7.3	2.4	5.2	4.8	4.6	4.6	6.5	2.6	4.7	5.3	4.4	6.2	1.6	5.8	12.9
2. Too little	17.6	19.6	15.5	18.1	15.9	13.2	16.1	23.3	13.9	18.0	16.7	16.3	16.4	18.3	20.0	17.9
3. About right	39.4	35.7	43.5	40.4	38.8	37.5	39.1	41.4	38.5	37.6	42.9	40.3	37.1	43.6	38.8	28.4
4. Too much	27.0	26.6	27.6	26.5	25.2	30.0	31.4	21.7	26.8	27.2	26.2	28.3	27.7	25.8	25.4	24.2
5. Far too much	11.1	10.8	11.0	9.8	15.2	14.6	8.8	7.2	18.2	12.5	8.8	10.7	12.6	10.7	10.0	16.6
Item 8510　Subject K03,L04　N	3209	1505	1596	2430	434	650	898	1089	571	1793	1227	1192	724	421	766	40

A27: Next are some questions which ask about your experiences and attitudes concerning particular drugs. First we want your answers about some drugs that can be bought at a drugstore without a doctor's prescription– sometimes called over-the-counter or non-prescription drugs.

DURING THE LAST 12 MONTHS, on how many occasions have you...

A27A: . . . used non-prescription drugs which are supposed to relieve pain (such as aspirin, Anacin, Bufferin, or Excedrin)?

	TOTAL	M	F	White	Black	NE	NC	S	W	Yes	No	None	Mar.	Few	More	Any
1. 0 occasions	7.8	10.4	4.9	5.0	20.0	8.1	6.8	7.6	9.2	6.7	7.9	10.8	7.4	4.7	4.8	-
2. 1-2	17.0	18.8	15.0	14.7	28.1	15.7	14.1	20.2	16.9	15.0	19.5	20.8	17.4	15.3	10.9	18.7
3. 3-5	18.5	20.6	16.7	17.6	21.6	20.1	17.7	16.7	21.7	17.3	20.0	20.0	22.5	17.0	13.4	19.5
4. 6-9	14.6	14.3	15.0	15.4	10.7	13.5	15.0	15.0	14.4	14.1	16.0	13.0	15.9	13.8	17.0	5.7
5. 10-19	17.3	16.4	18.4	19.3	8.9	17.8	18.1	16.1	17.6	19.8	14.7	16.5	14.8	22.6	19.2	8.7
6. 20-39	11.3	8.2	14.3	12.6	6.0	12.0	13.4	10.3	9.3	12.4	10.1	9.5	10.0	12.7	14.2	18.1
7. 40 or more	13.5	11.3	15.7	15.5	4.7	12.9	15.0	14.2	10.8	14.8	11.8	9.4	12.0	13.9	20.5	29.3
Item 8520　Subject A01b　　N	3254	1516	1628	2466	439	667	906	1107	574	1816	1247	1210	733	430	784	41

QUESTIONNAIRE FORM 3 1984	TOTAL	SEX		RACE		REGION				4YR COLLEGE PLANS		ILLICIT DRUG USE: LIFETIME				
		M	F	White	Black	NE	NC	S	W	Yes	No	None	Mari-juana Only	Few Pills	More Pills	Any Her-oin
N (Weighted No. of Cases): % of Weighted Total:	3287 100.0	1532 46.6	1632 49.6	2482 75.5	442 13.4	675 20.5	914 27.8	1116 33.9	582 17.7	1823 55.5	1254 38.1	1211 36.8	735 22.4	430 13.1	791 24.1	41 1.3
A27B: . . . used non-prescription drugs that are supposed to help people get to sleep (such as Sleep-Eze, Sominex, or Nytol)?																
1. 0 occasions	87.6	86.9	88.8	88.2	86.6	89.3	87.7	86.9	86.8	89.1	86.6	93.7	91.2	86.6	77.4	63.5
2. 1-2	6.0	6.3	5.4	5.9	6.9	5.0	5.9	6.5	6.3	5.4	6.2	3.7	4.7	8.3	9.0	15.3
3. 3-5	3.0	3.1	2.8	3.0	3.4	2.8	3.2	2.9	3.3	2.5	3.7	1.4	2.1	2.8	6.3	3.2
4. 6-9	1.5	1.6	1.5	1.3	1.2	0.8	1.6	1.8	1.6	1.4	1.7	0.7	1.0	0.7	3.4	3.7
5. 10-19	1.1	1.3	0.9	1.2	0.9	1.4	0.8	1.0	1.5	0.9	1.0	0.2	0.6	1.1	2.7	5.2
6. 20-39	0.2	0.1	0.3	0.3	-	-	0.2	0.3	0.4	0.1	0.4	0.2	0.2	0.3	0.2	-
7. 40 or more	0.5	0.6	0.2	0.2	0.9	0.7	0.6	0.5	0.1	0.5	0.4	0.1	0.2	0.3	1.1	9.1
Item 8530 Subject A01b N	3247	1511	1625	2462	435	666	904	1101	575	1815	1243	1208	733	428	782	41
A27C: . . . used non-prescription drugs that are supposed to help people stay awake (such as No-Doz, Wake, or Vivarin)?																
1. 0 occasions	83.1	81.9	84.4	81.8	92.3	85.0	83.4	83.6	79.8	83.6	83.4	93.8	89.1	84.9	62.5	45.0
2. 1-2	6.7	6.9	6.3	7.2	3.1	5.4	6.0	6.9	8.8	6.5	6.3	3.4	4.7	9.2	12.2	7.4
3. 3-5	3.6	4.2	3.2	4.0	1.8	3.5	2.6	4.0	4.4	3.6	3.6	1.3	2.4	2.9	8.2	11.3
4. 6-9	2.2	2.1	2.3	2.4	1.4	2.2	2.1	1.8	2.9	2.3	1.8	0.5	1.5	1.7	5.2	8.9
5. 10-19	2.0	2.3	1.8	2.3	0.3	1.6	2.9	1.7	1.6	2.0	1.9	0.5	1.8	0.7	4.7	9.0
6. 20-39	0.8	1.0	0.6	0.9	0.2	0.6	1.0	0.6	0.9	0.6	1.2	0.1	0.1	0.4	2.2	9.1
7. 40 or more	1.6	1.7	1.4	1.4	1.0	1.6	1.8	1.4	1.7	1.4	1.7	0.3	0.3	0.3	5.1	9.2
Item 8540 Subject A01b N	3249	1515	1625	2466	434	666	908	1099	577	1815	1244	1208	732	430	784	41
A27D: . . . used non-prescription drugs that are supposed to calm people down–keep them from being nervous or in a bad mood (such as Cope, Compoz, Devarex, or Miles Nervine)?																
1. 0 occasions	94.1	94.3	94.3	94.6	93.9	95.3	93.8	92.6	96.0	95.9	92.0	98.0	97.6	96.5	86.4	55.8
2. 1-2	2.5	2.5	2.5	2.6	2.0	2.0	2.9	3.2	1.3	2.0	3.2	0.9	0.9	1.8	6.0	13.5
3. 3-5	1.2	1.0	1.4	1.1	1.8	0.7	1.0	1.7	1.2	0.8	1.9	0.5	0.4	1.0	3.2	3.1
4. 6-9	0.7	0.6	0.7	0.5	0.7	0.3	0.9	0.8	0.6	0.6	0.8	0.1	0.7	0.2	1.4	4.1
5. 10-19	0.5	0.7	0.4	0.6	0.4	0.9	0.5	0.4	0.4	0.4	0.6	0.2	-	0.3	0.9	14.5
6. 20-39	0.3	0.2	0.4	0.2	0.2	-	0.4	0.5	0.3	0.1	0.7	0.1	0.3	0.3	0.5	3.2
7. 40 or more	0.6	0.7	0.3	0.3	0.9	0.8	0.4	0.8	0.2	0.4	0.8	0.1	0.2	-	1.6	5.8
Item 8550 Subject A01b N	3248	1513	1626	2466	435	666	905	1103	574	1815	1244	1207	733	428	784	41
A28: Individuals differ in whether or not they disapprove of people doing certain things. Do YOU disapprove of people (who are 18 or older) doing each of the following?																
A28A: Smoking one or more packs of cigarettes per day																
1. Don't disapprove	27.0	27.8	26.1	29.2	13.6	28.2	29.6	26.7	22.4	21.5	35.0	15.0	25.7	28.0	44.8	53.8
2. Disapprove	37.0	34.4	39.3	37.0	38.8	38.2	34.9	37.1	38.5	38.2	35.3	36.9	38.0	40.5	34.7	25.7
3. Strongly disapprove	36.0	37.8	34.5	33.8	47.6	33.6	35.5	36.2	39.2	40.3	29.6	48.1	36.3	31.4	20.4	20.5
Item 8560 Subject A11a N	3254	1519	1624	2470	439	666	907	1104	577	1816	1245	1208	732	430	787	40
A28B: Trying marijuana (pot, grass) once or twice																
1. Don't disapprove	50.7	51.9	49.2	52.5	39.1	60.9	47.8	43.1	58.2	49.6	52.4	17.0	64.3	62.4	83.4	67.2
2. Disapprove	22.2	21.1	23.5	22.2	25.0	19.4	25.0	23.1	19.2	23.1	20.7	29.1	22.0	23.6	9.7	26.5
3. Strongly disapprove	27.1	27.0	27.3	25.2	35.9	19.7	27.2	33.8	22.6	27.3	26.9	53.9	13.8	14.0	7.0	6.3
Item 8570 Subject A11a N	3247	1514	1624	2465	438	665	906	1103	573	1812	1244	1208	732	428	784	40
A28C: Smoking marijuana occasionally																
1. Don't disapprove	36.5	37.9	34.8	37.7	28.1	46.0	33.8	30.5	41.5	33.3	40.7	8.1	41.4	43.3	71.1	64.1
2. Disapprove	24.8	25.0	24.9	24.6	27.1	25.7	24.5	24.0	26.0	26.3	22.7	23.8	32.2	29.3	17.1	14.0
3. Strongly disapprove	38.6	37.2	40.4	37.8	44.8	28.4	41.7	45.5	32.4	40.4	36.6	68.1	26.5	27.4	11.8	22.0
Item 8580 Subject A11a N	3246	1515	1622	2465	437	664	903	1102	577	1813	1242	1204	731	430	785	40

QUESTIONNAIRE FORM 3 1984	TOTAL	SEX		RACE		REGION				4YR COLLEGE PLANS		ILLICIT DRUG USE: LIFETIME				
		M	F	White	Black	NE	NC	S	W	Yes	No	None	Mari- juana Only	Few Pills	More Pills	Any Her- oin
N (Weighted No. of Cases):	3287	1532	1632	2482	442	675	914	1116	582	1823	1254	1211	735	430	791	41
% of Weighted Total:	100.0	46.6	49.6	75.5	13.4	20.5	27.8	33.9	17.7	55.5	38.1	36.8	22.4	13.1	24.1	1.3
A28D: Smoking marijuana regularly																
1. Don't disapprove	15.3	17.6	12.8	15.3	11.7	21.0	12.6	13.1	17.0	11.0	21.2	2.7	11.4	13.8	37.0	53.9
2. Disapprove	25.1	26.6	23.0	25.5	23.9	27.1	23.7	23.2	28.3	25.6	24.2	12.7	31.7	31.7	33.8	25.8
3. Strongly disapprove	59.7	55.9	64.2	59.2	64.4	51.8	63.7	63.6	54.7	63.4	54.6	84.6	56.9	54.4	29.2	20.3
Item 8590 Subject A11a N	3244	1515	1620	2468	436	661	905	1102	577	1815	1237	1208	731	429	781	40
A28E: Trying LSD once or twice																
1. Don't disapprove	11.1	13.6	8.2	12.0	5.3	15.7	10.2	8.8	11.7	10.9	11.6	3.1	6.7	8.3	27.4	40.9
2. Disapprove	16.8	15.7	17.8	17.5	14.1	18.1	16.5	15.3	18.8	17.0	17.5	13.0	16.2	19.6	21.0	31.8
3. Strongly disapprove	72.0	70.6	74.0	70.5	80.6	66.2	73.3	75.9	69.5	72.1	70.9	83.9	77.1	72.2	51.6	27.3
Item 8600 Subject A11a N	3249	1517	1623	2468	438	664	906	1103	576	1816	1242	1208	731	430	785	40
A28F: Taking LSD regularly																
1. Don't disapprove	3.2	4.4	1.6	2.9	3.2	4.1	3.3	2.6	2.9	2.5	3.7	1.3	1.8	0.8	6.9	30.8
2. Disapprove	11.1	11.7	10.1	10.8	10.8	13.7	9.5	10.6	11.5	9.1	14.3	7.2	8.0	9.6	19.4	20.8
3. Strongly disapprove	85.8	84.0	88.3	86.3	86.0	82.2	87.2	86.8	85.6	88.4	81.9	91.5	90.1	89.6	73.7	48.4
Item 8610 Subject A11a N	3246	1516	1622	2465	439	663	904	1102	577	1813	1242	1206	731	428	787	39
A28G: Trying heroin (smack, horse) once or twice																
1. Don't disapprove	6.0	6.5	5.1	6.0	4.0	7.4	6.4	5.0	5.4	5.5	6.7	2.6	4.8	3.5	12.2	31.1
2. Disapprove	15.3	15.3	15.4	15.7	14.5	17.3	14.3	14.6	16.0	15.7	16.0	12.8	13.4	16.1	19.6	25.4
3. Strongly disapprove	78.7	78.2	79.5	78.3	81.4	75.3	79.4	80.3	78.6	78.9	77.3	84.6	81.8	80.5	68.2	43.5
Item 8620 Subject A11a N	3248	1516	1624	2468	437	665	905	1102	577	1816	1242	1207	729	430	787	40
A28H: Taking heroin occasionally																
1. Don't disapprove	2.9	3.6	1.8	2.5	3.4	3.6	3.2	2.0	3.2	2.4	3.4	1.7	1.9	1.1	5.0	26.3
2. Disapprove	10.7	10.6	10.8	10.8	10.3	12.3	9.6	11.3	9.4	9.5	12.8	7.8	9.7	8.9	15.7	22.5
3. Strongly disapprove	86.4	85.8	87.4	86.7	86.3	84.1	87.2	86.7	87.4	88.1	83.8	90.5	88.4	90.0	79.3	51.2
Item 8630 Subject A11a N	3246	1516	1622	2467	437	660	905	1104	577	1814	1242	1207	728	430	786	40
A28I: Taking heroin regularly																
1. Don't disapprove	2.0	2.5	1.1	1.6	2.8	2.4	2.2	1.7	1.6	1.5	2.4	1.1	1.5	0.8	2.8	25.1
2. Disapprove	8.2	8.7	7.6	7.7	9.4	10.6	6.6	8.2	7.8	6.6	11.0	6.6	6.4	5.8	12.8	12.7
3. Strongly disapprove	89.9	88.9	91.3	90.7	87.8	86.9	91.3	90.1	90.6	92.0	86.6	92.3	92.1	93.4	84.3	62.2
Item 8640 Subject A11a N	3239	1512	1619	2460	436	662	901	1100	576	1813	1236	1204	730	430	784	38
A28J: Trying a barbiturate (downer, goofball, red, yellow, etc.) once or twice																
1. Don't disapprove	15.9	17.0	14.3	17.4	7.7	19.2	15.4	14.8	14.7	14.0	18.3	4.4	7.8	13.2	40.2	66.2
2. Disapprove	23.1	21.6	25.0	24.9	18.3	24.1	22.3	20.5	28.1	23.9	22.9	16.2	23.9	28.9	29.7	21.0
3. Strongly disapprove	61.1	61.3	60.7	57.7	74.1	56.6	62.2	64.7	57.3	62.1	58.8	79.4	68.3	57.8	30.1	12.8
Item 8650 Subject A11a N	3252	1519	1625	2470	439	666	906	1105	576	1818	1244	1209	732	430	787	39
A28K: Taking barbiturates regularly																
1. Don't disapprove	4.9	6.0	3.3	4.8	4.0	4.8	5.2	5.0	4.3	3.3	6.6	1.4	2.3	2.1	12.6	35.2
2. Disapprove	22.2	23.6	21.0	22.1	20.5	25.6	18.2	22.1	24.8	19.1	27.6	12.6	19.3	23.7	37.9	35.6
3. Strongly disapprove	72.9	70.4	75.7	73.1	75.5	69.6	76.6	72.9	70.9	77.6	65.8	86.0	78.5	74.2	49.4	29.1
Item 8660 Subject A11a N	3239	1519	1612	2460	434	662	900	1101	576	1809	1238	1204	729	429	782	40
A28L: Trying an amphetamine (upper, pep pill, bennie, speed) once or twice																
1. Don't disapprove	27.2	27.1	27.1	29.8	12.9	30.8	27.3	23.9	29.5	25.3	29.9	6.0	19.1	26.8	66.1	75.2
2. Disapprove	24.4	23.4	25.4	25.3	22.8	26.2	25.8	22.0	24.5	25.0	23.8	22.1	27.8	32.2	20.8	15.1
3. Strongly disapprove	48.4	49.5	47.4	44.9	64.3	42.9	46.9	54.1	46.0	49.7	46.3	71.9	53.1	41.1	13.1	9.7
Item 8670 Subject A11a N	3241	1518	1614	2465	434	664	902	1100	574	1810	1240	1203	729	429	785	40

QUESTIONNAIRE FORM 3 1984	TOTAL	SEX		RACE		REGION				4YR COLLEGE PLANS		ILLICIT DRUG USE: LIFETIME				
		M	F	White	Black	NE	NC	S	W	Yes	No	None	Mari- juana Only	Few Pills	More Pills	Any Her- oin
N (Weighted No. of Cases):	3287	1532	1632	2482	442	675	914	1116	582	1823	1254	1211	735	430	791	41
% of Weighted Total:	100.0	46.6	49.6	75.5	13.4	20.5	27.8	33.9	17.7	55.5	38.1	36.8	22.4	13.1	24.1	1.3
A28M: Taking amphetamines regularly																
1. Don't disapprove	6.4	7.3	5.1	6.4	4.1	6.2	6.2	6.8	6.3	4.3	8.8	1.3	2.7	2.2	18.5	37.1
2. Disapprove	22.8	23.8	22.2	23.5	21.2	23.9	21.8	22.1	24.5	20.6	26.4	11.9	20.1	25.4	40.5	29.3
3. Strongly disapprove	70.8	68.9	72.7	70.1	74.7	69.9	72.0	71.1	69.1	75.0	64.8	86.8	77.2	72.4	41.0	33.6
Item 8680 Subject A11a N	3229	1509	1612	2453	431	662	896	1098	574	1806	1235	1202	723	427	784	39
A28N: Trying cocaine once or twice																
1. Don't disapprove	20.3	22.3	17.7	21.3	11.6	28.7	14.4	15.3	29.4	19.0	21.8	3.6	11.5	19.9	52.5	60.6
2. Disapprove	17.8	17.4	18.4	18.0	18.7	20.1	15.9	17.4	18.9	17.3	19.2	14.0	21.0	24.1	17.0	19.8
3. Strongly disapprove	61.9	60.3	63.9	60.7	69.7	51.2	69.7	67.2	51.7	63.7	59.1	82.4	67.5	56.0	30.4	19.6
Item 8690 Subject A11a N	3241	1515	1617	2465	433	662	902	1100	576	1810	1241	1206	727	430	783	40
A28O: Taking cocaine regularly																
1. Don't disapprove	5.5	7.3	3.2	5.2	3.9	9.4	3.8	3.9	6.4	4.0	6.7	1.3	2.3	2.3	14.5	39.1
2. Disapprove	15.8	17.2	14.4	16.3	13.0	19.5	11.5	14.5	21.0	14.8	17.8	6.8	13.5	15.6	31.4	26.9
3. Strongly disapprove	78.7	75.5	82.3	78.5	83.1	71.1	84.7	81.6	72.6	81.2	75.6	91.9	84.2	82.1	54.1	33.9
Item 8700 Subject A11a N	3222	1507	1606	2458	422	660	901	1088	573	1801	1233	1196	725	428	779	40
A28P: Trying one or two drinks of an alcoholic beverage (beer, wine, liquor)																
1. Don't disapprove	82.6	83.9	81.4	86.4	65.0	89.7	85.6	75.9	82.4	82.2	84.0	70.2	88.8	87.7	94.5	81.2
2. Disapprove	10.5	9.1	11.9	8.9	17.9	6.1	8.4	14.5	11.3	10.9	9.5	17.0	7.8	8.1	3.2	16.1
3. Strongly disapprove	6.9	7.0	6.7	4.8	17.1	4.2	6.0	9.5	6.4	6.8	6.5	12.8	3.4	4.2	2.2	2.7
Item 8710 Subject A11a N	3241	1516	1617	2466	434	664	902	1099	576	1810	1242	1207	726	430	784	40
A28Q: Taking one or two drinks nearly every day																
1. Don't disapprove	27.1	33.8	20.4	29.7	12.8	29.8	28.3	25.3	25.5	23.0	32.5	14.6	27.3	25.2	45.6	54.3
2. Disapprove	43.7	42.7	44.9	45.0	40.6	44.4	46.6	42.1	41.6	45.7	42.2	43.8	47.5	49.1	38.2	29.2
3. Strongly disapprove	29.1	23.5	34.7	25.3	46.6	25.7	25.1	32.6	32.9	31.3	25.3	41.5	25.3	25.6	16.2	16.4
Item 8720 Subject A11a N	3233	1512	1616	2461	433	664	903	1092	574	1807	1238	1205	726	427	782	40
A28R: Taking four or five drinks nearly every day																
1. Don't disapprove	9.0	13.0	4.8	8.9	5.4	8.7	9.4	8.9	8.7	5.7	13.4	3.4	7.4	4.9	19.6	31.7
2. Disapprove	26.0	29.1	22.9	28.3	17.5	28.5	25.7	24.8	26.1	24.0	28.3	19.4	28.3	26.9	33.7	22.9
3. Strongly disapprove	65.0	57.9	72.3	62.8	77.2	62.8	64.9	66.3	65.2	70.3	58.2	77.2	64.3	68.1	46.7	45.4
Item 8730 Subject A11a N	3232	1512	1614	2459	433	663	898	1095	577	1807	1235	1205	729	429	777	40
A28S: Having five or more drinks once or twice each weekend																
1. Don't disapprove	40.4	48.7	31.9	45.4	14.6	44.7	44.1	37.7	34.5	36.6	46.1	19.7	43.4	44.2	66.4	61.6
2. Disapprove	26.7	24.3	29.4	26.3	29.8	27.3	26.0	25.7	28.8	29.3	23.7	31.8	28.4	29.8	16.5	12.9
3. Strongly disapprove	33.0	27.1	38.7	28.3	55.7	28.0	29.9	36.6	36.7	34.1	30.2	48.6	28.2	26.0	17.1	25.5
Item 8740 Subject A11a N	3237	1512	1619	2463	433	664	901	1095	576	1808	1239	1207	727	429	781	40
A29: During the LAST 12 MONTHS, how often have you been around people who were taking each of the following to get high or for "kicks"?																
A29A: Marijuana (pot, grass) or hashish																
1. Not at all	25.6	23.1	28.1	26.4	22.2	18.3	29.7	27.8	23.5	27.6	23.3	48.9	13.6	16.1	7.8	9.2
2. Once or twice	23.2	22.7	23.8	22.8	26.0	18.3	23.2	26.0	23.5	24.2	21.3	28.8	24.9	24.2	12.7	7.0
3. Occasionally	26.4	27.9	25.1	25.7	30.9	28.4	24.7	25.6	28.2	26.4	26.8	16.1	38.2	32.2	27.5	24.9
4. Often	24.8	26.3	22.9	25.1	20.8	35.0	22.4	20.6	24.8	21.8	28.7	6.3	23.4	27.5	51.9	58.8
Item 20590 Subject A02b N	3238	1513	1618	2462	432	663	903	1098	575	1809	1241	1201	728	429	785	41

QUESTIONNAIRE FORM 3 1984	TOTAL	SEX		RACE		REGION				4YR COLLEGE PLANS		ILLICIT DRUG USE: LIFETIME				
		M	F	White	Black	NE	NC	S	W	Yes	No	None	Marijuana Only	Few Pills	More Pills	Any Heroin
N (Weighted No. of Cases):	3287	1532	1632	2482	442	675	914	1116	582	1823	1254	1211	735	430	791	41
% of Weighted Total:	100.0	46.6	49.6	75.5	13.4	20.5	27.8	33.9	17.7	55.5	38.1	36.8	22.4	13.1	24.1	1.3
A29B: LSD																
1. Not at all	87.5	84.5	90.8	86.2	95.6	83.8	89.3	88.6	86.7	88.6	86.2	95.9	93.5	88.3	70.5	46.5
2. Once or twice	7.7	9.3	5.9	8.5	2.2	9.4	6.5	7.4	7.9	7.6	7.9	3.1	5.0	8.6	15.5	29.3
3. Occasionally	3.4	4.4	2.6	3.9	1.5	5.0	2.7	3.3	3.0	2.8	4.3	0.7	1.2	2.3	10.3	8.2
4. Often	1.5	1.8	0.8	1.5	0.7	1.7	1.5	0.8	2.4	1.0	1.6	0.3	0.3	0.8	3.7	16.0
Item 20600 Subject A02b N	3199	1496	1597	2441	424	650	897	1083	569	1789	1224	1185	727	425	771	39
A29C: Other psychedelics (mescaline, peyote, PCP, etc.)																
1. Not at all	87.3	85.5	89.1	86.7	93.5	77.6	88.3	91.5	88.6	88.5	86.2	94.4	93.3	86.0	73.5	36.6
2. Once or twice	7.9	8.9	7.2	8.3	4.0	12.3	7.4	5.8	7.9	8.0	7.6	4.6	5.0	10.5	13.3	34.1
3. Occasionally	3.1	3.5	2.5	3.3	1.8	6.0	3.4	2.1	1.2	2.3	3.9	0.6	1.0	2.9	8.7	13.2
4. Often	1.7	2.1	1.2	1.6	0.6	4.1	0.9	0.6	2.3	1.2	2.2	0.4	0.7	0.7	4.5	16.1
Item 20610 Subject A02b N	3225	1508	1610	2451	431	658	898	1097	573	1798	1239	1193	729	427	782	41
A29D: Amphetamines (uppers, pep pills, bennies, speed)																
1. Not at all	55.0	53.3	56.6	50.2	77.4	48.8	52.1	59.1	59.0	58.0	50.5	78.7	59.9	46.1	20.4	13.0
2. Once or twice	21.7	23.8	19.6	23.3	15.9	24.9	19.8	20.5	23.0	22.3	21.1	14.3	27.1	31.8	23.5	14.9
3. Occasionally	14.3	14.0	14.8	16.4	4.6	17.5	17.0	12.0	11.0	12.6	17.1	5.2	9.6	15.3	31.1	29.6
4. Often	9.0	9.0	9.0	10.1	2.1	8.8	11.1	8.5	7.0	7.0	11.3	1.9	3.4	6.8	25.1	42.5
Item 20620 Subject A02b N	3231	1512	1614	2458	431	659	900	1098	574	1801	1243	1196	728	430	784	41
A29E: Barbiturates (downers, goofballs, reds, yellows, etc.)																
1. Not at all	78.8	76.6	81.1	76.5	92.2	73.3	79.1	79.4	83.4	81.7	75.3	91.5	87.2	77.5	54.7	22.7
2. Once or twice	13.3	15.3	11.5	15.1	4.9	17.6	12.1	12.7	11.4	12.8	14.1	6.1	10.5	15.8	25.7	23.5
3. Occasionally	5.2	4.7	5.5	5.7	1.3	6.5	5.7	4.8	3.5	3.9	7.0	1.7	1.2	5.1	12.8	29.1
4. Often	2.7	3.4	1.9	2.7	1.7	2.6	3.1	3.0	1.7	1.7	3.7	0.7	1.2	1.6	6.9	24.6
Item 20630 Subject A02b N	3228	1510	1612	2456	430	659	900	1097	573	1800	1242	1195	728	430	781	41
A29F: Tranquilizers (Librium, Valium, Miltown)																
1. Not at all	76.9	75.8	77.9	74.5	89.8	73.0	78.2	77.1	79.0	77.5	76.7	87.2	85.0	70.9	58.7	38.1
2. Once or twice	15.0	16.3	14.2	16.9	6.4	17.1	15.2	13.5	15.4	16.0	13.8	9.8	11.3	21.8	22.5	30.1
3. Occasionally	5.1	4.9	5.3	5.5	2.0	6.6	4.0	6.0	3.4	4.7	5.5	2.1	2.5	5.7	11.1	15.1
4. Often	2.9	3.0	2.5	3.0	1.7	3.3	2.6	3.4	2.1	1.8	4.0	1.0	1.2	1.6	7.7	16.7
Item 20640 Subject A02b N	3222	1507	1609	2455	429	657	900	1097	569	1798	1236	1194	725	429	780	41
A29G: Cocaine ("coke")																
1. Not at all	64.4	62.6	66.2	64.4	69.6	44.3	79.4	71.8	49.8	65.4	64.4	85.2	69.4	53.5	36.6	19.5
2. Once or twice	18.0	19.3	17.2	18.0	17.5	23.8	11.7	16.0	24.8	19.0	16.6	10.0	19.0	27.8	23.1	15.3
3. Occasionally	10.9	11.3	10.4	11.4	7.8	17.3	6.1	8.2	16.4	10.7	10.4	3.4	8.4	12.7	23.2	30.7
4. Often	6.7	6.8	6.2	6.2	5.1	14.6	2.8	4.0	9.0	4.9	8.5	1.5	3.2	6.0	17.1	34.4
Item 20650 Subject A02b N	3228	1508	1613	2457	430	658	901	1099	570	1799	1240	1194	727	429	784	41
A29H: Heroin (smack, horse)																
1. Not at all	94.0	92.4	95.7	94.3	96.3	91.3	95.0	95.3	93.1	95.2	93.2	96.0	96.8	93.6	91.2	41.8
2. Once or twice	3.9	4.8	3.1	3.8	1.8	6.2	2.5	3.1	5.0	3.6	4.0	2.6	2.3	4.6	5.9	27.2
3. Occasionally	1.0	1.2	0.7	0.9	0.7	1.3	0.8	1.3	0.3	0.6	1.4	0.7	0.5	0.8	1.9	6.4
4. Often	1.1	1.7	0.4	0.9	1.2	1.2	1.7	0.3	1.6	0.7	1.4	0.7	0.4	1.0	1.0	24.5
Item 20660 Subject A02b N	3215	1501	1607	2446	429	657	894	1095	569	1797	1232	1192	727	429	774	40
A29I: Other narcotics (methadone, opium, codeine, paregoric, etc.)																
1. Not at all	82.0	79.8	84.2	80.7	92.3	77.4	83.4	84.7	80.0	82.7	81.6	91.5	90.5	79.5	62.6	43.4
2. Once or twice	11.9	13.8	10.5	13.3	4.2	15.4	10.6	9.4	14.5	12.2	11.2	6.4	7.3	14.9	22.5	23.7
3. Occasionally	4.1	4.0	4.0	4.2	2.4	4.8	4.7	4.1	2.6	3.9	4.5	1.4	1.9	4.5	10.2	9.1
4. Often	2.0	2.4	1.4	1.8	1.1	2.4	1.3	1.8	2.9	1.2	2.7	0.7	0.3	1.1	4.7	23.7
Item 20670 Subject A02b N	3227	1508	1612	2454	431	658	899	1096	574	1799	1240	1194	728	429	781	41

QUESTIONNAIRE FORM 3 1984	TOTAL	SEX		RACE		REGION				4YR COLLEGE PLANS		ILLICIT DRUG USE: LIFETIME				
		M	F	White	Black	NE	NC	S	W	Yes	No	None	Mari-juana Only	Few Pills	More Pills	Any Her-oin
N (Weighted No. of Cases):	3287	1532	1632	2482	442	675	914	1116	582	1823	1254	1211	735	430	791	41
% of Weighted Total:	100.0	46.6	49.6	75.5	13.4	20.5	27.8	33.9	17.7	55.5	38.1	36.8	22.4	13.1	24.1	1.3
A29J: Alcoholic beverages (beer, wine, liquor)																
1. Not at all	6.0	5.4	6.4	4.5	10.5	6.3	5.5	5.6	7.2	6.4	4.6	12.1	2.1	2.8	1.9	2.4
2. Once or twice	9.5	8.7	10.5	7.5	19.5	7.5	8.6	10.5	11.0	10.8	7.3	17.0	6.5	5.4	2.2	8.5
3. Occasionally	25.8	25.7	25.9	24.3	34.4	20.3	25.4	28.6	27.7	25.0	27.4	34.5	30.3	23.6	11.3	4.8
4. Often	58.7	60.2	57.3	63.7	35.7	66.0	60.4	55.3	54.1	57.8	60.6	36.5	61.1	68.2	84.5	84.3
Item 20680 Subject A02b N	3237	1512	1620	2463	433	661	902	1100	574	1808	1242	1203	729	430	782	41

This section asks for your views and feelings about a number of different things.

D01: How satisfied are you with your life as a whole these days?

1. Completely dissatisfied	2.3	2.7	1.9	1.9	3.6	2.2	1.9	2.5	2.9	2.0	3.0	2.1	2.6	2.5	2.2	2.7
2. Quite dissatisfied	9.4	8.5	10.3	9.5	7.5	10.6	10.0	7.9	9.7	10.3	8.2	9.0	7.9	10.0	11.0	5.9
3. Somewhat dissatisfied	10.8	9.8	11.6	10.4	10.9	9.4	9.7	12.3	11.2	10.5	11.3	9.1	9.8	10.8	14.5	14.6
4. Neither, or mixed feelings	12.3	11.8	12.3	12.2	12.4	11.6	13.7	12.4	10.6	10.6	14.2	10.2	12.2	12.3	15.0	18.5
5. Somewhat satisfied	27.1	29.1	25.6	26.8	29.4	28.5	27.5	26.1	26.8	27.3	26.8	27.7	27.7	27.5	25.3	31.8
6. Quite satisfied	32.0	31.3	32.7	33.6	28.5	32.4	31.5	32.1	31.9	34.0	29.7	35.5	34.4	30.1	26.0	17.1
7. Completely satisfied	6.2	6.6	5.7	5.8	7.7	5.3	5.7	6.7	6.9	5.3	6.8	6.4	5.5	6.8	6.0	9.4
Item 6840 Subject P01,Q01 N	3092	1440	1569	2402	396	617	886	1040	549	1795	1210	1156	697	409	747	37

D02: These questions are about your health during the last MONTH.

D02A: Have you been bothered by shortness of breath when you were not exercising or working hard?

1. Never	72.7	77.0	69.1	72.6	75.0	72.1	71.6	75.1	70.5	76.0	68.1	79.2	77.2	66.5	62.4	59.6
2. Seldom	16.9	15.8	17.9	17.5	12.9	17.3	17.2	15.4	18.6	15.7	18.6	11.9	15.0	23.5	22.8	10.7
3. Sometimes	8.6	6.1	10.5	8.3	9.6	8.1	9.6	8.2	8.2	6.4	11.5	7.2	7.3	8.3	12.1	9.3
4. Often	1.9	1.1	2.6	1.6	2.5	2.5	1.6	1.3	2.7	1.9	1.7	1.6	0.4	1.7	2.8	20.4
Item 8850 Subject T N	3091	1436	1569	2403	392	619	886	1037	548	1788	1217	1157	692	409	749	37

D02B: Have you been bothered by your heart beating hard?

1. Never	73.5	78.3	69.3	73.3	76.8	73.3	72.4	73.0	76.4	75.9	70.3	78.1	78.7	69.2	64.4	56.8
2. Seldom	17.2	14.2	19.9	17.3	13.7	17.6	17.2	17.9	15.6	15.9	18.9	16.5	13.1	20.8	20.1	24.1
3. Sometimes	8.0	6.5	9.2	8.2	8.1	8.0	8.7	7.9	6.8	7.1	9.0	4.7	7.5	8.3	13.2	16.4
4. Often	1.3	1.0	1.5	1.2	1.4	1.1	1.7	1.2	1.2	1.0	1.8	0.7	0.8	1.7	2.3	2.7
Item 8860 Subject T N	3084	1433	1567	2400	391	617	885	1034	548	1787	1216	1156	690	409	747	37

D02C: Have you had spells of dizziness?

1. Never	61.2	71.7	51.6	60.5	66.1	64.2	60.2	61.2	59.5	62.1	59.7	66.4	64.6	59.6	51.8	46.4
2. Seldom	23.3	19.7	26.6	24.2	18.4	20.7	24.5	23.1	24.5	23.7	23.3	22.1	21.2	23.2	27.3	28.6
3. Sometimes	13.0	7.4	18.4	12.9	13.9	13.0	12.7	13.2	13.3	12.4	13.6	10.2	12.7	14.2	16.1	19.2
4. Often	2.5	1.3	3.4	2.5	1.6	2.1	2.7	2.5	2.7	1.9	3.5	1.3	1.5	3.0	4.9	5.9
Item 8870 Subject T N	3062	1426	1557	2386	389	613	883	1025	542	1779	1202	1145	689	407	739	37

D02D: Have your hands trembled enough to bother you?

1. Never	77.8	84.0	72.7	76.9	85.0	79.0	76.4	77.0	80.6	79.6	75.4	84.0	83.6	75.4	65.5	61.6
2. Seldom	13.0	9.4	16.2	13.7	7.3	11.5	13.8	13.6	12.2	12.3	14.0	10.4	10.2	15.5	18.6	13.3
3. Sometimes	6.9	4.6	8.9	7.0	6.6	7.2	7.0	7.6	4.9	6.4	7.7	4.7	5.3	6.4	11.7	12.7
4. Often	2.2	2.0	2.3	2.4	1.1	2.3	2.7	1.8	2.3	1.7	2.9	1.0	0.9	2.7	4.2	12.4
Item 8880 Subject T N	3068	1422	1564	2390	388	613	886	1027	543	1782	1204	1153	687	407	739	37

D02E: Have you been troubled by your hands sweating so that they felt damp and clammy?

1. Never	66.4	69.8	63.1	65.1	75.3	65.4	63.4	66.2	72.6	67.5	64.5	68.7	70.9	63.5	61.3	49.2
2. Seldom	21.1	19.0	23.4	22.3	14.9	23.6	22.5	20.8	16.8	21.6	20.7	19.6	20.8	22.2	23.0	30.5
3. Sometimes	8.8	7.7	9.6	9.1	6.4	8.1	9.7	9.3	7.3	7.6	10.5	8.2	6.0	11.1	11.0	7.9
4. Often	3.7	3.5	3.9	3.5	3.5	2.9	4.4	3.7	3.2	3.3	4.3	3.5	2.3	3.3	4.7	12.4
Item 8890 Subject T N	3078	1431	1565	2399	387	615	885	1031	547	1784	1212	1156	688	409	743	37

QUESTIONNAIRE FORM 3 1984	TOTAL	SEX		RACE		REGION				4YR COLLEGE PLANS		ILLICIT DRUG USE: LIFETIME				
		M	F	White	Black	NE	NC	S	W	Yes	No	None	Marijuana Only	Few Pills	More Pills	Any Heroin
N (Weighted No. of Cases):	3287	1532	1632	2482	442	675	914	1116	582	1823	1254	1211	735	430	791	41
% of Weighted Total:	100.0	46.6	49.6	75.5	13.4	20.5	27.8	33.9	17.7	55.5	38.1	36.8	22.4	13.1	24.1	1.3

D02F: Have there been times when you couldn't take care of things because you just couldn't get going?

1. Never	52.5	57.7	47.5	51.9	57.0	54.1	49.8	54.5	51.3	51.2	54.3	59.6	53.4	49.0	42.3	44.1
2. Seldom	27.7	28.3	27.3	29.0	23.1	26.5	28.8	27.3	28.0	29.4	25.3	24.3	28.9	31.4	30.0	32.8
3. Sometimes	15.6	11.4	19.7	15.4	15.3	14.6	16.7	14.2	17.6	15.5	15.7	13.2	15.4	15.8	19.7	16.6
4. Often	4.2	2.6	5.6	3.8	4.6	4.7	4.7	4.0	3.2	3.9	4.7	2.9	2.3	3.8	8.0	6.5
Item 8900 Subject T　N	3083	1432	1569	2400	389	618	886	1031	548	1786	1214	1156	692	410	743	37

D03: At any time during the LAST 12 MONTHS, have you felt in your own mind that you should REDUCE or STOP your use of . . .

D03A: Alcohol?

1. Yes	34.7	37.8	31.2	33.8	37.5	29.3	35.6	37.6	34.1	33.5	36.4	24.9	41.0	38.8	39.7	35.2
2. No	52.2	50.6	54.1	55.3	32.7	61.4	52.8	46.2	51.6	52.9	52.1	46.1	51.8	53.5	58.5	62.1
8. Haven't used in last 12 months	13.1	11.6	14.6	10.9	29.9	9.3	11.6	16.3	14.3	13.7	11.4	29.0	7.3	7.7	1.8	2.7
Item 8910 Subject A01i　N	2642	1241	1331	2148	263	529	776	863	474	1516	1033	886	610	369	712	31

D03B: Cigarettes?

1. Yes	24.2	20.2	27.5	25.2	16.3	26.2	24.2	25.9	19.0	19.6	31.2	8.1	26.7	26.0	45.0	43.7
2. No	15.3	15.4	15.3	15.6	15.0	16.7	16.1	14.5	14.1	13.8	17.4	9.6	13.8	15.7	23.1	35.8
8. Haven't used in last 12 months	60.5	64.3	57.3	59.2	68.6	57.1	59.8	59.7	67.0	66.6	51.4	82.3	59.5	58.3	31.9	20.5
Item 8920 Subject A01i　N	2966	1372	1519	2334	362	589	851	1001	526	1713	1153	1104	671	393	722	36

D03C: Marijuana?

1. Yes	20.6	24.6	16.5	19.8	23.5	20.7	17.2	21.3	24.4	18.5	24.0	-	33.3	26.8	38.4	45.1
2. No	18.6	18.2	18.8	19.4	14.8	28.3	16.3	15.1	18.4	16.2	22.0	-	23.0	23.5	40.0	39.6
8. Haven't used in last 12 months	60.8	57.2	64.7	60.8	61.7	51.0	66.4	63.6	57.2	65.3	54.0	100.0	43.7	49.7	21.7	15.3
Item 8930 Subject A01i　N	2653	1237	1352	2099	306	521	749	899	484	1551	1012	1034	567	341	654	29

D03D: Psychedelics (LSD, etc.)?

1. Yes	2.4	3.1	1.7	2.7	-	4.5	1.3	2.3	2.3	1.8	3.1	-	-	-	9.9	21.2
2. No	2.4	3.0	1.6	2.3	0.9	5.2	1.7	1.5	2.3	1.9	3.0	-	-	1.0	8.6	21.9
8. Haven't used in last 12 months	95.1	93.9	96.7	95.0	99.1	90.3	97.0	96.2	95.4	96.3	93.9	100.0	100.0	99.0	81.5	56.9
Item 8940 Subject A01i　N	2694	1239	1387	2152	302	519	775	914	486	1597	1013	1039	629	359	612	26

D03E: Amphetamines (uppers)?

1. Yes	6.0	5.6	6.4	6.8	0.4	6.2	7.4	5.6	4.2	4.2	8.1	-	-	4.2	25.8	35.7
2. No	6.9	6.9	6.9	7.6	2.1	8.4	6.5	6.2	7.1	5.5	8.8	-	-	2.9	31.5	24.2
8. Haven't used in last 12 months	87.1	87.6	86.7	85.6	97.5	85.4	86.1	88.1	88.6	90.3	83.0	100.0	100.0	92.9	42.8	40.1
Item 8950 Subject A01i　N	2509	1169	1273	1998	279	495	716	847	452	1505	922	1033	618	312	498	21

D03F: Tranquilizers?

1. Yes	1.5	1.9	1.0	1.7	-	2.2	0.7	2.3	0.7	1.0	2.2	-	-	0.5	5.5	26.1
2. No	2.4	1.9	2.5	2.2	2.7	1.6	2.0	3.2	2.1	2.0	2.8	-	-	1.3	8.6	22.3
8. Haven't used in last 12 months	96.1	96.2	96.5	96.1	97.3	96.2	97.3	94.5	97.2	97.0	94.9	100.0	100.0	98.2	85.8	51.6
Item 9005 Subject A01i　N	2628	1215	1345	2094	302	507	766	893	462	1565	988	1035	626	342	572	24

D03G: Barbiturates/Quaaludes (downers)?

1. Yes	1.7	2.1	1.1	1.8	-	2.6	1.2	2.2	0.4	1.1	2.4	-	-	-	6.3	24.4
2. No	2.9	3.5	2.1	2.9	2.0	2.8	2.6	3.2	2.8	1.7	4.1	-	-	1.2	10.8	21.9
8. Haven't used in last 12 months	95.5	94.5	96.8	95.3	98.0	94.6	96.2	94.6	96.8	97.2	93.5	100.0	100.0	98.8	82.9	53.6
Item 8970 Subject A01i　N	2664	1223	1373	2127	302	519	775	891	480	1579	1001	1038	630	359	583	26

D03H: Cocaine?

1. Yes	3.6	3.9	3.1	3.6	1.8	5.0	2.4	3.2	4.6	3.3	3.9	-	-	4.7	11.2	29.4
2. No	7.5	8.3	6.4	8.0	2.4	14.9	2.1	4.4	13.8	6.0	8.9	-	-	5.0	26.5	38.3
8. Haven't used in last 12 months	89.0	87.8	90.5	88.4	95.8	80.2	95.4	92.4	81.7	90.7	87.2	100.0	100.0	90.3	62.3	32.4
Item 8980 Subject A01i　N	2709	1239	1401	2171	299	525	780	912	493	1594	1026	1036	628	346	639	30

QUESTIONNAIRE FORM 3 1984	TOTAL	SEX		RACE		REGION				4YR COLLEGE PLANS		ILLICIT DRUG USE: LIFETIME				
		M	F	White	Black	NE	NC	S	W	Yes	No	None	Mari-juana Only	Few Pills	More Pills	Any Her-oin
N (Weighted No. of Cases):	3287	1532	1632	2482	442	675	914	1116	582	1823	1254	1211	735	430	791	41
% of Weighted Total:	100.0	46.6	49.6	75.5	13.4	20.5	27.8	33.9	17.7	55.5	38.1	36.8	22.4	13.1	24.1	1.3
D03I: Heroin?																
1. Yes	0.2	0.3	0.1	0.2	-	-	0.3	0.2	-	-	0.3	-	-	-	0.1	16.8
2. No	0.3	0.4	0.1	0.2	1.0	0.2	0.3	0.5	-	0.2	0.3	-	-	-	0.2	16.5
8. Haven't used in last 12 months	99.5	99.3	99.8	99.6	99.0	99.8	99.4	99.3	00.0	99.8	99.4	100.0	100.0	100.0	99.7	66.7
Item 8990 Subject A01i N	2731	1259	1405	2189	304	525	790	923	493	1617	1029	1038	628	367	645	25
D03J: Other narcotics?																
1. Yes	1.1	1.3	0.8	1.2	-	1.3	0.8	1.4	0.5	0.7	1.6	-	-	0.5	4.3	8.9
2. No	2.1	2.5	1.5	2.0	1.6	2.8	1.5	2.0	2.4	1.3	2.9	-	-	0.2	7.3	37.4
8. Haven't used in last 12 months	96.9	96.2	97.7	96.8	98.4	95.9	97.7	96.5	97.1	98.0	95.5	100.0	100.0	99.3	88.4	53.7
Item 9000 Subject A01i N	2624	1204	1355	2096	294	507	761	881	476	1552	992	1036	625	347	565	22
D04: How likely is it that you will use marijuana in the next 12 months?																
1. Definitely will-GO TO Q.D05	11.4	13.0	9.9	11.7	9.7	17.6	7.4	10.6	12.7	9.3	14.0	1.9	7.7	11.1	30.7	37.2
2. Probably will-GO TO Q.D05	14.1	14.4	13.5	14.5	9.5	17.4	14.8	11.1	15.1	14.0	14.6	0.5	22.0	21.2	25.6	20.4
3. Probably will not	18.9	19.8	18.3	18.9	18.6	20.9	20.7	15.9	19.6	19.8	18.0	10.1	28.5	25.0	21.4	7.5
4. Definitely will not	55.6	52.7	58.3	54.8	62.2	44.0	57.2	62.4	52.6	56.9	53.4	87.5	41.8	42.8	22.3	35.0
Item 9010 Subject A04a N	2794	1285	1446	2224	315	533	812	935	514	1643	1058	1108	616	370	640	30

Here are some reasons people give for not using marijuana, or for stopping use. If you have never used marijuana, or if you have stopped using it, please tell us which reasons are true for you. (Mark all that apply.)

	TOTAL	M	F	White	Black	NE	NC	S	W	Yes	No	None	Mari-juana Only	Few Pills	More Pills	Any Her-oin
A. Concerned about possible psychological damage	65.6	62.3	68.8	66.5	62.8	65.3	67.0	64.5	65.7	68.8	60.0	73.0	61.6	56.9	55.7	55.8
B. Concerned about possible physical damage	64.3	60.5	67.4	64.9	62.7	62.9	64.7	64.6	64.3	69.2	56.4	70.5	61.1	59.5	53.3	38.4
C. Concerned about getting arrested	38.8	41.5	36.1	39.3	39.0	32.7	39.7	43.4	33.9	41.4	35.5	40.1	42.0	36.5	31.9	55.9
D. Concerned about becoming addicted to marijuana	44.6	42.3	46.4	43.2	52.0	40.5	45.6	49.1	38.0	46.3	42.6	50.0	40.2	42.9	33.4	44.8
E. It's against my beliefs	53.1	48.3	57.1	54.7	47.2	49.4	52.3	56.3	51.8	57.0	46.4	67.4	36.7	45.5	34.5	42.8
F. Concerned about loss of energy or ambition	33.6	33.5	33.4	32.8	37.0	33.5	31.7	34.4	35.1	36.8	28.6	35.9	30.3	33.4	30.4	37.0
G. Concerned about possible loss of control of myself	48.1	43.9	51.8	48.5	47.4	46.3	49.0	48.7	46.9	51.9	41.7	55.4	41.9	40.6	39.1	25.9
H. It might lead to stronger drugs	48.6	47.6	49.7	48.0	51.4	46.4	47.2	52.2	45.9	48.7	48.4	52.6	46.2	50.0	37.6	64.4
I. Not enjoyable, I didn't like it	34.1	32.6	34.8	33.9	34.0	36.5	35.4	28.9	39.5	31.0	39.1	23.3	49.2	42.5	45.1	41.8
J. My parents would disapprove	56.8	53.8	60.1	57.3	55.3	52.5	58.5	59.3	53.2	59.4	52.4	61.3	54.9	53.7	46.4	81.6
K. My husband/wife (or boyfriend/girlfriend) would disapprove	29.8	28.3	31.2	30.2	30.1	26.9	30.1	33.5	24.9	28.9	31.0	28.7	32.1	29.0	31.8	49.3
L. I don't like being with the people who use it	42.2	36.8	46.3	42.5	40.7	31.0	41.0	48.5	42.6	43.2	40.2	50.6	33.9	42.7	24.9	31.8
M. My friends don't use it	34.7	30.5	38.1	37.0	21.3	26.6	40.2	33.6	35.1	38.1	29.3	41.2	26.6	35.2	23.1	30.7
N. I might have a bad trip	21.6	21.9	21.4	20.9	26.3	19.6	24.6	22.2	17.3	20.3	23.8	21.8	22.6	22.1	19.6	24.3
O. Too expensive	22.8	27.6	18.5	23.2	21.5	19.5	28.3	21.1	19.8	21.0	25.2	19.4	26.9	20.8	30.6	41.0
P. Not available	5.0	4.9	4.8	4.9	5.7	3.4	3.6	6.8	5.5	4.8	5.6	5.2	4.1	3.0	5.5	30.7
Q. Don't feel like getting high	59.3	53.1	64.6	59.3	58.9	61.8	57.1	55.7	67.5	58.9	59.5	63.1	56.2	57.8	51.8	52.6
Item 9020-9180 Subject A06a N★	2005	901	1063	1589	239	335	617	694	359	1209	732	1030	422	246	269	13

D05A: Has your use of alcohol ever caused any of the following problems for you?

Responses to this set of questions are not included because of complexities in the presentation and interpretation of the data.

Item 9190-9350 Subject A07b   N

★=excludes respondents for whom question was inappropriate.

QUESTIONNAIRE FORM 3 1984	TOTAL	SEX		RACE		REGION				4YR COLLEGE PLANS		ILLICIT DRUG USE: LIFETIME				
		M	F	White	Black	NE	NC	S	W	Yes	No	None	Mari- juana Only	Few Pills	More Pills	Any Her- oin
N (Weighted No. of Cases):	3287	1532	1632	2482	442	675	914	1116	582	1823	1254	1211	735	430	791	41
% of Weighted Total:	100.0	46.6	49.6	75.5	13.4	20.5	27.8	33.9	17.7	55.5	38.1	36.8	22.4	13.1	24.1	1.3

D05M: Has your use of marijuana ever caused any of the following problems for you? (Mark all that apply.)

Responses to this set of questions are not included because of complexities in the presentation and interpretation of the data.

Item 9360-9520 Subject A07b   N

D05O: Has your use of other drugs ever caused any of the following problems for you? (Mark all that apply.)

Responses to this set of questions are not included because of complexities in the presentation and interpretation of the data.

Item 9530-9690 Subject A07b   N

E01: Do you agree or disagree that most efforts to prevent (or clean up) pollution . . .

E01A: . . . are just too expensive

	TOTAL	M	F	White	Black	NE	NC	S	W	Yes	No	None	Mar. Only	Few Pills	More Pills	Any Heroin
1. Disagree	20.6	22.4	19.1	19.7	25.5	21.0	19.8	20.3	21.8	20.8	20.5	19.0	23.0	21.4	20.2	29.8
2. Mostly disagree	22.5	21.5	23.3	24.0	15.0	22.7	22.7	21.4	24.0	24.0	19.4	23.4	21.4	21.9	22.6	29.9
3. Neither	34.4	31.0	38.1	36.2	25.9	31.5	35.5	34.6	35.6	33.5	36.0	33.3	35.3	35.9	36.0	12.4
4. Mostly agree	16.1	17.4	14.5	15.1	20.9	17.6	16.6	16.4	13.2	16.1	16.4	17.7	14.3	17.1	14.4	14.7
5. Agree	6.4	7.6	5.0	5.0	12.8	7.2	5.4	7.4	5.5	5.5	7.6	6.5	6.0	3.7	6.8	13.2
Item 9700 Subject F04 N	2851	1318	1466	2254	348	553	838	944	516	1669	1094	1081	633	382	681	31

E01B: . . . cost more jobs than it's worth

	TOTAL	M	F	White	Black	NE	NC	S	W	Yes	No	None	Mar. Only	Few Pills	More Pills	Any Heroin
1. Disagree	24.9	26.4	23.9	25.5	21.2	24.9	25.0	23.4	27.6	26.4	22.6	24.2	26.5	26.6	23.7	39.5
2. Mostly disagree	26.0	25.7	26.1	27.3	21.6	25.7	26.6	24.9	27.5	27.9	23.0	28.4	23.4	25.1	25.4	27.1
3. Neither	34.0	31.6	36.3	35.3	28.3	32.9	34.2	35.1	32.8	32.8	35.9	31.9	36.3	37.3	37.3	10.8
4. Mostly agree	10.6	11.1	10.3	9.0	17.5	10.7	10.4	11.7	8.8	9.5	12.5	11.4	8.9	12.7	8.8	17.7
5. Agree	4.5	5.2	3.5	3.0	11.4	5.9	3.8	4.8	3.3	3.4	6.0	4.1	4.8	2.9	4.9	4.9
Item 9710 Subject F04 N	2830	1311	1453	2240	345	547	836	937	511	1657	1086	1075	628	380	673	31

E01C: . . . are proposed by people who usually don't know what they are talking about

	TOTAL	M	F	White	Black	NE	NC	S	W	Yes	No	None	Mar. Only	Few Pills	More Pills	Any Heroin
1. Disagree	17.3	18.3	16.4	17.4	17.2	18.7	17.0	15.5	19.6	19.2	14.5	15.9	19.2	20.1	16.3	18.6
2. Mostly disagree	24.1	21.3	26.7	25.7	18.5	24.8	25.4	22.6	24.2	28.0	19.1	26.5	22.2	23.8	22.4	36.4
3. Neither	35.1	32.5	37.6	35.8	30.3	36.2	36.0	34.6	33.3	33.2	36.8	34.2	35.3	34.9	36.7	23.3
4. Mostly agree	15.0	16.6	13.4	13.7	20.1	11.8	12.9	17.4	17.3	13.1	18.2	14.8	14.7	14.2	16.2	9.8
5. Agree	8.5	11.2	5.8	7.4	14.0	8.6	8.8	9.9	5.8	6.4	11.4	8.5	8.6	7.1	8.4	12.0
Item 9720 Subject F04 N	2808	1305	1437	2226	341	541	830	924	512	1645	1076	1073	620	378	666	29

E01D: . . . will not be enough anyhow

	TOTAL	M	F	White	Black	NE	NC	S	W	Yes	No	None	Mar. Only	Few Pills	More Pills	Any Heroin
1. Disagree	17.7	18.1	17.4	17.4	20.6	15.6	18.5	18.0	18.1	18.2	17.1	18.6	19.4	18.2	13.7	25.3
2. Mostly disagree	22.5	22.5	22.5	23.6	16.6	25.5	21.7	20.7	24.0	25.6	17.9	23.8	21.2	20.0	22.8	34.3
3. Neither	34.0	31.9	36.4	35.0	29.0	32.9	34.7	34.2	33.8	32.6	35.6	33.0	32.6	33.5	37.9	16.2
4. Mostly agree	18.2	18.9	17.4	17.8	19.6	18.2	17.9	18.5	17.8	17.6	19.5	17.8	17.8	21.9	17.7	17.7
5. Agree	7.6	8.7	6.3	6.2	14.3	7.9	7.2	8.6	6.3	6.0	9.9	6.8	9.1	6.4	8.0	6.5
Item 9730 Subject F04 N	2783	1290	1427	2215	330	543	821	911	508	1638	1060	1062	618	370	662	31

QUESTIONNAIRE FORM 3 1984	TOTAL	SEX		RACE		REGION				4YR COLLEGE PLANS		ILLICIT DRUG USE: LIFETIME				
		M	F	White	Black	NE	NC	S	W	Yes	No	None	Mari-juana Only	Few Pills	More Pills	Any Her-oin
N (Weighted No. of Cases):	3287	1532	1632	2482	442	675	914	1116	582	1823	1254	1211	735	430	791	41
% of Weighted Total:	100.0	46.6	49.6	75.5	13.4	20.5	27.8	33.9	17.7	55.5	38.1	36.8	22.4	13.1	24.1	1.3
E01E: . . . are useful because this society won't last long enough for such efforts to do any good																
1. Disagree	34.3	35.6	33.2	35.7	29.4	34.9	32.4	33.9	37.8	40.2	25.9	36.2	36.6	32.8	31.0	32.3
2. Mostly disagree	21.9	19.4	24.3	22.4	19.5	22.0	22.6	22.0	20.7	22.5	20.6	23.1	20.6	22.3	21.3	23.9
3. Neither	28.3	27.1	29.6	29.2	24.3	27.0	30.8	28.2	25.8	25.0	33.2	25.7	28.5	29.7	31.4	18.5
4. Mostly agree	9.0	10.3	7.9	7.9	12.6	10.0	8.0	9.2	9.4	7.4	11.9	8.9	7.6	8.4	10.7	8.7
5. Agree	6.4	7.6	5.0	4.8	14.2	6.1	6.3	6.7	6.3	4.9	8.3	6.1	6.6	6.8	5.6	16.7
Item 9740 Subject F04 N	2809	1299	1444	2231	338	544	831	920	514	1648	1073	1070	623	375	671	31
E02: There has been talk about shortages of energy, food, and raw materials in this country. Do you think that in the coming years we will have plenty to meet our needs, a sufficient amount, or will we have to consume less?																
1. Plenty to meet our needs	17.2	23.7	11.6	17.1	16.6	16.2	15.5	17.3	21.1	18.8	14.2	18.8	14.3	17.3	16.5	16.5
2. A sufficient amount	55.3	55.4	55.6	55.9	55.4	55.5	55.0	57.3	52.0	53.3	59.0	53.3	59.6	54.9	54.2	65.0
3. Will have to consume less	27.5	21.0	32.8	27.0	28.0	28.3	29.5	25.4	26.9	27.9	26.9	27.9	26.2	27.8	29.3	18.5
Item 9750 Subject F05 N	2722	1250	1416	2181	313	523	811	889	499	1613	1021	1036	608	371	642	26
E03: The questions in this section deal with population problems. How much do you agree or disagree with each statement?																
E03A: Our government should help other countries to control their population																
1. Disagree	25.7	30.6	21.5	25.0	32.5	24.7	25.4	26.0	26.9	24.6	27.8	25.6	26.2	23.9	25.2	56.0
2. Mostly disagree	19.0	16.6	20.9	20.3	12.6	17.1	20.5	18.0	20.7	19.4	18.5	18.5	20.7	23.1	17.1	2.4
3. Neither	26.2	23.6	28.8	26.6	20.7	29.6	28.1	23.4	24.4	26.5	25.4	28.7	22.4	23.7	27.5	20.1
4. Mostly agree	19.5	18.8	20.0	19.6	18.4	20.2	19.1	20.4	17.6	20.8	17.6	18.3	19.9	20.3	19.8	21.5
5. Agree	9.6	10.4	8.8	8.5	15.8	8.3	7.1	12.3	10.4	8.6	10.7	8.9	10.8	9.0	10.5	-
Item 9760 Subject E01,H02 N	2821	1310	1445	2237	340	550	829	931	511	1650	1080	1076	625	374	673	32
E03B: Governments should avoid making policy about population and let the individual decide																
1. Disagree	12.3	13.9	10.7	11.2	16.7	12.4	11.5	12.4	13.3	10.5	14.8	11.6	13.5	11.7	12.1	24.4
2. Mostly disagree	20.5	18.5	22.4	21.7	16.8	18.2	23.0	19.4	21.1	22.6	17.8	19.6	20.3	23.0	21.5	24.1
3. Neither	26.5	26.6	26.6	26.6	21.6	25.6	26.8	25.9	28.3	26.7	25.0	26.4	27.3	24.3	26.6	26.5
4. Mostly agree	25.4	24.0	26.4	26.2	23.4	29.6	23.6	25.1	24.2	25.3	25.9	25.9	24.9	28.6	23.2	18.5
5. Agree	15.3	17.0	13.9	14.3	21.5	14.2	15.2	17.2	13.2	14.9	16.6	16.5	14.0	12.4	16.6	6.5
Item 9770 Subject E01,H02 N	2796	1301	1431	2223	333	543	824	923	507	1635	1073	1064	626	369	668	30
E03C: I feel strongly enough about preventing overpopulation that I'd be willing to limit my family to two children																
1. Disagree	17.6	18.5	16.5	17.1	20.4	20.7	16.9	16.3	17.8	18.1	16.8	18.9	14.7	12.4	20.5	34.3
2. Mostly disagree	13.6	14.2	13.1	14.0	11.8	17.7	15.1	11.3	10.9	13.0	15.0	13.7	12.9	17.9	12.2	-
3. Neither	24.5	24.2	24.9	25.0	23.6	25.1	26.1	23.2	23.5	24.6	24.0	24.5	24.9	24.5	23.8	30.5
4. Mostly agree	21.4	20.0	22.6	21.7	18.7	18.6	21.8	22.7	21.5	22.5	19.7	21.4	21.8	23.4	20.5	6.9
5. Agree	22.9	23.2	22.8	22.2	25.5	17.9	20.0	26.5	26.4	21.8	24.6	21.6	25.7	21.8	22.9	28.4
Item 9780 Subject E01 N	2784	1288	1431	2215	329	542	823	915	504	1627	1068	1057	620	370	666	30
E03D: To prevent overpopulation, I might decide not to have any children of my own																
1. Disagree	55.2	52.7	57.6	56.2	50.1	58.6	55.5	55.4	51.0	56.2	54.2	55.6	54.2	57.0	55.4	44.6
2. Mostly disagree	17.4	17.4	17.2	18.1	14.9	15.5	18.0	16.5	19.7	18.5	16.2	17.0	17.8	22.3	15.2	26.8
3. Neither	16.8	19.0	15.2	16.4	18.1	15.1	16.7	17.1	18.2	16.3	17.1	17.4	17.0	13.0	17.6	6.2
4. Mostly agree	4.9	5.7	4.1	4.5	6.3	4.7	4.2	5.8	5.0	4.4	5.8	5.0	4.2	4.6	5.4	10.6
5. Agree	5.7	5.2	5.8	4.8	10.6	6.1	5.6	5.2	6.1	4.5	6.8	5.1	6.9	3.0	6.4	11.8
Item 9790 Subject E01 N	2782	1286	1431	2214	330	541	826	915	500	1628	1065	1055	617	371	669	30

QUESTIONNAIRE FORM 3 1984	TOTAL	SEX		RACE		REGION				4YR COLLEGE PLANS		ILLICIT DRUG USE: LIFETIME				
		M	F	White	Black	NE	NC	S	W	Yes	No	None	Mari-juana Only	Few Pills	More Pills	Any Her-oin
N (Weighted No. of Cases):	3287	1532	1632	2482	442	675	914	1116	582	1823	1254	1211	735	430	791	41
% of Weighted Total:	100.0	46.6	49.6	75.5	13.4	20.5	27.8	33.9	17.7	55.5	38.1	36.8	22.4	13.1	24.1	1.3

E03E: High schools should offer instruction in birth control methods

	TOTAL	M	F	White	Black	NE	NC	S	W	Yes	No	None	Mari-juana Only	Few Pills	More Pills	Any Her-oin
1. Disagree	8.0	9.4	6.6	7.5	8.2	8.6	7.1	8.0	8.9	7.7	8.5	9.8	5.9	6.1	7.1	20.9
2. Mostly disagree	5.2	5.3	4.8	5.3	4.5	5.8	6.6	4.7	3.4	4.4	6.6	6.4	5.2	3.7	3.8	14.6
3. Neither	14.6	17.6	12.1	14.7	12.4	15.0	14.3	15.4	13.3	13.6	15.9	18.5	13.1	8.8	12.6	9.8
4. Mostly agree	23.3	24.3	22.3	24.0	19.3	20.3	26.6	22.1	23.5	23.7	22.6	23.3	21.7	27.7	23.3	9.4
5. Agree	48.8	43.5	54.1	48.6	55.6	50.3	45.5	49.8	51.0	50.5	46.4	42.0	54.0	53.7	53.2	45.3
Item 9800 Subject E02 N	2780	1286	1429	2212	329	536	830	909	505	1630	1060	1049	621	371	668	30

E03F: I personally consider most methods of birth control to be immoral

	TOTAL	M	F	White	Black	NE	NC	S	W	Yes	No	None	Mari-juana Only	Few Pills	More Pills	Any Her-oin
1. Disagree	44.1	38.8	49.4	45.4	38.8	44.1	41.1	44.7	48.2	46.9	40.0	37.7	45.6	47.3	52.0	50.1
2. Mostly disagree	18.8	20.3	17.5	20.0	13.7	17.2	22.1	17.9	16.8	19.7	17.3	19.0	17.2	21.3	19.3	18.2
3. Neither	22.9	24.6	21.2	22.6	21.2	23.2	23.8	22.2	22.1	21.5	25.3	26.1	23.4	18.9	19.7	6.8
4. Mostly agree	7.1	8.4	5.9	6.4	12.4	6.8	8.0	7.0	6.0	5.8	8.6	8.0	7.4	6.1	4.8	16.3
5. Agree	7.1	7.9	6.1	5.6	13.9	8.7	4.9	8.2	6.9	6.1	8.8	9.1	6.4	6.3	4.2	8.6
Item 9810 Subject E02 N	2775	1279	1430	2209	329	537	827	909	502	1627	1059	1048	621	370	665	30

E03G: The government should make birth control information and services available without cost to anyone who wants them

	TOTAL	M	F	White	Black	NE	NC	S	W	Yes	No	None	Mari-juana Only	Few Pills	More Pills	Any Her-oin
1. Disagree	7.7	9.3	5.9	7.2	8.5	8.2	6.6	8.4	7.8	7.0	8.3	8.4	7.1	5.4	7.2	26.8
2. Mostly disagree	7.5	6.4	8.4	7.9	6.8	7.2	7.9	7.2	7.9	8.4	6.2	7.7	7.4	8.9	6.4	11.0
3. Neither	16.6	19.2	14.3	17.0	14.1	15.4	20.5	14.7	14.7	16.5	16.6	17.8	16.8	14.0	16.3	5.0
4. Mostly agree	24.6	24.4	25.0	25.7	17.1	24.7	23.4	24.8	26.0	25.9	23.1	26.7	22.7	30.7	21.0	8.7
5. Agree	43.6	40.7	46.4	42.3	53.5	44.5	41.6	44.9	43.6	42.3	45.8	39.5	46.0	41.1	49.1	48.6
Item 9820 Subject E02,H02 N	2774	1284	1424	2208	329	534	827	910	502	1625	1060	1046	620	371	667	30

E04: Did you have a unit on sex education when you were in high school?

	TOTAL	M	F	White	Black	NE	NC	S	W	Yes	No	None	Mari-juana Only	Few Pills	More Pills	Any Her-oin
1. No, and I'm glad I didn't	8.1	9.3	6.8	8.1	7.5	6.8	8.2	9.9	6.2	7.7	9.1	10.0	6.6	7.1	6.9	19.2
2. No, and I wish I had	23.4	22.6	24.0	23.8	25.7	15.6	24.0	30.9	17.2	23.7	23.6	24.2	24.0	21.1	23.3	13.9
3. Yes, and it was very worthwhile	27.3	24.2	30.3	25.1	36.9	26.6	26.6	26.0	31.3	25.0	30.3	26.2	28.5	28.9	26.9	27.9
4. Yes, and it was somewhat worthwhile	31.5	32.8	30.7	33.1	21.6	37.8	31.5	24.9	36.6	34.3	27.1	31.2	29.7	34.6	32.0	28.0
5. Yes, but it was not worthwhile at all	9.7	11.2	8.2	9.9	8.2	13.3	9.7	8.2	8.6	9.3	10.0	8.4	11.2	8.2	11.0	11.0
Item 9860 Subject B01,E02 N	2772	1280	1430	2194	332	541	820	907	505	1626	1056	1054	613	372	665	30

E05: Did you ever study about birth control methods in high school?

	TOTAL	M	F	White	Black	NE	NC	S	W	Yes	No	None	Mari-juana Only	Few Pills	More Pills	Any Her-oin
1. No, and I'm glad I didn't	11.7	15.8	7.5	12.0	8.6	11.1	12.5	13.5	7.8	10.1	14.5	15.5	9.1	8.0	10.2	13.7
2. No, and I wish I had	28.1	27.1	29.2	29.2	26.4	24.8	31.7	31.0	20.8	28.6	27.9	28.0	29.6	25.6	28.2	29.5
3. Yes, and it was very worthwhile	28.1	24.3	31.8	26.0	37.9	27.7	25.7	27.3	33.6	26.0	30.1	25.7	28.0	31.9	30.2	23.1
4. Yes, and it was somewhat worthwhile	25.1	25.5	24.9	26.1	21.4	28.2	24.3	21.4	29.6	27.5	22.0	24.5	26.6	26.4	24.2	18.3
5. Yes, but it was not worthwhile at all	7.0	7.4	6.5	6.8	5.8	8.2	5.9	6.7	8.1	7.9	5.6	6.3	6.7	8.2	7.2	15.4
Item 9870 Subject B01,E02 N	2740	1262	1415	2165	333	534	804	900	502	1610	1041	1040	605	370	660	30

E06: How important is each of the following for being looked up to or having high status in your school?

E06A: Coming from the right family

	TOTAL	M	F	White	Black	NE	NC	S	W	Yes	No	None	Mari-juana Only	Few Pills	More Pills	Any Her-oin
1. No importance	15.2	16.9	13.4	14.1	18.3	20.5	12.2	11.3	21.4	13.8	16.3	13.6	14.9	20.0	15.8	9.5
2. Little importance	18.1	18.6	18.0	19.0	14.2	20.9	15.6	18.0	19.4	20.7	14.8	18.9	16.3	16.8	18.7	37.0
3. Moderate importance	31.1	30.1	32.7	33.4	21.5	31.1	34.2	28.6	30.3	32.4	29.7	29.8	33.1	28.3	32.8	33.8
4. Great importance	17.2	16.4	17.3	16.9	19.7	13.2	18.4	20.7	13.4	16.3	18.6	17.5	17.9	16.8	16.7	10.1
5. Very great importance	18.4	18.0	18.6	16.6	26.2	14.3	19.5	21.4	15.5	16.7	20.7	20.3	17.8	18.1	16.1	9.6
Item 13580 Subject B04 N	2761	1280	1416	2194	330	532	821	906	501	1627	1048	1048	616	372	657	31

QUESTIONNAIRE FORM 3 1984	TOTAL	SEX		RACE		REGION				4YR COLLEGE PLANS		ILLICIT DRUG USE: LIFETIME				
		M	F	White	Black	NE	NC	S	W	Yes	No	None	Marijuana Only	Few Pills	More Pills	Any Heroin
N (Weighted No. of Cases):	3287	1532	1632	2482	442	675	914	1116	582	1823	1254	1211	735	430	791	41
% of Weighted Total:	100.0	46.6	49.6	75.5	13.4	20.5	27.8	33.9	17.7	55.5	38.1	36.8	22.4	13.1	24.1	1.3
E06B: Being a leader in student activities																
1. No importance	10.9	11.7	9.9	10.2	12.1	16.4	10.8	7.9	10.6	7.0	16.7	8.6	10.7	13.0	13.0	21.8
2. Little importance	17.1	18.2	16.1	17.0	17.1	19.4	16.6	15.7	18.3	15.1	20.2	16.2	14.5	20.0	19.9	20.7
3. Moderate importance	34.6	35.2	34.2	35.4	26.7	37.3	33.8	33.2	35.3	36.7	31.8	32.6	37.9	34.3	35.1	21.0
4. Great importance	24.5	23.1	26.0	25.1	25.9	16.4	26.2	27.4	25.2	27.7	19.9	28.6	23.5	21.0	21.1	24.8
5. Very great importance	12.9	11.8	13.8	12.2	18.2	10.4	12.6	15.7	10.8	13.6	11.4	14.2	13.4	11.8	10.9	11.7
Item 13590 Subject B04,M05 N	2753	1275	1414	2189	329	533	818	901	502	1627	1042	1048	612	369	656	31
E06C: Having a nice car																
1. No importance	14.4	12.2	16.3	13.0	19.5	18.6	13.4	13.3	13.4	13.2	15.7	15.1	14.7	15.3	12.6	14.0
2. Little importance	23.1	19.9	25.7	24.5	19.0	23.9	26.9	21.0	19.8	25.5	20.1	25.3	22.8	23.7	19.6	17.4
3. Moderate importance	31.8	32.8	31.8	32.9	26.2	30.0	31.8	32.7	32.3	33.4	29.4	31.1	33.2	32.4	32.0	31.5
4. Great importance	17.1	17.7	16.4	16.8	15.7	17.2	14.3	17.4	21.2	17.1	17.7	15.5	17.8	16.7	19.4	12.0
5. Very great importance	13.6	17.3	9.9	12.8	19.6	10.3	13.6	15.6	13.2	10.8	17.1	12.9	11.6	11.9	16.4	25.1
Item 13600 Subject B04,F01 N	2750	1275	1412	2188	328	532	821	896	501	1621	1043	1048	609	368	658	31
E06D: Getting good grades																
1. No importance	5.1	6.0	4.4	5.0	4.1	7.0	5.0	4.7	4.1	3.4	8.0	3.6	6.0	5.6	6.2	9.5
2. Little importance	12.5	12.3	12.9	13.8	7.5	13.6	11.0	13.4	12.2	12.4	12.9	11.9	11.8	12.7	13.7	27.3
3. Moderate importance	34.6	35.2	34.4	37.1	21.2	31.6	35.0	34.6	37.0	33.6	35.6	34.1	34.5	33.2	37.1	21.1
4. Great importance	26.9	26.5	26.8	27.2	23.5	27.7	29.5	24.2	26.3	30.2	22.3	27.4	26.3	29.3	25.3	20.4
5. Very great importance	20.9	20.1	21.5	16.9	43.7	20.1	19.5	23.0	20.4	20.4	21.2	23.0	21.5	19.2	17.6	21.6
Item 13610 Subject B04 N	2742	1268	1410	2184	328	532	816	896	497	1623	1035	1042	607	369	658	31
E06E: Being a good athlete																
1. No importance	9.8	8.2	10.9	8.9	12.1	12.0	8.5	10.5	8.2	6.1	15.5	9.8	9.4	10.6	9.1	19.9
2. Little importance	13.2	12.2	14.1	13.4	13.9	13.1	14.2	12.7	12.3	11.0	16.7	12.3	11.1	13.6	15.8	10.5
3. Moderate importance	28.5	27.1	29.7	29.0	22.8	31.6	28.0	29.0	25.3	29.6	26.4	28.3	27.8	32.2	28.4	29.9
4. Great importance	30.5	31.3	30.2	31.0	28.6	30.2	29.9	30.8	31.1	35.0	23.7	30.4	33.6	25.6	31.0	24.6
5. Very great importance	18.1	21.3	15.0	17.7	22.6	13.1	19.4	17.0	23.1	18.3	17.7	19.1	18.0	18.0	15.7	15.1
Item 13620 Subject B04 N	2735	1265	1406	2182	322	529	817	894	495	1617	1033	1040	606	368	655	31
E06F: Knowing a lot about intellectual matters																
1. No importance	11.8	11.3	12.3	12.1	9.7	12.7	10.6	12.3	11.9	9.7	15.2	9.6	11.3	14.1	14.4	15.5
2. Little importance	25.7	24.1	27.4	28.1	14.4	24.0	27.4	24.6	26.7	26.3	25.1	26.4	26.1	23.7	24.9	34.2
3. Moderate importance	38.6	38.4	38.8	40.5	27.3	39.1	41.8	36.0	37.4	39.8	36.4	38.1	39.8	41.0	37.8	31.2
4. Great importance	15.6	16.8	14.0	13.9	24.5	16.9	14.0	16.1	15.7	15.9	14.8	18.0	13.4	12.9	15.1	10.2
5. Very great importance	8.4	9.4	7.5	5.5	24.1	7.3	6.2	11.0	8.3	8.4	8.5	7.9	9.4	8.2	7.8	8.9
Item 13630 Subject B04 N	2739	1268	1408	2183	327	529	815	896	500	1622	1033	1040	610	368	655	31
E06G: Planning to go to college																
1. No importance	12.2	14.8	9.8	12.0	12.0	15.3	12.0	12.2	9.1	6.0	22.0	8.6	10.0	14.8	16.4	40.0
2. Little importance	16.4	16.5	16.4	18.2	8.0	16.6	19.2	14.0	16.0	15.2	18.8	16.4	17.1	13.8	17.5	15.3
3. Moderate importance	28.4	27.6	29.3	29.5	23.5	23.6	29.7	28.6	31.2	28.1	29.1	31.1	28.2	27.7	25.5	20.8
4. Great importance	24.3	22.7	25.7	24.5	23.3	25.2	22.8	23.7	26.8	27.5	18.7	22.7	27.0	26.3	23.5	12.5
5. Very great importance	18.7	18.3	18.8	15.9	33.2	19.3	16.3	21.6	16.9	23.1	11.4	21.1	17.7	17.4	17.1	11.4
Item 13640 Subject B04 N	2748	1270	1415	2186	330	529	820	900	499	1624	1036	1045	613	370	655	30
E07: How about using drugs (other than marijuana or alcohol)–does that cause a student to be looked up to or looked down on?																
E07A: Among the majority of students in my school, such drug use is . . .																
1. Looked down on a lot	23.0	25.3	20.5	23.4	24.6	17.4	27.4	24.4	19.2	24.4	20.8	28.6	22.9	17.6	17.3	17.9
2. Looked down on some	22.6	21.9	23.1	23.7	19.5	14.9	23.4	23.3	27.9	25.3	18.8	24.2	23.9	24.3	18.1	17.5
3. Neither, or mixed	44.7	43.0	46.6	44.6	42.4	56.2	40.7	42.5	43.2	42.6	47.8	36.9	44.7	49.9	54.1	51.6
4. Looked up to some	7.5	7.4	7.8	6.7	9.4	7.6	7.0	8.0	7.4	6.3	9.5	7.6	6.6	6.0	8.8	10.4
5. Looked up to a lot	2.2	2.4	2.0	1.7	4.1	3.9	1.5	2.0	2.3	1.5	3.1	2.7	1.9	2.3	1.7	2.6
Item 13650 Subject A12b N	2733	1264	1405	2173	329	523	812	900	497	1610	1034	1037	607	366	657	32

QUESTIONNAIRE FORM 3 1984	TOTAL	SEX		RACE		REGION				4YR COLLEGE PLANS		ILLICIT DRUG USE: LIFETIME				
		M	F	White	Black	NE	NC	S	W	Yes	No	None	Mari-juana Only	Few Pills	More Pills	Any Her-oin
N (Weighted No. of Cases):	3287	1532	1632	2482	442	675	914	1116	582	1823	1254	1211	735	430	791	41
% of Weighted Total:	100.0	46.6	49.6	75.5	13.4	20.5	27.8	33.9	17.7	55.5	38.1	36.8	22.4	13.1	24.1	1.3
E07B: Among my own group of friends, such drug use is . . .																
1. Looked down on a lot	39.2	37.0	41.3	40.5	35.7	31.6	41.1	41.9	39.4	45.6	29.6	59.4	35.3	32.2	17.2	12.8
2. Looked down on some	17.5	17.6	17.3	18.0	14.2	20.1	19.3	15.0	16.2	17.6	17.9	17.9	18.9	20.4	13.1	21.3
3. Neither, or mixed	33.8	34.0	33.6	32.9	36.6	36.0	30.6	34.3	36.0	29.7	39.6	20.4	35.1	38.9	51.0	34.5
4. Looked up to some	7.1	8.4	6.0	7.0	7.9	9.3	7.4	5.9	6.4	5.5	9.7	1.5	9.2	5.5	14.4	18.1
5. Looked up to a lot	2.3	3.0	1.7	1.6	5.6	3.0	1.5	2.9	2.0	1.6	3.2	0.8	1.5	3.0	4.3	13.3
Item 13660 Subject A12b N	2728	1263	1402	2168	328	520	813	899	495	1611	1029	1038	603	365	657	32
E07C: My own feelings about such drug use is that . . .																
1. I look down on it a lot	51.0	49.2	52.5	51.4	51.9	44.9	53.2	54.0	48.1	55.2	44.4	75.5	48.3	42.6	20.7	28.3
2. I look down on it some	18.0	17.5	18.5	18.6	15.1	17.1	18.2	17.2	19.7	19.3	16.8	11.2	22.7	23.9	21.1	8.9
3. Neither, or mixed	27.3	28.5	26.1	27.0	25.2	32.0	25.5	24.4	30.4	23.7	32.2	12.3	26.9	29.5	50.5	28.8
4. I look up to it some	2.9	3.5	2.3	2.4	5.3	4.4	2.7	3.3	0.8	1.3	5.0	0.7	1.9	3.1	6.0	24.0
5. I look up to it a lot	0.9	1.3	0.5	0.5	2.6	1.5	0.4	1.0	1.0	0.5	1.6	0.3	0.2	1.0	1.7	10.0
Item 13670 Subject A11c N	2732	1264	1404	2170	329	522	812	902	496	1611	1031	1042	603	366	656	32
E08: The next questions are about some things which may have happened TO YOU while you were at school (inside or outside or in a schoolbus). During the LAST 12 MONTHS, how often ...																
E08A: Has something of yours (worth under $50) been stolen?																
1. Not at all	64.8	61.4	68.1	64.0	69.9	62.2	67.2	64.9	63.6	62.9	68.1	71.0	65.4	61.0	57.3	59.6
2. Once	25.9	27.0	25.2	26.7	19.2	27.9	24.1	24.7	28.7	27.7	22.8	22.2	25.5	30.1	30.1	20.9
3. Twice	6.1	6.9	5.0	6.3	6.1	5.6	5.0	7.2	6.2	6.2	5.8	4.5	6.8	5.8	7.8	11.9
4. 3 or 4 times	2.1	3.2	1.2	2.1	2.6	2.7	2.6	2.1	0.9	2.1	2.4	1.4	1.6	2.1	3.1	7.6
5. 5 or more times	1.1	1.5	0.6	0.9	2.1	1.6	1.1	1.0	0.7	1.1	1.0	0.9	0.6	1.1	1.7	-
Item 9871 Subject B07,S03 N	2799	1305	1424	2221	335	536	833	921	509	1639	1062	1061	621	378	668	32
E08B: Has something of yours (worth over $50) been stolen?																
1. Not at all	88.2	86.3	90.5	89.9	80.6	87.3	90.4	87.0	87.8	87.9	89.4	91.4	86.9	89.8	85.0	79.4
2. Once	8.7	9.8	7.5	7.7	13.0	9.1	7.0	10.0	9.0	8.9	8.1	7.1	10.3	7.7	9.4	17.9
3. Twice	2.0	2.2	1.7	1.6	4.0	2.7	1.6	2.1	1.8	2.1	1.7	0.9	2.4	1.9	3.2	2.7
4. 3 or 4 times	0.7	0.9	0.3	0.4	2.0	0.4	0.6	0.6	1.2	0.8	0.2	0.6	0.2	0.6	1.2	-
5. 5 or more times	0.4	0.7	*	0.3	0.4	0.5	0.5	0.3	0.2	0.2	0.6	0.1	0.2	-	1.1	-
Item 9872 Subject B07,S03 N	2791	1301	1422	2217	333	534	831	918	508	1636	1059	1058	621	378	663	32
E08C: Has someone deliberately damaged your property (your car, clothing, etc.)?																
1. Not at all	75.8	68.9	82.4	75.7	78.2	78.4	75.8	76.7	71.3	76.2	75.7	80.7	77.1	75.7	68.9	46.5
2. Once	16.3	19.4	13.1	15.9	16.4	15.4	15.8	15.8	18.7	16.2	16.6	13.9	16.5	15.4	19.4	33.5
3. Twice	5.2	7.6	3.1	5.6	2.4	4.5	4.9	4.8	7.2	5.0	5.1	4.0	4.6	6.5	6.9	15.6
4. 3 or 4 times	2.1	3.0	1.3	2.2	2.4	1.0	2.6	2.4	2.2	2.1	2.1	1.0	1.4	2.2	4.1	4.4
5. 5 or more times	0.6	1.1	0.1	0.6	0.7	0.7	0.8	0.3	0.6	0.5	0.5	0.5	0.4	0.2	0.8	-
Item 9873 Subject B07,S03 N	2780	1295	1417	2213	330	531	830	910	508	1633	1051	1056	615	377	662	32
E08D: Has someone injured you with a weapon (like a knife, gun, or club)?																
1. Not at all	96.0	93.5	98.5	96.8	94.0	96.3	96.6	95.9	94.7	96.8	95.1	98.6	96.6	96.6	93.2	65.9
2. Once	2.8	4.5	1.0	2.4	3.7	2.3	2.2	3.1	3.8	2.2	3.6	1.0	2.7	3.0	4.1	24.2
3. Twice	0.6	0.9	0.3	0.4	0.8	0.4	0.4	0.6	0.7	0.3	0.7	0.2	0.4	0.3	1.4	4.2
4. 3 or 4 times	0.5	0.8	0.2	0.3	0.9	0.3	0.8	0.2	0.7	0.4	0.4	0.3	0.2	0.1	0.9	5.8
5. 5 or more times	0.2	0.4	*	0.1	0.6	0.6	-	0.3	-	0.2	0.2	*	0.2	-	0.5	-
Item 9874 Subject B07,S03 N	2781	1297	1416	2208	332	529	830	913	509	1631	1052	1058	617	375	660	32

*=less than .05 per cent.

	TOTAL	SEX		RACE		REGION				4YR COLLEGE PLANS		ILLICIT DRUG USE: LIFETIME				
QUESTIONNAIRE FORM 3 1984		M	F	White	Black	NE	NC	S	W	Yes	No	None	Mari- juana Only	Few Pills	More Pills	Any Her- oin
N (Weighted No. of Cases):	3287	1532	1632	2482	442	675	914	1116	582	1823	1254	1211	735	430	791	41
% of Weighted Total:	100.0	46.6	49.6	75.5	13.4	20.5	27.8	33.9	17.7	55.5	38.1	36.8	22.4	13.1	24.1	1.3
E08E: Has someone threatened you with a weapon, but not actually injured you?																
1. Not at all	88.1	82.4	93.2	89.1	83.3	87.5	88.5	87.4	89.3	90.5	84.6	93.4	88.4	86.7	81.7	67.6
2. Once	7.8	10.5	5.5	7.3	10.6	9.0	6.9	8.4	6.7	6.1	10.4	4.6	8.0	9.7	10.9	25.0
3. Twice	2.4	4.0	0.9	2.3	2.4	2.8	2.2	2.2	2.5	2.0	3.1	0.9	2.5	2.8	4.0	-
4. 3 or 4 times	1.2	2.2	0.2	0.9	2.5	0.3	1.7	1.1	1.4	1.0	1.1	0.7	0.8	0.8	2.6	-
5. 5 or more times	0.6	0.9	0.3	0.5	1.2	0.5	0.6	0.8	0.1	0.3	0.8	0.5	0.3	-	0.8	7.3
Item 9875 Subject B07,S03 N	2783	1299	1416	2210	332	530	831	915	508	1634	1054	1058	618	375	662	32
E08F: Has someone injured you on purpose without using a weapon?																
1. Not at all	87.5	84.2	91.0	87.9	86.7	86.8	88.1	88.7	85.2	88.8	86.2	93.0	86.3	86.2	82.8	65.4
2. Once	7.6	9.5	5.7	7.6	7.0	8.4	6.9	6.7	9.6	6.8	8.8	4.4	10.6	8.3	8.7	10.0
3. Twice	2.8	3.6	2.0	2.6	3.2	2.0	2.8	2.9	3.3	2.7	2.6	1.3	2.0	4.0	4.6	15.5
4. 3 or 4 times	1.3	1.8	0.6	1.3	1.2	1.8	1.7	0.7	1.2	1.2	1.2	0.6	0.4	1.4	2.7	3.1
5. 5 or more times	0.8	0.9	0.7	0.6	1.9	1.1	0.5	0.9	0.6	0.5	1.2	0.7	0.6	0.2	1.2	6.1
Item 9876 Subject B07,S03 N	2778	1298	1412	2205	331	528	830	912	508	1629	1053	1057	617	375	658	32
E08G: Has an unarmed person threatened you with injury, but not actually injured you?																
1. Not at all	77.1	68.8	85.0	77.0	75.6	76.8	75.3	77.8	78.9	77.4	76.6	84.7	75.8	74.4	69.3	59.8
2. Once	12.3	15.6	8.9	12.3	12.1	13.4	12.6	11.6	12.0	12.6	12.5	8.7	14.8	14.7	14.1	12.0
3. Twice	4.4	5.8	3.0	4.4	5.8	4.8	4.5	3.8	4.5	4.0	5.0	2.6	5.4	3.5	6.8	4.2
4. 3 or 4 times	3.1	3.9	2.3	2.8	4.7	2.1	3.2	3.5	3.0	2.7	3.4	2.3	1.8	4.0	4.4	6.7
5. 5 or more times	3.2	5.9	0.7	3.5	1.8	2.8	4.4	3.2	1.6	3.3	2.5	1.8	2.2	3.3	5.3	17.3
Item 9877 Subject B07,S03 N	2771	1292	1410	2201	330	527	830	909	505	1628	1049	1052	616	374	659	32
E09: Looking toward the future, how important would it be for you to have each of the following things?																
E09A: At least one car																
1. Not important	2.7	3.1	2.1	2.2	3.1	4.1	2.2	1.9	3.4	1.9	3.6	2.2	1.9	2.8	3.8	6.3
2. Somewhat important	16.5	15.8	16.9	15.5	22.1	15.9	15.6	17.9	16.0	18.0	14.5	18.2	18.3	14.3	13.1	15.9
3. Quite important	37.4	38.0	36.9	38.0	34.2	37.6	38.5	35.5	38.6	37.9	35.6	39.3	35.0	37.6	35.8	41.4
4. Extremely important	43.5	43.1	44.0	44.3	40.5	42.4	43.7	44.8	42.1	42.1	46.3	40.3	44.7	45.3	47.3	36.4
Item 13835 Subject F01 N	2761	1279	1414	2188	333	526	825	906	504	1627	1034	1048	612	377	656	32
E09B: At least two cars																
1. Not important	43.2	36.6	49.8	41.5	52.0	49.4	39.6	42.7	43.8	43.1	43.3	46.2	44.3	42.1	38.3	34.3
2. Somewhat important	32.2	33.1	31.0	34.0	23.8	29.4	34.1	32.6	31.6	32.0	32.9	31.5	33.2	32.6	33.4	27.2
3. Quite important	17.0	20.0	14.2	17.4	15.1	14.4	18.9	16.8	16.8	18.2	15.2	16.4	16.0	19.7	16.6	20.0
4. Extremely important	7.6	10.2	4.9	7.0	9.0	6.9	7.4	7.9	7.7	6.7	8.6	6.0	6.6	5.6	11.7	18.5
Item 13840 Subject F01 N	2762	1285	1410	2190	333	525	823	908	505	1628	1035	1047	617	377	653	31
E09C: A large (full-sized) car																
1. Not important	64.5	57.6	71.3	65.0	63.0	62.6	64.1	63.8	68.5	63.0	66.4	65.1	64.3	64.4	64.6	52.1
2. Somewhat important	22.9	25.7	19.9	23.5	20.1	23.7	24.5	22.8	19.7	23.1	23.1	22.6	23.4	25.1	22.5	15.4
3. Quite important	8.4	10.2	6.9	8.0	10.2	9.0	7.5	9.6	7.3	9.5	7.0	8.6	9.4	6.6	7.7	17.4
4. Extremely important	4.1	6.5	1.9	3.5	6.7	4.7	3.9	3.7	4.5	4.4	3.4	3.7	2.9	3.9	5.2	15.1
Item 13850 Subject F01 N	2734	1261	1406	2169	328	520	817	897	500	1613	1024	1036	613	371	647	30
E09D: A new car every two or three years																
1. Not important	63.5	56.4	70.1	63.2	65.4	64.3	62.2	61.8	68.2	62.3	66.5	66.8	64.0	59.1	60.8	63.1
2. Somewhat important	21.7	24.9	19.1	23.0	15.9	21.6	23.6	21.0	20.3	22.7	19.8	21.1	20.8	25.1	22.5	14.8
3. Quite important	9.0	10.8	7.5	8.8	10.8	10.1	8.2	10.6	6.4	10.4	6.8	7.4	9.0	11.7	10.0	1.6
4. Extremely important	5.7	8.0	3.4	5.1	7.9	4.0	6.1	6.7	5.1	4.6	6.9	4.7	6.2	4.1	6.7	20.5
Item 13860 Subject F01 N	2747	1272	1407	2178	330	522	822	904	499	1618	1029	1046	615	371	648	31

QUESTIONNAIRE FORM 3 1984	TOTAL	SEX		RACE		REGION				4YR COLLEGE PLANS		ILLICIT DRUG USE: LIFETIME				
		M	F	White	Black	NE	NC	S	W	Yes	No	None	Mari- juana Only	Few Pills	More Pills	Any Her- oin
N (Weighted No. of Cases):	3287	1532	1632	2482	442	675	914	1116	582	1823	1254	1211	735	430	791	41
% of Weighted Total:	100.0	46.6	49.6	75.5	13.4	20.5	27.8	33.9	17.7	55.5	38.1	36.8	22.4	13.1	24.1	1.3
E09E: Clothes in the latest style																
1. Not important	14.6	20.4	9.3	15.3	8.3	14.5	15.1	13.7	15.2	11.9	18.7	17.3	12.5	11.6	13.9	18.9
2. Somewhat important	37.2	37.2	37.4	38.5	29.6	34.8	39.4	35.3	39.5	36.8	37.7	38.3	37.7	35.7	36.1	34.9
3. Quite important	29.3	27.8	30.3	29.9	26.4	29.9	30.6	28.4	28.3	31.6	25.8	28.7	27.1	33.4	29.8	31.8
4. Extremely important	18.9	14.5	23.0	16.3	35.7	20.8	14.9	22.6	17.0	19.7	17.8	15.7	22.8	19.3	20.1	14.5
Item 13870 Subject F01 N	*2748*	*1278*	*1403*	*2179*	*330*	*522*	*825*	*901*	*501*	*1617*	*1031*	*1046*	*612*	*372*	*649*	*31*
E09F: A house of my own (instead of an apartment or condominium)																
1. Not important	15.5	12.3	18.5	15.9	14.6	16.4	14.6	15.4	16.2	15.2	15.6	17.1	14.2	11.7	15.9	20.7
2. Somewhat important	24.3	21.9	26.4	25.0	21.7	25.3	26.3	23.1	22.2	25.9	21.5	23.7	25.4	24.5	24.7	25.7
3. Quite important	30.7	31.6	30.0	31.4	25.3	28.2	31.4	31.5	31.0	31.6	30.2	30.8	29.8	34.4	29.1	23.1
4. Extremely important	29.5	34.2	25.1	27.6	38.4	30.1	27.7	30.0	30.6	27.3	32.6	28.4	30.6	29.4	30.3	30.5
Item 13880 Subject F01 N	*2750*	*1280*	*1404*	*2183*	*327*	*522*	*824*	*901*	*504*	*1624*	*1027*	*1045*	*612*	*377*	*649*	*31*
E09G: Lots of space around my house, a big yard																
1. Not important	15.0	13.1	16.9	14.1	18.6	14.2	12.0	16.2	18.4	14.4	15.0	16.7	13.4	12.3	14.5	21.0
2. Somewhat important	28.6	25.9	30.6	29.1	27.3	26.6	31.2	28.1	27.4	30.2	26.8	26.8	29.8	32.3	28.9	17.9
3. Quite important	30.8	32.3	29.8	31.9	25.9	31.9	32.3	29.5	29.5	31.0	30.9	30.9	32.9	30.5	28.7	26.6
4. Extremely important	25.6	28.7	22.7	25.0	28.2	27.3	24.6	26.2	24.6	24.4	27.2	25.6	23.8	24.8	27.9	34.6
Item 13890 Subject F01 N	*2754*	*1279*	*1408*	*2182*	*332*	*521*	*827*	*903*	*503*	*1625*	*1030*	*1046*	*615*	*377*	*648*	*31*
E09H: A well-kept garden and lawn																
1. Not important	12.5	13.0	11.8	11.8	14.8	14.2	11.9	12.8	10.9	11.4	13.9	12.3	11.6	11.0	13.9	20.4
2. Somewhat important	30.8	30.3	31.1	32.2	24.0	34.3	32.8	29.1	26.7	30.4	31.7	31.5	28.9	29.8	32.0	41.0
3. Quite important	34.7	34.0	35.5	35.6	30.6	30.9	35.8	33.9	38.2	36.7	31.7	34.1	36.1	36.3	33.6	21.5
4. Extremely important	22.1	22.7	21.6	20.4	30.6	20.6	19.5	24.2	24.2	21.4	22.7	22.1	23.3	22.9	20.4	17.1
Item 13900 Subject F01 N	*2740*	*1274*	*1401*	*2171*	*331*	*521*	*823*	*896*	*500*	*1618*	*1025*	*1041*	*613*	*374*	*647*	*30*
E09I: Major labor-saving appliances (washer, drier, dishwasher, etc.)																
1. Not important	7.8	8.3	7.5	7.2	9.3	7.8	9.0	7.4	6.7	6.0	10.0	7.9	7.2	8.0	7.6	10.9
2. Somewhat important	28.1	27.1	28.6	28.9	24.3	30.6	30.2	24.8	28.2	28.9	27.8	29.7	30.7	30.3	23.2	10.6
3. Quite important	37.3	38.6	36.8	38.5	32.4	36.5	38.4	36.3	38.1	37.8	36.5	38.6	35.5	32.7	39.0	53.8
4. Extremely important	26.7	26.0	27.2	25.5	34.0	25.1	22.4	31.5	27.0	27.3	25.6	23.8	26.7	29.0	30.2	24.7
Item 13910 Subject F01 N	*2741*	*1274*	*1401*	*2173*	*331*	*522*	*824*	*896*	*500*	*1618*	*1025*	*1041*	*612*	*374*	*646*	*31*
E09J: A high-quality stereo																
1. Not important	12.9	9.4	16.3	12.0	18.6	12.1	10.7	16.1	11.8	11.6	14.3	17.3	13.6	9.6	7.0	13.4
2. Somewhat important	32.0	25.8	37.5	32.6	30.9	30.9	33.1	33.2	29.4	32.5	32.2	35.8	29.3	33.1	28.5	21.5
3. Quite important	28.4	29.7	27.5	29.1	24.3	27.3	31.7	26.3	28.2	30.5	25.3	26.7	28.8	29.4	30.3	21.6
4. Extremely important	26.6	35.1	18.7	26.3	26.3	29.7	24.6	24.4	30.6	25.4	28.2	20.1	28.2	27.9	34.2	43.5
Item 13920 Subject F01 N	*2740*	*1276*	*1399*	*2173*	*331*	*521*	*822*	*895*	*501*	*1617*	*1024*	*1040*	*612*	*374*	*646*	*31*
E09K: A vacation house																
1. Not important	54.6	47.5	61.1	54.5	57.8	48.8	57.4	55.1	55.0	52.8	57.0	62.1	51.4	53.8	46.9	50.6
2. Somewhat important	25.3	28.8	22.2	26.1	20.0	25.9	25.5	24.3	26.3	26.5	24.0	22.0	27.9	27.6	26.5	27.5
3. Quite important	10.2	11.4	9.0	10.3	11.6	12.9	8.2	11.2	8.9	11.2	8.8	8.0	11.5	9.7	12.8	6.0
4. Extremely important	9.9	12.3	7.7	9.1	10.5	12.4	8.9	9.4	9.9	9.5	10.1	7.9	9.2	8.9	13.8	15.9
Item 13930 Subject F01 N	*2734*	*1271*	*1396*	*2167*	*331*	*521*	*820*	*893*	*501*	*1617*	*1020*	*1040*	*611*	*374*	*644*	*31*
E09L: A motor-powered, recreational vehicle (powerboat, snowmobile)																
1. Not important	48.4	35.1	60.8	45.5	66.6	47.5	42.0	54.0	49.6	49.3	47.6	56.6	46.5	45.9	38.7	56.0
2. Somewhat important	26.8	30.0	23.5	28.3	18.5	26.5	31.7	24.3	23.8	27.8	25.1	23.8	30.6	26.7	28.3	11.6
3. Quite important	13.0	17.4	9.4	14.6	5.2	14.2	12.7	12.3	13.7	13.4	12.3	9.7	11.7	15.3	18.1	12.5
4. Extremely important	11.8	17.5	6.4	11.6	9.7	11.9	13.6	9.5	12.9	9.5	15.0	9.8	11.2	12.1	15.0	19.9
Item 13940 Subject F01 N	*2734*	*1274*	*1394*	*2168*	*332*	*520*	*820*	*894*	*501*	*1619*	*1020*	*1039*	*608*	*375*	*644*	*31*

QUESTIONNAIRE FORM 3 1984	TOTAL	SEX		RACE		REGION				4YR COLLEGE PLANS		ILLICIT DRUG USE: LIFETIME				
		M	F	White	Black	NE	NC	S	W	Yes	No	None	Mari-juana Only	Few Pills	More Pills	Any Her-oin
N (Weighted No. of Cases):	3287	1532	1632	2482	442	675	914	1116	582	1823	1254	1211	735	430	791	41
% of Weighted Total:	100.0	46.6	49.6	75.5	13.4	20.5	27.8	33.9	17.7	55.5	38.1	36.8	22.4	13.1	24.1	1.3

E10: When (if ever) did you FIRST do each of the following things? Don't count anything you took because a doctor told you to.

E10A: Smoke cigarettes on a daily basis

	TOTAL	M	F	White	Black	NE	NC	S	W	Yes	No	None	Mari-juana Only	Few Pills	More Pills	Any Her-oin
8. Never	68.6	75.2	62.9	66.2	84.0	64.8	66.3	70.4	73.3	75.8	57.4	91.1	65.4	64.8	39.3	20.6
1. Grade 6 or below	4.5	4.5	4.7	4.8	2.7	3.4	5.4	4.4	4.5	3.1	6.8	1.9	4.2	2.0	9.9	18.9
2. Grade 7 or 8	8.5	6.9	9.8	9.3	2.3	8.3	10.4	7.6	7.1	5.8	12.9	1.4	9.4	10.9	17.3	17.2
3. Grade 9 (Freshman)	7.1	5.5	8.4	7.4	4.7	10.3	6.1	7.0	5.7	5.8	8.9	2.0	9.2	5.3	14.2	14.5
4. Grade 10 (Sophomore)	4.4	2.5	5.8	4.9	0.9	5.6	4.5	4.2	3.2	3.3	5.9	1.4	3.1	6.8	8.7	13.7
5. Grade 11 (Junior)	4.1	3.2	5.0	4.4	2.6	4.6	5.0	3.2	3.5	3.2	5.6	1.0	5.4	5.5	6.7	15.1
6. Grade 12 (Senior)	2.8	2.1	3.3	3.0	2.8	2.9	2.3	3.4	2.6	2.9	2.5	1.3	3.4	4.6	3.9	-
Item 5570　Subject A01g　N	2454	1137	1256	1964	292	465	739	798	451	1454	906	943	531	330	598	23

E10B: Try an alcoholic beverage - more than just a few sips

	TOTAL	M	F	White	Black	NE	NC	S	W	Yes	No	None	Mari-juana Only	Few Pills	More Pills	Any Her-oin
8. Never	7.0	6.7	7.2	5.8	14.9	5.8	6.5	7.8	7.6	7.3	5.6	17.4	1.1	1.6	0.5	-
1. Grade 6 or below	9.6	11.0	8.3	8.7	14.3	10.5	8.7	9.5	10.7	8.9	11.0	6.2	8.7	8.9	14.7	28.4
2. Grade 7 or 8	23.2	25.4	20.4	25.0	11.3	26.2	24.4	22.3	19.6	22.2	25.3	13.6	22.4	26.9	36.0	20.1
3. Grade 9 (Freshman)	23.7	22.3	25.3	24.9	15.5	26.5	21.9	22.7	25.5	24.1	23.0	17.8	27.8	25.5	27.7	27.0
4. Grade 10 (Sophomore)	19.6	19.5	20.1	20.2	19.8	16.9	21.1	20.0	19.3	20.9	17.6	18.9	24.7	23.8	13.2	12.3
5. Grade 11 (Junior)	11.2	10.4	12.2	11.0	14.4	10.0	11.1	11.1	13.0	11.0	12.1	16.0	11.5	10.4	5.1	12.2
6. Grade 12 (Senior)	5.6	4.8	6.5	4.5	9.9	4.1	6.3	6.6	4.3	5.6	5.6	10.2	3.9	3.0	2.8	-
Item 5580　Subject A01g　N	2485	1154	1273	2010	273	485	764	798	438	1458	939	876	572	350	629	28

E10C: Try marijuana or hashish

	TOTAL	M	F	White	Black	NE	NC	S	W	Yes	No	None	Mari-juana Only	Few Pills	More Pills	Any Her-oin
8. Never	46.7	43.3	50.1	45.3	56.1	37.5	47.3	54.2	42.0	51.7	38.9	100.0	-	29.7	11.2	-
1. Grade 6 or below	4.0	5.4	2.4	3.6	5.0	3.3	3.5	4.3	4.9	3.8	4.3	-	5.5	2.5	9.3	21.9
2. Grade 7 or 8	12.8	15.0	10.8	13.5	8.9	15.2	12.3	10.6	14.9	10.7	15.7	-	17.8	14.3	27.8	26.7
3. Grade 9 (Freshman)	14.1	13.7	14.3	14.7	9.4	21.1	12.9	10.1	15.8	13.1	15.9	-	22.8	21.6	25.1	29.2
4. Grade 10 (Sophomore)	11.2	10.2	12.4	11.9	6.7	13.0	11.6	9.7	11.3	9.9	13.1	-	22.5	17.3	15.5	16.8
5. Grade 11 (Junior)	7.3	7.8	6.5	7.3	8.3	4.9	8.3	7.7	7.3	6.5	8.3	-	19.0	9.7	8.2	5.4
6. Grade 12 (Senior)	4.0	4.6	3.5	3.7	5.5	4.9	4.1	3.4	3.7	4.2	3.7	-	12.5	4.9	2.8	-
Item 5590　Subject A01g　N	2560	1169	1329	2062	290	487	771	830	472	1524	938	1008	526	351	621	28

E10D: Try LSD

	TOTAL	M	F	White	Black	NE	NC	S	W	Yes	No	None	Mari-juana Only	Few Pills	More Pills	Any Her-oin
8. Never	93.3	92.4	94.6	92.5	99.7	89.7	94.4	94.4	93.4	94.8	91.5	100.0	100.0	95.5	75.5	52.5
1. Grade 6 or below	*	0.1	-	-	-	-	0.1	-	-	-	0.1	-	-	-	0.2	-
2. Grade 7 or 8	0.5	0.6	0.5	0.6	-	0.8	0.2	0.4	1.0	0.7	0.4	-	-	0.3	1.9	6.2
3. Grade 9 (Freshman)	1.6	1.8	1.3	1.8	0.3	3.1	1.1	1.3	1.5	1.2	2.3	-	-	1.4	5.5	20.4
4. Grade 10 (Sophomore)	1.8	2.0	1.4	2.0	-	2.7	1.7	1.6	1.5	1.2	2.7	-	-	0.4	6.9	18.3
5. Grade 11 (Junior)	1.6	1.9	1.4	1.9	-	2.0	2.0	1.1	1.5	1.3	1.7	-	-	0.5	6.7	2.6
6. Grade 12 (Senior)	1.0	1.2	0.9	1.2	-	1.7	0.4	1.2	1.0	0.8	1.2	-	-	1.8	3.3	-
Item 5600　Subject A01g　N	2650	1226	1364	2104	324	497	794	877	482	1581	975	1027	599	365	601	26

E10E: Try any psychedelic other than LSD

	TOTAL	M	F	White	Black	NE	NC	S	W	Yes	No	None	Mari-juana Only	Few Pills	More Pills	Any Her-oin
8. Never	96.3	96.0	97.1	96.0	99.0	92.5	97.9	97.6	95.0	96.7	95.8	100.0	100.0	98.2	86.1	58.2
1. Grade 6 or below	*	0.1	-	*	-	0.2	-	-	-	0.1	-	-	-	-	0.2	-
2. Grade 7 or 8	0.5	0.5	0.5	0.5	0.5	1.0	0.3	0.2	0.9	0.5	0.6	-	-	-	1.3	21.9
3. Grade 9 (Freshman)	0.7	0.6	0.8	0.9	0.2	0.8	0.6	0.6	1.0	0.4	1.1	-	-	0.1	2.9	5.5
4. Grade 10 (Sophomore)	1.1	1.2	0.8	1.0	0.3	2.2	0.7	0.9	1.2	1.1	1.1	-	-	-	4.5	14.4
5. Grade 11 (Junior)	0.8	1.1	0.5	1.0	-	1.7	0.5	0.6	0.8	0.7	1.0	-	-	0.6	3.3	-
6. Grade 12 (Senior)	0.5	0.5	0.4	0.6	-	1.6	-	-	1.2	0.5	0.4	-	-	1.1	1.6	-
Item 5610　Subject A01g　N	2623	1212	1346	2081	323	485	787	871	480	1557	970	1026	603	360	575	27

E10F: Try amphetamines

	TOTAL	M	F	White	Black	NE	NC	S	W	Yes	No	None	Mari-juana Only	Few Pills	More Pills	Any Her-oin
8. Never	82.6	83.4	81.8	79.9	98.2	80.2	82.2	83.9	83.5	85.4	78.9	100.0	100.0	74.0	22.3	29.9
1. Grade 6 or below	0.2	0.3	0.1	0.2	-	0.6	-	-	0.5	0.3	-	-	-	-	1.1	-
2. Grade 7 or 8	1.8	1.5	2.0	2.2	-	1.3	1.7	2.7	1.0	1.2	2.7	-	-	1.0	8.9	10.8
3. Grade 9 (Freshman)	5.6	5.7	5.4	6.5	0.3	6.5	5.4	5.0	5.8	4.7	6.0	-	-	5.4	26.8	18.7
4. Grade 10 (Sophomore)	5.0	3.7	6.2	5.7	0.9	6.9	5.2	3.8	4.7	3.8	7.2	-	-	7.4	21.6	29.5
5. Grade 11 (Junior)	3.1	3.5	2.8	3.7	0.2	2.8	3.4	3.2	2.6	3.0	3.1	-	-	6.9	12.6	11.1
6. Grade 12 (Senior)	1.8	1.9	1.7	2.0	0.5	1.7	2.1	1.4	2.0	1.5	2.1	-	-	5.2	6.7	-
Item 5620　Subject A01g　N	2330	1093	1177	1825	301	449	680	785	416	1419	829	1024	591	240	422	19

*=less than .05 per cent.

QUESTIONNAIRE FORM 3 1984	TOTAL	SEX		RACE		REGION				4YR COLLEGE PLANS		ILLICIT DRUG USE: LIFETIME				
		M	F	White	Black	NE	NC	S	W	Yes	No	None	Mari-juana Only	Few Pills	More Pills	Any Her-oin
N (Weighted No. of Cases):	3287	1532	1632	2482	442	675	914	1116	582	1823	1254	1211	735	430	791	41
% of Weighted Total:	100.0	46.6	49.6	75.5	13.4	20.5	27.8	33.9	17.7	55.5	38.1	36.8	22.4	13.1	24.1	1.3
E10G: Try quaaludes																
8. Never	93.7	92.8	94.8	92.8	98.9	92.5	95.1	92.3	94.8	94.9	92.5	100.0	100.0	95.6	76.2	53.2
1. Grade 6 or below	0.1	0.2	-	*	-	0.2	0.1	-	-	0.1	0.1	-	-	-	0.4	-
2. Grade 7 or 8	0.9	0.5	1.0	0.9	0.5	0.4	0.3	1.3	1.5	0.9	0.7	-	-	0.7	3.2	9.3
3. Grade 9 (Freshman)	1.8	2.6	1.1	2.0	0.5	2.6	1.5	1.8	1.6	1.4	2.1	-	-	0.8	6.8	22.6
4. Grade 10 (Sophomore)	2.0	2.1	1.6	2.3	-	2.8	1.9	1.9	1.3	1.4	2.8	-	-	1.4	7.5	8.9
5. Grade 11 (Junior)	1.3	1.2	1.4	1.5	-	1.2	0.9	2.2	0.3	0.9	1.5	-	-	1.1	4.7	5.9
6. Grade 12 (Senior)	0.3	0.6	0.1	0.4	-	0.2	0.1	0.5	0.5	0.4	0.2	-	-	0.4	1.2	-
Item 5630 Subject A01g N	2632	1213	1354	2088	323	498	786	862	487	1567	975	1024	602	360	591	22
E10H: Try barbiturates																
8. Never	94.5	93.7	95.4	93.9	99.4	93.1	94.7	94.6	95.6	96.0	92.8	100.0	100.0	98.1	77.7	45.2
1. Grade 6 or below	0.2	0.3	-	0.1	-	0.6	0.1	-	0.1	0.2	0.1	-	-	0.2	0.5	4.6
2. Grade 7 or 8	0.7	0.6	0.7	0.8	-	1.1	0.5	0.5	0.9	0.6	0.9	-	-	-	2.9	7.4
3. Grade 9 (Freshman)	1.7	2.0	1.3	1.7	-	2.2	1.9	1.4	1.1	1.0	2.6	-	-	0.6	7.3	2.5
4. Grade 10 (Sophomore)	1.6	1.9	1.3	1.8	0.6	1.6	1.7	1.5	1.5	1.1	2.1	-	-	-	6.5	25.4
5. Grade 11 (Junior)	1.0	1.0	1.0	1.2	-	1.0	0.7	1.7	0.2	0.8	1.2	-	-	0.3	3.8	15.0
6. Grade 12 (Senior)	0.4	0.6	0.3	0.5	-	0.3	0.4	0.3	0.6	0.4	0.3	-	-	0.8	1.3	-
Item 5640 Subject A01g N	2566	1187	1318	2034	314	484	769	837	475	1541	943	1024	601	341	545	22
E10I: Try tranquilizers																
8. Never	95.0	95.4	94.8	94.3	99.4	94.6	96.8	93.8	94.4	95.8	94.2	100.0	100.0	94.5	80.6	44.9
1. Grade 6 or below	0.1	0.1	0.1	0.1	-	0.2	0.1	0.2	-	0.2	0.1	-	-	-	0.6	-
2. Grade 7 or 8	0.5	0.6	0.5	0.5	-	0.2	0.4	0.8	0.6	0.6	0.5	-	-	-	1.9	15.9
3. Grade 9 (Freshman)	1.6	2.1	1.1	1.8	0.6	2.1	1.5	1.2	2.0	1.0	2.3	-	-	1.1	6.0	31.6
4. Grade 10 (Sophomore)	0.9	0.6	1.1	1.1	-	1.1	0.4	1.6	0.5	0.9	1.0	-	-	0.5	4.1	7.6
5. Grade 11 (Junior)	1.0	0.7	1.4	1.2	-	1.5	0.3	1.4	1.1	0.7	1.2	-	-	1.9	4.1	-
6. Grade 12 (Senior)	0.8	0.5	1.0	0.9	-	0.4	0.5	0.9	1.3	0.8	0.7	-	-	1.9	2.7	-
Item 5650 Subject A01g N	2486	1150	1274	1958	311	466	749	812	460	1494	903	1023	603	316	488	24
E10J: Try cocaine																
8. Never	86.3	84.2	88.4	85.2	93.6	77.4	92.7	91.2	76.4	87.9	84.7	100.0	100.0	79.5	55.9	25.2
1. Grade 6 or below	0.2	0.3	0.1	0.1	0.5	0.5	-	-	0.6	0.1	0.3	-	-	-	0.4	10.7
2. Grade 7 or 8	0.4	0.3	0.4	0.5	-	1.1	0.2	*	1.0	0.5	0.5	-	-	-	1.9	-
3. Grade 9 (Freshman)	2.0	2.1	1.8	2.1	1.2	3.4	1.3	1.2	3.1	1.4	2.7	-	-	0.8	6.6	34.5
4. Grade 10 (Sophomore)	2.9	3.9	1.9	3.3	0.4	5.4	1.2	2.0	4.8	2.6	2.9	-	-	2.5	10.7	11.2
5. Grade 11 (Junior)	4.2	5.0	3.6	4.6	2.8	6.1	2.7	2.5	8.0	3.6	5.1	-	-	5.9	14.2	15.6
6. Grade 12 (Senior)	3.9	4.2	3.7	4.2	1.5	6.2	2.0	3.0	6.1	3.9	3.8	-	-	11.4	10.1	2.7
Item 5660 Subject A01g N	2637	1210	1362	2097	319	502	788	871	476	1566	973	1022	597	349	611	26
E10K: Try heroin																
8. Never	99.4	99.2	99.7	99.5	99.2	99.2	99.4	99.6	99.4	99.5	99.3	100.0	100.0	100.0	100.0	-
1. Grade 6 or below	-	-	-	-	-	-	-	-	-	-	-	-	-	-	-	-
2. Grade 7 or 8	0.1	-	0.1	0.1	-	0.2	-	0.1	-	0.1	-	-	-	-	-	14.9
3. Grade 9 (Freshman)	0.1	*	0.2	0.1	-	0.1	0.1	0.2	-	0.1	0.1	-	-	-	-	19.3
4. Grade 10 (Sophomore)	0.2	0.4	-	0.1	0.8	0.2	0.3	-	0.4	0.1	0.3	-	-	-	-	32.3
5. Grade 11 (Junior)	0.1	0.1	0.1	0.1	-	0.2	-	0.1	-	*	0.1	-	-	-	-	13.5
6. Grade 12 (Senior)	0.1	0.2	-	0.1	-	-	0.3	-	0.2	0.1	0.2	-	-	-	-	20.1
Item 5670 Subject A01g N	2666	1234	1367	2118	326	507	801	873	485	1585	986	1021	598	369	631	15
E10L: Try any narcotic other than heroin																
8. Never	97.0	96.5	97.7	97.0	98.8	96.2	97.2	97.3	97.1	97.5	96.7	100.0	100.0	96.8	89.7	39.2
1. Grade 6 or below	*	-	*	-	0.2	-	-	0.1	-	*	-	-	-	0.2	-	-
2. Grade 7 or 8	0.1	0.3	-	0.2	-	0.3	0.2	0.1	-	0.2	0.1	-	-	-	0.7	-
3. Grade 9 (Freshman)	0.9	0.6	1.1	0.9	-	1.0	0.9	0.6	1.1	0.8	0.9	-	-	1.2	2.7	17.8
4. Grade 10 (Sophomore)	0.8	0.8	0.7	0.8	0.5	0.9	1.2	0.7	0.3	0.7	0.8	-	-	-	3.2	22.7
5. Grade 11 (Junior)	0.6	1.0	0.3	0.6	-	1.0	-	1.0	0.4	0.6	0.5	-	-	0.4	2.2	11.5
6. Grade 12 (Senior)	0.5	0.9	0.3	0.5	0.6	0.6	0.4	0.3	1.1	0.3	0.9	-	-	1.3	1.5	8.8
Item 5680 Subject A01g N	2511	1159	1289	1969	317	473	760	823	455	1492	929	1024	601	335	499	20

*=less than .05 per cent.

QUESTIONNAIRE FORM 3 1984	TOTAL	SEX		RACE		REGION				4YR COLLEGE PLANS		ILLICIT DRUG USE: LIFETIME				
		M	F	White	Black	NE	NC	S	W	Yes	No	None	Mari- juana Only	Few Pills	More Pills	Any Her- oin
N (Weighted No. of Cases):	3287	1532	1632	2482	442	675	914	1116	582	1823	1254	1211	735	430	791	41
% of Weighted Total:	100.0	46.6	49.6	75.5	13.4	20.5	27.8	33.9	17.7	55.5	38.1	36.8	22.4	13.1	24.1	1.3

E10M: Try inhalants

8. Never	92.0	88.9	94.8	90.9	98.6	89.9	93.8	93.2	89.3	92.9	91.6	98.8	95.9	92.2	76.6	62.1
1. Grade 6 or below	0.7	1.0	0.2	0.6	0.3	1.1	0.4	0.5	1.0	0.7	0.7	0.1	0.9	0.5	1.5	3.9
2. Grade 7 or 8	1.7	2.3	1.2	2.0	0.2	2.4	1.0	1.5	2.2	1.7	1.5	0.4	1.1	1.8	4.4	4.8
3. Grade 9 (Freshman)	1.5	2.2	0.9	1.8	0.3	2.2	0.6	1.6	2.1	1.2	1.6	-	0.8	1.5	4.9	4.6
4. Grade 10 (Sophomore)	1.6	2.5	0.9	1.8	0.7	1.5	2.0	1.4	1.6	1.3	2.3	0.2	0.4	1.2	5.3	14.1
5. Grade 11 (Junior)	1.1	1.7	0.7	1.2	-	1.8	1.0	0.4	2.0	0.8	1.2	0.1	0.9	1.0	3.3	2.1
6. Grade 12 (Senior)	1.3	1.5	1.3	1.6	-	1.1	1.2	1.3	1.8	1.4	1.1	0.4	-	1.8	3.9	8.5
Item 5685 Subject A01g N	2483	1133	1288	1962	304	463	751	821	448	1498	900	988	567	333	540	26

QUESTIONNAIRE FORM 4 1984	TOTAL	SEX		RACE		REGION				4YR COLLEGE PLANS		ILLICIT DRUG USE: LIFETIME				
		M	F	White	Black	NE	NC	S	W	Yes	No	None	Mari-juana Only	Few Pills	More Pills	Any Her-oin
N (Weighted No. of Cases):	3284	1588	1546	2489	414	679	909	1113	584	1830	1188	1253	675	426	806	39
% of Weighted Total:	100.0	48.4	47.1	75.8	12.6	20.7	27.7	33.9	17.8	55.7	36.2	38.1	20.6	13.0	24.5	1.2
A01: Taking all things together, how would you say things are these days-would you say you're very happy, pretty happy, or not too happy these days?																
3. Very happy	17.4	16.9	17.9	18.4	13.2	17.2	15.3	17.8	20.5	19.4	15.2	19.9	16.3	15.0	16.2	14.1
2. Pretty happy	70.2	70.6	70.1	71.0	69.0	68.5	70.9	71.5	68.5	70.8	69.9	68.9	71.2	71.3	71.5	56.4
1. Not too happy	12.4	12.5	12.1	10.6	17.9	14.4	13.8	10.7	11.0	9.8	14.9	11.1	12.5	13.8	12.3	29.5
Item 1190 Subject P01,Q01 N	3277	1585	1546	2487	414	678	906	1112	581	1827	1187	1251	674	426	806	39
A02: Looking ahead to the next five years, do you think that things in this country will get better or worse?																
1. Get much better	4.4	6.0	2.7	4.0	5.1	3.5	4.4	5.0	4.3	4.9	3.2	5.3	3.7	2.3	4.2	5.4
2. Get somewhat better	35.7	40.9	30.8	36.2	36.8	30.8	38.5	36.1	36.1	38.0	33.3	36.0	37.1	34.3	33.9	43.6
3. Stay about the same	30.8	30.7	30.7	32.8	20.6	35.1	28.8	28.6	33.2	31.2	30.5	30.1	33.6	34.1	29.3	14.3
4. Get somewhat worse	25.0	18.4	31.7	23.5	31.8	25.3	24.4	26.1	23.7	22.6	27.7	25.6	21.5	25.7	26.8	32.3
5. Get much worse	4.1	4.1	4.2	3.5	5.7	5.3	3.9	4.3	2.7	3.2	5.4	3.0	4.1	3.5	5.8	4.4
Item 9940 Subject I01 N	3275	1586	1544	2484	414	677	906	1111	581	1826	1188	1250	673	426	805	39
A03: Looking ahead to the next five years, do you think that things in the rest of the world will get better or worse?																
1. Get much better	1.9	2.5	1.4	1.5	2.3	1.3	1.9	2.4	1.7	2.1	1.7	2.3	1.9	1.3	1.5	5.9
2. Get somewhat better	18.9	19.4	18.1	16.6	30.6	16.6	21.7	18.2	18.4	18.2	20.2	18.8	20.5	17.8	17.2	18.1
3. Stay about the same	30.2	32.2	28.5	32.2	23.9	32.2	28.6	29.1	32.6	30.9	29.6	29.3	31.4	29.8	30.1	44.3
4. Get somewhat worse	40.7	38.2	42.8	42.2	33.1	41.3	40.6	40.4	40.6	41.0	39.4	42.1	37.5	43.1	41.7	23.1
5. Get much worse	8.3	7.7	9.2	7.5	10.2	8.6	7.2	9.9	6.6	7.8	9.0	7.5	8.7	8.0	9.5	8.6
Item 9950 Subject I01 N	3270	1580	1545	2482	414	672	906	1111	581	1824	1185	1251	668	426	806	39
A04: How do you think your own life will go in the next five years–do you think it will get better or worse?																
1. Get much better	43.5	42.9	44.3	42.0	50.6	41.6	41.4	44.6	46.8	43.3	42.9	41.8	44.0	44.9	45.1	28.9
2. Get somewhat better	46.1	45.6	46.5	47.5	40.4	48.8	47.0	44.4	44.9	47.9	45.3	46.2	48.3	44.3	45.7	56.5
3. Stay about the same	8.8	9.9	8.0	9.3	7.4	7.5	10.3	9.2	7.4	7.6	10.0	10.2	7.0	10.3	7.2	5.2
4. Get somewhat worse	1.2	1.3	1.1	1.1	1.7	1.5	1.1	1.5	0.7	1.1	1.5	1.6	0.7	0.5	1.3	5.1
5. Get much worse	0.3	0.3	*	0.1	-	0.6	0.2	0.3	0.2	*	0.4	0.2	0.1	-	0.7	4.3
Item 9960 Subject I01 N	3277	1585	1546	2486	414	677	907	1113	581	1828	1188	1251	674	426	806	39
A05: Some people think a lot about the social problems of the nation and the world, and about how they might be solved. Others spend little time thinking about these issues. How much do you think about such things?																
1. Never	2.9	3.5	1.9	2.5	3.3	5.1	2.3	2.2	2.9	2.0	4.2	2.2	2.4	4.1	3.4	6.5
2. Seldom	19.1	19.8	18.1	20.1	13.3	19.4	20.9	19.1	16.0	17.2	23.0	16.5	21.3	20.4	21.2	16.5
3. Sometimes	49.4	47.8	51.3	51.2	47.1	51.6	48.5	47.8	51.2	48.0	50.5	49.6	50.2	48.4	49.1	45.3
4. Quite often	23.8	23.6	24.2	22.4	27.8	20.9	23.6	25.3	24.7	27.2	18.5	26.5	20.7	24.0	22.1	23.3
5. A great deal	4.8	5.3	4.5	3.8	8.6	3.1	4.6	5.7	5.2	5.5	3.8	5.3	5.4	3.0	4.2	8.4
Item 6880 Subject J,Q08 N	3276	1585	1545	2486	414	677	906	1113	581	1827	1187	1251	675	426	805	39
A06: These questions are about pollution and the environment. Please mark the circle that shows how much you agree or disagree with each statement below.																
A06A: In general, pollution has increased in the U.S. in the last ten years																
1. Disagree	4.1	5.6	2.3	3.8	5.3	3.8	5.8	3.5	2.9	3.7	4.5	3.9	3.6	5.3	4.0	11.7
2. Mostly disagree	9.2	10.2	8.0	10.1	7.0	7.7	12.9	7.3	8.6	9.6	8.9	7.9	12.0	8.0	9.5	7.4
3. Neither	6.3	6.3	5.8	6.0	5.4	5.0	7.3	6.2	6.3	6.7	5.2	6.0	5.8	8.6	4.8	5.0
4. Mostly agree	34.3	32.4	36.9	35.2	31.4	34.4	35.8	32.8	34.5	36.3	32.8	34.9	35.3	33.9	34.2	36.1
5. Agree	46.2	45.5	47.0	44.9	51.0	49.1	38.2	50.3	47.7	43.7	48.6	47.3	43.4	44.2	47.5	39.7
Item 9970 Subject F04 N	3272	1586	1540	2483	412	675	909	1107	581	1825	1184	1247	675	426	803	39

*=less than .05 per cent.

QUESTIONNAIRE FORM 4 1984	TOTAL	SEX		RACE		REGION				4YR COLLEGE PLANS		ILLICIT DRUG USE: LIFETIME				
		M	F	White	Black	NE	NC	S	W	Yes	No	None	Marijuana Only	Few Pills	More Pills	Any Heroin
N (Weighted No. of Cases):	3284	1588	1546	2489	414	679	909	1113	584	1830	1188	1253	675	426	806	39
% of Weighted Total:	100.0	48.4	47.1	75.8	12.6	20.7	27.7	33.9	17.8	55.7	36.2	38.1	20.6	13.0	24.5	1.2
A06B: The dangers of pollution are not really as great as government, the media, and environmental groups would like us to believe																
1. Disagree	37.5	36.8	37.9	37.4	37.8	38.2	36.8	37.8	37.3	38.8	35.7	37.9	37.9	36.0	38.2	19.2
2. Mostly disagree	26.5	26.2	27.8	28.8	17.8	27.4	28.4	23.6	28.0	29.9	23.3	25.7	27.8	28.8	26.8	25.5
3. Neither	10.5	11.4	9.5	10.1	12.6	8.5	9.5	11.6	12.2	9.6	11.1	11.0	8.5	9.2	11.3	20.5
4. Mostly agree	16.4	16.5	16.0	15.9	17.9	15.8	16.4	16.6	17.0	14.6	18.4	15.7	16.2	18.1	15.8	28.2
5. Agree	9.1	9.1	8.8	7.8	13.9	10.1	8.9	10.4	5.6	7.1	11.5	9.8	9.6	7.9	8.0	6.5
Item 9980 Subject F04 N	3262	1582	1539	2482	408	671	909	1107	576	1818	1184	1248	669	424	801	39
A06C: America needs growth to survive, and that is going to require some increase in pollution																
1. Disagree	36.0	35.9	36.0	34.9	41.4	40.2	33.3	36.5	34.6	37.7	34.2	36.2	36.9	35.0	36.7	31.9
2. Mostly disagree	22.7	22.9	22.9	24.4	15.4	21.2	24.3	21.5	24.2	24.8	20.7	23.3	22.6	25.1	21.3	17.0
3. Neither	11.8	11.6	11.8	11.8	11.3	11.9	12.2	11.0	12.5	12.4	11.0	11.4	12.0	12.3	11.5	12.9
4. Mostly agree	17.4	17.0	17.9	18.5	12.7	14.9	20.0	16.8	17.2	15.7	19.6	17.5	15.5	16.1	18.7	24.2
5. Agree	12.1	12.6	11.4	10.3	19.2	11.7	10.1	14.3	11.5	9.4	14.6	11.6	13.0	11.6	11.8	14.0
Item 9990 Subject F04 N	3245	1572	1532	2464	412	668	899	1101	577	1816	1175	1239	671	421	798	38
A06D: People will have to change their buying habits and way of life to correct our environmental problems																
1. Disagree	13.7	15.0	12.0	12.6	17.0	15.4	11.1	15.5	12.2	12.0	15.7	12.6	15.6	13.2	13.5	10.7
2. Mostly disagree	14.1	13.8	13.9	14.3	11.9	12.9	15.0	14.9	12.6	14.6	13.4	14.3	13.6	12.4	14.8	17.1
3. Neither	15.3	16.1	14.8	16.2	12.3	16.9	14.9	14.2	16.3	16.2	13.7	12.6	16.7	16.0	17.3	13.8
4. Mostly agree	32.1	31.1	33.9	33.6	25.1	29.8	33.7	31.1	34.2	32.4	33.3	33.9	29.1	34.2	31.7	31.7
5. Agree	24.7	24.0	25.3	23.3	33.6	25.0	25.3	24.2	24.7	24.9	23.8	26.5	25.0	24.1	22.6	26.7
Item 10000 Subject F04 N	3251	1581	1531	2472	409	669	902	1100	580	1820	1173	1240	672	425	796	38
A06E: Government should take action to solve our environmental problems even if it means that some of the products we now use would have to be changed or banned																
1. Disagree	5.9	6.3	5.3	4.9	11.4	4.5	5.6	7.3	5.2	5.2	7.0	5.8	8.3	4.4	4.6	15.3
2. Mostly disagree	8.1	8.5	7.3	7.5	9.1	7.1	8.9	7.8	8.4	7.6	8.0	7.2	9.2	8.7	7.9	9.2
3. Neither	12.4	14.2	10.7	12.4	12.0	9.3	14.8	12.4	12.5	12.3	13.0	13.1	11.3	10.4	13.4	13.3
4. Mostly agree	34.4	33.2	36.0	36.4	26.7	32.2	37.8	31.4	37.3	35.0	35.1	34.5	35.6	37.0	31.3	38.7
5. Agree	39.2	37.8	40.7	38.8	40.9	46.9	33.0	41.1	36.6	39.9	36.9	39.5	35.6	39.5	42.8	23.4
Item 10010 Subject F04,H02 N	3260	1582	1539	2480	409	671	906	1106	578	1822	1181	1248	673	423	800	38
A06F: Government should place higher taxes on products which cause pollution in their manufacture or disposal, so that companies will be encouraged to find better ways to produce them																
1. Disagree	14.3	14.8	14.1	13.0	20.7	14.6	9.8	17.9	14.5	12.4	16.2	11.9	15.9	16.0	15.1	21.4
2. Mostly disagree	12.3	13.1	11.4	12.1	12.9	12.7	12.3	11.4	13.6	11.5	13.1	11.8	13.0	13.6	11.8	12.9
3. Neither	13.2	12.5	14.1	14.1	8.3	13.5	16.5	10.6	12.4	12.9	13.9	12.3	13.3	12.9	14.6	9.5
4. Mostly agree	27.6	27.1	28.0	29.1	20.8	25.3	30.9	27.4	25.7	29.7	26.5	28.8	25.3	28.7	26.7	31.5
5. Agree	32.6	32.6	32.4	31.6	37.4	33.9	30.6	32.8	33.8	33.5	30.3	35.1	32.6	28.8	31.7	24.7
Item 10020 Subject F04,H02 N	3257	1579	1537	2476	409	672	903	1105	578	1821	1179	1246	675	424	796	38
A06G: I wish that government would ban throwaway bottles and beverage cans																
1. Disagree	29.3	28.7	29.9	29.1	31.5	27.7	25.8	34.4	27.0	28.5	30.5	27.2	30.6	29.1	31.5	37.2
2. Mostly disagree	14.3	15.4	13.4	15.3	9.8	11.7	14.0	14.2	17.7	15.6	12.5	14.5	12.3	15.2	15.0	15.4
3. Neither	23.2	20.2	27.0	24.4	18.7	26.5	22.9	21.9	22.3	25.0	22.0	25.4	22.8	22.5	19.9	28.5
4. Mostly agree	14.4	14.4	14.1	14.1	15.7	14.5	16.3	12.8	14.2	14.6	13.6	14.4	14.7	15.8	13.7	8.6
5. Agree	18.9	21.4	15.6	17.1	24.4	19.6	21.0	16.7	18.8	16.3	21.4	18.4	19.6	17.3	19.9	10.3
Item 10030 Subject F04,H02 N	3249	1577	1529	2471	408	666	904	1105	574	1815	1177	1243	669	422	796	38

QUESTIONNAIRE FORM 4 1984	TOTAL	SEX		RACE		REGION				4YR COLLEGE PLANS		ILLICIT DRUG USE: LIFETIME				
		M	F	White	Black	NE	NC	S	W	Yes	No	None	Mari- juana Only	Few Pills	More Pills	Any Her- oin
N (Weighted No. of Cases):	3284	1588	1546	2489	414	679	909	1113	584	1830	1188	1253	675	426	806	39
% of Weighted Total:	100.0	48.4	47.1	75.8	12.6	20.7	27.7	33.9	17.8	55.7	36.2	38.1	20.6	13.0	24.5	1.2

A06H: T.V. commercials stimulate people to buy a lot of things they don't really need

	TOTAL	M	F	White	Black	NE	NC	S	W	Yes	No	None	Mari- juana Only	Few Pills	More Pills	Any Her- oin
1. Disagree	5.0	4.8	4.9	4.2	6.0	4.4	5.1	4.8	5.9	4.0	5.3	4.5	4.7	4.4	5.7	8.2
2. Mostly disagree	7.5	8.8	6.0	7.6	6.0	7.0	8.1	7.5	7.1	7.1	8.0	6.6	6.9	8.9	7.7	17.5
3. Neither	7.6	9.9	5.5	8.5	3.9	7.1	9.2	6.0	8.7	8.2	8.7	7.1	8.0	4.8	8.8	10.7
4. Mostly agree	27.0	29.1	24.3	27.5	24.3	28.2	29.5	25.2	24.9	28.2	26.0	28.4	27.2	27.1	25.1	26.5
5. Agree	53.0	47.4	59.3	52.2	59.7	53.3	48.2	56.5	53.4	52.5	53.7	53.4	53.2	54.8	52.7	37.2
Item 10040 Subject F02 N	3257	1578	1536	2476	410	673	904	1101	578	1823	1175	1244	674	419	802	38

A06I: T.V. commercials do a lot of good by showing new products that we might not know about otherwise

	TOTAL	M	F	White	Black	NE	NC	S	W	Yes	No	None	Mari- juana Only	Few Pills	More Pills	Any Her- oin
1. Disagree	5.7	5.9	5.5	5.8	5.1	9.9	5.2	4.3	4.5	5.4	5.5	5.8	5.4	7.2	5.2	7.6
2. Mostly disagree	10.8	10.8	10.6	11.3	7.6	12.5	10.9	8.1	13.6	11.9	9.0	10.1	9.8	11.0	12.3	12.1
3. Neither	15.0	16.8	13.7	16.8	5.9	15.4	16.7	11.4	19.0	17.3	12.8	15.2	15.1	12.6	16.2	15.1
4. Mostly agree	35.1	35.1	35.2	36.9	28.8	33.0	36.6	35.3	34.7	35.9	35.3	34.9	35.1	38.5	34.3	34.4
5. Agree	33.4	31.4	35.0	29.1	52.7	29.3	30.6	41.0	28.2	29.5	37.4	34.0	34.7	30.6	31.9	30.7
Item 10050 Subject F02 N	3257	1574	1540	2475	410	673	903	1105	577	1823	1176	1241	672	425	802	37

A06J: My family and I often buy things we don't really need; we could get along with much less

	TOTAL	M	F	White	Black	NE	NC	S	W	Yes	No	None	Mari- juana Only	Few Pills	More Pills	Any Her- oin
1. Disagree	13.7	13.1	13.9	11.6	23.2	19.8	10.3	13.9	11.9	12.9	14.3	12.3	15.4	14.3	13.8	8.7
2. Mostly disagree	15.4	16.9	13.2	15.2	16.0	13.8	18.1	12.0	19.8	16.0	14.4	15.1	14.7	14.6	15.9	34.4
3. Neither	13.8	16.5	11.6	14.9	9.5	13.7	12.9	14.0	14.9	14.1	13.8	14.0	13.7	16.0	12.5	12.5
4. Mostly agree	28.1	27.4	29.4	29.5	24.8	25.7	29.9	27.9	28.7	29.8	27.0	30.5	27.4	26.0	27.5	17.1
5. Agree	28.9	26.1	31.9	28.8	26.5	27.2	28.9	32.2	24.7	27.1	30.5	28.0	28.9	29.1	30.3	27.3
Item 10060 Subject F01 N	3247	1571	1534	2472	406	666	901	1102	579	1816	1173	1242	668	422	797	38

A06K: By the year 2000, engineers and scientists will probably have invented devices that will solve our pollution problems

	TOTAL	M	F	White	Black	NE	NC	S	W	Yes	No	None	Mari- juana Only	Few Pills	More Pills	Any Her- oin
1. Disagree	11.0	12.2	9.8	10.2	15.3	11.4	11.5	11.1	9.4	9.6	13.0	11.2	11.3	11.2	10.1	24.3
2. Mostly disagree	18.4	19.6	17.1	19.8	11.4	20.6	18.5	16.8	18.7	19.8	16.7	17.0	19.4	20.2	19.7	8.3
3. Neither	23.3	20.9	25.9	24.8	16.3	20.0	24.7	21.0	29.3	23.3	24.3	23.3	22.2	23.3	23.5	17.9
4. Mostly agree	30.4	30.5	30.7	30.5	33.3	30.0	30.3	31.3	29.6	32.1	27.6	31.1	29.5	31.2	29.9	33.5
5. Agree	16.9	16.8	16.6	14.6	23.7	18.0	15.0	19.9	12.9	15.1	18.3	17.4	17.5	14.2	16.8	16.0
Item 10070 Subject F04 N	3260	1580	1538	2479	409	672	904	1106	577	1823	1180	1246	673	424	799	38

A07: In your own actions–the things you buy and the things you do–how much of an effort do you make to conserve energy and protect the environment?

	TOTAL	M	F	White	Black	NE	NC	S	W	Yes	No	None	Mari- juana Only	Few Pills	More Pills	Any Her- oin
1. None	6.6	7.7	5.2	6.1	6.9	9.3	5.5	6.1	6.0	5.7	8.3	4.6	7.6	6.0	8.5	10.5
2. A little	27.0	25.7	28.1	27.5	26.9	27.8	26.7	26.9	26.5	27.2	26.0	24.0	29.0	28.7	29.6	29.2
3. Some	52.0	52.3	52.1	53.3	46.3	48.8	53.7	53.2	50.7	52.0	52.9	55.7	49.4	51.2	49.4	44.8
4. Quite a bit	14.5	14.3	14.6	13.1	19.9	14.1	14.1	13.8	16.8	15.1	12.8	15.8	14.0	14.1	12.6	15.5
Item 10080 Subject F04 N	3142	1507	1503	2417	382	647	885	1058	552	1766	1141	1200	648	412	774	37

The next questions are about work.

A08: Different people may look for different things in their work. Below is a list of some of these things. Please read each one, then indicate how important this thing is for you.

A08A: A job where you can see the results of what you do

	TOTAL	M	F	White	Black	NE	NC	S	W	Yes	No	None	Mari- juana Only	Few Pills	More Pills	Any Her- oin
1. Not important	0.9	1.2	0.5	0.7	2.2	1.4	0.7	1.0	0.6	0.9	0.9	1.1	0.4	1.3	0.6	2.3
2. A little important	7.6	9.1	6.5	8.8	2.7	8.3	11.0	5.2	6.1	6.5	10.0	7.4	6.5	5.9	9.1	14.4
3. Pretty important	34.2	36.3	32.1	36.7	22.5	29.4	37.9	32.3	37.8	34.4	33.8	33.2	34.0	39.4	32.9	44.6
4. Very important	57.2	53.3	60.9	53.7	72.6	60.9	50.3	61.6	55.5	58.1	55.4	58.2	59.1	53.5	57.4	38.7
Item 10090 Subject C04 N	3249	1574	1536	2470	413	671	901	1103	574	1817	1177	1244	668	424	803	38

QUESTIONNAIRE FORM 4 1984	TOTAL	SEX		RACE		REGION				4YR COLLEGE PLANS		ILLICIT DRUG USE: LIFETIME				
		M	F	White	Black	NE	NC	S	W	Yes	No	None	Mari-juana Only	Few Pills	More Pills	Any Her-oin
N (Weighted No. of Cases):	3284	1588	1546	2489	414	679	909	1113	584	1830	1188	1253	675	426	806	39
% of Weighted Total:	100.0	48.4	47.1	75.8	12.6	20.7	27.7	33.9	17.8	55.7	36.2	38.1	20.6	13.0	24.5	1.2
A08B: A job that has high status and prestige																
1. Not important	7.5	7.6	7.5	8.5	2.0	8.2	8.0	6.1	8.7	7.1	8.3	7.3	6.1	7.4	8.8	14.2
2. A little important	24.1	23.0	25.6	26.6	12.4	24.3	25.7	21.8	25.9	24.9	24.0	25.2	23.7	24.1	23.0	33.8
3. Pretty important	39.4	40.9	37.9	40.0	37.1	35.2	42.9	38.0	41.7	39.6	39.9	40.0	40.9	40.8	36.9	35.5
4. Very important	28.9	28.5	29.1	24.9	48.6	32.3	23.4	34.1	23.7	28.4	27.8	27.5	29.3	27.8	31.3	16.5
Item 10100 Subject C04 N	3240	1572	1532	2465	412	668	900	1101	571	1816	1173	1244	666	424	797	38
A08C: A job which is interesting to do																
1. Not important	0.3	0.3	*	0.1	0.1	0.4	0.1	0.3	0.3	0.1	0.2	0.3	0.2	0.1	0.1	2.7
2. A little important	1.5	1.6	1.3	1.3	2.9	1.8	1.9	1.5	0.5	1.0	2.0	1.4	0.4	1.4	2.1	4.2
3. Pretty important	11.1	12.0	9.7	11.4	9.1	10.6	12.6	9.6	12.1	10.0	12.5	9.8	11.4	11.2	12.3	19.3
4. Very important	87.2	86.1	89.0	87.2	87.8	87.2	85.4	88.6	87.1	88.9	85.3	88.6	88.0	87.3	85.4	73.8
Item 10110 Subject C04 N	3227	1562	1527	2453	409	670	888	1099	571	1809	1164	1234	667	420	796	38
A08D: A job where the chances for advancement and promotion are good																
1. Not important	1.2	1.4	1.0	1.2	0.4	1.5	1.5	1.1	0.6	1.1	1.3	1.5	0.7	0.6	1.4	3.9
2. A little important	6.3	5.5	7.3	6.6	2.9	4.7	8.9	5.0	6.4	6.3	6.4	6.6	5.3	8.7	5.2	4.4
3. Pretty important	26.9	26.2	27.3	29.0	16.1	25.2	30.5	23.6	29.4	28.2	25.6	30.3	26.1	27.9	21.6	32.5
4. Very important	65.7	67.0	64.3	63.1	80.5	68.7	59.1	70.3	63.7	64.4	66.7	61.6	67.9	62.7	71.8	59.2
Item 10120 Subject C04 N	3243	1572	1533	2469	408	673	896	1102	572	1816	1174	1240	670	424	799	38
A08E: A job that gives you an opportunity to be directly helpful to others																
1. Not important	2.8	4.3	1.1	2.5	2.2	4.6	1.9	2.1	3.4	3.0	2.3	1.9	1.6	3.8	4.3	3.9
2. A little important	14.7	20.4	8.9	16.1	7.6	16.4	15.3	12.8	15.3	13.5	16.2	11.3	16.1	11.5	19.6	30.4
3. Pretty important	36.0	39.3	32.8	37.4	31.8	32.7	37.5	37.5	34.4	35.5	36.7	33.7	36.7	41.2	36.0	36.5
4. Very important	46.6	35.9	57.2	44.0	58.4	46.4	45.3	47.5	46.9	47.9	44.9	53.2	45.5	43.5	40.0	29.2
Item 10130 Subject C04,O01 N	3250	1576	1536	2471	412	674	901	1103	573	1821	1175	1244	671	423	802	38
A08F: A job which provides you with a chance to earn a good deal of money																
1. Not important	1.5	1.2	1.8	1.6	0.5	1.0	1.5	1.3	2.4	1.6	1.1	2.1	1.0	0.4	1.5	-
2. A little important	7.7	7.6	7.9	8.3	2.6	7.6	8.3	6.5	9.4	9.4	5.5	10.0	6.2	8.8	5.0	3.1
3. Pretty important	33.2	30.7	36.6	36.5	22.0	29.1	40.0	30.9	32.1	36.6	30.6	37.6	33.0	29.1	29.9	29.7
4. Very important	57.6	60.5	53.7	53.7	74.8	62.3	50.3	61.3	56.2	52.4	62.9	50.3	59.7	61.7	63.6	67.2
Item 10140 Subject C04,F01 N	3245	1576	1531	2468	411	674	898	1101	572	1821	1170	1243	669	423	801	38
A08G: A job where you have the chance to be creative																
1. Not important	5.8	6.7	4.8	5.8	6.0	5.3	5.6	5.7	7.0	4.9	6.9	5.1	6.8	5.6	5.8	12.8
2. A little important	23.6	25.5	22.1	24.7	23.2	20.6	27.9	23.6	20.5	22.6	25.9	24.3	24.3	26.0	21.0	15.8
3. Pretty important	36.8	37.0	36.5	36.8	35.9	34.0	37.7	37.3	37.7	36.7	36.1	37.7	34.8	34.0	38.1	41.7
4. Very important	33.7	30.8	36.6	32.7	34.9	40.0	28.7	33.4	34.9	35.8	31.1	32.8	34.1	34.3	35.2	29.8
Item 10150 Subject C04 N	3249	1574	1535	2469	411	674	899	1102	574	1819	1175	1243	671	423	801	38
A08H: A job where the skills you learn will not go out of date																
1. Not important	3.6	3.2	3.7	3.5	4.7	2.4	3.6	3.5	5.3	4.2	2.7	3.2	3.2	4.1	3.6	8.3
2. A little important	9.4	8.9	10.0	9.5	8.5	9.6	8.8	9.8	9.7	10.0	9.7	9.8	7.8	10.9	9.0	10.8
3. Pretty important	31.1	31.2	30.8	33.8	21.2	29.9	34.4	28.9	31.5	32.7	28.7	33.8	29.3	29.8	28.6	32.3
4. Very important	55.9	56.6	55.5	53.2	65.6	58.1	53.2	57.9	53.5	53.1	58.9	53.3	59.7	55.2	58.8	48.6
Item 10160 Subject C04 N	3238	1568	1530	2465	408	669	898	1099	572	1811	1175	1242	667	422	796	38
A08I: A job that gives you a chance to make friends																
1. Not important	2.3	2.2	2.1	1.5	5.4	3.3	2.4	2.1	1.1	2.0	2.3	2.4	0.9	1.7	3.0	6.6
2. A little important	11.1	12.7	9.2	9.9	15.9	12.1	9.6	11.5	11.6	10.0	12.0	10.3	10.0	11.7	12.3	15.8
3. Pretty important	35.5	39.8	30.5	36.7	28.7	34.6	37.5	34.7	34.9	34.3	37.6	33.9	36.8	34.3	37.5	48.6
4. Very important	51.1	45.3	58.1	51.9	50.0	50.1	50.5	51.7	52.4	53.6	48.1	53.5	52.3	52.3	47.2	29.0
Item 10170 Subject C04,M04 N	3247	1577	1532	2470	411	672	900	1101	574	1819	1175	1241	669	423	803	38

*=less than .05 per cent.

QUESTIONNAIRE FORM 4 1984	TOTAL	SEX		RACE		REGION				4YR COLLEGE PLANS		ILLICIT DRUG USE: LIFETIME				
		M	F	White	Black	NE	NC	S	W	Yes	No	None	Marijuana Only	Few Pills	More Pills	Any Heroin
N (Weighted No. of Cases):	3284	1588	1546	2489	414	679	909	1113	584	1830	1188	1253	675	426	806	39
% of Weighted Total:	100.0	48.4	47.1	75.8	12.6	20.7	27.7	33.9	17.8	55.7	36.2	38.1	20.6	13.0	24.5	1.2

A08J: A job which uses your skills and abilities– lets you do the things you can do best

1. Not important	0.4	0.4	0.2	0.3	-	0.9	-	0.4	0.2	0.3	0.3	0.2	0.2	0.6	0.4	2.7
2. A little important	3.6	4.2	3.0	3.8	3.8	4.1	3.8	3.3	3.3	3.0	4.3	2.9	3.1	4.8	4.4	2.7
3. Pretty important	25.1	29.0	20.7	26.6	23.3	24.2	28.0	23.5	24.9	25.3	25.3	24.4	26.5	23.3	24.6	43.0
4. Very important	70.9	66.4	76.1	69.3	72.9	70.8	68.3	72.8	71.6	71.4	70.1	72.5	70.2	71.3	70.6	51.6
Item 10180 Subject C04 N	3250	1575	1537	2472	413	673	900	1104	573	1821	1175	1243	671	424	803	38

A08K: A job that is worthwhile to society

1. Not important	3.3	4.1	2.4	3.1	2.7	5.5	2.4	3.0	2.9	2.6	4.1	3.0	2.3	3.1	4.5	8.2
2. A little important	16.0	18.2	13.2	16.4	14.5	17.5	15.7	15.7	15.3	16.0	17.1	12.0	16.0	17.3	20.5	16.8
3. Pretty important	39.2	41.5	37.0	39.9	39.2	39.7	39.5	37.7	41.1	38.0	41.0	40.7	40.9	38.8	35.4	48.3
4. Very important	41.4	36.1	47.4	40.6	43.6	37.2	42.4	43.6	40.7	43.4	37.9	44.3	40.7	40.8	39.6	26.7
Item 10190 Subject C04,O01 N	3226	1571	1518	2456	404	667	898	1097	564	1808	1165	1231	666	422	797	38

A08L: A job where you have more than two weeks vacation

1. Not important	19.9	15.8	24.1	20.4	18.1	18.5	20.7	22.0	16.2	19.2	22.1	21.6	17.4	21.6	19.6	12.8
2. A little important	36.0	32.8	39.7	36.5	36.2	33.3	38.4	34.6	37.7	37.4	35.4	37.1	37.6	32.5	35.4	28.0
3. Pretty important	24.6	27.7	21.7	24.8	23.2	24.2	23.0	25.1	26.7	24.8	23.3	24.0	24.6	24.3	25.0	35.7
4. Very important	19.6	23.8	14.5	18.3	22.4	24.0	17.9	18.3	19.4	18.6	19.2	17.4	20.3	21.6	19.9	23.4
Item 10200 Subject C04 N	3245	1570	1536	2466	412	673	901	1101	569	1818	1175	1243	671	424	798	38

A08M: A job where you get a chance to partic- ipate in decision making

1. Not important	4.6	4.7	4.5	4.5	5.7	5.5	4.0	4.7	4.1	3.7	5.8	4.3	4.2	4.8	4.8	6.4
2. A little important	21.5	20.8	22.4	22.6	17.0	20.8	25.9	19.0	20.0	18.7	26.0	20.5	22.4	23.2	21.5	23.6
3. Pretty important	44.0	44.0	43.5	46.0	37.2	39.7	47.7	43.9	43.6	44.2	44.1	45.7	43.0	43.6	42.1	44.4
4. Very important	30.0	30.4	29.7	27.0	40.2	34.0	22.4	32.4	32.3	33.4	24.0	29.5	30.5	28.4	31.6	25.5
Item 10210 Subject C04 N	3244	1573	1534	2467	412	670	900	1099	575	1815	1176	1242	669	423	801	38

A08N: A job which leaves a lot of time for other things in your life

1. Not important	3.0	2.6	3.6	2.8	2.9	2.5	2.5	3.8	3.2	2.6	3.7	3.0	3.2	1.7	3.5	8.6
2. A little important	18.1	15.4	21.1	18.8	15.5	18.5	20.2	17.1	16.1	18.3	17.7	18.9	17.7	20.9	15.5	26.0
3. Pretty important	40.6	39.7	41.5	42.0	36.0	37.0	43.1	39.7	42.7	42.0	38.3	40.6	40.2	38.9	41.9	35.9
4. Very important	38.3	42.3	33.8	36.3	45.6	42.1	34.2	39.5	38.0	37.1	40.3	37.5	38.9	38.5	39.0	29.5
Item 10220 Subject C04 N	3243	1573	1531	2467	411	673	895	1099	575	1818	1173	1242	671	422	799	38

A08O: A job which allows you to establish roots in a community and not have to move from place to place

1. Not important	10.6	9.8	11.5	10.7	9.2	13.4	9.2	10.0	10.9	12.3	8.5	10.0	8.5	10.2	13.6	17.6
2. A little important	20.0	18.9	21.0	19.8	20.4	21.8	20.3	18.7	20.1	21.5	18.4	18.8	19.4	19.7	21.9	23.5
3. Pretty important	31.8	32.2	30.8	32.4	29.8	29.9	32.6	32.1	32.1	32.0	30.4	30.4	34.7	35.1	29.1	25.8
4. Very important	37.6	39.0	36.6	37.2	40.6	35.0	38.0	39.1	36.9	34.1	42.8	40.8	37.4	35.0	35.4	33.2
Item 10230 Subject C04 N	3249	1578	1533	2470	411	670	901	1104	574	1821	1174	1243	671	424	801	38

A08P: A job which leaves you mostly free of supervision by others

1. Not important	8.5	7.8	9.2	8.1	10.3	9.2	8.6	8.7	7.3	8.3	8.9	9.1	8.4	7.0	8.5	15.1
2. A little important	27.4	25.1	29.9	27.5	30.0	25.7	29.3	27.4	26.2	28.9	25.6	28.6	29.2	28.9	23.3	23.4
3. Pretty important	38.3	39.4	37.3	39.6	32.8	35.9	38.9	37.3	42.2	37.7	39.3	38.3	36.0	42.5	37.7	41.9
4. Very important	25.7	27.7	23.6	24.8	26.9	29.1	23.2	26.6	24.2	25.2	26.2	24.0	26.5	21.6	30.5	19.6
Item 10240 Subject C04 N	3250	1577	1537	2472	413	672	901	1103	573	1820	1178	1245	671	424	801	38

QUESTIONNAIRE FORM 4 1984	TOTAL	SEX		RACE		REGION				4YR COLLEGE PLANS		ILLICIT DRUG USE: LIFETIME				
		M	F	White	Black	NE	NC	S	W	Yes	No	None	Mari- juana Only	Few Pills	More Pills	Any Her- oin
N (Weighted No. of Cases):	3284	1588	1546	2489	414	679	909	1113	584	1830	1188	1253	675	426	806	39
% of Weighted Total:	100.0	48.4	47.1	75.8	12.6	20.7	27.7	33.9	17.8	55.7	36.2	38.1	20.6	13.0	24.5	1.2
A08Q: A job that offers a reasonably pre- dictable, secure future																
1. Not important	1.2	0.7	1.8	1.4	0.7	1.9	0.6	1.0	1.9	1.4	0.9	1.5	0.2	1.6	1.4	2.7
2. A little important	5.2	6.0	4.4	5.2	3.8	6.0	4.2	5.4	5.6	5.2	5.4	3.9	4.3	5.0	7.3	12.9
3. Pretty important	28.3	27.4	28.7	31.0	17.0	29.1	32.6	24.1	28.9	29.9	26.4	30.0	23.9	29.0	28.1	35.3
4. Very important	65.2	65.9	65.1	62.3	78.5	63.1	62.6	69.5	63.6	63.5	67.3	64.5	71.5	64.4	63.3	49.1
Item 10250 Subject C04 N	3248	1576	1534	2469	413	672	899	1103	574	1819	1176	1243	669	424	802	38
A08R: A job where you can learn new things, learn new skills																
1. Not important	1.6	2.2	1.0	1.6	0.7	2.0	1.6	1.6	1.3	1.9	1.3	1.6	1.0	1.4	2.2	2.8
2. A little important	11.9	14.3	9.4	13.2	5.9	10.3	14.6	10.9	11.7	13.5	10.2	12.9	12.3	8.8	12.1	9.3
3. Pretty important	40.7	43.6	37.5	43.4	27.2	41.0	42.7	39.6	39.1	40.3	40.8	40.1	40.1	44.9	39.6	47.4
4. Very important	45.8	40.0	52.1	41.7	66.1	46.7	41.1	48.0	47.8	44.3	47.7	45.4	46.6	44.8	46.2	40.5
Item 10260 Subject B02,C04 N	3245	1573	1534	2467	412	672	898	1102	573	1818	1175	1241	668	424	802	37
A08S: A job where you do not have to pretend to be a type of person that you are not																
1. Not important	5.2	6.8	3.6	4.4	6.7	5.1	3.7	6.4	5.5	4.4	5.9	4.6	5.5	5.1	5.5	14.1
2. A little important	5.1	7.1	2.9	5.0	4.3	5.5	5.7	4.0	5.9	4.8	5.4	4.5	4.9	4.7	5.5	9.4
3. Pretty important	20.3	26.3	13.8	21.4	16.2	21.1	23.1	18.5	18.4	20.3	20.5	21.1	20.3	19.5	19.1	26.6
4. Very important	69.4	59.8	79.6	69.2	72.8	68.3	67.5	71.0	70.3	70.5	68.2	69.7	69.2	70.8	69.9	49.9
Item 10270 Subject C04 N	3239	1567	1533	2460	411	668	896	1103	572	1811	1175	1237	667	424	800	38
A08T: A job that most people look up to and respect																
1. Not important	5.0	5.7	4.5	5.3	3.2	6.2	5.2	3.6	6.1	5.0	5.4	4.0	4.4	4.1	7.4	11.8
2. A little important	17.5	20.2	14.5	18.7	10.7	19.6	17.5	14.2	21.3	17.0	18.9	16.8	17.4	17.9	17.6	19.9
3. Pretty important	37.3	36.6	37.6	38.9	33.0	33.6	40.4	38.6	34.1	38.6	36.4	39.4	36.6	37.1	34.8	43.4
4. Very important	40.2	37.5	43.3	37.0	53.1	40.6	37.0	43.6	38.5	39.5	39.3	39.8	41.6	40.9	40.2	24.9
Item 10280 Subject C04 N	3239	1572	1529	2464	411	668	899	1099	573	1814	1173	1238	668	424	799	38
A08U: A job that permits contact with a lot of people																
1. Not important	7.5	9.2	5.4	7.2	8.4	7.9	7.4	7.8	6.6	7.6	7.5	7.8	6.1	5.1	8.9	12.3
2. A little important	24.2	30.8	16.9	23.4	27.1	22.2	24.4	25.0	24.9	20.4	30.0	23.5	23.8	24.0	23.8	49.5
3. Pretty important	35.6	34.3	37.2	36.4	34.0	34.8	38.4	34.7	34.1	36.5	33.2	35.7	38.4	34.2	34.8	16.3
4. Very important	32.6	25.6	40.5	32.9	30.5	35.1	29.8	32.5	34.4	35.4	29.2	33.0	31.7	36.7	32.5	21.9
Item 10290 Subject C04,M05 N	3241	1570	1534	2464	412	671	895	1101	574	1816	1173	1241	667	423	800	38
A08V: A job with an easy pace that lets you work slowly																
1. Not important	26.8	26.7	26.8	26.7	28.0	29.8	24.4	25.9	28.5	27.5	26.2	26.6	27.7	23.2	27.3	35.6
2. A little important	39.8	40.1	39.9	41.1	35.5	36.7	41.0	38.8	43.3	41.7	37.1	39.9	37.9	42.5	40.7	31.3
3. Pretty important	23.9	23.3	24.1	23.3	25.5	22.9	25.4	24.6	21.2	23.5	24.3	24.5	23.6	23.3	22.9	23.7
4. Very important	9.6	9.8	9.1	8.9	11.0	10.6	9.3	10.7	7.0	7.3	12.4	8.9	10.8	11.0	9.1	9.4
Item 10300 Subject C04 N	3239	1568	1534	2464	411	667	895	1103	574	1814	1173	1241	667	424	798	38
A08W: A job where most problems are quite difficult and challenging																
1. Not important	16.1	15.7	16.7	16.3	17.2	19.0	16.9	14.8	13.9	13.8	20.3	15.0	15.2	16.7	18.7	12.7
2. A little important	37.0	34.7	38.9	38.1	33.6	37.9	40.4	35.3	33.7	36.1	38.7	36.3	38.8	39.5	35.7	27.0
3. Pretty important	34.4	35.5	33.3	34.1	33.3	30.1	31.7	37.3	38.2	36.2	30.7	35.3	33.6	33.9	33.9	31.0
4. Very important	12.5	14.1	11.0	11.5	15.9	12.9	10.9	12.6	14.2	13.9	10.3	13.4	12.4	9.9	11.7	29.3
Item 10310 Subject C04 N	3239	1569	1532	2466	409	667	899	1102	571	1815	1173	1241	667	423	798	38

QUESTIONNAIRE FORM 4 1984	TOTAL	SEX		RACE		REGION				4YR COLLEGE PLANS		ILLICIT DRUG USE: LIFETIME				
		M	F	White	Black	NE	NC	S	W	Yes	No	None	Mari-juana Only	Few Pills	More Pills	Any Her-oin
N (Weighted No. of Cases):	3284	1588	1546	2489	414	679	909	1113	584	1830	1188	1253	675	426	806	39
% of Weighted Total:	100.0	48.4	47.1	75.8	12.6	20.7	27.7	33.9	17.8	55.7	36.2	38.1	20.6	13.0	24.5	1.2

A09: What kind of work do you think you will be doing when you are 30 years old? Mark the one that comes closest to what you expect to be doing.

	TOTAL	M	F	White	Black	NE	NC	S	W	Yes	No	None	Mari-juana Only	Few Pills	More Pills	Any Her-oin
01. Laborer (car washer, sanitary worker, farm laborer)	0.3	0.4	0.2	0.3	0.3	-	0.5	0.4	0.1	0.1	0.7	0.3	0.2	-	0.6	-
02. Service worker (cook, waiter, barber, janitor, gas station attendant, practical nurse, beautician)	3.5	1.1	5.8	3.2	4.8	4.0	5.0	3.1	1.1	1.3	5.9	3.0	4.6	2.4	3.3	4.1
03. Operative or semi-skilled worker (garage worker, taxicab, bus or truck driver, assembly line worker, welder)	2.4	4.0	0.5	2.3	1.7	2.1	3.2	2.6	1.1	0.4	5.2	1.6	2.2	2.4	3.4	5.6
04. Sales clerk in a retail store (shoe salesperson, department store clerk, drug store clerk)	1.5	0.7	2.1	1.1	4.1	1.1	0.9	2.2	1.3	0.9	2.3	1.6	1.5	1.9	0.9	-
05. Clerical or office worker (bank teller, bookkeeper, secretary, typist, postal clerk or carrier, ticket agent)	8.8	1.5	16.4	8.4	11.8	8.2	7.8	10.1	8.5	4.6	15.1	8.6	8.3	9.3	9.8	6.9
06. Protective service (police officer, fireman, detective)	3.0	4.9	1.1	3.1	2.0	3.0	2.7	2.3	5.1	2.3	4.2	2.3	3.6	2.9	3.8	1.1
07. Military service	5.0	8.4	1.1	3.7	9.9	3.3	4.9	7.1	3.3	3.3	6.2	5.4	4.7	4.7	4.6	6.6
08. Craftsman or skilled worker (carpenter, electrician, brick layer, mechanic, machinist, tool and die maker, telephone installer)	9.0	16.9	0.3	9.1	7.6	10.3	8.9	7.6	10.4	3.0	17.9	6.6	9.4	6.3	13.7	14.2
09. Farm owner, farm manager	1.3	2.3	0.3	1.6	-	0.6	1.6	1.8	0.9	1.0	1.9	1.9	1.1	1.2	0.8	-
10. Owner of small business (restaurant owner, shop owner)	5.5	6.9	4.0	5.6	4.2	6.8	5.0	5.5	5.1	5.0	6.4	4.8	5.7	5.2	6.9	5.2
11. Sales representative (insurance agent, real estate broker, bond salesman)	2.0	1.9	2.2	2.3	0.8	2.3	1.3	2.2	2.4	2.5	1.4	1.8	2.0	2.5	2.1	2.4
12. Manager or administrator (office manager, sales manager, school administrator, government official)	7.7	7.2	8.1	7.7	8.5	8.4	7.6	6.9	8.6	9.5	5.1	7.2	8.8	9.9	6.4	1.6
13. Professional without doctoral degree (registered nurse, librarian, engineer, architect, social worker, technician, accountant, actor, artist, musician)	28.9	25.6	33.0	29.6	29.4	29.2	29.3	27.8	29.7	39.0	14.7	31.9	28.2	29.7	24.2	32.7
14. Professional with doctoral degree or equivalent (lawyer, physician, dentist, scientist, college professor)	13.3	11.9	15.2	13.7	12.0	13.1	12.7	14.0	12.9	20.9	2.1	16.5	12.9	12.3	10.0	1.8
15. Full-time homemaker or housewife	2.2	0.1	4.3	2.3	0.3	1.8	3.0	1.8	2.0	0.8	4.4	2.0	1.8	2.0	2.9	1.8
16. Don't know-GO TO Q.A13	5.7	6.1	5.2	6.2	2.7	5.8	5.6	4.8	7.5	5.4	6.4	4.5	5.1	7.4	6.6	16.0
Item 10320 Subject C03 N	3085	1503	1465	2388	374	637	861	1041	547	1759	1107	1188	637	398	767	35

A10: How likely do you think it is that you will actually get to do this kind of work?

	TOTAL	M	F	White	Black	NE	NC	S	W	Yes	No	None	Mari-juana Only	Few Pills	More Pills	Any Her-oin
1. Not very likely	0.9	0.8	0.9	0.6	2.3	1.6	0.4	0.9	0.9	0.3	1.4	0.6	0.5	0.3	1.6	3.2
2. Somewhat likely	6.4	6.7	5.8	5.7	7.6	5.7	8.3	5.3	5.9	5.4	6.8	6.9	5.5	8.7	4.8	7.3
3. Fairly likely	20.9	22.2	19.7	21.5	21.8	20.1	23.6	20.7	17.9	20.7	21.0	18.6	22.2	25.8	20.4	26.6
4. Very likely	45.2	46.0	45.4	46.8	39.2	42.4	45.0	44.2	51.0	49.3	40.7	47.1	46.9	41.1	44.9	39.5
5. Certain	19.2	16.9	21.2	17.9	23.0	19.8	16.6	22.1	16.9	20.0	18.0	19.7	17.3	19.2	19.7	13.4
6. I already do this kind of work	7.4	7.4	7.2	7.5	6.0	10.4	6.1	6.8	7.3	4.2	12.0	7.1	7.6	4.9	8.7	10.1
Item 10330 Subject C03 N★	2999	1445	1429	2277	384	621	834	1023	520	1700	1065	1171	622	382	726	32

A11: How certain are you that this kind of work is a good choice for you?

	TOTAL	M	F	White	Black	NE	NC	S	W	Yes	No	None	Mari-juana Only	Few Pills	More Pills	Any Her-oin
1. Not at all certain	2.7	2.9	2.4	2.5	3.2	2.5	2.9	2.9	2.4	2.2	3.4	2.3	2.1	4.9	1.9	17.8
2. Somewhat certain	7.4	7.4	7.4	7.3	8.1	6.7	8.8	7.2	6.3	7.5	6.6	8.6	7.7	7.8	5.0	6.3
3. Fairly certain	29.8	32.1	27.9	32.0	23.4	27.6	32.0	28.7	30.8	31.7	27.5	28.1	30.3	32.3	31.1	28.6
4. Very certain	41.0	38.2	43.8	41.0	40.3	43.3	39.7	40.5	41.2	40.0	42.8	41.1	42.7	39.4	41.2	35.9
5. Completely certain	19.1	19.3	18.6	17.1	25.0	19.9	16.6	20.6	19.3	18.5	19.8	19.8	17.1	15.6	20.8	11.3
Item 10340 Subject C03 N★	3008	1453	1431	2285	386	623	836	1028	521	1702	1072	1175	622	383	732	32

★=excludes respondents for whom question was inappropriate.

QUESTIONNAIRE FORM 4 1984	TOTAL	SEX		RACE		REGION				4YR COLLEGE PLANS		ILLICIT DRUG USE: LIFETIME				
		M	F	White	Black	NE	NC	S	W	Yes	No	None	Mari-juana Only	Few Pills	More Pills	Any Her-oin
N (Weighted No. of Cases):	3284	1588	1546	2489	414	679	909	1113	584	1830	1188	1253	675	426	806	39
% of Weighted Total:	100.0	48.4	47.1	75.8	12.6	20.7	27.7	33.9	17.8	55.7	36.2	38.1	20.6	13.0	24.5	1.2

A12: How satisfying do you think this kind of work will be for you?

	TOTAL	M	F	White	Black	NE	NC	S	W	Yes	No	None	Mari-juana Only	Few Pills	More Pills	Any Her-oin
1. Not very satisfying	0.9	0.8	0.8	0.6	1.5	0.9	0.5	1.0	1.0	0.4	1.2	0.7	0.3	1.6	0.6	6.1
2. Somewhat satisfying	5.5	6.1	4.6	5.2	7.4	5.1	6.6	5.2	4.6	4.3	6.7	5.8	5.4	5.6	4.7	6.6
3. Quite satisfying	23.9	25.8	21.5	25.1	20.1	25.4	24.7	23.3	22.0	20.6	27.5	21.8	23.0	26.5	25.6	31.8
4. Very satisfying	42.4	42.2	43.2	42.3	41.6	39.8	46.1	40.8	42.7	44.8	40.4	41.9	46.9	37.9	42.8	48.3
5. Extremely satisfying	27.4	25.0	29.8	26.8	29.3	28.8	22.0	29.7	29.8	29.9	24.3	29.8	24.5	28.3	26.4	7.2
Item 10350 Subject C03,P02 N★	3007	1452	1431	2284	386	622	836	1028	521	1702	1071	1175	622	383	731	32

A13: To what extent do you think the things listed below will prevent you from getting the kind of work you would like to have?

A13A: Your religion

	TOTAL	M	F	White	Black	NE	NC	S	W	Yes	No	None	Mari-juana Only	Few Pills	More Pills	Any Her-oin
1. Not at all	91.1	91.4	91.5	93.1	87.1	91.4	92.1	89.7	91.7	93.0	90.3	89.7	92.6	92.6	94.5	72.5
2. Somewhat	4.3	4.2	4.1	3.9	3.9	3.5	4.9	4.8	3.6	3.7	4.4	4.4	4.4	3.9	3.1	13.1
3. A lot	1.5	1.5	1.2	0.8	2.9	0.7	1.1	2.2	1.5	0.9	1.9	2.3	0.3	0.5	0.6	7.7
8. Don't know	3.1	2.9	3.2	2.2	6.1	4.5	1.9	3.4	3.1	2.4	3.4	3.7	2.7	3.0	1.8	6.7
Item 10360 Subject C03,G N	3144	1519	1494	2399	396	650	871	1061	562	1781	1129	1201	648	415	776	39

A13B: Your sex

	TOTAL	M	F	White	Black	NE	NC	S	W	Yes	No	None	Mari-juana Only	Few Pills	More Pills	Any Her-oin
1. Not at all	77.9	89.1	66.0	78.5	74.3	76.3	75.6	79.4	80.3	76.9	79.6	76.3	79.0	77.9	79.7	70.5
2. Somewhat	16.7	6.8	27.5	16.7	16.5	17.4	18.9	14.4	16.7	19.0	13.5	18.0	17.1	17.2	14.9	14.7
3. A lot	3.6	2.7	4.2	3.5	4.1	3.3	3.8	4.3	2.3	2.9	4.5	3.3	2.7	3.3	4.5	8.4
8. Don't know	1.9	1.4	2.3	1.3	5.0	2.9	1.7	1.9	0.8	1.3	2.4	2.4	1.2	1.6	0.9	6.5
Item 10370 Subject C03,D06 N	3144	1519	1494	2398	395	649	872	1061	562	1781	1128	1200	648	415	777	39

A13C: Your race

	TOTAL	M	F	White	Black	NE	NC	S	W	Yes	No	None	Mari-juana Only	Few Pills	More Pills	Any Her-oin
1. Not at all	85.3	85.4	85.7	94.0	46.8	83.9	88.8	81.8	88.2	86.2	86.8	83.1	83.4	88.8	90.7	76.6
2. Somewhat	8.7	8.7	8.6	3.0	34.1	9.1	6.7	10.5	8.1	8.8	6.8	9.6	11.4	7.9	4.9	10.2
3. A lot	3.8	3.9	3.5	1.9	12.0	3.5	2.8	5.6	2.1	3.3	3.9	5.2	3.9	1.3	1.9	7.9
8. Don't know	2.2	2.0	2.3	1.0	7.1	3.4	1.7	2.1	1.5	1.7	2.5	2.2	1.3	2.0	2.4	5.3
Item 10380 Subject C03,N02 N	3143	1518	1493	2395	397	648	873	1062	560	1780	1129	1203	648	414	776	38

A13D: Your family background

	TOTAL	M	F	White	Black	NE	NC	S	W	Yes	No	None	Mari-juana Only	Few Pills	More Pills	Any Her-oin
1. Not at all	87.2	87.4	87.1	89.1	82.8	87.6	84.6	88.1	88.9	89.2	86.0	87.4	86.9	85.5	89.7	78.7
2. Somewhat	8.1	8.1	8.2	7.7	9.3	8.4	9.7	7.0	7.2	7.6	7.9	7.5	9.7	10.0	6.6	7.0
3. A lot	2.1	2.5	1.4	1.3	3.7	1.7	3.0	1.8	1.6	1.4	2.8	2.2	1.9	1.7	1.4	5.9
8. Don't know	2.7	2.0	3.3	2.0	4.2	2.2	2.7	3.1	2.4	1.9	3.3	2.9	1.4	2.8	2.4	8.4
Item 10390 Subject C03 N	3140	1517	1492	2393	396	648	868	1062	562	1782	1125	1198	648	415	775	39

A13E: Your political views

	TOTAL	M	F	White	Black	NE	NC	S	W	Yes	No	None	Mari-juana Only	Few Pills	More Pills	Any Her-oin
1. Not at all	82.9	83.7	82.5	85.5	70.1	82.2	81.6	83.6	84.1	84.6	81.6	82.4	84.8	83.0	84.0	69.7
2. Somewhat	9.3	10.2	8.0	8.9	11.9	7.3	12.1	8.2	9.3	8.8	9.7	8.6	9.7	10.5	9.1	18.5
3. A lot	1.1	1.0	1.3	0.7	3.1	2.0	0.4	1.4	0.7	0.7	1.3	1.2	1.0	1.2	0.7	2.7
8. Don't know	6.7	5.1	8.2	4.8	14.8	8.4	5.9	6.8	5.9	5.8	7.4	7.8	4.5	5.4	6.2	9.1
Item 10400 Subject C03,H01 N	3138	1517	1489	2395	395	648	870	1060	561	1780	1125	1200	647	414	775	38

A13F: Your education

	TOTAL	M	F	White	Black	NE	NC	S	W	Yes	No	None	Mari-juana Only	Few Pills	More Pills	Any Her-oin
1. Not at all	47.9	46.9	49.5	47.4	55.4	50.1	43.2	51.1	46.6	52.9	41.1	50.5	51.6	46.6	43.4	34.7
2. Somewhat	25.7	26.2	25.1	26.8	19.7	24.1	26.5	23.6	30.4	21.0	32.3	23.5	22.6	26.2	30.1	32.2
3. A lot	23.9	24.4	23.3	23.4	22.2	22.4	28.4	22.6	21.3	24.4	23.7	23.9	24.2	24.6	23.7	25.5
8. Don't know	2.5	2.5	2.1	2.4	2.7	3.3	1.9	2.8	1.7	1.6	2.9	2.0	1.6	2.5	2.9	7.6
Item 10410 Subject B09,C03 N	3147	1520	1496	2399	397	649	873	1063	562	1782	1127	1200	652	414	777	39

A13G: Lack of vocational training

	TOTAL	M	F	White	Black	NE	NC	S	W	Yes	No	None	Mari-juana Only	Few Pills	More Pills	Any Her-oin
1. Not at all	53.3	52.9	53.8	53.5	54.7	55.9	52.0	55.8	47.4	56.9	48.7	54.1	56.5	52.4	51.7	33.1
2. Somewhat	26.8	28.8	25.2	27.0	25.6	23.3	26.7	27.1	30.7	24.6	29.8	26.5	24.6	26.8	28.4	45.8
3. A lot	12.6	12.3	12.7	12.2	12.0	11.7	15.3	11.0	12.2	10.4	15.0	11.4	12.4	12.6	13.9	16.2
8. Don't know	7.3	6.1	8.3	7.2	7.7	9.1	6.0	6.1	9.7	8.0	6.6	8.0	6.6	8.2	6.0	4.9
Item 10420 Subject C03 N	3147	1522	1495	2399	400	649	873	1062	564	1780	1132	1203	647	416	778	39

	TOTAL	SEX		RACE		REGION				4YR COLLEGE PLANS		ILLICIT DRUG USE: LIFETIME				
QUESTIONNAIRE FORM 4 **1984**		M	F	White	Black	NE	NC	S	W	Yes	No	None	Mari-juana Only	Few Pills	More Pills	Any Her-oin
N (Weighted No. of Cases):	3284	1588	1546	2489	414	679	909	1113	584	1830	1188	1253	675	426	806	39
% of Weighted Total:	100.0	48.4	47.1	75.8	12.6	20.7	27.7	33.9	17.8	55.7	36.2	38.1	20.6	13.0	24.5	1.2
A13H: Lack of ability																
1. Not at all	59.3	59.0	59.7	59.1	62.2	59.5	56.6	60.6	60.7	60.7	57.8	57.8	61.2	55.8	61.8	54.0
2. Somewhat	15.9	16.3	15.6	16.0	14.5	15.4	18.1	15.2	14.3	13.6	19.4	15.3	15.0	16.8	16.5	26.5
3. A lot	21.1	21.1	21.1	21.3	20.1	20.4	21.9	20.6	21.5	22.6	18.8	22.7	21.6	23.9	18.0	11.8
8. Don't know	3.8	3.6	3.6	3.6	3.2	4.7	3.4	3.6	3.6	3.2	4.0	4.3	2.3	3.4	3.7	7.8
Item 10430 Subject C03 N	3138	1519	1491	2395	394	649	870	1060	559	1779	1126	1200	646	413	777	39
A13I: Not knowing the right people																
1. Not at all	46.4	45.0	47.9	46.0	46.1	47.5	43.7	47.2	47.6	43.3	51.6	45.9	45.6	45.4	49.1	42.3
2. Somewhat	37.3	36.8	37.1	38.0	37.2	33.4	39.1	38.4	36.9	40.6	32.5	38.2	39.1	35.3	36.1	36.8
3. A lot	10.3	11.8	9.1	10.3	10.7	11.5	11.0	9.3	9.4	10.5	9.2	9.2	9.7	13.7	9.9	13.9
8. Don't know	6.1	6.3	5.9	5.7	6.0	7.5	6.2	5.1	6.1	5.6	6.6	6.7	5.6	5.6	4.9	6.9
Item 10440 Subject C03 N	3140	1513	1496	2395	395	650	868	1060	561	1777	1129	1198	645	415	778	39
A13J: Not wanting to work hard																
1. Not at all	61.1	58.9	63.3	60.7	65.8	61.7	59.8	61.3	61.8	60.2	62.6	59.5	61.8	57.4	64.4	69.8
2. Somewhat	10.2	11.0	9.1	10.4	7.1	9.3	11.4	9.9	9.9	10.0	9.8	10.3	10.3	11.4	9.4	8.3
3. A lot	26.5	27.6	25.6	26.8	24.2	26.1	27.7	26.3	25.5	28.1	24.8	27.8	26.2	28.3	24.6	19.2
8. Don't know	2.3	2.5	2.0	2.1	2.9	2.9	1.1	2.5	2.8	1.7	2.8	2.5	1.8	2.9	1.7	2.6
Item 10450 Subject C03 N	3132	1515	1489	2390	396	647	867	1057	561	1776	1126	1200	644	413	772	39
A13K: Not wanting to conform																
1. Not at all	53.7	52.7	54.9	53.6	55.2	53.5	53.0	54.8	52.9	51.9	56.6	53.8	53.8	51.1	55.2	55.7
2. Somewhat	21.5	22.1	21.0	22.3	18.1	19.7	22.4	20.2	24.4	25.0	16.2	22.9	19.4	22.2	21.1	11.2
3. A lot	14.5	15.6	13.5	14.8	12.9	14.8	15.2	14.6	12.7	14.8	14.4	13.8	14.7	17.0	14.1	17.7
8. Don't know	10.3	9.6	10.6	9.4	13.8	11.9	9.5	10.3	9.9	8.4	12.8	9.4	12.1	9.7	9.5	15.4
Item 10460 Subject C03,Q08 N	3120	1504	1486	2384	392	643	863	1056	558	1770	1119	1193	642	412	771	38
A14: If you were to get enough money to live as comfortably as you'd like for the rest of your life, would you want to work?																
1. I would want to work	79.0	76.7	81.7	78.0	83.7	75.3	79.2	79.1	83.0	81.4	76.4	82.7	80.2	73.4	75.8	74.7
2. I would not want to work	21.0	23.3	18.3	22.0	16.3	24.7	20.8	20.9	17.0	18.6	23.6	17.3	19.8	26.6	24.2	25.3
Item 8100 Subject C06 N	3231	1571	1529	2463	409	670	896	1095	570	1813	1175	1240	669	420	799	38
A15: How much do you agree or disagree with each statement below?																
A15A: One sees so few good or happy marriages that one questions it as a way of life																
1. Disagree	29.0	29.8	28.9	30.4	19.8	27.8	32.3	25.4	32.4	32.4	25.4	33.3	29.0	28.6	23.7	25.1
2. Mostly disagree	17.9	17.6	18.5	19.8	12.6	19.4	18.0	17.1	17.4	19.7	16.4	17.5	18.1	21.6	16.7	16.0
3. Neither	20.3	23.1	17.5	20.7	19.5	19.6	20.6	20.2	21.1	19.2	21.2	19.2	20.4	18.1	23.3	5.8
4. Mostly agree	20.8	18.8	22.6	18.6	31.2	20.2	18.0	23.9	19.6	19.0	22.6	17.9	20.0	21.9	24.0	30.6
5. Agree	12.0	10.7	12.5	10.4	16.8	13.0	11.1	13.5	9.4	9.7	14.3	12.0	12.5	9.7	12.3	22.5
Item 10470 Subject D03 N	3220	1562	1529	2462	402	667	890	1091	572	1813	1165	1236	663	423	794	38
A15B: It is usually a good idea for a couple to live together before getting married in order to find out whether they really get along																
1. Disagree	27.9	21.8	35.3	28.5	29.4	21.7	27.4	33.5	25.4	31.2	24.6	41.1	24.2	23.4	13.9	17.4
2. Mostly disagree	13.4	14.2	12.8	14.0	9.6	12.1	15.0	13.3	12.4	14.2	12.2	14.6	11.4	13.6	13.6	11.6
3. Neither	15.4	17.1	14.3	16.4	11.5	15.5	17.1	14.2	15.2	17.5	13.5	15.1	18.8	14.5	13.4	15.2
4. Mostly agree	21.5	23.7	18.9	21.6	20.1	24.1	21.9	19.3	22.2	20.3	22.8	15.4	24.0	26.1	27.0	26.0
5. Agree	21.7	23.2	18.7	19.5	29.3	26.6	18.6	19.6	24.8	16.7	26.8	13.8	21.6	22.5	32.1	29.8
Item 10480 Subject D03 N	3243	1574	1536	2471	410	671	899	1099	574	1820	1176	1244	669	424	801	38

	TOTAL	SEX		RACE		REGION				4YR COLLEGE PLANS		ILLICIT DRUG USE: LIFETIME				
QUESTIONNAIRE FORM 4 1984		M	F	White	Black	NE	NC	S	W	Yes	No	None	Mari- juana Only	Few Pills	More Pills	Any Her- oin
N (Weighted No. of Cases):	3284	1588	1546	2489	414	679	909	1113	584	1830	1188	1253	675	426	806	39
% of Weighted Total:	100.0	48.4	47.1	75.8	12.6	20.7	27.7	33.9	17.8	55.7	36.2	38.1	20.6	13.0	24.5	1.2
A15C: Having a close intimate relationship with only one partner is too restrictive for the aver- age person																
1. Disagree	41.1	36.0	46.3	42.9	38.9	41.9	40.2	42.1	39.9	42.4	41.0	46.6	41.0	41.1	34.9	24.1
2. Mostly disagree	23.2	22.7	24.0	24.5	18.1	21.6	22.0	24.1	25.1	26.4	19.2	21.7	24.9	24.2	23.8	30.5
3. Neither	14.4	16.3	12.4	13.9	13.1	13.2	16.0	12.8	16.1	14.0	14.5	13.5	15.0	12.9	15.1	20.1
4. Mostly agree	12.8	14.9	10.4	12.0	16.2	13.8	13.0	12.1	12.6	10.6	15.0	9.6	12.1	13.4	17.4	3.9
5. Agree	8.5	10.1	6.9	6.7	13.6	9.5	8.7	8.9	6.4	6.7	10.2	8.6	7.0	8.4	8.8	21.3
Item 10490 Subject D03 N	*3230*	*1563*	*1536*	*2465*	*408*	*666*	*898*	*1093*	*573*	*1813*	*1174*	*1238*	*666*	*421*	*801*	*38*
A15D: Having a job takes away from a woman's relationship with her husband																
1. Disagree	46.8	35.8	58.1	45.1	59.6	51.8	44.2	45.8	47.2	48.3	45.5	48.1	45.3	45.9	48.6	27.4
2. Mostly disagree	27.3	28.2	26.8	28.7	21.4	24.3	27.8	27.7	29.5	28.2	26.3	27.4	27.9	28.1	26.2	29.0
3. Neither	12.5	17.9	7.1	12.8	10.3	12.8	12.9	13.4	10.0	12.0	13.1	11.3	13.7	13.3	12.3	23.0
4. Mostly agree	8.8	11.8	5.5	9.1	5.5	6.5	9.9	9.1	8.9	8.0	9.5	8.6	8.4	8.9	8.7	10.1
5. Agree	4.5	6.3	2.5	4.2	3.2	4.6	5.2	4.0	4.3	3.5	5.6	4.6	4.8	3.7	4.2	10.5
Item 10500 Subject D05 N	*3230*	*1567*	*1535*	*2466*	*407*	*666*	*896*	*1097*	*571*	*1815*	*1172*	*1239*	*668*	*423*	*799*	*38*
A15E: Having a job gives a wife more of a chance to develop herself as a person																
1. Disagree	2.9	3.3	2.3	2.6	3.6	3.1	3.5	3.0	1.6	2.2	3.5	3.5	3.0	1.7	2.2	3.9
2. Mostly disagree	3.9	5.8	1.7	4.0	2.6	2.2	4.3	4.5	3.8	3.1	4.5	3.5	3.8	2.7	4.5	6.1
3. Neither	9.5	13.2	5.4	9.6	8.1	8.1	9.0	10.1	10.9	9.0	10.3	8.7	10.3	9.4	9.7	7.5
4. Mostly agree	29.7	37.8	22.4	32.7	19.9	32.4	32.6	26.3	29.0	31.3	28.6	30.2	29.6	30.8	29.1	45.4
5. Agree	54.0	39.9	68.2	51.1	65.9	54.2	50.7	56.1	54.8	54.4	53.2	54.0	53.4	55.4	54.6	37.0
Item 10510 Subject D05 N	*3231*	*1567*	*1535*	*2470*	*406*	*666*	*895*	*1096*	*574*	*1812*	*1176*	*1240*	*669*	*423*	*797*	*38*
A15F: Being a father and raising children is one of the most fulfilling experiences a man can have																
1. Disagree	4.1	4.0	3.7	3.5	5.8	4.5	2.8	5.1	3.6	3.6	4.9	3.8	4.9	5.2	3.5	4.7
2. Mostly disagree	4.9	5.2	4.5	5.1	4.7	5.6	5.3	4.8	3.8	5.0	4.6	4.0	5.4	4.5	5.6	6.9
3. Neither	19.8	19.6	19.9	21.8	14.0	20.2	18.8	19.3	22.1	21.0	18.0	18.2	20.1	16.1	23.5	23.8
4. Mostly agree	30.4	30.2	30.9	31.6	25.0	31.0	31.1	27.4	34.7	30.8	30.8	29.2	33.4	32.0	29.6	30.3
5. Agree	40.7	40.9	40.8	38.0	50.5	38.7	42.0	43.5	35.8	39.7	41.6	44.9	36.2	41.4	37.8	34.2
Item 10520 Subject D05 N	*3202*	*1566*	*1510*	*2439*	*407*	*657*	*895*	*1080*	*569*	*1802*	*1162*	*1230*	*664*	*419*	*788*	*38*
A15G: Most mothers should spend more time with their children than they do now																
1. Disagree	4.4	3.9	4.6	3.9	5.7	6.3	3.6	4.5	3.3	4.0	4.5	4.3	4.9	5.5	3.5	7.4
2. Mostly disagree	10.2	9.0	11.3	11.1	5.9	9.4	10.8	8.3	14.0	11.3	9.0	9.3	10.5	9.5	12.3	7.7
3. Neither	26.4	31.2	21.1	28.3	18.0	28.9	28.4	21.6	29.7	28.4	24.2	23.6	25.5	27.5	31.1	19.9
4. Mostly agree	30.7	30.3	31.8	31.3	31.9	31.9	29.3	32.3	28.3	31.4	29.2	30.4	33.3	32.9	27.6	35.7
5. Agree	28.3	25.6	31.1	25.4	38.4	23.5	28.0	33.4	24.7	24.9	33.1	32.3	25.8	24.5	25.5	29.3
Item 10530 Subject D05 N	*3228*	*1567*	*1535*	*2469*	*405*	*667*	*898*	*1092*	*572*	*1816*	*1172*	*1241*	*667*	*423*	*797*	*38*
A15H: If a wife works, her husband should take a greater part in housework and child-care																
1. Disagree	5.8	6.4	5.0	5.8	3.2	6.5	5.8	5.1	6.3	4.9	6.9	5.2	6.6	5.8	5.6	9.9
2. Mostly disagree	5.9	6.1	5.5	5.5	6.3	4.9	5.1	7.0	6.1	4.8	7.2	5.6	5.5	6.6	5.7	10.4
3. Neither	13.9	16.1	11.8	13.9	13.5	12.4	14.6	13.4	15.6	13.4	14.7	13.4	12.0	13.7	16.1	14.0
4. Mostly agree	35.4	39.4	31.2	37.5	23.5	36.6	35.7	34.1	35.9	36.4	33.9	33.0	38.5	36.9	36.6	30.3
5. Agree	39.1	32.0	46.5	37.2	53.5	39.6	38.7	40.5	36.2	40.4	37.4	42.8	37.4	37.0	36.0	35.4
Item 10540 Subject D05 N	*3228*	*1570*	*1533*	*2468*	*407*	*666*	*896*	*1093*	*573*	*1815*	*1174*	*1242*	*665*	*424*	*797*	*38*

QUESTIONNAIRE FORM 4 1984	TOTAL	SEX		RACE		REGION				4YR COLLEGE PLANS		ILLICIT DRUG USE: LIFETIME				
		M	F	White	Black	NE	NC	S	W	Yes	No	None	Mari-juana Only	Few Pills	More Pills	Any Her-oin
N (Weighted No. of Cases):	3284	1588	1546	2489	414	679	909	1113	584	1830	1188	1253	675	426	806	39
% of Weighted Total:	100.0	48.4	47.1	75.8	12.6	20.7	27.7	33.9	17.8	55.7	36.2	38.1	20.6	13.0	24.5	1.2
A16: How much TV do you estimate you watch on an average weekday?																
1. None	3.2	2.3	3.6	3.2	0.7	3.0	3.0	2.6	5.3	3.4	2.4	2.4	2.5	4.1	4.2	5.1
2. Half-hour or less	11.8	11.5	12.5	13.4	5.9	14.1	10.0	10.2	15.2	13.0	10.3	11.4	9.1	11.0	14.8	7.5
3. About one hour	20.5	21.3	20.5	22.5	10.7	21.7	23.4	16.7	22.2	22.8	18.1	21.3	16.5	18.7	24.0	28.0
4. About two hours	22.7	22.6	22.8	23.8	17.9	21.8	20.0	23.3	26.5	24.8	20.0	23.9	23.2	21.3	21.0	24.9
5. About three hours	17.4	17.8	17.1	17.1	17.9	17.0	17.6	18.6	15.2	16.0	19.2	15.3	20.6	21.6	16.1	12.2
6. About four hours	12.1	12.0	12.0	10.9	16.7	11.7	13.1	13.0	9.3	10.3	14.0	12.8	11.2	12.6	11.2	9.7
7. Five hours or more	12.2	12.6	11.6	9.1	30.1	10.6	13.1	15.6	6.3	9.6	16.0	12.8	16.9	10.6	8.5	12.7
Item 10550　Subject C07　　N	3232	1568	1534	2466	408	670	896	1093	573	1815	1172	1244	663	424	800	39
A17: In the past year, how many books have you read just because you wanted to–that is, without their being assigned?																
1. None	17.7	24.1	9.9	17.5	14.5	21.5	17.7	16.2	16.2	12.7	24.4	14.5	18.6	17.6	20.7	32.6
2. One	13.2	13.8	12.4	13.6	11.2	13.6	12.9	12.8	13.7	12.8	12.7	11.0	17.2	12.8	13.5	7.6
3. Two to five	38.7	37.5	40.2	37.2	49.3	38.4	38.5	38.8	38.9	39.2	38.3	41.3	38.3	39.3	35.4	30.6
4. Six to ten	11.9	10.7	13.3	12.0	12.9	10.2	11.7	14.5	9.4	13.7	9.2	11.7	10.6	11.0	13.3	14.5
5. Ten or more	18.5	13.9	24.1	19.6	12.1	16.3	19.1	17.7	21.8	21.6	15.3	21.6	15.3	19.3	17.1	14.6
Item 10560　Subject C07　　N	3250	1580	1541	2483	410	673	902	1101	575	1825	1181	1250	675	421	800	38
A18: Some people think about what's going on in government very often, and others are not that interested. How much of an interest do you take in government and current events?																
1. No interest at all	4.4	4.7	3.6	4.2	2.8	7.2	4.7	3.4	2.5	2.1	7.2	3.1	4.6	5.9	5.5	5.2
2. Very little interest	18.8	14.7	22.9	18.7	19.5	21.0	17.5	17.9	20.1	14.6	25.2	17.0	17.1	22.7	21.1	18.6
3. Some interest	47.7	44.5	51.4	48.7	47.6	49.6	48.5	47.2	45.1	47.1	49.4	48.0	48.8	45.1	47.0	46.0
4. A lot of interest	20.0	23.8	16.1	20.0	19.6	15.7	21.2	20.2	22.9	23.6	14.2	20.8	21.3	20.7	17.9	21.3
5. A very great interest	9.1	12.2	5.9	8.4	10.5	6.6	8.1	11.2	9.4	12.5	4.0	11.0	8.1	5.7	8.6	8.9
Item 6330　Subject H01,Q08　　N	3245	1581	1540	2482	409	668	902	1101	575	1826	1181	1251	675	420	802	38
A19: Some people think that there ought to be changes in the amount of influence and power that certain organizations have in our society. Do you think the following organizations should have more influence, less influence, or about the same amount of influence as they have now?																
A19A: Large corporations?																
1. Much less	4.8	6.2	3.4	4.8	4.0	5.8	3.8	3.8	6.9	5.3	3.8	5.4	3.6	2.4	5.9	10.3
2. Less	27.0	28.3	25.4	30.2	13.4	28.2	30.5	23.0	27.7	31.3	21.4	30.8	24.0	24.5	25.5	26.9
3. Same as now	39.3	39.4	40.0	40.3	37.5	37.3	40.0	40.1	38.9	40.2	39.9	37.6	39.9	41.5	40.9	35.8
4. More	10.2	10.7	9.7	8.3	15.5	9.4	10.6	11.1	8.6	7.6	12.6	8.8	12.0	10.4	10.3	9.8
5. Much more	4.4	4.5	4.0	3.4	9.3	3.4	3.7	6.3	3.2	2.7	6.8	4.8	5.0	5.7	2.8	3.8
8. No opinion	14.3	10.9	17.5	13.0	20.3	15.9	11.3	15.6	14.7	12.9	15.5	12.5	15.6	15.6	14.7	13.3
Item 10570　Subject K03　　N	3225	1571	1534	2473	405	664	897	1093	572	1821	1171	1246	670	419	794	38
A19B: Major labor unions?																
1. Much less	9.6	14.3	5.1	11.3	2.3	6.6	9.6	11.5	9.3	11.5	7.3	11.7	7.6	8.8	8.0	19.3
2. Less	21.2	24.4	17.9	24.1	8.1	17.3	25.3	20.9	19.7	24.6	17.4	23.0	18.3	22.1	21.0	14.8
3. Same as now	30.7	30.0	31.5	31.4	26.1	31.4	31.1	28.0	34.3	31.9	29.3	29.2	35.7	27.4	31.1	26.0
4. More	17.3	13.9	20.4	15.1	28.4	18.1	15.2	18.4	17.6	15.6	18.6	16.5	18.1	19.4	16.7	12.0
5. Much more	7.3	7.8	6.7	4.6	16.7	9.2	6.9	7.8	4.7	4.3	11.0	6.0	6.8	7.3	8.5	15.2
8. No opinion	14.0	9.6	18.4	13.4	18.5	17.4	12.0	13.5	14.4	12.1	16.5	13.6	13.5	15.0	14.8	12.7
Item 10580　Subject K03　　N	3225	1574	1533	2474	404	665	897	1092	571	1822	1171	1246	670	420	793	38
A19C: Churches and religious organizations?																
1. Much less	5.8	7.1	4.3	6.4	1.5	6.9	4.2	4.7	8.9	6.4	4.4	5.0	5.1	6.3	7.3	8.1
2. Less	9.1	10.0	8.2	10.3	2.9	9.7	9.6	6.5	12.4	9.9	8.2	6.9	8.9	12.6	10.3	11.6
3. Same as now	33.3	35.9	30.6	35.6	20.4	36.0	36.6	27.8	35.3	34.4	32.0	30.6	33.3	31.2	38.9	31.3
4. More	25.4	23.4	27.2	25.3	30.6	21.9	27.8	28.5	19.7	26.5	24.6	28.1	26.6	25.1	20.6	20.3
5. Much more	17.4	15.3	19.8	14.0	35.3	13.4	14.3	25.5	11.3	16.1	18.0	22.2	17.6	14.8	11.3	11.8
8. No opinion	9.1	8.3	9.9	8.4	9.4	12.1	7.4	7.0	12.4	6.7	12.8	7.2	8.2	10.0	11.5	16.9
Item 10590　Subject G,K03　　N	3230	1576	1535	2475	406	666	899	1093	573	1823	1174	1248	671	421	794	38

QUESTIONNAIRE FORM 4 1984	TOTAL	SEX		RACE		REGION				4YR COLLEGE PLANS		ILLICIT DRUG USE: LIFETIME				
		M	F	White	Black	NE	NC	S	W	Yes	No	None	Mari-juana Only	Few Pills	More Pills	Any Her-oin
N (Weighted No. of Cases):	3284	1588	1546	2489	414	679	909	1113	584	1830	1188	1253	675	426	806	39
% of Weighted Total:	100.0	48.4	47.1	75.8	12.6	20.7	27.7	33.9	17.8	55.7	36.2	38.1	20.6	13.0	24.5	1.2
A19D: The national news media (TV, magazines, news services)?																
1. Much less	9.5	10.5	8.6	10.4	4.1	10.7	8.9	9.5	9.2	10.5	7.8	10.3	6.1	8.5	11.5	14.6
2. Less	25.2	25.8	24.6	27.1	16.6	23.9	26.9	23.5	27.2	27.9	22.0	25.9	25.4	25.2	24.8	19.1
3. Same as now	40.3	39.4	41.4	42.0	35.4	41.5	42.0	40.0	36.8	41.2	39.6	41.0	40.4	40.2	40.3	31.5
4. More	13.5	12.6	14.5	11.5	23.5	11.7	13.0	14.2	15.1	12.4	14.8	13.2	14.7	13.9	12.5	12.7
5. Much more	5.0	5.3	4.3	3.1	12.1	4.3	4.2	6.0	5.3	3.7	6.4	4.2	6.8	4.7	4.3	6.6
8. No opinion	6.5	6.4	6.7	5.9	8.4	7.9	5.0	6.9	6.5	4.4	9.4	5.3	6.7	7.6	6.6	15.6
Item 10600 Subject K03 N	3227	1574	1532	2472	405	666	897	1091	572	1823	1172	1247	671	420	793	38
A19E: The Presidency and the administration?																
1. Much less	4.3	4.1	4.2	3.7	7.8	5.0	4.0	4.5	3.6	3.2	6.1	4.2	3.1	2.3	6.4	11.4
2. Less	9.6	9.3	9.8	8.5	15.1	10.7	9.4	9.3	9.0	8.6	10.5	9.6	10.5	8.4	9.5	10.3
3. Same as now	40.7	39.9	41.4	41.6	39.1	40.0	40.0	38.6	46.3	44.1	35.8	41.6	40.2	38.2	41.7	35.1
4. More	23.2	24.9	21.8	24.9	14.7	21.5	25.5	23.8	20.4	25.0	20.3	26.1	20.3	26.4	19.3	27.6
5. Much more	12.2	14.1	9.9	12.2	10.9	11.6	11.5	14.0	10.4	12.1	12.9	10.3	15.0	13.9	11.7	7.0
8. No opinion	10.1	7.7	12.8	9.0	12.5	11.2	9.7	9.8	10.3	7.0	14.3	8.1	10.9	10.8	11.5	8.5
Item 10610 Subject H04,K03 N	3225	1573	1533	2472	405	666	897	1089	573	1821	1173	1247	667	421	795	38
A19F: The Congress–that is, the U.S. Senate and House of Representatives?																
1. Much less	3.4	4.1	2.1	3.0	4.8	3.7	4.1	3.4	1.7	2.4	4.4	3.3	2.7	3.3	3.9	11.4
2. Less	9.1	9.4	9.0	9.7	7.6	9.8	8.3	9.4	9.0	8.5	10.0	8.4	8.6	10.5	10.2	5.1
3. Same as now	43.1	43.7	42.3	44.3	38.0	42.3	41.9	43.6	45.1	46.0	38.7	45.2	43.2	41.0	41.8	37.8
4. More	23.3	24.2	23.0	23.8	22.4	21.2	26.4	21.3	24.5	26.4	19.6	25.7	21.0	23.4	21.1	21.3
5. Much more	9.3	9.6	8.7	8.2	12.7	9.1	8.1	10.8	8.5	8.1	10.8	7.9	12.6	8.5	9.0	11.6
8. No opinion	11.8	9.0	15.0	11.1	14.5	13.9	11.2	11.5	11.2	8.7	16.5	9.5	12.0	13.2	14.0	12.9
Item 10620 Subject H04,K03 N	3222	1571	1532	2469	404	665	897	1088	572	1822	1168	1248	667	420	792	38
A19G: The U.S. Supreme Court?																
1. Much less	2.1	2.2	1.7	2.1	2.1	2.8	2.2	2.2	1.0	1.4	3.0	2.0	2.3	1.9	2.4	2.7
2. Less	4.5	4.9	4.0	4.7	3.1	5.2	4.4	4.3	4.1	3.8	5.2	4.6	2.7	4.4	5.4	7.3
3. Same as now	44.1	45.3	42.7	46.3	37.1	44.5	43.9	43.5	44.9	47.5	39.1	44.1	44.5	47.2	43.0	39.1
4. More	25.3	25.3	25.8	25.1	26.9	22.8	25.4	25.1	28.6	27.9	22.5	28.8	24.9	22.3	22.1	26.6
5. Much more	11.3	12.2	10.2	10.1	13.1	10.2	11.8	12.4	9.6	9.8	13.1	9.7	11.8	11.6	12.8	13.4
8. No opinion	12.7	10.0	15.6	11.7	17.8	14.5	12.3	12.5	11.7	9.7	17.1	10.8	13.8	12.7	14.3	10.9
Item 10630 Subject H04,K03 N	3217	1566	1532	2470	401	664	895	1088	570	1817	1171	1248	666	419	789	38
A19H: All the courts and the justice system in general?																
1. Much less	2.2	2.5	1.5	2.3	1.9	2.6	1.9	2.5	1.6	1.6	2.7	2.1	2.5	2.1	2.2	6.1
2. Less	4.8	5.6	4.1	4.4	6.0	4.6	5.1	5.0	4.3	3.7	6.2	4.6	3.1	4.4	6.3	13.2
3. Same as now	40.5	42.1	38.4	42.7	32.2	37.4	43.0	38.8	43.5	43.0	37.4	39.2	43.8	41.7	40.8	28.4
4. More	28.4	27.3	30.2	28.3	30.6	29.3	27.4	28.5	29.0	31.3	25.4	32.6	25.3	29.6	23.9	20.8
5. Much more	12.4	13.3	11.6	11.2	14.9	12.8	11.8	12.8	11.8	10.9	14.4	11.2	13.7	12.2	12.6	19.8
8. No opinion	11.7	9.2	14.2	11.1	14.3	13.3	10.9	12.4	9.9	9.6	13.9	10.3	11.6	9.9	14.2	11.8
Item 10640 Subject H04,K03 N	3225	1573	1532	2473	405	666	897	1090	571	1822	1172	1248	670	420	793	37
A19I: The police and other law enforcement agencies?																
1. Much less	2.5	3.3	1.4	2.3	1.9	3.3	2.2	2.5	2.0	1.7	3.4	1.8	1.2	1.9	4.7	7.5
2. Less	7.7	9.1	6.4	8.3	6.1	7.6	8.3	6.2	9.7	7.7	7.6	5.9	6.9	9.3	9.9	15.7
3. Same as now	29.5	31.7	27.2	30.2	24.8	29.7	30.0	26.8	33.8	32.4	24.6	26.2	33.1	31.0	30.8	31.5
4. More	33.1	31.7	34.8	34.4	29.6	30.3	34.5	33.4	33.7	34.8	32.1	37.9	33.1	30.9	28.0	13.3
5. Much more	20.6	18.7	22.6	18.8	28.5	20.7	19.6	24.6	14.4	18.8	23.3	22.7	19.6	20.6	18.5	23.9
8. No opinion	6.6	5.6	7.6	6.0	9.2	8.5	5.4	6.6	6.3	4.5	8.9	5.5	6.1	6.3	8.2	8.0
Item 10650 Subject K03 N	3223	1569	1534	2470	405	665	899	1089	571	1820	1173	1247	670	418	792	38

QUESTIONNAIRE FORM 4 1984	TOTAL	SEX		RACE		REGION				4YR COLLEGE PLANS		ILLICIT DRUG USE: LIFETIME				
		M	F	White	Black	NE	NC	S	W	Yes	No	None	Mari- juana Only	Few Pills	More Pills	Any Her- oin
N (Weighted No. of Cases):	3284	1588	1546	2489	414	679	909	1113	584	1830	1188	1253	675	426	806	39
% of Weighted Total:	100.0	48.4	47.1	75.8	12.6	20.7	27.7	33.9	17.8	55.7	36.2	38.1	20.6	13.0	24.5	1.2
A19J: The U.S. military?																
1. Much less	4.8	4.9	4.6	4.7	4.5	5.0	3.5	3.4	9.2	5.0	4.5	4.1	3.9	2.4	8.2	2.7
2. Less	8.2	9.0	7.5	8.4	7.6	7.8	10.2	5.2	11.5	9.5	6.1	9.1	8.2	6.7	8.4	2.6
3. Same as now	37.7	35.1	40.5	39.8	30.0	38.3	38.7	34.9	40.7	40.9	34.1	37.2	43.0	38.1	35.3	14.3
4. More	22.4	22.8	22.0	22.7	22.4	21.6	22.4	25.4	17.3	23.3	20.8	24.6	19.7	23.7	20.2	33.1
5. Much more	16.9	21.3	12.1	15.2	21.9	14.7	15.3	21.6	12.9	13.1	21.5	15.5	15.8	17.8	17.7	33.3
8. No opinion	10.0	6.9	13.3	9.2	13.5	12.5	9.9	9.4	8.5	8.1	12.9	9.6	9.4	11.2	10.2	13.9
Item 10660 Subject K03,L04 N	3227	1574	1534	2474	405	666	898	1092	572	1824	1173	1248	669	420	795	38

The next questions ask your views about drugs.

A20: Do you think that people (who are 18 or older) should be prohibited by law from doing each of the following?

	TOTAL	M	F	White	Black	NE	NC	S	W	Yes	No	None	Mari- juana Only	Few Pills	More Pills	Any Her- oin
A20A: Smoking marijuana (pot, grass) in private																
1. No	42.2	41.8	42.4	41.2	41.6	49.9	37.7	38.7	47.2	39.1	46.2	24.8	43.6	43.8	67.5	60.7
2. Not sure	16.2	16.0	16.2	15.8	19.3	18.6	15.2	16.2	14.7	17.2	14.6	15.7	22.3	17.9	10.1	15.5
3. Yes	41.6	42.2	41.4	42.9	39.1	31.5	47.1	45.0	38.1	43.7	39.2	59.5	34.2	38.3	22.4	23.8
Item 10780 Subject A13a N	3236	1577	1538	2478	409	667	900	1095	575	1818	1180	1249	668	421	801	38
A20B: Smoking marijuana in public places																
1. No	15.8	17.0	13.4	13.0	20.3	14.5	16.6	15.9	15.8	11.4	20.2	11.4	14.6	15.7	21.5	34.6
2. Not sure	9.0	10.7	6.9	9.3	6.7	13.1	9.4	7.1	7.0	7.1	10.9	2.6	9.6	8.4	17.7	30.3
3. Yes	75.2	72.3	79.7	77.7	73.0	72.4	73.9	77.0	77.2	81.5	68.9	85.9	75.7	75.9	60.8	35.1
Item 10790 Subject A13a N	3236	1579	1537	2478	408	669	899	1095	574	1820	1179	1248	671	421	800	38
A20C: Taking LSD in private																
1. No	22.4	23.0	21.2	20.3	28.2	22.7	23.0	22.5	20.9	17.9	27.9	16.3	21.8	22.8	29.8	66.7
2. Not sure	9.7	9.6	10.0	8.1	16.7	10.1	8.5	11.3	8.2	9.3	9.6	10.2	8.5	7.4	10.4	12.4
3. Yes	67.9	67.4	68.8	71.6	55.1	67.3	68.4	66.2	70.9	72.8	62.5	73.5	69.7	69.8	59.8	20.9
Item 10800 Subject A13a N	3233	1577	1535	2473	408	668	899	1093	573	1820	1176	1248	669	421	798	38
A20D: Taking LSD in public places																
1. No	13.4	14.6	11.0	10.5	20.5	11.9	14.7	14.2	11.5	8.7	17.7	11.8	13.5	14.1	13.6	32.8
2. Not sure	4.2	5.0	3.3	3.5	6.7	5.5	3.5	4.4	3.5	3.7	4.7	2.5	4.8	2.1	6.5	13.3
3. Yes	82.4	80.4	85.7	86.0	72.8	82.7	81.8	81.5	85.0	87.6	77.6	85.8	81.7	83.8	79.9	53.9
Item 10810 Subject A13a N	3222	1574	1529	2468	404	665	896	1086	574	1818	1169	1246	668	419	793	38
A20E: Taking amphetamines (uppers) or barbi- turates (downers) in private																
1. No	29.3	29.1	29.4	28.2	32.0	29.4	28.6	29.0	31.0	24.6	35.5	18.7	26.2	27.0	47.9	66.6
2. Not sure	16.2	16.6	15.7	15.8	18.0	18.5	16.1	16.1	14.2	16.4	15.7	14.0	16.8	22.8	15.5	16.9
3. Yes	54.4	54.3	54.9	56.1	50.1	52.2	55.4	54.9	54.8	59.0	48.8	67.2	57.0	50.2	36.6	16.4
Item 10820 Subject A13a N	3232	1578	1535	2476	406	668	899	1091	574	1819	1178	1247	669	421	799	38
A20F: Taking amphetamines or barbiturates in public places																
1. No	15.6	16.6	13.5	13.2	20.1	15.2	17.2	15.5	13.9	10.7	20.9	12.0	13.6	14.5	22.0	38.4
2. Not sure	7.6	8.3	6.6	7.3	7.8	9.2	7.6	6.8	7.3	6.6	8.7	3.5	8.3	8.5	12.0	17.9
3. Yes	76.8	75.1	79.9	79.5	72.2	75.5	75.3	77.7	78.8	82.7	70.4	84.6	78.1	76.9	66.0	43.7
Item 10830 Subject A13a N	3229	1573	1537	2472	407	668	898	1090	573	1816	1178	1246	670	421	797	38
A20G: Taking heroin (smack, horse) in private																
1. No	21.1	21.5	19.8	18.5	29.3	20.4	21.2	21.9	20.3	16.7	26.1	16.4	21.5	23.3	24.5	53.0
2. Not sure	9.1	9.1	9.2	7.9	15.3	9.2	7.4	11.6	7.1	9.0	7.8	9.7	9.1	9.0	8.0	9.7
3. Yes	69.8	69.5	71.0	73.7	55.4	70.3	71.4	66.6	72.6	74.3	66.0	73.8	69.4	67.7	67.6	37.3
Item 10840 Subject A13a N	3226	1577	1530	2468	408	665	896	1093	572	1813	1178	1244	671	419	798	38

QUESTIONNAIRE FORM 4 1984	TOTAL	SEX		RACE		REGION				4YR COLLEGE PLANS		ILLICIT DRUG USE: LIFETIME				
		M	F	White	Black	NE	NC	S	W	Yes	No	None	Mari-juana Only	Few Pills	More Pills	Any Her-oin
N (Weighted No. of Cases):	3284	1588	1546	2489	414	679	909	1113	584	1830	1188	1253	675	426	806	39
% of Weighted Total:	100.0	48.4	47.1	75.8	12.6	20.7	27.7	33.9	17.8	55.7	36.2	38.1	20.6	13.0	24.5	1.2
A20H: Taking heroin in public places																
1. No	12.8	14.0	10.8	10.2	19.9	11.4	14.7	13.2	10.7	8.7	16.9	11.6	13.1	13.5	11.8	37.9
2. Not sure	3.8	4.3	2.8	2.9	6.7	5.5	2.1	5.0	2.2	3.2	3.6	3.1	5.1	2.6	3.9	8.0
3. Yes	83.4	81.7	86.4	86.9	73.4	83.1	83.1	81.8	87.1	88.2	79.5	85.3	81.8	83.9	84.3	54.1
Item 10850 Subject A13a N	*3221*	*1574*	*1530*	*2468*	*407*	*663*	*897*	*1090*	*571*	*1815*	*1174*	*1244*	*668*	*418*	*798*	*38*
A20I: Getting drunk in private																
1. No	64.9	66.0	64.4	68.2	47.9	69.0	65.1	62.5	64.6	65.7	65.2	51.0	67.9	71.3	81.5	66.5
2. Not sure	15.4	14.8	16.1	14.6	23.6	14.8	15.0	15.6	16.4	16.8	12.9	23.9	13.8	11.6	5.7	3.8
3. Yes	19.7	19.2	19.5	17.2	28.4	16.1	19.9	22.0	18.9	17.4	21.9	25.1	18.3	17.1	12.8	29.8
Item 10860 Subject A13a N	*3234*	*1580*	*1535*	*2476*	*408*	*669*	*900*	*1094*	*572*	*1818*	*1180*	*1246*	*672*	*422*	*800*	*38*
A20J: Getting drunk in public places																
1. No	27.3	28.2	26.5	27.6	21.1	27.4	32.1	23.9	26.3	25.0	29.7	19.1	28.4	24.5	39.4	51.4
2. Not sure	21.6	23.7	19.1	23.6	14.6	22.1	24.9	19.0	20.6	20.4	22.7	17.9	20.7	30.7	22.7	21.1
3. Yes	51.1	48.1	54.4	48.9	64.3	50.5	43.0	57.1	53.1	54.6	47.6	63.0	50.9	44.8	37.9	27.5
Item 10870 Subject A13a N	*3233*	*1579*	*1537*	*2477*	*407*	*668*	*898*	*1094*	*573*	*1822*	*1177*	*1246*	*671*	*421*	*799*	*38*
A20K: Smoking tobacco in certain specified public places																
1. No	43.5	42.7	43.9	45.2	33.0	42.6	45.1	42.4	44.2	40.4	48.6	33.6	44.5	44.6	58.0	37.4
2. Not sure	17.3	18.8	16.1	16.0	27.0	15.2	18.1	18.0	17.3	16.8	17.5	19.9	18.4	18.0	11.7	17.7
3. Yes	39.2	38.5	40.0	38.8	40.0	42.2	36.8	39.6	38.6	42.9	33.9	46.5	37.1	37.4	30.2	44.9
Item 10760 Subject A13a N	*3234*	*1577*	*1537*	*2476*	*408*	*669*	*899*	*1093*	*573*	*1821*	*1178*	*1248*	*672*	*422*	*797*	*38*
A21: In particular, there has been a great deal of public debate about whether marijuana use should be legal. Which of the following policies would you favor?																
1. Using marijuana should be entirely legal	18.6	21.4	15.1	19.6	11.4	20.7	17.9	17.3	19.9	16.1	22.0	5.9	18.3	16.5	38.6	47.3
2. It should be a minor violation –like a parking ticket– but not a crime	23.6	21.2	26.0	23.0	26.4	28.2	24.3	19.2	25.6	23.0	25.4	13.6	31.8	27.4	30.1	24.5
3. It should be a crime	40.6	40.7	41.1	41.3	40.4	32.0	44.0	45.0	36.9	43.4	36.4	65.1	29.9	33.7	17.0	13.1
4. Don't know	17.2	16.7	17.8	16.1	21.8	19.0	13.9	18.5	17.6	17.5	16.2	15.4	20.0	22.3	14.3	15.1
Item 10880 Subject A13b N	*3230*	*1575*	*1539*	*2477*	*404*	*670*	*899*	*1088*	*574*	*1819*	*1179*	*1245*	*671*	*422*	*799*	*38*
A22: If it were legal for people to USE marijuana, should it also be legal to SELL marijuana?																
1. No	30.9	30.9	30.7	29.8	32.0	28.4	32.3	30.2	32.8	32.5	28.6	42.7	28.9	29.7	15.7	15.1
2. Yes, but only to adults	45.8	47.8	43.8	47.2	41.0	44.8	46.8	44.5	47.6	45.8	46.0	34.9	46.8	46.1	62.1	49.9
3. Yes, to anyone	10.6	10.8	10.3	10.1	13.9	10.8	10.2	12.3	7.8	8.5	12.9	9.2	10.3	11.3	11.5	26.6
4. Don't know	12.8	10.6	15.2	12.8	13.2	16.0	10.7	13.0	11.7	13.2	12.5	13.3	14.0	12.9	10.7	8.5
Item 10890 Subject A13b N	*3222*	*1576*	*1532*	*2470*	*407*	*669*	*895*	*1086*	*573*	*1818*	*1175*	*1242*	*672*	*422*	*796*	*38*
A23: If marijuana were legal to use and legally available, which of the following would you be most likely to do?																
1. Not use it, even if it were legal and available	62.0	59.3	65.9	61.3	68.6	51.7	64.4	66.5	61.7	66.8	56.2	91.7	53.5	56.0	28.6	14.2
2. Try it	6.6	6.7	6.4	6.5	5.9	6.7	8.6	6.0	4.7	8.0	4.8	4.9	9.6	8.5	5.8	6.9
3. Use it about as often as I do now	19.1	20.6	17.3	20.4	11.1	25.7	16.7	14.8	23.2	16.6	22.5	0.3	22.1	21.4	43.8	46.1
4. Use it more often than I do now	4.7	5.7	3.4	4.8	3.5	6.8	4.9	3.2	4.7	3.4	6.2	0.1	4.3	4.7	11.1	22.8
5. Use it less than I do now	1.6	1.9	1.3	1.6	1.8	2.6	1.0	1.9	0.7	0.9	2.4	0.2	1.9	1.4	3.6	4.7
6. Don't know	6.0	5.8	5.8	5.3	9.1	6.5	4.3	7.6	5.0	4.3	7.9	2.8	8.7	8.0	7.0	5.2
Item 10900 Subject A13b N	*3224*	*1576*	*1534*	*2473*	*406*	*667*	*897*	*1087*	*573*	*1819*	*1177*	*1244*	*672*	*422*	*796*	*38*

This section asks for your views and feelings about a number of different things.

QUESTIONNAIRE FORM 4 1984	TOTAL	SEX		RACE		REGION				4YR COLLEGE PLANS		ILLICIT DRUG USE: LIFETIME				
		M	F	White	Black	NE	NC	S	W	Yes	No	None	Mari- juana Only	Few Pills	More Pills	Any Her- oin
N (Weighted No. of Cases):	3284	1588	1546	2489	414	679	909	1113	584	1830	1188	1253	675	426	806	39
% of Weighted Total:	100.0	48.4	47.1	75.8	12.6	20.7	27.7	33.9	17.8	55.7	36.2	38.1	20.6	13.0	24.5	1.2
D01: How satisfied are you with your life as a whole these days?																
1. Completely dissatisfied	2.1	2.1	2.2	1.7	2.6	2.8	2.3	1.9	1.5	1.7	2.9	1.9	2.6	2.1	1.9	5.0
2. Quite dissatisfied	8.3	8.4	8.5	8.3	8.0	9.7	8.5	6.7	9.7	8.5	8.1	7.7	8.4	8.7	9.0	15.8
3. Somewhat dissatisfied	11.3	10.7	11.9	10.9	13.9	11.5	10.8	10.7	13.2	12.0	10.4	11.0	10.3	13.7	11.8	9.0
4. Neither, or mixed feelings	15.0	14.8	15.5	15.1	16.5	15.7	15.9	14.9	13.0	12.6	18.8	13.3	14.0	15.7	20.0	33.6
5. Somewhat satisfied	24.3	26.5	22.0	24.3	23.8	19.8	26.0	25.2	24.6	24.3	24.2	23.4	26.1	26.3	22.4	14.4
6. Quite satisfied	33.5	32.9	34.1	35.1	27.3	35.3	33.0	34.3	31.1	36.6	29.2	35.9	36.2	30.7	30.2	15.9
7. Completely satisfied	5.4	4.7	5.8	4.6	7.9	5.2	3.5	6.4	6.9	4.4	6.5	6.8	5.2	2.9	4.6	6.2
Item 6840 Subject P01,Q01 N	3045	1479	1494	2399	364	595	866	1030	554	1801	1139	1189	625	406	751	35
D02: FOR THOSE WHO HAVE A JOB: All things considered, how satisfied are you with your present job?																
1. Completely dissatisfied	4.4	4.0	4.8	4.0	7.3	5.5	3.9	4.2	4.3	3.6	5.5	3.7	5.2	6.2	3.7	5.7
2. Quite dissatisfied	9.7	9.1	10.3	9.3	8.9	8.3	9.4	10.4	10.6	9.7	9.4	8.7	9.7	8.5	10.2	34.3
3. Somewhat dissatisfied	13.5	13.2	13.5	13.5	15.4	17.1	13.1	11.7	12.9	13.3	13.5	11.5	12.9	16.0	15.8	9.4
4. Neither, or mixed feelings	18.1	21.1	15.1	18.3	19.3	16.9	17.9	20.1	16.5	18.2	18.3	15.5	20.0	24.4	17.4	24.4
5. Somewhat satisfied	25.7	26.2	25.6	26.0	24.1	23.0	25.0	26.4	28.3	28.6	22.1	28.4	24.9	22.7	24.8	7.2
6. Quite satisfied	22.4	21.3	23.6	23.6	18.7	22.9	24.6	20.6	22.0	21.7	23.6	25.0	21.6	18.1	22.6	9.6
7. Completely satisfied	6.1	5.1	7.0	5.3	6.4	6.4	6.1	6.5	5.4	4.9	7.6	7.1	5.6	4.1	5.9	9.4
Item 10910 Subject C01,P02 N★	2002	1010	944	1669	167	420	543	640	399	1159	777	734	421	270	531	27
D03A: Which best describes your recent em- ployment experience?																
1. I have a paid job now.	64.9	65.8	64.5	67.9	44.8	68.6	60.9	63.6	69.3	64.1	66.4	61.6	65.8	64.9	70.3	60.6
2. No paid job now, but I had one during the past 3 months.	8.7	9.5	7.7	8.3	11.7	8.7	8.9	8.0	9.6	8.7	8.8	8.4	8.8	8.7	8.9	11.5
3. No paid job in the past 3 months –GO TO QUESTION D10	17.7	18.6	16.7	17.7	22.2	16.7	20.8	16.8	15.4	18.5	16.2	19.1	16.5	18.0	15.6	22.7
4. Never had a paid job–GO TO QUESTION D10	8.8	6.2	11.1	6.2	21.3	6.0	9.3	11.6	5.7	8.8	8.6	11.0	8.9	8.3	5.2	5.2
Item 21530 Subject C01 N	2749	1347	1337	2208	297	544	788	913	503	1640	1020	1060	568	367	689	30
The next questions are about your present or most recent paid job. (If you presently hold more than one paid job, answer for the more important one.)																
D03B: On the average, how many hours per week do (did) you work on this particular job?																
1. 5 or less hours	9.3	8.5	10.2	8.1	19.8	6.9	11.2	9.7	8.7	10.2	8.0	12.0	9.2	9.1	5.5	16.8
2. 6 to 10 hours	11.3	10.3	12.2	11.6	10.3	12.6	13.6	9.1	10.4	12.4	10.2	13.7	10.5	10.2	8.8	11.5
3. 11 to 15 hours	15.8	15.4	16.4	16.5	9.7	16.0	15.8	14.5	17.6	17.4	13.3	18.9	17.8	11.8	11.6	18.8
4. 16 to 20 hours	21.5	20.9	22.1	21.2	24.3	22.8	20.6	20.7	22.6	22.2	20.5	20.9	22.5	22.5	22.0	10.5
5. 21 to 25 hours	16.3	16.5	16.3	16.6	11.8	15.3	14.9	17.3	17.7	15.8	16.7	12.3	18.3	18.2	19.5	8.8
6. 26 to 30 hours	12.9	12.6	13.4	12.9	13.3	15.4	11.5	12.6	12.4	11.6	14.4	10.8	11.2	13.7	17.2	9.5
7. 31 to 35 hours	5.6	7.5	3.5	5.8	4.4	3.4	5.1	7.3	5.6	4.8	6.7	4.8	5.7	5.4	6.1	8.6
8. 36 or more hours	7.4	8.4	6.0	7.3	6.4	7.5	7.2	8.7	5.1	5.5	10.1	6.6	4.9	9.0	9.3	15.6
Item 21540 Subject C01 N★	2149	1084	1019	1772	192	451	593	695	410	1270	817	788	456	284	571	27
D04: About how old is (was) your supervisor?																
1. Age 20 or younger	2.5	2.8	2.2	1.9	6.4	3.6	1.1	2.7	2.8	2.3	2.4	2.6	2.0	4.0	1.4	9.8
2. 21 to 25	13.2	11.7	15.1	13.1	14.5	12.2	11.9	15.0	12.9	12.5	14.3	11.7	13.0	14.0	14.7	18.2
3. 26 to 30	25.2	23.8	26.8	26.2	19.2	22.3	27.3	26.7	23.0	25.0	25.9	27.2	23.5	23.2	24.9	16.0
4. 31 or older	59.2	61.7	55.9	58.8	59.8	61.9	59.7	55.7	61.3	60.2	57.4	58.6	61.5	58.7	59.0	56.0
Item 21550 Subject C01,M02 N★	2109	1063	999	1735	192	439	578	682	409	1231	810	767	447	281	565	26

★=excludes respondents for whom question was inappropriate.

QUESTIONNAIRE FORM 4 1984	TOTAL	SEX		RACE		REGION				4YR COLLEGE PLANS		ILLICIT DRUG USE: LIFETIME				
		M	F	White	Black	NE	NC	S	W	Yes	No	None	Marijuana Only	Few Pills	More Pills	Any Heroin
N (Weighted No. of Cases):	3284	1588	1546	2489	414	679	909	1113	584	1830	1188	1253	675	426	806	39
% of Weighted Total:	100.0	48.4	47.1	75.8	12.6	20.7	27.7	33.9	17.8	55.7	36.2	38.1	20.6	13.0	24.5	1.2

D05: How many of the other workers are within 2 or 3 years of your own age?

1. None	19.7	19.9	19.7	20.0	20.3	15.4	19.3	22.9	19.8	18.8	21.0	22.0	19.7	13.6	19.2	29.5
2. A few	29.1	28.4	29.9	29.2	30.4	27.6	29.2	27.9	32.5	28.9	29.9	30.7	25.7	32.7	28.3	22.8
3. About half	14.1	14.2	13.9	13.6	16.6	15.2	13.3	14.4	13.7	13.4	15.1	14.6	16.4	12.6	12.3	17.4
4. Most	14.6	15.0	13.9	15.0	13.1	16.3	14.7	14.2	13.4	14.4	14.5	14.5	14.8	14.6	14.8	7.4
5. Nearly all	16.0	15.9	16.5	15.7	14.3	17.7	18.0	14.1	14.6	17.2	14.9	13.8	16.0	18.5	18.0	10.4
6. All	6.4	6.7	6.1	6.6	5.3	7.7	5.5	6.5	6.1	7.4	4.6	4.5	7.3	7.9	7.3	12.6
Item 21560 Subject C01 N★	2106	1061	999	1736	189	434	584	683	406	1233	806	766	445	283	562	27

D06: To what extent does (did) this job . . .

D06A: Use your skills and abilities–let you do the things you do best?

1. Not at all	19.8	21.5	18.0	19.4	18.5	23.0	17.5	17.9	23.1	21.0	18.1	16.9	22.3	25.2	18.9	25.0
2. A little	31.5	33.2	29.9	32.4	28.9	32.2	33.4	32.1	27.0	35.4	26.5	31.6	32.3	28.1	32.7	21.7
3. Some extent	25.1	23.5	27.4	25.8	23.4	21.6	27.1	25.7	25.1	23.0	28.3	25.2	22.9	25.6	27.1	25.1
4. Considerable extent	12.7	10.7	14.4	12.9	10.4	12.3	12.5	11.7	15.1	10.8	14.6	13.3	13.1	13.1	11.8	10.2
5. A great extent	10.8	11.1	10.3	9.5	18.9	10.9	9.5	12.7	9.6	9.8	12.4	13.0	9.5	8.0	9.6	18.0
Item 21570 Subject C01 N★	2102	1053	1002	1729	195	426	588	685	404	1233	802	778	439	285	550	27

D06B: Teach you new skills that will be useful in your future work?

1. Not at all	23.4	25.7	21.0	23.9	18.7	26.5	22.6	21.1	25.4	24.4	22.3	21.5	25.3	24.4	23.8	28.5
2. A little	25.2	26.8	23.6	26.0	19.6	25.2	27.5	23.3	25.2	27.2	22.4	26.0	26.2	25.3	24.1	15.2
3. Some extent	21.7	20.8	22.4	21.8	22.4	20.0	20.6	25.1	19.6	21.6	22.3	20.7	21.6	22.6	23.1	23.0
4. Considerable extent	15.6	14.0	17.7	15.5	15.9	14.4	16.5	13.4	19.4	14.6	16.8	15.7	15.7	14.6	16.4	4.6
5. A great extent	14.0	12.7	15.3	12.7	23.4	14.0	12.8	17.1	10.4	12.2	16.1	16.1	11.2	13.1	12.6	28.8
Item 21580 Subject C01 N★	2098	1051	999	1727	195	426	585	684	403	1229	801	774	439	285	550	27

D06C: Make good use of special skills you learned in technical, vocational, business, or professional studies?

1. Not at all	50.1	50.5	50.2	52.3	34.8	54.9	48.4	46.2	53.9	55.1	43.3	47.5	50.8	55.7	50.3	46.5
2. A little	19.9	20.5	18.7	19.6	21.9	16.8	20.5	20.9	20.6	19.9	19.6	20.9	19.5	18.4	19.6	12.2
3. Some extent	13.5	13.3	13.8	13.4	13.9	10.2	15.7	14.2	12.7	12.5	15.0	13.5	13.4	13.1	13.7	22.9
4. Considerable extent	8.8	8.3	9.3	8.5	9.8	9.9	7.6	9.6	7.8	5.9	12.8	7.6	8.6	8.6	10.8	8.3
5. A great extent	7.8	7.4	8.1	6.2	19.6	8.2	7.8	9.1	5.1	6.7	9.2	10.5	7.7	4.2	5.6	10.1
Item 21590 Subject C01 N★	2084	1045	991	1715	193	423	584	680	397	1224	793	773	431	283	546	27

D06D: Let you get to know people with social backgrounds very different from yours?

1. Not at all	17.7	20.4	15.1	18.0	17.5	18.9	18.1	15.8	19.0	18.2	17.4	16.3	19.9	16.7	18.3	24.2
2. A little	24.3	25.7	22.7	24.6	22.5	22.0	24.8	24.2	26.2	24.7	23.3	24.4	27.9	22.6	22.1	22.5
3. Some extent	21.8	22.6	20.5	22.1	20.5	22.7	20.5	22.2	19.8	21.1	23.1	21.6	19.3	24.4	21.8	28.9
4. Considerable extent	17.8	17.1	18.7	18.2	14.1	16.4	18.1	17.6	19.3	18.1	17.3	18.2	14.4	19.6	20.0	5.5
5. A great extent	18.4	14.1	23.0	17.1	25.0	18.0	18.5	20.2	15.7	17.9	18.9	19.6	18.5	16.6	17.8	18.9
Item 21600 Subject C01,M05 N★	2081	1041	993	1711	194	423	581	681	396	1225	789	773	433	281	543	27

D06E: Let you get to know people over age 30?

1. Not at all	13.4	14.5	11.8	12.5	15.8	10.3	12.1	14.6	16.4	13.3	13.5	11.3	13.6	13.4	15.4	22.5
2. A little	17.3	19.4	14.9	17.9	15.1	15.8	18.5	14.8	21.5	16.9	17.6	18.5	19.3	18.8	13.7	18.1
3. Some extent	21.4	24.8	17.6	20.8	21.5	22.7	21.2	22.4	18.6	21.5	21.2	22.3	19.6	20.0	22.4	22.3
4. Considerable extent	20.6	20.7	21.3	21.5	18.2	24.9	17.8	20.1	21.1	21.7	19.3	20.0	19.0	23.7	21.1	17.7
5. A great extent	27.3	20.6	34.5	27.3	29.3	26.3	30.4	28.1	22.4	26.4	28.4	27.9	28.5	24.1	27.4	19.4
Item 21610 Subject C01,M02 N★	2081	1042	992	1711	194	422	580	681	397	1226	788	769	434	283	545	27

D06F: Cause you stress and tension?

1. Not at all	26.9	28.0	25.3	25.8	32.6	23.5	27.0	29.5	25.7	28.3	25.2	29.4	28.7	22.6	24.1	18.9
2. A little	31.8	32.7	31.1	33.0	26.0	32.4	29.9	29.5	37.6	31.6	32.8	33.3	32.4	33.4	29.2	25.5
3. Some extent	21.8	21.6	22.2	21.2	25.8	21.2	23.4	22.0	19.9	21.3	21.7	22.7	20.3	19.9	23.2	16.5
4. Considerable extent	10.9	11.2	10.9	11.4	7.2	11.9	12.8	9.1	10.4	11.1	10.3	6.8	12.0	12.7	14.1	21.2
5. A great extent	8.6	6.5	10.4	8.5	8.3	11.0	6.9	9.9	6.4	7.6	10.0	7.8	6.7	11.3	9.5	17.8
Item 21620 Subject C01 N★	2081	1041	994	1716	189	424	583	678	396	1225	792	772	432	280	547	27

★=excludes respondents for whom question was inappropriate.

QUESTIONNAIRE FORM 4 1984	TOTAL	SEX		RACE		REGION				4YR COLLEGE PLANS		ILLICIT DRUG USE: LIFETIME				
		M	F	White	Black	NE	NC	S	W	Yes	No	None	Mari- juana Only	Few Pills	More Pills	Any Her- oin
N (Weighted No. of Cases):	3284	1588	1546	2489	414	679	909	1113	584	1830	1188	1253	675	426	806	39
% of Weighted Total:	100.0	48.4	47.1	75.8	12.6	20.7	27.7	33.9	17.8	55.7	36.2	38.1	20.6	13.0	24.5	1.2
D06G: Interfere with your education?																
1. Not at all	49.8	48.1	51.5	50.6	48.4	53.4	53.6	46.4	46.3	48.2	52.6	54.2	50.8	46.3	45.8	35.0
2. A little	25.7	27.0	24.6	26.1	25.0	24.2	23.5	27.6	27.3	28.3	22.1	24.0	25.5	25.2	28.6	24.4
3. Some extent	14.9	16.2	13.7	14.7	14.0	12.2	15.1	16.2	15.5	14.8	15.0	14.7	14.9	16.8	14.4	20.3
4. Considerable extent	5.2	4.9	5.7	5.0	5.9	5.7	4.4	5.1	6.0	4.6	5.8	3.9	4.2	5.2	7.1	15.0
5. A great extent	4.3	3.8	4.6	3.6	6.6	4.4	3.4	4.7	4.9	4.0	4.4	3.1	4.7	6.5	4.1	5.4
Item 21630 Subject C01 N★	2079	1043	990	1713	190	422	583	679	396	1221	791	770	432	282	546	27
D06H: Interfere with your social life?																
1. Not at all	26.8	26.1	27.1	25.1	39.6	26.2	27.7	26.1	27.2	25.7	28.6	31.3	27.8	24.4	20.9	20.0
2. A little	30.0	29.9	30.4	30.6	27.5	30.2	29.1	30.6	30.0	30.5	29.9	31.7	29.3	25.0	32.1	15.2
3. Some extent	21.0	21.3	21.1	22.1	14.4	21.7	19.9	21.4	21.3	21.4	20.0	20.4	20.7	24.9	20.4	16.0
4. Considerable extent	13.1	13.9	12.3	13.3	11.9	13.1	14.5	12.8	11.3	13.6	11.8	9.9	13.5	13.5	16.7	10.8
5. A great extent	9.2	8.8	9.1	8.9	6.6	8.9	8.9	9.1	10.1	8.8	9.8	6.7	8.7	12.2	10.0	38.0
Item 21640 Subject C01 N★	2083	1044	993	1713	194	423	585	677	398	1225	794	773	434	282	544	27
D06I: Interfere with your family life?																
1. Not at all	48.2	45.5	50.9	47.5	59.7	49.7	50.6	47.2	44.9	49.3	47.3	51.0	49.8	46.6	45.2	31.5
2. A little	23.8	25.3	22.3	24.3	16.2	23.4	24.3	22.0	26.4	24.6	22.7	24.0	24.1	22.0	24.7	13.9
3. Some extent	16.4	17.3	15.2	17.0	14.5	16.4	14.2	18.9	15.3	15.7	16.9	16.0	16.6	16.3	15.7	29.1
4. Considerable extent	7.4	8.1	7.0	7.6	3.8	6.3	6.7	8.3	8.1	7.8	6.5	6.1	6.3	10.1	8.8	14.7
5. A great extent	4.2	3.9	4.6	3.7	5.8	4.1	4.3	3.6	5.2	2.6	6.5	3.0	3.1	5.1	5.6	10.8
Item 21650 Subject C01 N★	2081	1041	994	1713	193	421	585	677	398	1221	794	769	433	283	545	27
D07: To what extent is (was) this job . . .																
D07A: An interesting job to do?																
1. Not at all	17.1	19.1	15.0	17.0	16.0	21.6	17.0	13.0	19.7	17.0	17.5	13.7	18.4	21.0	19.0	18.4
2. A little	26.2	29.9	22.4	27.2	22.7	25.6	26.9	27.7	23.2	29.1	21.9	25.9	25.8	25.1	27.5	24.9
3. Some extent	24.8	23.2	26.6	25.6	20.5	26.0	22.4	24.9	26.9	24.8	25.2	26.7	24.6	23.1	23.1	26.9
4. Considerable extent	17.5	14.7	20.4	17.2	18.0	15.9	18.9	17.1	18.1	16.8	18.7	16.9	18.7	17.2	17.8	14.4
5. A great extent	14.3	13.1	15.5	13.0	22.8	11.0	14.8	17.2	12.1	12.4	17.5	16.8	12.5	13.6	12.6	15.4
Item 21660 Subject C01 N★	2071	1032	994	1706	190	420	582	675	394	1219	786	772	432	280	537	27
D07B: A job you COULD be happy doing for most of your life?																
1. Not at all	64.7	64.3	65.6	65.7	61.1	67.8	62.4	62.1	69.4	72.2	54.1	60.3	68.2	70.9	66.7	44.7
2. A little	11.1	11.5	10.7	11.7	5.6	9.2	12.8	10.8	11.5	10.7	11.7	13.0	9.9	6.9	10.5	25.8
3. Some extent	9.9	10.4	9.4	9.6	10.0	10.1	10.9	10.6	7.0	7.9	13.0	11.5	9.6	6.8	9.3	12.3
4. Considerable extent	7.4	7.6	7.1	6.6	13.9	6.3	7.6	9.0	5.8	4.9	11.1	7.4	6.3	8.6	7.6	7.4
5. A great extent	6.8	6.3	7.2	6.4	9.4	6.6	6.4	7.5	6.3	4.3	10.0	7.8	6.0	6.8	5.9	9.7
Item 21670 Subject C01 N★	2060	1026	992	1696	190	418	576	672	394	1217	779	768	430	279	532	27
D07C: The type of work you EXPECT to be doing for most of your life?																
1. Not at all	73.3	73.1	74.1	75.1	64.4	74.6	72.1	70.7	78.3	81.8	61.4	72.0	75.9	76.6	72.5	59.7
2. A little	8.8	9.3	8.3	8.5	11.3	6.7	10.5	8.6	9.1	7.2	11.0	8.7	7.6	8.3	10.1	9.6
3. Some extent	7.6	8.0	7.1	7.3	10.3	7.3	8.0	9.5	4.0	5.9	10.7	8.2	6.2	6.9	7.7	13.9
4. Considerable extent	5.2	4.8	5.3	4.5	6.4	5.9	6.2	4.5	4.1	2.0	9.3	5.1	6.1	3.4	4.9	11.8
5. A great extent	5.1	4.7	5.1	4.6	7.5	5.6	3.2	6.7	4.5	3.1	7.6	5.9	4.1	4.8	4.8	4.9
Item 21680 Subject C01 N★	2060	1029	989	1698	188	417	578	672	393	1216	781	769	429	277	534	27
D07D: A good stepping-stone toward the kind of work you want in the long run?																
1. Not at all	53.8	54.1	53.6	54.7	46.8	58.2	53.6	49.5	56.7	58.2	48.2	50.7	55.6	54.7	56.7	48.4
2. A little	16.7	17.0	16.4	17.7	12.7	15.3	18.4	17.5	14.4	17.8	15.2	18.0	17.1	16.6	14.7	18.2
3. Some extent	10.6	10.9	10.3	9.9	15.0	10.0	9.2	12.1	10.4	9.6	11.9	11.3	9.2	9.8	10.3	12.8
4. Considerable extent	8.4	9.0	7.8	8.0	11.7	7.2	8.6	9.1	8.1	6.1	11.2	8.1	8.3	9.5	8.8	5.2
5. A great extent	10.6	8.9	11.9	9.7	13.8	9.2	10.2	11.7	10.5	8.2	13.6	11.9	9.9	9.3	9.5	15.5
Item 21690 Subject C01 N★	2058	1028	989	1698	188	416	578	670	394	1213	781	768	427	280	533	27

★=excludes respondents for whom question was inappropriate.

QUESTIONNAIRE FORM 4 1984	TOTAL	SEX		RACE		REGION				4YR COLLEGE PLANS		ILLICIT DRUG USE: LIFETIME				
		M	F	White	Black	NE	NC	S	W	Yes	No	None	Mari-juana Only	Few Pills	More Pills	Any Her-oin
N (Weighted No. of Cases):	3284	1588	1546	2489	414	679	909	1113	584	1830	1188	1253	675	426	806	39
% of Weighted Total:	100.0	48.4	47.1	75.8	12.6	20.7	27.7	33.9	17.8	55.7	36.2	38.1	20.6	13.0	24.5	1.2
D07E: The kind of work people do just for the money?																
1. Not at all	21.0	18.8	22.8	20.4	22.8	16.2	26.0	20.8	19.1	19.3	24.3	23.8	20.6	16.8	18.6	33.0
2. A little	17.7	17.9	17.4	17.8	18.2	19.7	18.3	16.6	16.5	17.5	18.2	19.4	16.0	16.4	17.9	12.0
3. Some extent	19.3	20.5	17.9	19.3	19.0	17.2	19.1	20.6	19.7	18.3	20.9	18.7	17.9	18.9	20.6	35.4
4. Considerable extent	15.6	17.1	14.3	16.2	12.3	15.2	13.7	17.2	15.9	16.1	14.4	16.0	16.0	18.2	13.1	12.9
5. A great extent	26.4	25.6	27.6	26.3	27.7	31.7	22.9	24.8	28.9	28.9	22.2	22.1	29.5	29.6	29.9	6.7
Item 21700 Subject C01 N★	2052	1022	988	1688	191	417	571	670	393	1214	774	769	429	279	523	27
D08: To what extent did any high school teacher or counselor help you get this job?																
1. Not at all	78.2	80.7	76.6	80.7	62.5	85.1	75.7	73.0	83.6	81.3	72.7	77.8	80.7	76.8	78.0	75.4
2. A little	5.0	5.0	4.7	4.4	9.0	3.7	4.4	7.0	3.7	4.4	6.1	4.9	3.8	8.1	4.5	-
3. Some extent	4.9	5.4	4.1	4.4	7.8	3.3	4.4	6.2	5.0	3.5	7.1	4.3	4.5	5.2	5.4	9.4
4. Considerable extent	4.3	4.3	4.4	3.7	7.0	3.3	6.2	3.9	3.1	3.9	5.1	3.8	4.0	4.4	5.0	7.9
5. A great extent	7.7	4.7	10.1	6.7	13.7	4.6	9.4	10.0	4.6	6.8	9.0	9.1	7.1	5.4	7.2	7.4
Item 21710 Subject C01,M02 N★	2025	1009	975	1672	185	410	569	660	386	1199	763	754	421	274	527	27
D09: Is (was) this job part of a work-study program?																
1. Yes	16.5	13.3	19.4	14.9	23.4	8.7	18.4	21.1	13.9	12.7	22.3	14.6	14.1	14.7	22.4	18.8
2. No	83.5	86.7	80.6	85.1	76.6	91.3	81.6	78.9	86.1	87.3	77.7	85.4	85.9	85.3	77.6	81.2
Item 21720 Subject C01 N★	2004	984	982	1657	177	403	566	645	390	1195	746	753	415	269	523	26
D10: People have different opinions about world problems. How much do you agree or disagree with each of the following statements?																
D10A: I feel that I can do very little to change the way the world is today																
1. Disagree	9.7	9.9	9.5	8.5	14.7	8.3	8.2	11.2	10.6	10.5	8.3	11.7	7.6	7.3	9.2	8.5
2. Mostly disagree	19.2	19.4	18.9	19.3	17.4	18.8	18.6	19.9	19.2	22.0	15.0	21.6	15.5	15.8	19.9	24.6
3. Neither	23.0	23.2	22.7	23.9	20.0	21.8	22.8	23.1	24.5	22.1	24.9	20.5	25.5	25.7	24.1	19.5
4. Mostly agree	29.6	27.5	32.1	30.6	29.3	28.4	32.4	28.4	28.8	31.4	26.9	30.7	30.3	33.1	25.7	25.3
5. Agree	18.5	19.9	16.8	17.7	18.6	22.7	18.0	17.4	16.9	14.0	24.9	15.5	21.2	18.1	21.1	22.1
Item 10920 Subject I02,J N	2867	1380	1421	2268	347	539	835	982	511	1714	1054	1148	584	377	690	30
D10B: It does little good to clean up air and water pollution because this society will not last long enough for it to matter																
1. Disagree	41.3	41.3	41.5	42.5	33.2	43.6	40.0	39.4	44.9	44.6	35.9	43.1	42.6	38.0	41.0	19.4
2. Mostly disagree	27.7	26.7	28.7	28.9	25.2	26.0	27.8	28.4	28.0	30.8	23.6	27.6	28.0	27.9	27.0	26.2
3. Neither	17.8	18.8	16.9	18.0	17.5	13.8	18.9	18.9	17.8	15.5	21.5	15.1	17.6	23.0	19.5	19.1
4. Mostly agree	7.0	6.6	7.3	5.4	15.0	7.5	7.1	8.0	4.5	5.3	9.6	7.7	5.5	6.7	6.4	18.2
5. Agree	6.2	6.7	5.6	5.2	9.1	9.1	6.2	5.3	4.9	3.9	9.5	6.5	6.3	4.4	6.1	17.2
Item 10930 Subject F05,J N	2857	1378	1414	2260	345	535	834	979	509	1708	1051	1143	579	377	688	31
D10C: When things get tough enough, we'll put our minds to it and find a technological solution																
1. Disagree	5.8	5.7	5.8	5.4	6.7	8.0	6.1	5.3	4.2	4.7	7.8	6.0	5.9	5.5	5.8	2.3
2. Mostly disagree	10.7	9.9	11.4	11.1	8.6	12.8	11.8	9.8	8.5	11.4	9.9	10.3	9.7	11.0	12.3	12.2
3. Neither	22.7	22.5	23.0	23.4	20.2	22.7	22.8	23.3	21.1	22.2	23.3	18.5	27.9	24.4	23.2	32.2
4. Mostly agree	38.3	37.6	38.8	40.3	29.8	33.8	39.6	36.8	43.9	39.9	35.9	40.0	33.3	40.8	39.1	30.6
5. Agree	22.5	24.2	21.0	19.9	34.7	22.6	19.8	24.9	22.2	21.8	23.1	25.2	23.2	18.4	19.6	22.7
Item 10940 Subject I01,J N	2844	1372	1407	2254	339	530	833	975	506	1698	1047	1135	577	376	685	31

★=excludes respondents for whom question was inappropriate.

QUESTIONNAIRE FORM 4 1984	TOTAL	SEX		RACE		REGION				4YR COLLEGE PLANS		ILLICIT DRUG USE: LIFETIME				
		M	F	White	Black	NE	NC	S	W	Yes	No	None	Mari-juana Only	Few Pills	More Pills	Any Her-oin
N (Weighted No. of Cases):	3284	1588	1546	2489	414	679	909	1113	584	1830	1188	1253	675	426	806	39
% of Weighted Total:	100.0	48.4	47.1	75.8	12.6	20.7	27.7	33.9	17.8	55.7	36.2	38.1	20.6	13.0	24.5	1.2

D10D: When I think about all the terrible things that have been happening, it is hard for me to hold out much hope for the world

1. Disagree	18.1	18.6	17.7	18.1	19.4	17.6	18.2	18.9	16.9	19.8	15.8	21.1	17.7	15.1	15.6	12.4
2. Mostly disagree	28.4	30.3	26.7	30.2	21.0	28.5	26.0	27.4	34.5	31.6	24.1	28.8	28.9	26.5	28.9	24.1
3. Neither	25.7	27.4	23.7	26.7	21.3	23.2	29.0	24.7	25.0	23.9	27.9	22.3	27.8	31.9	26.1	30.2
4. Mostly agree	19.3	16.0	22.9	17.6	26.0	20.2	18.4	20.2	18.2	18.1	21.4	19.2	16.5	18.3	22.3	17.7
5. Agree	8.4	7.6	9.0	7.4	12.4	10.5	8.4	8.7	5.4	6.6	10.8	8.6	9.1	8.2	7.1	15.5
Item 10950 Subject J N	2839	1371	1402	2248	338	530	826	975	507	1699	1043	1135	579	372	685	30

D10E: I often wonder if there is any real purpose to my life in light of the world situation

1. Disagree	29.3	29.9	29.0	30.1	27.5	29.0	26.5	30.3	32.3	32.9	24.4	34.1	29.5	27.7	23.0	16.8
2. Mostly disagree	20.3	19.8	20.6	21.0	16.4	19.6	22.2	18.2	21.9	22.3	17.3	20.9	21.0	17.2	20.7	17.3
3. Neither	26.5	28.2	25.3	27.7	21.6	26.5	26.9	28.0	23.3	23.3	31.9	21.3	27.9	28.3	32.5	36.2
4. Mostly agree	15.7	13.8	17.2	14.6	21.3	15.9	17.2	13.9	16.3	14.0	18.1	15.7	13.6	17.2	16.3	18.1
5. Agree	8.2	8.3	7.9	6.5	13.3	9.0	7.2	9.6	6.2	7.5	8.3	8.0	8.0	9.5	7.5	11.7
Item 10960 Subject J N	2825	1369	1392	2239	337	526	823	971	505	1691	1036	1131	575	369	683	29

D10F: My guess is that this country will be caught up in a major world upheaval in the next 10 years

1. Disagree	13.9	16.6	11.3	13.8	15.0	17.2	13.2	12.8	13.8	14.9	12.2	14.4	16.0	10.9	13.2	4.7
2. Mostly disagree	14.5	15.2	14.1	14.3	14.9	15.3	13.6	14.6	15.0	15.4	13.6	14.6	13.8	14.2	15.4	9.0
3. Neither	35.0	33.6	35.8	35.5	32.5	31.4	39.5	33.8	33.6	34.1	36.6	35.0	32.9	38.9	35.0	32.2
4. Mostly agree	23.6	21.7	26.0	24.3	21.0	21.1	22.9	23.5	27.2	24.7	21.8	22.7	25.5	23.9	22.7	34.3
5. Agree	13.0	12.9	12.9	12.1	16.5	15.1	10.8	15.2	10.3	10.9	15.8	13.4	11.8	12.1	13.7	19.7
Item 10970 Subject J N	2820	1363	1394	2237	336	526	820	971	504	1690	1033	1130	573	371	679	29

D10G: Nuclear or biological annihilation will probably be the fate of all mankind, within my lifetime

1. Disagree	19.6	23.3	16.4	19.3	21.5	21.1	17.6	21.2	18.4	22.1	15.8	22.2	21.0	18.3	15.3	12.1
2. Mostly disagree	19.7	21.0	18.3	21.3	13.3	20.9	20.9	16.4	22.8	21.4	17.0	18.5	19.3	19.4	22.5	18.0
3. Neither	31.4	28.2	34.4	31.9	30.5	28.4	32.6	32.4	30.5	30.4	33.2	30.9	29.3	35.8	31.0	27.2
4. Mostly agree	16.3	14.5	17.9	15.8	17.6	14.6	16.3	16.9	16.8	15.5	17.8	15.7	17.7	16.1	16.3	27.7
5. Agree	13.0	13.0	13.0	11.6	17.1	15.0	12.7	13.1	11.5	10.6	16.2	12.7	12.7	10.4	14.8	14.9
Item 10980 Subject J N	2819	1365	1391	2237	336	525	823	968	502	1687	1035	1132	568	369	684	29

D10H: The human race has come through tough times before, and will do so again

1. Disagree	4.3	3.9	4.4	3.4	8.6	4.6	3.9	5.0	3.1	3.2	5.4	4.7	4.0	2.7	4.3	12.3
2. Mostly disagree	6.3	6.4	6.3	5.8	8.5	6.2	6.5	6.0	6.8	5.5	7.4	5.3	6.2	5.5	8.5	7.9
3. Neither	23.5	23.5	23.1	24.2	17.3	24.6	24.3	22.7	22.5	20.6	28.0	21.6	22.3	26.3	26.0	32.7
4. Mostly agree	34.4	32.9	36.1	35.2	31.4	32.0	34.3	33.9	38.2	36.2	31.1	34.5	32.3	36.6	35.4	22.4
5. Agree	31.5	33.3	30.0	31.4	34.1	32.5	31.0	32.4	29.4	34.4	28.0	33.8	35.2	28.9	25.8	24.6
Item 10990 Subject J N	2818	1363	1391	2236	335	524	820	972	503	1688	1032	1133	571	366	681	29

The next questions are about alcohol use–this time asking separately about beer, wine, and hard liquor.

D11: On how many occasions (if any) have you had a beer to drink . . .

D11A: . . . in your lifetime?

1. 0 occasions	11.6	8.6	14.3	9.6	23.5	7.2	9.6	14.1	14.4	12.5	9.9	25.1	3.3	4.0	1.3	13.9
2. 1-2	10.2	7.1	13.0	8.2	25.3	8.9	8.1	12.7	10.0	10.8	9.6	17.9	7.0	8.1	2.2	-
3. 3-5	7.5	6.4	8.5	6.9	11.1	7.0	8.5	7.7	6.3	7.6	7.7	9.9	8.6	7.7	2.8	10.0
4. 6-9	8.0	7.3	9.0	7.9	9.2	9.9	6.9	7.7	8.4	8.5	7.5	10.4	7.9	8.4	4.6	-
5. 10-19	10.6	9.4	11.9	10.6	10.5	8.8	11.4	11.6	9.3	12.0	8.5	11.5	13.3	10.2	7.8	7.2
6. 20-39	12.2	11.8	12.8	13.4	5.6	13.7	12.9	10.8	12.3	13.0	10.9	7.3	19.2	14.5	12.8	-
7. 40 or more	39.9	49.5	30.4	43.4	14.9	44.5	42.6	35.4	39.2	35.7	46.0	17.9	40.8	47.1	68.6	68.9
Item 11000 Subject A01a N	2724	1313	1345	2187	297	512	788	928	496	1646	984	1059	566	361	675	29

QUESTIONNAIRE FORM 4 1984	TOTAL	SEX M	SEX F	RACE White	RACE Black	REGION NE	REGION NC	REGION S	REGION W	4YR COLLEGE PLANS Yes	4YR COLLEGE PLANS No	None	Mari-juana Only	Few Pills	More Pills	Any Her-oin
N (Weighted No. of Cases):	3284	1588	1546	2489	414	679	909	1113	584	1830	1188	1253	675	426	806	39
% of Weighted Total:	100.0	48.4	47.1	75.8	12.6	20.7	27.7	33.9	17.8	55.7	36.2	38.1	20.6	13.0	24.5	1.2
D11B: . . . during the last 12 months?																
1. 0 occasions	23.3	17.2	29.2	19.6	47.8	17.4	18.1	28.4	28.1	24.1	21.7	42.6	13.5	16.6	5.7	20.6
2. 1-2	13.3	11.6	14.9	12.5	18.0	14.8	13.4	13.4	11.4	14.1	12.4	17.5	14.7	10.9	6.9	11.4
3. 3-5	8.9	7.7	10.1	9.1	8.8	8.3	9.2	8.8	9.2	8.9	9.0	9.9	8.9	10.6	6.1	1.7
4. 6-9	10.9	10.6	11.3	11.4	9.2	11.5	11.8	10.6	9.3	12.2	9.0	9.2	15.2	13.6	9.2	-
5. 10-19	13.6	14.4	12.9	14.9	6.9	14.5	12.8	13.8	13.4	13.4	13.9	8.5	17.7	14.8	17.4	8.0
6. 20-39	10.8	12.0	9.5	11.3	3.5	10.5	12.3	9.6	10.9	10.3	11.2	5.1	10.8	13.7	18.4	7.2
7. 40 or more	19.3	26.5	12.1	21.3	5.7	22.9	22.4	15.6	17.8	17.0	22.9	7.2	19.2	19.8	36.3	51.1
Item 11010 Subject A01b N	2693	1305	1324	2171	284	500	785	917	492	1631	974	1039	563	357	673	29
D11C: . . . during the last 30 days?																
1. 0 occasions	40.5	32.6	48.3	36.2	67.9	37.4	33.2	46.3	44.7	42.6	37.3	61.4	34.4	30.4	19.2	39.9
2. 1-2	17.9	17.2	19.0	19.2	13.4	17.4	18.9	17.0	18.3	18.7	16.4	17.5	18.8	24.9	14.8	-
3. 3-5	15.1	16.2	14.0	16.2	8.3	14.2	18.4	12.9	14.6	15.6	13.6	11.6	17.9	15.2	18.1	5.4
4. 6-9	12.0	14.7	9.4	13.3	4.3	11.5	13.7	11.1	11.6	10.8	14.4	5.0	15.8	14.7	18.3	7.6
5. 10-19	9.2	12.4	5.8	9.7	3.8	11.9	10.2	7.6	7.9	8.3	11.0	3.6	9.3	8.0	18.3	18.1
6. 20-39	3.1	3.6	2.4	3.2	0.8	3.9	3.2	3.3	1.5	2.2	4.0	0.4	1.7	3.8	7.3	18.0
7. 40 or more	2.3	3.3	1.1	2.1	1.4	3.7	2.5	1.8	1.3	1.7	3.3	0.5	2.0	3.0	4.1	11.0
Item 11020 Subject A01c N	2693	1308	1321	2168	286	502	783	918	490	1632	972	1038	565	357	672	30
D12: Think back over the LAST TWO WEEKS. How many times have you had five or more 12-ounce cans of beer (or the equivalent) in a row?																
1. None	63.8	52.3	75.0	61.0	82.2	60.2	56.4	68.5	70.6	66.4	58.8	82.6	59.9	58.4	41.3	38.3
2. Once	11.1	13.6	8.9	12.4	6.2	11.7	11.8	10.7	10.2	12.4	9.1	6.8	14.2	16.3	13.1	4.8
3. Twice	8.5	10.6	6.5	9.4	5.0	8.0	10.9	7.3	7.6	8.1	9.6	4.6	8.8	11.5	12.7	9.2
4. Three to five times	10.2	14.2	6.4	10.7	3.5	10.8	13.4	8.8	7.2	8.8	12.3	4.1	11.9	7.2	19.6	21.5
5. Six to nine times	3.5	4.6	2.4	3.6	0.9	6.1	3.8	2.7	1.9	2.4	5.6	1.0	2.1	3.2	8.6	7.8
6. Ten or more times	2.8	4.7	0.8	2.7	2.2	3.2	3.7	2.0	2.5	1.8	4.6	0.9	3.2	3.3	4.6	18.3
Item 11030 Subject A01d N	2685	1286	1337	2156	290	508	775	913	488	1627	962	1044	557	360	664	27
D13: On how many occasions (if any) have you had wine to drink . . .																
D13A: . . . in your lifetime?																
1. 0 occasions	14.6	16.1	13.1	12.6	28.2	8.9	12.6	18.2	17.0	13.6	15.9	25.8	9.2	8.7	4.8	12.0
2. 1-2	16.8	17.5	16.1	15.6	23.1	12.2	16.8	20.4	15.0	16.2	18.0	24.5	15.2	11.0	9.9	-
3. 3-5	16.3	16.2	16.2	16.0	15.1	13.2	17.4	17.2	16.0	17.7	14.8	16.7	20.1	18.4	11.8	6.4
4. 6-9	14.0	13.8	14.1	14.5	11.8	17.2	16.0	11.9	11.2	14.3	13.3	11.5	17.0	15.2	14.5	20.3
5. 10-19	15.7	15.3	16.1	17.0	8.7	18.0	16.2	13.4	16.6	15.9	15.6	11.5	17.0	19.9	19.0	17.3
6. 20-39	10.6	8.8	12.4	11.3	5.6	14.9	9.8	9.0	10.2	10.5	10.1	5.1	10.5	14.3	16.8	11.7
7. 40 or more	12.1	12.4	11.7	12.9	7.5	15.6	11.0	10.0	14.0	11.9	12.4	4.9	11.0	12.5	23.2	32.3
Item 11040 Subject A01a N	2719	1325	1332	2188	292	513	785	919	502	1648	976	1056	563	367	677	29
D13B: . . . during the last 12 months?																
1. 0 occasions	32.9	37.1	28.9	29.9	51.1	25.0	30.3	38.3	35.3	31.0	35.7	47.4	26.7	26.9	19.5	23.2
2. 1-2	25.1	25.0	25.1	25.4	22.7	23.3	28.3	25.2	21.3	25.6	25.2	27.3	27.8	24.0	20.6	8.3
3. 3-5	16.8	15.8	17.4	17.3	12.6	18.3	16.8	16.3	16.0	17.3	15.0	13.3	19.1	17.8	19.3	20.6
4. 6-9	11.3	10.0	12.7	12.1	6.6	15.1	10.9	9.7	10.8	12.0	10.3	6.5	13.6	14.8	14.9	10.9
5. 10-19	7.4	6.2	8.7	8.2	3.7	10.2	6.0	6.2	9.3	7.6	6.5	3.3	7.7	8.9	12.6	14.6
6. 20-39	3.4	2.4	4.3	3.8	1.5	4.2	3.6	2.6	3.6	3.2	3.6	1.1	2.6	5.9	6.1	1.9
7. 40 or more	3.2	3.6	2.8	3.3	1.8	3.9	4.2	1.8	3.6	3.2	3.6	1.2	2.5	1.8	7.0	20.5
Item 11050 Subject A01b N	2688	1309	1317	2167	286	503	780	905	500	1631	968	1036	557	367	672	29
D13C: . . . during the last 30 days?																
1. 0 occasions	65.9	69.7	61.9	64.2	78.6	58.5	65.7	70.5	65.3	66.0	66.3	80.9	63.9	55.8	51.1	45.1
2. 1-2	22.5	20.7	24.4	23.8	12.7	27.9	23.9	19.3	20.6	23.5	20.6	13.5	23.8	32.0	29.8	20.7
3. 3-5	7.2	5.7	9.0	7.7	5.0	7.9	5.9	6.8	9.2	6.8	7.5	3.7	7.7	8.6	11.2	14.7
4. 6-9	2.5	2.1	2.9	2.4	1.9	3.4	2.2	2.0	2.9	1.8	3.6	0.9	2.6	1.7	5.1	6.2
5. 10-19	1.2	0.9	1.5	1.2	1.5	1.0	1.4	0.8	1.9	1.3	0.9	0.6	1.1	1.8	2.1	-
6. 20-39	0.2	0.2	0.1	0.2	-	0.1	0.1	0.3	0.1	0.2	0.1	-	-	-	0.4	6.4
7. 40 or more	0.5	0.7	0.2	0.4	0.4	1.1	0.8	0.3	-	0.4	0.8	0.4	0.9	-	0.3	7.0
Item 11060 Subject A01c N	2680	1307	1311	2161	284	500	780	902	498	1628	966	1031	555	362	675	30

QUESTIONNAIRE FORM 4 1984	TOTAL	SEX		RACE		REGION				4YR COLLEGE PLANS		ILLICIT DRUG USE: LIFETIME				
		M	F	White	Black	NE	NC	S	W	Yes	No	None	Mari- juana Only	Few Pills	More Pills	Any Her- oin
N (Weighted No. of Cases):	3284	1588	1546	2489	414	679	909	1113	584	1830	1188	1253	675	426	806	39
% of Weighted Total:	100.0	48.4	47.1	75.8	12.6	20.7	27.7	33.9	17.8	55.7	36.2	38.1	20.6	13.0	24.5	1.2

D14: Think back over the LAST TWO WEEKS. How many times have you had five or more 4-ounce glasses of wine in a row (or the equivalent, which is about three-fourths of a bottle)?

	TOTAL	M	F	White	Black	NE	NC	S	W	Yes	No	None	Mari- juana Only	Few Pills	More Pills	Any Her- oin
1. None	87.0	87.4	86.9	86.6	91.8	83.1	85.9	89.0	89.2	88.1	85.6	94.1	86.5	83.8	79.5	63.2
2. Once	6.4	6.4	6.7	6.8	3.6	6.9	7.0	6.3	5.4	6.7	6.1	2.9	7.9	11.1	8.0	5.9
3. Twice	3.8	3.3	4.1	3.8	3.4	4.9	4.7	2.8	3.1	3.1	4.9	1.9	3.3	3.5	7.3	11.2
4. Three to five times	1.7	1.9	1.4	1.7	0.9	2.9	1.3	1.1	1.9	1.3	2.0	0.8	1.0	1.5	3.6	5.8
5. Six to nine times	0.6	0.4	0.5	0.5	-	0.9	0.7	0.4	0.2	0.4	0.8	0.2	0.5	0.2	1.2	-
6. Ten or more times	0.5	0.7	0.3	0.5	0.4	1.2	0.5	0.4	0.1	0.5	0.6	0.1	0.9	-	0.4	13.8
Item 11070 Subject A01d　　N	2645	1265	1319	2128	284	501	752	900	491	1619	930	1038	543	356	655	25

These next questions are about hard liquor. (Hard liquor includes whiskey, Scotch, bourbon, gin, vodka, rum, etc., or mixed drinks made with liquor.)

D15: On how many occasions (if any) have you had liquor to drink . . .

D15A: . . . in your lifetime?

	TOTAL	M	F	White	Black	NE	NC	S	W	Yes	No	None	Mari- juana Only	Few Pills	More Pills	Any Her- oin
1. 0 occasions	17.9	16.6	19.0	13.7	45.6	14.2	14.9	22.2	18.3	18.3	16.7	34.6	10.3	8.7	2.8	6.5
2. 1-2	12.9	12.3	13.7	12.6	16.6	12.4	12.0	13.8	12.9	14.0	11.6	21.8	12.6	7.8	2.9	-
3. 3-5	13.1	12.3	13.7	13.3	11.9	12.2	13.0	13.0	14.6	14.3	11.2	14.4	15.0	18.3	7.5	3.4
4. 6-9	11.0	9.9	11.8	11.2	7.8	9.3	14.3	9.5	10.1	10.3	11.8	8.2	15.2	13.5	10.4	3.9
5. 10-19	15.2	16.3	14.3	16.4	6.2	14.4	17.3	13.5	16.1	15.7	14.9	11.6	14.6	19.2	19.4	14.7
6. 20-39	13.1	11.8	14.5	14.3	5.6	16.0	13.1	11.3	13.5	12.7	13.5	5.0	15.5	17.0	21.5	21.8
7. 40 or more	16.8	20.8	12.9	18.4	6.3	21.4	15.4	16.7	14.5	14.6	20.2	4.5	16.8	15.5	35.5	49.7
Item 11080 Subject A01a　　N	2728	1323	1343	2191	299	512	786	928	503	1645	987	1057	567	366	677	28

D15B: . . . during the last 12 months?

	TOTAL	M	F	White	Black	NE	NC	S	W	Yes	No	None	Mari- juana Only	Few Pills	More Pills	Any Her- oin
1. 0 occasions	32.4	31.1	34.0	27.7	65.4	28.9	27.8	37.2	34.6	32.2	32.5	52.2	28.1	23.5	10.6	12.1
2. 1-2	18.5	16.4	20.0	19.0	14.3	18.0	19.9	18.3	17.1	20.3	15.7	22.0	17.8	21.0	13.0	8.2
3. 3-5	15.0	16.0	14.5	16.3	7.4	12.9	17.6	13.4	16.2	14.6	15.9	12.2	16.2	18.7	16.6	7.6
4. 6-9	11.3	11.7	10.8	11.9	6.5	12.5	12.4	9.9	11.0	11.6	11.4	5.6	16.3	14.0	14.9	6.4
5. 10-19	9.9	9.9	10.1	10.9	2.5	12.7	9.1	8.7	10.6	9.8	10.1	4.2	9.6	11.3	18.2	15.6
6. 20-39	6.8	7.2	6.5	7.7	1.0	7.6	7.2	6.3	6.0	5.9	7.7	1.4	6.1	8.1	14.5	20.8
7. 40 or more	6.0	7.7	4.1	6.5	2.9	7.3	6.0	6.2	4.4	5.5	6.7	2.3	5.9	3.4	12.1	29.2
Item 11090 Subject A01b　　N	2701	1313	1325	2172	293	509	782	915	496	1631	977	1043	564	362	670	28

D15C: . . . during the last 30 days?

	TOTAL	M	F	White	Black	NE	NC	S	W	Yes	No	None	Mari- juana Only	Few Pills	More Pills	Any Her- oin
1. 0 occasions	57.8	56.7	59.2	54.7	81.8	53.6	54.4	61.5	60.4	59.4	55.4	76.6	53.2	53.6	35.9	40.6
2. 1-2	21.5	20.8	22.3	22.8	12.0	23.6	24.5	17.0	23.1	21.6	21.5	16.2	24.0	23.5	26.7	16.5
3. 3-5	9.7	9.7	9.4	10.4	4.2	9.7	7.8	11.5	9.3	8.9	10.4	3.3	12.4	13.0	15.5	4.3
4. 6-9	6.1	7.2	5.2	6.9	0.9	6.7	8.0	5.1	4.6	6.0	6.6	2.4	5.7	6.8	11.5	15.1
5. 10-19	3.2	3.5	2.7	3.5	-	3.4	3.6	3.4	2.0	3.0	3.7	1.2	2.9	2.7	6.6	10.0
6. 20-39	0.9	1.0	0.7	0.9	-	1.1	0.8	1.0	0.6	0.6	1.3	0.1	0.3	0.4	2.4	9.7
7. 40 or more	0.9	1.0	0.5	0.7	1.1	2.0	1.0	0.6	-	0.6	1.3	0.3	1.5	-	1.5	3.8
Item 11100 Subject A01c　　N	2705	1313	1328	2176	293	512	783	914	496	1631	980	1041	563	364	674	29

D16: Think back over the LAST TWO WEEKS. How many times have you had five or more mixed drinks or shot-glasses of hard liquor in a row?

	TOTAL	M	F	White	Black	NE	NC	S	W	Yes	No	None	Mari- juana Only	Few Pills	More Pills	Any Her- oin
1. None	78.7	75.4	81.8	77.1	91.5	75.1	75.9	79.8	84.7	80.8	75.3	91.9	78.4	78.2	59.1	45.3
2. Once	8.6	8.9	8.2	9.5	3.0	8.1	9.1	8.4	8.3	8.4	8.6	4.0	10.2	9.4	14.1	6.2
3. Twice	5.8	7.2	4.5	6.4	2.5	8.4	6.7	4.9	3.1	4.9	6.8	2.0	6.4	6.7	10.9	9.0
4. Three to five times	4.6	5.4	3.8	4.6	2.6	4.8	4.9	5.3	2.7	4.1	5.6	1.2	2.7	4.5	11.3	15.0
5. Six to nine times	1.4	1.6	1.3	1.6	-	2.9	1.4	0.9	1.2	0.9	2.3	0.4	1.5	0.4	3.5	7.6
6. Ten or more times	0.9	1.5	0.4	0.9	0.3	0.7	2.0	0.7	-	0.8	1.2	0.5	0.8	0.9	1.1	16.9
Item 11110 Subject A01d　　N	2645	1275	1308	2124	287	503	756	897	489	1612	938	1036	550	356	646	23

These next questions ask for your opinions about the military services in the United States.

E01: To what extent do you think the following opportunities are available to people who work in the military services?

QUESTIONNAIRE FORM 4 1984	TOTAL	SEX		RACE		REGION				4YR COLLEGE PLANS		ILLICIT DRUG USE: LIFETIME				
		M	F	White	Black	NE	NC	S	W	Yes	No	None	Mari- juana Only	Few Pills	More Pills	Any Her- oin
N (Weighted No. of Cases):	3284	1588	1546	2489	414	679	909	1113	584	1830	1188	1253	675	426	806	39
% of Weighted Total:	100.0	48.4	47.1	75.8	12.6	20.7	27.7	33.9	17.8	55.7	36.2	38.1	20.6	13.0	24.5	1.2
E01A: A chance to get ahead																
1. To a very little extent	7.1	9.7	4.4	6.8	6.2	6.4	7.1	6.7	8.6	7.3	6.4	6.3	7.7	9.1	6.0	18.9
2. To a little extent	13.3	16.4	10.4	13.7	8.6	12.2	14.2	12.9	14.1	13.9	12.2	12.4	13.8	13.1	15.2	9.1
3. To some extent	42.1	39.4	44.9	43.4	34.8	42.2	42.4	39.6	46.5	43.4	40.6	43.2	40.1	41.9	42.4	22.7
4. To a great extent	23.3	20.8	26.1	23.5	26.0	24.4	24.7	23.6	19.6	22.4	24.8	24.5	24.1	24.3	19.7	33.0
5. To a very great extent	14.1	13.8	14.3	12.5	24.4	14.8	11.7	17.3	11.3	12.9	16.0	13.6	14.3	11.6	16.8	16.3
Item 11120 Subject L04 N	2757	1339	1354	2183	329	507	809	949	492	1660	1003	1113	554	369	657	27
E01B: A chance to get more education																
1. To a very little extent	5.0	7.4	2.8	4.9	5.0	5.4	4.4	5.1	5.3	4.7	5.0	4.2	6.0	7.0	4.1	3.6
2. To a little extent	8.0	9.0	6.9	8.1	6.2	7.6	7.8	7.5	8.3	7.9	8.3	7.3	7.2	7.5	10.2	3.3
3. To some extent	31.0	32.6	29.0	31.5	24.8	29.9	32.7	28.5	33.9	33.4	27.6	31.3	31.9	26.3	31.8	35.8
4. To a great extent	35.6	32.1	39.6	36.7	33.3	35.3	34.9	35.8	36.8	35.3	36.5	37.0	33.6	37.5	34.3	33.4
5. To a very great extent	20.4	18.9	21.7	18.8	30.6	21.7	19.3	23.1	15.7	18.8	22.6	20.2	21.3	21.7	19.6	23.9
Item 11130 Subject B10,L04 N	2753	1337	1352	2179	327	505	806	949	493	1660	997	1112	551	369	655	28
E01C: A chance to advance to a more respon- sible position																
1. To a very little extent	5.3	7.5	3.1	5.1	4.9	5.6	4.9	4.9	6.4	4.9	5.2	3.4	6.5	6.9	5.9	12.9
2. To a little extent	7.6	8.9	6.2	7.6	3.5	6.5	6.4	7.4	11.0	7.6	7.4	7.2	7.6	8.5	8.0	8.9
3. To some extent	32.0	33.8	30.6	33.0	27.4	31.6	35.7	29.8	30.2	32.9	30.9	32.6	30.2	29.7	33.7	27.1
4. To a great extent	34.8	30.2	39.1	35.6	33.3	34.2	32.8	35.4	37.7	35.8	33.8	35.7	36.5	35.3	31.5	25.2
5. To a very great extent	20.4	19.7	21.1	18.7	30.9	22.2	20.2	22.5	14.6	18.7	22.7	21.2	19.1	19.6	20.9	25.9
Item 11140 Subject L04 N	2752	1337	1352	2178	328	506	807	948	491	1659	999	1111	552	369	655	27
E01D: A chance to have a personally more ful- filling job																
1. To a very little extent	7.7	10.3	5.0	8.0	6.2	7.4	9.2	6.1	8.7	8.3	6.0	6.2	7.8	9.9	8.6	9.2
2. To a little extent	12.3	13.4	11.3	13.2	5.5	10.7	11.9	11.0	17.3	13.9	10.2	13.4	11.6	11.2	12.1	10.2
3. To some extent	35.7	35.3	36.2	36.8	27.9	37.1	36.6	34.5	35.4	37.7	33.1	36.0	36.1	33.2	36.4	39.1
4. To a great extent	28.2	25.3	31.0	28.1	30.8	25.9	29.1	29.3	26.8	26.1	31.9	27.9	30.6	30.5	25.2	19.2
5. To a very great extent	16.1	15.7	16.6	14.0	29.7	19.0	13.2	19.2	11.9	14.0	18.8	16.5	13.9	15.2	17.7	22.3
Item 11150 Subject C05,L04 N	2753	1340	1349	2177	329	505	807	949	492	1659	999	1112	555	369	653	27
E01E: A chance to get their ideas heard																
1. To a very little extent	17.1	21.9	12.6	18.3	9.7	15.8	18.1	14.1	22.6	20.0	12.5	16.3	19.2	16.7	17.0	18.5
2. To a little extent	23.8	24.8	23.0	25.4	16.4	24.3	23.2	22.4	26.8	26.1	20.4	24.0	23.6	24.8	23.6	21.3
3. To some extent	35.5	33.1	37.7	35.8	32.9	38.9	36.9	34.6	31.6	34.6	37.4	35.2	35.6	33.9	36.8	32.3
4. To a great extent	14.3	12.3	16.4	13.2	20.8	11.2	14.9	16.7	12.0	12.2	17.5	15.2	13.2	13.3	13.7	19.1
5. To a very great extent	9.3	7.8	10.4	7.3	20.3	9.8	6.8	12.2	7.0	7.1	12.2	9.2	8.4	11.2	8.8	8.8
Item 11160 Subject L04 N	2748	1333	1351	2175	328	505	804	947	491	1659	994	1112	552	369	653	25
E02: To what extent is it likely that a person in the military can get things changed and set right if he is being treated unjustly by a supe- rior?																
1. To a very little extent	22.6	26.4	18.7	23.6	13.0	24.4	22.5	21.1	23.6	24.8	19.6	22.6	24.9	21.2	21.3	18.7
2. To a little extent	27.8	27.8	28.2	28.2	24.1	29.8	27.9	25.6	30.1	29.6	24.6	27.7	25.7	25.2	31.5	28.6
3. To some extent	35.8	32.8	38.6	36.3	37.4	34.6	36.3	36.1	35.7	33.9	38.8	35.0	35.5	39.4	35.0	35.0
4. To a great extent	9.6	8.6	10.5	8.8	14.6	7.4	10.4	11.0	7.8	8.6	10.9	10.1	9.9	9.7	8.7	6.3
5. To a very great extent	4.2	4.4	4.0	3.1	10.9	3.9	2.8	6.3	2.9	3.0	6.1	4.5	4.0	4.5	3.6	11.4
Item 11170 Subject L04 N	2706	1318	1325	2149	319	493	802	932	479	1630	986	1101	532	362	646	29
E03: To what extent do you think there is any discrimination against women who are in the armed services?																
1. To a very little extent	15.8	17.8	13.8	15.1	20.5	16.8	16.4	15.4	14.8	15.4	16.1	15.6	17.1	18.3	13.9	13.2
2. To a little extent	26.0	26.9	25.4	27.1	20.6	23.0	25.8	26.9	27.7	26.7	25.2	25.7	25.5	24.8	27.8	15.6
3. To some extent	39.7	39.1	40.0	40.8	34.8	39.7	40.2	40.9	36.4	38.7	41.6	39.9	40.3	39.7	38.9	39.4
4. To a great extent	12.7	11.9	13.6	11.8	15.2	14.0	12.7	11.6	13.5	13.9	10.7	12.8	11.9	12.8	13.0	17.7
5. To a very great extent	5.7	4.3	7.2	5.3	9.0	6.5	4.9	5.2	7.5	5.3	6.4	6.0	5.1	4.3	6.4	14.1
Item 11180 Subject D06,L04 N	2709	1314	1332	2151	320	490	802	936	481	1628	988	1102	537	361	646	29

QUESTIONNAIRE FORM 4 1984	TOTAL	SEX		RACE		REGION				4YR COLLEGE PLANS		ILLICIT DRUG USE: LIFETIME				
		M	F	White	Black	NE	NC	S	W	Yes	No	None	Mari- juana Only	Few Pills	More Pills	Any Her- oin
N (Weighted No. of Cases):	3284	1588	1546	2489	414	679	909	1113	584	1830	1188	1253	675	426	806	39
% of Weighted Total:	100.0	48.4	47.1	75.8	12.6	20.7	27.7	33.9	17.8	55.7	36.2	38.1	20.6	13.0	24.5	1.2

E04: To what extent do you think there is any discrimination against black people who are in the armed services?

	TOTAL	M	F	White	Black	NE	NC	S	W	Yes	No	None	Mari-juana Only	Few Pills	More Pills	Any Heroin
1. To a very little extent	33.4	39.9	27.1	34.1	30.5	30.7	31.1	35.6	35.7	33.6	32.7	31.8	37.0	36.6	31.5	31.3
2. To a little extent	26.7	24.9	28.8	28.3	20.1	26.0	30.1	24.4	26.2	26.7	26.2	27.0	23.6	27.1	29.0	29.0
3. To some extent	30.1	26.8	32.9	29.4	32.1	33.0	29.6	29.0	30.3	30.1	30.8	31.0	29.9	29.2	28.6	28.3
4. To a great extent	5.9	5.1	6.8	5.4	7.8	7.1	6.1	5.8	4.8	6.6	5.1	5.6	6.3	4.6	6.9	6.4
5. To a very great extent	3.8	3.3	4.4	2.8	9.5	3.3	3.1	5.1	3.1	3.0	5.2	4.6	3.2	2.6	4.0	5.0
Item 11190 Subject L04,N02 N	2686	1303	1320	2138	311	481	799	928	477	1617	979	1094	532	361	637	28

E05: Do you personally feel that you would receive more just and fair treatment as a civilian or as a member of the military service?

	TOTAL	M	F	White	Black	NE	NC	S	W	Yes	No	None	Mari-juana Only	Few Pills	More Pills	Any Heroin
1. Much more fair in the military service	6.4	8.3	4.4	5.5	10.3	5.1	5.8	8.0	5.4	4.8	8.6	5.7	8.3	6.2	6.1	7.2
2. More fair in the military service	11.4	10.6	11.9	11.2	13.9	14.4	11.2	11.8	8.0	10.5	12.1	11.5	10.1	12.8	11.2	30.4
3. About the same	45.8	44.2	47.5	46.5	47.8	45.8	46.0	46.2	44.4	44.9	46.9	46.5	47.1	47.2	43.0	34.4
4. More fair as a civilian	13.8	13.9	13.5	14.5	8.5	13.4	14.8	12.5	14.8	14.9	12.6	14.6	12.5	13.0	14.4	2.7
5. Much more fair as a civilian	10.3	13.8	7.0	11.0	5.0	8.1	12.0	7.5	15.3	12.6	7.0	9.9	9.8	8.6	12.4	14.9
6. Question not appropriate for me	12.3	9.1	15.7	11.3	14.5	13.3	10.1	13.9	12.1	12.2	12.8	11.9	12.2	12.2	12.9	10.4
Item 11200 Subject L04 N	2694	1307	1325	2141	316	486	797	929	483	1628	977	1093	536	360	642	29

E06: If YOU felt that it was necessary for the U.S. to fight in some future war, how likely is it that you would volunteer for military service in that war?

	TOTAL	M	F	White	Black	NE	NC	S	W	Yes	No	None	Mari-juana Only	Few Pills	More Pills	Any Heroin
1. I'm sure that I would volunteer	14.9	23.8	6.3	15.5	10.7	13.6	13.5	17.7	13.3	12.6	17.9	13.2	17.6	11.6	17.1	23.8
2. I would very likely volunteer	7.3	10.4	4.0	7.5	4.7	6.0	5.3	9.7	7.3	6.8	7.9	6.5	6.2	10.1	7.4	15.0
3. I would probably volunteer	17.2	21.1	13.4	18.1	13.2	17.2	18.2	16.4	17.1	17.5	16.5	18.1	18.3	16.5	15.8	7.4
4. I would probably NOT volunteer	17.5	13.7	21.4	18.2	14.8	15.5	19.4	15.8	19.6	19.1	15.7	18.2	17.4	18.0	16.5	15.1
5. I would very likely NOT volunteer	6.6	4.9	8.4	6.9	5.4	7.2	7.1	5.7	7.0	7.0	5.6	6.7	6.3	6.4	6.9	5.1
6. I would definitely NOT volunteer	14.6	10.0	19.5	12.6	26.6	15.0	15.1	15.3	12.3	15.5	13.7	15.2	13.2	17.8	13.0	7.2
7. In my opinion, there is no such thing as a "necessary" war	21.8	16.0	27.0	21.1	24.5	25.5	21.4	19.4	23.5	21.5	22.7	22.1	21.0	19.7	23.2	26.3
Item 11220 Subject L03 N	2705	1307	1335	2151	318	491	799	928	486	1638	973	1092	541	366	641	29

E07: How closely do your ideas agree with your PARENTS' ideas about . . .

Our ideas are . . .

E07A: What you should do with your life.

	TOTAL	M	F	White	Black	NE	NC	S	W	Yes	No	None	Mari-juana Only	Few Pills	More Pills	Any Heroin
1. Very similar	29.9	28.2	31.5	29.4	30.5	31.1	30.0	30.0	28.4	34.4	21.8	33.6	31.0	26.4	25.6	19.8
2. Mostly similar	44.3	43.7	45.3	47.3	33.5	41.8	46.7	42.8	46.1	48.2	39.4	43.0	44.8	47.7	44.3	48.3
3. Mostly different	11.3	11.7	10.8	10.3	15.4	13.3	9.6	11.0	12.4	8.5	15.8	10.6	10.1	11.7	12.9	10.0
4. Very different	7.2	7.0	7.5	6.2	11.2	7.1	6.3	8.2	7.0	3.5	12.7	5.8	6.2	8.1	9.3	12.4
8. Don't know	7.3	9.3	4.9	6.9	9.4	6.7	7.4	8.1	6.0	5.4	10.4	7.0	7.9	6.0	7.9	9.5
Item 11230 Subject M03 N	2746	1324	1358	2180	325	504	807	942	494	1657	992	1102	553	367	660	29

E07B: What you do in your leisure time

	TOTAL	M	F	White	Black	NE	NC	S	W	Yes	No	None	Mari-juana Only	Few Pills	More Pills	Any Heroin
1. Very similar	10.2	8.1	11.7	9.6	14.3	11.6	7.5	11.3	11.0	10.6	8.9	11.6	10.6	12.0	6.8	2.1
2. Mostly similar	34.0	33.1	34.6	36.5	21.4	35.8	38.5	31.1	30.4	37.7	29.0	39.2	31.4	32.7	29.1	30.5
3. Mostly different	26.2	25.9	26.9	26.8	25.5	20.5	26.5	27.2	29.7	26.6	24.8	24.5	28.2	28.8	26.5	24.8
4. Very different	22.9	23.4	22.6	21.2	28.7	24.9	20.8	23.7	22.6	19.3	28.8	16.1	24.5	21.6	32.1	37.6
8. Don't know	6.7	9.4	4.3	5.9	10.2	7.1	6.7	6.8	6.3	5.7	8.5	8.6	5.4	5.0	5.5	4.9
Item 11240 Subject C08,M03 N	2735	1319	1354	2170	326	503	800	941	491	1654	984	1099	548	367	656	29

E07C: How you dress–what clothes you wear

	TOTAL	M	F	White	Black	NE	NC	S	W	Yes	No	None	Mari-juana Only	Few Pills	More Pills	Any Heroin
1. Very similar	25.2	21.0	29.4	24.5	29.9	25.9	23.0	26.7	25.3	26.6	23.6	27.2	25.1	26.5	21.8	13.7
2. Mostly similar	43.4	42.3	44.4	46.6	27.6	39.4	48.3	42.0	42.4	45.9	39.2	43.2	46.2	39.2	44.3	34.9
3. Mostly different	14.8	18.0	11.6	14.8	14.0	16.5	14.2	14.0	15.7	14.2	16.0	14.1	14.3	16.4	14.7	34.8
4. Very different	11.8	11.8	11.9	10.0	20.3	12.8	10.2	12.2	12.5	9.4	15.3	10.7	9.8	12.9	14.4	14.9
8. Don't know	4.8	6.8	2.6	4.1	8.1	5.4	4.4	5.1	4.1	3.9	5.8	4.9	4.6	5.1	4.8	1.7
Item 11250 Subject M03 N	2732	1316	1353	2169	324	502	800	937	492	1652	985	1097	548	366	658	29

QUESTIONNAIRE FORM 4 1984	TOTAL	SEX		RACE		REGION				4YR COLLEGE PLANS		ILLICIT DRUG USE: LIFETIME				
		M	F	White	Black	NE	NC	S	W	Yes	No	None	Marijuana Only	Few Pills	More Pills	Any Heroin
N (Weighted No. of Cases):	3284	1588	1546	2489	414	679	909	1113	584	1830	1188	1253	675	426	806	39
% of Weighted Total:	100.0	48.4	47.1	75.8	12.6	20.7	27.7	33.9	17.8	55.7	36.2	38.1	20.6	13.0	24.5	1.2
E07D: How you spend your money																
1. Very similar	13.9	11.9	15.5	12.7	20.8	10.5	12.2	16.5	15.2	14.8	12.2	16.8	15.1	12.6	8.8	14.3
2. Mostly similar	32.8	29.3	36.6	35.4	22.9	33.0	37.2	29.4	32.0	36.0	28.4	36.2	30.7	33.7	28.4	25.0
3. Mostly different	24.6	25.8	23.2	25.2	20.6	25.8	23.5	24.5	25.4	25.1	24.1	22.7	25.3	26.3	26.9	23.9
4. Very different	24.1	26.8	21.9	22.8	28.1	25.1	22.9	24.4	24.5	20.1	30.4	18.5	25.8	23.6	32.2	28.2
8. Don't know	4.6	6.2	2.8	3.9	7.6	5.6	4.3	5.2	2.8	4.0	5.0	5.9	3.1	3.7	3.8	8.6
Item 11260 Subject M03 N	2736	1320	1352	2172	325	502	800	942	492	1654	987	1101	548	364	659	29
E07E: What things are O.K. to do when you are on a date																
1. Very similar	16.9	14.3	19.5	16.8	17.1	10.9	16.8	18.8	19.5	17.6	15.4	21.5	14.7	15.0	13.0	3.2
2. Mostly similar	30.5	28.4	32.2	31.9	24.9	28.7	34.7	28.3	29.5	32.5	27.4	32.3	29.7	29.3	29.2	30.5
3. Mostly different	18.1	17.6	18.9	18.8	16.2	18.5	19.1	17.0	18.2	18.6	17.5	16.5	19.6	20.4	18.3	23.0
4. Very different	19.4	20.1	18.5	19.0	19.6	22.9	16.2	20.5	18.7	16.3	24.7	13.5	20.2	21.2	27.0	22.2
8. Don't know	15.2	19.6	10.9	13.4	22.3	19.0	13.3	15.3	14.2	15.0	14.9	16.3	15.8	14.1	12.6	21.2
Item 11270 Subject M03 N	2736	1318	1354	2172	326	503	801	939	492	1653	986	1101	548	364	659	29
E07F: Whether it is O.K. to drink																
1. Very similar	26.2	26.3	25.9	24.5	38.9	19.4	23.5	29.5	31.4	27.4	24.3	38.6	19.3	20.6	15.6	5.0
2. Mostly similar	31.9	28.9	34.8	33.8	22.1	35.6	33.9	28.6	31.4	34.0	29.2	30.6	31.0	34.8	33.1	22.9
3. Mostly different	17.6	18.4	17.0	19.4	8.8	19.7	18.5	16.8	15.6	17.6	17.8	11.3	24.3	18.5	22.8	19.3
4. Very different	18.7	19.6	18.0	18.5	16.6	20.0	19.5	18.7	16.3	16.9	21.6	13.8	18.7	19.9	25.1	43.1
8. Don't know	5.5	6.8	4.3	3.9	13.6	5.3	4.7	6.4	5.2	4.1	7.2	5.7	6.7	6.2	3.4	9.8
Item 11280 Subject M03 N	2775	1342	1369	2203	325	507	819	949	500	1674	1002	1115	555	371	667	29
E07G: Whether it is O.K. to use marijuana																
1. Very similar	50.2	45.9	54.6	51.7	48.7	40.0	53.2	55.1	46.1	55.0	43.3	75.0	41.1	44.8	21.2	3.1
2. Mostly similar	13.9	12.8	14.6	14.1	9.6	17.8	12.2	12.4	15.3	15.5	11.0	10.1	16.4	15.4	17.0	18.6
3. Mostly different	7.9	9.2	6.6	8.3	5.3	8.8	7.1	6.7	10.3	7.6	8.1	2.0	9.0	10.5	15.0	16.7
4. Very different	20.8	22.4	19.2	20.1	21.9	25.4	20.1	18.1	22.6	16.7	27.9	6.9	23.5	21.0	40.8	50.3
8. Don't know	7.3	9.7	5.1	5.9	14.4	7.9	7.4	7.7	5.7	5.2	9.7	6.0	10.0	8.3	6.0	11.2
Item 11290 Subject M03 N	2765	1337	1366	2197	323	504	817	948	498	1667	999	1111	551	371	664	30
E07H: Whether it is O.K. to use other drugs																
1. Very similar	58.6	54.5	62.8	60.0	57.1	52.5	59.4	63.1	54.8	64.9	49.4	78.3	59.3	59.1	27.0	6.8
2. Mostly similar	12.1	10.2	13.7	12.7	9.3	12.3	11.9	11.2	13.8	12.6	11.0	8.5	13.9	13.2	15.9	9.2
3. Mostly different	4.5	6.0	3.1	4.9	2.7	4.2	4.4	4.0	6.1	3.9	5.4	2.1	2.2	3.8	11.1	6.4
4. Very different	17.5	20.0	15.1	16.3	18.5	23.3	17.1	14.6	17.8	13.1	24.9	5.8	14.8	13.7	39.5	69.8
8. Don't know	7.3	9.3	5.2	6.1	12.3	7.8	7.1	7.0	7.6	5.4	9.4	5.4	9.8	10.2	6.5	7.7
Item 11300 Subject M03 N	2748	1325	1359	2185	321	499	808	943	498	1661	991	1101	550	370	659	30
E07I: What values are important in life																
1. Very similar	37.9	34.7	40.7	37.0	45.6	36.8	35.0	40.9	37.9	40.8	33.0	44.3	39.9	31.0	30.1	12.8
2. Mostly similar	38.9	39.4	38.7	41.2	28.3	39.7	42.6	36.1	37.2	40.2	37.8	37.5	36.7	42.4	41.7	42.1
3. Mostly different	11.7	12.2	11.3	11.9	10.7	11.7	11.6	11.7	12.1	10.0	14.5	8.9	11.6	13.8	15.3	14.5
4. Very different	6.0	6.8	5.5	5.3	5.9	7.0	5.0	5.3	8.3	4.6	8.4	4.0	6.5	7.1	7.6	19.3
8. Don't know	5.4	6.9	3.9	4.6	9.5	4.8	5.7	6.0	4.5	4.4	6.3	5.3	5.4	5.8	5.3	11.3
Item 11310 Subject M03 N	2743	1322	1357	2182	317	502	810	935	496	1659	986	1099	552	368	659	29
E07J: The value of education																
1. Very similar	56.8	53.2	60.8	55.9	66.7	56.1	54.5	59.9	55.2	65.9	41.7	61.7	57.4	54.5	51.1	27.0
2. Mostly similar	29.5	29.3	29.3	31.4	18.2	30.0	32.0	26.0	31.4	26.7	34.9	28.3	28.9	31.7	30.5	31.5
3. Mostly different	6.9	8.8	5.0	7.3	4.5	6.2	6.8	6.5	8.6	3.5	12.8	4.6	8.1	7.7	9.3	13.7
4. Very different	4.4	5.1	3.7	3.4	6.7	5.3	4.4	4.6	3.2	2.5	7.4	3.4	3.8	3.8	5.9	16.6
8. Don't know	2.4	3.5	1.2	2.0	3.9	2.4	2.2	3.0	1.5	1.4	3.3	2.0	1.9	2.3	3.3	11.4
Item 11320 Subject B09,M03 N	2749	1330	1355	2187	318	502	813	940	494	1662	989	1102	550	369	662	28

QUESTIONNAIRE FORM 4 1984	TOTAL	SEX		RACE		REGION				4YR COLLEGE PLANS		ILLICIT DRUG USE: LIFETIME				
		M	F	White	Black	NE	NC	S	W	Yes	No	None	Mari- juana Only	Few Pills	More Pills	Any Her- oin
N (Weighted No. of Cases):	3284	1588	1546	2489	414	679	909	1113	584	1830	1188	1253	675	426	806	39
% of Weighted Total:	100.0	48.4	47.1	75.8	12.6	20.7	27.7	33.9	17.8	55.7	36.2	38.1	20.6	13.0	24.5	1.2
E07K: What are appropriate roles for women																
1. Very similar	31.5	23.1	39.6	31.3	34.9	32.3	27.8	34.5	31.3	35.2	25.8	34.1	33.2	30.1	28.7	6.7
2. Mostly similar	36.6	37.8	35.5	38.6	28.6	36.8	38.2	34.5	37.9	37.4	36.3	37.1	37.8	35.5	36.4	32.1
3. Mostly different	10.9	11.7	10.4	10.8	10.8	8.8	11.8	11.3	10.9	10.3	12.2	10.6	8.8	11.4	11.9	19.0
4. Very different	6.5	7.1	5.7	5.8	6.4	6.2	6.9	6.0	7.3	4.1	10.0	4.1	5.0	8.7	9.3	20.7
8. Don't know	14.4	20.3	8.7	13.5	19.3	16.0	15.3	13.7	12.6	12.9	15.7	14.2	15.2	14.3	13.8	21.5
Item 11330 Subject D05,M03 N	2743	1323	1356	2177	321	505	805	939	494	1664	983	1102	549	366	661	28
E07L: Conservation and pollution issues																
1. Very similar	24.2	24.1	23.8	23.7	26.6	25.9	23.0	24.3	24.1	25.8	21.6	28.9	24.3	19.0	19.4	20.3
2. Mostly similar	29.7	32.6	27.3	31.9	18.1	27.8	29.1	28.2	35.8	31.9	26.5	29.1	29.0	31.0	30.4	35.2
3. Mostly different	6.5	7.3	5.7	6.2	8.8	5.5	6.9	7.7	4.4	5.9	7.5	6.6	6.4	5.1	6.9	12.8
4. Very different	4.5	5.7	3.2	3.4	6.8	4.9	4.8	4.3	3.9	3.2	6.4	3.7	4.3	6.3	4.7	9.0
8. Don't know	35.1	30.3	40.0	34.8	39.6	35.9	36.1	35.5	31.8	33.2	38.0	31.7	36.0	38.7	38.6	22.7
Item 11340 Subject F04,M03 N	2741	1325	1352	2178	317	506	805	934	496	1659	984	1100	548	367	659	29
E07M: Racial issues																
1. Very similar	31.7	31.9	31.2	30.9	37.8	32.3	28.8	33.5	32.5	34.6	27.3	34.7	32.4	28.3	29.2	21.6
2. Mostly similar	29.3	31.1	27.2	30.7	25.3	27.9	29.9	30.2	28.3	30.8	27.1	29.7	27.9	30.2	28.5	47.1
3. Mostly different	9.4	8.1	11.2	9.9	5.4	7.2	9.9	8.6	12.6	9.3	10.2	10.3	9.0	9.2	8.9	-
4. Very different	6.9	6.0	7.7	6.2	7.1	8.0	7.3	5.7	7.5	6.1	7.8	5.3	6.7	8.0	8.5	9.6
8. Don't know	22.6	22.9	22.7	22.4	24.3	24.6	24.0	22.0	19.1	19.1	27.6	20.0	24.1	24.3	24.9	21.7
Item 11350 Subject M03,N02 N	2747	1329	1354	2182	320	505	807	940	495	1663	987	1103	549	368	660	29
E07N: Religion																
1. Very similar	42.7	39.7	45.4	41.4	53.5	38.7	41.4	48.6	37.5	45.0	39.4	50.0	41.2	40.1	33.6	38.0
2. Mostly similar	28.6	27.5	29.4	29.8	21.5	31.8	28.8	25.8	30.2	29.7	27.4	28.0	26.2	30.4	30.3	33.3
3. Mostly different	9.5	9.8	9.3	10.3	6.1	8.5	9.7	8.9	11.1	9.2	9.4	8.9	9.8	11.5	8.9	-
4. Very different	7.4	8.6	6.3	6.9	8.0	8.8	7.3	6.6	7.5	6.6	8.7	5.8	7.3	5.7	10.7	17.5
8. Don't know	11.9	14.4	9.6	11.6	10.9	12.2	12.7	10.1	13.7	9.4	15.2	7.3	15.5	12.3	16.4	11.2
Item 11360 Subject G,M03 N	2744	1328	1352	2180	319	506	807	938	494	1660	986	1104	550	366	657	29
E07O: Politics																
1. Very similar	21.2	20.9	21.1	20.4	26.7	19.3	19.1	24.9	19.3	22.6	18.0	23.1	21.2	18.9	19.5	14.1
2. Mostly similar	28.1	29.7	26.3	29.8	21.3	26.0	28.4	28.1	29.8	31.1	23.5	30.0	26.8	31.6	24.4	26.7
3. Mostly different	9.6	10.0	9.1	10.0	7.1	8.5	11.1	8.8	9.8	9.5	10.0	8.7	8.6	9.7	11.6	21.3
4. Very different	6.2	8.0	4.4	5.2	7.9	8.7	3.9	6.2	7.4	4.8	8.7	5.4	6.1	6.5	7.0	14.2
8. Don't know	35.0	31.4	39.1	34.5	36.9	37.5	37.6	31.9	33.8	32.0	39.8	32.8	37.4	33.3	37.5	23.7
Item 11370 Subject H01,M03 N	2742	1327	1352	2178	320	503	807	938	494	1660	985	1102	549	368	656	29
E08: How do you think your CLOSE FRIENDS feel (or would feel) about YOU doing each of the following things?																
E08A: Smoking one or more packs of cigarettes per day																
1. Not disapprove	26.1	26.4	25.7	26.5	20.3	29.5	26.0	28.2	19.2	19.3	37.0	14.7	25.4	28.0	43.5	56.2
2. Disapprove	36.1	35.9	36.4	35.7	38.8	39.8	36.1	35.8	32.6	38.2	32.5	35.7	38.9	38.8	33.8	22.2
3. Strongly disapprove	37.8	37.7	37.9	37.8	40.8	30.7	37.9	36.0	48.2	42.5	30.5	49.6	35.7	33.2	22.8	21.6
Item 11470 Subject A12b N	2721	1310	1349	2165	313	501	807	920	493	1650	977	1095	541	367	652	31
E08B: Trying marijuana (pot, grass) once or twice																
1. Not disapprove	45.9	47.0	44.8	47.5	38.0	55.4	43.3	39.6	52.1	43.2	49.9	19.6	57.2	47.3	78.6	70.7
2. Disapprove	23.4	23.5	23.1	22.4	26.7	22.1	23.5	25.9	19.8	25.2	20.3	27.7	25.2	29.3	12.1	17.5
3. Strongly disapprove	30.7	29.6	32.1	30.1	35.2	22.5	33.2	34.5	28.1	31.5	29.8	52.8	17.6	23.3	9.3	11.7
Item 11480 Subject A12b N	2719	1307	1350	2164	316	500	806	921	493	1648	975	1092	540	367	656	30

QUESTIONNAIRE FORM 4 1984	TOTAL	SEX		RACE		REGION				4YR COLLEGE PLANS		ILLICIT DRUG USE: LIFETIME				
		M	F	White	Black	NE	NC	S	W	Yes	No	None	Marijuana Only	Few Pills	More Pills	Any Heroin
N (Weighted No. of Cases):	3284	1588	1546	2489	414	679	909	1113	584	1830	1188	1253	675	426	806	39
% of Weighted Total:	100.0	48.4	47.1	75.8	12.6	20.7	27.7	33.9	17.8	55.7	36.2	38.1	20.6	13.0	24.5	1.2
E08C: Smoking marijuana occasionally																
1. Not disapprove	37.1	39.9	34.3	38.0	28.8	46.9	32.6	34.0	40.3	32.9	43.5	13.5	42.1	39.4	69.5	76.5
2. Disapprove	25.3	24.4	26.0	24.9	31.3	24.6	24.4	26.5	25.3	27.6	21.6	26.3	30.8	28.8	18.3	8.1
3. Strongly disapprove	37.6	35.7	39.6	37.2	39.8	28.5	43.0	39.5	34.4	39.6	34.9	60.2	27.1	31.8	12.2	15.4
Item 11490 Subject A12b N	2718	1306	1350	2165	314	499	805	922	493	1647	975	1092	539	367	655	31
E08D: Smoking marijuana regularly																
1. Not disapprove	20.8	25.4	16.0	19.8	20.2	27.9	18.8	18.7	20.6	15.0	29.4	7.1	18.6	14.8	45.7	82.0
2. Disapprove	27.1	27.1	27.1	26.6	32.8	29.0	23.0	30.2	26.0	28.7	24.7	20.8	35.2	35.7	27.4	7.3
3. Strongly disapprove	52.2	47.5	56.9	53.6	47.0	43.1	58.1	51.1	53.4	56.3	45.9	72.2	46.2	49.6	27.0	10.7
Item 11500 Subject A12b N	2713	1305	1346	2161	314	498	805	919	491	1643	975	1091	538	365	653	31
E08E: Trying LSD once or twice																
1. Not disapprove	12.4	13.3	11.4	12.1	8.6	16.2	11.4	10.7	13.4	10.0	16.0	6.0	7.6	8.2	27.2	56.3
2. Disapprove	21.8	23.1	20.4	21.5	21.7	23.5	19.1	24.1	20.2	21.8	21.8	18.1	25.0	23.8	24.0	29.4
3. Strongly disapprove	65.8	63.6	68.2	66.3	69.7	60.2	69.5	65.2	66.5	68.2	62.1	76.0	67.4	68.0	48.8	14.2
Item 11510 Subject A12b N	2710	1304	1343	2155	316	497	801	921	491	1641	974	1087	540	365	652	31
E08F: Trying an amphetamine (upper, pep pill, bennie, speed) once or twice																
1. Not disapprove	23.0	22.7	23.4	25.1	8.7	26.6	22.2	19.1	27.9	20.4	26.7	9.2	14.1	22.7	51.7	64.4
2. Disapprove	25.2	27.9	22.4	25.1	22.1	27.1	24.3	25.0	25.1	25.9	24.0	21.4	28.3	32.2	24.7	28.6
3. Strongly disapprove	51.8	49.4	54.3	49.8	69.2	46.3	53.5	55.9	47.0	53.7	49.3	69.4	57.6	45.2	23.6	7.0
Item 11520 Subject A12b N	2712	1304	1346	2159	314	496	804	919	493	1642	973	1089	538	365	654	31
E08G: Taking one or two drinks nearly every day																
1. Not disapprove	26.4	34.9	18.0	26.6	20.4	28.7	27.5	27.2	21.1	21.7	34.6	17.7	26.1	23.8	40.6	68.5
2. Disapprove	34.1	32.7	35.7	36.0	24.1	37.1	33.7	33.5	33.1	34.6	33.5	31.2	36.0	39.1	35.5	17.6
3. Strongly disapprove	39.4	32.4	46.4	37.3	55.5	34.3	38.8	39.4	45.8	43.7	32.0	51.0	37.9	37.2	24.0	13.9
Item 11530 Subject A12b N	2705	1301	1342	2152	312	497	799	916	493	1640	969	1088	534	364	651	31
E08H: Taking four or five drinks nearly every day																
1. Not disapprove	13.9	19.8	7.6	13.0	12.6	14.7	16.3	13.4	9.9	9.7	20.8	9.7	10.6	12.5	21.7	60.4
2. Disapprove	27.0	31.1	23.0	27.5	23.8	30.2	26.5	29.0	21.0	25.8	28.4	22.5	29.2	30.5	31.0	22.2
3. Strongly disapprove	59.1	49.1	69.4	59.5	63.6	55.1	57.2	57.5	69.2	64.4	50.8	67.8	60.2	57.0	47.3	17.4
Item 11540 Subject A12b N	2706	1301	1343	2151	314	495	800	918	493	1641	970	1087	535	366	651	31
E08I: Having five or more drinks once or twice each weekend																
1. Not disapprove	48.7	56.9	40.6	53.4	21.0	49.7	57.0	43.6	43.7	45.8	52.9	32.1	52.3	55.0	69.0	71.5
2. Disapprove	21.5	18.6	24.4	20.6	26.4	23.3	18.9	23.0	21.3	22.9	19.1	23.4	21.0	21.7	18.4	17.0
3. Strongly disapprove	29.8	24.5	35.0	26.1	52.6	27.0	24.1	33.5	35.0	31.3	28.0	44.4	26.6	23.2	12.6	11.5
Item 11550 Subject A12b N	2705	1299	1343	2153	311	495	802	917	491	1638	972	1085	535	365	653	31
E08J: Driving a car after having 1-2 drinks																
1. Not disapprove	43.2	50.3	35.9	47.5	16.1	42.6	51.3	38.4	39.4	43.5	43.1	28.8	46.4	44.5	63.5	64.3
2. Disapprove	27.0	23.5	30.6	26.3	30.0	29.5	23.9	29.6	24.5	28.1	24.7	29.3	28.0	28.7	20.8	23.9
3. Strongly disapprove	29.8	26.2	33.4	26.3	53.8	27.9	24.8	31.9	36.1	28.4	32.2	42.0	25.6	26.8	15.6	11.7
Item 11551 Subject A12b N	2705	1302	1340	2152	314	495	802	917	491	1637	972	1087	537	365	649	31
E08K: Driving a car after having 5 or more drinks																
1. Not disapprove	11.2	16.5	5.9	11.3	7.3	8.6	14.6	10.6	9.4	8.7	14.4	5.7	9.9	13.7	18.8	34.8
2. Disapprove	26.2	29.6	22.5	27.0	19.2	26.3	28.7	26.5	21.4	25.7	27.2	22.7	28.6	24.7	29.7	34.5
3. Strongly disapprove	62.6	54.0	71.6	61.7	73.5	65.1	56.8	62.9	69.2	65.6	58.3	71.6	61.5	61.6	51.5	30.7
Item 11552 Subject A12b N	2706	1301	1342	2152	313	495	802	917	491	1639	972	1088	537	364	650	31

QUESTIONNAIRE FORM 4 1984	TOTAL	SEX		RACE		REGION				4YR COLLEGE PLANS		ILLICIT DRUG USE: LIFETIME				
		M	F	White	Black	NE	NC	S	W	Yes	No	None	Mari-juana Only	Few Pills	More Pills	Any Her-oin
N (Weighted No. of Cases):	3284	1588	1546	2489	414	679	909	1113	584	1830	1188	1253	675	426	806	39
% of Weighted Total:	100.0	48.4	47.1	75.8	12.6	20.7	27.7	33.9	17.8	55.7	36.2	38.1	20.6	13.0	24.5	1.2

E09: In some communities parents who are particularly concerned with drug or alcohol abuse among young people have formed groups of concerned parents to deal with these problems. In these groups parents try to become more informed and sometimes to set some common guidelines for young peoples' behavior. In general, what do you think of the idea of having parents get together in groups such as these?

	TOTAL	M	F	White	Black	NE	NC	S	W	Yes	No	None	Mari-juana Only	Few Pills	More Pills	Any Her-oin
1. A bad idea	6.6	8.6	4.3	6.1	8.3	7.1	6.9	7.5	3.8	5.4	8.5	5.1	5.7	4.8	9.4	28.0
2. More bad than good	7.9	8.4	7.4	8.0	7.6	7.0	9.9	7.3	6.5	7.3	9.0	4.6	7.5	10.0	12.4	16.3
3. Don't know or can't say	27.5	28.8	26.3	28.2	22.4	28.7	27.2	27.0	27.7	25.2	30.8	20.3	32.7	32.0	32.9	24.2
4. More good than bad	23.0	23.9	21.9	23.7	18.5	23.4	25.0	20.6	23.7	24.5	20.5	23.6	23.6	22.5	21.5	21.1
5. A good idea	35.1	30.2	40.1	33.9	43.2	33.9	31.0	37.6	38.4	37.6	31.1	46.5	30.4	30.7	23.8	10.4
Item 21730 Subject A16a N	2659	1276	1323	2122	308	481	793	906	479	1613	959	1081	526	357	633	27

E10: To the best of your knowledge, how many of your close friends have parents who are involved in such parent groups?

	TOTAL	M	F	White	Black	NE	NC	S	W	Yes	No	None	Mari-juana Only	Few Pills	More Pills	Any Her-oin
1. None	70.5	67.2	74.0	72.5	62.1	66.1	73.6	70.9	69.4	70.1	71.4	72.0	71.7	70.5	68.5	58.8
2. A few	20.3	21.9	19.0	19.6	23.1	22.0	18.4	20.3	21.8	20.9	19.7	19.4	18.5	20.6	22.7	28.0
3. Some	8.2	9.9	6.1	6.9	14.0	10.9	6.6	8.0	8.2	8.0	7.9	7.4	8.8	8.1	8.3	11.2
4. Most or all	1.0	1.1	0.9	1.0	0.8	1.0	1.3	0.9	0.6	0.9	1.0	1.3	1.0	0.9	0.4	2.0
Item 21740 Subject A16a N	2660	1276	1323	2112	313	482	791	905	482	1615	956	1081	527	357	632	27

E11: Has either (or both) of your own parents been involved in such a group?

	TOTAL	M	F	White	Black	NE	NC	S	W	Yes	No	None	Mari-juana Only	Few Pills	More Pills	Any Her-oin
1. No–GO TO QUESTION E14.	91.4	91.3	91.9	92.5	87.0	89.2	91.9	90.6	94.0	90.7	92.3	94.1	89.2	90.8	90.3	66.7
2. Yes, in the past, but not now	5.3	5.8	4.2	4.2	10.0	5.9	4.8	6.1	3.8	5.1	5.7	3.5	5.4	5.2	7.2	20.4
3. Yes, now	3.4	2.8	3.9	3.3	3.0	4.9	3.3	3.3	2.2	4.2	2.1	2.4	5.4	4.0	2.5	12.8
Item 21750 Subject A16a N	2597	1236	1302	2080	293	471	774	879	474	1593	921	1066	515	343	614	25

E12: Has the involvement of your parent(s) in such a group had any impact on your own feelings about drug or alcohol use?

	TOTAL	M	F	White	Black	NE	NC	S	W	Yes	No	None	Mari-juana Only	Few Pills	More Pills	Any Her-oin
1. Made me much less likely to use drugs or alcohol	23.0	18.8	27.5	18.5	36.1	22.1	19.5	26.7	21.4	24.5	20.3	26.8	23.7	18.6	21.4	9.3
2. Made me somewhat less likely to use drugs or alcohol	15.7	13.3	18.8	17.0	13.1	19.2	19.4	13.1	10.3	16.0	14.8	20.1	11.1	14.2	15.6	24.2
3. No impact either way	52.9	57.6	48.2	54.1	46.8	48.8	50.9	52.3	64.6	53.7	52.5	47.1	56.5	58.4	53.7	50.3
4. Made me somewhat more likely to use drugs or alcohol	5.9	7.5	3.7	7.8	2.6	4.4	8.7	6.1	2.4	5.3	7.3	6.1	5.9	8.8	3.3	8.4
5. Made me much more likely to use drugs or alcohol	2.4	2.8	1.7	2.5	1.4	5.5	1.6	1.9	1.2	0.6	5.1	-	2.7	-	6.1	7.8
Item 21760 Subject A16a N★	345	187	146	227	69	71	97	129	48	191	143	112	79	46	88	12

E13: What about your relationship with your parents? Has their involvement in the parent group made your relationship better or worse?

	TOTAL	M	F	White	Black	NE	NC	S	W	Yes	No	None	Mari-juana Only	Few Pills	More Pills	Any Her-oin
1. Much worse	8.6	10.6	5.8	7.0	7.4	13.3	10.4	5.2	8.5	4.1	15.2	6.3	4.7	5.8	15.1	16.2
2. Somewhat worse	14.5	18.3	9.8	14.6	13.0	17.2	18.6	14.4	2.9	10.1	19.5	10.3	14.3	14.6	11.5	39.7
3. No effect, don't know	50.0	48.4	54.6	55.6	38.9	48.9	51.8	47.5	55.7	57.6	40.6	53.7	54.9	64.0	42.0	24.7
4. Somewhat better	10.9	10.0	12.8	10.6	16.7	7.5	5.2	14.4	16.6	10.9	9.8	11.3	4.4	11.1	17.2	9.3
5. Much better	16.0	12.8	16.9	12.3	24.0	13.2	14.1	18.6	16.3	17.3	14.9	18.4	21.7	4.5	14.2	10.0
Item 21770 Subject A16a N★	340	179	148	220	71	68	91	135	47	188	143	114	75	43	87	12

★=excludes respondents for whom question was inappropriate.

	TOTAL	SEX		RACE		REGION				4YR COLLEGE PLANS		ILLICIT DRUG USE: LIFETIME				
QUESTIONNAIRE FORM 4 **1984**		M	F	White	Black	NE	NC	S	W	Yes	No	None	Mari-juana Only	Few Pills	More Pills	Any Her-oin
N (Weighted No. of Cases):	3284	1588	1546	2489	414	679	909	1113	584	1830	1188	1253	675	426	806	39
% of Weighted Total:	100.0	48.4	47.1	75.8	12.6	20.7	27.7	33.9	17.8	55.7	36.2	38.1	20.6	13.0	24.5	1.2
E14: In some communities young people themselves have formed groups aimed at avoiding drug use, such as Youth for Drug-Free Alternatives. How many of your close friends have been members of such a group?																
1. None	81.9	81.1	82.8	83.7	75.5	76.5	84.2	82.9	81.7	81.9	82.2	83.2	81.3	81.2	82.7	52.1
2. A few	13.2	13.2	13.1	12.6	14.0	16.0	11.8	11.9	15.0	13.8	12.3	12.5	12.8	13.5	13.1	28.6
3. Some	4.2	4.8	3.5	3.4	8.1	6.7	3.0	4.5	2.9	3.7	4.7	3.7	5.2	3.8	3.7	12.3
4. Most or all	0.8	0.9	0.6	0.3	2.3	0.9	1.0	0.7	0.4	0.6	0.8	0.6	0.6	1.5	0.5	6.9
Item 21780 Subject A16a N	2658	1272	1324	2116	308	478	790	907	482	1613	955	1081	524	358	631	27
E15: Have you ever participated in such a group?																
3. Yes, now	3.2	3.9	2.6	2.8	4.5	5.9	2.3	2.9	2.6	3.0	3.2	3.0	3.5	1.6	3.3	10.9
2. Yes, in the past, but not now	4.4	4.5	4.2	3.6	8.2	4.5	4.4	4.7	3.7	3.7	5.5	3.4	2.7	5.9	5.6	20.2
1. No	92.4	91.6	93.2	93.6	87.3	89.6	93.3	92.4	93.7	93.3	91.3	93.6	93.8	92.4	91.1	68.9
Item 21790 Subject A16a N	2616	1251	1304	2082	303	472	778	891	475	1587	942	1068	511	351	622	27

QUESTIONNAIRE FORM 5 1984	TOTAL	SEX		RACE		REGION				4YR COLLEGE PLANS		ILLICIT DRUG USE: LIFETIME				
		M	F	White	Black	NE	NC	S	W	Yes	No	None	Mari-juana Only	Few Pills	More Pills	Any Heroin
N (Weighted No. of Cases):	3294	1522	1656	2462	457	682	918	1107	587	1824	1282	1228	662	480	801	44
% of Weighted Total:	100.0	46.2	50.3	74.7	13.9	20.7	27.9	33.6	17.8	55.4	38.9	37.3	20.1	14.6	24.3	1.3

A01: Taking all things together, how would you say things are these days–would you say you're very happy, pretty happy, or not too happy these days?

	TOTAL	M	F	White	Black	NE	NC	S	W	Yes	No	None	Mari-juana Only	Few Pills	More Pills	Any Heroin
3. Very happy	18.7	18.4	19.0	19.7	13.5	16.6	14.8	21.3	22.0	21.4	15.6	20.0	18.1	18.1	16.9	24.3
2. Pretty happy	68.9	69.7	68.4	69.6	67.6	69.1	71.2	67.7	67.3	67.8	70.2	68.5	70.7	68.7	68.8	56.3
1. Not too happy	12.5	11.9	12.5	10.6	19.0	14.2	14.1	11.0	10.7	10.8	14.1	11.4	11.1	13.2	14.3	19.3
Item 1190 Subject P01,Q01 N	3285	1519	1654	2458	454	678	917	1104	586	1820	1282	1226	659	478	800	44

A02: Some people think a lot about the social problems of the nation and the world, and about how they might be solved. Others spend little time thinking about these issues. How much do you think about such things?

	TOTAL	M	F	White	Black	NE	NC	S	W	Yes	No	None	Mari-juana Only	Few Pills	More Pills	Any Heroin
1. Never	1.9	2.5	1.1	1.9	0.8	3.0	1.6	1.7	1.2	1.7	2.2	1.8	2.1	0.7	2.3	2.1
2. Seldom	14.8	13.5	15.9	15.1	12.6	18.8	13.5	13.8	14.0	12.9	17.2	13.4	13.5	15.9	16.3	31.4
3. Sometimes	54.5	53.1	55.9	55.6	49.1	52.6	58.8	51.5	55.4	51.7	58.4	55.4	53.6	53.8	54.6	46.7
4. Quite often	23.7	25.2	22.6	22.7	29.3	21.3	21.6	26.8	23.8	27.3	18.7	24.0	25.5	24.3	22.2	12.7
5. A great deal	5.2	5.7	4.5	4.6	8.2	4.3	4.6	6.2	5.5	6.4	3.5	5.4	5.3	5.4	4.6	7.0
Item 6880 Subject J,Q08 N	3284	1515	1655	2456	455	678	918	1104	584	1819	1281	1227	661	478	797	44

A03: Of all the problems facing the nation today, how often do you worry about each of the following?

A03A: Chance of nuclear war

	TOTAL	M	F	White	Black	NE	NC	S	W	Yes	No	None	Mari-juana Only	Few Pills	More Pills	Any Heroin
1. Never	8.1	8.5	7.5	7.3	11.0	10.1	7.9	7.4	7.4	6.7	9.4	8.8	6.4	5.4	9.3	10.2
2. Seldom	22.5	24.2	21.4	23.7	20.7	20.0	22.9	23.3	23.4	22.2	23.4	24.2	20.5	24.1	21.0	28.9
3. Sometimes	39.9	38.4	40.6	41.2	35.2	41.2	40.5	38.3	40.3	41.2	39.0	38.8	43.4	38.1	40.4	21.4
4. Often	29.5	28.9	30.4	27.8	33.0	28.8	28.7	31.0	28.8	30.0	28.2	28.2	29.7	32.3	29.4	39.5
Item 11660 Subject J N	3281	1517	1652	2457	451	676	917	1103	584	1819	1277	1225	660	478	797	44

A03B: Population growth

	TOTAL	M	F	White	Black	NE	NC	S	W	Yes	No	None	Mari-juana Only	Few Pills	More Pills	Any Heroin
1. Never	30.3	32.1	28.8	30.9	31.3	37.2	30.2	28.2	26.6	28.5	32.6	29.5	28.7	29.0	32.2	48.6
2. Seldom	44.4	43.8	45.2	46.6	36.2	43.1	50.0	42.2	41.1	47.0	41.9	46.0	43.5	44.3	44.5	24.4
3. Sometimes	20.3	20.0	20.4	18.5	22.9	15.9	17.7	22.8	24.7	20.6	19.0	19.5	21.9	21.1	18.9	25.2
4. Often	5.0	4.1	5.6	4.1	9.7	3.9	2.1	6.8	7.6	3.9	6.6	5.0	5.9	5.5	4.4	1.7
Item 11670 Subject E01,J N	3279	1517	1650	2456	448	676	917	1102	584	1821	1276	1223	660	478	798	44

A03C: Crime and violence

	TOTAL	M	F	White	Black	NE	NC	S	W	Yes	No	None	Mari-juana Only	Few Pills	More Pills	Any Heroin
1. Never	2.6	4.2	0.8	2.7	1.0	3.9	2.7	2.1	1.9	1.9	3.3	2.3	1.6	0.7	4.4	7.4
2. Seldom	13.5	18.4	8.8	14.1	8.6	13.5	13.7	11.9	16.3	12.6	14.7	10.1	14.4	12.7	17.2	22.9
3. Sometimes	42.5	47.4	38.6	44.8	32.1	44.2	41.8	41.5	43.6	44.5	40.8	44.7	45.9	40.9	39.0	34.1
4. Often	41.4	30.1	51.8	38.5	58.3	38.5	41.8	44.5	38.3	41.1	41.2	42.8	38.1	45.7	39.4	35.6
Item 11680 Subject J N	3275	1514	1649	2454	452	674	915	1103	583	1817	1275	1224	658	476	796	44

A03D: Pollution

	TOTAL	M	F	White	Black	NE	NC	S	W	Yes	No	None	Mari-juana Only	Few Pills	More Pills	Any Heroin
1. Never	13.1	12.6	13.2	12.5	14.6	14.3	13.2	13.4	10.8	12.2	14.4	11.4	13.1	12.8	14.9	18.4
2. Seldom	37.9	35.3	40.6	38.4	39.4	32.8	43.2	40.2	30.9	36.7	39.4	39.3	39.1	38.4	36.2	21.9
3. Sometimes	34.6	35.8	33.8	35.0	33.1	35.7	32.8	33.8	37.7	36.5	32.1	34.7	34.8	34.3	34.1	41.5
4. Often	14.5	16.3	12.5	14.1	12.9	17.2	10.8	12.6	20.6	14.6	14.2	14.7	13.0	14.4	14.7	18.2
Item 11690 Subject F04,J N	3263	1508	1644	2446	448	674	911	1097	581	1811	1270	1217	656	476	793	44

A03E: Energy shortages

	TOTAL	M	F	White	Black	NE	NC	S	W	Yes	No	None	Mari-juana Only	Few Pills	More Pills	Any Heroin
1. Never	18.9	16.3	21.2	18.1	23.9	22.3	17.1	20.5	14.9	17.4	20.8	16.8	19.1	19.8	20.7	28.4
2. Seldom	40.7	38.3	43.1	42.4	36.8	40.4	41.5	36.9	46.7	41.8	39.7	41.0	41.1	38.1	41.7	38.0
3. Sometimes	31.4	33.8	28.7	31.5	27.6	27.9	33.5	32.4	30.1	31.4	30.6	32.0	31.2	35.8	28.6	23.3
4. Often	9.0	11.6	7.0	8.1	11.7	9.4	7.9	10.1	8.4	9.4	8.9	10.2	8.6	6.4	8.9	10.3
Item 11700 Subject F05,J N	3269	1514	1645	2450	445	673	915	1098	583	1817	1272	1219	656	477	797	44

QUESTIONNAIRE FORM 5 1984	TOTAL	SEX		RACE		REGION				4YR COLLEGE PLANS		ILLICIT DRUG USE: LIFETIME				
		M	F	White	Black	NE	NC	S	W	Yes	No	None	Marijuana Only	Few Pills	More Pills	Any Heroin
N (Weighted No. of Cases):	3294	1522	1656	2462	457	682	918	1107	587	1824	1282	1228	662	480	801	44
% of Weighted Total:	100.0	46.2	50.3	74.7	13.9	20.7	27.9	33.6	17.8	55.4	38.9	37.3	20.1	14.6	24.3	1.3

A03F: Race relations

1. Never	22.5	23.1	22.0	24.4	13.4	24.1	25.9	18.0	23.5	18.2	28.7	20.2	20.6	20.8	27.3	37.0
2. Seldom	34.5	38.5	31.1	38.4	18.8	33.2	36.7	34.1	33.2	33.5	36.1	34.2	35.5	35.3	34.3	31.2
3. Sometimes	27.2	24.8	29.3	26.2	29.0	27.5	25.0	27.8	29.3	30.2	22.9	29.3	28.1	26.4	24.3	15.7
4. Often	15.9	13.6	17.6	11.0	38.8	15.3	12.5	20.1	14.0	18.1	12.3	16.3	15.9	17.4	14.2	16.1
Item 11710 Subject J,N02 N	3260	1510	1640	2447	444	671	915	1094	580	1813	1267	1216	654	475	797	44

A03G: Hunger and poverty

1. Never	10.1	13.6	6.5	10.5	7.4	12.8	9.7	8.9	9.6	8.2	12.5	8.9	9.5	8.1	12.9	10.9
2. Seldom	31.7	41.5	22.8	34.7	19.5	31.9	32.6	29.2	34.6	30.8	33.5	30.9	32.8	30.5	31.0	41.7
3. Sometimes	38.4	32.0	44.5	38.9	38.2	37.5	38.0	39.6	37.8	40.8	34.8	38.0	39.9	40.4	37.5	37.6
4. Often	19.9	12.9	26.2	15.9	34.9	17.8	19.7	22.3	18.0	20.2	19.2	22.1	17.8	20.9	18.6	9.9
Item 11720 Subject F03,J N	3266	1510	1645	2449	447	676	912	1093	585	1810	1272	1221	655	475	795	43

A03H: Using open land for housing or industry

1. Never	39.3	34.4	44.2	39.1	44.6	41.9	43.5	39.6	29.2	38.2	40.1	38.7	40.3	38.2	40.4	36.5
2. Seldom	30.6	30.2	31.1	31.5	30.0	31.2	32.3	30.0	28.6	32.3	29.5	29.9	33.3	32.8	29.9	21.6
3. Sometimes	18.9	20.7	17.0	18.9	15.7	17.1	15.9	19.2	25.4	19.0	18.6	19.8	17.1	18.7	17.9	27.6
4. Often	11.1	14.7	7.7	10.5	9.7	9.8	8.2	11.3	16.8	10.5	11.9	11.6	9.3	10.4	11.8	14.3
Item 11730 Subject F05,J N	3273	1513	1649	2452	449	673	917	1100	583	1814	1275	1220	659	478	797	44

A03I: Urban decay

1. Never	48.0	43.6	52.2	48.3	51.4	47.3	49.3	50.2	43.0	45.3	51.1	46.9	50.6	45.8	50.0	43.1
2. Seldom	34.0	35.7	32.8	34.2	31.8	30.5	37.6	32.1	35.8	35.3	33.2	35.6	31.0	36.3	32.8	31.3
3. Sometimes	14.2	16.6	11.6	14.2	11.9	16.6	10.5	13.8	17.9	14.9	13.0	13.5	14.5	14.7	13.7	20.6
4. Often	3.8	4.1	3.4	3.3	4.9	5.7	2.6	3.9	3.3	4.4	2.7	4.0	3.9	3.2	3.5	5.0
Item 11740 Subject J N	3243	1499	1635	2437	445	668	908	1089	577	1802	1262	1208	653	475	788	44

A03J: Economic problems

1. Never	7.8	7.7	7.8	7.5	8.4	12.0	6.0	7.0	7.2	6.2	9.5	6.7	8.0	4.6	10.4	16.5
2. Seldom	26.0	24.0	27.9	26.9	22.1	27.8	23.2	26.2	27.8	25.6	27.3	26.6	23.3	26.6	27.0	28.1
3. Sometimes	43.9	45.7	42.0	44.7	43.4	41.1	47.0	43.7	42.5	44.0	43.9	43.1	45.8	45.3	43.0	38.1
4. Often	22.3	22.6	22.3	20.9	26.1	19.0	23.9	23.0	22.5	24.1	19.3	23.6	23.0	23.6	19.6	17.3
Item 11750 Subject J N	3270	1515	1644	2452	446	675	917	1098	580	1817	1272	1218	660	478	794	44

A03K: Drug abuse

1. Never	9.3	13.7	5.2	9.0	7.6	10.6	7.5	8.7	11.9	7.7	11.2	8.3	9.6	5.4	12.1	11.4
2. Seldom	22.3	29.1	16.0	23.6	17.2	21.5	24.5	20.1	24.0	22.1	22.7	22.3	23.6	20.9	23.0	24.1
3. Sometimes	37.1	35.0	39.3	37.4	36.8	37.3	39.3	34.5	38.1	40.4	32.9	36.4	39.1	40.7	34.7	30.3
4. Often	31.3	22.2	39.5	29.9	38.4	30.6	28.7	36.6	26.0	29.8	33.2	33.0	27.7	33.1	30.2	34.2
Item 11760 Subject J N	3277	1515	1650	2455	450	675	917	1102	583	1817	1276	1223	660	478	797	44

A04: How well do you think your experiences and training (at home, school, work, etc.) have prepared you to be a good...

A04A: Husband or wife

1. Poorly	2.6	3.3	1.5	2.3	2.3	3.6	1.5	2.4	3.5	2.0	2.9	1.9	1.9	1.8	4.4	7.6
2. Not so well	4.4	4.7	4.2	4.3	4.8	5.2	3.5	3.9	6.2	4.6	4.2	4.9	3.2	3.9	5.2	2.7
3. Fairly well	22.5	26.6	18.2	23.0	19.1	21.4	24.3	20.3	24.8	21.1	23.7	20.6	20.8	22.1	25.1	34.7
4. Well	40.4	41.5	39.5	42.2	34.0	42.1	43.3	38.8	37.1	39.6	42.4	40.3	42.4	42.4	38.0	30.2
5. Very well	30.1	23.9	36.6	28.3	39.7	27.8	27.3	34.6	28.4	32.6	26.9	32.3	31.8	29.7	27.2	24.8
Item 11770 Subject D01 N	3212	1486	1618	2405	444	660	901	1080	572	1789	1249	1203	650	468	772	44

A04B: Parent

1. Poorly	2.2	2.6	1.5	1.9	2.1	2.1	1.0	2.5	3.7	1.6	2.9	1.3	1.3	1.8	4.6	4.7
2. Not so well	6.0	7.7	4.3	5.9	5.0	7.4	4.8	5.7	7.2	5.9	6.2	5.0	5.4	5.2	7.3	13.9
3. Fairly well	20.8	23.2	18.2	22.5	14.0	17.2	24.2	19.1	22.4	19.4	22.1	21.6	20.5	18.3	21.9	16.7
4. Well	37.5	39.9	35.5	39.1	28.9	38.3	41.6	35.5	33.9	37.8	37.9	37.5	39.0	39.1	35.3	32.8
5. Very well	33.5	26.6	40.5	30.6	49.9	35.0	28.4	37.2	32.9	35.4	31.0	34.6	33.8	35.5	30.8	31.8
Item 11780 Subject D02 N	3242	1496	1635	2429	444	669	907	1086	580	1808	1254	1212	655	476	780	44

QUESTIONNAIRE FORM 5 1984	TOTAL	SEX		RACE		REGION				4YR COLLEGE PLANS		ILLICIT DRUG USE: LIFETIME				
		M	F	White	Black	NE	NC	S	W	Yes	No	None	Mari-juana Only	Few Pills	More Pills	Any Her-oin
N (Weighted No. of Cases):	3294	1522	1656	2462	457	682	918	1107	587	1824	1282	1228	662	480	801	44
% of Weighted Total:	100.0	46.2	50.3	74.7	13.9	20.7	27.9	33.6	17.8	55.4	38.9	37.3	20.1	14.6	24.3	1.3

A04C: Worker on a job

1. Poorly	1.0	0.9	0.9	0.9	0.7	1.9	0.6	0.8	0.8	0.8	1.1	0.8	1.0	0.6	1.3	2.1
2. Not so well	2.4	2.2	2.3	1.9	2.3	2.2	3.0	1.7	3.1	2.2	2.3	2.4	2.4	2.1	2.5	2.6
3. Fairly well	14.3	13.7	15.1	14.7	12.4	13.9	15.0	12.6	16.9	13.3	15.8	13.6	16.3	11.9	15.8	6.7
4. Well	39.3	40.7	38.0	41.8	27.2	40.3	42.2	36.8	38.4	39.1	39.3	40.1	37.8	39.5	40.3	27.7
5. Very well	43.0	42.4	43.6	40.7	57.3	41.6	39.3	48.2	40.9	44.6	41.4	43.2	42.6	45.9	40.1	60.8
Item 11790 Subject C01 N	*3264*	*1512*	*1640*	*2446*	*448*	*679*	*911*	*1094*	*580*	*1809*	*1273*	*1219*	*658*	*473*	*793*	*44*

A05: Apart from the particular kind of work you want to do, how would you rate each of the following settings as a place to work?

A05A: Working in a large corporation

1. Not at all acceptable	4.4	4.2	4.3	4.2	3.5	4.7	4.3	4.5	4.3	3.6	5.4	4.6	3.2	3.0	5.5	2.1
2. Somewhat acceptable	21.7	20.9	22.7	22.7	14.1	22.4	23.2	19.8	21.9	17.8	26.0	20.7	21.1	23.5	21.7	31.4
3. Acceptable	47.3	49.7	45.1	48.3	46.9	46.2	47.3	48.0	47.2	47.1	48.2	48.9	48.4	46.4	45.8	37.9
4. Desirable	26.6	25.3	27.9	24.9	35.4	26.7	25.2	27.7	26.6	31.4	20.4	25.7	27.3	27.1	27.0	28.5
Item 11800 Subject C05 N	*3280*	*1515*	*1652*	*2457*	*450*	*677*	*916*	*1102*	*585*	*1820*	*1276*	*1222*	*660*	*478*	*798*	*44*

A05B: Working in a small business

1. Not at all acceptable	4.1	3.7	4.0	3.1	7.6	4.7	2.9	5.0	3.8	3.1	4.9	3.4	3.7	3.7	5.5	8.1
2. Somewhat acceptable	21.3	23.9	18.4	19.1	28.6	21.5	19.2	22.3	22.4	21.6	20.3	19.5	21.6	23.3	21.4	30.5
3. Acceptable	54.9	53.7	56.8	56.8	49.2	56.6	56.4	53.6	53.2	55.9	53.9	57.5	53.5	51.6	55.3	49.7
4. Desirable	19.6	18.7	20.8	21.0	14.6	17.2	21.4	19.1	20.7	19.5	20.9	19.6	21.2	21.3	17.8	11.8
Item 11810 Subject C05 N	*3279*	*1516*	*1650*	*2458*	*449*	*677*	*916*	*1102*	*585*	*1819*	*1276*	*1222*	*659*	*478*	*799*	*44*

A05C: Working in a government agency

1. Not at all acceptable	18.3	17.9	18.6	19.2	12.1	20.3	18.3	17.1	18.2	14.2	23.3	16.2	15.9	16.2	22.7	43.3
2. Somewhat acceptable	30.8	31.8	30.5	32.2	26.0	27.8	31.6	30.3	34.2	32.5	29.4	32.2	31.1	31.7	29.1	21.3
3. Acceptable	33.9	34.6	33.1	34.5	35.0	33.9	34.6	33.7	33.4	36.5	30.0	34.5	36.5	32.2	33.2	15.4
4. Desirable	16.9	15.8	17.8	14.2	26.9	18.0	15.5	18.9	14.1	16.8	17.3	17.1	16.4	20.0	15.0	20.0
Item 11820 Subject C05,H05 N	*3275*	*1513*	*1649*	*2454*	*450*	*675*	*914*	*1100*	*585*	*1816*	*1276*	*1220*	*659*	*478*	*797*	*43*

A05D: Working in the military service

1. Not at all acceptable	44.0	35.8	51.6	45.5	39.6	46.3	44.8	40.1	47.3	46.2	41.9	44.4	40.3	45.6	44.7	50.9
2. Somewhat acceptable	30.2	32.9	28.3	30.5	28.9	26.4	31.1	30.4	32.8	31.4	28.8	30.3	33.0	30.3	29.1	19.3
3. Acceptable	17.1	19.2	14.7	16.7	16.5	17.9	17.6	18.1	13.6	15.9	18.1	17.6	16.9	15.5	17.0	16.1
4. Desirable	8.7	12.1	5.5	7.3	15.0	9.4	6.5	11.4	6.3	6.5	11.2	7.7	9.8	8.6	9.2	13.7
Item 11830 Subject C05,L04 N	*3275*	*1515*	*1647*	*2457*	*449*	*677*	*913*	*1100*	*585*	*1816*	*1278*	*1220*	*659*	*478*	*799*	*44*

A05E: Working in a school or university

1. Not at all acceptable	24.5	30.1	18.5	24.4	21.0	26.8	24.7	25.3	20.3	17.8	33.3	18.9	24.6	23.3	31.5	38.9
2. Somewhat acceptable	36.5	36.1	36.8	37.0	36.2	38.3	38.4	35.9	32.2	36.0	36.9	37.1	36.8	36.4	35.9	35.0
3. Acceptable	26.5	24.2	29.2	26.2	26.3	23.9	24.9	25.6	33.4	29.4	22.9	29.0	26.2	26.3	23.9	20.7
4. Desirable	12.6	9.6	15.6	12.3	16.5	11.0	12.0	13.2	14.0	16.9	6.9	15.0	12.3	14.0	8.6	5.4
Item 11840 Subject B10,C05 N	*3272*	*1514*	*1646*	*2455*	*447*	*677*	*915*	*1097*	*583*	*1814*	*1275*	*1219*	*660*	*478*	*795*	*44*

A05F: Working in a police department or police agency

1. Not at all acceptable	29.8	29.5	29.9	28.4	34.9	29.0	28.3	31.4	30.0	30.4	28.5	29.4	29.5	27.9	31.0	28.7
2. Somewhat acceptable	32.9	32.0	33.8	33.3	33.3	32.8	34.4	33.3	30.2	35.3	29.5	35.0	32.3	32.1	32.7	21.1
3. Acceptable	27.2	27.6	27.0	28.8	21.6	28.2	27.1	25.5	29.6	25.4	30.2	27.1	28.9	30.5	24.0	29.3
4. Desirable	10.1	11.0	9.3	9.5	10.2	10.0	10.3	9.8	10.3	8.9	11.9	8.5	9.2	9.4	12.2	20.9
Item 11850 Subject C05 N	*3275*	*1514*	*1649*	*2456*	*448*	*678*	*915*	*1101*	*581*	*1816*	*1277*	*1217*	*660*	*478*	*799*	*44*

A05G: Working in a social service organization

1. Not at all acceptable	22.8	33.7	12.2	24.2	15.5	26.4	21.6	22.4	21.3	20.9	25.0	20.1	23.8	19.6	25.9	34.3
2. Somewhat acceptable	36.2	41.5	31.6	35.9	35.5	33.6	35.5	36.1	40.7	35.1	38.0	36.6	39.2	36.7	34.6	30.0
3. Acceptable	28.2	20.6	35.1	27.4	31.6	28.5	29.5	27.4	27.2	30.1	26.0	30.1	27.1	28.3	26.3	24.7
4. Desirable	12.8	4.2	21.1	12.5	17.4	11.5	13.4	14.1	10.9	13.9	11.0	13.2	9.9	15.4	13.2	10.9
Item 11860 Subject C05,O01 N	*3264*	*1509*	*1644*	*2450*	*447*	*676*	*913*	*1096*	*579*	*1813*	*1270*	*1214*	*659*	*476*	*798*	*44*

QUESTIONNAIRE FORM 5 1984	TOTAL	SEX		RACE		REGION				4YR COLLEGE PLANS		ILLICIT DRUG USE: LIFETIME				
		M	F	White	Black	NE	NC	S	W	Yes	No	None	Marijuana Only	Few Pills	More Pills	Any Heroin
N (Weighted No. of Cases):	3294	1522	1656	2462	457	682	918	1107	587	1824	1282	1228	662	480	801	44
% of Weighted Total:	100.0	46.2	50.3	74.7	13.9	20.7	27.9	33.6	17.8	55.4	38.9	37.3	20.1	14.6	24.3	1.3
A05H: Working with a small group of partners																
1. Not at all acceptable	9.1	9.0	8.6	7.4	15.9	9.0	8.8	9.6	8.5	7.5	10.8	7.0	10.4	8.3	10.6	9.8
2. Somewhat acceptable	28.5	28.6	28.3	28.0	32.6	29.7	27.9	29.6	26.1	26.5	31.2	28.6	29.8	29.8	27.6	20.3
3. Acceptable	43.3	41.8	44.9	44.8	35.4	45.1	44.7	40.7	44.0	43.9	43.2	44.2	41.0	42.7	44.5	47.5
4. Desirable	19.1	20.6	18.1	19.8	16.2	16.1	18.6	20.1	21.4	22.1	14.8	20.3	18.8	19.2	17.3	22.3
Item 11870 Subject C05 N	3272	1510	1650	2453	448	676	914	1098	583	1816	1274	1218	659	477	798	43
A05I: Working on your own (self-employed)																
1. Not at all acceptable	6.2	4.1	8.0	6.0	7.5	6.1	6.2	5.9	6.8	5.5	6.8	5.4	5.8	8.3	6.3	7.2
2. Somewhat acceptable	15.8	13.3	18.2	15.8	14.4	17.8	17.5	13.9	14.6	16.0	15.6	18.6	15.0	15.4	13.4	10.8
3. Acceptable	31.5	31.2	31.6	32.8	27.3	30.0	33.3	30.0	33.1	31.7	31.6	32.7	31.3	29.0	31.7	25.4
4. Desirable	46.5	51.4	42.2	45.4	50.9	46.0	43.0	50.2	45.4	46.7	46.1	43.3	47.9	47.3	48.6	56.6
Item 11880 Subject C05 N	3279	1515	1652	2456	452	677	916	1101	584	1819	1277	1221	662	478	797	44
A06: If you were to get enough money to live as comfortably as you'd like for the rest of your life, would you want to work?																
1. I would want to work	81.6	79.3	84.0	80.9	84.9	80.4	82.8	81.9	80.9	83.0	80.2	86.0	81.3	79.4	78.1	65.3
2. I would not want to work	18.4	20.7	16.0	19.1	15.1	19.6	17.2	18.1	19.1	17.0	19.8	14.0	18.7	20.6	21.9	34.7
Item 8100 Subject C06 N	3253	1503	1637	2438	447	670	909	1095	579	1802	1268	1214	653	471	796	44
A07: The next questions are about race relations. How much have you gotten to know people of other races...																
A07A: In school?																
1. Not at all	7.9	8.3	7.2	9.1	2.1	6.1	18.2	2.8	3.4	6.4	9.9	7.6	7.0	9.3	8.0	13.4
2. A little	19.6	20.5	19.0	22.8	10.0	21.6	27.4	13.5	16.8	18.9	21.2	18.9	19.4	19.7	21.3	14.9
3. Some	28.5	28.4	28.5	30.5	19.3	32.3	24.3	26.6	34.2	28.4	28.7	29.3	28.3	26.9	28.6	30.7
4. A lot	40.9	39.3	42.5	34.2	66.5	38.4	23.7	55.4	43.4	43.3	37.0	40.4	44.2	40.8	38.8	41.0
8. Does not apply to me	3.0	3.5	2.8	3.4	2.1	1.6	6.4	1.6	2.2	3.0	3.1	3.8	1.2	3.3	3.3	-
Item 11890 Subject B03,N03 N	3274	1512	1651	2450	454	680	912	1100	582	1813	1279	1221	660	478	795	44
A07B: In your neighborhood?																
1. Not at all	32.3	31.9	33.2	37.4	15.0	31.9	42.8	28.3	23.9	31.5	35.1	30.3	29.2	35.2	35.8	40.9
2. A little	23.0	22.6	23.6	23.6	21.2	25.5	18.2	23.8	26.3	23.7	22.2	22.3	26.3	20.2	23.4	24.6
3. Some	17.9	17.5	17.4	15.5	24.0	18.4	12.1	18.8	24.4	18.1	16.7	17.6	20.1	18.5	17.0	8.0
4. A lot	13.5	14.1	12.5	7.9	32.3	13.8	7.8	17.1	14.9	12.2	13.2	14.7	14.6	11.4	10.7	13.2
8. Does not apply to me	13.3	13.8	13.3	15.6	7.4	10.3	19.1	12.0	10.4	14.4	12.9	15.2	9.8	14.6	13.1	13.3
Item 11900 Subject N03 N	3267	1513	1645	2448	451	677	909	1097	584	1812	1274	1219	660	477	794	44
A07C: In church?																
1. Not at all	34.9	35.2	33.9	38.1	20.8	40.7	42.7	30.1	24.9	32.5	39.1	31.8	34.1	35.9	38.9	56.3
2. A little	21.9	21.9	22.3	21.2	26.4	22.0	19.6	23.2	23.0	22.1	20.5	22.7	22.3	23.9	19.5	14.8
3. Some	13.4	13.1	13.5	12.6	16.8	12.4	10.7	15.0	15.8	14.6	11.5	13.3	16.1	11.9	11.5	10.3
4. A lot	9.3	7.9	10.5	5.7	23.7	6.4	6.3	13.6	9.4	8.9	9.1	12.4	11.0	6.9	4.8	5.0
8. Does not apply to me	20.5	21.9	19.7	22.5	12.2	18.6	20.7	18.1	27.0	21.8	19.8	19.7	16.6	21.4	25.4	13.7
Item 11910 Subject G,N03 N	3262	1509	1643	2445	450	676	911	1094	582	1809	1275	1216	659	476	794	44
A07D: On sports teams?																
1. Not at all	18.4	15.3	21.1	20.2	10.8	21.2	28.1	11.6	12.9	14.5	24.1	17.5	18.4	16.6	21.2	22.0
2. A little	15.8	16.5	15.3	17.5	7.3	15.7	18.4	14.6	14.0	15.4	15.4	14.0	15.8	16.0	18.8	11.0
3. Some	19.3	21.2	17.2	19.9	15.8	18.1	18.0	18.2	24.9	20.4	17.7	19.5	18.9	19.7	18.5	21.0
4. A lot	27.6	34.3	21.3	22.8	49.5	26.1	16.7	35.8	31.0	31.1	23.0	26.4	33.1	29.2	23.0	37.2
8. Does not apply to me	18.9	12.6	25.2	19.6	16.7	19.0	18.9	19.9	17.2	18.5	19.8	22.6	13.8	18.4	18.5	8.8
Item 11920 Subject N03 N	3260	1510	1640	2441	452	676	912	1092	580	1808	1272	1214	661	476	792	44

QUESTIONNAIRE FORM 5 1984	TOTAL	SEX		RACE		REGION				4YR COLLEGE PLANS		ILLICIT DRUG USE: LIFETIME				
		M	F	White	Black	NE	NC	S	W	Yes	No	None	Mari- juana Only	Few Pills	More Pills	Any Her- oin
N (Weighted No. of Cases):	3294	1522	1656	2462	457	682	918	1107	587	1824	1282	1228	662	480	801	44
% of Weighted Total:	100.0	46.2	50.3	74.7	13.9	20.7	27.9	33.6	17.8	55.4	38.9	37.3	20.1	14.6	24.3	1.3
A07E: In clubs?																
1. Not at all	25.0	26.4	23.4	27.3	15.4	27.0	38.4	15.1	20.5	21.9	29.2	23.2	25.1	23.0	27.9	44.6
2. A little	18.7	18.8	19.3	20.5	12.5	20.3	17.3	18.8	18.9	19.7	17.2	17.6	20.7	20.6	19.2	10.6
3. Some	19.4	19.4	19.4	18.8	21.3	17.9	13.1	23.8	22.9	21.4	16.8	21.5	19.6	18.2	16.2	10.5
4. A lot	17.4	14.8	19.5	12.9	36.4	14.6	10.1	25.9	16.0	19.2	14.9	18.3	19.9	18.8	13.8	13.4
8. Does not apply to me	19.5	20.5	18.5	20.5	14.4	20.3	21.2	16.4	21.7	17.8	21.8	19.4	14.6	19.4	23.0	20.9
Item 11930 Subject N03 N	3258	1509	1642	2443	451	675	909	1095	579	1806	1272	1216	661	474	793	44
A07F: On a job?																
1. Not at all	16.5	17.0	16.1	19.2	6.9	14.4	27.6	11.0	11.9	15.4	18.4	17.5	16.9	15.9	15.4	23.0
2. A little	14.6	15.5	14.0	15.8	8.2	17.8	14.4	11.6	17.0	14.3	15.3	12.8	12.6	16.0	17.5	13.2
3. Some	21.9	22.8	20.8	22.9	17.5	23.1	19.1	21.6	25.5	23.8	19.3	21.0	21.8	20.8	23.9	28.2
4. A lot	30.1	30.3	29.4	25.5	47.2	30.7	20.3	37.9	30.2	27.7	32.8	27.2	34.9	30.4	30.1	28.8
8. Does not apply to me	16.9	14.4	19.6	16.6	20.2	14.0	18.6	17.9	15.3	18.7	14.2	21.5	13.9	16.9	13.1	6.7
Item 11940 Subject C01,N03 N	3263	1511	1643	2445	451	678	911	1094	581	1810	1273	1216	660	475	795	44
A08: Thinking about the country as a whole, would you say relations between white people and black people have been getting better, getting worse, or staying pretty much the same?																
1. Better	27.0	28.7	25.7	28.6	20.1	27.9	24.1	26.5	31.8	27.4	26.9	27.5	26.5	26.8	26.6	32.5
2. A little better	47.8	45.7	50.0	46.6	55.2	47.9	50.3	45.8	47.4	49.4	45.2	47.8	48.4	47.8	48.0	34.3
3. Same	19.6	20.2	18.8	19.6	18.1	18.6	19.8	21.1	17.7	18.8	20.6	19.6	19.9	20.3	19.0	24.7
4. A little worse	3.7	3.8	3.7	3.5	5.2	3.9	3.9	4.2	2.2	3.4	4.2	3.4	4.1	2.9	4.5	7.3
5. Worse	1.8	1.6	1.8	1.7	1.5	1.7	1.8	2.4	0.7	1.0	3.1	1.7	1.2	2.2	1.9	1.3
Item 11950 Subject N02 N	3267	1510	1647	2448	455	679	912	1097	579	1808	1279	1217	658	478	796	44
The next questions are about driving.																
A09: Do you have a driver's license?																
1. Yes	86.4	91.3	82.2	91.0	62.3	76.0	91.7	87.3	88.2	87.2	86.2	85.8	86.6	84.9	88.9	84.2
2. No, but I soon will– GO TO Q.A13	11.4	7.2	15.1	7.6	31.7	20.3	6.8	11.0	9.0	10.7	11.3	11.9	12.1	11.9	8.6	11.2
3. No–GO TO Q.A13	2.2	1.6	2.7	1.4	6.0	3.7	1.4	1.8	2.7	2.0	2.5	2.2	1.3	3.2	2.4	4.5
Item 11960 Subject F07 N	3154	1477	1579	2423	397	646	896	1053	560	1780	1218	1173	631	469	775	42
A10: Do you own a car?																
1. Yes	49.4	57.5	40.7	51.9	26.4	38.6	43.1	57.0	56.4	45.7	54.3	43.8	48.0	51.2	57.7	44.5
2. No, but I expect to own one in another year or two	34.3	30.3	38.7	32.2	52.8	38.9	38.0	31.4	28.8	32.5	36.6	33.3	34.8	37.8	33.4	35.9
3. No	16.3	12.2	20.7	15.9	20.8	22.5	18.9	11.6	14.7	21.8	9.1	22.9	17.2	11.0	8.9	19.6
Item 11970 Subject F07 N ★	2729	1351	1299	2206	248	491	822	923	494	1553	1050	1009	546	398	692	35
A11: Are you able to use someone else's car when you want to?																
1. Yes, whenever I wish	32.0	30.9	32.9	33.7	22.0	26.2	34.4	34.7	28.8	33.4	29.7	32.5	31.1	33.6	31.3	38.6
2. Yes, most of the time	44.5	44.5	44.8	44.3	50.1	46.0	44.3	42.8	46.4	45.7	43.5	43.4	46.9	46.9	43.8	30.6
3. Sometimes	16.6	17.6	15.4	15.7	17.3	19.7	13.5	15.7	20.3	15.3	18.0	16.7	16.0	15.6	17.3	8.4
4. Rarely	5.2	5.7	4.9	4.9	8.1	5.9	6.0	5.0	3.7	4.0	6.9	4.9	5.4	2.6	6.1	21.2
5. Never	1.7	1.4	2.0	1.4	2.5	2.3	1.8	1.9	0.9	1.6	1.7	2.6	0.6	1.3	1.5	1.2
Item 11980 Subject F07 N ★	2721	1349	1295	2201	248	487	822	919	494	1550	1048	1004	545	397	692	35
A12: Do you make an effort to cut down on driving, in order to save gasoline?																
1. Not at all	17.8	19.4	15.6	17.8	17.1	25.5	14.9	16.7	17.1	17.1	18.6	12.6	19.4	17.9	23.6	29.1
2. Not very much	33.2	32.7	33.8	34.7	24.0	34.2	33.5	32.9	32.6	34.9	30.8	32.1	33.6	33.2	36.0	12.4
3. Yes, to some extent	38.5	38.3	39.6	38.5	41.7	31.9	41.2	39.2	39.5	37.9	39.6	42.0	35.9	40.1	33.8	45.8
4. Yes, quite a bit	7.3	6.4	8.2	6.7	10.9	5.2	7.4	8.5	6.8	7.4	7.2	9.1	7.3	6.6	5.1	4.8
8. Don't know	3.2	3.3	2.8	2.3	6.3	3.3	3.0	2.8	4.1	2.7	3.7	4.2	3.8	2.3	1.4	7.9
Item 11990 Subject F07 N ★	2723	1348	1297	2204	248	489	822	918	494	1553	1048	1007	546	398	689	35

★=excludes respondents for whom question was inappropriate.

QUESTIONNAIRE FORM 5 1984	TOTAL	SEX		RACE		REGION				4YR COLLEGE PLANS		ILLICIT DRUG USE: LIFETIME				
		M	F	White	Black	NE	NC	S	W	Yes	No	None	Marijuana Only	Few Pills	More Pills	Any Heroin
N (Weighted No. of Cases):	3294	1522	1656	2462	457	682	918	1107	587	1824	1282	1228	662	480	801	44
% of Weighted Total:	100.0	46.2	50.3	74.7	13.9	20.7	27.9	33.6	17.8	55.4	38.9	37.3	20.1	14.6	24.3	1.3
A13: Do you make an effort to cut down on the amount of electricity you use in order to save energy?																
1. Not at all	7.9	9.2	6.5	7.9	7.1	9.8	9.0	6.3	7.1	7.7	7.9	5.7	8.0	7.2	10.6	22.9
2. Not very much	28.3	29.3	27.7	30.2	22.4	31.0	28.8	27.5	25.7	28.1	29.7	25.8	29.3	25.8	32.9	21.8
3. Yes, to some extent	46.2	45.1	47.6	46.7	46.7	45.8	46.0	47.2	44.9	46.9	46.0	48.8	45.6	47.6	43.8	31.7
4. Yes, quite a bit	15.3	14.3	16.0	13.2	21.4	11.1	13.9	16.2	20.5	15.5	13.9	17.3	14.2	17.4	11.0	19.0
8. Don't know	2.3	2.0	2.3	2.0	2.5	2.4	2.2	2.7	1.8	1.9	2.5	2.4	2.9	2.0	1.7	4.6
Item 12000 Subject F05　N	3279	1518	1650	2454	456	677	913	1104	585	1815	1280	1223	662	479	796	44
A14: In the house or apartment where you live, is an effort made to reduce heat during the winter, in order to save energy?																
1. Not at all	5.1	5.3	4.6	4.2	8.2	6.1	5.0	5.0	4.0	4.4	5.8	3.7	6.2	4.2	5.4	20.8
2. Not very much	14.6	14.9	14.0	13.7	16.4	13.1	13.3	16.4	14.8	13.2	16.6	12.5	13.6	14.7	18.2	10.8
3. Yes, to some extent	39.4	40.8	38.3	39.6	40.6	41.3	38.3	38.6	40.6	40.9	37.1	39.1	40.5	41.9	38.0	26.5
4. Yes, quite a bit	38.6	36.8	40.9	41.0	30.2	36.8	41.9	36.3	39.8	39.9	37.3	41.5	37.8	37.8	37.0	36.3
8. Don't know	2.3	2.2	2.2	1.5	4.7	2.7	1.4	3.7	0.7	1.6	3.2	3.1	2.0	1.4	1.5	5.5
Item 12010 Subject F05　N	3280	1519	1651	2455	456	678	914	1103	585	1817	1280	1223	662	479	797	44
A15: How do you feel about each of the following?																
A15A: How much do you enjoy shopping for things like clothes, records, sporting goods, and books?																
1. Not at all	1.7	3.3	0.2	1.9	1.0	1.8	1.3	1.8	2.1	1.5	2.0	1.8	2.0	0.6	1.8	4.9
2. Not very much	8.4	14.0	2.7	9.2	3.3	10.4	9.9	7.0	6.4	6.9	10.5	7.6	7.1	8.7	10.4	1.0
3. Pretty much	27.9	40.0	16.9	29.9	16.1	28.4	26.5	25.9	33.2	26.9	28.4	28.4	29.1	24.7	28.4	16.1
4. Very much	62.0	42.7	80.2	59.0	79.5	59.4	62.3	65.3	58.3	64.7	59.1	62.2	61.8	65.9	59.5	78.0
Item 12020 Subject F01　N	3281	1518	1652	2455	456	680	914	1102	585	1817	1281	1224	662	479	797	44
A15B: How much do you care about having the latest fashion in your clothes, records, leisure activities, and so on?																
1. Not at all	5.6	8.6	2.6	6.0	2.2	7.2	4.5	4.9	7.0	4.9	6.5	5.7	3.3	4.8	7.6	11.8
2. Not very much	25.1	29.2	21.1	26.1	17.5	24.3	24.7	21.6	33.0	23.7	27.2	26.5	23.9	25.4	24.7	12.4
3. Pretty much	39.4	40.0	39.7	41.1	32.9	36.6	42.0	39.9	37.5	40.3	38.4	42.8	40.1	35.7	36.6	34.8
4. Very much	29.9	22.2	36.6	26.7	47.3	31.9	28.7	33.6	22.5	31.0	27.9	25.0	32.8	34.1	31.0	40.9
Item 12030 Subject F01　N	3278	1517	1650	2453	455	679	914	1101	584	1815	1279	1222	662	479	797	44
A15C: How much do you care about whether your family has most of the things your friends and neighbors have?																
1. Not at all	24.9	23.7	25.7	22.6	32.1	29.2	18.3	25.6	28.7	23.4	26.4	23.6	25.8	22.3	27.0	33.0
2. Not very much	49.1	49.3	49.1	51.4	38.9	48.6	54.1	44.8	50.3	49.6	49.8	50.4	46.1	50.8	49.5	45.2
3. Pretty much	20.3	21.2	19.7	21.3	19.6	17.2	22.6	22.4	16.7	20.7	19.0	20.1	21.9	21.5	18.7	15.1
4. Very much	5.7	5.7	5.5	4.7	9.5	4.9	5.0	7.3	4.4	6.4	4.8	5.9	6.2	5.3	4.7	6.8
Item 12040 Subject F01　N	3272	1515	1646	2453	450	674	914	1101	583	1813	1278	1222	662	478	795	44
A16: When you are older, do you expect to own more possessions than your parents do now, or about the same, or less? I expect to own . . .																
1. Much less than my parents	1.8	2.3	1.2	1.5	3.2	1.4	1.8	2.3	1.5	1.0	2.6	2.0	1.0	0.9	2.2	4.9
2. Somewhat less than my parents	6.9	7.2	6.7	7.1	5.5	5.4	6.9	6.6	9.2	5.6	8.6	6.7	5.7	8.2	7.4	2.8
3. About as much as my parents	35.5	30.4	39.9	37.7	24.2	34.5	35.8	36.6	34.1	32.0	40.4	37.3	36.6	32.4	34.2	31.7
4. Somewhat more than my parents	38.1	38.5	37.9	38.3	38.2	38.4	41.4	36.6	35.4	41.3	34.5	38.4	38.2	38.3	38.9	17.9
5. Much more than my parents	17.7	21.5	14.3	15.4	28.9	20.2	14.2	18.0	19.8	20.1	13.9	15.6	18.5	20.2	17.3	42.8
Item 12050 Subject F01　N	3269	1510	1649	2446	456	675	913	1099	583	1812	1278	1222	660	478	791	44

QUESTIONNAIRE FORM 5 1984	TOTAL	SEX		RACE		REGION				4YR COLLEGE PLANS		ILLICIT DRUG USE: LIFETIME				
		M	F	White	Black	NE	NC	S	W	Yes	No	None	Mari-juana Only	Few Pills	More Pills	Any Her-oin
N (Weighted No. of Cases): % of Weighted Total:	3294 100.0	1522 46.2	1656 50.3	2462 74.7	457 13.9	682 20.7	918 27.9	1107 33.6	587 17.8	1824 55.4	1282 38.9	1228 37.3	662 20.1	480 14.6	801 24.3	44 1.3
A17: Compared with your parents, what is the smallest amount that you could be content or satisfied to own?																
The least I could be content to own is ...																
1. Much less than my parents	8.7	9.5	7.6	9.6	5.7	9.6	7.8	7.7	10.8	8.7	8.8	8.9	6.9	8.1	10.3	5.0
2. Somewhat less than my parents	31.0	30.3	32.0	34.7	18.2	29.4	33.2	29.8	31.8	32.7	29.7	31.9	30.8	30.2	31.3	28.7
3. About as much as my parents	42.9	42.1	43.9	42.2	42.9	41.9	44.3	43.3	41.3	41.8	45.0	42.0	46.3	44.2	41.8	24.8
4. Somewhat more than my parents	13.1	13.6	12.5	10.7	23.8	13.9	11.6	13.9	12.8	13.4	11.7	13.2	11.6	13.1	13.2	26.1
5. Much more than my parents	4.3	4.5	3.9	2.9	9.4	5.2	3.0	5.3	3.2	3.4	4.8	4.1	4.4	4.4	3.3	15.5
Item 12060 Subject F01 N	3250	1505	1635	2437	452	667	909	1093	581	1799	1275	1214	659	475	786	43
A18: These next questions ask your opinions about a number of different topics. How much do you agree or disagree with each statement below?																
A18A: We ought to worry about our own country and let the rest of the world take care of itself																
1. Disagree	22.1	23.3	21.4	21.1	23.6	21.3	20.5	23.1	23.8	25.3	18.3	23.2	24.5	22.3	18.6	12.1
2. Mostly disagree	24.6	22.9	26.2	26.6	19.2	24.1	25.7	23.7	24.8	27.4	20.5	27.7	23.1	24.0	21.7	25.8
3. Neither	13.5	12.6	14.5	13.4	13.3	13.4	13.1	13.2	15.1	13.2	14.0	13.8	13.0	12.1	14.9	5.9
4. Mostly agree	25.0	24.1	25.7	25.8	24.8	25.0	26.7	24.1	23.8	23.7	26.7	24.0	26.8	24.5	25.6	25.9
5. Agree	14.8	17.0	12.2	13.1	19.0	16.2	14.0	15.8	12.5	10.4	20.5	11.3	12.5	17.1	19.2	30.4
Item 12070 Subject O03 N	3273	1516	1648	2453	453	678	912	1101	582	1815	1279	1221	660	478	797	44
A18B: It would be better if we all felt more like citizens of the world than of any particular country																
1. Disagree	9.8	11.9	7.4	9.8	10.2	9.2	9.0	10.4	10.5	10.0	9.1	9.7	9.2	11.6	9.5	11.3
2. Mostly disagree	12.4	13.4	11.4	13.4	6.3	12.0	13.6	10.8	13.8	13.2	11.3	10.6	12.5	12.9	14.4	8.0
3. Neither	19.4	18.8	20.3	20.4	15.7	20.7	22.2	16.6	18.6	17.6	21.9	19.0	20.8	16.9	20.6	27.5
4. Mostly agree	29.7	28.3	31.1	30.9	25.6	29.1	30.3	29.4	29.8	30.0	29.1	31.3	29.5	32.0	26.0	23.6
5. Agree	28.8	27.5	29.9	25.5	42.1	28.8	24.8	32.8	27.4	29.2	28.6	29.4	28.0	26.6	29.5	29.6
Item 12080 Subject O03 N	3268	1513	1645	2447	453	673	913	1100	582	1813	1277	1219	659	479	794	44
A18C: I find it hard to be sympathetic toward starving people in foreign lands, when there is so much trouble in our own country																
1. Disagree	36.3	24.1	47.8	34.8	43.1	36.9	38.2	35.5	34.2	39.2	32.9	37.4	36.2	36.6	35.8	26.8
2. Mostly disagree	24.1	23.4	24.5	26.0	17.8	24.2	23.8	24.1	24.5	26.4	21.5	24.9	22.8	26.2	23.9	19.9
3. Neither	13.7	17.9	9.9	15.0	8.0	12.4	12.7	14.4	15.8	13.5	13.9	14.2	15.0	11.1	13.0	13.7
4. Mostly agree	14.9	19.5	10.5	14.4	15.7	15.6	14.1	14.2	16.5	13.1	16.7	13.9	15.5	13.9	15.9	13.8
5. Agree	11.0	15.0	7.3	9.8	15.5	10.9	11.3	11.8	9.0	7.9	15.0	9.6	10.5	12.2	11.4	25.8
Item 12090 Subject F03,O03 N	3273	1517	1647	2455	454	678	913	1100	582	1812	1281	1219	660	479	796	44
A18D: Maybe some minority groups do get unfair treatment, but that's no business of mine																
1. Disagree	41.1	31.7	50.2	38.1	54.7	39.3	39.3	42.4	43.7	48.4	31.1	45.0	42.9	42.4	34.4	30.2
2. Mostly disagree	27.1	27.8	26.4	30.0	17.0	26.2	29.8	25.6	26.6	28.4	26.1	27.8	27.1	27.1	27.0	14.7
3. Neither	18.4	23.2	14.0	19.4	13.2	20.4	17.7	17.2	19.5	15.0	22.9	15.6	18.0	18.9	22.2	22.5
4. Mostly agree	7.8	10.6	5.2	7.6	7.8	8.2	7.8	8.1	6.7	5.3	10.8	6.6	7.1	7.1	10.0	10.9
5. Agree	5.6	6.7	4.3	4.9	7.3	5.8	5.4	6.7	3.5	3.0	9.1	5.0	5.0	4.4	6.3	21.8
Item 12100 Subject N02,O03 N	3261	1510	1641	2448	450	674	913	1093	581	1809	1275	1217	655	477	794	44
A18E: I get very upset when I see other people treated unfairly																
1. Disagree	3.1	3.4	2.6	2.6	3.8	3.3	3.7	3.2	1.6	3.0	3.1	3.1	1.9	4.0	3.0	-
2. Mostly disagree	5.0	6.2	3.8	5.1	4.3	5.0	5.6	4.3	5.5	4.2	5.9	4.6	4.4	5.1	5.9	9.7
3. Neither	8.5	12.8	4.3	9.3	4.2	11.0	9.0	6.1	9.2	6.8	10.7	7.1	10.4	6.3	10.1	8.0
4. Mostly agree	31.4	36.4	26.4	33.0	25.0	31.1	32.8	31.1	30.0	30.2	33.0	29.5	32.3	31.1	33.6	35.4
5. Agree	52.1	41.1	62.9	50.1	62.7	49.7	49.0	55.4	53.7	55.8	47.2	55.7	51.0	53.5	47.4	46.8
Item 12110 Subject O03 N	3271	1511	1649	2450	452	676	913	1099	582	1814	1279	1220	658	479	796	43

QUESTIONNAIRE FORM 5 1984	TOTAL	SEX		RACE		REGION				4YR COLLEGE PLANS		ILLICIT DRUG USE: LIFETIME				
		M	F	White	Black	NE	NC	S	W	Yes	No	None	Marijuana Only	Few Pills	More Pills	Any Heroin
N (Weighted No. of Cases):	3294	1522	1656	2462	457	682	918	1107	587	1824	1282	1228	662	480	801	44
% of Weighted Total:	100.0	46.2	50.3	74.7	13.9	20.7	27.9	33.6	17.8	55.4	38.9	37.3	20.1	14.6	24.3	1.3
A18F: I would agree to a good plan to make a better life for the poor, even if it cost me money																
1. Disagree	6.9	10.2	3.9	7.3	3.2	7.5	7.5	6.6	5.8	5.6	8.9	4.7	7.6	7.5	9.3	8.1
2. Mostly disagree	10.7	13.4	8.0	12.0	5.6	12.4	9.8	9.4	12.3	11.1	9.6	8.6	11.5	10.4	12.5	15.1
3. Neither	22.7	25.3	20.3	24.6	14.6	24.6	25.0	19.9	22.3	21.9	24.1	21.6	22.8	22.7	24.2	29.9
4. Mostly agree	33.9	31.1	36.5	33.6	35.7	32.9	35.0	33.9	33.0	34.9	32.9	36.7	32.4	34.6	31.1	37.3
5. Agree	25.9	19.9	31.3	22.5	41.0	22.6	22.7	30.2	26.6	26.5	24.4	28.5	25.7	24.9	22.9	9.6
Item 12120 Subject O03 N	3267	1512	1644	2446	452	674	913	1098	581	1813	1276	1220	658	479	792	44
A18G: It's not really my problem if others are in trouble and need help																
1. Disagree	41.2	32.1	49.7	39.5	49.5	39.2	39.8	45.9	36.8	44.6	37.2	46.2	40.5	39.7	35.6	30.6
2. Mostly disagree	33.8	35.9	32.1	35.3	29.5	35.9	34.9	32.0	33.0	34.3	33.7	33.3	33.4	37.1	35.3	25.4
3. Neither	14.5	18.1	11.1	15.2	9.0	14.0	16.1	11.8	17.3	12.3	17.2	11.8	15.7	13.6	16.9	25.9
4. Mostly agree	6.7	8.7	4.6	6.7	5.9	7.5	5.7	5.5	9.6	6.1	6.5	5.9	6.6	5.9	8.1	8.0
5. Agree	3.8	5.0	2.4	3.2	6.2	3.4	3.4	4.7	3.2	2.7	5.3	2.8	3.8	3.7	4.1	10.2
Item 12130 Subject O03 N	3260	1507	1643	2449	446	675	909	1097	579	1807	1275	1216	655	476	795	44
A18H: Americans could change their eating habits to provide more food for the hungry people in other parts of the world, and at the same time be healthier themselves																
1. Disagree	10.2	14.0	6.3	9.6	11.0	10.8	8.7	10.8	10.8	8.5	12.1	8.8	9.9	9.6	12.9	13.3
2. Mostly disagree	11.5	14.4	8.9	12.0	9.8	10.5	12.9	11.7	10.1	12.4	10.6	11.7	9.7	11.7	13.1	11.5
3. Neither	17.7	20.8	14.5	17.7	16.7	19.0	17.7	17.2	17.1	17.3	17.9	17.2	17.7	14.4	19.1	26.6
4. Mostly agree	30.3	27.3	33.1	31.0	28.1	31.1	31.1	28.5	31.3	30.5	30.5	31.2	32.7	33.1	26.6	19.9
5. Agree	30.3	23.5	37.2	29.8	34.5	28.5	29.5	31.8	30.7	31.3	28.8	31.1	29.9	31.1	28.3	28.8
Item 12140 Subject F03,O03 N	3269	1514	1646	2450	453	676	913	1097	582	1813	1278	1219	659	479	794	44
A18I: My family and I often buy things we really don't need; we could get along with much less																
1. Disagree	14.7	15.6	13.8	11.9	25.5	19.0	10.2	14.8	16.3	12.6	17.3	13.3	15.1	15.0	15.4	26.4
2. Mostly disagree	16.1	18.5	13.6	16.0	16.1	16.3	15.6	15.6	17.9	16.0	16.4	16.4	15.8	14.8	17.2	17.1
3. Neither	16.4	18.6	14.3	17.0	11.4	17.1	17.8	13.9	18.2	16.9	16.0	17.1	16.5	14.4	16.2	18.2
4. Mostly agree	27.6	26.7	28.9	28.6	24.0	24.5	29.7	28.2	26.4	29.1	25.0	27.0	27.8	30.0	27.2	31.5
5. Agree	25.2	20.6	29.5	26.4	23.0	23.0	26.7	27.4	21.3	25.4	25.3	26.1	24.8	25.8	24.0	6.7
Item 10060 Subject F01 N	3266	1513	1645	2448	454	676	912	1096	582	1810	1280	1219	656	479	796	44
A18J: Most people will have fuller and happier lives if they choose legal marriage rather than staying single, or just living with someone																
1. Disagree	21.9	18.9	24.6	21.3	24.6	24.8	17.2	22.1	25.7	21.1	22.1	15.7	19.8	24.5	30.8	44.5
2. Mostly disagree	14.3	14.5	14.0	14.5	14.0	14.9	15.1	12.4	15.7	14.2	14.4	11.0	17.2	14.5	17.3	13.4
3. Neither	28.1	30.5	25.9	28.1	27.4	31.9	29.9	25.4	26.2	28.9	27.5	29.2	31.2	26.4	25.3	23.2
4. Mostly agree	15.2	16.4	14.0	15.5	14.8	12.7	15.8	17.2	13.4	15.5	15.1	18.2	13.4	16.5	11.5	7.7
5. Agree	20.5	19.7	21.4	20.7	19.2	15.8	22.0	22.9	18.9	20.3	20.9	25.9	18.4	18.0	15.1	11.2
Item 12150 Subject D03 N	3268	1512	1647	2449	453	675	912	1100	582	1812	1279	1220	657	478	795	44
A18K: Parents should encourage just as much independence in their daughters as in their sons																
1. Disagree	5.0	8.7	1.4	4.7	5.6	5.7	3.5	5.6	5.2	5.3	4.1	4.7	5.7	5.8	4.2	6.3
2. Mostly disagree	5.5	8.8	2.3	5.0	6.5	6.4	3.5	7.2	4.6	4.9	6.2	4.6	5.8	6.3	5.9	8.2
3. Neither	8.2	13.2	3.1	7.8	6.0	9.2	7.6	7.6	8.9	7.8	8.3	8.5	8.8	6.2	7.5	8.1
4. Mostly agree	24.0	29.6	18.8	24.6	20.4	22.4	26.4	21.9	25.9	23.3	24.4	25.2	23.1	22.7	23.8	31.5
5. Agree	57.4	39.7	74.4	57.9	61.4	56.3	58.9	57.7	55.4	58.6	57.0	57.0	56.7	59.0	58.6	45.9
Item 12160 Subject D05 N	3263	1512	1643	2445	453	673	911	1099	580	1814	1275	1220	654	478	794	44

QUESTIONNAIRE FORM 5 1984	TOTAL	SEX		RACE		REGION				4YR COLLEGE PLANS		ILLICIT DRUG USE: LIFETIME				
		M	F	White	Black	NE	NC	S	W	Yes	No	None	Mari-juana Only	Few Pills	More Pills	Any Her-oin
N (Weighted No. of Cases):	3294	1522	1656	2462	457	682	918	1107	587	1824	1282	1228	662	480	801	44
% of Weighted Total:	100.0	46.2	50.3	74.7	13.9	20.7	27.9	33.6	17.8	55.4	38.9	37.3	20.1	14.6	24.3	1.3

A18L: Being a mother and raising children is one of the most fulfilling experiences a woman can have

1. Disagree	6.0	4.4	7.3	5.6	5.9	7.8	4.8	5.1	7.1	6.1	5.5	4.0	5.8	6.5	8.6	6.3
2. Mostly disagree	5.7	4.8	6.3	5.6	5.9	7.0	6.1	4.6	5.5	5.9	5.4	5.0	5.1	6.0	7.2	4.9
3. Neither	27.7	43.3	14.0	30.5	17.9	28.1	27.0	26.0	31.6	29.7	26.0	26.4	30.0	23.6	30.3	34.9
4. Mostly agree	26.3	22.6	29.7	26.9	23.9	27.9	30.2	23.4	23.6	26.8	25.8	27.1	26.1	28.9	24.3	19.2
5. Agree	34.3	24.8	42.7	31.5	46.3	29.2	31.8	40.8	32.2	31.5	37.3	37.6	33.1	35.0	29.6	34.6
Item 12170 Subject D05 N	3227	1484	1640	2417	451	668	907	1081	570	1798	1260	1204	652	475	785	44

A18M: Most fathers should spend more time with their children than they do now

1. Disagree	1.5	1.5	1.1	1.2	1.3	1.9	1.5	1.2	1.7	1.3	1.6	1.2	1.1	1.2	2.4	5.1
2. Mostly disagree	3.1	3.9	2.1	3.0	2.6	4.9	2.4	2.5	3.1	2.3	3.7	2.1	4.5	1.8	3.7	6.6
3. Neither	15.0	17.1	12.9	15.6	11.0	19.4	12.9	13.0	17.0	16.1	13.7	13.5	15.5	15.3	15.6	23.7
4. Mostly agree	34.2	36.0	32.8	36.5	24.7	34.6	38.1	30.1	35.5	34.7	34.9	34.6	33.7	36.0	35.0	25.8
5. Agree	46.2	41.4	51.1	43.6	60.3	39.3	45.2	53.3	42.6	45.5	46.2	48.6	45.2	45.8	43.3	38.8
Item 12180 Subject D05 N	3258	1506	1646	2445	453	672	911	1098	577	1806	1278	1215	659	478	792	44

A18N: The husband should make all the important decisions in the family

1. Disagree	43.2	25.6	59.2	43.0	47.1	45.4	45.1	40.9	41.8	46.1	39.6	43.9	42.8	44.3	43.2	37.3
2. Mostly disagree	20.5	21.2	19.8	21.1	20.4	20.0	20.9	20.6	20.6	21.2	19.8	18.8	20.8	23.6	21.4	20.2
3. Neither	16.5	24.1	9.8	17.0	12.6	18.8	17.6	13.7	17.3	14.8	18.6	16.8	16.1	14.5	18.0	12.5
4. Mostly agree	11.9	16.5	7.8	11.7	10.8	9.4	10.7	14.0	12.6	11.6	12.3	13.1	10.5	10.6	10.7	16.1
5. Agree	8.0	12.6	3.4	7.1	9.0	6.4	5.8	10.8	7.7	6.3	9.7	7.5	9.8	7.0	6.7	13.9
Item 12190 Subject D05 N	3260	1506	1647	2447	453	672	911	1097	580	1810	1278	1214	659	478	795	43

A19: Some people think about what's going on in government very often, and others are not that interested. How much of an interest do you take in government and current events?

1. No interest at all	4.7	4.4	4.9	4.0	5.5	7.1	3.6	4.8	3.7	2.8	7.2	4.1	4.0	3.9	5.3	20.6
2. Very little interest	16.3	11.8	20.4	16.6	13.3	20.2	16.8	13.3	16.8	13.3	20.0	16.4	15.1	12.4	19.6	17.0
3. Some interest	49.2	46.1	52.3	49.0	51.2	47.2	50.7	49.0	49.6	47.2	52.8	48.2	50.4	49.9	49.6	35.2
4. A lot of interest	21.4	26.3	16.8	22.0	20.0	19.5	21.7	21.9	22.0	25.8	15.3	21.8	22.6	23.7	18.7	19.3
5. A very great interest	8.4	11.4	5.6	8.3	10.1	6.0	7.2	11.1	7.9	11.0	4.6	9.5	7.9	10.0	6.7	7.9
Item 6330 Subject H01,Q08 N	3259	1502	1649	2444	451	673	914	1096	576	1810	1275	1215	658	478	793	42

A20: If you have at least an average income in the future, how likely is it that you will contribute money to the following organizations? If you have already contributed, mark the last circle only. Are you likely to contribute to...

A20A: The United Fund or other community charities?

1. Definitely not	5.0	6.9	3.0	4.3	6.0	5.6	4.3	4.5	6.5	3.4	6.9	4.0	4.7	2.9	6.3	17.1
2. Probably not	16.0	19.5	13.1	17.6	9.5	18.8	16.8	13.3	16.6	14.0	18.6	14.2	15.0	17.4	18.7	25.0
3. Don't know	45.7	47.2	44.3	46.7	41.9	45.0	44.3	46.1	48.0	46.3	44.7	45.4	48.4	45.8	45.0	34.2
4. Probably will	24.0	18.1	29.7	22.8	30.4	22.8	26.1	24.2	21.7	26.6	21.1	26.2	25.5	24.5	19.5	14.2
5. Definitely will	2.8	2.3	2.9	2.1	5.1	1.7	2.7	3.6	2.4	3.2	2.1	4.0	1.9	1.7	2.3	-
6. Already have	6.5	6.0	7.0	6.4	7.0	6.1	5.8	8.2	4.9	6.5	6.6	6.1	4.5	7.8	8.2	9.5
Item 12200 Subject O02 N	3249	1499	1643	2438	447	672	906	1092	578	1806	1273	1214	655	476	792	42

A20B: International relief organizations (CARE, UNICEF, etc.)?

1. Definitely not	4.6	6.8	2.0	4.4	4.9	4.9	4.7	4.3	4.9	3.5	6.2	4.5	4.1	3.0	5.2	20.2
2. Probably not	15.5	19.2	12.3	17.4	7.2	14.3	18.3	13.2	16.9	13.7	17.4	15.3	14.7	14.2	16.9	19.9
3. Don't know	31.7	36.7	27.1	33.4	24.3	25.7	30.6	34.4	35.4	29.1	35.5	31.6	33.7	28.8	33.0	20.5
4. Probably will	33.4	26.9	39.5	31.2	43.1	34.7	33.6	32.7	32.7	35.6	30.8	32.9	33.2	37.9	31.3	22.5
5. Definitely will	7.2	4.7	9.6	5.4	16.2	7.4	5.5	9.5	5.5	8.5	5.2	8.7	6.4	6.7	6.4	5.7
6. Already have	7.6	5.7	9.5	8.3	4.3	13.1	7.3	6.0	4.6	9.5	4.9	7.0	7.9	9.3	7.3	11.0
Item 12210 Subject O02 N	3242	1500	1635	2433	448	673	908	1090	571	1801	1270	1210	653	477	793	40

QUESTIONNAIRE FORM 5 1984	TOTAL	SEX		RACE		REGION				4YR COLLEGE PLANS		ILLICIT DRUG USE: LIFETIME				
		M	F	White	Black	NE	NC	S	W	Yes	No	None	Marijuana Only	Few Pills	More Pills	Any Heroin
N (Weighted No. of Cases):	3294	1522	1656	2462	457	682	918	1107	587	1824	1282	1228	662	480	801	44
% of Weighted Total:	100.0	46.2	50.3	74.7	13.9	20.7	27.9	33.6	17.8	55.4	38.9	37.3	20.1	14.6	24.3	1.3

A20C: Minority group organizations (NAACP, SCLC, etc.)?

	TOTAL	M	F	White	Black	NE	NC	S	W	Yes	No	None	Marijuana Only	Few Pills	More Pills	Any Heroin
1. Definitely not	10.7	14.6	6.6	11.9	4.3	10.9	10.5	11.9	8.2	9.7	11.9	10.5	8.1	8.9	13.1	34.2
2. Probably not	26.9	28.6	26.3	32.1	6.5	26.2	29.8	25.7	25.6	27.6	27.1	26.1	26.0	27.1	30.5	17.7
3. Don't know	39.5	37.0	41.9	43.8	18.7	39.7	41.7	35.3	43.7	37.1	43.1	38.8	39.6	41.5	41.2	22.7
4. Probably will	15.3	13.1	17.3	10.0	35.5	16.2	12.2	16.9	16.1	16.7	12.8	17.0	18.3	13.6	10.7	18.5
5. Definitely will	6.0	5.0	6.5	1.6	29.0	5.3	4.6	8.2	4.9	7.3	3.7	6.3	5.9	6.9	3.7	6.8
6. Already have	1.6	1.7	1.5	0.6	6.0	1.7	1.1	2.0	1.5	1.6	1.4	1.3	2.1	1.9	0.8	-
Item 12220 Subject N02,O02 N	3239	1495	1637	2433	446	669	907	1089	574	1803	1267	1207	655	476	790	42

A20D: Church or religious organizations?

	TOTAL	M	F	White	Black	NE	NC	S	W	Yes	No	None	Marijuana Only	Few Pills	More Pills	Any Heroin
1. Definitely not	4.9	6.6	3.2	5.1	2.6	5.1	3.9	3.9	8.3	4.6	5.5	3.6	4.9	4.3	6.2	18.5
2. Probably not	9.7	10.9	9.0	10.5	4.1	11.1	9.1	7.4	13.4	9.1	10.9	8.2	8.9	7.6	13.7	10.7
3. Don't know	12.8	15.1	10.7	12.8	10.7	16.0	9.0	11.9	16.9	11.0	14.8	10.0	15.2	9.3	16.7	7.9
4. Probably will	24.8	25.6	23.9	25.1	23.2	27.5	27.2	23.5	20.0	22.7	27.5	23.4	22.1	28.3	26.8	26.4
5. Definitely will	16.6	14.3	18.4	14.2	30.4	12.2	16.2	21.4	13.4	18.1	14.3	19.4	20.1	15.4	10.9	7.4
6. Already have	31.1	27.5	34.8	32.3	29.0	28.0	34.6	31.9	28.0	34.5	27.1	35.4	28.8	35.0	25.7	29.1
Item 12230 Subject G,O02 N	3242	1501	1636	2431	449	670	906	1093	573	1802	1270	1212	653	475	794	42

A20E: Political parties or organizations?

	TOTAL	M	F	White	Black	NE	NC	S	W	Yes	No	None	Marijuana Only	Few Pills	More Pills	Any Heroin
1. Definitely not	17.9	19.3	16.1	17.4	18.6	20.9	19.0	16.3	15.8	15.1	21.9	16.0	16.4	15.8	21.4	44.4
2. Probably not	27.7	24.5	31.2	29.8	20.6	28.2	28.7	27.2	26.5	27.0	29.0	28.6	26.5	28.1	27.5	19.4
3. Don't know	33.9	33.5	34.3	32.5	40.0	31.6	32.9	34.6	36.8	34.1	32.7	34.8	36.9	33.6	31.6	22.8
4. Probably will	14.6	15.8	13.3	14.5	14.4	13.9	13.9	15.1	15.6	16.8	12.1	14.4	15.7	15.8	13.5	5.1
5. Definitely will	3.1	3.6	2.8	2.9	4.6	2.4	2.3	4.1	3.6	3.6	2.5	4.0	2.7	2.4	2.3	6.6
6. Already have	2.8	3.3	2.3	2.9	1.8	3.0	3.2	2.8	1.8	3.5	1.7	2.1	1.8	4.3	3.6	1.6
Item 12240 Subject H05,O02 N	3241	1498	1637	2435	444	667	907	1092	575	1801	1270	1208	654	476	792	42

A20F: Citizen lobbies (Common Cause, Public Citizen, etc.)?

	TOTAL	M	F	White	Black	NE	NC	S	W	Yes	No	None	Marijuana Only	Few Pills	More Pills	Any Heroin
1. Definitely not	9.9	10.8	8.4	9.2	10.4	10.1	9.8	9.5	10.4	8.0	11.6	8.3	9.6	8.6	11.2	34.3
2. Probably not	25.2	24.9	26.2	27.8	17.1	28.4	28.2	20.5	25.7	26.2	24.6	23.9	23.5	29.3	27.0	12.4
3. Don't know	47.0	45.9	48.2	47.9	45.0	45.7	47.2	49.2	43.9	48.6	45.6	50.1	50.2	45.6	42.2	39.3
4. Probably will	14.0	14.5	13.2	12.1	19.3	12.7	11.0	15.5	17.3	13.9	13.3	13.5	13.4	13.2	15.7	8.7
5. Definitely will	2.8	2.6	3.0	2.0	6.3	1.6	3.0	3.8	1.8	2.2	3.6	3.3	2.7	1.8	2.2	4.3
6. Already have	1.2	1.3	1.1	1.0	2.0	1.5	0.9	1.5	0.8	1.1	1.2	1.0	0.6	1.5	1.6	1.0
Item 12250 Subject H05,I02,O02 N	3236	1493	1636	2432	444	670	904	1087	575	1797	1269	1206	652	477	791	42

A20G: Charities to help fight diseases (Cancer, Heart Disease, etc.)?

	TOTAL	M	F	White	Black	NE	NC	S	W	Yes	No	None	Marijuana Only	Few Pills	More Pills	Any Heroin
1. Definitely not	2.0	2.6	1.0	1.4	2.5	2.3	1.6	2.1	2.2	1.2	2.9	1.5	2.6	1.4	1.7	12.3
2. Probably not	3.7	5.5	1.9	4.2	2.0	3.3	3.7	3.0	5.4	2.8	4.7	4.0	2.5	3.3	3.8	8.4
3. Don't know	13.8	18.6	9.2	14.5	8.5	13.4	13.4	12.8	16.8	12.2	15.2	13.5	15.0	9.6	15.0	14.8
4. Probably will	37.1	38.7	35.8	37.4	35.5	36.2	39.0	35.7	37.6	37.9	36.9	36.4	38.4	37.8	37.3	27.8
5. Definitely will	27.7	21.2	33.6	25.8	38.1	28.6	26.5	29.3	25.5	28.3	26.4	28.9	28.1	29.0	25.2	27.6
6. Already have	15.7	13.3	18.5	16.7	13.5	16.3	15.9	17.0	12.5	17.6	13.9	15.6	13.5	18.9	17.0	9.0
Item 12260 Subject O02 N	3245	1500	1637	2433	450	673	907	1089	576	1804	1271	1210	657	474	792	42

A20H: Organizations concerned with population problems (Planned Parenthood, ZPG, etc.)?

	TOTAL	M	F	White	Black	NE	NC	S	W	Yes	No	None	Marijuana Only	Few Pills	More Pills	Any Heroin
1. Definitely not	9.0	11.0	6.5	8.6	9.1	10.5	9.7	8.7	6.7	8.5	9.3	8.4	8.2	7.1	10.0	26.2
2. Probably not	23.0	26.7	19.8	25.5	13.8	21.1	25.4	22.4	22.3	23.6	22.4	25.0	19.8	22.7	23.3	13.0
3. Don't know	41.5	43.4	40.1	42.6	38.3	41.0	41.7	42.1	40.7	42.0	40.8	42.7	44.4	41.7	39.1	27.3
4. Probably will	18.0	13.1	22.8	15.9	24.8	18.8	16.4	18.5	18.8	17.9	18.1	16.7	20.4	19.5	17.5	19.4
5. Definitely will	7.0	4.4	9.1	6.0	11.7	6.9	6.1	6.6	9.4	6.6	7.4	6.1	6.3	6.5	8.9	9.2
6. Already have	1.5	1.3	1.7	1.3	2.3	1.7	0.8	1.7	2.0	1.3	2.0	1.1	1.0	2.5	1.3	4.8
Item 12270 Subject E01,O02 N	3248	1501	1640	2441	449	672	908	1092	577	1805	1275	1212	657	477	791	42

QUESTIONNAIRE FORM 5 1984	TOTAL	SEX		RACE		REGION				4YR COLLEGE PLANS		ILLICIT DRUG USE: LIFETIME				
		M	F	White	Black	NE	NC	S	W	Yes	No	None	Mari- juana Only	Few Pills	More Pills	Any Her- oin
N (Weighted No. of Cases):	3294	1522	1656	2462	457	682	918	1107	587	1824	1282	1228	662	480	801	44
% of Weighted Total:	100.0	46.2	50.3	74.7	13.9	20.7	27.9	33.6	17.8	55.4	38.9	37.3	20.1	14.6	24.3	1.3

A20I: Organizations concerned with environmental problems (Sierra Club, Friends of Earth, etc.)?

1. Definitely not	9.2	9.6	8.6	8.1	12.8	9.1	10.6	8.9	7.8	7.4	11.4	8.0	10.2	7.9	9.4	24.8
2. Probably not	23.2	21.1	25.8	24.7	18.0	21.7	24.5	24.0	21.5	24.2	22.4	23.3	20.1	24.4	25.0	25.2
3. Don't know	40.4	37.3	43.2	40.7	40.4	37.9	40.7	42.1	39.7	39.1	41.2	41.4	41.7	39.5	39.5	23.1
4. Probably will	18.0	20.7	15.5	17.6	19.2	21.3	17.9	15.6	18.8	18.6	17.6	18.1	18.4	20.1	16.3	17.5
5. Definitely will	7.2	8.8	5.6	7.0	6.9	8.3	5.4	7.0	8.9	8.2	6.0	7.2	7.7	6.8	7.3	7.6
6. Already have	2.0	2.5	1.4	1.8	2.8	1.6	0.8	2.4	3.2	2.5	1.4	1.9	1.9	1.3	2.5	1.8
Item 12280　Subject F04,O02　N	3250	1501	1643	2442	448	673	908	1093	577	1808	1274	1214	656	477	793	42

Now we have a different kind of question.

A21: How satisfied are you with your life as a whole these days?

1. Completely dissatisfied	1.6	1.2	1.6	1.5	1.5	1.7	1.7	1.5	1.3	1.6	1.6	1.9	0.6	1.1	2.1	6.3
2. Quite dissatisfied	5.5	4.7	6.1	5.8	4.1	5.5	5.2	4.8	7.3	6.1	4.9	5.3	5.8	5.7	4.9	12.8
3. Somewhat dissatisfied	8.4	7.4	9.2	8.1	9.6	10.1	7.8	8.3	7.4	8.1	8.9	7.5	8.2	9.3	8.3	13.4
4. Neither, or mixed feelings	14.3	14.7	13.6	13.2	14.8	15.0	16.6	12.1	13.9	12.6	15.9	11.9	14.9	16.9	15.9	20.8
5. Somewhat satisfied	26.6	28.9	24.8	26.2	29.2	26.0	28.5	25.9	25.6	25.0	28.3	25.4	26.7	24.9	29.5	17.6
6. Quite satisfied	36.5	36.5	37.3	38.8	30.2	35.8	33.5	38.6	38.1	39.5	32.7	39.2	35.3	35.8	35.3	17.9
7. Completely satisfied	7.2	6.6	7.4	6.4	10.6	5.9	6.6	8.8	6.5	7.1	7.7	8.8	8.6	6.3	4.0	11.2
Item 6840　Subject P01,Q01　N	3265	1513	1647	2452	452	673	911	1097	584	1814	1276	1221	659	478	799	44

A22: These questions are about whether you think women are discriminated against in each of the following areas. To what extent are women discriminated against...

A22A: In getting a college education?

1. Not at all	44.9	50.7	39.7	45.2	43.4	48.5	41.9	46.8	41.8	43.7	46.0	41.9	46.2	43.8	49.2	47.5
2. Very little	31.2	28.3	34.4	34.3	22.5	29.1	36.4	27.7	32.1	34.2	28.5	33.3	32.3	31.6	28.5	21.6
3. Some	12.7	8.8	16.1	12.2	12.9	11.6	12.5	12.6	14.3	13.5	11.3	13.3	9.5	14.9	12.6	15.7
4. A good deal	2.1	1.4	2.5	1.5	4.9	1.9	1.4	2.9	1.8	1.7	2.3	1.9	2.6	2.2	1.5	9.7
5. A great deal	1.6	1.4	2.0	0.7	4.8	1.2	1.2	2.0	2.3	0.9	2.6	2.0	1.7	1.2	1.0	-
8. Don't know	7.5	9.5	5.3	6.1	11.4	7.7	6.5	8.1	7.7	5.9	9.3	7.6	7.6	6.2	7.4	5.4
Item 12290　Subject D06　N	3260	1510	1648	2451	450	672	910	1095	583	1814	1275	1218	659	478	799	44

A22B: In gaining positions of leadership over men and women?

1. Not at all	5.4	7.9	2.8	5.2	5.0	6.0	5.9	5.5	3.7	3.9	7.1	5.2	5.2	4.8	6.0	9.6
2. Very little	11.8	14.4	9.3	12.0	9.5	14.0	9.7	12.4	11.4	10.6	13.3	11.7	11.9	10.9	11.8	21.8
3. Some	34.4	37.0	32.2	36.6	26.8	35.6	36.2	31.6	35.6	36.5	32.3	34.7	34.1	36.1	34.1	34.2
4. A good deal	26.9	23.1	30.6	28.2	21.7	24.0	28.7	26.2	28.8	29.5	23.0	26.4	25.3	29.2	27.7	16.7
5. A great deal	15.7	10.1	21.0	13.3	27.6	15.9	14.5	17.2	14.2	15.1	16.5	15.8	18.3	13.6	14.7	11.7
8. Don't know	5.9	7.6	4.1	4.8	9.4	4.7	5.0	7.1	6.3	4.4	7.8	6.2	5.2	5.4	5.6	6.0
Item 12300　Subject D06　N	3262	1513	1647	2451	452	672	912	1094	583	1814	1276	1218	661	478	799	44

A22C: In obtaining executive positions in business?

1. Not at all	7.0	9.2	4.8	6.3	7.2	8.2	7.1	7.5	4.6	5.0	9.5	6.2	6.4	8.1	7.2	19.9
2. Very little	15.5	18.2	13.0	16.6	11.4	15.6	14.5	15.0	17.9	13.8	18.1	13.9	15.9	17.2	17.3	8.2
3. Some	31.2	31.0	31.7	33.9	20.3	31.8	32.4	28.9	32.7	33.2	28.2	32.2	31.2	28.0	31.6	37.4
4. A good deal	25.7	23.5	27.8	25.4	27.5	25.4	26.7	24.0	27.5	28.7	22.4	26.3	24.9	27.6	25.4	16.7
5. A great deal	13.2	8.4	17.4	11.5	22.9	13.2	12.7	15.5	9.9	13.4	12.6	13.6	15.5	12.8	10.0	11.2
8. Don't know	7.4	9.8	5.3	6.3	10.8	5.9	6.7	9.1	7.4	5.9	9.2	7.7	6.1	6.2	8.3	6.6
Item 12310　Subject D06　N	3255	1509	1646	2448	451	670	908	1093	583	1813	1274	1218	659	475	797	44

A22D: In obtaining top jobs in the professions?

1. Not at all	8.9	11.3	6.4	8.5	10.9	10.0	9.0	9.5	6.5	7.2	10.5	7.1	10.7	8.5	10.2	18.4
2. Very little	17.8	20.1	15.3	18.4	13.3	18.5	15.9	16.9	21.5	17.7	18.4	17.1	16.8	18.6	18.9	16.1
3. Some	30.9	30.5	31.8	33.1	20.5	31.3	33.2	28.5	31.6	31.9	30.0	34.5	23.1	32.5	32.0	26.6
4. A good deal	22.4	21.4	23.9	22.9	21.8	21.4	25.1	22.3	19.4	25.3	19.0	20.9	27.3	21.8	22.2	10.5
5. A great deal	13.7	8.3	18.4	11.8	23.5	13.4	11.2	15.8	13.8	13.1	14.0	14.3	15.8	13.7	10.1	20.2
8. Don't know	6.3	8.4	4.2	5.4	10.0	5.4	5.7	7.0	7.0	4.7	8.1	6.1	6.2	5.0	6.6	8.2
Item 12320　Subject D06　N	3257	1509	1646	2448	451	671	908	1095	583	1813	1274	1218	660	475	797	44

QUESTIONNAIRE FORM 5 1984	TOTAL	SEX		RACE		REGION				4YR COLLEGE PLANS		ILLICIT DRUG USE: LIFETIME				
		M	F	White	Black	NE	NC	S	W	Yes	No	None	Mari-juana Only	Few Pills	More Pills	Any Her-oin
N (Weighted No. of Cases):	3294	1522	1656	2462	457	682	918	1107	587	1824	1282	1228	662	480	801	44
% of Weighted Total:	100.0	46.2	50.3	74.7	13.9	20.7	27.9	33.6	17.8	55.4	38.9	37.3	20.1	14.6	24.3	1.3

A22E: In getting skilled labor jobs?

1. Not at all	10.1	11.4	8.7	9.5	11.2	12.0	9.4	10.2	8.5	9.3	11.0	9.8	10.4	9.0	10.8	16.6
2. Very little	19.6	20.8	18.6	20.7	14.8	19.8	19.8	18.2	21.4	18.7	20.8	17.6	19.9	20.0	21.8	15.5
3. Some	32.4	33.1	31.8	33.3	29.7	35.6	33.3	28.5	34.7	33.8	30.8	34.5	32.0	33.3	30.4	26.6
4. A good deal	18.2	17.2	19.3	19.1	18.0	15.5	20.3	19.0	16.5	19.2	17.5	18.3	17.9	17.9	18.6	18.4
5. A great deal	9.2	6.5	11.4	7.6	15.8	8.0	8.4	11.7	7.3	8.9	9.4	8.5	10.0	10.4	8.0	16.4
8. Don't know	10.6	10.9	10.3	9.9	10.6	9.1	8.8	12.5	11.6	10.1	10.5	11.4	9.7	9.4	10.3	6.5
Item 12330 Subject D06 N	3247	1503	1642	2443	449	668	906	1091	582	1810	1267	1215	656	474	795	44

A22F: In getting elected to political office?

1. Not at all	4.9	7.3	2.4	4.5	5.3	5.1	5.1	5.5	2.9	3.8	5.9	4.8	4.6	4.4	4.6	16.3
2. Very little	10.1	13.6	6.8	10.0	9.2	10.9	9.9	9.4	10.7	9.0	11.5	10.5	10.6	10.1	8.9	8.8
3. Some	23.5	27.6	20.1	24.6	19.7	20.2	23.6	23.8	26.5	24.5	22.5	24.3	22.0	22.8	24.8	25.6
4. A good deal	24.9	23.2	26.1	26.9	17.6	25.6	26.9	23.4	23.8	27.0	22.5	25.5	24.1	24.2	25.5	15.7
5. A great deal	30.9	21.2	40.3	29.3	39.2	32.6	29.3	31.7	29.8	31.8	29.8	29.3	32.6	33.9	30.5	24.9
8. Don't know	5.8	7.1	4.3	4.7	9.1	5.5	5.2	6.1	6.3	3.8	7.7	5.7	6.1	4.5	5.7	8.7
Item 12340 Subject D06,H02 N	3259	1509	1648	2448	452	673	909	1096	581	1813	1274	1220	660	476	796	44

A22G: In getting equal pay for equal work?

1. Not at all	12.3	17.2	7.5	11.7	12.8	12.5	10.6	13.9	11.5	10.9	13.8	12.2	13.8	9.6	12.6	15.4
2. Very little	17.3	21.4	13.9	18.9	11.4	17.5	18.4	15.6	18.3	17.6	17.2	17.7	16.8	18.5	16.6	15.6
3. Some	25.9	25.9	26.1	26.9	23.7	25.6	26.0	25.7	26.4	28.7	22.2	25.6	25.0	26.9	26.8	25.9
4. A good deal	19.5	17.8	21.1	19.8	16.9	21.1	19.7	17.7	20.9	21.0	17.9	18.9	21.4	18.4	20.1	12.9
5. A great deal	18.7	9.8	27.0	17.1	27.7	16.1	19.7	21.2	15.7	16.9	21.2	19.6	17.8	20.9	16.7	20.4
8. Don't know	6.3	7.9	4.3	5.8	7.4	7.2	5.7	5.9	7.2	4.9	7.6	6.0	5.2	5.7	7.2	9.9
Item 12350 Subject D06 N	3259	1509	1648	2448	451	672	909	1094	584	1815	1273	1218	660	477	797	44

A23: The next questions ask for your opinions on the effects of using certain drugs and other substances. First, how much do you think people risk harming themselves (physically or in other ways), if they...

A23A: Smoke one or more packs of cigarettes per day

1. No risk	1.7	2.0	1.1	0.8	4.6	1.8	1.1	2.5	1.2	0.8	2.6	2.0	1.6	0.9	1.3	2.2
2. Slight risk	6.1	6.4	5.5	5.6	8.6	6.1	6.5	6.5	4.8	3.8	9.5	4.3	5.3	4.7	9.4	14.8
3. Moderate risk	27.0	27.6	26.4	29.4	15.0	29.1	27.7	26.7	23.9	24.6	30.2	22.7	25.9	27.1	35.6	20.7
4. Great risk	63.8	62.0	66.4	63.5	68.8	61.7	63.8	62.3	68.8	70.0	55.7	68.9	66.6	66.5	53.1	60.2
5. Can't say, drug unfamiliar	1.4	2.1	0.7	0.7	3.0	1.2	0.9	2.0	1.3	0.8	1.9	2.0	0.6	0.9	0.5	2.2
Item 12360 Subject A14a N	3262	1512	1649	2449	452	672	911	1098	581	1815	1274	1222	659	476	797	43

A23B: Try marijuana (pot, grass) once or twice

1. No risk	35.1	39.0	31.2	37.1	25.9	47.6	29.7	30.0	38.8	33.9	36.5	12.6	43.8	39.0	60.0	57.6
2. Slight risk	34.5	32.0	37.2	36.1	33.2	30.6	39.0	33.0	34.6	35.3	33.3	38.1	34.1	39.4	27.0	21.0
3. Moderate risk	12.8	12.2	13.6	12.1	15.4	9.7	15.1	13.8	11.0	14.2	11.4	19.4	9.3	11.2	7.1	10.5
4. Great risk	14.7	13.8	15.2	12.7	20.6	9.8	14.1	19.2	12.7	14.9	14.5	24.7	12.4	8.7	4.9	8.7
5. Can't say, drug unfamiliar	2.9	3.1	2.6	2.0	4.9	2.4	2.1	4.0	2.8	1.7	4.3	5.2	0.4	1.7	1.0	2.1
Item 12370 Subject A14a N	3259	1510	1648	2447	451	671	912	1095	581	1815	1273	1220	660	477	796	44

A23C: Smoke marijuana occasionally

1. No risk	9.2	10.8	7.4	8.9	8.1	14.2	6.9	8.2	9.0	7.0	11.8	2.8	7.2	9.2	19.5	21.0
2. Slight risk	29.0	30.4	27.9	30.6	22.7	34.7	25.5	25.4	34.8	28.7	30.6	14.4	34.6	32.1	44.1	51.9
3. Moderate risk	36.2	34.2	38.3	38.4	32.7	31.3	41.2	35.7	34.8	37.6	33.4	41.0	38.1	39.2	27.1	19.8
4. Great risk	22.6	21.4	23.9	20.1	31.2	17.0	24.2	26.9	18.5	24.7	20.2	36.8	19.2	16.7	8.5	7.3
5. Can't say, drug unfamiliar	2.9	3.2	2.5	2.0	5.4	2.7	2.2	3.7	2.9	1.9	4.2	5.0	1.0	2.7	0.9	-
Item 12380 Subject A14a N	3248	1505	1642	2443	449	667	906	1095	580	1804	1272	1212	659	475	795	44

QUESTIONNAIRE FORM 5 1984	TOTAL	SEX		RACE		REGION				4YR COLLEGE PLANS		ILLICIT DRUG USE: LIFETIME				
		M	F	White	Black	NE	NC	S	W	Yes	No	None	Marijuana Only	Few Pills	More Pills	Any Heroin
N (Weighted No. of Cases):	3294	1522	1656	2462	457	682	918	1107	587	1824	1282	1228	662	480	801	44
% of Weighted Total:	100.0	46.2	50.3	74.7	13.9	20.7	27.9	33.6	17.8	55.4	38.9	37.3	20.1	14.6	24.3	1.3
A23D: Smoke marijuana regularly																
1. No risk	3.1	3.6	2.1	1.9	5.4	4.2	2.4	3.2	2.4	1.6	4.6	2.3	2.4	2.2	4.6	6.4
2. Slight risk	7.5	9.6	5.4	7.8	6.3	9.1	6.4	7.3	7.8	5.4	10.8	1.7	5.3	6.6	17.9	17.7
3. Moderate risk	19.7	21.8	17.8	20.7	16.2	26.0	18.4	16.0	21.3	19.1	20.3	8.1	22.1	23.7	32.4	36.9
4. Great risk	66.9	61.8	72.2	67.7	66.5	58.2	70.6	69.7	65.7	72.1	60.3	83.0	69.2	65.4	44.2	36.8
5. Can't say, drug unfamiliar	2.8	3.1	2.5	1.9	5.6	2.5	2.1	3.7	2.7	1.8	4.0	4.8	1.0	2.2	0.8	2.1
Item 12390 Subject A14a N	3252	1509	1643	2444	451	666	912	1095	579	1812	1269	1218	656	476	796	44
A23E: Try LSD once or twice																
1. No risk	4.2	4.7	3.4	3.5	4.7	5.5	4.6	3.4	3.7	3.6	4.5	2.2	4.4	2.2	7.3	20.1
2. Slight risk	16.0	16.2	15.8	17.2	10.3	17.3	18.4	13.8	15.2	16.3	16.4	10.8	14.2	17.8	23.9	35.6
3. Moderate risk	24.0	23.9	24.7	25.8	16.2	25.8	23.3	22.3	26.1	25.8	22.1	24.3	21.1	28.8	24.4	11.9
4. Great risk	45.4	44.4	46.2	44.9	51.8	40.7	44.6	48.4	46.6	46.2	44.2	52.0	48.7	39.8	36.9	32.4
5. Can't say, drug unfamiliar	10.3	10.9	9.8	8.5	16.9	10.7	9.2	12.1	8.3	8.0	12.9	10.8	11.6	11.3	7.5	-
Item 12400 Subject A14a N	3260	1513	1648	2450	452	671	913	1096	580	1817	1274	1221	660	476	797	44
A23F: Take LSD regularly																
1. No risk	1.8	1.9	1.4	0.4	5.5	1.6	1.1	2.9	1.0	0.8	2.8	2.2	1.7	1.3	1.3	3.6
2. Slight risk	0.8	1.0	0.5	0.6	1.1	1.5	0.7	0.9	0.4	0.5	1.3	0.4	0.1	1.2	1.1	7.5
3. Moderate risk	4.1	4.8	3.4	4.1	3.1	5.8	4.5	2.9	3.7	4.0	4.3	2.7	2.0	3.2	7.1	22.9
4. Great risk	83.8	82.2	85.7	87.2	74.4	80.9	85.5	82.2	87.4	87.2	80.0	84.7	85.3	83.3	83.9	66.0
5. Can't say, drug unfamiliar	9.5	10.1	9.0	7.7	15.9	10.2	8.3	11.2	7.5	7.4	11.7	10.0	10.9	10.9	6.5	-
Item 12410 Subject A14a N	3251	1511	1641	2447	447	667	910	1094	580	1811	1272	1214	658	477	797	44
A23G: Try heroin (smack, horse) once or twice																
1. No risk	3.0	3.0	2.4	1.8	5.0	4.6	2.9	2.8	1.5	2.2	3.8	2.2	2.8	2.9	3.4	19.7
2. Slight risk	12.9	11.5	14.4	13.6	10.6	15.3	13.4	11.3	12.1	13.0	12.5	11.4	10.8	13.9	16.1	20.4
3. Moderate risk	23.3	22.0	24.9	25.3	17.1	20.9	24.3	23.9	23.4	25.1	21.9	24.1	22.2	25.6	21.6	30.2
4. Great risk	49.8	52.4	47.2	49.7	49.6	48.0	48.1	50.1	53.8	51.1	48.1	51.4	52.2	45.0	49.9	29.7
5. Can't say, drug unfamiliar	11.1	11.0	11.0	9.6	17.7	11.2	11.3	11.8	9.1	8.7	13.8	10.9	12.1	12.5	8.9	-
Item 12420 Subject A14a N	3253	1511	1643	2444	451	665	913	1095	581	1813	1270	1219	659	477	795	42
A23H: Take heroin occasionally																
1. No risk	1.8	2.0	1.4	0.6	5.0	1.7	1.3	3.0	0.6	1.0	2.8	1.9	1.7	1.4	1.4	12.3
2. Slight risk	1.3	1.0	1.7	1.0	1.8	2.1	0.9	1.3	1.1	1.1	1.8	1.1	0.6	1.4	1.4	7.1
3. Moderate risk	16.0	14.0	17.9	17.0	12.8	18.5	16.9	14.5	14.5	16.4	15.7	14.9	14.0	17.4	18.2	30.2
4. Great risk	70.7	73.2	68.7	72.8	64.4	67.3	70.4	70.1	76.4	73.5	67.3	72.1	72.9	68.1	70.9	50.4
5. Can't say, drug unfamiliar	10.1	9.8	10.3	8.7	16.0	10.5	10.5	11.0	7.3	8.1	12.4	10.1	10.8	11.6	8.0	-
Item 12430 Subject A14a N	3256	1513	1645	2448	451	669	913	1095	579	1816	1272	1217	660	477	796	44
A23I: Take heroin regularly																
1. No risk	1.8	2.0	1.3	0.5	4.6	1.5	1.4	2.8	1.0	0.8	2.9	2.0	1.5	1.2	1.6	8.4
2. Slight risk	0.4	0.5	0.3	0.3	1.1	0.7	0.1	0.6	0.2	0.3	0.6	0.3	0.2	0.6	0.1	5.2
3. Moderate risk	1.0	1.1	0.8	0.7	1.7	1.9	0.6	0.9	0.7	0.7	1.2	0.7	0.8	1.5	1.0	2.4
4. Great risk	87.2	86.8	88.1	90.2	77.4	85.8	88.1	85.4	90.8	90.6	83.4	87.5	86.9	85.9	89.6	84.0
5. Can't say, drug unfamiliar	9.6	9.6	9.5	8.4	15.1	10.0	9.7	10.4	7.3	7.6	11.9	9.5	10.6	10.8	7.6	-
Item 12440 Subject A14a N	3248	1511	1639	2444	448	668	910	1091	580	1811	1269	1217	657	476	794	44
A23J: Try barbiturates (downers, goofballs, reds, yellows, etc.) once or twice																
1. No risk	9.9	10.6	9.0	10.2	4.8	12.9	8.9	9.5	8.8	9.0	10.8	3.7	6.2	9.5	21.8	36.1
2. Slight risk	25.0	24.0	25.9	28.0	14.3	28.1	26.1	22.3	24.7	24.5	26.1	18.8	20.6	29.0	35.4	29.7
3. Moderate risk	27.0	26.9	27.6	28.3	23.5	26.7	26.7	25.7	30.5	29.8	23.7	29.7	27.4	30.5	22.7	13.0
4. Great risk	27.4	27.0	27.5	25.6	35.9	22.3	27.2	30.6	27.4	28.0	26.6	35.5	32.6	20.3	14.7	21.2
5. Can't say, drug unfamiliar	10.7	11.5	10.0	7.9	21.6	10.0	11.0	11.9	8.6	8.7	12.7	12.3	13.2	10.7	5.5	-
Item 12450 Subject A14a N	3252	1510	1646	2449	453	667	913	1093	579	1813	1273	1217	659	476	797	44

QUESTIONNAIRE FORM 5 1984	TOTAL	SEX		RACE		REGION				4YR COLLEGE PLANS		ILLICIT DRUG USE: LIFETIME				
		M	F	White	Black	NE	NC	S	W	Yes	No	None	Marijuana Only	Few Pills	More Pills	Any Heroin
N (Weighted No. of Cases):	3294	1522	1656	2462	457	682	918	1107	587	1824	1282	1228	662	480	801	44
% of Weighted Total:	100.0	46.2	50.3	74.7	13.9	20.7	27.9	33.6	17.8	55.4	38.9	37.3	20.1	14.6	24.3	1.3

A23K: Take barbiturates regularly

1. No risk	1.9	2.1	1.4	0.9	3.9	1.7	1.3	3.0	0.6	1.1	2.8	1.6	1.3	0.9	2.6	10.3
2. Slight risk	4.1	4.9	3.5	4.4	1.5	5.7	4.3	3.2	3.8	2.9	5.8	1.5	2.2	3.0	9.4	21.1
3. Moderate risk	15.2	15.7	14.4	17.0	9.9	17.8	14.6	14.4	15.0	13.8	17.2	8.8	12.8	16.6	26.0	28.3
4. Great risk	68.5	66.5	70.9	70.4	63.7	64.8	69.7	68.0	71.8	73.6	62.2	76.3	71.2	69.3	56.5	40.3
5. Can't say, drug unfamiliar	10.3	10.9	9.8	7.4	20.9	10.0	10.1	11.3	8.8	8.6	12.0	11.8	12.5	10.1	5.5	-
Item 12460 Subject A14a N	3236	1501	1640	2437	450	660	911	1090	575	1805	1265	1214	654	474	792	43

A23L: Try amphetamines (uppers, pep pills, bennies, speed) once or twice

1. No risk	14.2	15.3	13.3	15.1	6.4	17.0	13.1	14.0	13.2	12.7	15.9	4.4	8.7	15.2	32.4	40.4
2. Slight risk	26.3	24.8	27.8	29.4	14.7	27.7	28.2	23.3	27.2	26.3	26.8	20.6	21.7	30.6	36.8	26.1
3. Moderate risk	27.0	28.2	26.2	27.3	27.5	28.2	26.3	25.8	28.8	29.9	23.5	31.5	29.1	28.8	18.3	16.4
4. Great risk	25.4	24.7	25.7	23.1	37.6	20.0	25.0	29.5	24.7	25.6	25.1	34.7	31.0	19.0	10.5	15.0
5. Can't say, drug unfamiliar	7.1	7.0	7.0	5.1	13.9	7.1	7.4	7.4	6.1	5.6	8.6	8.8	9.6	6.3	2.0	2.1
Item 12470 Subject A14a N	3249	1508	1646	2448	449	667	911	1093	578	1813	1272	1218	658	476	795	44

A23M: Take amphetamines regularly

1. No risk	2.6	3.1	2.0	1.7	4.6	2.0	2.5	4.0	0.8	1.7	3.9	1.7	1.3	1.9	4.8	9.8
2. Slight risk	5.4	6.2	4.6	5.9	2.0	7.6	5.9	4.1	4.7	3.9	7.5	1.5	3.0	5.4	12.6	16.3
3. Moderate risk	17.3	18.4	16.2	19.4	10.0	21.8	16.5	15.4	16.9	16.4	18.8	9.8	14.3	18.7	30.4	28.8
4. Great risk	67.1	64.8	69.7	67.5	69.1	61.0	67.0	68.7	71.1	72.0	60.5	77.4	71.2	67.3	49.7	42.9
5. Can't say, drug unfamiliar	7.7	7.4	7.5	5.4	14.3	7.6	8.1	7.8	6.5	6.0	9.4	9.6	10.3	6.7	2.5	2.2
Item 12480 Subject A14a N	3239	1503	1641	2439	447	661	910	1092	576	1807	1270	1215	653	476	795	43

A23N: Try cocaine once or twice

1. No risk	11.8	13.3	10.2	11.9	8.0	18.7	8.9	9.5	12.7	10.4	13.7	3.0	6.7	11.1	28.5	43.6
2. Slight risk	21.4	23.1	20.1	22.2	17.8	28.0	19.1	16.6	26.3	21.8	20.8	14.1	21.1	25.8	30.3	23.7
3. Moderate risk	25.1	22.0	28.1	26.4	22.2	22.8	26.4	25.5	25.2	26.7	23.9	29.5	25.9	27.9	17.4	13.9
4. Great risk	35.7	34.9	36.3	34.4	42.5	25.1	39.6	41.5	30.7	36.3	34.7	46.2	39.4	29.4	21.0	17.9
5. Can't say, drug unfamiliar	6.0	6.7	5.3	5.1	9.5	5.4	6.0	6.8	5.0	4.7	6.9	7.2	6.8	5.8	2.7	1.0
Item 12490 Subject A14a N	3243	1504	1644	2443	447	667	906	1092	578	1810	1269	1217	655	477	793	44

A23O: Take cocaine regularly

1. No risk	2.3	2.6	1.7	1.1	4.6	2.9	1.6	2.8	1.6	1.3	3.5	1.8	1.8	1.4	2.8	16.8
2. Slight risk	3.5	4.7	2.4	3.8	1.9	6.6	2.6	2.7	3.0	2.5	5.1	0.6	1.3	2.5	9.7	12.0
3. Moderate risk	9.8	11.9	7.9	10.1	8.2	16.6	6.7	6.5	13.2	9.1	11.1	4.3	7.1	10.3	19.8	22.9
4. Great risk	78.8	74.4	83.2	80.3	76.5	68.1	83.9	81.7	77.8	82.5	74.1	86.8	83.4	80.0	64.8	47.3
5. Can't say, drug unfamiliar	5.5	6.4	4.8	4.7	8.8	5.8	5.2	6.2	4.4	4.6	6.2	6.4	6.3	5.9	2.8	1.0
Item 12500 Subject A14a N	3231	1506	1630	2438	445	665	907	1083	576	1795	1273	1203	656	474	796	44

A23P: Try one or two drinks of an alcoholic beverage (beer, wine, liquor)

1. No risk	51.9	56.2	48.5	55.7	34.1	63.5	51.1	44.7	53.1	52.3	51.5	36.2	56.0	55.5	70.7	71.2
2. Slight risk	33.9	30.7	36.8	33.6	38.2	27.5	38.5	34.8	32.7	34.0	34.1	42.3	31.7	35.0	22.8	19.8
3. Moderate risk	8.6	6.7	10.3	7.2	14.0	4.5	7.3	12.7	7.7	8.3	8.9	13.0	7.7	6.3	4.4	-
4. Great risk	4.6	5.2	3.8	3.1	10.4	3.2	2.5	6.3	6.2	4.8	4.2	6.7	4.1	2.8	2.0	9.0
5. Can't say, drug unfamiliar	1.0	1.3	0.7	0.4	3.3	1.4	0.6	1.5	0.3	0.5	1.3	1.8	0.5	0.3	0.1	-
Item 12510 Subject A14a N	3251	1509	1647	2447	450	669	909	1095	578	1815	1271	1219	658	477	795	44

A23Q: Take one or two drinks nearly every day

1. No risk	8.7	11.8	5.4	8.1	8.3	12.3	6.7	9.4	6.1	6.7	11.0	4.8	7.4	7.2	15.0	22.5
2. Slight risk	26.2	29.0	23.7	27.7	21.3	28.0	27.3	24.7	25.5	23.2	30.2	20.2	26.6	33.2	30.7	36.3
3. Moderate risk	40.9	38.7	43.5	42.3	37.1	40.2	42.8	40.8	39.1	44.3	36.6	43.6	44.3	39.2	37.0	31.0
4. Great risk	23.0	19.0	26.6	21.5	30.1	18.2	22.2	23.6	28.7	25.3	20.5	29.3	21.3	20.0	17.2	9.3
5. Can't say, drug unfamiliar	1.2	1.5	0.7	0.5	3.2	1.3	1.1	1.5	0.6	0.6	1.7	2.1	0.4	0.3	0.1	1.0
Item 12520 Subject A14a N	3250	1510	1645	2447	450	668	910	1095	577	1812	1273	1218	659	477	795	44

QUESTIONNAIRE FORM 5 1984	TOTAL	SEX		RACE		REGION				4YR COLLEGE PLANS		ILLICIT DRUG USE: LIFETIME				
		M	F	White	Black	NE	NC	S	W	Yes	No	None	Mari-juana Only	Few Pills	More Pills	Any Her-oin
N (Weighted No. of Cases):	3294	1522	1656	2462	457	682	918	1107	587	1824	1282	1228	662	480	801	44
% of Weighted Total:	100.0	46.2	50.3	74.7	13.9	20.7	27.9	33.6	17.8	55.4	38.9	37.3	20.1	14.6	24.3	1.3
A23R: Take four or five drinks nearly every day																
1. No risk	3.2	4.1	2.1	2.1	5.3	3.6	2.5	4.4	1.5	1.8	4.6	2.4	2.8	2.7	4.0	9.4
2. Slight risk	5.7	8.3	3.2	6.2	3.6	6.5	6.5	5.5	4.3	4.2	7.9	3.5	4.6	6.1	9.7	6.6
3. Moderate risk	21.5	24.6	18.6	22.6	15.9	24.4	20.5	21.5	19.8	19.2	24.3	17.6	22.9	22.5	25.1	47.3
4. Great risk	68.4	61.6	75.1	68.7	71.6	64.1	69.5	67.3	73.6	74.3	61.3	74.5	68.8	68.3	61.0	36.8
5. Can't say, drug unfamiliar	1.2	1.4	0.9	0.4	3.6	1.4	1.1	1.3	0.7	0.5	1.9	2.0	0.9	0.3	0.2	-
Item 12530 Subject A14a N	3250	1509	1646	2447	449	667	910	1095	578	1814	1272	1219	658	477	796	44
A23S: Have five or more drinks once or twice each weekend																
1. No risk	9.6	12.7	6.1	9.1	9.4	12.9	9.1	8.5	8.6	7.0	12.6	4.3	8.9	8.2	17.4	33.8
2. Slight risk	17.5	22.5	13.2	19.7	9.9	22.7	18.9	14.7	14.6	16.1	19.8	10.2	19.9	20.2	25.6	16.7
3. Moderate risk	30.0	29.7	30.7	32.0	21.8	30.2	28.5	29.0	34.2	32.4	26.9	29.4	31.6	32.0	29.8	11.8
4. Great risk	41.7	33.6	49.0	38.8	55.5	32.8	42.3	46.4	42.1	43.7	38.9	53.9	39.0	39.2	26.8	37.8
5. Can't say, drug unfamiliar	1.2	1.4	0.9	0.4	3.5	1.4	1.2	1.4	0.6	0.7	1.7	2.2	0.6	0.3	0.3	-
Item 12540 Subject A14a N	3251	1510	1646	2448	450	668	910	1094	578	1813	1273	1219	658	477	797	44

This section asks for your views and feelings about a number of different things.

D01: Do you agree or disagree with each of the following?

D01A: I take a positive attitude toward myself																
1. Disagree	1.8	1.3	2.0	1.6	2.2	1.6	1.5	2.5	0.9	0.9	2.8	2.3	1.1	0.9	1.4	12.6
2. Mostly disagree	6.4	4.1	8.1	6.7	3.0	6.7	7.7	5.7	5.3	6.2	6.6	5.3	5.8	6.4	8.3	4.0
3. Neither	6.7	6.9	6.5	7.3	1.2	10.0	6.4	4.6	7.7	5.4	8.8	5.6	6.0	7.7	8.4	14.3
4. Mostly agree	46.6	43.0	50.5	49.4	34.6	48.5	48.5	42.3	49.6	46.9	46.6	46.3	46.3	48.6	48.0	36.8
5. Agree	38.5	44.8	32.9	35.0	59.1	33.2	35.9	44.9	36.6	40.7	35.1	40.5	40.8	36.4	34.0	32.3
Item 12550 Subject Q01 N	3123	1453	1595	2392	417	619	903	1046	556	1787	1259	1174	627	463	769	42

D01B: Good luck is more important than hard work for success																
1. Disagree	37.4	34.6	40.1	37.1	39.8	33.0	38.5	39.3	37.0	39.0	35.3	40.0	37.6	35.8	33.6	40.0
2. Mostly disagree	36.9	36.8	36.6	39.9	26.3	38.5	35.6	35.5	39.6	38.9	34.7	37.0	38.5	35.3	38.7	20.9
3. Neither	15.4	16.6	14.5	15.0	14.0	18.2	15.4	13.7	15.3	14.8	15.8	13.9	14.8	15.8	17.4	23.2
4. Mostly agree	7.4	8.7	6.0	6.1	12.5	7.3	7.2	8.0	6.4	5.5	9.6	6.3	6.4	9.9	7.6	1.8
5. Agree	3.0	3.3	2.7	1.8	7.3	3.0	3.3	3.5	1.6	1.8	4.7	2.8	2.7	3.2	2.8	14.1
Item 12560 Subject Q02 N	3122	1451	1596	2392	416	620	901	1045	556	1787	1258	1173	627	463	770	42

D01C: I feel I am a person of worth, on an equal plane with others																
1. Disagree	1.3	1.3	1.1	1.1	1.4	1.2	1.0	1.7	1.1	0.5	2.1	1.2	0.8	0.7	1.4	11.1
2. Mostly disagree	3.3	3.3	3.2	3.5	2.1	5.0	4.2	2.3	1.6	2.8	3.9	2.9	1.9	4.3	4.3	4.3
3. Neither	8.5	9.2	7.8	8.9	3.9	11.5	8.9	7.3	6.7	6.7	11.0	6.9	9.7	7.4	10.7	9.0
4. Mostly agree	40.4	37.9	42.2	41.2	33.4	43.0	42.5	35.3	43.4	38.0	44.0	39.4	40.1	41.8	42.4	28.7
5. Agree	46.6	48.3	45.7	45.2	59.2	39.3	43.4	53.4	47.2	52.0	39.0	49.7	47.5	45.9	41.2	46.9
Item 12570 Subject Q01 N	3109	1444	1592	2386	416	616	900	1039	555	1781	1255	1169	626	462	764	42

D01D: I am able to do things as well as most other people																
1. Disagree	1.0	1.4	0.6	0.8	0.8	1.1	1.0	1.2	0.6	0.6	1.5	1.1	0.6	0.4	0.9	5.6
2. Mostly disagree	2.6	1.8	3.0	2.5	2.4	2.9	2.7	2.6	2.1	1.3	4.4	2.3	2.6	0.6	4.2	4.5
3. Neither	5.6	5.0	6.2	5.8	3.2	6.7	6.1	4.8	5.0	5.2	6.3	4.6	6.1	4.9	6.3	19.3
4. Mostly agree	41.5	38.3	44.4	43.7	29.8	45.7	43.4	37.9	40.8	40.0	43.3	40.2	38.1	45.8	44.7	33.2
5. Agree	49.3	53.5	45.8	47.2	63.8	43.6	46.7	53.6	51.5	52.8	44.6	51.7	52.7	48.3	43.8	37.3
Item 12580 Subject Q01 N	3106	1443	1589	2382	416	613	899	1039	555	1779	1252	1166	626	460	766	41

QUESTIONNAIRE FORM 5 1984	TOTAL	SEX		RACE		REGION				4YR COLLEGE PLANS		ILLICIT DRUG USE: LIFETIME				
		M	F	White	Black	NE	NC	S	W	Yes	No	None	Mari- juana Only	Few Pills	More Pills	Any Her- oin
N (Weighted No. of Cases):	3294	1522	1656	2462	457	682	918	1107	587	1824	1282	1228	662	480	801	44
% of Weighted Total:	100.0	46.2	50.3	74.7	13.9	20.7	27.9	33.6	17.8	55.4	38.9	37.3	20.1	14.6	24.3	1.3
D01E: Every time I try to get ahead, something or somebody stops me																
1. Disagree	19.4	19.4	19.6	18.2	25.3	20.0	16.1	20.9	21.6	22.1	15.7	22.5	20.1	13.1	17.8	22.6
2. Mostly disagree	32.4	30.1	34.7	35.1	22.3	31.5	33.1	30.6	35.9	36.1	27.8	33.0	32.4	33.8	32.0	25.9
3. Neither	24.1	26.3	22.4	25.4	17.2	24.5	26.3	22.1	23.5	23.2	25.0	21.3	26.7	27.7	25.0	19.9
4. Mostly agree	17.8	18.0	17.2	16.6	24.4	18.9	17.9	19.0	14.3	14.0	23.2	17.4	12.9	20.5	19.7	20.8
5. Agree	6.2	6.2	6.1	4.7	10.8	5.1	6.6	7.3	4.8	4.6	8.3	5.7	8.0	4.9	5.4	10.7
Item 12590 Subject Q02 N	3102	1439	1590	2377	415	610	899	1040	553	1775	1253	1166	625	461	764	42
D01F: Planning only makes a person unhappy since plans hardly ever work out anyway																
1. Disagree	31.9	30.3	34.1	32.6	31.0	24.1	32.8	34.2	34.8	36.1	26.1	36.4	32.1	27.5	28.5	16.5
2. Mostly disagree	31.5	28.6	33.8	33.3	24.9	30.8	33.2	29.2	33.6	33.3	29.4	31.8	30.2	35.0	31.8	10.6
3. Neither	17.0	19.8	14.4	17.4	13.3	19.9	15.4	15.6	18.9	16.0	17.8	15.5	18.8	17.8	16.4	31.2
4. Mostly agree	12.9	14.9	11.0	11.8	17.0	16.6	12.4	12.9	9.3	9.9	16.8	10.2	11.1	13.0	17.1	23.6
5. Agree	6.8	6.3	6.8	4.8	13.7	8.7	6.2	8.1	3.4	4.7	9.9	6.1	7.9	6.6	6.2	18.0
Item 12600 Subject Q02 N	3102	1441	1587	2378	416	613	900	1038	550	1776	1252	1166	623	461	762	42
D01G: People who accept their condition in life are happier than those who try to change things																
1. Disagree	18.7	20.8	17.0	18.2	24.1	17.3	18.4	19.6	18.9	22.3	13.3	19.3	21.6	17.7	16.5	22.1
2. Mostly disagree	23.3	21.1	25.1	24.8	17.3	23.2	25.9	20.1	25.2	25.9	20.0	24.2	20.7	23.3	24.8	18.7
3. Neither	21.1	21.7	20.4	22.1	14.5	24.7	21.1	19.1	20.7	19.8	23.0	20.5	22.9	19.4	21.6	26.5
4. Mostly agree	21.6	21.8	21.5	21.5	21.0	20.3	20.8	22.2	23.1	19.2	24.9	20.6	20.4	25.0	22.1	16.9
5. Agree	15.3	14.5	16.0	13.5	23.1	14.5	13.8	18.9	12.1	12.9	18.8	15.5	14.5	14.5	15.0	15.9
Item 12610 Subject Q02 N	3091	1438	1579	2371	412	610	899	1032	551	1771	1245	1159	623	460	760	42
D01H: On the whole, I'm satisfied with myself																
1. Disagree	2.7	2.3	2.8	2.4	4.3	2.5	3.1	3.0	1.6	2.0	3.5	3.7	2.3	1.3	2.0	10.1
2. Mostly disagree	6.2	6.0	6.2	6.5	4.5	6.6	6.1	6.0	6.3	5.9	6.6	4.1	4.9	7.2	9.9	2.0
3. Neither	8.2	9.2	7.3	8.7	4.9	11.4	9.6	5.7	7.1	7.2	9.6	6.6	7.6	7.7	11.1	19.5
4. Mostly agree	39.1	35.7	42.1	40.0	34.9	37.7	39.6	38.9	40.1	39.5	38.4	36.9	41.0	44.5	37.9	33.7
5. Agree	43.8	46.8	41.6	42.4	51.4	41.8	41.6	46.4	44.9	45.3	41.9	48.7	44.2	39.3	39.0	34.8
Item 12620 Subject P01,Q01 N	3090	1435	1582	2368	412	610	897	1032	551	1773	1242	1162	622	457	759	42
D01I: People like me don't have much of a chance to be successful in life																
1. Disagree	60.6	59.6	62.3	60.1	67.9	55.2	56.7	64.3	65.9	68.7	49.3	62.4	63.6	59.8	57.1	43.5
2. Mostly disagree	23.9	23.3	24.1	25.9	14.4	27.1	26.6	20.4	22.7	21.5	27.8	22.8	22.9	27.3	25.0	27.0
3. Neither	8.5	9.3	7.8	8.9	5.2	11.2	9.5	8.3	4.4	5.9	11.9	7.9	6.6	7.0	11.3	20.0
4. Mostly agree	4.5	5.3	3.7	3.6	7.4	4.4	4.9	4.0	5.0	2.4	7.4	4.3	4.6	3.9	4.6	4.6
5. Agree	2.4	2.5	2.1	1.5	5.1	2.1	2.2	3.0	2.0	1.5	3.6	2.5	2.3	2.0	2.0	5.0
Item 12630 Subject Q02 N	3092	1438	1580	2368	415	610	899	1034	549	1772	1245	1164	621	459	759	42
D01J: When I make plans, I am almost certain that I can make them work																
1. Disagree	2.1	2.0	2.0	1.7	2.6	2.5	2.1	2.4	1.1	1.2	3.4	2.2	2.2	1.0	2.3	8.6
2. Mostly disagree	5.9	5.2	6.5	5.3	6.7	6.3	6.1	5.8	5.2	5.2	6.4	5.0	5.1	5.3	7.6	9.7
3. Neither	14.2	15.2	13.3	15.4	6.8	11.8	13.1	12.7	12.9	11.6	18.0	12.8	14.3	12.9	15.8	40.8
4. Mostly agree	46.2	44.6	48.0	48.1	41.5	46.6	50.1	42.6	46.4	49.9	41.7	47.3	46.1	48.1	45.3	29.4
5. Agree	31.5	33.0	30.3	29.5	42.4	24.7	28.7	36.5	34.3	32.1	30.4	32.7	32.3	32.6	29.0	11.5
Item 12640 Subject Q02 N	3094	1436	1584	2370	415	609	900	1034	551	1775	1245	1164	621	459	761	42
D01K: A lot of times I feel lonely																
1. Disagree	19.1	21.1	16.6	16.8	28.1	20.4	17.2	20.1	18.9	17.4	21.2	18.0	22.1	18.2	17.5	28.1
2. Mostly disagree	29.4	28.7	30.4	32.0	22.5	29.5	30.7	26.4	32.9	33.3	24.3	30.4	27.7	29.8	31.2	10.3
3. Neither	17.3	21.2	13.8	19.3	7.2	19.1	19.2	14.0	18.5	15.7	19.3	15.1	18.7	17.7	19.3	20.9
4. Mostly agree	22.9	19.8	26.1	22.8	20.8	21.6	22.6	24.5	21.8	23.9	21.9	23.1	21.8	25.2	23.0	18.5
5. Agree	11.3	9.1	13.1	9.1	21.3	9.5	10.4	15.0	7.9	9.7	13.3	13.4	9.7	9.1	9.1	22.2
Item 12650 Subject Q03 N	3047	1410	1562	2335	407	606	886	1013	542	1742	1215	1144	617	450	751	42

QUESTIONNAIRE FORM 5 1984	TOTAL	SEX		RACE		REGION				4YR COLLEGE PLANS		ILLICIT DRUG USE: LIFETIME				
		M	F	White	Black	NE	NC	S	W	Yes	No	None	Mari- juana Only	Few Pills	More Pills	Any Her- oin
N (Weighted No. of Cases):	3294	1522	1656	2462	457	682	918	1107	587	1824	1282	1228	662	480	801	44
% of Weighted Total:	100.0	46.2	50.3	74.7	13.9	20.7	27.9	33.6	17.8	55.4	38.9	37.3	20.1	14.6	24.3	1.3
D01L: I feel I do not have much to be proud of																
1. Disagree	45.8	46.0	45.5	44.4	55.3	40.9	41.8	50.2	49.3	49.6	40.4	49.3	46.0	44.5	40.8	44.1
2. Mostly disagree	31.3	31.0	31.8	33.7	21.2	33.2	33.8	27.8	31.7	32.9	29.4	29.9	31.3	34.4	33.5	20.9
3. Neither	9.4	10.6	8.4	9.8	6.0	12.0	10.4	8.2	7.3	7.6	11.7	8.7	10.3	7.8	9.9	19.7
4. Mostly agree	9.2	8.6	9.7	8.9	9.3	9.9	9.1	9.2	8.6	6.8	12.5	7.3	8.9	10.2	11.4	8.6
5. Agree	4.3	3.8	4.6	3.3	8.3	4.1	5.0	4.6	3.1	3.1	6.1	4.8	3.4	3.2	4.4	6.7
Item 12660 Subject Q01 N	3040	1410	1557	2333	402	602	886	1012	540	1740	1211	1143	617	445	749	42
D01M: There is always someone I can turn to if I need help																
1. Disagree	3.8	4.4	3.0	3.1	6.1	4.0	3.4	5.1	1.9	3.3	4.5	4.4	3.8	1.7	3.6	14.2
2. Mostly disagree	5.3	5.3	5.3	5.2	5.9	5.8	5.0	4.6	6.3	5.4	5.3	4.9	5.6	3.7	6.7	1.5
3. Neither	5.1	6.4	3.8	5.3	4.3	6.1	6.3	4.7	2.6	5.2	4.9	4.5	6.8	4.4	4.6	4.0
4. Mostly agree	28.3	31.9	24.8	29.8	19.3	30.3	28.7	24.5	32.5	29.2	26.8	25.8	27.3	30.8	31.7	37.2
5. Agree	57.6	52.0	63.0	56.7	64.4	53.9	56.7	61.1	56.7	57.0	58.5	60.4	56.5	59.4	53.5	43.2
Item 12670 Subject Q03 N	3031	1404	1555	2329	401	598	886	1010	538	1734	1209	1141	617	443	746	42
D01N: Sometimes I think that I am no good at all																
1. Disagree	35.3	38.7	32.4	32.8	50.5	38.1	30.4	39.4	32.7	36.4	33.3	37.9	38.0	33.6	30.3	39.7
2. Mostly disagree	24.9	24.1	25.5	27.1	15.8	24.3	26.7	21.2	29.5	26.7	22.9	23.3	26.0	27.0	26.7	7.6
3. Neither	15.6	17.0	14.7	16.4	10.0	15.4	15.5	16.0	15.1	15.4	16.1	15.7	13.1	16.2	17.1	24.9
4. Mostly agree	15.0	13.2	16.7	15.4	13.1	13.8	17.2	14.3	14.1	13.9	16.7	13.3	16.0	13.4	17.5	11.4
5. Agree	9.2	6.9	10.8	8.3	10.6	8.4	10.2	9.1	8.6	7.6	11.0	9.7	6.9	9.8	8.5	16.3
Item 12680 Subject Q01 N	3028	1404	1551	2324	403	595	885	1010	538	1733	1206	1140	616	443	746	42
D01O: I often feel left out of things																
1. Disagree	21.2	23.2	19.3	19.2	32.5	24.6	16.8	23.4	20.6	21.1	21.1	21.2	24.3	17.5	21.8	9.4
2. Mostly disagree	26.8	26.2	27.5	28.5	19.2	25.0	25.9	25.0	33.5	29.2	23.3	25.7	25.0	30.3	28.2	30.4
3. Neither	19.4	21.4	17.7	20.3	14.6	19.6	21.2	18.5	18.2	18.7	20.7	19.6	19.7	18.6	19.1	20.5
4. Mostly agree	22.2	20.5	23.9	22.5	20.0	21.0	24.0	21.7	21.2	22.5	22.1	22.0	20.5	25.1	22.1	17.4
5. Agree	10.4	8.8	11.5	9.6	13.6	9.8	12.0	11.4	6.4	8.6	12.8	11.5	10.5	8.5	8.8	22.3
Item 12690 Subject Q03 N	3025	1400	1552	2322	401	594	884	1009	538	1733	1203	1142	614	440	744	42
D01P: I believe a person is master of his/her own fate																
1. Disagree	5.1	6.2	4.0	4.9	4.2	4.9	4.6	6.3	3.7	4.9	5.2	6.5	4.9	3.3	3.7	8.1
2. Mostly disagree	5.1	4.6	5.4	5.4	3.0	6.4	5.1	3.9	5.7	4.7	5.3	5.4	7.3	3.3	4.0	2.8
3. Neither	18.0	15.6	19.8	19.4	10.2	19.8	19.7	16.1	16.6	17.1	19.7	17.7	15.8	16.9	20.3	26.2
4. Mostly agree	33.9	32.4	35.6	34.9	28.9	32.7	35.7	30.3	39.3	34.8	32.6	32.2	33.5	39.4	34.4	30.8
5. Agree	37.9	41.2	35.2	35.3	53.8	36.2	34.9	43.4	34.7	38.5	37.1	38.2	38.6	37.1	37.5	32.0
Item 12700 Subject Q02 N	3013	1396	1544	2316	397	590	880	1007	536	1727	1197	1136	612	439	743	42
D01Q: There is usually someone I can talk to, if I need to																
1. Disagree	2.8	2.7	2.6	2.2	5.0	3.6	2.6	3.3	1.1	2.0	3.9	2.7	3.1	1.5	3.0	9.9
2. Mostly disagree	4.0	4.6	3.4	3.9	3.2	4.0	3.3	4.4	4.6	4.1	4.0	3.4	5.0	2.9	5.0	3.8
3. Neither	4.9	7.0	2.9	5.1	3.7	6.2	4.9	4.8	3.7	4.1	5.8	4.4	5.6	3.0	5.4	8.4
4. Mostly agree	27.2	29.2	25.4	28.0	20.6	27.6	29.4	22.1	32.5	29.8	24.0	27.0	26.4	27.6	28.6	21.5
5. Agree	61.1	56.5	65.7	60.8	67.4	58.6	59.8	65.4	58.1	60.0	62.3	62.5	59.9	65.1	58.0	56.4
Item 12710 Subject Q03 N	3017	1397	1548	2317	398	590	884	1005	538	1730	1199	1140	613	439	742	42
D01R: I feel that I can't do anything right																
1. Disagree	47.2	49.2	46.0	46.6	55.0	46.8	46.3	47.4	48.9	51.8	40.7	49.9	50.0	42.8	43.9	37.6
2. Mostly disagree	27.8	26.8	28.7	29.5	19.5	27.9	28.0	27.2	28.6	27.6	28.5	26.0	26.6	32.3	30.5	18.5
3. Neither	12.2	11.3	12.9	12.8	8.1	13.4	12.6	11.7	11.2	10.1	14.7	11.7	11.4	12.6	12.8	20.2
4. Mostly agree	8.7	7.9	9.1	8.2	9.0	8.1	9.0	9.0	8.2	7.1	11.1	8.2	6.4	9.1	9.5	19.5
5. Agree	4.1	4.7	3.4	2.9	8.4	3.8	4.1	4.7	3.1	3.5	5.0	4.2	5.6	3.1	3.2	4.1
Item 12720 Subject Q01 N	2995	1384	1539	2306	391	583	877	1000	535	1716	1191	1133	610	435	736	42

QUESTIONNAIRE FORM 5 1984	TOTAL	SEX		RACE		REGION				4YR COLLEGE PLANS		ILLICIT DRUG USE: LIFETIME				
		M	F	White	Black	NE	NC	S	W	Yes	No	None	Marijuana Only	Few Pills	More Pills	Any Heroin
N (Weighted No. of Cases):	3294	1522	1656	2462	457	682	918	1107	587	1824	1282	1228	662	480	801	44
% of Weighted Total:	100.0	46.2	50.3	74.7	13.9	20.7	27.9	33.6	17.8	55.4	38.9	37.3	20.1	14.6	24.3	1.3
D01S: I often wish I had more good friends																
1. Disagree	18.4	16.6	20.0	17.7	19.3	22.9	16.7	17.9	17.1	17.4	18.5	16.7	19.8	20.7	18.2	19.6
2. Mostly disagree	15.4	15.5	15.4	17.1	8.6	13.5	18.1	14.1	15.7	17.1	13.3	14.4	15.2	14.7	18.1	15.1
3. Neither	16.8	18.5	15.1	17.8	11.4	16.6	17.2	15.4	18.9	16.0	18.4	16.4	15.3	17.2	18.3	27.7
4. Mostly agree	27.0	27.4	26.6	27.6	26.5	26.6	26.1	26.4	30.3	26.9	27.1	26.0	28.7	27.7	27.3	16.6
5. Agree	22.3	21.9	22.9	19.9	34.2	20.4	21.9	26.2	18.0	22.5	22.7	26.5	21.0	19.7	18.1	21.0
Item 12730 Subject Q03 N	2998	1386	1541	2302	399	586	876	1001	535	1717	1192	1131	611	437	737	42
D01T: Planning ahead makes things turn out better																
1. Disagree	3.9	3.6	4.0	2.8	6.6	5.8	3.8	3.8	2.0	2.5	5.8	2.9	5.3	4.2	3.5	11.9
2. Mostly disagree	6.4	5.7	6.8	6.1	8.9	11.8	4.5	5.3	5.8	5.7	7.5	4.0	10.1	5.0	7.9	13.4
3. Neither	17.7	17.7	17.4	18.6	12.4	22.5	16.5	16.2	17.1	16.4	19.1	16.1	17.5	13.5	22.1	29.2
4. Mostly agree	39.6	39.4	40.0	42.6	28.8	34.6	44.9	37.1	41.2	41.6	37.6	40.3	35.5	46.6	39.2	21.9
5. Agree	32.4	33.5	31.7	30.0	43.3	25.4	30.2	37.7	33.8	33.7	30.1	36.7	31.6	30.7	27.3	23.6
Item 12740 Subject Q02 N	3010	1391	1546	2313	397	590	879	1004	537	1726	1195	1137	611	438	740	42
D01U: I feel that my life is not very useful																
1. Disagree	53.8	53.0	54.9	52.4	65.4	53.2	50.2	56.0	56.4	59.5	45.9	56.5	58.2	50.6	48.8	48.9
2. Mostly disagree	26.7	27.5	26.6	28.4	16.6	27.7	28.0	24.2	28.2	25.2	28.9	24.6	24.7	31.4	29.2	15.8
3. Neither	10.5	10.5	10.5	11.4	6.3	10.2	12.3	10.8	7.2	8.1	13.7	9.7	8.2	12.3	11.8	19.1
4. Mostly agree	5.7	5.7	5.1	5.2	5.6	5.1	6.4	5.7	5.3	4.7	7.3	5.5	5.9	4.5	6.6	6.0
5. Agree	3.3	3.3	3.0	2.6	6.1	3.7	3.2	3.3	2.9	2.6	4.3	3.8	3.1	1.2	3.6	10.2
Item 12750 Subject Q01 N	3000	1385	1543	2306	395	588	875	1003	534	1723	1190	1135	611	436	735	42
D01V: I usually have a few friends around that I can get together with																
1. Disagree	4.5	4.3	4.5	3.8	5.6	4.6	4.6	4.2	4.6	4.0	5.2	4.2	5.2	3.3	4.6	5.0
2. Mostly disagree	5.4	4.1	6.6	5.1	6.9	4.9	5.1	5.5	6.3	5.2	5.7	5.6	6.7	4.5	4.9	1.0
3. Neither	6.5	6.7	6.2	6.5	5.1	7.4	7.5	5.8	5.1	6.1	6.9	7.0	6.3	5.1	6.0	18.5
4. Mostly agree	35.8	36.4	35.4	37.1	28.6	33.2	37.6	33.5	39.8	35.3	37.3	35.7	34.3	39.7	36.5	15.4
5. Agree	47.9	48.5	47.3	47.5	53.8	49.9	45.2	51.0	44.2	49.4	45.0	47.6	47.5	47.4	47.9	60.2
Item 12760 Subject Q03 N	3000	1386	1542	2308	394	588	877	998	537	1722	1191	1133	612	435	736	42
D01W: I am eager to leave home and live on my own–independent from my parents																
1. Disagree	9.1	9.8	8.5	7.9	15.9	10.7	7.6	9.7	8.8	7.6	11.1	12.3	8.1	7.1	5.8	7.9
2. Mostly disagree	11.3	11.2	10.9	11.5	8.3	11.6	12.2	11.7	8.5	11.0	11.2	13.6	11.6	9.3	8.9	3.4
3. Neither	18.6	22.1	15.8	19.8	12.6	18.7	22.3	15.9	17.5	18.6	18.8	21.3	19.0	16.3	15.5	15.9
4. Mostly agree	28.5	27.0	29.9	29.4	24.7	28.6	27.2	28.7	30.2	30.5	26.5	27.9	29.6	28.7	30.1	11.0
5. Agree	32.5	29.9	34.9	31.4	38.5	30.4	30.7	34.0	34.9	32.4	32.4	24.9	31.7	38.6	39.7	61.8
Item 13950 Subject I03,Q01 N	2998	1384	1541	2303	397	586	874	1002	536	1719	1190	1132	612	436	734	42
D01X: I feel hesitant about taking a full-time job and becoming part of the "adult world"																
1. Disagree	34.2	34.4	34.0	32.2	44.5	39.1	29.3	35.5	34.2	31.8	37.8	31.0	34.7	33.2	37.8	44.3
2. Mostly disagree	22.2	23.3	21.2	23.5	15.2	20.9	23.8	20.6	23.9	23.0	20.9	22.8	20.0	24.3	22.8	9.6
3. Neither	13.4	14.2	12.6	14.1	7.8	13.1	13.6	12.4	15.0	14.0	12.7	14.8	13.9	12.9	11.3	19.5
4. Mostly agree	20.3	20.0	20.4	21.4	16.9	16.2	22.4	21.6	18.7	21.7	18.4	21.1	20.5	20.3	19.5	9.7
5. Agree	10.0	8.2	11.7	8.8	15.6	10.6	10.9	9.9	8.2	9.5	10.3	10.3	10.9	9.3	8.8	16.9
Item 13960 Subject I03,Q01 N	2999	1386	1540	2306	397	585	878	1000	536	1722	1191	1136	612	435	732	42

The next two questions ask your views about different lifestyles that have been in the news lately.

QUESTIONNAIRE FORM 5 1984	TOTAL	SEX		RACE		REGION				4YR COLLEGE PLANS		ILLICIT DRUG USE: LIFETIME				
		M	F	White	Black	NE	NC	S	W	Yes	No	None	Mari- juana Only	Few Pills	More Pills	Any Her- oin
N (Weighted No. of Cases):	3294	1522	1656	2462	457	682	918	1107	587	1824	1282	1228	662	480	801	44
% of Weighted Total:	100.0	46.2	50.3	74.7	13.9	20.7	27.9	33.6	17.8	55.4	38.9	37.3	20.1	14.6	24.3	1.3

D02: A man and a woman who live together without being married are . . . (Mark ONE circle.)

1. Experimenting with a worthwhile alternative lifestyle	21.0	22.5	20.1	20.5	23.8	24.4	21.1	18.1	22.7	19.6	23.2	16.8	24.7	21.6	23.7	24.5
2. Doing their own thing and not affecting anyone else	50.7	52.1	49.5	52.3	45.5	54.9	50.3	47.8	52.0	49.9	51.2	43.9	52.1	54.2	58.2	49.6
3. Living in a way that could be destructive to society	6.0	5.9	6.0	5.5	10.2	4.5	5.7	7.7	5.1	6.1	5.9	6.4	7.4	5.8	4.3	10.3
4. Violating a basic principle of human morality	15.1	11.4	18.2	15.3	13.7	8.4	14.8	20.7	12.5	17.2	12.2	23.5	10.6	12.8	7.6	4.2
8. None of the above	7.2	8.1	6.2	6.4	6.8	7.9	8.2	5.7	7.6	7.2	7.4	9.5	5.1	5.6	6.2	11.4
Item 12770 Subject D03 N	2945	1357	1517	2277	383	567	866	982	530	1696	1164	1121	602	423	719	40

D03: A man and a woman who decide to have and raise a child out of wedlock are . . .

1. Experimenting with a worthwhile alternative lifestyle	8.4	7.9	8.5	7.0	13.7	10.1	7.2	8.3	9.1	7.8	9.0	6.0	12.1	6.9	10.0	10.9
2. Doing their own thing and not affecting anyone else	33.3	36.4	30.5	32.0	42.5	35.5	31.1	31.6	37.5	31.6	35.2	28.2	34.9	34.5	38.7	33.8
3. Living in a way that could be destructive to society	18.3	17.1	19.3	19.1	14.8	17.8	19.6	17.7	17.8	18.8	18.0	18.1	18.3	19.6	17.9	16.5
4. Violating a basic principle of human morality	27.4	26.5	28.6	29.6	18.2	22.5	29.4	30.2	24.3	29.5	24.7	33.1	24.1	29.1	21.0	19.7
8. None of the above	12.6	12.1	13.0	12.3	10.7	14.2	12.6	12.2	11.4	12.3	13.0	14.6	10.5	9.9	12.3	19.0
Item 12775 Subject D03 N	2924	1347	1505	2262	381	567	853	977	527	1689	1152	1112	597	423	714	40

D04: These next questions ask how you feel about your present financial situation and your future financial security.

D04A: I feel that I have enough money to get along pretty well

1. Never	11.4	9.7	12.6	9.8	17.8	11.5	11.4	11.3	11.5	9.2	14.4	9.6	11.1	10.9	14.4	14.0
2. Seldom	18.3	17.4	19.1	18.7	17.5	21.5	20.4	16.3	15.4	15.6	22.4	18.7	18.4	16.3	19.2	24.2
3. Sometimes	36.2	35.3	37.0	36.4	35.6	35.0	39.2	32.3	40.0	35.2	38.2	34.5	36.7	40.7	36.3	38.0
4. Often	24.7	27.6	22.4	26.0	19.8	24.0	22.4	26.5	25.7	28.5	19.0	25.8	25.4	24.1	22.9	15.3
5. Always	9.3	10.0	8.9	9.1	9.3	8.0	6.6	13.5	7.4	11.5	6.1	11.3	8.5	8.1	7.3	8.6
Item 12990 Subject C02 N	2943	1354	1516	2269	383	563	867	981	532	1687	1171	1120	598	428	717	39

D04B: I get very concerned about how I am going to be able to pay my next bills

1. Never	25.4	22.9	27.7	22.7	36.9	25.5	21.1	29.9	23.7	27.9	21.6	25.6	29.0	22.7	22.9	33.1
2. Seldom	26.5	27.1	25.8	29.3	17.3	27.8	25.0	24.9	30.3	27.9	24.5	26.9	26.1	28.3	25.9	17.4
3. Sometimes	27.0	27.9	26.0	27.4	23.7	26.5	28.7	25.3	27.5	27.1	26.8	26.8	28.0	26.8	27.0	22.9
4. Often	14.9	15.1	14.8	15.2	11.2	14.5	17.5	13.6	13.4	12.4	18.4	14.0	12.3	16.4	17.2	17.2
5. Always	6.3	7.0	5.7	5.4	10.8	5.6	7.7	6.3	5.1	4.7	8.7	6.7	4.6	5.8	7.0	9.4
Item 13000 Subject C02 N	2914	1339	1503	2253	377	555	858	973	529	1676	1154	1111	592	423	711	39

D04C: I worry whether I will have any job at all in a few months

1. Never	35.9	35.1	36.6	36.7	31.9	37.3	30.6	38.9	37.1	39.6	30.2	34.6	36.5	35.3	38.1	43.1
2. Seldom	24.5	25.6	23.9	26.4	17.5	26.4	23.7	23.5	26.0	27.2	21.0	24.8	24.3	24.8	25.4	16.9
3. Sometimes	18.6	20.3	16.9	18.2	19.9	19.1	17.7	19.7	17.6	16.2	22.1	19.0	17.1	20.2	17.1	24.3
4. Often	12.8	12.3	13.2	12.9	12.1	11.6	16.7	10.2	12.7	11.2	15.2	13.0	13.3	12.8	12.4	8.6
5. Always	8.2	6.7	9.4	5.9	18.6	5.6	11.4	7.7	6.6	5.8	11.5	8.7	8.8	6.9	7.0	7.1
Item 13010 Subject C02 N	2901	1340	1489	2243	372	556	852	968	525	1665	1151	1102	586	421	713	39

D04D: I feel sure that I could go out and get a new job (with decent pay) whenever I want one

1. Never	11.8	8.2	14.6	10.2	19.2	11.6	15.0	11.5	7.7	9.3	15.3	12.8	11.0	9.1	11.9	24.6
2. Seldom	23.1	20.7	25.1	23.5	20.7	23.5	27.2	19.9	21.9	22.7	24.0	22.0	22.9	25.4	23.9	19.6
3. Sometimes	33.7	32.7	34.9	34.3	31.2	34.3	35.0	31.8	34.4	33.3	34.5	34.1	32.0	34.8	34.7	30.1
4. Often	20.1	24.3	16.8	21.6	14.8	20.5	14.8	21.6	25.4	22.7	15.9	19.8	22.4	18.5	20.1	14.6
5. Always	11.3	14.1	8.6	10.3	14.2	10.1	8.1	15.2	10.6	12.0	10.3	11.3	11.8	12.3	9.4	11.2
Item 13020 Subject C02 N	2896	1333	1491	2238	377	553	852	962	529	1664	1152	1101	589	418	710	39

QUESTIONNAIRE FORM 5 1984	TOTAL	SEX		RACE		REGION				4YR COLLEGE PLANS		ILLICIT DRUG USE: LIFETIME				
		M	F	White	Black	NE	NC	S	W	Yes	No	None	Mari- juana Only	Few Pills	More Pills	Any Her- oin
N (Weighted No. of Cases):	3294	1522	1656	2462	457	682	918	1107	587	1824	1282	1228	662	480	801	44
% of Weighted Total:	100.0	46.2	50.3	74.7	13.9	20.7	27.9	33.6	17.8	55.4	38.9	37.3	20.1	14.6	24.3	1.3

FOR THOSE WHO HAVE A JOB:

D04E: I feel sure I that can keep working steadily with my present employer as long as I want to

	TOTAL	M	F	White	Black	NE	NC	S	W	Yes	No	None	Mari- juana Only	Few Pills	More Pills	Any Her- oin
1. Never	6.4	5.8	6.7	4.8	17.7	6.3	7.3	6.0	5.8	5.9	6.3	6.2	7.8	6.2	5.4	8.4
2. Seldom	5.1	5.1	4.9	4.4	5.8	7.2	5.2	4.4	3.7	3.9	6.3	5.1	4.9	6.1	4.7	9.5
3. Sometimes	13.9	14.2	13.2	12.9	20.0	15.8	15.1	11.7	13.5	10.8	18.0	12.1	16.8	11.1	14.0	27.7
4. Often	26.9	27.6	26.6	27.4	22.0	21.5	27.4	29.4	27.7	28.8	24.4	27.7	27.9	27.4	25.4	16.4
5. Always	47.8	47.2	48.5	50.5	34.5	49.2	44.9	48.5	49.4	50.6	44.9	48.9	42.6	49.1	50.5	38.0
Item 13030 Subject C02 N★	1886	924	920	1514	199	391	530	618	347	1066	762	658	396	262	517	28

D04F: I worry about getting fired or laid-off from my job

	TOTAL	M	F	White	Black	NE	NC	S	W	Yes	No	None	Mari- juana Only	Few Pills	More Pills	Any Her- oin
1. Never	56.6	52.7	61.1	58.5	56.0	59.1	58.2	54.4	55.1	58.1	54.4	57.7	54.6	56.8	57.8	58.6
2. Seldom	24.8	27.4	22.0	26.0	16.8	23.1	24.1	24.8	27.9	27.2	22.1	23.7	25.6	26.8	25.6	5.5
3. Sometimes	12.1	13.1	10.6	10.6	15.7	12.8	10.7	13.2	11.4	9.1	15.9	11.1	14.7	10.4	10.4	27.4
4. Often	3.7	3.9	3.4	2.9	6.7	2.5	4.6	4.2	2.6	2.8	5.0	3.7	2.6	3.1	4.2	2.7
5. Always	2.9	2.8	2.8	2.0	4.7	2.6	2.4	3.5	3.0	2.8	2.6	3.7	2.5	2.9	1.9	5.7
Item 13040 Subject C02 N★	1881	921	918	1511	197	391	528	619	342	1067	757	655	395	261	517	28

D05: Please think about all the money you earned during the past year, including last summer.

About how much of your past year's earnings have gone into:

D05A: Savings for your future education

	TOTAL	M	F	White	Black	NE	NC	S	W	Yes	No	None	Mari- juana Only	Few Pills	More Pills	Any Her- oin
1. None	49.7	50.0	49.3	48.7	51.8	46.3	47.6	53.3	50.2	40.4	63.3	44.0	51.5	45.1	59.4	64.0
2. A little	21.4	22.4	20.5	22.4	17.2	21.5	20.9	19.2	25.9	23.3	18.5	21.5	20.5	27.1	18.2	13.5
3. Some	11.5	10.9	12.1	11.5	12.6	11.8	12.6	11.6	9.4	13.5	8.7	12.6	10.6	11.4	11.1	2.2
4. About half	7.2	6.4	7.8	7.2	7.0	7.9	8.6	6.5	5.4	9.2	4.2	7.8	7.3	6.3	6.7	4.7
5. Most	5.6	5.9	5.4	5.6	6.6	8.9	4.5	5.1	4.7	7.7	2.4	8.1	5.6	4.9	2.2	6.9
6. Almost all	3.5	3.1	4.1	3.9	3.2	3.2	4.1	3.2	3.6	4.8	1.7	4.3	4.2	5.1	1.0	5.6
7. All	1.1	1.4	0.9	0.8	1.6	0.4	1.8	1.1	0.9	1.1	1.2	1.6	0.4	0.1	1.5	3.1
Item 20830 Subject C02 N	2786	1286	1432	2183	334	544	829	914	499	1613	1100	1045	572	406	689	39

D05B: Savings or payments for a car or car expenses

	TOTAL	M	F	White	Black	NE	NC	S	W	Yes	No	None	Mari- juana Only	Few Pills	More Pills	Any Her- oin
1. None	46.8	38.6	53.6	43.3	63.0	51.6	47.6	46.6	40.4	50.2	41.9	50.8	46.5	46.3	41.6	44.1
2. A little	16.7	16.6	17.3	18.2	10.5	14.9	16.9	16.5	18.8	17.4	15.5	17.0	16.7	17.7	16.1	18.8
3. Some	14.4	16.4	12.9	15.5	10.4	13.1	14.5	15.1	14.4	14.0	14.9	13.1	15.1	14.4	16.0	18.4
4. About half	9.1	11.6	6.5	9.4	5.9	7.3	8.4	8.9	12.6	8.9	9.9	7.1	9.8	8.8	11.8	3.8
5. Most	7.3	9.5	5.4	8.0	5.9	7.7	6.5	7.0	8.7	5.5	10.0	6.6	7.1	9.4	7.0	9.2
6. Almost all	3.9	5.0	3.0	4.0	2.6	4.0	3.9	4.0	3.7	3.0	5.3	3.6	3.8	2.7	5.0	-
7. All	1.7	2.2	1.3	1.6	1.7	1.4	2.1	1.8	1.3	1.1	2.6	1.7	1.0	0.7	2.5	5.7
Item 20840 Subject C02 N	2777	1282	1427	2175	336	544	827	908	499	1606	1097	1044	568	405	687	39

D05C: Other savings for long-range purposes

	TOTAL	M	F	White	Black	NE	NC	S	W	Yes	No	None	Mari- juana Only	Few Pills	More Pills	Any Her- oin
1. None	48.5	47.2	49.5	47.4	55.1	46.1	51.8	46.8	48.8	47.7	49.5	46.2	51.9	46.9	50.8	50.3
2. A little	23.5	26.3	21.2	24.8	16.0	23.6	25.4	21.5	23.9	25.3	21.1	23.5	19.7	27.4	23.8	23.2
3. Some	13.5	12.3	14.9	14.1	11.3	15.2	11.0	14.9	13.5	13.5	13.9	14.3	14.0	12.5	13.2	6.2
4. About half	6.0	6.0	5.8	5.8	6.4	6.2	5.1	7.2	5.2	5.3	6.9	5.7	5.3	6.5	6.2	6.3
5. Most	4.4	4.3	4.6	4.5	4.4	5.5	4.1	4.4	4.0	4.2	4.7	5.2	4.8	4.2	3.4	4.3
6. Almost all	2.6	2.8	2.6	2.4	3.3	2.2	1.7	3.2	3.5	2.8	2.4	3.4	3.0	2.0	1.4	4.8
7. All	1.4	1.1	1.5	0.9	3.6	1.2	1.0	2.0	1.1	1.2	1.6	1.7	1.2	0.5	1.2	4.9
Item 20850 Subject C02 N	2766	1277	1420	2169	332	545	823	904	494	1597	1095	1037	565	405	685	39

★=excludes respondents for whom question was inappropriate.

QUESTIONNAIRE FORM 5 1984	TOTAL	SEX		RACE		REGION				4YR COLLEGE PLANS		ILLICIT DRUG USE: LIFETIME				
		M	F	White	Black	NE	NC	S	W	Yes	No	None	Marijuana Only	Few Pills	More Pills	Any Heroin
N (Weighted No. of Cases):	3294	1522	1656	2462	457	682	918	1107	587	1824	1282	1228	662	480	801	44
% of Weighted Total:	100.0	46.2	50.3	74.7	13.9	20.7	27.9	33.6	17.8	55.4	38.9	37.3	20.1	14.6	24.3	1.3

D05D: Spending on your own needs and activities – things such as clothing, stereo, TV, records, other possessions, movies, eating out, other recreation, hobbies, gifts for others, and other personal expenses

	TOTAL	M	F	White	Black	NE	NC	S	W	Yes	No	None	Mari Only	Few Pills	More Pills	Any Her
1. None	5.5	5.7	4.7	3.8	12.8	5.0	5.7	6.1	4.5	4.3	7.3	6.1	5.7	4.4	4.3	15.3
2. A little	19.0	21.3	17.3	20.4	10.9	21.4	19.4	16.0	21.0	19.5	19.1	21.9	19.1	18.3	15.5	13.9
3. Some	17.1	18.1	15.9	18.1	11.6	16.6	17.7	17.9	15.3	18.1	15.9	17.9	16.6	18.9	15.3	9.1
4. About half	18.5	17.3	19.6	18.4	18.0	18.8	17.6	18.2	20.2	18.2	18.6	18.3	19.2	20.3	17.1	19.6
5. Most	16.8	17.4	16.7	17.7	15.6	17.6	16.9	17.1	15.3	18.0	15.2	16.3	15.1	15.9	20.0	14.6
6. Almost all	13.8	12.4	15.7	13.6	14.4	10.5	14.4	13.9	16.2	13.3	14.0	12.6	12.0	15.2	16.2	15.4
7. All	9.3	7.8	10.2	7.9	16.7	10.1	8.3	10.7	7.6	8.7	9.8	6.9	12.3	7.0	11.6	12.1
Item 20860 Subject C02 N	2769	1279	1420	2175	333	540	825	907	497	1598	1096	1037	566	407	684	39

D05E: Helping to pay family living expenses (groceries, housing, etc.)

	TOTAL	M	F	White	Black	NE	NC	S	W	Yes	No	None	Mari Only	Few Pills	More Pills	Any Her
1. None	55.8	57.5	54.4	60.4	36.5	55.4	62.1	50.0	56.3	61.2	48.7	56.0	56.3	53.6	57.5	54.6
2. A little	25.5	25.5	25.9	25.9	21.7	26.6	22.5	26.5	27.2	23.6	28.0	25.6	23.7	25.3	27.7	23.9
3. Some	8.9	7.8	9.4	6.8	17.5	7.2	7.1	11.1	9.7	7.7	10.3	8.0	8.0	12.3	7.7	5.9
4. About half	4.3	3.9	4.7	3.4	9.8	4.4	4.9	5.0	1.9	3.1	6.0	4.8	5.8	4.0	2.4	9.8
5. Most	2.2	2.3	2.1	1.4	6.0	3.2	1.6	2.4	1.8	2.0	2.5	1.9	2.3	1.4	2.7	5.8
6. Almost all	1.9	1.9	1.9	1.0	5.6	1.7	0.9	3.3	1.4	1.4	2.7	1.7	2.9	1.8	1.4	-
7. All	1.4	1.2	1.5	1.0	3.0	1.3	0.9	1.6	1.7	0.9	1.9	1.9	1.0	1.6	0.7	-
Item 20870 Subject C02 N	2769	1275	1425	2172	333	541	824	907	497	1601	1094	1044	563	407	682	37

The next questions ask about characteristics which some people associate with the use of particular drugs. We want to know what you think.

E01: Do YOU think that people who smoke marijuana several times a week tend to be . . .

E01A: More creative than average

	TOTAL	M	F	White	Black	NE	NC	S	W	Yes	No	None	Mari Only	Few Pills	More Pills	Any Her
1. No	64.9	63.3	66.8	67.6	54.3	58.4	67.1	64.3	69.3	69.1	59.4	72.1	63.2	64.9	55.8	42.4
2. Yes	13.0	16.0	10.1	11.7	16.7	17.7	12.3	12.0	11.1	10.1	16.9	6.9	10.4	12.7	22.9	52.2
3. Not sure, no opinion	22.1	20.6	23.1	20.7	29.0	23.9	20.6	23.7	19.6	20.8	23.8	21.0	26.5	22.3	21.4	5.3
Item 13060 Subject A11c N	2915	1339	1505	2260	371	556	865	969	525	1682	1152	1113	583	431	709	39

E01B: Less sensible than average

	TOTAL	M	F	White	Black	NE	NC	S	W	Yes	No	None	Mari Only	Few Pills	More Pills	Any Her
1. No	20.9	23.2	18.5	20.4	23.6	26.4	18.3	20.7	19.6	18.3	24.8	12.8	16.9	20.4	36.1	38.4
2. Yes	62.4	61.6	63.0	64.6	53.4	59.4	64.5	60.1	66.1	66.2	57.0	69.6	63.9	65.1	48.1	59.2
3. Not sure, no opinion	16.8	15.3	18.4	15.0	23.0	14.2	17.1	19.2	14.3	15.5	18.3	17.5	19.2	14.5	15.9	2.4
Item 13070 Subject A11c N	2911	1334	1505	2258	369	556	865	967	523	1682	1152	1110	584	430	709	39

E01C: More interesting people than average

	TOTAL	M	F	White	Black	NE	NC	S	W	Yes	No	None	Mari Only	Few Pills	More Pills	Any Her
1. No	66.4	63.5	69.5	69.6	54.8	61.7	68.1	66.6	68.5	70.6	61.5	75.0	63.9	66.6	56.5	50.5
2. Yes	15.1	18.5	11.5	13.4	21.0	20.6	13.6	13.7	14.1	12.3	18.0	7.0	16.9	14.2	25.1	37.6
3. Not sure, no opinion	18.5	18.0	19.0	17.0	24.2	17.7	18.3	19.7	17.4	17.0	20.5	18.0	19.2	19.2	18.4	12.0
Item 13080 Subject A11c N	2903	1328	1502	2251	371	554	863	966	520	1678	1146	1105	582	431	709	39

E01D: Less hard-working than average

	TOTAL	M	F	White	Black	NE	NC	S	W	Yes	No	None	Mari Only	Few Pills	More Pills	Any Her
1. No	24.6	26.2	22.6	24.3	25.7	30.7	21.4	23.2	26.1	21.0	30.0	16.3	23.7	23.1	38.4	41.8
2. Yes	57.8	56.8	59.0	60.1	50.0	54.6	61.8	56.2	57.3	62.0	51.5	63.4	57.7	62.1	47.6	45.6
3. Not sure, no opinion	17.6	17.0	18.4	15.6	24.2	14.7	16.8	20.6	16.6	16.9	18.5	20.3	18.6	14.8	14.0	12.6
Item 13090 Subject A11c N	2905	1331	1501	2252	370	551	865	966	523	1677	1147	1103	585	430	709	39

E01E: More independent than average

	TOTAL	M	F	White	Black	NE	NC	S	W	Yes	No	None	Mari Only	Few Pills	More Pills	Any Her
1. No	54.2	49.7	58.5	55.7	50.4	51.0	54.0	56.2	54.0	55.7	52.7	56.5	54.4	57.2	49.5	45.3
2. Yes	25.1	30.9	20.0	25.5	21.2	29.2	25.6	22.3	25.3	23.6	27.0	20.4	23.5	26.8	32.0	42.4
3. Not sure, no opinion	20.7	19.4	21.5	18.8	28.4	19.7	20.4	21.4	20.7	20.7	20.3	23.0	22.1	16.0	18.6	12.2
Item 13100 Subject A11c N	2895	1320	1503	2245	370	552	862	960	521	1674	1141	1104	578	428	707	39

QUESTIONNAIRE FORM 5 1984	TOTAL	SEX		RACE		REGION				4YR COLLEGE PLANS		ILLICIT DRUG USE: LIFETIME				
		M	F	White	Black	NE	NC	S	W	Yes	No	None	Mari-juana Only	Few Pills	More Pills	Any Her-oin
N (Weighted No. of Cases):	3294	1522	1656	2462	457	682	918	1107	587	1824	1282	1228	662	480	801	44
% of Weighted Total:	100.0	46.2	50.3	74.7	13.9	20.7	27.9	33.6	17.8	55.4	38.9	37.3	20.1	14.6	24.3	1.3
E01F: More emotionally unstable than average																
1. No	20.3	24.3	16.4	20.3	18.5	25.0	18.8	18.9	20.4	17.5	24.4	10.7	18.5	23.3	33.9	35.1
2. Yes	62.3	57.9	66.5	63.5	58.4	59.3	65.3	62.2	60.8	66.2	56.5	70.9	61.4	63.3	49.5	62.4
3. Not sure, no opinion	17.4	17.8	17.1	16.2	23.1	15.7	15.9	18.9	18.8	16.2	19.1	18.3	20.1	13.5	16.6	2.4
Item 13110 Subject A11c N	2900	1325	1504	2249	371	553	863	964	520	1674	1146	1106	582	430	708	39
E01G: More concerned about other people than average																
1. No	70.3	69.7	71.5	73.0	62.2	69.8	70.3	70.5	70.6	72.7	67.8	74.3	68.2	74.2	63.6	72.8
2. Yes	9.5	10.9	7.7	8.5	10.4	12.6	9.2	7.5	10.1	7.3	11.8	5.2	8.9	8.4	16.7	19.3
3. Not sure, no opinion	20.2	19.4	20.8	18.5	27.3	17.5	20.5	22.0	19.3	20.0	20.4	20.5	22.8	17.4	19.6	7.9
Item 13120 Subject A11c N	2888	1319	1498	2244	362	548	860	959	521	1665	1142	1100	580	428	704	39
E01H: More weak-willed than average																
1. No	23.4	25.2	21.6	23.9	17.9	29.8	21.5	22.7	21.2	20.0	28.0	12.8	22.9	23.5	38.5	49.0
2. Yes	55.8	54.7	57.0	56.9	55.2	51.1	56.9	55.5	59.6	61.1	48.9	65.5	55.5	58.8	40.6	44.8
3. Not sure, no opinion	20.7	20.1	21.4	19.2	26.9	19.1	21.6	21.8	19.2	18.8	23.1	21.7	21.5	17.7	20.8	6.2
Item 13130 Subject A11c N	2891	1319	1501	2242	369	549	858	963	521	1667	1144	1098	581	428	707	39
E01I: More criminal than average																
1. No	26.0	27.6	24.6	26.5	21.8	34.3	21.5	25.2	26.1	24.9	27.7	14.3	27.2	25.7	42.5	46.4
2. Yes	53.5	53.8	53.1	54.6	52.3	45.0	59.0	53.3	53.9	55.4	51.7	63.0	51.4	55.6	40.6	33.6
3. Not sure, no opinion	20.5	18.6	22.3	19.0	25.9	20.7	19.5	21.6	20.0	19.8	20.6	22.7	21.4	18.7	16.9	20.0
Item 13140 Subject A11c N	2891	1321	1499	2244	367	550	860	963	518	1670	1141	1101	581	428	706	37

The next questions are similar, but ask about illegal drugs other than marijuana–like psychedelics, barbiturates, narcotics, and amphetamines.

E02: Do YOU think that people who use illegal drugs (other than marijuana) several times a week tend to be . . .

	TOTAL	M	F	White	Black	NE	NC	S	W	Yes	No	None	Mari-juana Only	Few Pills	More Pills	Any Her-oin
E02A: More creative than average																
1. No	65.4	62.9	67.5	68.0	55.5	61.6	66.5	64.0	69.9	68.4	61.6	70.5	61.9	65.2	61.2	56.0
2. Yes	10.0	11.8	8.2	8.4	13.2	14.3	9.8	8.8	7.8	8.5	11.9	7.4	6.6	9.0	15.6	34.2
3. Not sure, no opinion	24.7	25.4	24.3	23.7	31.3	24.0	23.7	27.2	22.3	23.1	26.4	22.1	31.5	25.8	23.2	9.8
Item 13330 Subject A11c N	2851	1303	1477	2213	360	540	850	952	509	1658	1114	1093	568	419	695	39
E02B: Less sensible than average																
1. No	14.2	15.4	13.2	13.2	18.5	15.7	14.1	13.0	15.2	11.7	17.7	10.1	9.6	12.3	23.7	39.8
2. Yes	65.7	63.1	67.7	68.0	55.2	65.3	67.5	63.2	67.7	70.4	59.5	72.1	66.0	67.5	55.7	53.6
3. Not sure, no opinion	20.1	21.5	19.1	18.8	26.4	19.0	18.4	23.9	17.1	17.8	22.8	17.8	24.4	20.2	20.6	6.6
Item 13340 Subject A11c N	2849	1301	1477	2209	363	539	849	952	509	1657	1112	1088	566	421	696	39
E02C: More interesting people than average																
1. No	67.8	65.0	70.4	70.9	55.8	65.8	69.6	65.7	70.7	71.6	63.2	74.7	62.6	67.6	62.4	60.7
2. Yes	8.7	9.8	7.4	7.4	12.4	12.4	7.9	7.6	8.1	6.8	11.1	4.1	9.4	8.5	14.3	27.3
3. Not sure, no opinion	23.5	25.2	22.1	21.8	31.8	21.8	22.5	26.7	21.2	21.7	25.7	21.2	28.0	23.9	23.3	12.0
Item 13350 Subject A11c N	2850	1299	1480	2209	363	538	849	952	511	1658	1113	1091	566	421	695	39
E02D: Less hard-working than average																
1. No	15.7	17.7	13.8	14.8	18.9	16.5	16.5	14.7	15.3	13.3	19.5	11.7	13.9	13.2	24.2	25.9
2. Yes	61.6	58.9	63.9	63.9	50.9	62.5	63.0	58.8	63.6	65.6	56.0	66.0	61.1	65.0	54.0	59.5
3. Not sure, no opinion	22.7	23.4	22.3	21.3	30.2	21.0	20.5	26.4	21.1	21.1	24.5	22.3	25.0	21.8	21.8	14.6
Item 13360 Subject A11c N	2852	1301	1480	2211	363	540	849	952	511	1659	1113	1091	568	421	695	39

QUESTIONNAIRE FORM 5 1984	TOTAL	SEX		RACE		REGION				4YR COLLEGE PLANS		ILLICIT DRUG USE: LIFETIME				
		M	F	White	Black	NE	NC	S	W	Yes	No	None	Mari- juana Only	Few Pills	More Pills	Any Her- oin
N (Weighted No. of Cases):	3294	1522	1656	2462	457	682	918	1107	587	1824	1282	1228	662	480	801	44
% of Weighted Total:	100.0	46.2	50.3	74.7	13.9	20.7	27.9	33.6	17.8	55.4	38.9	37.3	20.1	14.6	24.3	1.3
E02E: More independent than average																
1. No	56.2	52.5	59.8	57.3	53.9	57.1	55.7	55.6	57.3	57.5	54.4	57.4	54.9	57.9	55.1	49.4
2. Yes	18.6	21.8	15.6	18.6	15.4	21.0	19.9	17.1	16.9	17.8	20.1	17.2	17.2	18.7	21.1	37.2
3. Not sure, no opinion	25.1	25.7	24.5	24.0	30.8	21.9	24.4	27.3	25.8	24.7	25.6	25.4	27.9	23.4	23.9	13.4
Item 13370 Subject A11c N	*2842*	*1294*	*1478*	*2208*	*360*	*539*	*849*	*943*	*511*	*1653*	*1112*	*1090*	*563*	*420*	*692*	*39*
E02F: More emotionally unstable than average																
1. No	12.2	15.3	9.6	11.5	12.8	12.9	12.0	12.4	11.2	9.4	16.1	8.4	11.5	12.3	17.3	29.7
2. Yes	67.3	62.2	71.5	69.4	58.3	69.0	67.9	64.6	69.4	72.3	60.7	71.7	64.8	68.3	62.6	66.1
3. Not sure, no opinion	20.5	22.6	19.0	19.1	28.8	18.0	20.0	23.0	19.4	18.3	23.2	19.8	23.7	19.4	20.1	4.2
Item 13380 Subject A11c N	*2847*	*1299*	*1478*	*2206*	*363*	*538*	*849*	*950*	*510*	*1657*	*1110*	*1089*	*568*	*421*	*692*	*39*
E02G: More concerned about other people than average																
1. No	69.6	67.8	71.5	72.0	60.4	69.8	69.2	69.2	70.7	71.7	67.0	72.8	65.2	71.3	67.4	71.0
2. Yes	6.0	6.8	5.0	5.1	8.6	8.3	7.0	4.6	4.6	4.3	8.5	4.1	6.0	5.4	8.8	19.3
3. Not sure, no opinion	24.4	25.4	23.5	23.0	31.0	21.9	23.7	26.2	24.7	24.0	24.5	23.1	28.8	23.2	23.8	9.8
Item 13390 Subject A11c N	*2844*	*1295*	*1479*	*2207*	*359*	*538*	*849*	*946*	*511*	*1653*	*1112*	*1088*	*566*	*420*	*693*	*39*
E02H: More weak-willed than average																
1. No	13.4	15.1	11.7	13.0	12.3	16.0	12.6	13.7	11.7	11.5	16.1	8.8	10.7	13.7	21.0	42.0
2. Yes	62.2	60.0	64.4	64.0	56.4	61.9	62.9	59.3	67.0	66.7	56.6	69.0	60.6	64.8	53.0	50.4
3. Not sure, no opinion	24.3	25.0	23.9	23.0	31.3	22.0	24.5	27.0	21.4	21.9	27.3	22.1	28.7	21.5	26.1	7.6
Item 13400 Subject A11c N	*2847*	*1298*	*1478*	*2210*	*362*	*539*	*849*	*950*	*508*	*1657*	*1110*	*1090*	*568*	*421*	*693*	*37*
E02I: More criminal than average																
1. No	14.8	14.6	15.0	14.1	16.1	19.5	14.1	13.1	14.3	13.8	16.4	10.5	14.4	12.3	22.2	33.5
2. Yes	62.3	62.7	62.0	64.3	54.0	58.4	64.6	61.6	63.5	64.8	59.2	67.4	60.5	64.5	55.4	59.3
3. Not sure, no opinion	22.9	22.7	23.0	21.6	29.9	22.1	21.3	25.3	22.1	21.4	24.4	22.1	25.1	23.2	22.3	7.2
Item 13410 Subject A11c N	*2849*	*1300*	*1480*	*2210*	*362*	*539*	*848*	*951*	*511*	*1656*	*1114*	*1092*	*568*	*421*	*692*	*39*
The next few questions ask how YOU view cigarette smoking.																
E03: In my opinion, when a guy my age is smoking a cigarette, it makes him look . . .																
E03A: Cool, calm, in-control																
1. Disagree	63.1	63.6	62.7	62.9	62.8	59.7	60.7	62.8	71.0	68.7	55.2	75.2	60.2	60.1	49.5	53.6
2. Mostly disagree	12.0	12.3	11.9	12.6	7.7	12.3	13.7	10.2	12.4	10.4	14.5	9.9	13.3	12.1	14.4	19.5
3. Neither	17.8	16.5	19.0	18.7	17.3	21.4	19.6	17.9	10.9	15.7	21.0	9.2	20.5	21.2	26.5	21.1
4. Mostly agree	4.2	4.3	4.0	3.8	5.4	4.9	3.7	4.9	3.3	3.4	5.5	3.2	3.7	4.2	6.4	1.8
5. Agree	2.8	3.3	2.4	1.8	6.7	1.8	2.3	4.2	2.3	1.8	3.8	2.5	2.3	2.4	3.3	4.0
Item 20880 Subject A11c N	*2832*	*1292*	*1469*	*2200*	*356*	*536*	*848*	*938*	*510*	*1649*	*1102*	*1080*	*562*	*420*	*693*	*39*
E03B: Insecure																
1. Disagree	15.7	14.5	16.5	14.3	20.2	19.8	16.4	15.3	10.8	12.5	20.1	12.6	12.7	14.6	22.6	29.4
2. Mostly disagree	8.7	8.1	9.4	8.9	9.2	8.9	9.7	8.4	6.9	7.6	10.3	5.1	9.1	9.5	13.5	9.8
3. Neither	30.6	28.7	31.3	31.3	31.4	32.7	28.6	32.6	27.8	29.6	32.0	25.9	33.6	32.4	34.9	24.7
4. Mostly agree	21.9	23.4	21.2	23.0	13.1	18.8	23.1	20.6	25.5	24.5	17.9	26.1	22.9	21.5	16.7	7.3
5. Agree	23.2	25.2	21.6	22.6	26.2	19.8	22.1	23.0	29.0	25.8	19.7	30.2	21.7	22.1	12.3	28.8
Item 20890 Subject A11c N	*2824*	*1289*	*1465*	*2195*	*357*	*536*	*846*	*932*	*510*	*1646*	*1097*	*1078*	*561*	*419*	*692*	*38*
E03C: Rugged, tough, independent																
1. Disagree	54.1	54.1	53.8	54.3	51.9	52.7	51.5	54.1	59.6	56.5	50.7	62.9	49.7	50.8	46.8	43.3
2. Mostly disagree	14.6	15.7	14.0	14.9	12.1	11.7	16.6	13.6	16.3	14.5	14.9	14.5	15.6	16.7	13.4	9.6
3. Neither	21.1	20.5	21.4	21.7	19.6	27.0	20.9	19.6	17.8	19.6	23.7	14.1	23.3	22.1	29.2	24.4
4. Mostly agree	6.5	6.1	6.9	6.4	7.8	6.0	6.8	7.8	4.0	6.4	6.0	5.2	8.0	7.2	6.5	10.4
5. Agree	3.8	3.7	3.9	2.7	8.6	2.6	4.2	5.0	2.2	3.0	4.7	3.4	3.4	3.2	4.0	12.2
Item 20900 Subject A11c N	*2819*	*1282*	*1465*	*2192*	*356*	*534*	*840*	*934*	*511*	*1642*	*1096*	*1075*	*562*	*418*	*689*	*38*

QUESTIONNAIRE FORM 5 1984	TOTAL	SEX		RACE		REGION				4YR COLLEGE PLANS		ILLICIT DRUG USE: LIFETIME				
		M	F	White	Black	NE	NC	S	W	Yes	No	None	Mari-juana Only	Few Pills	More Pills	Any Her-oin
N (Weighted No. of Cases):	3294	1522	1656	2462	457	682	918	1107	587	1824	1282	1228	662	480	801	44
% of Weighted Total:	100.0	46.2	50.3	74.7	13.9	20.7	27.9	33.6	17.8	55.4	38.9	37.3	20.1	14.6	24.3	1.3
E03D: Conforming																
1. Disagree	29.4	29.6	29.4	27.8	36.6	28.7	27.4	31.3	29.8	27.8	31.7	31.8	25.5	27.2	30.5	27.6
2. Mostly disagree	9.9	9.6	10.0	9.8	10.6	9.6	10.4	9.5	9.9	8.6	11.4	7.7	11.3	11.0	11.6	11.4
3. Neither	37.5	35.6	38.9	38.7	32.7	41.4	37.2	36.7	35.3	34.8	41.6	33.1	41.6	38.5	40.1	41.3
4. Mostly agree	11.2	12.8	9.9	11.7	8.3	10.8	11.5	10.3	12.9	13.4	8.0	12.5	10.1	11.3	10.5	6.0
5. Agree	12.0	12.3	11.7	12.0	11.9	9.5	13.5	12.2	12.1	15.4	7.3	15.0	11.5	12.0	7.3	13.8
Item 20910 Subject A11c N	2775	1268	1438	2160	350	527	831	923	494	1626	1070	1052	551	415	684	38
E03E: Mature, sophisticated																
1. Disagree	61.2	59.1	62.7	60.9	59.4	58.3	58.1	60.8	69.8	65.1	55.3	72.7	55.0	58.2	51.4	53.1
2. Mostly disagree	13.4	14.2	13.1	14.2	9.9	11.8	17.0	12.5	10.9	12.9	14.5	11.5	16.4	15.1	13.4	4.3
3. Neither	19.5	19.9	19.1	19.9	20.1	25.8	18.7	19.2	14.7	17.2	22.9	12.1	21.9	20.0	27.7	29.9
4. Mostly agree	3.9	4.3	3.3	3.5	6.4	3.2	3.7	4.9	3.2	3.1	4.7	2.5	4.0	3.9	5.8	8.5
5. Agree	2.1	2.4	1.8	1.4	4.2	0.9	2.6	2.6	1.4	1.7	2.7	1.2	2.6	2.7	1.7	4.1
Item 20920 Subject A11c N	2807	1275	1461	2186	357	531	834	931	511	1642	1089	1071	561	416	685	38
E03F: Like he's TRYING to appear mature and sophisticated																
1. Disagree	14.5	12.8	15.9	13.6	17.7	16.7	13.7	15.6	11.4	10.3	20.5	11.3	14.6	11.4	20.1	26.2
2. Mostly disagree	4.4	4.6	4.4	4.4	4.3	5.4	4.7	4.3	3.3	3.0	6.4	2.4	5.4	6.7	5.6	2.9
3. Neither	17.4	17.7	16.9	18.2	14.3	20.7	17.5	17.4	13.8	14.9	21.2	9.9	19.8	17.1	26.2	28.3
4. Mostly agree	21.1	20.1	22.3	22.4	18.1	20.4	20.6	21.0	23.1	23.5	17.9	22.5	19.5	23.3	20.1	15.9
5. Agree	42.6	44.8	40.6	41.5	45.6	36.8	43.6	41.8	48.5	48.3	34.0	53.9	40.6	41.5	28.0	26.7
Item 20930 Subject A11c N	2811	1283	1457	2192	351	535	837	929	511	1645	1089	1070	565	417	684	38
E04: In my opinion, when a girl my age is smoking a cigarette, it makes her look . . .																
E04A: Cool, calm, in-control																
1. Disagree	69.1	69.5	68.8	68.9	70.0	62.7	68.0	69.2	77.7	73.1	62.9	81.2	67.5	66.1	55.3	52.2
2. Mostly disagree	10.3	10.4	10.3	10.7	7.9	11.4	11.6	9.3	8.9	9.7	11.2	7.2	12.1	13.4	12.2	8.8
3. Neither	14.8	14.0	15.6	15.7	13.1	18.4	15.4	15.4	9.0	12.6	18.4	7.2	15.3	13.7	25.8	27.2
4. Mostly agree	3.0	2.8	3.1	2.7	3.9	4.9	2.8	2.6	2.1	2.9	3.2	1.5	3.8	4.7	3.7	8.4
5. Agree	2.7	3.3	2.2	2.0	5.2	2.6	2.2	3.5	2.3	1.7	4.3	2.9	1.3	2.1	3.0	3.4
Item 20940 Subject A11c N	2776	1249	1455	2164	351	521	836	926	492	1622	1074	1057	556	411	676	38
E04B: Insecure																
1. Disagree	18.1	17.3	18.9	15.8	27.6	20.1	17.9	19.4	14.0	15.1	22.4	15.9	17.1	16.3	22.4	31.6
2. Mostly disagree	7.8	7.8	7.7	7.7	8.2	8.8	8.7	7.3	6.1	6.4	9.7	4.6	8.0	10.9	11.0	10.5
3. Neither	24.4	23.0	25.1	25.3	22.8	27.6	23.4	25.7	20.0	22.9	26.7	18.6	25.9	24.2	32.6	15.1
4. Mostly agree	18.0	18.4	18.1	18.9	12.4	17.8	17.6	18.1	19.0	20.8	14.0	20.4	19.2	19.5	13.5	7.8
5. Agree	31.7	33.5	30.3	32.3	29.0	25.7	32.4	29.5	40.9	34.7	27.2	40.5	29.8	29.0	20.5	35.0
Item 20950 Subject A11c N	2769	1245	1454	2165	346	521	834	924	491	1617	1074	1052	555	412	677	38
E04C: Independent and liberated																
1. Disagree	56.4	55.4	57.2	56.0	57.2	53.7	54.9	56.1	62.5	59.7	51.6	67.5	52.6	50.6	47.1	41.8
2. Mostly disagree	13.7	13.9	13.6	14.6	9.6	12.0	15.3	12.7	14.9	13.2	14.7	11.9	14.4	18.8	14.1	4.5
3. Neither	19.6	19.8	19.4	20.6	17.6	24.9	19.3	19.4	14.8	18.1	22.0	13.2	21.0	19.7	27.1	31.3
4. Mostly agree	6.0	6.1	6.0	5.7	5.6	5.9	6.4	6.7	3.8	5.7	6.1	3.7	7.5	6.7	7.1	15.0
5. Agree	4.3	4.9	3.7	3.0	10.0	3.4	4.1	5.2	4.0	3.2	5.6	3.6	4.6	4.3	4.6	7.5
Item 20960 Subject A11c N	2766	1244	1451	2162	347	520	835	921	490	1618	1070	1053	554	410	676	38
E04D: Conforming																
1. Disagree	33.6	33.4	33.9	31.7	41.3	31.7	31.7	36.3	33.9	31.1	37.6	35.7	30.3	30.3	35.0	34.9
2. Mostly disagree	8.5	7.9	8.8	8.2	10.1	8.8	8.8	8.2	8.3	7.0	10.4	5.2	9.9	11.3	11.0	8.4
3. Neither	33.3	31.6	34.6	34.6	29.0	37.2	34.1	31.0	32.2	31.8	36.0	30.4	37.6	32.2	35.4	37.4
4. Mostly agree	10.6	12.5	9.1	10.9	7.6	10.9	10.0	10.8	10.8	12.6	7.3	10.7	9.8	13.4	8.8	6.9
5. Agree	14.0	14.6	13.5	14.5	12.1	11.3	15.4	13.8	14.8	17.4	8.8	17.9	12.3	12.7	9.7	12.4
Item 20970 Subject A11c N	2726	1229	1428	2133	342	515	824	910	477	1603	1048	1032	548	406	667	38

QUESTIONNAIRE FORM 5 1984	TOTAL	SEX		RACE		REGION				4YR COLLEGE PLANS		ILLICIT DRUG USE: LIFETIME				
		M	F	White	Black	NE	NC	S	W	Yes	No	None	Mari-juana Only	Few Pills	More Pills	Any Her-oin
N (Weighted No. of Cases):	3294	1522	1656	2462	457	682	918	1107	587	1824	1282	1228	662	480	801	44
% of Weighted Total:	100.0	46.2	50.3	74.7	13.9	20.7	27.9	33.6	17.8	55.4	38.9	37.3	20.1	14.6	24.3	1.3

E04E: Mature, sophisticated

	TOTAL	M	F	White	Black	NE	NC	S	W	Yes	No	None	Mari-juana Only	Few Pills	More Pills	Any Her-oin
1. Disagree	65.2	65.1	65.1	65.2	63.5	61.0	62.6	65.7	73.0	70.8	56.8	76.9	62.3	62.0	52.8	52.4
2. Mostly disagree	12.2	12.3	12.3	12.3	11.0	11.6	14.3	11.2	11.1	11.5	13.2	9.7	13.5	14.1	13.9	5.0
3. Neither	16.3	15.5	16.9	17.1	14.7	20.2	15.9	16.2	12.8	13.0	21.2	10.0	16.0	16.3	25.7	23.5
4. Mostly agree	4.0	4.3	3.7	3.7	5.8	5.0	3.8	4.4	2.4	3.5	4.9	1.9	5.5	5.1	4.8	10.9
5. Agree	2.4	2.8	1.9	1.7	5.0	2.1	3.3	2.6	0.7	1.3	3.9	1.6	2.7	2.5	2.8	8.1
Item 20980 Subject A11c N	2761	1239	1452	2161	345	521	834	917	488	1615	1071	1051	553	412	670	38

E04F: Like she's TRYING to appear mature and sophisticated

	TOTAL	M	F	White	Black	NE	NC	S	W	Yes	No	None	Mari-juana Only	Few Pills	More Pills	Any Her-oin
1. Disagree	14.3	13.1	15.1	12.6	20.5	15.2	13.3	15.7	12.4	10.3	20.1	11.4	14.3	11.8	18.8	30.0
2. Mostly disagree	4.4	4.3	4.3	4.2	4.3	5.7	4.6	4.1	3.1	2.9	6.5	2.4	5.7	6.4	5.3	4.4
3. Neither	15.4	15.8	15.0	16.3	12.5	17.5	15.3	15.7	12.6	13.7	18.2	9.4	16.9	14.6	23.1	22.5
4. Mostly agree	17.9	17.4	18.5	18.6	16.0	20.6	17.2	17.2	17.6	19.0	16.5	18.4	17.0	19.2	18.3	9.4
5. Agree	48.0	49.5	47.1	48.3	46.6	41.0	49.6	47.3	54.3	54.2	38.7	58.5	46.1	48.0	34.4	33.6
Item 20990 Subject A11c N	2755	1239	1448	2161	339	519	833	914	489	1611	1068	1049	558	411	667	36

E05: Do you agree or disagree..

E05A: Smokers know how to enjoy life more than nonsmokers

	TOTAL	M	F	White	Black	NE	NC	S	W	Yes	No	None	Mari-juana Only	Few Pills	More Pills	Any Her-oin
1. Disagree	73.7	70.2	77.3	73.6	75.0	71.7	71.2	75.7	76.1	77.4	68.3	82.7	70.5	70.8	64.9	64.5
2. Mostly disagree	8.9	9.8	8.2	9.5	5.3	9.2	10.7	7.5	8.1	8.5	9.4	7.1	11.5	9.4	9.6	3.8
3. Neither	13.8	15.8	12.0	14.3	12.0	15.9	14.0	12.5	13.9	11.8	16.9	7.6	14.8	15.8	21.1	26.1
4. Mostly agree	1.6	1.4	1.7	1.4	3.7	1.5	1.4	2.3	0.9	1.2	2.3	1.3	1.2	1.5	2.1	-
5. Agree	1.9	2.7	0.8	1.2	4.0	1.7	2.7	1.9	1.1	1.0	3.0	1.3	2.0	2.4	2.2	5.6
Item 21000 Subject A11c N	2799	1267	1461	2183	345	530	839	930	499	1631	1091	1063	561	419	680	38

E05B: I prefer to date people who don't smoke

	TOTAL	M	F	White	Black	NE	NC	S	W	Yes	No	None	Mari-juana Only	Few Pills	More Pills	Any Her-oin
1. Disagree	8.5	7.8	8.9	7.8	10.1	8.8	9.3	9.1	5.6	5.5	12.6	6.2	6.3	5.7	14.4	16.2
2. Mostly disagree	4.1	3.4	4.6	4.4	3.5	6.1	4.2	3.5	2.9	2.6	6.5	2.7	4.4	3.9	6.4	6.1
3. Neither	17.3	15.2	19.1	17.9	14.7	24.5	17.9	14.0	14.8	14.9	20.9	8.1	18.5	20.9	28.1	25.0
4. Mostly agree	10.9	11.0	10.7	11.1	10.5	10.9	11.0	10.8	11.0	11.6	10.2	8.6	13.2	11.4	12.7	6.1
5. Agree	59.2	62.7	56.7	58.8	61.3	49.7	57.7	62.6	65.7	65.5	49.7	74.5	57.6	58.1	38.4	46.6
Item 21010 Subject A11c N	2795	1265	1461	2179	347	530	839	930	497	1631	1085	1063	561	419	678	38

E05C: The harmful effects of cigarettes have been exaggerated

	TOTAL	M	F	White	Black	NE	NC	S	W	Yes	No	None	Mari-juana Only	Few Pills	More Pills	Any Her-oin
1. Disagree	46.6	45.0	48.4	47.8	42.0	42.8	47.6	45.6	50.8	51.2	39.8	56.1	43.7	44.5	37.7	21.4
2. Mostly disagree	20.2	19.5	20.6	22.0	11.0	21.9	18.9	19.7	21.6	22.4	17.4	19.7	19.2	24.2	20.9	8.1
3. Neither	15.2	14.3	15.9	14.4	17.7	17.8	14.7	14.3	14.9	13.1	18.1	11.6	18.2	14.5	17.8	37.2
4. Mostly agree	9.9	10.8	9.0	10.0	9.7	10.3	10.6	10.5	7.3	7.6	13.0	6.0	9.3	10.6	14.9	20.9
5. Agree	8.1	10.4	6.0	5.7	19.7	7.2	8.4	9.9	5.5	5.6	11.7	6.7	9.6	6.2	8.7	12.4
Item 21020 Subject A11c N	2764	1247	1449	2168	338	526	831	917	491	1621	1069	1048	556	416	669	37

E05D: I think that becoming a smoker reflects poor judgment

	TOTAL	M	F	White	Black	NE	NC	S	W	Yes	No	None	Mari-juana Only	Few Pills	More Pills	Any Her-oin
1. Disagree	11.6	9.9	12.6	10.2	17.6	14.8	11.6	11.0	9.4	9.2	15.6	7.1	12.8	9.8	17.3	33.6
2. Mostly disagree	8.2	7.4	8.9	8.3	6.0	9.1	8.8	7.6	7.3	6.8	10.4	5.7	8.8	9.4	11.1	7.5
3. Neither	21.9	20.6	23.3	23.1	18.8	21.7	23.0	22.2	19.5	20.3	23.9	18.1	22.6	23.8	25.6	28.3
4. Mostly agree	16.1	15.0	17.0	17.2	12.0	17.5	17.0	14.4	16.4	18.3	13.0	16.0	15.4	16.2	16.8	13.3
5. Agree	42.2	47.0	38.2	41.2	45.5	36.8	39.6	44.8	47.5	45.3	37.2	53.1	40.3	40.7	29.2	17.3
Item 21030 Subject A11c N	2783	1255	1458	2175	347	527	836	925	495	1630	1079	1060	558	415	677	38

E05E: I personally don't mind being around people who are smoking

	TOTAL	M	F	White	Black	NE	NC	S	W	Yes	No	None	Mari-juana Only	Few Pills	More Pills	Any Her-oin
1. Disagree	34.7	35.5	33.9	33.4	44.6	31.0	34.7	35.1	37.9	37.9	30.2	49.3	31.9	29.4	19.2	8.8
2. Mostly disagree	15.5	16.0	15.1	15.9	10.8	13.6	14.1	14.9	20.8	18.1	11.5	18.1	14.6	16.8	11.6	17.2
3. Neither	13.2	14.9	11.7	14.0	11.3	14.0	13.4	13.7	11.2	13.4	12.6	10.3	14.3	15.2	15.1	25.2
4. Mostly agree	17.4	16.8	18.2	18.4	13.9	21.6	17.2	16.2	15.8	17.0	18.4	12.8	18.0	22.3	21.9	9.0
5. Agree	19.1	16.8	21.1	18.3	19.4	19.8	20.4	20.2	14.2	13.6	27.4	9.6	21.2	16.3	32.2	39.9
Item 21040 Subject A11c N	2786	1257	1459	2179	343	527	835	928	496	1629	1080	1057	558	416	680	38

QUESTIONNAIRE FORM 5 1984	TOTAL	SEX		RACE		REGION				4YR COLLEGE PLANS		ILLICIT DRUG USE: LIFETIME				
		M	F	White	Black	NE	NC	S	W	Yes	No	None	Mari- juana Only	Few Pills	More Pills	Any Her- oin
N (Weighted No. of Cases):	3294	1522	1656	2462	457	682	918	1107	587	1824	1282	1228	662	480	801	44
% of Weighted Total:	100.0	46.2	50.3	74.7	13.9	20.7	27.9	33.6	17.8	55.4	38.9	37.3	20.1	14.6	24.3	1.3
E05F: Smoking is a dirty habit																
1. Disagree	11.1	11.3	10.2	10.2	14.6	11.3	12.1	11.2	9.2	8.5	15.0	7.5	10.1	10.3	17.2	21.0
2. Mostly disagree	6.2	5.5	7.0	5.6	7.2	8.0	5.8	6.4	4.9	5.0	8.1	3.7	7.5	5.0	10.0	7.6
3. Neither	14.4	13.8	14.9	14.4	14.9	16.4	14.3	14.1	12.7	14.2	14.5	10.0	17.9	15.8	17.1	21.1
4. Mostly agree	15.8	15.8	15.9	16.9	12.3	18.5	15.8	14.1	16.0	16.7	14.1	15.3	16.5	17.0	16.1	10.6
5. Agree	52.5	53.6	52.1	53.0	51.0	45.8	52.0	54.1	57.2	55.7	48.3	63.5	48.0	51.9	39.6	39.6
Item 21050 Subject A11c N	*2789*	*1259*	*1460*	*2179*	*346*	*527*	*836*	*930*	*496*	*1631*	*1080*	*1059*	*558*	*416*	*680*	*38*
E06: The next questions ask how you feel about the amount of supervision that you re- ceived from your parents (or guardians) during your high school years. For each of the follow- ing areas, do you feel that you received about the right amount of supervision, too little, or too much?																
E06A: What kinds of parties, dances or other events you could go to																
1. Far too little supervision	10.5	13.6	7.3	9.2	15.4	12.7	10.9	10.3	7.9	8.0	13.6	6.0	11.0	10.8	15.5	23.3
2. Too little	7.6	8.0	7.4	6.7	10.8	7.7	6.8	8.5	7.5	6.8	8.8	6.2	8.3	7.4	9.2	5.2
3. About right	65.2	63.6	67.0	66.8	61.6	62.2	62.3	65.3	73.0	69.2	60.0	74.1	64.7	61.5	55.5	47.6
4. Too much supervision	11.7	9.7	13.5	12.5	8.5	14.8	13.1	10.4	8.6	11.3	12.2	9.9	12.3	16.3	11.9	10.7
5. Far too much	5.0	5.1	4.8	4.9	3.7	2.7	6.9	5.5	3.1	4.6	5.5	3.8	3.8	4.0	7.8	13.1
Item 21800 Subject M03 N	*2794*	*1264*	*1461*	*2183*	*353*	*529*	*838*	*928*	*499*	*1624*	*1090*	*1065*	*568*	*411*	*673*	*38*
E06B: How late you stayed out on dates																
1. Far too little supervision	5.6	7.8	3.3	4.7	6.9	7.4	6.1	4.8	4.4	4.1	7.6	3.6	5.6	6.2	7.8	13.8
2. Too little	7.3	7.7	7.2	6.4	11.1	7.8	5.7	8.2	8.1	7.0	7.5	6.5	8.6	7.5	6.9	15.7
3. About right	61.1	64.5	58.6	61.8	61.9	57.4	60.1	62.6	63.9	62.4	59.9	65.9	61.1	56.6	57.1	41.5
4. Too much supervision	18.0	12.8	22.3	19.5	12.0	19.8	19.7	15.8	17.4	18.9	16.6	18.0	15.2	21.5	19.3	12.4
5. Far too much	8.0	7.2	8.6	7.5	8.1	7.6	8.5	8.7	6.2	7.6	8.3	6.1	9.5	8.3	8.9	16.7
Item 21810 Subject M03 N	*2774*	*1250*	*1455*	*2177*	*343*	*526*	*835*	*919*	*493*	*1619*	*1078*	*1054*	*563*	*412*	*670*	*37*
E06C: The way you dressed																
1. Far too little supervision	5.5	6.8	3.9	4.2	8.0	7.8	4.9	5.1	5.0	4.1	7.2	3.6	5.8	6.8	7.2	14.6
2. Too little	4.4	5.8	3.3	3.7	7.1	6.7	3.9	4.6	2.3	3.4	5.5	4.3	5.2	2.6	5.0	2.2
3. About right	79.3	75.6	82.5	81.6	70.8	73.5	79.9	78.2	86.3	82.5	75.1	84.0	77.2	77.1	76.5	59.3
4. Too much supervision	7.5	8.5	6.9	7.7	7.8	8.7	8.0	7.5	5.4	7.2	7.9	5.3	9.7	9.9	7.4	14.7
5. Far too much	3.4	3.3	3.4	2.8	6.3	3.4	3.3	4.6	1.1	2.7	4.2	2.9	2.1	3.7	4.0	9.1
Item 21820 Subject M03 N	*2782*	*1252*	*1461*	*2176*	*350*	*522*	*834*	*928*	*499*	*1623*	*1082*	*1068*	*564*	*409*	*669*	*34*
E06D: What you did with your money																
1. Far too little supervision	5.3	5.7	4.7	4.5	6.2	6.2	5.6	5.3	4.0	3.2	8.0	3.6	5.0	4.4	8.5	14.0
2. Too little	10.1	11.1	8.9	9.7	9.2	12.2	9.6	9.2	10.2	9.4	11.0	9.5	9.5	10.1	11.1	13.1
3. About right	62.9	58.9	66.4	64.3	58.9	57.2	64.1	62.9	67.2	66.7	57.6	69.2	64.0	56.5	58.0	28.6
4. Too much supervision	15.6	17.7	14.2	15.8	17.9	17.3	15.6	15.3	14.1	15.6	15.5	13.5	14.7	21.9	14.8	27.9
5. Far too much	6.1	6.5	5.7	5.7	7.9	7.0	5.1	7.3	4.5	5.1	7.9	4.2	6.9	7.1	7.6	16.5
Item 21830 Subject M03 N	*2778*	*1250*	*1459*	*2178*	*348*	*522*	*833*	*927*	*495*	*1623*	*1079*	*1063*	*563*	*409*	*669*	*35*
E06E: How often you went out in the evening																
1. Far too little supervision	4.8	5.6	3.7	3.8	8.2	7.1	4.3	4.5	3.7	3.0	7.3	3.3	4.9	4.1	6.9	15.7
2. Too little	6.0	7.2	5.0	4.8	11.3	8.3	4.2	6.8	5.3	5.7	6.5	5.6	5.9	5.2	7.0	1.3
3. About right	61.9	63.0	61.3	63.9	57.8	56.6	63.6	63.0	62.9	63.2	59.7	67.5	63.0	58.2	56.4	35.9
4. Too much supervision	19.7	17.9	21.6	20.5	15.7	20.2	18.9	18.2	23.5	21.5	17.6	18.1	18.4	23.6	20.6	29.2
5. Far too much	7.5	6.3	8.4	7.1	7.0	7.9	9.0	7.5	4.6	6.7	8.9	5.4	7.8	8.9	9.1	17.9
Item 21840 Subject M03 N	*2771*	*1249*	*1453*	*2174*	*345*	*523*	*831*	*926*	*492*	*1614*	*1079*	*1055*	*561*	*410*	*670*	*37*
E06F: How much time you spent on homework																
1. Far too little supervision	8.1	9.5	6.7	7.7	6.5	9.1	9.4	6.9	7.1	5.7	11.4	4.5	9.3	7.3	12.9	17.1
2. Too little	19.9	22.6	17.6	20.2	18.7	19.6	19.9	19.8	20.7	19.7	20.2	18.7	20.4	22.3	21.2	3.4
3. About right	55.6	50.2	60.3	56.6	52.1	54.1	55.6	55.3	57.8	58.4	51.9	62.9	53.4	52.1	48.3	48.7
4. Too much supervision	10.6	10.6	10.9	10.3	14.5	12.3	9.6	11.1	9.5	11.0	9.8	9.9	11.5	12.9	9.2	17.7
5. Far too much	5.7	7.2	4.5	5.2	8.1	4.8	5.6	6.8	5.0	5.1	6.7	4.0	5.5	5.4	8.5	13.1
Item 21850 Subject M03 N	*2772*	*1247*	*1457*	*2173*	*348*	*520*	*832*	*922*	*497*	*1614*	*1080*	*1061*	*560*	*406*	*670*	*37*

QUESTIONNAIRE FORM 5 1984	TOTAL	SEX		RACE		REGION				4YR COLLEGE PLANS		ILLICIT DRUG USE: LIFETIME				
		M	F	White	Black	NE	NC	S	W	Yes	No	None	Marijuana Only	Few Pills	More Pills	Any Heroin
N (Weighted No. of Cases):	3294	1522	1656	2462	457	682	918	1107	587	1824	1282	1228	662	480	801	44
% of Weighted Total:	100.0	46.2	50.3	74.7	13.9	20.7	27.9	33.6	17.8	55.4	38.9	37.3	20.1	14.6	24.3	1.3

E06G: What courses you took in school

1. Far too little supervision	5.3	6.0	4.6	4.6	5.6	6.8	6.0	5.0	3.0	3.6	7.2	3.3	5.0	4.8	8.7	16.2
2. Too little	12.5	13.1	12.0	11.4	16.7	10.4	12.0	12.1	16.4	11.0	14.8	11.6	13.9	12.0	14.1	-
3. About right	70.7	69.3	72.3	74.1	60.2	72.9	73.4	68.4	68.0	73.9	67.2	75.6	69.1	71.7	64.1	53.2
4. Too much supervision	7.2	7.6	6.7	6.6	9.6	7.2	4.6	8.1	9.9	7.4	6.7	6.7	6.9	7.4	7.4	19.1
5. Far too much	4.3	4.0	4.5	3.4	7.8	2.8	3.9	6.4	2.7	4.0	4.2	2.8	5.1	4.0	5.6	11.5
Item 21860 Subject M03 N	2767	1242	1458	2173	346	522	832	919	494	1618	1071	1061	560	408	668	36

E06H: The hours you could work during the school year

1. Far too little supervision	6.1	5.8	6.1	4.7	8.9	8.5	6.3	5.4	4.5	4.3	7.9	3.5	6.4	5.9	9.5	15.7
2. Too little	9.4	10.2	8.8	8.3	13.5	8.9	10.0	9.4	9.1	8.2	11.9	8.5	8.9	8.5	11.2	5.2
3. About right	71.5	71.7	71.8	75.1	60.6	71.1	73.1	69.2	73.6	75.3	66.9	75.7	72.9	72.0	65.2	55.3
4. Too much supervision	8.5	8.5	8.5	8.6	8.4	8.4	7.5	9.1	9.4	8.3	8.5	8.1	7.2	10.5	9.2	6.8
5. Far too much	4.4	3.7	4.8	3.3	8.6	3.1	3.1	6.9	3.4	3.9	4.8	4.2	4.6	3.1	4.9	17.0
Item 21870 Subject M03 N	2745	1235	1443	2157	344	518	825	915	487	1596	1070	1048	557	404	661	37

E06I: How much TV you watched

1. Far too little supervision	8.3	8.8	7.3	6.6	12.1	10.6	8.2	6.8	8.5	6.3	10.9	5.6	9.7	8.6	11.0	15.7
2. Too little	10.9	12.7	9.7	10.1	14.2	10.7	9.2	11.7	12.3	11.1	10.5	12.2	9.6	11.4	10.3	3.4
3. About right	70.2	66.8	73.3	74.0	57.1	67.8	72.8	68.9	70.5	72.9	66.7	70.8	69.2	72.1	69.6	62.9
4. Too much supervision	6.6	7.2	6.3	6.3	7.0	7.3	6.3	7.3	5.3	6.2	7.1	7.3	6.6	5.6	5.6	9.7
5. Far too much	4.0	4.6	3.4	3.0	9.6	3.5	3.4	5.2	3.4	3.4	4.8	4.1	4.9	2.3	3.5	8.2
Item 21880 Subject M03 N	2763	1245	1451	2165	347	521	830	918	494	1614	1070	1060	560	406	663	37

E06J: What kinds of TV programs you watched

1. Far too little supervision	9.2	10.5	7.7	7.7	13.8	10.8	9.1	9.1	7.9	7.1	12.2	6.2	10.8	7.3	13.8	15.2
2. Too little	8.3	9.3	7.3	6.8	13.9	8.0	6.7	8.6	10.5	7.7	8.9	8.4	9.5	8.2	7.5	-
3. About right	72.4	69.2	75.3	76.0	59.4	69.7	74.6	70.8	74.4	75.6	68.0	75.4	69.6	76.0	69.5	53.3
4. Too much supervision	6.8	6.8	6.9	6.7	6.6	7.5	6.4	7.4	5.5	6.9	6.6	7.3	6.6	6.0	5.9	12.3
5. Far too much	3.4	4.2	2.7	2.9	6.3	3.9	3.2	4.0	1.8	2.8	4.3	2.7	3.5	2.5	3.3	19.2
Item 21890 Subject M03 N	2757	1240	1450	2162	345	519	831	915	493	1610	1069	1056	558	406	663	37

E07: Over the LAST 12 MONTHS, about how often have you gone to parties?

1. Not at all–GO TO Q.9	14.4	13.3	15.1	12.3	23.7	6.9	14.2	17.9	15.9	12.7	17.6	23.2	12.2	8.3	6.2	9.9
2. Once a month or less	33.9	31.7	36.2	35.7	23.3	32.4	33.3	35.4	33.8	37.1	28.9	46.9	27.7	37.2	18.9	5.6
3. 2 or 3 times a month	26.8	27.6	26.0	27.8	26.4	28.7	27.6	25.1	26.6	26.3	27.0	19.3	32.7	32.1	30.0	32.8
4. About once a week	15.0	16.5	14.0	15.0	16.5	17.8	16.5	12.3	14.7	14.2	16.5	7.9	17.6	13.0	24.7	16.9
5. 2 or 3 times a week	7.0	7.7	6.5	6.9	6.2	10.2	5.9	6.0	7.5	7.8	6.1	1.6	7.4	8.0	14.5	13.9
6. Over 3 times a week	2.8	3.3	2.3	2.3	3.9	4.0	2.5	3.3	1.5	2.0	4.0	1.1	2.4	1.4	5.7	20.9
Item 21900 Subject C07 N	2705	1210	1433	2123	331	502	817	901	485	1588	1033	1028	548	399	652	35

E08: Now think about the parties you went to in the last 12 months. How often...

E08A: Were people over age 30 present at least some of the time?

1. Never	41.8	41.9	41.6	41.1	47.4	43.0	46.1	40.2	35.7	39.8	45.3	38.0	50.6	38.1	42.5	34.6
2. Seldom	29.3	30.6	28.4	30.5	21.8	30.1	28.2	28.2	32.6	31.7	25.7	27.7	27.1	34.1	29.9	41.0
3. Sometimes	17.8	18.0	17.7	17.7	20.7	17.5	15.3	20.2	17.8	17.4	18.0	17.5	14.1	17.8	20.3	18.4
4. Most times	7.5	6.8	8.3	7.3	6.3	6.7	6.9	7.7	9.0	7.7	7.1	10.9	6.4	7.1	4.9	-
5. Always	3.6	2.8	4.1	3.4	4.0	2.6	3.5	3.7	4.8	3.5	4.0	5.9	1.8	2.9	2.4	6.0
Item 21910 Subject C07,M02 N★	2403	1087	1258	1907	279	480	723	781	420	1413	913	818	498	381	631	34

E08B: Did someone get high on alcohol?

1. Never	9.1	7.0	11.2	8.7	11.8	6.6	8.7	11.0	9.2	10.3	7.5	20.2	3.8	4.8	2.0	-
2. Seldom	6.0	6.8	5.2	4.5	11.1	7.3	5.9	5.5	6.0	5.5	6.6	11.1	3.6	4.7	2.4	3.4
3. Sometimes	16.9	17.6	16.0	15.5	21.7	18.0	16.2	18.3	14.0	16.4	17.5	20.2	16.4	17.1	12.5	12.4
4. Most times	26.8	26.8	27.3	28.2	23.3	29.0	26.5	25.0	28.4	28.0	25.5	23.6	32.1	29.1	26.2	18.5
5. Always	41.1	41.8	40.4	43.1	32.0	39.2	42.8	40.1	42.3	39.8	42.9	24.9	44.1	44.4	56.9	65.7
Item 21920 Subject A02b,C07 N★	2401	1088	1256	1902	283	481	723	778	419	1411	910	815	500	382	630	34

★=excludes respondents for whom question was inappropriate.

QUESTIONNAIRE FORM 5 1984	TOTAL	SEX		RACE		REGION				4YR COLLEGE PLANS		ILLICIT DRUG USE: LIFETIME				
		M	F	White	Black	NE	NC	S	W	Yes	No	None	Mari- juana Only	Few Pills	More Pills	Any Her- oin
N (Weighted No. of Cases):	3294	1522	1656	2462	457	682	918	1107	587	1824	1282	1228	662	480	801	44
% of Weighted Total:	100.0	46.2	50.3	74.7	13.9	20.7	27.9	33.6	17.8	55.4	38.9	37.3	20.1	14.6	24.3	1.3
E08C: Did most people get high on alcohol?																
1. Never	12.3	10.5	14.2	11.5	14.8	10.4	11.6	13.7	13.4	14.3	9.3	27.2	4.5	6.6	3.4	-
2. Seldom	11.2	11.8	10.6	9.8	15.1	11.6	9.6	12.5	11.0	11.9	9.9	16.6	10.2	10.2	5.6	11.0
3. Sometimes	20.0	21.3	18.7	19.5	24.9	21.1	21.9	18.6	18.2	21.2	18.3	22.5	20.0	20.7	16.5	4.9
4. Most times	29.4	27.6	30.7	31.6	23.2	31.2	28.6	28.4	30.3	28.2	31.4	21.3	34.9	35.9	32.1	26.3
5. Always	27.1	28.9	25.8	27.6	22.0	25.8	28.3	26.8	27.0	24.3	31.1	12.4	30.4	26.5	42.3	57.9
Item 21930 Subject A02b,C07 N★	2381	1074	1250	1889	279	476	715	774	417	1399	902	808	493	380	627	34
E08D: Did you get high on alcohol?																
1. Never	29.0	23.9	33.5	24.2	53.8	26.4	26.7	34.6	25.6	33.1	22.8	57.2	18.2	18.9	8.8	7.8
2. Seldom	16.8	17.2	16.8	17.7	13.1	13.6	18.0	15.8	20.4	16.2	18.3	17.8	20.7	18.6	11.0	8.6
3. Sometimes	24.4	22.5	26.0	25.6	20.3	24.9	25.9	24.8	20.4	25.0	23.2	15.7	29.3	29.1	29.0	23.9
4. Most times	17.2	19.3	15.4	19.1	7.7	22.0	15.7	13.6	21.2	16.4	18.7	6.3	21.5	23.9	25.3	14.0
5. Always	12.5	17.1	8.3	13.3	5.0	13.1	13.8	11.1	12.4	9.4	17.0	3.0	10.3	9.5	26.0	45.8
Item 21940 Subject A05c,C07 N★	2388	1077	1254	1896	279	480	716	776	415	1406	904	808	495	381	629	34
E08E: Did you feel pressure to drink alcohol?																
1. Never	64.7	59.6	69.2	63.9	71.6	68.3	61.9	64.1	66.7	63.0	67.5	67.9	60.0	61.3	66.2	78.2
2. Seldom	18.1	19.6	17.1	19.2	7.9	17.4	18.8	17.3	19.5	19.9	15.5	16.0	19.5	20.2	19.2	13.7
3. Sometimes	11.1	13.1	9.4	11.5	9.8	9.3	11.9	13.3	7.5	11.5	10.0	10.0	11.4	13.0	10.7	4.3
4. Most times	3.2	4.1	2.4	3.1	5.8	3.0	3.7	2.6	3.9	3.2	3.5	3.9	5.3	1.8	1.5	3.9
5. Always	2.8	3.6	2.0	2.3	4.9	2.1	3.6	2.7	2.4	2.4	3.5	2.2	3.8	3.7	2.4	-
Item 21950 Subject A02b,C07 N★	2391	1080	1254	1894	282	481	718	779	414	1410	904	812	498	380	627	34
E08F: Did you feel pressure to drink enough to get high?																
1. Never	72.6	66.6	78.3	72.7	74.9	73.0	72.2	73.2	72.1	73.4	72.2	79.3	69.1	68.8	69.2	81.7
2. Seldom	15.8	18.9	12.8	16.7	8.2	15.9	15.6	15.4	16.7	16.7	14.1	12.1	17.6	17.3	19.0	7.3
3. Sometimes	7.4	9.0	6.3	7.3	8.9	7.1	7.2	7.8	7.5	6.6	8.6	5.3	8.2	9.7	7.6	7.7
4. Most times	1.9	2.8	1.0	1.7	3.5	2.2	2.0	2.0	1.2	1.5	2.2	1.7	2.5	2.0	1.7	-
5. Always	2.2	2.7	1.6	1.7	4.5	1.8	2.9	1.7	2.5	1.8	3.0	1.7	2.5	2.2	2.5	3.4
Item 21960 Subject A02b,C07 N★	2390	1079	1254	1894	281	480	719	775	416	1408	904	811	497	381	626	34
E08G: Did someone get high on marijuana?																
1. Never	32.5	31.2	33.4	33.5	23.7	24.4	35.1	37.0	29.0	34.8	29.8	57.1	22.7	28.3	12.1	4.3
2. Seldom	14.8	16.8	13.3	15.3	11.6	16.1	14.7	13.7	15.3	15.7	13.6	16.5	18.0	13.9	10.9	4.8
3. Sometimes	22.6	23.1	22.1	23.4	18.4	24.5	23.7	20.8	21.7	24.2	20.6	13.2	27.5	26.7	28.4	18.1
4. Most times	15.1	13.0	17.2	15.0	20.4	17.8	12.2	15.0	17.3	13.7	17.2	7.6	18.7	17.7	20.6	23.4
5. Always	15.0	15.9	14.1	12.8	26.0	17.1	14.3	13.5	16.6	11.6	18.9	5.6	13.1	13.4	28.0	49.3
Item 21970 Subject A02b,C07 N★	2386	1078	1249	1890	280	482	718	773	413	1405	903	808	495	380	628	34
E08H: Did most people get high on marijuana?																
1. Never	40.6	39.7	41.3	43.1	24.6	33.3	46.1	44.2	32.8	44.7	35.4	66.2	32.0	34.3	20.2	6.4
2. Seldom	22.2	24.3	21.0	23.9	14.8	20.8	23.9	19.0	27.3	24.0	19.8	16.3	28.4	27.7	22.5	13.3
3. Sometimes	16.2	15.6	16.7	16.4	16.1	18.3	13.7	15.7	19.1	16.3	16.2	8.1	19.5	20.0	21.7	27.2
4. Most times	10.5	9.5	11.5	9.4	19.6	14.7	8.0	10.6	9.8	8.1	13.9	4.4	9.9	12.5	17.3	12.5
5. Always	10.4	11.0	9.6	7.3	24.9	12.9	8.3	10.5	11.0	6.8	14.7	5.0	10.2	5.5	18.2	40.7
Item 21980 Subject A02b,C07 N★	2383	1078	1247	1887	280	479	718	773	413	1405	900	809	494	382	625	34
E08I: Did you get high on marijuana?																
1. Never	68.0	64.8	71.4	67.8	71.3	57.1	73.3	71.3	65.4	73.0	60.8	98.6	65.9	65.1	34.2	20.1
2. Seldom	12.7	14.5	11.4	13.5	9.8	18.1	9.6	11.1	15.0	12.3	13.6	0.9	19.0	18.8	19.9	5.7
3. Sometimes	9.9	9.4	10.1	10.1	8.1	12.7	9.3	8.8	9.9	8.1	12.6	0.1	9.2	9.8	22.5	32.0
4. Most times	4.4	5.2	3.9	4.0	7.3	5.6	3.0	5.1	4.5	3.1	6.4	0.3	3.3	4.5	10.1	12.3
5. Always	4.9	6.2	3.3	4.6	3.4	6.4	4.8	3.7	5.3	3.5	6.6	-	2.6	1.7	13.2	29.9
Item 21990 Subject A05c,C07 N★	2382	1077	1248	1889	281	475	717	778	413	1410	894	811	494	379	624	34

★=excludes respondents for whom question was inappropriate.

QUESTIONNAIRE FORM 5 1984	TOTAL	SEX		RACE		REGION				4YR COLLEGE PLANS		ILLICIT DRUG USE: LIFETIME				
		M	F	White	Black	NE	NC	S	W	Yes	No	None	Mari-juana Only	Few Pills	More Pills	Any Her-oin
N (Weighted No. of Cases):	3294	1522	1656	2462	457	682	918	1107	587	1824	1282	1228	662	480	801	44
% of Weighted Total:	100.0	46.2	50.3	74.7	13.9	20.7	27.9	33.6	17.8	55.4	38.9	37.3	20.1	14.6	24.3	1.3

E08J: Did you feel pressure to use marijuana?

1. Never	84.9	81.0	89.0	85.6	83.4	83.0	86.3	85.4	83.8	85.5	84.8	92.9	81.1	83.7	78.9	80.9
2. Seldom	7.7	9.1	6.3	8.1	5.7	10.1	6.5	6.8	8.7	7.9	6.7	3.3	8.8	7.7	12.1	14.0
3. Sometimes	4.6	6.2	3.2	4.5	4.5	5.0	4.6	4.6	4.3	4.4	5.1	1.8	6.4	5.8	6.5	1.7
4. Most times	1.0	1.6	0.3	0.7	2.0	0.9	0.6	1.0	1.6	0.7	1.4	0.9	0.7	1.5	1.0	-
5. Always	1.8	2.1	1.2	1.2	4.4	1.0	1.9	2.2	1.6	1.4	2.0	1.1	3.1	1.2	1.5	3.5
Item 22000 Subject A02b,C07 N★	2376	1075	1242	1886	278	471	715	777	413	1404	894	809	492	378	622	34

E08K: Did someone get high on other drugs?

1. Never	55.1	54.9	55.4	56.0	49.5	49.3	58.8	59.3	47.5	57.2	52.8	71.5	59.3	53.8	32.1	26.0
2. Seldom	19.6	19.6	20.0	21.0	14.1	21.4	16.8	19.7	22.1	20.7	18.0	15.2	19.0	22.0	25.2	13.4
3. Sometimes	15.7	16.4	14.8	15.0	19.4	18.0	15.8	12.0	19.8	15.4	15.7	8.4	13.5	17.0	26.0	22.0
4. Most times	5.0	4.5	5.3	4.8	5.9	6.0	4.1	4.4	6.8	3.4	7.3	2.6	3.4	4.8	8.8	20.0
5. Always	4.5	4.6	4.4	3.3	11.1	5.2	4.5	4.5	3.8	3.3	6.1	2.2	4.8	2.4	7.9	18.5
Item 22010 Subject A02b,C07 N★	2357	1070	1227	1871	274	470	714	766	407	1389	892	804	489	373	618	34

E08L: Did most people get high on other drugs?

1. Never	62.2	62.3	62.3	64.7	49.1	58.0	66.3	65.2	54.1	66.4	57.4	77.6	64.8	60.4	41.8	31.2
2. Seldom	19.4	19.9	19.3	20.3	15.5	20.5	17.5	17.2	25.9	19.7	19.0	11.6	20.1	22.2	28.2	18.6
3. Sometimes	11.2	11.3	10.8	9.9	17.9	12.6	9.7	10.3	14.1	9.4	13.2	6.3	9.0	12.7	18.3	19.8
4. Most times	3.6	2.7	4.4	2.9	8.8	4.6	3.5	3.7	2.8	2.3	5.5	2.3	3.3	3.3	5.7	9.9
5. Always	3.5	3.8	3.3	2.2	8.8	4.2	3.1	3.8	3.1	2.2	4.9	2.2	2.8	1.4	6.0	20.5
Item 22020 Subject A02b,C07 N★	2353	1064	1230	1869	271	467	713	767	407	1387	889	807	485	374	615	34

E08M: Did you get high on other drugs?

1. Never	86.0	82.9	89.4	86.7	90.9	79.9	88.0	89.4	83.3	88.7	82.5	97.3	96.5	93.3	61.8	32.8
2. Seldom	6.6	7.7	5.6	6.9	1.4	9.6	5.9	4.6	8.4	6.0	7.4	1.0	1.1	4.5	19.2	14.6
3. Sometimes	4.3	5.8	2.8	4.1	3.3	6.2	3.0	3.6	5.6	3.4	5.4	0.7	1.2	0.7	12.6	17.9
4. Most times	1.6	1.9	1.2	1.3	1.7	1.8	1.4	1.3	2.1	1.0	2.5	0.2	0.3	1.5	3.5	19.7
5. Always	1.4	1.7	1.0	0.9	2.7	2.5	1.6	1.1	0.6	0.9	2.2	0.7	1.0	-	2.8	15.1
Item 22030 Subject A05c,C07 N★	2368	1070	1239	1881	273	468	715	772	412	1400	890	809	488	376	621	34

E08N: Did you feel pressure to use other drugs?

1. Never	91.4	88.4	94.2	92.6	87.4	88.4	92.7	92.3	90.6	93.3	89.7	94.0	92.1	93.1	87.1	84.3
2. Seldom	4.1	5.6	2.9	4.4	2.1	5.7	3.8	3.0	5.1	3.4	4.9	2.6	1.8	4.0	7.7	8.5
3. Sometimes	2.2	2.9	1.6	1.7	3.9	3.6	2.0	1.5	2.6	1.7	2.6	1.1	2.9	1.8	3.6	-
4. Most times	0.7	1.4	0.1	0.3	1.6	1.2	-	1.1	0.6	0.6	0.9	0.8	1.2	0.4	0.1	2.2
5. Always	1.6	1.7	1.3	0.9	5.0	1.2	1.5	2.1	1.2	1.1	1.9	1.5	2.0	0.7	1.5	5.0
Item 22040 Subject A02b,C07 N★	2367	1070	1239	1881	273	468	715	771	412	1396	892	807	488	378	620	34

E09: Now think about how you would LIKE parties to be. At the parties you go to, how often...

E09A: Would you like people over age 30 to be present at least some of the time?

1. Never	40.2	43.0	37.6	39.1	50.6	40.7	42.5	39.4	37.6	39.0	42.1	33.6	46.5	39.4	44.7	47.1
2. Seldom	28.5	27.9	29.4	29.5	20.2	29.7	29.4	26.2	30.2	29.5	27.1	27.6	27.0	33.0	30.1	17.3
3. Sometimes	23.1	22.0	24.2	23.7	20.4	22.9	19.8	25.8	24.1	23.7	22.4	28.3	21.7	19.8	18.1	23.2
4. Most times	4.5	3.5	5.4	4.4	4.7	3.2	4.7	4.8	4.9	4.9	3.9	6.8	0.9	4.0	4.4	1.7
5. Always	3.6	3.6	3.4	3.3	4.0	3.5	3.6	3.8	3.2	2.9	4.6	3.7	3.9	3.7	2.8	10.7
Item 22050 Subject C08,M02 N	2698	1211	1420	2109	342	503	818	898	480	1586	1036	1024	545	405	647	37

E09B: Would you like to get high on alcohol?

1. Never	36.8	33.1	40.0	30.6	66.9	28.6	33.8	45.2	34.7	40.0	32.6	62.9	28.8	23.1	11.9	11.4
2. Seldom	18.0	16.5	19.1	19.0	15.3	18.8	19.6	16.5	17.2	17.2	19.6	17.1	17.4	23.2	16.9	8.6
3. Sometimes	26.5	26.1	27.1	29.4	13.2	29.3	27.5	22.9	28.4	25.5	27.6	15.0	31.5	35.1	35.0	29.1
4. Most times	11.0	13.4	9.0	12.5	3.8	13.0	10.4	9.7	12.6	11.3	10.6	3.4	15.9	12.7	17.9	21.9
5. Always	7.7	11.0	4.8	8.5	0.8	10.3	8.8	5.7	7.1	6.0	9.6	1.5	6.6	5.9	18.2	29.0
Item 22060 Subject A05c,C08 N	2688	1207	1415	2105	339	499	817	896	476	1581	1031	1020	543	402	646	36

★=excludes respondents for whom question was inappropriate.

QUESTIONNAIRE FORM 5 1984	TOTAL	SEX		RACE		REGION				4YR COLLEGE PLANS		ILLICIT DRUG USE: LIFETIME				
		M	F	White	Black	NE	NC	S	W	Yes	No	None	Marijuana Only	Few Pills	More Pills	Any Heroin
N (Weighted No. of Cases):	3294	1522	1656	2462	457	682	918	1107	587	1824	1282	1228	662	480	801	44
% of Weighted Total:	100.0	46.2	50.3	74.7	13.9	20.7	27.9	33.6	17.8	55.4	38.9	37.3	20.1	14.6	24.3	1.3
E09C: Would you like other people to get high on alcohol?																
1. Never	35.5	31.0	39.3	29.6	61.8	28.0	32.6	43.1	34.3	37.5	33.2	59.4	27.3	22.6	13.4	13.3
2. Seldom	18.9	18.3	19.5	20.3	15.4	18.9	19.9	17.8	19.0	18.4	19.9	18.4	18.2	25.1	16.8	8.4
3. Sometimes	28.5	28.4	28.9	31.2	16.9	31.9	29.7	25.0	29.4	29.1	27.5	16.9	34.8	36.7	36.2	39.0
4. Most times	9.9	11.3	8.3	10.9	3.6	12.2	9.6	7.9	11.6	9.8	9.9	3.4	13.6	10.2	16.8	19.3
5. Always	7.3	10.9	4.0	8.0	2.4	9.0	8.3	6.1	5.6	5.2	9.6	1.9	6.1	5.5	16.8	20.0
Item 22070 Subject A11d,C08 N	2670	1193	1410	2088	338	494	813	890	473	1570	1024	1016	535	400	642	37
E09D: Would you like to use marijuana?																
1. Never	70.8	68.3	73.3	70.5	74.8	58.3	74.3	74.4	71.2	75.0	65.0	97.1	68.1	68.0	36.7	17.0
2. Seldom	11.3	11.4	11.1	11.3	11.3	16.1	10.0	10.4	9.9	10.1	12.8	1.8	16.8	14.1	19.5	16.3
3. Sometimes	9.6	10.7	8.6	10.2	7.8	12.9	8.1	8.6	10.8	8.5	11.8	0.5	9.5	11.8	21.3	29.9
4. Most times	4.1	4.1	4.1	3.9	4.7	5.9	3.4	3.4	4.8	3.1	5.3	0.3	3.2	3.9	10.6	16.1
5. Always	4.2	5.5	2.9	4.1	1.4	6.8	4.1	3.2	3.3	3.3	5.1	0.3	2.4	2.2	11.8	20.7
Item 22080 Subject A05c,C08 N	2693	1209	1418	2105	341	499	818	898	478	1582	1032	1024	542	405	644	37
E09E: Would you like other people to use marijuana?																
1. Never	66.4	64.3	68.5	65.3	72.5	52.1	70.1	71.9	64.4	71.0	60.5	91.8	64.0	62.5	33.5	13.6
2. Seldom	14.2	13.8	14.4	14.8	11.8	19.9	12.6	13.0	13.2	13.7	14.8	5.2	17.2	17.9	23.5	14.5
3. Sometimes	12.6	14.1	11.2	13.3	10.0	17.2	11.3	9.7	15.6	10.4	16.0	2.4	15.1	14.4	23.9	39.1
4. Most times	3.4	3.0	3.7	3.1	4.3	5.4	2.0	2.9	4.6	2.1	5.2	0.4	1.7	3.1	9.2	14.1
5. Always	3.4	4.8	2.2	3.5	1.4	5.4	4.0	2.5	2.2	2.9	3.6	0.2	2.0	2.0	9.9	18.8
Item 22090 Subject A11d,C08 N	2675	1200	1408	2092	337	495	813	893	474	1572	1027	1022	538	398	640	37
E09F: Would you like to use other drugs?																
1. Never	86.4	84.2	88.9	86.3	91.7	77.6	89.2	90.0	84.3	89.0	82.9	98.1	93.0	91.5	62.4	28.2
2. Seldom	6.1	6.6	5.6	6.8	3.0	10.6	4.4	4.3	7.8	5.2	7.4	0.7	3.2	4.9	17.4	26.4
3. Sometimes	4.4	5.7	3.1	4.1	4.1	6.5	3.3	3.9	5.3	3.4	5.8	0.8	2.2	2.9	12.2	12.8
4. Most times	1.4	1.7	1.1	1.2	1.0	2.4	0.9	0.8	2.5	1.1	2.0	0.3	0.7	0.5	3.7	15.3
5. Always	1.6	1.9	1.3	1.6	0.2	2.9	2.2	1.0	0.2	1.3	1.9	0.1	1.0	0.2	4.3	17.3
Item 22100 Subject A05c,C08 N	2686	1208	1411	2102	340	500	818	894	475	1577	1033	1022	543	404	640	37
E09G: Would you like other people to use other drugs?																
1. Never	83.7	81.0	86.4	83.7	86.3	74.5	84.5	87.7	84.3	86.6	79.8	94.8	89.7	87.3	61.6	37.1
2. Seldom	7.9	8.7	7.3	8.3	5.7	11.4	8.7	6.0	6.6	7.3	9.0	3.5	4.4	7.4	17.6	20.7
3. Sometimes	5.5	6.6	4.2	5.4	5.0	8.7	3.8	4.0	7.9	4.1	7.4	1.1	3.6	3.6	14.0	20.3
4. Most times	1.4	1.7	1.0	1.2	1.8	3.0	0.8	1.2	1.1	1.0	1.9	0.4	1.0	1.3	3.2	4.8
5. Always	1.6	2.0	1.1	1.4	1.2	2.4	2.2	1.2	0.2	1.1	1.9	0.2	1.2	0.5	3.6	17.0
Item 22110 Subject A11d,C08 N	2667	1199	1402	2088	335	495	808	890	474	1564	1028	1016	536	400	637	37
E10: If you had ever used marijuana or hashish, do you think that you would have said so in this questionnaire?																
1. No	6.9	8.7	4.9	5.2	14.4	5.0	6.2	8.9	6.5	5.1	9.6	10.5	4.3	3.6	4.6	13.5
2. Not sure	5.4	4.9	5.7	4.9	8.4	5.3	5.8	6.4	3.0	4.3	6.8	7.7	3.9	4.7	3.3	3.2
3. Yes	57.7	56.0	59.8	58.9	55.0	52.3	62.0	57.0	57.0	61.2	52.7	78.6	51.3	50.6	35.8	36.2
4. I did say so	30.0	30.4	29.5	30.9	22.1	37.3	26.0	27.8	33.4	29.4	30.9	3.3	40.5	41.1	56.2	47.1
Item 20800 Subject A15a N	2660	1188	1406	2082	337	492	819	884	466	1567	1014	1000	541	402	641	36
E11: If you had ever used amphetamines (without a doctor's orders), do you think that you would have said so in this questionnaire?																
1. No	8.9	11.0	6.4	6.1	22.3	6.6	7.7	11.8	7.7	6.2	12.6	10.9	8.4	7.2	5.5	13.5
2. Not sure	6.0	5.4	6.4	5.7	7.9	6.6	5.5	6.4	5.2	5.2	6.8	8.3	5.6	5.8	2.9	2.0
3. Yes	69.0	67.3	71.1	70.8	63.1	69.0	70.6	66.8	70.3	74.1	61.9	77.3	81.3	69.3	47.8	47.2
4. I did say so	16.2	16.2	16.2	17.4	6.8	17.8	16.2	14.9	16.8	14.5	18.7	3.5	4.7	17.7	43.7	37.3
Item 20810 Subject A15a N	2658	1188	1404	2080	336	488	819	882	469	1564	1015	998	539	402	642	36

	TOTAL	SEX		RACE		REGION				4YR COLLEGE PLANS		ILLICIT DRUG USE: LIFETIME				
QUESTIONNAIRE FORM 5 1984		M	F	White	Black	NE	NC	S	W	Yes	No	None	Mari- juana Only	Few Pills	More Pills	Any Her- oin
N (Weighted No. of Cases):	3294	1522	1656	2462	457	682	918	1107	587	1824	1282	1228	662	480	801	44
% of Weighted Total:	100.0	46.2	50.3	74.7	13.9	20.7	27.9	33.6	17.8	55.4	38.9	37.3	20.1	14.6	24.3	1.3
E12: If you had ever used heroin, do you think that you would have said so in this question- naire?																
1. No	9.7	12.6	6.7	7.2	20.2	9.3	7.4	11.9	10.4	6.9	13.4	11.0	9.6	6.5	9.2	6.4
2. Not sure	8.7	8.2	8.9	8.9	10.0	8.8	9.7	8.7	6.7	7.6	9.9	9.8	8.4	9.3	7.2	3.2
3. Yes	74.2	71.5	77.4	77.0	64.1	72.1	76.7	72.7	75.0	79.0	68.4	75.8	77.1	78.0	70.1	37.9
4. I did say so	7.3	7.7	6.9	6.9	5.8	9.7	6.2	6.8	7.9	6.4	8.3	3.4	4.9	6.2	13.5	52.4
Item 20820 Subject A15a N	2655	1186	1405	2077	337	487	819	882	468	1563	1016	1001	541	401	636	36

Cross-Time Index of Questionnaire Items, 1975-1985

Introduction to the Indexing Conventions

Beginning with the 1982 volume, the cross-time index of question locations is organized first by subject area (see Table 3 for complete listing). Within each subject area, questions are listed in numerical sequence according to item reference number, which is the unique numerical identifier assigned to each question in the study.

The Question Index may be used in two major ways:

1. **Locating a Question Across Years.** Having located a question of interest in the Descriptive Results section, the reader may determine in what other years that same question has appeared by simply looking it up by subject area and item reference number. The Index will show all years in which that item has appeared and also show its location each year (by questionnaire form, section, and item number). All items will retain their unique reference numbers in future years as well, and thus may be located in exactly the same way in subsequent volumes in this series.

EXAMPLE: A reader interested in a particular item about the nation needing more long-range planning would note that it has been classified under subject area I01 ("Expectations concerning social change") and that it has been assigned item reference number 1200. The index entry for item 1200 shows that this item has appeared in Section A of questionnaire Form 1 in all annual surveys in the series. Its question number was 4A in 1975 and 2A thereafter.

2. **Locating Questions by Subject Area.** Given an interest in some particular subject area, one can quickly scan the Index to locate all questions dealing with that area. Table 3 lists all the subject areas into which items are classified, along with the alphanumeric code assigned to each area.

EXAMPLE: A reader interested in items dealing with religion should first locate the relevant code in Table 3: Code G, "Religion." The second step is to scan that section of the item index, noting for every item its item reference number and page location in this volume. The reader may or may not find the abbreviated description of the item (given in the third column of the index and further described below) helpful in deciding whether to look up a particular item in the Descriptive Results section. Some of these descriptions are rather clear as to their meaning, but others are less so.

Definition of the Column Headings

The definitions of column headings, and the conventions used for the entries in each column, are given below under the numbers indicated in the following key.

①**Item Reference Number.** A unique identification number is assigned to each question for the duration of this research and reporting series. It appears below that question in the Descriptive Results section, as well as in this index and the indices of all other volumes in this series.

②**Page Location.** The second column of the Question Index gives the page number of the present volume on which a verbatim statement of the question may be found along with this year's descriptive results.

③**Item Description (Abbreviated).** This is a brief mnemonic description — up to 16 characters in length — that attempts to characterize the content of the question. Originally developed for question identification on OSIRIS computer files, it may in many cases allow one to determine the relevance of the question to one's own interest and thus reduce the number of irrelevant questions that must be looked up in the Descriptive Results section.

④Questionnaire Location by Year. An entry is provided for every year in which an item appeared in one of the study's questionnaire forms. The six (or fewer) characters comprising the entry indicate the form in which the question appeared, the section of that form, and the question number. Take as an example the questionnaire location 1A004A. This location code indicates that the question appeared in Form 1, Section A, and was labeled as Question 4a.

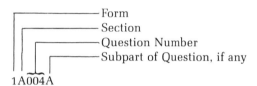

Occasionally an entry will be enclosed in parentheses. This indicates that there was a change (usually minor) in the wording of the question and/or the answer alternatives in subsequent years.

A form number (ranging from 1 to 5) is usually shown in the first character location. However, two substitute characters will replace the form number at times:

+ A plus sign indicates that the item appeared in all five forms that year and that it appeared in the same location on all forms.
* An asterisk indicates that the item appeared in four forms (Forms 2 through 5) and in the same location on all forms.

⑤ Subject Area. Table 3 shows the subject content areas that have been distinguished here and gives the alphanumeric code assigned to each of them. Every question item in the index has been classified into (and listed under) one or more of the subject areas, and the index (beginning with the 1982 volume) has been organized by subject area.

Figure 2

Guide to Cross-Time Index

| ① | ② | ③ | ④ | | | | | | | | |

Item Refer-ence Number	Page Loc. in this Volume	ITEM DESCRIPTION (ABBREVIATED)	QUESTIONNAIRE LOCATION BY YEAR (FORM, SECTION, AND QUESTION NUMBER)								
			1975	1976	1977	1978	1979	1980	1981	1982/83	1984/85

⑤ A01a: DRUGS. Number of uses in lifetime

Item Ref.	Page	Description	1975	1976	1977	1978	1979	1980	1981	1982/83	1984/85
760	25	EVR SMK CIG,REGL	1A018 *B01	+B01	+B01	+B01	+B01	+B01	+B01	+B01	+B01
790	25	EVER DRINK	1A026 *B03	*B03	*B03	*B03	*B03	*B03	*B03	*B03	*B03
810	41	#X DRNK/LIFETIME	1A028A	1B007A	1B007A	1B007A	1B007A	1B007A	1B007A	1B007A	1B007A
	25		*B04A	*B04A	*B04A	*B04A	*B04A	*B04A	*B04A	*B04A	*B04A
860	26	#XMJ+HS/LIFETIME	1A044A *B07A	*B07A	*B07A	*B07A	*B07A	*B07A	*B07A	*B07A	*B07A
890	50	#X LSD/LIFETIME	1A057A	1B029A	1B029A	1B029A	1B029A	1B029A	1B029A	1B033A	1B033A
	27		*B08A	*B08A	*B08A	*B08A	*B08A	*B08A	*B08A	*B08A	*B08A
920	53	#X PSYD/LIFETIME	1A071A	1B038A	1B038A	1B038A	1B038A	1B038A	1B038A	1B042A	1B042A
	27		*B09A	*B09A	*B09A	*B09A	*B09A	*B09A	*B09A	*B09A	*B09A
950	70	#X COKE/LIFETIME	1A144A	1B076A	1B076A	1B076A	1B076A	1B076A	1B076A	1B083A	1B083A
	28		*B10A	*B10A	*B10A	*B10A	*B10A	*B10A	*B10A	*B10A	*B10A
980	56	#X AMPH/LIFETIME	1A087A	1B043A	1B043A	1B043A	1B043A	1B043A	1B043A	1B050A	1B050A
	28		*B11A	*B11A	*B11A	*B11A	*B11A	*B11A	(*B11A)	*B11A	*B11A
1010	60	#X QUAD/LIFETIME	1A102A	1B053A	1B053A	1B053A	1B053A	1B053A	1B053A	1B060A	1B060A
	29		*B12A	*B12A	*B12A	*B12A	*B12A	*B12A	*B12A	*B12A	*B12A
1040	61	#X BRBT/LIFETIME	1A116A	1B057A	1B057A	1B057A	1B057A	1B057A	1B057A	1B064A	1B064A
	30		*B13A	*B13A	*B13A	*B13A	*B13A	*B13A	*B13A	*B13A	*B13A
1070	66	#X TRQL/LIFETIME	1A131A	1B067A	1B067A	1B067A	1B067A	1B067A	1B067A	1B074A	1B074A
	30		*B14A	*B14A	*B14A	*B14A	*B14A	*B14A	*B14A	*B14A	*B14A
1100	74	#X "H"/LIFETIME	1A158A	1B085A	1B085A	1B085A	1B085A	1B085A	1B085A	1B092A	1B092A
	31		*B15A	*B15A	*B15A	*B15A	*B15A	*B15A	*B15A	*B15A	*B15A
1130	75	#X NARC/LIFETIME	1A173A	1B095A	1B095A	1B095A	1B095A	1B095A	1B095A	1B094A	1B094A
	31		*B16A	*B16A	*B16A	*B16A	*B16A	*B16A	*B16A	*B16A	*B16A
1160	32	#X INHL/LIFETIME		*B17A	*B17A	*B17A	*B17A	*B17A	*B17A	*B17A	*B17A
1181	111	#X PCP/LIFETIME								2E02A	2E02A
1184	112	#X PPRS/LIFETIME								2E03A	2E03A
2040	45	#X HASH/LIFETIM		1B018A							1B018A
2070	46	#X MARJ/LIFETIME		1B							1B019A
11000	164	#X BEER/LIFETIME									
11040	165	#X WINE/LIFETIME									
11080	166	#X LIQR/LIFETIME									
21180	49	MJ/HSH EVR DLY									
	49	REGE									

Table 3

Subject Area Key
(Referenced by letter in the Question Index)

A. **Drugs.** Drug use and related attitudes and beliefs, drug availabilty and exposure, surrounding conditions and social meaning of drug use. Views of significant others regarding drugs.

A01 Use of Drugs
 A01a — . . . in lifetime
 A01b — . . . in the last 12 months
 A01c — . . . in the last 30 days
 A01d —Quantity used
 A01e —How high? (How often?)
 A01f —How long high?
 A01g —Incidence of first use
 A01h —Use with other drugs
 A01i —Try to stop?
 A01j — . . . on doctor's orders?
 A01k —Bad trip?
 A01l —Kinds of drugs

A02 Exposure to Drug Use
 A02a —Friends' use of drugs
 A02b —Exposure to users

A03 Availability of Drugs

A04 Expected Future Use

A05 Conditions of Use
 A05a —Alone
 A05b —With others
 A05c —Settings
 A05d —Mode of drug administration

A06 Reasons for Use, Abstention, and Stopping

A07 Problems with Drugs

A08 Sources of Help regarding Drugs

A09 Parental Awareness of Use

A10 Drug Education

A11 Own Attitudes regarding Drugs and Drug Users
 A11a —For adults
 A11b —For own children
 A11c —Perception of drug users

A12 Others' Attitudes regarding Drugs and Drug Users

A12a —Parents
A12b —Friends and students
A12c —Perception of drug users

A13 Legal Issues regarding Drugs
 A13a —Preferred legality for adults
 A13b —Own response to legalization
 A13c —Knowledge of marijuana laws

A14 Risk of Drug Harm
 A14a —To self
 A14b —To others

B. **Education.**

B01 High school: scholastic status, objectives, experiences

B02 Combining work and school: attitudes, experiences

B03 Interracial contact at school

B04 Student norms

B05 Counseling

B06 Absenteeism and truancy

B07 Delinquency and victimization at school

B08 Opinions regarding competency testing

B09 Post high school: status, plans, characteristics

B10 Attitudes regarding educational institutions

C. **Work and Leisure.**

C01 Present or recent work experience

C02 Income sources; financial security

C03 Vocational plans, aspiration, expectations

C04 Preferences regarding job characteristics

Table 3 (continued)

C05 Desirability of different working arrangements and settings

C06 Work ethic/success orientation

C07 Leisure time: extent, activities

C08 Attitudes toward leisure time

D. Sex Roles and Family.

D01 Dating and marriage: status, attitudes, expectations

D02 Parenthood: status, attitudes, expectations

D03 Values surrounding marriage and family

D04 Preferences regarding marital/familial arrangements

D05 Sex role attitudes

D06 Opinions regarding sex discrimination

E. Population Concerns.

E01 Overpopulation

E02 Birth control

F. Conservation, Materialism, Equity, etc.

F01 Personal materialism

F02 Societal materialism and advertising

F03 Concern with world hunger and poverty

F04 Ecological concerns

F05 Concern with conservation of resources

F06 Preferences regarding dwelling type and urbanicity

F07 Driving and use of mass transit

G. Religion.   **Religious preferences, activities, views.**

H. Politics.

H01 Political interest and preferences

H02 Attitudes toward governmental policies and practices

H03 Views about the role of citizens in government. (See also I02: Attitudes regarding activism)

H04 Confidence in government

H05 Voting, political activism

I. Social Change.

I01 Expectations concerning societal change

I02 Attitudes regarding activism

I03 Reactions to personal and social change

J. Social Problems. Interest and concerns.

K. Major Social Institutions

K01 Trust (See also C05: Institutions as work settings)

K02 Satisfaction with performance

K03 Preferred influence

L. Military.

L01 Plans for military service

L02 Attitudes toward a draft

L03 Views about the use of military force

L04 Attitudes toward the military as an institution and occupation

M. Interpersonal Relationships.

M01 Dating

M02 Cross-age relationships with adults outside the family (See also B05)

M03 Agreement/disagreement with parents

Table 3 (continued)

M04 Friendships (See also Q03: Loneliness)

M05 Community at large

N. Race Relations.

N01 Preferred interracial contact

N02 Attitudes about discrimination

N03 Actual interracial contacts

O. Concern for Others.

O01 Attitudes regarding social service, charitable activism

O02 Involvement in community, altruistic activities

O03 Concern with the problems of others

P. Happiness.

P01 Happiness; satisfaction with life and self

P02 Satisfaction with specific life domains

Q. Other Personality Variables.

Q01 Attitudes about self, self-esteem

Q02 Locus of control

Q03 Loneliness

Q04 Risk taking

Q05 Trust in others

Q06 (Changed to Subject Area T.)

Q07 Importance placed on various life goals

Q08 Social, political, cultural orientation

Q09 Hostility

R. Background.

R01 Age, sex, race, and marital status

R02 Family characteristics

R03 Living arrangements and household characteristics

S. Deviance and Victimization.

S01 Delinquent behaviors

S02 Driving violations and accidents

S03 Victimization experiences

T. Health Habits and Symptoms.

Item Reference Number	Page Loc. in this Volume	ITEM DESCRIPTION (ABBREVIATED)	QUESTIONNAIRE LOCATION BY YEAR (FORM, SECTION, AND QUESTION NUMBER)								
			1975	1976	1977	1978	1979	1980	1981	1982/83	1984/85

A01a: DRUGS. Number of uses in lifetime

Item Reference Number	Page Loc.	ITEM DESCRIPTION	1975	1976	1977	1978	1979	1980	1981	1982/83	1984/85
760	25	EVR SMK CIG,REGL	1A018 *B01	+B01	+B01	+B01	+B01	+B01	+B01	+B01	+B01
790	25	EVER DRINK	1A026 *B03	*B03	*B03	*B03	*B03	*B03	*B03	*B03	*B03
810	41	#X DRNK/LIFETIME	1A028A	1B007A	1B007A	1B007A	1B007A	1B007A	1B007A	1B007A	1B007A
	25		*B04A	*B04A	*B04A	*B04A	*B04A	*B04A	*B04A	*B04A	*B04A
860	26	#XMJ+HS/LIFETIME	1A044A *B07A	*B07A	*B07A	*B07A	*B07A	*B07A	*B07A	*B07A	*B07A
890	50	#X LSD/LIFETIME	1A057A	1B029A	1B029A	1B029A	1B029A	1B029A	1B029A	1B033A	1B033A
	27		*B08A	*B08A	*B08A	*B08A	*B08A	*B08A	*B08A	*B08A	*B08A
920	53	#X PSYD/LIFETIME	1A071A	1B038A	1B038A	1B038A	1B038A	1B038A	1B038A	1B042A	1B042A
	27		*B09A	*B09A	*B09A	*B09A	*B09A	*B09A	*B09A	*B09A	*B09A
950	70	#X COKE/LIFETIME	1A144A	1B076A	1B076A	1B076A	1B076A	1B076A	1B076A	1B083A	1B083A
	28		*B10A	*B10A	*B10A	*B10A	*B10A	*B10A	*B10A	*B10A	*B10A
980	56	#X AMPH/LIFETIME	1A087A	1B043A	1B043A	1B043A	1B043A	1B043A	(1B043A)	1B050A	1B050A
	28		*B11A	*B11A	*B11A	*B11A	*B11A	*B11A	(*B11A)	*B11A	*B11A
1010	60	#X QUAD/LIFETIME	1A102A	1B053A	1B053A	1B053A	1B053A	1B053A	1B053A	1B060A	1B060A
	29		*B12A	*B12A	*B12A	*B12A	*B12A	*B12A	*B12A	*B12A	*B12A
1040	61	#X BRBT/LIFETIME	1A116A	1B057A	1B057A	1B057A	1B057A	1B057A	1B057A	1B064A	1B064A
	30		*B13A	*B13A	*B13A	*B13A	*B13A	*B13A	*B13A	*B13A	*B13A
1070	66	#X TRQL/LIFETIME	1A131A	1B067A	1B067A	1B067A	1B067A	1B067A	1B067A	1B074A	1B074A
	30		*B14A	*B14A	*B14A	*B14A	*B14A	*B14A	*B14A	*B14A	*B14A
1100	74	#X "H"/LIFETIME	1A158A	1B085A	1B085A	1B085A	1B085A	1B085A	1B085A	1B092A	1B092A
	31		*B15A	*B15A	*B15A	*B15A	*B15A	*B15A	*B15A	*B15A	*B15A
1130	75	#X NARC/LIFETIME	1A173A	1B095A	1B095A	1B095A	1B095A	1B095A	1B095A	1B094A	1B094A
	31		*B16A	*B16A	*B16A	*B16A	*B16A	*B16A	*B16A	*B16A	*B16A
1160	32	#X INHL/LIFETIME		*B17A	*B17A	*B17A	*B17A	*B17A	*B17A	*B17A	*B17A
1181	111	#X PCP/LIFETIME					2E02A	2E02A	2E02A	2E02A	2E02A
1184	112	#X PPRS/LIFETIME					2E03A	2E03A	2E03A	2E03A	2E03A
2040	45	#X HASH/LIFETIM		1B018A	1B018A	1B018A	1B018A	1B018A	1B018A	1B018A	1B018A
2070	46	#X MARJ/LIFETIME		1B019A	1B019A	1B019A	1B019A	1B019A	1B019A	1B019A	1B019A
11000	164	#X BEER/LIFETIME		4D04A	4D04A	4D04A	4D04A	4D04A	4D04A	4D11A	4D11A
11040	165	#X WINE/LIFETIME		4D06A	4D06A	4D06A	4D06A	4D06A	4D06A	4D13A	4D13A
11080	166	#X LIQR/LIFETIME		4D08A	4D08A	4D08A	4D08A	4D08A	4D08A	4D15A	4D15A
21180	49	MJ/HSH EVR DLY								1B028	1B028
21200	49	RECENT DAILY MJ								1B030	1B030
21210	49	#X DAILY MJ/LFT								1B031	1B031
21220	54	#X DIETPILL/LFT								1B046A	1B046A
21250	55	#X STA-AWAK/LFT								1B047A	1B047A
21280	55	#X LOOKALIK/LFT								1B048A	1B048A

A01b: DRUGS. Number of uses in last 12 months

Item Reference Number	Page Loc.	ITEM DESCRIPTION	1975	1976	1977	1978	1979	1980	1981	1982/83	1984/85
820	42	#X DRNK/LAST12MO	1A028B	1B007B	1B007B	1B007B	1B007B	1B007B	1B007B	1B007B	1B007B
	25		*B04B	*B04B	*B04B	*B04B	*B04B	*B04B	*B04B	*B04B	*B04B
870	26	#XMJ+HS/LAST12MO	1A044B *B07B	*B07B	*B07B	*B07B	*B07B	*B07B	*B07B	*B07B	*B07B
900	50	#X LSD/LAST 12MO	1A057B	1B029B	1B029B	1B029B	1B029B	1B029B	1B029B	1B033B	1B033B
	27		*B08B	*B08B	*B08B	*B08B	*B08B	*B08B	*B08B	*B08B	*B08B
930	53	#X PSYD/LAST12MO	1A071B	1B038B	1B038B	1B038B	1B038B	1B038B	1B038B	1B042B	1B042B
	27		*B09B	*B09B	*B09B	*B09B	*B09B	*B09B	*B09B	*B09B	*B09B
960	70	#X COKE/LAST12MO	1A144B	1B076B	1B076B	1B076B	1B076B	1B076B	1B076B	1B083B	1B083B
	28		*B10B	*B10B	*B10B	*B10B	*B10B	*B10B	*B10B	*B10B	*B10B
990	56	#X AMPH/LAST12MO	1A087B	1B043B	1B043B	1B043B	1B043B	1B043B	(1B043B)	1B050B	1B050B
	29		*B11B	*B11B	*B11B	*B11B	*B11B	*B11B	(*B11B)	*B11B	*B11B
1020	60	#X QUAD/LAST12MO	1A102B	1B053B	1B053B	1B053B	1B053B	1B053B	1B053B	1B060B	1B060B
	29		*B12B	*B12B	*B12B	*B12B	*B12B	*B12B	*B12B	*B12B	*B12B
1050	62	#X BRBT/LAST12MO	1A116B	1B057B	1B057B	1B057B	1B057B	1B057B	1B057B	1B064B	1B064B
	30		*B13B	*B13B	*B13B	*B13B	*B13B	*B13B	*B13B	*B13B	*B13B
1080	66	#X TRQL/LAST12MO	1A131B	1B067B	1B067B	1B067B	1B067B	1B067B	1B067B	1B074B	1B074B
	30		*B14B	*B14B	*B14B	*B14B	*B14B	*B14B	*B14B	*B14B	*B14B
1110	74	#X "H"/LAST 12MO	1A158B	1B085B	1B085B	1B085B	1B085B	1B085B	1B085B	1B092B	1B092B
	31	(continued)	*B15B	*B15B	*B15B	*B15B	*B15B	*B15B	*B15B	*B15B	*B15B

A01b: DRUGS. Number of uses in last 12 months (continued)

Item Reference Number	Page Loc. in this Volume	ITEM DESCRIPTION (ABBREVIATED)	QUESTIONNAIRE LOCATION BY YEAR (FORM, SECTION, AND QUESTION NUMBER)								
			1975	1976	1977	1978	1979	1980	1981	1982/83	1984/85
1140	75	#X NARC/LAST12MO	1A173B	1B095B	1B095B	1B095B	1B095B	1B095B	1B095B	1B094B	1B094B
	31		*B16B	*B16B	*B16B	*B16B	*B16B	*B16B	*B16B	*B16B	*B16B
1170	32	#X INHL/LAST12MO		*B17B	*B17B	*B17B	*B17B	*B17B	*B17B	*B17B	*B17B
1182	112	#X PCP/LAST12MO					2E02B	2E02B	2E02B	2E02B	2E02B
1185	112	#X PPRS/LAST12MO					2E03B	2E03B	2E03B	2E03B	2E03B
2050	45	#X HASH/LAST12M		1B018B	1B018B	1B018B	1B018B	1B018B	1B018B	1B018B	1B018B
2080	46	#X MARJ/LAST12MO		1B019B	1B019B	1B019B	1B019B	1B019B	1B019B	1B019B	1B019B
8520	128	12MO,#OCC PAINRF	3A48A	3A27A	3A27A	3A27A	3A27A	3A27A	3A27A	3A27A	3A27A
8530	129	12MO,#OCC SLP PL	3A48B	3A27B	3A27B	3A27B	3A27B	3A27B	3A27B	3A27B	3A27B
8540	129	12MO,#OCC AWK PL	3A48C	3A27C	3A27C	3A27C	3A27C	3A27C	3A27C	3A27C	3A27C
8550	129	12MO,#OCC CALM P	3A48D	3A27D	3A27D	3A27D	3A27D	3A27D	3A27D	3A27D	3A27D
11010	165	#X BEER/LAST12MO		4D04B	4D04B	4D04B	4D04B	4D04B	4D04B	4D11B	4D11B
11050	165	#X WINE/LAST12MO		4D06B	4D06B	4D06B	4D06B	4D06B	4D06B	4D13B	4D13B
11090	166	#X LIQR/LAST12MO		4D08B	4D08B	4D08B	4D08B	4D08B	4D08B	4D15B	4D15B
21230	54	#X DIETPILL/12M								1B046B	1B046B
21260	55	#X STA-AWAK/12M								1B047B	1B047B
21290	56	#X LOOKALIK/12M								1B048B	1B048B

A01c: DRUGS. Number of uses in last 30 days

Item Reference Number	Page Loc. in this Volume	ITEM DESCRIPTION (ABBREVIATED)	1975	1976	1977	1978	1979	1980	1981	1982/83	1984/85
780	41	#CIGS SMKD/30DAY	1A020	1B003	1B003	1B003	1B003	1B003	1B003	1B003	1B003
	25		*B02	*B02	*B02	*B02	*B02	*B02	*B02	*B02	*B02
830	42	#X DRNK/LAST30DA	1A028C	1B007C	1B007C	1B007C	1B007C	1B007C	1B007C	1B007C	1B007C
	25		*B04C	*B04C	*B04C	*B04C	*B04C	*B04C	*B04C	*B04C	*B04C
880	27	#XMJ+HS/LAST30DA	1A044C	*B07C	*B07C	*B07C	*B07C	*B07C	*B07C	*B07C	*B07C
			*B07C								
910	50	#X LSD/LAST 30DA	1A057C	1B029C	1B029C	1B029C	1B029C	1B029C	1B029C	1B033C	1B033C
	27		*B08C	*B08C	*B08C	*B08C	*B08C	*B08C	*B08C	*B08C	*B08C
940	53	#X PSYD/LAST30DA	1A071C	1B038C	1B038C	1B038C	1B038C	1B038C	1B038C	1B042C	1B042C
	28		*B09C	*B09C	*B09C	*B09C	*B09C	*B09C	*B09C	*B09C	*B09C
970	70	#X COKE/LAST30DA	1A144C	1B076C	1B076C	1B076C	1B076C	1B076C	1B076C	1B083C	1B083C
	28		*B10C	*B10C	*B10C	*B10C	*B10C	*B10C	*B10C	*B10C	*B10C
1000	57	#X AMPH/LAST30DA	1A087C	1B043C	1B043C	1B043C	1B043C	1B043C	(1B043C)	1B050C	1B050C
	29		*B11C	*B11C	*B11C	*B11C	*B11C	*B11C	(*B11C)	*B11C	*B11C
1030	60	#X QUAD/LAST30DA	1A102C	1B053C	1B053C	1B053C	1B053C	1B053C	1B053C	1B060C	1B060C
	29		*B12C	*B12C	*B12C	*B12C	*B12C	*B12C	*B12C	*B12C	*B12C
1060	62	#X BRBT/LAST30DA	1A116C	1B057C	1B057C	1B057C	1B057C	1B057C	1B057C	1B064C	1B064C
	30		*B13C	*B13C	*B13C	*B13C	*B13C	*B13C	*B13C	*B13C	*B13C
1090	66	#X TRQL/LAST30DA	1A131C	1B067C	1B067C	1B067C	1B067C	1B067C	1B067C	1B074C	1B074C
	30		*B14C	*B14C	*B14C	*B14C	*B14C	*B14C	*B14C	*B14C	*B14C
1120	74	#X "H"/LAST 30DA	1A158C	1B085C	1B085C	1B085C	1B085C	1B085C	1B085C	1B092C	1B092C
	31		*B15C	*B15C	*B15C	*B15C.	*B15C	*B15C	*B15C	*B15C	*B15C
1150	75	#X NARC/LAST30DA	1A173C	1B095C	1B095C	1B095C	1B095C	1B095C	1B095C	1B094C	1B094C
	32		*B16C	*B16C	*B16C	*B16C	*B16C	*B16C	*B16C	*B16C	*B16C
1180	32	#X INHL/LAST30DA		*B17C	*B17C	*B17C	*B17C	*B17C	*B17C	*B17C	*B17C
1183	112	#X PCP/LAST30DA					2E02C	2E02C	2E02C	2E02C	2E02C
1186	112	#X PPRS/LAST30DA					2E03C	2E03C	2E03C	2E03C	2E03C
2060	45	#X HASH/LAST30D		1B018C	1B018C	1B018C	1B018C	1B018C	1B018C	1B018C	1B018C
2090	46	#X MARJ/LAST30DA		1B019C	1B019C	1B019C	1B019C	1B019C	1B019C	1B019C	1B019C
11020	165	#X BEER/LAST30DA		4D04C	4D04C	4D04C	4D04C	4D04C	4D04C	4D11C	4D11C
11060	165	#X WINE/LAST30DA		4D06C	4D06C	4D06C	4D06C	4D06C	4D06C	4D13C	4D13C
11100	166	#X LIQR/LAST30DA		4D08C	4D08C	4D08C	4D08C	4D08C	4D08C	4D15C	4D15C
21240	54	#X DIETPILL/30D								1B046C	1B046C
21270	55	#X STA-AWAK/30D								1B047C	1B047C
21300	56	#X LOOKALIK/30D								1B048C	1B048C

A01d: DRUGS. Quantity used

Item Reference Number	Page Loc. in this Volume	ITEM DESCRIPTION (ABBREVIATED)	1975	1976	1977	1978	1979	1980	1981	1982/83	1984/85
850	44	5+DRK ROW/LST 2W	1A035	1B012	1B012	1B012	1B012	1B012	1B012	1B012	1B012
	26		*B06	*B06	*B06	*B06	*B06	*B06	*B06	*B06	*B06
1990	44	#X/2W,3-4 DR RW	1A036	1B013	1B013	1B013	1B013	1B013	1B013	1B013	1B013
2000	44	#X/2WK,2 DRK RW	1A037	1B014	1B014	1B014	1B014	1B014	1B014	1B014	1B014
2010	45	#X/2WK,JST 1DRK	1A038	1B015	1B015	1B015	1B015	1B015	1B015	1B015	1B015
		(continued)									

Item Reference Number	Page Loc. in this Volume	ITEM DESCRIPTION (ABBREVIATED)	QUESTIONNAIRE LOCATION BY YEAR (FORM, SECTION, AND QUESTION NUMBER)								
			1975	1976	1977	1978	1979	1980	1981	1982/83	1984/85

A01d: DRUGS. Quantity used (continued)

2360	48	JOINT/DA LST MO		1B025	1B025	1B025	1B025	1B025	1B025	1B025	1B025
2370	48	OZS.MJ LST MO/6		1B026	1B026	1B026	1B026	1B026	1B026	1B026	1B026
11030	165	5+BR/LST2WK,10+X		4D05	4D05	4D05	4D05	4D05	4D05	4D12	4D12
11070	166	#X 20OZ+ WN/2 WK		4D07	4D07	4D07	4D07	4D07	4D07	4D14	4D14
11110	166	#X 5+LIQ/LST 2WK		4D09	4D09	4D09	4D09	4D09	4D09	4D16	4D16
21100		#CANS COLA/DAY							5E10		
21110		#CUPS COFFEE/DAY							5E11		
21120		#CUPS TEA/DAY							5E12		
21130		#12OZ CAF DRK/DA								5E08	
21140		#12OZ OTH DRK/DA								5E09	
21150		#CUPS COFFEE/DA								5E10	
21160		#CUPS OF TEA/DAY								5E11	
21170		#CUPS DECAFF/DAY								5E12	

A01e: DRUGS. How high, how often high

840	26	#X DRK ENF FL HI	*B05	*B05	*B05	*B05	*B05	*B05	*B05	*B05	*B05
1970	44	#X DRK ENF FL 4	1A033	1B010	1B010	1B010	1B010	1B010	1B010	1B010	1B010
2340	48	MJ/HSH,VRY HIGH	1A050	1B023	1B023	1B023	1B023	1B023	1B023	1B023	1B023
2650	52	LSD,GET VERY HI	1A063	1B033	1B033	1B033	1B033	1B033	1B033	1B037	1B037
2700	53	PSYD,GT VERY HI	1A077	1B039	1B039	1B039	1B039	1B039	1B039	1B043	1B043
3100	59	AMPH,GT VERY HI	1A093	1B047	1B047	1B047	1B047	1B047	1B047	1B054	1B054
3260	61	QUAD GT VERY HI	1A108	1B054	1B054	1B054	1B054	1B054	1B054	1B061	1B061
3590	64	BARB,GT VERY HI	1A122	1B061	1B061	1B061	1B061	1B061	1B061	1B068	1B068
4050	69	TRNQ,GT VERY HI	1A137	1B071	1B071	1B071	1B071	1B071	1B071	1B078	1B078
4520	73	COK,GET VERY HI	1A150	1B080	1B080	1B080	1B080	1B080	1B080	1B087	1B087
4930		HER,GT VERY HI	1A164	1B089	1B089	1B089	1B089	1B089	1B089		
5380	79	NARC,GT VERY HI	1A179	1B099	1B099	1B099	1B099	1B099	1B099	1B098	1B098

A01f: DRUGS. How long high

1980	44	DRK AL,HI24+HR	1A034	1B011	1B011	1B011	1B011	1B011	1B011	1B011	1B011
2350	48	MJ/HSH,HI 24+HR	1A051	1B024	1B024	1B024	1B024	1B024	1B024	1B024	1B024
2660	52	LSD,HIGH 24+ HR	1A064	1B034	1B034	1B034	1B034	1B034	1B034	1B038	1B038
2710	54	PSYD,HI 24+ HRS	1A078	1B040	1B040	1B040	1B040	1B040	1B040	1B044	1B044
3110	59	AMPH,HI 24+ HRS	1A094	1B048	1B048	1B048	1B048	1B048	1B048	1B055	1B055
3270	61	QUAD,HI 24+ HRS	1A109	1B055	1B055	1B055	1B055	1B055	1B055	1B062	1B062
3600	65	BARB,HI 24+ HRS	1A123	1B062	1B062	1B062	1B062	1B062	1B062	1B069	1B069
4060	69	TRNQ,HI 24+ HRS	1A138	1B072	1B072	1B072	1B072	1B072	1B072	1B079	1B079
4530	73	COK,HIGH 24+ HR	1A151	1B081	1B081	1B081	1B081	1B081	1B081	1B088	1B088
4940		HER,HI 24+ HRS	1A165	1B090	1B090	1B090	1B090	1B090	1B090		
5390	79	NARC,HI 24+ HRS	1A180	1B100	1B100	1B100	1B100	1B100	1B100	1B099	1B099

A01g: DRUGS. Incidence of first use

1680	40	SMK CIG DLY/12G	1A019	1B002	(1B002)	1B002	1B002	1B002	1B002	1B002	1B002
5570	80	GR 1ST SMOK DLY	1A019	1B105A	1B105A	1B105A	1B105A	1B105A	1B105A	1B104A	1B104A
	143				3E12A	3E12A	3E12A	3E12A	3E12A	3E10A	3E10A
5580	80	GR 1ST TRY ALC	1A027	1B105B	1B105B	1B105B	1B105B	1B105B	1B105B	1B104B	1B104B
	143				3E12B	3E12B	3E12B	3E12B	3E12B	3E10B	3E10B
5590	80	GR 1ST TRY MJ	1A043	1B105C	1B105C	1B105C	1B105C	1B105C	1B105C	1B104C	1B104C
	143				3E12C	3E12C	3E12C	3E12C	3E12C	3E10C	3E10C
5600	80	GR 1ST TRY LSD	1A056	1B105D	1B105D	1B105D	1B105D	1B105D	1B105D	1B104D	1B104D
	143				3E12D	3E12D	3E12D	3E12D	3E12D	3E10D	3E10D
5610	80	GR 1ST TRY PSY	1A070	1B105E	1B105E	1B105E	1B105E	1B105E	1B105E	1B104E	1B104E
	143				3E12E	3E12E	3E12E	3E12E	3E12E	3E10E	3E10E
5620	80	GR 1ST TRY AMP	1A086	1B105F	1B105F	1B105F	1B105F	1B105F	1B105F	1B104F	1B104F
	143				3E12F	3E12F	3E12F	3E12F	3E12F	3E10F	3E10F
5630	81	GR 1ST TRY QUA	1A101	1B105G	1B105G	1B105G	1B105G	1B105G	1B105G	1B104G	1B104G
	144				3E12G	3E12G	3E12G	3E12G	3E12G	3E10G	3E10G
5640	81	GR 1ST TRY BRB	1A115	1B105H	1B105H	1B105H	1B105H	1B105H	1B105H	1B104H	1B104H
	144				3E12H	3E12H	3E12H	3E12H	3E12H	3E10H	3E10H
5650	81	GR 1ST TRY TRN	1A130	1B105I	1B105I	1B105I	1B105I	1B105I	1B105I	1B104I	1B104I
		(continued)									

Item Reference Number	Page Loc. in this Volume	ITEM DESCRIPTION (ABBREVIATED)	QUESTIONNAIRE LOCATION BY YEAR (FORM, SECTION, AND QUESTION NUMBER)								
			1975	1976	1977	1978	1979	1980	1981	1982/83	1984/85

A01g: DRUGS. Incidence of first use (continued)

Item Reference Number	Page Loc. in this Volume	ITEM DESCRIPTION (ABBREVIATED)	1975	1976	1977	1978	1979	1980	1981	1982/83	1984/85
	144				3E12I	3E12I	3E12I	3E12I	3E12I	3E10I	3E10I
5660	81	GR 1ST TRY COK	1A143	1B105J	1B105J	1B105J	1B105J	1B105J	1B105J	1B104J	1B104J
	144				3E12J	3E12J	3E12J	3E12J	3E12J	3E10J	3E10J
5670	81	GR 1ST TRY HER	1A157	1B105K	1B105K	1B105K	1B105K	1B105K	1B105K	1B104K	1B104K
	144				3E12K	3E12K	3E12K	3E12K	3E12K	3E10K	3E10K
5680	81	GR 1ST TRY NRC	1A172	1B105L	1B105L	1B105L	1B105L	1B105L	1B105L	1B104L	1B104L
	144				3E12L	3E12L	3E12L	3E12L	3E12L	3E10L	3E10L
5685	145	GR 1ST TRY INHAL				3E12M	3E12M	3E12M	3E12M	3E10M	3E10M
5686	112	GR 1ST TRY PCP						2E04A	2E04A	2E04A	2E04A
5687	113	GR 1ST TRY PPRS						2E04B	2E04B	2E04B	2E04B
21190	49	GR 1ST DAILY MJ								1B029	1B029

A01h: DRUGS. Use with other drugs

Item Reference Number	Page Loc. in this Volume	ITEM DESCRIPTION (ABBREVIATED)	1975	1976	1977	1978	1979	1980	1981	1982/83	1984/85
2200	47	#X OVL MJ+ ALC		1B021	1B021	1B021	1B021	1B021	1B021	1B021	1B021
2500	51	#X OVL LSD+ ALC		1B031A	1B031A	1B031A	1B031A	1B031A	1B031A	1B035A	1B035A
2510	52	#X OVL LSD+ MJ		1B031B	1B031B	1B031B	1B031B	1B031B	1B031B	1B035B	1B035B
2900	58	#X OVL AMPH+ALC		1B045A	1B045A	1B045A	1B045A	1B045A	1B045A	1B052A	1B052A
2910	58	#X OVL AMPH+MJ		1B045B	1B045B	1B045B	1B045B	1B045B	1B045B	1B052B	1B052B
2920	58	#X OVL AMPH+LSD		1B045C	1B045C	1B045C	1B045C	1B045C	1B045C	1B052C	1B052C
2930	59	#X OVL AMPH+PSY		1B045D	1B045D	1B045D	1B045D	1B045D	1B045D	1B052D	1B052D
3390	63	#X OVL BARB+ALC		1B059A	1B059A	1B059A	1B059A	1B059A	1B059A	1B066A	1B066A
3400	63	#X OVL BARB+MJ		1B059B	1B059B	1B059B	1B059B	1B059B	1B059B	1B066B	1B066B
3410	64	#X OVL BARB+LSD		1B059C	1B059C	1B059C	1B059C	1B059C	1B059C	1B066C	1B066C
3420	64	#X OVL BARB+PSY		1B059D	1B059D	1B059D	1B059D	1B059D	1B059D	1B066D	1B066D
3430	64	#X OVL BARB+AMP		1B059E	1B059E	1B059E	1B059E	1B059E	1B059E	1B066E	1B066E
3440	64	#X OVL BARB+QUA		1B059F	1B059F	1B059F	1B059F	1B059F	1B059F	1B066F	1B066F
3840	68	#X OVL TRQL+ALC		1B069A	1B069A	1B069A	1B069A	1B069A	1B069A	1B076A	1B076A
3850	68	#X OVL TRQL+MJ		1B069B	1B069B	1B069B	1B069B	1B069B	1B069B	1B076B	1B076B
3860	68	#X OVL TRQL+LSD		1B069C	1B069C	1B069C	1B069C	1B069C	1B069C	1B076C	1B076C
3870	68	#X OVL TRQL+PSY		1B069D	1B069D	1B069D	1B069D	1B069D	1B069D	1B076D	1B076D
3880	68	#X OVL TRQL+AMP		1B069E	1B069E	1B069E	1B069E	1B069E	1B069E	1B076E	1B076E
3890	68	#X OVL TRQL+QUA		1B069F	1B069F	1B069F	1B069F	1B069F	1B069F	1B076F	1B076F
3900	68	#X OVL TRQL+BRB		1B069G	1B069G	1B069G	1B069G	1B069G	1B069G	1B076G	1B076G
4290	72	#X OVL COKE+ALC		1B078A	1B078A	1B078A	1B078A	1B078A	1B078A	1B085A	1B085A
4300	72	#X OVL COKE+MJ		1B078B	1B078B	1B078B	1B078B	1B078B	1B078B	1B085B	1B085B
4310	72	#X OVL COKE+LSD		1B078C	1B078C	1B078C	1B078C	1B078C	1B078C	1B085C	1B085C
4320	72	#X OVL COKE+PSY		1B078D	1B078D	1B078D	1B078D	1B078D	1B078D	1B085D	1B085D
4330	72	#X OVL COKE+AMP		1B078E	1B078E	1B078E	1B078E	1B078E	1B078E	1B085E	1B085E
4340	72	#X OVL COKE+QUA		1B078F	1B078F	1B078F	1B078F	1B078F	1B078F	1B085F	1B085F
4350	73	#X OVL COKE+BRB		1B078G	1B078G	1B078G	1B078G	1B078G	1B078G	1B085G	1B085G
4360	73	#X OVL COKE+TRN		1B078H	1B078H	1B078H	1B078H	1B078H	1B078H	1B085H	1B085H
4710		#X OVL HER +ALC		1B087A	1B087A	1B087A	1B087A	1B087A	1B087A		
4720		#X OVL HER +MJ		1B087B	1B087B	1B087B	1B087B	1B087B	1B087B		
4730		#X OVL HER +LSD		1B087C	1B087C	1B087C	1B087C	1B087C	1B087C		
4740		#X OVL HER +PSY		1B087D	1B087D	1B087D	1B087D	1B087D	1B087D		
4750		#X OVL HER +AMP		1B087E	1B087E	1B087E	1B087E	1B087E	1B087E		
4760		#X OVL HER +QUA		1B087F	1B087F	1B087F	1B087F	1B087F	1B087F		
4770		#X OVL HER +BRB		1B087G	1B087G	1B087G	1B087G	1B087G	1B087G		
4780		#X OVL HER +TRN		1B087H	1B087H	1B087H	1B087H	1B087H	1B087H		
4790		#X OVL HER +COK		1B087I	1B087I	1B087I	1B087I	1B087I	1B087I		
5130	77	#X OVL NARC+ALC		1B097A	1B097A	1B097A	1B097A	1B097A	1B097A	1B096A	1B096A
5140	77	#X OVL NARC+MJ		1B097B	1B097B	1B097B	1B097B	1B097B	1B097B	1B096B	1B096B
5150	77	#X OVL NARC+LSD		1B097C	1B097C	1B097C	1B097C	1B097C	1B097C	1B096C	1B096C
5160	77	#X OVL NARC+PSY		1B097D	1B097D	1B097D	1B097D	1B097D	1B097D	1B096D	1B096D
5170	77	#X OVL NARC+AMP		1B097E	1B097E	1B097E	1B097E	1B097E	1B097E	1B096E	1B096E
5180	77	#X OVL NARC+QUA		1B097F	1B097F	1B097F	1B097F	1B097F	1B097F	1B096F	1B096F
5190	78	#X OVL NARC+BRB		1B097G	1B097G	1B097G	1B097G	1B097G	1B097G	1B096G	1B096G
5200	78	#X OVL NARC+TRN		1B097H	1B097H	1B097H	1B097H	1B097H	1B097H	1B096H	1B096H
5210	78	#X OVL NARC+COK		1B097I	1B097I	1B097I	1B097I	1B097I	1B097I	1B096I	1B096I
5220	78	#X OVL NARC+HER		1B097J	1B097J	1B097J	1B097J	1B097J	1B097J	1B096J	1B096J

Item Reference Number	Page Loc. in this Volume	ITEM DESCRIPTION (ABBREVIATED)	QUESTIONNAIRE LOCATION BY YEAR (FORM, SECTION, AND QUESTION NUMBER)								
			1975	1976	1977	1978	1979	1980	1981	1982/83	1984/85

A01i: DRUGS. Tried to stop

Item Reference Number	Page Loc. in this Volume	ITEM DESCRIPTION (ABBREVIATED)	1975	1976	1977	1978	1979	1980	1981	1982/83	1984/85
1690	41	*TRY STP SMK&FL	1A021	1B004	1B004	1B004	1B004	1B004	1B004	1B004	1B004
1700	41	*WNT STP SMK NW	1A022	1B005	1B005	1B005	1B005	1B005	1B005	1B005	1B005
2020	45	*TRY STP ALC&FL	1A039	1B016	1B016	1B016	1B016	1B016	1B016	1B016	1B016
2380	49	*TRY STP MJ &FL	1A052	1B027	1B027	1B027	1B027	1B027	1B027	1B027	1B027
2680	52	*TRY STP LSD&FL	1A066	1B036	1B036	1B036	1B036	1B036	1B036	1B040	1B040
3240	60	*TRY STP AMP&FL	1A096	1B051	1B051	1B051	1B051	1B051	1B051	1B058	1B058
3710	65	TRY STP BARB&FL	1A125	1B064	1B064	1B064	1B064	1B064	1B064	1B071	1B071
4170	69	*TRY STP TRQ&FL	1A139	1B074	1B074	1B074	1B074	1B074	1B074	1B081	1B081
4540	73	*TRY STP COK&FL	1A152	1B082	1B082	1B082	1B082	1B082	1B082	1B089	1B089
4950		TRY STP HER& FL	1A166	1B091	1B091	1B091	1B091	1B091	1B091		
5500	79	TRY STP NARC&FL	1A182	1B102	1B102	1B102	1B102	1B102	1B102	1B101	1B101
8910	134	12MO REDUCE ALCL		3D03A	3D03A	3D03A	3D03A	3D03A	3D03A	3D03A	3D03A
8920	134	12MO REDUCE CIG		3D03B	3D03B	3D03B	3D03B	3D03B	3D03B	3D03B	3D03B
8930	134	12MO REDUCE MARJ		3D03C	3D03C	3D03C	3D03C	3D03C	3D03C	3D03C	3D03C
8940	134	12MO REDUCE PSYC		3D03D	3D03D	3D03D	3D03D	3D03D	3D03D	3D03D	3D03D
8950	134	12MO REDUCE AMPH		3D03E	3D03E	3D03E	3D03E	3D03E	3D03E	3D03E	3D03E
8960		12MO REDUCE QUAL		3D03F	3D03F	3D03F					
8970	134	12MO REDUCE BARB		3D03G	3D03G	(3D03G)	3D03G	3D03G	3D03G	3D03G	3D03G
8980	134	12MO REDUCE COKE		3D03H	3D03H	3D03H	3D03H	3D03H	3D03H	3D03H	3D03H
8990	135	12MO REDUCE HRN		3D03I	3D03I	3D03I	3D03I	3D03I	3D03I	3D03I	3D03I
9000	135	12MO REDUCE NARC		3D03J	3D03J	3D03J	3D03J	3D03J	3D03J	3D03J	3D03J
9005	134	12MO REDUCE TRQL					3D03F	3D03F	3D03F	3D03F	3D03F

A01j: DRUGS. Use on doctor's orders

Item Reference Number	Page Loc. in this Volume	ITEM DESCRIPTION (ABBREVIATED)	1975	1976	1977	1978	1979	1980	1981	1982/83	1984/85
2790	56	DR TOLD TK AMPH	1A085	1B042	1B042	1B042	1B042	1B042	1B042	1B049	1B049
3280	61	DR TOLD TK BARB	1A114	1B056	1B056	1B056	1B056	1B056	1B056	1B063	1B063
3730	65	DR TOLD TK TRNQ	1A129	1B066	1B066	1B066	1B066	1B066	1B066	1B073	1B073
5020	75	DR TOLD TK NARC	1A171	1B094	1B094	1B094	1B094	1B094	1B094	1B093	1B093

A01k: DRUGS. Bad trip

Item Reference Number	Page Loc. in this Volume	ITEM DESCRIPTION (ABBREVIATED)	1975	1976	1977	1978	1979	1980	1981	1982/83	1984/85
2670	52	1+ BAD TRIP LSD	1A065	1B035	1B035	1B035	1B035	1B035	1B035	1B039	1B039

A01l: DRUGS. Specific kinds of drugs

Item Reference Number	Page Loc. in this Volume	ITEM DESCRIPTION (ABBREVIATED)	1975	1976	1977	1978	1979	1980	1981	1982/83	1984/85
2720	54	TKN YR,MESCALIN	1A079A	1B041A	1B041A	1B041A	1B041A	1B041A	1B041A	1B045A	1B045A
2730	54	TKN YR,PEYOTE	1A079B	1B041B	1B041B	1B041B	1B041B	1B041B	1B041B	1B045B	1B045B
2740	54	TKN YR,PSILOCYB	1A079C	1B041C	1B041C	1B041C	1B041C	1B041C	1B041C	1B045C	1B045C
2750	54	TKN YR,PCP		1B041D	1B041D	1B041D	1B041D	1B041D	1B041D	1B045D	1B045D
2760	54	TKN YR,CNCT THC	1A079D	1B041E	1B041E	1B041E	1B041E	1B041E	1B041E	1B045E	1B045E
2770	54	TKN YR,OTH PSYD	1A079E	1B041F	1B041F	1B041F	1B041F	1B041F	1B041F	1B045F	1B045F
2780	54	TKN YR,DK NAME	1A079F	1B041G	1B041G	1B041G	1B041G	1B041G	1B041G	1B045G	1B045G
3120	59	TKN YR,BENZDRIN	1A095A	1B049A	1B049A	1B049A	1B049A	1B049A	1B049A	1B056A	1B056A
3130	59	TKN YR,DEXEDRIN	1A095B	1B049B	1B049B	1B049B	1B049B	1B049B	1B049B	1B056B	1B056B
3140	59	TKN YR,METHDRIN	1A095C	1B049C	1B049C	1B049C	1B049C	1B049C	1B049C	1B056C	1B056C
3150	59	TKN YR,RITALIN	1A095D	1B049D	1B049D	1B049D	1B049D	1B049D	1B049D	1B056D	1B056D
3160	59	TKN YR,PRELUDIN	1A095E	1B049E	1B049E	1B049E	1B049E	1B049E	1B049E	1B056E	1B056E
3170	59	TKN YR,DEXAMYL	1A095F	1B049F	1B049F	1B049F	1B049F	1B049F	1B049F	1B056F	1B056F
3180	59	TKN YR,METHAMPH	1A095G	1B049G	1B049G	1B049G	1B049G	1B049G	1B049G	1B056G	1B056G
3190	59	TKN YR,OTH AMPH	1A095H	1B049H	1B049H	1B049H	1B049H	1B049H	1B049H	1B056H	1B056H
3200	59	TKN YR,DNT KN N	1A095I	1B049I	1B049I	1B049I	1B049I	1B049I	1B049I	1B056I	1B056I
3610	65	TKN YR,PHNOBARB	1A124A	1B063A	1B063A	1B063A	1B063A	1B063A	1B063A	1B070A	1B070A
3620	65	TKN YR,SECONAL	1A124B	1B063B	1B063B	1B063B	1B063B	1B063B	1B063B	1B070B	1B070B
3630	65	TKN YR,TUINAL	1A124C	1B063C	1B063C	1B063C	1B063C	1B063C	1B063C	1B070C	1B070C
3640	65	TKN YR,NEMBUTAL	1A124D	1B063D	1B063D	1B063D	1B063D	1B063D	1B063D	1B070D	1B070D
3650	65	TKN YR,LUMINAL	1A124E	1B063E	1B063E	1B063E	1B063E	1B063E	1B063E	1B070E	1B070E
3660	65	TKN YR,DESBUTAL	1A124F	1B063F	1B063F	1B063F	1B063F	1B063F	1B063F	1B070F	1B070F
3670	65	TKN YR,AMYTAL	1A124G	1B063G	1B063G	1B063G	1B063G	1B063G	1B063G	1B070G	1B070G
3680	65	TKN YR,ADRNOCAL	1A124H	1B063H	1B063H	1B063H	1B063H	1B063H	1B063H	1B070H	1B070H
3690	65	TKN YR,OTH BRBT	1A124I	1B063I	1B063I	1B063I	1B063I	1B063I	1B063I	1B070I	1B070I
3700	65	TKN YR,DNT KNOW	1A124J	1B063J	1B063J	1B063J	1B063J	1B063J	1B063J	1B070J	1B070J
4070	69	TKN YR,LIBRIUM		1B073A	1B073A	1B073A	1B073A	1B073A	1B073A	1B080A	1B080A
		(continued)									

Item Reference Number	Page Loc. in this Volume	ITEM DESCRIPTION (ABBREVIATED)	QUESTIONNAIRE LOCATION BY YEAR (FORM, SECTION, AND QUESTION NUMBER)								
			1975	1976	1977	1978	1979	1980	1981	1982/83	1984/85

A01l: DRUGS. Specific kinds of drugs *(continued)*

4080	69	TKN YR,VALIUM		1B073B	1B073B	1B073B	1B073B	1B073B	1B073B	1B080B	1B080B
4090	69	TKN YR,MILTOWN		1B073C	1B073C	1B073C	1B073C	1B073C	1B073C	1B080C	1B080C
4100	69	TKN YR,EQUANIL		1B073D	1B073D	1B073D	1B073D	1B073D	1B073D	1B080D	1B080D
4110	69	TKN YR,MEPRBMTE		1B073E	1B073E	1B073E	1B073E	1B073E	1B073E	1B080E	1B080E
4120	69	TKN YR,SERAX		1B073F	1B073F	1B073F	1B073F	1B073F	1B073F	1B080F	1B080F
4130	69	TKN YR,ATARAX		1B073G	1B073G	1B073G	1B073G	1B073G	1B073G	1B080G	1B080G
4140	69	TKN YR,TRANXENE		1B073H	1B073H	1B073H	1B073H	1B073H	1B073H	1B080H	1B080H
4150	69	TKN YR,VISTARIL		1B073I	1B073I	1B073I	1B073I	1B073I	1B073I	1B080I	1B080I
4160	69	TKN YR,DNT KNW		1B073J	1B073J	1B073J	1B073J	1B073J	1B073J	1B080J	1B080J
5400	79	NARC TKN MTHDNE	1A181A	1B101A	1B101A	1B101A	1B101A	1B101A	1B101A	1B100A	1B100A
5410	79	NARC TKN OPIUM	1A181B	1B101B	1B101B	1B101B	1B101B	1B101B	1B101B	1B100B	1B100B
5420	79	NARC TKN MRPHNE	1A181C	1B101C	1B101C	1B101C	1B101C	1B101C	1B101C	1B100C	1B100C
5430	79	NARC TKN CODEIN	1A181D	1B101D	1B101D	1B101D	1B101D	1B101D	1B101D	1B100D	1B100D
5440	79	NARC TKN DEMROL	1A181E	1B101E	1B101E	1B101E	1B101E	1B101E	1B101E	1B100E	1B100E
5450	79	NARC TKN PARGRC	1A181F	1B101F	1B101F	1B101F	1B101F	1B101F	1B101F	1B100F	1B100F
5460	79	NARC TKN TALWIN	1A181G	1B101G	1B101G	1B101G	1B101G	1B101G	1B101G	1B100G	1B100G
5470	79	NARC TKN LDANUM	1A181H	1B101H	1B101H	1B101H	1B101H	1B101H	1B101H	1B100H	1B100H
5480	79	NARC TKN OTHER	1A181I	1B101I	1B101I	1B101I	1B101I	1B101I	1B101I	1B100I	1B100I
5490	79	NARC TKN DNT KN	1A181J	1B101J	1B101J	1B101J	1B101J	1B101J	1B101J	1B100J	1B100J

A02a: DRUGS. Friends' use

7070	109	ALL FRD SMK CIGS	2A41A	2D06A	2D06A	2D06A	2D06A	2D06A	2D06A	2D06A	2D06A
7080	109	ALL FRD SMK MARJ	2A41B	2D06B	2D06B	2D06B	2D06B	2D06B	2D06B	2D06B	2D06B
7090	109	ALL FRD TAKE LSD	2A41C	2D06C	2D06C	2D06C	2D06C	2D06C	2D06C	2D06C	2D06C
7100	109	ALL FRD TK PSYDL	2A41D	2D06D	2D06D	2D06D	2D06D	2D06D	2D06D	2D06D	2D06D
7110	110	ALL FRD TK AMPH	2A41E	2D06E	2D06E	2D06E	2D06E	2D06E	2D06E	2D06E	2D06E
7120	110	ALL FRD TK QUALD	2A41F	2D06F	2D06F	2D06F	2D06F	2D06F	2D06F	2D06F	2D06F
7130	110	ALL FRD TK BARBT	2A41G	2D06G	2D06G	2D06G	2D06G	2D06G	2D06G	2D06G	2D06G
7140	110	ALL FRD TK TRNQL	2A41H	2D06H	2D06H	2D06H	2D06H	2D06H	2D06H	2D06H	2D06H
7150	110	ALL FRD TK COKE	2A41I	2D06I	2D06I	2D06I	2D06I	2D06I	2D06I	2D06I	2D06I
7160	110	ALL FRD TK HERON	2A41J	2D06J	2D06J	2D06J	2D06J	2D06J	2D06J	2D06J	2D06J
7170	110	ALL FRD TK NARC	2A41K	2D06K	2D06K	2D06K	2D06K	2D06K	2D06K	2D06K	2D06K
7180	111	ALL FRD TK INHL	2A41L	2D06L	2D06L	2D06L	2D06L	2D06L	2D06L	2D06L	2D06L
7190	111	ALL FRD DRK ALCL	2A41M	2D06M	2D06M	2D06M	2D06M	2D06M	2D06M	2D06M	2D06M
7200	111	ALL FRD GT DRUNK	2A41N	2D06N	2D06N	2D06N	2D06N	2D06N	2D06N	2D06N	2D06N
7201	111	# FRNDS TAKE PCP					2E01A	2E01A	2E01A	2E01A	2E01A
7202	111	# FRNDS TK PPRS					2E01B	2E01B	2E01B	2E01B	2E01B

A02b: DRUGS. Exposure to users

8750		OFT W PL TK MARJ	3A55A	5E07A	5E08A	5E08A					
8760		OFT W PL TK LSD	3A55B	5E07B	5E08B	5E08B					
8770		OFT W PL TK PSYC	3A55C	5E07C	5E08C	5E08C					
8780		OFT W PL TK QUAL		5E07D	5E08D	5E08D					
8790		OFT W PL TK BARB	3A55E	5E07E	5E08E	5E08E					
8800		OFT W PL TK TRQL	3A55F	5E07F	5E08F	5E08F					
8810		OFT W PL TK COKE	3A55G	5E07G	5E08G	5E08G					
8820		OFT W PL TK HRN	3A55H	5E07H	5E08H	5E08H					
8830		OFT W PL TK NARC	3A55I	5E07I	5E08I	5E08I					
8835		OFT W PL TK INHL		5E07J	5E08J	5E08J					
8840		OFT W PL TK ALCL	3A55K	5E07K	5E08K	5E08K					
20590	131	12MO NR OTH MARJ		3A29A	3A29A	3A29A	3A29A	3A29A	3A29A	3A29A	3A29A
20600	132	12MO NR OTH LSD		3A29B	3A29B	3A29B	3A29B	3A29B	3A29B	3A29B	3A29B
20610	132	12MO NR OTH PSYC		3A29C	3A29C	3A29C	3A29C	3A29C	3A29C	3A29C	3A29C
20620	132	12MO NR OTH AMPH		3A29D	3A29D	3A29D	3A29D	3A29D	3A29D	3A29D	3A29D
20630	132	12MO NR OTH BARB		3A29E	3A29E	3A29E	3A29E	3A29E	3A29E	3A29E	3A29E
20640	132	12MO NR OTH TRQL		3A29F	3A29F	3A29F	3A29F	3A29F	3A29F	3A29F	3A29F
20650	132	12MO NR OTH COKE		3A29G	3A29G	3A29G	3A29G	3A29G	3A29G	3A29G	3A29G
20660	132	12MO NR OTH HRN		3A29H	3A29H	3A29H	3A29H	3A29H	3A29H	3A29H	3A29H
20670	132	12MO NR OTH NARC		3A29I	3A29I	3A29I	3A29I	3A29I	3A29I	3A29I	3A29I
20680	133	12MO NR OTH ALCL		3A29J	3A29J	3A29J	3A29J	3A29J	3A29J	3A29J	3A29J
21920	200	PARTY-ONE HI ALC									5E08B
		(continued)									

Item Reference Number	Page Loc. in this Volume	ITEM DESCRIPTION (ABBREVIATED)	QUESTIONNAIRE LOCATION BY YEAR (FORM, SECTION, AND QUESTION NUMBER)								
			1975	1976	1977	1978	1979	1980	1981	1982/83	1984/85

A02b: DRUGS. Exposure to users *(continued)*

21930	201	PARTY-OTH HI ALC									5E08C
21950	201	PARTY-PRESS ALCL									5E08E
21960	201	PARTY-PRS HI ALC									5E08F
21970	201	PARTY-ONE HI MJ									5E08G
21980	201	PARTY-OTH HI MJ									5E08H
22000	202	PARTY-PRESS MJ									5E08J
22010	202	PARTY-ONE HI OTD									5E08K
22020	202	PARTY-OTH HI OTD									5E08L
22040	202	PARTY-PRESS OTDG									5E08N

A03a: DRUGS. Availability

6750	103	EASY GT MARIJUAN	2A40A	2A21A	2A21A	2A21A	2A21A	2A21A	2A21A	2A21A	2A21A
6760	103	EASY GT LSD	2A40B	2A21B	2A21B	2A21B	2A21B	2A21B	2A21B	2A21B	2A21B
6770	103	EASY GT PSYDELIC	2A40C	2A21C	2A21C	2A21C	2A21C	2A21C	2A21C	2A21C	2A21C
6780	103	EASY GT AMPHTMNS	2A40D	2A21D	2A21D	2A21D	2A21D	2A21D	2A21D	2A21D	2A21D
6790	103	EASY GT BBTUATES	2A40F	2A21E	2A21E	2A21E	2A21E	2A21E	2A21E	2A21E	2A21E
6800	103	EASY GT TRANQLIZ	2A40G	2A21F	2A21F	2A21F	2A21F	2A21F	2A21F	2A21F	2A21F
6810	104	EASY GT COCAINE	2A40H	2A21G	2A21G	2A21G	2A21G	2A21G	2A21G	2A21G	2A21G
6820	104	EASY GT HEROIN	2A40I	2A21H	2A21H	2A21H	2A21H	2A21H	2A21H	2A21H	2A21H
6830	104	EASY GT NARCOTIC	2A40J	2A21I	2A21I	2A21I	2A21I	2A21I	2A21I	2A21I	2A21I

A04a: DRUGS. Expected future use

1710	41	NO SMK IN 5 YR	1A023	1B006	1B006	1B006	1B006	1B006	1B006	1B006	1B006
2030	45	NO ALC IN 5 YR	1A040	1B017	1B017	1B017	1B017	1B017	1B017	1B017	1B017
2390	49	NO MJ/HSH IN5YR	1A053	1B028	1B028	1B028	1B028	1B028	1B028	1B032	1B032
2690	53	NO LSD IN 5 YRS	1A067	1B037	1B037	1B037	1B037	1B037	1B037	1B041	1B041
3250	60	NO AMPH IN 5YR	1A097	1B052	1B052	1B052	1B052	1B052	1B052	1B059	1B059
3720	65	NO BARB IN 5YR	1A126	1B065	1B065	1B065	1B065	1B065	1B065	1B072	1B072
4180	70	NO TRNQ IN 5YR	1A140	1B075	1B075	1B075	1B075	1B075	1B075	1B082	1B082
4600	74	NO COKE IN 5YR	1A154	1B084	1B084	1B084	1B084	1B084	1B084	1B091	1B091
5010		NO HER IN 5 YR	1A168	1B093	1B093	1B093	1B093	1B093	1B093		
5560	79	NO NARC IN 5YR	1A184	1B104	1B104	1B104	1B104	1B104	1B104	1B103	1B103
9010	135	NXT 12MOS USE MJ			3D04	3D04	3D04	3D04	3D04	3D04	3D04

A05a: DRUGS. Use alone

1720	42	#X/YR ALC ALONE		1B008A	1B008A	1B008A	1B008A	1B008A	1B008A	1B008A	1B008A
2100	46	#X/YR MJ ALONE	1A045	1B020A	1B020A	1B020A	1B020A	1B020A	1B020A	1B020A	1B020A
2400	50	#X/YR LSD ALONE		1B030A	1B030A	1B030A	1B030A	1B030A	1B030A	1B034A	1B034A
2800	57	#X/YR AMPH ALNE		1B044A	1B044A	1B044A	1B044A	1B044A	1B044A	1B051A	1B051A
3290	62	#X/YR BRBT ALNE		1B058A	1B058A	1B058A	1B058A	1B058A	1B058A	1B065A	1B065A
3740	66	#X/YR TRQL ALNE		1B068A	1B068A	1B068A	1B068A	1B068A	1B068A	1B075A	1B075A
4190	70	#X/YR COKE ALNE		1B077A	1B077A	1B077A	1B077A	1B077A	1B077A	1B084A	1B084A
4610		#X/YR HER ALONE		1B086A	1B086A	1B086A	1B086A	1B086A	1B086A		
5030	75	#X/YR NARC ALNE		1B096A	1B096A	1B096A	1B096A	1B096A	1B096A	1B095A	1B095A

A05b: DRUGS. Use with others

1730	42	#X/YR ALC-2 PPL		1B008B	1B008B	1B008B	1B008B	1B008B	1B008B	1B008B	1B008B
1750	42	#X/YR ALC-DT/SP		1B008D	1B008D	1B008D	1B008D	1B008D	1B008D	1B008D	1B008D
1760	43	#X/YR ALC-ADLTS		1B008E	1B008E	1B008E	1B008E	1B008E	1B008E	1B008E	1B008E
2110	46	#X/YR MJ-2 PPL		1B020B	1B020B	1B020B	1B020B	1B020B	1B020B	1B020B	1B020B
2130	47	#X/YR MJ-DT/SP		1B020D	1B020D	1B020D	1B020D	1B020D	1B020D	1B020D	1B020D
2140	47	#X/YR MJ-ADLTS		1B020E	1B020E	1B020E	1B020E	1B020E	1B020E	1B020E	1B020E
2410	50	#X/YR LSD-2 PPL		1B030B	1B030B	1B030B	1B030B	1B030B	1B030B	1B034B	1B034B
2430	51	#X/YR LSD-DT/SP		1B030D	1B030D	1B030D	1B030D	1B030D	1B030D	1B034D	1B034D
2440	51	#X/YR LSD-ADLTS		1B030E	1B030E	1B030E	1B030E	1B030E	1B030E	1B034E	1B034E
2810	57	#X/YR AMPH-2PPL		1B044B	1B044B	1B044B	1B044B	1B044B	1B044B	1B051B	1B051B
2830	57	#X/YR AMPH-DT/S		1B044D	1B044D	1B044D	1B044D	1B044D	1B044D	1B051D	1B051D
2840	57	#X/YR AMPH-ADLT		1B044E	1B044E	1B044E	1B044E	1B044E	1B044E	1B051E	1B051E
3300	62	#X/YR BRBT-2PPL		1B058B	1B058B	1B058B	1B058B	1B058B	1B058B	1B065B	1B065B
		(continued)									

Item Reference Number	Page Loc. in this Volume	ITEM DESCRIPTION (ABBREVIATED)	QUESTIONNAIRE LOCATION BY YEAR (FORM, SECTION, AND QUESTION NUMBER)								
			1975	1976	1977	1978	1979	1980	1981	1982/83	1984/85

A05b: DRUGS. Use with others (continued)

3320	62	#X/YR BRBT-DT/S		1B058D	1B058D	1B058D	1B058D	1B058D	1B058D	1B065D	1B065D
3330	63	#X/YR BRBT-ADLT		1B058E	1B058E	1B058E	1B058E	1B058E	1B058E	1B065E	1B065E
3750	66	#X/YR TRQL-2PPL		1B068B	1B068B	1B068B	1B068B	1B068B	1B068B	1B075B	1B075B
3770	67	#X/YR TRQL-DT/S		1B068D	1B068D	1B068D	1B068D	1B068D	1B068D	1B075D	1B075D
3780	67	#X/YR TRQL-ADLT		1B068E	1B068E	1B068E	1B068E	1B068E	1B068E	1B075E	1B075E
4200	71	#X/YR COKE-2PPL		1B077B	1B077B	1B077B	1B077B	1B077B	1B077B	1B084B	1B084B
4220	71	#X/YR COKE-DT/S		1B077D	1B077D	1B077D	1B077D	1B077D	1B077D	1B084D	1B084D
4230	71	#X/YR COKE-ADLT		1B077E	1B077E	1B077E	1B077E	1B077E	1B077E	1B084E	1B084E
4620		#X/YR HER-2 PPL		1B086B	1B086B	1B086B	1B086B	1B086B	1B086B		
4640		#X/YR HER-DA/SP		1B086D	1B086D	1B086D	1B086D	1B086D	1B086D		
4650		#X/YR HER-ADULT		1B086E	1B086E	1B086E	1B086E	1B086E	1B086E		
5040	76	#X/YR NARC-2PPL		1B096B	1B096B	1B096B	1B096B	1B096B	1B096B	1B095B	1B095B
5060	76	#X/YR NARC-DT/S		1B096D	1B096D	1B096D	1B096D	1B096D	1B096D	1B095D	1B095D
5070	76	#X/YR NARC-ADLT		1B096E	1B096E	1B096E	1B096E	1B096E	1B096E	1B095E	1B095E

A05c: DRUGS. Settings of use

1740	42	#X/YR ALC@PARTY		1B008C	1B008C	1B008C	1B008C	1B008C	1B008C	1B008C	1B008C
1770	43	#X/YR ALC-DATIM		1B008F	1B008F	1B008F	1B008F	1B008F	1B008F	1B008F	1B008F
1780	43	#X/YR ALC@HOME		1B008G	1B008G	1B008G	1B008G	1B008G	1B008G	1B008G	1B008G
1790	43	#X/YR ALC@SCHL		1B008H	1B008H	1B008H	1B008H	1B008H	1B008H	1B008H	1B008H
1810	43	#X/YR ALCIN CAR		1B008I	1B008I	1B008I	1B008I	1B008I	1B008I	1B008I	1B008I
2120	46	#X/YR MJ@PARTY		1B020C	1B020C	1B020C	1B020C	1B020C	1B020C	1B020C	1B020C
2150	47	#X/YR MJ-DATIME		1B020F	1B020F	1B020F	1B020F	1B020F	1B020F	1B020F	1B020F
2160	47	#X/YR MJ@HOME		1B020G	1B020G	1B020G	1B020G	1B020G	1B020G	1B020G	1B020G
2170	47	#X/YR MJ@SCHL		1B020H	1B020H	1B020H	1B020H	1B020H	1B020H	1B020H	1B020H
2190	47	#X/YR MJIN CAR		1B020I	1B020I	1B020I	1B020I	1B020I	1B020I	1B020I	1B020I
2420	50	#X/YR LSD@PARTY		1B030C	1B030C	1B030C	1B030C	1B030C	1B030C	1B034C	1B034C
2450	51	#X/YR LSD-DATIM		1B030F	1B030F	1B030F	1B030F	1B030F	1B030F	1B034F	1B034F
2460	51	#X/YR LSD@HOME		1B030G	1B030G	1B030G	1B030G	1B030G	1B030G	1B034G	1B034G
2470	51	#X/YR LSD@SCHL		1B030H	1B030H	1B030H	1B030H	1B030H	1B030H	1B034H	1B034H
2490	51	#X/YR LSDIN CAR		1B030I	1B030I	1B030I	1B030I	1B030I	1B030I	1B034I	1B034I
2820	57	#X/YR AMPH@PRTY		1B044C	1B044C	1B044C	1B044C	1B044C	1B044C	1B051C	1B051C
2850	58	#X/YR AMPH-DATM		1B044F	1B044F	1B044F	1B044F	1B044F	1B044F	1B051F	1B051F
2860	58	#X/YR AMPH@HOME		1B044G	1B044G	1B044G	1B044G	1B044G	1B044G	1B051G	1B051G
2880	58	#X/YR AMPH@SCHL		1B044H	1B044H	1B044H	1B044H	1B044H	1B044H	1B051H	1B051H
2890	58	#X/YR AMPH@CAR		1B044I	1B044I	1B044I	1B044I	1B044I	1B044I	1B051I	1B051I
3310	62	#X/YR BRBT@PRTY		1B058C	1B058C	1B058C	1B058C	1B058C	1B058C	1B065C	1B065C
3340	63	#X/YR BRBT-DATM		1B058F	1B058F	1B058F	1B058F	1B058F	1B058F	1B065F	1B065F
3350	63	#X/YR BRBT@HOME		1B058G	1B058G	1B058G	1B058G	1B058G	1B058G	1B065G	1B065G
3360	63	#X/YR BRBT@SCHL		1B058H	1B058H	1B058H	1B058H	1B058H	1B058H	1B065H	1B065H
3380	63	#X/YR BRBT@CAR		1B058I	1B058I	1B058I	1B058I	1B058I	1B058I	1B065I	1B065I
3760	67	#X/YR TRQL@PRTY		1B068C	1B068C	1B068C	1B068C	1B068C	1B068C	1B075C	1B075C
3790	67	#X/YR TRQL-DATM		1B068F	1B068F	1B068F	1B068F	1B068F	1B068F	1B075F	1B075F
3800	67	#X/YR TRQL@HOME		1B068G	1B068G	1B068G	1B068G	1B068G	1B068G	1B075G	1B075G
3810	67	#X/YR TRQL@SCHL		1B068H	1B068H	1B068H	1B068H	1B068H	1B068H	1B075H	1B075H
3830	67	#X/YR TRQL@CAR		1B068I	1B068I	1B068I	1B068I	1B068I	1B068I	1B075I	1B075I
4210	71	#X/YR COKE@PRTY		1B077C	1B077C	1B077C	1B077C	1B077C	1B077C	1B084C	1B084C
4240	71	#X/YR COKE-DATM		1B077F	1B077F	1B077F	1B077F	1B077F	1B077F	1B084F	1B084F
4250	71	#X/YR COKE@HOME		1B077G	1B077G	1B077G	1B077G	1B077G	1B077G	1B084G	1B084G
4260	71	#X/YR COKE@SCHL		1B077H	1B077H	1B077H	1B077H	1B077H	1B077H	1B084H	1B084H
4280	72	#X/YR COKE@CAR		1B077I	1B077I	1B077I	1B077I	1B077I	1B077I	1B084I	1B084I
4630		#X/YR HER@PARTY		1B086C	1B086C	1B086C	1B086C	1B086C	1B086C		
4660		#X/YR HER-DATIM		1B086F	1B086F	1B086F	1B086F	1B086F	1B086F		
4670		#X/YR HER@HOME		1B086G	1B086G	1B086G	1B086G	1B086G	1B086G		
4680		#X/YR HER@SCHL		1B086H	1B086H	1B086H	1B086H	1B086H	1B086H		
4700		#X/YR HER@CAR		1B086I	1B086I	1B086I	1B086I	1B086I	1B086I		
5050	76	#X/YR NARC@PRTY		1B096C	1B096C	1B096C	1B096C	1B096C	1B096C	1B095C	1B095C
5080	76	#X/YR NARC-DATM		1B096F	1B096F	1B096F	1B096F	1B096F	1B096F	1B095F	1B095F
5090	76	#X/YR NARC@HOME		1B096G	1B096G	1B096G	1B096G	1B096G	1B096G	1B095G	1B095G
5100	76	#X/YR NARC@SCHL		1B096H	1B096H	1B096H	1B096H	1B096H	1B096H	1B095H	1B095H
5120	77	#X/YR NARC @CAR		1B096I	1B096I	1B096I	1B096I	1B096I	1B096I	1B095I	1B095I
21940	201	PARTY-YOU HI ALC									5E08D
		(continued)									

Item Reference Number	Page Loc. in this Volume	ITEM DESCRIPTION (ABBREVIATED)	QUESTIONNAIRE LOCATION BY YEAR (FORM, SECTION, AND QUESTION NUMBER)								
			1975	1976	1977	1978	1979	1980	1981	1982/83	1984/85

A05c: DRUGS. Settings of use *(continued)*

21990	201	PARTY-YOU HI MJ									5E08I
22030	202	PARTY-YOU HI OTD									5E08M
22060	202	PRF PTY-U HI ALC									5E09B
22080	203	PRF PTY-U USE MJ									5E09D
22100	203	PR PTY-U USE OTD									5E09F

A05d: DRUGS. Mode of administration

3210	60	MTHD AMPH-MOUTH		1B050A	1B050A	1B050A	1B050A	1B050A	1B050A	1B057A	1B057A
3220	60	MTHD AMPH-INJCT		1B050B	1B050B	1B050B	1B050B	1B050B	1B050B	1B057B	1B057B
3230	60	MTHD AMPH-OTHER		1B050C	1B050C	1B050C	1B050C	1B050C	1B050C	1B057C	1B057C
4550	74	MTHD COKE SNORT	1A153A	1B083A	1B083A	1B083A	1B083A	1B083A	1B083A	1B090A	1B090A
4560	74	MTHD COKE-SMOKE	1A153B	1B083B	1B083B	1B083B	1B083B	1B083B	1B083B	1B090B	1B090B
4570	74	MTHD COKE-INJCT	1A153C	1B083C	1B083C	1B083C	1B083C	1B083C	1B083C	1B090C	1B090C
4580	74	MTHD COKE-MOUTH	1A153D	1B083D	1B083D	1B083D	1B083D	1B083D	1B083D	1B090D	1B090D
4590	74	MTHD COKE-OTHER	1A153E	1B083E	1B083E	1B083E	1B083E	1B083E	1B083E	1B090E	1B090E
4960		METHD HRN SNORT	1A167A	1B092A	1B092A	1B092A	1B092A	1B092A	1B092A		
4970		METHD HRN-SMOKE	1A167B	1B092B	1B092B	1B092B	1B092B	1B092B	1B092B		
4980		METHD HRN-INJCT	1A167C	1B092C	1B092C	1B092C	1B092C	1B092C	1B092C		
4990		METHD HRN-MOUTH	1A167D	1B092D	1B092D	1B092D	1B092D	1B092D	1B092D		
5000		METHD HRN-OTHER	1A167E	1B092E	1B092E	1B092E	1B092E	1B092E	1B092E		
5510	79	METH NARC SNORT	1A183A	1B103A	1B103A	1B103A	1B103A	1B103A	1B103A	1B102A	1B102A
5520	79	METH NARC SMOKE	1A183B	1B103B	1B103B	1B103B	1B103B	1B103B	1B103B	1B102B	1B102B
5530	79	METH NARC INJCT	1A183C	1B103C	1B103C	1B103C	1B103C	1B103C	1B103C	1B102C	1B102C
5540	79	METH NARC MOUTH	1A183D	1B103D	1B103D	1B103D	1B103D	1B103D	1B103D	1B102D	1B102D
5550	79	METH NARC OTHER	1A183E	1B103E	1B103E	1B103E	1B103E	1B103E	1B103E	1B102E	1B102E

A06a: DRUGS. Reasons for use, abstention, and stopping

1820	43	ALC EXPERIMENT		1B009A	1B009A	1B009A	1B009A	1B009A	1B009A	1B009A	1B009A
1830	43	ALC RELAX	1A032A	1B009B	1B009B	1B009B	1B009B	1B009B	1B009B	1B009B	1B009B
1840	43	ALC GET HIGH	1A032B	1B009C	1B009C	1B009C	1B009C	1B009C	1B009C	1B009C	1B009C
1850	43	ALC SEEK INSGHT	1A032C	1B009D	1B009D	1B009D	1B009D	1B009D	1B009D	1B009D	1B009D
1860	43	ALC GD TM FRNDS	1A032D	1B009E	1B009E	1B009E	1B009E	1B009E	1B009E	1B009E	1B009E
1870	43	ALC FIT IN GRP	1A032E	1B009F	1B009F	1B009F	1B009F	1B009F	1B009F	1B009F	1B009F
1880	43	ALC GET AWY PRB	1A032F	1B009G	1B009G	1B009G	1B009G	1B009G	1B009G	1B009G	1B009G
1890	43	ALC BOREDOM	1A032G	1B009H	1B009H	1B009H	1B009H	1B009H	1B009H	1B009H	1B009H
1900	43	ALC ANGR&FRSTRN	1A032H	1B009I	1B009I	1B009I	1B009I	1B009I	1B009I	1B009I	1B009I
1910	43	ALC GT THRU DAY	1A032J	1B009J	1B009J	1B009J	1B009J	1B009J	1B009J	1B009J	1B009J
1920	43	ALC INCRS EF DR	1A032K	1B009K	1B009K	1B009K	1B009K	1B009K	1B009K	1B009K	1B009K
1930	43	ALC DECRS EF DR	1A032L	1B009L	1B009L	1B009L	1B009L	1B009L	1B009L	1B009L	1B009L
1940	43	ALC GET SLEEP		1B009M	1B009M	1B009M	1B009M	1B009M	1B009M	1B009M	1B009M
1950	43	ALC TASTES GOOD	1A032N	1B009N	1B009N	1B009N	1B009N	1B009N	1B009N	1B009N	1B009N
1960	43	ALC I AM HOOKED	1A032M	1B009O	1B009O	1B009O	1B009O	1B009O	1B009O	1B009O	1B009O
2210	48	MJ EXPERIMENT	1A049A	1B022A	1B022A	1B022A	1B022A	1B022A	1B022A	1B022A	1B022A
2220	48	MJ RELAX	1A049B	1B022B	1B022B	1B022B	1B022B	1B022B	1B022B	1B022B	1B022B
2230	48	MJ GET HIGH	1A049C	1B022C	1B022C	1B022C	1B022C	1B022C	1B022C	1B022C	1B022C
2240	48	MJ SEEK INSIGHT	1A049D	1B022D	1B022D	1B022D	1B022D	1B022D	1B022D	1B022D	1B022D
2250	48	MJ GD TM FRNDS	1A049E	1B022E	1B022E	1B022E	1B022E	1B022E	1B022E	1B022E	1B022E
2260	48	MJ FIT IN GRP	1A049F	1B022F	1B022F	1B022F	1B022F	1B022F	1B022F	1B022F	1B022F
2270	48	MJ GET AWY PRB	1A049G	1B022G	1B022G	1B022G	1B022G	1B022G	1B022G	1B022G	1B022G
2280	48	MJ BOREDOM	1A049H	1B022H	1B022H	1B022H	1B022H	1B022H	1B022H	1B022H	1B022H
2290	48	MJ ANGR&FRUSTRN	1A049I	1B022I	1B022I	1B022I	1B022I	1B022I	1B022I	1B022I	1B022I
2300	48	MJ GET THRU DAY	1A049K	1B022J	1B022J	1B022J	1B022J	1B022J	1B022J	1B022J	1B022J
2310	48	MJ INCRS EF DRG	1A049L	1B022K	1B022K	1B022K	1B022K	1B022K	1B022K	1B022K	1B022K
2320	48	MJ DECRS EF DRG	1A049M	1B022L	1B022L	1B022L	1B022L	1B022L	1B022L	1B022L	1B022L
2330	48	MJ I AM HOOKED		1B022M	1B022M	1B022M	1B022M	1B022M	1B022M	1B022M	1B022M
2520	52	LSD EXPERIMENT	1A062A	1B032A	1B032A	1B032A	1B032A	1B032A	1B032A	1B036A	1B036A
2530	52	LSD RELAX	1A062B	1B032B	1B032B	1B032B	1B032B	1B032B	1B032B	1B036B	1B036B
2540	52	LSD GET HIGH	1A062C	1B032C	1B032C	1B032C	1B032C	1B032C	1B032C	1B036C	1B036C
2550	52	LSD SEEK INSGHT	1A062D	1B032D	1B032D	1B032D	1B032D	1B032D	1B032D	1B036D	1B036D
2560	52	LSD GD TM FRNDS	1A062E	1B032E	1B032E	1B032E	1B032E	1B032E	1B032E	1B036E	1B036E
2570	52	LSD FIT IN GRP	1A062F	1B032F	1B032F	1B032F	1B032F	1B032F	1B032F	1B036F	1B036F
		(continued)									

Item Reference Number	Page Loc. in this Volume	ITEM DESCRIPTION (ABBREVIATED)	QUESTIONNAIRE LOCATION BY YEAR (FORM, SECTION, AND QUESTION NUMBER)								
			1975	1976	1977	1978	1979	1980	1981	1982/83	1984/85

A06a: DRUGS. Reasons for use, abstention, and stopping (continued)

Item Reference Number	Page Loc. in this Volume	ITEM DESCRIPTION (ABBREVIATED)	1975	1976	1977	1978	1979	1980	1981	1982/83	1984/85
2580	52	LSD GT AWY PRB	1A062G	1B032G	1B032G	1B032G	1B032G	1B032G	1B032G	1B036G	1B036G
2590	52	LSD BOREDOM	1A062H	1B032H	1B032H	1B032H	1B032H	1B032H	1B032H	1B036H	1B036H
2600	52	LSD ANGR&FRSTRN	1A062I	1B032I	1B032I	1B032I	1B032I	1B032I	1B032I	1B036I	1B036I
2610	52	LSD GT THRU DAY	1A062K	1B032J	1B032J	1B032J	1B032J	1B032J	1B032J	1B036J	1B036J
2620	52	LSD INCRS EF DR	1A062L	1B032K	1B032K	1B032K	1B032K	1B032K	1B032K	1B036K	1B036K
2630	52	LSD DCRS EF DRG	1A062M	1B032L	1B032L	1B032L	1B032L	1B032L	1B032L	1B036L	1B036L
2640	52	LSD I AM HOOKED		1B032M	1B032M	1B032M	1B032M	1B032M	1B032M	1B036M	1B036M
2940	59	AMPH EXPERIMENT	1A092A	1B046A	1B046A	1B046A	1B046A	1B046A	1B046A	1B053A	1B053A
2950	59	AMPH RELAX	1A092B	1B046B	1B046B	1B046B	1B046B	1B046B	1B046B	1B053B	1B053B
2960	59	AMPH GET HIGH	1A092C	1B046C	1B046C	1B046C	1B046C	1B046C	1B046C	1B053C	1B053C
2970	59	AMPH SK INSIGHT	1A092D	1B046D	1B046D	1B046D	1B046D	1B046D	1B046D	1B053D	1B053D
2980	59	AMPH GD TM FRND	1A092E	1B046E	1B046E	1B046E	1B046E	1B046E	1B046E	1B053E	1B053E
2990	59	AMPH FIT IN GRP	1A092F	1B046F	1B046F	1B046F	1B046F	1B046F	1B046F	1B053F	1B053F
3000	59	AMPH GT AWY PRB	1A092G	1B046G	1B046G	1B046G	1B046G	1B046G	1B046G	1B053G	1B053G
3010	59	AMPH BOREDOM	1A092H	1B046H	1B046H	1B046H	1B046H	1B046H	1B046H	1B053H	1B053H
3020	59	AMPH ANGR&FRSTN	1A092I	1B046I	1B046I	1B046I	1B046I	1B046I	1B046I	1B053I	1B053I
3030	59	AMPH GT THRU DA	1A092K	1B046J	1B046J	1B046J	1B046J	1B046J	1B046J	1B053J	1B053J
3040	59	AMPH INCR EF DR	1A092L	1B046K	1B046K	1B046K	1B046K	1B046K	1B046K	1B053K	1B053K
3050	59	AMPH DCRS EF DR	1A092M	1B046L	1B046L	1B046L	1B046L	1B046L	1B046L	1B053L	1B053L
3060	59	AMPH STAY AWAKE	1A092N	1B046M	1B046M	1B046M	1B046M	1B046M	1B046M	1B053M	1B053M
3070	59	AMPH GET >ENERGY	1A092O	1B046N	1B046N	1B046N	1B046N	1B046N	1B046N	1B053N	1B053N
3080	59	AMPH LOSE WGHT	1A092P	1B046O	1B046O	1B046O	1B046O	1B046O	1B046O	1B053O	1B053O
3090	59	AMPH I AM HOOKD	1A092Q	1B046P	1B046P	1B046P	1B046P	1B046P	1B046P	1B053P	1B053P
3450	64	BARB EXPERIMENT	1A121A	1B060A	1B060A	1B060A	1B060A	1B060A	1B060A	1B067A	1B067A
3460	64	BARB RELAX	1A121B	1B060B	1B060B	1B060B	1B060B	1B060B	1B060B	1B067B	1B067B
3470	64	BARB GET HIGH	1A121C	1B060C	1B060C	1B060C	1B060C	1B060C	1B060C	1B067C	1B067C
3480	64	BARB SK INSIGHT	1A121D	1B060D	1B060D	1B060D	1B060D	1B060D	1B060D	1B067D	1B067D
3490	64	BARB GD TM FRND	1A121E	1B060E	1B060E	1B060E	1B060E	1B060E	1B060E	1B067E	1B067E
3500	64	BARB FIT IN GRP	1A121F	1B060F	1B060F	1B060F	1B060F	1B060F	1B060F	1B067F	1B067F
3510	64	BARB GT AWY PRB	1A121G	1B060G	1B060G	1B060G	1B060G	1B060G	1B060G	1B067G	1B067G
3520	64	BARB BOREDOM	1A121H	1B060H	1B060H	1B060H	1B060H	1B060H	1B060H	1B067H	1B067H
3530	64	BARB ANGR&FRSTN	1A121I	1B060I	1B060I	1B060I	1B060I	1B060I	1B060I	1B067I	1B067I
3540	64	BARB GT THRU DA	1A121K	1B060J	1B060J	1B060J	1B060J	1B060J	1B060J	1B067J	1B067J
3550	64	BARB INCR EF DR	1A121L	1B060K	1B060K	1B060K	1B060K	1B060K	1B060K	1B067K	1B067K
3560	64	BARB DCRS EF DR	1A121M	1B060L	1B060L	1B060L	1B060L	1B060L	1B060L	1B067L	1B067L
3570	64	BARB GET SLEEP	1A121N	1B060M	1B060M	1B060M	1B060M	1B060M	1B060M	1B067M	1B067M
3575	64	BARB RLV PHYS PN				1B060N	1B060N	1B060N	1B060N	1B067N	1B067N
3580	64	BARB I AM HOOKD	1A121O	1B060N	1B060N	1B060O	1B060O	1B060O	1B060O	1B067O	1B067O
3910	69	TRNQ EXPERIMENT	1A136A	1B070A	1B070A	1B070A	1B070A	1B070A	1B070A	1B077A	1B077A
3920	69	TRNQ RELAX	1A136B	1B070B	1B070B	1B070B	1B070B	1B070B	1B070B	1B077B	1B077B
3930	69	TRNQ GET HIGH	1A136C	1B070C	1B070C	1B070C	1B070C	1B070C	1B070C	1B077C	1B077C
3940	69	TRNQ SK INSIGHT	1A136D	1B070D	1B070D	1B070D	1B070D	1B070D	1B070D	1B077D	1B077D
3950	69	TRNQ GD TM FRND	1A136E	1B070E	1B070E	1B070E	1B070E	1B070E	1B070E	1B077E	1B077E
3960	69	TRNQ FIT IN GRP	1A136F	1B070F	1B070F	1B070F	1B070F	1B070F	1B070F	1B077F	1B077F
3970	69	TRNQ GT AWY PRB	1A136G	1B070G	1B070G	1B070G	1B070G	1B070G	1B070G	1B077G	1B077G
3980	69	TRNQ BOREDOM	1A136H	1B070H	1B070H	1B070H	1B070H	1B070H	1B070H	1B077H	1B077H
3990	69	TRNQ ANGR&FRSTN	1A136I	1B070I	1B070I	1B070I	1B070I	1B070I	1B070I	1B077I	1B077I
4000	69	TRNQ GT THRU DA	1A136K	1B070J	1B070J	1B070J	1B070J	1B070J	1B070J	1B077J	1B077J
4010	69	TRNQ INCR EF DR	1A136L	1B070K	1B070K	1B070K	1B070K	1B070K	1B070K	1B077K	1B077K
4020	69	TRNQ DCRS EF DR	1A136M	1B070L	1B070L	1B070L	1B070L	1B070L	1B070L	1B077L	1B077L
4030	69	TRNQ GET SLEEP	1A136N	1B070M	1B070M	1B070M	1B070M	1B070M	1B070M	1B077M	1B077M
4035	69	TRNQ RLV PHYS PN				1B070N	1B070N	1B070N	1B070N	1B077N	1B077N
4040	69	TRNQ I AM HOOKD	1A136O	1B070N	1B070N	1B070O	1B070O	1B070O	1B070O	1B077O	1B077O
4370	73	COKE EXPERIMENT	1A149A	1B079A	1B079A	1B079A	1B079A	1B079A	1B079A	1B086A	1B086A
4380	73	COKE RELAX	1A149B	1B079B	1B079B	1B079B	1B079B	1B079B	1B079B	1B086B	1B086B
4390	73	COKE GET HIGH	1A149C	1B079C	1B079C	1B079C	1B079C	1B079C	1B079C	1B086C	1B086C
4400	73	COKE SK INSIGHT	1A149D	1B079D	1B079D	1B079D	1B079D	1B079D	1B079D	1B086D	1B086D
4410	73	COKE GD TM FRND	1A149E	1B079E	1B079E	1B079E	1B079E	1B079E	1B079E	1B086E	1B086E
4420	73	COKE FIT IN GRP	1A149F	1B079F	1B079F	1B079F	1B079F	1B079F	1B079F	1B086F	1B086F
4430	73	COKE GT AWY PRB	1A149G	1B079G	1B079G	1B079G	1B079G	1B079G	1B079G	1B086G	1B086G
4440	73	COKE BOREDOM	1A149H	1B079H	1B079H	1B079H	1B079H	1B079H	1B079H	1B086H	1B086H
4450	73	COKE ANGR&FRSTN	1A149I	1B079I	1B079I	1B079I	1B079I	1B079I	1B079I	1B086I	1B086I
4460	73	COKE GT THRU DA	1A149K	1B079J	1B079J	1B079J	1B079J	1B079J	1B079J	1B086J	1B086J

(continued)

Item Reference Number	Page Loc. in this Volume	ITEM DESCRIPTION (ABBREVIATED)	QUESTIONNAIRE LOCATION BY YEAR (FORM, SECTION, AND QUESTION NUMBER)								
			1975	1976	1977	1978	1979	1980	1981	1982/83	1984/85

A06a: DRUGS. Reasons for use, abstention, and stopping (continued)

4470	73	COKE INCR EF DR	1A149L	1B079K	1B079K	1B079K	1B079K	1B079K	1B079K	1B086K	1B086K
4480	73	COKE DCRS EF DR	1A149M	1B079L	1B079L	1B079L	1B079L	1B079L	1B079L	1B086L	1B086L
4490	73	COKE STAY AWAKE		1B079M	1B079M	1B079M	1B079M	1B079M	1B079M	1B086M	1B086M
4500	73	COKE GET>ENERGY	1A149N	1B079N	1B079N	1B079N	1B079N	1B079N	1B079N	1B086N	1B086N
4510	73	COKE I AM HOOKD	1A149O	1B079O	1B079O	1B079O	1B079O	1B079O	1B079O	1B086O	1B086O
4800		HERIN EXPERMENT	1A163A	1B088A	1B088A	1B088A	1B088A	1B088A	1B088A		
4810		HERIN RELAX	1A163B	1B088B	1B088B	1B088B	1B088B	1B088B	1B088B		
4820		HERIN GET HIGH	1A163C	1B088C	1B088C	1B088C	1B088C	1B088C	1B088C		
4830		HERIN SK INSIGT	1A163D	1B088D	1B088D	1B088D	1B088D	1B088D	1B088D		
4840		HERIN GD TM FRN	1A163E	1B088E	1B088E	1B088E	1B088E	1B088E	1B088E		
4850		HERIN FT IN GRP	1A163F	1B088F	1B088F	1B088F	1B088F	1B088F	1B088F		
4860		HERIN GT AWY PB	1A163G	1B088G	1B088G	1B088G	1B088G	1B088G	1B088G		
4870		HERIN BOREDOM	1A163H	1B088H	1B088H	1B088H	1B088H	1B088H	1B088H		
4880		HERIN ANGR&FRST	1A163I	1B088I	1B088I	1B088I	1B088I	1B088I	1B088I		
4890		HERIN GT THR DA	1A163K	1B088J	1B088J	1B088J	1B088J	1B088J	1B088J		
4900		HERIN INC EF DG	1A163L	1B088K	1B088K	1B088K	1B088K	1B088K	1B088K		
4910		HERIN DEC EF DG	1A163M	1B088L	1B088L	1B088L	1B088L	1B088L	1B088L		
4920		HERIN I AM HOOK	1A163N	1B088M	1B088M	1B088M	1B088M	1B088M	1B088M		
5230	78	NARC EXPERIMENT	1A178A	1B098A	1B098A	1B098A	1B098A	1B098A	1B098A	1B097A	1B097A
5240	78	NARC RELAX	1A178B	1B098B	1B098B	1B098B	1B098B	1B098B	1B098B	1B097B	1B097B
5250	78	NARC GET HIGH	1A178C	1B098C	1B098C	1B098C	1B098C	1B098C	1B098C	1B097C	1B097C
5260	78	NARC SK INSIGTS	1A178D	1B098D	1B098D	1B098D	1B098D	1B098D	1B098D	1B097D	1B097D
5270	78	NARC GD TM FRND	1A178E	1B098E	1B098E	1B098E	1B098E	1B098E	1B098E	1B097E	1B097E
5280	78	NARC FIT IN GRP	1A178F	1B098F	1B098F	1B098F	1B098F	1B098F	1B098F	1B097F	1B097F
5290	78	NARC GT AWY PBM	1A178G	1B098G	1B098G	1B098G	1B098G	1B098G	1B098G	1B097G	1B097G
5300	78	NARC BOREDOM	1A178H	1B098H	1B098H	1B098H	1B098H	1B098H	1B098H	1B097H	1B097H
5310	78	NARC ANGR&FRSTN	1A178I	1B098I	1B098I	1B098I	1B098I	1B098I	1B098I	1B097I	1B097I
5320	78	NARC GT THRU DA	1A178K	1B098J	1B098J	1B098J	1B098J	1B098J	1B098J	1B097J	1B097J
5330	78	NARC INC EF DG	1A178L	1B098K	1B098K	1B098K	1B098K	1B098K	1B098K	1B097K	1B097K
5340	78	NARC DEC EF DG	1A178M	1B098L	1B098L	1B098L	1B098L	1B098L	1B098L	1B097L	1B097L
5350	78	NARC GET SLEEP		1B098M	1B098M	1B098M	1B098M	1B098M	1B098M	1B097M	1B097M
5360	78	NARC SBST HERIN	1A178O	1B098N	1B098N	1B098N	1B098N	1B098N	1B098N	1B097N	1B097N
5363	78	NARC RLV PHYS PN				1B098O	1B098O	1B098O	1B098O	1B097O	1B097O
5366	78	NARC RLV COUGHNG				1B098P	1B098P	1B098P	1B098P	1B097P	1B097P
5370	78	NARC I AM HOOKD	1A178N	1B098O	1B098O	1B098Q	1B098Q	1B098Q	1B098Q	1B097Q	1B097Q
9020	135	CNCRN PSYCH DAMG		(3D04A)	(3D04A)	3D04A	3D04A	3D04A	3D04A	3D04A	3D04A
9030	135	CNCRN PHYSCL DMG		(3D04B)	(3D04B)	3D04B	3D04B	3D04B	3D04B	3D04B	3D04B
9040	135	CNCRN GT ARRESTD		(3D04C)	(3D04C)	3D04C	3D04C	3D04C	3D04C	3D04C	3D04C
9050	135	CNCRN BECOM ADCT		(3D04D)	(3D04D)	3D04D	3D04D	3D04D	3D04D	3D04D	3D04D
9060	135	AGST MY BELIEFS		(3D04E)	(3D04E)	3D04E	3D04E	3D04E	3D04E	3D04E	3D04E
9070	135	CNCRN LEGY&AMBTN		(3D04F)	(3D04F)	3D04F	3D04F	3D04F	3D04F	3D04F	3D04F
9080	135	CNCRN LOSS CNTRL		(3D04G)	(3D04G)	3D04G	3D04G	3D04G	3D04G	3D04G	3D04G
9090	135	MJ ->STRNGR DRGS		(3D04H)	(3D04H)	3D04H	3D04H	3D04H	3D04H	3D04H	3D04H
9100	135	MJ NOT ENJOYABLE		(3D04I)	(3D04I)	3D04I	3D04I	3D04I	3D04I	3D04I	3D04I
9110	135	PRNTS DISAPPROVE		(3D04J)	(3D04J)	3D04J	3D04J	3D04J	3D04J	3D04J	3D04J
9120	135	HS/WF DISAPPROVE		(3D04K)	(3D04K)	3D04K	3D04K	3D04K	3D04K	3D04K	3D04K
9130	135	DONT LIKE USERS		(3D04L)	(3D04L)	3D04L	3D04L	3D04L	3D04L	3D04L	3D04L
9140	135	FRNDS DNT USE IT		(3D04M)	(3D04M)	3D04M	3D04M	3D04M	3D04M	3D04M	3D04M
9150	135	PSSBLY BAD TRIP		(3D04N)	(3D04N)	3D04N	3D04N	3D04N	3D04N	3D04N	3D04N
9160	135	TOO EXPENSIVE			3D04O	3D04O	3D04O	3D04O	3D04O	3D04O	3D04O
9170	135	NOT AVAILABLE			3D04P	3D04P	3D04P	3D04P	3D04P	3D04P	3D04P
9180	135	NOT WNT GET HIGH			3D04Q	3D04Q	3D04Q	3D04Q	3D04Q	3D04Q	3D04Q

A07a: DRUGS. Tickets, accidents after use

660	22	#TCKTS AFT DRNK		+C29A	+C29A	+C29A	+C29A	+C29A	+C29A	+C29A	+C29A
670	23	#TCKTS AFT MARJ		+C29B	+C29B	+C29B	+C29B	+C29B	+C29B	+C29B	+C29B
680	23	#TCKTS AFT OTDG		+C29C	+C29C	+C29C	+C29C	+C29C	+C29C	+C29C	+C29C
700	23	#ACDTS AFT DRNK		+C31A	+C31A	+C31A	+C31A	+C31A	+C31A	+C31A	+C31A
710	23	#ACDTS AFT MARJ		+C31B	+C31B	+C31B	+C31B	+C31B	+C31B	+C31B	+C31B
720	23	#ACDTS AFT OTDG		+C31C	+C31C	+C31C	+C31C	+C31C	+C31C	+C31C	+C31C
1811	116	#X/2W DRIVE+ALCL									2E19A
1812	117	#X/2W DRIVE+5DRK									2E19B
		(continued)									

Item Reference Number	Page Loc. in this Volume	ITEM DESCRIPTION (ABBREVIATED)	QUESTIONNAIRE LOCATION BY YEAR (FORM, SECTION, AND QUESTION NUMBER)								
			1975	1976	1977	1978	1979	1980	1981	1982/83	1984/85

A07a: DRUGS. Tickets, accidents after use *(continued)*

1815	117	#X/2W RIDE+ALCL									2E20A
1816	117	#X/2W RIDE+5DRK									2E20B

A07b: DRUGS. Problems after use

9190	135	AL CS BEHV REGRT		3D05A	3D05A	3D05A	3D05A	3D05A	3D05A	3D05A	3D05A
9200	135	AL HURT REL PRNT		3D05A	3D05A	3D05A	3D05A	3D05A	3D05A	3D05A	3D05A
9210	135	AL HURT REL SPSE		3D05A	3D05A	3D05A	3D05A	3D05A	3D05A	3D05A	3D05A
9220	135	AL HURT REL FRND		3D05A	3D05A	3D05A	3D05A	3D05A	3D05A	3D05A	3D05A
9230	135	AL HURT REL TCHR		3D05A	3D05A	3D05A	3D05A	3D05A	3D05A	3D05A	3D05A
9240	135	AL INV PL BD INF		3D05A	3D05A	3D05A	3D05A	3D05A	3D05A	3D05A	3D05A
9250	135	AL HURT PERF JOB		3D05A	3D05A	3D05A	3D05A	3D05A	3D05A	3D05A	3D05A
9260	135	AL CAUS<INTERSTD		3D05A	3D05A	3D05A	3D05A	3D05A	3D05A	3D05A	3D05A
9270	135	AL CS<STABL EMTN		3D05A	3D05A	3D05A	3D05A	3D05A	3D05A	3D05A	3D05A
9280	135	AL CS HAV<ENERGY		3D05A	3D05A	3D05A	3D05A	3D05A	3D05A	3D05A	3D05A
9290	135	AL INTF THNK CLR		3D05A	3D05A	3D05A	3D05A	3D05A	3D05A	3D05A	3D05A
9300	135	AL BD PSYCH EFCT		3D05A	3D05A	3D05A	3D05A	3D05A	3D05A	3D05A	3D05A
9310	135	AL CS HEALTH BAD		3D05A	3D05A	3D05A	3D05A	3D05A	3D05A	3D05A	3D05A
9320	135	AL CS DRIV UNSAF		3D05A	3D05A	3D05A	3D05A	3D05A	3D05A	3D05A	3D05A
9330	135	AL GT TRBL W POL		3D05A	3D05A	3D05A	3D05A	3D05A	3D05A	3D05A	3D05A
9340	135	AL CS NO PROBLEM			3D05A	3D05A	3D05A	3D05A	3D05A	3D05A	3D05A
9350	135	AL NEVER USED DG			3D05A	3D05A	3D05A	3D05A	3D05A	3D05A	3D05A
9360	136	MJ CS BEHV REGRT		3D05M	3D05M	3D05M	3D05M	3D05M	3D05M	3D05M	3D05M
9370	136	MJ HURT REL PRNT		3D05M	3D05M	3D05M	3D05M	3D05M	3D05M	3D05M	3D05M
9380	136	MJ HURT REL SPSE		3D05M	3D05M	3D05M	3D05M	3D05M	3D05M	3D05M	3D05M
9390	136	MJ HURT REL FRND		3D05M	3D05M	3D05M	3D05M	3D05M	3D05M	3D05M	3D05M
9400	136	MJ HURT REL TCHR		3D05M	3D05M	3D05M	3D05M	3D05M	3D05M	3D05M	3D05M
9410	136	MJ INV PL BD INF		3D05M	3D05M	3D05M	3D05M	3D05M	3D05M	3D05M	3D05M
9420	136	MJ HURT PERF JOB		3D05M	3D05M	3D05M	3D05M	3D05M	3D05M	3D05M	3D05M
9430	136	MJ CAUS<INTERSTD		3D05M	3D05M	3D05M	3D05M	3D05M	3D05M	3D05M	3D05M
9440	136	MJ CS<STABL EMTN		3D05M	3D05M	3D05M	3D05M	3D05M	3D05M	3D05M	3D05M
9450	136	MJ CS HAV<ENERGY		3D05M	3D05M	3D05M	3D05M	3D05M	3D05M	3D05M	3D05M
9460	136	MJ INTF THNK CLR		3D05M	3D05M	3D05M	3D05M	3D05M	3D05M	3D05M	3D05M
9470	136	MJ BD PSYCH EFCT		3D05M	3D05M	3D05M	3D05M	3D05M	3D05M	3D05M	3D05M
9480	136	MJ CS HEALTH BAD		3D05M	3D05M	3D05M	3D05M	3D05M	3D05M	3D05M	3D05M
9490	136	MJ CS DRIV UNSAF		3D05M	3D05M	3D05M	3D05M	3D05M	3D05M	3D05M	3D05M
9500	136	MJ GT TRBL W POL		3D05M	3D05M	3D05M	3D05M	3D05M	3D05M	3D05M	3D05M
9510	136	MJ CS NO PROBLEM			3D05M	3D05M	3D05M	3D05M	3D05M	3D05M	3D05M
9520	136	MJ NEVER USED DG			3D05M	3D05M	3D05M	3D05M	3D05M	3D05M	3D05M
9530	136	OT CS BEHV REGRT		3D05O	3D05O	3D05O	3D05O	3D05O	3D05O	3D05O	3D05O
9540	136	OT HURT REL PRNT		3D05O	3D05O	3D05O	3D05O	3D05O	3D05O	3D05O	3D05O
9550	136	OT HURT REL SPSE		3D05O	3D05O	3D05O	3D05O	3D05O	3D05O	3D05O	3D05O
9560	136	OT HURT REL FRND		3D05O	3D05O	3D05O	3D05O	3D05O	3D05O	3D05O	3D05O
9570	136	OT HURT REL TCHR		3D05O	3D05O	3D05O	3D05O	3D05O	3D05O	3D05O	3D05O
9580	136	OT INV PL BD INF		3D05O	3D05O	3D05O	3D05O	3D05O	3D05O	3D05O	3D05O
9590	136	OT HURT PERF JOB		3D05O	3D05O	3D05O	3D05O	3D05O	3D05O	3D05O	3D05O
9600	136	OT CAUS<INTERSTD		3D05O	3D05O	3D05O	3D05O	3D05O	3D05O	3D05O	3D05O
9610	136	OT CS<STABL EMTN		3D05O	3D05O	3D05O	3D05O	3D05O	3D05O	3D05O	3D05O
9620	136	OT CS HAV<ENERGY		3D05O	3D05O	3D05O	3D05O	3D05O	3D05O	3D05O	3D05O
9630	136	OT INTF THNK CLR		3D05O	3D05O	3D05O	3D05O	3D05O	3D05O	3D05O	3D05O
9640	136	OT BD PSYCH EFCT		3D05O	3D05O	3D05O	3D05O	3D05O	3D05O	3D05O	3D05O
9650	136	OT CS HEALTH BAD		3D05O	3D05O	3D05O	3D05O	3D05O	3D05O	3D05O	3D05O
9660	136	OT CS DRIV UNSAF		3D05O	3D05O	3D05O	3D05O	3D05O	3D05O	3D05O	3D05O
9670	136	OT GT TRBL W POL		3D05O	3D05O	3D05O	3D05O	3D05O	3D05O	3D05O	3D05O
9680	136	OT CS NO PROBLEM			3D05O	3D05O	3D05O	3D05O	3D05O	3D05O	3D05O
9690	136	OT NEVER USED DG			3D05O	3D05O	3D05O	3D05O	3D05O	3D05O	3D05O

A08a: DRUGS. Sources of help

7540		TRN FA/MO DRG HP			2E05A		2E07A				
7550		TRN SR/BR DRG HP			2E05B		2E07B				
7560		TRN RLTVS DRG HP			2E05C		2E07C				
7570		TRN FRND DRG HP			2E05D		2E07D				
		(continued)									

Item Reference Number	Page Loc. in this Volume	ITEM DESCRIPTION (ABBREVIATED)	QUESTIONNAIRE LOCATION BY YEAR (FORM, SECTION, AND QUESTION NUMBER)								
			1975	1976	1977	1978	1979	1980	1981	1982/83	1984/85

A08a: DRUGS. Sources of help *(continued)*

Item Reference Number	Page Loc.	ITEM DESCRIPTION	1975	1976	1977	1978	1979	1980	1981	1982/83	1984/85
7580		TRN DOCTR DRG HP			2E05E		2E07E				
7590		TRN CLINC DRG HP			2E05F		2E07F				
7600		TRN CNSLR DRG HP			2E05G		2E07G				
7610		TRN TCHR DRG HP			2E05H		2E07H				
7620		TRN MNSTR DRG HP			2E05I		2E07I				

A09a: DRUGS. Parental awareness of use

Item Reference Number	Page Loc.	ITEM DESCRIPTION	1975	1976	1977	1978	1979	1980	1981	1982/83	1984/85
7510	113	PRNT THK U DRINK			2E02	2E01	2E04	2E05	2E05	2E05	2E05
7520	113	PRNT THK U SM MJ			2E03	2E02	2E05	2E06	2E06	2E06	2E06
7530		PRNT THK USE DRG			2E04	2E03	2E06	2E07	2E07		

A10a: DRUGS. Education

Item Reference Number	Page Loc.	ITEM DESCRIPTION	1975	1976	1977	1978	1979	1980	1981	1982/83	1984/85
7690	116	HAD DRUG EDUCATN		2E05	2E09	2E09	2E11	2E12	2E12	2E15	2E15
7840	116	DG ED,>DG INTRST		2E06	2E10	2E10	2E12	2E13	2E13	2E16	2E16
7850	116	DG ED,SPC COURSE		2E07A	2E11A	2E11A	2E13A	2E14A	2E14A	2E17A	2E17A
7860	116	DG ED,IN REG CRS		2E07B	2E11B	2E11B	2E13B	2E14B	2E14B	2E17B	2E17B
7870	116	DG ED,NT REG CRS		2E07C	2E11C	2E11C	2E13C	2E14C	2E14C	2E17C	2E17C
7880	116	DG ED,SPC DISCUS		2E07D	2E11D	2E11D	2E13D	2E14D	2E14D	2E17D	2E17D
7890	116	DG ED,GRT VALUE		2E08	2E12	2E12	2E14	2E15	2E15	2E18	2E18

A11a: DRUGS. Own attitudes about use by adults

Item Reference Number	Page Loc.	ITEM DESCRIPTION	1975	1976	1977	1978	1979	1980	1981	1982/83	1984/85
8560	129	DAP SMK 1PCK CIG	(3A53A)	3A28A	3A28A	3A28A	3A28A	3A28A	3A28A	3A28A	3A28A
8570	129	DAP TRY MRJ 1-2T	(3A53B)	3A28B	3A28B	3A28B	3A28B	3A28B	3A28B	3A28B	3A28B
8580	129	DAP SMK MRJ OCCS	(3A53C)	3A28C	3A28C	3A28C	3A28C	3A28C	3A28C	3A28C	3A28C
8590	130	DAP SMK MRJ REGL	(3A53D)	3A28D	3A28D	3A28D	3A28D	3A28D	3A28D	3A28D	3A28D
8600	130	DAP TRY LSD 1-2T	(3A53E)	3A28E	3A28E	3A28E	3A28E	3A28E	3A28E	3A28E	3A28E
8610	130	DAP TKG LSD REGL	(3A53F)	3A28F	3A28F	3A28F	3A28F	3A28F	3A28F	3A28F	3A28F
8620	130	DAP TRY HRN 1-2T	(3A53G)	3A28G	3A28G	3A28G	3A28G	3A28G	3A28G	3A28G	3A28G
8630	130	DAP TKG HRN OCCS	(3A53H)	3A28H	3A28H	3A28H	3A28H	3A28H	3A28H	3A28H	3A28H
8640	130	DAP TKG HRN REGL	(3A53I)	3A28I	3A28I	3A28I	3A28I	3A28I	3A28I	3A28I	3A28I
8650	130	DAP TRY BRB 1-2T	(3A53J)	3A28J	3A28J	3A28J	3A28J	3A28J	3A28J	3A28J	3A28J
8660	130	DAP TKG BRB REGL	(3A53K)	3A28K	3A28K	3A28K	3A28K	3A28K	3A28K	3A28K	3A28K
8670	130	DAP TRY AMP 1-2T	(3A53L)	3A28L	3A28L	3A28L	3A28L	3A28L	3A28L	3A28L	3A28L
8680	131	DAP TKG AMP REGL	(3A53M)	3A28M	3A28M	3A28M	3A28M	3A28M	3A28M	3A28M	3A28M
8690	131	DAP TRY COC 1-2T	(3A53N)	3A28N	3A28N	3A28N	3A28N	3A28N	3A28N	3A28N	3A28N
8700	131	DAP TKG COC REGL	(3A53O)	3A28O	3A28O	3A28O	3A28O	3A28O	3A28O	3A28O	3A28O
8710	131	DAP TRY DRK ALCL	(3A53P)	3A28P	3A28P	3A28P	3A28P	3A28P	3A28P	3A28P	3A28P
8720	131	DAP 1-2 DRK/DAY	(3A53Q)	3A28Q	3A28Q	3A28Q	3A28Q	3A28Q	3A28Q	3A28Q	3A28Q
8730	131	DAP 4-5 DRK/DAY	(3A53R)	3A28R	3A28R	3A28R	3A28R	3A28R	3A28R	3A28R	3A28R
8740	131	DAP 5+ DRK WKNDS	(3A53S)	3A28S	3A28S	3A28S	3A28S	3A28S	3A28S	3A28S	3A28S

A11b: DRUGS. Own attitudes about use by own children

Item Reference Number	Page Loc.	ITEM DESCRIPTION	1975	1976	1977	1978	1979	1980	1981	1982/83	1984/85
7210		FBD CHLD CIG RGL			2E01A						
7220		FBD CHLD MJ OCCS			2E01B						
7230		FBD CHLD MJ RGLY			2E01C						
7240		FBD CHLD LSD OCC			2E01D						
7250		FBD CHLD AMPH OC			2E01E						
7260		FBD CHLD BARB OC			2E01F						
7270		FBD CHLD COKE OC			2E01G						
7280		FBD CHLD HRN OCC			2E01H						
7290		FBD CHLD DRNK OC			2E01I						
7300		FBD CHLD DRNK RG			2E01J						
7310		FBD CHLD DRUNKOC			2E01K						

A11c: DRUGS. Own perceptions of users

Item Reference Number	Page Loc.	ITEM DESCRIPTION	1975	1976	1977	1978	1979	1980	1981	1982/83	1984/85
13060	194	I/MJ USR,>CREATV			5E01A	5E01A	5E01A	5E01A	5E01A	5E01A	5E01A
13070	194	I/MJ USR,<SENSBL			5E01B	5E01B	5E01B	5E01B	5E01B	5E01B	5E01B
13080	194	I/MJ USR,>INTRST			5E01C	5E01C	5E01C	5E01C	5E01C	5E01C	5E01C
		(continued)									

Item Reference Number	Page Loc. in this Volume	ITEM DESCRIPTION (ABBREVIATED)	QUESTIONNAIRE LOCATION BY YEAR (FORM, SECTION, AND QUESTION NUMBER)								
			1975	1976	1977	1978	1979	1980	1981	1982/83	1984/85

A11c: DRUGS. Own perceptions of users (continued)

Item Reference Number	Page Loc. in this Volume	ITEM DESCRIPTION (ABBREVIATED)	1975	1976	1977	1978	1979	1980	1981	1982/83	1984/85
13090	194	I/MJ USR,<HRDWKG			5E01D	5E01D	5E01D	5E01D	5E01D	5E01D	5E01D
13100	194	I/MJ USR,>INDPND			5E01E	5E01E	5E01E	5E01E	5E01E	5E01E	5E01E
13110	195	I/MJ USR,>UNSTBL			5E01F	5E01F	5E01F	5E01F	5E01F	5E01F	5E01F
13120	195	I/MJ USR,>CNCRND			5E01G	5E01G	5E01G	5E01G	5E01G	5E01G	5E01G
13130	195	I/MJ USR,>WKWLD			5E01H	5E01H	5E01H	5E01H	5E01H	5E01H	5E01H
13140	195	I/MJ USR,>CRMNL			5E01I	5E01I	5E01I	5E01I	5E01I	5E01I	5E01I
13330	195	I/DG USR,>CREATV			5E03A	5E03A		5E03A		5E03A	5E02A
13340	195	I/DG USR,<SENSBL			5E03B	5E03B		5E03B		5E03B	5E02B
13350	195	I/DG USR,>INTRST			5E03C	5E03C		5E03C		5E03C	5E02C
13360	195	I/DG USR,<HRDWKG			5E03D	5E03D		5E03D		5E03D	5E02D
13370	196	I/DG USR,>INDPND			5E03E	5E03E		5E03E		5E03E	5E02E
13380	196	I/DG USR,>UNSTBL			5E03F	5E03F		5E03F		5E03F	5E02F
13390	196	I/DG USR,>CNCRND			5E03G	5E03G		5E03G		5E03G	5E02G
13400	196	I/DG USR,>WKWLD			5E03H	5E03H		5E03H		5E03H	5E02H
13410	196	I/DG USR,>CRMNL			5E03I	5E03I		5E03I		5E03I	5E02I
13670	140	DRG USE+,MY FLGS			5E07C	5E07C	5E05C	5E07C		3E07C	3E07C
20880	196	GUY SMK COOL							5E03A	5E05A	5E03A
20890	196	GUY SMK INSECURE							5E03B	5E05B	5E03B
20900	196	GUY SMK INDPNDNT							5E03C	5E05C	5E03C
20910	197	GUY SMK CONFORMG							5E03D	5E05D	5E03D
20920	197	GUY SMK MATURE							5E03E	5E05E	5E03E
20930	197	GUY SM TRY MATUR							5E03F	5E05F	5E03F
20940	197	GIRL SMK COOL							5E04A	5E06A	5E04A
20950	197	GRL SMK INSECURE							5E04B	5E06B	5E04B
20960	197	GRL SMK INDPNDNT							5E04C	5E06C	5E04C
20970	197	GRL SMK CONFORMG							5E04D	5E06D	5E04D
20980	198	GRL SMK MATURE							5E04E	5E06E	5E04E
20990	198	GRL SM TRY MATUR							5E04F	5E06F	5E04F
21000	198	SMKRS ENJOY LIFE							5E05A	5E07A	5E05A
21010	198	PRFR DATE N-SMKR							5E05B	5E07B	5E05B
21020	198	HARMFUL CIG EXAG							5E05C	5E07C	5E05C
21030	198	SMKR POOR JDGMNT							5E05D	5E07D	5E05D
21040	198	DONT MIND SMOKNG							5E05E	5E07E	5E05E
21050	199	SMKG DIRTY HABIT							5E05F	5E07F	5E05F

A11d: DRUGS. Own attitudes about use by people of high school age

Item Reference Number	Page Loc. in this Volume	ITEM DESCRIPTION (ABBREVIATED)	1975	1976	1977	1978	1979	1980	1981	1982/83	1984/85
22070	203	PR PTY-OTH HI AL									5E09C
22090	203	PR PTY-OT USE MJ									5E09E
22110	203	PR PTY-OT USE OT									5E09G

A12a: DRUGS. Parents' attitudes about use

Item Reference Number	Page Loc. in this Volume	ITEM DESCRIPTION (ABBREVIATED)	1975	1976	1977	1978	1979	1980	1981	1982/83	1984/85
11380		PRNT DAP CIGS	4A35A	4E09A	4E09A	4E08A	4E08A				
11390		PRNT DAP TRY MRJ	4A35B	4E09B	4E09B	4E08B	4E08B				
11400		PRNT DAP MJ OCC	4A35C	4E09C	4E09C	4E08C	4E08C				
11410		PRNT DAP MJ REG	4A35D	4E09D	4E09D	4E08D	4E08D				
11420		PRNT DAP TRY LSD	4A35E	4E09E	4E09E	4E08E	4E08E				
11430		PRNT DAP TRY AMP	4A35F	4E09F	4E09F	4E08F	4E08F				
11440		PRNT DAP 1-2DR/D	4A35G	4E09G	4E09G	4E08G	4E08G				
11450		PRNT DAP 4-5DR/D	4A35H	4E09H	4E09H	4E08H	4E08H				
11460		PRNT DAP 5+DR/WE	4A35I	4E09I	4E09I	4E08I	4E08I				

A12b: DRUGS. Friends' and students' attitudes about use

Item Reference Number	Page Loc. in this Volume	ITEM DESCRIPTION (ABBREVIATED)	1975	1976	1977	1978	1979	1980	1981	1982/83	1984/85
11470	170	FRD DAP CIGS			4E10A		4E09A	4E08A	4E08A	4E08A	4E08A
11480	170	FRD DAP TRY MARJ			4E10B		4E09B	4E08B	4E08B	4E08B	4E08B
11490	171	FRD DAP MJ OCC			4E10C		4E09C	4E08C	4E08C	4E08C	4E08C
11500	171	FRD DAP MJ REG			4E10D		4E09D	4E08D	4E08D	4E08D	4E08D
11510	171	FRD DAP TRY LSD			4E10E		4E09E	4E08E	4E08E	4E08E	4E08E
11520	171	FRD DAP TRY AMP			4E10F		4E09F	4E08F	4E08F	4E08F	4E08F
11530	171	FRD DAP 1-2DR/DA			4E10G		4E09G	4E08G	4E08G	4E08G	4E08G
11540	171	FRD DAP 4-5DR/DA			4E10H		4E09H	4E08H	4E08H	4E08H	4E08H

(continued)

Item Reference Number	Page Loc. in this Volume	ITEM DESCRIPTION (ABBREVIATED)	QUESTIONNAIRE LOCATION BY YEAR (FORM, SECTION, AND QUESTION NUMBER)								
			1975	1976	1977	1978	1979	1980	1981	1982/83	1984/85

A12b: DRUGS. Friends' and students' attitudes about use (continued)

Item Reference Number	Page Loc. in this Volume	ITEM DESCRIPTION (ABBREVIATED)	1975	1976	1977	1978	1979	1980	1981	1982/83	1984/85
11550	171	FRD DAP 5+DR/WKD			4E10I		4E09I	4E08I	4E08I	4E08I	4E08I
11551	171	FRD DAP DRIV+2DR									4E08J
11552	171	FRD DAP DRIV+5DR									4E08K
13650	139	DRG USE+,MAJ STD		5E06A	5E07A	5E07A	5E05A	5E07A		3E07A	3E07A
13660	140	DRG USE+,MY FRND		5E06B	5E07B	5E07B	5E05B	5E07B		3E07B	3E07B

A12c: DRUGS. Others' perceptions of users

Item Reference Number	Page Loc. in this Volume	ITEM DESCRIPTION (ABBREVIATED)	1975	1976	1977	1978	1979	1980	1981	1982/83	1984/85
12780		PSN TKG MJ/AMBTS		5D02A							
12790		PSN TKG MJ/-SOCL		5D02B							
12800		PSN TKG MJ/CNFMG		5D02C							
12810		PSN TKG MJ/CRMNL		5D02D							
12820		PSN TKG MJ/-STBL		5D02E							
12830		PSN TKG MJ/INTRS		5D02F							
12840		PSN TKG MJ/RBLS		5D02G							
12850		PSN TKG MJ/SNSBL		5D02H							
12860		PSN TKG MJ/SX PR		5D02I							
12870		PSN TKG MJ/WKWLD		5D02J							
12890		PSN TKG DG/AMBTS		5D03A							
12900		PSN TKG DG/-SOCL		5D03B							
12910		PSN TKG DG/CNFMG		5D03C							
12920		PSN TKG DG/CRMNL		5D03D							
12930		PSN TKG DG/-STBL		5D03E							
12940		PSN TKG DG/INTRS		5D03F							
12950		PSN TKG DG/RBLS		5D03G							
12960		PSN TKG DG/SNSBL		5D03H							
12970		PSN TKG DG/SX PR		5D03I							
12980		PSN TKG DG/WKWLD		5D03J							
13190		PPL/MJUSR>CREATV			5E02A	5E02A		5E02A	5E02A	5E02A	
13200		PPL/MJUSR<SENSBL			5E02B	5E02B		5E02B	5E02B	5E02B	
13210		PPL/MJUSR>INTRST			5E02C	5E02C		5E02C	5E02C	5E02C	
13220		PPL/MJUSR<HRDWKG			5E02D	5E02D		5E02D	5E02D	5E02D	
13230		PPL/MJUSR>INDPND			5E02E	5E02E		5E02E	5E02E	5E02E	
13240		PPL/MJUSR>UNSTBL			5E02F	5E02F		5E02F	5E02F	5E02F	
13250		PPL/MJUSR>CNCRND			5E02G	5E02G		5E02G	5E02G	5E02G	
13260		PPL/MJUSR>WKWLD			5E02H	5E02H		5E02H	5E02H	5E02H	
13270		PPL/MJUSR>CRMNL			5E02I	5E02I		5E02I	5E02I	5E02I	
13490		PPL/DGUSR>CREATV			5E04A	5E04A		5E04A		5E04A	
13500		PPL/DGUSR<SENSBL			5E04B	5E04B		5E04B		5E04B	
13510		PPL/DGUSR>INTRST			5E04C	5E04C		5E04C		5E04C	
13520		PPL/DGUSR<HRDWKG			5E04D	5E04D		5E04D		5E04D	
13530		PPL/DGUSR>INDPND			5E04E	5E04E		5E04E		5E04E	
13540		PPL/DGUSR>UNSTBL			5E04F	5E04F		5E04F		5E04F	
13550		PPL/DGUSR>CNCRND			5E04G	5E04G		5E04G		5E04G	
13560		PPL/DGUSR>WKWLD			5E04H	5E04H		5E04H		5E04H	
13570		PPL/DGUSR>CRMNL			5E04I	5E04I		5E04I		5E04I	

A13a: DRUGS. Preferred legality for adults

Item Reference Number	Page Loc. in this Volume	ITEM DESCRIPTION (ABBREVIATED)	1975	1976	1977	1978	1979	1980	1981	1982/83	1984/85
10760	159	LAW 4 SMK TOBPUB			4A20K	4A20K	4A20K	4A20K	4A20K	4A20K	4A20K
10770		ILGL AD SMK CIG		4A20A							
10780	158	ILGL AD MRJ PRIV		4A20B	4A20A	4A20A	4A20A	4A20A	4A20A	4A20A	4A20A
10790	158	ILGL AD MRJ PUBL		4A20C	4A20B	4A20B	4A20B	4A20B	4A20B	4A20B	4A20B
10800	158	ILGL AD LSD PRIV		4A20D	4A20C	4A20C	4A20C	4A20C	4A20C	4A20C	4A20C
10810	158	ILGL AD LSD PUBL		4A20E	4A20D	4A20D	4A20D	4A20D	4A20D	4A20D	4A20D
10820	158	ILGL AD AMP PRIV		4A20F	4A20E	4A20E	4A20E	4A20E	4A20E	4A20E	4A20E
10830	158	ILGL AD AMP PUBL		4A20G	4A20F	4A20F	4A20F	4A20F	4A20F	4A20F	4A20F
10840	158	ILGL AD HRN PRIV		4A20H	4A20G	4A20G	4A20G	4A20G	4A20G	4A20G	4A20G
10850	159	ILGL AD HRN PUBL		4A20I	4A20H	4A20H	4A20H	4A20H	4A20H	4A20H	4A20H
10860	159	ILGL AD DRNK PRV		4A20J	4A20I	4A20I	4A20I	4A20I	4A20I	4A20I	4A20I
10870	159	ILGL AD DRNK PBL		4A20K	4A20J	4A20J	4A20J	4A20J	4A20J	4A20J	4A20J

Item Reference Number	Page Loc. in this Volume	ITEM DESCRIPTION (ABBREVIATED)	QUESTIONNAIRE LOCATION BY YEAR (FORM, SECTION, AND QUESTION NUMBER)								
			1975	1976	1977	1978	1979	1980	1981	1982/83	1984/85

A13b: DRUGS. Own response to legalization

10880	159	CRIME 2 USE MARJ	4A32	4A21	4A21	4A21	4A21	4A21	4A21	4A21	4A21
10890	159	LEGAL 2 SELL MRJ	4A33	4A22	4A22	4A22	4A22	4A22	4A22	4A22	4A22
10900	159	USE<MJ IF LEGAL	4A34	4A23	4A23	4A23	4A23	4A23	4A23	4A23	4A23

A13c: DRUGS. Knowledge of marijuana laws

13050		R'S STATE LAW/MJ		5D04	5D05	5D05	5D05	5D05			

A14a: DRUGS. Risk of harm to self

12360	185	RSK OF CIG1+PK/D	5A41A	5A23A	5A23A	5A23A	5A23A	5A23A	5A23A	5A23A	5A23A
12370	185	RSK OF MJ 1-2 X	5A41B	5A23B	5A23B	5A23B	5A23B	5A23B	5A23B	5A23B	5A23B
12380	185	RSK OF MJ OCSNLY	5A41C	5A23C	5A23C	5A23C	5A23C	5A23C	5A23C	5A23C	5A23C
12390	186	RSK OF MJ REGLY	5A41D	5A23D	5A23D	5A23D	5A23D	5A23D	5A23D	5A23D	5A23D
12400	186	RSK OF LSD 1-2 X	5A41E	5A23E	5A23E	5A23E	5A23E	5A23E	5A23E	5A23E	5A23E
12410	186	RSK OF LSD REGLY	5A41F	5A23F	5A23F	5A23F	5A23F	5A23F	5A23F	5A23F	5A23F
12420	186	RSK OF 'H' 1-2 X	5A41G	5A23G	5A23G	5A23G	5A23G	5A23G	5A23G	5A23G	5A23G
12430	186	RSK OF 'H' OCSNL	5A41H	5A23H	5A23H	5A23H	5A23H	5A23H	5A23H	5A23H	5A23H
12440	186	RSK OF 'H' REGLY	5A41I	5A23I	5A23I	5A23I	5A23I	5A23I	5A23I	5A23I	5A23I
12450	186	RSK OF BARB 1-2X	5A41J	5A23J	5A23J	5A23J	5A23J	5A23J	5A23J	5A23J	5A23J
12460	187	RSK OF BARB REGY	5A41K	5A23K	5A23K	5A23K	5A23K	5A23K	5A23K	5A23K	5A23K
12470	187	RSK OF AMPH 1-2X	5A41L	5A23L	5A23L	5A23L	5A23L	5A23L	5A23L	5A23L	5A23L
12480	187	RSK OF AMPH REG	5A41M	5A23M	5A23M	5A23M	5A23M	5A23M	5A23M	5A23M	5A23M
12490	187	RSK OF COKE 1-2X	5A41N	5A23N	5A23N	5A23N	5A23N	5A23N	5A23N	5A23N	5A23N
12500	187	RSK OF COKE REG	5A41O	5A23O	5A23O	5A23O	5A23O	5A23O	5A23O	5A23O	5A23O
12510	187	RSK OF 1-2 DRINK	5A41P	5A23P	5A23P	5A23P	5A23P	5A23P	5A23P	5A23P	5A23P
12520	187	RSK OF 1-2 DR/DA	5A41Q	5A23Q	5A23Q	5A23Q	5A23Q	5A23Q	5A23Q	5A23Q	5A23Q
12530	188	RSK OF 4-5 DR/DA	5A41R	5A23R	5A23R	5A23R	5A23R	5A23R	5A23R	5A23R	5A23R
12540	188	RSK OF 5+DR/WKND	5A41S	5A23S	5A23S	5A23S	5A23S	5A23S	5A23S	5A23S	5A23S

A14b: DRUGS. Risk of harm to others

7320		RSK/OT CIG1+PK/D		2E01A							
7330		RSK/OT MJ 1-2 X		2E01B							
7340		RSK/OT MJ OCSNLY		2E01C							
7350		RSK/OT MJ REGLY		2E01D							
7360		RSK/OT LSD 1-2 X		2E01E							
7370		RSK/OT LSD REGLY		2E01F							
7380		RSK/OT 'H' 1-2 X		2E01G							
7390		RSK/OT 'H' OCSNL		2E01H							
7400		RSK/OT 'H' REGLY		2E01I							
7410		RSK/OT BARB 1-2X		2E01J							
7420		RSK/OT BARB REGY		2E01K							
7430		RSK/OT AMPH 1-2X		2E01L							
7440		RSK/OT AMPH REG		2E01M							
7450		RSK/OT COKE 1-2X		2E01N							
7460		RSK/OT COKE REG		2E01O							
7470		RSK/OT 1-2 DRINK		2E01P							
7480		RSK/OT 1-2 DR/DA		2E01Q							
7490		RSK/OT 4-5 DR/DA		2E01R							
7500		RSK/OT 5+DR/WKND		2E01S							

A15a: DRUGS. Admitting use in questionnaire

20800	203	WLD ADMT USE MJ					5E09	5E09	5E14	5E13	5E10
20810	203	WLD ADMT USE AMP					5E10	5E10	5E15	5E14	5E11
20820	204	WLD ADMT USE HER					5E11	5E11	5E16	5E15	5E12

A16a: DRUGS. Parent groups

21730	172	IDEA PARENTS GRP								4E09†	4E09
21740	172	#FRNDS PRNTS GRP								4E10†	4E10
21750	172	OWN PRNTS IN GRP								4E11†	4E11
		(continued)									

† This question appears in 1983 but does not appear in 1982.

Item Reference Number	Page Loc. in this Volume	ITEM DESCRIPTION (ABBREVIATED)	QUESTIONNAIRE LOCATION BY YEAR (FORM, SECTION, AND QUESTION NUMBER)								
			1975	1976	1977	1978	1979	1980	1981	1982/83	1984/85

A16a: DRUGS. Parent groups *(continued)*

Item Reference Number	Page Loc. in this Volume	ITEM DESCRIPTION (ABBREVIATED)	1975	1976	1977	1978	1979	1980	1981	1982/83	1984/85
21760	172	GP IMPCT OWN FLG								4E12†	4E12
21770	172	GP CHG RELP PRNT								4E13†	4E13
21780	173	#FRNDS ANTIDG GP								4E14†	4E14
21790	173	EVR IN ANTIDG GP								4E15†	4E15

B01: EDUCATION. High school: scholastic status, objectives, experiences

Item Reference Number	Page Loc. in this Volume	ITEM DESCRIPTION (ABBREVIATED)	1975	1976	1977	1978	1979	1980	1981	1982/83	1984/85
390	19	WHEN R XPCT GRAD		+C14	+C14	+C14	+C14	+C14	+C14	+C14	+C14
400	19	R'S HS PROGRAM		+C15	+C15	+C15	+C15	+C15	+C15	+C15	+C15
410	19	RT SF SCH AB>AVG		+C16	+C16	+C16	+C16	+C16	+C16	+C16	+C16
420	19	RT SF INTELL>AVG		+C17	+C17	+C17	+C17	+C17	+C17	+C17	+C17
470	20	R HS GRADE/D=1		+C20	+C20	+C20	+C20	+C20	+C20	+C20	+C20
1310	35	SAT EDUC EXPRNCS	1A009E	1A006E	1A006E	1A006E	1A006E	1A006E	1A006E	1A006E	1A006E
1660	40	GO SCH ENJY XPR	1A013I	1A011I	1A011I	1A011I	1A011I	1A011I	1A011I	1A011I	1A011I
1670	40	DO WL SC IMP/JB	1A013H	1A011J	1A011J	1A011J	1A011J	1A011J	1A011J	1A011J	1A011J
5700	82	*SC WRK NVR MNG		1D002	1D002	1D002	1D002	1D002	1D002	1D002	1D002
5710	82	*MST COUR V DUL		1D003	1D003	1D003	1D003	1D003	1D003	1D003	1D003
5720	82	*LRN SCH NT IMP		1D004	1D004	1D004	1D004	1D004	1D004	1D004	1D004
7630	82	R LIKES SCHOOL		1D001	1D001	1D001	1D001	1D001	1D001	1D001	1D001
	115			2E02	2E06	2E06	2E08	2E09	2E09	2E12	2E12
				3E08	3E07	3E07	3E07	3E07	3E07		
				4E10	5E05	5E05	5E03	5E05			
				5E04							
7640	115	HRS/WK SPND HMWK		2E03	2E07	2E07	2E09	2E10	2E10	2E13	2E13
9860	138	HAD SEX ED IN HS		3E09	3E08	3E08	3E08	3E08	3E08	3E04	3E04
9870	138	STUDY BC IN HS		3E10	3E09	3E09	3E09	3E09	3E09	3E05	3E05

B02: EDUCATION. Combining work and school: attitudes, experiences

Item Reference Number	Page Loc. in this Volume	ITEM DESCRIPTION (ABBREVIATED)	1975	1976	1977	1978	1979	1980	1981	1982/83	1984/85
5770	83	R IN WK-STDY PG		1D009	1D009	1D009	1D009	1D009	1D009	1D009	1D009
10260	151	JOB IMPC LRNING	4A08R	4A08R	4A08R	4A08R	4A08R	4A08R	4A08R	4A08R	4A08R

B03: EDUCATION. Interracial contact at school

Item Reference Number	Page Loc. in this Volume	ITEM DESCRIPTION (ABBREVIATED)	1975	1976	1977	1978	1979	1980	1981	1982/83	1984/85
8220	124	DES AL CHL SM RC	3A19L	3A10A	3A10A	3A10A	3A10A	3A10A	3A10A	3A10A	3A10A
8230	124	DES SM CHL OT RC	3A19M	3A10B	3A10B	3A10B	3A10B	3A10B	3A10B	3A10B	3A10B
8240	124	DES MS CHL OT RC	3A19N	3A10C	3A10C	3A10C	3A10C	3A10C	3A10C	3A10C	3A10C
8270	124	ELEMSCH AL OT RC	3A21	3A13	3A13	3A13	3A13	3A13	3A13	3A13	3A13
8280	124	HISCH AL OT RC	3A20	3A14	3A14	3A14	3A14	3A14	3A14	3A14	3A14
11890	177	RCL CNTCT SCHOOL		5A07A	5A07A	5A07A	5A07A	5A07A	5A07A	5A07A	5A07A

B04: EDUCATION. Student norms

Item Reference Number	Page Loc. in this Volume	ITEM DESCRIPTION (ABBREVIATED)	1975	1976	1977	1978	1979	1980	1981	1982/83	1984/85
5730	82	LOT CMPTN GRADE		1D005	1D005	1D005	1D005	1D005	1D005	1D005	1D005
5740	82	STDTS DSLK CHTG		1D006	1D006	1D006	1D006	1D006	1D006	1D006	1D006
5750	83	ST -LK PROV TCH		1D007	1D007	1D007	1D007	1D007	1D007	1D007	1D007
5760	83	FRD NCG/TCH -LK		1D008	1D008	1D008	1D008	1D008	1D008	1D008	1D008
13580	138	STS SCH RT FAMLY		5E05A	5E06A	5E06A	5E04A	5E06A		3E06A	3E06A
13590	139	STS SCH LDS STU		5E05B	5E06B	5E06B	5E04B	5E06B		3E06B	3E06B
13600	139	STS SCH NIC CAR		5E05C	5E06C	5E06C	5E04C	5E06C		3E06C	3E06C
13610	139	STS SCH HI GRDE		5E05D	5E06D	5E06D	5E04D	5E06D		3E06D	3E06D
13620	139	STS SCH GD ATHLT		5E05E	5E06E	5E06E	5E04E	5E06E		3E06E	3E06E
13630	139	STS SCH INTLCTL		5E05F	5E06F	5E06F	5E04F	5E06F		3E06F	3E06F
13640	139	STS SCH PLN CLG		5E05G	5E06G	5E06G	5E04G	5E06G		3E06G	3E06G

B05: EDUCATION. Counseling

Item Reference Number	Page Loc. in this Volume	ITEM DESCRIPTION (ABBREVIATED)	1975	1976	1977	1978	1979	1980	1981	1982/83	1984/85
5780	83	#X/YR COUNS IND		1D010	1D010	1D010	1D010	1D010	1D010	1D010	1D010
5790	83	#X/YR COUNS GRP		1D011	1D011	1D011	1D011	1D011	1D011	1D011	1D011
5800	83	R LK C COUNS MR		1D012	1D012	1D012	1D012	1D012	1D012	1D012	1D012
5810	84	CSLNG VRY HLPFL		(1D013)	1D013	1D013	1D013	1D013	1D013	1D013	1D013
5811	84	CNSL COURSES					1D014A	1D014A	1D014A	1D014A	1D014A
5812	84	CNSL CL PROB					1D014B	1D014B	1D014B	1D014B	1D014B
		(continued)									

† This question appears in 1983 but does not appear in 1982.

Item Reference Number	Page Loc. in this Volume	ITEM DESCRIPTION (ABBREVIATED)	QUESTIONNAIRE LOCATION BY YEAR (FORM, SECTION, AND QUESTION NUMBER)								
			1975	1976	1977	1978	1979	1980	1981	1982/83	1984/85

B05: EDUCATION. Counseling *(continued)*

Item Reference Number	Page Loc. in this Volume	ITEM DESCRIPTION (ABBREVIATED)	1975	1976	1977	1978	1979	1980	1981	1982/83	1984/85
5813	84	CNSL TRBL R IN					1D014C	1D014C	1D014C	1D014C	1D014C
5814	84	CNSL MILTRY PLN					1D014D	1D014D	1D014D	1D014D	1D014D
5815	84	CNSL EDUC PLANS					1D014E	1D014E	1D014E	1D014E	1D014E
5816	84	CNSL CAREER PLN					1D014F	1D014F	1D014F	1D014F	1D014F
5817	85	CNSL PRNL PROB					1D014G	1D014G	1D014G	1D014G	1D014G

B06: EDUCATION. Absenteeism and truancy

Item Reference Number	Page Loc. in this Volume	ITEM DESCRIPTION (ABBREVIATED)	1975	1976	1977	1978	1979	1980	1981	1982/83	1984/85
430	19	#DA/4W SC MS ILL		+C18A	+C18A	+C18A	+C18A	+C18A	+C18A	+C18A	+C18A
440	20	#DA/4W SC MS CUT		+C18B	+C18B	+C18B	+C18B	+C18B	+C18B	+C18B	+C18B
450	20	#DA/4W SC MS OTH		+C18C	+C18C	+C18C	+C18C	+C18C	+C18C	+C18C	+C18C
460	20	#DA/4W SKP CLASS		+C19	+C19	+C19	+C19	+C19	+C19	+C19	+C19

B07: EDUCATION. Delinquency and victimization at school

Item Reference Number	Page Loc. in this Volume	ITEM DESCRIPTION (ABBREVIATED)	1975	1976	1977	1978	1979	1980	1981	1982/83	1984/85
6540	100	FRQ FGT WRK/SCHL	2A39C	2A19C	2A19C	2A19C	2A19C	2A19C	2A19C	2A19C	2A19C
6650	101	FRQ DMG SCH PPTY	2A39N	2A19N	2A19N	2A19N	2A19N	2A19N	2A19N	2A19N	2A19N
9871	140	SM1 SCL ROB <$50		4E11A	3E10A	3E10A	5E06A	5E08A	5E13A	3E08A	3E08A
9872	140	SM1 SCL ROB >$50		4E11B	3E10B	3E10B	5E06B	5E08B	5E13B	3E08B	3E08B
9873	140	SM1 SCL DMG PRTY		4E11C	3E10C	3E10C	5E06C	5E08C	5E13C	3E08C	3E08C
9874	140	SM1 SCL IN U W/W		4E11D	3E10D	3E10D	5E06D	5E08D	5E13D	3E08D	3E08D
9875	141	SM1 SCL TH U W/W		4E11E	3E10E	3E10E	5E06E	5E08E	5E13E	3E08E	3E08E
9876	141	SM1 SCL IN U -WP		4E11F	3E10F	3E10F	5E06F	5E08F	5E13F	3E08F	3E08F
9877	141	SM1 SCL TH U W/I		4E11G	3E10G	3E10G	5E06G	5EO8G	5E13G	3E08G	3E08G

B08: EDUCATION. Opinions regarding competency testing

Item Reference Number	Page Loc. in this Volume	ITEM DESCRIPTION (ABBREVIATED)	1975	1976	1977	1978	1979	1980	1981	1982/83	1984/85
7900		16YR+,TEST->DIPL				2E13A	(2E13A)	5E07A	2E16A	2E16A	2E19A	
7910		14YR+,TEST->DIPL				2E13B	(2E13B)	5E07B	2E16B	2E16B	2E19B	
7920		ALL STD H.S.TEST				2E13C	(2E13C)	5E07C	2E16C	2E16C	2E19C	

B09: EDUCATION. Post high school: status, plans, characteristics

Item Reference Number	Page Loc. in this Volume	ITEM DESCRIPTION (ABBREVIATED)	1975	1976	1977	1978	1979	1980	1981	1982/83	1984/85
480	20	R WL DO VOC/TEC		+C21A	+C21A	+C21A	+C21A	+C21A	+C21A	+C21A	+C21A
490	20	R WL DO ARMD FC		+C21B	+C21B	+C21B	+C21B	+C21B	+C21B	+C21B	+C21B
500	21	R WL DO 2YR CLG		+C21C	+C21C	+C21C	+C21C	+C21C	+C21C	+C21C	+C21C
510	21	R WL DO 4YR CLG		+C21D	+C21D	+C21D	+C21D	+C21D	+C21D	+C21D	+C21D
520	21	R WL DO GRD/PRF		+C21E	+C21E	+C21E	+C21E	+C21E	+C21E	+C21E	+C21E
530	21	R WNTDO VOC/TEC		+C22A	+C22A	+C22A	+C22A	+C22A	+C22A	+C22A	+C22A
540	21	R WNTDO ARMD FC		+C22B	+C22B	+C22B	+C22B	+C22B	+C22B	+C22B	+C22B
550	21	R WNTDO 2YR CLG		+C22C	+C22C	+C22C	+C22C	+C22C	+C22C	+C22C	+C22C
560	21	R WNTDO 4YR CLG		+C22D	+C22D	+C22D	+C22D	+C22D	+C22D	+C22D	+C22D
570	21	R WNTDO GRD/PRF		+C22E	+C22E	+C22E	+C22E	+C22E	+C22E	+C22E	+C22E
580	21	R WNTDO NONE		+C22F	+C22F	+C22F	+C22F	+C22F	+C22F	+C22F	+C22F
10410	153	JOB OBSTC EDUCTN		4A13F	4A13F	4A13F	4A13F	4A13F	4A13F	4A13F	4A13F
11320	169	P'IDEA OF EDUC	4A27J	4E08J	4E08J	4E07J	4E07J	4E07J	4E07J	4E07J	4E07J

B10: EDUCATION. Attitudes regarding educational institutions

Item Reference Number	Page Loc. in this Volume	ITEM DESCRIPTION (ABBREVIATED)	1975	1976	1977	1978	1979	1980	1981	1982/83	1984/85
6910	105	DHNSTY COLL&UNIV	2A20C	2D04C	2D04C	2D04C	2D04C	2D04C	2D04C	2D04C	2D04C
6920	105	DHNSTY PBLC SCHL	2A20D	2D04D	2D04D	2D04D	2D04D	2D04D	2D04D	2D04D	2D04D
7650	115	PRCL INFL SCL RN		2E04A	2E08A	2E08A	2E10A	2E11A	2E11A	2E14A	2E14A
7660	115	TCHR INFL SCL RN		2E04B	2E08B	2E08B	2E10B	2E11B	2E11B	2E14B	2E14B
7670	115	STDS INFL SCL RN		2E04C	2E08C	2E08C	2E10C	2E11C	2E11C	2E14C	2E14C
7680	116	PRTS INFL SCL RN		2E04D	2E08D	2E08D	2E10D	2E11D	2E11D	2E14D	2E14D
8400	126	GD JB COLLG&UNIV	3A27C	3A24C	3A24C	3A24C	3A24C	3A24C	3A24C	3A24C	3A24C
8410	127	GD JB PBLC SCHOL	3A27D	3A24D	3A24D	3A24D	3A24D	3A24D	3A24D	3A24D	3A24D
11130	167	MLTRY MORE ED		4E01B	4E01B	4E01B	4E01B	4E01B	4E01B	4E01B	4E01B
11840	176	PLC WRK SCH/UNIV	5A09E	5A05E	5A05E	5A05E	5A05E	5A05E	5A05E	5A05E	5A05E

Item Reference Number	Page Loc. in this Volume	ITEM DESCRIPTION (ABBREVIATED)	QUESTIONNAIRE LOCATION BY YEAR (FORM, SECTION, AND QUESTION NUMBER)								
			1975	1976	1977	1978	1979	1980	1981	1982/83	1984/85

C01: WORK and LEISURE. Present or recent work experience

Item Reference Number	Page Loc. in this Volume	ITEM DESCRIPTION (ABBREVIATED)	1975	1976	1977	1978	1979	1980	1981	1982/83	1984/85
590	21	HRS/W WRK SCHYR		+C23	+C23	+C23	+C23	+C23	+C23	+C23	+C23
1270	34	SAT PRESENT JOB	1A009A	1A006A	1A006A	1A006A	1A006A	1A006A	1A006A	1A006A	1A006A
5770	83	R IN WK-STDY PG		1D009	1D009	1D009	1D009	1D009	1D009	1D009	1D009
6540	100	FRQ FGT WRK/SCHL	2A39C	2A19C	2A19C	2A19C	2A19C	2A19C	2A19C	2A19C	2A19C
6660	101	FRQ DMG WK PRPTY	2A39O	2A19O	2A19O	2A19O	2A19O	2A19O	2A19O	2A19O	2A19O
10910	160	CMP SATFD W/JOB		4D02	4D02	4D02	4D02	4D02	4D02	4D02	4D02
11790	176	XPRC MK R GD WKR		5A04C	5A04C	5A04C	5A04C	5A04C	5A04C	5A04C	5A04C
11940	178	RCL CNTCT JOB		5A07F	5A07F	5A07F	5A07F	5A07F	5A07F	5A07F	5A07F
21530	160	RCNT EMPLYMT EXP								4D03A	4D03A
21540	160	JOB-#HRS/WEEK								4D03B	4D03B
21550	160	JOB-SUPERVSR AGE								4D04	4D04
21560	161	JOB-#WKRS OWN AG								4D05	4D05
21570	161	JOB-USE BEST SKL								4D06A	4D06A
21580	161	JOB-TEACH SKILLS								4D06B	4D06B
21590	161	JOB-USE LRND SKL								4D06C	4D06C
21600	161	JOB-DIF SOC BKGD								4D06D	4D06D
21610	161	JOB-OVER AGE 30								4D06E	4D06E
21620	161	JOB->STRESS								4D06F	4D06F
21630	162	JOB-INTRFR W ED								4D06G	4D06G
21640	162	JOB-INTRFR W SOC								4D06H	4D06H
21650	162	JOB-INTRFR W FAM								4D06I	4D06I
21660	162	JOB-INTERESTING								4D07A	4D07A
21670	162	JOB-HAPPY FR LIF								4D07B	4D07B
21680	162	JOB-EXPCT FR LIF								4D07C	4D07C
21690	162	JOB-STEP STONE								4D07D	4D07D
21700	163	JOB-DO JST FOR $								4D07E	4D07E
21710	163	JOB-TCHR HELP GT								4D08	4D08
21720	163	JOB-WORK STUDY								4D09	4D09

C02: WORK and LEISURE. Income sources; financial security

Item Reference Number	Page Loc. in this Volume	ITEM DESCRIPTION (ABBREVIATED)	1975	1976	1977	1978	1979	1980	1981	1982/83	1984/85
600	21	R$/AVG WEEK JOB		+C24A	+C24A	+C24A	+C24A	+C24A	(+C24A)	+C24A	+C24A
610	22	R$/AVG WEEK OTH		+C24B	+C24B	+C24B	+C24B	+C24B	(+C24B)	+C24B	+C24B
12990	192	I HAVE ENOUGH $			5D04A	5D04A	5D04A	5D04A	5D02A	5D04A	5D04A
13000	192	I LACK $FR BILL			5D04B	5D04B	5D04B	5D04B	5D02B	5D04B	5D04B
13010	192	I WRY@-FINDG JOB			5D04C	5D04C	5D04C	5D04C	5D02C	5D04C	5D04C
13020	192	I CAN FIND JOB			5D04D	5D04D	5D04D	5D04D	5D02D	5D04D	5D04D
13030	193	I CAN KEEP MYJOB			5D04E	5D04E	5D04E	5D04E	5D02E	5D04E	5D04E
13040	193	I WRY@LOSS MYJOB			5D04F	5D04F	5D04F	5D04F	5D02F	5D04F	5D04F
20830	193	%$SAVE FUTR EDUC							5D03A	5D05A	5D05A
20840	193	%$SAVE/SPEND CAR							5D03B	5D05B	5D05B
20850	193	%$SAVE OTHER							5D03C	5D05C	5D05C
20860	194	%$SPEND ON SELF							5D03D	5D05D	5D05D
20870	194	%$SPEND HELP FAM							5D03E	5D05E	5D05E

C03: WORK and LEISURE. Vocational plans, aspirations, expectations

Item Reference Number	Page Loc. in this Volume	ITEM DESCRIPTION (ABBREVIATED)	1975	1976	1977	1978	1979	1980	1981	1982/83	1984/85
480	20	R WL DO VOC/TEC		+C21A	+C21A	+C21A	+C21A	+C21A	+C21A	+C21A	+C21A
530	21	R WNTDO VOC/TEC		+C22A	+C22A	+C22A	+C22A	+C22A	+C22A	+C22A	+C22A
6870	105	HOW GD AS WORKER	2A19C	2D02C	2D02C	2D02C	2D02C	2D02C	2D02C	2D02C	2D02C
8090	122	SAME JOB MST LIF	3A08I	3A05E	3A05E	3A05E	3A05E	3A05E	3A05E	3A05E	3A05E
10320	152	KIND OF WORK @30	4A09	4A09	4A09	4A09	4A09	4A09	4A09	4A09	4A09
10330	152	R SURE GT THS WK		4A10	4A10	4A10	4A10	4A10	4A10	4A10	4A10
10340	152	R SURE WK GD CHC		4A11	4A11	4A11	4A11	4A11	4A11	4A11	4A11
10350	153	R THNK WK BE SAT		4A12	4A12	4A12	4A12	4A12	4A12	4A12	4A12
10360	153	JOB OBSTC RELGN		4A13A	4A13A	4A13A	4A13A	4A13A	4A13A	4A13A	4A13A
10370	153	JOB OBSTC SEX		4A13B	4A13B	4A13B	4A13B	4A13B	4A13B	4A13B	4A13B
10380	153	JOB OBSTC RACE		4A13C	4A13C	4A13C	4A13C	4A13C	4A13C	4A13C	4A13C
10390	153	JOB OBSTC BKGRND		4A13D	4A13D	4A13D	4A13D	4A13D	4A13D	4A13D	4A13D
10400	153	JOB OBSTC POL VW		4A13E	4A13E	4A13E	4A13E	4A13E	4A13E	4A13E	4A13E
10410	153	JOB OBSTC EDUCTN		4A13F	4A13F	4A13F	4A13F	4A13F	4A13F	4A13F	4A13F
10420	153	JOB OBSTC -VOC T		4A13G	4A13G	4A13G	4A13G	4A13G	4A13G	4A13G	4A13G
10430	154	JOB OBSTC -ABLTY		4A13H	4A13H	4A13H	4A13H	4A13H	4A13H	4A13H	4A13H

(continued)

Item Reference Number	Page Loc. in this Volume	ITEM DESCRIPTION (ABBREVIATED)	QUESTIONNAIRE LOCATION BY YEAR (FORM, SECTION, AND QUESTION NUMBER)								
			1975	1976	1977	1978	1979	1980	1981	1982/83	1984/85

C03: WORK and LEISURE. Vocational plans, aspirations, expectations *(continued)*

10440	154	JOB OBSTC - PULL		4A13I	4A13I	4A13I	4A13I	4A13I	4A13I	4A13I	4A13I
10450	154	JOB OBSTC -WK HD		4A13J	4A13J	4A13J	4A13J	4A13J	4A13J	4A13J	4A13J
10460	154	JOB OBSTC -CONFM		4A13K	4A13K	4A13K	4A13K	4A13K	4A13K	4A13K	4A13K

C04: WORK and LEISURE. Preferences regarding job characteristics

1460	37	IMP STEADY WORK		1A007F	1A007F	1A007F	1A007F	1A007F	1A007F	1A007F	1A007F
8050	121	LIK WRK CAN FRGT	3A08D	3A05A	3A05A	3A05A	3A05A	3A05A	3A05A	3A05A	3A05A
10090	148	JOB IMPC SE RSLT	4A08A	4A08A	4A08A	4A08A	4A08A	4A08A	4A08A	4A08A	4A08A
10100	149	JOB IMPC STATUS	4A08B	4A08B	4A08B	4A08B	4A08B	4A08B	4A08B	4A08B	4A08B
10110	149	JOB IMPC INTRSTG	4A08C	4A08C	4A08C	4A08C	4A08C	4A08C	4A08C	4A08C	4A08C
10120	149	JOB IMPC ADVNCMT	4A08D	4A08D	4A08D	4A08D	4A08D	4A08D	4A08D	4A08D	4A08D
10130	149	JOB IMPC HLP OTH	4A08E	4A08E	4A08E	4A08E	4A08E	4A08E	4A08E	4A08E	4A08E
10140	149	JOB IMPC EARN $	4A08F	4A08F	4A08F	4A08F	4A08F	4A08F	4A08F	4A08F	4A08F
10150	149	JOB IMPC CREATVY	4A08G	4A08G	4A08G	4A08G	4A08G	4A08G	4A08G	4A08G	4A08G
10160	149	JOB IMPC UTILITY	4A08H	4A08H	4A08H	4A08H	4A08H	4A08H	4A08H	4A08H	4A08H
10170	149	JOB IMPC MK FRND	4A08I	4A08I	4A08I	4A08I	4A08I	4A08I	4A08I	4A08I	4A08I
10180	150	JOB IMPC USE SKL	4A08J	4A08J	4A08J	4A08J	4A08J	4A08J	4A08J	4A08J	4A08J
10190	150	JOB IMPC WRTHWLE	4A08K	4A08K	4A08K	4A08K	4A08K	4A08K	4A08K	4A08K	4A08K
10200	150	JOB IMPC VACATN	4A08L	4A08L	4A08L	4A08L	4A08L	4A08L	4A08L	4A08L	4A08L
10210	150	JOB IMPC MK DCSN	4A08M	4A08M	4A08M	4A08M	4A08M	4A08M	4A08M	4A08M	4A08M
10220	150	JOB IMPC FRE TIM		4A08N	4A08N	4A08N	4A08N	4A08N	4A08N	4A08N	4A08N
10230	150	JOB IMPC NO MVNG	4A08O	4A08O	4A08O	4A08O	4A08O	4A08O	4A08O	4A08O	4A08O
10240	150	JOB IMPC NO SPRV	4A08P	4A08P	4A08P	4A08P	4A08P	4A08P	4A08P	4A08P	4A08P
10250	151	JOB IMPC SECURTY	4A08Q	4A08Q	4A08Q	4A08Q	4A08Q	4A08Q	4A08Q	4A08Q	4A08Q
10260	151	JOB IMPC LRNING	4A08R	4A08R	4A08R	4A08R	4A08R	4A08R	4A08R	4A08R	4A08R
10270	151	JOB IMPC BE SELF	4A08S	4A08S	4A08S	4A08S	4A08S	4A08S	4A08S	4A08S	4A08S
10280	151	JOB IMPC RESPECT	4A08T	4A08T	4A08T	4A08T	4A08T	4A08T	4A08T	4A08T	4A08T
10290	151	JOB IMPC CNTC PL	4A08U	4A08U	4A08U	4A08U	4A08U	4A08U	4A08U	4A08U	4A08U
10300	151	JOB IMPC EZ PACE		4A08V	4A08V	4A08V	4A08V	4A08V	4A08V	4A08V	4A08V
10310	151	JOB IMPC HRD PRB		4A08W	4A08W	4A08W	4A08W	4A08W	4A08W	4A08W	4A08W

C05: WORK and LEISURE. Desirability of different working arrangements and settings

6160	94	-CHL,HB WK1.,W=0	2A15A	2A08A	2A08A	2A08A	2A08A	2A08A	2A08A	2A08A	2A08A
6170	94	-CHL,HB WK1.,W.5	2A15B	2A08B	2A08B	2A08B	2A08B	2A08B	2A08B	2A08B	2A08B
6180	94	-CHL,HB&WF WK 1.	2A15C	2A08C	2A08C	2A08C	2A08C	2A08C	2A08C	2A08C	2A08C
6190	94	-CHL,HB&WF WK .5	2A15D	2A08D	2A08D	2A08D	2A08D	2A08D	2A08D	2A08D	2A08D
6200	94	-CHL,W WK 1.,H.5	2A15E	2A08E	2A08E	2A08E	2A08E	2A08E	2A08E	2A08E	2A08E
6210	94	-CHL,W WK 1.,H=0	2A15F	2A08F	2A08F	2A08F	2A08F	2A08F	2A08F	2A08F	2A08F
6220	95	PSCH,HB WK1.,W=0	2A16A	2A09A	2A09A	2A09A	2A09A	2A09A	2A09A	2A09A	2A09A
6230	95	PSCH,HB WK1.,W.5	2A16B	2A09B	2A09B	2A09B	2A09B	2A09B	2A09B	2A09B	2A09B
6240	95	PSCH,HB&WF WK 1.	2A16C	2A09C	2A09C	2A09C	2A09C	2A09C	2A09C	2A09C	2A09C
6250	95	PSCH,HB&WF WK .5	2A16D	2A09D	2A09D	2A09D	2A09D	2A09D	2A09D	2A09D	2A09D
6260	95	PSCH,WF WK1.,H.5	2A16E	2A09E	2A09E	2A09E	2A09E	2A09E	2A09E	2A09E	2A09E
6270	95	PSCH,WF WK1.,H=0	2A16F	2A09F	2A09F	2A09F	2A09F	2A09F	2A09F	2A09F	2A09F
8120	122	DES SUPVR DIF RC	3A19B	3A07B	3A07B	3A07B	3A07B	3A07B	3A07B	3A07B	3A07B
8160	123	DES AL WKS SM RC	3A19F	3A08A	3A08A	3A08A	3A08A	3A08A	3A08A	3A08A	3A08A
8170	123	DES SO WKS DF RC	3A19G	3A08B	3A08B	3A08B	3A08B	3A08B	3A08B	3A08B	3A08B
8180	123	DES MS WKS DF RC	3A19H	3A08C	3A08C	3A08C	3A08C	3A08C	3A08C	3A08C	3A08C
11150	167	MLTRY >FLFLLG JB		4E01D	4E01D	4E01D	4E01D	4E01D	4E01D	4E01D	4E01D
11800	176	PLC WRK LG CORPN	5A09A	5A05A	5A05A	5A05A	5A05A	5A05A	5A05A	5A05A	5A05A
11810	176	PLC WRK SM BSNSS	5A09B	5A05B	5A05B	5A05B	5A05B	5A05B	5A05B	5A05B	5A05B
11820	176	PLC WRK GVT AGCY	5A09C	5A05C	5A05C	5A05C	5A05C	5A05C	5A05C	5A05C	5A05C
11830	176	PLC WRK MLTY SVC	5A09D	5A05D	5A05D	5A05D	5A05D	5A05D	5A05D	5A05D	5A05D
11840	176	PLC WRK SCH/UNIV	5A09E	5A05E	5A05E	5A05E	5A05E	5A05E	5A05E	5A05E	5A05E
11850	176	PLC WRK PLC DEPT	5A09F	5A05F	5A05F	5A05F	5A05F	5A05F	5A05F	5A05F	5A05F
11860	176	PLC WRK SOC SVCS	5A09G	5A05G	5A05G	5A05G	5A05G	5A05G	5A05G	5A05G	5A05G
11870	177	PLC WRK SML GRP	5A09H	5A05H	5A05H	5A05H	5A05H	5A05H	5A05H	5A05H	5A05H
11880	177	PLC WRK SLF EMPL	5A09I	5A05I	5A05I	5A05I	5A05I	5A05I	5A05I	5A05I	5A05I

Item Reference Number	Page Loc. in this Volume	ITEM DESCRIPTION (ABBREVIATED)	QUESTIONNAIRE LOCATION BY YEAR (FORM, SECTION, AND QUESTION NUMBER)								
			1975	1976	1977	1978	1979	1980	1981	1982/83	1984/85

C06: WORK and LEISURE. Work ethic/success orientation

Item Reference Number	Page Loc. in this Volume	ITEM DESCRIPTION (ABBREVIATED)	1975	1976	1977	1978	1979	1980	1981	1982/83	1984/85
1410	36	IMP B SUCCSS WK		1A007A	1A007A	1A007A	1A007A	1A007A	1A007A	1A007A	1A007A
8060	121	WRK=ONLY MK LVNG	3A08E	3A05B	3A05B	3A05B	3A05B	3A05B	3A05B	3A05B	3A05B
8070	121	WRK CNTRL PRT LF	3A08G	3A05C	3A05C	3A05C	3A05C	3A05C	3A05C	3A05C	3A05C
8080	121	OVTM 2DO BST JOB	3A08H	3A05D	3A05D	3A05D	3A05D	3A05D	3A05D	3A05D	3A05D
8100	122	ENUF$,NT WNT WRK	3A10	3A06	3A06	3A06	3A06	3A06	3A06	3A06	3A06
	154		4A09A	4A14	4A14	4A14	4A14	4A14	4A14	4A14	4A14
	177		5A11	5A06	5A06	5A06	5A06	5A06	5A06	5A06	5A06

C07: WORK and LEISURE. Leisure time: extent, activities

Item Reference Number	Page Loc. in this Volume	ITEM DESCRIPTION (ABBREVIATED)	1975	1976	1977	1978	1979	1980	1981	1982/83	1984/85
620	22	#X/AV WK GO OUT		+C25	+C25	+C25	+C25	+C25	+C25	+C25	+C25
630	22	#X DATE 3+/WK		+C26	+C26	+C26	+C26	+C26	+C26	+C26	+C26
5820	89	DALY WATCH TV		2A02A	2A02A	2A02A	2A02A	2A02A	2A02A	2A02A	2A02A
5830	89	DALY GO TO MOVIE		2A02B	2A02B	2A02B	2A02B	2A02B	2A02B	2A02B	2A02B
5840		DALY ART,MSC,PLA		2A02C	2A02C	2A02C	2A02C	2A02C	2A02C	2A02C	
5845	89	DALY ROCK CONCRT									2A02C
5850	89	DALY RIDE FORFUN			2A02D	2A02D	2A02D	2A02D	2A02D	2A02D	2A02D
5860	89	DALY CMNTY AFFRS		2A02E	2A02E	2A02E	2A02E	2A02E	2A02E	2A02E	2A02E
5870	89	DALY PLA MSC,SNG		2A02F	2A02F	2A02F	2A02F	2A02F	2A02F	2A02F	2A02F
5880	90	DALY CREAT WRTNG		2A02G	2A02G	2A02G	2A02G	2A02G	2A02G	2A02G	2A02G
5890	90	DALY ACTV SPORTS		2A02H	2A02H	2A02H	2A02H	2A02H	2A02H	2A02H	2A02H
5900	90	DALY ART/CRAFTS		2A02I	2A02I	2A02I	2A02I	2A02I	2A02I	2A02I	2A02I
5910	90	DALY WRK HSE,CAR		2A02J	2A02J	2A02J	2A02J	2A02J	2A02J	2A02J	2A02J
5920	90	DALY VIST W/FRDS		2A02K	2A02K	2A02K	2A02K	2A02K	2A02K	2A02K	2A02K
5930	90	DALY GO SHOPPING		2A02L	2A02L	2A02L	2A02L	2A02L	2A02L	2A02L	2A02L
5940	90	DALY ALONE LEISR		(2A02M)	2A02M	2A02M	2A02M	2A02M	2A02M	2A02M	2A02M
5950	91	DALY READ BK,MAG		2A02N	2A02N	2A02N	2A02N	2A02N	2A02N	2A02N	2A02N
5960	91	DALY GO TO BARS		2A02O	2A02O	2A02O	2A02O	2A02O	2A02O	2A02O	2A02O
5970	91	DALY GO TO PARTY		2A02P	2A02P	2A02P	2A02P	2A02P	2A02P	2A02P	2A02P
5980		DALY GO CHURCH		2A02D							
10550	156	#HRS TV/DAY/5+		4A16	4A16	4A16	4A16	4A16	4A16	4A16	4A16
10560	156	#BKS LAST YR/10+		4A17	4A17	4A17	4A17	4A17	4A17	4A17	4A17
21900	200	#X/LAST12M PARTY									5E07
21910	200	PARTY-PPL OVR 30									5E08A
21920	200	PARTY-ONE HI ALC									5E08B
21930	201	PARTY-OTH HI ALC									5E08C
21940	201	PARTY-YOU HI ALC									5E08D
21950	201	PARTY-PRESS ALCL									5E08E
21960	201	PARTY-PRS HI ALC									5E08F
21970	201	PARTY-ONE HI MJ									5E08G
21980	201	PARTY-OTH HI MJ									5E08H
21990	201	PARTY-YOU HI MJ									5E08I
22000	202	PARTY-PRESS MJ									5E08J
22010	202	PARTY-ONE HI OTD									5E08K
22020	202	PARTY-OTH HI OTD									5E08L
22030	202	PARTY-YOU HI OTD									5E08M
22040	202	PARTY-PRESS OTDG									5E08N

C08: WORK and LEISURE. Attitudes toward leisure time

Item Reference Number	Page Loc. in this Volume	ITEM DESCRIPTION (ABBREVIATED)	1975	1976	1977	1978	1979	1980	1981	1982/83	1984/85
1370	36	SAT SPD LEISR	1A009K	1A006K	1A006K	1A006K	1A006K	1A006K	1A006K	1A006K	1A006K
1440	37	IMP TM RCRN&HBY		1A007D	1A007D	1A007D	1A007D	1A007D	1A007D	1A007D	1A007D
9880		DK DO W LEISR TM			3E11A		3E11A	3E11A	3E11A		
9890		TM QUIK/LEIS HRS			3E11B		3E11B	3E11B	3E11B		
9900		WASTE LEIS TIME			3E11C		3E11C	3E11C	3E11C		
9910		ENUF TIME FR THG			3E11D		3E11D	3E11D	3E11D		
11240	168	P'IDEA OF LSR TM	4A27B	4E08B	4E08B	4E07B	4E07B	4E07B	4E07B	4E07B	4E07B
22050	202	PRFR PTY-PPL >30									5E09A
22060	202	PRF PTY-U HI ALC									5E09B
22070	203	PR PTY-OTH HI AL									5E09C
22080	203	PRF PTY-U USE MJ									5E09D
22090	203	PR PTY-OT USE MJ									5E09E
22100	203	PR PTY-U USE OTD									5E09F
22110	203	PR PTY-OT USE OT									5E09G

Item Reference Number	Page Loc. in this Volume	ITEM DESCRIPTION (ABBREVIATED)	QUESTIONNAIRE LOCATION BY YEAR (FORM, SECTION, AND QUESTION NUMBER)								
			1975	1976	1977	1978	1979	1980	1981	1982/83	1984/85

D01: SEX ROLES and FAMILY. Dating and marriage: status, attitudes, expectations

Item Reference Number	Page Loc. in this Volume	ITEM DESCRIPTION (ABBREVIATED)	1975	1976	1977	1978	1979	1980	1981	1982/83	1984/85
60	16	R NOT MARRIED		+C06	+C06	+C06	+C06	+C06	+C06	+C06	+C06
6120	93	DFNTLY PRFR MATE	2A10	2A05	2A05	2A05	2A05	2A05	2A05	2A05	2A05
6130	93	THINK WILL MARRY	2A11	2A06	2A06	2A06	2A06	2A06	2A06	2A06	2A06
6140	93	LIKLY STAY MARRD	2A12A	2A07A	2A07A	2A07A	2A07A	2A07A	2A07A	2A07A	2A07A
6850	104	HOW GD AS SPOUSE	2A19A	2D02A	2D02A	2D02A	2D02A	2D02A	2D02A	2D02A	2D02A
8320	125	MARRD OR ENGAGED	3A41	3A18	3A18	3A18	3A18	3A18	3A18	3A18	3A18
8330	125	WHN WANT GT MARR	3A42	3A19	3A19	3A19	3A19	3A19	3A19	3A19	3A19
11770	175	XPRC MK R GD SPS		5A04A	5A04A	5A04A	5A04A	5A04A	5A04A	5A04A	5A04A

D02: SEX ROLES and FAMILY. Parenthood: status, attitudes, expectations

Item Reference Number	Page Loc. in this Volume	ITEM DESCRIPTION (ABBREVIATED)	1975	1976	1977	1978	1979	1980	1981	1982/83	1984/85
6150	93	LIKLY HAVE KIDS	2A12B	2A07B	2A07B	2A07B	2A07B	2A07B	2A07B	2A07B	2A07B
6860	104	HOW GD AS PARENT	2A19B	2D02B	2D02B	2D02B	2D02B	2D02B	2D02B	2D02B	2D02B
8340	125	THGT LOT HAV CHL	3A43	3A20	3A20	3A20	3A20	3A20	3A20	3A20	3A20
8350	125	# CHLDN WANT(6+)	3A44	3A21	3A21	3A21	3A21	3A21	3A21	3A21	3A21
8360	126	IF -POP, MR CHLD	3A45	3A22	3A22	3A22	3A22	3A22	3A22	3A22	3A22
8370	126	WHN 1ST CHL(5+Y)	3A46	3A23	3A23	3A23	3A23	3A23	3A23	3A23	3A23
11780	175	XPRC MK R GD PRT		5A04B	5A04B	5A04B	5A04B	5A04B	5A04B	5A04B	5A04B

D03: SEX ROLES and FAMILY. Values surrounding marriage and family

Item Reference Number	Page Loc. in this Volume	ITEM DESCRIPTION (ABBREVIATED)	1975	1976	1977	1978	1979	1980	1981	1982/83	1984/85
1420	37	IMP GD MRRG&FAM		1A007B	1A007B	1A007B	1A007B	1A007B	1A007B	1A007B	1A007B
10470	154	FEW GD MAR, ? IT	4A11A	4A15A	4A15A	4A15A	4A15A	4A15A	4A15A	4A15A	4A15A
10480	154	GD LIV TG BF MRG	4A11B	4A15B	4A15B	4A15B	4A15B	4A15B	4A15B	4A15B	4A15B
10490	155	1 PRTNR=RSTRCTVE	4A11C	4A15C	4A15C	4A15C	4A15C	4A15C	4A15C	4A15C	4A15C
12150	181	FULLR LVS IF MRY	5A12A	5A18J	5A18J	5A18J	5A18J	5A18J	5A18J	5A18J	5A18J
12770	192	LV TGTH=BD MRLTY		5D05	5D02	5D02	5D02	5D02		5D02	5D02
12775	192	FAM-MAR=BD MRLTY		5D06	5D03	5D03	5D03	5D03		5D03	5D03

D04: SEX ROLES and FAMILY. Preferences regarding marital/familial arrangements

Item Reference Number	Page Loc. in this Volume	ITEM DESCRIPTION (ABBREVIATED)	1975	1976	1977	1978	1979	1980	1981	1982/83	1984/85
6160	94	-CHL,HB WK1.,W=0	2A15A	2A08A	2A08A	2A08A	2A08A	2A08A	2A08A	2A08A	2A08A
6170	94	-CHL,HB WK1.,W.5	2A15B	2A08B	2A08B	2A08B	2A08B	2A08B	2A08B	2A08B	2A08B
6180	94	-CHL,HB&WF WK 1.	2A15C	2A08C	2A08C	2A08C	2A08C	2A08C	2A08C	2A08C	2A08C
6190	94	-CHL,HB&WF WK .5	2A15D	2A08D	2A08D	2A08D	2A08D	2A08D	2A08D	2A08D	2A08D
6200	94	-CHL,W WK 1.,H.5	2A15E	2A08E	2A08E	2A08E	2A08E	2A08E	2A08E	2A08E	2A08E
6210	94	-CHL,W WK 1.,H=0	2A15F	2A08F	2A08F	2A08F	2A08F	2A08F	2A08F	2A08F	2A08F
6220	95	PSCH,HB WK1.,W=0	2A16A	2A09A	2A09A	2A09A	2A09A	2A09A	2A09A	2A09A	2A09A
6230	95	PSCH,HB WK1.,W.5	2A16B	2A09B	2A09B	2A09B	2A09B	2A09B	2A09B	2A09B	2A09B
6240	95	PSCH,HB&WF WK 1.	2A16C	2A09C	2A09C	2A09C	2A09C	2A09C	2A09C	2A09C	2A09C
6250	95	PSCH,HB&WF WK .5	2A16D	2A09D	2A09D	2A09D	2A09D	2A09D	2A09D	2A09D	2A09D
6260	95	PSCH,WF WK1.,H.5	2A16E	2A09E	2A09E	2A09E	2A09E	2A09E	2A09E	2A09E	2A09E
6270	95	PSCH,WF WK1.,H=0	2A16F	2A09F	2A09F	2A09F	2A09F	2A09F	2A09F	2A09F	2A09F
6280	95	H WK,W -WK,W CCR	2A17A	2A10A	2A10A	2A10A	2A10A	2A10A	2A10A	2A10A	2A10A
6290	96	H WK,W -WK,W>CCR	2A17B	2A10B	2A10B	2A10B	2A10B	2A10B	2A10B	2A10B	2A10B
6300	96	H WK,W -WK,=CHCR	2A17C	2A10C	2A10C	2A10C	2A10C	2A10C	2A10C	2A10C	2A10C
6310	96	H WK,W -WK,H>CCR	2A17D	2A10D	2A10D	2A10D	2A10D	2A10D	2A10D	2A10D	2A10D
6320	96	H WK,W -WK,H CCR	2A17E	2A10E	2A10E	2A10E	2A10E	2A10E	2A10E	2A10E	2A10E
11560		H&W WK,WF AL HWK			4E11A	4E10A	4E10A	4E10A	4E10A		
11570		H&W WK,WF MS HWK			4E11B	4E10B	4E10B	4E10B	4E10B		
11580		H&W WK,DO = HWRK			4E11C	4E10C	4E10C	4E10C	4E10C		
11590		H&W WK,HB MS HWK			4E11D	4E10D	4E10D	4E10D	4E10D		
11600		H&W WK,HB AL HWK			4E11E	4E10E	4E10E	4E10E	4E10E		
11610		H&W WK+CH,W CHCR			4E12A	4E11A	4E11A	4E11A	4E11A		
11620		H&W WK+CH,W>CHCR			4E12B	4E11B	4E11B	4E11B	4E11B		
11630		H&W WK+CH,=CHCAR			4E12C	4E11C	4E11C	4E11C	4E11C		
11640		H&W WK+CH,H>CHCR			4E12D	4E11D	4E11D	4E11D	4E11D		
11650		H&W WK+CH,H CHCR			4E12E	4E11E	4E11E	4E11E	4E11E		
13150		FAM+REL GD/CHILD		5E01A							
13160		FAM+REL GD/PARNT		5E01B							
13170		FAM+REL GD/GRPNT		5E01C							
13180		FAM+REL,R LIK/PT		5E01D							
13280		FAM+CPL GD/CHILD		5E02A							

(continued)

D04: SEX ROLES and FAMILY. Preferences regarding marital/familial arrangements (continued)

Item Reference Number	Page Loc. in this Volume	ITEM DESCRIPTION (ABBREVIATED)	1975	1976	1977	1978	1979	1980	1981	1982/83	1984/85
13290		FAM+CPL GD/PARNT		5E02B							
13300		FAM+CPL GD/CPLS		5E02C							
13310		FAM+CPL,LIK/PRNT		5E02D							
13320		FAM+CPL,LIK/-CHD		5E02E							
13420		CPL+OTH +CHD MAR		5E03A							
13430		CPL+OTH +CHD DVC		5E03B							
13440		CPL+OTH +MAR CPL		5E03C							
13450		CPL+OTH +DIV PRT		5E03D							
13460		CPL+OTH +UNMARRD		5E03E							
13470		CPL+OTH,LK,MR PT		5E03F							
13480		CPL+OTH,LK,DVC P		5E03G							

D05: SEX ROLES and FAMILY. Sex role attitudes

Item Reference Number	Page Loc. in this Volume	ITEM DESCRIPTION (ABBREVIATED)	1975	1976	1977	1978	1979	1980	1981	1982/83	1984/85
7970	120	MN=ACHV/WMN=HOME	3A17H	3A03E	3A03E	3A03E	3A03E	3A03E	3A03E	3A03E	3A03E
7980	120	CHL SUFF W WK MO	3A17I	3A03F	3A03F	3A03F	3A03F	3A03F	3A03F	3A03F	3A03F
7990	120	WK MO AS WRM REL	3A17J	3A03G	3A03G	3A03G	3A03G	3A03G	3A03G	3A03G	3A03G
10500	155	JB INTFR REL HBD	4A11E	4A15D	4A15D	4A15D	4A15D	4A15D	4A15D	4A15D	4A15D
10510	155	JB DVLP WF PERSN	4A11G	4A15E	4A15E	4A15E	4A15E	4A15E	4A15E	4A15E	4A15E
10520	155	RS CHLD + FR MAN	4A11H	4A15F	4A15F	4A15F	4A15F	4A15F	4A15F	4A15F	4A15F
10530	155	MO SH B W CHL>TM	4A11I	4A15G	4A15G	4A15G	4A15G	4A15G	4A15G	4A15G	4A15G
10540	155	WF WK,HBD SHD>HW	4A11K	4A15H	4A15H	4A15H	4A15H	4A15H	4A15H	4A15H	4A15H
11330	170	P'IDEA OF SX RLS	4A27K	4E08K	4E08K	4E07K	4E07K	4E07K	4E07K	4E07K	4E07K
12160	181	ENCRG=INDP DT/SN	5A12B	5A18K	5A18K	5A18K	5A18K	5A18K	5A18K	5A18K	5A18K
12170	182	BNG MOTH V FULFL	5A12D	5A18L	5A18L	5A18L	5A18L	5A18L	5A18L	5A18L	5A18L
12180	182	FTHR>TIME W CHLD	5A12G	5A18M	5A18M	5A18M	5A18M	5A18M	5A18M	5A18M	5A18M
12190	182	HSB MAK IMP DCSN	5A12H	5A18N	5A18N	5A18N	5A18N	5A18N	5A18N	5A18N	5A18N

D06: SEX ROLES and FAMILY. Opinions regarding sex discrimination

Item Reference Number	Page Loc. in this Volume	ITEM DESCRIPTION (ABBREVIATED)	1975	1976	1977	1978	1979	1980	1981	1982/83	1984/85
7930	119	MEN&WOMN/=$,=WRK	3A17A	3A03A	3A03A	3A03A	3A03A	3A03A	3A03A	3A03A	3A03A
7940	119	CNSDR WMN/HI JOB	3A17B	3A03B	3A03B	3A03B	3A03B	3A03B	3A03B	3A03B	3A03B
7950	119	WMN SHD =JOB OPP	3A17C	3A03C	3A03C	3A03C	3A03C	3A03C	3A03C	3A03C	3A03C
7960	119	WMN SHD =ED OPP	3A17D	3A03D	3A03D	3A03D	3A03D	3A03D	3A03D	3A03D	3A03D
10370	153	JOB OBSTC SEX		4A13B	4A13B	4A13B	4A13B	4A13B	4A13B	4A13B	4A13B
11180	167	MLTRY DSCRM WOMN		4E03	4E03	4E03	4E03	4E03	4E03	4E03	4E03
12290	184	DSCM WN COLLG ED	5A21A	5A22A	5A22A	5A22A	5A22A	5A22A	5A22A	5A22A	5A22A
12300	184	DSCM WN LDRSHP	5A21B	5A22B	5A22B	5A22B	5A22B	5A22B	5A22B	5A22B	5A22B
12310	184	DSCM WN EXEC/BSN	5A21C	5A22C	5A22C	5A22C	5A22C	5A22C	5A22C	5A22C	5A22C
12320	184	DSCM WN TOP/PRFN	5A21D	5A22D	5A22D	5A22D	5A22D	5A22D	5A22D	5A22D	5A22D
12330	185	DSCM WN SKL LABR	5A21E	5A22E	5A22E	5A22E	5A22E	5A22E	5A22E	5A22E	5A22E
12340	185	DSCM WN PLTCL OF	5A21F	5A22F	5A22F	5A22F	5A22F	5A22F	5A22F	5A22F	5A22F
12350	185	DSCM WN =PAY =WK	5A21G	5A22G	5A22G	5A22G	5A22G	5A22G	5A22G	5A22G	5A22G

E01: POPULATION CONCERNS. Overpopulation

Item Reference Number	Page Loc. in this Volume	ITEM DESCRIPTION (ABBREVIATED)	1975	1976	1977	1978	1979	1980	1981	1982/83	1984/85
8360	126	IF -POP, MR CHLD	3A45	3A22	3A22	3A22	3A22	3A22	3A22	3A22	3A22
9760	137	GOV HP PRB POPL	3A32N	3E04A	3E04A	3E04A	3E04A	3E04A	3E04A	3E03A	3E03A
9770	137	GOV NO POP PLCY	3A32A	3E04B	3E04B	3E04B	3E04B	3E04B	3E04B	3E03B	3E03B
9780	137	STR OVPOP,LMT FM	3A32B	3E04C	3E04C	3E04C	3E04C	3E04C	3E04C	3E03C	3E03C
9790	137	PRV OVPOP,NO CHL	3A32C	3E04D	3E04D	3E04D	3E04D	3E04D	3E04D	3E03D	3E03D
9830		US POP SZ LRGER	3A34	3E06	3E05	3E05	3E05	3E05	3E05		
9840		GVNG FOOD O CNTY	3A33	3E05							
9850		WRLD POP SZ LRGR	3A35	3E07	3E06	3E06	3E06	3E06	3E06		
11670	174	WR/NT POP GROWTH	5A04B	5A03B	5A03B	5A03B	5A03B	5A03B	5A03B	5A03B	5A03B
12270	183	CTB TO POP PRBMS	5A20H	5A20H	5A20H	5A20H	5A20H	5A20H	5A20H	5A20H	5A20H

E02: POPULATION CONCERNS. Birth control

Item Reference Number	Page Loc. in this Volume	ITEM DESCRIPTION (ABBREVIATED)	1975	1976	1977	1978	1979	1980	1981	1982/83	1984/85
9800	138	HISCH INS BRTH C	3A32E	3E04E	3E04E	3E04E	3E04E	3E04E	3E04E	3E03E	3E03E
9810	138	BRTH CNT IMMORAL	3A32I	3E04F	3E04F	3E04F	3E04F	3E04F	3E04F	3E03F	3E03F
9820	138	GOV BRTHC NO CST	3A32M	3E04G	3E04G	3E04G	3E04G	3E04G	3E04G	3E03G	3E03G
9860	138	HAD SEX ED IN HS		3E09	3E08	3E08	3E08	3E08	3E08	3E04	3E04
9870	138	STUDY BC IN HS		3E10	3E09	3E09	3E09	3E09	3E09	3E05	3E05

Item Reference Number	Page Loc. in this Volume	ITEM DESCRIPTION (ABBREVIATED)	1975	1976	1977	1978	1979	1980	1981	1982/83	1984/85
						QUESTIONNAIRE LOCATION BY YEAR (FORM, SECTION, AND QUESTION NUMBER)					

F01: CONSERVATION, MATERIALISM, EQUITY, ETC. Personal materialism

Item Reference Number	Page Loc. in this Volume	ITEM DESCRIPTION (ABBREVIATED)	1975	1976	1977	1978	1979	1980	1981	1982/83	1984/85
1350	35	SAT STD OF LVG	1A009I	1A006I	1A006I	1A006I	1A006I	1A006I	1A006I	1A006I	1A006I
1430	37	IMP LOTS OF $		1A007C	1A007C	1A007C	1A007C	1A007C	1A007C	1A007C	1A007C
5930	90	DALY GO SHOPPING		2A02L	2A02L	2A02L	2A02L	2A02L	2A02L	2A02L	2A02L
7700		NOW OWN HAIR DRY		2E09A							
7710		NOW OWN WT/S SKI		2E09B							
7720		NOW OWN CAMERA		2E09C							
7730		NOW OWN WATCH		2E09D							
7740		NOW OWN HKG BKPK		2E09E							
7750		NOW OWN CK RADIO		2E09F							
7760		NOW OWN EL SHAVR		2E09G							
7770		NOW OWN TENIS RQ		2E09H							
7780		NOW OWN TV SET		2E09I							
7790		NOW OWN BICYCLE		2E09J							
7800		NOW OWN CAR		2E09K							
7810		NOW OWN TAPE REC		2E09L							
7820		NOW OWN ELT CALC		2E09M							
7830		NOW OWN BT/SNMBL		2E09N							
8020	120	MR$FR LASTG THG	3A31E	3A04C	3A04C	3A04C	3A04C	3A04C	3A04C	3A04C	3A04C
10060	148	FAM BUYS THG -ND	4A22L	4A06J	4A06J	4A06J	4A06J	4A06J	4A06J	4A06J	4A06J
	181			5A18I	5A18I	5A18I	5A18I	5A18I	5A18I	5A18I	5A18I
10140	149	JOB IMPC EARN $		4A08F	4A08F	4A08F	4A08F	4A08F	4A08F	4A08F	4A08F
12020	179	ENJOY SHOPPING	5A35A	5A15A	5A15A	5A15A	5A15A	5A15A	5A15A	5A15A	5A15A
12030	179	CARE LATST FASHN	5A35B	5A15B	5A15B	5A15B	5A15B	5A15B	5A15B	5A15B	5A15B
12040	179	CR FAM HV NBR HV	5A35C	5A15C	5A15C	5A15C	5A15C	5A15C	5A15C	5A15C	5A15C
12050	179	XPCT 2 OWN>PRNTS	5A36	5A16	5A16	5A16	5A16	5A16	5A16	5A16	5A16
12060	180	LST CNT OWN>PRNT	5A37	5A17	5A17	5A17	5A17	5A17	5A17	5A17	5A17
13600	139	STS SCH NIC CAR		5E05C	5E06C	5E06C	5E04C	5E06C		3E06C	3E06C
13700		BY SOON HAIR DRY		2E10A							
13710		BY SOON WT/S SKI		2E10B							
13720		BY SOON CAMERA		2E10C							
13730		BY SOON WATCH		2E10D							
13740		BY SOON HKG BKPK		2E10E							
13750		BY SOON CK RADIO		2E10F							
13760		BY SOON EL SHAVR		2E10G							
13770		BY SOON TENIS RQ		2E10H							
13780		BY SOON TV SET		2E10I							
13790		BY SOON BICYCLE		2E10J							
13800		BY SOON CAR		2E10K							
13810		BY SOON TAPE REC		2E10L							
13820		BY SOON ELT CALC		2E10M							
13830		BY SOON BT/SNMBL		2E10N							
13835	141	IMP HAV 1 CAR		3E12A		3E11A	3E10A	3E10A	3E10A	3E09A	3E09A
13840	141	IMP HAV 2 CARS		3E12B		3E11B	3E10B	3E10B	3E10B	3E09B	3E09B
13850	141	IMP HAV LARG CAR		3E12C		3E11C	3E10C	3E10C	3E10C	3E09C	3E09C
13860	141	IMP HAV NW CR OF		3E12D		3E11D	3E10D	3E10D	3E10D	3E09D	3E09D
13870	142	IMP HAV NW CLTHS		3E12E		3E11E	3E10E	3E10E	3E10E	3E09E	3E09E
13880	142	IMP HAV OWN HSE		3E12F		3E11F	3E10F	3E10F	3E10F	3E09F	3E09F
13890	142	IMP HAV BIG YARD		3E12G		3E11G	3E10G	3E10G	3E10G	3E09G	3E09G
13900	142	IMP HAV NEAT LWN		3E12H		3E11H	3E10H	3E10H	3E10H	3E09H	3E09H
13910	142	IMP HAV APPLINCS		3E12I		3E11I	3E10I	3E10I	3E10I	3E09I	3E09I
13920	142	IMP HAV G STEREO		3E12J		3E11J	3E10J	3E10J	3E10J	3E09J	3E09J
13930	142	IMP HAV VAC HSE		3E12K		3E11K	3E10K	3E10K	3E10K	3E09K	3E09K
13940	142	IMP HAV REC VEH		3E12L		3E11L	3E10L	3E10L	3E10L	3E09L	3E09L

F02: CONSERVATION, MATERIALISM, EQUITY, ETC. Societal materialism and advertising

Item Reference Number	Page Loc. in this Volume	ITEM DESCRIPTION (ABBREVIATED)	1975	1976	1977	1978	1979	1980	1981	1982/83	1984/85
6000	91	2MUCH CNCRN MTRL	2A23K	2A03B	2A03B	2A03B	2A03B	2A03B	2A03B	2A03B	2A03B
6010	91	ENCOURG PPL BUY>	2A23L	2A03C	2A03C	2A03C	2A03C	2A03C	2A03C	2A03C	2A03C
6020	92	-WRNG ADVERTISNG	2A23M	2A03D	2A03D	2A03D	2A03D	2A03D	2A03D	2A03D	2A03D
6030	92	MOR SHORTGS FUTR	2A23N	2A03E	2A03E	2A03E	2A03E	2A03E	2A03E	2A03E	2A03E
10040	148	TV COMM CRT NDS	4A22H	4A06H	4A06H	4A06H	4A06H	4A06H	4A06H	4A06H	4A06H
10050	148	TV COMMRCLS GOOD	4A22I	4A06I	4A06I	4A06I	4A06I	4A06I	4A06I	4A06I	4A06I

Item Reference Number	Page Loc. in this Volume	ITEM DESCRIPTION (ABBREVIATED)	QUESTIONNAIRE LOCATION BY YEAR (FORM, SECTION, AND QUESTION NUMBER)								
			1975	1976	1977	1978	1979	1980	1981	1982/83	1984/85

F03: CONSERVATION, MATERIALISM, EQUITY, ETC. Concern with world hunger and poverty

Item Reference Number	Page Loc. in this Volume	ITEM DESCRIPTION (ABBREVIATED)	1975	1976	1977	1978	1979	1980	1981	1982/83	1984/85
5990	91	US 2 MUCH PROFIT	2A23J	2A03A	2A03A	2A03A	2A03A	2A03A	2A03A	2A03A	2A03A
8040	121	EAT DIF->FD STRV	3A31G	3A04E	3A04E	3A04E	3A04E	3A04E	3A04E	3A04E	3A04E
11720	175	WR/NT HNGR&PVRTY	5A04G	5A03G	5A03G	5A03G	5A03G	5A03G	5A03G	5A03G	5A03G
12090	180	-SYMP TWD STARVG	5A19E	5A18C	5A18C	5A18C	5A18C	5A18C	5A18C	5A18C	5A18C
12140	181	RB CHNG ETG HABT		5A18H	5A18H	5A18H	5A18H	5A18H	5A18H	5A18H	5A18H
16440		SAT EAT<BEEF>GRN				2E05B					
19470		EAT<FD,>OWN CITY					5E08A				
19480		EAT<FD,>NRBY STT					5E08B				
19490		EAT<FD,>DIF REGN					5E08C				
19500		EAT<FD,>ASIAN CN					5E08D				

F04: CONSERVATION, MATERIALISM, EQUITY, ETC. Ecological concerns

Item Reference Number	Page Loc. in this Volume	ITEM DESCRIPTION (ABBREVIATED)	1975	1976	1977	1978	1979	1980	1981	1982/83	1984/85
1640	40	US NEEDS GROWTH	1A013E	1A011G	1A011G	1A011G	1A011G	1A011G	1A011G	1A011G	1A011G
8000	120	POLLUT INCREASED	3A31A	3A04A	3A04A	3A04A	3A04A	3A04A	3A04A	3A04A	3A04A
8010	120	GOVT DEAL ENV PR	3A31D	3A04B	3A04B	3A04B	3A04B	3A04B	3A04B	3A04B	3A04B
9700	136	PRVNT POL TOO >$		3E02A	3E02A	3E02A	3E02A	3E02A	3E02A	3E01A	3E01A
9710	136	PRVNT POL CST JB		3E02B	3E02B	3E02B	3E02B	3E02B	3E02B	3E01B	3E01B
9720	136	PRVNT POL PPL DK		3E02C	3E02C	3E02C	3E02C	3E02C	3E02C	3E01C	3E01C
9730	136	PRVNT POL -ENUF		3E02D	3E02D	3E02D	3E02D	3E02D	3E02D	3E01D	3E01D
9740	137	PRVNT POL USELSS		3E02E	3E02E	3E02E	3E02E	3E02E	3E02E	3E01E	3E01E
9970	146	PLLTN INCR IN US	4A22A	4A06A	4A06A	4A06A	4A06A	4A06A	4A06A	4A06A	4A06A
9980	147	PLLTN NT SO DANG	4A22B	4A06B	4A06B	4A06B	4A06B	4A06B	4A06B	4A06B	4A06B
9990	147	PLLTN NEC 4 GRTH	4A22C	4A06C	4A06C	4A06C	4A06C	4A06C	4A06C	4A06C	4A06C
10000	147	INDVL RESP 4 ENV	4A22D	4A06D	4A06D	4A06D	4A06D	4A06D	4A06D	4A06D	4A06D
10010	147	GOVT RESP 4 ENV	4A22E	4A06E	4A06E	4A06E	4A06E	4A06E	4A06E	4A06E	4A06E
10020	147	GOVT TAX PLLTRS	4A22F	4A06F	4A06F	4A06F	4A06F	4A06F	4A06F	4A06F	4A06F
10030	147	GOVT BAN DSPSBLE	4A22G	4A06G	4A06G	4A06G	4A06G	4A06G	4A06G	4A06G	4A06G
10070	148	POL SLVD BY 2000	4A22M	4A06K	4A06K	4A06K	4A06K	4A06K	4A06K	4A06K	4A06K
10080	148	R EFRT 2 HLP ENV	4A23	4A07	4A07	4A07	4A07	4A07	4A07	4A07	4A07
11340	170	P'IDEA OF ECLOGY	4A27L	4E08L	4E08L	4E07L	4E07L	4E07L	4E07L	4E07L	4E07L
11690	174	WR/NT POLLUTION	5A04D	5A03D	5A03D	5A03D	5A03D	5A03D	5A03D	5A03D	5A03D
12280	184	CTB TO ENVIR PBM	5A20I	5A20I	5A20I	5A20I	5A20I	5A20I	5A20I	5A20I	5A20I
16450		SAT TAX FR ECLGY					2E05C				

F05: CONSERVATION, MATERIALISM, EQUITY, ETC. Concern with conservation of resources

Item Reference Number	Page Loc. in this Volume	ITEM DESCRIPTION (ABBREVIATED)	1975	1976	1977	1978	1979	1980	1981	1982/83	1984/85
9750	137	FUTR,HAV2 CNSUM<		3E03	3E03	3E03	3E03	3E03	3E03	3E02	3E02
10930	163	SOCTY WONT LAST	4A28B	4D03B	4D03B	4D03B	4D03B	4D03B	4D03B	4D10B	4D10B
11700	174	WR/NT ENRGY SHRT	5A04E	5A03E	5A03E	5A03E	5A03E	5A03E	5A03E	5A03E	5A03E
11730	175	WR/NT USE OPN LD	5A04H	5A03H	5A03H	5A03H	5A03H	5A03H	5A03H	5A03H	5A03H
12000	179	R CUT ELECTRICTY		5A13	5A13	5A13	5A13	5A13	5A13	5A13	5A13
12010	179	RDCE HEAT R'S HM		5A14	5A14	5A14	5A14	5A14	5A14	5A14	5A14

F06: CONSERVATION, MATERIALISM, EQUITY, ETC. Preferences regarding dwelling type and urbanicity

Item Reference Number	Page Loc. in this Volume	ITEM DESCRIPTION (ABBREVIATED)	1975	1976	1977	1978	1979	1980	1981	1982/83	1984/85
17860		DESRD LVG RURAL				4E09A		4E09A	4E09A	4E09A‡	
17870		DESRD LVG SM TWN				4E09B		4E09B	4E09B	4E09B‡	
17880		DESRD LVG SM CTY				4E09C		4E09C	4E09C	4E09C‡	
17890		DESRD LVG SUBURB				4E09D		4E09D	4E09D	4E09D‡	
17900		DESRD LVG LG CTY				4E09E		4E09E	4E09E	4E09E‡	
17910		DSRD HSG 1 FAMLY				4E09F		4E09F	4E09F	4E09F‡	
17920		DSRD HSG 2 FAMLY				4E09G		4E09G	4E09G	4E09G‡	
17930		DSRD HSG CNDMINM				4E09H		4E09H	4E09H	4E09H‡	
17940		DSRD HSG APT BLD				4E09I		4E09I	4E09I	4E09I‡	
17950		DSRD HSG HI RISE				4E09J		4E09J	4E09J	4E09J‡	

F07: CONSERVATION, MATERIALISM, EQUITY, ETC. Driving and use of mass transit

Item Reference Number	Page Loc. in this Volume	ITEM DESCRIPTION (ABBREVIATED)	1975	1976	1977	1978	1979	1980	1981	1982/83	1984/85
640	22	DRIVE>200 MI/WK		+C27	+C27	+C27	+C27	+C27	+C27	+C27	+C27
8030	121	USE BYC/MAS TRAN	3A31F	3A04D	3A04D	3A04D	3A04D	3A04D	3A04D	3A04D	3A04D
11960	178	DNT HV DRVR LCNS	5A22	5A09	5A09	5A09	5A09	5A09	5A09	5A09	5A09
11970	178	DONT OWN CAR	5A23	5A10	5A10	5A10	5A10	5A10	5A10	5A10	5A10
		(continued)									

‡ This question appears in 1982 but does not appear in 1983.

Item Refer-ence Number	Page Loc. in this Volume	ITEM DESCRIPTION (ABBREVIATED)	QUESTIONNAIRE LOCATION BY YEAR (FORM, SECTION, AND QUESTION NUMBER)								
			1975	1976	1977	1978	1979	1980	1981	1982/83	1984/85

F07: CONSERVATION, MATERIALISM, EQUITY, ETC. Driving and use of mass transit *(continued)*

11980	178	NEVR USE OTHS CR	5A24	5A11	5A11	5A11	5A11	5A11	5A11	5A11	5A11
11990	178	R CUT DRIVING		5A12	5A12	5A12	5A12	5A12	5A12	5A12	5A12
16430		SAT EVB CAR POOL				2E05A					

G: RELIGION. Religious preferences, activities, views

360	18	R'S RELGS PRFNC		+C13A	+C13A	+C13A	+C13A	+C13A	(+C13A)	+C13A	+C13A
370	18	R'ATTND REL SVC		+C13B	+C13B	+C13B	+C13B	+C13B	+C13B	+C13B	+C13B
380	19	RLGN IMP R'S LF		+C13C	+C13C	+C13C	+C13C	+C13C	+C13C	+C13C	+C13C
5980		DALY GO CHURCH		2A02D							
6930	106	DHNSTY CHURCHES	2A20E	2D04E	2D04E	2D04E	2D04E	2D04E	2D04E	2D04E	2D04E
8420	127	GD JB CHURCHES	3A27E	3A24E	3A24E	3A24E	3A24E	3A24E	3A24E	3A24E	3A24E
10360	153	JOB OBSTC RELGN		4A13A	4A13A	4A13A	4A13A	4A13A	4A13A	4A13A	4A13A
10590	156	>INFLC CHURCHES	4A14C	4A19C	4A19C	4A19C	4A19C	4A19C	4A19C	4A19C	4A19C
11360	170	P'IDEA OF RLGION	4A27N	4E08N	4E08N	4E07N	4E07N	4E07N	4E07N	4E07N	4E07N
11910	177	RCL CNTCT CHURCH		5A07C	5A07C	5A07C	5A07C	5A07C	5A07C	5A07C	5A07C
12230	183	CTB TO RELGS ORG	5A20D	5A20D	5A20D	5A20D	5A20D	5A20D	5A20D	5A20D	5A20D

H01: POLITICS. Political interest and preferences

340	18	R'S POLTL PRFNC		+C11	+C11	+C11	+C11	+C11	+C11	+C11	+C11
350	18	R'POL BLF RADCL		+C12	+C12	+C12	+C12	+C12	+C12	+C12	+C12
6330	96	INTEREST IN GOVT	2A31	2A11	2A11	2A11	2A11	2A11	2A11	2A11	2A11
	156		4A29	3E01	3E01	3E01	3E01	3E01	3E01	4A18	4A18
	182		5A40	4A18	4A18	4A18	4A18	4A18	4A18	5A19	5A19
				5A19	5A19	5A19	5A19	5A19	5A19		
10400	153	JOB OBSTC POL VW		4A13E	4A13E	4A13E	4A13E	4A13E	4A13E	4A13E	4A13E
11370	170	P'IDEA OF PLTICS	4A27O	4E08O	4E08O	4E07O	4E07O	4E07O	4E07O	4E07O	4E07O

H02: POLITICS. Attitudes toward governmental policies and practices

1390	36	SAT GOVT OPRTNG		1A006M	1A006M	1A006M	1A006M	1A006M	1A006M	1A006M	1A006M
5690	98	US GO WAR FR OTH	2A38B	2A18B	2A18B	2A18B	2A18B	2A18B	2A18B	2A18B	2A18B
6450	98	US SHD DISARM	2A38A	2A18A	2A18A	2A18A	2A18A	2A18A	2A18A	2A18A	2A18A
6460	98	US WAR PRTCT ECN	2A38C	2A18C	2A18C	2A18C	2A18C	2A18C	2A18C	2A18C	2A18C
6470	98	US ONLY WAR DFNS	2A38D	2A18D	2A18D	2A18D	2A18D	2A18D	2A18D	2A18D	2A18D
6480	99	-US MIL PWR>USSR	2A38E	2A18E	2A18E	2A18E	2A18E	2A18E	2A18E	2A18E	2A18E
6490	99	US NEED>PWR OTHS	2A38F	2A18F	2A18F	2A18F	2A18F	2A18F	2A18F	2A18F	2A18F
6500	99	US FRN PLCY NRRW	2A38G	2A18G	2A18G	2A18G	2A18G	2A18G	2A18G	2A18G	2A18G
7940	119	CNSDR WMN/HI JOB	3A17B	3A03B	3A03B	3A03B	3A03B	3A03B	3A03B	3A03B	3A03B
8010	120	GOVT DEAL ENV PR	3A31D	3A04B	3A04B	3A04B	3A04B	3A04B	3A04B	3A04B	3A04B
9760	137	GOV HP PRB POPL	3A32N	3E04A	3E04A	3E04A	3E04A	3E04A	3E04A	3E03A	3E03A
9770	137	GOV NO POP PLCY	3A32A	3E04B	3E04B	3E04B	3E04B	3E04B	3E04B	3E03B	3E03B
9820	138	GOV BRTHC NO CST	3A32M	3E04G	3E04G	3E04G	3E04G	3E04G	3E04G	3E03G	3E03G
10010	147	GOVT RESP 4 ENV	4A22E	4A06E	4A06E	4A06E	4A06E	4A06E	4A06E	4A06E	4A06E
10020	147	GOVT TAX PLLTRS	4A22F	4A06F	4A06F	4A06F	4A06F	4A06F	4A06F	4A06F	4A06F
10030	147	GOVT BAN DSPSBLE	4A22G	4A06G	4A06G	4A06G	4A06G	4A06G	4A06G	4A06G	4A06G
11210		-MLTRY COUP U.S.		4E06	4E06						
12340	185	DSCM WN PLTCL OF	5A21F	5A22F	5A22F	5A22F	5A22F	5A22F	5A22F	5A22F	5A22F

H03: POLITICS. Views about the role of citizens in government (See also I02: Attitudes regarding activism)

1580	39	-OBY LW=-GD CTZN		1A011A	1A011A	1A011A	1A011A	1A011A	1A011A	1A011A	1A011A
1590	39	GD CTZN ALG GOVT		1A011B	1A011B	1A011B	1A011B	1A011B	1A011B	1A011B	1A011B
1600	39	GD CTZN CHG GOVT	1A013B	1A011C	1A011C	1A011C	1A011C	1A011C	1A011C	1A011C	1A011C
1620	39	CTZN GRP HV EFCT		1A011E	1A011E	1A011E	1A011E	1A011E	1A011E	1A011E	1A011E

H04: POLITICS. Confidence in government

1630	39	OUR SYST ST BS	1A013C	1A011F	1A011F	1A011F	1A011F	1A011F	1A011F	1A011F	1A011F
6340	96	GOVT PPL -DSHNST	2A32	2A12	2A12	2A12	2A12	2A12	2A12	2A12	2A12
6350	96	GOVT DSNT WASTE$	2A33	2A13	2A13	2A13	2A13	2A13	2A13	2A13	2A13
6360	97	NEVER TRUST GOVT	2A34	2A14	2A14	2A14	2A14	2A14	2A14	2A14	2A14
		(continued)									

Item Reference Number	Page Loc. in this Volume	ITEM DESCRIPTION (ABBREVIATED)	QUESTIONNAIRE LOCATION BY YEAR (FORM, SECTION, AND QUESTION NUMBER)								
			1975	1976	1977	1978	1979	1980	1981	1982/83	1984/85

H04: POLITICS. Confidence in government (continued)

6370	97	GVT PPL DK DOING	2A35	2A15	2A15	2A15	2A15	2A15	2A15	2A15	2A15
6380	97	GOVT RUN FOR PPL	2A36	2A16	2A16	2A16	2A16	2A16	2A16	2A16	2A16
6950	106	DHNSTY PRES&ADMN	2A20G	2D04G	2D04G	2D04G	2D04G	2D04G	2D04G	2D04G	2D04G
6960	106	DHNSTY CONGRESS	2A20H	2D04H	2D04H	2D04H	2D04H	2D04H	2D04H	2D04H	2D04H
6970	106	DHNSTY SUPRM CRT	2A20I	2D04I	2D04I	2D04I	2D04I	2D04I	2D04I	2D04I	2D04I
6980	106	DHNSTY JUSTC SYS	2A20J	2D04J	2D04J	2D04J	2D04J	2D04J	2D04J	2D04J	2D04J
8440	127	GD JB PRES&ADMIN	3A27G	3A24G	3A24G	3A24G	3A24G	3A24G	3A24G	3A24G	3A24G
8450	127	GD JB CONGRESS	3A27H	3A24H	3A24H	3A24H	3A24H	3A24H	3A24H	3A24H	3A24H
8460	127	GD JB SUPRM CRT	3A27I	3A24I	3A24I	3A24I	3A24I	3A24I	3A24I	3A24I	3A24I
8470	127	GD JB JUSTC SYST	3A27J	3A24J	3A24J	3A24J	3A24J	3A24J	3A24J	3A24J	3A24J
10610	157	>INFLC PRES&ADMN	4A14E	4A19E	4A19E	4A19E	4A19E	4A19E	4A19E	4A19E	4A19E
10620	157	>INFLC CONGRESS	4A14F	4A19F	4A19F	4A19F	4A19F	4A19F	4A19F	4A19F	4A19F
10630	157	>INFLC SUPRM CRT	4A14G	4A19G	4A19G	4A19G	4A19G	4A19G	4A19G	4A19G	4A19G
10640	157	>INFLC JUSTC SYS	4A14H	4A19H	4A19H	4A19H	4A19H	4A19H	4A19H	4A19H	4A19H

H05: POLITICS. Voting, political activism

1610	39	VOTE->MAJ IMPCT		1A011D	1A011D	1A011D	1A011D	1A011D	1A011D	1A011D	1A011D
6390	97	DO OR PLN VOTE	2A37A	2A17A	2A17A	2A17A	2A17A	2A17A	2A17A	2A17A	2A17A
6400	97	DO OR PLN WRITE	2A37B	2A17B	2A17B	2A17B	2A17B	2A17B	2A17B	2A17B	2A17B
6410	97	DO OR PLN GIVE $	2A37C	2A17C	2A17C	2A17C	2A17C	2A17C	2A17C	2A17C	2A17C
6420	98	DO OR PLN WK CPG	2A37D	2A17D	2A17D	2A17D	2A17D	2A17D	2A17D	2A17D	2A17D
6430	98	DO OR PLN DEMNST	2A37E	2A17E	2A17E	2A17E	2A17E	2A17E	2A17E	2A17E	2A17E
6440	98	DO OR PLN BOYCOT	2A37F	2A17F	2A17F	2A17F	2A17F	2A17F	2A17F	2A17F	2A17F
9920		R WL VOTE IN '76		3E11							
11820	176	PLC WRK GVT AGCY	5A09C	5A05C	5A05C	5A05C	5A05C	5A05C	5A05C	5A05C	5A05C
12240	183	CTB TO PLTCL PTY	5A20E	5A20E	5A20E	5A20E	5A20E	5A20E	5A20E	5A20E	5A20E
12250	183	CTB TO CTZN LBBY	5A20F	5A20F	5A20F	5A20F	5A20F	5A20F	5A20F	5A20F	5A20F
16340		EFCTV VOTING				2E04C					

I01: SOCIAL CHANGE. Expectations concerning societal change

1200	33	US NEEDS PLANNG	1A004A	1A002A	1A002A	1A002A	1A002A	1A002A	1A002A	1A002A	1A002A
1230	33	X AHEAD TOUGHER	1A004G	1A002D	1A002D	1A002D	1A002D	1A002D	1A002D	1A002D	1A002D
9940	146	FUTR CNTRY WORSE	+A01	4A02	4A02	4A02	4A02	4A02	4A02	4A02	4A02
9950	146	FUTR WORLD WORSE	+A02	4A03	4A03	4A03	4A03	4A03	4A03	4A03	4A03
9960	146	FUTR R LIFE WRSE	+A03	4A04	4A04	4A04	4A04	4A04	4A04	4A04	4A04
10940	163	THG TUF,TCHN SLV	4A28C	4D03C	4D03C	4D03C	4D03C	4D03C	4D03C	4D03C	4D10C

I02: SOCIAL CHANGE. Attitudes regarding activism

1610	39	VOTE->MAJ IMPCT		1A011D	1A011D	1A011D	1A011D	1A011D	1A011D	1A011D	1A011D
1620	39	CTZN GRP HV EFCT		1A011E	1A011E	1A011E	1A011E	1A011E	1A011E	1A011E	1A011E
1650	40	LV THNGS TO GOD	1A004C	1A011H	1A011H	1A011H	1A011H	1A011H	1A011H	1A011H	1A011H
6040	92	APRV PETITIONS	2A21A	2A04A	2A04A	2A04A	2A04A	2A04A	2A04A	2A04A	2A04A
6050	92	APRV BOYCOTT	2A21B	2A04B	2A04B	2A04B	2A04B	2A04B	2A04B	2A04B	2A04B
6060	92	APRV LWFL DMSTN	2A21C	2A04C	2A04C	2A04C	2A04C	2A04C	2A04C	2A04C	2A04C
6070	92	APRV OCCUPY BLDG	2A21D	2A04D	2A04D	2A04D	2A04D	2A04D	2A04D	2A04D	2A04D
6080	92	APRV WLDCAT STRK	2A21E	2A04E	2A04E	2A04E	2A04E	2A04E	2A04E	2A04E	2A04E
6090	93	APRV BLK TRAFFIC	2A21F	2A04F	2A04F	2A04F	2A04F	2A04F	2A04F	2A04F	2A04F
6100	93	APRV DAMAG THING	2A21G	2A04G	2A04G	2A04G	2A04G	2A04G	2A04G	2A04G	2A04G
6110	93	APRV PSNL VIOLNC	2A21H	2A04H	2A04H	2A04H	2A04H	2A04H	2A04H	2A04H	2A04H
6390	97	DO OR PLN VOTE	2A37A	2A17A	2A17A	2A17A	2A17A	2A17A	2A17A	2A17A	2A17A
6400	97	DO OR PLN WRITE	2A37B	2A17B	2A17B	2A17B	2A17B	2A17B	2A17B	2A17B	2A17B
6410	97	DO OR PLN GIVE $	2A37C	2A17C	2A17C	2A17C	2A17C	2A17C	2A17C	2A17C	2A17C
6420	98	DO OR PLN WK CPG	2A37D	2A17D	2A17D	2A17D	2A17D	2A17D	2A17D	2A17D	2A17D
6430	98	DO OR PLN DEMNST	2A37E	2A17E	2A17E	2A17E	2A17E	2A17E	2A17E	2A17E	2A17E
6440	98	DO OR PLN BOYCOT	2A37F	2A17F	2A17F	2A17F	2A17F	2A17F	2A17F	2A17F	2A17F
10920	163	I CNT CHNG WORLD	4A28A	4D03A	4D03A	4D03A	4D03A	4D03A	4D03A	4D10A	4D10A
12250	183	CTB TO CTZN LBBY	5A20F	5A20F	5A20F	5A20F	5A20F	5A20F	5A20F	5A20F	5A20F
16320		EFCTV WRIT OFCLS				2E04A					
16330		EFCTV WRK PL CPN				2E04B					
16340		EFCTV VOTING				2E04C					

(continued)

Item Reference Number	Page Loc. in this Volume	ITEM DESCRIPTION (ABBREVIATED)	QUESTIONNAIRE LOCATION BY YEAR (FORM, SECTION, AND QUESTION NUMBER)								
			1975	1976	1977	1978	1979	1980	1981	1982/83	1984/85

I02: SOCIAL CHANGE. Attitudes regarding activism *(continued)*

16350		EFCTV PETITIONS				2E04D					
16360		EFCTV BOYCOTT				2E04E					
16370		EFCTV LWFL DMSTN				2E04F					
16380		EFCTV OCPY BLDGS				2E04G					
16390		EFCTV WLDCT STRK				2E04H					
16400		EFCTV BLK TRAFIC				2E04I					
16410		EFCTV DAMAG THNG				2E04J					
16420		EFCTV PSNL VLNC				2E04K					

I03: SOCIAL CHANGE. Reactions to personal and social change

1210	33	ENJOY FAST PACE	1A004B	1A002B	1A002B	1A002B	1A002B	1A002B	1A002B	1A002B	1A002B
1220	33	THG CHG 2 QUICK	1A004D	1A002C	1A002C	1A002C	1A002C	1A002C	1A002C	1A002C	1A002C
13950	191	EAGR TO LEAV HOM						5D01W	5D01W	5D01W	5D01W
13960	191	HEST PRT ADLT WL						5D01X	5D01X	5D01X	5D01X

J: SOCIAL PROBLEMS. Interest and concerns

1230	33	X AHEAD TOUGHER	1A004G	1A002D	1A002D	1A002D	1A002D	1A002D	1A002D	1A002D	1A002D
6880	105	THK ABT SOC ISSU	*A06	2D03	2D03	2D03	2D03	2D03	2D03	2D03	2D03
	119			3A02	3A02	3A02	3A02	3A02	3A02	3A02	3A02
	146			4A05	4A05	4A05	4A05	4A05	4A05	4A05	4A05
	174			5A02	5A02	5A02	5A02	5A02	5A02	5A02	5A02
10920	163	I CNT CHNG WORLD	4A28A	4D03A	4D03A	4D03A	4D03A	4D03A	4D03A	4D10A	4D10A
10930	163	SOCTY WONT LAST	4A28B	4D03B	4D03B	4D03B	4D03B	4D03B	4D03B	4D10B	4D10B
10940	163	THG TUF,TCHN SLV	4A28C	4D03C	4D03C	4D03C	4D03C	4D03C	4D03C	4D10C	4D10C
10950	164	NO HOPE 4 WORLD	4A28D	4D03D	4D03D	4D03D	4D03D	4D03D	4D03D	4D10D	4D10D
10960	164	WNDR PURPS 2 LIF	4A28E	4D03E	4D03E	4D03E	4D03E	4D03E	4D03E	4D10E	4D10E
10970	164	WRLD UPHVL 10 YR	4A28F	4D03F	4D03F	4D03F	4D03F	4D03F	4D03F	4D10F	4D10F
10980	164	ANNIHLTN IN LFTM	4A28G	4D03G	4D03G	4D03G	4D03G	4D03G	4D03G	4D10G	4D10G
10990	164	HMN RCE RSILIENT	4A28H	4D03H	4D03H	4D03H	4D03H	4D03H	4D03H	4D10H	4D10H
11660	174	WR/NT NUCLER WAR	5A04A	5A03A	5A03A	5A03A	5A03A	5A03A	5A03A	5A03A	5A03A
11670	174	WR/NT POP GROWTH	5A04B	5A03B	5A03B	5A03B	5A03B	5A03B	5A03B	5A03B	5A03B
11680	174	WR/NT CRIME&VLNC	5A04C	5A03C	5A03C	5A03C	5A03C	5A03C	5A03C	5A03C	5A03C
11690	174	WR/NT POLLUTION	5A04D	5A03D	5A03D	5A03D	5A03D	5A03D	5A03D	5A03D	5A03D
11700	174	WR/NT ENRGY SHRT	5A04E	5A03E	5A03E	5A03E	5A03E	5A03E	5A03E	5A03E	5A03E
11710	175	WR/NT RACE RELTN	5A04F	5A03F	5A03F	5A03F	5A03F	5A03F	5A03F	5A03F	5A03F
11720	175	WR/NT HNGR&PVRTY	5A04G	5A03G	5A03G	5A03G	5A03G	5A03G	5A03G	5A03G	5A03G
11730	175	WR/NT USE OPN LD	5A04H	5A03H	5A03H	5A03H	5A03H	5A03H	5A03H	5A03H	5A03H
11740	175	WR/NT URBN DECAY	5A04I	5A03I	5A03I	5A03I	5A03I	5A03I	5A03I	5A03I	5A03I
11750	175	WR/NT ECON PRBLM	5A04J	5A03J	5A03J	5A03J	5A03J	5A03J	5A03J	5A03J	5A03J
11760	175	WR/NT DRUG ABUSE	5A04K	5A03K	5A03K	5A03K	5A03K	5A03K	5A03K	5A03K	5A03K

K01: MAJOR SOCIAL INSTITUTIONS. Trust (See also C05: Institutions as work settings)

6340	96	GOVT PPL -DSHNST	2A32	2A12	2A12	2A12	2A12	2A12	2A12	2A12	2A12
6350	96	GOVT DSNT WASTE$	2A33	2A13	2A13	2A13	2A13	2A13	2A13	2A13	2A13
6360	97	NEVER TRUST GOVT	2A34	2A14	2A14	2A14	2A14	2A14	2A14	2A14	2A14
6370	97	GVT PPL DK DOING	2A35	2A15	2A15	2A15	2A15	2A15	2A15	2A15	2A15
6380	97	GOVT RUN FOR PPL	2A36	2A16	2A16	2A16	2A16	2A16	2A16	2A16	2A16
6890	105	DHNSTY LARG CORP	2A20A	2D04A	2D04A	2D04A	2D04A	2D04A	2D04A	2D04A	2D04A
6900	105	DHNSTY LBR UNION	2A20B	2D04B	2D04B	2D04B	2D04B	2D04B	2D04B	2D04B	2D04B
6910	105	DHNSTY COLL&UNIV	2A20C	2D04C	2D04C	2D04C	2D04C	2D04C	2D04C	2D04C	2D04C
6920	105	DHNSTY PBLC SCHL	2A20D	2D04D	2D04D	2D04D	2D04D	2D04D	2D04D	2D04D	2D04D
6930	106	DHNSTY CHURCHES	2A20E	2D04E	2D04E	2D04E	2D04E	2D04E	2D04E	2D04E	2D04E
6940	106	DHNSTY NEWS MDIA	2A20F	2D04F	2D04F	2D04F	2D04F	2D04F	2D04F	2D04F	2D04F
6950	106	DHNSTY PRES&ADMN	2A20G	2D04G	2D04G	2D04G	2D04G	2D04G	2D04G	2D04G	2D04G
6960	106	DHNSTY CONGRESS	2A20H	2D04H	2D04H	2D04H	2D04H	2D04H	2D04H	2D04H	2D04H
6970	106	DHNSTY SUPRM CRT	2A20I	2D04I	2D04I	2D04I	2D04I	2D04I	2D04I	2D04I	2D04I
6980	106	DHNSTY JUSTC SYS	2A20J	2D04J	2D04J	2D04J	2D04J	2D04J	2D04J	2D04J	2D04J
6990	107	DHNSTY POLICE	2A20K	2D04K	2D04K	2D04K	2D04K	2D04K	2D04K	2D04K	2D04K
7000	107	DHNSTY MILITARY	2A20L	2D04L	2D04L	2D04L	2D04L	2D04L	2D04L	2D04L	2D04L

Item Reference Number	Page Loc. in this Volume	ITEM DESCRIPTION (ABBREVIATED)	QUESTIONNAIRE LOCATION BY YEAR (FORM, SECTION, AND QUESTION NUMBER)								
			1975	1976	1977	1978	1979	1980	1981	1982/83	1984/85

K02: MAJOR SOCIAL INSTITUTIONS. Satisfaction with performance

Item Reference Number	Page Loc. in this Volume	ITEM DESCRIPTION (ABBREVIATED)	1975	1976	1977	1978	1979	1980	1981	1982/83	1984/85
1390	36	SAT GOVT OPRTNG		1A006M	1A006M	1A006M	1A006M	1A006M	1A006M	1A006M	1A006M
8380	126	GD JB LARG CORPS	3A27A	3A24A	3A24A	3A24A	3A24A	3A24A	3A24A	3A24A	3A24A
8390	126	GD JB LBR UNIONS	3A27B	3A24B	3A24B	3A24B	3A24B	3A24B	3A24B	3A24B	3A24B
8400	126	GD JB COLLG&UNIV	3A27C	3A24C	3A24C	3A24C	3A24C	3A24C	3A24C	3A24C	3A24C
8410	127	GD JB PBLC SCHOL	3A27D	3A24D	3A24D	3A24D	3A24D	3A24D	3A24D	3A24D	3A24D
8420	127	GD JB CHURCHES	3A27E	3A24E	3A24E	3A24E	3A24E	3A24E	3A24E	3A24E	3A24E
8430	127	GD JB NEWS MEDIA	3A27F	3A24F	3A24F	3A24F	3A24F	3A24F	3A24F	3A24F	3A24F
8440	127	GD JB PRES&ADMIN	3A27G	3A24G	3A24G	3A24G	3A24G	3A24G	3A24G	3A24G	3A24G
8450	127	GD JB CONGRESS	3A27H	3A24H	3A24H	3A24H	3A24H	3A24H	3A24H	3A24H	3A24H
8460	127	GD JB SUPRM CRT	3A27I	3A24I	3A24I	3A24I	3A24I	3A24I	3A24I	3A24I	3A24I
8470	127	GD JB JUSTC SYST	3A27J	3A24J	3A24J	3A24J	3A24J	3A24J	3A24J	3A24J	3A24J
8480	128	GD JB POLICE	3A27K	3A24K	3A24K	3A24K	3A24K	3A24K	3A24K	3A24K	3A24K
8490	128	GD JB MILITARY	3A27L	3A24L	3A24L	3A24L	3A24L	3A24L	3A24L	3A24L	3A24L

K03: MAJOR SOCIAL INSTITUTIONS. Preferred influence

Item Reference Number	Page Loc. in this Volume	ITEM DESCRIPTION (ABBREVIATED)	1975	1976	1977	1978	1979	1980	1981	1982/83	1984/85
8500	128	MIL TOO MCH INFL	3A28	3A25	3A25	3A25	3A25	3A25	3A25	3A25	3A25
8510	128	US TOO MCH$MILT	3A29	3A26	3A26	3A26	3A26	3A26	3A26	3A26	3A26
10570	156	>INFLC LARG CORP	4A14A	4A19A	4A19A	4A19A	4A19A	4A19A	4A19A	4A19A	4A19A
10580	156	>INFLC LBR UNION	4A14B	4A19B	4A19B	4A19B	4A19B	4A19B	4A19B	4A19B	4A19B
10590	156	>INFLC CHURCHES	4A14C	4A19C	4A19C	4A19C	4A19C	4A19C	4A19C	4A19C	4A19C
10600	157	>INFLC NEWS MDIA	4A14D	4A19D	4A19D	4A19D	4A19D	4A19D	4A19D	4A19D	4A19D
10610	157	>INFLC PRES&ADMN	4A14E	4A19E	4A19E	4A19E	4A19E	4A19E	4A19E	4A19E	4A19E
10620	157	>INFLC CONGRESS	4A14F	4A19F	4A19F	4A19F	4A19F	4A19F	4A19F	4A19F	4A19F
10630	157	>INFLC SUPRM CRT	4A14G	4A19G	4A19G	4A19G	4A19G	4A19G	4A19G	4A19G	4A19G
10640	157	>INFLC JUSTC SYS	4A14H	4A19H	4A19H	4A19H	4A19H	4A19H	4A19H	4A19H	4A19H
10650	157	>INFLC POLICE	4A14I	4A19I	4A19I	4A19I	4A19I	4A19I	4A19I	4A19I	4A19I
10660	158	>INFLC MILITARY	4A14J	4A19J	4A19J	4A19J	4A19J	4A19J	4A19J	4A19J	4A19J

L01: MILITARY. Plans for military service

Item Reference Number	Page Loc. in this Volume	ITEM DESCRIPTION (ABBREVIATED)	1975	1976	1977	1978	1979	1980	1981	1982/83	1984/85
490	20	R WL DO ARMD FC		+C21B	+C21B	+C21B	+C21B	+C21B	+C21B	+C21B	+C21B
540	21	R WNTDO ARMD FC		+C22B	+C22B	+C22B	+C22B	+C22B	+C22B	+C22B	+C22B
730	24	R'S BRANCH SERV		+C32	+C32	+C32	+C32	+C32	+C32	+C32	+C32
740	24	R XPCTS B OFFCR		+C33	+C33	+C33	+C33	+C33	+C33	+C33	+C33
750	24	R XPCTS MLTR CR		+C34	+C34	+C34	+C34	+C34	+C34	+C34	+C34

L02: MILITARY. Attitudes toward a draft

Item Reference Number	Page Loc. in this Volume	ITEM DESCRIPTION (ABBREVIATED)	1975	1976	1977	1978	1979	1980	1981	1982/83	1984/85
21060	114	FAVOR MLTY DRAFT							5E06	2E08	2E08
21070	114	DRAFT INCL WOMEN							5E07	2E09	2E09

L03: MILITARY. Views about the use of military force

Item Reference Number	Page Loc. in this Volume	ITEM DESCRIPTION (ABBREVIATED)	1975	1976	1977	1978	1979	1980	1981	1982/83	1984/85
5690	98	US GO WAR FR OTH	2A38B	2A18B	2A18B	2A18B	2A18B	2A18B	2A18B	2A18B	2A18B
6450	98	US SHD DISARM	2A38A	2A18A	2A18A	2A18A	2A18A	2A18A	2A18A	2A18A	2A18A
6460	98	US WAR PRTCT ECN	2A38C	2A18C	2A18C	2A18C	2A18C	2A18C	2A18C	2A18C	2A18C
6470	98	US ONLY WAR DFNS	2A38D	2A18D	2A18D	2A18D	2A18D	2A18D	2A18D	2A18D	2A18D
6480	99	-US MIL PWR>USSR	2A38E	2A18E	2A18E	2A18E	2A18E	2A18E	2A18E	2A18E	2A18E
6490	99	US NEED>PWR OTHS	2A38F	2A18F	2A18F	2A18F	2A18F	2A18F	2A18F	2A18F	2A18F
6500	99	US FRN PLCY NRRW	2A38G	2A18G	2A18G	2A18G	2A18G	2A18G	2A18G	2A18G	2A18G
6510	99	SRVCMEN SHD OBEY	2A38H	2A18H	2A18H	2A18H	2A18H	2A18H	2A18H	2A18H	2A18H
11210		-MLTRY COUP U.S.		4E06	4E06						
11220	168	NT VOL 4 NEC WAR		4E07	4E07	4E06	4E06	4E06	4E06	4E06	4E06

L04: MILITARY. Attitudes toward the military as an institution and occupation

Item Reference Number	Page Loc. in this Volume	ITEM DESCRIPTION (ABBREVIATED)	1975	1976	1977	1978	1979	1980	1981	1982/83	1984/85
7000	107	DHNSTY MILITARY	2A20L	2D04L	2D04L	2D04L	2D04L	2D04L	2D04L	2D04L	2D04L
8490	128	GD JB MILITARY	3A27L	3A24L	3A24L	3A24L	3A24L	3A24L	3A24L	3A24L	3A24L
8500	128	MIL TOO MCH INFL	3A28	3A25	3A25	3A25	3A25	3A25	3A25	3A25	3A25
8510	128	US TOO MCH$MILT	3A29	3A26	3A26	3A26	3A26	3A26	3A26	3A26	3A26
10660	158	>INFLC MILITARY	4A14J	4A19J	4A19J	4A19J	4A19J	4A19J	4A19J	4A19J	4A19J
11120	167	MLTRY GET AHEAD		4E01A	4E01A	4E01A	4E01A	4E01A	4E01A	4E01A	4E01A
		(continued)									

Item Reference Number	Page Loc. in this Volume	ITEM DESCRIPTION (ABBREVIATED)	QUESTIONNAIRE LOCATION BY YEAR (FORM, SECTION, AND QUESTION NUMBER)								
			1975	1976	1977	1978	1979	1980	1981	1982/83	1984/85

L04: MILITARY. Attitudes toward the military as an institution and occupation (continued)

Item Reference Number	Page Loc. in this Volume	ITEM DESCRIPTION (ABBREVIATED)	1975	1976	1977	1978	1979	1980	1981	1982/83	1984/85
11130	167	MLTRY MORE ED		4E01B	4E01B	4E01B	4E01B	4E01B	4E01B	4E01B	4E01B
11140	167	MLTRY ADVNC RESP		4E01C	4E01C	4E01C	4E01C	4E01C	4E01C	4E01C	4E01C
11150	167	MLTRY >FLFLLG JB		4E01D	4E01D	4E01D	4E01D	4E01D	4E01D	4E01D	4E01D
11160	167	MLTRY IDEAS HERD		4E01E	4E01E	4E01E	4E01E	4E01E	4E01E	4E01E	4E01E
11170	167	EXTNT MLTRY JSTC		4E02	4E02	4E02	4E02	4E02	4E02	4E02	4E02
11180	167	MLTRY DSCRM WOMN		4E03	4E03	4E03	4E03	4E03	4E03	4E03	4E03
11190	168	MLTRY DSCRM BLKS		4E04	4E04	4E04	4E04	4E04	4E04	4E04	4E04
11200	168	>FAIR MLTRY CVLN		4E05	4E05	4E05	4E05	4E05	4E05	4E05	4E05
11830	176	PLC WRK MLTY SVC	5A09D	5A05D	5A05D	5A05D	5A05D	5A05D	5A05D	5A05D	5A05D
21080	114	MLTRY PAY CLG GD							5E08	2E10	2E10
21090	115	R WD DO MLTY/CLG							5E09	2E11	2E11

M01: INTERPERSONAL RELATIONSHIPS. Dating

Item Reference Number	Page Loc. in this Volume	ITEM DESCRIPTION (ABBREVIATED)	1975	1976	1977	1978	1979	1980	1981	1982/83	1984/85
620	22	#X/AV WK GO OUT		+C25	+C25	+C25	+C25	+C25	+C25	+C25	+C25
630	22	#X DATE 3+/WK		+C26	+C26	+C26	+C26	+C26	+C26	+C26	+C26

M02: INTERPERSONAL RELATIONSHIPS. Cross-age relationships with adults outside the family (See also B05)

Item Reference Number	Page Loc. in this Volume	ITEM DESCRIPTION (ABBREVIATED)	1975	1976	1977	1978	1979	1980	1981	1982/83	1984/85
1240	33	TM SPT ADLT MST	1A006	1A003	1A003	1A003	1A003	1A003	1A003	1A003	1A003
1250	34	LK MR TM ADLT	1A007	1A004	1A004	1A004	1A004	1A004	1A004	1A004	1A004
1260	34	LK MR TM YG CHD	1A008	1A005	1A005	1A005	1A005	1A005	1A005	1A005	1A005
6530	99	FRQ HIT SUPRVISR	2A39B	2A19B	2A19B	2A19B	2A19B	2A19B	2A19B	2A19B	2A19B
21550	160	JOB-SUPERVSR AGE								4D04	4D04
21610	161	JOB-OVER AGE 30								4D06E	4D06E
21710	163	JOB-TCHR HELP GT								4D08	4D08
21910	200	PARTY-PPL OVR 30									5E08A
22050	202	PRFR PTY-PPL >30									5E09A

M03: INTERPERSONAL RELATIONSHIPS. Agreement/disagreement with parents

Item Reference Number	Page Loc. in this Volume	ITEM DESCRIPTION (ABBREVIATED)	1975	1976	1977	1978	1979	1980	1981	1982/83	1984/85
1330	35	SAT GT ALNG PRNT	1A009G	1A006G	1A006G	1A006G	1A006G	1A006G	1A006G	1A006G	1A006G
1500	38	IMP LIV CLS PRNT		1A007J	1A007J	1A007J	1A007J	1A007J	1A007J	1A007J	1A007J
6520	99	FRQ FIGHT PARNTS	2A39A	2A19A	2A19A	2A19A	2A19A	2A19A	2A19A	2A19A	2A19A
11230	168	P'IDEA OF DO LIF	4A27A	4E08A	4E08A	4E07A	4E07A	4E07A	4E07A	4E07A	4E07A
11240	168	P'IDEA OF LSR TM	4A27B	4E08B	4E08B	4E07B	4E07B	4E07B	4E07B	4E07B	4E07B
11250	168	P'IDEA OF CLTHES	4A27C	4E08C	4E08C	4E07C	4E07C	4E07C	4E07C	4E07C	4E07C
11260	169	P'IDEA OF SPND $	4A27D	4E08D	4E08D	4E07D	4E07D	4E07D	4E07D	4E07D	4E07D
11270	169	P'IDEA OF DATE	4A27E	4E08E	4E08E	4E07E	4E07E	4E07E	4E07E	4E07E	4E07E
11280	169	P'IDEA OF OK DRK	4A27F	4E08F	4E08F	4E07F	4E07F	4E07F	4E07F	4E07F	4E07F
11290	169	P'IDEA OF OK MRJ	4A27G	4E08G	4E08G	4E07G	4E07G	4E07G	4E07G	4E07G	4E07G
11300	169	P'IDEA OF OK DRG	4A27H	4E08H	4E08H	4E07H.	4E07H	4E07H	4E07H	4E07H	4E07H
11310	169	P'IDEA OF VALUES	4A27I	4E08I	4E08I	4E07I	4E07I	4E07I	4E07I	4E07I	4E07I
11320	169	P'IDEA OF EDUC	4A27J	4E08J	4E08J	4E07J	4E07J	4E07J	4E07J	4E07J	4E07J
11330	170	P'IDEA OF SX RLS	4A27K	4E08K	4E08K	4E07K	4E07K	4E07K	4E07K	4E07K	4E07K
11340	170	P'IDEA OF ECLOGY	4A27L	4E08L	4E08L	4E07L	4E07L	4E07L	4E07L	4E07L	4E07L
11350	170	P'IDEA OF RCL IS	4A27M	4E08M	4E08M	4E07M	4E07M	4E07M	4E07M	4E07M	4E07M
11360	170	P'IDEA OF RLGION	4A27N	4E08N	4E08N	4E07N	4E07N	4E07N	4E07N	4E07N	4E07N
11370	170	P'IDEA OF PLTICS	4A27O	4E08O	4E08O	4E07O	4E07O	4E07O	4E07O	4E07O	4E07O
13150		FAM+REL GD/CHILD		5E01A							
13160		FAM+REL GD/PARNT		5E01B							
13170		FAM+REL GD/GRPNT		5E01C							
13180		FAM+REL,R LIK/PT		5E01D							
19530	113	3MO/DLY ARG PRNT						2E08A	2E08A	2E07A	2E07A
21800	199	PRNT SUPRV PARTY									5E06A
21810	199	PRNT SUPRV DATES									5E06B
21820	199	PRNT SUPRV DRESS									5E06C
21830	199	PRNT SUPRV MONEY									5E06D
21840	199	PRNT SUPRV EVENG									5E06E
21850	199	PRNT SUPRV HOMWK									5E06F
21860	200	PRN SUPRV COURSE									5E06G
21870	200	PRNT SUPRV WORK									5E06H
21880	200	PRN SUPR TV QNTY									5E06I
21890	200	PRN SUPR TV QLTY									5E06J

Item Reference Number	Page Loc. in this Volume	ITEM DESCRIPTION (ABBREVIATED)	QUESTIONNAIRE LOCATION BY YEAR (FORM, SECTION, AND QUESTION NUMBER)								
			1975	1976	1977	1978	1979	1980	1981	1982/83	1984/85

M04: INTERPERSONAL RELATIONSHIPS. Friendships (See also Q03: Loneliness)

Item Reference Number	Page Loc. in this Volume	ITEM DESCRIPTION (ABBREVIATED)	1975	1976	1977	1978	1979	1980	1981	1982/83	1984/85
1320	35	SAT OWN FRIENDS	1A009F	1A006F	1A006F	1A006F	1A006F	1A006F	1A006F	1A006F	1A006F
1450	37	IMP STRG FRDSHP		1A007E	1A007E	1A007E	1A007E	1A007E	1A007E	1A007E	1A007E
5920	90	DALY VIST W/FRDS		2A02K	2A02K	2A02K	2A02K	2A02K	2A02K	2A02K	2A02K
10170	149	JOB IMPC MK FRND	4A08I	4A08I	4A08I	4A08I	4A08I	4A08I	4A08I	4A08I	4A08I

M05: INTERPERSONAL RELATIONSHIPS. Community at large

Item Reference Number	Page Loc. in this Volume	ITEM DESCRIPTION (ABBREVIATED)	1975	1976	1977	1978	1979	1980	1981	1982/83	1984/85
1480	37	IMP LDR COMUNTY		1A007H	1A007H	1A007H	1A007H	1A007H	1A007H	1A007H	1A007H
10290	151	JOB IMPC CNTC PL	4A08U	4A08U	4A08U	4A08U	4A08U	4A08U	4A08U	4A08U	4A08U
13590	139	STS SCH LDS STU		5E05B	5E06B	5E06B	5E04B	5E06B		3E06B	3E06B
21600	161	JOB-DIF SOC BKGD								4D06D	4D06D
21730	172	IDEA PARENTS GRP								4E09†	4E09
21740	172	#FRNDS PRNTS GRP								4E10†	4E10
21750	172	OWN PRNTS IN GRP								4E11†	4E11
21760	172	GP IMPCT OWN FLG								4E12†	4E12
21770	172	GP CHG RELP PRNT								4E13†	4E13
21780	173	#FRNDS ANTIDG GP								4E14†	4E14
21790	173	EVR IN ANTIDG GP								4E15†	4E15

N01: RACE RELATIONS. Preferred interracial contact

Item Reference Number	Page Loc. in this Volume	ITEM DESCRIPTION (ABBREVIATED)	1975	1976	1977	1978	1979	1980	1981	1982/83	1984/85
8110	122	DES FRND OTH RC	3A19A	3A07A	3A07A	3A07A	3A07A	3A07A	3A07A	3A07A	3A07A
8120	122	DES SUPVR DIF RC	3A19B	3A07B	3A07B	3A07B	3A07B	3A07B	3A07B	3A07B	3A07B
8130	122	DES FAM NX DF RC	3A19C	3A07C	3A07C	3A07C	3A07C	3A07C	3A07C	3A07C	3A07C
8140	122	DES CHL FD SM RC	3A19D	3A07D	3A07D	3A07D	3A07D	3A07D	3A07D	3A07D	3A07D
8150	123	DES CHL FD OT RC	3A19E	3A07E	3A07E	3A07E	3A07E	3A07E	3A07E	3A07E	3A07E
8160	123	DES AL WKS SM RC	3A19F	3A08A	3A08A	3A08A	3A08A	3A08A	3A08A	3A08A	3A08A
8170	123	DES SO WKS DF RC	3A19G	3A08B	3A08B	3A08B	3A08B	3A08B	3A08B	3A08B	3A08B
8180	123	DES MS WKS DF RC	3A19H	3A08C	3A08C	3A08C	3A08C	3A08C	3A08C	3A08C	3A08C
8190	123	DES AL NGB SM RC	3A19I	3A09A	3A09A	3A09A	3A09A	3A09A	3A09A	3A09A	3A09A
8200	123	DES SO NGB OT RC	3A19J	3A09B	3A09B	3A09B	3A09B	3A09B	3A09B	3A09B	3A09B
8210	123	DES MS NGB OT RC	3A19K	3A09C	3A09C	3A09C	3A09C	3A09C	3A09C	3A09C	3A09C
8220	124	DES AL CHL SM RC	3A19L	3A10A	3A10A	3A10A	3A10A	3A10A	3A10A	3A10A	3A10A
8230	124	DES SM CHL OT RC	3A19M	3A10B	3A10B	3A10B	3A10B	3A10B	3A10B	3A10B	3A10B
8240	124	DES MS CHL OT RC	3A19N	3A10C	3A10C	3A10C	3A10C	3A10C	3A10C	3A10C	3A10C

N02: RACE RELATIONS. Attitudes about discrimination

Item Reference Number	Page Loc. in this Volume	ITEM DESCRIPTION (ABBREVIATED)	1975	1976	1977	1978	1979	1980	1981	1982/83	1984/85
1520	38	IMP CRRCT INEQL		1A007L	1A007L	1A007L	1A007L	1A007L	1A007L	1A007L	1A007L
10380	153	JOB OBSTC RACE		4A13C	4A13C	4A13C	4A13C	4A13C	4A13C	4A13C	4A13C
11190	168	MLTRY DSCRM BLKS		4E04	4E04	4E04	4E04	4E04	4E04	4E04	4E04
11350	170	P'IDEA OF RCL IS	4A27M	4E08M	4E08M	4E07M	4E07M	4E07M	4E07M	4E07M	4E07M
11710	175	WR/NT RACE RELTN		5A04F	5A03F	5A03F	5A03F	5A03F	5A03F	5A03F	5A03F
11950	178	B/W RLTNS WRSE		5A15	5A08	5A08	5A08	5A08	5A08	5A08	5A08
12100	180	MNRTY NT MY BSNS		5A19F	5A18D	5A18D	5A18D	5A18D	5A18D	5A18D	5A18D
12220	183	CTB TO MNRTY GRP		5A20C	5A20C	5A20C	5A20C	5A20C	5A20C	5A20C	5A20C

N03: RACE RELATIONS. Actual interracial contacts

Item Reference Number	Page Loc. in this Volume	ITEM DESCRIPTION (ABBREVIATED)	1975	1976	1977	1978	1979	1980	1981	1982/83	1984/85
8250	124	FRNDS AL OT RC	3A22	3A11	3A11	3A11	3A11	3A11	3A11	3A11	3A11
8260	124	NGBHD AL OT RC	3A23	3A12	3A12	3A12	3A12	3A12	3A12	3A12	3A12
8270	124	ELEMSCH AL OT RC	3A21	3A13	3A13	3A13	3A13	3A13	3A13	3A13	3A13
8280	124	HISCH AL OT RC	3A20	3A14	3A14	3A14	3A14	3A14	3A14	3A14	3A14
8290	125	WRKRS AL OT RC		3A15	3A15	3A15	3A15	3A15	3A15	3A15	3A15
8300	125	DO LOT THG OT RC	3A24	3A16	3A16	3A16	3A16	3A16	3A16	3A16	3A16
8310	125	VRY GD EXP OT RC	3A25	3A17	3A17	3A17	3A17	3A17	3A17	3A17	3A17
11890	177	RCL CNTCT SCHOOL		5A07A	5A07A	5A07A	5A07A	5A07A	5A07A	5A07A	5A07A
11900	177	RCL CNTCT NGHBHD		5A07B	5A07B	5A07B	5A07B	5A07B	5A07B	5A07B	5A07B
11910	177	RCL CNTCT CHURCH		5A07C	5A07C	5A07C	5A07C	5A07C	5A07C	5A07C	5A07C
11920	177	RCL CNTCT SPORTS		5A07D	5A07D	5A07D	5A07D	5A07D	5A07D	5A07D	5A07D
11930	178	RCL CNTCT CLUBS		5A07E	5A07E	5A07E	5A07E	5A07E	5A07E	5A07E	5A07E
11940	178	RCL CNTCT JOB		5A07F	5A07F	5A07F	5A07F	5A07F	5A07F	5A07F	5A07F

† This question appears in 1983 but does not appear in 1982.

Item Reference Number	Page Loc. in this Volume	ITEM DESCRIPTION (ABBREVIATED)	QUESTIONNAIRE LOCATION BY YEAR (FORM, SECTION, AND QUESTION NUMBER)								
			1975	1976	1977	1978	1979	1980	1981	1982/83	1984/85

O01: CONCERN FOR OTHERS. Attitudes regarding social service, charitable activism

Item Ref	Page	Description	1975	1976	1977	1978	1979	1980	1981	1982/83	1984/85
1470	37	IMP CNTRBTN SOC		1A007G	1A007G	1A007G	1A007G	1A007G	1A007G	1A007G	1A007G
1520	38	IMP CRRCT INEQL		1A007L	1A007L	1A007L	1A007L	1A007L	1A007L	1A007L	1A007L
10130	149	JOB IMPC HLP OTH	4A08E	4A08E	4A08E	4A08E	4A08E	4A08E	4A08E	4A08E	4A08E
10190	150	JOB IMPC WRTHWLE	4A08K	4A08K	4A08K	4A08K	4A08K	4A08K	4A08K	4A08K	4A08K
11860	176	PLC WRK SOC SVCS	5A09G	5A05G	5A05G	5A05G	5A05G	5A05G	5A05G	5A05G	5A05G

O02: CONCERN FOR OTHERS. Involvement in community, altruistic activities

Item Ref	Page	Description	1975	1976	1977	1978	1979	1980	1981	1982/83	1984/85
5860	89	DALY CMNTY AFFRS		2A02E	2A02E	2A02E	2A02E	2A02E	2A02E	2A02E	2A02E
12200	182	CTB TO UNTD FUND	5A20A	5A20A	5A20A	5A20A	5A20A	5A20A	5A20A	5A20A	5A20A
12210	182	CTB TO INTL RELF	5A20B	5A20B	5A20B	5A20B	5A20B	5A20B	5A20B	5A20B	5A20B
12220	183	CTB TO MNRTY GRP	5A20C	5A20C	5A20C	5A20C	5A20C	5A20C	5A20C	5A20C	5A20C
12230	183	CTB TO RELGS ORG	5A20D	5A20D	5A20D	5A20D	5A20D	5A20D	5A20D	5A20D	5A20D
12240	183	CTB TO PLTCL PTY	5A20E	5A20E	5A20E	5A20E	5A20E	5A20E	5A20E	5A20E	5A20E
12250	183	CTB TO CTZN LBBY	5A20F	5A20F	5A20F	5A20F	5A20F	5A20F	5A20F	5A20F	5A20F
12260	183	CTB TO VS DISEAS	5A20G	5A20G	5A20G	5A20G	5A20G	5A20G	5A20G	5A20G	5A20G
12270	183	CTB TO POP PRBMS	5A20H	5A20H	5A20H	5A20H	5A20H	5A20H	5A20H	5A20H	5A20H
12280	184	CTB TO ENVIR PBM	5A20I	5A20I	5A20I	5A20I	5A20I	5A20I	5A20I	5A20I	5A20I

O03: CONCERN FOR OTHERS. Concern with the problems of others

Item Ref	Page	Description	1975	1976	1977	1978	1979	1980	1981	1982/83	1984/85
5990	91	US 2 MUCH PROFIT	2A23J	2A03A	2A03A	2A03A	2A03A	2A03A	2A03A	2A03A	2A03A
8040	121	EAT DIF->FD STRV	3A31G	3A04E	3A04E	3A04E	3A04E	3A04E	3A04E	3A04E	3A04E
9840		GVNG FOOD O CNTY	3A33	3E05							
12070	180	WRRY ABT OW CTRY	5A19A	5A18A	5A18A	5A18A	5A18A	5A18A	5A18A	5A18A	5A18A
12080	180	BTTR IF CTZ WRLD	5A19C	5A18B	5A18B	5A18B	5A18B	5A18B	5A18B	5A18B	5A18B
12090	180	-SYMP TWD STARVG	5A19E	5A18C	5A18C	5A18C	5A18C	5A18C	5A18C	5A18C	5A18C
12100	180	MNRTY NT MY BSNS	5A19F	5A18D	5A18D	5A18D	5A18D	5A18D	5A18D	5A18D	5A18D
12110	180	UPST PL TR -FAIR	5A19G	5A18E	5A18E	5A18E	5A18E	5A18E	5A18E	5A18E	5A18E
12120	181	HELP POOR W MY $	5A19I	5A18F	5A18F	5A18F	5A18F	5A18F	5A18F	5A18F	5A18F
12130	181	-MY PRB OT ND HP	5A19K	5A18G	5A18G	5A18G	5A18G	5A18G	5A18G	5A18G	5A18G
12140	181	RB CHNG ETG HABT		5A18H	5A18H	5A18H	5A18H	5A18H	5A18H	5A18H	5A18H
16430		SAT EVB CAR POOL				2E05A					
16440		SAT EAT <BEEF>GRN				2E05B					
19470		EAT <FD,>OWN CITY					5E08A				
19480		EAT <FD,>NRBY STT					5E08B				
19490		EAT <FD,>DIF REGN					5E08C				
19500		EAT <FD,>ASIAN CN					5E08D				

P01: HAPPINESS. Happiness; satisfaction with life and self

Item Ref	Page	Description	1975	1976	1977	1978	1979	1980	1981	1982/83	1984/85
1190	33	VRY HPY THS DAYS		1A001	1A001	1A001	1A001	1A001	1A001	1A001	1A001
	89			2A01	2A01	2A01	2A01	2A01	2A01	2A01	2A01
	119			3A01	3A01	3A01	3A01	3A01	3A01	3A01	3A01
	146			4A01	4A01	4A01	4A01	4A01	4A01	4A01	4A01
	174			5A01	5A01	5A01	5A01	5A01	5A01	5A01	5A01
1340	35	SAT YOURSELF	1A009H	1A006H	1A006H	1A006H	1A006H	1A006H	1A006H	1A006H	1A006H
1380	36	SAT LIFE AS WHLE	1A009L	1A006L	1A006L	1A006L	1A006L	1A006L	1A006L	1A006L	1A006L
6840	104	CMP SATFD W/LIFE		2D01	2D01	2D01	2D01	2D01	2D01	2D01	2D01
	133			3D01	3D01	3D01	3D01	3D01	3D01	3D01	3D01
	160			4D01	4D01	4D01	4D01	4D01	4D01	4D01	4D01
	184			5A21	5A21	5A21	5A21	5A21	5A21	5A21	5A21
12620	108	SATISFD W MYSELF	5A39H	5D01H	5D01H	5D01H	5D01H	5D01H	5D01H	5D01H	2D05J
	189										5D01H

P02: HAPPINESS. Satisfaction with specific life domains

Item Ref	Page	Description	1975	1976	1977	1978	1979	1980	1981	1982/83	1984/85
1270	34	SAT PRESENT JOB	1A009A	1A006A	1A006A	1A006A	1A006A	1A006A	1A006A	1A006A	1A006A
1280	34	SAT NEIGHBORHOD	1A009B	1A006B	1A006B	1A006B	1A006B	1A006B	1A006B	1A006B	1A006B
1290	34	SAT PRSNL SAFTY	1A009C	1A006C	1A006C	1A006C	1A006C	1A006C	1A006C	1A006C	1A006C
1300	35	SAT OWN PROP SF	1A009D	1A006D	1A006D	1A006D	1A006D	1A006D	1A006D	1A006D	1A006D
1310	35	SAT EDUC EXPRNCS	1A009E	1A006E	1A006E	1A006E	1A006E	1A006E	1A006E	1A006E	1A006E
1320	35	SAT OWN FRIENDS	1A009F	1A006F	1A006F	1A006F	1A006F	1A006F	1A006F	1A006F	1A006F

(continued)

Item Reference Number	Page Loc. in this Volume	ITEM DESCRIPTION (ABBREVIATED)	QUESTIONNAIRE LOCATION BY YEAR (FORM, SECTION, AND QUESTION NUMBER)								
			1975	1976	1977	1978	1979	1980	1981	1982/83	1984/85

P02: HAPPINESS. Satisfaction with specific life domains (continued)

Item Reference Number	Page Loc. in this Volume	ITEM DESCRIPTION (ABBREVIATED)	1975	1976	1977	1978	1979	1980	1981	1982/83	1984/85
1330	35	SAT GT ALNG PRNT	1A009G	1A006G	1A006G	1A006G	1A006G	1A006G	1A006G	1A006G	1A006G
1350	35	SAT STD OF LVG	1A009I	1A006I	1A006I	1A006I	1A006I	1A006I	1A006I	1A006I	1A006I
1360	36	SAT TIME FR THGS	1A009J	1A006J	1A006J	1A006J	1A006J	1A006J	1A006J	1A006J	1A006J
1370	36	SAT SPD LEISR	1A009K	1A006K	1A006K	1A006K	1A006K	1A006K	1A006K	1A006K	1A006K
1400	36	SAT AMT OF FUN		1A006N	1A006N	1A006N	1A006N	1A006N	1A006N	1A006N	1A006N
10350	153	R THNK WK BE SAT		4A12	4A12	4A12	4A12	4A12	4A12	4A12	4A12
10910	160	CMP SATFD W/JOB		4D02	4D02	4D02	4D02	4D02	4D02	4D02	4D02

Q01: OTHER PERSONALITY VARIABLES. Attitudes about self, self-esteem

Item Reference Number	Page Loc. in this Volume	ITEM DESCRIPTION (ABBREVIATED)	1975	1976	1977	1978	1979	1980	1981	1982/83	1984/85
1190	33	VRY HPY THS DAYS		1A001	1A001	1A001	1A001	1A001	1A001	1A001	1A001
	89			2A01	2A01	2A01	2A01	2A01	2A01	2A01	2A01
	119			3A01	3A01	3A01	3A01	3A01	3A01	3A01	3A01
	146			4A01	4A01	4A01	4A01	4A01	4A01	4A01	4A01
	174			5A01	5A01	5A01	5A01	5A01	5A01	5A01	5A01
1340	35	SAT YOURSELF	1A009H	1A006H	1A006H	1A006H	1A006H	1A006H	1A006H	1A006H	1A006H
1400	36	SAT AMT OF FUN		1A006N	1A006N	1A006N	1A006N	1A006N	1A006N	1A006N	1A006N
6840	104	CMP SATFD W/LIFE		2D01	2D01	2D01	2D01	2D01	2D01	2D01	2D01
	133			3D01	3D01	3D01	3D01	3D01	3D01	3D01	3D01
	160			4D01	4D01	4D01	4D01	4D01	4D01	4D01	4D01
	184			5A21	5A21	5A21	5A21	5A21	5A21	5A21	5A21
6850	104	HOW GD AS SPOUSE	2A19A	2D02A	2D02A	2D02A	2D02A	2D02A	2D02A	2D02A	2D02A
6860	104	HOW GD AS PARENT	2A19B	2D02B	2D02B	2D02B	2D02B	2D02B	2D02B	2D02B	2D02B
6870	105	HOW GD AS WORKER	2A19C	2D02C	2D02C	2D02C	2D02C	2D02C	2D02C	2D02C	2D02C
12550	108	POS ATT TWD SELF	5A39A	5D01A	5D01A	5D01A	5D01A	5D01A	5D01A	5D01A	2D05G
	188											5D01A
12570	108	AM PRSN OF WORTH	5A39C	5D01C	5D01C	5D01C	5D01C	5D01C	5D01C	5D01C	2D05H
	188											5D01C
12580	108	DO WELL AS OTHRS	5A39D	5D01D	5D01D	5D01D	5D01D	5D01D	5D01D	5D01D	2D05I
	188											5D01D
12620	108	SATISFD W MYSELF	5A39H	5D01H	5D01H	5D01H	5D01H	5D01H	5D01H	5D01H	2D05J
	189											5D01H
12660	108	-MUCH TO B PROUD			5D01L	5D01L	5D01L	5D01L	5D01L	5D01L	2D05K
	190											5D01L
12680	109	I AM NO GOOD			5D01N	5D01N	5D01N	5D01N	5D01N	5D01N	2D05L
	190											5D01N
12720	109	I DO WRONG THING			5D01R	5D01R	5D01R	5D01R	5D01R	5D01R	2D05M
	190											5D01R
12750	109	MY LIFE NT USEFL			5D01U	5D01U	5D01U	5D01U	5D01U	5D01U	2D05N
	191											5D01U
13950	191	EAGR TO LEAV HOM						5D01W	5D01W	5D01W	5D01W
13960	191	HEST PRT ADLT WL						5D01X	5D01X	5D01X	5D01X

Q02: OTHER PERSONALITY VARIABLES. Locus of control

Item Reference Number	Page Loc. in this Volume	ITEM DESCRIPTION (ABBREVIATED)	1975	1976	1977	1978	1979	1980	1981	1982/83	1984/85
1210	33	ENJOY FAST PACE	1A004B	1A002B	1A002B	1A002B	1A002B	1A002B	1A002B	1A002B	1A002B
1220	33	THG CHG 2 QUICK	1A004D	1A002C	1A002C	1A002C	1A002C	1A002C	1A002C	1A002C	1A002C
12560	188	LUCK>IMP HRD WRK	5A39B	5D01B	5D01B	5D01B	5D01B	5D01B	5D01B	5D01B	5D01B
12590	189	TRY GT AHD,STOPD	5A39E	5D01E	5D01E	5D01E	5D01E	5D01E	5D01E	5D01E	5D01E
12600	189	PLNNG MKS UNHPPY	5A39F	5D01F	5D01F	5D01F	5D01F	5D01F	5D01F	5D01F	5D01F
12610	189	ACPT LIFE->HAPPR	5A39G	5D01G	5D01G	5D01G	5D01G	5D01G	5D01G	5D01G	5D01G
12630	189	PPL LK ME -CHANC	5A39I	5D01I	5D01I	5D01I	5D01I	5D01I	5D01I	5D01I	5D01I
12640	189	MY PLANS DO WORK			5D01J	5D01J	5D01J	5D01J	5D01J	5D01J	5D01J
12700	190	PPL MASTER FATE			5D01P	5D01P	5D01P	5D01P	5D01P	5D01P	5D01P
12740	191	PLANS->BTR RSLTS			5D01T	5D01T	5D01T	5D01T	5D01T	5D01T	5D01T

Q03: OTHER PERSONALITY VARIABLES. Loneliness

Item Reference Number	Page Loc. in this Volume	ITEM DESCRIPTION (ABBREVIATED)	1975	1976	1977	1978	1979	1980	1981	1982/83	1984/85
12650	189	OFTN FEEL LONELY			5D01K	5D01K	5D01K	5D01K	5D01K	5D01K	5D01K
12670	190	ALWYS SM1 HELP R			5D01M	5D01M	5D01M	5D01M	5D01M	5D01M	5D01M
12690	190	OFTN FL LEFT OUT			5D01O	5D01O	5D01O	5D01O	5D01O	5D01O	5D01O
12710	190	USLY SM1 TALK TO			5D01Q	5D01Q	5D01Q	5D01Q	5D01Q	5D01Q	5D01Q
12730	191	OFT WSH MOR FRND			5D01S	5D01S	5D01S	5D01S	5D01S	5D01S	5D01S
12760	191	USLY FRDS BE WTH			5D01V	5D01V	5D01V	5D01V	5D01V	5D01V	5D01V

Item Reference Number	Page Loc. in this Volume	ITEM DESCRIPTION (ABBREVIATED)	QUESTIONNAIRE LOCATION BY YEAR (FORM, SECTION, AND QUESTION NUMBER)								
			1975	1976	1977	1978	1979	1980	1981	1982/83	1984/85

Q04: OTHER PERSONALITY VARIABLES. Risk taking

Item Reference Number	Page Loc.	ITEM DESCRIPTION	1975	1976	1977	1978	1979	1980	1981	1982/83	1984/85
7050	108	KICK DO DANGR TH		2D05E	2D05E	2D05E	2D05E	2D05E	2D05E	2D05E	2D05E
7060	108	LIKE RISK SOME X		2D05F	2D05F	2D05F	2D05F	2D05F	2D05F	2D05F	2D05F

Q05: OTHER PERSONALITY VARIABLES. Trust in others

Item Reference Number	Page Loc.	ITEM DESCRIPTION	1975	1976	1977	1978	1979	1980	1981	1982/83	1984/85
1550	38	PPL CAN B TRSTD	1A010	1A008	1A008	1A008	1A008	1A008	1A008	1A008	1A008
1560	38	PPL TRY B HLPFL	1A011	1A009	1A009	1A009	1A009	1A009	1A009	1A009	1A009
1570	38	PPL TRY BE FAIR	1A012	1A010	1A010	1A010	1A010	1A010	1A010	1A010	1A010

Q06: OTHER PERSONALITY VARIABLES. See Subject Area T: HEALTH HABITS AND SYMPTOMS

Q07: OTHER PERSONALITY VARIABLES. Importance placed on various life goals

Item Reference Number	Page Loc.	ITEM DESCRIPTION	1975	1976	1977	1978	1979	1980	1981	1982/83	1984/85
1410	36	IMP B SUCCSS WK		1A007A	1A007A	1A007A	1A007A	1A007A	1A007A	1A007A	1A007A
1420	37	IMP GD MRRG&FAM		1A007B	1A007B	1A007B	1A007B	1A007B	1A007B	1A007B	1A007B
1430	37	IMP LOTS OF $		1A007C	1A007C	1A007C	1A007C	1A007C	1A007C	1A007C	1A007C
1440	37	IMP TM RCRN&HBY		1A007D	1A007D	1A007D	1A007D	1A007D	1A007D	1A007D	1A007D
1450	37	IMP STRG FRDSHP		1A007E	1A007E	1A007E	1A007E	1A007E	1A007E	1A007E	1A007E
1460	37	IMP STEADY WORK		1A007F	1A007F	1A007F	1A007F	1A007F	1A007F	1A007F	1A007F
1470	37	IMP CNTRBTN SOC		1A007G	1A007G	1A007G	1A007G	1A007G	1A007G	1A007G	1A007G
1480	37	IMP LDR COMUNTY		1A007H	1A007H	1A007H	1A007H	1A007H	1A007H	1A007H	1A007H
1490	37	IMP CHLD BTR OPP		1A007I	1A007I	1A007I	1A007I	1A007I	1A007I	1A007I	1A007I
1500	38	IMP LIV CLS PRNT		1A007J	1A007J	1A007J	1A007J	1A007J	1A007J	1A007J	1A007J
1510	38	IMP GT AWY AREA		1A007K	1A007K	1A007K	1A007K	1A007K	1A007K	1A007K	1A007K
1520	38	IMP CRRCT INEQL		1A007L	1A007L	1A007L	1A007L	1A007L	1A007L	1A007L	1A007L
1530	38	IMP NEW XPRNCE		1A007M	1A007M	1A007M	1A007M	1A007M	1A007M	1A007M	1A007M
1540	38	IMP FND PRPS LF		1A007N	1A007N	1A007N	1A007N	1A007N	1A007N	1A007N	1A007N

Q08: OTHER PERSONALITY VARIABLES. Social, political, cultural orientation

Item Reference Number	Page Loc.	ITEM DESCRIPTION	1975	1976	1977	1978	1979	1980	1981	1982/83	1984/85
6330	96	INTEREST IN GOVT	2A31	2A11	2A11	2A11	2A11	2A11	2A11	2A11	2A11
	156		4A29	3E01	3E01	3E01	3E01	3E01	3E01	4A18	4A18
	182		5A40	4A18	4A18	4A18	4A18	4A18	4A18	5A19	5A19
				5A19	5A19	5A19	5A19	5A19	5A19		
6880	105	THK ABT SOC ISSU	*A06	2D03	2D03	2D03	2D03	2D03	2D03	2D03	2D03
	119			3A02	3A02	3A02	3A02	3A02	3A02	3A02	3A02
	146			4A05	4A05	4A05	4A05	4A05	4A05	4A05	4A05
	174			5A02	5A02	5A02	5A02	5A02	5A02	5A02	5A02
7010	107	2MCH COMPTN SCTY	2A23C	2D05A	2D05A	2D05A	2D05A	2D05A	2D05A	2D05A	2D05A
7020	107	2MANY YNG SLOPPY	2A23H	2D05B	2D05B	2D05B	2D05B	2D05B	2D05B	2D05B	2D05B
7030	107	2MUCH HARD ROCK	2A23I	2D05C	2D05C	2D05C	2D05C	2D05C	2D05C	2D05C	2D05C
7040	107	SHD DO OWN THING	2A23A	2D05D	2D05D	2D05D	2D05D	2D05D	2D05D	2D05D	2D05D
7630	82	R LIKES SCHOOL		1D001	1D001	1D001	1D001	1D001	1D001	1D001	1D001
	115			2E02	2E06	2E06	2E08	2E09	2E09	2E12	2E12
				3E08	3E07	3E07	3E07	3E07	3E07		
				4E10	5E05	5E05	5E03	5E05			
				5E04							
10460	154	JOB OBSTC -CONFM		4A13K	4A13K	4A13K	4A13K	4A13K	4A13K	4A13K	4A13K
17570		PPL SHD CONFORM					5E02A				
17580		PPL SHD LV HRMNY					5E02B				
17590		PPL SHD B FRANK					5E02C				
17600		PPL SHD THK FREE					5E02D				
17610		PPL SHD B INDPNT					5E02E				

Q09: OTHER PERSONALITY VARIABLES. Hostility

Item Reference Number	Page Loc.	ITEM DESCRIPTION	1975	1976	1977	1978	1979	1980	1981	1982/83	1984/85
19530	113	3MO/DLY ARG PRNT						2E08A	2E08A	2E07A	2E07A
19540	113	3MO/DLY ARG AUTH						2E08B	2E08B	2E07B	2E07B
19550	113	3MO/DLY MAD						2E08C	2E08C	2E07C	2E07C
19560	114	3MO/DLY MAD,SMSH						2E08D	2E08D	2E07D	2E07D
19570	114	3MO/DLY WANT FGT						2E08E	2E08E	2E07E	2E07E
19580	114	3MO/DLY DID FGHT						2E08F	2E08F	2E07F	2E07F

Item Reference Number	Page Loc. in this Volume	ITEM DESCRIPTION (ABBREVIATED)	QUESTIONNAIRE LOCATION BY YEAR (FORM, SECTION, AND QUESTION NUMBER)								
			1975	1976	1977	1978	1979	1980	1981	1982/83	1984/85

R01: BACKGROUND. Age, sex, race, and marital status

Item Reference Number	Page Loc. in this Volume	ITEM DESCRIPTION (ABBREVIATED)	1975	1976	1977	1978	1979	1980	1981	1982/83	1984/85
10	16	R'S BIRTH YEAR		+C01	+C01	+C01	+C01	+C01	+C01	+C01	+C01
20	16	R'S BIRTH MONTH		+C02	+C02	+C02	+C02	+C02	+C02	+C02	+C02
30	16	R'S SEX		+C03	+C03	+C03	+C03	+C03	+C03	+C03	+C03
40	16	R'S RACE		+C04	+C04	+C04	+C04	+C04	+C04	+C04	+C04
60	16	R NOT MARRIED		+C06	+C06	+C06	+C06	+C06	+C06	+C06	+C06
8320	125	MARRD OR ENGAGED	3A41	3A18	3A18	3A18	3A18	3A18	3A18	3A18	3A18

R02: BACKGROUND. Family characteristics

Item Reference Number	Page Loc. in this Volume	ITEM DESCRIPTION (ABBREVIATED)	1975	1976	1977	1978	1979	1980	1981	1982/83	1984/85
75	17	# OLDER BR/SIS									+C07A
76	17	# YOUNGER BR/SR									+C07B
310	17	FATHR EDUC LEVEL		+C08	+C08	+C08	+C08	+C08	+C08	+C08	+C08
320	17	MOTHR EDUC LEVEL		+C09	+C09	+C09	+C09	+C09	+C09	+C09	+C09
330	18	MOTH PD JB R YNG		+C10	+C10	+C10	+C10	+C10	+C10	+C10	+C10

R03: BACKGROUND. Living arrangements and household characteristics

Item Reference Number	Page Loc. in this Volume	ITEM DESCRIPTION (ABBREVIATED)	1975	1976	1977	1978	1979	1980	1981	1982/83	1984/85
50	16	R SPD >TIM R-URB		+C05	+C05	+C05	+C05	+C05	+C05	+C05	+C05
80	17	R'S HSHLD ALONE		+C07A	+C07A	+C07A	+C07A	+C07A	+C07A	+C07A	+C07Ca
90	17	R'S HSHLD FATHER		+C07B	+C07B	+C07B	+C07B	+C07B	+C07B	+C07B	+C07Cb
100	17	R'S HSHLD MOTHER		+C07C	+C07C	+C07C	+C07C	+C07C	+C07C	+C07C	+C07Cc
110	17	R'S HSHLD BR/SR		+C07D	+C07D	+C07D	+C07D	+C07D	+C07D	+C07D	+C07Cd
120	17	R'S HSHLD GRPRNT		+C07E	+C07E	+C07E	+C07E	+C07E	+C07E	+C07E	+C07Ce
130	17	R'S HSHLD SPOUSE		+C07F	+C07F	+C07F	+C07F	+C07F	+C07F	+C07F	+C07Cf
140	17	R'S HSHLD CHLDRN		+C07G	+C07G	+C07G	+C07G	+C07G	+C07G	+C07G	+C07Cg
150	17	R'S HSHLD RELTVS		+C07H	+C07H	+C07H	+C07H	+C07H	+C07H	+C07H	+C07Ch
160	17	R'S HSHLD NONRLT		+C07I	+C07I	+C07I	+C07I	+C07I	+C07I	+C07I	+C07Ci

S01: DEVIANCE AND VICTIMIZATION. Delinquent behaviors

Item Reference Number	Page Loc. in this Volume	ITEM DESCRIPTION (ABBREVIATED)	1975	1976	1977	1978	1979	1980	1981	1982/83	1984/85
6520	99	FRQ FIGHT PARNTS	2A39A	2A19A	2A19A	2A19A	2A19A	2A19A	2A19A	2A19A	2A19A
6530	99	FRQ HIT SUPRVISR	2A39B	2A19B	2A19B	2A19B	2A19B	2A19B	2A19B	2A19B	2A19B
6540	100	FRQ FGT WRK/SCHL	2A39C	2A19C	2A19C	2A19C	2A19C	2A19C	2A19C	2A19C	2A19C
6550	100	FRQ GANG FIGHT	2A39D	2A19D	2A19D	2A19D	2A19D	2A19D	2A19D	2A19D	2A19D
6560	100	FRQ HURT SM1 BAD	2A39E	2A19E	2A19E	2A19E	2A19E	2A19E	2A19E	2A19E	2A19E
6570	100	FRQ THREAT WEAPN	2A39F	2A19F	2A19F	2A19F	2A19F	2A19F	2A19F	2A19F	2A19F
6580	100	FRQ STEAL <$50	2A39G	2A19G	2A19G	2A19G	2A19G	2A19G	2A19G	2A19G	2A19G
6590	100	FRQ STEAL >$50	2A39H	2A19H	2A19H	2A19H	2A19H	2A19H	2A19H	2A19H	2A19H
6600	100	FRQ SHOPLIFT	2A39I	2A19I	2A19I	2A19I	2A19I	2A19I	2A19I	2A19I	2A19I
6610	101	FRQ CAR THEFT	2A39J	2A19J	2A19J	2A19J	2A19J	2A19J	2A19J	2A19J	2A19J
6620	101	FRQ STEAL CAR PT	2A39K	2A19K	2A19K	2A19K	2A19K	2A19K	2A19K	2A19K	2A19K
6630	101	FRQ TRESPAS BLDG	2A39L	2A19L	2A19L	2A19L	2A19L	2A19L	2A19L	2A19L	2A19L
6640	101	FRQ ARSON	2A39M	2A19M	2A19M	2A19M	2A19M	2A19M	2A19M	2A19M	2A19M
6650	101	FRQ DMG SCH PPTY	2A39N	2A19N	2A19N	2A19N	2A19N	2A19N	2A19N	2A19N	2A19N
6660	101	FRQ DMG WK PRPTY	2A39O	2A19O	2A19O	2A19O	2A19O	2A19O	2A19O	2A19O	2A19O
6670	101	FRQ TRUBL POLICE	2A39P	2A19P	2A19P	2A19P	2A19P	2A19P	2A19P	2A19P	2A19P

S02: DEVIANCE AND VICTIMIZATION. Driving violations and accidents

Item Reference Number	Page Loc. in this Volume	ITEM DESCRIPTION (ABBREVIATED)	1975	1976	1977	1978	1979	1980	1981	1982/83	1984/85
650	22	#X/12MO R TCKTD		+C28	+C28	+C28	+C28	+C28	+C28	+C28	+C28
660	22	#TCKTS AFT DRNK		+C29A	+C29A	+C29A	+C29A	+C29A	+C29A	+C29A	+C29A
670	23	#TCKTS AFT MARJ		+C29B	+C29B	+C29B	+C29B	+C29B	+C29B	+C29B	+C29B
680	23	#TCKTS AFT OTDG		+C29C	+C29C	+C29C	+C29C	+C29C	+C29C	+C29C	+C29C
690	23	#ACCIDNTS/12 MO		+C30	+C30	+C30	+C30	+C30	+C30	+C30	+C30
700	23	#ACDTS AFT DRNK		+C31A	+C31A	+C31A	+C31A	+C31A	+C31A	+C31A	+C31A
710	23	#ACDTS AFT MARJ		+C31B	+C31B	+C31B	+C31B	+C31B	+C31B	+C31B	+C31B
720	23	#ACDTS AFT OTDG		+C31C	+C31C	+C31C	+C31C	+C31C	+C31C	+C31C	+C31C

S03: DEVIANCE AND VICTIMIZATION. Victimization experiences

Item Reference Number	Page Loc. in this Volume	ITEM DESCRIPTION (ABBREVIATED)	1975	1976	1977	1978	1979	1980	1981	1982/83	1984/85
6680	102	SM1 ROB YRS <$50		2A20A	2A20A	2A20A	2A20A	2A20A	2A20A	2A20A	2A20A
6690	102	SM1 ROB YRS >$50		2A20B	2A20B	2A20B	2A20B	2A20B	2A20B	2A20B	2A20B
6700	102	SM1 DMG YR PRPTY		2A20C	2A20C	2A20C	2A20C	2A20C	2A20C	2A20C	2A20C
		(continued)									

Item Reference Number	Page Loc. in this Volume	ITEM DESCRIPTION (ABBREVIATED)	QUESTIONNAIRE LOCATION BY YEAR (FORM, SECTION, AND QUESTION NUMBER)								
			1975	1976	1977	1978	1979	1980	1981	1982/83	1984/85

S03: DEVIANCE AND VICTIMIZATION. Victimization experiences *(continued)*

Item Reference Number	Page Loc. in this Volume	ITEM DESCRIPTION	1975	1976	1977	1978	1979	1980	1981	1982/83	1984/85
6710	102	SM1 INJR U W/WPN		2A20D	2A20D	2A20D	2A20D	2A20D	2A20D	2A20D	2A20D
6720	102	SM1 THRTN U W/WP		2A20E	2A20E	2A20E	2A20E	2A20E	2A20E	2A20E	2A20E
6730	102	SM1 INJR YU -WPN		2A20F	2A20F	2A20F	2A20F	2A20F	2A20F	2A20F	2A20F
6740	103	SM1 THRT U W/INJ		2A20G	2A20G	2A20G	2A20G	2A20G	2A20G	2A20G	2A20G
9871	140	SM1 SCL ROB <$50		4E11A	3E10A	3E10A	5E06A	5E08A	5E13A	3E08A	3E08A
9872	140	SM1 SCL ROB >$50		4E11B	3E10B	3E10B	5E06B	5E08B	5E13B	3E08B	3E08B
9873	140	SM1 SCL DMG PRTY		4E11C	3E10C	3E10C	5E06C	5E08C	5E13C	3E08C	3E08C
9874	140	SM1 SCL IN U W/W		4E11D	3E10D	3E10D	5E06D	5E08D	5E13D	3E08D	3E08D
9875	141	SM1 SCL TH U W/W		4E11E	3E10E	3E10E	5E06E	5E08E	5E13E	3E08E	3E08E
9876	141	SM1 SCL IN U -WP		4E11F	3E10F	3E10F	5E06F	5E08F	5E13F	3E08F	3E08F
9877	141	SM1 SCL TH U W/I		4E11G	3E10G	3E10G	5E06G	5E08G	5E13G	3E08G	3E08G

T: HEALTH HABITS AND SYMPTOMS

Item Reference Number	Page Loc. in this Volume	ITEM DESCRIPTION	1975	1976	1977	1978	1979	1980	1981	1982/83	1984/85
8850	133	OFTN SHRTNS BRTH		(3D02A)	3D02A	3D02A	3D02A	3D02A	3D02A	3D02A	3D02A
8860	133	OFTN HEART BEATG		(3D02B)	3D02B	3D02B	3D02B	3D02B	3D02B	3D02B	3D02B
8870	133	OFTN SPLLS DZZNS		(3D02C)	3D02C	3D02C	3D02C	3D02C	3D02C	3D02C	3D02C
8880	133	OFTN HNDS TRMBLE		(3D02D)	3D02D	3D02D	3D02D	3D02D	3D02D	3D02D	3D02D
8890	133	OFTN HNDS SWEATG		(3D02E)	3D02E	3D02E	3D02E	3D02E	3D02E	3D02E	3D02E
8900	134	OFTN CDNT GT GNG		(3D02F)	3D02F	3D02F	3D02F	3D02F	3D02F	3D02F	3D02F
20690		ATTN TO NUTRITON					2E15A				
20700		MIN CHOLESTEROL					2E15B				
20710		AVOID ADDITIVES					2E15C				
20720		TRY GET EXERCISE					2E15D				
20730		CNTRL OWN HEALTH					2E16				
20740	117	OFTN EAT BRKFST					2E17A	2E17A	2E17A	2E20A	2E21A
20750	117	OFTN EAT GN VEG					2E17B	2E17B	2E17B	2E20B	2E21B
20760	117	OFTN EAT FRUIT					2E17C	2E17C	2E17C	2E20C	2E21C
20770	118	OFTN EXERCISE					2E17D	2E17D	2E17D	2E20D	2E21D
20780	118	OFTN 7HRS SLEEP					2E17E	2E17E	2E17E	2E20E	2E21E
20790	118	OFTN SLEEP <SHLD					2E17F	2E17F	2E17F	2E20F	2E21F
21310	85	#DA HEADACHE								1D015A	1D015A
21320	85	#DA SORE THROAT								1D015B	1D015B
21330	85	#DA SINUS CONG								1D015C	1D015C
21340	85	#DA COUGHING								1D015D	1D015D
21350	85	#DA CHEST COLD								1D015E	1D015E
21360	86	#DA COUGH PHLM								1D015F	1D015F
21370	86	#DA SHORT BRTH								1D015G	1D015G
21380	86	#DA WHEEZING								1D015H	1D015H
21390	86	#DA TRBL REMEM								1D015I	1D015I
21400	86	#DA DFCT THINK								1D015J	1D015J
21410	86	#DA TRBL LEARN								1D015K	1D015K
21420	87	#DA TRBL SLEEP								1D015L	1D015L
21430	87	#DA TRBL START								1D015M	1D015M
21440	87	#DA STAY HOME								1D015N	1D015N
21450	87	#X/12M DOC-CHEK								1D016A	1D016A
21460	87	#X/12M DOC-FGHT								1D016B	1D016B
21470	87	#X/12M DOC-INJ								1D016C	1D016C
21480	88	#X/12M DOC-ILL								1D016D	1D016D
21490	88	#X/12M DOC-PSY								1D016E	1D016E
21500	88	#X/12M HSP-INJ								1D017A	1D017A
21510	88	#X/12M HSP-ILL								1D017B	1D017B
21520	88	RLTV PHY HEALTH								1D018	1D018

Appendix A
Sampling Error Estimates and Tables

All of the percentages reported in this volume are really *estimates* of the response percentages that would have been obtained if, instead of using a sample survey, we had asked all high schools throughout the United States to participate, and in all schools that agreed to participate we had invited the whole senior class to fill out the questionnaires. The question naturally arises: How accurate are the present percentage estimates based on a limited number of schools and seniors? For any particular percentage resulting from a sample survey we cannot know exactly how much error has resulted from sampling, but we can make reasonably good estimates of "confidence intervals" — ranges within which the "true" population value is very likely to fall. The word "true" in this context is defined quite narrowly; it refers only to the value that would be found if we had set out to survey the total population — all high school seniors in the United States. Thus this concept of "true" population value does *not* take account of biases that might occur due to refusals, distortion of responses, faulty question wording, and other factors. Each of these sources of possible error is discussed in the "Representativeness and Validity" section of the Introduction to this volume. The reader is urged to review this material and take it into account along with the sampling error estimates included in this appendix.

The estimation of confidence intervals in surveys involving complex samples can be a highly complicated combination of statistical science plus informed judgment. It is an area in which there is no single "right answer" or "best approach." We suspect that many of those using this volume will not be especially interested in *how* we have chosen to solve the problems involved in estimating confidence intervals, so long as we provide guidelines that can be applied in a fairly simple and straightforward manner. This appendix is designed to accomplish that. Appendix B provides a more extensive discussion of how we obtained the confidence intervals shown here, and it also provides guidelines for computing specific confidence intervals for a wider range of possible applications than can be covered in the tables provided in this appendix.

A very rough example of a confidence interval can be stated in these terms: For percentages based on the total sample (all five questionnaire forms), the "true" values are rarely more than 1.5 percent higher or lower than the percentage estimates reported in this volume. How rarely? The chances are much lower than 1 in 20. Indeed, many of the percentages reported for the total sample are accurate to within one percent.

Of course, most of the data reported here are based on items included only in one or another of the five questionnaire forms. Since such percentages are based on only one-fifth of the total sample, they are somewhat less accurate. The loss in accuracy is less than might be imagined, however, for reasons spelled out in Appendix B. For present purposes, it is enough to say that percentages based on 3,000 or more seniors responding to one questionnaire form are rarely (less than 1 in 20) farther than 2.4 percent away from the "true" value.

We have thus far provided two very rough illustrations of confidence intervals — a range of ± 1.5 percent for percentages based on the total sample, and a range of ± 2.4 percent for percentages based on the number of seniors responding to one questionnaire form. While these two intervals provide some notion of the overall range of accuracy of the sample, they fall short of our needs in a number of respects. We need to be able to assign confidence intervals for subgroups such as males, females, those who plan to complete college, and so forth, all of which involve smaller numbers of cases and thus some reduction in accuracy. We also need to take account of the fact that, other things equal, confidence intervals grow smaller when one moves from the middle of the scale (percentages near 50 percent) to the extremes (e.g., 4 percent or 96 percent). Further, we need to provide guidelines for evaluating the *difference* between two percentages; for example, we may wish to know whether the difference between male and female percentages in response to a particular question is large enough so that it is not likely to be merely the result of sampling error. Another type of difference of considerable interest is that between percentages from two different years; for example, we may wish to know whether an increase in the percentage of daily marijuana users from one year to the next is large enough to be considered a statistically significant change.

Each of the requirements mentioned above is taken into account in the tables of confidence intervals which follow.

Confidence Intervals for Single Percentages

Table A-1 provides confidence intervals for single percentages that are reasonably good approximations for most *variables* and for most *subgroups* (as well as for the total sample). The table entries slightly underestimate the confidence intervals for regional subgroups and for blacks. These underestimates can be corrected reasonably well by multiplying the entries in Table A-1 by a factor of 1.1 for data based on a single form and by a factor of 1.33 for data based on all five forms. A more serious problem is that the table entries substantially underestimate the confidence intervals for certain variables which tend to be somewhat homogeneous within schools, as well as other factors likely to show clustering according to geographical area or socioeconomic level. A discussion of some of these variables is provided at the end of this appendix.

Table A-1 accommodates various numbers of cases (presented as different columns in the table), and various percentages (presented as different rows in the table). The table entries, when added to and subtracted from the observed percentage, establish the 95 percent confidence interval (calculated as 1.96 sampling errors). Thus, for example, to determine the accuracy of a result of 67.4 percent based on a sample of 1,632 cases, one should first look for the closest values in the table (in this case, about 70 percent and a number of cases approximately equal to 1,500); next determine the values to be added to and subtracted from the observed percentage (in this case the values

would be + 2.8 percent and − 2.9 percent); and then compute the confidence interval around the observed percentage of 67.4 percent (in this case an interval ranging from 64.5 percent to 70.2 percent). This procedure yields an interval such that, for most variables, the chances are 95 in 100 that if all high school seniors in the country had been asked to participate in the survey the resulting percentage would fall within the interval.

Confidence Intervals for Differences between Two Percentages

Table A-2 provides confidence intervals for differences between certain percentages. Specifically, the table can be used for *comparisons* between males and females, between those who do and do not plan to complete four years of college, and between those falling into different categories of the five-level index of drug usage. The above comparisons are appropriate for data from any single year (e.g., male seniors in 1976 compared with female seniors in 1976, or the "marijuana only" seniors in 1977 compared with the "no illicit drugs" seniors in 1977). Table A-2 is also useful in assessing *one-year* trends for any of the above subgroups as well as for the total sample. For example, one may be interested in a confidence interval (or significance level) for the difference between the percentage of female seniors in 1977 who used marijuana and the percentage of female seniors in 1978 who did so. The values in Table A-2 are appropriate for confidence intervals across adjacent years (e.g., 1976 compared with 1977), provided the same subgroup (e.g., females) is being considered both years. The confidence intervals for comparisons across non-adjacent years (e.g., 1976 compared with 1978), are slightly larger.

With appropriate corrections, the entries in Table A-2 can be used for trends covering more than one year and for trends or comparisons involving regional subgroups and blacks. Each of these applications requires some upward adjustment of the table entries; guidelines for such adjustments are provided in the notes accompanying Table A-2.

For information on the derivation of Table A-2 and for guidelines to be used in computing confidence intervals not covered in that table, the reader is referred to Appendix B.

In order to find the appropriate confidence interval in Table A-2, one must first locate that portion of the table which deals with percentage values closest to the two percentages being compared (for example, if one wished to compare a value of 28.1 percent with one of 35.4 percent, the "p = 30 percent or 70 percent" portion of the table would be closest). The next step is to locate the specific table entry which corresponds most closely to the numbers of cases involved in the two percentages being compared (e.g., if those numbers were 1,478 and 1,563 for 28.1 percent and 35.4 percent, the correct table entry would be 3.9 percent). That table entry, when added to and subtracted from the difference between the two percentages, yields the 95 percent confidence interval for the difference. (In the above illustration that would be 7.3 percent ± 3.9 percent or an interval from 3.4 percent to 11.2 percent.) The chances are only 1 in 20 that the "true" difference between two percentages lies outside of this interval.

Another use of Table A-2 is to test whether a difference between two percentages is "statistically significant." If the table entry is smaller than the difference between the two percentages (as is true in the above illustration), then the difference is statistically significant at the 95 percent level (sometimes indicated as $p < .05$).

Some Cautions

The tables provided here are based on averages of large numbers of sampling errors computed across a wide range of the variables which appear in this volume, as well as across all of the subgroups for which data are reported here. We are confident that the values in the tables are reasonably accurate for most purposes, but we must repeat the caution that the tables slightly underestimate confidence intervals for the following groups and comparisons:

> Blacks
> Regions (Northeast, North Central,
>   South, West)
> Comparisons among regions
> Comparisons across non-adjacent years
>   (e.g., 1976 vs. 1978)

A more important problem is that the tables substantially underestimate the confidence intervals for certain variables that, for various reasons, show greater than average homogeneity within schools. After an extensive, but by no means exhaustive, sampling of the kinds of variables which might show such clustering by school, we can provide the following examples of the kinds of variables for which Tables A-1 and A-2 substantially underestimate the confidence intervals.

Variables Related to Educational Background and Aspirations. The questionnaire items dealing with father's education, mother's education, high school curriculum (college preparatory versus all other), and plans for completing four years of college, all show an appreciable amount of clustering by school. Accordingly, for such variables the confidence intervals provided in the tables should be doubled.

Other items dealing with plans for technical/vocational schooling, a two-year college program, or graduate/professional study, also require adjustment. The confidence intervals in the tables should be multiplied by a factor of 1.5 in order to be applicable to these variables.

It seems clear that the common factor underlying these particular variables is the tendency for family socioeconomic level to be somewhat homogeneous within school districts — some schools serve wealthier populations than others. That makes the form of sampling we use somewhat less efficient for measuring those variables (like those listed above) which are closely associated with family socioeconomic level. Therefore, we urge the reader to treat with caution any variables which are likely to be strongly linked to socioeconomic factors. In the absence of more specific computations of sampling errors, a good rule of thumb for dealing with such variables would be to double the confidence intervals provided in Tables A-1 and A-2.

Variables Related to Geographic Location. Another category of variables which are somewhat homogeneous within schools and school districts consists of those things which reflect differences in region and/or urbanicity. An obvious example is a background question asking where the respondent grew up; the response category "on a farm" shows a very high degree of clustering within schools. One would have to more than double the confidence intervals in the tables to deal with such a measure. Similarly high clustering was found for some responses about religious preference; for example, those whose preference is Baptist are located primarily in the South (and probably heavily in rural areas), whereas those whose preference is Jewish are located primarily in the Northeast (especially in larger cities). The confidence intervals in Tables A-1 and A-2 should be multiplied by a factor as large as 3 in order to be applicable to such variables.

Other variables which show some greater than average homogeneity within schools include such ideologically related dimensions as frequency of attending religious services, importance of religion, and political preference. Still other variables showing high homogeneity, probably because of their association with urbanicity, include driving (percentage who usually do not drive at all), working (percentage with no job), and household composition (percentage with father not living in the home). For each of the variables mentioned in this paragraph, the confidence intervals shown in Tables A-1 and A-2 should be multiplied by a factor of about 1.5.

Variables Involving Use of Alcohol and Marijuana. Extensive work has been done to compute sampling errors and confidence intervals for the drug use measures included in this volume (see Johnston, Bachman, and O'Malley, 1977, 1979, especially Appendix B). Most drug use variables show sampling errors which lie within the range of those provided in Tables A-1 and A-2. Usage levels for alcohol and marijuana, however, show some degree of homogeneity within schools, thus requiring that the table levels be adjusted. For items dealing with alcohol use, the entries in Table A-1 should be multiplied by a factor

of 1.6; for items dealing with marijuana use, the correction factor is 1.35.

As noted earlier, this appendix has presented guidelines for using the tables of confidence intervals provided herein. Those readers interested in learning more about the rationale underlying such tables, the procedures used to derive the particular tables presented here, and guidelines for further computations of confidence intervals may consult Appendix B of this volume.

Notes to Table A-1

Caution: The entries in this table systematically underestimate confidence intervals for regional subgroups and for blacks. In order to correct these underestimates, the table entries should be multiplied by a factor of 1.10 for data from a single form and by a factor of 1.33 for data based on five forms. Further cautions and corrections are required for some specific variables which relate to educational background and aspirations, geographic location, and the use of alcohol and marijuana (see discussion in the final sections of Appendix A).

The values in this table, when added to and subtracted from an observed percentage, establish the 95 percent confidence interval around that percentage, incorporating a design effect. Table values were calculated using the following formula (adapted from Hays, 1973, p. 379):

$$\text{lower limit} = p - \frac{2N'p + (1.96)^2 - 1.96\sqrt{4N'p\,(1-p) + (1.96)^2}}{2[N' + (1.96)^2]}$$

$$\text{upper limit} = \frac{2N'p + (1.96)^2 + 1.96\sqrt{4N'p\,(1-p) + (1.96)^2}}{2[N' + (1.96)^2]} - p$$

where p = the percentage, and N' is the "effective N," N' = N/(1.3 + .00015N).
(See Appendix B for a discussion of the concept of "effective N.")

Table A-1

Confidence Intervals (95% Level) around Percentage Values

Number of Cases

	100	200	300	400	500	700	1000	1500	2000	2500	3000	3500	4000	5000	7000	10000	15000	20000
99%+	0.9	0.8	0.7	0.7	0.6	0.6	0.5	0.5	0.4	0.4	0.4	0.4	0.3	0.3	0.3	0.3	0.3	0.2
−	5.6	3.2	2.4	1.9	1.7	1.3	1.1	0.8	0.7	0.6	0.6	0.6	0.5	0.5	0.4	0.4	0.3	0.3
97%+	2.1	1.8	1.6	1.4	1.3	1.2	1.0	0.9	0.8	0.8	0.7	0.7	0.6	0.6	0.6	0.5	0.5	0.5
−	6.6	4.1	3.2	2.6	2.3	1.9	1.6	1.3	1.1	1.0	0.9	0.9	0.8	0.8	0.7	0.6	0.6	0.5
95%+	3.1	2.5	2.2	2.0	1.8	1.6	1.4	1.2	1.1	1.0	0.9	0.9	0.9	0.8	0.7	0.7	0.6	0.6
−	7.4	4.7	3.7	3.1	2.7	2.3	1.9	1.5	1.4	1.2	1.1	1.1	1.0	0.9	0.8	0.8	0.7	0.7
90%+	4.9	3.8	3.3	2.9	2.7	2.3	2.0	1.7	1.5	1.4	1.3	1.3	1.2	1.1	1.0	0.9	0.9	0.8
−	8.8	5.8	4.6	4.0	3.5	2.9	2.5	2.0	1.8	1.6	1.5	1.4	1.4	1.3	1.1	1.0	0.9	0.9
85%+	6.6	4.8	4.1	3.6	3.3	2.9	2.5	2.1	1.9	1.7	1.6	1.5	1.5	1.4	1.2	1.1	1.0	1.0
−	9.7	6.6	5.3	4.5	4.0	3.4	2.9	2.4	2.1	1.9	1.8	1.7	1.6	1.5	1.3	1.2	1.1	1.1
80%+	7.4	5.6	4.7	4.2	3.8	3.3	2.8	2.4	2.1	2.0	1.8	1.7	1.7	1.5	1.4	1.3	1.2	1.1
−	10.3	7.1	5.7	4.9	4.4	3.7	3.1	2.6	2.3	2.1	2.0	1.8	1.8	1.6	1.5	1.3	1.2	1.2
70%+	9.1	6.8	5.6	5.0	4.5	3.9	3.3	2.8	2.5	2.3	2.1	2.0	1.9	1.8	1.6	1.5	1.4	1.3
−	11.1	7.7	6.3	5.5	4.9	4.2	3.5	2.9	2.6	2.4	2.2	2.1	2.0	1.8	1.7	1.5	1.4	1.3
50%+	11.0	7.9	6.5	5.7	5.1	4.4	3.7	3.1	2.8	2.5	2.4	2.2	2.1	2.0	1.8	1.6	1.5	1.4
−	11.0	7.9	6.5	5.7	5.1	4.4	3.7	3.1	2.8	2.5	2.4	2.2	2.1	2.0	1.8	1.6	1.5	1.4
30%+	11.1	7.7	6.3	5.5	4.9	4.2	3.5	2.9	2.6	2.4	2.2	2.1	2.0	1.8	1.7	1.5	1.4	1.3
−	9.1	6.8	5.6	5.0	4.5	3.9	3.3	2.8	2.5	2.3	2.1	2.0	1.9	1.8	1.6	1.5	1.4	1.3
20%+	10.3	7.1	5.7	4.9	4.4	3.7	3.1	2.6	2.3	2.1	2.0	1.8	1.8	1.6	1.5	1.3	1.2	1.2
−	7.4	5.6	4.7	4.2	3.8	3.3	2.8	2.4	2.1	2.0	1.6	1.7	1.7	1.5	1.4	1.3	1.2	1.1
15%+	9.7	6.6	5.3	4.5	4.0	3.4	2.9	2.4	2.1	1.9	1.8	1.7	1.6	1.5	1.3	1.2	1.1	1.1
−	6.3	4.8	4.1	3.6	3.3	2.9	2.5	2.1	1.9	1.7	1.6	1.5	1.5	1.4	1.2	1.1	1.0	1.0
10%+	8.8	5.8	4.6	4.0	3.5	2.9	2.5	2.0	1.8	1.6	1.5	1.4	1.4	1.3	1.1	1.0	0.9	0.9
−	4.9	3.8	3.3	2.9	2.7	2.3	2.0	1.7	1.5	1.4	1.3	1.3	1.2	1.1	1.0	0.9	0.9	0.8
5%+	7.4	4.7	3.7	3.1	2.7	2.3	1.9	1.5	1.4	1.2	1.1	1.1	1.0	0.9	0.8	0.8	0.7	0.7
−	3.1	2.5	2.2	2.0	1.8	1.6	1.4	1.2	1.1	1.0	0.9	0.9	0.9	0.8	0.7	0.7	0.6	0.6
3%+	6.6	4.1	3.2	2.6	2.3	1.9	1.6	1.3	1.1	1.0	0.9	0.9	0.8	0.8	0.7	0.6	0.6	0.5
−	2.1	1.8	1.6	1.4	1.3	1.2	1.0	0.9	0.8	0.8	0.7	0.7	0.6	0.6	0.6	0.5	0.5	0.5
1%+	5.6	3.2	2.4	1.9	1.7	1.3	1.1	0.8	0.7	0.6	0.6	0.6	0.5	0.5	0.4	0.4	0.3	0.3
−	0.9	0.8	0.7	0.7	0.6	0.6	0.5	0.5	0.4	0.4	0.4	0.4	0.3	0.3	0.3	0.3	0.3	0.2

Notes to Table A-2

The entries in this table (which appear on the next two pages) are appropriate for *comparisons* between (a) males and females, (b) those who do and do not plan four years of college, and (c) those falling into different categories of the five-level index of drug usage. The table entries are also appropriate for *one-year trends* for the total sample and any of the subgroups except region. Most other trends and subgroup comparisons require that the table entries be multiplied by an adjustment factor, given below.

Outline of Steps to Follow (see text of appendix for illustrations)

1. Locate the portion of the table with "p" values closest to the two percentages being compared.

2. Locate the specific entry closest to the weighted Ns for the two percentages.

3. Multiply that entry by any necessary adjustment factor (see below).

4. That table value (or adjusted table value), when added to and subtracted from the difference between the two percentages, yields the 95 percent confidence interval for the difference.

5. Also, if the table value (or adjusted table value) is smaller than the difference between the two percentages, then the difference may be described as "statistically significant at the 95 percent level."

	Adjustment Factor (to be multiplied by table entry)
Adjustment Factors	
For comparisons between blacks and whites	
based on single form data	*
based on five form data	1.25
For comparisons between any two regions	
based on single form data	1.15
based on five form data	1.50
For one-year trends involving any region	
based on single form data	*
based on five form data	1.25
For trends over two or more years involving any region	
based on single form data	*
based on five form data	1.35
For trends over two or more years involving all other groups	
based on single form data	*
based on five form data	1.15

*indicates that no adjustment is necessary for category shown

NOTE: The table entries were calculated using the following formula: $1.96\sqrt{p(1-p)}\,\frac{1}{N'_1}+\frac{1}{N'_2}$

where $N'_1=N_1/DEFF$, and $N'_2=N_2/DEFF$, $DEFF=1.3+.000075\left[\frac{N_1 N_2}{N_1+N_2}\right]$

Table A-2

Confidence Intervals (95% Confidence Level) for Differences Between Two Percentages

$N_1 =$	100	200	300	400	500	700	1000	1500	2000	3000	4000	5000	7000	10000	15000	20000
$N_2 = 100$	3.2															
200	2.7	2.2														
300	2.6	2.0	1.8													
400	2.5	1.9	1.7	1.6												
500	2.4	1.9	1.6	1.5	1.4											
700	2.4	1.8	1.6	1.4	1.3	1.2										
1000	2.3	1.7	1.5	1.3	1.2	1.1	1.0									
1500	2.3	1.7	1.4	1.3	1.2	1.0	0.9	0.8								
2000	2.3	1.7	1.4	1.2	1.1	1.0	0.9	0.8	0.7							
3000	2.3	1.6	1.4	1.2	1.1	1.0	0.8	0.7	0.7	0.6						
4000	2.3	1.6	1.4	1.2	1.1	0.9	0.8	0.7	0.7	0.6	0.6					
5000	2.3	1.6	1.3	1.2	1.1	0.9	0.8	0.7	0.6	0.6	0.5	0.5				
7000	2.3	1.6	1.3	1.2	1.1	0.9	0.8	0.7	0.6	0.5	0.5	0.5	0.4			
10000	2.2	1.6	1.3	1.2	1.0	0.9	0.8	0.7	0.6	0.5	0.5	0.5	0.4	0.4		
15000	2.2	1.6	1.3	1.2	1.0	0.9	0.8	0.6	0.6	0.5	0.5	0.4	0.4	0.4	0.4	
20000	2.2	1.6	1.3	1.1	1.0	0.9	0.8	0.6	0.6	0.5	0.5	0.4	0.4	0.4	0.3	0.3

p = 1% or 99%

$N_1 =$	100	200	300	400	500	700	1000	1500	2000	3000	4000	5000	7000	10000	15000	20000
$N_2 = 100$	5.4															
200	4.7	3.8														
300	4.4	3.5	3.1													
400	4.3	3.3	2.9	2.7												
500	4.2	3.2	2.8	2.6	2.4											
700	4.1	3.1	2.7	2.4	2.3	2.1										
1000	4.0	3.0	2.5	2.3	2.1	1.9	1.8									
1500	4.0	2.9	2.4	2.2	2.0	1.8	1.6	1.5								
2000	3.9	2.9	2.4	2.1	1.9	1.7	1.5	1.4	1.3							
3000	3.9	2.8	2.3	2.1	1.9	1.7	1.5	1.3	1.2	1.1						
4000	3.9	2.8	2.3	2.0	1.9	1.6	1.4	1.2	1.1	1.0	0.9					
5000	3.9	2.8	2.3	2.0	1.8	1.6	1.4	1.2	1.1	1.0	0.9	0.9				
7000	3.9	2.8	2.3	2.0	1.8	1.6	1.4	1.2	1.0	0.9	0.9	0.8	0.8			
10000	3.9	2.8	2.3	2.0	1.8	1.5	1.3	1.1	1.0	0.9	0.8	0.8	0.7	0.7		
15000	3.8	2.7	2.3	2.0	1.8	1.5	1.3	1.1	1.0	0.9	0.8	0.7	0.7	0.6	0.6	
20000	3.8	2.7	2.3	2.0	1.8	1.5	1.3	1.1	1.0	0.9	0.8	0.7	0.7	0.6	0.6	0.6

p = 3% or 97%

Table A-2 (continued)

$N_1 =$	100	200	300	400	500	700	1000	1500	2000	3000	4000	5000	7000	10000	15000	20000
$N_2 = 100$	6.9															
200	6.0	4.9														
300	5.6	4.5	4.0													
400	5.5	4.3	3.8	3.5												
500	5.4	4.1	3.6	3.3	3.1											
700	5.2	3.9	3.4	3.1	2.9	2.7							$p = 5\%$ or 95%			
1000	5.1	3.8	3.2	2.9	2.7	2.5	2.2									
1500	5.1	3.7	3.1	2.8	2.6	2.3	2.1	1.9								
2000	5.0	3.6	3.1	2.7	2.5	2.2	2.0	1.7	1.6							
3000	5.0	3.6	3.0	2.6	2.4	2.1	1.9	1.6	1.5	1.4						
4000	5.0	3.6	3.0	2.6	2.4	2.1	1.8	1.6	1.4	1.3	1.2					
5000	4.9	3.6	2.9	2.6	2.3	2.0	1.8	1.5	1.4	1.2	1.2	1.1				
7000	4.9	3.5	2.9	2.6	2.3	2.0	1.7	1.5	1.3	1.2	1.1	1.0	1.0			
10000	4.9	3.5	2.9	2.5	2.3	2.0	1.7	1.4	1.3	1.1	1.1	1.0	0.9	0.9		
15000	4.9	3.5	2.9	2.5	2.3	2.0	1.7	1.4	1.3	1.1	1.0	1.0	0.9	0.8	0.8	
20000	4.9	3.5	2.9	2.5	2.3	1.9	1.7	1.4	1.3	1.1	1.0	0.9	0.9	0.8	0.7	0.7

$N_1 =$	100	200	300	400	500	700	1000	1500	2000	3000	4000	5000	7000	10000	15000	20000
$N_1 = 100$	9.5															
200	8.2	6.7														
300	7.8	6.2	5.5													
400	7.5	5.9	5.2	4.8												
500	7.4	5.7	4.9	4.6	4.3											
700	7.2	5.4	4.7	4.3	4.0	3.7							$p = 10\%$ or 90%			
1000	7.1	5.2	4.5	4.0	3.7	3.4	3.1									
1500	7.0	5.1	4.3	3.8	3.5	3.2	2.8	2.6								
2000	6.9	5.0	4.2	3.7	3.4	3.0	2.7	2.4	2.2							
3000	6.9	4.9	4.1	3.6	3.3	2.9	2.6	2.2	2.1	1.9						
4000	6.8	4.9	4.1	3.6	3.3	2.8	2.5	2.2	2.0	1.8	1.7					
5000	6.8	4.9	4.0	3.6	3.2	2.8	2.4	2.1	1.9	1.7	1.6	1.5				
7000	6.8	4.9	4.0	3.5	3.2	2.8	2.4	2.0	1.8	1.6	1.5	1.4	1.3			
10000	6.8	4.8	4.0	3.5	3.2	2.7	2.3	2.0	1.8	1.6	1.4	1.4	1.3	1.2		
15000	6.8	4.8	4.0	3.5	3.1	2.7	2.3	2.0	1.8	1.5	1.4	1.3	1.2	1.1	1.1	
20000	6.8	4.8	4.0	3.5	3.1	2.7	2.3	1.9	1.7	1.5	1.4	1.3	1.2	1.1	1.0	1.0

Table A-2 (continued)

p = 15% or 85%

	N₁ = 100	200	300	400	500	700	1000	1500	2000	3000	4000	5000	7000	10000	15000	20000
N₂ = 100	11.3															
200	9.8	8.0														
300	9.3	7.3	6.6													
400	9.0	7.0	6.2	5.7												
500	8.8	6.7	5.9	5.4	5.1											
700	8.6	6.5	5.6	5.1	4.8	4.4										
1000	8.4	6.2	5.3	4.8	4.5	4.0	3.7									
1500	8.3	6.1	5.1	4.6	4.2	3.8	3.4	3.0								
2000	8.2	6.0	5.0	4.5	4.1	3.6	3.2	2.9	2.7							
3000	8.2	5.9	4.9	4.3	3.9	3.5	3.0	2.7	2.5	2.2						
4000	8.1	5.8	4.9	4.3	3.9	3.4	2.9	2.6	2.3	2.1	2.0					
5000	8.1	5.8	4.8	4.2	3.8	3.3	2.9	2.5	2.3	2.0	1.9	1.8				
7000	8.1	5.8	4.8	4.2	3.8	3.3	2.8	2.4	2.2	1.9	1.8	1.7	1.6			
10000	8.1	5.8	4.8	4.2	3.8	3.2	2.8	2.4	2.1	1.9	1.7	1.6	1.5	1.4		
15000	8.1	5.7	4.7	4.1	3.7	3.2	2.7	2.3	2.1	1.8	1.7	1.6	1.4	1.3	1.3	
20000	8.0	5.7	4.7	4.1	3.7	3.2	2.7	2.3	2.1	1.8	1.6	1.5	1.4	1.3	1.2	1.2

p = 20% or 80%

	N₁ = 100	200	300	400	500	700	1000	1500	2000	3000	4000	5000	7000	10000	15000	20000
N₂ = 100	12.7															
200	11.0	9.0														
300	10.4	8.2	7.4													
400	10.0	7.8	6.9	6.4												
500	9.8	7.5	6.6	6.1	5.7											
700	9.6	7.2	6.2	5.7	5.3	4.9										
1000	9.4	7.0	6.0	5.4	5.0	4.5	4.1									
1500	9.3	6.8	5.7	5.1	4.7	4.2	3.8	3.4								
2000	9.2	6.7	5.6	5.0	4.6		3.6	3.2	3.0							
3000	9.1	6.6	5.5	4.9	4.4	3.9	3.4	3.0	2.8	2.5						
4000	9.1	6.5	5.4	4.8	4.3	3.8	3.3	2.9	2.6	2.4	2.2					
5000	9.1	6.5	5.4	4.7	4.3	3.7	3.2	2.8	2.6	2.3	2.1	2.0				
7000	9.1	6.5	5.4	4.7	4.2	3.7	3.2	2.7	2.5	2.2	2.0	1.9	1.8			
10000	9.0	6.5	5.3	4.7	4.2	3.6	3.1	2.7	2.4	2.1	1.9	1.8	1.7	1.6		
15000	9.0	6.4	5.3	4.6	4.2	3.6	3.1	2.6	2.3	2.0	1.9	1.7	1.6	1.5	1.4	
20000	9.0	6.4	5.3	4.6	4.2	3.6	3.1	2.6	2.3	2.0	1.8	1.7	1.6	1.5	1.4	1.3

Table A-2 (continued)

p = 30% or 70%

N₂ \ N₁ =	100	200	300	400	500	700	1000	1500	2000	3000	4000	5000	7000	10000	15000	20000
100	14.5															
200	12.6	10.3														
300	11.9	9.4	8.4													
400	11.5	8.9	7.9	7.3												
500	11.3	8.6	7.6	7.0	6.6											
700	11.0	8.3	7.2	6.5	6.1	5.6										
1000	10.8	8.0	6.8	6.2	5.7	5.2	4.7									
1500	10.6	7.8	6.6	5.9	5.4	4.8	4.3	3.9								
2000	10.6	7.7	6.4	5.7	5.2	4.6	4.1	3.7	3.4							
3000	10.5	7.6	6.3	5.6	5.1	4.4	3.9	3.4	3.2	2.9						
4000	10.4	7.5	6.2	5.5	5.0	4.3	3.8	3.3	3.0	2.7	2.5					
5000	10.4	7.5	6.2	5.4	4.9	4.3	3.7	3.2	2.9	2.6	2.4	2.3				
7000	10.4	7.4	6.1	5.4	4.9	4.2	3.6	3.1	2.5	2.3	2.2	2.1				
10000	10.4	7.4	6.1	5.3	4.8	4.2	3.6	3.0	2.7	2.4	2.2	2.1	1.9	1.8		
15000	10.3	7.4	6.1	5.3	4.8	4.1	3.5	3.0	2.7	2.3	2.1	2.0	1.8	1.7	1.6	
20000	10.3	7.4	6.1	5.3	4.8	4.1	3.5	3.0	2.6	2.3	2.1	2.0	1.8	1.7	1.6	1.5

p = 35% or 65%

N₂ \ N₁ =	100	200	300	400	500	700	1000	1500	2000	3000	4000	5000	7000	10000	15000	20000
100	15.8															
200	13.7	11.2														
300	13.0	10.3	9.2													
400	12.6	9.8	8.6	8.0												
500	12.3	9.4	8.2	7.6	7.2											
700	12.0	9.0	7.8	7.1	6.7	6.1										
1000	11.8	8.7	7.5	6.7	6.2	5.6	5.1									
1500	11.6	8.5	7.2	6.4	5.9	5.3	4.7	4.3								
2000	11.5	8.4	7.0	6.2	5.7	5.1	4.5	4.0	3.7							
3000	11.4	8.2	6.9	6.1	5.5	4.8	4.3	3.7	3.4	3.1						
4000	11.4	8.2	6.8	6.0	5.4	4.7	4.1	3.6	3.3	3.0	2.8					
5000	11.3	8.1	6.7	5.9	5.4	4.7	4.1	3.5	3.2	2.8	2.7	2.5				
7000	11.3	8.1	6.7	5.9	5.3	4.6	4.0	3.4	3.1	2.7	2.5	2.4	2.2			
10000	11.3	8.1	6.7	5.8	5.3	4.5	3.9	3.3	3.0	2.6	2.4	2.3	2.1	2.0		
15000	11.3	8.0	6.6	5.8	5.2	4.5	3.8	3.3	2.9	2.5	2.3	2.2	2.0	1.9	1.8	
20000	11.3	8.0	6.6	5.8	5.2	4.5	3.8	3.2	2.9	2.5	2.3	2.1	2.0	1.8	1.7	1.6

Appendix B
Procedures Used to Derive Design Effects and Sampling Errors

Appendix A provided a very brief and relatively nontechnical explanation of sampling error estimates, accompanied by two tables of confidence intervals which can be used to ascertain the accuracy of most percentages reported in this volume. The present appendix is intended to provide some background concerning the strategy and rationale involved in computing these confidence intervals. It also offers guidance for those wishing to make sampling computations beyond those contained in Appendix A.

This appendix, like the first, is intended to be readable and usable by the nonstatistician. For that reason, we take the time to outline (albeit briefly) a number of relatively elementary factors involved in estimating confidence intervals.

Factors Influencing the Size of Confidence Intervals

The most straightforward types of samples, from a statistical standpoint at least, are simple random samples. In such samples the confidence limits for a proportion are influenced by the size of the sample or subgroups being considered and also by the size of the proportion. For example, the 95 percent confidence interval for a proportion p based on a simple random sample of N cases is approximated by:
$p \pm 1.96 \sqrt{p(1-p)/N}$. In a complex probability sample such as the present one, there are a number of other factors which influence the size of confidence limits. This section lists all of the factors which have been taken into account in calculating confidence intervals for use with the data in this volume, beginning with the most simple factors and then proceeding to the more complex.

Number of Cases (N). Other things equal, the larger a sample (or subgroup within a sample), the smaller or more precise will be the confidence interval for a percentage based on that sample. One of the factors determining the size of the confidence interval is $1/\sqrt{N}$. Thus, for example, if all other things were equal, a sample of 400 would have confidence intervals half as large (or twice as precise) as a sample of 100, because $1/\sqrt{400}$ is half as large as $1/\sqrt{100}$.

Size of Percentage. Other things equal, percentage values around 50 percent have larger confidence intervals than higher or lower percentage values. This is because another of the factors determining the size of the confidence interval is $\sqrt{p(1-p)}$ where p is a proportion ranging from 0 to 1.0 (or, to put it in percentage terms, the factor is $\sqrt{x\%(100-x\%)}$). Thus, for example, a proportion of either .1 or .9 (a percentage of either 10 percent or 90 percent) will have a confidence interval only three-fifths as large as the confidence interval around a proportion of .5 (or 50 percent), because $\sqrt{.1(1-.1)}$ is three-fifths as large as $\sqrt{.5(1-.5)}$.

Design Effects in Complex Samples. Under conditions of simple random sampling, a confidence interval can be determined solely on the basis of the number of cases and the percentage value involved. More complex samples such as the one used in the present study make use of stratification and clustering and often differential weighting of respondent scores, and these all influence sampling error. While stratification tends to heighten the precision of a sample, the effects of clustering and weighting reduce precision (compared with a simple random sample of the same size). Therefore, it is not appropriate to apply the

257

standard, simple random sampling formulas to such complex samples in order to obtain estimates of sampling errors, because they would almost always underestimate the actual sampling errors.

Methods exist for correcting for this underestimation, however. Kish (1965, p. 258) defines a correction term called the design effect (DEFF), where:

$$DEFF = \frac{\text{actual sampling variance}}{\begin{array}{l}\text{expected sampling variance} \\ \text{from a simple random sample} \\ \text{with same number of elements}\end{array}}$$

Thus, if the actual sampling variance in a complex sample is four times as large as the expected sampling variance from a simple random sample with the same number of cases, the DEFF is 4.0. Since confidence intervals are proportionate to the square root of variance, the confidence intervals for such a sample would be twice as large (because the square root of 4 is 2) as the confidence interval for a simple random sample with the same number of cases. A fairly simple and straightforward way of applying the concept of design effect may be to note that an increase in design effect has the same impact on precision as a reduction in the number of cases in a simple random sample. For example, a sample of 16,000 cases with a design effect of 4.0 would have the same degree of precision (the same size confidence intervals around various percentages) as a simple random sample of 4,000.

In principle, every different statistic resulting from a complex sample can have its own design effect, and different statistics in the same sample may have quite different design effects. However, it is not feasible to compute every design effect, nor would it be feasible to report every one. Thus, in practice, design effects are averaged across a number of statistics and these average values are used to estimate the design effects for other statistics based on the same sample. Sometimes a single design effect is applied to all statistics of a given type (e.g., percentages) for a given sample. In the present study, however, a rather extensive exploration of design effects revealed a number of systematic differences. These systematic differences have to do with the particular measures being examined, the subgroups involved, and the question of whether a trend over time is being considered. The most consistent difference involves the number of cases in the group or subgroup for which the design effect is computed.

The Relationship between Subgroup Size and Design Effects. Kish et al. (1976) have observed that design effects tend to be smaller for subgroups than for total samples; moreover, the smaller the subgroup the smaller the design effect is likely to be. The ex-

planation for this widespread phenomenon is that the average number of cases in each sampling cluster is an important factor in determining the size of the design effect, and as subgroup size decreases so does this average number of cases per cluster. This point is illustrated by several subgroups treated in the present volume — males, females, those planning four years of college, and those not planning four years of college. All (or virtually all) of the schools in the sample have both male and female students, as well as some students who plan four years of college and others who do not. Thus, each of these four subgroups is spread more or less evenly across the full number of clusters (schools). Since each of these subgroups includes roughly half of the total sample, the average number of cases per cluster is about half as large as for the total sample, and this leads to a smaller design effect than is found for the total sample. Other subgroups involving different patterns of drug use are also distributed more or less evenly across all clusters and thus are subject to the same phenomenon of smaller design effects because of the smaller number of cases per cluster.

One very important exception to the pattern of smaller design effects for subgroups involves the four geographic region subgroups presented in this volume. These subgroups do not cut across all clusters; instead, regions have been described as "segregated" subgroups, in contrast to the "cross-class" subgroups discussed above. For such segregated subgroups the average number of cases per cluster is about the same as is found in the total sample, and thus the design effects are not lower than those for the total sample (Kish et al., 1976). Another subgroup which is in some respects similar to regional subgroups is the category of blacks. Black respondents are not found equally across high schools throughout the United States. There are, of course, regional differences in proportions of blacks, and these contribute substantially to this lack of equal distribution. In addition, there are patterns of segregation in housing which continue to be reflected in the unequal distribution of blacks in high schools. The net effect of these several factors is that the black subgroup in our sample is "partially segregated" in a sampling sense as well as in the more usual usage of that word. For that reason, the design effects for blacks are somewhat larger than for other subgroups of approximately similar size.

Because the subgroups consisting of blacks and the four regional groups all have larger design effects than other subgroups of the same size, it is necessary to adjust the confidence intervals for these subgroups as indicated in Appendix A. (At a later point in the present appendix we will say more about these adjustment factors.)

One other kind of "subgroup" must be noted in this discussion of the relationship between subgroup size and design effects. One-fifth of the total sample filled out each of the five separate questionnaire forms, and thus the respondents to each of these forms may be viewed as a "cross-class" subgroup of the total sample. The average cluster size for a single form is exactly 20 percent of the average cluster size for the total sample. That means, of course, that the single form samples (which are the basis for the large majority of the data presented in this volume) are distinctly more "efficient" than the sample based on all five forms. Accordingly, single form data have much smaller design effects (as displayed later in this appendix).

Design Effects for Comparisons between Subgroups. We noted above that a number of subgroups treated in this volume can be described as "cross-class" subgroups, meaning that members of the subgroup are distributed more or less evenly across sampling clusters. For these kinds of subgroups, it turns out that *comparisons* are relatively efficient, from a sampling standpoint. The technical explanation for this phenomenon is that there is a higher degree of covariance between such subgroup pairs than would be the case in a comparison of independent subgroups. Now let us offer a fairly nontechnical illustration to indicate why this is so. Suppose that a researcher interested in use of marijuana during the senior year of high school obtained data from five high schools concerning female seniors' marijuana use and data from five other high schools concerning male seniors' marijuana use. Suppose that the percentage values for marijuana use during senior year were as follows:

Female seniors (five schools): 60%, 20%, 65%, 30%, 50%

Male seniors (five other schools): 40%, 80%, 25%, 70%, 60%

Even though there is a difference of ten percentage points between males and females (if the five schools in each case are averaged), there is still so much variability among schools that one would not conclude with very much confidence that females in general are less likely than males to use marijuana during the senior year of high school. Suppose, on the other hand, that the researcher had obtained data from a total of only five schools and had obtained data concerning both male and female seniors in each school as follows:

	Females	Males
School A	60%	70%
School B	20%	25%
School C	65%	80%
School D	30%	40%
School E	50%	60%

The same group of percentages, this time based on five pairings of males and females rather than independent observations, are much more strongly suggestive of systematic differences between the sexes.

A process analogous to that illustrated above is involved when "cross-class" subgroups are compared, and the increased accuracy or sampling efficiency is reflected in relatively small sampling errors and design effects.

Design Effects for Trends. Thus far this discussion of factors influencing design effects and confidence intervals has focused only on groups and subgroups within a single year. But one of the central purposes of the Monitoring the Future project is to monitor trends over time; indeed, the study procedures have been standardized across years insofar as possible in order to provide the opportunity for sensitive measurement of change. One of the factors designed to produce an added degree of consistency from one year to the next is the use of each school for two data collections, which means that for any two successive years half of the sample of schools is the same. This, plus the fact that the other half of the school sample in a given year is from the same primary sampling units as the half sample it replaced, means that there is a good deal of consistency in the sampling and clustering of the sample from one year to the next. As a result, when cross-year comparisons are made (say, between 1976 and 1977), the design effects are appreciably smaller (i.e., the efficiency is greater) than if completely independent samples of schools had been drawn each year. In other words, the 1976 and 1977 samples are not independent; on the contrary, there is a considerable degree of covariance between them. A similar level of covariance occurs between any pair of adjacent-year samples (e.g., 1977 and 1978), because about half of the schools in both samples were the same. This covariance, or partial "matching," reduces the design effect for differences observed between adjacent years, compared to what they would have been with totally independent samples.

It follows from the discussion above that a trend over an interval greater than one year (e.g., a comparison between 1976 and 1978 which involves totally non-overlapping school samples) is likely to have a design effect which is larger than that for a comparison between adjacent-year samples.

Variables with Unusually Large Design Effects. Kish et al. (1976) stress the importance of computing sampling errors for many kinds of variables, and they point out that they have found "very wide ranges in values of sampling errors (standard errors and design effects) between diverse variables within the same survey" (p. 21). Our own experience has been that, among most variables, the variation in sampling errors and design effects seems more random than consistent, and thus we are reasonably comfortable with the use of averaging procedures (described below) in order to derive a set of general purpose tables. There are some important exceptions to the above generalization, however. Variables which are likely to be grouped according to geographical area (region and/or urbanicity), as well as variables that may differ systematically from one school to another, show much higher than usual amounts of homogeneity within sample clusters. It follows necessarily that such variables also have much higher than usual design effects. The variables in the Monitoring the Future study which seem most likely to show such high design effects tend to be grouped into the questionnaire segment dealing with background 'factors and educational aspirations (Section C of all questionnaire forms). These variables were excluded from the process of computing overall design effects and the confidence intervals provided in Tables A-1 and A-2. Appendix A provides a further discussion of some of these variables and offers some suggestions for adjusting the confidence interval tables to deal with them.

Procedures Used in Deriving Design Effects and Tables of Confidence Intervals

Having taken some pains to review the several factors which can influence design effects and confidence intervals, it is now a fairly simple matter for us to summarize the steps followed to compute the tables of confidence intervals shown in Appendix A. We were heavily influenced in this effort by the work of Kish and his colleagues (Kish, 1965; Kish et al., 1976) in two ways. First, we followed their recommendation that sampling errors be computed and averaged across a goodly number of variables and subgroups. Second, we paid particular attention to their observation that design effects tend to be smaller for subgroups than for total samples (a point discussed earlier in this appendix).

Confidence Intervals for Single Percentages. Our procedure was to compute sampling errors and design effects for most of the variables which are common to all five forms (those in the C sections of all questionnaires, and those in the B sections of Forms 2 through 5), and for every twentieth variable in the A, D, and E sections of Forms 2 through 5. (Form 1 was omitted because most of this form is comprised of drug-related items, and such items involve high proportions of missing data because respondents are instructed to skip over many questions which are not applicable to them). Design effects were computed for each of the subgroups reported in this volume, as well as for the total sample. Design effects for each subgroup and for the total were averaged across variables for the C sec-

tion material (all five forms), the B section material (drug use measures, all five forms), and the sampling of variables from the A, D, and E sections (single form data). As noted earlier, the variables which showed unusually high levels of homogeneity within sample clusters were excluded from the C section variables when they were averaged. The 1977 data were used for this analysis. Later replication using 1976 data provided nearly identical values.

The averaging process consisted of taking a mean of the *square roots* of the design effects. Kish and his colleagues (1976) refer to the design effect as DEFF, and to the square root of the design effect as DEFT; thus, $\sqrt{\text{DEFF}} = \text{DEFT}$. We will find it useful to use this terminology in what follows. The rationale for computing means of DEFT rather than DEFF is that the former value is directly proportionate to the size of confidence intervals. A further reason for doing so is that the values of DEFT approximate a normal distribution much more closely than the values of DEFF, which are skewed upward. (A comparison of mean DEFTs and median DEFTs showed them to be quite similar, something which certainly is not true of mean and median DEFFs).

Bearing in mind that design effects tend to be smaller for subgroups than for total samples, and bearing in mind also that confidence intervals are directly proportional to DEFT and to $\sqrt{N}$, we plotted the mean DEFT values for the total sample and for all subgroups, in each case relating DEFT to $\sqrt{N}$. The results are shown in Figure B-1. Note that distinctions are made between "cross-class" and "segregated" subgroups, and between mean DEFTs based on five forms and those based on single forms (the $\sqrt{N}$ values for the latter are, of course, much smaller).*

Setting aside the "segregated" subgroups (regions and blacks) for the moment, it is clear that the rest of the mean DEFTs in Figure B-1 show a very clear and consistent pattern: the higher the value $\sqrt{N}$ the higher the mean DEFT. It turns out that these mean DEFT values are very closely approximated by the function $\text{DEFT} = \sqrt{1.3 + .00015N}$, as shown by the solid line in the figure. (The function can also be stated as $\text{DEFF} = 1.3 + .00015N$.) The particular parameters in that function were derived empirically, but the basic function (i.e., $\text{DEFT} = \sqrt{a + bN}$) was adapted directly from the work of Kish et al. (1976).

Given the above function that fitted the mean DEFT values for the total sample and the "cross-class" subgroups, we returned to the problem of assigning DEFT values for the "segregated" subgroups. The simplest solution was to select two adjustment factors which could be multiplied by the confidence interval values in Table A-1. These adjustment factors are shown by the dashed lines in Figure B-1; they cor-

---

* The five form data consisted of C section material, excluding those variables related to region, urbanicity, and/or socioeconomic level.

Figure B-1
Design Effects for Single Percentages

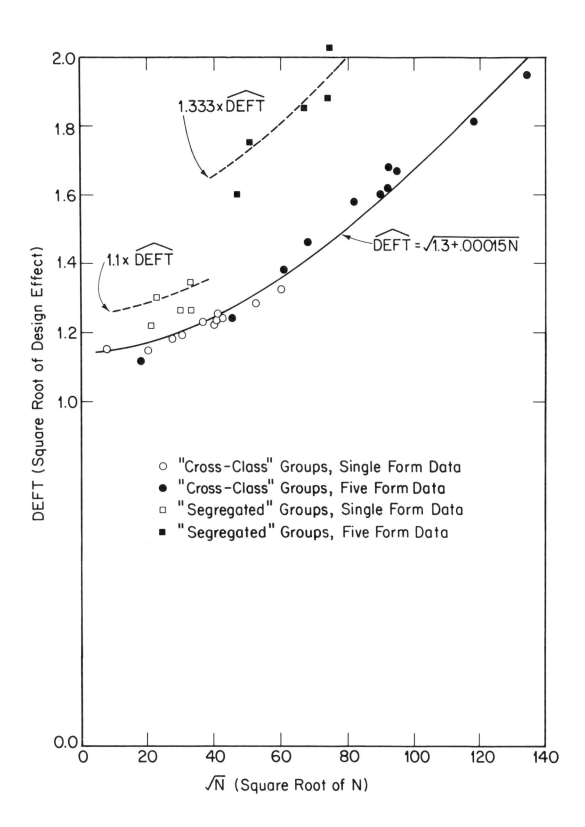

respond to multiplying the "standard" DEFT (solid line) by a factor of 1.1 for single form data and by a factor of 1.33 for five form data. These adjustments, which were selected on empirical grounds, yield design effects for the "segregated" subgroups which are approximately equal to the design effects for the total sample (treating single form and five form data separately, of course). This is reassuring, since Kish et al. (1976) have reported that "segregated" subgroups can in general be expected to show design effects approximately equivalent to the design effects for the total sample.

After the data in Figure B-1 were plotted and the form of the main function (indicated by the solid line) was determined, DEFT values for drug use measures (material in Section B of all forms) were checked. It was found that the DEFTs for only two drug categories, alcohol and marijuana, exceeded the values indicated by the function; accordingly, adjustment factors were developed for these two drugs (1.6 and 1.35, respectively).

Confidence Intervals for Differences between Two Percentages. Our procedure here was directly parallel to that followed in determining confidence intervals for single percentages. DEFT values for the differences between 1977 and 1976 percentages were computed using virtually the same set of items as used earlier. Also computed were mean DEFT values for comparisons in the same year between subgroups such as males and females, those who did and did not plan to complete four years of college, blacks and whites, pairings of regions, and pairings of drug use groups. It was found that, for any given level of N, the mean DEFT values for subgroup comparisons were quite similar to the mean DEFT values for one-year trends; accordingly, all of these mean DEFTs were included in Figure B-2, which plots mean DEFTs for differences between percentages. In this figure, as in Figure B-1, the strong relationship was evident between mean DEFTs and the numbers of cases in the two groups being compared. This relationship can be very closely approximated by the function DEFT = $\sqrt{1.3 + .000075N}$ (which can also be stated DEFF = 1.3 + .000075N), where N = $2N_1N_2/N_1 + N_2$.

It was expected on grounds of sampling theory that as we found earlier, the function which fit most differences between percentages would not fit differences involving regions and differences involving blacks. In fact, the data indicated that some adjustment is necessary for black-white comparisons using data from all five forms, and also for comparisons as well as trends involving any region. We have not tried to show those adjustments in Figure B-2, but the several values involved are shown in the guidelines to Table A-2.

It was also expected on the grounds of sampling theory that trends across an interval of two or more years would show somewhat higher values of DEFT than one-year trends. It turned out that this was true only for data from all five forms; data based on one form only did not show significantly higher values. The adjustment factors for trends involving five forms over two or more years are shown in Table A-2.

Use of Weighted Numbers of Cases in Entering Confidence Interval Tables. We should mention in passing that the recommendations for using the tables in Appendix A indicate that *weighted* N values should be used. The computer program which generated our design effect statistics makes use of weights in calculating percentages and actual sampling variances. But in computing the DEFF ratio, defined as the actual sampling variance divided by the expected sampling variance from a simple random sample with the same number of elements, the program makes use of the *unweighted* numbers of cases to determine "the same number of elements." Since the mean weights used in the 1975, 1976, and 1977 data tables are slightly lower than 1.0, this means that when entering the tables in Appendix A with weighted data from those years, one is being very slightly "conservative" (slightly reduced risk of a Type 1 error, slightly increased risk of a Type 2 error). It is important to realize that if one took the trouble to make corrections for this "conservatism," the correction would rarely be as great as multiplying the Table A-1 and Table A-2 entries by a factor of .95; and in the large majority of cases the correction would involve multiplying by a factor of about .98. We find such discrepancies to be trivially small, particularly when compared with what Kish et al. (1976, p. 12) describe as the "heroic simplifications" required in some of the steps leading to general purpose tables of design effects and confidence intervals.

Before the 1978 data tables were produced we had come to realize the advantages in having weighted values which averaged 1.0; accordingly, beginning with the 1978 data, the weighted N values in the tables do approximate the actual numbers of cases quite closely. But it was impractical to redo the 1975 through 1977 data tables to incorporate this refinement. Another alternative would have been to employ slightly different versions of Tables A-1 and A-2, containing slightly different confidence intervals for each of those three years; however, we felt that such an approach could introduce confusion when cross-year comparisons were made. Thus, we opted for the solution which seems to us to be most simple and manageable, even though it involves the slight degree of "conservatism" noted above. For readers who find this solution undesirable, we have included Tables B-1 and B-2, which present weighted and unweighted Ns for the various subgroups for each year. Table B-1 contains Ns for all five forms (except for 1975 which shows Ns for Forms 2 through 5), and Table B-2 con-

Figure B-2
Design Effects for Differences Between Percentages

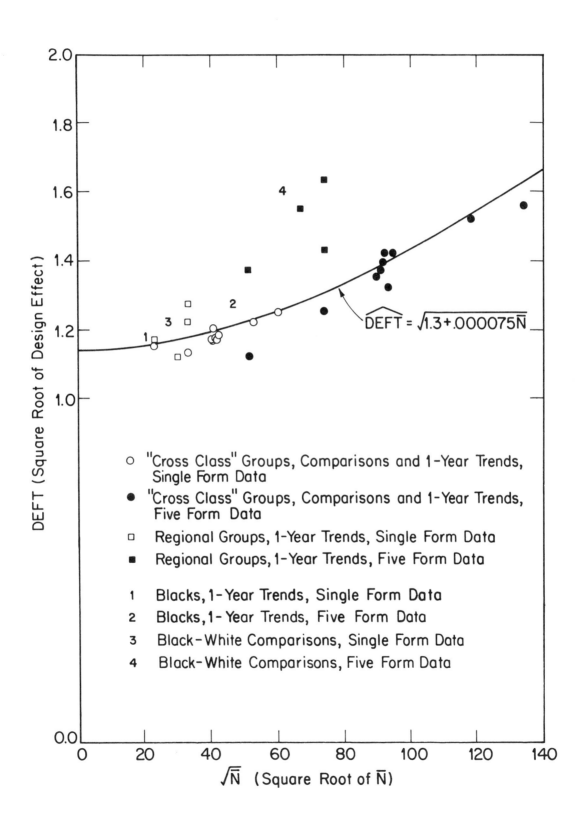

tains approximate Ns for a single form. Thus, readers who wish to avoid the slight "conservatism" (and also to be more precise for subgroups in 1978 and later whose average weight is not exactly 1.0) may determine the unweighted Ns. Some correction for missing data should be made in this case; this can be accomplished by calculating the percentage of missing data (using the weighted Ns from the data table and the weighted N from Table B-1 or B-2) and adjusting the unweighted N accordingly. These adjusted unweighted Ns can then be used in Appendix A.

TABLE B-1
Sample Sizes (Unweighted and Weighted) in Subgroups by Year

Number of Cases

	Class of 1975*		Class of 1976		Class of 1977		Class of 1978		Class of 1979		Class of 1980		Class of 1981		Class of 1982		Class of 1983		Class of 1984	
	Unwtd	Wtd	Unwtd	Wtd	Unwtd	Wtd	Unwtd	Wtd	Unwtd	Wtd	Unwtd	Wtd	Unwtd	Wtd	Unwtd	Wtd	Unwtd	Wtd	Unwtd	Wtd
Total Sample	12627	12108	16678	15138	18436	15830	18924	18916	16662	16662	16524	16524	18267	18267	18348	18348	16947	16947	16499	16499
Sex:																				
Male	5799	5571	7999	7241	8449	7358	8603	8779	7889	7778	7935	7744	8775	8725	8979	8828	8106	8074	7653	7800
Female	6371	6100	7924	7257	9188	7850	9416	9266	8139	8232	7874	8078	8752	8865	8610	8788	8160	8227	8144	8029
Race:																				
White	**	**	12933	11796	13818	12240	14663	14847	13432	13299	12894	12846	13625	13985	13753	13887	12697	12806	12223	12337
Black	**	**	1806	1716	2500	1938	2205	2096	1617	1742	1939	2098	2495	2265	2203	2080	2191	2067	2281	2244
Region:																				
Northeast	3014	2695	4034	3570	4760	3959	4841	4607	3926	4016	4281	3877	4269	4290	4719	4741	4130	4056	3658	3387
North Central	3951	3832	5098	4687	5697	4758	5576	5411	5385	4874	4340	4873	5069	5484	5223	5383	4245	4784	4018	4612
South	3366	3857	4177	4597	4908	4820	5566	6292	4713	5055	4667	5049	5513	5600	5191	5551	5522	5434	5726	5568
West	2296	1724	3369	2284	3071	2294	2941	2605	2638	2717	3236	2726	3416	2893	3215	2672	3050	2673	3097	2932
College Plans:																				
Complete 4 yrs	**		7963	6994	8933	7407	9264	8844	8571	8203	9191	8658	10256	9878	9851	9360	9342	9062	9114	9103
None or under 4 yrs	**		7179	6877	7764	7048	7857	8413	6715	7063	5995	6578	6486	7008	6971	7507	6214	6555	6002	6124
Illicit Drug Use:																				
None	4329	4400	6532	6091	6672	5878	6400	6595	5426	5654	5322	5591	5954	6148	6157	6328	6001	6082	6124	6199
Marijuana Only	2044	1894	3950	3457	4955	4050	5354	5214	4756	4610	4480	4357	4313	4179	4127	4040	3657	3599	3585	3529
Few Pills	1163	1113	1942	1736	2173	1813	2329	2304	2171	2168	2150	2104	2297	2306	2449	2439	2308	2315	2198	2196
More Pills	2157	1989	3427	2987	3857	3266	3906	3885	3622	3543	3873	3760	4972	4925	4896	4839	4333	4306	3946	3936
Any Heroin	231	216	319	268	321	280	289	302	193	186	186	180	183	189	212	210	210	206	206	207

*The number of cases shown for 1975 is based on Forms 2 through 5 only, because the data from Form 1 are intentionally not included in tabulations based on drug and demographic items which appeared in all forms.

**Missing data problems were severe for race and college plans in 1975; accordingly, these data have been excluded from all tables in the 1975 report.

TABLE B-2
Sample Sizes (Unweighted and Weighted) in Subgroups by Year
for Questions on a Single Form*

Number of Cases

	Class of 1975		Class of 1976		Class of 1977		Class of 1978		Class of 1979		Class of 1980		Class of 1981		Class of 1982		Class of 1983		Class of 1984	
	Unwtd	Wtd	Unwtd	Wtd	Unwtd	Wtd	Unwtd	Wtd	Unwtd	Wtd	Unwtd	Wtd	Unwtd	Wtd	Unwtd	Wtd	Unwtd	Wtd	Unwtd	Wtd
Total Sample	3157	3027	3336	3028	3687	3166	3785	3783	3332	3332	3305	3305	3653	3653	3670	3670	3389	3389	3300	3300
Sex:																				
Male	1450	1393	1600	1488	1690	1472	1721	1756	1578	1556	1587	1549	1755	1745	1796	1766	1621	1615	1531	1560
Female	1593	1525	1585	1451	1838	1570	1883	1853	1628	1646	1575	1616	1750	1773	1722	1758	1632	1645	1629	1606
Race:																				
White	**	**	2587	2359	2764	2448	2933	2969	2686	2660	2579	2569	2725	2797	2751	2777	2540	2561	2445	2467
Black	**	**	361	343	500	388	441	419	323	348	388	420	499	453	441	416	438	413	456	449
Region:																				
Northeast	754	674	807	714	952	792	968	921	785	803	856	775	854	858	944	948	826	811	732	677
North Central	988	958	1020	937	1139	952	1115	1082	1077	975	868	975	1014	1097	1045	1077	849	957	804	922
South	842	964	835	919	982	964	1113	1258	943	1011	933	1010	1103	1120	1038	1110	1104	1087	1145	1114
West	574	431	674	457	614	459	588	521	528	543	647	545	683	579	643	534	610	535	619	586
College Plans:																				
Complete 4 yrs	**	**	1593	1399	1787	1481	1853	1769	1714	1641	1838	1732	2051	1976	1970	1872	1868	1812	1823	1821
None or under 4 yrs	**	**	1436	1375	1553	1410	1571	1683	1343	1413	1199	1316	1297	1402	1394	1501	1243	1311	1200	1225
Illicit Drug Use																				
None	1082	1100	1306	1218	1334	1176	1280	1319	1085	1131	1064	1118	1191	1230	1231	1266	1200	1216	1225	1240
Marijuana Only	511	474	790	691	991	810	1071	1043	951	922	896	871	863	836	825	808	731	720	717	706
Few Pills	291	278	388	347	435	363	466	461	434	434	430	421	459	461	490	488	462	463	440	439
More Pills	539	497	685	597	771	653	781	777	724	709	775	752	994	985	979	968	867	861	789	787
Any Heroin	58	54	64	54	64	56	58	60	39	37	37	36	37	38	42	42	42	41	41	41

*The Ns given here are very close approximations of the N in the given subgroup for any of the five different questionnaire forms used in the year.

**Missing data problems were severe for race and college plans in 1975; accordingly, these data have been excluded from all tables in the 1975 report.

Further Applications of these Design Effects and Sampling Errors

One of the reasons for providing the above review of the factors influencing design effects and confidence intervals, and the procedures used in computing our confidence interval tables, is to provide sufficient background and data to permit the interested reader to go beyond the material provided in Appendix A. In this section we consider two specific extensions, the calculation of levels of "statistical significance" higher than 95 percent and the computation of means and their confidence intervals.

Calculating Confidence Intervals for Higher Levels of Statistical Significance. The entries contained in Tables A-1 and A-2 provide the 95 percent confidence level (also referred to as the .05 level of significance). These entries were computed by multiplying the standard error (square root of sample variance) by a factor of 1.96. The 99 percent confidence interval (.01 level of significance) uses a factor of 2.58 standard errors, and the 99.9 percent confidence interval (.001 level of significance) uses a factor of 3.29 standard errors. To convert the entries in Tables A-1 and A-2 to these higher levels, it is necessary only to multiply the entries by the appropriate constant shown below (keeping in mind that any other adjustments required in the tables must also be applied):

Confidence Interval	Significance Level	Multiply entries in Tables A-1 and A-2 by the following:
99%	.01	2.58/1.96= 1.32
99.9%	.001	3.29/1.96= 1.68

Computing Means and Their Confidence Intervals. Many of the questionnaire items included in this volume have ordinal response scales (e.g., agree, agree mostly, neither, disagree mostly, disagree), and it is often the case that a survey analyst will be willing to treat such scales as if they involved equal intervals. In such cases, means and standard deviations are more "efficient" in their use of information than are dichotomies which yield a single percentage or a pair of percentages (e.g., those who respond "agree" or "agree mostly," versus all others). It is a relatively straightforward matter to compute means and standard deviations for the total sample or any of the subgroups treated in this volume. The problem, then, is to be able to specify confidence intervals for the means, or for the differences between pairs of means. In the case of simple random samples, one needs only the means, standard deviations (or variances), and numbers of cases in order to compute confidence intervals. But in complex samples such as the present one,

it is also necessary to take account of design effects. If an estimate of design effect is available, one of the simplest procedures to follow is to divide the actual numbers of cases by the design effect (thereby "depreciating" the actual number to its equivalent value in simple random sample terms) and then employ the standard statistical procedures which have been developed for application to simple random samples. Thus, for example, if the design effect (DEFF) for a sample of 18,000 were 4.0, then one could divide the 18,000 by 4.0 and the result, 4,500, could be entered as the value of "N" in statistical tables and formulas designed for use with simple random samples. To take another example, if one were comparing means based on two subgroups, each involving about 9,000 cases, and if DEFF (for both subgroups) was 2.0, then one could compute the significance of the difference between the two means as if the N for each group were 4,500 (i.e., 9,000 divided by 2.0).

In short, the strategy involves dividing the actual number of cases by the appropriate DEFF in order to get a "simple random sampling equivalent N" or, more simply, an "effective N" for use in statistical procedures designed for random samples.

Design Effects for Use in Computing "Effective Ns." In order to employ the strategy outlined above, one must have estimates of design effects which are judged to be appropriate for one's purposes. In the case of means based on the percentages reported in this volume, we are confident (based on personal communications with Kish) that it is appropriate to use the same DEFF values as were used in developing Tables A-1 and A-2. For other, more complex statistics, we cannot make the same assertion, although it is generally the case that design effects for such statistics are not larger than those for means and percentages (Kish and Frankel, 1970; Frankel, 1971).

In Table B-3 we provide guidelines for computing DEFF values for single percentages (or means) and for differences between two percentages (or means). For reasons discussed elsewhere in this appendix, we must provide for different (and somewhat higher) DEFFs for "segregated" subgroups (regional subgroups and sometimes also blacks), and for trends over two or more years (in contrast to one-year trends). And in all instances, of course, the DEFF values are very much influenced by the average size of sampling clusters, which is always dependent on the number of cases (N). Accordingly, all of the design effect formulas in Table B-3 require computations which take account of N. (It should also be noted that the formulas in Table B-3 correspond exactly to the values of design effects and adjustment factors used in Tables A-1 and A-2 in Appendix A.

A Concluding Note. In their very useful paper dealing with sampling errors for fertility surveys, Kish

Table B-3
Guidelines for Computing Design Effects (DEFFs) for Percentages
and Means Derived from Monitoring the Future Samples

DEFINITIONS

$$\text{DEFF (design effect} = \frac{\text{(estimated sampling variance}}{\begin{array}{l}\text{expected sampling variance from simple}\\\text{random sample with same number of elements}\end{array}}$$

N = number of respondents on whom a single percentage or mean is based

$\overline{N}$ = $2N_1N_2/(N_1 + N_2)$, for use in comparisons of two percentages or means, based on two groups of sizes N_1 and N_2.

DESIGN EFFECT FORMULAS

1. For single percentages or means involving . . .
    a. regional subgroups or blacks
       DEFF for single form data ....(1.3 + .00015N) (1.21)
       DEFF for five form data ....(1.3 + .00015N) (1.78)

    b. all other subgroups or total sample
       DEFF for single form or five form data ....1.3 + .00015N

2. For comparisons between . . .
    a. any two regions
       DEFF for single form data ....(1.3 + .000075$\overline{N}$) (1.32)
       DEFF for five form data ....(1.3 + .000075$\overline{N}$) (2.25)

    b. blacks and whites
       DEFF for single form data..1.3 + .000075$\overline{N}$
       DEFF for five form data ....(1.3 + .000075$\overline{N}$) (1.56)

    c. genders, college plans groups, or any two "drug use" subgroups
       DEFF for single form or five form data ....1.3 + .000075$\overline{N}$

3. For one-year trends involving . . .
    a. any region
       DEFF for single form data..1.3 + .000075$\overline{N}$
       DEFF for five form data ....(1.3 + .000075$\overline{N}$) (1.56)
    b. all other subgroups or total sample
       DEFF for single form or five form data ....1.3 + .000075$\overline{N}$

4. For trends over two or more years involving . . .
    a. any region
       DEFF for single form data..1.3 + .000075$\overline{N}$
       DEFF for five form data ....(1.3 + .000075$\overline{N}$) (1.82)
    b. all other subgroups or total sample
       DEFF for single form data..1.3 + .000075$\overline{N}$
       DEFF for five form data ....(1.3 + .000075$\overline{N}$) (1.32)

et al. (1976) commented that some of the methods they used ". . . emerged after several false starts." They went on to say that the volume and diversity of the data they were dealing with ". . . presented new challenges and opportunities." And they added, "Our methods are subject to further developments and modifications, and we invite participation and suggestions" (p. 10). Our own attempts to apply the methods of Kish and his colleagues to the data reported in this volume have been challenged by the diversity of the data, have involved several false starts, and we hope are subject to further developments and modifications. We invite readers to offer their suggestions, and we also encourage readers to inquire about further work that we and/or others may carry out during the coming months and years.

Appendix C
Questionnaire Covers, Instructions, and Sample Page

monitoring the future
a continuing study of the lifestyles and values of youth

This questionnaire is part of a nationwide study of high school seniors, conducted each year by the University of Michigan's Institute for Social Research. The questions ask your opinions about a number of things — the way things are now and the way you think they ought to be in the future. In a sense, many of your answers on this questionnaire will count as "votes" on a wide range of important issues.

If this study is to be helpful, it is important that you answer each question as thoughtfully and frankly as possible. All your answers will be kept strictly confidential, and will never be seen by anyone who knows you.

This study is completely voluntary. If there is any question that you or your parents would find objectionable for any reason, just leave it blank.

In a few months, we would like to mail each of you a summary of the nationwide results from this study. Also, in about a year we would like to mail another questionnaire to some of you, asking about how your plans have worked out and what's happening in your lives.

In order to include you in these mailings, we ask for your name and address on a special form at the end of this questionnaire. This form is to be torn out and handed in separately. Once the address form and the questionnaire have been separated, there is no way they can be matched again, except by using a special computer tape at the University of Michigan. The only purpose for that tape is to match a follow-up questionnaire with this one.

Other seniors have said that these questionnaires are very interesting and that they enjoy filling them out. We hope you will too. Be sure to read the instructions on the other side of this cover page before you begin to answer. Thank you very much for being an important part of this project.

INSTITUTE FOR SOCIAL RESEARCH
THE UNIVERSITY OF MICHIGAN
ANN ARBOR, MICHIGAN

271

INSTRUCTIONS

1. This is not a test, so there are no right or wrong answers; we would
    like you to work fairly quickly, so that you can finish.

2. All of the questions should be answered by marking one of the answer spaces.
    If you don't always find an answer that fits exactly, use the one that comes
    closest. If any question does not apply to you, or you are not sure of what it
    means, just leave it blank.

3. Your answers will be read automatically by a machine called an optical mark
    reader. Please follow these instructions carefully:

    • Use only the black lead pencil you have been given.

    • Make heavy black marks inside the circles.

    • Erase cleanly any answer you wish to change.   These kinds of markings
                                                          will work: ●   ◖   ◕

    • Make no other markings or comments on the   These kinds of markings
      answer pages, since they interfere with the   will NOT work: ⊙   ✦   ○
      automatic reading. (If you want to add a
      comment about any question, please use the
      space provided below.)

(THIS SPACE FOR WRITTEN COMMENTS)

WHY YOUR NAME AND ADDRESS?

As we told you earlier, we'd like to send you a summary of the nationwide results of the present study, and in about a year we want to mail a shorter questionnaire to some of you. In order to include you in these follow-ups, we would like to have an address where information will be sure to reach you during the coming year.

HOW IS CONFIDENTIALITY PROTECTED?

- The information on this page will be used ONLY for mailing, and will always be kept separate from your answers. A special Grant of Confidentiality from the U.S. government protects all information gathered in this research project.

- The questionnaire and address pages will be collected separately, sealed immediately in separate envelopes, and sent to two different cities for processing.

- Once a questionnaire and address page have been separated, there is no way they can be matched, except by using a special computer tape at the University of Michigan. That tape contains the two DIFFERENT numbers that appear on the back of this address page and on the back of the questionnaire. These numbers will be used ONLY to match a follow-up questionnaire with this one.

> Before filling out this address page, please separate it from the rest of the questionnaire by FOLDING ALONG THE PERFORATED LINE AND TEARING CAREFULLY.

Please **PRINT** your name and the address where you can most likely be reached during the coming year.

Mr.
Miss _
Ms.   FIRST NAME   INITIAL   LAST NAME
Mrs.

STREET _

CITY _

STATE _ _ _ _ _ _ _ _ _ _ _ _ _ _ _ _ _ _ ZIP _ _ _ _ _ _ _ _

TELEPHONE NO.   (   ) — _ _ _ _ _ _ _ _ _ _ _ _ _ _ _
                      AREA

In case we should have trouble getting mail to you, if you move, please **PRINT** the name and address of one other person (with a different address than your own) who will know where to reach you in the future. (Examples of such a person: aunt or uncle, older sister or brother, or close friend.)

Mr.
Miss _
Ms.   FIRST NAME   INITIAL   LAST NAME
Mrs.

STREET _

CITY _

STATE _ _ _ _ _ _ _ _ _ _ _ _ _ _ _ _ _ _ ZIP _ _ _ _ _ _ _ _

TELEPHONE NO.   (   ) — _ _ _ _ _ _ _ _ _ _ _ _ _ _ _
                      AREA

THANK YOU AGAIN FOR YOUR HELP

PART A

* **BEFORE BEGINNING BE SURE YOU HAVE
  READ THE INSTRUCTIONS ON THE COVER.**

1. Taking all things together, how would you say things are
   these days--would you say you're very happy, pretty
   happy, or not too happy these days?

   ○ Very happy
   ○ Pretty happy
   ○ Not too happy

2. Some people think a lot about the social problems of the
   nation and the world, and about how they might be solved.
   Others spend little time thinking about these issues. How
   much do you think about such things?

   ① Never
   ② Seldom
   ③ Sometimes
   ④ Quite often
   ⑤ A great deal

3. **Of all the problems facing the nation
   today, how often do you worry about
   each of the following?** (Mark one
   circle for each line.)

   Never   Seldom   Sometimes   Often

   a. Chance of nuclear war .... ①②③④

   b. Population growth .... ①②③④

   c. Crime and violence .... ①②③④

   d. Pollution .... ①②③④

   e. Energy shortages .... ①②③④

   f. Race relations .... ①②③④

   g. Hunger and poverty .... ①②③④

   h. Using open land for housing or
       industry .... ①②③④

   i. Urban decay .... ①②③④

   j. Economic problems .... ①②③④

   k. Drug abuse .... ①②③④

4. How well do you think your experiences
   and training (at home, school, work, etc.)
   have prepared you to be a good...

   Poorly   Not So Well   Fairly Well   Well   Very Well

   a. ...husband or wife? .... ①②③④⑤

   b. ...parent? .... ①②③④⑤

   c. ...worker on a job? .... ①②③④⑤

5. Apart from the particular kind of work
   you want to do, how would you rate each
   of the following settings as a place to
   work? (Mark one circle for each line.)

   Not At All Acceptable   Somewhat Acceptable   Acceptable   Desirable

   a. Working in a large corporation .... ①②③④

   b. Working in a small business .... ①②③④

   c. Working in a government agency .... ①②③④

   d. Working in the military service .... ①②③④

   e. Working in a school or university .... ①②③④

   f. Working in a police department or police
       agency .... ①②③④

   g. Working in a social service organization .. ①②③④

   h. Working with a small group of partners ... ①②③④

   i. Working on your own (self-employed) ..... ①②③④

6. **If you were to get enough money to live as comfortably as
   you'd like for the rest of your life, would you want to
   work?**

   ① I would want to work
   ② I would not want to work

References

Adelson, J. "What Generation Gap?" *New York Times Magazine*, January 18, 1970, pp. 1–11.

Adelson, J. "Adolescence and the Generation Gap." *Psychology Today*, February 1979, pp. 33–37.

Bachman, J.G., and Johnston, L.D. "The Monitoring the Future Project Design and Procedures," (Occasional Paper #1). Institute for Social Research, The University of Michigan, Ann Arbor, 1978.

Bachman, J.D., and Johnston, L.D. "The Freshmen, 1979." *Psychology Today*, September 1979, pp. 79–87.

Bachman, J.G.; Johnston, L.D.; and O'Malley, P.M. "Smoking, Drinking, and Drug Use Among American High School Students: Correlates and Trends, 1975–1979." *American Journal of Public Health* 71 (1981):59–69.

Bachman, J.G., and O'Malley, P.M. "When Four Months Equal a Year: Inconsistencies in Students' Reports of Drug Use." *Public Opinion Quarterly* 45 (1981):536–548.

Bachman, J.G., and O'Malley, P.M. "Yea-saying, Nay-saying, and Going to Extremes: Are Black-White Differences in Survey Results Due to Response Styles?" *Public Opinion Quarterly*, 48 (1984):409–427.

Bachman, J.G.; O'Malley, P.M.; and Johnston, J. Youth in Transition, Volume VI: *Adolescence to Adulthood – A Study of Change and Stability in the Lives of Young Men.* Ann Arbor: Institute for Social Research, The University of Michigan, 1978.

Dearman, N.B., and Plisko, V.W. *The Condition of Education.* (National Center for Education Statistics). Washington, D.C.: U.S. Government Printing Office, 1982.

Frankel, M.R. *Inference from Survey Samples: An Empirical Investigation.* Ann Arbor: Institute for Social Research, The University of Michigan, 1971.

Hays, W.L. *Statistics for the Social Sciences* (2nd ed.). New York: Holt, Rinehart, & Winston, 1973.

Johnston, L.D. *Drugs and American Youth.* Ann Arbor: Institute for Social Research, The University of Michigan, 1973.

Johnston, L.D.; Bachman, J.G.; and O'Malley, P.M. *Drug Use Among American High School Students, 1975–1977* (National Institute on Drug Abuse). Washington, D.C.: U.S. Government Printing Office, 1977.

Johnston, L.D.; Bachman, J.G.; and O'Malley, P.M. *Drugs and the Class of 1978: Behaviors, Attitudes, and Recent National Trends* (National Institute on Drug Abuse). Washington, D.C.: U.S. Government Printing Office, 1979(a).

Johnston, L.D.; Bachman, J.G.; and O'Malley, P.M. *1979 Highlights: Drugs and the Nation's High School Students, Five Year National Trends* (National Institute on Drug Abuse). Washington, D.C.: U.S. Government Printing Office, 1979(b).

Johnston, L.D.; Bachman, J.G.; and O'Malley, P.M. *Highlights from Student Drug Use in America: 1975–1980* (National Institute on Drug Abuse). Washington, D.C.: U.S. Government Printing Office, 1981.

Johnston, L.D.; Bachman, J.G.; and O'Malley, P.M. *Student Drug Use in America, 1975–1981.* (National Institute on Drug Abuse). Washington, D.C.: U.S. Government Printing Office, 1982.

Johnston, L.D.; Bachman, J.G.; and O'Malley, P.M. *Student Drug Use, Attitudes and Beliefs: National Trends 1975–1982.* (National Institute on Drug Abuse). Washington, D.C.: U.S. Government Printing Office, 1983.

Johnston, L.D.; O'Malley, P.M.; and Bachman, J.G. *Highlights from Drugs and American High School Students, 1975–1983.* (National Institute on Drug Abuse). Washington, D.C.: U.S. Government Printing Office, 1984.

Johnston, L.D.; O'Malley, P.M.; and Bachman, J.G. *Drugs and American High School Students, 1975–1983.* (National Institute on Drug Abuse). Washington, D.C.: U.S. Government Printing Office, 1984.

Kish, L. *Survey Sampling.* New York: John Wiley & Sons, 1965.

Kish, L., and Frankel, M.R. "Balanced Repeated Replication for Standard Errors." *Journal of the American Statistical Association* 65 (1970):1071–1094.

Kish, L.; Groves, R.M.; and Krotki, K.P. *Sampling Errors for Fertility Surveys* (Occasional Papers Series No. 17). Voorburg, The Netherlands: International Statistical Institute, 1976.

U.S. Bureau of the Census, *Current Population Reports.* Series P-20, No. 319, School enrollment – social and economic characteristics of students, October 1976. Washington, D.C.: U.S. Government Printing Office, 1978.

275